DICTIONARY
of
QUOTATIONS

COLLECTED AND ARRANGED
AND WITH COMMENTS BY

Bergen Evans

AVENEL BOOKS · NEW YORK

Contents

In this edition the Topical Index, Quotations, and Index of Authors
have been included. The Subject Index has been omitted.

Copyright © MCMLXVIII by Bergen Evans
All rights reserved
Manufactured in the United States of America

This edition published by Avenel Books,
distributed by Crown Publishers, Inc.,
by arrangement with Delacorte Press

g h i j k l m

AVENEL BOOKS • 1978 PRINTING

Library of Congress Cataloging in Publication Data

Evans, Bergen, 1904-
Dictionary of quotations.

Reprint of the ed. published by Delacorte Press, New York.
1. Quotations, English. I. Title.
PN6081.E9 1978   808.88'2   66-20131
ISBN 0-517-26280-0 lib. bdg.
ISBN 0-517-268094

❦ On Looking It Up ❦

THERE ARE MANY PLEASURES to be derived from a dictionary of quotations.

First, there is the relief of finding something that has been buzzing in our minds, something which we know is incomplete or imperfect and which demands to be completed or corrected. The attempt to recollect and complete a quotation which we have in only a fragmentary and distorted form soon passes from the tantalizing to the irritating to the obsessive. And then—blessed release!—there it is. It's the equivalent of hearing the other shoe drop, of having the aching tooth out at last.

But there are greater pleasures. To find some thought of which we approve but which we have not managed to express clearly—to come upon this thought brilliantly expressed, with all the humor, bitterness or tenderness that its full expression requires—is a deep and complex satisfaction. It comforts us with the assurance, for one thing, that we are not alone, that others—the famous and respected—have agreed with us. And it lets us know that the idea we wanted to express with our poor stammering tongue has already been sent abroad on winged words. Then gnomic wisdom confers a wonderful sense of superiority. For a moment we stand above the battle "and see the errors and wanderings and mists and tempests in the vale below" (to quote Bacon quoting Lucretius quoting God knows who).

It's a purely retrospective delight, of course; for, unfortunately, wisdom is meaningless until our own experience has given it meaning. It's not that experience keeps a dear school—no tuition would be too high—but she keeps a daft school. As Vernon Law put it, she gives the test first and the lesson afterward. And most of what passes as human wisdom is merely the post-examination gabble of the excited students trying to guess how the new lesson will explain the old questions.

When we *do* see the relation, however, the perception is one of life's keenest satisfactions. No man was ever made wise by reading Koheleth or cynical by reading La Rochefoucauld. But the wise—the burnt children—delight in Ecclesiastes and the cynical in the *Maxims*.

They further delight in taunting the teacher. For there is a folly in wisdom and a wisdom in perceiving this folly. To every proverb there seems to be an anti-proverb. Thus Proverbs 26:4 warns us not to answer a fool according to his folly, lest we be like unto him; but the next verse, Proverbs 26:5, urges us to answer a fool according to his folly, lest he be wise in his own conceit. So that, plainly, there is a wisdom in the selection of wisdom.

Or even in its rejection—which may, indeed, be the *summa cum laude* of Experience's curriculum. The literature of wisdom, for example, is crammed with comments on the folly of fear: "our fears do make us traitors" (Shakespeare), "fear doubleth danger" (Fuller), "makes men believe the worst" (Quintus Rufus) and there is "no passion so contagious" (Montaigne). But despite "all we have to fear is fear" (Thoreau, F.D.R., and countless others), every wise man's son doth know that there are very real things to be afraid of and fear is an essential guarantor of life. Without it we would be destroyed, and even with it we may not be preserved, for there is no certainty of salvation: "He that fleeth from the fear shall fall into the pit; and he that getteth up out of the pit shall be taken in the snare" (Jeremiah).

And there is a baseness in wisdom, too, especially in that shrewd practical wisdom our fathers set such store by. A penny saved *is* a penny got, but this is a "scoundrel maxim" (Thomson). Honesty *is* the best policy, but Archbishop Whately was right in asserting that anyone who acts on that principle is not an honest man. And Chesterfield's letters to his son, crammed with worldly wisdom, do indeed "teach the manners of a dancing master and the morals of a whore."

Not that it matters, for no one ever schooled himself by reading aphorisms. They are more allied to pleasure than profit, material or moral, and one of the pleasures they offer is the watching of a phrase change—sometimes for the better, sometimes for the worse—as it passes through successive pens. To see, for example, Locke's "life, liberty, health . . . and the possession of outward things" become Jefferson's "life, liberty and the pursuit of happiness." Or to see Daniel Webster's "The people's government, made for the people, made by the people, and answerable to the people" refined into Theodore Parker's "government of all the people, by all the people, for all the people," achieve its perfection in Lincoln's final form.

Then there is a delight in the happy application of wit. An apt quotation can be as brilliant as an original coinage. Sometimes more so, for the wit of a quotation caroms its meaning off not only the original but off an accreted complex of attitudes toward the original.

Thus "He gives twice that gives quickly" was proverbial by the first century B.C., since it appeared in the maxims of Publilius Syrus, and had been echoed in every adjuration to the charitable through the ensuing centuries. And it was this aura of established virtue, of respectable, almost hackneyed, piety that gave piquancy to Ben Franklin's dry comment (in *Poor Richard's Almanack*, 1752) that he who gives quickly gives twice because he is soon called upon to give again.

So the full humor of the saying attributed to Philip Guedalla that "any stigma will do to beat a dogma" lies in part in the contrast between the homeliness of the original and the sophistication of its application. The distortion adds to it, like the mirrors in a sideshow. "You don't change barrels while going over Niagara Falls"—a comment on the re-election of Franklin D. Roosevelt commonly attributed to Al Smith—not only echoes Lincoln's backwoodsy saying about not changing horses while crossing a stream but implies that under Roosevelt's control of the election machinery any change was ludicrously impossible, even though—in the opinion of the speaker—we were plunging into a roaring abyss.

An apt quotation or an echo of a quotation can range from the scornfully flippant (as in Byron's "Go, little book") to the almost unendurably poignant (as in T. S. Eliot's "Good night, sweet ladies, good night, good night").

Or it can be a nest of Chinese boxes, each evocation evoking still another. Thus when Lord David Cecil entitled his biography of the poet Cowper *The Stricken Deer* he was alluding to Cowper's description of himself as "a stricken deer that had left the herd long since." As a college student Cowper had suffered what we would call a severe nervous breakdown and spent the rest of his life in retirement, poised on the dreadful edge of complete collapse. In so describing himself Cowper, of course, expected his reader to remember Hamlet's

> Why, let the stricken deer go weep,
>   The hart ungalled play;
> For some must watch, while some must sleep:
>   So runs the world away.

Hamlet's words suited him, for they were wild and whirling, bordering on madness, bitter. Cowper's use of them was sad and Lord Cecil's echo of Cowper's echo moving and pitiful. And the reader's pleasure in such a complex interplay, subtle and manifold.

When, on looking up a quotation, one finds that one has remembered it exactly, there is a thrill of triumph. But there is also a pleasure, even though it is often mingled with annoyance, in finding, sometimes, that one has *not* remembered a quotation exactly, that the original is significantly, often startlingly, different from the commonly accepted version. To find, for instance, that it is not a little *knowledge* that is "a dangerous thing" but a little *learning;* that the lion will not, at the millennium, lie down with the lamb, but with the fatling—it is the wolf that will have the pleasure of dwelling with the lamb; that the Israelites were not compelled to "make bricks without straw" but to furnish their own straw; that the mysterious writing is not to be such "that he that runs may read" but the more spooky "that he that reads may run"; that the famous image in Nebuchadnezzar's dream did not have "feet of clay" but "part of iron and part of clay"; that it is not "a drop *in* the bucket" but "a drop *of* the bucket"; that it is not "the right hand of fellowship" but "the right hands of fellowship"; that Saint Paul did not say that he was "born free" but that he was "free born."

In many of these established misquotations we find that two parts of a passage have been run together. Thus, as a trope of unnecessary embellishment, we speak of "gilding the lily," though a moment's reflection would tell us that there was something wrong, since lilies aren't gold-colored. And on consulting the original we see what has happened. Shakespeare, in a passage stating a series of supererogatory acts, had listed "To gild refined gold, to paint the lily" and in our collective minds "gild" has jumped over from "gold" to replace the more fitting "paint" in front of "lily." So also when Commencement orators speak of "the bright lexicon of youth" (in which "there is no such word as 'fail' ") they have moved "bright" back from the next line where, in the original, it applies to manhood. Even the golden rule, as commonly stated ("Do unto others as you would have them do unto you"), is a blend, with a slight modernization of the language, of two passages, Matthew 7:12 and Luke 6:31.

Nor are these changes invariably "mistakes." Sometimes they are improvements, fine strokes of emendation, for we all have the stuff of poetry in our subliminal depths. Thus the accurate "with the skin of my teeth" is merely mystifying, but the popular "by the skin of my teeth" is a masterstroke of humorous exaggeration, like "skinflint." Most users of the expression "not room enough to swing a cat" would be surprised to learn that it probably refers to a cat-o'-nine-tails, not to *Felix domestica*. But for our purposes, since flogging has happily been banished from the Navy, the popular misconception is an improvement: one would want plenty of room (and courage!) to swing an alley cat or a Siamese.

One of the commonest reasons for consulting a dictionary of quotations is to "find out who said it." But ascription of origin is a ticklish business. When, for instance, Lydgate said, in 1412, that a certain man was "as bald as a coot," had he coined an amusing simile or was he merely using a hackneyed comparison? Who can say? All we know is that this is the earliest record of the phrase known. And so with Richard Brome's "You rose on the wrong side of the bed today" (1652) or Royal Tyler's "left holding the bag" (1787) and a thousand other well-known expressions.

Acknowledgment is no safe guide, for the acknowledger may innocently assume that his informant was the creator, instead of the tenth transmitter, of a foolish phrase. Anything is fresh on the first hearing even though others may have heard it a thousand times through a score of generations.

Thus we often find "Give us the luxuries of life and we will dispense with the necessities" ascribed to Oliver Wendell Holmes. But Holmes, in *The Autocrat of the Breakfast Table,* where the statement appears, acknowledges that he got it from John Lathrop Motley. But Motley could have got it from John Gay's *Polly* and Gay could have had it from Voltaire (or Voltaire from Gay), though it is more likely that they both borrowed it from Plutarch's *Morals.* But even Plutarch isn't the source, for he says that he was merely quoting "Scopas of Thessaly." But whether this otherwise unknown worthy made it up or was quoting someone even more obscure, we shall probably never know.

These skeins and pedigrees at once distress and fascinate the compiler. There's always the urge to look further and the hope and fear that if one does one may find something. The hope is for the triumph of accomplishment; the fear is that one thing will lead to another and there will be no end to it and three score and ten are the years of a man's life.

Consider John William Burgon's *A rose-red city—"half as old as time."* The line comes from Burgon's "Petra," a prize poem recited and published at Oxford in 1845. Many poets owe their fame to a single poem, but Burgon has the almost comic distinction of owing his to a single line. Or, more accurately, to a half line, for the quotation marks show that the better half of the famous line is someone else's. But whose? Most anthologies just assign the whole line to Burgon and hurry by. But some indefatigable scholar has shown that the quotation is from the 1838 revision of Samuel Rogers's *Italy*. And an even more indefatigable scholar has shown that Rogers borrowed it from a satirical poem—"Heroic Epistle to Burke"—published anonymously in 1791.

This would seem to take it back to its source were it not that the anonymous satirist affirms in a preface that there is "scarcely a single image" in his poem "which is not extracted from Mr. Burke's celebrated *Reflections*." But a perusal of the celebrated *Reflections* fails to discover this particular image, and one is left wondering whether the anonymous poet's memory deceived him or whether he had modestly failed to recognize a jewel of his own creation.

There is even greater difficulty in assigning an expression to its originator when we are dealing with a translation, for then we have to decide whether the passage in question is in the original or whether the translator has added it. And, even more difficult, whether the translator chose to translate the passage into some accepted phraseology.

Thus, to illustrate, in the twelfth book of the *Odyssey*, when Odysseus brings his narrative to the point that he had already covered in an earlier talk with King Alcinous, he breaks off, saying (in T. E. Shaw's translation), "It goes against my grain to repeat a tale already plainly told." Pope, in his translation, rendered this: "What is so tedious as a twice-told tale?", an echo of Shakespeare's "Life is as tedious as a twice-told tale." No deception was intended. Pope could not have thought that the line would be taken as his own. He wrote for educated readers and must have assumed that every educated reader would recognize the passage and would have the added pleasure —a pleasure much esteemed and catered to in the eighteenth century—of recognition.

But all of his readers were probably not as familiar with Shakespeare as he assumed them to be and many must have taken for granted that the words were his or Homer's. And while we may smile at such simplicity, we have to face the fact that there is no man living learned enough to know just what in, say, Burton's *Anatomy of Melancholy* is the author's, what is quoted and what, in the quoting, is deliberately or accidentally distorted.

There are a number of books, indeed, much relied on as sources of gnomic wisdom which are, really, not sources at all but unacknowledged compilations. Burton's book is one of these, the more difficult in that it is not *wholly* a compilation. And so, to a lesser degree, is *Don Quixote*. Hundreds of proverbs, in all anthologies, are ascribed to Cervantes. But he is their transmitter, not their creator; for much of the comedy of Sancho Panza lies in the fact that his conversation is a tissue of proverbs—some straight, some distorted and some wittily adapted.

Even more amazing is the listing of Swift's *Polite Conversation* as an original source. Much has been made of the ironical fact that *Gulliver,* the most savage attack on the human race ever written, is sold chiefly as a children's storybook. As much or more could be made of the fact that the most scathing denunciation of clichés and hackneyed commonplaces, of that moldy wit, veiled malice and tittering vacuity that passes for sprightly chitchat in high society, that has ever been made should be solemnly accepted for centuries as a compendium of cleverness.

But these are problems for the scholar. The layman is free from any such enervating doubts. To him it's simple: ascribe a saying to whatever folk hero or villain *might* have said it. Marie Antoinette did not say, or at least did not originate, "Let 'em eat cake." But all the king's lexicographers will never free her from the saying. Horace Greeley insisted repeatedly that he had borrowed "Go west, young man" from John Babson Soule of Terre Haute. But it was the sort of thing the public thought Greeley would have said, and that settled it. And, anyway, who was John Babson Soule? And even if he did say it, maybe he got it from a copy boy. Things attributed to great ones *have* been cribbed from the lowly. We learned in our youth that a certain Ernest Hemingway had coined a poignant phrase, "the lost generation," only to learn in our maturity that he hadn't coined it at all, that it was the product of one of Gertrude Stein's lucid intervals. Only to learn still further, in our senescence, that she hadn't coined it either but had cribbed it from a Parisian garage mechanic, some *Milton muet et inglorieux.*

The simple fact is that authors are magpies, echoing each other's words and seizing avidly on anything that glitters. From Seneca through Montaigne to Kipling they have openly avowed the principle of plagiary—though most are indignant when accused of any specific appropriation.

The commonest justification is that creation is frequently a matter of growth and hence " 'tis his at last that says it best." And this is true often enough to warrant the assertion. Marlowe's "Infinite riches in a little room" is certainly pure gold compared to its leaden original, William Harrison's "great commoditie in a little room." And the Elizabethans, who were unconscionable thieves, plundered Marlowe like cormorants. Shakespeare has "a great reckoning in a little room," Ben Jonson "sacred treasures in this blessed room," and Chapman "riches in a little room." But Marlowe's mighty imprint was too much for them and the line remains forever his.

So Webster's "They that have the yellow Jaundeise thinke all objects they looke on to bee yellow" is the dross which Pope, a hundred years later, transmuted into the famous

> All seems infected that th' infected spy,
> As all looks yellow to the jaundic'd eye.

The honors here are plainly and deservedly Pope's and the thought forever his. And Goldsmith deserves full credit for

Man wants but little here below,
Nor wants that little long,

even though he had only added "here below" to Young's "Man wants but little, nor that little long."

But all appropriation is not improvement and immortality does not always go to merit. Sometimes, perhaps in order to disguise the theft, the thought is disfigured ("as gypsies do stolen children to make 'em pass for their own")— though more often it is merely banalized by being passed through a commonplace mind—and the public prefers the disfigurement.

Thus Lord Acton has acquired a reputation for oracular wisdom for his trite observation, in a letter to Bishop Creighton, in 1887, that power corrupts and absolute power corrupts absolutely. From the reverential care always taken to ascribe this sentiment to Acton ("as Lord Acton said") one would assume that by some miracle it had thitherto escaped the observation of mankind.

But nothing could be further from the truth and many of its previous statements were more memorably expressed. Tacitus had observed that "the lust for power inflames the heart more than any other passion." Shakespeare had seen it as a universal wolf that makes "perforce an universal prey." William Pitt said that "unlimited power is apt to corrupt the minds of those who possess it" and Burke said that it "gradually extirpates from the mind every humane and gentle virtue." The finest statement is probably Bacon's remark that "every wand or staff of empire is curved at the top." Though since Bishop Creighton himself bore such a staff, he might have failed to see the exquisiteness of Bacon's wit.

An amusing instance of " 'tis his at last who says it *worst*" is furnished by the cliché "few and far between." In 1700 John Norris had written in "The Parting": "Like angels' visits, short and bright." Forty-three years later Robert Blair, in his lugubrious poem "The Grave," referred to "Visits, like those of Angels, short and far between." And it was this line that Thomas Campbell in "The Pleasures of Hope" adapted to "Like angel-visits, few and far between." The line became popular, but Hazlitt in his *Lectures on the English Poets* (1818) pointed out that Campbell had not only cribbed the line but had messed it up, since "few" and "far between" are the same, whereas "short" had conveyed an additional idea. Campbell was angry with Hazlitt. But he need not have been, for the last laugh, however unwarranted, has been Campbell's: the corrupted, meaningless line has passed into general speech and the sensible original into oblivion!

Familiar quotations are fine and satisfying. But the unfamiliar are delightful and stimulating. And one of the difficulties in compiling a volume such as this is to strike a balance between the quoted and the quotable, seeing that the present gets its due as well as the past. Juvenal and Erasmus were very clever fellows and are well worth quoting. But so are Ogden Nash and Adlai Stevenson, and their wit is more likely to be sought for by the contemporary reader.

Every user will be amused, indignant or triumphant, according to his nature, at finding omissions. But that is as much to be expected as regretted. It is inevitable; a volume that held every quotation that every reader hoped to find would have to be fifty times this size and would have to be revised every year.

But if the user is pleased to find most expected and delighted to find some unexpected sayings, the book will have served its purpose.

⤷ How to Use This Book ⤶

In seeking quotations that illustrate or develop an idea, the reader should turn to the Topical Index, which is cross-indexed.

The quotations under each topical heading are arranged in chronological order to show the development of an idea, the perfecting of its wording and, often, the attitude of different periods toward certain thoughts and values.

The Index of Authors serves to give a more exact date to the individual quotations. Where the dates of an author's life are enclosed in parentheses immediately after his name at the end of a quotation, they serve to distinguish him from another author of the same name. Where a date is given with a quotation, it is to call the reader's attention, for a specific reason, to the time of the appearance of that particular quotation.

The reader who wishes to pursue an individual author's contribution to the world's quoted and quotable sayings will find, under the author's name in the Index of Authors, a list of all the pages on which he is quoted.

The notes to some of the quotations seek to make their meaning clearer, to show their development, or to comment on their significance.

Where it has been deemed a convenience to the reader, a quotation appears more than once. The Ten Commandments, the Twenty-third Psalm, the Seven Ages of Man and the Gettysburg Address, for example, are given in their entirety because the common reader expects to find them. But much-quoted phrases from them are also given under separate topical headings since, merely as phrases, they are a part of our intellectual inheritance and many users may not, offhand, connect them with their source. Then there are some phrases that are repeated under different topics because they are applied to more than one meaning in popular use.

TOPICAL INDEX

A

ADVICE
See also COUNSEL
AESTHETE
AFFAIRS
See also ADULTERY, BUSINESS, GAL-
LANTRY
AFFECTATION
See also HYPOCRISY, MINCING,
SENTIMENTALITY
AFFECTION
See also LIKING, LOVE,
AFFLICTION
See also MISERY, PERSECUTION, PLAGUE,
SORROW, TROUBLE
AFFRONT
See also INSULT, SLIGHT
AFTERNOON
See also EVENING
AFTON
AGE: general
See also DOTAGE, GRAY HAIR, MARRIAGE:
January and May, MARRIED LOVE,
OLD, OLD AGE, SENILITY, WOMAN: and
age, YOUTH: and age
AGE: its beauty and dignity
AGE: contemptible and despised
AGE: its fears
AGE: its garrulity
AGE: growing old
See also ARTERIES
AGE: its loneliness
AGE: a lusty and vital old age
AGE: its mellowing, wisdom, insights
AGE: its moral decline
AGE: its pleasures and compensations
AGE: its weakness and miseries
AGE (PERIOD)
AGNOSTIC
See also ATHEIST, INFIDEL, SKEPTIC, UN-
BELIEVER
AGONY
See also MISERY, PAIN, SUFFERING, TOR-
MENT, WOE
AGREEABLE
See also AMIABILITY, PLEASING, WILLING
AGREEMENT
See also COMPLIANCE, CONCORD, OBLIGA-
TION, O.K., PROMISE, YIELDING
AGRICULTURE
See also CORN, FARMERS, FARMING, HAR-
VEST, PLOW
AIMLESSNESS
See also FICKLENESS, RANDOM
AIMS
See OBJECTIVE

AIR
AIRCRAFT
ALBATROSS
ALEXANDER
ALIBI
See also EXCUSE
ALICE
ALIMONY
See also DIVORCE, MARRIAGE, WIFE
ALLEGIANCE
See also DUTY, OBEDIENCE, SUBMISSION
ALLEGORY
See also METAPHOR, SIMILE, STORY
ALLEY
ALLIANCE
ALLITERATION
ALL THINGS
ALONE
See also ISOLATION, LONELINESS, SOLI-
TARY, SOLITUDE
ALPH
ALTAR
ALTERATION
See also CHANGE, INNOVATION, NOVELTY
AMAZEMENT
See also ADMIRATION, WONDER
AMBASSADOR
AMBER
AMBITION
See also ASPIRATION, ENVY, FAME: glory
of and desire for
AMBITION: not wholly evil
AMEN
AMERICA
See also COUNTRY, MELTING POT, MON-
ROE DOCTRINE
AMERICAN(S)
AMIABILITY
See also FRIENDSHIP, LOVABLE, SOCIA-
BILITY, SWEETNESS
AMMUNITION
See also GUNS, WAR
AMUSED
See also TICKLE
AMUSEMENT(S)
See also FUN, PLEASURE
ANALYSIS
See also EXAMINATION, LOGIC, PROVE
ANCESTOR(S)
ANCESTRY
See also ANCESTOR(S)
ANCIENT
See also OLD
ANGEL(S)

See also ARCHANGEL, LUCIFER

ANGER

See also CROSS, CROSS PATCH, FURY, MADNESS, PASSION, SLEEVE, TEMPER, WRATH

ANIMAL(S)

See also ADDER, APE, ASS, BEAR, BEAST, BIRDS, BULLOCKS, CAT, CATTLE, COWS, CROCODILE, DEER, DOG, ELEPHANT, EQUAL, FISH, FOXES, HART, HOG, HOLINESS, HORSE, INSECTS, LAMB, LEOPARD, LEVIATHAN, LION, MOLE, MONKEY, MOUSE, MULE, OX, OYSTERS, PIG, PORPOISE, RATS, SHARK, SHEEP, SNAIL, TIGER, TOAD, WEASEL, WILDCAT, WORM, ZOOS

ANNABEL LEE

(QUEEN) ANNE

ANNIE LAURIE

ANNIHILATION

See also DEATH, DESTRUCTION, HEREAFTER, RUIN

ANONYMITY

ANSWER(S)

See also RETORT

ANT

ANTAGONIST

See also ADVERSARY, ENEMY, FOE

ANTHEMS

ANTICIPATION

See also EXPECTATION, PROSPECT

ANTI-CLIMAX

ANTONY

ANVIL

ANXIETY

See also DREAD, FEAR, MISERY, PERPLEXITY, WORRY

AONIAN MOUNT

See also PARNASSUS, POETRY

APE

See also IMITATION, MONKEY

APHORISMS

See also EPIGRAM, MAXIMS, PRECEPT, PROVERBS, WISDOM

APHRODISIAC(S)

APOLOGY

APPAREL

See also CLOTHING, GARMENT

APPARITION

See also DELUSION, HALLUCINATION, PHANTOM, VISION

APPEAL

See also ASKED, PRAYER, SUIT

APPEARANCES

See also COUNTENANCE, SEEMING, SIGHT

APPETITE

See also DESIRE, HUNGER, LUST

APPLAUSE

See also APPROBATION, CHEER, PRAISE

APPLE(S)

APPLIANCES

APPROBATION

See also APPLAUSE, DISLIKE

APRIL

See also SPRING

ARCHANGEL

See also ANGEL

ARCHITECTURE

See also BUILDING, WREN

ARGOT

See also DIALECT, LANGUAGE, SPEECH

ARGUMENT

See also DIFFERENCE OF OPINION, QUARREL, REASON, TELLING, UNDERSTANDING

ARISING

See also EARLY TO BED

ARISTIDES

ARISTOCRACY

See also FOUR HUNDRED, GENTRY, HIGH BIRTH, NOBILITY, SOCIETY, SUPERIOR PEOPLE

ARISTOTLE

ARITHMETIC

See also FIGURES

ARM

ARMCHAIR

ARMED

ARMS (WEAPONS)

See also GUNS, SWORD, WAR

ARMY

See BATTLE, HOST, MILITARY, SOLDIER, STOMACH, TERRIBLE

ARROGANCE

See also CONCEIT, IMPUDENCE, INSOLENCE, PRIDE, RUDENESS, VANITY

ARROW

See also BOLT, BOW

ARSENIC

See also POISON

ART(S)

See also LIMITATION, MICHELANGELO, NATURE, PAINTING, PICTURE, SKILL, STYLE

ARTERIES

ARTHUR

ARTIFICIAL

See also NATURAL, UNNATURAL

ARTIST

See also ART

ASCENT

B

BABBLE
BABE(S)
See also CHILDREN, INFANT
BABY
BABYLON
BACH
BACHELOR
See also BENEDICK, SINGLE LIFE, UN-
MARRIED
BACON
See also MARRIAGE: happiness in
BACON, FRANCIS
BAD NEWS
See also NEWS
BAG
See also SUCKER
BAG AND BAGGAGE
BAIT
See also SEDUCTION, TEMPTATION
BALANCE OF POWER
BALD
BALLAD
See also SONGS
BALLOONISTS
See also AIRCRAFT
BALLOT
BALM
See also CURE, HEALING, REMEDY
BANBURY
BANISHMENT
See also EXILE
BANKRUPT
See also RUIN
BANNER
See also FLAG, STANDARD, TERRIBLE
BARD(S)
See also MINSTREL, POET
BARGAIN
See also NEGOTIATION
BARGE
BARK (OF A DOG)
See also DOG
BARK (SHIP)
See also SHIP
BARNEY BODKIN
BARONETS
BASHFULNESS
See also DIFFIDENCE, MODESTY, SHYNESS
BASSOON

BASTARDS
See also NUTS
BAT(S)
BATHING
See also BATHTUB
BATHOS: illustrations of
See also STYLE
BATHTUB
BATTALIONS
BATTLE
See also FIGHT, WAR, WATERLOO
BAUBLE
BAWDY-HOUSE
See also BROTHEL
BEANS
BEAR
See also STAKE
BEARD(S)
BEAST
See also ANIMALS
BEAT
BEATITUDES
BEAUTY: its follies, ills and dangers.
BEAUTY: its power
BEAUTY: but skin deep
See also COSMETICS
BEAUTY: its transitory nature
BEAUTY: in various women
See also FAIR
BEAUTY: miscellaneous
BED
See also REPOSE, REST, SLEEP
BEDFELLOWS
BEE(S)
See also HONEY, SWEETNESS
BEEF
BEETLE
See also PAIN, SUFFERING
BEGGAR(S)
BEGGING
See also ASKED, PRAYER, SUIT
BEGINNING(S)
See also BIRTH, SOURCE
BEHAVIOR
See also CONDUCT, MANNERS, POLITE-
NESS
BEING
BELIEF

See also CREDENCE, CREDULITY, DOUBT, FAITH, RELIGION

BELL(S)
See also CHIMES, ISLAND, NEW YEAR

BELLE
See also BEAUTY, GIRLS

BELLY
See also GUTS, STOMACH

BENEDICK
See also BACHELOR

BENEDICTION
See also BLESSING, GRACE, PRAYER

BENEFITS
See also GIFTS, PROFIT

BENEFITS: arouse affection in benefactor

BENEFITS: in excess excite animosity

BENT

BERMUDA

BERRY

BEST
See also GOOD

BET
See also WAGER

BETHLEHEM

BETRAYAL
See also TREACHERY

BETTER
See also IMPROVEMENT

BETTER 'OLE

BETTY MARTIN

BEWARE
See also CAUTION

BEWITCHED
See APHRODISIAC, SEDUCTION

BIBLE
See also CHRISTIANITY, RELIGION, SCRIPTURES

BICYCLE

BIGAMY
See also ADULTERY, MARRIAGE, MONOGAMY

BIG BROTHER
See also DESPOTISM, TYRANNY

BIGOT
See also FANATIC, FANATICISM

BIOGRAPHY
See also AUTOBIOGRAPHY

BIRCHES

BIRD(S)
See also ALBATROSS, CASSOWARY, COCK, COCK ROBIN, CROW, CUCKOO, DOVES, EAGLE, FALCON, MARTLET, NET, NIGHTINGALE, OWL, PEACOCK, PELICANS,

PHOEBES, PHOENIX, PIGEONS, RAVEN, ROBIN, SIBLINGS, SKYLARK, SPARROWS, STORK, SWALLOW, SWAN, THRUSH, WREN

BIRDS: fly together and agree in their nests

BIRD: in a gilded cage

BIRD: in the hand
See also CARPE DIEM

BIRD: an ill, that fouls its own nest

BIRTH
See also CRADLE, DEATH, NATIVITY, SHAVING

BIRTH: the beginning of woe

BIRTHRIGHT

BISHOP
See also CLERGY, PARSON

BITTER
See also SWEET

BITTERNESS
See also SWEETNESS

BLACKBIRD(S)

BLACK SHEEP
See also DISGRACE, ROGUE

BLACKSMITH

BLAME
See also ACCUSATION, CENSURE, DISGRACE, FAULT

BLASPHEMY(IES)
See also GOD: some irreverent comments on, SACRILEGE, SIN

BLEMISHED
See also DEFECT, FAULT, IMPERFECTION

BLESSED
See also HOLY

BLESSING
See also BENEDICTION, CURSE, GRACE

BLIND
See also EYELESS, SIGHT

BLINDNESS
See also EYELESS

BLISS
See also DELIGHT, ECSTASY, HAPPINESS

BLOCKHEAD(S)
See also DUNCE

BLONDE(S)

BLOOD

BLOODY

BLOOM
See also FLOWER

BLOT
See also BLEMISHED, DEFECT, FAULT

BLOW
See also ATTACK, EVEN

BLUE

BROADWAY
BROOK
See also RIVER, STREAM
BROOM
BROTHELS
See also BAWDY HOUSE
BROTHER(S)
See also FAMILY, MANKIND,
BROWN, JOHN
See also SLAVERY
BROWNING
BRUTUS
BRYAN, WILLIAM JENNINGS
BUCKET
See also WELL
BUCKINGHAM PALACE
BUGBEARS
See also TERROR
BUGS
See also BUGBEARS, TERROR
BUILDING
See also ARCHITECTURE, WREN
BULK
BULL
See also BLUNDER, IMPUDENCE
BULLET
See also BALLOT
BULLOCKS
BUM
See also LOAFING, WANDERERS
BUNK
See also ABSURDITY, DRIVEL, NONSENSE
BURDEN(S)

See also LOAD
BURGLAR
See also CHEAT, ROBBERY, ROGUE, THIEF
BURIAL
See also DEATH, GRAVE, SHROUD
BURIAL SERVICE
BURIED
BURKE, EDMUND
BURNS, ROBERT
See also JOIE DE VIVRE
BURY
BUSINESS
See also BUYER, COMMERCE, CORPORA-
TIONS, GETTING AND SPENDING, MAR-
KET, MOTION, SELLING, SHOPKEEPERS,
TRADE
BUSINESSMAN
See also COMMERCE, GETTING AND
SPENDING, MERCHANT
BUSY
See also ACTIONS, DOING
BUTTER
BUTTERCUP
BUTTERFLY
BUYER
See also COMMERCE, GETTING AND SPEND-
ING, MARKET, PRICE, SELLING
BUYING
See also BUSINESS, BUYER, COMMERCE,
GETTING AND SPENDING, MARKET,
TRADE
BYRON

CAD
See also SCOUNDREL, VILLAIN
CAESAR
See also RUBICON, VENI VIDI VICI
CAIN
CAKE
CALAIS
CALAMITY(IES)
See also MISFORTUNE, TROUBLE
CALIFORNIA
CALM

See also COMPOSURE, EQUANIMITY,
PATIENCE, PEACE, PHILOSOPHIC,
REPOSE, SMOOTH, TRANQUILITY
CALUMNY
See also RUMOR, SCANDAL, SLANDER,
LIBEL
CALVINISM
CAMOMILE
CANDID
See also FRANKNESS, JUST, OUTSPOKEN
CANDLE(S)

See also KNAVERY, PLAGIARY, PYRA-
MIDS, THEFT
CHEEK
CHEER
See also APPLAUSE, REJOICE, ROAR,
SHOUT, TOAST
CHEERFULNESS
See also MIRTH, OPTIMISM, SERENITY
CHESTERFIELD
See also PATRON
CHESTNUT
See also PLATITUDE
CHICAGO
CHICKEN(S)
See also HEN, SLIP
CHIEF
See also KING, LEADER, MASTER, RULER
CHIEFTAIN
CHILD
See also BABE, BABY, CHILDREN, FEAR:
the burnt child, INFANT, ROD
CHILDHOOD
CHILDREN
See also CHILD, DISCIPLINE, FAMILY,
GOLF, PARENTS: and children, PRO-
GENY, WIFE: and children
CHILDREN: their drawbacks
CHIMAERA
See also ILLUSION
CHIMES
See also BELLS
CHINEE
CHIP OFF THE OLD BLOCK
CHIVALRY
See also COURTESY, GALLANTRY, GOOD
MANNERS
CHOICE
See also CALLED, HOBSON'S CHOICE,
ROADS
CHORTLING
See also LAUGHTER
CHRIST
See JESUS CHRIST
CHRISTIAN(S)
CHRISTIANITY
See also BIBLE, FAITH, GOSPEL, JESUS
CHRIST, RELIGION
CHRISTMAS
CHRONICLER
See also HISTORIANS
CHURCH(ES)
See also CATHEDRALS, CLERGY, PAPACY,
RELIGION, SALUTATION, THEOLOGY
CICERO
CIGAR

See also TOBACCO
CIRCLE
See also GIOTTO'S O
CIRCUMSTANCE(S)
CITIZEN
CITY(IES)
See also, CHICAGO, COLOGNE, GOTHAM,
LONDON, MANDALAY, MANHATTAN,
PARIS, ROME, TOWN, VENICE
CIVILIAN
CIVILITIES
See also COURTESY, MANNERS, POLITE-
NESS, RESPECT
CIVILIZATION
CIVILIZE
CLARET
CLARITY
See also LUCID
CLASSICS
See also LITERATURE
CLAWS
CLAY
See also CORPSE
CLEANLINESS
See also PURITY
CLEAR
See also LUCID
CLEOPATRA
CLERGY
See also BISHOP, CURATE, PARSON,
PIETY, PRIEST, RELIGION, THEOLOGIAN
CLEVER
See also EXPERT, WIT
CLIFFS OF DOVER
CLOCK
See also TIMEPIECE
CLOTHING
See also APPAREL, GARMENT, LINEN,
PANTS, PETTICOAT, ROBE
CLOUD(S)
See also PILLAR, RAIN
CLUB
See also SOCIABILITY
COALS
COALS OF FIRE
See also SELF-REPROACH
COAST
See also SHORE
COCK
COCK A DOODLE DOO
COCK ROBIN
COEDUCATION
See also EDUCATION
COFFEE
COFFEE SPOONS

See also TIMIDITY
COGITATION
See also CONTEMPLATION, DRINKING:
and thinking, PHILOSOPHY, THOUGHT
COITION
See also CONCEPTION, FORNICATION
COLD
See also FROST, ICE, ICICLES, SNOW
COLERIDGE
COLLAPSE
COLLEGE
See also EDUCATION, LEARNING
COLOGNE
COLONIZING
COLOSSUS
COLUMBIA
See also AMERICA, UNITED STATES
COLUMBUS
COMEDY
See also TRAGEDY
COMFORT
See also CONSOLATION, LUXURY, SNUG,
SYMPATHY
COMFORTERS
See also ROD
COMING
COMMAND
See also AUTHORITY, DECREE, PRECEPT
COMMANDMENTS
COMMERCE
See also BUSINESS, BUYER, GETTING
AND SPENDING, MARKET, RECIPROCITY,
SELLING, SHOPKEEPERS, TRADE
COMMERCIALISM
See also ECONOMICS, GETTING AND
SPENDING, MARKET, SELLING, SHOP-
KEEPERS
COMMON
See also VULGAR
COMMONALTY
COMMONPLACE
See also DULL, STALE
COMMON SENSE
See also HORSE SENSE
COMMUNICATION(S)
COMMUNIST
COMPANION
COMPANY
COMPARISONS: are odious
COMPASSION
See also KINDNESS, MILDNESS, PITY,
SYMPATHY
COMPETITION
See also EMULATION, RACE
COMPLACENCY

See also ASSURANCE, SELF-CONFIDENCE,
SMUGNESS
COMPLAIN(ING)
See also CRYING, FAULT FINDING,
LAMENTATION, PEEVISHNESS, WEEPING
COMPLEXION
COMPLIANCE
See also AGREEMENT, OBEDIENCE,
YIELDING
COMPLIMENT
See also PRAISE, TOAST
COMPOSING
COMPOSURE
See also CALM, EQUANIMITY, PHILOSO-
PHY, SELF-CONTROL
COMPROMISE
COMPUNCTION
See also REGRET, REMORSE
CONCEALMENT
CONCEIT
See also ARROGANCE, PRIDE, VANITY
CONCEPTION
See also COITION, FORNICATION
CONCESSIONS
See also PRIVILEGE
CONCLUSION
See also END
CONCORD
See also AGREEMENT, HARMONY
CONDEMNATION
See also CENSURE
CONDESCENSION
See also ARROGANCE, CONCEIT, IN-
SOLENCE, PRIDE
CONDUCT
See also BEHAVIOR, MANNERS
CONFESS
CONFESSION
See also OMISSION
CONFIDENCE
See also ASSURANCE, EXPECTATION,
HOPE, OPTIMISM
CONFINEMENT
CONFLICT
See also INTERFERENCE, STRIFE
CONFORMITY
See also AGREEMENT
CONFUSION
See also CHAOS, RIOT
CONGREGATION
See also AUDIENCE
CONGRESS
CONNUBIALITY
See also MARRIAGE
CONQUER

See also DEFEAT
CONSCIENCE
See also GUILT, MORALITY, SCRUPLES,
SELF-REPROACH
CONSCIENCE: cynical and worldly
views of
CONSECRATION
See also HOLINESS, PIETY
CONSENT
See AGREEMENT, PERMISSION,
YIELDING
CONSEQUENCES
See also END, HARVEST
CONSERVATISM
See also LIBERALISM
CONSERVATIVES
CONSIDERATION
See also MILDNESS, RESPECT
CONSISTENCY
See also CONSTANCY, HARMONY
CONSOLATION
See also COMFORT
CONSPICUOUS
See OSTENTATION
CONSTANCY
See also CONSISTENCY, FICKLENESS,
FLIRTATION, LOVE: capricious and un-
certain, LOVE: constancy in, PER-
SEVERANCE, TENACITY
CONSTANT
See also RESOLUTE
CONSTITUTION: of the U.S., Fifth
Amendment
CONSTITUTION: of the U.S.,
Preamble
CONSUMPTION
See also ECONOMICS, GETTING AND
SPENDING
CONTEMPLATION
See also COGITATION
CONTEMPT
See also FAMILIARITY: breeds contempt,
RIDICULE, SATIRE, SCORN, YOUTH AND
AGE: their mutual contempt
CONTENT(ED)
See also RICH: and content
CONTENTION
See also ARGUMENT, STRIFE, QUARREL-
ING, CONTRADICTION
CONTENTMENT
See also PEACE, SATISFACTION
CONTRADICTION
See also DEFIANCE, OPPOSITION, PARA-
DOXES, PROTEST, QUARREL
CONTRITE

See HEART: the sad and broken
heart, PENANCE, REGRET, REPENTENT-
ANCE
CONVENTIONALITY
See also ORTHODOXY, RESPECTABLE
CONVERSATION
See also ARGUMENT, DEBATE, DISCOURSE,
SPEECH, TOPICS
CONVERSION
CONVICTION(S)
See also CERTAINTY, TRUST
COOK
COOKING
See also FOOD
COQUETTE
See also FLIRTATION
CORD
See also UNITY
CORIOLANUS
CORN
CORPORATIONS
CORPSE
See also BODY, CLAY, DEAD, DEATH
CORRECTION
See also REPROOF
CORRESPONDENCE
See also LETTERS
CORROBORATION
See also PROOF
CORRUPTION
See also DECAY, KNAVERY, POISON,
POWER: corrupts, ROTTEN
CORTEZ
COSMETICS
See also BEAUTY: but skin deep
COSMOPOLITAN
COSMOPOLITE
COST
See also EXPENDITURE, PRICE
COUGH
COUNSEL
See also ADVICE
COUNTENANCE
See also APPEARANCES
COUNTING
COUNTRY (PATRIOTISM)
See also PATRIOTISM, STATE
COURAGE
See also AUDACITY, BOLDNESS, FEAR,
FORTITUDE, HEROISM, TEMERITY, VALOR
COURIERS
COURSE
See also SELF-REPROACH
COURT
COURTESY

See also CIVILITIES, MANNERS, POLITENESS,
RESPECT, RUDENESS

COURTING
See also FLIRTATION, GALLANTRY, KISSES,
MARRIAGE, PHILANDERING, ROMANCE

COVENTRY

COVET
See also COMMANDMENTS, DESIRES,
ENVY, LONGINGS

COVETOUS

COVETOUSNESS
See also ENVY

COW(S)

COWARD(S)
See also FIGHT: he who fights and
runs away

COWARDICE
See also COURAGE, DISCRETION, PRU-
DENCE, TERROR, TIMIDITY, VALOR

COYNESS
See also SHYNESS

CRADLE

CRAFT
See also CUNNING, KNAVERY, SKILL

CREATION

CREDENCE
See also BELIEF, FAITH, TRUST

CREDO

CREDULITY
See also BELIEF, DISBELIEF, DOUBT, FAITH

CRICKET

CRIME
See also OFFENSE, SIN

CRIMINAL
See also FELON, OUTLAW, SINNER,
TRANSGRESSOR

CRISIS

CRITIC(S)
See also AMBER

CRITICAL
See also CENSURE

CRITICISM
See also BOOK REVIEW

CROCODILE
See also HYPOCRISY

CROMWELL
See also MISTAKEN

CROSS

CROSS (ANGRY)
See also PEEVISHNESS

CROSS-PATCH

CROSS-WORD PUZZLES

CROW

CROWD
See also HERD, POPULACE, VULGAR

CROWN

CRUCIFIXION
See also CROSS, JESUS CHRIST

CRUELTY
See also FISHING, INHUMANITY, NATURE:
wise, eternal, mysterious, cruel,
RUTHLESSNESS, UNKINDNESS

CRUSADER
See also WARRIOR

CRUST
See also BREAD, PROVIDENCE

CRY(ING)
See also LAMENTATION, TEARS, WAILING,
WEEPING

CUCKOLD(S)
See also ADULTERY, MARRIAGE: regrets,
dangers, and woes

CUCKOO

CUCUMBER

CULTURE

CUNNING
See also CRAFT, KNAVERY, SKILL, WISDOM

CUP

CUPID

CURATE
See also CLERGY, PARSON

CURE
See also DOCTORS, HEALING, MEDICINE,
PHYSICIANS, REMEDY, SICKNESS

CURFEW

CURIOSITY: admirable

CURIOSITY: dangerous and wicked

CURIOUS

CURLY LOCKS

CURSE(S)(ING)
See also BLESSING, OATHS, PROFANITY,
SACRILEGE, SWEARING

CURTAIN LECTURE
See also HENPECKED, HUSBANDS AND
WIVES

CURZON

CUSTOM(S)
See also DISHONESTY, HABIT, LAW,
MANNERS, MANNER BORN

CYNIC

CYNICISM

D

DAFFODILS
DAGGER
DAISY
DALHOUSIE
DALLIANCE
See also: GALLANTRY, PHILANDERING,
ROMANCE
DAMNED
See also HELL, LOST
DAMP
DAMSEL
See also DULCIMER, GIRLS, MAIDENS,
WENCH
DAN
DANCE(ING)
See also WALTZ
DANGER(S)
See also ADVENTURE, FEAR: the danger
of, PERILS, RISK, TRUTH: dangers of
telling, WOMAN: danger of her
allure
DANIEL
DAPPLED THINGS
DARE(ING)
See also COURAGE, DEFIANCE, FEAR
DARK(NESS)
See also LIGHT, OBSCURITY
DARLING(S)
DARWIN
See also EVOLUTION
DAUGHTER(S)
See also CHILDREN, FAMILY, FATHER,
MOTHER
DAWN
See also DAY, MORNING, SUNRISE
DAY(S)
See also AFTERNOON, DAWN, EVENING,
MORNING, NOON, SUNRISE DAY: and
night
DAY: day and night
DAYLIGHT
See also SUN, SUNSHINE
DEAD
See also DOORNAIL, LOST
DEAF(NESS)
See also EARS, HEAR, LISTEN
DEAR
DEATH
See also ANNIHILATION, BIRTH, BURIAL,
DROWNING, DUST, DYING, GUILLOTINE,

LIFE: and death, LIVING, LOVE: and
death, MARRIED LOVE, MORTALITY,
SLEEP: and death, SUICIDE, VALLEY,
WAR: and death
DEATH: the act of dying
DEATH: brings oblivion
DEATH: brings peace
DEATH: comes to all
DEATH: its compensations and rewards
DEATH: the conqueror
DEATH: devoutly to be wished
DEATH: the end of woe
DEATH: an enigma
DEATH: fears and terrors
DEATH: its finality
DEATH: the grisly specter
DEATH: implacable
DEATH: inevitable
DEATH: the leveller
DEATH: loneliness
DEATH: longing for
DEATH OF KINGS
DEATH: peaceful
DEATH: proud death
DEATH: readiness for
DEATH: reunion in
DEATH: a sleep
DEATH: sudden
DEATH: triumph over
DEATH: general and miscellaneous
DEATHBED UTTERANCES
DEBATE
See also ARGUMENT, DIALOGUE,
REASON
DEBT(S)
See also LIABILITIES
DEBTORS
DECAY
See also CORRUPTION, ROTTEN
DECEMBER
DECENCY
See also CHASTITY, MODESTY, PROPER,
PURITY
DECEPTION
See also DISSEMBLE, DISSIMULATION,
FRAUD, HOAX, KNAVERY, LYING,
SIMULATION, SOPHISTRY
DECISION
See also CONCLUSION, RESOLVE, ROADS
DECLINE

See also AVERNUS

DECREE
See also COMMAND, ORDER, STATUTES

DEE
See MILLER

DEED(S)
See also ACTIONS, ANONYMITY, DOING, EVENTS, NAUGHTY

DEEP

DEER

DEFEAT
See also CONQUER, FAILURE, LOSS, RUIN, VANQUISHED, VICTORY

DEFECT
See also FAULT, FEET OF CLAY, IMPERFECTION

DEFENSE
See also PROTECTION

DEFIANCE
See also DARE, IMPUDENCE, OPPOSITION, REBELLION

DEFILE
See also PITCH

DEFORMITY
See also CRAFT

DEGREE
See also ORDER

DEJECTION
See also DESPAIR, DESPONDENCY, HOPE: deferred, MELANCHOLY

DELAY
See also PROCRASTINATION

DELIBERATION
See also COGITATION, THOUGHTS: second

DELICACY
See also MODESTY, TACT

DELICATELY

DELIGHT(S)
See also DRINKING: delights of, ECSTASY, JOY, LOVE: its delights, MARRIAGE: delights and compensations, MONEY: its delights, PLEASURE, REJOICE, TRAVEL: delights of, WOMAN: man's delight in, YOUTH: its glory and delights

DELIVERANCE
See also HELP, RELIEF, SALVATION

DELIVERER

DELUGE
See also RAIN, STORM

DELUSION
See also HALLUCINATION, HOPE: the delusion of, ILLUSION, WILL-O-THE-WISP

DEMOCRACY

See also ARISTOCRACY, EQUAL, EQUALITARIANISM, EQUALITY, LEVELLING

DENIAL
See also PROHIBITION, REFUSAL, REJECTION

DENMARK

DEPARTURE
See also FAREWELL, FRENCH LEAVE, PARTING

DEPENDENCE

DEPTH(S)
See also DEEP, PROFUNDITY

DERISION
See also CONTEMPT, RAILLERY, RIDICULE, SARCASM, SATIRE, SCORN

DESCENT INTO AVERNUS
See AVERNUS

DESCRIPTION

DESERT
See also URGENCY, WILDERNESS

DESERTION
See also LONELINESS, PARTING, TREACHERY

DESIGN
See also MEANING, PATTERNS, PLAN, SYSTEM, TELEOLOGY

DESIRE(S)
See also COVET, IMPULSE, WISHES

DESIRE (SEXUAL)
See also APPETITE, FORBIDDEN, LUST, PASSION

DESOLATION
See also DESERT, DREARY, WILDERNESS

DESPAIR
See also DEJECTION, HOPE: deferred, HOPE: and despair, MELANCHOLY, SUICIDE

DESPERATE MEN

DESPERATION
See also PESSIMISM

DESPONDENCY
See also DEJECTION, HOPE: deferred, MELANCHOLY, PESSIMISM

DESPOT
See also TYRANTS

DESPOTISM
See also FRANCE, POWER, RULE

DESTINY
See also FATE, FREE WILL, LUCK

DESTRUCTION
See also ANNIHILATION, DEFEAT, LOSS, PERDITION, RUIN

DETAIL(S)

DETERMINATION

See also LINE, PERSEVERANCE, RESOLUTE, RESOLVE

DETESTATION
See also HATE, REVULSION

DETRACTION
See also ENVY, LIBEL, SLANDER

DEVIL
See also FIEND, LEGION, LUCIFER, SATAN, SHADOW

DEVOTION
See also FAITHFULNESS, PIETY, SELF-SACRIFICE, SUNFLOWER

DEW-DROPS

DEWEY
See also FIRE, PRESIDENCY

DIALECT

DIALOGUE
See also ARGUMENT, CONVERSATION, DE-BATE, DISCOURSE

DIAMONDS

DIANA

DIARIES

DICE
See also CHANCE, GAMBLING, HAZARD

DICKENS

DICKINSON, EMILY

DICTATORS
See also DESPOT, TYRANTS

DICTIONARY(IES)
See also LEXICOGRAPHER

DIE
See also CHANCE, DICE, HAZARD

DIET
See also DINNER, FEAST, GOOD CHEER, HUNGER, ROAST BEEF

DIFFER
See also PROTEST

DIFFERENCE(S)
See also DISTINCTION, INCONSISTENCY

DIFFERENCE OF OPINION
See ARGUMENT

DIFFICULTY
See also TROUBLE

DIFFIDENCE
See also BASHFUNESS, COWARDICE, FEAR, MODESTY, PRUDENCE, SHYNESS, TIMID-ITY

DIGNITY
See also AGE: its beauty and dignity, AUTHORITY, PRIDE, SOLEMNITY, SUB-LIMITY

DILIGENCE
See also CELERITY, INDUSTRY, PERSEVER-ANCE, SPEED, STRENUOUS

DINING

See also EATING

DINING OUT
See also SOCIABILITY, SOCIETY

DINNER

DIPLOMACY
See also TACT

DIRT
See also OBSCENITY, VILE

DISADVANTAGE
See also FAULT, WEAKNESS

DISAPPOINTMENT
See also CONTRITE, FAILURE, HOPE: de-ferred, REGRET, REMORSE

DISAPPROBATION
See also FROWN, PROTEST, REPREHENSION

DISBELIEF
See also BELIEF, DOUBT, FAITH, REJEC-TION

DISCIPLINE
See also COMMAND, EDUCATION, PUN-ISHMENT, RESTRAINT, ROD, TRAINING

DISCONTENT(S)
See also DISSATISFACTION

DISCORD
See also CONFLICT, HARMONY, STRIFE

DISCOURSE
See also ARGUMENT, DEBATE, DIALOGUE, TOPICS

DISCOVERY
See also INVENTION

DISCRETION
See also COWARDICE, FIGHT: he who fights and runs away, PRUDENCE

DISCRETION: the better part of valor

DISDAIN
See CONTEMPT, SCORN

DISGRACE
See also BLACK SHEEP, HUMILIATION, INFAMY, ROGUE, SHAME, VILE

DISHES

DISHONESTY
See also LYING

DISHONOR
See also DISGRACE, HUMILIATION, INFAMY, SHAME

DISLIKE
See also AVERSION, DISGUST, DOCTOR FELL HATE, HATRED, REVULSION

DISOBEDIENCE
See also OBEDIENCE, REBELLION

DISORDER
See also TROUBLE

DISSATISFACTION
See also INGRATITUDE, RESTLESSNESS

DISSEMBLE(ING)

See also CONCEALMENT
DISSENSION
See also ARGUMENT, DIFFERENCE OF
OPINION, DISCOURSE, STRIFE
DISSIMULATION
See also DECEPTION, DISSEMBLE, DISSIM-
ULATION, FRAUD, HOAX, HYPOCRISY,
LYING
DISTANCE
See also FORMALITY
DISTINCTION
See also DIFFERENCE
DIVORCE
See also ALIMONY, MARRIAGE, WIFE
DIXIE
See also KENTUCKY, THE SOUTH, VIR-
GINNY
DO
See also ACTIONS, DEEDS
DOCTOR(S)
See also PHYSICIANS
DOCTOR FELL
DOCTRINES
See also DOGMA, PROPAGANDA, TEACH-
ING
DOG
See also CERBERUS, HOUNDS, MOTHER
HUBBARD, PREACHING, VOMIT
DOG: love me, love my dog
DOG: man's best friend
DOG: unfavorable.
DOG: general and favorable
DOGGEREL
See also POETRY, rhyme
DOGMA
See also DOCTRINES, ORTHODOXY, PROPA-
GANDA, RELIGION, THEOLOGY
DOGMATISM
See also CERTAINTY, CONVICTION,
FANATICISM
DOING
See also ACTIONS, DEEDS, GOOD: doing
good
DO-IT-YOURSELF
See also SELF-RELIANCE
DOLLAR
DOMESTICITY
See also FAMILY, HOME, MARRIAGE: de-
lights and compensations
DOMINANCE
See also MASTER(S), RULE
DOMINION
See also AUTHORITY, MASTER, POWER,
RULE
DOORNAIL

See also DEAD
DOORS
See also KNOCK, MOUSETRAP
DOTAGE
See also AGE, SENILITY
DOTS
DOUBT(S)
See also DISBELIEF, FAITH: and doubt,
MISTRUST, SCRUPLES, SUSPENSE
DOUGHNUT
DO UNTO OTHERS
DOVE(S)
See also PIGEONS
DOWN
DRAGONS
DRAMA
See also COMEDY, PLAYS, THEATER, TRAG-
EDY
DREAD
See also FEAR, FRIGHT, TERROR
DREAM(S)
See also ASPIRATION, NIGHTMARE, SLEEP,
VISIONS
DREAMER(S)
DREAMING
See also SLEEP, STARGAZING
DREARY
See also DESOLATION, STALE
DRESSING TABLE
DRINKER
DRINKING
See CLARET, DRUNK, DRUNKENNESS,
GOUT, LIQUOR, TOAST, WINE
DRINKING: delights of
DRINKING: and thinking
DRINKING: woes and perils
DRINKING: miscellaneous
DRIVEL
See also BUNK, CANT, NONSENSE
DROP
See also SOCIETY
DROWNING
DRUNK
See also APPEAL
DRUNKARD(S)
DRUNKENNESS
See also DRINKING
DRYDEN
See also POPE, ALEXANDER
DUCHESS
DULCIMER
DULL
See also SLOW, STALE, TEDIOUS
DULLNESS

See also WEARINESS
DUNCE
See also BLOCKHEAD, FOOL, INTENTIONS,
   MORON, WAG
DUST
See also CLAY, DEATH
DUTY

See also MORALITY, OBLIGATION, RIGHT,
   WIFE: the dutiful wife
DWARF
DYING
See also DEATH, LIVING
DYING WORDS
See also SALUTATION

EAGLE
EAR(S)
See also DEAF, HEAR
EARLY TO BED
EARNEST
See also RESOLUTE, SERIOUS, SINCERITY,
   SOLEMNITY
EARTH
See also UNIVERSE, WORLD
EASE
See also IDLENESS, LEISURE, LUXURY, RE-
   POSE, REST, SLOTH
EAST
EAST AND WEST
See also WEST
EAT, DRINK AND BE MERRY
See also DRINKING, FEAST, ORGIES, REV-
   ELRY
EATEN
EATING
See also DINING, DINING OUT, DINNER,
   FOOD, GLUTTONY, HUNGER
ECCENTRICITY
See also INDIVIDUALISM, ODDITIES
ECHOES
ECLIPSE
See also OBSCURITY
ECONOMICS
See also CONSUMPTION, INCREMENT, MAR-
   KET
ECONOMY
See FRUGALITY, THRIFT
ECSTASY
See also DELIGHT, FALCON, JOY, PLEAS-
   URE
EDEN
See also ADAM AND EVE, PARADISE, PARA-
   DISE LOST

EDUCATION
See also COEDUCATION, GAMALIEL,
   KNOWLEDGE, LEARNING, LIBERAL EDU-
   CATION, MARK HOPKINS, NATURE: the
   great teacher, PEDANTRY, PHILOSO-
   PHY, SCHOLARS, SCIENCE, TEACHER,
   TRAINING, TWIG
EFFEMINACY
See also FOP
EFFICIENCY
EGG(S)
See also HEN
EGOISM
EGOTISM
See also APOLOGY, CONCEIT, MYSELF,
   PRIDE, PROUD, SELF-LOVE, SELF-ESTEEM
ELEPHANT(S)
ELEVATION
See also GREATNESS, HEIGHT, SUBLIMITY
EL GRECO
ELISHA
ELIZABETH
ELOQUENCE
See also ACTION: in eloquence, SILENCE:
   its eloquence, SPEECH, VERBOSITY
ELOQUENT
ELVES
See FAIRIES, GLOW WORM, GOBLINS
EMBERS
See also LIGHT
EMBRYO(S)
EMERSON
EMINENCE
See also ELEVATION, GREATNESS, HEIGHT,
   REPUTATION, SUBLIMITY
EMPEROR
See also MARCUS AURELIUS, MISCHIEF,
   MYSTERIES, NECK

EMPHASIS
EMPIRE
See also ADMIRALTY, PAPACY, RHODES
(CECIL), RULE
EMPTY(INESS)
See also PURGE, STERILITY, VACUUM, VAN-
ITY
EMULATION
See also ENVY, RIVALRY
ENCOURAGEMENT
See ADMIRAL, ASSURANCE, CONFIDENCE,
HOPE, PERSUASION, STIMULATION
END(S)
See also CONCLUSION, MEANS, NEVER-
MORE, OBJECTIVE, RUST
ENDURANCE
See also FORTITUDE, HEROISM, PATIENCE,
PERSEVERANCE, RESIGNATION,
STOICISM, SUBMISSION, SUFFERANCE,
TOLERATION
ENDURE(D)
See also ABIDE, KEEP, SURVIVAL
ENEMY(IES)
See also ADVERSARY, ANTAGONIST, FOE,
FRIENDS: and enemies, FRIGHT
ENGLAND
See also BRITTANIA, HOMES
ENGLISH (LANGUAGE)
See also LANGUAGE, SPEECH
ENGLISH (PEOPLE)
ENJOY
ENJOYMENT
See also AIMS, CARPE DIEM, DELIGHT,
PLEASURE
ENLIGHTENMENT
ENMITY
See also ENEMIES, HATE, MALICE, RAN-
COR
ENOUGH
See also PLENTY, RICH: and content,
SATIETY, SUFFICIENT
ENTHUSIASM
See also ZEAL
ENVY
See also COVETOUSNESS, EMULATION,
JEALOUSY, SOUR GRAPES
EPICS
EPICURUS
EPIDEMICS
See also PLAGUE
EPIGRAM
See also WIT, APHORISM(S), PROVERBS
EPITAPHS: comment on
EPITAPHS: famous and curious
EPITAPHS: mock and literary

EPITAPHS: self-written
E PLURIBUS UNUM
EQUAL
EQUALITARIANISM
See also ARISTOCRACY, DEMOCRACY,
EQUAL, EQUALITY, LEVELLING
EQUALITY
See also EQUAL, EQUALITARIANISM
EQUANIMITY
See also CALM, COMPOSURE, SELF-CON-
TROL
EQUESTRIANISM
EQUITY
See also INJUSTICE, JUSTICE, LAW, REC-
TITUDE, RIGHT
EQUIVOCATION
See also DISSIMULATION, LYING,
SOPHISTRY, WEASEL WORDS
ERASMUS
ERR
See also MISTAKEN, MISTAKES
ERRANDS
ERROR
See also BLUNDERS, MISTAKES
ESTATE
See also HERITAGE, PROPERTY
ETERNAL
ETERNITY
See also FOREVER, TIME: and eternity
ETYMOLOGY
See also WORD
EUNUCHS
EUREKA
EUROPE
EUXINE
EVANGELISM
See also GOSPEL, PROPAGANDA, RELIGION,
ZEAL
EVASION
See also SECRECY, WEASEL WORDS
EVEN
EVENING
See also AFTERNOON, GLOAMING, SUNSET,
TWILIGHT
EVENT(S)
See also DEED(S)
EVER
See also ETERNAL, ETERNITY, FOREVER,
TIME: and eternity
EVERYONE
EVIDENCE
See also EXPERIENCE, FACTS, PROOF
EVIL
See also GOOD: and evil, HARM, HEART:

the evil heart, MISCHIEF, NAUGHTY, SIN, VICE, VILE, WICKED, WRONG

EVOLUTION
See also DARWIN, MAN: evolution and his animal nature, NATURAL SELECTION, PROGRESS, TADPOLE

EXAGGERATION
See also HYPERBOLE

EXAMINATION(S)
See also OBSERVATION, QUESTIONING, RESEARCH

EXAMPLE(S)
See also GLASS, MODEL, PRECEPT, STANDARD

EXCELLENCE
See also SUPERIORITY

EXCELSIOR
See AMBITION, ASPIRATION, IDEALS, STRIVING

EXCEPTION
See also RARENESS

EXCESS
See also LUXURY, PLENTY, SATIETY, SUPERFLUOUS, SURFEIT, TOO MUCH

EXCHANGE
See also RECIPROCITY, SWAP

EXCISE
See also TAXATION

EXCUSE(S)
See also ALIBI, EXTENUATE, ORPHAN, PARDON

EXECUTION
See also GUILLOTINE, HANGING, NECK VERSE, TACT

EXECUTIONER

EXERCISE
See also PRACTICE

EXILE
See also ARISTIDES, BANISHMENT, REJECTION

EXPECTATION
See also ANTICIPATION, DISAPPOINTMENT, HOPE

EXPEDIENCE
See also VICAR OF BRAY

EXPENDITURE
See also COST, PAYMENT, PRICE, WOMAN: expensive to maintain

EXPERIENCE
See also PROOF

EXPERIENCE: keeps a dear school

EXPERT
See also CLEVER, SKILL

EXPLANATION
See also GLOSSING, MEANING

EXPLORATION
See also PURSUIT

EXPRESSION
See FACES, LANGUAGE, SPEECH, STYLE, WORDS

EXTENUATE
See also EXCUSE, VINDICATION

EXTREME(S)

EYE(S)
See also HYPNOTISM, SIGHT

EYE FOR AN EYE

EYELESS
See also BLIND, BLINDNESS

FACE(S)
See also WRINKLE

FACTS
See also EVIDENCE, EXPERIENCE, PROOF

FAERY
See also FAIRIES

FAILINGS
See also WEAKNESS

FAILURE(S)
See also DISAPPOINTMENT, GREATEST, REGRET

FAIN
See also GLADNESS

FAINT
See also WEAKNESS

FAIR
See also BEAUTY, JUST, RIGHT

FAIRIES

See also ELVES, FAERY, GOBLINS
FAIRY TALES
See also FICTION, NARRATIVE, STORY,
TALES
FAITH
See also BELIEF, CREDULITY, DISBELIEF,
DOUBT, EVIDENCE, HERESY,
ORTHODOXY, SCIENTIFIC SPIRIT,
TRUST
FAITH: and doubt
FAITH: in the impossible
FAITHFUL
See also FALSE, LOVE: faithful and
faithless, TRUE
FAITHFULNESS
See also DEVOTION, SUNFLOWER
FALCON
FALL
See also HUMPTY-DUMPTY, STUMBLE
FALSE
See also MISTAKEN, TRUE, UNFAITHFUL,
WRONG
FALSEHOOD
See also LYING
FALSE SECURITY
See also DANGER, SAFETY, SECURITY
FAME
See CELEBRITY, GLORY, HONOR, IM-
MORTALITY, NAME, POPULARITY, REPU-
TATION
FAME: absurdity, impermanence, inad-
equacy, injustice, and irony of
FAME: glory of and desire for
FAME: miscellaneous
FAMILIAR
FAMILIARITY
See also EASE
FAMILIARITY BREEDS CONTEMPT
FAMILY(IES)
See also CHILDREN, DAUGHTERS, FATHER,
FATHER AND SON, GRANDPARENTS, HUS-
BANDS AND WIVES, KIN, MOTHER,
PARENTS, RELATIONS, RELATIVES, SONS,
WIFE
FAMINE
See also FEAST, HUNGER
FANATIC
FANATICISM
See also DOGMATISM, OBSESSION, RELI-
GION, ZEAL
FANCY
See also IMAGINATION, ROMANCE
FANCY-FREE
See also INDEPENDENT
FAREWELL(S)

See also ADIEU, DEPARTURE, BOOK:
l'envoi, PARTING
FARMER(S)
See also RUSTICS, PEASANTS, SHOT
FARMING
See also AGRICULTURE, PLOW
FASHION
See also CUSTOM, REJECTION, STYLE,
TASTE
FAST(ING)
See also HUNGER
FAT
See also STOUTNESS
FATALISM
See also KISMET, RESIGNATION
FATALITY
See ACCIDENT, CHANCE, DEATH, MO-
RALITY
FATE(S)
See also CHANCE, DESTINY, FREE WILL,
NECESSITY
FATHER(S)
See also CHILDREN, DAUGHTER(s),
SON(s)
FATHER AND SON
See also RAINBOW, SONS
FATHER WILLIAM
FATTED CALF
FAULT(S)
See also DEFECT, DISADVANTAGE, GENER-
OUS, IMPERFECTION, WEAKNESS
FAULT-FINDING
See also COMPLAINING
FAVOR(S)
See also TURN
FAVORITE
See also DARLINGS
FAWNING
See also FLATTERY
FEAR
See also AGE: its fears, ANXIETY, CON-
CESSIONS, DARE, DEATH: fears and ter-
rors, DEATH: the grisly specter, DREAD,
FOREBODING, FRIGHT, HOPE: and fear,
TERROR, TIMIDITY
FEAR: the burnt child
FEAR: the danger of
FEAR: excessive and overrated
FEAR: and hate
See also HATE
FEARED
FEAST
See also DIET, DINING OUT, FAMINE, REV-
ELRY
FEATHER(S)

See also BIRDS
FEEDING
   See also DIET, FOOD
FEELING
   See also ANGER, FEAR, GAMUT, HATE,
     LOVE, LUST, PASSION, PITY, SORROW
FEET
FEET OF CLAY
FELICITY
   See also DELIGHT, HAPPINESS, JOY, PROS-
     PERITY
FELL
   See DOCTOR FELL
FELLOW(S)
FELLOWMEN
FELLOWSHIP
   See also ACQUAINTANCE, FRIENDSHIP, SO-
     CIETY
FELON
   See also CRIMINAL
FEMALE
   See also MALE
FENCES
   See also NEIGHBOR, WALLS
FERRY
FEVER
   See also SICKNESS
FEW
FICKLENESS
   See also AIMLESSNESS, CONSTANCY,
     TREACHERY
FICTION
   See also FAIRY TALES, NARRATIVE, STORY,
     TALE, TRUTH
FIDDLE
FIDDLER
FIEND
   See also DEVIL, SATAN
FIERCE
   See also CRUELTY, SAVAGE
FIFTH OF NOVEMBER
FIFTY
FIFTY-FOUR FORTY
FIGHT
   See CONFLICT, DISADVANTAGE,
     STRIFE, WAR
FIGHT: he who fights and runs away
FIGHT ON
FIGURES
   See also ARITHMETIC
FINEST HOUR
FINGER(S)
FIRE
   See also ASHES, BRAND, FLAME, FRYING
     PAN, KINDLED, MOVING, SMOKE

FIRMNESS
   See also RESOLUTION, SECURITY
FIRST
   See also LAST
FIRST COME
   See also PRECEDENCE, PRECEDENCY
FIRST PLACE
FISH
FISHBALL
FISHERMAN
FISHERS
FISHING
FIT
   See also PROPER, RIGHT
FITS
FITTEST
FITZGERALD, F. SCOTT
FLAG
   See also BANNER, STANDARD, STAR-
     SPANGLED BANNER
FLAME
   See also FIRE
FLATTERY
   See also FAWNING, PRAISE: faint and ex-
     cessive, UNCTION, YES-MAN
FLATTERY: self-flattery
FLEA
FLESH
FLIGHT
   See also PURSUIT, RETREAT
FLIRTATION
   See also ADULTERY, COQUETTE, GLANCES
FLOTSAM AND JETSAM
FLOWER(S)
   See also DAFFODILS, DAISY, GEM, LILACS,
     LILY, MARIGOLD, POPPIES, PRIMROSE,
     ROSE, SUNFLOWER, VIOLET, WEEDS
FLY(IES)
   See also AMBER, JAMES I
FOAM
FOE(S)
   See also ADVERSARY, ENEMY
FOG
FOLLY
   See also ABSURDITY, GRAVITY, LEARNING:
     pains and follies, LOVE: its folly,
     NONSENSE, SIEVE, WISDOM: and folly,
     WIT: and folly, YOUTH: its folly
FOLLY: in praise of
FOOD
   See also BIRTHRIGHT, BREAD, CAKE, COOK,
     DIET, DOUGHNUT, FEEDING, GOOD
     CHEER, MEAT, PEASE PORRIDGE, PIE,
     ROAST BEEF, SOUP

FOOL(S)
See also ASS, BLOCKHEAD, DERISION,
DUNCE, EXPERIENCE: keeps a dear
school, FOREIGNERS, FORTUNE: fa-
vors the foolish, MORTALS, WISE MEN:
and fools
FOOTBALL
FOOTMAN(MEN)
FOOTPRINT(S)
FOP
See also AFFECTATION, MINCING
FORBEARANCE
See also ABSTINENCE, SELF-CONTROL, SUF-
FERANCE, STOICISM, TEMPERANCE, TOL-
ERANCE
FORBIDDEN
FORCE
See also MIGHT, POWER,
STRENGTH
FOREBODING
See also FEAR, OMENS
FOREGONE CONCLUSION
See also CERTAINTY
FOREIGNERS
FORESIGHT
See also PROPHECY, PROSPECT
FOREST
See also TREES, WOODS
FORETHOUGHT
See also NAIL, PLAN, PROVIDENCE,
PRUDENCE, VIGILANCE
FOREVER
See also ETERNAL, ETERNITY, INFINITY,
TIME: and eternity
FOREWARNED
FORGET(TING)
See also FORGIVE: and forget
FORGETFULNESS
See also MEMORY, OBLIVION
FORGIVE
See also PARDON
FORGIVE: and forget
FORGIVENESS
See also CHARITY, MERCY, PARDON
FORGOTTEN MAN
FORLORN
See also DESPAIR, MELANCHOLY
FORM
See also SHAPE
FORMALITY
See also CEREMONY, DISTANCE, FAMILI-
ARITY, SOLEMNITY
FORNICATION
See also ADULTERY, COITION

FORTITUDE
See also AUDACITY, BOLDNESS, COURAGE,
ENDURANCE, PATIENCE, RESOLUTION,
STIFF UPPER LIP, STOICISM, STRENGTH
FORTUNATE
See also LUCK
FORTUNE
See CHANCE, HAZARD, LUCK, VICISSITUDES
FORTUNE: favors the bold and the
foolish
FORTUNE: never perfect
FORTY
FORWARD
See also OFFICIOUS
FOUNDATION
FOUR HUNDRED
See also SOCIETY, SUPERIOR PEOPLE
FOURTH ESTATE
See also JOURNALISM, NEWSWRITERS
FOXES
FRAGRANCE
See also PERFUME, SMELL
FRAILTY
See also WEAKNESS, WOMAN: frail
FRANCE
See also BOURBONS, NAPOLEON
FRANKNESS
See also CANDOR, OUTSPOKEN, PLAIN
SPEAKING, SPADE, TRUTH, VERACITY
FRAUD
See also CRAFT, CUNNING, DECEPTION,
KNAVERY, PLAGIARY, THEFT
FRAY
See also BATTLE, CONFLICT, STRIFE, WAR
FREE
See also EDUCATION
FREEDOM
See also INDEPENDENCE, LIBERATION,
LIBERTY, MARATHON, WHISKEY
FREEDOM OF SPEECH
FREE THOUGHT
FREE WILL
See also DESTINY, FATE, WILL
FRENCH
FRENCH LEAVE
FRENCHMEN
FREUD
FRIEND(S)
See also DOG: man's best friend, ENEMY
FRIEND(S): and enemies
FRIEND: in need
FRIEND(S): need of and desire for
FRIEND: a rarity
FRIEND(S): treachery and malice of

GENTILITY
  See also GOOD MANNERS, MANNERS,
    POLITENESS
GENTLE
GENTLEMAN(MEN)
GENTLENESS
  See also MILDNESS
GENTRY
  See also ARISTOCRACY, NOBILITY,
    SUPERIOR PEOPLE
GEORGE
GEORGE III
GEORGE IV
GEORGIA
GERMANY
GETTING AND SPENDING
  See also BUSINESS, BUYER, COMMERCE,
    MARKET, PROFIT, SELLING, THINGS,
    TRADE
GETTING INTO
GETTYSBURG ADDRESS
GHOST(S)
  See also APPARITION, PHANTOM, SPIRITS
GIANT(S)
  See also DWARF
GIBBON, EDWARD
GIFT(S)
  See also BENEFITS
GIFT HORSE
GILBERT, W. S.
GIOTTO'S O
GIRDLE
GIRL(S)
  See also DAMSEL, LASSES, MAIDENS,
    VIRGINS, WENCH
GIVER(S)
GIVING
  See also CHARITY, LIBERALITY
GLADNESS
  See also DELIGHT, ECSTASY, FAIN, HAP-
    PINESS, JOY, REJOICE
GLANCES
GLASS(ES)
  See also MIRROR
GLIBNESS
  See also SPEAKING, TALKING, VERBOSITY
GLITTERS
GLOAMING
  See also EVENING, TWILIGHT
GLORY
  See also CELEBRITY, FAME, GOD: his glory
    and majesty, HONOR, IMMORTALITY,
    MAN: his glory, REPUTATION, WAR:
    its appeal and excitement, YOUTH:
    its glory

GLORY: hollow and soon fading
GLORY: paths of, lead but to the grave
GLOSSING
  See also EXPLANATION, LUCUS A NON
    LUCENDO, PEDANTRY
GLOVE(S)
  See also MITTENS
GLOWWORM
GLUTTONY
  See also HUNGER, SURFEIT
GNATS
GO
GOBLINS
  See also ELVES, FAIRIES
GOD
  See BATTALIONS, MONOTHEISM,
    NATURE: and God, PERSONS, PROPOSES,
    WORD OF GOD
GOD: attempts at definition of
GOD: His demise
GOD: His glory and mystery
GOD: His grace and love
GOD: some irreverent comments on
GOD: our refuge and strength
GOD: His ubiquity
GOD: His wrath and justice
GOD: miscellaneous
GODS
  See also CUPID, DIANA, HYPERION,
    IDOLS, IMAGE, MAMMON, MOLOCH,
    PAN, SATURN, TRITON, VENUS
GOETHE
GOLD
  See also GLITTERS, MONEY, RICHES,
    TREASURE, WEALTH
GOLDEN AGE
GOLDEN RULE
  See also DO UNTO OTHERS, NEIGHBOR
GOLF
GONE
GOOD
GOOD: and bad
GOOD: doing good
GOOD: and evil
GOOD: the good
GOOD BEHAVIOR
  See also MORALITY, VIRTUE
GOOD BREEDING
  See also MANNERS, POLITENESS, WELL-
    BRED
GOOD CHEER
  See also DIET, FOOD, GLUTTONY
GOOD INTENTIONS
  See also HELL
GOOD LUCK

See also FORTUNATE, LUCK, PROSPERITY

GOOD MAN(MEN)

GOOD MANNERS

See also CHIVALRY, GENTILITY, MANNERS, POLITENESS, RUDENESS

GOOD NAME

See also FAME, HONOR, REPUTATION

GOODNESS

See also MERIT, RECTITUDE, VIRTUE

GOOSE (GEESE)

GOSPEL

See also EVANGELISM

GOSSIP

See also RUMOR, SCANDAL, SLANDER

GOSSIPS

See also TALEBEARER

GOTHAM

GOUT

GOVERNMENT

See also DEMOCRACY, POLITICS, STATE, TYRANNY

GOVERNMENT: overrated

GRACE: in act

See also GOD: His grace and love

GRACE: of God

GRACE: before meat

GRADUALNESS

See also INEVITABLE, SLOW

GRAMMAR

See also ADJECTIVES, ADVERBS, LAN-GUAGE, PREPOSITION, RHETORIC, SEN-TENCE, SPLIT INFINITIVE, USAGE

GRANDFATHER'S CLOCK

GRANDPARENTS

See also FAMILY

GRASS

GRASS ROOTS

GRATIFICATION

See also PLEASURE, SATISFACTION

GRATITUDE

See also THANKS

GRAVE(S)

See also GLORY: paths of, lead but to the grave, MONUMENT, SEPULCHRE, SHROUD, TOMB

GRAVEYARD

GRAVITY

See also SOLEMNITY

GRAY HAIR

See also AGE

GREAT

GREATEST

GREATNESS

See also ELEVATION, EMINENCE, HEIGHT, SUBLIMITY

GREECE

See also MARATHON, SPARTANS

GREEK(S)

GREETING

See also SALUTATION

GRENVILLE

GRIEF

See also MISERY, SORROW, TROUBLE

GROANING

See also COMPLAINING, LAMENTATION

GROWED

GROWING UP

See also MATURITY

GRUESOME

See also HORROR

GRUNDY, MRS.

See also GOSSIP, PUBLIC OPINION, THEY

GUARD(S)

GUARDIANS

See also PROTECTION

GUEST(S)

See also HOSPITALITY, HOST, VISITORS

GUIDE

See also PILOT

GUILLOTINE

GUILT

See also BLAME, CONSCIENCE, INNOCENCE, SELF-REPROACH

GULF

GUNGA DIN

GUNS

See also AMMUNITION, SOLDIER, WAR

GUTS

H

HEAVEN: and Hell
  See also HELL
HEAVEN: the way to
HEAVEN: miscellaneous
HEBRIDES
  See also LONELINESS, REMOTENESS,
    SOLITUDE
HECUBA
HEEDLESS
  See also INATTENTION, RASHNESS,
    RECKLESSNESS, UNAWARENESS
HEIGHT
  See also ELEVATION, PERFECTION
HEIR(ESS)
HELEN OF TROY
HELL
  See AVERNUS, HEAVEN: and hell,
    KANSAS, PERDITION, TEXAS
HELL: definitions, descriptions and
    topography
HELL: miscellaneous
HELLENISM AND HEBRAISM
HELP
  See also PATRON, REMEDY, SERVE,
    SUCCOR
HELPMATE/HELPMEET
HEN
  See also CHICKEN, EGG(S)
HENPECKED
  See also CURTAIN LECTURE, HUSBANDS
    AND WIVES, SCOLD, SHREW, XANTIPPE
HERD
  See also CROWD, ROGUE, VULGAR
HEREAFTER
  See also HEAVEN, HELL, DEATH: brings
    oblivion, DEATH: the end of woe,
    DEATH: its finality, DEATH: reunion
    in, DEATH: a sleep, DEATH: triumph
    over, IMMORTALITY, MANSIONS,
    PERHAPS, PURGATORY, ZION
HEREDITY
  See also ANCESTRY
HERESY
  See also DOUBT, FAITH, ORTHODOXY,
    RELIGION, TRUTH
HERETIC
  See also ORTHODOX
HERITAGE
  See also ANCESTRY, INHERITANCE
HERO(ES)
  See also CHAMPIONS, CLARET, VALET
HEROD
HEROISM
  See also BOLDNESS, COURAGE, FORTITUDE
HESITATION

See also INDECISION, IRRESOLUTION,
    PERPLEXITY, SLOW, STOOLS, SUSPENSE
HESPERUS
HICKORY DICKORY DOCK
HIDING PLACE
  See also REFUGE, RETREAT, SECURITY
HIGH BIRTH
  See also ARISTOCRACY,
    NOBILITY
HIGHBROW
  See also INTELLECTUAL
HIGHEST
HIGHLAND LASS
HIGHLANDS
HIGHWAYMAN
  See also OUTLAW, ROBBERY
HILARITY
  See also JOLLITY, LEVITY, MERRIMENT,
    REVELRY
HILLS
  See also MOUNTAINS
HINDMOST
  See also LAST
HINDSIGHT
  See also LOOKING BACK, WISDOM
HIP
HISTORIANS
  See also CHRONICLER
HISTORY
HISTORY: definitions
HIT
HITCH
  See AMBITION, REACH, STRIVING
HOBBY
  See also AVOCATION, OCCUPATION,
    PURSUIT
HOBBY-HORSE
HOBSON'S CHOICE
  See also NECESSITY
HOG
  See also PEARLS BEFORE SWINE, PIG(S)
HOLD
  See also KEEP
HOLINESS
  See also CONSECRATION, PIETY,
    RELIGION
HOLMES, OLIVER WENDELL
HOLY
  See also BLESSED
HOLY ROMAN EMPIRE
HOME(S)
  See HEARTH, LONGEST, MANSIONS
HOME: definitions
HOME: is best
HOME: miscellaneous

HOMECOMING
See also RETURN
HOMELINESS
See also THIRTY, UGLY
HOMEMADE
HOMER
HOMES
HOMESICK
See also NOSTALGIA
HONEST
See also JUST, RIGHT, TRUE
HONESTY
See also INTEGRITY, JUSTICE, MORALITY,
RECTITUDE, TRUTH, VERACITY
HONESTY: its drawbacks
HONEY
See also BEES, SWEETNESS
HONOR
See also CELEBRITY, FAME, GARTER,
GLORY, GOOD NAME, IMMORTALITY,
MORALITY, NAME, RECTITUDE, REPU-
TATION, RIGHT, SELF-RESPECT, TITLES
HONOR: some cynical observations on
HOOK
HOPE
See CONFIDENCE, EXPECTATION,
LOVE: and hope, OPTIMISM,
PROSPECT
HOPE: deferred
See also SUIT
HOPE: definition
HOPE: the delusion of
HOPE: and despair
See also DESPAIR
HOPE: and fear
See also FEAR
HOPE: miscellaneous
HOPKINS
See MARK HOPKINS
HORATIUS
HORN(S)
See also TRUMPETS
HORNER, JACK
HORROR
See also FEAR, GRUESOME, TERROR
HORSE
See also GALLOPING, NAIL, NOD, OATS,
SWAP
HORSEMAN
See also KNIGHT
HORSE SENSE
See also COMMON SENSE
HOSPITALITY
See also EAT DRINK AND BE MERRY,

GENIALITY, GOOD CHEER, GUEST,
SOCIABILITY, WELCOME
HOST
See also GUEST
HOTEL
See also INN, TAVERN
HOT WEATHER
HOUNDS
See also DOG
HOUR(S)
See also TIME
HOUSE(S)
See also HOME
HOUSE DIVIDED
See also REBELLION
HOUSE OF COMMONS
See also PARLIAMENT
HOUSEWIFE
See also HUSBANDS AND WIVES
HUBBARD, MOTHER
HUCKLEBERRY FINN
HUMANITARIANISM
See also CHARITY, GENEROUS
GIVING, KINDNESS, LOVE, PHILANTHROPY
HUMANITY
See also INHUMANITY, MANKIND
HUMAN NATURE
HUMAN RACE
See also MANKIND
HUMBLE
See also MEEK
HUMILIATION
See also DISGRACE, DROP, REBUFF, SHAME
HUMILITY
See also MEEKNESS, MODESTY, PATIENCE,
PRIDE
HUMOR
See also FUNNY, JEST, LAUGHTER,
MERRIMENT, MOOD, SATIRE, WIT
HUMPTY-DUMPTY
HUNGER
See also APPETITE, FAMINE, FASTING,
FOOD, GLUTTONY, LUST
HUNGRY
See also INSATIATE
HUNTER
See also (JOHN) PEEL
HUNTING
See also PURSUIT, SPORT
HURRY
See also CELERITY, HASTE, SPEED
HURT
See also HARM, INJURY, MISCHIEF, PAIN
HUSBANDS
See also FAMILY, HUSBANDS AND WIVES,

MARRIAGE, WIFE
HUSBANDS AND WIVES
See also BLOW, HENPECKED, WIFE
HYGIENE
See also HEALTH
HYPERBOLE
See also EXAGGERATION
HYPERION

HYPNOTISM
HYPOCRISY
See also DISSEMBLE, DISSIMULATION,
FRAUD, SMILER
HYPOCRITE(S)
HYPOTHESIS
See also THEORY, SPECULATE, SYSTEM

∽ **I** ∽

IBSEN
See also NECK
ICE
ICICLES
IDEAS
See also OPINIONS, PHILOSOPHY,
THOUGHT, SENTIMENTS
IDEAL(S)
See also EXCELSIOR, PHILOSOPHY
IDEALIST(S)
See also PHILOSOPHER
IDENTITY
See also MYSELF, STRIVING
IDIOM
See also SPEECH
IDIOT
See also FOOL, MORON
IDLE
IDLENESS
See also INACTION, LEISURE, LOAFING,
PASSIVITY, SLOTH
IDLER
IDOLS
IF
IGNORANCE
See also KNOWLEDGE, STUPIDITY, WISDOM
IGNORANT
See also UNEDUCATED
ILL
See also EVIL
ILL-FAVORED
See also HOMELINESS, UGLY
ILL-GOTTEN GAIN
ILLICIT
ILLUSION
See also DELUSION, HALLUCINATION,
MITTY, PHANTOM

IMAGE
See also LIKENESS, METAPHOR, PICTURE,
SIMILE
IMAGINATION
See also FANCY, FICTION, MIND, POETRY
IMITATION
See also APE
IMMORAL
See WICKED
IMMORALITY
See also EVIL, IMPROPRIETY
IMMORTALITY
See CELEBRITY, DEATH: reunion in,
FAME, GLORY, HEREAFTER, HONOR,
REPUTATION
IMMORTALITY: doubt and fear of
**IMMORTALITY: hope for and affir-
mation of**
IMMORTALITY: miscellaneous
IMPARTIALITY
See also JUSTICE, RIGHT
IMPATIENCE
See also HASTE, IMPETUOSITY, PATIENCE,
RESTLESSNESS
IMPERFECTION
See also BLEMISHED, DEFECT, FAULT,
FEET OF CLAY, FORTUNE: never
perfect, HAPPINESS: imperfect
IMPETUOSITY
See also HASTE, HEADSTRONG, HURRY
IMPIETY
See also ATHEISM, DISBELIEF, DOUBT,
HERESY, SACRILEGE, SIN
IMPOSSIBLE
IMPOSSIBILITIES
IMPROPRIETY
See also IMMORALITY

IMPROVEMENT
See also BETTER, PROGRESS
IMPUDENCE
See also ARROGANCE, AUDACITY, BOLD-
NESS, BULL, CONCEIT, DEFIANCE,
INSOLENCE
IMPULSE
See also DESIRE
INACTION
See also IDLENESS, LOAFING, PASSIVITY,
SLOTH
INATTENTION
See also HEEDLESS, RECKLESSNESS
INCENTIVE
See also MOTIVE, REWARD, STIMULATION
INCONSISTENCY
See also DIFFERENCE
INCREASE
See also ACCUMULATION, INCREMENT
INCREMENT
See also INCREASE
INDECISION
See also DOUBT, HESITATION, PERPLEXITY,
SUSPENSE
INDEPENDENCE
See also FREEDOM, HOG, LIBERTY, SELF-
RELIANCE
INDEPENDENT
See also FANCY FREE, SELF-RELIANCE
INDEX
INDIAN(S)
INDICTMENT
See also ACCUSATION, BLAME
INDIFFERENCE
INDIGESTION
INDISPENSABLE
See also NECESSITY, NEEDFUL
INDIVIDUALISM
See also ECCENTRICITY, INDEPENDENCE
INDOMITABLE
See also RESOLUTE, SECURE, UNBOWED,
UNCONQUERABLE
INDUSTRY
See also DILIGENCE, LABOR, TOIL, WORK
INEVITABLE
See FATE, GRADUALNESS
INFAMY
See also DISGRACE, DISHONOR
INFANT
See also BABE, CHILDREN
INFATUATION
See also FOLLY, LOVE, PASSION, ROMANCE
INFIDELITY
See also ATHEISM, SKEPTICISM,
TREACHERY

INFINITY
See also FOREVER
INFORMATION
See also KNOWLEDGE, NEWS
INGRATIATION
See also PLEASING
INGRATITUDE
See also DISSATISFACTION, GRATITUDE,
THANKS
INHERITANCE
See also ANCESTRY, HERITAGE, LEGACY,
WILLS
INHUMANITY
See also CRUELTY, MAN: a wolf to man,
RUTHLESSNESS, SAVAGE, UNKINDNESS
INIQUITY
See also EVIL, INFAMY, WICKEDNESS
INJURY(IES)
See also HURT, OFFENSE, WRONG
INJUSTICE
See also JUSTICE, WRONG, INJURY
INN
See also HOTEL, TAVERN
INNISFREE
INNOCENCE
See also GUILT, SIMPLICITY
INNOCENT
INNOCUOUS DESUETUDE
INNOVATION
See ALTERATION, CHANGE, NOVELTY
INSANE
See MAD
INSANITY
See also ABSURDITY, FOLLY, MADNESS
INSATIATE
See HUNGRY
INSECTS
See ANTS, BEES, BEETLE, BUGS, BUTTER-
FLY, CRICKET, FLEA, FLY, GNAT,
LOCUST, MOTH, SPIDER
INSECURITY
See also DOUBT, HESITATION, PERPLEXITY
INSIGHT
See also INTUITION, PERCEPTION, UN-
DERSTANDING
INSIGNIFICANCE
See also TRIFLES, UNIMPORTANCE
INSOLENCE
See also ARROGANCE, CONCEIT, OFFENSE,
PRIDE, PROUD, RUDENESS
INSTINCT(S)
INSTITUTION(S)
INSTRUMENTS
See also MACHINES, TOOLS
INSUBSTANTIAL

INSULT(S)
See also AFFRONT
INTEGRITY
See also HONESTY, MORALITY, RECTITUDE,
SELF-RESPECT
INTELLECTUAL
See also HIGHBROW
INTELLIGENCE
See also INSIGHT, MIND, PERCEPTION,
REASON, STUPIDITY, WISDOM, WIT
INTELLIGIBLE
See also CLEAR, LUCID, OBVIOUS, PLAIN-
SPEAKING
INTENT
See also MOTIVE, PURPOSE, RESOLVE
INTENTIONS
INTERDEPENDENCE
See also INDEPENDENCE, RECIPROCITY
INTEREST
INTERFERENCE
See also CONFLICT, MEDDLING
INTERPRETATION
See also UNDERSTANDING
INTOLERABLE
INTOXICATION
See also DRINKING, DRUNKENNESS, WINE
INTRUSIVE
See also MEDDLING, OFFICIOUS
INTUITION
See also INSIGHT, KNOWLEDGE, PERCEP-
TION, UNDERSTANDING
INUNDATION
INVENTION(S)
See also DISCOVERY, IMAGINATION,

NECESSITY: the mother of invention
INVITATION
See also ASK, ASKING
INVOCATION
See also PRAYER
INVULNERABLE
See also SECURE
IRELAND
IRESON
IRISH
IRISH BULL
See BULL
IRON(S)
See also MANACLES
IRON CURTAIN
IRONIES
See also SARCASM
IRRESOLUTION
See also DOUBT, HESITATION, INDECISION
ISHMAEL
See also OUTLAW
ISLAND(S)
See also ENGLISH PEOPLE
ISOLATION
See also ALONE, LONELINESS, SOLITUDE
ISRAEL
ISRAFEL
ITALY
ITERATION
I TOLD YOU SO
IVORY TOWER(S)
See also GUTTER

JABBERWOCKE
JACK AND JILL
JACK ROBINSON
JACKSON, STONEWALL
See also ARM, NICKNAME
JACK SPRAT
JAIL
See also PRISON
JAKES
JAM
JAMES I
JAMES, JESSE

JAUNDICED
See also PEEVISHNESS, PREJUDICE
JAWBONE
JEALOUSY
See also ENVY, MISTRUST, SOUR GRAPES,
SUSPICION
JEANIE
JEHU
JERUSALEM
JEST
See also EARNEST, HUMOR, JOKE,
LAUGHTER, WIT

K

See also EDUCATION, INFORMATION, INTUITION, LEARNING, NEWS, PERCEPTION, SCHOOLBOY, SCIENCE, UNDERSTANDING, WISDOM: and knowledge

KNOWLEDGE: and wisdom
HAD I ONLY KNOWN
   See also REGRET
KOSCIUSKO

L

LA BELLE DAME SANS MERCI
LABOR
   See also DILIGENCE, GENIUS: infinite capacity for taking pains, INDUSTRY, SERVICE, SWEAT, TOIL, WORK
LABORER
   See also WORKER
LADY(IES)
   See WOMAN
LADYBIRD
LADY MONDEGREEN
LAFAYETTE
LAMB(S)
   See also SHEEP
LAMENTATION
   See also COMPLAINING, GROANING, MOURNING, TEARS, WEEPING
LAMP(S)
   See also LIGHT
LAND
LANGUAGE(S)
   See also DIALECT, ENGLISH LANGUAGE, GRAMMAR, SPEECH
LANGUAGE: usage
LARK
   See also SKYLARK
LASSES
   See also DAMSEL, GIRLS, WENCH
LAST
   See also FIRST
LATE
   See also TARDY
LATIN AND GREEK
LAUGH(TER) (noun)
   See also CHORTLING, FUNNY, HUMOR, JEST, RIDICULE, SMILE, WEEPING, WIT
LAUGH(ING) (verb)
LAVENDER
LAW
   See also CUSTOM, EQUITY, JUDGES, JURY, JUSTICE, LEGISLATION, LEGISLATOR,

NECESSITY: knows no law, PRECEDENT, STATUTES
LAWYER(S)
   See also ATTORNEY
LAZY
   See also HABIT, IDLENESS, INACTION, SLOTH
LEADER
   See also CHIEF, KING, LORD, RULER, MASTER
LEAR
LEARNED
   See also EDUCATION, PEDANTRY, TEACHER, TEACHING
LEARNING
   See EDUCATION, EXPERIENCE: keeps a dear school, KNOWLEDGE, PEDANTRY, RESEARCH, ROYAL ROAD, SELF-IMPROVEMENT, SCIENTIFIC SPIRIT, STUDIES, TEACHER, TEACHING, WOMAN: and learning
LEARNING: and action
LEARNING: its pains and follies
LEARNING: and wisdom and virtue
LEARNING: miscellaneous
LEAVES
   See also AUTUMN, FALL, TREES
LECHERY
   See also LEWD, LUST, TURK
LEE, GENERAL ROBERT E.
   See ARM, WAR: its appeal
LEGACY
   See also INHERITANCE, WILLS
LEGION
LEGISLATION
   See also LAW
LEGISLATOR
LEISURE
   See also EASE, IDLENESS, LOAFING
LENDING
   See also BORROWER

LEOPARD
LET GEORGE DO IT
  See GEORGE
LETHE
  See also FORGIVENESS, OBLIVION
LETTER(S)
  See also CORRESPONDENCE, LITERATURE
LETTERS (MISSIVES)
LEVELING
  See also DEATH: the leveler, DEMOC-
  RACY
LEVIATHAN
LEVITY
  See also FOLLY, HILARITY, JOLLITY
LEWD
  See also LECHERY, OBSCENITY, VILE,
  VULGAR
LEXICOGRAPHER
  See also DICTIONARY, JOHNSON (DR.
  SAMUEL)
LIABILITIES
  See also DEBTS, OBLIGATION
LIAR(S)
LIBEL
  See also CALUMNY, SCANDAL, SLANDER
LIBERAL AND CONSERVATIVE
LIBERAL EDUCATION
LIBERALISM
  See also CONSERVATISM
LIBERALITY
  See also BOUNTY, CHARITY, GIVING
LIBERATION
LIBERTY(IES)
  See also FREEDOM, INDEPENDENCE
LIBRARY(IES)
  See also BOOKS
LICENSE
  See also EXCESS, PERMISSION, PRIVILEGE
LIE
  See also LYING, TRUTH
LIFE
  See LIVING, LONGEVITY, SURVIVAL
LIFE: annoyance, boredom and misery
  of
LIFE: the art of
LIFE: its brevity and unreality
LIFE: dear to us
LIFE: and death
LIFE: definitions of
LIFE: mysterious and incredible
LIFE: real and earnest
LIFE: triviality of
LIFE: miscellaneous
LIGHT

  See also CANDLE, DAYLIGHT, EMBERS,
  LAMP, MOONLIGHT, NAUGHTY, SUN
LIGHT (LEVITY)
LIGHTNING
  See also STORM, THUNDER
LIKELIHOOD
  See also PROBABILITY
LIKENESS
  See also IMAGE, PICTURE, SIMILE
LIKING
  See also AFFECTION, LOVE, SYMPATHY
LILACS
LILY(IES)
  See also WEEDS
LIMBO
  See also PARADISE OF FOOLS
LIMITATION
  See also ART, MONEY: its limitations,
  RESTRAINT
LINCOLN, ABRAHAM
LINE
LINEN
  See also CLOTHING
LION(S)
LIP(S)
  See also KISS(ES)
LIQUOR
  See also CLARET, DRINK, DRINKING, RUM,
  SHERRY, WHISKEY, WINE
LIST
  See also CATALOG
LISTEN
  See also EARS, HEAR
LITERARY MEN
  See also AUTHORS, BOOKS: the book and
  the author, WRITERS
LITERATURE
  See also CLASSICS, LETTERS
LITTLE
LITTLE BILLEE
LITTLENESS
LIVING
  See also DEATH, DYING
LIVINGSTONE
LOAD
  See also BURDEN
LOAFING
  See BUM, EASE, IDLENESS, INACTION,
  LEISURE, LOITERING, REPOSE
LOAN
  See also BORROWER, BORROWING
LOCHINVAR
LOCKS
LOCK, STOCK AND BARREL
LOCUST

LOGIC
See also ANALYSIS, ONE HOSS SHAY, PHI-
  LOSOPHY, REASON, ROPE OF SAND
LOINS
LOITERING
See also LOAFING
LONDON
See also MANACLES
LONDON BRIDGE
LONELINESS
See also AGE: its loneliness, DEATH: loneli-
  ness, FRIENDS: need of and desire for,
  ISOLATION, REMOTENESS, SOLITUDE
LONGEST
LONGEVITY
See AGE, LIVING
LONGING(S)
See also ANTICIPATION, ASPIRATION, DE-
  SIRES, HEARTACHE, HOMESICK,
  LOVE: longings, NOSTALGIA, SIGHING,
  WISHES
LOOK
See also APPEARANCE, SEEING, SIGHT
LOOKING BACK
See also HINDSIGHT, NOSTALGIA
LORD
See also HARROW, LEADER, MASTER,
  RULER
THE LORD'S PRAYER
LOSS
See also ABSENCE, DEFEAT, DESTRUCTION,
  NAIL, RUIN, SACRIFICE, WRECK
LOST
See also DAMNED, DEAD
LOTHARIO
See also RAKE
LOVABLE
See also AMIABLE, LIKING, SWEET
LOVE
See AFFECTION, CHARITY, COURTING,
  DESIRE (SEXUAL), GALLANTRY, GOD:
  His grace and love, ILLICIT, INFATU-
  ATION, MARRIAGE: and love, MONEY:
  and love, PASSION, ROMANCE, WOMAN:
  and love, WOOING, YOUTH: and love
LOVE: at first sight
LOVE: its beginnings
LOVE: is best
LOVE: is blind
LOVE: capricious and uncertain
LOVE: constancy in
LOVE: and death
LOVE: definitions of
LOVE: its delights

LOVE: its departure
LOVE: faithful and faithless
LOVE: its folly
LOVE: and hate
LOVE: and hope
LOVE: longings
LOVE: and lust
LOVE: and madness
LOVE: and marriage
LOVE: of men, and of women
LOVE: nature of
LOVE: new love
LOVE: its permanence
LOVE: and poverty
LOVE: its power
LOVE: its quarrels and reconciliations
LOVE: its regrets
LOVE: divine and spiritual love
LOVE: its torments and pains
LOVE: miscellaneous
LOVER(S)
See also LOCHINVAR, LOTHARIO, ROMEO
LUCID
See also CERTAIN, CLEAR, INTELLIGIBLE,
  SANE
LUCIFER
See also SATAN
LUCK
See also ADVENTURE, CHANCE, DESTINY,
  FATE, FORTUNE, GAMBLING, HAZARD,
  KISMET, MARRIAGES: made in heaven,
  SUCCESS
LUCUS A NON LUCENDO
LUCY LOCKET
LULLABY
LUNATIC FRINGE
See also ENTHUSIASM, ZEAL
LUNATIC, LOVER, AND POET
LUST
See also ADULTERY, APPETITE, CHASTITY,
  DESIRE (sexual), FORBIDDEN, LECHERY,
  LOVE: and lust, PASSION
LUTHER
LUXURY(IES)
See also COMFORT, EASE, EXCESS, PLEAS-
  URE, RILEY, SLOTH, VOLUPTUOUSNESS
LYING
See also DISSEMBLING, DISSIMULATION,
  EQUIVOCATION, FALSEHOOD, LIE, SIMU-
  LATION, TRUTH
LYING: and truth
See also TRUTH: and lies
LYRICS
See also MELODIES

M

MARRIAGE: man and wife
MARRIAGE: marry in haste, repent at leisure
MARRIAGE: the negative view
MARRIAGE: proper time and place
MARRIAGE: regrets, dangers, and woes
MARRIAGE: second marriage
MARRIAGE: and single life
MARRIAGE: without love
MARRIAGE: miscellaneous
MARRIED LOVE
MARTLET
MARTYR(S)
  See also SAINTS, SELF-SACRIFICE
MARY(S)
MASSES
  See also CROWD, HERD, POPULACE, VULGAR
MASTER(S)
  See also AUTHORITY, CHIEF, LEADER, RULER, SERVANTS, VALET
MATE
MATRIMONY
  See also MARRIAGE
MATTER
MATTER-OF-FACTNESS
MATURITY
  See also GROWING UP, PRECOCITY, RIPENESS
MAXIM(S)
  See also APHORISM, EPIGRAM, PROVERB
MAY (MONTH)
MAY QUEEN
MEANDERING
  See also PROLIXITY
MEANING
  See also DESIGN, EXPLANATION, PLAN, SOUND, TELEOLOGY
MEANS
  See also ENDS
MEAT
  See also FOOD, GRACE: before meat
MEAT: one man's
MEDDLESOME MATTY
MEDDLING
  See also INTERFERENCE, INTRUSIVE, OFFICIOUS
MEDES AND PERSIANS
MEDICINE
  See also BALM, CURE, HEALING, NARCOTICS, PHYSICIAN, REMEDY, SICKNESS
MEEK
  See also HUMBLE
MEEKNESS

  See also CHEEK, HUMILITY, MODESTY, RESIGNATION, SUFFERANCE
MEETING
  See also RENDEZVOUS
MELANCHOLY
  See also DEJECTION, DESPONDENCY, DESPAIR, FORLORN, HOPE: and despair, HOPE: deferred, IDLE
MELANCHOLY: its pleasures
MELODIES
  See also LYRICS, STRAINS
MELTING POT
MEMORY
  See also NO SOAP, RECOLLECTION, REMEMBRANCE
MENACE
  See also CLOUDS, THREAT, WARNING
MEN AND WOMEN
  See also WOMAN: should be subject to man
MENE, MENE
MERCENARIES
  See also SOLDIERS
MERCHANT(S)
  See also BUSINESSMAN, COMMERCIALISM, GETTING AND SPENDING, MARKET, SELLING
MERCY
  See also CHARITY, FORGIVENESS, KINDNESS, ORPHAN, PITY, SYMPATHY, TOLERANCE
MERIT
  See also GARTER, GOODNESS, VIRTUE
MERMAID(S)
  See also SIRENS
MERMAID TAVERN
MERRIMENT
  See also HILARITY, JOCULARITY, JOLLITY, KING COLE, LEVITY, MIRTH, REJOICE
MERRY
MESSAGE TO GARCIA
METAL
  See also GOLD, IRON
METAPHOR
  See also IMAGE, LIKENESS, SIMILE
METAPHYSICS
  See also THEOLOGY
METEOR
METER
  See also POETRY: rhythm, POETRY: rhyme, VERSE
METHOD
  See also ORDER, PLAN, SYSTEM
MEXICO
MICHELANGELO

MICROSCOPES
MIDDLE AGE
MIDNIGHT
See also NIGHT
MIGHT
See also FORCE, MORALITY, POWER,
STRENGTH
MIGHT HAVE BEEN
See also REMEMBERING HAPPIER THINGS
MIGHTY
See also INDOMITABLE, POWERFUL,
STRONG, SUPERIOR PEOPLE, UNCON-
QUERABLE
MILDNESS
See also COMPASSION, CONSIDERATION,
GENTLENESS, KINDNESS, MILK OF
HUMAN KINDNESS, MODERATION, PITY,
SWEETNESS, TEMPERANCE
MILITARY
See also ARMY, NAVY, SOLDIERS, WAR
MILK
MILKMAID
MILK OF HUMAN KINDNESS
See also GENTLENESS, KINDNESS, MILD-
NESS, PITY, SYMPATHY
MILL(ER)
MILLS OF THE GODS
See also JUSTICE, RETRIBUTION, VENGE-
ANCE
MILLSTONE
See also RETRIBUTION
MILTON, JOHN
MINCING
See also AFFECTATION, FOP, PRUDERY
MIND
See also BRAINS, IMAGINATION, INTELLI-
GENCE, JUDGMENT, PERCEPTION, REA-
SON, UNDERSTANDING
MIND AND BODY
MINE OWN
MINIVER CHEEVY
MINORITY
See also MAJORITY
MINSTREL
See also BARD, POET
MIRACLE(S)
See also EVIDENCE, MYSTERY, PRODIGY,
SUPERSTITION, WONDERS
MIRROR(S)
See also GLASS
MIRTH
See also JOLLITY, JOY, MERRIMENT, REJOICE
MISCHIEF
See also EVIL, HARM
MISER

See also AVARICE, GOLD, THRIFT
MISERY(IES)
See also AGONY, ANXIETY, GRIEF, HEART-
ACHE, HEARTBREAK, POVERTY: its mis-
eries, SORROW, SUFFERING, TORMENTS,
UNHAPPINESS, WRETCHEDNESS, WOE
MISFORTUNE(S)
See also ADVERSITY, BOTTOM, CALAMITY,
CATASTROPHE, TROUBLE
MISOGYNIST
See also MEN AND WOMEN
MISSOURI
MISTAKEN
See also ERR, FALSE, WRONG
MISTAKES
See also ERROR
MISTRESS(ES)
See also HARLOT, POMPADOUR, PROSTI-
TUTE, SHE, WHORE
MISTRUST
See also DOUBT, JEALOUSY, SUSPICION
MITTENS
See also GLOVES
MITTY
MIZPAH
MOBLED
MODEL
See EXAMPLE, PATTERN, STANDARD
MODERATION
See also MILDNESS, TEMPERANCE
MODERN
See also NEW
MODERN LIFE
MODESTY
See also BASHFULNESS, DECENCY, DIFFI-
DENCE, HUMILITY, MEEKNESS
MOHAMMED AND THE MOUN-
TAIN
MOHICANS
MOLE
MOLOCH
MOMENT
See also OPPORTUNITY
MONARCH
See also KING, RULER
MONEY
See AVARICE, CASH, GLITTERS, GOLD,
POVERTY, PRIMITIVE, RICHES,
TREASURE, WEALTH, YOU CAN'T TAKE
IT WITH YOU
MONEY: its delights
MONEY: filthy lucre
MONEY: the lack of it
MONEY: its limitations
MONEY: and love

MONEY: the love of
MONEY: its power
MONEY: put money in thy purse
MONEY: miscellaneous
MONKEY(S)
See also APE
MONOGAMY
See also BIGAMY, MARRIAGE
MONOTHEISM
See also GOD, RELIGION
MONROE DOCTRINE
MONSTER(S)
See also PRODIGY
MONTREAL
MONUMENT(S)
See also GRAVE, TOMB
MOOD
See also HUMOR
MOON
MOONLIGHT
MOORE, TOM
MORAL
MORALITY
See also AGE: its moral decline, CON-
SCIENCE, DISHONESTY, DUTY, GATE,
GOOD BEHAVIOR, HONOR, HONESTY,
INDIGESTION, INTEGRITY, JUSTICE,
MIGHT AND RIGHT, MONTREAL, PHI-
LOSOPHY, PRINCIPLE, VIRTUE, WAR:
morality of, YOUTH AND AGE: their
morality
MORALS AND MANNERS
MORE
MORNING
See also DAWN, DAY, DAYLIGHT
MORON
See also FOOL, IDIOT, STUPIDITY
MORTALITY
See also DEATH, FATALITY
MORTAL(S)
MOSES
See MEEK
MOTE(S)
MOTH(S)
MOTHER
See also CHILDREN, CRADLE, DAUGH-
TER(S), SON(S)
MOTION
See also MOVE, MOVING
MOTIVE(S)

See also CAUSE, INCENTIVE, INTENT, IN-
TENTION, PURPOSE, REASON, STIMULA-
TION
MOUNTAIN(S)
See also HIGHLANDS, HILLS, MOHAMMED,
OSSA
MOURNING
See also LAMENTATION
MOUSE (MICE)
See also CAT, RAT, SCHEMES
MOUSETRAP
MOUTH(S)
See also GIFT HORSE
MOVE
See also MOTION
MOVING
See also MOTION
MUCKRAKER(S)
See also REFORM
MUFFET
MULE
See also ASS
MUMMY
MURDER
See also KILL(ING), SLAUGHTER, SUICIDE
MUSEUMS
MUSIC
See ANTHEMS, BACH, BASSOON,
CHORD, DULCIMER, FIDDLE, FIDDLER,
HANDEL, HARMONY, HARPS, HORNS,
LULLABY, LYRICS, MADRIGALS, MELO-
DIES, MINSTREL, PIANIST, RIFT, SINGING,
SONGS, STRAINS, TONE
MUSIC: descriptions of
MUSIC: its power
MUSIC: miscellaneous
MUST
See also NECESSITY: needs must
MUTABILITY
See also CHANGE
MUTE
See also SILENT
MYRTLES
MYSELF
See also EGOISM
MYSTERY(IES)
See also GOD: His glory and mystery,
LIFE: mysterious, and incredible, NA-
TURE: wise, eternal, mysterious, cruel,
RIDDLE OF THE SPHINX, SECRECY

1

N

NAGGING
  See also SCOLD
NAILS
NAKED(NESS)
NAMBY-PAMBY
NAME(S)
  See also NICKNAME, REPUTATION
NAPOLEON
NARCOTICS
  See also MEDICINE
NARRATIVE
  See also FICTION, NOVEL, STORY, TALES,
    WRITING
NATIVITY
  See also BIRTH
NATURAL
  See also ARTIFICIAL, UNNATURAL
NATURAL SELECTION
  See also EVOLUTION
NATURE: and art
NATURE: and God
NATURE: the great teacher
NATURE: wise, eternal, mysterious,
    cruel
NATURE: miscellaneous
NAUGHTY
  See also EVIL, WICKED
NAVAL
  See SAILING, SEA, SHIPS, WAR
NAVEL
NAVY
  See also SAILORS, SAILING, SHIPS, WAR
NAZARETH
  See also JESUS CHRIST
NEAR
NEARER
NEAT
  See also SNUG, TIDYING UP
NECESSITY
  See FATE, INDISPENSABLE, MUST,
    POVERTY
NECESSITY: knows no law
NECESSITY: making a virtue of
NECESSITY: the mother of invention
NECESSITY: needs must
  See also MUST
NECESSITY: supreme
NECESSITY: the tyrant's plea
NECESSITY: miscellaneous
NECK

NECK VERSE
NEED(S)
  See also FRIEND: in need, NECESSITY,
    POVERTY, WANT
NEEDFUL
  See also INDISPENSABLE, NECESSITY
NEEDLE
  See also NAKED
NEGATIVE(S)
  See also NO
NEGLECT
  See also INACTION, OMISSION
NEGOTIATING
NEGOTIATION
  See also BARGAIN
NEGRO
  See also NIGGER, OLD BLACK JOE
NEIGHBOR
NELL GWYNN
NET
NETWORK
  See also WEB
NEVERMORE
NEW
  See also MODERN, NOVEL, UNKNOWN
NEW DEAL
NEWS
  See also BAD NEWS, INFORMATION, NOV-
    ELTY, TIDINGS
NEWSPAPER(S)
NEWSWRITERS
  See also FOURTH ESTATE, JOURNALISM
NEWTON, SIR ISAAC
NEW YEAR
NEW YORK
  See also GOTHAM, MANHATTAN
NICE
  See also WATERLOO
NICKNAME
  See also JACKSON (STONEWALL)
NIGGER
  See also NEGRO
NIGHT
  See also MIDNIGHT, MOON, MOONLIGHT
NIGHTINGALE
  See also IMAGE
NIGHTINGALE, FLORENCE
NIGHTMARE
  See also DREAMS, TERROR
NO

See also NEGATIVE, YES
NOBILITY
See also ARISTOCRACY, DUCHESS, GENTRY,
HIGH BIRTH, PRINCES, SUBLIMITY
NOBODY
NOD
NOISE
See also QUIET, ROAR, SOUND
NONCONFORMIST
See also DISSENSION, NOBODY, PROTES-
TANTISM, RADICAL, REBELLION
NONEXISTENTS
NONSENSE
See also ABSURDITY, BUNK, DRIVEL,
FOLLY, NO SOAP
NOON
NORMALCY
NOSE
NO SOAP

NOSTALGIA
See also AULD LANG SYNE, HOMESICK,
LONGING, PAST: sadness of and
longing for, RECOLLECTION
NOTE(S)
NOTHING
See also VACUUM
NOVEL(S)
See also NARRATIVE, NEW, ROMANCE,
WRITING
NOVELTY
See also ALTERATION, CHANGE, INNOVA-
TION, ORIGINALITY
NOVEMBER
NOWHERE
NURSE
NUTS
See WAR: famous utterances

O

OATH(S)
See also PROFANITY, SWEARING, SWORN
OATS
OBEDIENCE
See also ALLEGIANCE, CHARGE OF THE
LIGHT BRIGADE, COMPLIANCE, DISOBE-
DIENCE, SUBMISSION
OBJECTIVE
See also AIMS, END, JUST
OBLIGATION
See also AGREEMENT, DUTY, LIABILITIES,
OWE, PROMISE
OBLIGING
OBLIVION
See also FORGETFULNESS, LETHE
OBSCENITY
See also DIRT, LECHERY, LEWD,
VILE
OBSCURITY
See also DARKNESS, ECLIPSE, LUCID,
SHADOW, UNKNOWN, UNWEPT
OBSERVATION
See also ATTENTION, ELEPHANT, EX-
AMINATION, NOTES, OPINION, SEEING,
UTTERANCE WATCH
OBSERVER

See also SPECTATOR, WITNESSES
OBSESSION
See also CARTHAGE, (KING) CHARLES'S
HEAD, FANATICISM, FANCY, ZEAL
OBSTINACY
See also DETERMINATION, STUBBORN,
TENACITY
OBVIOUS
See also CLEAR, LUCID, INTELLIGIBLE
OCCUPATION
See also HOBBY, PROFESSION, PURSUIT,
SERVICE, WORK
OCEAN
See also DEEP, SEA
OCTOBER
ODDITIES
See also ECCENTRICITY
ODYSSEY
See also OCEAN, SCYLLA AND CHARYBDIS,
WEB
OFF AGIN
OFFEND(ING)
OFFENSE
OFFICE
OFFICIAL

OFFICIOUS
  See also FORWARD, INTRUSIVE, MEDDLING
OIL
OINTMENT
O.K.
OLD
  See also AGE, SENILITY
OLD BLACK JOE
OLD KENTUCKY HOME
OMENS
  See also AUGURS, FOREBODING, WARNING
OMISSION
  See also NEGLECT
ONCE
ONE
  See also UNIQUE
ONE-HOSS SHAY
ONION
ONOMATOPOEIA
OPEN MIND
  See also RECEPTIVITY, TOLERANCE,
    TOLERATION
OPINION(S)
  See also JUDGMENTS, OBSERVATION, SEN-
    TIMENTS, VERDICT
OPPORTUNITY
  See also BIRD: in the hand, CARPE DIEM,
    CHANCE, MOMENT, TIME: and action,
    VICAR OF BRAY
OPPOSITION
  See also CONTRADICTION, DEFIANCE, EN-
    MITY
OPPRESSION
  See ABUSE, CRUELTY, PERSECUTION,
    SEVERITY, TYRANNY
OPTIMISM
  See also CHEERFULNESS, HOPE

OPTIMIST
ORACLE(S)
  See also AUTHORITY
ORDER
  See also COMMAND, DECREE, DEGREE,
    METHOD, SYSTEM
ORGIES
  See also DRINKING, FEAST, REVELRY
ORIGINALITY
  See also NOVELTY
ORPHAN
ORTHODOX
  See also DOGMATISM, HERETIC, RESPECT-
    ABLE, RIGHT
ORTHODOXY
  See also HERESY, RELIGION
OSSA
OSTENTATION
  See also CONSPICUOUS, POMP, SPECTACLE,
    VANITY
OURSELVES
OUT
OUTLAW
  See also CRIMINAL, DESPERATE MEN, HIGH-
    WAYMAN, ISHMAEL, JAMES (JESSE),
    PIRACY
OUTSPOKEN
  See also BLUNTNESS, CANDID, FRANKNESS,
    PLAIN SPEAKING, SINCERITY, TACT
OWE
  See also DUTY, OBLIGATION
OWL
OX(EN)
  See also PLOW, YOKE
OXFORD
OYSTER(S)
OZYMANDIAS

P

PA
PAGAN
  See also HEATHEN, IDOLS
PAIN
  See also AGONY, BEETLE, GRIEF, HURT,
    MISERY, PLEASURE: and pain, SUFFER-
    ING, WOE
PAINTING

  See also ART, DUCHESS, EL GRECO, PIC-
    TURE
PAN
PANTHEISM
  See also GOD, His ubiquity, NATURE:
    and God
PANTS
PAPACY

PAPERWORK
PARADISE
  See also EDEN, HEAVEN
PARADISE LOST
PARADISE OF FOOLS
  See also LIMBO
PARADOXES
  See also CONTRADICTION
PARDON
  See also EXCUSE, FORGIVE
PARENTS
  See also FAMILY
PARENTS: and children
  See also CHILDREN
PARIS
PARKINSON'S LAW
PARLIAMENTS
  See also HOUSE OF COMMONS
PARNASSUS
  See also AONIAN MOUNT, POETRY
PARSON
  See also CLERGY, CURATE
PARTING
  See also ADIEU, BOOK: l'envoi, DEPAR-
    TURE, FAREWELL
PARTY
  See also POLITICS, POLITICIAN
PASS(ING)
PASSION(S)
  See also ANGER, DESIRE (sexual), FEEL-
    ING, HATE, INFATUATION, LOVE, LUST,
    SUFFERING, ZEAL
PASSIVITY
  See IDLENESS, INACTION, PATIENCE,
    REPOSE
PAST: and future
PAST: and present
THE PAST: irrevocable
THE PAST: sadness of and longing for
  See also NOSTALGIA
THE PAST: miscellaneous
  See also GOLDEN AGE, YESTERDAY
PATIENCE
  See also CALM, ENDURANCE, FORBEAR-
    ANCE, FORTITUDE, HUMILITY, IMPA-
    TIENCE, PASSIVITY, STOICISM, SUBMIS-
    SION, SUFFERANCE, WAITING, WRITING:
    labor and patience
PATRIOT(ISM)
  See also COSMOPOLITE, COUNTRY, ENG-
    LAND, JINGO, PENSIONER, TREASON
PATRON
PATTERNS
  See also EXAMPLE, STANDARD
PAUPER

  See also BEGGAR, POOR, POORHOUSE,
    POVERTY, WRETCH
PAYMENT
  See also EXPENDITURE, FORGOTTEN MAN,
    PENANCE, PRICE, PUNISHMENT, REMU-
    NERATION, REWARD, SATISFACTION,
    TRIBUTE
PEACE
  See also CALM, CONTENTMENT, DEATH:
    brings peace, QUIET, REPOSE, REST,
    SERENITY, STILLNESS, TRANQUILITY,
    WAR: and peace
PEACOCK
PEARL
PEARLS BEFORE SWINE
PEASANT
  See also FARMERS, RUSTICS
PEASE PORRIDGE
PEDANTRY
  See also EDUCATION, LEARNING, KNOWL-
    EDGE, PROFESSORS, TEACH, TEACHER
PEDESTRIAN
PEEL, JOHN
PEERS
  See also EQUAL, EQUALITARIANISM,
    JURY, LORD
PEEVISHNESS
  See also COMPLAINING, CROSS, CROSS-
    PATCH, JAUNDICED
PELICAN(S)
PEN
PEN: and sword
PENANCE
  See also CONTRITE, PUNISHMENT, REGRET
PENNY(IES)
PENSION
PENSIONER
PENURY
  See POVERTY, WRETCHEDNESS
PEOPLE(S)
  See also MANKIND
PERCEPTION
  See also INSIGHT, KNOWLEDGE, MIND,
    SENSITIVITY, UNDERSTANDING
PERDITION
  See also DESTRUCTION, HELL, RUIN
PERFECTION
  See also ABSOLUTE, COMPLETION, GIOT-
    TO'S O, HEIGHT, MATURITY, PURE
PERFUME(S)
  See also FRAGRANCE, LAVENDER, ODOR,
    SMELL
PERHAPS
PERILS
  See also DANGER, HAZARD, RISK

PERISH
PERJURY
PERMISSION
See also CONSENT, LICENSE
PERPLEXITY
See also ANXIETY, DOUBT, HESITATION,
INDECISION, SUSPENSE
PERSECUTION
See also AFFLICTION, PUNISHMENT,
TORMENTS, TYRANNY
PERSEVERANCE
See also CONSTANCY, DETERMINATION,
DILIGENCE, ENDURANCE, OBSTINACY,
PERSISTENCE, RESOLUTION
PERSISTENCE
See PERSEVERANCE
PERSONS
PESSIMISM
See also DESPERATION, DESPONDENCY
PESSIMIST
See OPTIMIST
PETARD
PETTICOAT
PHANTOM
See also APPARITION, GHOST, HALLUCINA-
TION, ILLUSION, SPIRIT
PHILADELPHIA LAWYER
PHILANDERING
See also ADULTERY, COURTING, GAL-
LANTRY, WOOING
PHILANTHROPY
See also CHARITY, GENEROUS, GIVING,
HUMANITARIANISM, KINDNESS
PHILISTINES
See also ANTI-INTELLECTUALISM
PHILISTINISM
PHILOSOPHER(S)
See also ARISTOTLE, CICERO, EPICURUS,
GUIDE, IDEALIST, SOCRATES, VOLTAIRE
PHILOSOPHIC
See also CALM, SELF-CONTROL, SPECU-
LATE, STOICISM
PHILOSOPHY
See also CALM, COGITATION, COMPOSURE,
DEATH: readiness for, IDEALS, IDEAS,
LOGIC, MORALITY, SELF-CONTROL, SELF-
KNOWLEDGE, SELF-RESPECT, STOICISM,
THINKING, THOUGHT
PHOEBES
PHOENIX
PHYSICIAN(S)
See also CURE, DOCTORS, HEALING,
HEALTH, MEDICINE
PIANIST
PICKING

See also STEALING
PICKWICKIAN
PICTURE
See also ART, IMAGE, LIKENESS, PAINTING
PIE
See also HORNER
PIED PIPER
PIETY
See also CLERGY, CONSECRATION, DE-
VOTION, EUNUCHS, HOLINESS, RAINBOW,
RELIGION, RIGHTEOUSNESS
PIG(S)
See also HOG
PIGEONS
See also DOVE(s)
PILGRIMS
See also TRAVELER, WAYFARING
PILGRIM'S PROGRESS
PILLAR
PILOT
PINE
PIONEERS
PIOUS
See also PURE, RIGHTEOUS, VIRTUOUS
PIRACY
See also PLAGIARY, ROBBERY, THEFT
PIT
See also HELL
PITCH
PITCHER
PITIFUL
See also WRETCHED
PITY
See also CHARITY, COMPASSION,
COMPUNCTION, CRIMINAL, KINDNESS,
LOVE, MERCY, MILK OF HUMAN
KINDNESS, RUE, SYMPATHY
PLACE(S)
PLACE: position
PLAGIARISM
PLAGIARY
See also CHEATING, ROBBERY, STEALING,
THEFT
PLAGUE
See also AFFLICTION, EPIDEMIC, PER-
PLEXITY, SICKNESS, TORMENT, WORRY
PLAIN SPEAKING
See also CANDOR, FRANKNESS, OUT-
SPOKEN, SPADE, VERACITY
PLAN
See also DESIGN, FORETHOUGHT, MEAN-
ING, METHOD, RESOLVE, SYSTEM,
TELEOLOGY
PLANETS
PLATITUDE(S)

See also CHESTNUT
PLAY
  See WORK
PLAY(S)
  See also DRAMA, THEATER
PLEASING
  See also AMIABILITY, INGRATIATION
PLEASURE
  See also AGE: its pleasures, AMUSE-
    MENT, DELIGHT, DIVERTING, ECSTASY,
    ENJOYMENT, FUN, GRATIFICATION,
    JOY, LOVE: its delights, LUXURY,
    MARRIAGE: delights, SATISFACTION
PLEASURE: and pain
  See also SCRATCHING
PLEASURE-DOME
PLENTY
  See also EXCESS, LUXURY,
    SATIETY, SUFFICIENT, SUPERFLUOUS
PLODDERS
  See also GENIUS, SLOW
PLOT
PLOW(S)
  See also OXEN, SENTENCE, YOKE
POBBLE
POCKET
POE
POEM
POET(S)
  See BARD, BROWNING, BURNS, CHAUCER,
    COLERIDGE, DRYDEN, GOETHE,
    HARDY, JONSON, KIPLING, MARLOWE,
    MERMAID TAVERN, MILTON, MOORE,
    POE, POPE, SHAKESPEARE, SHELLEY,
    SPENSER, VERGIL, WORDSWORTH,
    YEATS
POET: less favorable views
POET: to madness near allied
POET: his power
POET: his sensitivity, ecstasy and pains
POET: miscellaneous
POETRY
  See BATHOS, DOGGEREL, METER,
    ONOMATOPOEIA, PROSE, RHYME,
    SONNET, TONE, TRANSLATION, VERSE
POETRY: attempts at definition
POETRY: and prose
  See also PROSE
POETRY: rhyme
POETRY: rhythm
POETRY: suggests more than it states
POETRY: its uses
POETRY: miscellaneous
POINT

POINT OF VIEW
POISON
  See also ARSENIC, CORRUPTION, FEVER,
    MATE, MEAT: one man's
POLICEMAN
POLITENESS
  See also AFFRONT, CHIVALRY, COURTESY,
    GENTILITY, GOOD BREEDING, GOOD
    MANNERS, RUDENESS
POLITICAL ASPIRANT
POLITICIAN(S)
  See also PARTY, STATESMAN
POLITICS
  See also PARTY, RADICAL, SPOILS
POLYGAMY
  See also MARRIAGE, SERAGLIO
POMP
  See also CEREMONY, GRAVITY,
    SOLEMNITY
POMPADOUR
POOR
  See also PAUPER, POORHOUSE,
    POVERTY, RICH: and poor
POORHOUSE
  See also PAUPER, PENURY, POVERTY
POOR RELATION(S)
POPE
POPE, ALEXANDER, AND
  DRYDEN, JOHN
POPPIES
POPULACE
  See also MASSES, PEOPLE, PUBLIC
POPULARITY
  See also ADMIRATION, CELEBRITY, FAME,
    LIKING, LOVABLE
POPULATION
  See also POPULACE
PORPOISE
POSSIBILITIES
  See also LIKELIHOOD, PROBABILITY
POSTERITY
  See also CHILDREN, PROGENY
POSTSCRIPT
POTENTIALITY
  See also POSSIBILITY, POWER
POUND OF FLESH
  See also JUSTICE, SEVERITY, VENGEANCE
POVERTY
  See LOVE: and poverty, MONEY: the
    lack of it, NECESSITY, NEED, PAUPER,
    PENURY, POOR, POORHOUSE,
    WRETCHEDNESS
POVERTY: its advantages
POVERTY: some definitions
POVERTY: its miseries

POVERTY: its shame
POVERTY: miscellaneous
POWDER
   See also WAR: famous utterances
POWER
   See also AUTHORITY, DELICACY, DO-
      MINION, MONEY: its power, MUSIC:
      its power, POTENTIALITY, STRENGTH,
      WOMAN: her power and sway, WORDS:
      their power
POWER: corrupts
POWERFUL
   See also MIGHTY
PRACTICE
   See also EXERCISE
PRACTICE WHAT YOU PREACH
PRAIRIE
PRAISE
   See also APPLAUSE, APPROBATION,
      COMPLIMENT, FLATTERY
PRAISE: faint and excessive
PRAISE: reciprocal
   See also FLATTERY
PRAY
PRAYER(S)
   See also APPEAL, GOD, RELIGION
PREACHING
   See also CLERGY, PULPIT, THEOLOGY,
      RANT
PRECEDENCE
   See also ADVANTAGE, FIRST COME
PRECEDENCY
   See also FIRST, FIRST COME, FIRST PLACE
PRECEDENT
   See also AUTHORITY
PRECEPT
   See also APHORISM, COMMAND, EXAMPLE,
      MAXIM, WISDOM
PRECISION
   See also CLARITY, EQUIVOCATION,
      LUCID, P'S AND Q'S
PRECOCITY
   See also PRODIGY
PREGNANCY
   See also BIRTH
PREGNANT
PREJUDICE
   See also JAUNDICED
PREPOSITION
PRESBYTERIAN
PRESENT
   See also PAST, FUTURE
PRESIDENCY
   See also LINCOLN, PA, WASHINGTON
      (GEORGE), WILSON (WOODROW)

PRESS
   See also FOURTH ESTATE,
      JOURNALISM
PREVENT
PREVENTION
   See also PROHIBITION
PREY
PRICE
   See also BUYER, COST, EXPENDITURE,
      PAYMENT, VALUE
PRIDE
   See also ARROGANCE, DIGNITY, EGOTISM,
      MILITARY, PROUD, REASON (verb),
      UNHAPPINESS
PRIEST
   See also CLERGY
PRIMITIVE
PRIMROSE
PRIMROSE PATH
PRINCE(S)
PRINCIPLE(S)
   See also MORALITY, VALUE
PRINT(ING)
PRISON(S)
   See also JAIL
PRIVACY
   See also SECRECY
PRIVILEGE
   See also ADVANTAGE, CONCESSION,
      LICENSE, RIGHT
PROBABILITY
   See also LIKELIHOOD, POSSIBILITIES
PROCRASTINATION
   See also DELAY
PRODIGAL
   See also WASTE
PRODIGY
   See also GENIUS, MIRACLE, MONSTER,
      PRECOCITY, SPECTACLE
PROFANITY
   See also BLASPHEMY, CURSING, OATHS,
      SACRILEGE, SIN, SWEARING
PROFESSION(S)
   See also OCCUPATION, VOCATION, WORK
PROFESSORS
   See also EDUCATION, KNOWLEDGE,
      LEARNING, PEDANTRY, TEACHING
PROFIT
   See also ADVANTAGE, BENEFIT, GETTING
      AND SPENDING, PROSPERITY, REMU-
      NERATION
PROFUNDITY
   See also DEPTH, WISDOM
PROGENY
   See also CHILDREN, POSTERITY

PROGRESS
See also ADVANCEMENT, EVOLUTION, IMPROVEMENT

PROHIBITION
See also DENIAL, PREVENTION

PROLIXITY
See BOREDOM, MEANDERING, TALKING, TEDIOUS, VERBOSITY

PROLOGUE

PROMISE(S)
See also AGREEMENT, ASSURANCE, VOW

PROOF
See also CORROBORATION, EVIDENCE, EXPERIENCE, WITNESSES

PROPAGANDA
See also DOCTRINE, DOGMA, EVANGELISM, TEACHING

PROPER
See also FIT, HANDSOME, RIGHT

PROPERTY
See also ESTATE, RICHES, WEALTH

PROPHECY
See also AIRCRAFT, FORESIGHT, WARNING

PROPHET(S)
See also SEER

PROPOSAL
See also PLAN, SCHEME

PROPOSES

PROSE
See also POETRY: and prose

PROSPECT
See also ANTICIPATION, FORESIGHT, HOPE, PROBABILITY

PROSPERITY
See also FELICITY, PROFIT, SUCCESS, WEALTH

PROSTITUTE
See also BAWDY HOUSE, HARLOT, MISTRESS, WHORE

PROTECTION
See also CARE, DEFENSE, GUARDIANS, REFUGE, SHIELD, SUPPORT

PROTEST
See also CONTRADICTION, DIFFER, DIS-APPROBATION, REPREHENSION

PROTESTANTISM
See also NONCONFORMIST

PROUD
See also ARROGANCE, CONCEIT, CONDE-SCENSION, EGOTISM, INSOLENCE

PROVE
See also ANALYSIS, CORROBORATION, EVIDENCE, PROOF, SUPPORT

PROVERBS
See also APHORISMS, EPIGRAMS, MAXIMS

PROVIDENCE
See also FORETHOUGHT, NAIL, PRU-DENCE, SPARROWS

PRUDE

PRUDENCE
See also CAUTION, COWARDICE, DISCRE-TION, FIGHT: he who fights and runs away, FORETHOUGHT, MISTRUST, PROVIDENCE, TIMIDITY, VALOR, VIGILANCE

PRUDERY
See also AFFECTATION, MINCING, MODESTY

PRUNES AND PRISMS

P'S AND Q'S

PUBLIC
See also POPULACE, SOCIETY

PUBLICITY
See also ADVANCEMENT, ADVERTISING, PUFF

PUBLIC OPINION
See also GOSSIP, GRUNDY, MRS.

PUBLIC SCHOOLS
See also DISCIPLINE, EDUCATION, LEARN-ING, TEACHING

PUBLIC SPEAKING
See ACTION, PROLIXITY, RHETORIC, TALKING, VERBOSITY

PUBLISHING
See also BOOKS, LIBEL, UTTERANCE

PUFF
See also ADVERTISING

PULL

PULPIT
See also CLERGY, PREACHING, SERMONS, THEOLOGY

PULSE
See also HEART

PUN(NING)

PUNCTUALITY
See also READINESS

PUNISHMENT
See also CORRECTION, DISCIPLINE, IRESON, PAYMENT, PENANCE, PERSECUTION, REVENGE, ROD, VENGEANCE, WHIPS

PURE
See also CHASTITY, PIOUS, PURITY, VESTAL, VIRGIN

PURGATORY
See HEAVEN, HELL, LIMBO

PURGE

See also ABSOLUTION, EMPTY
PURITAN(S)
PURITANISM
  See also NONCONFORMIST, PROTESTANT-
    ISM
PURITY
  See also CHASTITY, CLEANLINESS,
    DECENCY, VESTAL, VIRGINITY
PURPLE COW
PURPOSE

See also INTENT, INTENTION, MOTIVE,
  RESOLVE
PURSE
  See also MONEY, NAME
PURSUIT
  See also EXPLORATION, HOBBY, HUNT-
    ING, OCCUPATION, SEEKING, SPORT,
    WORK
PYRAMID(S)

QUALITY
  See also CHARACTER
QUARREL(S) (noun)
  See also LOVE: its quarrels and recon-
    ciliations
QUARREL(ING) (verb)
QUEER
  See also ODDITIES, STRANGE
QUESTION(S)

See also ASK
QUESTIONING
  See also EXAMINATION
QUIET
  See also CALM, NOISE, REPOSE, RETI-
    CENCE, SERENITY, SILENCE, SILENT,
    STILLNESS, TRANQUILLITY
QUOTATION
  See also PLAGIARY

R

RACE
  See also COMPETITION
RACING
RADICAL
  See also CONSERVATIVE, NONCONFORMIST
RADICALISM
  See SOCIALISM
RAILLERY
  See also DERISION, RIDICULE, SARCASM,
    SATIRE
RAILROADS
RAIN
  See also CLOUDS, DELUGE, STORM
RAINBOW
RAKE
  See also ADULTERY, LECHERY, LOTHARIO
RANCOR

See also ENMITY, HATE, MALICE, RESENT-
  MENT
RANDOM
  See also AIMLESSNESS, CHANCE, HAZARD
RANT(ING)
  See also BOASTING, BOMBAST, VERBOSITY
RAPE
  See DEFILE, FORCE, SEDUCTION,
    VIOLATE
RARENESS
  See also EXCEPTION, SCARCITY, STRANGE
RARITIES
RASHNESS
  See also AUDACITY, HEEDLESS, RECK-
    LESSNESS
RAT(S)
  See also ALLEY, MOUSE

RAVEN(S)

REACH
See AMBITION, ASPIRATION, HITCH

READ(ING)
See also BOOKS: and reading, NECK
VERSE

READER

READINESS
See also PUNCTUALITY

REALISM
See also TWO AND TWO

REALITY
See also ACTUALITY

REASON (noun)
See also INTELLIGENCE, LOGIC, MIND,
MOTIVE

REASON (verb)

REBELLION
See also DEFIANCE, DISOBEDIENCE, NON-
CONFORMIST, REVOLUTION, RESENT-
MENT, RIOT

REBUFF
See also HUMILIATION, REJECTION,
REPREHENSION, REPROOF

RECEPTIVITY
See also BROAD-MINDED, OPEN MIND

RECIPROCITY
See also COMMERCE, EXCHANGE, INTER-
DEPENDENCE, PRAISE: reciprocal

RECKLESSNESS
See also HEEDLESS, RASHNESS

RECOLLECTION
See also MEMORY, NOSTALGIA, REMEM-
BERING HAPPIER THINGS, REMEM-
BRANCE

RECTITUDE
See also EQUITY, GOODNESS, HONESTY,
HONOR, INTEGRITY, RIGHT, RIGHTEOUS-
NESS, VIRTUE

REED

REELING
See also STUMBLE

REFORM
See also MUCKRAKERS

REFUGE
See also GOD: our refuge, PROTECTION,
RETREAT, ROCK, SAFETY, SECURITY

REFUSAL
See also DENIAL, REJECTION

REGRET
See also COMPUNCTION, CONTRITE, DIS-
APPOINTMENT, FAILURE, HAD I ONLY
KNOWN, LOVE: its regrets, MIGHT HAVE
BEEN, PENANCE, REMORSE, RUE,
TOO LATE

REIGN
See also DOMINION, RULE

REJECTION
See also ARISTIDES, DENIAL, DISBELIEF,
EXILE, REBUFF, REFUSAL, UNWORTHY

REJOICE
See also CHEER, DELIGHT, GLADNESS,
HAPPINESS, JOY, MERRIMENT, MIRTH

RELATIONS
See also FAMILY, KIN, POOR RELATIONS,
RELATIVES

RELATIVES
See also FAMILY, KIN, RELATIONS

RELATIVISM

RELATIVITY

RELIEF
See also DELIVERANCE, HELP, REMEDY

RELIGION
See also ALTARS, ATHEISM, BELIEF, BIBLE,
CHRISTIANITY, DEATH: triumph over,
DEVIL, DINING, DISBELIEF, DOCTRINES,
EVANGELISM, FAITH, FANATICISM,
GOD, GODS, GOSPEL, JESUS CHRIST,
MOHAMMED, MONOTHEISM, PIETY,
PROTESTANTISM, PURITANISM,
SCRIPTURES, SECTS, SENSIBLE, SUPER-
STITION, THEOLOGY, WORSHIP

RELIGION: negative comments

REMEDY(IES)
See also CURE, MEDICINE, RELIEF

REMEMBERING HAPPIER THINGS
See also MIGHT HAVE BEEN

REMEMBRANCE
See also FORGETTING, MEMORY,
OBLIVION, RECOLLECTION

REMORSE
See also PENANCE, REGRET, REPENTANCE

REMOTENESS
See also DISTANCE, HEBRIDES, LONELI-
NESS, SOLITUDE

REMUNERATION
See also PAYMENT, PROFIT, REWARD

RENDEZVOUS
See also MEETING

RENEWAL

RENUNCIATION
See also REJECTION

REPENT
See also MARRIAGE: marry in haste,
repent at leisure

REPENTANCE
See also CONTRITE, PENANCE, REGRET,
REMORSE, RUE, SELF-REPROACH

REPLACEMENT

REPOSE

See also CALM, EASE, LOAFING, PASSIVITY, PEACE, QUIET, REST, SLEEP, SLOTH, STILL WATERS, TRANQUILLITY

REPREHENSION
See also BLAME, CENSURE, DISAPPROBA- TION, PROTEST, REBUFF, REPROOF, SCOLD

REPROOF
See also CENSURE, CORRECTION, REPRE- HENSION, SCOLD

REPUTATION
See also CELEBRITY, EMINENCE, FAME, GLORY, GOOD NAME, IMMORTALITY

RESEARCH
See also EDUCATION, EXAMINATION, PEDANTRY, STUDY, UNIVERSITY

RESENTMENT
See also BENEFITS, HATE, MALICE, RANCOR

RESIGNATION
See also ACCEPTANCE, ENDURANCE, FATALISM, FORTITUDE, MEEKNESS, PATIENCE, SUBMISSION, SUFFERANCE, SURRENDER, TOLERANCE

RESOLUTE
See also CONSTANT, DETERMINATION, EARNEST, INDOMITABLE

RESOLUTION
See also DETERMINATION, FIRMNESS, FORTITUDE, PERSEVERANCE, SELF- RELIANCE, TENACITY

RESOLVE
See also CONCLUSION, DECISION, INTENT, LINE, PLAN, PURPOSE

RESPECT
See also ADMIRATION, ATTENTION, CIVILITY, CONSIDERATION, COURTESY, PERSONS

RESPECTABLE
See also ORTHODOX, WELL-BRED

REST
See also DEATH: brings peace, REPOSE, SABBATH

RESTLESSNESS
See also DISSATISFACTION, IMPATIENCE, TUMULT, WANDERLUST

RESTRAINT
See also DISCIPLINE, LIMITATION

RESURRECTION

RETICENCE
See also SECRECY, SILENCE, STILLNESS, VERBOSITY, TACITURNITY

RETIREMENT
See also REPOSE, RETREAT, SOLITUDE

RETORT
See ANSWER

RETREAT
See also FLIGHT, REFUGE

RETRIBUTION
See EYE FOR AN EYE, FRYING, JUSTICE, MILLS OF THE GODS, PUNISH- MENT, REVENGE, VENGEANCE

RETURN
See also HOMECOMING, RETREAT

REUNION
See also JOIN

REVELRY
See also DRINKING, EAT DRINK AND BE MERRY, FEAST, HILARITY, ORGIES, WINE: women and song

REVENGE
See also JUSTICE, PUNISHMENT, RETRI- BUTION, TIME: reveals, VENGEANCE

REVERE, PAUL

REVOLUTION
See also REBELLION, RIOT

REVULSION
See also AVERSION, DETESTATION, DISLIKE

REWARD(S)
See also INCENTIVE, PAYMENT, REMU- NERATION, SUCCESS

RHETORIC
See also GRAMMAR, PUBLIC SPEAKING, VERBOSITY

RHINE

RHODES, CECIL

RHYME NOR REASON
See POETRY

RICH: and content

RICH: dangers of being

RICH: and poor
See also POOR

RICH: miscellaneous
See also POOR, POVERTY, RICHES, WEALTH

RICHARDSON, SAMUEL

RICHELIEU

RICHES
See also GOLD, MONEY, POVERTY, PROPERTY, TREASURE, WEALTH

RICHES: the baggage of virtue

RIDDLE OF THE SPHINX

RIDICULE
See also CONTEMPT, DERISION, RAILLERY, SARCASM, SATIRE, SCORN

RIFT
See also BREACH

RIGHT
See also DUTY, EQUITY, FAIR, FIT, HONEST, HONOR, IMPARTIALITY, JUST,

ORTHODOX, PRIVILEGE, PROPER, RECTI-
TUDE, TRUE, TRUTH, VIRTUE, WRONG

RIGHTEOUS
See also PIOUS

RIGHTEOUSNESS
See also DOGMATISM, HOLINESS, PIETY,
RECTITUDE, RIGHT

RIGHTS
See also DUTY, PRIVILEGE

RILEY

RIOT
See also CONFUSION, REBELLION, REVO-
LUTION, TUMULT

RIPENESS
See also MATURITY

RISE AND FALL

RISING
See also ASCENT

THE RISING MAN

RISK
See also ADVENTURE, CHANCE, DANGER,
GAMBLING, HAZARD, PERILS, WAGER

RIVALRY
See also EMULATION, STRIFE

RIVER
See also AFTON, DEE, POTOMAC, RUBICON,
STREAM, WABASH, YARROW

ROADS
See also HIGHWAY, TRAVEL, WAY, WAY-
FARING

ROAR
See also CHEER, NOISE, SHOUT, TUMULT

ROAST BEEF

ROBBERY
See also EXCHANGE, PIRACY, PLAGIARY,
STEALING, THEFT, THIEF

ROBBING PETER

ROBE

ROBESPIERRE

ROBIN

ROBIN OSTLER

ROBINSON CRUSOE

ROCK
See also REFUGE, STONE

ROD
See also EDUCATION, DISCIPLINE, PUNISH-
MENT, STAFF

RODERICK

ROGUE
See also BLACK SHEEP, CHEAT, KNAVERY,
SCOUNDREL, THIEF, VILLAIN, WAG

ROLAND

ROMAN(S)

ROMANCE
See also COURTING, DALLIANCE, EXAG-

GERATION, FANTASY, GALLANTRY,
INFATUATION, LOVE, NOVEL, PHI-
LANDERING, WOOING

ROMAN HOLIDAY

ROMANTIC SPIRIT

ROME

ROMEO

ROOM

ROOTS
See also CAUSE

ROPE(S)
See also TACT

ROPE OF SAND

ROSARY

ROSE(S)

ROSE AYLMER

ROSEBUDS

ROTTEN
See also CORRUPTION, DECAY, DENMARK,
LILY

ROUGHNESS
See CRUELTY, INHUMANITY, SEVERITY,
UNKINDNESS

ROUSSEAU

ROW (verb)

ROYAL ROAD

RUBICON
See also CAESAR

RUDENESS
See also ARROGANCE, BLUNTNESS,
CIVILITY, COURTESY, GOOD MANNERS,
VULGAR

RUE
See also PITY, REGRET, REPENTANCE,
SORROW

RUGGED INDIVIDUALISM

RUIN(S)
See also ANNIHILATION, BANKRUPT,
DEFEAT, DESTRUCTION, PERDITION

RULE
See also DOMINANCE, DOMINION, EMPIRE,
EXCEPTION, REIGN, SOVEREIGNTY,
TYRANNY

RULER(S)
See also DESPOT, EMPEROR, KING, LEADER,
LORD, MASTER, MONARCH, TYRANTS

RUM
See also LIQUOR

RUMOR
See also GOSSIP, SCANDAL, WHISPERINGS

RUSSIA

RUSSIAN

RUST

RUSTICS
See also FARMERS, PEASANTS

RUTH
RUTHLESSNESS

See also CRUELTY, INHUMANITY, SEVERITY

S

SABBATH
See also SUNDAY
SACRAMENT
SACRIFICE
See also LOSS
SACRILEGE
See also BLASPHEMY, CURSE, GOD: some
irreverent comments on, IMPIETY,
PROFANITY, SIN, SWEARING
SADDER
See also WISER
SAFETY
See also REFUGE, SECURITY, SURETY
SAILING
See also SEA, SHIPS
SAILORS
See also MARINERS, MARINES, NAVY
SAINT(S)
See also MARTYRS
SALAD
See also ONION
SALLY
SALT
SALUTATION
See also GREETING, HAIL
SALVATION
See also DELIVERANCE
SAMSON
SAND(S)
See also SHORE
SANE
See also HEALTH, LUCID, MAD
SANITY
See also MADNESS
SANTA CLAUS
SARCASM
See also CONTEMPT, DERISION, IRONIES,
RAILLERY, RIDICULE, SATIRE, SCORN,
SNEER
SATAN
See also DEVIL, FIEND, LUCIFER
SATIETY

See also ENOUGH, EXCESS, PLENTY,
SUPERFLUOUS, SURFEIT
SATIRE
See also CONTEMPT, HUMOR, RAILLERY,
RIDICULE, SARCASM, SCORN, WIT
SATISFACTION
See also CONTENTMENT, DELIGHT,
GRATIFICATION, PLEASURE, SUFFICIENT
SATURN
SAUL
SAVAGE(S)
See also CANNIBALS, RUDENESS
SCANDAL
See also CALUMNY, GOSSIP, LIBEL,
RUMOR, SLANDER
SCAPEGOAT
SCARCITY
See also NEED, RARENESS, WANT
SCARS
See also WOUNDS
SCHEMES
See also DESIGN, PLAN, PROPOSAL
SCHOLAR(S)
See also EDUCATION, LEARNING, STUDY,
TEACHER
SCHOOL(S)
See also EDUCATION, LEARNING, TEACH-
ING
SCHOOLBOY
SCIENCE
See also KNOWLEDGE
SCIENTIFIC SPIRIT
See also EDUCATION, LEARNING, STUDY,
TEACHER
SCOLD
See also CURTAIN LECTURE, NAGGING,
REPREHENSION, SHREW
SCORN
See also CONTEMPT, DERISION, DISDAIN,
RIDICULE, SARCASM, SATIRE, SNEER,
THOU
SCOTCHMAN
SCOTLAND

SCOTS
SCOUNDREL
See also CHEAT, KNAVERY, ROGUE,
   TRANSGRESSOR, VILLAIN, WRETCH
SCRATCHING
SCRIPTURE(S)
See also BIBLE
SCRUPLE(S)
See also CONSCIENCE, DOUBTS
SCYLLA AND CHARYBDIS
SEA
See also DEEP, FOAM, OCEAN, SETTING
   OUT TO SEA, SHELL, SHIPS, SHORE,
   STORM, WAVES
SEAL
SEASONS
See also APRIL, AUTUMN, DECEMBER,
   MAY, JUNE, SPRING, SUMMER, WINTER
SECOND PLACE
SECRECY
See also EVASION, MYSTERY, PRIVACY,
   RETICENCE, SHYNESS, SOLITUDE,
   STEALTH, TACITURNITY
SECRET(S)
See also MYSTERY, SNUG
SECTS
See also RELIGION
SECURE
See also ASSURANCE, CERTAIN, CONFI-
   DENCE, INDOMITABLE, INVULNERABLE
SECURITY
See also FALSE SECURITY, FIRMNESS,
   REFUGE, SAFETY, SURETY, TRUST
SEDUCTION
See also PHILANDERING, TEMPTATION,
   WOOING
SEEING
See also LOOK, OBSERVATION, SIGHT
SEEK(ING)
See also ASK, LOOK, PURSUIT
SEEMING
See also APPEARANCES
SEER
See also AUGURS, PROPHET
SELF-CONFIDENCE
See also ASSURANCE, COMPLACENCY
SELF-CONTROL
See also COMPOSURE, PATIENCE,
   PHILOSOPHY, STOICISM
SELF-DEFENSE
SELF-ESTEEM
See also ARROGANCE, EGOTISM, VANITY
SELF-IMPROVEMENT
SELF-INTEREST
See also VICAR OF BRAY

SELF-KNOWLEDGE
See also PHILOSOPHY
SELF-LOVE
See also EGOTISM, FLATTERY
SELF-PITY
SELF-PRAISE
See also BOASTING, VANITY
SELF-RELIANCE
See also ASSURANCE, DO-IT-YOURSELF,
   RESOLUTION
SELF-REPROACH
See also COALS OF FIRE, CONSCIENCE,
   COURSE
SELF-RESPECT
See also HONOR, INTEGRITY
SELF-SACRIFICE
See also DEVOTION, GENEROSITY
SELLING
See also BUSINESS, BUYER, COMMERCIAL-
   ISM, GETTING AND SPENDING, MARKET,
   MERCHANTS, TRADE
SENILITY
See also AGE, DOTAGE
SENSATION(S)
See also FEELING
SENSIBLE
See also WISE
SENSITIVITY
See also PERCEPTION
SENTENCE
SENTIMENTALITY
See also AFFECTATION, EMOTION
SENTIMENTS
See also IDEA, OPINIONS, THOUGHT
SEPULCHRE
See also GRAVE, TOMB
SERAGLIO
See also EUNUCHS, POLYGAMY, WIVES
SERENITY
See also CALM, CHEERFULNESS, PEACE,
   QUIET, TRANQUILLITY
SERIOUS
See also EARNEST, LIFE: real and ear-
   nest, SINCERITY, SOLEMNITY
SERMONS
See also CLERGY, PULPIT, THEOLOGY
SERPENT
See also ADDER, SNAKE
SERVANT(S)
See also COOK, MAID, SLAVE(S), UNDER-
   LINGS, VALET
SERVE
See also HELP
SERVICE
See also LABOR, OCCUPATION

SESAME
SETTING OUT TO SEA
SEVEN
SEVEN AGES OF MAN
SEVERITY
See CRUELTY, OPPRESSION, PURITY, RUTHLESSNESS
SEX
See also ADULTERY, COITION, FORNICATION, HUSBANDS AND WIVES, MARRIAGE, MEN AND WOMEN
SHADOW(S)
See also OBSCURITY
SHAKESPEARE
See also TIGER
SHALOTT, LADY OF
SHAME
See also BASHFULNESS, DISGRACE, DISHONOR, HUMILIATION, POVERTY: its shame
SHAPE
See also FORM
SHARING
SHARK
SHAVING
SHAW, G. B.
SHE
SHEEP
See also BO-PEEP, HERD, LAMB(S), SHEPHERD
SHELL
SHELLEY
SHEPHERD(S)
See also LAMB(S), SHEEP
SHERIDAN, GENERAL PHILIP
SHERRY
SHIBBOLETH
SHIELD
See also PROTECTION
SHIP(S)
See also BARGE, BARK, FERRY, OCEAN, PASSING, SAILING, SAILORS, SEA
SHOE(S)
See also BOOTS, NAIL
SHOP
SHOPKEEPERS
See also BUYER, COMMERCIALISM, GETTING AND SPENDING, MERCHANTS, TRADE
SHORE
See also FOAM, SAND, SEA, SURF
SHOUT
See also CHEER, NOISE, ROAR, TUMULT, YAWP
SHREW

See also SCOLD, HENPECKED, HUSBANDS AND WIVES, XANTIPPE
SHROUD
See also BURIAL, DEATH, GRAVE
SHUDDER
See also HORROR
SHYNESS
See also BASHFULNESS, COYNESS, DIFFIDENCE, MODESTY
SIBLINGS
See BROTHERS, CHILDREN, FAMILY, KIN, PARENTS, RELATIVES, SISTERS
SICKNESS
See also CURE, EPIDEMICS, FEVER, GOUT, HEALTH, HEALING, MEDICINE, PLAGUE, PHYSICIAN, REMEDY
SIDNEY [HILLMAN]
SIEVE
SIGH(ING)
See also LONGING, LOVE, REGRET, REPENTANCE, SORROW, WOE
SIGHT(S)
See also APPEARANCE, EYES, LOOK, OBSERVATION, SEEING, SPECTACLE, VISION, WATCH
SIGN(S)
SILENCE
See also NOISE, QUIET, RETICENCE, STILLNESS, TACITURNITY
SILENCE: its eloquence
SILENCE: is golden
SILENT
See also MUTE
SILK
SILK PURSE
SILVER AND GOLD
See also GOLD
SIMILE(S)
See also LIKENESS, METAPHOR
SIMON PURE
SIMPLICITY
See also INNOCENCE
SIMPLIFY
SIMULATION
See also DECEPTION
SIN(S)
See also BLASPHEMY, CRIME, EVIL, IMPIETY, SACRILEGE, VICE, WHORING, WICKEDNESS, WRONG
SINCERITY
See also INTEGRITY, EARNEST, OUTSPOKEN
SING(ING)
See also ISRAFEL, SONGS
SINGLE LIFE

See also BACHELOR, CELIBACY, MAR-
RIAGE: and single life, THE UNMAR-
RIED

SINK(ING)
See also BATHOS

SINNER
See also CRIMINAL,
TRANSGRESSOR

SIREN(S)
See LOVE: is blind, MERMAIDS

SISTER(S)

SKATING

SKELETON

SKEPTICISM
See also ATHEISM, DOUBT, INFIDELITY,
NONCONFORMIST, SALT

SKILL
See also ABILITY(IES), CRAFT, CUNNING,
EXPERT

SKIN

SKIN OF MY TEETH

SKULL

SKY

SKYLARK
See also LARK

SLANDER
See also ABUSE, CALUMNY, DETRACTION,
GOSSIP, LIBEL, SCANDAL

SLAUGHTER
See also ASSASSINATION, MURDER, SAUL,
WAR: violence

SLAVE(S)
See also SERVANT

SLAVERY
See also DIXIE, (JOHN) BROWN, NEGRO,
TOIL

SLEEP
See also BED, DREAMING, DREAMS, RE-
POSE, REST, SNORING, UNHAPPINESS

SLEEP: and death
See DEATH: a sleep

SLEEVE

SLEIGH

SLIGHT

SLIP
See also CHICKENS

SLOTH
See also EASE, IDLENESS, INACTION, RE-
POSE, REST

SLOW
See also DULL, GRADUALNESS, HESITA-
TION, PLODDERS, TARDY

SLUGGARD
See also ANT

SMELL

See also FRAGRANCE, ODOR, OINTMENT,
PERFUME, STINK

SMILE(S)
See also LAUGHTER

SMILER
See also HYPOCRISY

SMOKE(ING)
See also TOBACCO

SMOOTH
See also CALM

SMUGNESS
See also COMPLACENCY

SNAIL

SNAKE
See also ADDER, SERPENT

SNARK

SNEER(ING)
See also CONTEMPT, SARCASM, SCORN

SNEEZE(ING)

SNOB
See also INSOLENCE, SELF-ESTEEM

SNORING
See also NURSE, SLEEP

SNOW
See also SLEIGH, WINTER

SNUG
See also COMFORT, NEAT, SECRET

SOCIABILITY
See also AMIABILITY, DINING OUT, FRIEND-
SHIP, HOSPITALITY

SOCIALISM
See also RADICALISM

SOCIALIST

SOCIETY
See also ARISTOCRACY, DINING OUT, DROP,
FELLOWSHIP, FOUR HUNDRED, FRIEND-
SHIP, SUPERIOR PEOPLE

SOCRATES

SOCRATIC

SODA WATER

SOLDIER(S)
See also ARM, BRITISH GRENADIER, CAE-
SAR, CROMWELL, GUARD, GUNS, MER-
CENARIES, MILITARY, NAPOLEON, SHER-
IDAN, WAR, WARRIORS, WELLINGTON

SOLEMNITY
See also CEREMONY, DIGNITY, EARNEST,
FORMALITY, FUNERAL, GRAVITY, MAJ-
ESTY, POMP, SERIOUS

SOLITARY
See also ALONE

SOLITUDE
See also ALONE, ISOLATION, LONELINESS,
REMOTENESS, SECRECY

SOMEBODY

SON(S)
  See also CHILDREN, FATHER AND SON,
    MOTHER
SONG(S)
  See also BALLADS, LULLABY, MADRIGALS,
    SINGING
SONNET
SON OF A BITCH
SOPHISTRY
  See also DECEPTION, EQUIVOCATION
SOPHOCLES
SOPHONISBA
SORE EYES
  See SIGHT(s)
SORROW(S)
  See also GRIEF, HEART: the sad and
    broken heart, HEARTBREAK, MISERY,
    RUE, TROUBLE, WISDOM: and sorrow,
    WOE
SOUL
  See also BODY, SPIRIT
SOULFUL
SOUND
  See also HEAR, MEANING, NOISE, ONO-
    MATOPOEIA, TONE
SOUP
SOURCE
  See also BEGINNINGS
SOUR GRAPES
  See also ENVY, JEALOUSY
THE SOUTH
  See also DIXIE
SOUTHERNERS
SOVEREIGNTY
  See also DOMINION, REIGN, RULE
SOWING AND REAPING
  See also HARVEST
SPADE
  See also CANDOR, FRANKNESS, PLAIN
    SPEAKING
SPAIN
SPARROWS
  See also PROVIDENCE
SPARTANS
SPEAK(ING)
  See also GLIBNESS, PROLIXITY, PRUNES
    AND PRISMS, PUBLIC SPEAKING, TALK-
    ING, VERBOSITY
SPECTACLE
  See also MONSTER, OSTENTATION, PROD-
    IGY, SIGHT
SPECTATOR
  See also OBSERVER, WITNESS
SPECULATE
  See also GAMBLING, THEORY

SPEECH(ES)
  See also ACCENT, ACTION: in eloquence,
    ADVERBS, ARGOT, DIALECT, DISCOURSE,
    ELOQUENCE, EXPRESSION, GLIBNESS,
    HEART: thought, speech and action,
    IDIOM, LANGUAGE, PROLIXITY, RANT,
    SILENCE, TEDIOUS, TONGUE, UTTERANCE,
    VERBOSITY
SPEED
  See also CELERITY, GALLOPING, HASTE,
    HURRY
SPELLING
  See also WORDS
SPENS, SIR PATRICK
SPENSER, EDMUND
SPHERICAL
SPIDER(S)
  See also MARRIED LOVE
SPIRIT(S)
  See also GHOST, PHANTOM, SOUL
SPLIT INFINITIVE
SPOILS
  See also POLITICS
SPORT
  See also FALCON, FISHING, FOOTBALL,
    GOLF, HUNTING, PETARD, PURSUIT, RO-
    MAN HOLIDAY, SALUTATION
SPOT
SPRING
  See also APRIL, MAY
SQUARE PEGS
STAFF
  See also ROD
STAG
STAKE
STALE
  See also DULL, DREARY
STAND
STANDARD
  See also BANNER, FLAG, EXAMPLE, PAT-
    TERN
STAR(S)
  See also IMPOSSIBILITIES
STARGAZING
  See also DREAMING
STAR-SPANGLED BANNER
STATE
  See also BODY POLITIC, COUNTRY, DO-
    MINION, GOVERNMENT, RULE
STATESMAN
  See also POLITICIAN
STATUTES
  See also DECREE, LAW
STEAL(ING)

See also PICKING, PLAGIARY, ROBBERY, THEFT

STEALTH
See also SECRECY

STEAM

STEIN

STEP

STEPMOTHERS
See also FAMILY

STERILITY
See also EMPTY, FUTILITY, UNFULFILLMENT

STICKS

STIFF UPPER LIP
See also STOICISM, WAR: famous utterances

STILLNESS
See also CALM, NOISE, PEACE, QUIET, SILENCE, SILENT

STILL WATERS
See also PEACE, REPOSE, SECURITY

STIMULATION(S)
See also HOPE, INCENTIVE, MOTIVE

STINK
See also SMELL, OINTMENT

STOICISM
See also ENDURANCE, FORBEARANCE, FORTITUDE, PHILOSOPHY, SELF-CONTROL, STIFF UPPER LIP, STORIES, SUFFERANCE

STOMACH
See also BELLY, GUTS, LIKING

STONE
See also ROCK

STOOLS
See also HESITATION, INDECISION, PERPLEXITY, SUSPENSE

STORK

STORM
See also DELUGE, LIGHTNING, RAIN, SEA, TEMPEST, THUNDER, WIND

STORY
See also FICTION, NARRATIVE, NOVEL, TALE, WRITING

STOUTNESS
See also FAT

STOWE, HARRIET BEECHER

STRAIGHT

STRAIN

STRAINS
See MELODIES, MUSIC, TUNES

STRANGE
See also ECCENTRICITY, QUEER, RARENESS

STRANGER(S)

STRAW

See also BRICKS

STRAWBERRY
See also FISHING

STREAM(S)
See also BROOK, RIVER

STRENGTH
See also FORCE, FORTITUDE, MIGHT, POWER, VITALITY

STRENUOUS
See also DILIGENCE

STRIFE
See also BATTLE, CONFLICT, CONTENTION, DISSENSION, FIGHT, QUARREL, RIVALRY, STRUGGLE, WAR

STRIKE

STRIVINGS
See also ASPIRATION, LONGINGS, TRY

STRONG
See also MIGHTY

STRUCK

STRUGGLE
See also STRIFE, TRY

STUBBORN
See also HEADSTRONG, OBSTINACY, TENACITY

STUDY(IES)
See also EDUCATION, LEARNING, RESEARCH, SCHOLAR(S), TEACHER

STUMBLE
See also FALL, REELING

STUPIDITY
See also ANTI-INTELLECTUALISM, FOLLY, IGNORANCE, INTELLIGENCE, MORON

STYLE
See also ACADEMY, ADDISON, ADJECTIVES, ALLITERATION, ART, BATHOS, BREVITY, CLARITY, COMPOSING, CUSTOM, ELOQUENCE, FASHION, IDIOM, METAPHOR, METER, NARRATIVE, SENTENCES, TASTE, WORDS: hard words, WRITING

SUBDUED
See also MELANCHOLY

SUBLIME AND RIDICULOUS

SUBLIMITY
See also DIGNITY, ELEVATION, EMINENCE, GREATNESS, MAJESTY, NOBILITY

SUBMISSION
See also OBEDIENCE, PATIENCE, RESIGNATION, SUFFERANCE, SURRENDER

SUBWAY

SUCCESS
See ADVENTURE, CHANCE, FAILURE, FAME, FORTUNE, HAZARD, LUCK, PROSPERITY, REWARD, (THE) RISING MAN, TRIUMPH

SUCCESS: definitions
SUCCESS: how to achieve
SUCCESS: miscellaneous
SUCCOR
   See also HELP, RELIEF, SUPPORT
SUCKER
   See also BAG, CAT'S PAW
SUEZ
SUFFERANCE
   See also CHEEK, ENDURANCE, PATIENCE,
     RESIGNATION, STOICISM
SUFFERING
   See also AFFLICTION, AGONY, BEETLE,
     MISERY, PAIN, PASSION, TORMENTS,
     TROUBLE, WOE
SUFFICIENT
   See also ENOUGH, LITTLE, PLENTY, RICH:
     and content, SATISFACTION, WELL
     ENOUGH, WORD: to the wise
SUICIDE(S)
   See also DEATH: longing for, KILLING,
     MURDER
SUIT
   See also ASK, ASKED, BEGGING,
     FRUSTRATION, HOPE: deferred,
     PRAYER
SUMMER
   See also JUNE, LINE, SWALLOW
SUM OF THINGS
SUN
   See also DAWN, DAY, MORNING, SUNRISE,
     SUNSET
SUNDAY
   See also SABBATH
SUNDIAL
   See also TIME
SUNFLOWER
   See also DEVOTION, FAITHFULNESS
SUNRISE
   See also DAWN, DAY, MORNING, SUN
SUNSET
   See also AFTERNOON, EVENING, GLOAM-
     ING, NIGHT, TWILIGHT
SUNSHINE
   See also DAWN, DAYLIGHT, SUN
SUPERFLUOUS
   See also COALS, EXCESS, PLENTY, SATIETY
SUPERIORITY
   See also EXCELLENCE
SUPERIOR PEOPLE
   See also CURZON, FOUR HUNDRED,
     MIGHTY, NOBILITY, OFFICIAL, PATRON,
     SALT, SNOB, SOCIETY, STATE, WHEELS
SUPERLATIVE

   See also ABSOLUTE, EXCELLENCE
SUPERNUMERARY
   See also EXCESSIVE, SUPERFLUOUS
SUPERSTITION
   See also EVIDENCE, FAIRY TALES, RELI-
     GION
SUPPORT
   See also PROOF, PROTECTION, SUCCOR
SUPREME COURT
   See also JUSTICE, LAW
SURETY
   See also ASSURANCE, BOND, CERTAINTY,
     SAFETY, SECURITY, TRUST
SURF
   See also SHORE
SURFEIT
   See also EXCESS, GLUTTONY, SATIETY
SURGEON
   See also CURE, HEALTH, MEDICINE, PHY-
     SICIAN
SURMISE
   See also THINK, SUSPICION
SURRENDER
   See also BAG AND BAGGAGE, RESIGNATION,
     SUBMISSION, YIELDING
SURVIVAL
   See also ENDURE, LIFE, LONGEVITY
SURVIVORS
SUSANNA
SUSPENSE
   See also DOUBT, HESITATION, INDECISION,
     PERPLEXITY, STOOLS
SUSPICION(S)
   See also JEALOUSY, MISTRUST, SURMISE,
     VIGILANCE
SWALLOW
SWAN(S)
   See also GOOSE
SWAP
   See also EXCHANGE
SWEARING
   See also BLASPHEMY, CURSING, OATHS,
     OBSCENITY, PROFANITY, SACRILEGE,
     VOW
SWEAR-WORD
SWEAT
   See also LABOR, TOIL
SWEET(NESS)
   See also AMIABILITY, BEES, HONEY, LOV-
     ABLE, MILDNESS
SWORD
   See also DEATH, FORCE, PEN: and sword,
     POWER, RULE
SWORN
   See also OATHS

SYLVIA
SYMBOL
  See also TYPES
SYMPATHY
  See also COMFORT, COMPASSION, KIND-
NESS, MERCY, MILK OF HUMAN KIND-
NESS, PITY, TENDERNESS
SYSTEM(S)
  See also DESIGN, HYPOTHESIS, ORDER,
  PLAN, THEORY

T

TACITURNITY
  See also RETICENCE, SECRECY, SILENCE,
    VERBOSITY
TACT
  See also CANDOR, DIPLOMACY
TADPOLE
TAKEN
TALE(S)
  See also FAIRY TALES, FICTION, NARRA-
    TIVE, STORY
TALEBEARER
  See also GOSSIPS
TALENT(S)
  See also ABILITY, GENIUS
TALK(ING)
  See also CONVERSATION, GLIBNESS, PUBLIC
    SPEAKING, SPEAKING, SPEECH,
    VERBOSITY, WOMAN: and talk
TALKER
TAR-BABY
TARDY
  See also LATE, SLOW
TARN
TARTNESS
TASTE
  See also CUSTOM, FASHION, STYLE
TAVERN(S)
  See also HOTEL, INN
TAXATION
  See also EXCISE
TAXED
TAX(ES)
  See also EXCISE, TRIBUTE
TEA
TEACH(ING)
  See also EXAMPLE, EXPERIENCE, KNOWL-
    EDGE, LEARNING, PEDANTRY, PRECEPT,
    PROPAGANDA, TRAINING
TEACHER
  See also EDUCATION, LEARNED, LEARN-
ING, NATURE: the great teacher, PED-
ANTRY, SCHOLAR(S), SCIENTIFIC SPIRIT,
STUDIES
TEAR(S)
  See also CRYING, LAMENTATION, WEEP-
ING
TEDIOUS
  See also BOREDOM, DULL, PROLIXITY
TEETH
  See TOOTH
TELEOLOGY
  See also DESIGN, MEANING, PLAN, RELI-
GION
TELEVISION
TELLING
  See also ARGUMENT
TEMPER
  See also ANGER, FURY, MADNESS, WRATH
TEMPERAMENTS
TEMPERANCE
  See also ABSTINENCE, FORBEARANCE,
    FRUGALITY, MILDNESS, MODERATION
TEMPERATE
TEMPEST
  See also STORM, WHIRLWIND, WIND
TEMPTATION
  See also BAIT, BEWITCHED, SEDUCTION
TEMPTING FATE
TENACITY
  See also CONSTANCY, FIGHT ON, OBSTI-
    NACY, PERSEVERANCE, RESOLUTION,
    STUBBORN, TRY
TENDER-HEARTEDNESS
  See also MILDNESS, MILK OF HUMAN
    KINDNESS, PITY
TENDERNESS
  See also KINDNESS, PITY, SYMPATHY
TENNYSON
TENTING
TERRIBLE

TERROR
See also BUGBEARS, COWARDICE, DREAD, FEAR, FRIGHT, HORROR, NIGHTMARE
TEXAS
TEXT
THANKS
See also GRATITUDE
THANK YOU
THEATER
See also ACTING, ACTORS, ACTRESSES, BROADWAY, COMEDY, DRAMA, GARRICK, HEROD, IBSEN, KEAN, PLAYS, SHAKESPEARE, SOPHOCLES, TRAGEDY
THEFT
See also CHEATING, FRAUD, PIRACY, PLAGIARY, ROBBERY, THIEF
THEOLOGIAN
See also CLERGY, RELIGION
THEOLOGY
See also CLERGY, DOGMA, METAPHYSICS, SERMONS
THEORY(IES)
See also DESIGN, HYPOTHESIS, PLAN, SPECULATE, SYSTEM
THEY
See also GRUNDY, PUBLIC OPINION
THICK
THIEF(VES)
See also BURGLAR, CHEAT, PIRACY, ROBBERY, ROGUE, THEFT
THINGS
See also GETTING AND SPENDING
THINK(ING)
See also DRINKING: and thinking, PHILOSOPHY, SURMISE, THOUGHT
THINKERS
See also MINIVER CHEEVY, PHILOSOPHERS
THIRST
THIRTEEN
THIRTY
THIRTY-FIVE
THIRTY-THREE
THOREAU
THORN(S)
THOU
THOUGHT(S)
See also COGITATION, DELIBERATION, DRINKING: and thinking, FREE THOUGHT, HEART: thought, ideas, speech and action, IDEAS, OPINIONS, PHILOSOPHY, SECOND THOUGHTS, SENTIMENTS
THOUGHTS: second thoughts
See also DELIBERATION
THREAT(S)

See also MENACE, MENE, MENE, WARNING
THRESHING
THRIFT
See also AVARICE, ECONOMY, EXPENDITURE, FRUGALITY, MISER
THRONE
THRUSH
THULE
THUMBS
THUNDER
See also LIGHTNING, STORM
THUS
TICKETS
TICKLE
See also AMUSED
TIDE
See also SEA, TIME
TIDINGS
See NEWS
TIDYING UP
See also NEAT
TIE
See also BOND
TIGER
TIGHT
TIME
See AGE, DAYS, FUTURE, HOURS, NEW YEAR, SEASONS, TIDE, TOMORROW, URGENCY, YEARS
TIME: and action
See also OPPORTUNITY, TIDE
TIME: brings change
TIME: brings our own end
TIME: the destroyer
TIME: and eternity
TIME: flies
TIME: reveals, consoles, revenges
TIME: the waste of
TIME: miscellaneous
TIMEPIECE
See also CLOCK, GRANDFATHER'S CLOCK, HICKORY DICKORY DOCK, IDLER
TIMES
See also AGE (PERIOD), GOLDEN AGE
TIMIDITY
See also BASHFULNESS, COFFEE SPOONS, COWARDICE, DIFFIDENCE, FEAR
TIPPERARY
TIRED
See also WEARY
TITLE(S)
See also NOBILITY
TOAD
See HARROW, UGLY

TOAST
See also CHEER, COMPLIMENT, DRINKING
TOBACCO
See also CIGAR, SMOKING
TOBACCO: against
TOBACCO: for
TOES
TOIL
See also DILIGENCE, INDUSTRY, LABOR, SLAVERY, SWEAT, WORK
TOLERANCE
See FORBEARANCE, MILDNESS, OPEN MIND, RESIGNATION, SUFFERANCE
TOLERANCE: general and favorable
TOLERATION: an evil
TOMB
See also GRAVE, MONUMENT, SEPULCHRE
TOMORROW
TONE
See also MUSIC, POETRY, SOUND
TONGUE
See also SPEECH
TOO LATE
See also MIGHT HAVE BEEN, REGRETS
TOOLS
See also INSTRUMENTS
TOO MUCH
See EXCESS, SUPERFLUOUS, SURFEIT
TOOTH (TEETH)
TOPICS
See also CONVERSATION, DISCOURSE, SPEECH
TOPSY
See GROWED
TORMENTS
See also AGONY, LOVE: its torments and pains, MISERY, NAGGING, PLAGUE, SUFFERING, WOMAN: man's distraction and damnation, WORRY
TORPEDOES
TOUCH
TOWN
See also CITY
TOWN AND COUNTRY
TOYS
TRADE
See also BUSINESS, COMMERCE, GETTING AND SPENDING, MARKET, SELLING
TRAGEDY
See also DRAMA, SORROW
TRAINING
See also DISCIPLINE, EDUCATION, TEACHING, TWIG
TRANQUILLITY

See also CALM, PEACE, PHILOSOPHY, QUIET, REPOSE, REST, STILLNESS
TRANSGRESSOR(S)
See also CRIMINAL, FELON, SCOUNDREL, SINNER, VILLAIN
TRANSLATION(S)
TRAPEZE
TRAVEL
See DIARIES, DUNCE, GIRDLE, JOURNEYS, ROAD, WANDERLUST, WAY, WAYFARING
TRAVEL: delights and rewards of
TRAVEL: illusions, hardships and futility of
TRAVEL: miscellaneous
TRAVELER
See also PILGRIMS, WANDERER, WAYFARING
TREACHERY
See also BETRAYAL, BREACH, FRIENDS: treachery and malice of, HYPOCRISY, INFIDELITY, REBELLION, UNFAITHFUL, WOMAN: frail . . . treacherous
TREASON
See also FIFTH OF NOVEMBER, INDICTMENT, PATRIOTISM, TREACHERY
TREASURE(S)
See also GOLD, MONEY, RICHES, WEALTH
TREE(S)
See also AUTUMN, BRANCH, FALL, FOREST, LEAVES, WILLOW, WOODS
TRELAWNY
TRIBUTE
See also PAYMENT, TAX
TRICK(S)
TRIFLE(S)
See also BAUBLE
TRINITY
See also GOD
TRITON
TRIUMPH
See also SUCCESS, VICTORY
TROUBLE(S)
See also AFFLICTION, ADVERSITY, CALAMITY, DIFFICULTY, DISORDER, GRIEF, HASTE: causes trouble, MISFORTUNE, SORROW, SUFFERING
TROWEL
TRUE
See also CERTAIN, FAITHFUL, FALSE, HONEST, RIGHT
TRUMPET(S)
See also HORNS
TRUST
See also CERTAINTY, CONVICTION, CRE-

DENCE, BELIEF, DUTY, FAITH, SECURITY, SURETY

TRUTH
See also CANDOR, FALSEHOOD, FICTION, FRANKNESS, HONESTY, INTEGRITY, LIBEL, LIE, LYING, RIGHT, VERACITY

TRUTH: dangers and difficulties of telling

TRUTH: and lies

TRUTH: our obligation to

TRUTH: will prevail

TRUTH: miscellaneous

TRY
See also STRIVINGS, STRUGGLE

TUMULT
See also RESTLESSNESS, RIOT, ROAR, STORM

TUNE(S)
See also MELODIES, MUSIC, STRAINS

TURK

TURN

See also FAVOR

TURNING

TURNIP

TWEEDLEDUM AND TWEEDLEDEE

TWENTY-THREE, SKIDDOO

TWIG
See also EDUCATION, TEACHING, TRAINING

TWILIGHT
See also EVENING, GLOAMING

TWINKLING

TWO AND TWO
See also REALISM

TYPES
See also SYMBOL

TYRANNY
See also BRICKS, NECESSITY: the tyrant's plea, OZYMANDIAS, PERSECUTION

TYRANTS
See also BIG BROTHER, DESPOT, DICTATORS

U

UGLY
See also HOMELINESS, ILL-FAVORED

UNAWARENESS
See also HEEDLESS, UNCONSCIOUS

UNBOWED
See also INDOMITABLE, UNCONQUERABLE

UNCLE SAM
See also AMERICA, COLUMBIA

UNCONQUERABLE
See also INDOMITABLE, UNBOWED

UNCONSCIOUS
See also UNAWARENESS

UNCTION
See also FAWNING, FLATTERY

UNDERLINGS
See also SERVANTS, SLAVE(S)

UNDERSTAND

UNDERSTANDING
See also INSIGHT, INTERPRETATION, INTUITION, KNOWLEDGE, PERCEPTION, REASON, WISDOM

UNEDUCATED
See also IGNORANT

UNFAITHFUL
See also FALSE, TREACHERY

UNFORTUNATE
See DOWN, WRETCHED

UNFULFILLMENT
See also FUTILITY, STERILITY

UNHAPPINESS
See also GRIEF, HAPPINESS, MISERY, SORROW, SUFFERING

UNIFORM
See also GARMENT

UNIMPORTANCE
See also INSIGNIFICANCE

UNION

UNIQUE
See also ONE

UNITED STATES
See also AMERICA

UNITY
See also CORD, E PLURIBUS UNUM, PULL, UNION

UNIVERSE

See also EARTH, WORLD

UNIVERSITY
See also COEDUCATION, EDUCATION,
KNOWLEDGE, LEARNING, LIBERAL EDU-
CATION, MARK HOPKINS, RESEARCH,
SCHOLAR(S), STUDY

UNKINDNESS
See also CRUELTY, INHUMANITY, ROUGH-
NESS, SEVERITY

UNKNOWN
See also NEW, OBSCURITY

UNMARRIED
See also BACHELOR, CELIBACY,
MARRIAGE: and single life, SINGLE LIFE

UNNATURAL
See also ARTIFICIAL

UNPARTICULAR
UNWEPT
UNWORTHY
See also REJECTION
UP-HILL
UPLIFTING
URGENCY
USAGE
See also ACADEMY, CUSTOM, GRAMMAR
USE
USELESS
UTILITY
UTOPIA
UTTERANCE
See also OBSERVATION, PUBLISHING,
SPEECH

VACUUM
See also EMPTINESS, NOTHING

VALET
See also HERO, MASTER, SERVANTS

VALLEY

VALOR
See also AUDACITY, BOLDNESS, COURAGE,
COWARDICE, DISCRETION, FORTITUDE,
HERO, HORATIUS

VALUE
See also PRICE, PRINCIPLE, WORTH

VANITY(IES)
See also ARROGANCE, BOASTING, CONCEIT,
EGOTISM, EMPTINESS, OSTENTATION,
SELF-ESTEEM, SELF-PRAISE

VANITY FAIR

VANQUISHED
See also DEFEAT, LOSS, RUIN, VICTORY

VARIETY

VENGEANCE
See also EYE FOR AN EYE, JUSTICE,
MILLS OF THE GODS, RETRIBUTION,
REVENGE

VENICE

VENI, VIDI, VICI

VENUS

VERACITY
See also CANDOR, FALSEHOOD, FRANK-

NESS, HONESTY, PLAIN-SPEAKING,
SPADE

VERBOSITY
See also GLADSTONE, GLIBNESS, PRO-
LIXITY, PUBLIC SPEAKING, RANTING,
RETICENCE, TALKING

VERDICT
See also JUDGMENT, JURY, OPINION

VERGIL

VERSATILITY

VERSE
See also METER, POETRY, PROSE, RHYME

VESTAL
See also VIRGINS

VICAR OF BRAY

VICE(S)
See also EVIL, SIN, VIRTUE: and vice,
WICKED, WOMAN: vices, WRONG

VICISSITUDES
See also CHANGE, FORTUNE, HAZARD

VICTORY
See also DEFEAT, FUSTEST, TRIUMPH,
VANQUISHED

VIGILANCE
See also CARE, CAUTION, FORETHOUGHT,
PRUDENCE, SUSPICION, WATCH

VILE
See also DIRT, DISGRACE, EVIL, LEWD,
OBSCENITY, VICE

VILLAGE
See also AUBURN, TOWN, TOWN AND
COUNTRY
VILLAIN
See also CAD, ROGUE, SCOUNDREL, TRANS-
GRESSOR
VILLAINY
See also CRAFT, CUNNING, DECEPTION,
FRAUD, KNAVERY
VINDICATION
See also EXCUSE, EXTENUATE
VINE
See also BACCHUS, WINE
VINTAGE
See also WINE
VIRGIL
See VERGIL
VIRGINITY
See also CHASTITY, FANCY FREE, MAIDEN-
HEADS, VESTAL
VIRGINNY
VIRGINS
See also MAIDENS, VESTALS
VIRTUE
See GOODNESS, INTEGRITY, MERIT,
MORALITY, NECESSITY: making a
virtue of, RECTITUDE, RICHES: the
baggage of virtue, RIGHT, RIGHTEOUS-
NESS
VIRTUE: its nature

VIRTUE: its rewards and penalties
VIRTUE: and vice
VIRTUE: miscellaneous
VIRTUOUS
See also PIOUS, PURE
VISION
See also APPARITION, DELUSION, DREAMS,
HALLUCINATION, RUIN, SIGHT
VISIT
VISITOR(S)
See also GUEST
VITALITY
See also HEALTH, JOIE DE VIVRE, LIVING,
STRENGTH
VOCATION
See also OCCUPATION, PROFESSION,
WORK
VOICE(S)
See also HEAR, SPEECH
VOLTAIRE
VOLUPTUOUSNESS
See also LUXURY
VOMIT
See AUTHORITY, DISGUST, DOG, SICKNESS
VOW(S)
See also OATH, PROMISE, SWEARING
VULGAR
See also COMMON, CROWD, FAMILIAR,
GENTILITY, HERD, LEWD, POPULACE

WABASH
WAG
See also BLOCKHEAD, JESTERS, ROGUE,
WIT
WAGER(S)
See also BET, GAMBLING, GAMING,
HAZARD, RISK
WAILING
See also CRYING, LAMENTATION, WEEPING
WAITING
See also IMPATIENCE, PATIENCE
WAKE
See also FUNERAL
WALKING

See also DELICATELY, GAIT, MARCHING,
MINCING
WALL(S)
See also FENCES, NEIGHBOR
WALTZ
WANDERERS
See also BUM, PILGRIMS, TRAVELER,
WAYFARING
WANDERING
WANDERLUST
See also BUM, TRAVEL
WANT(S)
See also NECESSITY, NEED, SCARCITY
WAR

See ARMS, ARMY, BATTALIONS,
   BATTLES, CONFLICT, FAIR, FIGHT, FRAY,
   MILITARY, NAVY, PEACE, SOLDIER,
   STRIFE, WARRIOR
WAR: its appeal, excitement, glory
WAR: causes of
WAR: famous utterances
   See also CHEER, DIE, DUTY, ENEMY, FIRE,
   GUARD, POWDER, RUBICON
WAR: morality of
WAR: and peace
   See also PEACE
WAR: violence, danger, death, slaughter
WAR: miscellaneous
WARNING
   See also MENACE, OMEN, THREAT
WARRIOR(S)
   See also CRUSADER, MERCENARIES,
   SOLDIERS
WASH(ING)
WASHINGTON, GEORGE
WASTE
   See also LOSS, PINE
WATCH
   See also OBSERVATION, VIGILANCE,
   WAKE
WATER(S)
   See also MILL, WELL
WATERLOO
   See also WAR: famous utterances
WATTLE, CAPTAIN
WAVES
   See also FOAM, OCEAN, SEA, SHORE
WAY
   See also LONGEST, OUT, ROAD, TRAVEL
WAYFARING
   See also ROAD, STRANGER, WANDERER,
   TRAVEL, TRAVELER
WEAKNESS
   See also FAILINGS, FAINT, FEET OF CLAY,
   FRAILTY
WEALTH
   See also GOLD, MONEY, POVERTY,
   PROPERTY, RICH, RICHES, TREASURE
WEARINESS
   See also BOREDOM, DULLNESS, SURFEIT,
   TEDIOUS
WEARY
   See also TIRED
WEASEL
WEASEL WORDS
   See also EQUIVOCATION, EVASION
WEATHER
   See also FOG, FROST, RAIN, RAINBOW,
   SNOW, STORM, SUN, WIND, WINTER

WEB
   See also NET, NETWORK, SPIDER
WEDDING
   See also BASSOON, MARRIAGE
WEED(S)
WEEPING
   See also CRYING, LAMENTATION,
   LAUGHTER, TEARS, WAILING
WEE WILLIE WINKIE
WELCOME
   See also HOSPITALITY, SOCIABILITY
WELL
   See also BUCKET
WELL-BRED
   See also COURTESY, GOOD BREEDING,
   MANNERS, POLITENESS, RESPECTABLE
WELL DRESSED
WELL ENOUGH
   See also SUFFICIENT
WELLINGTON, DUKE OF
WENCESLAS
WENCH
   See also DAMSEL, GIRLS, LASSES, LOOK
WERTHER
WEST
   See also EAST AND WEST
WHEEL(S)
WHEREFORE
WHIMPER
WHIPS
   See also PUNISHMENT
WHIRLWIND
   See also STORM, TEMPEST
WHISKEY
WHISPERINGS
   See also SCANDAL, GOSSIP
WHISTLE
WHITE
WHITHER
WHORE
   See also BAWDY-HOUSE, HARLOT,
   PROSTITUTE
WHORING
   See also ADULTERY, FORNICATION,
   PHILANDERING, SIN
WICKED
   See also EVIL, IMMORAL, NAUGHTY, SIN,
   VICE
WICKEDNESS
   See also INIQUITY
WIDOW
WIFE
   See ALIMONY, FAMILY, HELPMATE/
   HELPMEET, HUSBANDS AND WIVES,

MARRIAGE: man and wife, SHREW,
WIVES
WIFE: and children
WIFE: the dutiful wife
WIFE: pro
WIFE: con
WIFE(VES): miscellaneous
WILDCATS
WILDERNESS
  See also DESERT, DESOLATION
WILL
  See also FREE WILL
WILLING
  See also AGREEABLE
WILL-O-THE-WISP
  See also DELUSION
WILLOW
WILLS
  See also INHERITANCE, LEGACY
WILSON, WOODROW
WIND
  See also GONE, STORM, TEMPEST, WHIRL-
    WIND
WINDMILLS
WINDOW(S)
WINE
  See BOTTLES, CLARET, DRINKING,
    DRUNKENNESS, GOUT, INTOXICATION,
    SHERRY, VINE, VINTAGE
WINE: its allure
WINE: bad
WINE: good
WINE: women, and song
WINE: miscellaneous
WINEPRESS
WINGS
WINTER
  See also COLD, FROST, ICE, ICICLES, SNOW
WISDOM
  See AGE: its wisdom, CUNNING,
    EARLY TO BED, FOLLY, HINDSIGHT,
    IMAGINATION, INSIGHT, INTELLIGENCE,
    INTUITION, KNOWLEDGE, NEGLECT,
    PERCEPTION, PHILOSOPHY,
    PROFUNDITY, UNDERSTANDING
WISDOM: and folly
WISDOM: of hindsight
WISDOM: and knowledge
WISDOM: its limitations
WISDOM: and sorrow
WISDOM: miscellaneous
WISE
  See also PHILOSOPHIC, SENSIBLE, WORD:
    to the wise
WISE MEN: and fools

See also FOOL
WISER
  See also SADDER
WISH(ES)
  See also DESIRES, LONGINGS
WISHERS
WIT
  See APHORISM, EPIGRAM, HUMOR,
    IMPROPRIETY., INTELLIGENCE, JEST,
    MALICE, RAILLERY, RAZORS, SATIRE,
    WITTY
WIT: its dangers
WIT: and folly
WIT: and madness
WIT: and malice
WIT: its power
WIT: some praises of
WIT: its skill and techniques
WIT: miscellaneous
WITCH(ES)
  See also WIZARDS
WITHERS
WITNESSES
  See also EVIDENCE, EXPERIENCE, OB-
    SERVER, SPECTATOR
WIZARDS
  See also WITCHES
WOE(S)
  See also AGONY, DEATH: the end of woe,
    GRIEF, MARRIAGE: regrets, dangers
    and woes, MISERY, SORROW,
    SUFFERING, TROUBLES, UNHAPPINESS,
    WOMAN: woes, WRETCHEDNESS,
    YOUTH: woes
WOLF(VES)
  See also MAN: a wolf to man
WOLSEY
WOMAN
  See BEAUTY, FRAILTY, FURY, LADY,
    LASSES, LOVE: of men, and of women,
    MAIDENS, PREACHING
WOMAN: and age
WOMAN: all alike
WOMAN: danger of her allure
WOMAN: definitions
  See also MAIDENS
WOMAN: expensive to maintain
WOMAN: frail, shifting, treacherous
WOMAN: illogical and trivial
WOMAN: and learning
WOMAN: and love
WOMAN: her malice
WOMAN: man's delight in
WOMAN: man's distraction and
    damnation

WOMAN: her power and sway
WOMAN: praise of
WOMAN: should be subject to man
WOMAN: and talk
WOMAN: vices
WOMAN: woes
WOMAN: miscellaneous
WONDER(S)
See also EVIDENCE, MIRACLES
WOODS
See also FOREST, TREES
WOOING
See also COURTING, FLIRTATION, GAL-
LANTRY, GLANCES, PHILANDERING,
ROMANCE, WIDOW
WOOL
WOOLGATHERING
See also ABSENCE
WORD(S)
See ACTIONS: and words, ETYMOLOGY,
PUN, SPEECH
WORD: of God
WORD: to the wise
WORDS: their futility
WORDS: hard words
WORDS: and meaning
WORDS: their power
WORDS: proper and seasonable
WORDS: saddest of tongue or pen
WORDS: use and abuse of
WORDS: wild, whirling and bitter
WORDS: miscellaneous
WORDSWORTH
WORK
See also DILIGENCE, INDUSTRY, LABOR,
OCCUPATION, PARKINSON'S LAW, PRIM-
ITIVE, PROFESSION, PURSUIT, TOIL,
VALUE, VOCATION
WORKERS
See also LABORER
WORKING GIRL
WORLD: society and its values
WORLD: the terrestrial globe, man's
dwelling place
See also EARTH, UNIVERSE
WORLDLINESS

See also AMBITION, PRIDE, VANITY FAIR
WORLDLY
WORM
WORM WILL TURN
WORRY
See also ANXIETY, CARE, DREAD, FEAR,
PLAGUE, TORMENTS
WORSE
See also FURTHER
WORSHIP
See also PRAYER, RELIGION
WORST
WORTH
See also COST, VALUE
WOULD
WOUND(S)
See also SCARS
WRATH
See also ANGER, FURY, GOD: His wrath
and justice, MADNESS, TEMPER
See also DESTRUCTION, HESPERUS
WREN
WREN, SIR CHRISTOPHER
See also ARCHITECTURE
WRETCH(ED)
See also PAUPER, PITIFUL, SCOUNDREL,
UNFORTUNATE
WRETCHEDNESS
See also GRIEF, SORROW
WRINKLE
WRITER(S)
See also AUTHOR(S)
WRITING
See AUTHOR(S), BOOKS, DESCRIPTION,
DIALOGUE, EPICS, NARRATIVE, POETRY,
PROSE, STYLE
WRITING: the art of it
WRITING: the itch to scribble
See also GIBBON
WRITING: labor and patience
WRITING: motives
WRITING: miscellaneous
WRONGS
See also INJURIES, OFFENSE
WYCLIF, JOHN
WYNKEN, BLYNKEN, AND NOD

X

XANADU:
  See PLEASURE DOME
XANTIPPE

See also HENPECKED, SCOLD, SHREW,
SOCRATES

Y

YARROW
YAWN(ING)
YAWP
  See SHOUT
YEAR(S)
  See also SEASONS, TIME
YEATS, WILLIAM BUTLER
YES
  See also NO, O.K.
YES-MAN
  See also AGREEABLE, FAWNING, FLATTERY
YES AND NO
YESTERDAY
  See also PAST, TODAY, TOMORROW
YIELDING
  See also SURRENDER
YOKE
  See also BURDEN, OXEN, PLOW
YONGHY-BONGHY-BO
YORICK

See also JESTERS, SKULL, WAG
YOU CAN'T TAKE IT WITH YOU
  See also MONEY
YOUNG
  See also YOUTH
YOUTH: its confidence and assertiveness
YOUTH: its folly, heedlessness and
  illusions
YOUTH: its glory and delight
  See also YOUNG
YOUTH: inexperience, woes, problems
  and longings
YOUTH: and love
YOUTH: will not endure
YOUTH AND AGE: their conduct of
  affairs
YOUTH AND AGE: their morality
YOUTH AND AGE: their mutual con-
  tempt
YOUTH AND AGE: miscellaneous

Z

Z
ZEAL
  See also ENTHUSIASM, EUNUCHS,
    EVANGELISM, LUNATIC FRINGE, OBSES-

SION, PASSION, STRENUOUS
ZION
ZOOS

QUOTATIONS
A

ABBREVIATION
1 It is one thing to abbreviate by contracting, another by cutting off. [Francis Bacon: *Of Dispatch*]

ABIDE
2 Abide with me! Fast falls the eventide;
The darkness deepens; Lord, with me abide!
When other helpers fail, and comforts flee,
Help of the helpless, oh, abide with me!
[H. F. Lyte: *Abide with Me*]

ABILITY(IES)
3 I have never learned . . . to play the lyre, but I know how to make a small and obscure city rich and great. [Themistocles (when taunted with his lack of cultural accomplishments): in Plutarch's *Lives*, "Themistocles" II.3.]
4 Natural ability without education has more often raised a man to glory and virtue than education without natural ability. [Cicero: *Pro Archia*]
5 It is a great ability to be able to conceal one's ability. [La Rochefoucauld: *Maxims*]
6 As we advance in life, we learn the limits of our abilities. [J. A. Froude: *Short Studies*, "Education"]
7 From each according to his abilities, to each according to his needs. [Karl Marx: *Critique of the Gotha Programme*]
8 In the last analysis, ability is commonly found to consist mainly in a high degree of solemnity. [Ambrose Bierce: *The Devil's Dictionary*]

ABOMINATION
9 These six things doth the Lord hate: yea, seven are an abomination unto him:
A proud look, a lying tongue, and hands that shed innocent blood,
An heart that deviseth wicked imaginations, feet that be swift in running to mischief,
A false witness that speaketh lies, and he that soweth discord among brethren.
[Proverbs 6:16-19]

ABOU BEN ADHEM
10 Abou Ben Adhem (may his tribe increase!)
Awoke one night from a deep dream of peace.
[Leigh Hunt: *Abou Ben Adhem*]
11 And lo! Ben Adhem's name led all the rest.
[Leigh Hunt: *Abou Ben Adhem*]

ABSENCE
12 How like a winter hath my absence been
From thee, the pleasure of the fleeting year!
What freezings have I felt, what dark days seen!
What old December's bareness everywhere!
[Shakespeare: *Sonnets* XCVII]
13 I dote on his very absence. [Shakespeare: *The Merchant of Venice* I.ii.]
14 What, keep a week away? seven days and nights?
Eight score eight hours? and lovers' absent hours,
More tedious than the dial eight score times?
O weary reckoning!
[Shakespeare: *Othello* III.iv.]
15 Wives in their husbands' absences grow subtler,
And daughters sometimes run off with the butler.
[Byron: *Don Juan* III.xxii.]
16 We shall meet, but we shall miss him,
There will be one vacant chair;
We shall linger to caress him
When we breathe our evening prayer.
[Henry Stevenson Washburn: *The Vacant Chair*]

ABSENCE: conspicuous by
17 One provision was conspicuous by its absence. [Lord John Russell: speaking

1

to the electors of London, April 1859]
*Lord Russell was referring to a provi-
sion in Lord Derby's Reform Bill. He
later said that he had not coined the
expression but had taken it from "one
of the greatest historians of antiquity."*
   *The historian was Tacitus, who in his
Annals (III.76.ii.), speaking of the funeral procession of Junia, the sister of
Brutus and wife of Cassius, says that,
although the images of twenty of the
greatest families were borne before her
bier, "Those of Brutus and Cassius were
not displayed; but for that very reason
they shone with pre-eminent lustre."*

ABSENCE: makes the heart grow
                                fonder
1   Out of sight, out of mind. [Old English proverb, going back to at least the
13th century]
2   Absence doth sharpen love, presence
strengthens it; the one brings fuel, the
other blowes it till it burnes cleare. [Sir
Thomas Overbury: *Newes of My Morning Worke* (1616)]
3   Absence diminishes little passions and
increases great ones, just as the wind
blows out a candle and fans a fire. [La
Rochefoucauld: *Maxims*]
4   Friendship, like love, is destroyed by
long absence, though it may be increased
by short intermissions. [Samuel Johnson: *The Idler* No. 23]
5   Absence makes the heart grow fonder.
[Thomas Haynes Bayly: *Isle of Beauty*]
6   Absence is the death of love. [Cal-
derón: *El Jardín de Falerina* I]

ABSENT
7   Absent in body, but present in spirit.
[I Corinthians 5:3]
8   It is commonly known that the absent
know by a ringing in their ears that they
are being talked about. [Pliny: *Natural
History* XXVIII. 2]
9   The absent are always in the wrong.
[Philippe Néricault: *L'Obstacle Imprévu*
I.vi. (1720)]
   *Though Néricault, who was better known
   under the name of* Destouches, *is credited with the first statement of this
   thought in this form, the idea is old and,
   in other forms, universal.*

ABSOLUTION
10   Full swetely herde he confessioun,
    And pleasaunt was his absolucioun.
[Chaucer: Prologue to *The Canterbury
   Tales*]
   he = *the Friar*

ABSTINENCE
11   Abstinence from doing is often as
generous as doing, but it is not so apparent. [Montaigne: *Essays* III.x.]

ABSURDITY
12   There is no absurdity so palpable but
that it may be firmly planted in the human head if you only begin to inculcate
it before the age of five, by constantly
repeating it with an air of great solemnity. [Schopenhauer: *Studies in Pessimism,* "Psychological Observations"]

ABUSE
13   The abuse of a thing is no argument
against the use of it. [Jeremy Collier:
Introduction to *Immorality of the English Stage*]
14   Abuse is an indirect species of homage. [William Hazlitt: *Characteristics*]

ACADEMY
15   If an academy should be established
for the cultivation of our style, I . . .
hope the spirit of English liberty will
hinder or destroy [it]. [Samuel Johnson:
Preface to the *Dictionary*]

ACCENT
16   The accent of one's country remains
in the mind and in the heart as much
as in one's speech. [La Rochefoucauld:
Maxims]

ACCEPTANCE
17   Yet I argue not
    Against Heav'n's hand or will, nor
                                bate one jot
    Of heart or hope; but still bear up
                                and steer
    Right onward.
[John Milton: *Sonnet* XVII, "To Cyriack
   Skinner, Upon His Blindness"]
18   I accept the universe! [Margaret Ful-
ler]
   *The remark has been attributed to Mar-
   garet Fuller, and the comment "By God,*

she'd better!" to Carlyle.

1 When you came, you were like red
wine and honey,
And the taste of you burnt my mouth
with its sweetness.
Now you are like morning bread,
Smooth and pleasant.
I hardly taste you at all, for I know
your savor;
But I am completely nourished.
[Amy Lowell: *A Decade*]

2 Ah, when to the heart of man
Was it ever less than a treason
To go with the drift of things,
To yield with a grace to reason,
And bow and accept the end
Of a love or a season?
[Robert Frost: *Reluctance*]

ACCIDENT(S)

3 Moving accidents by flood and field.
[Shakespeare: *Othello* I.iii.]

4 There is no such thing as an accident.
What we call by that name is the effect
of some cause which we do not see. [Voltaire: *Lettres de Memmius* III]

5 Accidents will happen—best regulated families. [Dickens: *Pickwick Papers* II (1836)]

> With the insertion of "in the," the form
> Dickens gave to this commonplace observation has been accepted as the proverbial one. George Colman had stated
> sixty years before that accidents happen
> and Scott, thirteen years before, had
> observed that irregularities "befall in the
> best regulated families." The thought
> unquestionably goes back to the Stone
> Age and must have been expressed in the
> intervening millennia in every conceivable combination of words in every language.

6 ACCIDENT. An inevitable occurrence
due to the action of immutable natural
laws. [Ambrose Bierce: *The Devil's Dictionary*]

ACCOMPLISHMENT

7 Wha does the utmost that he can,
Will whyles do mair.
[Burns: *To Dr. Blacklock*]
whyles = *at times;* mair = *more*

8 Somebody said that it couldn't be
done,
But he with a chuckle replied

That "maybe it couldn't," but he
would be one
Who wouldn't say so till he'd tried.
So he buckled right in with the trace
of a grin
On his face. If he worried he hid it.
He started to sing as he tackled the
thing
That couldn't be done, and he did
it.
[Edgar A. Guest: *It Couldn't Be Done*]

ACCORD

9 Two souls with but a single thought,
Two hearts that beat as one.
[Maria Lovell: *Ingomar the Barbarian*]

ACCUMULATION

10 For the proverb saith that many small
maken a great. [Chaucer: *The Parson's Tale*]

ACCUSATION

11 Accuse not a servant unto his master.
[Proverbs 30:10]

12 No man is bound to accuse himself.
[John Selden: *Table Talk*, "Law"]

13 *J'accuse*. [Émile Zola: open letter to
the President of France, accusing various
persons of complicity in the Dreyfus case
(1898)]

ACHILLES

14 Achilles absent was Achilles still.
[Homer: *Iliad* XXII]

ACQUAINTANCE

15 The art of life is to keep down acquaintances. One's friends one can manage, but one's acquaintances can be the
devil. [E. V. Lucas: *Over Bremerton's*]

ACTING

16 All the world doth practise stageplaying. [Montaigne: *Essays* III.x.]

17 I can counterfeit the deep tragedian;
Speak and look back, and pry on every side,
Tremble and start at wagging of a
straw,
Intending deep suspicion.
[Shakespeare: *Richard III* III.v.]

18 Oh, it offends me to the soul to hear
a robustious periwig-pated fellow tear a
passion to tatters, to very rags, to split

the ears of the groundlings, who for the most part are capable of nothing but inexplicable dumb-shows and noise. I would have such a fellow whipped for o'erdoing Termagant; it out-herods Herod. [Shakespeare: *Hamlet* III.ii.]
See HEROD.

1 Speak the speech, I pray you, as I pronounced it to you, trippingly on the tongue; but if you mouth it, as many of your players do, I had as lief the town-crier spoke my lines. Nor do not saw the air too much with your hand, but use all gently; for in the very torrent, tempest, and, as I may say, the whirlwind of passion, you must acquire and beget a temperance that may give it smoothness. [Shakespeare: *Hamlet* III.ii.]

2 Suit the action to the word, the word to the action; with this special observance, that you o'erstep not the modesty of nature. [Shakespeare: *Hamlet* III.ii.]

3 To hold, as 'twere, the mirror up to nature; to show virtue her own feature, scorn her own image, and the very age and body of the time his form and pressure. [Shakespeare: *Hamlet* III.ii.]

4 On this great stage, the world, no
      monarch e'er
Was half so haughty as a monarch
      player.
[Charles Churchill: *The Apology* 254]

5 Everybody has his own theatre, in which he is manager, actor, prompter, playwright, sceneshifter, boxkeeper, doorkeeper, and audience. [J. C. and A. W. Hare: *Guesses at Truth*, Series ii.]

6 Acting is the lowest of the arts, if it is an art at all. [George Moore: *Mummer-Worship*]

ACTION: in eloquence

7 Action! Action! Action! [Demosthenes: when asked to name the three most important things in oratory; quoted by Plutarch in *Lives of the Ten Orators*]
The idea of listing the same thing three times over as the three most important things has been much imitated. The most famous of its imitations is Danton's De l'audace, encore de l'audace, et toujours de l'audace (1792).

8 Action is eloquence. [Shakespeare: *Coriolanus* III.ii.]

9 Action [in public speaking] can have no effect upon reasonable minds. It may augment noise, but it can never enforce argument. [Samuel Johnson: in Boswell's *Life,* April 3, 1773]

ACTION(S)

10 It is too late to look for instruments when the work calls for execution. [Samuel Johnson: Preface to the *Dictionary*]

11 We never do anything well till we cease to think about the manner of doing it. [William Hazlitt: *On Prejudice*]

12 Each morning sees some task begun,
    Each evening sees it close;
Something attempted, something
               done,
    Has earned a night's repose.
[Longfellow: *The Village Blacksmith*]

13 In base times active men are of more use than virtuous. [Francis Bacon: *Of Followers and Friends*]

14 Thoughts were given for action's gov-
      ernment;
Where action ceases, thought's im-
      pertinent.
Our sphere of action is life's hap-
      piness,
And he that thinks beyond, thinks
      like an ass.
[John Wilmot, Earl of Rochester: *A Satyr Against Mankind*]

15 A generous action is its own reward. [William Walsh: *Upon Quitting His Mistress* (1692)]

16 Think that day lost whose descending
      sun
Views from thy hand no noble action
      done.
[Jacob Bobart: *Virtus sua Gloria*]
Signed "James Bobart" and dated 1697, this famous couplet (commonly misquoted "Count that day lost . . .") is in an autograph album of David Krieg in the British Museum.

The various versions of this sentiment all stem from the statement in Suetonius (A.D. 70-140) that the Emperor Titus was accustomed to exclaim (no doubt to murmurs of admiration and much uplifting of hands and eyes from his courtiers) that he had "lost a day" on those days when he had failed to perform some noble act.

The sentiment, which is echoed in Pope, Young and other poets, was prob-

ably drawn directly from Suetonius until the 19th century.

ACTIONS: and words

1 Such things are easier said than done. [Plautus: *Asinaria* I.iii.]

2 No sooner said than done, so acts your man of worth. [Ennius: *Annals* IX. Fragment 315]

3 We think according to nature; we speak according to rules; we act according to custom. [Francis Bacon: *The Advancement of Learning*, "Nature"]

4 'Tis better said than done. [Shakespeare: *III Henry VI* III.ii.]

5 Suit the action to the word, the word to the action. [Shakespeare: *Hamlet* III.ii.]

6 Thy actions to thy words accord. [John Milton: *Paradise Lost* III.9.]

7 I have always thought the actions of men the best interpreters of their thoughts. [John Locke: *An Essay Concerning Human Understanding* I.3.]

ACT OF GOD

8 An act of God was defined as *something which no reasonable man could have expected.* [A. P. Herbert: *Uncommon Law*]

ACTORS

9 Like a strutting player, whose conceit
Lies in his hamstring, and doth think
it rich
To hear the wooden dialogue and
sound
'Twixt his stretch'd footing and the
scaffoldage.
[Shakespeare: *Troilus and Cressida* I.iii.]
conceit = *power of imagination;* hamstring = *used here collectively for the tendons which form the ham or space at the back of the knee.*

The passage so aptly describes the "ham" that it is hard to feel it doesn't have something to do with the application of that word to certain fatuous, exhibitionistic actors. But the origin of ham *in this sense is obscure. Some think it derives from Hamlet, a favorite role of such players. Some think it derives from the ham fat which the minstrel troupers used as cold cream.*

10 They are the abstracts and brief chronicles of the time. [Shakespeare: *Hamlet* II.ii.]

11 There be players that I have seen play, and heard others praise, and that highly, not to speak it profanely, that neither have the accent of Christian, pagan, nor man, have so strutted and bellowed, that I have thought some of nature's journeymen had made men, and not made them well, they imitated humanity so abominably. [Shakespeare: *Hamlet* III.ii.]

12 Whence are we, and why are we? Of
what scene
The actors or spectators?
[Shelley: *Adonais*]

ACTRESSES

13 I'll come no more behind your scenes, David; for the silk stockings and white bosoms of your actresses excite my amorous propensities. [Samuel Johnson: in Boswell's *Life* (1750)]

There is evidence that Boswell, who had the story from Hume who had it from Garrick, bowdlerized Johnson a little here, that the actual words were more fervent.

ACTUALITY

14 An acre in Middlesex is better than a principality in Utopia. The smallest actual good is better than the most magnificent promises of impossibilities. [Macaulay: *Francis Bacon*]

ADAM AND EVE

15 The hye god, whan he hadde Adam
maked,
And saugh him al allone, belly-naked,
God of his grete goodnesse seyde
than,
"Lat us now make an help un-to this
man
Lyk to him-self;" and thanne he made
him Eve.
[Chaucer: *The Merchant's Tale*]

16 And Adam was a gardener. [Shakespeare: *II Henry VI* IV.ii.]

17 In Adam's fall
We sinned all.
[Anon.: *The New England Primer*]

5

1 Adam the goodliest man of men since
born
His sons, the fairest of her daughters
Eve.
[John Milton: *Paradise Lost* IV.323.]

2 For contemplation he and valour
form'd,
For softness she and sweet attractive
grace;
He for God only, she for God in him.
[John Milton: *Paradise Lost* IV.297.]

3 And therefore though Adam was
framed without this part [the navel],
as having no other womb than that of
his proper principles, yet was not his
posterity without the same: for the sem-
inality of his fabrick contained the power
thereof; and was endued with the science
of those parts whose predestinations
upon succession it did accomplish. [Sir
Thomas Browne: *Pseudodoxia Epidemica* V]

> proper principles = *own origins*
>
> *Sir Thomas's chief argument against
> Adam's having had a navel was that it
> would carry the imputation that "the
> Creator affected superfluities, or ordained
> parts without use or office."*
>
> *This is generally regarded as the de-
> finitive statement on the nonomphalic
> side. If the reader is unable to grasp Sir
> Thomas's meaning at first perusal, he
> may reread.*

4 When Eve upon the first of Men
The apple press'd with specious
cant,
Oh! what a thousand pities then
That Adam was not Adamant!
[Thomas Hood: *A Reflection*]

5 Whoever has lived long enough to
find out what life is, knows how deep a
debt of gratitude we owe to Adam, the
first great benefactor of our race. He
brought death into the world. [Mark
Twain: *Pudd'nhead Wilson's Calendar*]

6 Adam
Had 'em.
[Strickland Gillilan: *On the Antiquity
of Microbes* (1912)]

ADDER

7 They are like the deaf adder that
stoppeth her ear;
Which will not hearken to the voice

of charmers, charming never so wisely.
[Psalms 58:4-5]

ADDISON

8 He from the taste obscene reclaims
our youth,
And sets the passions on the side of
Truth,
Forms the soft bosom with the gen-
tlest Art,
And pours each human virtue in the
heart.
[Alexander Pope: *Imitations of Horace*
Bk. II. *Epistle* I, 217-220.]

9 Whoever wishes to attain an English
style, familiar but not coarse, and elegant but not ostentatious, must give his
days and nights to the volumes of Addison. [Samuel Johnson: *Lives of the Poets,*
"Addison"]

ADJECTIVE(S)

10 As to the Adjective: when in doubt,
strike it out. [Mark Twain: *Pudd'nhead
Wilson's Calendar*]

11 But why wasn't I born, alas, in an
age of Adjectives; why can one no longer
write of silver-shedding Tears and moon-
tailed Peacocks, of eloquent Death, of
the Negro and star-enamelled Night?
[Logan Pearsall Smith: *More Trivia,*
"Adjectives"]

ADMIRAL

12 It is good, from time to time, to kill
an admiral, in order to encourage the
others. [Voltaire: *Candide* XXIII]

> *Voltaire was alluding, with the pity and
> horror at the thought of human stupid-
> ity that underlay most of his jesting, to
> the case of the British admiral, John
> Byng, who was executed in 1757 for not
> having engaged the enemy with sufficient
> vigor. By modern standards the execu-
> tion was unwarranted. Voltaire had been
> active in trying to save Byng's life. This
> witticism may, in the long run, have
> done more good than his humane efforts.*

ADMIRALTY

13 If blood be the price of admiralty,
Lord God, we ha' paid in full!
[Kipling: *The Song o' the Dead*]

ADMIRATION

1 Season your admiration for a while. [Shakespeare: *Hamlet* I.ii.]

2 Admiration is the daughter of ignorance. [Thomas Fuller (1608-1661): *The Holy State*, "The Embassadour"]

admiration = *astonishment, surprise, wondering, marveling*

3 Things not understood are admired. [Thomas Fuller (1654-1734): *Gnomologia* (1732)]

admired = *wondered at*

4 We are willing to be pleased but are not willing to admire; we favor the mirth or officiousness that solicits our regard but oppose the worth or spirit that enforces it. [Samuel Johnson: *The Rambler* No. 188]

5 ADMIRATION. Our polite recognition of another's resemblance to ourselves. [Ambrose Bierce: *The Devil's Dictionary*]

ADULTERY

6 Whosoever looketh on a woman to lust after her hath committed adultery with her already in his heart. [Matthew 5:28]

7 Whosoever shall marry her that is divorced committeth adultery. [Matthew 5:32]

8 Of the same paper whereon a judge writ but even now the condemnation against an adulterer, he will tear a scantling, thereon to write some love-lines to his fellow-judge's wife. [Montaigne: *Essays* III.ix.]

9   And easy it is
Of a cut loaf to steal a shive.
[Shakespeare: *Titus Andronicus* II.i.]

shive = *slice*

The saying, a common one, implies that adultery might be easy to arrange and would pass unnoticed.

10   What was thy cause? Adultery?
Thou shalt not die: die for adultery?
No!
The wren goes to 't, and the small
gilded fly
Does lecher in my sight. Let copulation thrive.
[Shakespeare: *King Lear* IV.vi.]

11 A wanton and lascivious eye betrays
the heart's adultery.

[Robert Herrick: *Hesperides*, "The Eye" (1648)]

12 What men call gallantry, and gods
adultery,
Is much more common where the climate's sultry.
[Byron: *Don Juan* I.lxiii.]

13 Do not adultery commit;
Advantage rarely comes of it.
[Arthur Hugh Clough: *The Latest Decalogue*]

14 Democracy applied to love. [H. L. Mencken: *A Book of Burlesques*]

ADVANCEMENT

15 If you wish in this world to advance
Your merits you're bound to enhance;
You must stir it and stump it,
And blow your own trumpet,
Or, trust me, you haven't a chance.
[W. S. Gilbert: *Ruddigore* I]

ADVANTAGE

16 To whose advantage would it be?
(*Cui bono fuerit?*)

Cui bono? *was the principle on which the severe Roman judge, Lucius Cassius Longinus (2nd century* B.C.*) decided his cases. He was convinced that the crime was committed by the person who profited, or would have profited, by it. He was probably right much of the time and when he was wrong it was not to the advantage of the guilty to correct him.*

17 It's them as take advantage that get advantage i' this world. [George Eliot: *Adam Bede* XXXII]

ADVENTURE

18 With the woman-adventurer all is love or hate. Her adventure is man; her type is not the prospector, but the courtesan. That is, her adventure is an escape, developing inevitably into a running fight with the institution of marriage. [William Bolitho: *Twelve Against the Gods*, "Lola Montez"]

ADVERBS

19 God loveth adverbs. [Bishop Joseph Hall: *Holy Observations* (1607)]

20 I'm glad you like adverbs—I adore them. [Henry James: Letter to Miss Edwards, Jan. 5, 1912]

ADVERSARY

1 Agree with thine adversary quickly, whiles thou art in the way with him. [Matthew 5:25]

2 Treating your adversary with respect is giving him an advantage to which he is not entitled. [Samuel Johnson: in Boswell's *Life* (1779)]

ADVERSITY

3 If thou faint in the day of adversity, thy strength is small. [Proverbs 24:10]

4 The bread of adversity and the water of affliction. [Isaiah 30:20]

5 Sweet are the uses of adversity;
Which, like the toad, ugly and venomous,
Wears yet a precious jewel in his head.
[Shakespeare: *As You Like It* II.i.]

6 He knows not his own strength that hath not met adversity. [Francis Bacon: *Of Fortune*]

7 Prosperity doth best discover vice, but adversity doth best discover virtue. [Francis Bacon: *Of Adversity*]
discover = *reveal, bring to light, uncover*

8 The virtue of prosperity is temperance; the virtue of adversity is fortitude; which in morals is the more heroical virtue. [Francis Bacon: *Of Adversity*]

9 The greatest object in the universe, says a certain philosopher, is a good man struggling with adversity; yet there is a still greater, which is the good man that comes to relieve it. [Oliver Goldsmith: *The Vicar of Wakefield* XXX]

10 For one man who can stand prosperity, there are a hundred that will stand adversity. [Thomas Carlyle: *Heroes and Hero Worship*, "The Hero as Man of Letters"]
This is one of the commonest of the utterances of the wise. But does observation support it? Is it not possible that in adversity men are humble, obsequious, respectful—even to philosophers—and that this attitude makes them seem "better" men to those who dislike independence in others?

ADVERTISING

11 Promise, large promise, is the soul of an advertisement. [Samuel Johnson: *The Idler* No. 40]

12 Advertisements contain the only truths to be relied on in a newspaper. [Thomas Jefferson: Letter to Nathaniel Macon]
Journalists and ad men agree that this is a half truth but are unable to agree which half is truthful.

13 Advertising is a racket . . . its constructive contribution to humanity is exactly minus zero. [F. Scott Fitzgerald: *The Crack-Up*]
Fitzgerald worked for a while as a young man in an advertising company.

14 Doing business without advertising is like winking at a girl in the dark. You know what you are doing, but nobody else does. [Steuart Henderson Britt, quoted *New York Herald Tribune*, Oct. 30, 1956]

ADVICE

15 Advice is judged by results, not by intentions. [Cicero: *Ad Atticum* IX]

16 Whatever advice you give, be short. [Horace: *Ars poetica*]

17 Many receive advice, only the wise profit by it. [Publilius Syrus: *Maxims*]

18 One who is not wise himself cannot be well advised. [Machiavelli: *The Prince* XXIII]

19 Who cannot give good counsel? 'Tis cheap, it costs them nothing. [Robert Burton: *The Anatomy of Melancholy* II.2.3.]

20 Ask counsel of both times: of the ancient time what is best; and of the latter time what is fittest. [Francis Bacon: *Of Great Place*]

21 It is a rare thing, except it be from a perfect and entire friend, to have counsel given but such as shall be bowed and crooked to some ends which he hath that giveth it. [Francis Bacon: *Of Friendship*]

22 He that will not be counselled cannot be helped. [John Clarke: *Paroemiologia*]
A proverb listed in many collections, including Poor Richard's Almanack, *and in many languages.*

23 If a man love to give advice, it is a sure sign that he himself wanteth it. [Lord Halifax: *Works*]

24 How is it possible to expect that man-

8

kind will take advice, when they will not so much as take warning? [Jonathan Swift: *Thoughts on Various Subjects*]

1 He that refuseth to buy counsel cheap, shall buy repentance dear. [Anon.: *The Country-mans New Commonwealth* (1647)]

> counsel = *advice*

2 Counsel is as welcome to him as a Shoulder of Mutton to a sick Horse. [Thomas Fuller (1654-1734): *Gnomologia* (1732)]

> counsel = *advice*

3 I give myself admirable advice, but I am incapable of taking it. [Lady Mary Wortley Montagu: Letter to the Countess of Mar]

4 Advice is seldom welcome; and those who want it the most always like it the least. [Lord Chesterfield: *Letters,* January 29, 1748]

> want = *need, desire*

5 It is not often that any man can have so much knowledge of another as is necessary to make instruction [i.e. advice] useful. [Samuel Johnson: *The Rambler* No. 87]

6 Advice, as it always gives a temporary appearance of superiority, can never be grateful, even when it is most necessary or most judicious. [Samuel Johnson: *The Rambler* No. 87]

> grateful = *acceptable, welcome, pleasing to the mind*

7 Vanity is so frequently the apparent motive of advice that we, for the most part, summon our powers to oppose it without any very accurate inquiry whether it is right. It is sufficient that another is growing great in his own eyes at our expense and assumes authority over us without our permission; for many would contentedly suffer the consequences of their own mistakes rather than the insolence of him who triumphs as their deliverer. [Samuel Johnson: *The Rambler* No. 87]

8 Advice is offensive—because it shows us that we are known to others as well as to ourselves. [Samuel Johnson: *The Rambler* No. 155]

9 We ask advice, but we mean approbation. [C. C. Colton: *Lacon*]

10 I have lived some thirty years on this planet, and I have yet to hear the first syllable of valuable or even earnest advice from my seniors. [Thoreau: *Walden I*]

11 It is always a silly thing to give advice, but to give good advice is absolutely fatal. [Oscar Wilde: *Portrait of Mr. W.H.*]

12 A good scare is worth more to a man than good advice. [E. W. Howe: *Country Town Sayings*]

13 Perhaps one of the only positive pieces of advice that I was ever given was that supplied by an old courtier who observed: Only two rules really count. Never miss an opportunity to relieve yourself; never miss a chance to sit down and rest your feet. [Edward, Duke of Windsor: *A King's Story* (1951)]

14 Never play cards with a man called Doc. Never eat at a place called Mom's. Never sleep with a woman whose troubles are worse than your own. [Nelson Algren, in *Newsweek,* July 2, 1956]

> *Mr. Algren said he had the advice from a convict.*

AESTHETE

15 A greenery-yallery, Grosvenor Gallery, Foot-in-the-grave young man!
[W. S. Gilbert: *Patience* II]

AFFAIRS

16 Every man's affairs, however little, are important to himself. [Samuel Johnson: Letter to the Earl of Bute, Nov. 3, 1762]

> *For every man hath business and desire,*
> *Such as it is.*
>
> Shakespeare: Hamlet *I.v.*

AFFECTATION

17 The qualities we have do not make us so ridiculous as those we affect to have. [La Rochefoucauld: *Maxims*]

18 Affectation is always to be distinguished from hypocrisy, as being the art of counterfeiting those qualities which we might with innocence and safety be known to want. [Samuel Johnson: *The Rambler* No. 20]

19 Affectation is as necessary to the mind as dress is to the body. [William Hazlitt: *Characteristics*]

AFFECTION
1 Yet still he fills affection's eye,
Obscurely wise, and coarsely kind.
[Samuel Johnson: *On the Death of Dr. Robert Levet*]

AFFLICTION
2 The bread of affliction. [Deuteronomy 16:31]
The phrase occurs also in I Kings 22:27 and II Chronicles 18:26, where is also found "water of affliction."
3 Are afflictions aught
But blessings in disguise?
[David Mallet: *Amyntor and Theodora*]

AFFRONT
4 A moral, sensible, and well-bred man
Will not affront me, and no other can.
[William Cowper: *Conversation*]

AFTERNOON
5 In the posteriors of this day, which the rude multitude call the afternoon.
[Shakespeare: *Love's Labour's Lost* V.i.]
6   A land
In which it seemed always afternoon.
[Tennyson: *The Lotos-Eaters*]

AFTON
7 Flow gently, sweet Afton, among thy green braes!
Flow gently, I'll sing thee a song in thy praise.
[Burns: *Flow Gently, Sweet Afton*]

AGE: general
8 What else is an old man but voice and shadow? [Euripides: *Melanippe*, Fragment 18]
9 Remember now thy Creator in the days of thy youth, while the evil days come not, nor the years draw nigh, when thou shalt say, I have no pleasure in them;
While the sun, or the light, or the moon, or the stars, be not darkened, nor the clouds return after the rain:
In the day when the keepers of the house shall tremble, and the strong men shall bow themselves, and the grinders cease because they are few, and those that look out of the windows be darkened,
And the doors shall be shut in the streets, when the sound of the grinding is low, and he shall rise up at the voice of the bird, and all the daughters of music shall be brought low;
Also when they shall be afraid of that which is high, and fears shall be in the way, and the almond tree shall flourish, and the grasshopper shall be a burden, and desire shall fail: because man goeth to his long home, and the mourners go about the streets:
Or ever the silver cord be loosed, or the golden bowl be broken, or the pitcher be broken at the fountain, or the wheel broken at the cistern.
Then shall the dust return to the earth as it was: and the spirit shall return unto God who gave it. [Ecclesiastes 12:1-7]
Scholars are agreed that these verses are a description of physical old age, but there is dispute about the significance of many details. Some have claimed, for instance, that the silver cord is the spinal cord; others maintain that it is merely a figure of speech for that which binds us to life.
10 Old age is an incurable disease. [Seneca: *Ad Lucilium*, Epist. cviii.]
11 With one foot in the ferry boat. [Lucian: *Apologia I*]
12 For Age, with stealing steps,
Hath clawed me with his clutch.
[Thomas, Lord Vaux: *The Aged Lover Renounceth Love. A Ditty . . . Representing the Image of Death*]
The gravedigger in Hamlet sings this song as he digs, to Hamlet's horror.
13 When forty winters shall besiege thy brow,
And dig deep trenches in thy beauty's field.
[Shakespeare: *Sonnets*, "Dedication"]
14 That time of year thou mayst in me behold
When yellow leaves, or none, or few, do hang
Upon those boughs which shake against the cold,
Bare ruined choirs where late the sweet birds sang.
[Shakespeare: *Sonnets* LXXIII]

1   The sixth age shifts
Into the lean and slipper'd panta-
            loon,
With spectacles on nose and pouch
            on side,
His youthful hose, well saved, a world
            too wide
For his shrunk shank; and his big
            manly voice,
Turning again toward childish treble,
            pipes
And whistles in his sound.
[Shakespeare: *As You Like It* II.vii.]

2   You are old;
Nature in you stands on the very
            verge
Of her confine.
[Shakespeare: *King Lear* II.iv.]

3 I am a very foolish fond old man,
Fourscore and upward; not an hour
            more nor less,
And, to deal plainly,
I fear I am not in my perfect mind.
[Shakespeare: *King Lear* IV.vii.]

4 The oldest man he seemed that ever
            wore grey hairs.
[Wordsworth: *Resolution and Independence*]

5 Upon the margin of that moorish
            flood
Motionless as a cloud the old man
            stood,
That heareth not the loud winds
            when they call;
And moveth all together, if it move
            at all.
[Wordsworth: *Resolution and Independence*]

6 Nature abhors the old.
[Emerson: *Circles*]

7 Little of all we value here
Wakes on the morn of its hundredth
            year
Without both feeling and looking
            queer.
[O. W. Holmes: *The Deacon's Masterpiece*]

8 She may very well pass for forty-three
In the dusk with a light behind
            her!
[W. S. Gilbert: *Trial by Jury*]

9 By the time a man gets well into the
seventies his continued existence is a
mere miracle. [R. L. Stevenson: *Aes Triplex*]

AGE: its beauty and dignity

10 An age that melts with unperceiv'd
            decay,
And glides in modest innocence away.
[Samuel Johnson: *Vanity of Human Wishes*]

11 The day becomes more solemn and
            serene
When noon is past; there is a har-
            mony
In Autumn, and a lustre in its sky
Which through the Summer is not
            heard or seen,
As if it could not be, as if it had not
            been!
[Shelley: *Hymn to Intellectual Beauty*]

12 As a white candle
In a holy place,
So is the beauty
Of an aged face.
[Joseph Campbell: *The Old Woman*]

13 There are people who, like houses,
are beautiful in dilapidation. [Logan
Pearsall Smith: *Afterthoughts*]

14 The heads of strong old age are beau-
            tiful
Beyond all grace of youth.
[Robinson Jeffers: *Promise of Peace*]

AGE: contemptible and despised

15 Nothing is less worthy of honor than
an old man who has no other evidence
of having lived long except his age.
[Seneca: *De Tranquillitate*]

16 Do you set down your name in the
scroll of youth, that are written down old
with all the characters of age? Have you
not a moist eye? a dry hand? a yellow
cheek? a white beard? a decreasing leg?
an increasing belly? is not your voice
broken? your wind short? your chin double? your wit single? and every part
about you blasted with antiquity? and
will you yet call yourself young? Fie, fie!
[Shakespeare: *II Henry IV* I.ii.]

17 How ill white hairs become a fool
            and jester!
[Shakespeare: *II Henry IV* V.v.]

18 The satirical rogue says here, that old
men have grey beards; that their faces
are wrinkled; their eyes purging thick
amber and plum-tree gum; and that they
have a plentiful lack of wit, together
with most weak hams. [Shakespeare:
Hamlet II.ii.]

1 An old man is twice a child.
[Shakespeare: *Hamlet* II.ii.]
2 A poor, infirm, weak, and despised
old man.
[Shakespeare: *King Lear* III.ii.]
3 Superfluous lags the veteran on the
stage.
[Samuel Johnson: *The Vanity of Human Wishes* (1749)]

> *Age is unnecessary.*
> Shakespeare: King Lear *II.iv.*
> *If I should live to be*
> *The last leaf upon the tree*
> *In the spring,*
> *Let them smile, as I do now,*
> *At the old forsaken bough*
> *Where I cling.*
> O. W. Holmes: The Last Leaf

4 The old draw upon themselves the
greatest part of those insults which they
so much lament; age is rarely despised
but when it is contemptible. [Samuel
Johnson: *The Rambler* No. 50]
5 He's always compleenin' frae mornin'
to e'enin',
He hoasts and he hirples the weary
day lang;
He's doylt and he's dozin', his bluid
it is frozen,
O dreary's the night wi' a crazy auld
man!
[Burns: *What Can a Young Lassie Do Wi' an Auld Man?*]

hoasts = *coughs, clears his throat;* hirples
= *walks as if crippled, limps;* doylt =
stupid; bluid = *blood.*

AGE: its fears
6 Old age, more to be feared than
death. [Juvenal: *Satires* XI]
7 Every man desires to live long, but no
man would be old. [Jonathan Swift:
Thoughts on Various Subjects]
8 One evil in old age is that, as your
time is come, you think every little illness is the beginning of the end. When
a man expects to be arrested, every
knock at the door is an alarm. [Sydney
Smith: Letter (1836)]
9 In old age we live under the shadow
of Death, which, like the sword of Damo-
cles, may descend at any moment, but we
have so long found life to be an affair of
being rather frightened than hurt that
we have become like the people who live

under Vesuvius, and chance it without
much misgiving. [Samuel Butler (1835-
1902): *The Way of All Flesh*]

AGE: its garrulity
10 A good old man, sir; he will be talking: as they say, "when the age is in, the
wit is out." [Shakespeare: *Much Ado About Nothing* III.v.]
11 It was near a miracle to see an old
man silent, since talking is the disease of
age. [Ben Jonson: *Explorata,* "Homeri
Ulysses"]

AGE: growing old
12 Alas, Posthumus, the years go by!
Piety cannot delay wrinkles and the
approach of age
Nor hold back irresistible death.
[Horace: *Odes* II.xiv.]
13 For you and I are past our dancing
days.
[Shakespeare: *Romeo and Juliet* I.v.]
14 And so from hour to hour we ripe
and ripe,
And then from hour to hour we rot
and rot;
And thereby hangs a tale.
[Shakespeare: *As You Like It* II.vii.]
15 My way of life
Is fall'n into the sere, the yellow leaf;
And that which should accompany
old age,
As honour, love, obedience, troops of
friends,
I must not look to have; but in their
stead,
Curses, not loud but deep; mouth-
honour, breath,
Which the poor heart would fain
deny, and dare not.
[Shakespeare: *Macbeth* V.iii.]
16 When we are old as you? When we
shall hear
The rain and wind beat dark December.
[Shakespeare: *Cymbeline* III.iii.]
17 Age is like love, it cannot be hid.
[Thomas Dekker: *Old Fortunatus* II.i.]
18 Discern of the coming on of years,
and think not to do the same things still;
for age will not be defied. [Francis
Bacon: *Of Regimen of Health*]
19 How soon hath Time, the subtle thief
of youth,

Stolen on his wing my three and
twentieth year!
[John Milton: *On His being Arrived at
the Age of Twenty-three* (1631)]
Compare A. E. Housman's:
May will be fine next year as like as
not:
Oh, aye, but then we shall be twenty-
four.
Milton's lament is for the delay of
fruition; Housman's is for the passing
of joy.

1   Few people know how to be old.
[La Rochefoucauld: *Maxims*]
2   John Anderson my jo, John,
When we were first acquent,
Your locks were like the raven,
Your bonnie brow was brent;
But now your brow is beld, John,
Your locks are like the snaw;
But blessings on your frosty pow,
John Anderson my jo.
[Burns: *John Anderson My Jo*]
jo = *sweetheart, joy;* brent = *smooth, un-*
wrinkled; beld = *bald;* pow = *poll, head.*

3   Why with such earnest pains dost
thou provoke
The years to bring the inevitable
yoke,
Thus blindly with thy blessedness at
strife?
[Wordsworth: *Intimations of Immortal-*
ity]
4   Oh! the joys that came down shower-
like,
Of Friendship, Love, and Liberty
Ere I was old!
[Coleridge: *Youth and Age*]
5   *Ere* I was old? Ah, woful Ere,
Which tells me, Youth's no longer
here!
[Coleridge: *Youth and Age*]
6   As boy, I thought myself a clever fellow,
And wish'd that others held the
same opinion;
They took it up when my days grew
more mellow,
And other minds acknowledged my
dominion:
Now my sere fancy 'falls into the yellow
Leaf,' and Imagination droops her
pinion,
And the sad truth which hovers o'er

my desk
Turns what was once romantic to
burlesque.
[Byron: *Don Juan* IV.iii.]
7   My days are in the yellow leaf;
The flowers and fruits of love are
gone;
The worm, the canker and the grief
Are mine alone.
[Byron: *On This Day I Complete my*
Thirty-sixth Year (1824)]
Byron, of course, is echoing Macbeth's:
I have liv'd long enough. My way of
life
Is fall'n into the sere, the yellow leaf.
Shakespeare: Macbeth V.iii.
See **THIRTY-THREE**
8   It is to spend long days
And not once feel that we were ever
young;
It is to add, immured
In the hot prison of the present,
month
To month with weary pain.
[Matthew Arnold: *Growing Old*]
9   Grow old along with me!
The best is yet to be,
The last of life, for which the first
was made.
[Robert Browning: *Rabbi Ben Ezra*]
10   I'm growing fonder of my staff;
I'm growing dimmer in the eyes;
I'm growing fainter in my laugh;
I'm growing deeper in my sighs;
I'm growing careless of my dress;
I'm growing frugal of my gold;
I'm growing wise; I'm growing—yes—
I'm growing old.
[J. G. Saxe: *I'm Growing Old*]
11   Darling, I am growing old,
Silver threads among the gold
Shine upon my brow today;
Life is fading fast away.
[E. E. Rexford: *Silver Threads Among*
the Gold]
12   A little more tired at close of day,
A little less anxious to have our way;
A little less ready to scold and blame,
A little more care of a brother's name;
And so we are nearing our journey's
end,
Where time and eternity meet and
blend.
[Rollin John Wells: *Growing Old*]
13   She was a faded but still lovely

woman of twenty-seven. [F. Scott Fitzgerald: written in 1920, when Mr. Fitzgerald himself lacked three years of that state of decrepitude]

Fitzgerald commented on the youthfulness of the line, in Early Success (1937).

1 I don't believe one grows older. I think that what happens early on in life is that at a certain age one stands still and stagnates. [T. S. Eliot, quoted in the *New York Times*, Sept. 21, 1958]

Not entirely; Mr. Eliot, for example, did not pick up the idiom "early on" in his youthful years in America.

AGE: its loneliness

2 Old age is a dreary solitude. [Plato: *Laws*]

3 Decrepitude is a solitary quality. [Montaigne: *Essays* III.ix.]

4 When all the world is old, lad,
    And all the trees are brown;
    And all the sport is stale, lad,
    And all the wheels run down:
Creep home, and take your place
                                there,
    The spent and maimed among:
God grant you find one face there
    You loved when all was young.
[Charles Kingsley: *Water Babies*]

5 One aged man—one man—can't fill a
                                house.
[Robert Frost: *An Old Man's Winter Night*]

6 But the old men know when an old
                          man dies.
[Ogden Nash: *Old Men*]

AGE: a lusty and vital old age

7 Nobody loves life like an old man. [Sophocles: *Acrisius*]

8 Become old early if you wish to stay old long. [Cato the Censor: quoted by Cicero, in *De Senectute* X.xxxii.]

Cato felt that a long life depended upon the early abandonment of the dissipations of youth. Whether this is so is as questionable as whether it is desirable.

Oliver Wendell Holmes once said that the best recipe he knew for longevity was the contraction of an incurable disease in youth. And certainly many sickly people live to a great age.

My age is as a lusty winter,
Frosty, but kindly.
[Shakespeare: *As You Like It* II.iii.]

10 Young I was, but now am old,
    But I am not yet grown cold;
    I can play, and I can twine
    'Bout a virgin like a vine:
    In her lap too I can lie
    Melting, and in fancy die:
    And return to life, if she
    Claps my cheek, or kisseth me;
    Thus, and thus it now appears
    That our love outlasts our years.
[Robert Herrick: *Hesperides:* "On Himselfe"]

11 Old as I am, for ladies' love unfit,
    The power of beauty I remember yet.
[Dryden: *Cymon and Iphigenia*]

Note the pronunciation which the rhyme suggests for yet. It is still the general pronunciation in southern USA and widely heard everywhere.

12 A stout healthy old man is like a tower undermined. [Samuel Johnson: in Boswell's *Life*, May 16, 1784]

stout = vigorous, strong, sturdy

Johnson attributes the saying to Bacon.

13 Old age hath yet his honour and his
                                toil;
    Death closes all: but something ere
                            the end,
    Some work of noble note, may yet be
                                done,
    Not unbecoming men that strove
                        with Gods.
[Tennyson: *Ulysses*]

14 Tho' much is taken, much abides;
                        and tho'
    We are not now that strength which
                        in old days
    Moved earth and heaven; that which
                    we are, we are—
    One equal temper of heroic hearts,
    Made weak by time and fate, but
                        strong in will
    To strive, to seek, to find, and not to
                            yield.
[Tennyson: *Ulysses*]

15 An aged man is but a paltry thing,
    A tattered coat upon a stick, unless
    Soul clap its hands and sing.
[William Butler Yeats: *Sailing to Byzantium*]

AGE: its mellowing, wisdom, insights

16 As you are old and reverend, you
                    should be wise.
[Shakespeare: *King Lear* I.iv.]

1 Old age consoles itself by giving good precepts for being unable to give bad examples. [La Rochefoucauld: *Maxims*]

2 The seas are quiet when the winds
      give o'er;
So calm are we when passions are no
      more.
For then we know how vain it was to
      boast
Of fleeting things, so certain to be
      lost.
Clouds of affection from our younger
      eyes
Conceal that emptiness which age
      descries.
[Edmund Waller: *Of the Last Verses in the Book*]

3 The soul's dark cottage, batter'd and
      decay'd,
Lets in new light through chinks that
      Time hath made;
Stronger by weakness, wiser men be-
      come,
As they draw near to their eternal
      home.
Leaving the old, both worlds at once
      they view,
That stand upon the threshold of the
      new.
[Edmund Waller: *On the Divine Poems*]

4 Then old age and experience, hand
      in hand,
Lead him to death, and make him
      understand,
After a search so painful and so long,
That all his life he has been in the
      wrong.
[John Wilmot, Earl of Rochester: *A Satyr Against Mankind*]

5 Old age takes from the intellectual man no qualities save those which are useless to wisdom. [Joseph Joubert: *Pensées*]

6 Years that bring the philosophic mind. [Wordsworth: *Intimations of Immortality*]

7 Old we grow, indeed, but who grows wise? [Goethe: *Faust* II.ii.]

8 How earthy old people become— mouldy as the grave! Their wisdom smacks of the earth. There is no fore-taste of immortality in it. They remind me of earthworms and mole crickets. [Thoreau: *Journal,* August 16, 1853]

9 Many a man that cudden't direct ye to th' drug store on th' corner whin he was thirty will get a respectful hearin' whin age has further impaired his mind. [Finley Peter Dunne: *Old Age*]

10 We get too soon old, and too late smart. [Anon.]

11 The older I grow the more I distrust the familiar doctrine that age brings wisdom. [H. L. Mencken: *Prejudices: Third Series*]

AGE: its moral decline

12 Old men have more regard for ex-pediency than for honor. [Aristotle: *Rhetoric* II]

13 Age doth profit rather in the powers of understanding than in the virtues of the will and affections. [Francis Bacon: *Of Youth and Age*]
    doth profit = *gains, or makes progress*

14 But age doth not rectifie but incur-vate our natures, turning bad disposi-tions into worser habits and brings on incurable vices; for every day as we grow weaker in age, we grow stronger in sin. [Sir Thomas Browne: *Religio Medici* I.xlii.]

15 The heart never grows better by age; I fear rather worse; always harder. A young liar will be an old one; and a young knave will only be a greater knave as he grows older. [Lord Chesterfield: *Letters,* May 17, 1750]

16 Every man over forty is a scoundrel. [G. B. Shaw: *Maxims for Revolutionists*]
    Though age never ceases to deplore the moral degeneracy of youth, many seers feel that youth is far more moral than age—though whether this arises from inexperience, excessive vitality, or an innocent acceptance of the advice of its elders may be disputed.
    Cf. Bacon: For the moral part, perhaps youth will have the preeminence.
    Hood: But now 'tis little joy
              To know I'm farther off
                  from Heaven
              Than when I was a boy.

17 We grow with years more fragile in body, but morally stouter, and we can throw off the chill of a bad conscience

almost at once. [Logan Pearsall Smith: *Afterthoughts*]

AGE: its pleasures and compensations
1 Old age has a great sense of calm and freedom. When the passions have relaxed their hold you have escaped, not from one master, but from many. [Plato: *The Republic*]
2 I am very grateful to old age because it has increased my desire for conversation and lessened my desire for food and drink. [Cicero: *De Senectute* XIV.xlvi.]
3 When a man has said, "I have lived," every morning he arises he receives a bonus. [Seneca: *Ad Lucilium* XII]
"Bonus time" might be a better phrase than our present "borrowed time." Borrowed time more accurately expresses the time given to the excesses of youth which, as Bacon says, "are owing a man" until his age.
4 Alonso of Aragon was wont to say in commendation of age, that age appears to be best in four things—old wood best to burn, old wine to drink, old friends to trust, and old authors to read. [Francis Bacon: *Apothegms*]
The saying is much quoted, but no one has been able to identify the geriaphilic Alonso of Aragon. Mencken labels him "mysterious and probably mythical."
5 An old man in the house is a good sign. [Benjamin Franklin: *Poor Richard's Almanack* (1744)]
6 Alas! What do the compensations of age after all amount to? What joy can the years bring half so sweet as the unhappiness they take away? [Logan Pearsall Smith: *Afterthoughts*]
7 Old age isn't so bad when you consider the alternative. [Maurice Chevalier, quoted in the *New York Times,* Oct. 9, 1960]
Mr. Chevalier, meditating on his having passed the biblical threescore and ten.

AGE: its weakness and miseries
8 Old people have fewer diseases than the young, but their diseases never leave them. [Hippocrates: *Aphorisms*]
9 All ills gather together in old age. [Bion of Borysthenes: in Diogenes Laertius, IV.vii.]
10 The days of our years are threescore and ten; and if by reason of strength they be fourscore years, yet is their strength labor and sorrow; for it is soon cut off, and we fly away. [Psalms 90:10]
11 When thou shalt be old, thou shalt stretch forth thy hands, and another shall gird thee, and carry thee whither thou wouldest not. [John 21:18]
12 Old age and happiness seldom go together. [Seneca: *Hercules Oetaeus*]
13 God doth them a grace from whom little by little he subtracts their life. It is the only benefit of old age. Their last death shall be so much the less full, languishing and painful: it shall then kill but one half or a quarter of a man. [Montaigne: *Essays* III.xiii.]
14 Strength of nature in youth passeth over many excesses which are owing a man till his age. [Francis Bacon: *Of Regimen of Health*]
15 Men of age object too much, consult too long, adventure too little, repent too soon. [Francis Bacon: *Of Youth and Age*]
16 Old age is a tyrant who forbids, upon pain of death, all the pleasures of youth. [La Rochefoucauld: *Maxims*]
17 Life protracted is protracted woe. [Samuel Johnson: *The Vanity of Human Wishes*]
18 My diseases are an asthma and a dropsy, and what is less curable, seventy-five. [Samuel Johnson: Letter to W. G. Hamilton, Oct. 20, 1784]
19 Old age, a second child, by Nature curst,
With more and greater evils than the first:
Weak, sickly, full of pains, in every breath
Railing at life and yet afraid of death.
[Charles Churchill: *Gotham*]
20 Two causes, the abbreviation of time and the failure of hope, will always tinge with a browner shade the evening of life. [Edward Gibbon: *Autobiography*]
21 . . . the uselessness of men above sixty years of age, and the incalculable benefit it would be in commercial, political, and in professional life if, as a matter of course, men stopped work at this age. [Sir William Osler: in a speech at Johns Hopkins University, 1905]

This was presented in a large part of the press as advocating euthanasia for all men over sixty and caused an uproar.
1 To deprive elderly people of their bogeys is as bad as snatching from babies their big stuffed bears. [Logan Pearsall Smith: *Afterthoughts*]

See also YOUTH AND AGE

AGE (PERIOD)
2   How many ages hence
Shall this our lofty scene be acted
      o'er,
In states unborn and accents yet un-
      known!
[Shakespeare: *Julius Caesar* III.i.]
3 This Age will serve to make a very
      pretty farce for the next.
[Samuel Butler (1612-1680): *Remains* II]

AGNOSTIC
4 I took thought, and invented what I conceived to be the appropriate title of "agnostic." [T. H. Huxley: *Science and Christian Tradition* VII]

AGONY
5 Ay, many flowering islands lie
In the waters of wide Agony.
[Shelley: *Lines written amongst the Euganean Hills*]

AGREEABLE
6 I do not want people to be very agreeable, as it saves me the trouble of liking them a great deal. [Jane Austen: Letter to her sister Cassandra, Dec. 24, 1798]
7 My idea of an agreeable person is a person who agrees with me. [Benjamin Disraeli: *Lothair* XLI]

AGREEMENT
8 Can two walk together, except they be agreed? [Amos 3:3]
9 Agreed to differ. [Robert Southey: *Life of Wesley*]

AGRICULTURE
10 He gave it for his opinion, that whoever could make two ears of corn or two blades of grass to grow upon a spot of ground where only one grew before, would deserve better of mankind, and do more essential service to his country than the whole race of politicians put together. [Jonathan Swift: *Gulliver's Travels* II.vi.]

AIMLESSNESS
11 He trudg'd along unknowing what he
      sought,
And whistled as he went, for want of
      thought.
[Dryden: *Cymon and Iphigenia*]

AIR
12 The empty, vast, and wandering air. [Shakespeare: *Richard III* I.iv.]
13 This castle hath a pleasant seat; the
      air
Nimbly and sweetly recommends it-
      self
Unto our gentle senses.
[Shakespeare: *Macbeth* I.vi.]
14 A nipping and an eager air.
[Shakespeare: *Hamlet* I.iv.]
15 Now fades the glimmering landscape
      on the sight,
And all the air a solemn stillness
      holds.
[Thomas Gray: *Elegy Written in a Country Churchyard*]

AIRCRAFT
16 For I dipt into the future, far as hu-
      man eye could see,
Saw the Vision of the world, and all
      the wonder that would be;
Saw the heavens fill with commerce,
      argosies of magic sails,
Pilots of the purple twilight, drop-
      ping down with costly bales;
Heard the heavens fill with shouting,
      and there rain'd a ghastly dew
From the nations' airy navies grap-
      pling in the central blue.
[Tennyson: *Locksley Hall*]

ALBATROSS
17 "God save thee, ancient Mariner!
From fiends, that plague thee thus!—
Why look'st thou so?"—"With my
      cross-bow
I shot the Albatross."
[Coleridge: *The Ancient Mariner* I]
18 Instead of the cross, the Albatross
About my neck was hung.
[Coleridge: *The Ancient Mariner* II]

1 He thought he saw an Albatross
That fluttered round the lamp:
He looked again, and found it was
A penny-postage-stamp.
"You'd best be getting home," he
said,
"The nights are very damp."
[Lewis Carroll: *Sylvie and Bruno* XII]

ALEXANDER
2 If I were not Alexander, I would be
Diogenes. [Plutarch: *Lives*, "Alexander"
XIV.iii.]
*Alexander's patrician and patronizing
but fairly feeble riposte to one of the
all-time-masterly strokes of one-upmanship.*
*Alexander, a simple-minded warrior
having the misfortune to live in the days
before every general was protected with
a bodyguard of public-relations advisers,
innocently went to see Diogenes the
Cynic. He loftily asked Diogenes if there
were anything he could do for him, and
the currish old rascal said, "Yes, get out
from between me and the sun."*

ALIBI
3 Oh, Sammy, Sammy, vy worn't there
a alleybi! [Dickens: *The Pickwick Papers*
II]

ALICE
4 Don't you remember sweet Alice, Ben
Bolt?
Sweet Alice, whose hair was so
brown?
Who wept with delight when you
gave her a smile
And trembled with fear at your
frown?
[T. D. English: *Ben Bolt*]

ALIMONY
5 She is as implacable an adversary as a
wife suing for alimony. [William Wycherley: *The Plain-Dealer* I (1676)]

ALLEGIANCE
6 I pledge allegiance to the flag of the
United States of America and to the republic for which it stands, one nation,
under God, indivisible, with liberty and
justice for all. [Francis M. Bellamy: *The*

Pledge of Allegiance to the Flag]
*In the early days of the Republic alle-
giance to the flag was taken for granted
and, in time of danger, heroically demonstrated. Whether an enforced daily reci-
tation increases a sense of the dignity or
of the obligations of citizenship has been
argued. "Under God" was inserted during former President Eisenhower's second
term. That, too, was formerly taken for
granted.*

ALLEGORY
7 As headstrong as an allegory on the
banks of the Nile. ["Mrs. Malaprop": in
Richard Brinsley Sheridan's *The Rivals*
III.iii.]

ALLEY
8 I think we are in rats' alley
Where the dead men lost their bones.
[T. S. Eliot: *The Waste Land* II]

ALLIANCE
9 It is our true policy to steer clear of
permanent alliance with any portion of
the foreign world. [George Washington:
Farewell Address, Sept. 17, 1796]
10 Peace, commerce and honest friendship with all nations—entangling alli-
ances with none. [Thomas Jefferson: *Inaugural Address*, March 4, 1801]

ALLITERATION
11 Apt Alliteration's artful aid. [Charles
Churchill: *Prophecy of Famine*]

ALL THINGS
12 I am made all things to all men. [I
Corinthians 9:22]

ALONE
13 Alone, alone, all all alone,
Alone on a wide, wide sea!
And never a saint took pity on
My soul in agony.
[Coleridge: *The Ancient Mariner* IV]
14 I feel like one who treads alone
Some banquet-hall deserted,
Whose lights are fled, whose garlands
dead,
And all but he departed.
[Thomas Moore: *Oft in the Stilly Night*]
15 The man who goes alone can start
today, but he who travels with another

must wait till that other is ready. [Thoreau: *Walden* V]

1 Down to Gehenna or up to the Throne,
He travels the fastest who travels alone.
[Kipling: *The Winners*]

2 The strongest man in the world is he who stands alone. [Henrik Ibsen: *An Enemy of the People* V]

ALPH

3 Where Alph, the sacred river, ran
Through caverns measureless to man
Down to a sunless sea.
[Coleridge: *Kubla Khan*]

ALTAR

4 The great world's altar-stairs
That slope thro' darkness up to God.
[Tennyson: *In Memoriam* LV]

ALTERATION

5 He's full of alteration and self-reproving.
[Shakespeare: *King Lear* V.i.]

AMAZEMENT

6   Ye gods, it doth amaze me
A man of such a feeble temper should
So get the start of the majestic world
And bear the palm alone.
[Shakespeare: *Julius Caesar* I.ii.]

AMBASSADOR

7 An ambassador is an honest man, sent to lie abroad for the good of his country.
[Sir Henry Wotton]

> lie abroad = *settle, take up his residence
> The pun, the wit of the saying, depends wholly on the proper placement of lie. Those who misquote the saying as "sent abroad to lie for the good of his country" are undiscerning oafs, unfit to be entrusted with wit. Wotton wrote the famous witticism in the album of a friend in 1604. It was intended as a private joke. Unfortunately it attracted attention and several years later was published and caused Wotton to lose favor with King James I.*

AMBER

8 Pretty, in amber, to observe the forms
Of hairs, or straws, or dirt, or grubs,
or worms;
The things, we know, are neither rich
nor rare,
But wonder how the devil they got
there.
[Alexander Pope: *Epistle to Dr. Arbuthnot*]

> *Pope is alluding satirically to
> . . . small critics
> Preserv'd in Milton's or in Shakespeare's
> name.*

AMBITION

9 Hew not too high,
Lest the chips fall in thine eye.
[14th-century proverb]

> *A very old warning against the dangers of ambition.*

10 Ill-weav'd ambition, how much art
thou shrunk!
When that this body did contain a
spirit,
A kingdom for it was too small a
bound;
But now, two paces of the vilest earth
Is room enough.
[Shakespeare: *I Henry IV* V.iv.]

11 Chok'd with ambition of the meaner
sort.
[Shakespeare: *I Henry VI* II.v.]

12 When the poor have cried, Caesar
hath wept:
Ambition should be made of sterner
stuff.
[Shakespeare: *Julius Caesar* III.ii.]

13 That's villainous, and shows a most pitiful ambition in the fool that uses it.
[Shakespeare: *Hamlet* III.ii.]

> *Prince Hamlet is instructing the players in their art, a passage of great interest because, of course, Shakespeare is speaking through the Prince's mouth and airing some of the dramatic author's perennial grievances. One of these—then as now—was the ad libbing of comedians, and it is to this the passage alludes.*

14 Vaulting ambition, which o'erleaps
itself
And falls on the other [side].
[Shakespeare: *Macbeth* I.vii.]

> *The last word is omitted in many texts— as Macbeth is cut off by the entrance of Lady Macbeth. But since he is not speaking, but in soliloquy, it is hard to see how a single word could be cut short.*

1 No man's pie is freed
From his ambitious finger.
[Shakespeare: *Henry VIII* I.i.]
2 I charge thee, fling away ambition.
By that sin fell the angels; how can
man then,
The image of his Maker, hope to win
by it?
[Shakespeare: *Henry* VIII III.ii.]
3 He that plots to be the only figure
among ciphers, is the decay of a whole
age. [Francis Bacon: *Of Ambition*]
4 Ambitious men, if they find the way
open for their rising and still get forward, they are rather busy than dangerous; but if they be checked in their desires, they become secretly discontent,
and look upon men and matters with an
evil eye, and are best pleased when
things go backward. [Francis Bacon: *Of
Ambition*]
still = *continuously*
5 Ambition, a proud covetousness, or a
dry thirst of honour, a great torture of
the mind, composed of envy, pride, and
covetousness, a gallant madness, one defines it a pleasant poison. [Robert Burton: *Anatomy of Melancholy* I.ii.3.11]
6 The ambitious climbs up high and
perilous stairs, and never cares how to
come down; the desire of rising hath
swallowed up his fear of a fall. [Thomas
Adams: *Diseases of the Soul*]
7 One often passes from love to ambition, but one rarely returns from ambition to love. [La Rochefoucauld: *Maxims*]
8 Wild ambition loves to slide, not
stand,
And Fortune's ice prefers to Virtue's
land.
[Dryden: *Absalom and Achitophel* I.198
(1681)]
*"Greatness on goodness loves to slide,
not stand,
And leaves for Fortune's ice Virtue's
firm land."*
Knolles: History of the Turks (*1570*)
*The similarity is too great to be acci-
dental, but Dryden may not have been
aware of it at the time of writing. The
idea and its rime are catchy and could
have caught in his mind and sunk out
of conscious memory.*
9 Ambition often puts men upon doing

the meanest offices: so climbing is performed in the same posture with creeping. [Jonathan Swift: *Thoughts on Various Subjects*]
10 The slave has but one master; the
man of ambition has as many as there
are people useful to his fortune. [La
Bruyère: *Les Caractères*]
11 Ambition is the only power that combats love. [Colley Cibber: *Caesar in
Egypt* I]
12 Ambition can creep as well as soar.
[Edmund Burke: *Letters on a Regicide
Peace* No. 3]
13   Ambition
Is like the sea wave, which the more
you drink
The more you thirst—yea—drink too
much, as men
Have done on rafts of wreck—it
drives you mad.
[Tennyson: *The Cup* I.iii.]
14 Ambition is but avarice on stilts and
masked.
[Walter Savage Landor: *Imaginary Conversations,* "Lord Brooke and Sir P.
Sidney"]
15 I had Ambition, by which sin
The angels fell;
I climbed and, step by step, O Lord,
Ascended into Hell.
[W. H. Davies: *Ambition*]
16 AMBITION. An overmastering desire to
be vilified by enemies while living and
made ridiculous by friends when dead.
[Ambrose Bierce: *The Devil's Dictionary*]
17 Talk of love making people jealous
and suspicious—it's nothing to social ambition. [Edith Wharton: *The House of
Mirth* II]

AMBITION: not wholly evil
18 Though ambition in itself is a vice,
yet it is often the parent of virtues.
[Quintilian: *Institutio Oratoria* II.xxii.]
19 Who does i' the wars more than his
captain can,
Becomes his captain's captain: and
ambition,
The soldier's virtue, rather makes
choice of loss,
Than gain which darkens him.
[Shakespeare: *Antony and Cleopatra*
III.i.]

1 Power to do good is the true and lawful end of aspiring.
[Francis Bacon: *Of Great Place*]

2 Ambition first sprung from your blest abodes,
The glorious fault of angels and of gods.
[Alexander Pope: *Elegy to the Memory of an Unfortunate Lady*]

3 To be happy at home is the ultimate result of all ambition, the end to which every enterprise and labor tends, and of which every desire prompts the prosecution. [Samuel Johnson: *The Rambler* No. 68]

4 I would sooner fail than not be among the greatest. [Keats: Letter to James Hessey, October 9, 1818]

AMEN

5 But I struck one chord of music,
Like the sound of a great Amen.
[Adelaide Ann Procter: *A Lost Chord*]

AMERICA

6 My country, 'tis of thee,
Sweet land of liberty,
Of thee I sing;
Land where my fathers died,
Land of the pilgrims' pride,
From every mountain side
Let freedom ring.
[Samuel Francis Smith: *America*]

7 I hear America singing, the varied carols I hear.
[Walt Whitman: *Leaves of Grass*, "I Hear America Singing"]

8 It was wonderful to find America, but it would have been more wonderful to miss it. [Mark Twain: *Pudd'nhead Wilson's Calendar*]

9 The youth of America is their oldest tradition. It has been going on now for three hundred years. [Oscar Wilde: *A Woman of No Importance* I]

10 Our whole duty, for the present at any rate, is summed up in the motto: America first. [Woodrow Wilson: in a speech in New York, April 20, 1915]

11 O beautiful for spacious skies,
For amber waves of grain,
For purple mountain majesties
Above the fruited plain!
America! America!
God shed his grace on thee
And crown thy good with brotherhood
From sea to shining sea!
[Katharine Lee Bates: *America the Beautiful*]

12 Wider still and wider shall thy bounds be set;
God, who made thee mighty, make thee mightier yet.
[A. C. Benson: *Land of Hope and Glory*]

13 American life is a powerful solvent. It seems to neutralise every intellectual element, however tough and alien it may be, and to fuse it in the native good-will, complacency, thoughtlessness, and optimism. [James Harvey Robinson: *Character and Opinion in the United States*]

14 Providence, that watches over children, drunkards, and fools
With silent miracles and other esoterica,
Continue to suspend the ordinary rules
And take care of the United States of America.
[Arthur Guiterman: *Gaily the Troubadour*]

15 Q. If you find so much that is unworthy of reverence in the United States, then why do you live here?
A. Why do men go to zoos? [H. L. Mencken: *Prejudices: Fifth Series*]

16 America Was Promises. [Title of a poem by Archibald MacLeish]

AMERICAN(S)

17 They [the American colonists] are a race of convicts, and ought to be thankful for anything we allow them short of hanging. [Samuel Johnson: in Boswell's *Life*, March 21, 1775]

18 Good Americans, when they die, go to Paris. [Attr. to Thomas G. Appleton]

19 It's a complex fate, being an American. [Henry James: Letter (1872)]
This was one of James's basic thoughts. In Lady Barberina *he wrote "It is not simple to be an American." It is the theme of many of his novels, including* The Ambassadors.

20 Enslaved, illogical, elate,
He greets the embarrassed gods, nor fears
To shake the iron hand of fate
Or match with destiny for beers.

[Kipling: *An American*]

1 A sound American is simply one who has put out of his mind all doubts and questionings, and who accepts instantly, and as incontrovertible gospel, the whole body of official doctrine of his day, whatever it may be and no matter how often it may change. The instant he challenges it, no matter how timorously and academically, he ceases by that much to be a loyal and creditable citizen of the Republic. [H. L. Mencken: in the *Baltimore Evening Sun,* March 12, 1923]

2 Every third American devotes himself to improving and uplifting his fellow-citizens, usually by force. [H. L. Mencken: *Prejudices: First Series*]

3 There are no second acts in American lives. [F. Scott Fitzgerald: *The Last Tycoon*]

AMIABILITY

4 I never met a man I didn't like. [Will Rogers: in a speech at Boston, June 1930]

Except for such avowals, one would have no idea of how few people a public figure gets to meet.

AMMUNITION

5 Praise the Lord and pass the ammunition. [Chaplain Howell M. Forgy: at Pearl Harbor, December 7, 1942]

A good saying, but not one of the great ones. It's a little too jaunty for the occasion. And then an incentive to combat isn't entirely proper in a clergyman, although an urging to piety gives a soldier a little extra something. Cromwell's "Trust in God and keep your powder dry" is grade A.

AMUSED

6 We are not amused. [Queen Victoria's blood-chilling rebuke to any off-color remark or improper levity]

The remark was ascribed to her while she was still living.

There is a story that it was spoken to a young gentleman who was imitating her mannerisms at the royal table, but such bold ill manners in the Presence seems scarcely credible.

AMUSEMENT(S)

7 The English amuse themselves sadly after the custom of their country. [Duc de Sully: *Memoirs* (1630)]

Often attr. to Froissart, but it cannot be found in his writings.

8 Amusement is the happiness of those who cannot think. [Alexander Pope: *Thoughts on Various Subjects*]

9 I am a great friend to public amusements; for they keep people from vice. [Samuel Johnson: in Boswell's *Life,* March 31, 1772]

10 What a pity it is that we have no amusements in England but vice and religion! [Sydney Smith: in Lady Holland's *Memoir* X]

ANALYSIS

11 The habit of analysis has a tendency to wear away the feelings. [John Stuart Mill: *Autobiography* V]

With most people it works, rather, the other way round: as long as their feelings are involved, they are incapable of analysis.

ANCESTOR(S)

12 He who boasts of his ancestry praises the deeds of another. [Seneca: *Hercules Furens*]

13 The man who has not anything to boast of but his illustrious ancestors is like a potato—the only good belonging to him is under ground. [Sir Thomas Overbury: *Characters*]

14 Our ancestors are very good kind of folks; but they are the last people I should choose to have a visiting acquaintance with. [Richard Brinsley Sheridan: *The Rivals* IV.i.]

15 I am my own ancestor. [Marshal Junot: on being created a Duke and being asked, with a sneer, by a member of the old French nobility, who his ancestors were.]

A similar statement has been attributed to many others. Plutarch, in the Apothegms, ascribes such a statement to Iphicrates, a shoemaker's son.

Frederick Edwin Smith, on being created Lord Birkenhead, chose as his motto Faber mea fortuna ("I am the smith of my fortunes").

16 If I am to live only with my equals, then I must go down into the tomb of my ancestors, and stay there forever.

[Francis II of Austria]

1 There were human beings aboard the Mayflower, Not merely ancestors.

[Stephen Vincent Benét: *Western Star* I]

2 GENEALOGIST: One who traces back your family as far as your money will go. [Anon.]

3 Nothing is so soothing to our self-esteem as to find our bad traits in our forbears. It seems to absolve us. [Van Wyck Brooks: *From a Writer's Notebook*]

ANCESTRY

4 My father was a Creole, his father a Negro, and his father a monkey; my family, it seems, begins where yours left off.

Attr. to Alexander Dumas père, *when someone asked him with a sneer who his father was.*

5 I can trace my ancestry back to a protoplasmal primordial atomic globule. [W. S. Gilbert: *The Mikado* I]

ANCIENT

6 The ancient and honourable. [Isaiah 9:15]

7 The Ancient of days. [Daniel 7:9,13, 22]

ANGEL(S)

8 He shall give his angels charge over thee, to keep thee in all thy ways. [Psalms 91:11]

9 And, lo, the angel of the Lord came upon them, and the glory of the Lord shone round about them: and they were sore afraid. [Luke 2:9]

10 Not Angles, but Angels. [Attr. to Gregory the Great: on his seeing some blond English captives offered for sale at Rome and being told they were Angles.]

The Pontifical pun is related in Bede's Ecclesiastical History, *II.i. The version there is fuller: "It is well [that they are called Angles], for they have the faces of angels." The Latin of the better-known shorter form is:* Non Angli, sed Angeli. -

The Romans were greatly excited by blonds. Roman ladies dyed their hair blond and Caesar, who had had the mis-fortune to capture some swarthy Celts in Britain, had his captives' hair dyed so the populace would see what they expected to see.

11 Angels are bright still, though the brightest fell. [Shakespeare: *Macbeth* IV.iii.]

12 Angels and ministers of grace, defend us! [Shakespeare: *Hamlet* I.iv.]

13 And flights of angels sing thee to thy rest! [Shakespeare: *Hamlet* V.ii.]

14 At the round earth's imagin'd corners, blow
Your trumpets, angels, and arise, arise
From death, you numberless infinities
Of souls.
[Donne: *Holy Sonnets* VII]

15 Every man hath a good and a bad angel attending on him in particular all his life long. [Robert Burton: *The Anatomy of Melancholy* I.ii.1.2]

16 Look homeward, angel. [John Milton: *Lycidas*]
Used as the title of a novel by Thomas Wolfe in 1929

17 As far as angels' ken. [John Milton: *Paradise Lost* I.59]

18 He, above the rest
In shape and gesture proudly eminent,
Stood like a tower. His form had not yet lost
All her original brightness, nor appeared
Less than Archangel ruined, and the excess
Of glory obscured.
[John Milton: *Paradise Lost* I.589]

19 Darkened so, yet shone
Above them all the Archangel: but his face
Deep scars of thunder had intrenched, and care
Sat on his faded cheek, but under brows
Of dauntless courage, and considerate pride
Waiting revenge.
[John Milton: *Paradise Lost* I.599]
considerate = *deliberate*

20 Some who are far from atheists, may

make themselves merry with that conceit of thousands of spirits dancing at once upon a needle's point. [Ralph Cudworth: *The True Intellectual System of the Universe* III. (1678)]

conceit = *imaginative thought*

Cudworth is plainly alluding to some assertion or passage in literature which he assumes is fairly well known. But no one has ever been able to find, in theological discussions, the question of how many angels can "dance on the point of a pin" (the modern form).

Some of the propositions that were discussed, however, seem even more bizarre: What do angels do with material bodies that they used on some mission, but no longer require? Do angels defecate? If a cannibal family has for generations eaten nothing but human beings, so that the entire substance of their bodies is made up of the absorbed bodies of others, what will they do at the Resurrection for bodies of their own to suffer in hell?

1 Why, a spirit is such a little thing, that I have heard a man, who was a great scholar, say that he'll dance ye a hornpipe upon the point of a needle. [Joseph Addison: *The Drummer* I.i. (1716)]

2 He rais'd a mortal to the skies,
  She drew an angel down.
[Dryden: *Alexander's Feast*]

3 Like angel-visits, few and far between. [Thomas Campbell: *Pleasures of Hope* II (1799)]

The phrase had been almost a hundred years a-forming. In 1700 John Norris had written: Like angels' visits, short and bright (The Parting); in 1743 Robert Blair, in his lugubrious long poem The Grave (II.586) had referred to: Visits/ Like those of angels, short and far between. Hazlitt, in his Lectures on the English Poets (1818), pointed out that Campbell had taken the line from Blair and spoiled it in the taking, since "few" and "far between" are the same. But Campbell (who was angry with Hazlitt) has had the last laugh. Spoiled or not, "few and far between" is the form that has caught the popular fancy and achieved immortality.

4 Is man an ape or an angel? Now I am on the side of the angels. [Benjamin Disraeli: at a meeting at Oxford, 1864]

The blandness of "Dizzy's" support of the Heavenly Powers tickled the fancy of his contemporaries, many of whom would not have assigned him to the side he selected for himself.

The saying is often quoted with slight variations.

5 I want to be an angel,
  And with the angels stand,
  A crown upon my forehead,
  A harp within my hand.
[Urania Bailey: *I Want to be an Angel*]

6 In Heaven an angel is nobody in particular. [G. B. Shaw: *Maxims for Revolutionists*]

ANGER

7 Do not do to others that which would anger you if others did it to you. [Isocrates: *Nicocles* XIII]

8 Anyone can become angry—that is easy, but to be angry with the right person, to the right degree, at the right time, for the right purpose, and in the right way—this is not easy. [Aristotle: *Nicomachean Ethics* II.ix]

9 A soft answer turneth away wrath. [Proverbs 15:1]

10 Ambition and resentment are bad advisers. [Sallust: *Bellum Iugurthinum* LXIV.v. (40 B.C.)]

11 Anger is momentary insanity. [Horace: *Epistolae* I.ii.]

12 The greatest remedy for anger is delay. [Seneca: *De Ira* II.xxviii.]

13 Anger is brief madness and, unchecked, becomes protracted madness, bringing shame and even death. [Petrarch: *Sonetti sopra Vari Argomenti* XIX]

14 Touch me with noble anger. [Shakespeare: *King Lear* II.iv.]

15 Never anger/ Made good guard for itself.
[Shakespeare: *Antony and Cleopatra* IV.i.]

16 Anger's my meat; I sup upon myself. [Shakespeare: *Coriolanus* IV.ii.]

17 Anger makes dull men witty, but it keeps them poor. [Francis Bacon: *Apothegms*]

Quoted as by Queen Elizabeth

18 Valour's whetstone, anger. [Thomas Randolph: *The Muses' Looking-Glass*

III.ii.]

1 Anger may repast with thee for an hour, but not repose for a night; the continuance of anger is hatred, the continuance of hatred turns malice. That anger is not warrantable which hath seen two suns. [Francis Quarles: *Enchiridion* II.lx.]
turns = *turns into*

2 Anger is one of the sinews of the soul; he that wants it hath a maimed mind. [Thomas Fuller (1608-1661): *Holy and Profane State*, "Of Anger"]
wants = *lacks*

3 Anger makes a rich man hated and a poor man scorned. [Thomas Fuller (1654-1734): *Gnomologia*]

4 Two to one in all things, against the angry man. [Thomas Fuller: (1654-1734): *Gnomologia*]

5 Angry men make themselves beds of nettles. [Samuel Richardson: *Clarissa Harlowe* VII (1748)]

6 Whate'er's begun in anger, ends in shame. [Benjamin Franklin: *Poor Richard's Almanack* (1734)]

7 When angry, count ten before you speak; if very angry, an hundred. [Thomas Jefferson: *A Decalogue of Canons for Observation in Practical Life*]

8 I was angry with my friend:
I told my wrath, my wrath did end.
I was angry with my foe:
I told it not, my wrath did grow.
[William Blake: *A Poison Tree*]

ANIMAL(S)

9 Animals are nothing but the forms of our virtues and vices, wandering before our eyes, the visible phantoms of our souls. [Victor Hugo: *Les Misérables* V.v.]

10 I think I could turn and live with animals, they are so placid and self-contain'd;
I stand and look at them long and long.
They do not sweat and whine about their condition;
They do not lie awake in the dark and weep for their sins;
They do not make me sick discussing their duty to God.
[Walt Whitman: *Leaves of Grass*, "Song of Myself" 32]

11 I never saw a wild thing
Sorry for itself.
[D. H. Lawrence: *Self-Pity*]

12 Be a good animal, true to your animal instincts. [D. H. Lawrence: *The White Peacock* II.ii.]

ANNABEL LEE

13 And neither the angels in Heaven above
Nor the demons down under the sea,
Can ever dissever my soul from the soul
Of the beautiful Annabel Lee.
[Edgar Allan Poe: *Annabel Lee*]

(Queen) ANNE

14 Queen Anne's dead. [George Colman the Younger: *The Heir-at-Law* I.i.]
A proverb for something everybody knows which someone is advancing as a piece of news.
A generation ago in a popular song the American version was "George Washington is dead."

ANNIE LAURIE

15 And for bonnie Annie Laurie
I'd lay me doun an' dee.
[William Douglas: *Annie Laurie*]

ANNIHILATION

16 . . . when many that feared to die shall groan that they can die but once. The dismal state is the second and living death, when life puts despair on the damned; when men shall wish the coverings of Mountains, not of Monuments, and annihilation shall be courted. [Sir Thomas Browne: *Urn-Burial* V]

ANONYMITY

17 A deed without a name. [Shakespeare: *Macbeth* IV.i.]

18 To be namelesse in worthy deeds exceeds an infamous history. [Sir Thomas Browne: *Urn-Burial* V]

ANSWER(S)

19 I am not bound to please thee with my answer.
[Shakespeare: *The Merchant of Venice* IV.i.]

20 Had I as many mouths as Hydra,

such an answer would stop them all. [Shakespeare: *Othello* II.iii.]

1 When a man says, "Get out of my house! what would you have with my wife?" there's no answer to be made. [Cervantes: *Don Quixote* II.IV.38]

2 It isn't very intelligent to find answers to questions which are unanswerable. [Fontenelle: *La Pluralité des Mondes*, "Cinquième Soir"]

3 But answer came there none—
And this was scarcely odd, because
They'd eaten every one.
[Lewis Carroll: *Through the Looking-Glass*, "The Walrus and the Carpenter"]

4 His answer trickled through my head,
Like water through a sieve.
[Lewis Carroll: *Through the Looking-Glass* VIII]

ANT

5 Go to the ant, thou sluggard; consider her ways, and be wise. [Proverbs 6:6]

The ant, as Clarence Day has said, is a monkey's idea of industriousness. Its furious aimlessness and busy and bossy inefficiency so resemble "administrative talent" that we have accepted the ant as the type of admirable energy.

Nothing, actually, would be worse for a sluggard than to contemplate ants. Their small accomplishment for so enormous an expenditure of energy would reconcile him to his own indolence. Their infatuation for and indulgence of their parasites would lead him to parasitism. The only thing he might admire would be their thieving and their periodic orgies, the most wasteful saturnalias in nature.

6 An ant is a wise creature for itself but it is a shrewd thing in an orchard or garden. [Francis Bacon: *Of Wisdom for a Man's Self*]

shrewd = *evil, pernicious*

ANTAGONIST

7 He that wrestles with us strengthens our nerves, and sharpens our skill. Our antagonist is our helper. [Edmund Burke: *Reflections on the Revolution in France*]

ANTHEMS

8 For my voice, I have lost it with hollaing and singing of anthems. [Shakespeare: *II Henry IV* I.ii.]

ANTICIPATION

9 We are never in our selves, but beyond. Fear, desire, and hope draw us ever towards that which is to come and remove our sense and consideration from that which is. [Montaigne: *Essays* I.iii.]

10 Oft expectation fails, and most oft there
Where most it promises; and oft it hits
Where hope is coldest and despair most fits.
[Shakespeare: *All's Well That Ends Well* II.i.]

11 I have known him [Mr. Micawber] come home to supper with a flood of tears, and a declaration that nothing was now left but a jail; and go to bed making a calculation of the expense of putting bow-windows to the house, "in case anything turned up," which was his favorite expression. [Dickens: *David Copperfield* II]

ANTI-CLIMAX: illustrations of

12 The rest of all the acts of Asa, and all his might, and all that he did, and the cities which he built, are they not written in the book of the chronicles of the Kings of Judah? Nevertheless in the time of his old age he was diseased in his feet. [I Kings, 15:23]

13 "For God, for Country, and for Yale." [Yale University Anthem]

14 Once every month Joseph Self, an investment analyst by profession, takes a jet fighter plane up to 40,000 feet and from that height looks down on Wall Street, "in a larger perspective."

"From there you can see the relationship of things," he said, "and on clear nights you can see Philadelphia." [from the *New York Herald Tribune*, quoted *The New Yorker*, July 15, 1961]

15 Charges of practising medicine without a license, carrying an unauthorized gun and making an improper left turn were filed against him . . . [*Chicago Sun-Times*, Jan. 1, 1955, p. 23]

ANTONY

1 O! wither'd is the garland of the war,
The soldier's pole is fall'n; young boys and girls
Are level now with men; the odds is gone,
And there is nothing left remarkable
Beneath the visiting moon.
[Shakespeare: *Antony and Cleopatra* IV.xiii.]

ANVIL

2 To find oneself between the anvil and the hammers.
[Rabelais: *Pantagruel* IV.xxix.]
3 In this world a man must either be anvil or hammer.
[Longfellow: *Hyperion* IV.vii.]

ANXIETY

4 Huge and mighty forms that do not live
Like living men, moved slowly through the mind
By day, and were a trouble to my dreams.
[Wordsworth: *The Prelude* I]

AONIAN MOUNT

5 I thence
Invoke thy aid to my adventurous song,
That with no middle flight intends to soar
Above the Aonian mount.
[John Milton: *Paradise Lost* I.12-15]
The Aonian mount is Helicon, in Boeotia, sacred to the Muses. Milton states that he intends to outsoar the classic poets.

APE

6 How like to us is that filthy beast the ape. [Cicero: *De natura deorum* I]
7 Man is God's ape, and an ape is zany to a man. [Thomas Dekker: *The Seven Deadly Sins of London* V]
8 Of beasts, it is confess'd, the ape
Comes nearest us in human shape;
Like man he imitates each fashion,
And malice is his ruling passion.
[Jonathan Swift: *The Logicians Refuted*]
9 I have thus played the sedulous ape to Hazlitt, to Lamb, to Wordsworth, to Sir Thomas Browne, to Defoe, to Hawthorne, to Montaigne, to Baudelaire and to Obermann. [R. L. Stevenson: *Memories and Portraits* IV]

APHORISMS

10 Aphorisms are salted, not sugared, almonds at Reason's feast. [Logan Pearsall Smith: *Afterthoughts*]
11 I love them, because it is a joy to find thoughts one might have, beautifully expressed with much authority by someone recognizedly wiser than oneself. [Marlene Dietrich: *Marlene Dietrich's ABC*]

APHRODISIAC(S)

12 I am bewitched with the rogue's company. If the rascal have not given me medicines to make me love him, I'll be hanged. [Shakespeare: *I Henry IV* II.ii.]

APOLOGY

13 Apologizing—a very desperate habit —one that is rarely cured. Apology is only egotism wrong side out. [O. W. Holmes: *The Professor at the Breakfast-Table* VI]

APPAREL

14 Costly thy habit as thy purse can buy,
But not express'd in fancy; rich, not gaudy;
For the apparel oft proclaims the man.
[Shakespeare: *Hamlet* I.iii.]

APPARITION

15 The earth hath bubbles, as the water has,
And these are of them.
[Shakespeare: *Macbeth* I.iii.]
16 Anno 1670, not far from Cirencester, was an apparition: being demanded, whether a good spirit, or a bad? returned no answer, but disappeared with a curious perfume and most melodious twang. [John Aubrey: *Miscellanies*, "Apparitions"]
17 A dancing shape, an Image gay,
To haunt, to startle, and way-lay.
[Wordsworth: *She was a Phantom of Delight*]

APPEAL

18 To appeal from Philip drunk to Philip sober.

The proverb derives from an anecdote of Philip of Macedon given in the second chapter of Book 6 of the Memorabilia *of Valerius Maximus (1st century A.D.).*

The story is that an old woman against whom Philip had passed an unjust judgment after dinner, cried out, "I appeal!" Philip, an absolute monarch, was astonished and asked her to whom she intended to appeal. "To Philip," she said, "but to Philip sober." The king granted the appeal and, when sober, reversed his decision.

APPEARANCES

1 It is only shallow people who do not judge by appearances. [Oscar Wilde: *Picture of Dorian Gray* II]

APPETITE

2 Put a knife to thy throat, if thou be a man given to appetite. [Proverbs 23:2]

3   Who riseth from a feast
With that keen appetite that he sits
          down?
[Shakespeare: *The Merchant of Venice* II.vi.]

4 A sick man's appetite, who desires
          most that
Which would increase his evil.
[Shakespeare: *Coriolanus* I.i.]

5 The eye is bigger than the belly.
[George Herbert: *Jacula Prudentum*]

APPLAUSE

6 The applause of listening senates to
          command.
[Thomas Gray: *Elegy Written in a Country Churchyard* (1750)]
*While listening senates hang upon thy
          tongue.*
James Thomson: The Seasons, "Autumn"
          (*1730*)

7 Applause is the spur of noble minds, the end and aim of weak ones. [C. C. Colton: *Lacon*]

8 To hear the world applaud the hol-
          low ghost
Which blamed the living man.
[Matthew Arnold: *Growing Old*]

9 I sat down amid the cheers of the uncomprehending little audience. [Logan Pearsall Smith: *Trivia*, "The Coming of Fate"]

APPLE(S)

10 The woman whom thou gavest to be with me, she gave me of the tree, and I did eat. [Genesis 3:12]

11 The apple of his eye. [Deuteronomy 32:10]
Apple in this phrase is a translation into English of the Latin pupillam. *The pupil of the eye was called the apple in older English because it was thought to be a solid, spherical body. The old meaning of apple was almost any fruit. The old word for pine cone, for instance, was pineapple. It was transferred to what we now call a pineapple* (Ananas cosmosus) *because of the tropical fruit's resemblance to a pine cone. Nowhere does the Bible say that the fruit of the forbidden tree of which Adam and Eve ate was an apple in the sense in which it is now commonly conceived: the pome fruit of any tree of the genus* Malus.

12 Keep me as the apple of the eye; hide me under the shadow of thy wings. [Psalms 17:8]

13 There's small choice in rotten apples. [Shakespeare: *The Taming of the Shrew* I.i.]

14 Like to the apples on the Dead Sea's
          shore,
All ashes to the taste.
[Byron: *Childe Harold* III.xxxiv.]

APPLIANCES

15 With all appliances and means to
          boot.
[Shakespeare: *II Henry IV* III.i.]

APPROBATION

16 The desire for approbation is perhaps the most deeply seated instinct of civilized man. [W. Somerset Maugham: *The Moon and Sixpence*]

APRIL

17 April showers do bring May flowers. [Thomas Tusser: *Five Hundred Points of Good Husbandry*]

18 The uncertain glory of an April day. [Shakespeare: *Two Gentlemen of Verona* I.iii.]

19 'Tis a month before the month of
          May,
And the spring comes slowly up this
          way.
[Coleridge: *Christabel* I]

1 Oh, to be in England
Now that April's there.
[Robert Browning: *Home Thoughts from Abroad*]

2 The sun was warm but the wind was chill.
You know how it is with an April day:
When the sun is out and the wind is still,
You're one month on in the middle of May.
But if you so much as dare to speak,
A cloud comes over the sunlit arch,
A wind comes off a frozen peak,
And you're two months back in the middle of March.
[Robert Frost: *Two Tramps in Mud-Time*]

3 April is the cruelest month, breeding
Lilacs out of the dead land, mixing
Memory and desire, stirring
Dull roots with spring rain.
[T. S. Eliot: *The Waste Land* I]

4 April prepares her green traffic light and the world thinks Go. [Christopher Morley: *John Mistletoe*]

5 It is not enough that yearly, down this hill, April
Comes like an idiot, babbling and strewing flowers.
[Edna St. Vincent Millay: *Spring*]

ARCHANGEL
6 An archangel a little damaged. [Charles Lamb: description of Samuel Taylor Coleridge, in a letter to Wordsworth (1816)]

ARCHITECTURE
7 No architecture can be truly noble which is *not* imperfect. [John Ruskin: *The Stones of Venice* II.vi.]

ARGOT
8 Argot is nothing more nor less than a wardrobe in which language, having some bad deed to do, disguises itself. It puts on word-masks and metaphoric rags. [Victor Hugo: *Les Misérables* VII.i.]

ARGUMENT
9 Disputation cannot be held without reprehension. [Montaigne: *Essays* III. viii.]

Naturally, we find those who do not agree with us disagreeable; and since they insist on being this way in disputation, they are much to blame.

10 Therefore I'll darkly end the argument. [Shakespeare: *Love's Labour's Lost* V.ii.]
An early recognition of the principle of one-upmanship.

11 Be calm in arguing: for fierceness makes
Errour a fault, and truth discourtesy.
[George Herbert: *The Church-Porch*]

12 Don't take the wrong side of an argument just because your opponent has taken the right side. [Gracián: *Oráculo Manual*]

13 The argument of the stronger party is always the best. [La Fontaine: *The Wolf and the Lamb*]
In the fable the wolf and the lamb argue. The lamb's points are reasonable, just, and modestly stated. None the less, the wolf eats the lamb.

14 I have found you an argument; I am not obliged to find you an understanding. [Samuel Johnson: in Boswell's *Life*, June, 1784]
Johnson had become involved in a prolonged argument with "a pertinacious gentleman" who had talked "in a very puzzling manner." To one of Johnson's points the gentleman had said, "I don't understand you, Sir." Upon which Johnson, exasperated, replied as above.

15 In arguing, too, the parson own'd his skill,
For even though vanquished he could argue still.
[Oliver Goldsmith: *The Deserted Village*]

16 There is no arguing with Johnson: for if his pistol misses fire, he knocks you down with the butt end of it. [Oliver Goldsmith: in Boswell's *Life of Johnson*, October 26, 1769]
Boswell states that the image was borrowed from "one of Cibber's comedies."
Goldsmith scored several times against Johnson, no mean accomplishment. On another occasion (April 27, 1773) he was talking of the difficulty of writing fables and instanced the necessity if one were including little fishes of making them talk like fishes. Johnson laughed

and Goldsmith, annoyed at the laughter,
said, "Why, Dr. Johnson, this is not so
easy as you seem to think; for if you
were to make little fishes talk, they
would talk like WHALES."

1 We may convince others by our arguments; but we can only persuade them by their own. [Joseph Joubert: *Pensées*]

2 Myself when young did eagerly frequent
Doctor and Saint, and heard great argument
About it and about; but evermore
Came out by the same door wherein
I went.
[Rubáiyát of Omar Khayyám (trans. Edward FitzGerald)]

3 There is no good in arguing with the inevitable. The only argument available with an east wind is to put on your overcoat. [James Russell Lowell: *Democracy and Addresses*]

4 "In my youth," said his father, "I took to the law,
And argued each case with my wife;
And the muscular strength, which it gave to my jaw,
Has lasted the rest of my life."
[Lewis Carroll: *Alice's Adventures in Wonderland* VI]

5 He argued high, he argued low,
He also argued round about him.
[W. S. Gilbert: *Sir Macklin*]

ARISING

6 Up roos the sonne, and up roos Emelye.
[Chaucer: *The Knight's Tale*]

7 You rose on the wrong side of the bed today. [Richard Brome: *The Court-Beggar* II (1652)]

8 I have, all my life long, been lying till noon; yet I tell all young men, and tell them with great sincerity, that nobody who does not rise early will ever do any good. [Samuel Johnson: in Boswell's *Tour to the Hebrides*, Sept. 15, 1773]

9 Its habit of getting up late you'll agree
That it carries too far when I say
That it frequently breakfasts at five o'clock tea,
And dines on the following day.
[Lewis Carroll: *The Hunting of the*

Snark, Fit 1]

10 A birdie with a yellow bill
Hopped upon the window sill,
Cocked his shining eye and said:
"Ain't you 'shamed, you sleepy-head?"
[R. L. Stevenson: *Time to Rise*]

11 Even if a farmer intends to loaf, he gets up in time to get an early start. [E. W. Howe: *Country Town Sayings*]

12 O! it's nice to get up in the mornin'
But it's nicer to lie in bed.
[Sir Harry Lauder: *It's Nice to Get Up in the Mornin'*]

13 I forget who it was that recommended men for their soul's good to do each day two things they disliked: . . . it is a precept that I have followed scrupulously, for every day I have got up and I have gone to bed. [W. Somerset Maugham: *The Moon and Sixpence* II]

ARISTIDES

14 I'm just tired of hearing him called "the Just."
Plutarch relates that, when ostracism
was being voted against Aristides, "an
illiterate clownish fellow" who obvi-
ously did not know to whom he was
speaking, asked Aristides to write the
name Aristides *for him on his ostrakon.*
Aristides did so but asked him if Aris-
tides had ever done him any injury.
"None at all," said he, "neither know
I the man; but I am tired of hearing
him everywhere called the Just."
  About 1930, in the course of some
excavations in Athens, an ostrakon was
actually discovered with the name Aris-
tides on it.

ARISTOCRACY

15 Aristocracy is that form of government in which education and discipline are qualifications for suffrage or office-holding. [Aristotle: *Rhetoric* I.viii.]

16 Plutocracy lacks all the essential characters of a true aristocracy: a clean tradition, culture, public spirit, honesty, honor, courage—above all, courage. [H. L. Mencken: *Notes on Democracy*]

ARISTOTLE

17 The master of them that know. [Dante: *Divine Comedy*, "Inferno" I]

1 Aristotle, that hath an oar in every water and meddleth with all things. . . . [Montaigne: *Essays* I.iii.]

ARITHMETIC

2 Multiplication is vexation,
  Division is as bad;
  The Rule of Three perplexes me,
  And practice drives me mad.
[Anon.]
This wail of resentment, which has been scribbled in a million arithmetic books, has been traced back to 1570.

ARM

3 You are better off than I am, for while you have lost your *left,* I have lost my *right* arm. [Robert E. Lee: Letter to Stonewall Jackson, May 4, 1863]
Jackson had been wounded by one of his own sentries at Chancellorsville on May 2. His arm was amputated on May 3 and he died May 10.
Puns were used formerly, as here, to convey subtle shades of meaning and emotion. The touch of playfulness did not conceal, nor was it meant to conceal, Lee's anguish. It gave a touch of grace to despair and gilded horror with tenderness.

ARMCHAIR

4 I love it, I love it; and who shall dare
  To chide me for loving that old armchair?
[Eliza Cook: *The Old Arm Chair*]

ARMED

5 Thrice is he armed that hath his quarrel just.
[Shakespeare: *II Henry VI* III.ii.]

ARMS (WEAPONS)

6 Arms and the man I sing.
  (*Arma virumque cano*)
[Vergil: *Aeneid* I.i.]
7 The principal foundations of all states are good laws and good arms; and there cannot be good laws where there are not good arms. [Machiavelli: *The Prince* XII]
8   The arms are fair,
  When the intent of bearing them is just.
[Shakespeare: *I Henry IV* V.ii.]
9   And weaponless himself,

Made arms ridiculous.
[John Milton: *Samson Agonistes*]
10 A Farewell to Arms.
  Hemingway borrowed the title for his famous novel (1929) from a lyric of the same title by George Peele, an Elizabethan poet. In it the aged warrior accepts the fact that
    His helmet now shall make a hive for bees.

ARROGANCE

11 No doubt but ye are the people and wisdom shall die with you. [Job 12:2]

ARROW

12 I have shot mine arrow o'er the house
  And hurt my brother.
[Shakespeare: *Hamlet* V.ii.]
13 I shot an arrow into the air,
  It fell to earth, I know not where.
[Longfellow: *The Arrow and the Song*]

ARSENIC

14 Arsenic and Old Lace. [Title of play by Joseph Kesselring]
  Adapted from the cliché used to describe ultra-respectable, charming old ladies: "lavender and old lace."

ART(S)

15 The perfection of art is to conceal art. [Quintilian]
16 I hate all Boets and Bainters. [George II, King of England, quoted in Lord Campbell's *Lives of the Chief Justices* 30]
  The "boets" have always reciprocated the sentiment and "unwilling, unwieldy, unwanted George" has suffered at their hands.
17 All Nature is but Art, unknown to thee;
  All Chance, Direction, which thou canst not see.
[Alexander Pope: *An Essay on Man,* Epist. I 289-90]
18 'Tis to create, and in creating live
  A being more intense, that we endow
  With form our fancy, gaining as we give
  The life we image.
[Byron: *Childe Harold* III.vi.]
19 Art is long and Time is fleeting.
[Longfellow: *A Psalm of Life*]

Longfellow gave the now-accepted form to an aphorism that dates back to Hippocrates (460?-?377 B.C.) where the art alluded to was the art of healing. One of the best-known statements of it in English is Chaucer's:

The life so short, the craft so long to learn,
Th' assay so hard, so sharp the conquering.

The Parlement of Foules, "Proem" (1380)

1 Great art is produced by men who feel acutely and nobly; and it is in some sort an expression of this personal feeling. [John Ruskin: *Modern Painters* III.iv.]

2 Listen! There never was an artistic period. There never was an art-loving nation. [Whistler: *Ten O'Clock*]

3 All art does but consist in the removal of surplusage. [Walter Pater: *Appreciations*, "Style"]

4 Art comes to you proposing frankly to give nothing but the highest quality to your moments as they pass. [Walter Pater: *The Renaissance*]

5 Nothing is so poor and melancholy as art that is interested in itself and not in its subject. [George Santayana: *Life of Reason* IV]

6 There is nothing but art. Art is living. To attempt to give an object of art life by dwelling on its historical, cultural, or archaeological associations is senseless. [W. Somerset Maugham: *The Summing Up*]

7 An artist's saddest secrets are those that have to do with his artistry. [Willa Cather: *Youth and the Bright Medusa*, "The Diamond Mine"]

8 Life rushes from within, not from without. There is no work of art so big or so beautiful that it was not all once contained in some youthful body. [Willa Cather: *The Song of the Lark* I.xviii.]

9 What was any art but a mould in which to imprison for a moment the shining, elusive element which is life itself—life hurrying past us and running away, too strong to stop, too sweet to lose. [Willa Cather: *The Song of the Lark* IV.iii.]

10 The true function of art is to . . . edit nature and so make it coherent and lovely. The artist is a sort of impassioned proofreader, blue-penciling the bad spelling of God. [H. L. Mencken]

11 Art is one of the means whereby man seeks to redeem a life which is experienced as chaotic, senseless, and largely evil. [Aldous Huxley: *Themes and Variations*]

12 The finest works of art are precious, among other reasons, because they make it possible for us to know, if only imperfectly and for a little while, what it actually feels like to think subtly and feel nobly. [Aldous Huxley: *Ends and Means* XII]

13 Art is the terms of an armistice signed with fate. [Bernard De Voto: *Mark Twain at Work*]

14 All art is a revolt against man's fate. [André Malraux: *Voices of Silence*]

15 Art is not a pastime but a priesthood. [Jean Cocteau, quoted *New York Times*, Sept. 8, 1957]

16 Writers write for themselves and not for their readers. Art has nothing to do with communication between person and person, only with communication between different parts of a person's mind. [Rebecca West: "The Art of Skepticism," *Vogue*, Nov. 1, 1952]

17 A product of the untalented, sold by the unprincipled to the utterly bewildered. [Al Capp (on abstract art), quoted *National Observer*, July 1, 1963]

ARTERIES

18 A man is as old as his arteries. [Dr. Thomas Sydenham (attr.)]

ARTHUR

19 Nay, sure, he's not in hell; he's in Arthur's bosom, if ever man went to Arthur's bosom. [Shakespeare: *Henry V* II.iii.]

ARTIFICIAL

20 All things are artificial, for nature is the art of God. [Sir Thomas Browne: *Religio Medici* I.xvi.]

21 If the artificial is not better than the natural, to what end are all the arts of life? To dig, to plough, to build, to wear clothes, are direct infringements of the injunction to follow nature. [John Stuart Mill: *Three Essays on Religion* (Essay 1: "Nature")]

ARTIST

1 The artist, like the God of the creation, remains within or behind or beyond or above his handiwork, invisible, refined out of existence, indifferent, paring his fingernails. [James Joyce: *Portrait of the Artist as a Young Man*]

2 An artist is always alone—if he *is* an artist . . . the artist needs loneliness. [Henry Miller: *Tropic of Cancer*]

ASCENT

3   Long is the way
And hard, that out of Hell leads up
        to light.
[John Milton: *Paradise Lost* II.432-433]

ASCETICISM

4 Alas! what boots it with uncessant
        care
To tend the homely slighted shep-
        herd's trade,
And strictly meditate the thankless
        Muse?
Were it not better done as others use,
To sport with Amaryllis in the shade,
Or with the tangles of Neaera's hair?
[John Milton: *Lycidas*]

ASHES

5 Yet in our asshen old is fire y-reke. [Chaucer: Prologue to *The Reeve's Tale*]

6 Earth to earth, ashes to ashes, dust to dust, in sure and certain hope of the resurrection. [*Book of Common Prayer*, "Burial of the Dead"]

7 E'en in our ashes live their wonted
        fires.
[Thomas Gray: *Elegy Written in a Country Churchyard*]

ASK

8 Ask, and it shall be given you; seek, and ye shall find; knock, and it shall be opened unto you. [Matthew 7:7]

ASKED

9 You asked for it, Georges Dandin, you asked for it. [Molière: *Georges Dandin* I.ix.]

ASPIRATION

10   Raise thy head;
Take stars for money.
[George Herbert: *The Church-Porch* XXIX]

11 The shades of night were falling fast,
As through an Alpine village passed
A youth, who bore, 'mid snow and ice,
A banner with the strange device,
    Excelsior!
[Longfellow: *Excelsior*]
Longfellow's poem appeared in 1841. In 1868 U.S. Patent No. 75728 connected excelsior *with wood shavings, to be used as stuffing or packing material. The manufacturer may have profited by the exploitation of Longfellow's word, but the poem suffered. It now evokes associations inconsistent with dignity, let alone nobility; and the poem that inspired one generation, by a trick of fate, serves only to amuse another.*

12 Build thee more stately mansions, O
        my soul,
As the swift seasons roll!
Leave thy low-vaulted past!
Let each new temple, nobler than the
        last,
Shut thee from heaven with a dome
        more vast,
Till thou at length art free,
Leaving thine outgrown shell by life's
        unresting sea!
[O. W. Holmes: *The Chambered Nautilus*]

13 Death closes all: but something ere
        the end,
Some work of noble note, may yet be
        done,
Not unbecoming men that strove with
        gods.
[Tennyson: *Ulysses*]

14 I hold it truth, with him who sings
    To one clear harp in divers tones,
    That men may rise on stepping-
        stones
Of their dead selves to higher things.
[Tennyson: *In Memoriam* I]

15 That low man seeks a little thing
        to do,
    Sees it and does it:
This high man, with a great thing to
        pursue,
    Dies ere he knows it.
This low man goes on adding one to
        one,
    His hundred's soon hit:
This high man, aiming at a million,
    Misses an unit.
[Robert Browning: *A Grammarian's Fu-*

neral]
1 What I aspired to be,
And was not, comforts me.
[Robert Browning: *Rabbi Ben Ezra*]
2 Ah, but a man's reach should exceed
his grasp,
Or what's a heaven for?
[Robert Browning: *Andrea del Sarto*]
3 The youth gets together his materials
to build a bridge to the moon, or perchance, a palace or temple on earth, and,
at length, the middle-aged man concludes
to build a woodshed with them. [Thor-
eau: *Journal* July 14, 1852]

ASS

4 Egregiously an ass.
[Shakespeare: *Othello* II.i.]
5 The Nightingale of Brutes. [Jona-
than Swift: *The Beasts' Confession*
(1732)]
6 He that makes himself an Ass, must
not take it ill if Men ride him. [Thomas
Fuller (1654-1734): *Gnomologia* (1732)]
7 An ass may bray a good while before
he shakes the stars down. [George Eliot:
Romola III.l.]
8 Instead of feeling complimented
when we are called an ass, we are left
in doubt. [Mark Twain: *Pudd'nhead
Wilson's Calendar*]

ASSASSINATION

9 Let's carve him as a dish fit for the
gods,
Not hew him as a carcass fit for
hounds.
[Shakespeare: *Julius Caesar* II.i.]

ASSURANCE

10 They thinke they haue God almightie
by the toe. [Ariosto: *Orlando Furioso*
(trans. Sir John Harington)]
11 I'll make assurance double sure,
And take a bond of fate.
[Shakespeare: *Macbeth* IV.i.]
12 It generally happens that assurance
keeps an even pace with ability. [Samuel
Johnson: *The Rambler* No. 159]
13 He did not object to Gladstone's always having the ace of trumps up his
sleeve, but only to his pretense that God
put it there. [Henry Labouchere: as
quoted in the *Dictionary of National
Biography*, "Gladstone"]

ASSYRIAN

14 The Assyrian came down like the
wolf on the fold,
And his cohorts were gleaming in
purple and gold;
And the sheen of their spears was
like stars on the sea,
When the blue wave rolls nightly
on deep Galilee.
[Byron: *The Destruction of Sennacherib*]

ASTROLOGY

15 This is the excellent foppery of the
world, that, when we are sick in fortune
—often the surfeit of our own behaviour
—we make guilty of our disasters the sun,
the moon, and the stars: as if we were
villains by necessity; fools by heavenly
compulsion; knaves, thieves, and treach-
ers, by spherical predominance; drunkards, liars, and adulterers by an enforced
obedience of planetary influence; and all
that we are evil in, by a divine thrusting
on. . . . [Shakespeare: *King Lear* I.ii.]
16   There's some ill planet reigns:
I must be patient till the heavens look
With an aspect more favourable.
[Shakespeare: *The Winter's Tale* II.i.]

ASTRONOMER

17 An undevout astronomer is mad.
[Edward Young: *Night Thoughts* (1742)]
*But, of course, he would be even madder
to espouse any sect, and it would be
very hard for him to regard man as only
a little lower than the angels.*

ATHEISM

18 The fool hath said in his heart, There
is no God. [Psalms 14:1 and 53:1]
19 All that impugn a received religion
or superstition are, by the adverse part,
branded with the name of atheists. [Fran-
cis Bacon: *Of Atheism*]
20 Atheism leaves a man to sense, to philosophy, to natural piety, to laws, to
reputation: all which may be guides to
an outward moral virtue, though religion
were not; but superstition dismounts all
these and erecteth an absolute monarchy
in the minds of men. [Francis Bacon:
Of Superstition]
*though religion were not = even if reli-
gion did not exist*
21 It is true, that a little philosophy in-

clineth man's mind to atheism, but depth in philosophy bringeth men's minds about to religion. [Francis Bacon: *Of Atheism*]

1 Atheism is hateful in that it depriveth human nature of the means to exalt itself above human frailty. [Francis Bacon: *Of Atheism*]

2 Atheism is the vice of a few intelligent people. [Voltaire: *Philosophical Dictionary*]

3 It is easier to suppose that the universe has existed from all eternity than to conceive a Being beyond its limits capable of creating it. [Shelley: Notes to *Queen Mab*]

4 The three great apostles of practical atheism, that make converts without persecuting, and retain them without preaching, are wealth, health and power. [C. C. Colton: *Lacon*]

5 My atheism, like that of Spinoza, is true piety towards the universe and denies only gods fashioned by men in their own image, to be servants of their human interests. [George Santayana: *Soliloquies in England*]

6 The spread of Atheism among the young is awful; I give no credit, however, to the report that some of them do not believe in Mammon. [Logan Pearsall Smith: *Afterthoughts*]

7 The man who is thoroughly convinced of the universal operation of the law of causation cannot for a moment entertain the idea of a being who interferes in the course of events . . . He has no use for the religion of fear and equally little for social or moral religion. [Albert Einstein: "Religion and Science," *New York Times Magazine,* Nov. 9, 1930]

ATHEIST

8 No one has ever died an atheist. [Plato: *Laws* X]
But unless one equates Zeus with Jehovah—an equivalence which no Christian would countenance—then, surely, Plato's believers had better have died atheists.

9 Where there are three physicians there are two atheists. [Medieval Latin proverb]
The hostility of the Church to medicine was reciprocated. Chaucer says of his

Doctor of Physic that "His studie was but litel on the Bible."

10 There are no atheists in foxholes. [Attr. William Thomas Cummings, Lt. Col. Warren J. Clear, and various unidentified chaplains, sergeants and other philosophers]
The statement, exceedingly popular during World War II and extended to include cockpits, life rafts and sundry other positions and vessels, was simply meant to be an emphatic way of saying that all men in time of fear seek religion. Whether they do or not is as much a question as whether it is creditable to religion to claim they do. It rather ranks with death-bed conversions which, as John Selden said, was as much something to boast of as seducing a woman when she was drunk.

11 An atheist is a man who has no invisible means of support. [Fulton Sheen: *Look,* Dec. 14, 1955]

ATHENS

12 Athens, the eye of Greece, mother of arts
And eloquence.
[John Milton: *Paradise Regained* IV. 240]

13 Ancient of days! august Athena! where,
Where are thy men of might? thy grand in soul?
Gone—glimmering through the dream of things that were:
First in the race that led to Glory's goal,
They won, and pass'd away—is this the whole?
[Byron: *Childe Harold* II.ii.]

ATHLETICS

14 The popular belief in [college] athletics is grounded upon the theory that violent exercise makes for bodily health, and that bodily health is necessary to mental vigor. Both halves of this theory are highly dubious. . . . The truth is that athletes, as a class, are not above the normal in health, but below it. [H. L. Mencken: in *The American Mercury,* June 1931]

ATOM(S)

1 A blind, fortuitous concourse of atoms. [John Locke: *An Essay Concerning Human Understanding* IV.20]

2 $E = mc^2$ [Albert Einstein: *Annalen der Physik*, 1905]
   $E = energy$
   $m = the\ mass\ of\ the\ atom$
   $c = the\ speed\ of\ light$

ATTACK

3 There is always more spirit in attack than in defense. [Livy: *Histories* XXI. xliv.]

ATTEMPT

4   The attempt and not the deed Confounds us.
[Shakespeare: *Macbeth* II.ii.]

ATTENTION

5 And listens like a three years' child. [Coleridge: *The Ancient Mariner* I]

ATTICUS

6   Peace to all such! but were there One
                  whose fires
True Genius kindles, and fair Fame
                 inspires;
Blest with each talent and each art
              to please,
And born to write, converse, and live
             with ease:
Should such a man, too fond to rule
              alone,
Bear, like the Turk, no brother near
           the throne,
View him with scornful, yet with jealous eyes,
And hate for arts that caus'd himself
           to rise;
Damn with faint praise, assent with
           civil leer,
And without sneering, teach the rest
           to sneer;
Willing to wound, and yet afraid to
           strike,
Just hint a fault, and hesitate dislike;
Alike reserv'd to blame, or to commend,
A tim'rous foe, and a suspicious
           friend;
Dreading ev'n fools, by Flatterers besieg'd,
And so obliging, that he ne'er
           obliged;
Like *Cato*, give his little Senate laws,
And sit attentive to his own applause;
While Wits and Templars ev'ry sentence raise,
And wonder with a foolish face of
           praise—
Who but must laugh, if such a man
           there be?
Who would not weep, if ATTICUS
           were he?
[Alexander Pope: *Epistle to Dr. Arbuthnot*]

converse = move graciously in polite society; besieg'd — note the rime and the pronunciation of "obliged" as "obleeged"; wonder = admire

Pope had at first written:
   Who would not smile if such a
          man there be?
   Who would not laugh if Addison
          were he?

This, however, was merely a continuation of the clever, cold derision of the preceding lines and had the weakness, in the last line, of showing malice openly.
   So he changed it to:
   Who would not grieve if such a
          man there be?
   Who would not laugh if Addison
          were he?

This suggests more real detestation and conceals the derision under an assumption of shocked humanity. But the last line remains openly contemptuous of the demigod of the age. So he finally changed it to the form given above and thus made it one of the most brilliantly cruel satirical passages in any language. Light jesting was turned to bitter earnest. Pope himself seems shocked at what he has to tell, grief stricken to have to confess that the idol of his youth was a petty, cold, mean, contemptible man.
   The lines were published after Addison's death. Pope said that he showed them to Addison, but this is doubted.

ATTORNEY

7 He did not care to speak ill of any man behind his back, but he believed the gentleman was an attorney. [Samuel Johnson: in Boswell's *Life* (1770), of one who had just left the room]

In American English attorney is almost

synonymous with lawyer. *In England lawyers are classified as* barristers *and* solicitors. *An attorney is a lawyer considerably beneath these in dignity, and the word is tainted with opprobrium and rarely used. Johnson's remark would strike many Americans as a gratuitous insult. An English lawyer, on the other hand, would be taken aback at the sign in many American office buildings, even in the courts, "Solicitors not allowed."*

ATTRACTION

1 Long custom, a manly appearance, faultless boots and clothes, and a happy fierceness of manner, will often help a man as much as a great balance at the banker's. [W. M. Thackeray: *Vanity Fair* XXII]

AUBURN

2 Sweet Auburn! loveliest village of the plain.
[Oliver Goldsmith: *The Deserted Village*]

AUDACITY

3 Stubborn audacity is the last refuge of guilt. [Samuel Johnson: *Journey to the Western Islands of Scotland*]
Johnson was alluding to James Macpherson's continued insistence that the poems of Ossian were genuine, though he refused to submit to anyone's inspection of the manuscripts which he averred he possessed. Time has completely vindicated Johnson.

4 Audacity, more audacity, and always audacity! (*De l'audace, encore de l'audace, et toujours de l'audace!*) [Danton: in a speech before the French National Assembly, August, 1792]
Before the young are carried away by the inspiration of these glorious words, it is well for the teacher to point out that Danton was guillotined two years later.

AUDIENCE

5 Fit audience find, though few.
[John Milton: *Paradise Lost* VII. 31]

AUGURS

6 Got the ill name of augurs, because

they were bores. [James Russell Lowell: *A Fable for Critics*]

AULD LANG SYNE

7 Should auld acquaintance be forgot,
And never brought to min'?
Should auld acquaintance be forgot,
And auld lang syne?
  For auld lang syne, my dear,
  For auld lang syne,
  We'll tak a cup o' kindness yet,
  For auld lang syne.
[Burns: *Auld Lang Syne*]
Burns took the title from a song by Allan Ramsay, but little else. The song is a song of reunion, but often sung at parting.

AUTHOR(S)

8 He that I am reading seems always to have the most force. [Montaigne: *Essays* II.xii.]

9 Discouraged, scorn'd, his writings vilified,
Poorly—poor man—he liv'd; poorly
—poor man—he died.
[Phineas Fletcher: *The Purple Island* IV.xix.]

10 No author ever spar'd a brother;
Wits are gamecocks to one another.
[John Gay: *The Elephant and the Bookseller*]

11 Authors are partial to their wit, 'tis true,
But are not critics to their judgment too?
[Alexander Pope: *An Essay on Criticism* I, 17-18]

12 Just writes to make his barrenness appear,
And strains from hard-bound brains eight lines a year.
[Alexander Pope: *Epistle to Dr. Arbuthnot*]

13 The chief glory of every people arises from its authors. [Samuel Johnson: Preface to the *Dictionary*]

14 The best part of every author is in general to be found in his book, I assure you. [Samuel Johnson: in Boswell's *Life*, July 21, 1763]

15 Authors—essayist, atheist, novelist, realist, rhymester, play your part,
Paint the mortal shame of nature with the living hues of Art.

Rip your brothers' vices open, strip
your own foul passions bare;
Down with Reticence, down with Reverence—forward—naked—let them
stare.
[Tennyson: *Locksley Hall Sixty Years
After*]
1 There is probably no hell for authors
in the next world—they suffer so much
from critics and publishers in this. [C. N.
Bovee: *Authors*]
2 What I like in a good author is not
what he says, but what he whispers.
[Logan Pearsall Smith: *Afterthoughts*]
3 Every author, however modest, keeps
a most outrageous vanity chained like a
madman in the padded cell of his breast.
[Logan Pearsall Smith: *Afterthoughts*]

AUTHORITY

4 For he taught them as one having
authority. [Matthew 7:29]
5 I am a man under authority, having
soldiers under me: and I say to this man,
Go, and he goeth; and to another,
Come, and he cometh; and to my servant,
Do this, and he doeth it. [Matthew 8:9]
 *The speaker was a centurion, a Roman
 military officer commanding a century,
 approximately one hundred men.*
6 Nothing overshadows truth so completely as authority. [Alberti: *Del Prin-
cipe* III]
7   But man, proud man,
Drest in a little brief authority,
Most ignorant of what he's most assur'd,
His glassy essence, like an angry ape,
Plays such fantastic tricks before high
heaven,
As make the angels weep.
[Shakespeare: *Measure for Measure* II.ii.]
8 Thou hast seen a farmer's dog bark at
a beggar,
And the creature run from the cur:
There, thou might'st behold the great
image of authority;
A dog's obeyed in office.
[Shakespeare: *King Lear* IV.vi.]
9 Nothing destroyeth authority so much
as the unequal and untimely interchange
of power pressed too far and relaxed too
much. [Francis Bacon: *Of Empire*]
10 The vices of authority are chiefly
four: delays, corruption, roughness and

facility. [Francis Bacon: *Of Great Place*]
 facility = *overreadiness to yield, weakness*
11 Reproofs from authority ought to be
grave and not taunting. [Francis Bacon:
Of Great Place]
12 In the name of the great Jehovah and
the Continental Congress. [Ethan Allen:
on being asked by what authority he demanded the surrender of Ticonderoga,
May 10, 1775]
13 All authority belongs to the people.
[Thomas Jefferson: Letter to Spencer
Roane]
14 Authority forgets a dying king. [Ten-
nyson: *Morte d'Arthur*]
15 To despise legitimate authority, no
matter in whom it is invested, is unlawful; it is rebellion against God's will.
[Leo XIII: *Immortale Dei,* Nov. 1, 1885]
 But what makes authority "legitimate"?

AUTOBIOGRAPHY

16 The writer of his own life has, at
least, the first qualification of an historian, the knowledge of the truth; and
though it may be plausibly objected that
his temptations to disguise it are equal to
his opportunities of knowing it, yet I
cannot but think that impartiality may
be expected with equal confidence from
him that relates the passages of his own
life as from him that delivers the trans-
actions of another. [Samuel Johnson:
The Idler No. 84]

AUTOSUGGESTION

17 Every day, in every way, I'm growing
better and better. [Émile Coué: a slogan
to aid healing]
 First announced in 1910.

AUTUMN

18 The teeming autumn, big with rich
increase.
[Shakespeare: *Sonnets* XCVII]
19 The day becomes more solemn and
serene
When noon is past: there is a harmony
In Autumn, and a lustre in its sky
Which through the Summer is not
heard or seen,
As if it could not be, as if it had not
been!
[Shelley: *Hymn to Intellectual Beauty*]

1 The melancholy days are come, the
saddest of the year,
Of wailing winds and naked woods,
and meadows brown and sear.
[William Cullen Bryant: *The Death of
the Flowers*]

2 Season of mists and mellow fruitful-
ness,
Close bosom-friend of the maturing
sun;
Conspiring with him how to load and
bless
With fruit the vines that round the
thatch-eaves run;
To bend with apples the moss'd cot-
tage-trees,
And fill all fruit with ripeness to the
core.
[Keats: *To Autumn*]

3 When the frost is on the punkin and
the fodder's in the shock.
[James Whitcomb Riley: *When the Frost
Is on the Punkin*]

4 A haze on the far horizon,
The infinite, tender sky,
The ripe, rich tint of the cornfields,
And the wild geese sailing high—
And all over upland and lowland
The charm of the goldenrod—
Some of us call it Autumn,
And others call it God.
[W. H. Carruth: *Each in His Own
Tongue*]

5 The beautiful and death-struck year.
[A. E. Housman: *A Shropshire Lad* XLI]

AVALANCHE
6 "Beware the pine-tree's withered
branch!
Beware the awful avalanche!"
[Longfellow: *Excelsior*]

AVALON
7 I am going a long way
With these thou seest—if indeed I go
(For all my mind is clouded with a
doubt)—
To the island-valley of Avilion;
Where falls not hail, or rain, or any
snow,
Nor ever wind blows loudly; but it
lies
Deep-meadow'd, happy, fair with or-
chard lawns
And bowery hollows crown'd with

summer sea,
Where I will heal me of my grievous
wound.
[Tennyson: *The Passing of Arthur*]

AVARICE
8 The love of gold knows no fear of
sword or death. [Lucan: *Pharsalia* III]

9 The miser is as much in want of what
he has as of what he has not. [Publilius
Syrus: *Maxims*]

10 Poverty wants much; but avarice, everything. [Publilius Syrus: *Maxims*]

11 Avarice is likerousness in herte to
have erthely things. [Chaucer: *The Parson's Tale*]
likerousness = *lechery*
*Chaucer is paraphrasing St. Augustine.
In* The Last Tycoon, *F. Scott Fitzgerald
speaks of an ambitious underling in
Hollywood eying one of the Great Ones
there "with open economic lechery."*

12 He that maketh haste to be rich shall
not be innocent. [Proverbs 28:20]

13 Greedy of filthy lucre. [I Timothy
3:3]

14 Bell, book, and candle shall not drive
me back,
When gold and silver becks me to
come on.
[Shakespeare: *King John* III.iii.]

15 That disease
Of which all old men sicken, avarice.
[Thomas Middleton: *The Roaring Girl*
I.1.]

16 A mere madness, to live like a wretch,
and die rich. [Robert Burton: *Anatomy
of Melancholy* I.2.3.13.]

17 Avarice is more opposed to thrift
than liberality is. [La Rochefocauld:
Maxims]

18 Avarice, sphincter of the heart. [Mat-
thew Green: *The Spleen*]

19 Avarice is generally the last passion
of those lives of which the first part has
been squandered in pleasure, and the
second devoted to ambition. [Samuel
Johnson: *The Rambler* No. 151]

20 Avarice is a uniform and tractable
vice: other intellectual distempers are
different in different constitutions of
mind; that which soothes the pride of
one will offend the pride of another; but
to the favor of the covetous there is a
ready way; bring money, and nothing is

denied. [Samuel Johnson: *Rasselas* XXXIX]

1 There are few ways in which a man can be more innocently employed than in getting money. [Samuel Johnson: in Boswell's *Life,* March 27, 1775]

2 Avarice, the spur of industry. [David Hume: *Of Civil Liberty*]

3 My days of love are over; me no more
    The charms of maid, wife, and still
        less of widow,
Can make the fool of which they
        made before—
In short, I must not lead the life I
        did do;
The credulous hope of mutual minds
        is o'er,
The copious use of claret is forbid
        too,
So for a good old-gentlemanly vice,
    I think I must take up with avarice.
[Byron: *Don Juan* I.ccxvi.]

4 Novel: the man who realizes that one needs to be rich in order to live, who devotes himself completely to the acquisition of money, who succeeds, lives and dies *happy.* [Albert Camus: *Notebooks 1935-1942* Ch. 1, p. 50]

AVERAGE SENSUAL MAN

5 In M. Victor Hugo we have . . . the average sensual man impassioned and grandiloquent; in M. Zola we have the average sensual man going near the ground. [Matthew Arnold: *Discourses in America,* Discourse 2]

AVERNUS

6 Easy is the descent to Avernus. [Vergil: *Aeneid* VI]

> *The entire passage reads:*
> *The way is easy to the Avernian flood,*
> *Black Pluto's gates stand open day and*
> *   night:*
> *But to return, and view etherial light,*
> *That is a work, a labor.*
> *   Ogilby's translation*

AVERSION

7 Some men there are love not a gaping
        pig;
Some that are mad if they behold a
        cat;
And others, when the bag-pipe sings
        i' the nose,
Cannot contain their urine.
[Shakespeare: *The Merchant of Venice* IV.i.]

8   O, he's as tedious
As is a tir'd horse, a railing wife;
Worse than a smoky house; I had
        rather live
With cheese and garlic in a windmill,
        far,
Than feed on cates, and have him
        talk to me,
In any summer-house in Christen-
        dom.
[Shakespeare: *I Henry IV* III.i.]
cates = delicacies—*whence our word* caterer

AVOCATION

9 I want to know a butcher paints,
    A baker rhymes for his pursuit,
Candlestick-maker much acquaints
    His soul with song, or, haply mute,
Blows out his brains upon the flute!
[Robert Browning: *Shop*]

AWAKENING

10 Clay lies still, but blood's a rover;
    Breath's a ware that will not keep.
Up, lad: when the journey's over
    There'll be time enough to sleep.
[A. E. Housman: *A Shropshire Lad* IV]

11 It is as painful perhaps to be awakened from a vision as to be born. [James Joyce: *Ulysses*]

AWARENESS

12 The unexamined life is not worth living. [Socrates: in Plato's *Apology*]

AXE

13 An axe to grind.

> *The phrase, used to suggest a hidden personal advantage concealed in a seemingly disinterested proposal, is hard to account for. Some trace it to a story by Benjamin Franklin of a man who agreed to turn a grindstone for one who wanted to polish an axe. But since the motive was plain from the beginning, this seems, rather, to suggest: "Don't bite off more than you can chew."*
>
> *Others attribute it to Charles Miner's* Who'll Turn the Grindstone? *(1810). This is a story of a boy who is flattered into turning a grindstone while a stran-*

ger sharpens his axe. The boy not only finds the task much harder than he thought it would be, but at its conclusion he is dismissed not with thanks but with a warning that he'd better not be late to school. Miner ends the story by saying that whenever he sees a merchant overpolite to a customer, he says to himself, "That man has an axe to grind." But since the stranger makes his intention plain from the beginning, this doesn't explain it either and one suspects that Miner made up the story, ineptly, to explain the saying.

B

BABBLE

1 Babble, babble; our old England may go down in babble at last. [Tennyson: *Locksley-Hall Sixty Years After*]

BABE(S)

2 Out of the mouths of babes and sucklings hast thou ordained strength. [Psalms 8:2]

3 As I in hoary winter night stood
    shivering in the snow,
Surprised was I with sudden heat
    which made my heart to glow;
And lifting up a fearful eye to view
    what fire was near
A pretty Babe all burning bright did
    in the air appear.
[Robert Southwell: *The Burning Babe*]

4   I have given suck, and know
How tender 'tis to love the babe that
    milks me.
[Shakespeare: *Macbeth* I.vii.]

BABY

5 Mewling and puking in the nurse's
    arms.
[Shakespeare: *As You Like It* II.viii.]

6 Bye, baby bunting,
Daddy's gone a-hunting,
Gone to get a rabbit skin
To wrap up baby bunting in.
[Nursery rhyme, with many variants: oldest known printed form 1784, but the rhyme itself probably many centuries older]

    bunting = *short and thick (cf. "dumpling"), a term of endearment*

7 A tight little bundle of wailing and flannel. [Frederick Locker-Lampson: *The Old Cradle*]

8 Where did you come from, baby dear? Out of the everywhere into here. [George Macdonald: *At the Back of the North Wind*]

BABYLON

9 By the rivers of Babylon, there we sat down, yea, we wept, when we remembered Zion. [Psalms: 137:1]

    By the waters of Babylon we sat down
and wept: when we remembered thee, O Sion.
Book of Common Prayer, *Psalm 137:1*

10 Babylon is fallen, is fallen. [Isaiah 21:9]

11 Babylon is fallen, is fallen, that great city. [Revelation 14:8]

12 Or ever the knightly years were gone
    With the old world to the grave,
I was a King in Babylon
    And you were a Christian Slave.
[W. E. Henley: *Echoes* XXXVII, "To W. A."]

BACH

13 Bach, sir? Bach's concert? And pray, sir, who is Bach? Is he a piper? [Samuel Johnson: quoted by Fanny Burney in *Memoirs of Dr. Burney*, II.90, 93]

BACHELOR

14 Bachelors' wives and maids' children are always well taught. [John Heywood: *Proverbs* (1546)]

15 The world must be peopled. When I said I would die a bachelor, I did not think I should live till I were married. [Shakespeare: *Much Ado About Nothing* II.iii.]

16 The unsettled, thoughtless condition of a bachelor. [Samuel Johnson: *The Rambler* No. 18]

17 Nobody knows how to manage a wife but a bachelor. [George Colman the Elder: *The Jealous Wife* IV]

18 It is a truth universally acknowledged, that a single man in possession of a good fortune must be in want of a wife. [Jane Austen: *Pride and Prejudice* I]

19 The old bachelor don't die at all—he sort of rots away, like a pollywog's tail. [Artemus Ward: *The Draft in Baldinsville*]

20 Single men in barracks don't grow into plaster saints. [Kipling: *Tommy*]
    It is interesting that the lower-class pronunciation would be emphasized by the spelling Kipling assigns to it; the upper-class pronunciation "barrucks" would be

spelled barracks.

1 Bachelors know more about women than married men. If they didn't they'd be married, too. [H. L. Mencken: *Chrestomathy* 621]

BACON

2 The bacon was not fat for them, I trow,
That some men have in Essex at Dunmowe.

[Chaucer: Prologue to *The Wife of Bath's Tale*]

The Wife of Bath is saying that she nagged her husbands and led them a wretched life. The allusion is to a flitch of bacon which was offered annually at Dunmow, a village in Essex, England, to any couple that would kneel at the church door and swear that for a year and a day they had not quarreled and that at no time during the preceding year had either wished himself or herself unmarried. Between 1244 and 1772, a period of more than 500 years, the flitch was awarded only eight times.

BACON, FRANCIS

3 His hearers could not cough, or look aside from him, without loss. . . . The fear of every man that heard him was, lest he should make an end. [Ben Jonson: *Discoveries* lxxviii.]

4 If parts allure thee, think how Bacon shin'd,
The wisest, brightest, meanest of mankind.

[Alexander Pope: *An Essay on Man* IV]

5 The art which Bacon taught was the art of inventing arts. [Macaulay: *Francis Bacon*]

BAD NEWS

6 Here are a few of the unpleasant'st words
That ever blotted paper.

[Shakespeare: *The Merchant of Venice* III.ii.]

7 Though it be honest, it is never good
To bring bad news.

[Shakespeare: *Antony and Cleopatra* II.v.]

BAG

8 . . . since General Shays has sneaked off and given us the bag to hold. [Royall Tyler: *The Contrast* II.ii.]

BAG AND BAGGAGE

9 Come . . . let us make an honorable retreat; though not with bag and baggage. . . . [Shakespeare: *As You Like It* III.ii.]

Bag and baggage was a military term denoting the collective property of the army (baggage) and the property of the individual soldiers. The expression was used chiefly in relation to a besieged garrison which, though compelled to surrender, marched out with honor. There was an established procedure to mark such a surrender. The soldiers retained their arms, their drums were beating and their colors flying. Each musketeer carried a bullet in his mouth, bandoliers full of powder, and matches lighted at both ends. That is, though the army was surrendering and retreating, it was in a posture of defence, in instant readiness to protect itself and avenge perfidy. It was far from a demoralized army and something of its bristling defiance in retreat survives in the contemporary use of the expression.

BAIT

10 BAIT. A preparation that renders the hook more palatable. The best kind is beauty. [Ambrose Bierce: *The Devil's Dictionary*]

BALANCE OF POWER

11 The balance of power. [Sir Robert Walpole, Speech in the House of Commons, Feb. 13, 1741]

BALD

12 And he [Elisha] went up from thence unto Bethel: and as he was going up by the way, there came forth little children out of the city, and mocked him, and said unto him, Go up, thou bald head; go up, thou bald head.

And he turned back, and looked on them, and cursed them in the name of the Lord. And there came forth two she bears out of the wood, and tare forty and two children of them. [II Kings 2:23-24]

Men are very sensitive about the loss of their hair and the passage may have been dictated by the Holy Spirit to show us the deeply human being under the prophet's mantle.

1 He was as ballid as a cote.

[John Lydgate: *Troy Book* II (1412-20)]
ballid = bald; cote = coot

2 As bald as a coot.

[Robert Burton: *The Anatomy of Melancholy* III.3.1.2. (1621)]

BALLAD

3 I had rather be a kitten and cry mew,
Than one of these same meter ballad-mongers.

[Shakespeare: *I Henry IV* III.i.]
Glendower had boasted of his skill in singing and Hotspur, baiting him, replied in the above words. They are a good example, by the way, of the danger of prefacing a quotation from the plays with "Shakespeare says."

4 The farmer's daughter hath soft brown hair
(Butter and eggs and a pound of cheese)
And I met with a ballad, I can't say where,
That wholly consisted of lines like these.

[Charles Stuart Calverley: *Ballad, after William Morris*]

BALLOONISTS

5 Balloonists have an unsurpassed view of the scenery, but there is always the possibility that it may collide with them.

[H. L. Mencken: *The Bend in the Tube*]

BALLOT

6 Among free men there can be no successful appeal from the ballot to the bullet. [Abraham Lincoln: Letter to James C. Conkling, August 26, 1863]
Ballot and bullet are etymologically the same word.
And, of course, if the bullet is successful, the free men are no longer free.

BALM

7 Is there no balm in Gilead? [Jeremiah 8:22]

BANBURY

8 Ride a cock-horse to Banbury Cross,
To see a fine lady upon a white horse;
Rings on her fingers and bells on her toes,
And she shall have music wherever she goes.

[Nursery rhyme]
Older version had the lady an old woman: "The strangest old woman that ever you saw." The big cross at Banbury was destroyed in 1601. The "fine lady" is believed by some to have been Queen Elizabeth.

BANISHMENT

9 Eating the bitter bread of banishment.

[Shakespeare: *Richard II* III.i.]

BANKRUPT

10 Bankrupt of life, yet prodigal of ease.
[Dryden: *Absalom and Achitophel* I.168]

BANNER

11 Th' imperial ensign, which, full high advanc'd,
Shone like a meteor, streaming to the wind.

[John Milton: *Paradise Lost* I.536]

BARD(S)

12 A bard here dwelt, more fat than bard beseems,
Who, void of envy, guile, and lust of gain,
On virtue still, and nature's pleasing themes,
Pour'd forth his unpremeditated strain.

[James Thomson (1700-1748): *The Castle of Indolence* I.68]

Shelley's skylark,

> *That from heaven, or near it,*
> *Pourest thy full heart*
> *In profuse strains of unpremeditated art*

unquestionably echoes this passage.

13 Bards of Passion and of Mirth,
Ye have left your souls on earth!
Have ye souls in heaven too?

[Keats: Ode written on the blank page before Beaumont and Fletcher's *Fair Maid of the Inn*]

BARGAIN

14 It is naught, it is naught, saith the buyer: but when he is gone his way, then

he boasteth. [Proverbs 20:14]

1 I'll give thrice so much land
To any well-deserving friend;
But in the way of bargain, mark ye
me,
I'll cavil on the ninth part of a hair.
[Shakespeare: *I Henry IV* III.i.]
cavil = *raise captious and frivolous ob-
jections*

BARGE

2 The barge she sat in, like a burnish'd
throne,
Burn'd on the water; the poop was
beaten gold;
Purple the sails, and so perfumed that
The winds were love-sick with them;
the oars were silver,
Which to the tune of flutes kept
stroke, and made
The water which they beat to follow
faster,
As amorous of their strokes.
[Shakespeare: *Antony and Cleopatra*
II.ii.]

BARK (OF A DOG)

3 His bark is worse than his bite.
[George Herbert: *Jacula Prudentum*]

BARK (SHIP)

4 Though his bark cannot be lost,
Yet it shall be tempest-tost.
[Shakespeare: *Macbeth* I.iii.]

5 It was that fatal and perfidious bark,
Built in th' eclipse, and rigg'd with
curses dark,
That sunk so low that sacred head of
thine.
[John Milton: *Lycidas*]

BARNEY BODKIN

6 Barney Bodkin broke his nose,
Without feet we can't have toes;
Crazy folks are always mad,
Want of money makes us sad.
[Nursery rhyme: earliest known date
1812]

BARONETS

7 All baronets are bad.
[W. S. Gilbert: *Ruddigore* I]

BASHFULNESS

8 A maiden never bold;

Of spirit so still and quiet, that her
motion
Blush'd at herself.
[Shakespeare: *Othello* I.iii.]
motion = *emotion*

9 To get thine ends, lay bashfulness
aside;
Who fears to ask, doth teach to be
deny'd.
[Robert Herrick: *No Bashfulness in Begging*]

10 Though modesty be a virtue, yet
bashfulness is a vice. [Thomas Fuller
(1654-1734): *Gnomologia*]

11 No cause more frequently produces
bashfulness than too high an opinion of
our own importance. [Samuel Johnson:
The Rambler No. 159]

12 I pity bashful men, who feel the pain
Of fancied scorn and undeserv'd dis-
dain,
And bear the marks, upon a blushing
face,
Of needless shame, and self-impos'd
disgrace.
[William Cowper: *Conversation*]

BASSOON

13 The Wedding-Guest here beat his
breast,
For he heard the loud bassoon.
[Coleridge: *The Ancient Mariner* I]

BASTARDS

14 There are no illegitimate children—
only illegitimate parents. [Judge Leon
R. Yankwich: *Zipkin vs. Mozon*, June
1928]

*Judge Yankwich's dictum does honor to
his heart, but it does not express the
attitude of the law in most European
countries through the ages. Filius nul-
lius ("nobody's child") was the legal
designation and the common law proceeded on the principle that "Once a
bastard, always a bastard." A child born
out of wedlock could not be legitima-
tized except by an act of Parliament.
He could not be adopted or legitima-
tized by adoption by his parents or by
his parents' marriage. He could not inherit as heir and could have no heirs
but of his own body. Many American
states now make the child legitimate if*

the parents marry, but not all states do. In most states, but again not all, parents may adopt their illegitimate child. And all of this amounts to a considerable recognition by the law of illegitimacy in children.

BAT(S)

1   Ere the bat hath flown
His cloister'd flight.
[Shakespeare: *Macbeth* III.ii.]
2 His father's sister had bats in the belfry and was put away. [Eden Phillpotts: *Peacock House*]

BATHING
3 Against the rigors of a damp cold
                              heav'n
To fortify their bodies, some frequent
The gelid cistern.
[Dr. John Armstrong: *The Art of Preserving Health* (1744)]
i.e., some people think cold baths are healthful

BATHOS: illustrations of
4 Worms lurk in all: yet, pronest they
                            to worms,
Who from Mundingo sail.
[James Grainger: *The Sugar-Cane* III]
The Sugar-Cane is one of the longest, flattest poems in English. Lewis and Lee, in The Stuffed Owl, select this passage as one of the worst in the language. Tennyson once invented a line of Wordsworth's:
A Mr. Wilkinson, a clergyman.
The "they" in whom the worms lurk, by the way, are slaves.
5 And now, kind friends, what I have
                              wrote,
I hope you will pass o'er,
And not criticise as some have done
Hitherto herebefore.
[Julia A. Moore, "The Sweet Singer of Michigan"]
6 Entrapt inside a submarine,
With death approaching on the scene,
The crew composed their minds to
                              dice,
More for the pleasure than the vice.
[Congressman H. C. Canfield: *Elegy on the Loss of the U.S. Submarine S-4*]

BATHTUB
7 The first American bathtub was installed and dedicated so recently as December 20, 1842. [H. L. Mencken: in the *New York Evening Mail*, December 28, 1917]
The above statement constitutes the most successful hoax ever perpetrated in America. Mencken himself stated that the article enlarging on it was "of spoofing all compact . . . a tissue of heavy absurdities, all of them deliberate and most of them obvious." He issued at least four formal denials, but his history of the bathtub has passed into solemn works of reference, the Congressional Record, *sermons and editorials and is no longer to be stopped merely by the truth. It has taken its place in our national mythology beside Washington's cherry tree and Lincoln's conversion. Mencken has been denounced as a meddler and a liar for daring to expose his own hoax.*

BATTALIONS
8 God is always on the side of the big battalions. [Voltaire: Letter to M. le Riche, Feb. 6, 1770]
Voltaire says, "as they say." He does not pretend that it was an original thought. It had occurred in various letters and statements, in various forms, a good hundred years before Voltaire's time—indeed, thousands of years before, since Tacitus (Histories IV) had observed that the gods are on the side of the stronger.

BATTLE
9 When the hurly-burly's done,
When the battle's lost and won.
[Shakespeare: *Macbeth* I.i.]
10 The battle is lost, but there is time to win another. [Marshal Louis Charles Desaix: at Marengo, June 14, 1800]
At four o'clock in the afternoon it looked as if the French were defeated, but the resistance of Desaix's division saved the day and turned defeat into victory. Desaix himself was killed.
11 But hark!—that heavy sound breaks
                        in once more,
As if the clouds its echo would re-
                              peat;
And nearer, clearer, deadlier than be-
                              fore!
Arm! Arm! it is—it is—the cannon's

opening roar!
[Byron: *Childe Harold* III.xxii.]
1 So all day long the noise of battle
roll'd
Among the mountains by the winter
sea.
[Tennyson: *The Passing of Arthur*]

BAUBLE
2 Take away that bauble. [Oliver
Cromwell: instructions to a soldier as
he was dismissing Parliament, April 20,
1653]
*The "bauble" was the Mace, the pres-
ence of which marks the legality of
Parliament. By having the bauble taken
away, Cromwell removed the last ves-
tige of historical continuity in his government and simply ruled by the sword.*

BAWDY-HOUSE
3 Sir, your wife *under pretence of keeping a bawdy-house,* is a receiver of stolen
goods. [Samuel Johnson: in Boswell's
Life (1780)]
*"It is well known," Boswell writes, "that
there was formerly a rude custom for
those who were sailing upon the Thames,
to accost each other as they passed, in
the most abusive language they could
invent, generally, however, with as much
satirical humour as they were capable
of producing." Addison gives a specimen
of this ribaldry in No. 383 of* The Spectator.
*As Johnson was on the river one day,
"a fellow" called to him something to
the effect, one gathers, that his wife was
a bawd. Johnson answered him as above.
Boswell felt that the sage had been
"eminently successful" in the exchange.*
*This strange custom of offering gratui-
tous insults is preserved at Oxford and
Cambridge, where one who is being
awarded an honorary degree may find
himself attacked with ribaldry by the
undergraduates. Tennyson was very angry when it happened to him. The custom is ancient and may have something
to do with averting the evil eye.*

BEANS
4 Abstain from beans. [A famous
maxim of the philosopher Pythagoras
(6th century B.C.): quoted by Plutarch,
Cicero, Lucian, Erasmus, Swift and hundreds of other writers]
*What is interesting is the variety of
interpretations that, through the ages,
has been placed on this admonition.
Some say it means just what it says and
adduce many hurtful qualities of beans.
Others say it is a parable and means
"Be chaste!" Still others say it means
"Stay out of politics!"*
5 Full o' beans and benevolence! [R. S.
Surtees: *Handley Cross*]

BEAR
6 　　　Thou'ldst shun a bear;
But if thy flight lay toward the raging
sea,
Thou'ldst meet the bear i' the mouth.
[Shakespeare: *King Lear* III.iv.]
7 Exit, pursued by a bear.
[Shakespeare: *The Winter's Tale* III.iii.
A stage direction]
8 So watchful Bruin forms, with plastic
care,
Each growing lump, and brings it to
a bear.
[Alexander Pope: *The Dunciad* I]
*From the time of Plutarch and Pliny,
and probably long before, it was believed that young bears were brought
forth as shapeless lumps and that the
mother licked them into shape. From
this came the idea of licking some young
"cub" into shape, and since the chief
shaping object, formerly, was the rod,
the word "licking" came to mean a beating.*
9 Never sell the bear's skin until you
have killed the bear. [La Fontaine:
Fables, "L'Ours et les Deux Compag-
nons" (1668)]
*The saying occurs in many forms in all
European languages. It is the origin, by
the way, of our use of bear to designate
one who sells short on the Stock Exchange with the expectation of covering
at a lower price. The implications of
this are made clear in a reference to the
fable in Lyly's* Euphues and His England, *almost 100 years before La Fontaine:*
*I solde the skinne before the Beaste
was taken, reconing with-out mine
hoast, and setting down that in my*

*bookes as ready money, which after-
wards I found to be a desperate debt.*

1 No dancing bear was so genteel,
Or half so *dégagé*.
[William Cowper: *On Himself*]
2 The captain was as savage as a bear
with a sore head. [Frederick Marryat:
The King's Own XXVI]

BEARD(S)
3 With many a tempest hadde his berd
been shake.
[Chaucer: Prologue to *The Canterbury
Tales*]
4 Stay, friend, until I put aside my
beard, for that never committed treason.
[Thomas More: on the scaffold, to the
executioner, July 7, 1535]
5 I could not endure a husband with a
beard on his face:
I had rather lie in the woollen.
[Shakespeare: *Much Ado About Nothing*
II.i.]
6 There was an Old Man with a beard,
Who said: "It is just as I feared!
Two Owls and a Hen,
Four Larks and a Wren
Have all built their nests in my
beard."
[Edward Lear: *The Book of Nonsense*]

BEAST
7 Some evil beast hath devoured him.
[Genesis 37:20]
8 A very gentle beast, and of a good
conscience.
[Shakespeare: *A Midsummer Night's
Dream* V.i.]
9 If his chief good and market of his
time
Be but to sleep and feed? a beast, no
more.
[Shakespeare: *Hamlet* IV.iv.]
10 He that will not be merciful to his
beast, is a beast himself. [Thomas Fuller
(1608-1661): *The Holy State* I.9]

BEAT
11 A woman, a dog, and a walnut-tree,
The more you beat 'em the better
they be.
[Thomas Fuller (1654-1734): *Gnomologia* (1732)]
Fuller gives what was, apparently, a 17th-

*century English version of a very old and
very widespread aphorism. It has been
traced back to 1560 and found in several
languages where, however, an ass, rather
than a dog, makes up the trio.*
*Though he may or may not sympa-
thize with the sentiment, a modern can
understand what is intended in regard
to the woman and the dog, but why the
walnut-tree? The universality of the
proverb makes it plain that, for some
reason, a nut tree was beaten as a part
of its proper care. There is a statement
of the fact in Book II of* The Holy War
*by (by chance) the other Thomas Fuller
(1608-1661): "a nut-tree must be manured
by beating, or else would never bear
fruit." "Manured" here, as Archbishop
Trench specifically points out, means
"cultivated."*

BEATITUDES
12 Blessed are the poor in spirit: for
theirs is the kingdom of heaven.
Blessed are they that mourn: for they
shall be comforted.
Blessed are the meek: for they shall
inherit the earth.
Blessed are they which do hunger and
thirst after righteousness: for they
shall be filled.
Blessed are the merciful: for they
shall obtain mercy.
Blessed are the pure in heart: for they
shall see God.
Blessed are the peacemakers: for
they shall be called the children of
God.
[Matthew 5:3-9]

BEAUTY: its follies, ills and dangers
13 Beauty—a deceitful bayte with a
deadly hooke. [John Lyly: *Euphues*]
14 There was never yet fair woman but
she made mouths in a glass. [Shake-
speare: *King Lear* III.ii.]
15 A poor beauty finds more lovers than
husbands. [George Herbert: *Jacula Prudentum*]
16 Beauty and folly are generally companions. [Gracián: *The Art of Worldly
Wisdom*]
*No wonder. For there are few human
things to which so much license and
indulgence and special privilege are*

granted as to beauty.

1 Beauty and folly are old companions. [Benjamin Franklin: *Poor Richard's Almanack* (1734)]

2 What ills from beauty spring. [Samuel Johnson: *The Vanity of Human Wishes*]

3 The fatal gift of beauty. [Byron: *Childe Harold* IV.xlii.]

4 What a strange illusion it is to suppose that beauty is goodness. [Tolstoy: *Kreutzer Sonata* V]

BEAUTY: its power

5 Personal beauty is a greater recommendation than any letter of reference. [Aristotle: quoted by Diogenes Laertius, "Aristotle" V.18]

The sentiment has been echoed or, more likely, conceived afresh every generation since Aristotle. It is one of the facts of life that the able, but unattractive, have to put up with.

6 Who is she that looketh forth as the morning, fair as the moon, clear as the sun, and terrible as an army with banners? [Song of Solomon 6:10]

7 As the Adamant draweth the heavie yron, the Harpe the fleete Dolphin, so beautie allureth the chast minds to love, and the wisest witte to lust. [John Lyly: *Euphues*]

8 All orators are dumb when beauty pleadeth.
[Shakespeare: *The Rape of Lucrece*]

9 She never yet was foolish that was fair.
[Shakespeare: *Othello* II.i.]

10 Yet beauty, though injurious, hath strange power,
After offence returning, to regain
Love once possess'd.
[John Milton: *Samson Agonistes*]

11 Fair maidens wear no purses. [James Kelly: *Scottish Proverbs* (1721)]

That is, their beauty makes it unnecessary; some man is always willing to pay their bill.

12 Loveliness
Needs not the foreign aid of ornament.
But is, when unadorned, adorned the most.
[James Thomson (1700-1748): *The Seasons*, "Autumn"]

13 Beauty in distress is much the most affecting beauty. [Edmund Burke: *The Sublime and the Beautiful*]

14 'Tis the eternal law
That first in beauty should be first in might.
[Keats: *Hyperion* II.ccxxviii.]

15 Beauty is truth, truth beauty—that is all
Ye know on earth, and all ye need to know.
[Keats: *Ode on a Grecian Urn*]

16 Beauty is its own excuse for being. [Emerson: *The Rhodora*]

17 Beauty is the index of a larger fact than wisdom. [O. W. Holmes: *The Professor at the Breakfast-Table* II]

18 Everything beautiful impresses us as sufficient to itself.
[Thoreau: *Autumn* (1892)]

19 BEAUTY. The power by which a woman charms a lover and terrifies a husband. [Ambrose Bierce: *The Devil's Dictionary*]

BEAUTY: but skin deep

20 Beauty is but skin-deep. [Old English Proverb]

21 All the carnall beauty of my wife
Is but skin-deep, but to two senses known.
[Sir Thomas Overbury: *A Wife*]

22 All the beauty of the world, 'tis but skin deep. [Ralph Venning: *Orthodoxe Paradoxes*, "The Triumph of Assurance"]

23 The saying that beauty is but skin deep is a skin-deep saying. [Herbert Spencer: *Personal Beauty*]

BEAUTY: its transitory nature

24 Beauty is but a flower
Which wrinkles will devour;
Brightness falls from the air;
Queens have died young and fair;
Dust hath closed Helen's eye.
[Thomas Nashe: *In Time of Pestilence*]

25 Ah! yet doth beauty, like a dial-hand,
Steal from his figure and no pace perceived.
[Shakespeare: *Sonnets* CIV]

26 Beauty is as summer fruits which are easy to corrupt and cannot last; and, for the most part, it makes a dissolute youth

and an age a little out of countenance.
[Francis Bacon: *Of Beauty*]
out of countenance = *dissatisfied with
itself*

1 Art quickens nature; care will make a
face;
Neglected beauty perisheth apace.
[Robert Herrick: *Neglect*]

2 After-comers cannot guess the beauty
been. [Gerard Manley Hopkins: *Binsey
Poplars Felled (1879)*]

3 Beauty is all very well at first sight;
but who ever looks at it when it has been
in the house three days? [G. B. Shaw:
Man and Superman IV]

BEAUTY: in various women and men

4 To me, fair friend, you never can be
old,
For as you were when first your eye
I ey'd
Such seems your beauty still.
[Shakespeare: *Sonnets* CIV]

5 Hear this thou age unbred:
Ere you were born was beauty's sum-
mer dead.
[Shakespeare: *Sonnets* CIV]

6 When in the chronicle of wasted
time
I see descriptions of the fairest
wights,
And beauty making beautiful old
rhyme
In praise of ladies dead and lovely
knights,
Then, in the blazon of sweet beauty's
best,
Of hand, of foot, of lip, of eye, of
brow,
I see their antique pen would have
expressed
Even such a beauty as you master
now.
[Shakespeare: *Sonnets* CVI]

7 Oh, she doth teach the torches to
burn bright;
It seems she hangs upon the cheek
of night
Like a rich jewel in an Ethiop's ear.
[Shakespeare: *Romeo and Juliet* I.v.]

8 Beauty too rich for use, for earth too
dear.
[Shakespeare: *Romeo and Juliet* I.v.]

9 Death, that hath suck'd the honey
of thy breath,

Hath had no power yet upon thy
beauty;
Thou art not conquer'd; beauty's ensign yet
Is crimson in thy lips and in thy
cheeks,
And death's pale flag is not advanced
there.
[Shakespeare: *Romeo and Juliet* V.iii.]

10 Towers and battlements it sees
Bosom'd high in tufted trees,
Where perhaps some beauty lies,
The cynosure of neighboring eyes.
[John Milton: *L'Allegro*]

11 Grace was in all her steps, heav'n in
her eye,
In every gesture dignity and love.
[John Milton: *Paradise Lost* VIII 488]

12 Sacharissa's beauty's wine,
Which to madness doth incline:
Such a liquor as no brain
That is mortal can sustain.
[Edmund Waller: *Amoret*]

13 On Richmond Hill there lives a lass,
More bright than May-day morn,
Whose charms all other maids sur-
pass—
A rose without a thorn.
[James Upton: *The Lass of Richmond
Hill*]

14 Her gentle limbs did she undress,
And lay down in her loveliness.
[Coleridge: *Christabel* I]

15 There be none of Beauty's daughters
With magic like thee;
And like music on the waters
Is thy sweet voice to me.
[Byron: *Stanzas for Music*]

16 She walks in Beauty, like the night
Of cloudless climes and starry skies;
And all that's best of dark and bright
Meet in her aspect and her eyes:
Thus mellowed to that tender light
Which Heaven to gaudy day denies.
[Byron: *She Walks in Beauty*]
*The lady who inspired these famous
lines was Byron's second cousin, Mrs.
John Wilmot.*
*It comes as a slight shock, however,
to learn how literal the glorious first line
is—for when he first saw her, at Lady
Sitwell's party (1814), she was dressed
"in mourning with numerous spangles
in her dress."*

17 A pard-like spirit, beautiful and swift.

[Shelley: *Adonais* XXXII]

1 On desperate seas long wont to roam,
Thy hyacinth hair, thy classic face,
Thy Naiad airs have brought me
home
To the glory that was Greece
And the grandeur that was Rome.
[Edgar Allan Poe: *To Helen*]

2 Helen, thy beauty is to me
Like those Nicaean barks of yore,
That gently, o'er a perfumed sea,
The weary, wayworn wanderer bore
To his own native shore.
[Edgar Allan Poe: *To Helen*]

3 A daughter of the gods, divinely tall,
And most divinely fair.
[Tennyson: *A Dream of Fair Women*]
*The English have never seemed to like
them petite. Chaucer rejoices that his
Prioress "was nat undergrowe." But one
detects a certain longing under W. S.
Gilbert's chivalry:*
*A wonderful joy our eyes to bless,
In her magnificent comeliness,
Is an English girl of eleven stone two,
And five foot ten in her dancing shoe!*
Utopia, Limited *II*

BEAUTY: miscellaneous

4 O beloved Pan, and all ye other gods
of this place, grant me to become beautiful in the inner man. [Socrates: in
Plato's *Phaedrus*]

5 There is no woman so deformed, who
hearing herself called beautiful, believeth it not. [Stefano Guazzo: *Civile
Conversation* I.lxxxvi.]

6 In bed, beauty before goodness.
[Montaigne: *Essays* I.xxvii.]

7 He hath a daily beauty in his life
That makes me ugly.
[Shakespeare: *Othello* V.i.]

8 There is no excellent beauty that
hath not some strangeness in the proportion. [Francis Bacon: *Of Beauty*]

9 There's no use being young without
being beautiful, and no use being beautiful without being young. [La Rochefoucauld: *Maxims*]

10 All heiresses are beautiful. [Dryden:
King Arthur I.i.]

11 He injures a fair Lady, that beholds
her not. [Thomas Fuller (1654-1734):
Gnomologia]

12 Beauty, like supreme dominion,

Is but supported by opinion.
[Benjamin Franklin: *Poor Richard's Almanack* (1741)]

13 A thing of beauty is a joy for ever;
Its loveliness increases; it will never
Pass into nothingness.
[Keats: *Endymion* I]

14 If you get simple beauty and nought
else,
You get about the best thing God
invents.
[Robert Browning: *Fra Lippo Lippi*]

15 It is better to be beautiful than to be
good, but it is better to be good than
to be ugly. [Oscar Wilde: *The Picture
of Dorian Gray* XVII]

16 To be born a woman is to know—
Although they do not talk of it at
school—
That we must labor to be beautiful.
[William Butler Yeats: *Adam's Curse*]

17 Clarence had the Fatal Gift of Beauty
and he was Wise to the Fact. He hated
to turn out the light at Night and have
all his Good Looks go to waste for Hours
at a stretch. [George Ade: *True Bills*]

18 Euclid alone has looked on Beauty
bare.
[Edna St. Vincent Millay: *The HarpWeaver*, IV. Sonnet xxii.]

BED

19 The difference is wide that the sheets
will not decide. [John Ray: *English
Proverbs*]

20 Item, I give unto my wife my second
best bed. [Specific bequest in Shakespeare's will]

21 Early to bed and early to rise, makes
a man healthy, wealthy and wise. [John
Clarke: *Paroemiologia* (1639)]
*The proverb, in slightly different forms,
is very old. Franklin copied Clarke's
wording in* Poor Richard's Almanack
*(1735) and repeated it in 1758, and most
Americans simply ascribe the saying to
Franklin.*
*Such enormous popularity as this
aphorism has enjoyed is bound to produce parodies and anti-comments. Of
these one of the best-known is George
Ade's "Early to bed and early to rise
and you won't meet many prominent
people." One of the shrewdest is James
Howell's (1659): "He that hath the name.*

to be an early riser may sleep till noon."
1 And so to bed. [Samuel Pepys: *Diary*,
20 April 1660 and *passim*]
2 In bed we laugh, in bed we cry;
And born in bed, in bed we die;
The near approach a bed may show
Of human bliss to human woe.
[Isaac de Benserade: *À son Lit* (trans.
Samuel Johnson)]
3 Loth to bed and loth out of it. [James
Kelly: *Scottish Proverbs*]
4 In winter I get up at night
And dress by yellow candle-light.
In summer, quite the other way,
I have to go to bed by day.
[R. L. Stevenson: *A Child's Garden of
Verses*, "Bed in Summer"]
5 Oh, it's nice to get up in the mornin',
But it's nicer to lie in bed.
[Sir Harry Lauder: *Song*]
6 I should of stood in bed. [Joe Jacobs:
in October 1935]

> *Mr. Jacobs had risen from a sickbed to
> attend the World Series in Detroit
> where, to his chagrin, the team he bet
> on was defeated.*

BEDFELLOWS

7 Misery acquaints a man with strange
bedfellows.
[Shakespeare: *The Tempest* II.ii.]
See POLITICS

BEE(S)

8 What is not good for the swarm is
not good for the bee. [Marcus Aurelius:
Meditations VI]
9 Lyk a bisy bee, with-outen gyle.
[Chaucer: *The Second Nun's Tale*]
10   For so work the honey-bees,
Creatures that by a rule in nature
teach
The act of order to a peopled king-
dom.
They have a king and officers of sorts;
Where some, like magistrates, correct
at home,
Others, like merchants, venture trade
abroad,
Others, like soldiers, armèd in their
stings,
Make boot upon the summer's velvet
buds;
Which pillage they with merry march
bring home
To the tent-royal of their emperor:

Who, busied in his majesty, surveys
The singing masons building roofs of
gold,
The civil citizens kneading up the
honey,
The poor mechanic porters crowding
in
Their heavy burdens at his narrow
gate,
The sad-eyed justice, with his surly
hum,
Delivering o'er to executors pale
The lazy yawning drone.
[Shakespeare: *Henry V* I.ii.]
*This famous passage is an interesting
illustration of the way men read their
customs into nature and then find confirmation for them in "natural" order.
For ages it was simply assumed that the
principal figure in a hive* must *be a
king—and the hive was then instanced
as proof of the "natural" order of a
monarchy.*

11 Where the bee sucks, there suck I:
In a cowslip's bell I lie;
There I couch when owls do cry.
On the bat's back I do fly
After summer merrily:
Merrily, merrily shall I live now
Under the blossom that hangs on the
bough.
[Shakespeare: *The Tempest* V.i.]
12 How doth the little busy bee
Improve each shining hour,
And gather honey all the day
From every opening flower.
[Isaac Watts: *Divine Songs for Children*]
*Parodied by Lewis Carroll: "How doth
the little crocodile/ Improve his shining
tail,/ And pour the waters of the Nile/
On every golden scale." Watt's little
poems were excellent—simple, innocent
and sincere. But they were forced on
children by parents and teachers until
they became loathsome to the young.
And when these young grew up they
had their revenge. But Time has had
the final—and cruelest—revenge, oblit-
erating parodee and parodist alike.*

13 A bee in his bonnet. [David Moir:
The Life of Mansie Waugh XXIV
(1824)]
*The idea, as a humorous term for mad-
ness, was much older. Herrick alludes to
it in* The Mad Maids Song *(1648), and*

Sir Walter Scott alludes to it; and the 19th century, after Scott and Moir, seemed very fond of the expression.

1 His labor is a chant,
His idleness a tune;
Oh, for a bee's experience
Of clovers and of noon!
[Emily Dickinson: *The Bee*]

2 For among Bees and Ants are social
systems found
so complex and well-order'd as to invite offhand
a pleasant fable enough: that once
upon a time,
or ever a man were born to rob their
honeypots,
bees were fully endow'd with Reason
and only lost it
by ordering so their life as to dispense
with it;
whereby it pined away and perish'd
of disuse.
[Robert Bridges: *The Testament of Beauty* II]

3 And yet, hang it all, who by rights should be the teacher and who the learners? For those peevish, over-toiled utilitarian insects, was there no lesson to be derived from the spectacle of Me? Gazing out at me with composite eyes from their joyless factories, might they not learn at last—could I not finally teach them—a wiser and more generous-hearted way to improve the shining hours? [Logan Pearsall Smith: *Trivia*, "The Busy Bees"]

BEEF
4 I am a great eater of beef, and I believe that does harm to my wit. [Shakespeare: *Twelfth Night* I.iii.]

BEETLE
5 The poor beetle that we tread upon
In corporal sufferance finds a pang as
great
As when a giant dies.
[Shakespeare: *Measure for Measure* III.i.]
There is a firm conviction among many fishermen that a hooked fish is not suffering any real discomfort.

BEGGAR(S)
6 Beggars should be no choosers. [John Heywood: *Proverbs*]

Beggars must be no choosers.
Beaumont and Fletcher:
Scornful Lady
V.iii.

7 Beggars mounted run their horse to
death.
[Shakespeare: *III Henry VI* I.iv.]

8 Set a beggar on horseback, and he will gallop. [William Camden: *Remains* (1605)]
Camden is using a proverbial saying. There are many sayings, before and after Camden, that state, in one way or another, that if a beggar is set on horseback he will make the most of it, abuse the privilege, damage the horse, etc.

9 Beg from beggars and you'll never be rich. [James Kelly: *Scottish Proverbs*]

10 BEGGAR. One who has relied on the assistance of his friends. [Ambrose Bierce: *The Devil's Dictionary*]

BEGGING
11 I cannot dig; to beg I am ashamed. [Luke 16:3]

12 Three things another's modest wishes
bound,
My friendship, and a Prologue, and
ten pound.
[Alexander Pope: *Epistle to Dr. Arbuthnot*]

13 The roads are very dirty,
My boots are very thin,
I have a little pocket
To put a penny in.
If you haven't got a penny
A ha'penny will do.
If you haven't got a ha'penny,
God bless you!
[English children's Christmas begging rhyme.]

BEGINNING(S)
14 Into the midst of things. (*In medias res*) [Horace: *Ars poetica* I.cxlviii.]
Usually used of a narrative which commences in the midst of the action and, by various techniques, reveals, as it goes along, the antecedent action.

15 Well begun is half done. [Horace: *Epistles* I.ii.]
From Horace on, the proverb appears in many forms in almost every European language.

1 Every beginning is hard. [German proverb]
2 I am Alpha and Omega, the beginning and the end, the first and the last. [Revelation 21:6]
3 Things bad begun make strong themselves by ill. [Shakespeare: *Macbeth* III.ii.]
4 Ah, but in such matters it is only the first step that is difficult. [Madame du Deffand: to Cardinal de Polignac, when the Cardinal told her that St. Denis, after being decapitated, had picked up his head and carried it two leagues.]
Voltaire relates the incident in a note to the first canto of La Pucelle. *See also her letters to D'Alembert, July 7, 1763 and to Horace Walpole, June 6, 1767.*
5   You're searching, Joe,
For things that don't exist; I mean
    beginnings.
Ends and beginnings—there are no
    such things.
There are only middles.
[Robert Frost: *In the Home Stretch*]

BEHAVIOR
6 For behaviour, men learn it, as they take diseases, one of another. [Francis Bacon: *The Advancement of Learning* II]
7 Put himself upon his good behaviour. [Byron: *Don Juan* V.xlvii.]

BEING
8 For in him we live, and move, and have our being. [Acts 17:28]
9 The centre that I cannot find
Is known to my Unconscious Mind;
I have no reason to despair
Because I am already there.
[W. H. Auden: *The Labyrinth*]

BELIEF
10 One does not have to believe everything one hears. [Cicero: *De Divinatione* II.xiii.]
11 Men quite gladly believe what they want to believe. [Caesar: *De Bello Gallico* III.xviii.]
12 Where belief is painful, we are slow to believe. [Ovid: *Heroides* II.ix.]
13 I believe it because it is impossible. (*Credo, quia impossibile.*) [Commonly ascribed to Tertullian]
14 Nothing is so firmly believed as that which we least know. [Montaigne: *Essays* I.xxxi.]
15 Lord, I believe; help thou mine unbelief. [Mark 9:24]
16 We soone beleeve the thing we would have so. [Ariosto: *Orlando Furioso* I. lvi. (trans. Sir John Harington)]
17 Man prefers to believe what he prefers to be true. [Francis Bacon: *Aphorisms*]
18 He does not believe, that does not live according to his belief. [Thomas Fuller (1654-1734): *Gnomologia*]
19 Every man who attacks my belief diminishes in some degree my confidence in it, and therefore makes me uneasy, and I am angry with him who makes me uneasy. [Samuel Johnson: in Boswell's *Life,* April 3, 1776]
20 Each man's belief is right in his own eyes. [William Cowper: *Hope*]
21 I am always at a loss to know how much to believe of my own stories. [Washington Irving: Preface to *Tales of a Traveller*]
22 Believing where we cannot prove. [Tennyson: Prologue to *In Memoriam*]
23 It is not disbelief that is dangerous to our society; it is belief. [G. B. Shaw: Preface to *Androcles and the Lion*]
24 We are incredibly heedless in the formation of our beliefs, but find ourselves filled with an illicit passion for them when anyone proposes to rob us of their companionship. [James Harvey Robinson: *The Mind in the Making*]
25 It is easier to believe than to doubt. [E. D. Martin: *The Meaning of a Liberal Education* V]

BELL(S)
26   The bell invites me.
Hear it not, Duncan; for it is a knell
That summons thee to heaven or to
    hell.
[Shakespeare: *Macbeth* II.i.]
27 Like sweet bells jangled, out of tune
    and harsh.
[Shakespeare: *Hamlet* III.i.]
28 Any man's death diminishes me, because I am involved in Mankinde; And therefore never send to know for whom the bell tolls; It tolls for thee. [John

Donne: *Devotions upon Emergent Occasions* XVII]

> *It was from this passage, of course, that Hemingway took the title for his novel on the Spanish Civil War,* For Whom the Bell Tolls *(1940).*

1 Oranges and lemons,
 Say the bells of St. Clement's.

 You owe me five farthings,
 Say the bells of St. Martin's.

 When will you pay me?
 Say the bells of Old Bailey.

 When I get rich,
 Say the bells of Shoreditch.

 When will that be?
 Say the bells of Stepney.

 I don't know,
 Says the big bell of Bow.

 Here comes a candle to light you to
  bed,
 Here comes a chopper to chop off
  your head.

[Nursery rhyme: earliest known printed version, 1744]

> *The assigning of words to the rhythm of certain bells is widespread. These are all bells of London churches. The sound of Bow Bell marked the limit of cockneydom. It is also believed to be the bell that told Whittington to "turn again, Lord Mayor of London."*

2 How soft the music of those village
  bells
 Falling at intervals upon the ear
 In cadence sweet!

[William Cowper: *The Task* VI]

3 Bells, the poor man's only music.

[Coleridge: *Frost at Midnight*]

4 The Cardinal rose with a dignified
  look,
 He called for his candle, his bell, and
  his book!
 In holy anger and pious grief,
 He solemnly cursed that rascally
  thief!

[R. H. Barham: *The Jackdaw of Rheims*]

> *The thief turns out to be a jackdaw and, in consequence of the curse, his feathers fall out. Barham paraphrases the famous curse of Bishop Ernulph, preserved in Rochester Cathedral—the curse that plays so large a part in Laurence Sterne's* Tristram Shandy.
>
> *Bell, book and candle marked the*

Greater Excommunication, introduced into the Roman Catholic Church in the 8th century. After the reading of the curse, a bell was rung, a book closed and a candle extinguished. This marked the formal separation of the cursed one "from all good deeds and prayers of Holy Church . . . within or without, sleeping or waking, going and sitting, lying above earth and under earth . . . in wood, in water, in field, in town . . . that the pains of Hell be their meed with Judas that betrayed our Lord Jesus Christ! and the life of them be put out of the book of life. . . ." (*A curse, from* Instructions for Parish Priests *(1420), by John Myrc, Canon Regular of Lilleshall.*)

> *The fear of such a curse was a strong deterrent to evil doers, but, at the same time, marked the determination of the bold who were willing to flout it: "Bell, book and candle shall not drive me back/ When gold and silver becks me to come on" (Shakespeare:* King John *III.iii.)*

5 The bells, the iron dogs of the air,
 Lift up their joyful barking.

[Heine: *Kobes* I]

6 His death, which happen'd in his
  berth,
  At forty-odd befell:
 They went and told the sexton, and
 The sexton toll'd the bell.

[Thomas Hood: *Faithless Sally Brown*]

7 Keeping time, time, time,
 In a sort of Runic rhyme,
 To the tintinnabulation that so mu-
  sically wells
 From the bells . . .

[Edgar Allan Poe: *The Bells*]

8 Hear the mellow wedding bells,
  golden bells!
 What a world of happiness their
  harmony foretells.

[Edgar Allan Poe: *The Bells*]

9 Ring out, wild bells, to the wild sky.

[Tennyson: *In Memoriam* CVI]

10 In the middle of the night it rang a little silver bell in my ear. [George Meredith: *The Egoist* XXV]

11 He was a rationalist, but he had to confess that he liked the ringing of church bells. [Anton Chekhov: *Notebooks*]

BELLE

1 Where none admire, 'tis useless to
excel;
Where none are beaux, 'tis vain to
be a belle.
[George Lyttelton: *Soliloquy on a Beauty
in the Country*]

BELLY

2 There is no part of man
more like a dog than brazen Belly,
crying to be remembered.
[Homer: *Odyssey* VII (trans. Robert Fitz-
Gerald)]
3 For their cursed belly's sake men endure evil woes.
[Homer: *Odyssey* XV]
*Elsewhere Homer speaks of the "shame-
less" belly and the "insatiate" belly.*
4 The belly will not listen to advice.
[Seneca: *Ad Lucilium* XXI]
*There are many proverbs that comment
on the fact that hunger is unreasonable.
The commonest English form is that
"The belly has no ears"—Izaak Walton:
The Compleat Angler (1653).*
5 It once happened that all the other
members of a man mutinied against the
stomach, which they accused as the only
idle, uncontributing part in the whole
body, while the rest were put to hardships and the expense of much labor to
supply and minister to its appetites. The
stomach, however, merely ridiculed the
silliness of the members, who appeared
not to be aware that the stomach certainly does receive the general nourishment, but only to return it again, and
redistribute it amongst the rest. [Me-
nenius Agrippa: in Plutarch's *Life of
Coriolanus*]
Plutarch calls it "the celebrated fable."
6 Whose God is their belly. [Philip-
pians 3:19]
7 A mannerly belly is a great part of a
man's liberty. [Montaigne: *Essays* III.
xiii.]
*Montaigne is quoting Seneca. That man
only is free whose appetites are under
his control. If the belly domineers, then
the man has no freedom at all; he is
his belly's slave and, as Odysseus said,
"The belly is a shameless thing."*
8 The belly carries the legs, and not the
legs the belly. [Cervantes: *Don Quixote*

II.34]
9 My belly thinks my throat's cut.
*This fine old expression of hunger dates
back to at least the 16th century. It was
a proverb then.*
10 When the lank hungry belly barks for
food. [Ben Jonson: *Every Man Out of
His Humour* I.i.]
11 Such as for their bellies' sake
Creep and intrude, and climb into
the fold.
[John Milton: *Lycidas*]
12 He who does not mind his belly will
hardly mind anything else. [Samuel
Johnson: in Boswell's *Life*, August 5,
1763]
*A cheerful and good heart will have a
care of his meat and drink.*
Ecclesiasticus 30:25
*Wherever the dinner is ill got there is
poverty, or there is avarice, or there is
stupidity; in short, the family is somehow grossly wrong: for a man seldom
thinks with more earnestness of any
thing than he does of his dinner.*
Samuel Johnson: in Mrs. Piozzi's Anecdotes
13 An army marches on its belly. [In
various forms, attr. Napoleon, Frederick
the Great, and other commanders]
14 He had a broad face and a little
round belly,
That shook, when he laughed, like a
bowlful of jelly.
[Clement Clarke Moore: *A Visit from
St. Nicholas*]

BENEDICK

15 Here you may see Benedick the married man.
[Shakespeare: *Much Ado About Nothing*
I.i.]
*Newly married men are frequently
called* benedicts, *because of this line.
Purists insist it must be* benedick—
*and so, in reference to Shakespeare's
character, it must be—but the variant
spelling is no great crime.*

BENEDICTION

16 The benediction of these covering
heavens
Fall on their heads like dew!
[Shakespeare: *Cymbeline* V.v.]
17 God be with you, till we meet again,
By his counsel's guide, uphold you,

With his sheep securely fold you;
God be with you, till we meet again.
[Jeremiah Eames Rankin: *Mizpah*]
See MIZPAH

BENEFITS
1 They are either rogues or fools who think benefits are merely gifts. [Publilius Syrus: *Maxims*]
2 Let him who has conferred the benefit conceal it; let him who has accepted it disclose it. [Seneca: *De Beneficiis* II]
3 He who believes that new benefits make great men forget old injuries deceives himself. [Machiavelli: *The Prince* VII]
4 The obligation of a benefit has wholly reference to the will of the giver. [Montaigne: *Essays* III.v.]
5 There is a hook in every benefit, that sticks in his jaws that takes that benefit, and draws him whither the benefactor will. [Donne: *Sermons*]

BENEFITS: arouse affection in benefactor
6 Benefactors seem to love those whom they benefit more than those who receive benefits love their benefactors. [Aristotle: *Nicomachean Ethics* IX:vii.]
7 Human nature causes men to feel as much obligation when they confer benefits as when they receive them. [Machiavelli: *The Prince* X]
8 We naturally endear to ourselves those to whom we impart any kind of pleasure, because we imagine their affection and esteem secured to us by the benefits which they receive. [Samuel Johnson: *The Rambler* No. 148]

BENEFITS: in excess excite animosity
9 Benefits are only so far acceptable as they seem capable of being requited; beyond that point, they excite hatred instead of gratitude. [Tacitus: *Annals* IV. xviii.]
10 Benefits are so long welcome as we think they may be requited, but when they much exceed all power of recompense, hate is returned for thanks and good will. [Montaigne: *Essays* III.viii.]
Montaigne is quoting from Tacitus, Annals, above.
11 Benefits which cannot be repaid and obligations which cannot be discharged are not commonly found to increase affection. [Samuel Johnson: *The Rambler* No. 64]
12 Benefits too great
To be repaid, sit heavy on the soul,
As unrequited wrongs.
[Thomas Gray: *Agrippina* I.i.]

BENT
13 John Gilpin kissed his loving wife;
O'er joyed was he to find,
That though on pleasure she was bent,
She had a frugal mind.
[William Cowper: *John Gilpin*]
14 Still bent to make some port he knows not where,
Still standing for some false impossible shore.
[Matthew Arnold: *A Summer Night*]

BERMUDA
15 Where the remote Bermudas ride,
In th' ocean's bosom unespied.
[Andrew Marvell: *Bermudas*]

BERRY
16 His palfrey was as broun as is a berye.
[Chaucer: Prologue to *The Canterbury Tales*]
No one knows a brown berry. Some have suggested a coffee berry, but coffee in any form was unknown to Chaucer. It's one of the minor mysteries of the language, and not the least of its mysteries is that it goes vigorously on; we hear it every day. One more illustration of the power of alliteration.

BEST
17 He wishes not to seem, but to be, the best. [Aeschylus: *Seven Against Thebes*]
18 I woot wel clerkes wol seyn as hem leste
By arguments, that al is for the beste.
[Chaucer: *The Franklin's Tale*]
clerkes = clerics, a general term with Chaucer, and his contemporaries, for learned men
The "clerkes" little wotted that in the lair of things to come Voltaire was lying in wait for them.
19 The best oil is on the top; the best wine in the middle; and the best honey is on the bottom. [Thomas Fuller (1608-

1661): *Worthies of England*, "Hants" VI.iii.]

> *Fuller gives the statement as "an old and true rule."*

1 All is best, though we oft doubt
What the unsearchable dispose
Of Highest Wisdom brings about,
And ever best found in the close.
[John Milton: *Samson Agonistes*]
2 The best is the enemy of the good.
[Voltaire: *Philosophical Dictionary*, "Dramatic Art"]
3 All is for the best in the best of possible worlds. [Voltaire: *Candide*, Ch. 30]
4 My business is not to remake myself,
But make the absolute best of what God made.
[Robert Browning: *Bishop Blougram's Apology*]

BET

5 If there were two birds sitting on a fence, he would bet you which one would fly first. [Mark Twain: *The Celebrated Jumping Frog of Calaveras County*]

BETHLEHEM

6 O little town of Bethlehem,
How still we see thee lie;
Above thy deep and dreamless sleep
The silent stars go by.
[Phillips Brooks: *O Little Town of Bethlehem*]

BETRAYAL

7 And oftentimes, to win us to our harm,
The instruments of darkness tell us truths,
Win us with honest trifles, to betray 's
In deepest consequence.
[Shakespeare: *Macbeth* I.iii.]
8 Just for a handful of silver he left us,
Just for a riband to stick in his coat.
[Robert Browning: *The Lost Leader*]
9 Frankie and Johnny were lovers, my God, how they could love,
Swore to be true to each other, true as the stars above;
He was her man, but he done her wrong.
[Anon.: *Frankie and Johnny*]

BETTER

10 I could have better spared a better man.
[Shakespeare: *I Henry IV* V.iv.]
11 No better than she should be. [Cervantes: *Don Quixote* I.iii.6.]
12 Every day, in every way, I'm getting better and better. [Émile Coué: formula for self-cure through faith]

BETTER 'OLE

13 Well, if you knows of a better 'ole, go to it. [Bruce Bairnsfather: caption of cartoon, 1915]

BETTY MARTIN

14 All my eye and Betty Martin. [R. D. Blackmore: *Perlycross* XXI (1894)]

> *Miss Martin had been in the language, together with the speaker's eye, as an expression of skepticism for more than a hundred years before Blackmore, though his wording is the one now most used.*
>
> *No one knows how the phrase originated or exactly what it means (other than "Nonsense!"). "All my eye" was combined with several other words to express scornful doubt, and Betty Martin may be a corruption of some forgotten phrase. One ingenious scholar has suggested Oh, mihi, beate Martine, but there is nothing to support this and it is equally meaningless.*

BEWARE

15 And all should cry, Beware! Beware!
His flashing eyes, his floating hair!
Weave a circle round him thrice,
And close your eyes with holy dread,
For he on honey-dew hath fed,
And drunk the milk of Paradise.
[Coleridge: *Kubla Khan*]

> *The reason for the "holy dread" is that "he" is one of the fanatical followers of Hassan-ben-Sabah, the Old Man of the Mountain, who, having been deluded by hashish into thinking he has tasted the delights of Paradise, is reckless of his life in his eager desire to return there.*

BIBLE

16 His studie was but litel on the Bible.
[Chaucer: Prologue to *The Canterbury Tales*]

> *The reference is to the Physician.*

1 Prosperity is the blessing of the Old Testament; adversity is the blessing of the New. [Francis Bacon: *Of Adversity*]
2 Whenever we read the obscene stories, the voluptuous debaucheries, the cruel and tortuous executions, the unrelenting vindictiveness, with which more than half the Bible is filled, it would be more consistent that we called it the word of a demon than the word of God. It is a history of wickedness that has served to corrupt and brutalize mankind. [Thomas Paine: *The Age of Reason* I]
3 Both read the Bible day and night,
But thou read'st black where I read white.
[William Blake: *The Everlasting Gospel*]
4 Within that awful volume lies
The mystery of mysteries! . . .
And better had they ne'er been born,
Who read to doubt, or read to scorn.
[Sir Walter Scott: *The Monastery* I.xii.]
5 The English Bible, a book which, if everything else in our language should perish, would alone suffice to show the whole extent of its beauty and power. . . . [Macaulay: *On John Dryden*]

BICYCLE
6 Daisy, Daisy, give me your answer, do!
I'm half crazy, all for the love of you!
It won't be a stylish marriage,
I can't afford a carriage,
But you'll look sweet upon the seat
Of a bicycle built for two!
[Harry Dacre: *Daisy Bell*]

BIGAMY
7 How happy I could be with either,
Were t'other dear charmer away!
[John Gay: *The Beggar's Opera* I]

BIG BROTHER
8 Big Brother is watching you. [George Orwell: *1984* I]

BIGOT
9 Ne se, bigot! ["Not I, by God!"]
The origin of the word bigot (*as told by Wace, a 12th-century chronicler*) *is that when Rollo, a Norman Baron, was required to kiss the foot of King Charles the Simple, as an act of homage, he roared "Ne se, bi got!" If that is true, the word, while keeping all its fervor of disdain, has since reversed its practical application, bigots today being fond of these acts of ritual homage.*
10 A bigot is a person who, under an atheist king, would be an atheist. [La Bruyère: *Les Caractères*]
11 I am a Bible-bigot. [John Wesley: *Journal*, June 2, 1766]
12 How it infuriates a bigot, when he is forced to drag out his dark convictions! [Logan Pearsall Smith: *Afterthoughts*]

BIOGRAPHY
13 There has rarely passed a life of which a judicious and faithful narrative would not be useful. [Samuel Johnson: *The Rambler* No. 60]
14 No species of writing seems more worthy of cultivation than biography, none can be more delightful or more useful, none can more certainly enchain the heart by irresistible interest, or more widely diffuse instruction to every diversity of condition. [Samuel Johnson: *The Rambler* No. 60]
15 The business of the biographer is often to pass slightly over those performances and incidents which produce vulgar greatness, to lead the thoughts into domestic privacies and display the minute details of daily life. [Samuel Johnson: *The Rambler* No. 60]
16 Biography is, of the various kinds of narrative writing, that which is most eagerly read and most easily applied to the purposes of life. [Samuel Johnson: *The Idler* No. 84]
17 A well-written Life is almost as rare as a well-spent one. [Thomas Carlyle: *Critical Essays*, "Richter"]
18 There is properly no history; only biography. [Emerson: *History*]
19 Geography is about maps,
But biography is about chaps.
[E. C. Bentley: *Biography for Beginners*]

BIRCHES
20 I'd like to go by climbing a birch tree,
And climb black branches up a snow-

white trunk
Toward heaven, till the tree could
bear no more,
But dipped its top and set me down
again.
That would be good both going and
coming back.
One could do worse than be a swinger
of birches.
[Robert Frost: *Birches*]

BIRD(S)

1 A rare bird on earth, like a black
swan. [Juvenal: *Satires* VI]
2 The time of the singing of birds is
come, and the voice of the turtle is heard
in our land. [*The Song of Solomon* 2:12]
turtle = *the turtle dove*
3 He's in great want of a bird that will
give a groat for an owl. [John Ray: *English Proverbs*]
4 'Tis true; the raven doth not hatch
a lark.
[Shakespeare: *Titus Andronicus* II.iii.]
5 The early bird catches the worm.
[William Camden: *Remains*]
The early worm, of course, gets caught.
6 Every crow thinks her own bird fairest. [Robert Burton: *The Anatomy of
Melancholy* III.1.2.3]
bird = *what we would call a young bird,
a chick or a nestling. The old word for
a mature bird was "fowl."*
7 Call for the robin redbreast and the
wren,
Since o'er shady groves they hover,
And with leaves and flowers do cover
The friendless bodies of unburied
men.
[John Webster: *The White Devil* V.iv.]
8 I heard a little bird say so. [Jonathan
Swift: Letter to Stella, May 23, 1711]
*To say of some piece of information
that "a little bird told me" is very old.
It may derive from a passage in the
Bible:*
Curse not the king, no not in thy
thought; and curse not the rich in thy
bedchamber: for a bird of the air shall
carry the voice, and that which hath
wings shall tell the matter.
Ecclesiastes 10:20
9 I shall not ask Jean Jacques Rousseau,
If birds confabulate or no.
[William Cowper: *Pairing Time Antici-*

pated]
10 The feather'd race with pinions skim
the air—
Not so the mackerel, and still less the
bear!
[John Hookham Frere: *Progress of Man*]
11 A bird appears a thoughtless
thing. . . .
No doubt he has his little cares,
And very hard he often fares,
The which so patiently he bears.
[Charles Lamb: *Crumbs to the Birds*]
12 A bird knows nothing of gladness,
Is only a song machine.
[George MacDonald: *A Book of Dreams*]
13 These are brand new birds of twelve-
months' growing,
Which a year ago, or less than twain,
No finches were, nor nightingales,
Nor thrushes,
But only particles of grain,
And earth, and air, and rain.
[Thomas Hardy: *Proud Songsters*]

**BIRDS: fly together and agree in
their nests**

14 Byrds of a fether, best flye together.
[George Whetstone: *Promos and Cassandra* (1578)]
15 Birds of a feather will gather together. [Robert Burton: *Anatomy of
Melancholy* III.1.2.1]
*This is a proverb that has been found
in almost every language from the beginning of the written record.*
16 Birds in their little nests agree;
And 'tis a shameful sight
When children of one family
Fall out, and chide, and fight.
[Isaac Watts: *Divine Songs*]
*Nothing is more sadly at variance with
the facts than the famous first line of
this quatrain. Birds in their little nests,
as elsewhere throughout their lives, live
in a hierarchy of force maintained by
ceaseless violence. It is a rare thing for
a brood to be reared without at least one
nestling being killed by the others.*
See W. C. Allee: The Social Life of
Animals, *N.Y., 1938, pp. 176-184, and
see the researches of Schjelderup-Ebbe,
which have established the term "pecking order."*
17 Birds in their little nests agree
With Chinamen, but not with me.

[Hilaire Belloc: *New Cautionary Tales,* "On Food"]

BIRD: in a gilded cage
1 Tak any brid, and put it in a cage,
And do al thyn entente and thy cor-
age
To fostre it tendrely with mete and
drinke,
Of alle deyntees that thou canst bi-
thinke,
And keep it al-so clenly as thou may;
Al-though his cage of gold be never
so gay.
Yet hath this brid, by twenty thou-
sand fold,
Lever in a forest, that is rude and
cold,
Gon ete wormes and swich wrecched-
nesse.
[Chaucer: *The Manciple's Tale*]
Strange as it seems to us, brid *was the old form of the word. The* r *shifted its position—as it has in the common pronunciation* hunderd.
2 A robin redbreast in a cage
Puts all heaven in a rage.
[William Blake: *Auguries of Innocence*]
3 Her beauty was sold for an old man's
gold,
She's a bird in a gilded cage.
[Arthur J. Lamb: *A Bird in a Gilded Cage* (c. 1900)]

BIRD: in the hand
4 He is a fool who lets slip a bird in
the hand for a bird in the bush. [Plu-
tarch: *Of Garrulity*]
5 A feather in hand is better than a
bird in the air. [George Herbert: *Jacula Prudentum*]
6 One bird in the hand is worth two
in the bush. [Nathaniel Woods: *The Conflict of Conscience* IV]
With variations on the number of birds in the bush, the proverb appears in many forms from the 14th century on. The 19th century was a little uneasy, lest the saying suggest that the Present was to be preferred to the Hereafter, but the 20th has accepted it without qualms.

BIRD: an ill, that fouls its own nest
7 It's an ill bird that fouls its own nest.

[13th-century proverb]
8 Old proverbe says,
That byrd ys not honest
That fyleth hys owne nest.
[John Skelton: *Poems against Garnesche* III]
honest = *pure;* fyleth = *defiles*
9 It is a foule byrd that fyleth his owne
nest. [John Heywood: *Proverbs* (1546)]
The proverb has been traced back to the 11th century and is probably much older.

BIRTH
10 Being born, we die; our end is the
consequence of our beginning. [Manil-
ius: *Astronomican* IV.xvi.]
11 Death, like birth, is a secret of
Nature. [Marcus Aurelius: *Meditations* IV.v.]
12 Unto us a child is born, unto us a son
is given. [Isaiah 9:6]
13 For we brought nothing into this
world, and it is certain we can carry
nothing out. [I Timothy 6:7]
14 My lord, I was born about three of
the clock in the afternoon, with a white
head, and something of a round belly.
For my voice, I have lost it with hollaing,
and singing of anthems. [Shakespeare:
II Henry IV I.ii.]
15 Bring forth men children only.
[Shakespeare: *Macbeth* I.vii.]
16 Macduff was from his mother's
womb
Untimely ripped.
[Shakespeare: *Macbeth* V.vii.]
17 It is as natural to die as to be born;
and to a little infant, perhaps, the one is
as painful as the other. [Francis Bacon:
Of Death]
18 Born of a Monday, fair in the face,
Born of a Tuesday, full of God's
grace,
Born of a Wednesday, merry and
glad,
Born of a Thursday, sour and sad,
Born of a Friday, Godly given,
Born of a Saturday, work for your
living.
Born of a Sunday, ne'er shall you
want,
So ends the week, and there's an end
on 't.
[Unknown: (Brand, *Popular Antiquities.*

Notes and Queries, ser. V, VII, 424.)]

1 Our birth is but a sleep and a for-
getting:
The soul that rises with us, our life's
star,
Hath had elsewhere its setting,
And cometh from afar.
Not in entire forgetfulness,
And not in utter nakedness,
But trailing clouds of glory do we
come
From God, who is our home.
[Wordsworth: *Intimations of Immortal-
ity*]

2 Every moment dies a man,
Every moment one is born.
[Tennyson: *The Vision of Sin* IV]

BIRTH: the beginning of woe

3 Let the day perish wherein I was
born, and the night in which it was said,
There is a man child conceived. [Job
3:3]

4 And when I was born, I drew in the
common air, and fell upon the earth,
which is of like nature, and the first
voice which I uttered was crying, as all
others do. . . . For all men have one
entrance into life, and the like going out.
[*Apocrypha: Wisdom of Solomon* 7:3-6]

5 We begin with cries, and end with
cares. [George Pettie: *Petite Pallace*]

6 A grievous burthen was thy birth to
me;
Tetchy and wayward was thy infancy.
[Shakespeare: *Richard III* IV.iv.]

7 Thou know'st, the first time that we
smell the air
We wawl and cry. . . .
When we are born, we cry that we are
come
To this great stage of fools.
[Shakespeare: *King Lear* IV.vi.]
*It is unlikely that Lear would have
thought of the world as a stage of any
kind. But, of course, Shakespeare would,
and his use of the metaphor here is interesting and revealing.*

8 The infant, as soon as Nature with
great pangs of travail hath sent it forth
from the womb of its mother into the
regions of light, lies, like a sailor cast out
from the waves, naked upon the earth, in
utter want and helplessness, and fills every place around with mournful wailings
and piteous lamentations, as is natural
for one who has so many ills of life in
store for him, so many evils which he
must pass through and suffer. [Lucretius:
De Rerum Natura V.ccxxiii.]

9 He is born naked, and falls a whining
at the first. [Robert Burton: *Anatomy of
Melancholy* I.2.3.10]

10 When I was born, I did lament and
cry,
And now each day doth show the reason why.
[Richard Watkyns: *Flamma Sine Fumo*
(1662)]

11 We should weep for men at their
birth, not at their death. [Montesquieu:
Lettres Persanes XL]

12 We are born crying, live complaining,
and die disappointed. [Thomas Fuller:
(1654-1734): *Gnomologia*]

13 My mother groan'd, my father wept;
Into the dangerous world I leapt,
Helpless, naked, piping loud,
Like a fiend hid in a cloud.
[William Blake: *Infant Sorrow*]

BIRTHRIGHT

14 Esau selleth his birthright for a mess
of potage. [Chapter heading to Genesis
25 in the *Geneva Bible*]
*It is interesting that this exact phrase-
ology, though often heard, is not in the
King James version. The Geneva Bible
was published in 1560 and reprinted in
200 editions. Still, by the end of the 17th
century it had been almost completely
displaced by the King James version, and
the retention of this phrase is a remarkable instance of the transmitting power
of speech.*

BISHOP

15 I should as soon think of contradicting a bishop. [Samuel Johnson: in Boswell's *Life*, May 15, 1784]

16 It was a Bishop bold,
And London was his see,
He was short and stout and round
about
And zealous as could be.
[W. S. Gilbert: *Bab Ballads*, "The Bishop
and the Busman"]

BITTER

1 A bitter heart that bides its time and
bites.
[Robert Browning: *Caliban upon Sete-bos*]

BITTERNESS

2 But hushed be every thought that
springs
From out the bitterness of things.
[Wordsworth: *Elegiac Stanzas*]

3 He thought he saw an Elephant,
That practised on a fife:
He looked again, and found it was
A letter from his wife.
"At length I realize," he said,
"The bitterness of Life!"
[Lewis Carroll: *Sylvie and Bruno* V]

BLACKBIRD(S)

4 Sing a song of sixpence,
A pocket full of rye;
Four and twenty blackbirds,
Baked in a pie.

When the pie was opened,
The birds began to sing;
Wasn't that a dainty dish
To set before a king?
[Nursery rhyme: first versions, c. 1744,
1780]
*Fragments of this famous rhyme are
known as early as the 16th century.
There have been many attempts at eluci-
dation, mostly fantastic. The theory that
it relates to the first productions of
Henry James Pye as Poet Laureate (1790)
is disproved by the fact that the nursery
rhyme was in print before that date. The
Opies, editors of* The Oxford Dictionary
of Nursery Rimes *(pp. 394-5), are of the
opinion that it is simply a merry account
of an actual event. They quote recipes
for arranging pies so that live birds
might fly out of them, causing a "diverting Hurley-Burley amongst the Guests."*

5 The nightingale has a lyre of gold,
The lark's is a clarion call,
And the blackbird plays but a box-
wood flute,
But I love him best of all.
[W. E. Henley: *Echoes* XVIII]

6 The blackbird in the coppice
Looked out to see me stride,
And hearkened as I whistled
The trampling team beside,

And fluted and replied.
[A. E. Housman: *A Shropshire Lad* VII]

BLACK SHEEP

7 Baa, baa, black sheep,
Have you any wool?
Yes, sir, yes, sir,
Three bags full;
One for the master,
And one for the dame,
And one for the little boy
Who lives in the lane.
[Nursery rhyme]
*Sometimes the little boy "cries in the
lane."*
*Earliest known printed version, 1744.
But the rhyme is thought to be much
older. The division of the bags is thought,
somehow, to refer to the export tax on
wool.*

BLACKSMITH

8 Under a spreading chestnut tree
The village smithy stands;
The smith, a mighty man is he,
With large and sinewy hands;
And the muscles of his brawny arms
Are strong as iron bands.
[Longfellow: *The Village Blacksmith*]

BLAME

9 This is the excellent foppery of the
world, that, when we are sick in fortune
—often the surfeit of our own behaviour
—we make guilty of our disasters the sun,
the moon, and the stars; as if we were villains by necessity; fools by heavenly compulsion. [Shakespeare: *King Lear* I.ii.]
10 No blame on that account can be laid
at my door. [George III: letter to Shel-
burne, 1782]
*"that account" = loss of the American
colonies*
*On further consideration his Majesty
added that the Americans were such
knaves that it was probably a good thing
not to have to have any further connection with them.*
11 Before we blame, we should first see
if we can't excuse. [G. C. Lichtenberg:
*Nachtrag zu den moralischen Bemerk-
ungen*]

BLASPHEMY(IES)

12 That in the captain's but a choleric

word,
Which in the soldier is flat blasphemy.
[Shakespeare: *Measure for Measure* II.ii.]
1 (Blasphemy is) denying the being or providence of God, contumelious reproaches of our Saviour Christ, profane scoffing at the Holy Scripture, or exposing it to contempt or ridicule. [William Blackstone: *Commentaries on the Laws of England* IV]
2 Shrink not from blasphemy—'twill pass for wit. [Byron: *English Bards and Scotch Reviewers*]
3 All great truths begin as blasphemies. [G. B. Shaw: *Annajanska*]

BLEMISHED

4 He that is wounded in the stones or hath his privy member cut off, shall not enter into the congregation of the Lord. [Deuteronomy 23:1]
Only those who are unblemished can present themselves before God (Leviticus 21:16-23).

BLESSED

5 Blessed is the man that walketh not in the counsel of the ungodly, nor standeth in the way of sinners, nor sitteth in the seat of the scornful. [Psalms 1:1]
6 Blessed is he who has found his work; let him ask no other blessedness. [Thomas Carlyle: *Past and Present* III.ii.]

BLESSING

7 I will not let thee go, except thou bless me. [Genesis 32:26]
8 The Lord bless thee, and keep thee: The Lord make his face shine upon thee, and be gracious unto thee: The Lord lift up his countenance upon thee, and give thee peace. [Numbers 6:24-26]
9 He that blesseth his friend with a loud voice, rising early in the morning, it shall be counted a curse to him. [Proverbs 27:14]
10 Our King and Queen, the Lord-God bless,
The Paltzgrave, and the Lady Besse,
And God bless every living thing
That lives and breathes and loves the King.

God bless the Council of Estate,
And Buckingham, the fortunate.
God bless them all, and keep them safe,
And God bless me, and God bless Raph.
[Ben Jonson: *Extempore Blessing before King James I*]
The Lady Bess was the Princess Elizabeth, daughter of James and married to the Pfalzgrave Frederick, Elector Palatine. The Duke of Buckingham, George Villiers, was James's favorite. The Elizabethans pronounced Ra(l)ph as Rafe.
Aubrey (Brief Lives, "Ben Jonson") says: "The king was mighty enquisitive to know who this Raph was. Ben told him 'twas the drawer at the Swanne tavernne, by Charing-crosse, who drew him good Canarie. For this drollery his majestie gave him an hundred poundes."
11 Matthew, Mark, Luke and John,
Bless the bed that I lie on.
Four corners to my bed,
Four angels round my head;
One to watch and one to pray
And two to bear my soul away.
[Nursery prayer—or, more accurately, a night-spell, one of the few remnants of what was once a very common form of magic.]
Though first referred to in print in 1656, it is there called a "Popish charm" learned "in Queen Marie's time." It is probably very old, and is sometimes called the "White Paternoster."
12 Matthew, Mark, Luke and John,
The bed be blest that I lye on.
[Thomas Ady: *A Candle in the Dark*]
13 A spring of love gush'd from my heart,
And I blessed them unaware.
[Coleridge: *Ancient Mariner* IV]
14 Blessed is the corpse that the rain falls on;
Blessed is the bride that the sun shines on.
[William Hone: *Table-Book*]
15 "God bless us every one," said Tiny Tim. [Dickens: *A Christmas Carol*, "Stave Three"]
16 Wherefore, Christian men, be sure,
Wealth or rank possessing,
Ye who now do bless the poor
Shall yourselves find blessing.

[John Mason Neale: *Good King Wenceslas*]

BLIND

1 In the land of the blind, the one-eyed is king. [Apostolius: *Paroemiae* VII.xxiii.]

2 I was eyes to the blind, and feet was I to the lame. [Job 29:15]

3 If the blind lead the blind, both shall fall into the ditch. [Matthew 15:14]

4 The blind eat many a fly.
[John Lydgate: *Balade* (c.1430)]
The proverb appears in many forms— as, no doubt, did the flies. The Host, in Chaucer's Canterbury Tales *tells Hogge of Ware, the Cook:*

    Of many a pilgrim hastow Cristes curs,
    For of thy persly yet they fare the
                   wors,
    That they han eten with thy stubbel-
                   goos;
    For in thy shoppe is many a flye loos.

5 In the land of the blind the one-eyed man is lord. [Machiavelli: *La Mandragola* III (1524)]
In the kingdom of the blind, the one-eyed are kings.
Jean Jacques Rousseau: Confessions *I.v.*

6 Who is blinder than he that will not see? [Andrew Boorde: *Breviary of Helthe* II.vi. (1547)]
This was a proverb and appeared in many other works. It appears in Peter Heylin's Animadversions, Matthew Henry's *Commentaries, etc. By 1738 Swift listed it as hackneyed.*

7 Now and then a blinde man may hit a crow. [Robert Armin: *A Nest of Ninnies*]

8 Mettle is dangerous in a blind horse. [John Ray: *English Proverbs* (1670)]

9 When the blind leads the blind, no wonder they both fall into—matrimony. [George Farquhar: *Love and a Bottle* V.i.]

10 A blind Man will not thank you for a Looking Glass. [Thomas Fuller (1654-1734): *Gnomologia*]

BLINDNESS

11   These eyes, though clear
  To outward view of blemish or of
                   spot,
  Bereft of light, their seeing have for-
                   got;
Nor to their idle orbs doth sight ap-
                   pear
Of sun, or moon, or star, throughout
                the year,
Or man, or woman.
[John Milton: *Sonnet XXII*]

12   Thus with the year
Seasons return; but not to me returns
Day, or the sweet approach of even or
                morn,
Or sight of vernal bloom or summer's
                rose,
Or flocks, or herds, or human face
                divine;
But cloud instead, and ever-during
                dark
Surrounds me; from the cheerful ways
                of men
Cut off, and for the book of knowl-
                edge fair
Presented with a universal blank
Of Nature's works, to me expung'd
                and raz'd,
And wisdom at one entrance quite
                shut out.
[John Milton: *Paradise Lost* III.40]

13 O loss of sight, of thee I most com-
                plain!
Blind among enemies, O worse than
                chains,
Dungeon, or beggary, or decrepit age!
[John Milton: *Samson Agonistes*]

14 The sun to me is dark
  And silent as the moon,
When she deserts the night
  Hid in her vacant interlunar cave.
[John Milton: *Samson Agonistes*]

BLISS

15 I, who move and breathe and place one foot before the other, who watch the Moon wax and wane, and put off answering my letters, where shall I find the Bliss which dreams and blackbirds' voices promise, of which the waves whisper, and hand organs in streets near Paddington faintly sing? [Logan Pearsall Smith: *Trivia,* "Where?"]

16 Grishkin is nice: her Russian eye
  Is underlined for emphasis;
Uncorseted, her friendly bust
  Gives promise of pneumatic bliss.
[T. S. Eliot: *Whispers of Immortality*]
The last line was the suggestion for the

impersonal "pneumatic" charm of the unindividualized women in Aldous Huxley's Brave New World.

BLOCKHEADS

1 Let blockheads read what blockheads wrote. [Lord Chesterfield: *Letters,* November 1, 1750]

BLONDE(S)

2 Casey would waltz with a strawberry blonde,
And the band played on.
[John F. Palmer: *The Band Played On*]
3 Gentlemen Prefer Blondes. [Anita Loos: title of a book, 1925]

BLOOD

4 His blood be on us, and on our children. [Matthew 27:25]
5 Your blood be upon your own heads. [Acts 18:6]
6   O! The blood more stirs
To rouse a lion than to start a hare!
[Shakespeare: *I Henry IV* I.iii.]
7 Why should a man, whose blood is warm within,
Sit like his grandsire cut in alabaster?
[Shakespeare: *The Merchant of Venice* I.i.]
i.e., like his grandfather's alabaster image on his tomb in the church.
8 As dear to me as are the ruddy drops
That visit my sad heart.
[Shakespeare: *Julius Caesar* II.i.]
9 What bloody man is that?
[Shakespeare: *Macbeth* I.ii.]
10 Will all great Neptune's ocean wash this blood
Clean from my hand? No, this my hand will rather
The multitudinous seas incarnadine,
Making the green one red.
[Shakespeare: *Macbeth* II.ii.]
11   I am in blood
Stepp'd in so far, that, should I wade no more,
Returning were as tedious as go o'er.
[Shakespeare: *Macbeth* III.iv.]
12 It will have blood; they say, blood will have blood.
[Shakespeare: *Macbeth* III.v.]
13 Yet who would have thought the old man to have had so much blood in him?
[Shakespeare: *Macbeth* V.i.]

14 Your antient but ignoble blood
Has crept thro' Scoundrels ever since the Flood.
[Alexander Pope: *An Essay on Man* IV]
15 There is a fountain fill'd with blood
Drawn from Emmanuel's veins;
And sinners, plung'd beneath that flood,
Lose all their guilty stains.
[William Cowper: *There is a Fountain*]
16 Just as I am, without one plea
But that Thy blood was shed for me,
And that Thou bid'st me come to Thee,
O Lamb of God, I come!
[Charlotte Elliott: *Just As I Am*]
17 There's no getting blood out of a turnip. [Frederick Marryat: *Japhet in Search of a Father* IV]
This was an old proverb. Sometimes it was a stone from which blood could not be had.
18 Blood is thicker than water.
The saying had appeared as a proverb in John Ray's collection (1670) and had been used in Scott's Guy Mannering *XXXVIII.*
But it had fallen into disuse until revived by Commodore Josiah Tatnall in a despatch to the U.S. Secretary of the Navy (June, 1859) explaining why he had gone to the assistance of an English squadron in the Pei-Ho river in China.
19 I have nothing to offer but blood, toil, tears and sweat. [Sir Winston Churchill: in a speech, to the House of Commons, May 13, 1940]
The famous phrase had its antecedents through the ages: Donne had spoken of "teares, or sweat, or blood" (1611); Byron (in 1823) of "Blood, sweat, and tear-wrung millions."

BLOODY

20 Not bloody likely! [G. B. Shaw: *Pygmalion* III]
Eliza Doolittle's use of the intensive bloody *caused a gasp of horror when Shaw's play was first presented (1913). Since World War II the word has become so common in England that it would now be shrugged off, but it still is an improper word.*
Linguistically, it is exceedingly interesting because it demonstrates that im-

propriety is whatever a society deems improper. The word is neither profanity nor obscenity. Some have attempted to trace it to "by our Lady," but phonetically this won't hold up and historically it doesn't ring true. The Oxford English Dictionary *thinks that it was at first a reference to the habits of "bloods" or aristocratic rowdies in the late 17th and early 18th centuries. Thus "bloody drunk" = "as drunk as a blood." It was extended and became a lower-class word, and that is what made it evil.*

BLOOM
1 And since to look at things in bloom
Fifty springs are little room,
About the woodlands I will go
To see the cherry hung with snow.
[A. E. Housman: *A Shropshire Lad* II]

BLOT
2 The fairer the Paper, the fouler the Blot. [Thomas Fuller (1654-1734): *Gnomologia*]
3 Cleaning a Blot with blotted Fingers, maketh a greater Blur. [Thomas Fuller (1654-1734): *Gnomologia*]

BLOW
4 The first blow makes the Wrong, but the second makes the Fray. [Donne: *Sermons*]
5 "Thrice is he armed that hath his quarrel just"—
And four times he who gets his fist in fust.
[Artemus Ward: *Shakespeare Up-to-Date*]

BLUE
6 'Twas Presbyterian true blue. [Samuel Butler (1612-1680): *Hudibras*]
Of all the old dyes, blue was the fastest and was called "true blue." The Scotch Covenanters adopted blue as their color, as opposed to the King's color, red, and "true blue" came to be applied to the Presbyterians.

BLUESTOCKING
7 A Blue Stocking.
Bluestocking was first used to describe a lady of literary tastes in the 18th cen-

tury. A Mrs. Edward Montagu sought distinction by having intellectual parties and, to show their disdain of luxury and frivolity, her guests dressed plainly. Plainest was Mr. Benjamin Stillingfleet who even wore a tradesman's homely blue-gray stockings instead of the white silk stockings a gentleman would be expected to wear on formal occasions. Society at once dubbed the intellectuals "bluestockings" and the name stuck—though to the ladies.

BLUNDER(S)
8 It is worse than a crime; it is a blunder. [Boulay de la Meurthe: commenting on the execution of the Duc d'Enghien, March 21, 1804]
On a suspicion—now generally believed by historians to have been unwarranted —Napoleon decided that the Duke of Enghien, a scion of the great Bourbon-Condé family, a Royalist emigré, was involved in a plot against his life. He had d'Enghien kidnapped in Baden, carried forcibly across the frontier into France, tried by drumhead court martial, and summarily executed. This brutal procedure aroused feelings of profound horror throughout Europe. The saying is sometimes attributed to Fouché and sometimes to Talleyrand.
9 Someone had blundered.
[Tennyson: *The Charge of the Light Brigade*]
The phrase "someone had blundered" in the account in the Times *of the charge of the Light Brigade was the genesis of Tennyson's famous poem.*
10 The pain others give passes away in their later kindness, but that of our own blunders, especially when they hurt our vanity, never passes away. [William Butler Yeats: *Dramatis Personae*]

BLUNTNESS
11   This is some fellow
Who, having been prais'd for bluntness, doth affect
A saucy roughness, and constrains the garb
Quite from his nature.
[Shakespeare: *King Lear* II.ii.]
affect = assume an affectation of; from = away from

BLUSH

1 And of his own thought he wex all
reed.

[Chaucer: *The Shipman's Tale* I]
2 Men blush less for their crimes than
for their weaknesses and vanity. [La
Bruyère: *Les Caractères*]
3 So sweet the blush of bashfulness,
E'en pity scarce can wish it less!
[Byron: *The Bride of Abydos* I.viii.]
4 There's a blush for won't, and a blush
for shan't,
And a blush for having done it;
There's a blush for thought and a
blush for nought,
And a blush for just begun it.
[Keats: Letter to J. H. Reynolds, Jan. 13,
1818]
*In the letter, Keats refers to these lines
as "the old song."*
5 The question [with Mr. Podsnap]
about everything was, would it bring a
blush into the cheek of the young person? [Dickens: *Our Mutual Friend* XI]
*"The young person" is Podsnap's daughter, Georgiana. Podsnap, one of Dickens's
greatest creations, is a pompous, self-satisfied man, burdened with a sense of
his own importance who, by a fortunate
chance, always knew exactly what Providence wanted in any situation. Even
more remarkable, what Providence
wanted was always what Mr. Podsnap
wanted.*

BOARDS

6 The warping boards pull out their
own old nails.
[Robert Frost: *The Black Cottage*]

BOASTING

7 A vantour and a lyere, al is on.
[Chaucer: *Troilus and Criseyde* III]
vantour = *boaster*
8 Such boastings as the Gentiles use,
Or lesser breeds without the Law.
[Kipling: *Recessional*]

BOBBY SHAFTOE

9 Bobby Shaftoe's gone to sea,
Silver buckles at his knee;
He'll come back and marry me,
Bonny Bobby Shaftoe!
[Nursery rhyme]
Much sung in the Irish elections of 1761.

BODY

10 I am fearfully and wonderfully made.
[Psalms 139:14]
11 No one is free who is a slave to the
body. [Seneca: *Epistolae* XCII.xxxiii.]
12 Love's mysteries in souls do grow,
But yet the body is his book.
[Donne: *The Extasie*]
13 This house of clay not built with
hands. [Coleridge: *Youth and Age*]
14 If anything is sacred the human body
is sacred.
[Walt Whitman: *Leaves of Grass*, "I
Sing the Body Electric"]

BODY POLITIC

15 The body politic, like the human
body, begins to die from its birth, and
bears in itself the causes of its destruction. [Jean Jacques Rousseau: *The Social Contract* III.xi.]

BOG

16 A gulf profound as that Serbonian
bog
Betwixt Damiata and Mount Casius
old,
Where armies whole have sunk.
[John Milton: *Paradise Lost* II. 592-594]

BOLD

17 Fortune favors the bold.
[Vergil: *Aeneid* X]
*A sentiment echoed, in varying phrases,
by writers in every nation for millennia.
Sometimes it's the brave, sometimes—
and more often—the bold. It's not
merely courage; there must be an element of impertinence in it—especially in
relation to love.*
See FORTUNE
18 And as she lookt about, she did behold
How over that same door was likewise writ,
Be bold, be bold, and everywhere Be
bold.
[Edmund Spenser: *The Faerie Queene*
III.xi.]
19 Only the bold have good luck in love.
[Carlo Goldoni: *Belisario* I.ix.]

BOLDNESS

20 In desperate matters the boldest counsels are the safest. [Livy: *Histories* XXV.
xxxviii.]

1 By boldness great fears are concealed.
[Lucan: *De Bello Civili* IV]
2 A bold bad man.
[Edmund Spenser: *The Faerie Queene* I.i.37]
3 Things out of hope are compassed oft with venturing.
[Shakespeare: *Venus and Adonis*]
4 This bold bad man.
[Shakespeare: *Henry VIII* II.ii.]
5 Boldness is an ill keeper of promise.
[Francis Bacon: *Of Boldness*]
6 Great boldness is seldom without some absurdity. [Francis Bacon: *Of Boldness*]
7 Boldness is ever blind; for it seeth not dangers and inconveniences: therefore it is ill in counsel, good in execution; so that the right use of bold persons is that they never command in chief, but be seconds and under the direction of others; for in counsel it is good to see dangers and in execution not to see them except they be very great. [Francis Bacon: *Of Boldness*]
8 Boldness is a child of ignorance and baseness, far inferior to other parts; but, nevertheless, it doth fascinate and bind hand and foot those that are either shallow in judgment or weak in courage, which are the greatest part; yea, and prevaileth with wise men at weak times. [Francis Bacon: *Of Boldness*]
   parts = *abilities, capacities, talents*
9 Boldness in business is the first, second, and third thing. [Thomas Fuller (1654-1734): *Gnomologia*]
10 Bolder words and more timorous meaning, I think were never brought together. [Samuel Johnson: in Boswell's *Life*, 1780]
   Johnson was referring to The Jesuit *by George Marriott.*
11 If I could dwell
   Where Israfel
Hath dwelt, and he where I,
He might not sing so wildly well
A mortal melody,
While a bolder note than this might swell
From my lyre within the sky.
[Edgar Allan Poe: *Israfel*]

BOLT
12 You have shot your bolt. [Jonathan Swift: *Polite Conversation* I (1738)]
Swift is alluding to the proverb: "A fool's bolt is soon shot."

A bolt or quarrel was a short, thick arrow shot from a crossbow. The crossbow was more deadly than the longbow but it took longer to prepare it to shoot; once the quarrel was released—that is, the bolt was shot—the crossbowman was not to be feared, was indeed highly vulnerable as he labored to reload and wind. The crossbowman had therefore to hold his aim until it could be most effective and to resist excited urges to shoot the bolt too soon.

BOMBAST
13 And he whose fustian's so sublimely bad,
   It is not poetry, but prose run mad.
[Alexander Pope: *Epistle to Dr. Arbuthnot*]
   fustian = *inflated, turgid, inappropriately lofty language*

BOND
14 Is it so nominated in the bond?
[Shakespeare: *The Merchant of Venice* IV.i.]
15 An honest man's word is as good as his bond. [Cervantes: *Don Quixote* III.ii.34]

BONES
16 Don't make any bones about it. [R. L. Stevenson: *St. Ives* XXV (1894)]
Stevenson didn't invent the expression. It's been in the language and literature for 500 years. Now it means to show no reluctance, make no opposing fuss, have no scruples about. Nicholas Udall, in 1548, said that Abraham "made no manner of bones nor sticking" when God commanded him to offer up Isaac. John Marbeck (1581) speaks of one who "never made bones in it" when required to do something. The expression referred, apparently, to finding or pretending to find bones in soup as an obstacle to swallowing it. There are many terms in the language wherein acceptability is spoken of in terms of eating, such as "That won't go down," "It sticks in my craw," "He won't swallow that," "I can't stomach it." The same Nicholas Udall quoted above

—with whom it seems to have been a favorite term—says (Ralph Roister Doister *I.iii. (1553)*):

Sweet male maketh jolly good ale for the nones,
Which will slide down the lane without any bones. . . .

BOOK(S)

1 Oh that mine adversary had written a book. [Job 31:35]
book = *bill of charges*
The King James version (given above) is misleading to the modern reader. The Revised Standard Version renders it indictment.
Job wishes that God had written out a libel or bill of indictment, stating specifically what the charges against him are. Only if he knows them can he hope to refute them and prove his innocence.
2 Books being once called in and forbidden become more saleable and public. [Montaigne: *Essays* III.v.]
3 Was ever book containing such vile matter
So fairly bound?
[Shakespeare: *Romeo and Juliet* III.ii.]
4 The gentleman is not in your books.
[Shakespeare: *Much Ado about Nothing* I.i.]
5 And deeper than did ever plummet sound
I'll drown my book.
[Shakespeare: *The Tempest* V.i.]
6 Learning hath gained most by those books by which the printers have lost. [Thomas Fuller (1608-1661): *The Holy and Profane State,* "Of Books"]
7 It is with books as with men: a very small number play a great part, the rest are lost in the multitude. [Voltaire: *Philosophical Dictionary,* "Books"]
8 Any fool may write a most valuable book by chance, if he will only tell us what he heard and saw with veracity. [Thomas Gray: Letter to Horace Walpole, February 25, 1768]
9 Great collections of books are subject to certain accidents besides the damp, the worms, and the rats; one not less common is that of the borrowers, not to say a word of the purloiners. [Isaac D'Israeli: *Curiosities of Literature,* "The Bibliomania"]
10 Beware the man of one book. [Isaac D'Israeli: *Curiosities of Literature*]
11 There is no such thing as a moral or an immoral book. Books are well written, or badly written. That is all. [Oscar Wilde: Preface to *The Picture of Dorian Gray*]
12 When I am dead, I hope it may be said:
"His sins were scarlet, but his books were read."
[Hilaire Belloc: *On His Books*]
13 I may as well confess myself the author
Of several books against the world in general.
[Robert Frost: *New Hampshire*]

BOOK(S): the book and the author

14 I have not made my book more than my book has made me. [Montaigne: *Essays* II.xviii.]
15 Reader, look
Not on his picture, but his book.
[Ben Jonson: lines on Shakespeare's portrait, prefaced to the Folio of 1623]
16 As good almost kill a man as kill a good book: who kills a man kills a reasonable creature, God's image; but he who destroys a good book, kills reason itself, kills the image of God, as it were, in the eye. [John Milton: *Areopagitica*]
17 A presentation copy . . . is a copy of a book which does not sell, sent you by the author, with his foolish autograph at the beginning of it; for which, if a stranger, he only demands your friendship; if a brother author, he expects from you a book of yours, which does not sell, in return. [Charles Lamb: *Last Essays of Elia,* "Popular Fallacies: XI. That We Must Not Look a Gift-Horse in the Mouth"]
18 'Tis pleasant, sure, to see one's name in print;
A book's a book, although there's nothing in 't.
[Byron: *English Bards and Scotch Reviewers*]
19 Camerado, this is no book,
Who touches this touches a man.
[Walt Whitman: *Leaves of Grass,* "So Long"]

BOOK(S): dispraise of

1 Of making many books there is no end; and much study is a weariness of the flesh. [Ecclesiastes 12:12]

2 There's more ado to interpret interpretations, than to interpret things: and more books upon books, than upon any other subject. [Montaigne: *Essays* III. xiii.]

3 The wise are above books. [Samuel Daniel: *A Defense of Rhyme* (1602)]

4   Who reads
Incessantly, and to his reading brings
                      not
A spirit and judgment equal or superior,
(And what he brings what needs he
                elsewhere seek?)
Uncertain and unsettled still remains,
Deep-versed in books and shallow in
                himself.
[John Milton: *Paradise Regained* IV. 322]

5 He [Thomas Hobbes] was wont to say that if he had read as much as other men, he should have known no more than other men. [John Aubrey: *Brief Lives* I.349]

6 He was naturally learn'd; he needed not the spectacles of books to read Nature; he looked inwards, and found her there. [Dryden: *Essay of Dramatic Poesy*]

7 Unlearned men of books assume the
                care,
As eunuchs are the guardians of the
                fair.
[Edward Young: *Love of Fame* II.lxxxiii.]

8 The multitude of books is making us ignorant. [Voltaire: (attr.)]

9 Books without the knowledge of life are useless. [Samuel Johnson: in Mrs. Piozzi's *Johnsoniana*]

10 I hate books, for they only teach people to talk about what they do not understand. [Jean Jacques Rousseau: *Émile* I]

11 Some books are lies frae end to end. [Burns: *Death and Dr. Hornbook*]

12 Up! up! my friend, and quit your
                books;
Or surely you'll grow double.
[Wordsworth: *The Tables Turned*]

13 Books are fatal: they are the curse of the human race. Nine-tenths of existing books are nonsense, and the clever books are the refutation of that nonsense. The greatest misfortune that ever befell man was the invention of printing. [Benjamin Disraeli: *Lothair* XXIV]

14 Most books, indeed, are records less
Of fulness than of emptiness.
[William Allingham: *Writing*]

15 Books are good enough in their own way, but they are a mighty bloodless substitute for life. [R. L. Stevenson: *An Apology for Idlers*]

16 A best-seller is the gilded tomb of a mediocre talent. [Logan Pearsall Smith: *Afterthoughts*]

BOOK: l'envoi

17 Go, litel book, go litel myn tragedie,
  Ther God thy maker yet, er that he
                dye,
So sende might to make in som comedie!
But litel book, no making thou nenvye,
But subgit be to alle poesye;
And kis the steppes, wher-as thou
                seest pace
Virgile, Ovyde, Omer, Lucan, and
                Stace.
[Chaucer: *Troilus and Criseyde* V]
nenvye = *no envy;* subgit = *subject;* Omer = *Homer;* Stace = *Statius Caecilius, Roman comic poet who adapted the plays of the Greek poet Menander*

18 Go, little Book! from this my solitude;
I cast thee on the waters—go thy ways:
And if, as I believe, thy vein be good,
The World will find thee after many
                days.
Be it with thee according to thy worth;
Go, little Book! in faith I send thee
                forth.
[Robert Southey: *Lay of the Laureate,* "L'Envoi"]

19 "Go little book, from this my solitude!
I cast thee on the waters—go thy
                ways!
And if, as I believe, thy vein be good,
The world will find thee after many
                days."
When Southey's read, and Wordsworth understood,
I can't help putting in my claim to
              praise—
The first four rhymes are Southey's,

every line:
For God's sake, reader! take them not
for mine.
[Byron: *Don Juan* I.ccxxii.]
*The contrast between Chaucer's humility
and Southey's arrogance justifies Byron's
mockery.*

BOOK(S): praise of

1 And as for me, thogh that I can but
lyte,
On bokes for to rede I me delyte,
And to hem yeve I feyth and ful
credence,
And in myn herte have hem in reverence.
[Chaucer: Prologue to *The Legend of
Good Women*]
can but lyte = *know but little;* yeve =
give

2 For out of olde feldes, as men seith,
Cometh al this newe corn fro yeer to
yere;
And out of olde bokes, in good feith,
Cometh al this newe science that men
lere.
[Chaucer: *The Parlement of Foules*]

3 For him was lever have at his beddes
heed
Twenty bokes, clad in blak or reed,
Of Aristotle and his philosophye,
Than robes riche, or fithele, or gay
sautrye.
[Chaucer: Prologue to *The Canterbury
Tales*]
fithele = *fiddle;* sautrye = *psaltery, harp*
*Twenty books would have been an im-
possible dream for a poor scholar in the
Middle Ages. Musical instruments were
forbidden in the colleges—yet, apparently, they were what most of the other
students desired rather than books.*

4 But the images of men's wits and
knowledges remain in books, exempted
from the wrong of time, and capable of
perpetual renovation. Neither are they
fitly to be called images, because they
generate still, and cast their seeds in the
minds of others, provoking and causing
infinite actions and opinions in succeeding ages. [Francis Bacon: *Advancement
of Learning* I]

5 A good book is the precious life-blood
of a master-spirit, embalmed and treas-
ured up on purpose to a life beyond life.

[John Milton: *Areopagitica*]

6 Books are not absolutely dead things,
but do contain a potency of life in them
to be as active as that soul was whose
progeny they are; nay, they do preserve
as in a vial the purest efficacy and ex-
traction of that living intellect that bred
them. [John Milton: *Areopagitica*]

7 The true University of these days is
a collection of books. [Thomas Carlyle:
On Heroes and Hero Worship V]

8 There is no frigate like a book
To take us lands away,
Nor any coursers like a page
Of prancing poetry.

This traverse may the poorest take
Without oppress of toll;
How frugal is the chariot
That bears a human soul.
[Emily Dickinson: *Part I, Life* XCIX]

BOOK(S): and reading

9 Every abridgment of a good book is a
stupid abridgment. [Montaigne: *Essays*
III.viii.]

10 Bookes give not wisdome where none
was before,
But where some is, there reading
makes it more.
[Sir John Harington: *Epigrams* I]

11 Some books are to be tasted, others to
be swallowed, and some few to be
chewed and digested: that is, some books
are to be read only in parts, others to be
read, but not curiously, and some few to
be read wholly, and with diligence and
attention. [Francis Bacon: *Of Studies*]

12 Alonso of Arragon was wont to say of
himself, "That he was a great necromancer, for that he used to ask counsel of the
dead," meaning books. [Francis Bacon:
Apothegms]

13 Books should to one of these four
ends conduce,
For wisdom, piety, delight, or use.
[John Denham: *Of Prudence*]

14 There are the men who pretend to
understand a book by scouting through
the index: as if a traveler should go
about to describe a palace when he had
seen nothing but the privy. [Jonathan
Swift: *On the Mechanical Operation of
the Spirit*]

15 The great drawback in new books is

that they prevent our reading the old ones. [Joseph Joubert: *Pensées*]

1 My days among the Dead are passed,
    Around me I behold,
    Where'er these casual eyes are cast,
      The mighty minds of old:
    My never-failing friends are they,
    With whom I converse day by day.
[Robert Southey: *My Days Among the Dead Are Passed*]

2 I love to lose myself in other men's minds. [Charles Lamb: *Detached Thoughts on Books and Reading*]

3 Never read any book that is not a year old. [Emerson: *In Praise of Books*]

4 There are some books which cannot be adequately reviewed for twenty or thirty years after they come out. [John Morley: *Recollections* I]

BOOK REVIEW

5 I read the "Christabel"; Very well:
I read the "Missionary"; Pretty—
        very.
I tried at "Ilderim"; Ahem!
I read a sheet of "Marg'ret of *An-jou*"; Can you?
I turn'd a page of Scott's "Waterloo";
        Pooh! pooh!
I look'd at Wordsworth's milk-white "Rylstone Doe"; Hillo!
I read "Glenarvon" too by Caroline Lamb; God damn!
[Byron: *Versicles*]
  Glenarvon, by Lady Caroline Lamb, was a highly-wrought and romanticized account, in a thin fictional disguise, of her love affair with Byron. She was, of course, wild to know Byron's opinion of it, and in this sort of "Saturday review" of the week's fiction, he expressed it.

BOOTS

6 Boots—boots—boots—boots—movin' up and down again! There's no discharge in the war!
[Kipling: *Boots*]
  There is no discharge in that war.
             Ecclesiastes 8:8

BO-PEEP

7 Little Bo-peep has lost her sheep,
    And doesn't know where to find
        them;
    Leave them alone, and they'll come
        home,

Wagging their tails behind them.
[Nursery rhyme: many versions.]
  Probably very old, though the oldest known printed version goes back only to the 19th century.
  The Elizabethan game of Bo-peep, played with babies, was what we call Peek-a-Boo.

LIZZIE BORDEN

8 Lizzie Borden took an axe
And gave her mother forty whacks;
When she saw what she had done
She gave her father forty-one!
[Anon.]
  This jingle swept the country after the trial of Lizzie Borden for the murder of her parents, at Fall River, Mass., June, 1893. Miss Borden was acquitted.
  Next to "Let them eat cake," the rhyme must stand as one of the most devastating pieces of propaganda known. Despite the verdict, it has convinced most people of her guilt. A serious study of the case—Lizzie Borden, by Edward Radin, N. Y., 1961—affirms her innocence.

BORE(S)

9 We often pardon those who bore us, but never those whom we bore. [La Rochefoucauld: *Maxims*]

10 Faith! he must make his stories
        shorter
  Or change his comrades once a quar-
        ter.
[Jonathan Swift: *On the Death of Dr. Swift*]

11 The secret of being a bore is to tell everything. [Voltaire: *L'enfant prodigue*]

12 He says a thousand pleasant things—
  But never says, "Adieu."
[J. G. Saxe: *My Familiar*]

13 There was one feudal custom worth
        keeping, at least,
  Roasted bores made a part of each
        well-ordered feast.
[James Russell Lowell: *A Fable for Critics*]

14 BORE. A person who talks when you wish him to listen. [Ambrose Bierce: *The Devil's Dictionary*]

BOREDOM

15   Oh, he's as tedious

As is a tir'd horse, a railing wife;
Worse than a smoky house; I had
    rather live
With cheese and garlic in a windmill
    far
Than feed on cates and have him
    talk to me
In any summer house in Christendom.
[Shakespeare: *I Henry IV* III.i.]
    cates = *delicacies. The word is akin to*
caterer *and derived from a word mean-
ing* "to purchase."

    *There's an innocent implication in the
word that* "boughten" *things are much
finer than homemade.* "Homemade," *as
a term of commendation, came into use
only after most things had become factory made.*

1 How weary, stale, flat and unprofita-
    ble,
Seem to me all the uses of this world!
[Shakespeare: *Hamlet* I.ii.]
2 A man would die, though he were
neither valiant nor miserable, only upon
a weariness to do the same thing so oft
over and over. [Francis Bacon: *Of
Death*]
3 One is almost always bored by those
persons with whom one is not permitted
to be bored. [La Rochefoucauld: *Maxims*]
4 Time hangs heavy on my hands, and
my money burns in my pocket. [George
Farquhar: *The Inconstant* V.iii.]
5 Their only labour was to kill the
    time;
    And labour dire it is, and weary woe.
[James Thomson (1700-1748): *The Castle of Indolence* I.lxxii.]
6 After three days men grow weary of
a wench, a guest, and rainy weather.
[Benjamin Franklin: *Poor Richard's Almanack (1733)*]
7 Time, with all its celerity, moves
slowly to him whose whole employment
is to watch its flight. [Samuel Johnson:
The Idler No. 21]
8 A scholar knows no boredom. [Jean
Paul Richter: *Hesperus* VIII.]
9 Boredom is a vital problem for the
moralist, since at least half the sins of
mankind are caused by the fear of it.
[Bertrand Russell: *The Conquest of
Happiness* IV]

BORROWER
10 I must become a borrower of the
    night
    For a dark hour or twain.
[Shakespeare: *Macbeth* III.i.]
11 Neither a borrower nor a lender be;
    For loan oft loses both itself and
        friend,
    And borrowing dulls the edge of hus-
        bandry.
[Shakespeare: *Hamlet* I.iii.]
12 The human species, according to the
best theory I can form of it, is composed
of two distinct races, the men who borrow and the men who lend. [Charles
Lamb: *The Two Races of Men*]
    *Of these two, Lamb says, the borrowers
are the greater race.*
13 The borrower is servant to the
lender. [Proverbs 22:7]

BORROWING
14 Be not made a beggar by banqueting upon borrowing. [Ecclesiasticus
18:33]
15 He that goes a-borrowing, goes a-
sorrowing. [Benjamin Franklin: *Poor
Richard's Almanack (1758)*]
    *Who goeth a-borrowing, goeth a-sorrow-
ing.*

    Thomas Tusser: Five Hundred Points
of Good Husbandry, *June's Abstract
(1580). Poor Richard was not original.*
16 Let us all be happy and live within
our means, even if we have to borrow the
money to do it with. [Artemus Ward:
Science and Natural History]

BOSOMS
17 . . . come home to men's businesses
and bosoms. [Francis Bacon: *Essays,
"Dedication"*]
    Speaking of the essays themselves.

BOSTON
18 And this is good old Boston,
    The home of the bean and the cod,
    Where the Lowells talk to the Cabots,
    And the Cabots talk only to God.
[John Collins Bossidy: *On the Aristocracy of Harvard*]
    *Then here's to the City of Boston,
    The town of the cries and the groans,
    Where the Cabots can't see the Kabot-
        schniks,*

And the Lowells won't speak to the
Cohns.
Franklin Pierce Adams (1881-1960):
Revised.
FPA's contribution to the humorous
furor that arose when one of the Cabots
attempted to get an injunction to pre-
vent a certain Kabotschnik from legally
changing his name to Cabot. Another
contribution ran:
> *Here's to good old Boston,*
> *The home of the bean and the cod,*
> *Where the Lowell's can't speak to the*
> *Cabots,*
> *For the Kabots speak Yiddish, by God!*

BOTANIST
1   A fingering slave,
One that would peep and botanize
Upon his mother's grave.
[Wordsworth: *A Poet's Epitaph*]

BOTTLES
2 Neither do men put new wine into
old bottles; else the bottles break, and
the wine runneth out, and the bottles
perish: but they put new wine into new
bottles, and both are preserved. [Mat-
thew 9:17]
> bottle = *wineskin*
> *Old wineskins are dry and brittle and*
> *the residual fermentation which would*
> *be in new wine would burst old skins.*
> *New skins have considerable "give" to*
> *them.*

3 It is with narrow-souled people as
with narrow-necked bottles; the less they
have in them the more noise they make
in pouring out. [Alexander Pope:
Thoughts on Various Subjects]

BOTTOM
4 I am not now in fortune's power;
He that is down can fall no lower.
[Samuel Butler: (1612-1680): *Hudibras*]
> *This is a common proverbial sentiment.*
> *But it is fallacious. As Shakespeare ob-*
> *serves (Lear IV.i), as long as a man can*
> *say "This is the worst that can happen*
> *to me," it isn't the worst; when the worst*
> *comes, he won't be able to comment on*
> *it or to boast of his strength to endure*
> *it.*

BOUNCE
5 He speaks plain cannon fire, and

smoke and bounce.
[Shakespeare: *King John* II.i.]
> *Bounce was the Elizabethan word for*
> *the sound of a cannon, in some ways*
> *better than our* boom *or* bang.

BOUNTY
6   For his bounty,
There was no winter in 't; an autumn 'twas
That grew the more by reaping.
[Shakespeare: *Antony and Cleopatra* V.
ii.]

BOURBONS
7 They (the Bourbons) have learned
nothing and forgotten nothing. [Attr.
various Frenchmen, including C. M. Tall-
eyrand]

BOW (GESTURE)
8 Mr. Seward saw him [Johnson] presented to the Archbishop of York, and
described his *Bow to an ARCH-BISHOP,*
as such a studied elaboration of homage,
such an extension of limb, such a flexion
of body, as have seldom or ever been
equalled. [Boswell: *Life of Johnson*
(1783)]
> extension of limb = *thrusting the right*
> *foot forward was a part of the formal*
> *bow in the 18th century. It was some-*
> *times known as "making a leg."*

BOW (WEAPON)
9 Who seaketh two strings to one bowe,
he may shute strong but never strait.
[Queen Elizabeth: to James VI of Scot-
land]
10 Bring me my bow of burning gold:
Bring me my arrows of desire:
Bring me my spear: O clouds unfold!
Bring me my chariot of fire.
[William Blake: *Milton*]

BOWELS
11 My bowels shall sound like an harp.
[Isaiah 16:11]
> *RSV gives a more elegant rendition: "My*
> *soul moans like a lyre."*

BOY(S)
12 Of all the animals, the boy is the most
unmanageable. [Plato: *Phaedrus*]

1 He's an ill Boy, that goes like a Top; no longer than 'tis whipt. [Thomas Fuller (1654-1734): *Gnomologia*]
2 A ragged colt may prove a good horse. And so may an untoward slovenly boy prove a decent and useful man. [James Kelly: *Scottish Proverbs*]
3 What are little boys made of?
What are little boys made of?
Frogs and snails,
And puppy-dogs' tails,
That's what little boys are made of.

What are little girls made of?
What are little girls made of?
Sugar and spice
And all that's nice,
That's what little girls are made of.
[Nursery rhyme: earliest known version, 19th century]
Attr. Southey, but not to be found in his works.
4 Boys are capital fellows in their own way, among their mates; but they are unwholesome companions for grown people. [Charles Lamb: *The Old and the New Schoolmaster*]
5 A boy's will is the wind's will,
And the thoughts of youth are long, long thoughts.
[Longfellow: *My Lost Youth*]
6 Blessings on thee, little man,
Barefoot boy, with cheek of tan.
[J. G. Whittier: *The Barefoot Boy*]
7 Boys will be boys. [E. G. Bulwer-Lytton: *The Caxtons* XV.i.]
This is a fairly recent proverb but, apparently, it was established by 1849.
8 When I was a boy with never a crack in my heart.
[William Butler Yeats: *The Meditation of the Old Fisherman*]

BOY BLUE
9 Little Boy Blue,
Come blow your horn,
The sheep's in the meadow,
The cow's in the corn;
But where is the boy
Who looks after the sheep?
He's under a haycock,
Fast asleep.
[Nursery rhyme: earliest printed version, 1760]
Some scholars think the poem is a veiled allusion to Cardinal Wolsey (1475?-1530). There is a definite allusion to the poem in King Lear *(III.vi.) (1607).*

BRAGGART
10 A' never broke any man's head but his own, and that was against a post when he was drunk. [Shakespeare: *Henry V* III.ii.]

BRAIN
11 Proceeding from the heat-oppressed brain.
[Shakespeare: *Macbeth* II.i.]
12 BRAIN. An apparatus with which we think that we think. [Ambrose Bierce: *The Devil's Dictionary*]

BRANCH
13 Cut is the branch that might have grown full straight,
And burned is Apollo's laurel bough,
That sometime grew within this learned man.
[Christopher Marlowe: *Doctor Faustus*: Concluding chorus]
sometime = *formerly*

BRAND
14 And ye were as a firebrand plucked out of the burning. [Amos IV:11]
15 Is not this a brand plucked out of the fire? [Zechariah 3:2]
Usually heard as "a brand plucked from the burning." A brand was a live coal.

BRAVE
16 Fortune favors the brave. [Terence: *Phormio* I.iv.]
Terence's wording is: Fortes fortuna adjuvat. *The same thought appears in Vergil* (Aeneid *X.284.*): Audentes fortuna juvat (*"Fortune helps the daring"*), *and Claudianus* (Epistolae *IV.9.*): Fors juvat audentes.
17 None but the brave deserves the fair. [Dryden: *Alexander's Feast*]
None but the brave desert the fair.
Addison Mizner
18 How sleep the brave, who sink to rest
By all their country's wishes bless'd!
[William Collins: *Ode Written in the Year 1746* I]

BREACH

1 Ye shall know my breach of promise.
[Numbers 14:34]

> *The translators of the Revised Stand-
> ard Version, shocked at God's perfidy,
> changed this to "you shall know my dis-
> pleasure." If we may rely on Job 42:7,
> they very well may.*

2 Once more unto the breach, dear
friends.
[Shakespeare: *Henry V* III.i.]

> *When the walls of a besieged town had
> been breached, either by sapping or di-
> rect battering, the besiegers faced their
> most dangerous moment, for the breach
> had to be entered and would be fiercely
> defended by the besieged who, in such
> an action, were usually desperate and
> had all the advantages.*
>
> *This was "the imminent deadly
> breach" in which the warrior Othello
> had had hairbreadth escapes, the account
> of which so fascinated the gentle Des-
> demona. It was in Badajoz's breaches
> that Hood's Ben Battle left his legs and
> earned the scorn of faithless Nelly Gray.*
>
> *King Henry's "dear friends" reminds
> us that in his* Dictionary for the Use of
> Kings *Voltaire defined my dear friend as
> "I have need of you."*

3 A custom more honored in the breach
than the observance.
[Shakespeare: *Hamlet* I.iv.]

> *i.e., a custom which is more honorable
> to disregard than to continue.*
> *See* TO THE MANNER BORN

BREAD

4 Cast thy bread upon the waters: for
thou shalt find it after many days. [Ec-
clesiastes 11:1]

5 But he answered and said, It is written, Man shall not live by bread alone,
but by every word that proceedeth out of
the mouth of God. [Matthew 4:4]

> *It is so written in Deuteronomy 8:3:
> Man doth not live by bread only, but by
> every word that proceedeth out of the
> mouth of the Lord doth man live.*
> *The statement is repeated in Luke 4:4.*

6 What man is there of you, whom if
his son ask bread, will he give him a
stone? [Matthew 7:9]

7 The people that had once bestowed
commands, consulships, legions, and all

else, now . . . longs eagerly for just two
things, bread and circus games. [Juve-
nal: *Satires* X.lxxviii.]

> *The Latin is* panem et circenses.

8 I know on which side my bread is
buttered. [John Heywood: *Proverbs*
(1546)]

9 Better halfe a loafe than no bread.
[William Camden: *Remains,* "Proverbs"]

10 I won't quarrel with my bread and
butter. [Jonathan Swift: *Polite Conversation* I (1738)]

> *The appearance of some well-known ex-
> pression in Jonathan Swift's* A Complete
> Collection of Genteel and Ingenious Con-
> versation *(1738) does not mean, as many
> collections of quotations would lead
> their readers to assume, that the phrase
> originated* there, *but that it was already
> threadbare in 1738. For the* Polite Con-
> versation *is a pastiche of clichés. That's
> its whole point—that the upper classes,
> those who set the tone of court and po-
> lite society, haven't a fresh thought or
> a fresh expression but think and speak
> only in stereotypes.*

11 A loaf of bread, the Walrus said,
  Is what we chiefly need:
Pepper and vinegar besides
  Are very good indeed.
[Lewis Carroll: *Through the Looking
Glass,* "The Walrus and the Carpen-
ter," IV]

BREAST

12 The yielding marble of her snowy
breast.
[Edmund Waller: *On a Lady Passing
through a Crowd*]

BREATH

13 I'll keep my breath to cool my porridge. [Thomas Deloney: *Gentle Craft*
II.iii.]

14 Spare your breath to cool your porridge. [Cervantes: *Don Quixote* II.v.]

> *And also Rabelais:* Works *V.28. —show-
> ing that it was an established proverb
> in France and Spain by the end of the
> 16th century.*
>
> *This sentence, however, is an inter-
> polation by the English translator (1693).
> The older form of the proverb in Eng-
> lish had been* pottage. Porridge *is a
> "corruption" of* pottage.

BREECH

1 There is nothing more vayne . . .
Than to beg a breeche of a bare arst
man.

[John Heywood: *Proverbs* (1546)]

BREVITY

2 I labor to be brief—and manage to
be obscure.
[Horace: *Ars poetica* XXV]
3 What's the use of brevity when there's
a whole book of it? [Martial: *Epigrams*
VIII.xxix.]
4 Brevity is the soul of wit.
[Shakespeare: *Hamlet* II.ii.]
5 Dear Sir, be short and sweet.
[John Fletcher: *The Scornful Lady*
II.i.]
6 For brevity is very good,
Where we are, or are not understood.
[Samuel Butler (1612-1680): *Hudibras*]
7 Brevity is the soul of lingerie.
*Attr. Dorothy Parker, when she was
working in an advertising agency, 1920.*

BRIAR PATCH

8 Bred en bawn in a brier-patch, Brer
Fox. [Joel Chandler Harris: *Uncle Remus* IV]

BRICKS

9 Ye shall no more give the people straw
to make brick as heretofore: let them go
and gather straw for themselves. [Exo-
dus 5:7]
*Pharaoh so commanded his taskmasters
in order to make things even harder for
the overworked Israelites; they had to
make the same number of bricks as before, but they must now gather their
own straw, formerly furnished them. But
the passage is often misquoted today as
"bricks without straw" or "making bricks
without straw." The bricks were still
made with straw, but the Israelites had
to provide the straw.*

BRIDE

10 The bride hath paced into the hall,
Red as a rose is she.
[Coleridge: *The Ancient Mariner* I]

BRIDGE

11 Now who will stand on either hand,
And keep the bridge with me?

[Macaulay: *Lays of Ancient Rome*, "Horatius," XXIX]
12 By the rude bridge that arched the
flood,
Their flag to April's breeze un-
furl'd;
Here once the embattl'd farmers
stood,
And fired the shot heard round the
world.
[Emerson: *Hymn sung at the completion
of the Concord Monument*]
13 Don't cross the bridge till you come
to it,
Is a proverb old, and of excellent wit.
[Longfellow: *The Golden Legend*, VI.
"The School of Salerno"]

BRIGHTNESS

14 Brightness falls from the air;
Queens have died young and fair.
[Thomas Nashe: *In Time of Pestilence*]
15 Dark with excessive bright.
[John Milton: *Paradise Lost* III.380]

BRILLIG

16 'Twas brillig, and the slithy toves
Did gyre and gimble in the wabe;
All mimsy were the borogoves,
And the mome raths outgrabe.
[Lewis Carroll: *Through the Looking
Glass*, "Jabberwocky"]
*Humpty Dumpty explained to Alice that
brillig = four o'clock in the afternoon,
that slithy was a "portmanteau" combination of lithe and slimy, that to gyre was
to go round and round like a gyroscope
and that to gimble is to make holes like
a gimlet. Wabe is the open space that
goes way before a sun dial, etc.*
*Though Lewis Carroll was being ra-
ther laboriously funny, the tendencies of
the language which he uses in Jabberwocky are legitimate tendencies. Words
are made in just these ways.*

BRINKMANSHIP

17 Dryden delighted to tread upon the
brink of meaning. [Samuel Johnson:
Life of Dryden]
18 We're eye-ball to eye-ball and the
other fellow just blinked. [Dean Rusk,
Saturday Evening Post, Dec. 8, 1962]
*The incident referred to was the con-
frontation with Russia concerning the
missile crisis in Cuba.*

1 Local defense must be reinforced by the further deterrent of massive retaliatory power. [John Foster Dulles, speaking before the Council on Foreign Relations, Jan. 12, 1954]

Mr. Dulles, President Eisenhower's Secretary of State, invented a form of diplomatic Russian roulette known as brinkmanship. He was a master of fascinating and frightening phraseology, threatening our allies with "agonizing re-appraisal" and our enemies with "massive retaliation." Tension dissolved into laughter, however, when he threatened to "unleash Chiang Kai-shek."

BRITANNIA

2 When Britain first, at Heaven's command,
    Arose from out the azure main,
This was the charter of the land,
    And guardian angels sung this strain—
"Rule, Britannia, rule the waves;
Britons never will be slaves."
[James Thomson (1700-1748): "Rule Britannia," in *Alfred, A Masque* (1740)]

3 Britannia, the pride of the ocean,
    The home of the brave and the free,
The shrine of the sailor's devotion,
    No land can compare unto thee!
[David Taylor Shaw: *The Red, White, and Blue*]

Sung with great success in England. In America, the first line was changed to "Columbia, the gem of the Ocean," and the song was an even greater success. But one is a little shocked by the facility of the change.

BRITISH

4 Pride in their port, defiance in their eye,
I see the lords of humankind pass by.
[Oliver Goldsmith: *The Traveller*]

The reference—with their full approval —was to the 18th-century British.

5 And curving a contumelious lip,
Gorgonized me from head to foot
With a stony British stare.
[Tennyson: *Maud* XIII.ii.]

BRITISH GRENADIER

6 Some talk of Alexander, and some of Hercules;
Of Hector and Lysander, and such great names as these;
But of all the world's brave heroes, there's none that can compare,
With a tow, row, row, row, row, row, for the British Grenadier.
[Anon.: *The British Grenadier*]

BROAD-MINDED

7 Broad-mindedness is the result of flattening high-mindedness out. [George Saintsbury (attr.)]

BROADWAY

8 Give my regards to Broadway,
    Remember me to Herald Square,
Tell all the gang at Forty-second Street
    That I will soon be there.
[George M. Cohan: *Give My Regards to Broadway*]

BROOK

9 A noise like of a hidden brook
In the leafy month of June,
That to the sleeping woods all night
Singeth a quiet tune.
[Coleridge: *The Ancient Mariner* V]

10 I come from haunts of coot and hern,
    I make a sudden sally,
And sparkle out among the fern,
    To bicker down a valley.
[Tennyson: *The Brook*]

11 For men may come and men may go,
But I go on forever.
[Tennyson: *The Brook*]

BROOM

12 New Brome swepth cleene. [John Heywood: *Proverbs* (1546)]

BROTHELS

13 Keep thy foot out of brothels, thy hand out of plackets, thy pen from lenders' books, and defy the foul fiend. [Shakespeare: *King Lear* III.iv.]

placket = an opening in a woman's dress

BROTHER(S)

14 Am I my brother's keeper? [Genesis 4:9]

Cain's answer to God, when God de-

mands of him *"Where is thy brother Abel?"*

1 The younger brother hath the more wit. [John Ray: *English Proverbs*]
In the times when primogeniture was the rule, the younger brother was resentful but dependent; wit was likely to be his sole resource. Our word cad originally meant a younger brother.

2 Then let us pray that come it may,
As come it will for a' that;
That sense and worth o'er a' the earth,
May bear the gree, and a' that.
For a' that and a' that,
It's coming yet, for a' that,
That man to man the warld o'er
Shall brothers be for a' that.
[Burns: *For a' that and a' that*]
bear the gree = *bear off the prize*

JOHN BROWN

3 John Brown's body lies a-mouldering in the grave,
His soul is marching on!
[Attr. Thomas Brigham Bishop, H. H. Brownell, Frank E. Jerome and Charles Sprague Hall, and sometimes listed—and perhaps most wisely—as anonymous.]
The tune was an old one, and apparently the original words were altered and added to by many.

BROWNING

4 Meredith is a prose Browning, and so is Browning. [Oscar Wilde: *The Critic as Artist*]

BRUTUS

5 *Et tu, Brute?* ("And thou, Brutus?")
[Shakespeare: *Julius Caesar* III.i.]
It is from Shakespeare that these, Caesar's reputed last words, have passed into the vocabulary of the ordinary speaker of English. Shakespeare took the Latin phrase from North's translation of Plutarch, though the actual words, as recorded in Suetonius (Divus Julius, LXXXII), are said to have been spoken in Greek and to have been "And thou, Brutus, my child!"
Plutarch's Life of Marcus Brutus *says that Caesar had had a love affair with Servilia, Brutus's mother, and believed*

Brutus to be his own son. Others believed so too. See Suetonius, Divus Julius L.

6 Brutus seemed no more than a resounding set of vocal cords wrapped up in a toga. [John Mason Brown: *Two on the Aisle*]

BRYAN, WILLIAM JENNINGS

7 A somewhat greasy bald-headed man with his mouth open. [H. L. Mencken: *Damn! A Book of Calumny*]

BUCKET

8 The nations are as a drop of a bucket, and are counted as the small dust of the balance. [Isaiah 40:15]

9 Now up, now doun, as boket in a welle.
[Chaucer: *The Knight's Tale*]

10 The old oaken bucket, the iron-bound bucket,
The moss-covered bucket, which hung in the well.
[Samuel Woodworth: *The Old Oaken Bucket*]

BUCKINGHAM PALACE

11 They're changing guard at Buckingham Palace—
Christopher Robin went down with Alice.
[A. A. Milne: *When We Were Very Young*, "Buckingham Palace"]

BUGBEARS

12 It is the test of reason and refinement to be able to exist without bugbears. [William Hazlitt: *Emancipation of the Jews*]

BUGS

13 Thou shalt not nede to be afrayed for eny bugges by night. [Psalms 91:5]
The Coverdale (1535) translation. The King James version (1611) has: "Thou shalt not be afraid for the terror by night." And the Revised Standard (1952) has: "You will not fear the terror of the night." In Great Britain the word bug *has now become specialized to mean bedbug and this throws on Coverdale a meaning never intended.*
A bug *was a bugaboo, something frightening, and it was, as here, capable*

of serious and even solemn use. In Shakespeare's III Henry VI *(V.ii.), King Edward says of the Earl of Warwick, "Warwick was a bug that fear'd us all," meaning "Warwick was a bugaboo that frightened us all."*

BUILDING

1 He that buys a house ready wrought
Hath many a pin and nail for nought.
[William Camden: *Remains*]
   That is, it is cheaper to buy than to build.

BULK

2 It is not growing like a tree
   In bulk, doth make men better be.
[Ben Jonson: *Ode on the Death of Sir H. Morison*]

BULL

3 There is one distinguishing peculiarity of the Irish bull—its horns are tipped with brass. [Maria Edgeworth: *Essay on Irish Bulls* (1802)]
   These ludicrous incongruities now generally ascribed to the Irish ("I'm an atheist, God help me!"; "Me mother had no children, God rest her soul!"; "God bless the Trinity!") were formerly called simply bulls *(possibly from O. Fr.* boule, *deceit). Under the English tyranny the Irish peasant often played the fool and loosed his shafts of resentment only when hidden in a joke or made to seem absurd. Yet there was frequently impertinence under the absurdity—as Maria Edgeworth states. There was also likely to be a serious meaning, as Professor Tyrrell wittily remarked when he said that an Irish bull differed from other bulls in that it was always pregnant.*

BULLET

4 Every bullet has its billet.
   In Laurence Sterne's Tristram Shandy *(VIII.XIX. 1760) this is assigned to King William III of England (1689-1702). William was a soldier and a fatalist and may well have said it. The actual form given above appears, as a quotation and ascribed to William, in John Wesley's* Journal *(1765).*

BULLOCKS

5 How can he get wisdom that holdeth the plough . . . and whose talk is of bullocks? [Ecclesiasticus 38:25]

BUM

6 Oh, why don't you work like other men do?
   How the hell can I work when there's no work to do?
   Hallelujah, I'm a bum, hallelujah, bum again,
   Hallelujah, give us a handout to revive us again.
[Anon.: *Hallelujah, I'm a Bum*]

BUNK

7 Parliament speaking through reporters to Buncombe. [Thomas Carlyle: *Latter-Day Pamphlets*, VI, "Parliaments"]
   Our bunk ("dishonest nonsense") is a contraction of Buncombe. It came into the language in 1820 when Representative Felix Walker, from Buncombe County, North Carolina, justified the irrelevance of one of his speeches in Congress by saying that it wasn't intended for his colleagues but for his constituents, that he was talking "only for Buncombe."
   Carlyle's Latter-Day Pamphlets *were published in 1850. It is interesting that American slang was, even then, crossing the Atlantic.*

8 When a statesman is not talking bunk he is making trouble for himself. [G. B. Shaw: *On the Rocks*]

BURDEN(S)

9 Borne the burden and heat of the day. [Matthew 20:12]
10 Bear ye one another's burdens. [Galatians 6:2]
11 Take up the White Man's burden—
    Send forth the best ye breed—
   Go bind your sons to exile
    To serve your captives' need;
   To wait, in heavy harness,
    On fluttered folk and wild—
   Your new-caught, sullen peoples,
    Half-devil and half-child.
[Kipling: *The White Man's Burden*]

BURGLAR

12 When the enterprising burglar's not a-burgling,
   When the cutthroat isn't occupied in crime,

He loves to hear the little brook
a-gurgling,
And to listen to the merry village
chime.
[W. S. Gilbert: *The Pirates of Penzance* II]

BURIAL

1 Earth to earth, ashes to ashes, dust to dust; in sure and certain hope of the Resurrection. [*The Book of Common Prayer:* Burial of the Dead]
2 Call for the robin redbreast and the
wren,
Since o'er shady groves they hover,
And with leaves and flowers do cover
The friendless bodies of unburied
men.
[John Webster: *The White Devil* V.iv. (dirge)]
3 Slowly and sadly we laid him down,
From the field of his fame fresh and
gory;
We carved not a line, and we raised
not a stone,
But we left him alone with his
glory.
[Charles Wolfe: *The Burial of Sir John Moore*]

BURIAL SERVICE

4 One of the crying needs of the time is for a suitable Burial Service for the admittedly damned. [H. L. Mencken: *Prejudices: Sixth Series*]

BURIED

5 And those who husbanded the
Golden grain,
And those who flung it to the winds
like Rain,
Alike to no such aureate Earth are
turned
As, buried once, Men want dug up
again.
[*Rubáiyát of Omar Khayyám* (trans. Edward FitzGerald)]

BURKE, EDMUND

6 Burke, sir, is such a man, that if you met him for the first time in a street where you were stopped by a drove of oxen, and you and he stepped aside to take shelter but for five minutes, he'd talk to you in such a manner, that, when you parted, you would say, this is an extraordinary man. [Samuel Johnson: in Boswell's *A Tour to the Hebrides,* August 15, 1773]

BURNS, ROBERT

7 The poor inhabitant below
Was quick to learn and wise to
know,
And keenly felt the friendly glow,
And softer flame;
But thoughtless follies laid him low,
And stain'd his name.
[Burns: *A Bard's Epitaph*]

BURY

8 History is on our side. We will bury you! [Nikita Khrushchev, to Western ambassadors at a reception in the Kremlin, Nov. 17, 1956]
This remark was widely and persistently exploited by anti-communists who interpreted it to mean "We will kill you—and then bury you." Khrushchev himself repeatedly insisted (as at the National Press Club in Washington, Sept. 17, 1959) that he simply meant that, in his opinion, Communism was more vital than Capitalism and would outlive it.

BUSINESS

9 To business that we love we rise betime,
And go to 't with delight.
[Shakespeare: *Antony and Cleopatra* IV.iv.]
10 In business the keeping close to the matter and not taking of it too much at once, procureth dispatch. [Francis Bacon: *Of Dispatch*]
11 I remember that a wise friend of mine did usually say, "That which is everybody's business is nobody's business." [Izaak Walton: *The Compleat Angler* I.ii.]
12 The first Mistake in public Business, is the going into it. [Benjamin Franklin: *Poor Richard's Almanack* (1758)]
13 No man can see all with his own eyes or do all with his own hands. Whoever is engaged in multiplicity of business must transact much by substitution and leave something to hazard, and he who attempts to do all will waste his life in do-

ing little. [Samuel Johnson: *The Idler* No. 19]

1 Business is business. [George Colman the Younger: *The Heir-at-Law* III]

2 "If everybody minded their own business," the Duchess said, in a hoarse growl, "the world would go round a great deal faster than it does." [Lewis Carroll: *Alice's Adventures in Wonderland* Ch. VI]

3 Perpetual devotion to what a man calls his business, is only to be sustained by perpetual neglect of many other things. [R. L. Stevenson: *An Apology for Idlers,* III.]

4 The maxim of the British people is "Business as usual." [Sir Winston Churchill: in a speech at the Guild-hall, London, Nov. 9, 1914]

5 The business of America is business. [Calvin Coolidge: in a speech before the Society of American Newspaper Editors, Washington, Jan. 17, 1925]

BUSINESSMAN

6 He [the businessman] is the only man above the hangman and the scavenger who is forever apologizing for his occupation. He is the only one who always seeks to make it appear, when he attains the object of his labors, *i.e.*, the making of a great deal of money, that it was not the object of his labors. [H. L. Mencken: in the *Smart Set*, February 1921]

BUSY

7 No-wher so bisy a man as he ther nas,
And yet he semed bisier than he was.
[Chaucer: Prologue to *The Canterbury Tales*]
nas = *was not. The feeling against double negatives is very recent.*
Several likenesses to George F. Babbitt can be detected in Chaucer's businessman.

BUTTER

8 She brought forth butter in a lordly dish. [Judges 5:25]

9 It is not all butter that the cow drops. [John Heywood: *Proverbs* (1546)]

10 She looketh as butter would not melte in hir mouth. [John Heywood: *Proverbs* (1546)]
Today it is always a feminine mouth

that butter won't melt in, but formerly the expression was applied to men and women. It is spoken of someone who, in the speaker's opinion, is nowhere near so demure as he—and for the past 200 years more especially she—looks. Swift, in Polite Conversation (1738), a collection of jaded phrases, gives it as "She looks as if butter wouldn't melt in her mouth but, I warrant, cheese won't choke her." That is, "She appears to be cold and fastidious but, in reality, nothing's too strong or gross for her."*

BUTTERCUP

11 I'm called little Buttercup,
Dear little Buttercup,
Though I could never tell why.
[W. S. Gilbert: *H. M. S. Pinafore* I]

BUTTERFLY

12 Who breaks a butterfly upon a wheel? [Alexander Pope: *Epistle to Dr. Arbuthnot*]

BUYER

13 Let the buyer beware. (*Caveat emptor*) [Roman legal maxim]
In many ways a noble and manly statement.

BUYING

14 A woman is always buying something. [Ovid: *Ars amatoria* I]

BYRON

15 Even I—albeit I'm sure I did not know it,
Nor sought of foolscap subjects to be king—
Was reckon'd, a considerable time,
The grand Napoleon of the realms of rhyme.
[Byron: *Don Juan* XI.lv.]

16 Lord Byron is only great as a poet; as soon as he reflects, he is a child. [Goethe: *Conversations with Eckermann*, Jan. 18, 1825]

17 The Pilgrim of Eternity. [Shelley: *Adonais* XXX]

18 From the poetry of Lord Byron they drew a system of ethics compounded of misanthropy and voluptuousness—a system in which the two great commandments were to hate your neighbour and to love your neighbour's wife. [Macaulay: *On Moore's Life of Lord Byron*]

1 What helps it now, that Byron bore,
  With haughty scorn which mock'd the
                                smart,
  Through Europe to the Aetolian
                                shore
  The pageant of his bleeding heart?
  That thousands counted every groan,
  And Europe made his woe her own?
[Matthew Arnold: *The Grande Chartreuse*]

2 The power of Byron's personality lies in the splendid and imperishable excellence which covers all his offences and outweighs all his defects: *the excellence of sincerity and strength.* [Swinburne: *Byron*]

3 "Lord Byron" was an Englishman,
    A poet I believe,
  His first works in old England
    Was poorly received.
  Perhaps it was "Lord Byron's" fault
    And perhaps it was not.
  His life was full of misfortunes,
    Ah, strange was his lot.
[Julia A. Moore: *Sketch of Lord Byron's Life*]

C

CAD

1 The most disgusting cad in the world is the man who, on the grounds of decorum and morality, avoids the game of love. [H. L. Mencken: in *Smart Set*, May 1919]

CAESAR

2 Render therefore unto Caesar the things which are Caesar's; and unto God the things that are God's. [Matthew 22:21]
> *The same thought is expressed also in Mark 12:17 and Luke 20:25.*

3 I appeal unto Caesar. [Acts 25:11]

4 Caesar or nothing? We're nothing loath
So to acclaim him: Caesar Borgia's both.
[Jacopo Sannazaro: *De Cesare Borgia*]
> *Aut Caesar aut nihil ("Either Caesar or nothing") was Caesar Borgia's motto. Fate's final answer was: nothing.*

5 Upon what meat doth this our Caesar feed,
That he is grown so great?
[Shakespeare: *Julius Caesar* I.ii]

6 Imperious Caesar, dead and turn'd to clay,
Might stop a hole to keep the wind away.
[Shakespeare: *Hamlet* V.i.]

CAIN

7 As the inventor of murder, and the father of art, Cain must have been a man of first-rate genius. [Thomas De Quincey: *On Murder Considered as One of the Fine Arts*]

CAKE

8 Dost thou think, because thou art virtuous, there shall be no more cakes and ale? [Shakespeare: *Twelfth Night* II.iii.]

9 Couldst thou both eat thy cake and have it? [George Herbert: *The Church*, "The Size"]
> *This was an established proverb.*

10 Pat-a-cake, pat-a-cake, baker's man,
Bake me a cake as fast as you can;
Pat it and prick it, and mark it with B,
And put it in the oven for Baby and Me.
[Nursery rhyme: child's clapping rhyme; earliest known date, 1698]

11 Let them eat cake.
> *The ascription of this saying to Marie Antoinette, on her being told that the poor had no bread, has been one of the supreme successes of propaganda.*
>
> *The famous saying first appeared in the sixth book of Rousseau's* Confessions, *where it is attributed to "a great princess." The date of composition of the* Confessions *is uncertain, but 1766 is commonly accepted for at least this part of it. This was four years before Marie Antoinette, then a child of eleven, came to France. And from the context it is plain that Rousseau had heard the saying by 1740, eleven years before her birth.*
>
> *"Cake" is an improvement on the original, which was* brioche.

CALAIS

12 When I am dead and opened, you shall find "Calais" lying in my heart. [Queen Mary I (of England): in Holinshed's *Chronicle* III]
> *The English held Calais from 1347 to 1558 and as long as they held it dreamed of conquering France again. All kings of England in their official titles designated themselves as Kings of France, down through George III (d. 1820). The loss of this seaport-fortress was one of the worst blows that Mary sustained in her brief and tragic reign (1553-1558).*

CALAMITY(IES)

13 Affliction is enamour'd of thy parts,
And thou art wedded to calamity.
[Shakespeare: *Romeo and Juliet* III. iii.]

14 If Mr. Gladstone fell in the Thames, that would be a misfortune. If someone fished him out, that would be a calamity.

[Attr. Benjamin Disraeli: when someone asked him the difference between a calamity and a misfortune.]

1 Calamities are of two kinds: misfortune to ourselves, and good fortune to others. [Ambrose Bierce: *The Devil's Dictionary*]

CALIFORNIA

2 I met a Californian who would
  Talk California—a state so blessed,
He said, in climate, none had ever
              died there
A natural death, and Vigilance Committees
  Had had to organize to stock the
              graveyards
And vindicate the state's humanity.
[Robert Frost: *New Hampshire*]

CALM

3 His servants He, with new acquist
  Of true experience from this great
              event,
With peace and consolation hath dismissed,
  And calm of mind, all passion spent.
[John Milton: *Samson Agonistes* (concluding lines)]

4 The seas are quiet, when the winds
              give o'er;
So calm are we, when passions are no
              more.
[Edmund Waller: *Of the Last Verses in the Book*]

5 Ne'er saw I, never felt, a calm so
              deep!
The river glideth at his own sweet
              will:
Dear God! the very houses seem
              asleep;
And all that mighty heart is lying
              still!
[Wordsworth: *Composed Upon Westminster Bridge*]

6 And, through the heat of conflict,
              keeps the law
In calmness made, and sees what he
              foresaw.
[Wordsworth: *Character of the Happy Warrior*]

7 There is no joy but calm.
[Tennyson: *The Lotos-Eaters*]

8 Calm's not life's crown, though calm
              is well.

'Tis all perhaps which man acquires,
But 'tis not what our youth desires.
[Matthew Arnold: *Youth and Calm*]

CALUMNY

9 Nothing is so swift as calumny; nothing is more easily uttered; nothing more readily received; nothing more widely dispersed. [Cicero: *Pro Cnaeo Plancio* XXIII]

10 Be thou as chaste as ice, as pure as snow, thou shalt not escape calumny. [Shakespeare: *Hamlet* III.i.]

11 To spread suspicion, to invent calumnies, to propagate scandal, requires neither labor nor courage. It is easy for the author of a lie, however malignant, to escape detection, and infamy needs very little industry to assist its circulation. [Samuel Johnson: *The Rambler* No. 183]

12 A man's reputation is not in his own keeping, but lies at the mercy of the profligacy of others. Calumny requires no proof. The throwing out of malicious imputations against any character leaves a stain, which no after-refutation can wipe out. To create an unfavorable impression, it is not necessary that certain things should be *true,* but that they *have been said.* [William Hazlitt: *Essays, Characteristics*]

CALVINISM

13 You will and you won't—You'll be
              damned if you do—
  And you'll be damned if you don't.
[Lorenzo Dow (1777-1834): *Reflections on the Love of God*]
  A definition of Calvinism.

CAMOMILE

14 The camomile, the more it is trodden on the faster it grows. [Shakespeare: *I Henry IV* II.iv.]
  This was a conviction of medieval pseudo-botany that persisted because it was a useful parable applied with unremitting cheerfulness by the unscathed to the unfortunate. See also: BEAT.

CANDID

15 Whenever one has anything unpleasant to say, one should always be quite candid. [Oscar Wilde: *The Importance of Being Earnest* II]

CANDLE(S)

1 Neither do men light a candle, and put it under a bushel. [Matthew 5:15]
2 The game is not worth the candle. [Montaigne: *Essays* II.xvii.]
A saying which appeared in many slightly varying forms in English before and after Montaigne (1580). The meaning is that there is not enough at stake, or to be gained, to pay the necessary expenses of the undertaking. Or, more generally, the risks are far too great for any possible gain.
3 How far that little candle throws his beams!
So shines a good deed in a naughty world.
[Shakespeare: *The Merchant of Venice* V.i.]
4 It is a poor sport that is not worth the candle. [George Herbert: *Jacula Prudentum*]
5 To burn the candle at both ends. [Alain René Le Sage: *Gil Blas* VII.xv.]
6 My candle burns at both ends;
It will not last the night;
But, ah, my foes, and, oh, my friends—
It gives a lovely light.
[Edna St. Vincent Millay: *Figs from Thistles*, "First Fig"]
7 She would rather light candles than curse the darkness. [Adlai Stevenson: in a eulogy to Eleanor Roosevelt in the United Nations General Assembly, November 9, 1962]
Mr. Stevenson was paraphrasing the motto of The Christophers, a religious organization: "Better to light one candle than to curse the darkness." The Christophers identify the sentiment as "an old Chinese proverb."

CANDOR

8 Candor and generosity, unless tempered by due moderation, lead to ruin. [Tacitus: *History* III.lxxxvi.]
9 I hate him that my vices telleth me. [Chaucer: Prologue to *The Wife of Bath's Tale*]
10 A man that should call everything by its right name, would hardly pass the streets without being knocked down as a common enemy. [Lord Halifax: *Works*]
11 Give me the avowed, the erect, the manly foe,
Bold I can meet—perhaps may turn his blow;
But of all plagues, good Heaven, thy wrath can send,
Save, save, oh, save me from the Candid Friend!
[George Canning: *The New Morality*]

CANNIBALS

12 The cannibals that each other eat,
The Anthropophagi, and men whose heads
Do grow beneath their shoulders.
[Shakespeare: *Othello* I.iii.]
13 I have been assured by a very knowing American of my acquaintance in London, that a young healthy child well nursed is at a year old a most delicious, nourishing, and wholesome food, whether stewed, roasted, baked or boiled, and I make no doubt that it will equally serve in a fricassee or a ragout. [Jonathan Swift: *A Modest Proposal*]
14 For a month we'd neither wittles nor drink,
Till a-hungry we did feel,
So we drawed a lot, and, accordin',
shot
The captain for our meal.
[W. S. Gilbert: *The Yarn of the "Nancy Bell"*]

CANOE

15 I think it much better that . . . every man paddle his own canoe. [Frederick Marryat: *Settlers in Canada* VIII]

CANT

16 My dear friend, clear your *mind* of cant. [Samuel Johnson: in Boswell's *Life*, May 15, 1783]

CAPTAIN

17 Who does i' the wars more than his captain can
Becomes his captain's captain.
[Shakespeare: *Antony and Cleopatra* III.i.]
18 O Captain! my Captain! our fearful trip is done!
The ship has weather'd every rack, the prize we sought is won,
The port is near, the bells I hear, the people all exulting.

[Walt Whitman: *Leaves of Grass*, "O Captain! My Captain!"]

CARDS

1 There be that can pack the cards, and yet cannot play well. [Francis Bacon: *Of Cunning*]

CARE

2 Care, looking grim and black, doth sit
Behind his back that rides from it.
[Montaigne: *Essays* I.xxxviii. (trans. John Florio)]
A passage from Horace.

3 Care keeps his watch in every old man's eye,
And where care lodges, sleep will never lie.
[Shakespeare: *Romeo and Juliet* II.iii.]

4 Euripides did well and wisely say
Man's life and care are twins, and born one day.
[Alexander Craig: *The Misery of Man*]

5   Care
Sat on his faded cheek, but under brows
Of dauntless courage, and considerate pride
Waiting revenge.
[John Milton: *Paradise Lost* I, 601-603]
considerate = *thoughtfully patient*

6 I care for nobody, no, not I,
If no one cares for me.
[Isaac Bickerstaffe: *Love in a Village* I.v.]

7 Ye banks and braes o' bonnie Doon,
How can ye bloom sae fresh and fair;
How can ye chant, ye little birds,
And I sae weary fu' o' care!
[Burns: *The Banks o' Doon*]

8 I could lie down like a tired child,
And weep away the life of care
Which I have borne and yet must bear.
[Shelley: *Stanzas written in dejection, near Naples*]

9 Irks care the crop-full bird? Frets doubt the maw-crammed beast?
[Robert Browning: *Rabbi Ben Ezra*]

CARGO

10 Once in three years came the navy of Tharshish, bringing gold, and silver, ivory, and apes, and peacocks. [I Kings 10:22]
Repeated in II. Chron. 10:21.

11 Quinquireme of Nineveh from distant Ophir,
Rowing home to haven in sunny Palestine,
With a cargo of ivory,
And apes and peacocks,
Sandalwood, cedarwood, and sweet white wine.
[John Masefield: *Cargoes*]
In the next stanza Masefield compares this gorgeous and romantic cargo with the "firewood, ironware, and cheap tin trays" of a modern coaster. A quinquireme *was a galley with five banks of oars.*

CARPE DIEM

12 Seize the day. (*Carpe diem*) [Horace: *Odes* I.xi.]
One of the most famous of quotations. The meaning is: Live in the immediate present, since you have no assurance of the future.

13 He that will not when he may,
When he will he shall have nay.
[Robert Burton: *The Anatomy of Melancholy* III.ii.5]
Where it is quoted as a popular jingle.

14 Gather ye rosebuds while ye may,
Old Time is still a-flying:
And this same flower that smiles today,
To-morrow will be dying.
[Robert Herrick: *To the Virgins, to Make Much of Time*]

15 Then be not coy, but use your time,
And while ye may, go marry:
For having lost but once your prime,
You may for ever tarry.
[Robert Herrick: *To the Virgins, to Make Much of Time*]

16 Now therefore, while the youthful hue
Sits on thy skin like morning dew,
And while thy willing soul transpires
At every pore instant fires,
Now let us sport us while we may,
And now, like amorous birds of prey,
Rather at once our time devour
Than languish in his slow-chapt power.
Let us roll all our strength and all
Our sweetness up into one ball,

And tear our pleasures with rough
                strife
Through the iron gates of life.
[Andrew Marvell: *To His Coy Mistress*]
1 Ah, my Beloved, fill the Cup that
                clears
To-day of past Regret and future
                Fears:
To-morrow!—Why, To-morrow I
                may be
Myself with Yesterday's Seven thou-
                sand Years.
[*Rubáiyát of Omar Khayyám* (trans. Ed-
ward FitzGerald)]

CARTHAGE
2 Carthage must be destroyed. (*Delenda
est Carthago*) [Marcus Cato: in Plutarch's *Lives,* "Marcus Cato"]
    *The destruction of Carthage became an
    obsession with Cato and he concluded
    all speeches and even signed letters with
    this formula.*

CASEY
3 Oh! somewhere in this favored land
        the sun is shining bright;
The band is playing somewhere, and
        somewhere hearts are light;
And somewhere men are laughing
        and somewhere children shout,
But there is no joy in Mudville—
        mighty Casey has struck out.
[E. L. Thayer: *Casey at the Bat*]

CASEY JONES
4 Casey Jones, he mounted to the cabin,
Casey Jones, with his orders in his
        hand!
Casey Jones, he mounted to the cabin,
Took his farewell trip into the pro-
        mised land.
[*Casey Jones:* author unknown]
    *John Luther Jones (called Casey because
    he came from Cayce, Kentucky) was the
    engineer of the ill-fated Illinois Cen-
    tral's "Cannonball" Express and was
    killed in the wreck of that famous train
    on April 30, 1900. The song is believed
    to have been composed by his Negro
    engine-wiper, Wallace Saunders, but this
    cannot be definitely established. The
    comfort his widow offers her children
    in the concluding lines ("You got another
    daddy on the Salt Lake Line") was, late*

*in her life, considered libellous by Mrs.
Jones and is discreetly dropped from
some versions.*

CASH
5 Cash-payment is not the sole nexus of
man with man. [Thomas Carlyle: *Past
and Present* III.ix.]
6 Some for the Glories of this World;
        and some
Sigh for the Prophet's Paradise to
        come;
Ah, take the cash, and let the Credit
        go,
Nor heed the rumble of a distant
        Drum!
[*Rubáiyát of Omar Khayyám* (trans. Edward FitzGerald)]

CASSOWARY
7 If I were a Cassowary
    On the plains of Timbuctoo,
I would eat a missionary,
    Coat and bands and hymn-book
        too.
[Bishop Samuel Wilberforce: *Epigram*]

CASTLES
8 Thou shalt make castles then in
        Spain,
And dream of joy, all but in vain.
[Chaucer: *Romaunt of the Rose*]
    *The first known use of the phrase "cas-
    tles in Spain." But the text makes it
    evident that it was already a phrase with
    its present meaning.*
9 Build castles in the air. [Robert Burton: *Anatomy of Melancholy* I.2.1.3.]
10 Castles in the air—they are so easy to
take refuge in. And so easy to build, too.
[Henrik Ibsen: *The Master Builder* III]
11 A neurotic is the man who builds a
castle in the air. A psychotic is the man
who lives in it. And a psychiatrist is the
man who collects the rent. [Lord Webb-
Johnson, *Look,* October 4, 1955]

CAT(S)
12 Who'll bell the cat? [Attr. Aesop,
though not known before *Piers Plowman*
(1362-1399)]
    *The fable is alluded to today as if its
    moral was that heroism conquers all
    difficulties. But the earlier moral was
    "It's easy to propose impossible reme-
    dies."*

1 Lat take a cat, and fostre him wel
with milk
And tendre flesh, and make his couche
of silk,
And lat him see a mouse go by the
wal,
Anon he weyveth milk, and flesh, and
al,
And every deyntee which is in that
hous,
Swich appetyt hath he to ete a mous.
[Chaucer: *The Manciple's Tale*]

2 A cat may looke on a King. [John Heywood: *Proverbs* (1546)]

3 A Cat May Look at a King. [Title of a pamphlet (published 1652)]

4 The cat would eat fish but would not wet her feet.
This is "the poor cat i' th' adage" to which Lady Macbeth (I.vii.) scornfully compared her lord for "Letting 'I dare not' wait upon 'I would.' "

5 When I am playing with my cat, who knows whether she have more sport in dallying with me than I have in gaming with her? [Montaigne: *Essays* II.xii.]

6 A cat in gloves catches no mice. [16th-century proverb]

7 Nothing's more playful than a young cat, nor more grave than an old one. [Thomas Fuller (1654-1734): *Gnomologia*]

8 Hey diddle diddle,
The cat and the fiddle,
The cow jumped over the moon;
The little dog laughed
To see such sport,
And the dish ran away with the
spoon.
[Nursery rhyme: earliest printed form about 1765]
There are references, as early as 1569, which seem to point to this rhyme. But they are not certain and—despite learned efforts—no meaning or origin for it has been proved.

9 What female heart can gold despise? What cat's averse to fish?
[Thomas Gray: *On the Death of a Favourite Cat*]

10 I am pent up in frowsy lodgings, where there is not room enough to swing a cat. [Tobias Smollett: *Humphry Clinker*, June 8, 1771]
Smollett had served as a surgeon aboard

a man-of-war and cat *here* = *cat-o'-nine-tails. It was, apparently, a seaman's expression.*
Most who use the phrase assume that it refers to Felix domestica *and, it must be confessed, this is an improvement; one would want plenty of room (and courage!) to swing an alley cat or a Siamese!*

11 The woman grins like a Cheshire cat. [W. M. Thackeray: *The Newcomes* XXIV (1855)]
Lewis Carroll did not invent the Cheshire cat. Alice did not appear until ten years after the quotation above. When Alice encountered the creature in the Duchess's kitchen, its smile was already as much an enigma as the Mona Lisa's. One of the sanest conjectures of the expression's origin is that some painter of inn signs in Cheshire had depicted lions rampant—a very common inn sign—with snarls so amiable that they were taken for smiles.

12 There are more ways of killing a cat than choking her with cream. [Charles Kingsley: *Westward Ho XX*]
One hears today "There are more ways than one to skin a cat." But this merely states the obvious. The older saying, however, implies that someone has gone about some task in an expensive, foolish way—and one particularly unlikely to accomplish its purpose.

13 Cats and monkeys, monkeys and cats —all human life is there. [Henry James: *The Madonna of the Future*]

CATALOG

14 There is no stronger evidence of a crazy understanding than the making too large a catalog of things necessary. [George Savile: *Advice to a Daughter*]

CATASTROPHE

15 Pat! he comes like the catastrophe of the old comedy. [Shakespeare: *King Lear* I.ii.]

CATEGORICAL IMPERATIVE

16 There is . . . but one categorical imperative: Act only on that maxim whereby thou canst at the same time will that it should become a universal law.

[Immanuel Kant: *Fundamental Principles of Morals,* "The Categorical Imperative" Ch. I.]

CATERPILLARS
1 The caterpillars of the commonwealth. [Shakespeare: *Richard II* II.iii.]
Caterpillars is used here as a type of devouring vermin.

CATHAY
2 Better fifty years of Europe than a cycle of Cathay. [Tennyson: *Locksley Hall*]
Cathay was an old name for China. The Chinese do not applaud this sentiment.

CATHEDRALS
3   Cathedrals,
Luxury liners laden with souls,
Holding to the east their hulls of
                    stone.
[W. H. Auden: *On This Island* XVII]

CAT'S PAW
4 Pull out the chestnuts with the cat's paw. [Molière: *L'Étourdi* III.v.]
The expression, which antedates Molière and occurs in most European languages, derives from the fable of a monkey that persuaded a cat to pull a chestnut out of the fire for him. The cat got a burned paw and the monkey enjoyed the chestnut. From the same story comes the use of catspaw for one who is used by another to serve his purposes. In older versions of the fable, it was a puppy that was persuaded to take the fruitless risk, and this is so much more suitable that it is believed that cat *is simply a misunderstanding or mistranslation of the Latin* catellus, *"puppy."*

CATTLE
5 The cattle upon a thousand hills. [Psalms 50:10]
6 More than sixscore thousand persons that cannot discern between their right hand and their left hand; and also much cattle. [Jonah 4:11]
7 "O Mary, go and call the cattle home,
And call the cattle home,
And call the cattle home,
Across the sands of Dee;"
The western wind was wild and dank
                    with foam,

And all alone went she.
[Charles Kingsley: *The Sands of Dee*]

CAUSE
8 The cause is hidden, but the result is known. [Ovid: *Metamorphoses* IV]
9   And now remains
That we find out the cause of this effect;
Or rather say, the cause of this defect,
For this effect defective comes by
                    cause.
[Shakespeare: *Hamlet* II.ii.]
10 That evil is half-cured whose cause
                    we know.
[Charles Churchill: *Gotham* III]
11 Then conquer we must, for our cause
                    it is just—
And this be our motto—"In God is
                    our trust!"
[Francis Scott Key: *The Star-Spangled Banner*]

CAUTION
12 Wisely and slow; they stumble that
                    run fast.
[Shakespeare: *Romeo and Juliet* II.iii.]
13 Have more than thou showest,
Speak less than thou knowest,
Lend less than thou owest,
Ride more than thou goest,
Learn more than thou trowest,
Set less than thou throwest.
[Shakespeare: *King Lear* I.iv.]
owest = *ownest;* goest = *proceed on foot;* trowest = *believest*
The whole saying means: Don't show everything you have,| Don't tell everything you know,| Don't give away everything you have,| Don't wear yourself out any more than you have to,| Don't believe everything you hear,| Don't set everything on one throw of the dice.
14 He that cannot see well, let him go softly. [Francis Bacon: *Baconiana*]
15 What ever men for Loyalty pretend,
'Tis Wisdomes part to doubt a faithfull friend.
[Robert Herrick: *Distrust*]
16 Know, one false step is ne'er retriev'd,
And be with caution bold.
[Thomas Gray: *On the Death of a Favourite Cat*]

CAVE
17 Behold! human beings living in an

underground den . . . their legs and necks chained so that they cannot move . . . they see only their own shadows, or the shadows of one another, which the fire throws on the opposite wall of the cave. [Plato: *The Republic* VII (opening lines)]

This is the famous simile of the cave that has kept other philosophers busy interpreting it. The "lesson" is that those who are familiar with only shadows will find realities, should they be liberated and forced to face them, painful and confusing, and difficult to comprehend.

CAVIAR
1 Caviar to the general.
[Shakespeare: *Hamlet* II.ii.]
Hamlet, speaking to the players at Elsinore, recollects a play that was never acted or, if acted, only once, "for the play . . . pleas'd not the million, 'twas caviar to the general." That is, it was like caviar (a strange delicacy for which a taste must be acquired), esteemed by epicures but repugnant to the generality, to the general public.

CELEBRITY
2 When once a man has made celebrity necessary to his happiness, he has put it in the power of the weakest and most timorous malignity, if not to take away his satisfaction, at least to withhold it. His enemies may indulge their pride by airy negligence and gratify their malice by quiet neutrality. [Samuel Johnson: *The Rambler* No. 146]
3 A celebrity is one who is known to many persons he is glad he doesn't know. [H. L. Mencken: *Chrestomathy* 617]
4 A celebrity is a person who works hard all his life to become well known, then wears dark glasses to avoid being recognized. [Fred Allen: *Treadmill to Oblivion*]

CELERITY
5 Celerity is never more admired
Than by the negligent.
[Shakespeare: *Antony and Cleopatra* III.vii.]
6 And generally it is good to commit the beginnings of all great actions to Ar-

gus with his hundred eyes, and the ends to Briareus with his hundred hands; first to watch and then to speed; for the helm of Pluto, which maketh the politic man go invisible, is secrecy in the council, and celerity in the execution; for when things are once come to the execution, there is no secrecy comparable to celerity. [Francis Bacon: *Of Delays*]

CELIBACY
7 Marriage has many pains, but celibacy has no pleasures. [Samuel Johnson: *Rasselas* XXVI]
8 To live without feeling or exciting sympathy, to be fortunate without adding to the felicity of others, or afflicted without tasting the balm of pity, is a state more gloomy than solitude: it is not retreat, but exclusion from mankind. [Samuel Johnson: *Rasselas* XXVI]

CENSORSHIP
9 Give me six lines written by the most honorable of men, and I will find an excuse in them to hang him. [Cardinal Richelieu: *Mirame*]
10 If we think we regulate printing, thereby to rectify manners, we must regulate all recreations and pastimes, all that is delightful to man. [John Milton: *Areopagitica*]
11 Knowledge cannot defile, nor consequently the books, if the will and conscience be not defiled. . . . Wholesome meats to a vitiated stomach differ little or nothing from unwholesome; and best books to a naughty mind are not unappliable to occasions of evil. [John Milton: *Areopagitica*]
12 Every society has a right to preserve public peace and order, and therefore has a good right to prohibit the propagation of opinions which have a dangerous tendency. . . . No member of a society has a right to teach any doctrine contrary to what the society holds to be true. [Samuel Johnson: in Boswell's *Life*, May 7, 1773]
13 Assassination is the extreme form of censorship. [G. B. Shaw: *The Rejected Statement*]
14 Did you ever hear anyone say, "That work had better be banned because I might read it and it might be very dam-

aging to me"? [Joseph Henry Jackson: in the *San Francisco Chronicle*]

CENSURE

1 Censure is the tax a man pays to the public for being eminent. [Jonathan Swift: *Thoughts on Various Subjects*]
2 All censure of a man's self is oblique praise. It is in order to show how much he can spare. It has all the invidiousness of self-praise, and all the reproach of falsehood. [Samuel Johnson: in Boswell's *Life*, April 28, 1778]

CERBERUS

3 A sop for Cerberus. [Congreve: *Love for Love* I.iv.]
In the sixth Book of Vergil's Aeneid (ll.417 and ff.), Aeneas was able to enter the underworld only because his guide, the Sibyl, threw "a morsel drowsy with honey and drugged meal" to the three-headed dog, Cerberus, that guarded the entrance.

CEREMONY

4   To feed were best at home;
From thence the sauce to meat is
                            ceremony;
Meeting were bare without it.
[Shakespeare: *Macbeth* III.iv.]
5 When love begins to sicken and de-
                            cay,
It useth an enforcèd ceremony.
There are no tricks in plain and sim-
                            ple faith.
[Shakespeare: *Julius Caesar* IV.ii.]

CERTAIN

6 Nothing is certain but death and taxes. [Benjamin Franklin: Letter to M. Leroy (1789)]
7 I am certain of nothing but the holiness of the heart's affections and the truth of imagination. [Keats: Letter to Benjamin Bailey, Nov. 22, 1817]

CERTAINTY

8 Certainty generally is illusion, and repose is not the destiny of man. [O. W. Holmes, Jr.: *The Path of the Law*]
9 Ah, what a dusty answer gets the soul
When hot for certainties in this our
                            life!
[George Meredith: *Modern Love*, Sonnet L]

CERVANTES

10 Cervantes smiled Spain's chivalry
                            away;
A single laugh demolished the right
                            arm
Of his own country.
[Byron: *Don Juan* XIII.xi.]
Don Quixote appeared in 1605 and 1615. Spain's chivalry, like everyone else's, was on the way out long before that.
Byron's idea was a common one: "I am sorry Cervantes laughed chivalry out of fashion," Horace Walpole wrote to Sir Horace Mann, July 10, 1774.

CHAIRS

11 I had three chairs in my house: one for solitude, two for friendship, three for society. [Thoreau: *Walden* VI]

CHAM

12 That great Cham of literature. [Tobias Smollett: in a letter to John Wilkes, March 16, 1759, referring to Samuel Johnson]
Cham is an obsolete form of Khan, the title formerly applied to the rulers of the Tartars and Mongols. Smollett's sobriquet was a good one; it acknowledged Johnson's supremacy, but implied that it was dictatorial and barbarous, in a splendid way. It also suggested that the men of letters were wild hordes. All this tickled the popular fancy and the name caught on.
James Burnett (Lord Monboddo, 1714-1799), an eccentric Scotsman, has been called "the lesser Cham."

CHAMPIONS

13 The meeting of these champions
                            proud
Seem'd like the bursting thunder-
                            cloud.
[Sir Walter Scott: *The Lay of the Last Minstrel* III.v.]

CHANCE(S)

14 I returned and saw under the sun, that the race is not to the swift, nor the battle to the strong, neither yet bread to the wise, nor yet riches to men of un-

derstanding, nor yet favor to men of skill; but time and chance happeneth to them all. [Ecclesiastes 9:11]

George Orwell (in "Politics and the English Language") says that the famous passage from Ecclesiastes would have appeared in a government report as:

Objective consideration of contemporary phenomena compels the conclusion that success or failure in competitive activities exhibits no tendency to be commensurate with innate capacity, but that a considerable element of the unpredictable must be taken into account.

1 How often things occur by mere chance which we dared not even hope for. [Terence: *Phormio* V.i.]

2 Wherein I spake of most disastrous chances,
Of moving accidents by flood and field,
Of hair-breadth 'scapes i' th' imminent deadly breach.
[Shakespeare: *Othello* I.iii.]

Othello's account to the Venetian senators of his wooing of Desdemona. Iago characterized it as "bragging and telling her fantastical lies." See 77:2.

3 By wondrous accident perchance one may
Grope out a needle in a load of hay;
And though a white crow be exceeding rare,
A blind man may (by fortune) catch a hare.
[John Taylor, the "Water Poet": *A Kicksy Winsey* VII]

4 That power which erring men call chance.
[John Milton: *Comus* 587]

5   Next him high arbiter Chance governs all.
[John Milton: *Paradise Lost* II, 909-910]

6 All chance, direction, which thou canst not see. [Alexander Pope: *An Essay on Man* I]

7 Chance is a word void of sense; nothing can exist without a cause. [Voltaire: *Philosophical Dictionary*, "Chance"]

8 He seldom lives frugally who lives by chance. [Samuel Johnson: *Life of Dryden*]

9 A fool must now and then be right by chance.
[William Cowper: *Conversation*]

10 Every night and every morn
Some to misery are born;
Every morn and every night
Some are born to sweet delight.
[William Blake: *Auguries of Innocence*]

11 One man, says the auld proverb, is born wi' a silver spoon in his mouth, and another wi' a wudden ladle. [John Wilson: *Noctes Ambrosianae* (November, 1831)]

12 Discouragement seizes us only when we can no longer count on chance.
[George Sand: *Handsome Lawrence* II]

CHANGE(S)

13 Can the Ethiopian change his skin, or the leopard his spots? [Jeremiah 13:23]

14 Presume not that I am the thing I was.
[Shakespeare: *II Henry IV* V.v.]

15 Nothing of him that doth fade,
But doth suffer a sea-change
Into something rich and strange.
[Shakespeare: *The Tempest* I.ii.]

16 When change itself can give no more,
'Tis easy to be true.
[Sir Charles Sedley: *Reasons for Constancy*]

17 When men are easy in their circumstances, they are naturally enemies to innovations. [Joseph Addison: *The Freeholder* No. 42]

18 Change and decay in all around I see;
O Thou, who changest not, abide with me!
[H. F. Lyte: *Eventide*]

19 Let the great world spin for ever down the ringing grooves of change.
[Tennyson: *Locksley Hall*]

Of this famous line Tennyson wrote the following note:

"When I went by the first train from Liverpool to Manchester (1830), I thought that the wheels ran in a groove. It was a black night and there was such a vast crowd round the train at the station that we could not see the wheels. Then I made this line . . ."

Hallam Tennyson: Tennyson: A Memoir I.

See also 50:16.

1 Earth changes, but thy soul and God
stand sure.
[Robert Browning: *Rabbi Ben Ezra*]

CHANGE: inevitable and desirable
2 There is nothing permanent except
change. [Heraclitus: *Fragment*]
3 All things change; nothing perishes.
[Ovid: *Metamorphoses* XV]
4 Observe constantly that all things
take place by change, and accustom thyself to consider that the nature of the
Universe loves nothing so much as to
change the things which are, and to make
new things like them. [Marcus Aurelius:
Meditations IV]
5 It is a secret both in nature and state,
that it is safer to change many things
than one. [Francis Bacon: *Of Regimen
of Health*]
6 Tomorrow to fresh woods and pastures new.
[John Milton: *Lycidas*]
7 The world's a scene of changes, and
to be
Constant, in Nature were inconstancy.
[Abraham Cowley: *Inconstancy*]
8 A man used to vicissitudes is not easily dejected. [Samuel Johnson: *Rasselas*
XII]
9 The old order changeth, yielding
place to new;
And God fulfils himself in many ways,
Lest one good custom should corrupt
the world.
[Tennyson: *Passing of Arthur*]

CHANGE: undesirable
10 Keep what you have; the known evil
is best. [Plautus: *Trinummus* I.ii.]
11 A rolling stone gathers no moss. [Pub-
lilius Syrus: *Maxims*]
12 Changes never answer the end.
[Roger North: *Examen* (1740)]
*One reason is that when men propose
changes they always think of them as
taking place in a static situation, whereas
the making of the change of necessity
alters the situation so that the change
really takes place in another situation.
And then many changes are dynamic
and set in motion many other changes.*
13 This sad vicissitude of things. [Lau-
rence Sterne: *Sermons*, XVI, "The Character of Shimel"]

14 It is a maxim here (at Venice) that
change breeds more mischief from its
novelty than advantage from its utility.
[Mrs. Piozzi: *Observations on a Journey
Through Italy*]
15 It is best not to swap horses while
crossing the river. [Abraham Lincoln: in
an address to a delegation from the National Union League, June 9, 1864]

CHAOS
16 Chaos is come again.
[Shakespeare: *Othello* III.iii.]
17 Through the palpable obscure find
out
His uncouth way.
[John Milton: *Paradise Lost* II, 406-
407]
uncouth = *unknown*
18 This wild abyss,
The womb of nature and perhaps her
grave.
[John Milton: *Paradise Lost* II, 910-
911]
19 Chaos umpire sits,
And by decision more embroils the
fray
By which he reigns.
[John Milton: *Paradise Lost* II, 907-909]
20 The whole world is in a state of chas-
sis. [Sean O'Casey: *Juno and the Pay-
cock* I.i.]

CHARACTER(S)
21 Character is destiny. [Heraclitus:
Fragment]
22 Character is simply habit long continued. [Plutarch: *On Moral Virtue* IV]
23 Look thou character.
[Shakespeare: *Hamlet* I.iii.]
look = *look out for, search for*
24 What is character but the determination of incident? What is incident but
the illustration of character? [Henry
James: *The Art of Fiction*]
25 When writing a novel a writer should
create living people; people not characters. A *character* is a caricature. [Ernest
Hemingway: *Death in the Afternoon*
XVI]

CHARGE OF THE LIGHT BRIGADE
26 Half a league, half a league,
Half a league onward,
All in the valley of Death
Rode the six hundred.

[Tennyson: *The Charge of the Light Brigade*]

This famous poem has suffered the frequent fate of poems that are too popular; it has come to be regarded as humorous. But at the time of its appearance its impact was enormous. Tennyson himself had a thousand copies struck off and sent to the wounded in the Crimea upon whom they were said to have exercised remarkable restorative powers. An American clergyman wrote Tennyson that he had read the poem from his pulpit, instead of the regular sermon, and that, although some members of the congregation had been shocked, one dissipated roué was immediately reformed. Not everyone was pleased, however. Lord Cardigan, who had led the charge, said to one going to England: "If you see Tennyson, ask him how he came to write all that rot about Balaclava!"

CHARIOT(S)

1 And the Lord was with Judah; and he drave out the inhabitants of the mountain; but could not drive out the inhabitants of the valley, because they had chariots of iron. [Judges 1:19]

2 Swing low, sweet chariot—
Comin' for to carry me home;
I looked over Jordan and what did I see?
But a band of angels comin' after me,
Comin' for to carry me home.
[Anon.]

American Negro spiritual.

CHARITY

3 I was hungered, and ye gave me meat: I was thirsty, and ye gave me drink: I was a stranger, and ye took me in. [Matthew 25:35]

4 Though I speak with the tongues of men and of angels, and have not charity, I am become as sounding brass, or a tinkling cymbal. [I Corinthians 13:1]

The Revised Standard Version renders this as:

If I speak in the tongues of men and of angels, but have not love, I am a noisy gong or a clanging cymbal.

5 Charity suffereth long, and is kind; charity envieth not; charity vaunteth not itself, is not puffed up. [I Corinthians 13:4]

6 And now abideth faith, hope, charity, these three; but the greatest of these is charity. [I Corinthians 13:13]

7 Charity shall cover the multitude of sins. [I Peter 4:8]

Commonly spoken as: "Charity covers a multitude of sins."

8 That which we give to the wretched, we lend to fortune. [Seneca: *Troades*]

9 An old man, broken with the storms of state,
Is come to lay his weary bones among ye;
Give him a little earth for charity!
[Shakespeare: *Henry VIII* IV.ii.]

10 The noblest works and foundations have proceeded from childless men. [Francis Bacon: *Of Parents and Children*]

11 In charity there is no excess. [Francis Bacon: *Of Goodness and Goodness of Nature*]

12 Charity and Pride have different aims, yet both feed the poor. [Thomas Fuller (1654-1734): *Gnomologia*]

13 Alas! for the rarity
Of Christian charity
Under the sun!
[Thomas Hood: *The Bridge of Sighs*]

14 With malice toward none, with charity for all, with firmness in the right, as God gives us to see the right. [Abraham Lincoln: *Second Inaugural Address* (1865)]

Lincoln seems to have unconsciously echoed here a passage from a letter by John Quincy Adams to Bronson Alcott, July 30, 1838. Adams had written: "In charity to all mankind, bearing no malice or ill-will to any human being. . . ."

Lincoln's reversal of the order is just the sort of thing we all do with something we have read and then "forgotten."

15 Tenderness and generosity are the manly forms of these female virtues, charity and love. [Albert Camus: *Notebooks 1935-1942* III, p. 181]

CHARITY: begins at home

16 Charity and beating begins at home. [Beaumont and Fletcher: *Wit without Money* V.ii.]

17 But how shall we expect charity to-

wards others, when we are uncharitable to our selves? Charity begins at home, is the voice of the world; yet is every man his greatest enemy, and, as it were, his own executioner. [Sir Thomas Browne: *Religio Medici* II.iv.]

1 And charity begins at home,
  And mostly ends where it begins.
[Horace Smith: *Horace in London* II. xv.]

CHARITY: organized, cautious, imperfect

2 He that defers his charity until he is dead is, if a man weighs it rightly, rather liberal of another man's than of his own. [Francis Bacon: *Collection of Sentences*]

3 A man may give his body to be burnt, and yet not have charity. [Thomas Fuller (1608-1661): *The Holy State*, IV.2.]

4 And in charity-meetings it stands at the door,
  And collects—though it does not subscribe.
[Lewis Carroll: *The Hunting of the Snark*, Fit 5]

5 Remember the poor—it costs nothing. [Mark Twain: *Pudd'nhead Wilson's Calendar*]

6 The organized charity, scrimped and iced,
  In the name of a cautious, statistical Christ.
[John Boyle O'Reilly: *In Bohemia*]

KING CHARLES'S HEAD

7 Mr. Dick had been for upwards of ten years endeavoring to keep King Charles the First out of the Memorial; but he was constantly getting into it, and was there now. [Dickens: *David Copperfield* XIV]
  It's particularly King Charles's head that obsesses Mr. Dick, a gentle madman.

CHARLES XII OF SWEDEN

8 His fall was destined to a barren strand,
  A petty fortress, and a dubious hand;
  He left the name, at which the world grew pale,
  To point a moral, or adorn a tale.
[Samuel Johnson: *The Vanity of Human Wishes*]
  The reference is to Charles XII of Swe-

den *(1682-1718)*, *"The Madman of the North," whose meteoric military career that had all Europe alarmed suddenly collapsed. He was killed by a chance shot at the siege of Fredrikshald.*

CHARLIE

9 Oh, Charlie is my darling, my darling, my darling,
  Oh, Charlie is my darling, the young Chevalier.
[Carolina Oliphant, Lady Nairne: *Charlie is my Darling*]

CHARM

10 She is pretty to walk with,
  And witty to talk with,
  And pleasant, too, to think on.
[Sir John Suckling: *The Brennoralt*]

11 If to her share some female errors fall
  Look on her face, and you'll forget 'em all.
[Alexander Pope: *The Rape of the Lock* II]

12 All charming people, I fancy, are spoiled. That is the secret of their attraction. [Oscar Wilde: *The Portrait of Mr. W. H.*]

13 It's a sort of bloom on a woman. If you have it, you don't need to have anything else; and if you don't have it, it doesn't much matter what else you have. [J. M. Barrie: *What Every Woman Knows* I]
  Barrie is referring to "charm." A generation later Elinor Glyn was to narrow its range and increase its tension to "It."

14 Charming people live up to the very edge of their charm, and behave as outrageously as the world will let them. [Logan Pearsall Smith: *Afterthoughts*]

CHARMER

15 How happy could I be with either
  Were t'other dear charmer away.
[John Gay: *The Beggar's Opera* II.xiii.]

CHASTITY

16 An unattempted woman cannot boast of her chastity. [Montaigne: *Essays* III. v.]

17 Husbands would have their wives sound, healthy, strong and plump, well-fed and chaste at the same time—that is to say, hot and cold. [Montaigne: *Essays* III.v.]

1 The fair, the chaste and unexpressive she.
[Shakespeare: *As You Like It* III.ii.]
2 The chariest maid is prodigal enough
If she unmask her beauty to the moon.
[Shakespeare: *Hamlet* I.iii.]
3 Banish all objects of lust, shut up all youth into the severest discipline that can be exercised in any hermitage, ye cannot make them chaste, that came not thither so. [John Milton: *Areopagitica*]
4   In part to blame is she
Which hath without consent been only tried;
He comes too near, that comes to be denied.
[Sir Thomas Overbury: *A Wife* XXXVI]
  only = *even so much as*
5 The maiden who listens [to an improper proposal] is—like a besieged city that consents to parley—half-way towards surrender. [Adrien de Montluc: *La Comédie de Proverbes* I.iii.]
6 The woman that deliberates is lost. [Joseph Addison: *Cato* IV.i.]
7 A woman's chastity consists, like an onion, in a series of coats. [Nathaniel Hawthorne: *Journal,* March 16, 1854]

CHASTITY: some unfavorable comments
8 Chaste women are often proud and froward, as presuming upon the merit of their chastity. [Francis Bacon: *Of Marriage and Single Life*]
  froward = *perverse, wilfully contrary, not easily managed*
9 There are few chaste women who are not tired of their trade. [La Rochefoucauld: *Maxims*]
10 Chaste to her husband, frank to all beside,
A teeming mistress, but a barren bride.
[Alexander Pope: *Moral Essays* II]
11 Chastity is a monkish and evangelical superstition, a greater foe to natural temperance even than unintellectual sensuality; it strikes at the root of all domestic happiness, and consigns more than half of the human race to misery. [Shelley: Notes to *Queen Mab*]
12 Our vocabulary is defective: we give the same name to a woman's lack of temptation and a man's lack of opportunity. [Ambrose Bierce: *The Devil's Dictionary*]
13 Chastity—the most unnatural of the sexual perversions. [Aldous Huxley: *Eyeless in Gaza* XXVII]
  He is quoting Remy de Gourmont.

CHAUCER
14 Dan Chaucer, well of English undefyled,
On Fames eternall beadroll worthie to be fyled.
[Edmund Spenser: *The Faerie Queene* IV.ii.]
  Dan = "Master." It is akin to the Spanish Don *and the Portuguese* Dom, *derived from the Latin* dominus.
15 Or call up him that left half told
The story of Cambuscan bold.
[John Milton: *Il Penseroso*]
  The "story of Cambuscan bold" is the Squire's Tale, which Chaucer left unfinished.
16 Here is God's plenty.
[Dryden: Preface to the *Fables* (1700)]
17 Dan Chaucer, the first warbler, whose sweet breath
Preluded those melodious bursts that fill
The spacious times of great Elizabeth.
[Tennyson: *A Dream of Fair Women*]

CHEAPENING
18 Alas! 'tis true I have gone here and there,
And made myself a motley to the view,
Gored mine own thoughts, sold cheap what is most dear.
[Shakespeare: *Sonnets* CX]
  Motley, a cloth of mixed colors, was worn by fools; hence motley *came to mean "fool."*

CHEAPNESS
19 Never buy what you do not want, because it is cheap; it will be dear to you. [Thomas Jefferson: *A Decalogue of Canons for Observation in Practical Life*]

CHEAT
20 I hope I shall never be deterred from detecting what I think a cheat, by the

menaces of a ruffian. [Samuel Johnson: Letter to James Macpherson, Jan. 20, 1775]

Macpherson had published a hoax called Ossian which had been and for a generation after the time of Johnson's letter was accepted as genuine by some of the greatest minds of the age. Johnson had firmly maintained that the whole thing was an imposition and demanded that Macpherson produce the evidence that he claimed he had. Macpherson wrote Johnson a threatening letter, "a foolish and impudent letter," Johnson called it. Johnson's answer is in some ways even better than his more famous letter to Lord Chesterfield.

CHEATING

1 Nothing is easier than to cheat an honest man. [Gracián: *Oráculo Manual*]

A good example of proverb and anti-proverb is furnished by this saying and the equally common assertion that "You can't cheat an honest man." Both have validity. This says that an honest man suspects no duplicity in others. The other states the equally true fact that many men enter the deals in which they are cheated with dishonest intent; they're lured by the hope of improper gains.

2 Doubtless the pleasure is as great
Of being cheated as to cheat.
[Samuel Butler (1612-1680): *Hudibras*]

3 'Tis no sin to cheat the devil. [Daniel Defoe: *History of the Devil* II.x.]

4 Cheat me in the price but not in the goods. [Thomas Fuller (1654-1734): *Gnomologia*]

5 It is better to suffer wrong than to do it, and happier to be sometimes cheated than not to trust. [Samuel Johnson: *The Rambler* No. 79]

6 He'll cheat without scruple, who can without fear. [Benjamin Franklin: *Poor Richard's Almanack* (1743)]

An interesting glimpse into the depths of Franklin's pecksniffian morality.

7 Thou shalt not steal; an empty feat,
When it's so lucrative to cheat.
[Arthur Hugh Clough: *The Latest Decalogue*]

8 Don't steal; thou'lt never thus compete

Successfully in business. Cheat.
[Ambrose Bierce: *The Devil's Dictionary*]

9 It is almost worth while to be cheated; people's little frauds have an interest which amply repays what they cost us. [Logan Pearsall Smith: *Afterthoughts*]

CHEEK

10 Whosoever shall smite thee on thy right cheek, turn to him the other also. [Matthew 5:39]

CHEER

11 I have not that alacrity of spirit,
Nor cheer of mind, that I was wont to have.
[Shakespeare: *Richard III* V.iii.]

12 And even the ranks of Tuscany
Could scarce forbear to cheer.
[Macaulay: *Lays of Ancient Rome*, "Horatius"]

The doings at the bridge are mythical. But there was a Porsena, who, head of the united forces of Etruria, led an attack on Rome, at the end of the 6th century B.C. Macaulay's poem is a delightful illustration of the manner in which an age interprets the past in its own image. Prehistoric tribal warfare is assumed to have been conducted in the sporting spirit of a good public school.

Horatius Cocles, the splendid defender of the bridge, is thought by some scholars to be no less than Polyphemus.

13 No, at noonday in the bustle of man's work-time
Greet the unseen with a cheer!
[Robert Browning: Epilogue to *Asolando*]

CHEERFULNESS

14 A merry heart maketh a cheerful countenance. [Proverbs 15:13]

15 A merry heart doeth good like a medicine. [Proverbs 17:22]

16 A light heart lives long.
[Shakespeare: *Love's Labour's Lost* V.ii.]

17 To be free minded and cheerfully disposed at hours of meat and sleep and of exercise is one of the best precepts of long lasting. [Francis Bacon: *Of Regimen of Health*]

1 I have always preferred Cheerfulness to Mirth. The latter I consider as an Act, the former as a Habit of the Mind. Mirth is short and transient, Cheerfulness fixed and permanent. [Joseph Addison: *The Spectator* No. 381]

2 A cheerful temper, joined with innocence will make beauty attractive, knowledge delightful, and wit good-natured. [Joseph Addison: *The Tatler* No. 192]

3 I went out to Charing Cross, to see Major-general Harrison hanged, drawn, and quartered; which was done there, he looking as cheerful as any man could do in that condition. [Samuel Pepys: *Diary*, October 13, 1660]

Cheerfulness's finest hour!

4 Cheered up himself with ends of verse
And sayings of philosophers.
[Samuel Butler (1612-1680): *Hudibras* I.iii.1011]

5 How often it seems the chief good to be born with a cheerful temper. [Emerson: *Society and Solitude*, "Success"]

6 The cheerful clatter of Sir James Barrie's cans as he went round with the milk of human kindness. [Philip Guedalla: *Some Critics*]

CHESTERFIELD

7 They teach the morals of a whore, and the manners of a dancing master. [Samuel Johnson: in Boswell's *Life* (1754)]

Johnson's opinion of Lord Chesterfield's Letters to His Son.

CHESTNUT

8 A chestnut. I have heard you tell the joke twenty-seven times, and I am sure it was a chestnut. [William Dimond (1780-1837): *The Broken Sword* (1816)]

Captain Xavier, a tedious blowhard, is always repeating himself. He starts to tell a yarn that involves a cork tree when another character, Pablo, corrects him. Pablo says it was a chestnut tree. The captain is enraged and insists that it was a cork tree and that he ought to know because it's his story. Pablo says he ought to know: he's heard it twenty-seven times before and it was always a chestnut. It is from this that we derive the term "an old chestnut" for a worn-out joke.

CHICAGO

9 Hog Butcher for the World,
Tool Maker, Stacker of Wheat,
Player with Railroads and the Nation's Freight Handler;
Stormy, husky, brawling,
City of the Big Shoulders.
[Carl Sandburg: *Chicago*]

CHICKEN(S)

10 Thou hast been considering whether the chicken came first from the egg or the egg from the chicken. [Macrobius (c. A.D. 400): *Saturnalia* VII.xvi.]

The context implies that the problem was a byword even then.

11 To swallow gudgeons ere they're catch'd,
And count their chickens ere they're hatch'd.
[Samuel Butler (1612-1680): *Hudibras*]

The saying is very old. It occurs in Don Quixote, in the Colloquies of Erasmus, and many other places. Ultimately it seems to be derived from one of the fables attributed to Aesop which tells of a milkmaid who, dreaming of the money she was going to make from some eggs she had under a setting hen, didn't watch what she was doing and spilled her milk. But it's equally probable that the fable was built upon the proverb.

12 A hen is only an egg's way of making another egg. [Samuel Butler (1835-1902): *Life and Habit* VIII]

13 A chicken in every pot. [Republican campaign slogan, 1932]

I hope to make France so prosperous that every peasant will have a chicken in his pot on Sunday.

Henri IV, King of France (1589-1610), speaking at his coronation.

CHIEF

14 Hail to the chief who in triumph advances!
[Sir Walter Scott: *The Lady of the Lake* II]

CHIEFTAIN

15 A chieftain to the Highlands bound
Cries, "Boatman, do not tarry!
And I'll give thee a silver pound
To row us o'er the ferry."

[Thomas Campbell: *Lord Ullin's Daughter*]

CHILD

1 Train up a child in the way he should go: and when he is old, he will not depart from it. [Proverbs 22:6]

2 When I was a child, I spake as a child, I understood as a child, I thought as a child: but when I became a man, I put away childish things. [I Corinthians 13:11]

3 Sweet invocation of a child; most pretty and pathetical. [Shakespeare: *Love's Labour's Lost* I.ii.]

4 Woe to that land that's govern'd by a child!
[Shakespeare: *Richard III* II.iii.]

5   Wife and child
Those precious motives, those strong knots of love.
[Shakespeare: *Macbeth* IV.iii.]

6 I had rather to adopt a child than get it. [Shakespeare: *Othello* I.iii.]
get = *to beget*

7 The burnt child dreads the fire. [Ben Jonson: *The Devil is an Ass* I.ii.]

8 Come when you're called,
And do as you're bid;
Shut the door after you,
And you'll never be chid.
[Maria Edgeworth: *The Contrast*]

9   A simple child,
That lightly draws its breath,
And feels its life in every limb,
What should it know of death?
[Wordsworth: *We Are Seven*]

10 Three years she grew in sun and shower,
Then Nature said, 'A lovelier flower
On earth was never sown;
This Child I to myself will take;
She shall be mine, and I will make
A Lady of my own.'
[Wordsworth: *Three Years She Grew*]

11 The sweetest thing that ever grew
Beside a human door.
[Wordsworth: *Lucy Gray*]

12 The child is father of the man.
[Wordsworth: *My Heart Leaps Up*]

13 Respect the child. Be not too much his parent. Trespass not on his solitude.
[Emerson: *Education*]

14 A child should always say what's true,
And speak when he is spoken to,
And behave mannerly at table:
At least as far as he is able.
[R. L. Stevenson: *Whole Duty of Children*]

15 The child that is not plain and neat,
With lots of toys and things to eat,
He is a naughty child, I'm sure—
Or else his dear papa is poor.
[R. L. Stevenson: *System*]

16 If you strike a child . . . strike it in anger. . . . A blow in cold blood neither can nor should be forgiven. [G. B. Shaw: *Maxims for Revolutionists*]

17 The nicest child I ever knew
Was Charles Augustus Fortescue.
[Hilaire Belloc: *Charles Augustus Fortescue*]

18 And he who gives a child a treat
Makes joy-bells ring in Heaven's street,
But he who gives a child a home
Builds palaces in Kingdom come,
And she who gives a baby birth
Brings Saviour Christ again to Earth.
[John Masefield: *The Everlasting Mercy*]
But, alas, who could have foreseen that the touching sentiment of the first two lines could lead to the hysterical horrors of contemporary Christmas!

CHILDHOOD

19   The childhood shows the man
As morning shows the day.
[John Milton: *Paradise Regained* IV. 220]

20 There was an old woman who lived in a shoe,
She had so many children she didn't know what to do;
She gave them some broth without any bread;
She whipped them all soundly and put them to bed.
[Nursery rhyme: earliest known version, 1797; but probably much older]
The shoe is well recognized as a fertility symbol—vide its being thrown at weddings—but aside from this vaguely suggestive fact no one has been able to unravel the mystery of this well-known verse.

21 Sweet childish days, that were as long
As twenty days are now.
[Wordsworth: *To a Butterfly*]

1 Heaven lies about us in our infancy!
Shades of the prison-house begin to
close
Upon the growing boy,
But he beholds the light, and whence
it flows,
He sees it in his joy;
The youth, who daily farther from
the east
Must travel, still is Nature's priest,
And by the vision splendid
Is on his way attended;
At length the man perceives it die
away,
And fade into the light of common
day.
[Wordsworth: *Intimations of Immortality*]

2 The smiles, the tears of boyhood's
years,
The words of love then spoken.
[Thomas Moore: *Oft in the Stilly Night*]

3 How dear to this heart are the
scenes of my childhood,
When fond recollection presents
them to view.
[Samuel Woodworth: *The Old Oaken
Bucket*]

4 I remember, I remember,
The house where I was born,
The little window where the sun
Came peeping in at morn.
[Thomas Hood: *I Remember, I Remember*]

5 Backward, turn backward, O Time,
in thy flight;
Make me a child again, just for to-
night.
[Elizabeth Akers Allen: *Rock Me to
Sleep*]

CHILDREN

6 Happy is the man that hath his quiver
full of them. [Psalms 127:5]
7 Suffer the little children to come unto
me, and forbid them not: for of such is
the kingdom of God. [Mark 10:14]
8 For the children of this world are in
their generation wiser than the children
of light. [Luke 16:8]
9 Children's playings are not sports and
should be deemed as their most serious
actions. [Montaigne: *Essays* I.xxii.]
10 'Tis an old said saw. Children and
fools speak true. [John Lyly: *Endimion*
IV.2.]
11 Children have neither past nor future; they enjoy the present, which very
few of us do. [La Bruyère: *Les Caractères*]
12 Children pick up words as pigeons
pease,
And utter them again as God shall
please.
[John Ray: *English Proverbs* (1670)]
13 Children are poor men's riches.
[John Ray: *English Proverbs* (1670)]
14 Children have more need of models
than of critics. [Joseph Joubert: *Pensées*]
15 Between the dark and the daylight,
When the night is beginning to
lower,
Comes a pause in the day's occupations,
That is known as the Children's
Hour.
[Longfellow: *The Children's Hour*
(1860)]
*What an enviable picture of the life
of a well-to-do Victorian this poem conjures up for us: the little girls, washed,
fed and neatly dressed, were allowed to
visit Papa and romp a little with him
towards evening, when his work was
done. What sustaining illusions must
have been nurtured on both sides!*

16 Little children are still the symbol of
the eternal marriage between love and
duty. [George Eliot: Proem to *Romola*]
17 The golf links lie so near the mill
That almost every day
The laboring children can look out
And see the men at play.
[Sarah N. Cleghorn: *Quatrain*]

CHILDREN: their drawbacks

18 Children sweeten labors; but they
make misfortunes more bitter. [Francis
Bacon: *Of Parents and Children*]
19 Children when they are little make
parents fools, when they are great they
make them mad. [George Herbert: *Jacula Prudentum*]
20 When children stand quiet, they have
done some ill. [George Herbert: *Jacula
Prudentum*]
21 Children blessings seem, but torments are;
When young, our folly, and when

old, our fear.
[Thomas Otway: *Don Carlos*]
1 Children suck the mother when they are young and the father when they are old. [John Ray: *English Proverbs* (1670)]
2 *Les enfants terribles!* ("Those dreadful children!") [Gavarni: title of a series of sketches published in 1865]
3 Children begin by loving their parents. After a time they judge them. Rarely, if ever, do they forgive them. [Oscar Wilde: *A Woman of No Importance* II]

CHIMAERA
4 A chimaera buzzing in a vacuum. [Rabelais: *Pantagruel* II.vii.]
In Greek mythology the chimaera was a monster with the head of a lion, the body of a goat, and the tail of a dragon. Hence, an unreal creature of the imagination, an idle fantasy. Rabelais's phrase for futility is something like Matthew Arnold's description of Shelley (in part taken from Shelley) as "an ineffectual angel beating in the void his luminous wings in vain."

CHIMES
5 We have heard the chimes at midnight.
[Shakespeare: *II Henry IV* III.ii.]

CHINEE
6 Which I wish to remark,
   And my language is plain,
That for ways that are dark
   And for tricks that are vain,
The heathen Chinee is peculiar.
[Bret Harte: *Plain Language from Truthful James*]

CHIP OFF THE OLD BLOCK
7 He's a chip o' th' old block. [William Rowley: *A Match at Midnight* I]
8 How well dost thou now appear to be a chip of the old block? [John Milton: *Apology for Smectymnuus* (1642)]
Most commonly heard today as a chip off the old block. Milton accepted the English version of the old saying. Theocritus (270 B.C.) had it as a chip of the old flint, but then he was nearer to the

Old Stone Age, when the figure no doubt originated.

CHIVALRY
9 It is now sixteen or seventeen years since I saw the Queen of France . . . at Versailles; and surely never lighted on this orb a more delightful vision . . . glittering like the morning star, full of life, and splendor, and joy. . . . Little did I dream that I should have lived to see disasters fallen upon her in a nation of gallant men, in a nation of men of honor, and of cavaliers. I thought ten thousand swords must have leaped from their scabbards to avenge even a look that threatened her with insult. But the age of chivalry is gone. That of sophisters, economists, and calculators, has succeeded; and the glory of Europe is extinguished for ever. [Burke: *Reflections on the Revolution in France* (1790)]
Burke lived to see far worse things happen to Marie Antoinette.

CHOICE
10 But one thing is needful; and Mary hath chosen that good part. [Luke 10:42]
11 Sometimes it is a good choice not to choose at all. [Montaigne: *Essays* III.ix.]
12 Life often presents us with a choice of evils, rather than of goods. [C. C. Colton: *Lacon*]
13 Life's business being just the terrible choice.
[Robert Browning: *The Ring and the Book*, "The Pope"]
14 The strongest principle of growth lies in human choice. [George Eliot: *Daniel Deronda* VI. 42]
15 Where there is no choice, we do well to make no difficulty. [George MacDonald: *Sir Gibbie* XI]
16 The difficulty in life is the choice. [George Moore: *The Bending of the Bough* IV]

CHORTLING
17 "And hast thou slain the Jabberwock?
   Come to my arms, my beamish boy!
O frabjous day! Callooh! Callay!"
   He chortled in his joy.
[Lewis Carroll: *Through the Looking-Glass*, "Jabberwocky"]

CHRISTIAN(S)

1 Almost thou persuadest me to be a Christian. [Acts 26:28]

The Revised Standard Version renders this famous passage: "In a short time you think to make me a Christian!" The New English Bible: "You think it will not take much to win me over and make a Christian of me."

2 Lord, I ascribe it to Thy grace,
    And not to chance, as others do,
That I was born of Christian race,
    And not a Heathen or a Jew.
[Isaac Watts: *Divine Songs for Children,* "Praise for the Gospel"]

3 If the Tiber reaches the walls, if the Nile does not rise . . . if the sky doesn't move or the earth does, if there is a famine or a plague, the cry is "The Christians to the lions!" [Tertullian: *Apologeticus* XL.ii.]

Well, turn about is fair play. After the terrible earthquake that shattered Lisbon in 1755, a number of heretics were publicly burned, the University of Coimbra having declared, as Voltaire phrased it, "that the sight of several persons being slowly burned in great ceremony is an infallible secret for preventing earthquakes."

4 Truly, sir, when a man is ruined, 'tis but the duty of a Christian to tell him of it. [George Farquhar: *Twin-Rivals* I.i.]

5 I think all Christians, whether papists or Protestants, agree in the essential articles, and that their differences are trivial, and rather political than religious. [Samuel Johnson: in Boswell's *Life,* June 25, 1763]

6 Christians have burnt each other,
    quite persuaded
That all the Apostles would have
    done as they did.
[Byron: *Don Juan* I.lxxxiii.]

7 My object will be, if possible, to form Christian men, for Christian boys I can scarcely hope to make. [Thomas Arnold: Letter, written in 1828 when appointed headmaster of Rugby]

8 And hated all for love of Jesus Christ. [Christina Rossetti: *A Portrait*]

9 Onward, Christian soldiers!
    Marching as to war,
With the cross of Jesus
    Going on before.
[Sabine Baring-Gould: *Onward, Christian Soldiers*]

10 In truth, there was only *one* Christian, and he died on the cross. [Friedrich Nietzsche: *The Antichrist*]

CHRISTIANITY

11 Thou hast conquered, O Galilean. (*Vicisti, Galilaee!*) [Attr. the Roman Emperor Julian on his deathbed, but probably apocryphal]

Julian was called "the Apostate"—and for centuries heaped with obloquy—because, reared a Christian, he renounced Christianity on his accession to the purple and published an edict of tolerance.

12 But Cristes loore, and his Apostles
    twelve,
He taughte, but first he folowed it
    hymselfe.
[Chaucer: Prologue to *The Canterbury Tales*]

13 No nations are more warlike than those which profess Christianity. [Pierre Bayle: *Pensées sur la Comète*]

14 Christianity, and nothing short of it, must be made the element and principle of all education. [John Henry Newman: *The Tamworth Reading Room* III]

15 His Christianity was muscular. [Benjamin Disraeli: *Endymion* XIV]

16 Thou hast conquered, O pale Galilean; the world has grown grey
    from thy breath;
We have drunken of things Lethean,
    and fed on the fullness of death.
[Swinburne: *Hymn to Proserpine*]

17 Popular Christianity has for its emblem a gibbet, for its chief sensation a sanguinary execution after torture, for its central mystery an insane vengeance bought off by a trumpery expiation. But there is a nobler and profounder Christianity which affirms the sacred mystery of equality and forbids the glaring futility and folly of vengeance. [G. B. Shaw: Preface to *Major Barbara*]

18 Civilization is perhaps approaching one of those long winters that overtake it from time to time. Romantic Christendom—picturesque, passionate, unhappy episode—may be coming to an end. Such a catastrophe would be no reason for despair. [George Santayana: *Character and Opinion in the United States*]

CHRISTMAS

1 Away in a manger, no crib for a bed,
The little Lord Jesus laid down His
sweet head.
[Martin Luther: *Cradle Hymn*]

2 At Christmas play, and make good
cheer,
For Christmas comes but once a year.
[Thomas Tusser: *Five Hundred Points
of Good Husbandry* (1557)]

3 Some say that ever 'gainst that season
comes
Wherein our Saviour's birth is celebrated,
The bird of dawning singeth all night
long:
And then, they say, no spirit can walk
abroad;
The nights are wholesome; then no
planets strike,
No fairy takes, nor witch hath power
to charm,
So hallow'd and so gracious is the
time.
[Shakespeare: *Hamlet* I.i.]
strike = *with apoplexy; cf. our "stroke"*
takes = *afflicts with disease*

4 The first day of Christmas
My true love sent to me
A partridge in a pear tree.
[Nursery rhyme]
*Apparently a very old fireside memory
game, with forfeits to be paid by those
who, when it was their turn, could not
repeat accurately all the preceding lines
with their accumulating gifts.*

5 God rest you merry, gentlemen,
Let nothing you dismay,
For Jesus Christ, our Saviour,
Was born upon this day.
[Unknown: *Old Carol*]
*Note the punctuation. It is not: God rest
you, merry gentlemen. It means: God
keep you happy, gentlemen.*

6 While shepherds watched their flocks
by night
All seated on the ground,
The angel of the Lord came down
And glory shone around.

"Fear not," said he; for mighty dread
Had seized their troubled mind;
"Glad tidings of great joy I bring
To you and all mankind."
[Nahum Tate and Nicholas Brady:
Christmas Hymn]

7 Coming! ay, so is Christmas. [Jona-
than Swift: *Polite Conversation* I]
*All that the appearance of the phrase in
Swift's book tells us is that it was hackneyed as long ago as 1738.*

8 I have often thought, says Sir Roger,
it happens very well that Christmas
should fall out in the middle of winter.
[Joseph Addison: *The Spectator* No. 269]

9 Christians awake! Salute the happy
morn,
Whereon the Saviour of the world
was born!
[John Byrom: *Hymn for Christmas
Day*]

10 Hark! the herald angels sing
Glory to the new-born King;
Peace on earth, and mercy mild,
God and sinners reconciled!
Joyful all ye nations rise,
Join the triumph of the skies;
With th' angelic host proclaim
Christ is born in Bethlehem.
[Charles Wesley: *Hark! the Herald An-
gels Sing*]

11 'Twas the night before Christmas,
when all through the house
Not a creature was stirring—not even
a mouse;
The stockings were hung by the chimney with care,
In hopes that St. Nicholas soon would
be there.
[Clement Moore: *A Visit from St. Nicholas* (1823)]

12 I heard the bells on Christmas Day
Their old, familiar carols play,
And wild and sweet
The words repeat
Of peace on earth, good-will to men!
[Longfellow: *Christmas Bells*]

13 The time draws near the birth of
Christ.
[Tennyson: *In Memoriam* XXVIII]

14 It came upon the midnight clear,
That glorious song of old,
From Angels bending near the earth
To touch their harps of gold;
"Peace on the earth, good will to men
From Heaven's all gracious King."
The world in solemn stillness lay
To hear the angels sing.
[Edmund Hamilton Sears: *The Angels'
Song*]

1   O little town of Bethlehem!
       How still we see thee lie;
     Above thy deep and dreamless sleep
       The silent stars go by;
     Yet in thy dark streets shineth
       The everlasting Light;
     The hopes and fears of all the years
       Are met in thee tonight.
[Phillips Brooks: *O Little Town of Bethlehem*]

CHRONICLER

2   After my death I wish no other herald,
     No other speaker of my living ac-
                    tions,
     To keep mine honor from corrup-
                    tion,
     Than such an honest chronicler as
                    Griffith.
[Shakespeare: *Henry VIII* IV.ii.]
*Griffith, Queen Katherine's Gentleman
Usher, after listening to her enumeration
of Cardinal Wolsey's faults, had begged
her permission "to speak his good" and
had listed his merits. The Queen was
moved by the fairness of the praise.*

CHURCH(ES)

3   Thou art Peter, and upon this rock I
will build my church. [Matthew 16:18]
4   The nearer the church, the farther
from God. [John Heywood: *Proverbs
(1546)*]
*Quoted by Bishop Lancelot Andrewes:
Sermon on the Nativity*
5   And storied windows richly dight,
     Casting a dim religious light.
     There let the pealing organ blow,
     To the full-voiced quire below,
     In service high, and anthems clear
     As may, with sweetness, through mine
                    ear
     Dissolve me into ecstasies,
     And bring all Heaven before mine
                    eyes.
[John Milton: *Il Penseroso*]
6   Thunders are observed oftener to
break upon churches than upon any
other buildings. [Cotton Mather: *The
Wonders of the Invisible World*]
*Church steeples, often surmounted by a
metal vane and rising to a high point
over all other buildings in their vicinity
were, of course, repeatedly struck by
lightning. This was explained as the*
work of the Devil or as a manifestation
of Divine wrath against heresy or hidden
sins among the congregation. One of the
more spectacular of such rebukes was the
collapse of the tower of Shrewsbury
church after it had been proposed that
a memorial to Darwin be erected there.
7   A man must have very little to do at
church that can give an account of the
sermon. [John Vanbrugh: *The Relapse*
I]
8   Some to church repair
     Not for the doctrine, but the music
                    there.
[Alexander Pope: *An Essay on Criticism*
II]
9   Who builds a church to God, and not
                    to fame,
     Will never mark the marble with his
                    name.
[Alexander Pope: *Moral Essays* III]
10   *Deo erexit Voltaire.* (Voltaire built
[it] for God) [Voltaire: inscription on
a church which he built at Ferney, 1761]
*The inscription—as it was no doubt
meant to—puzzled the age. Did it show
faith under skepticism? Or was it a
crowning blasphemy? Cowper commented that Voltaire "Built God a
church and laugh'd His word to scorn"
—Retirement.*

11   To be of no church is dangerous. Religion, of which the rewards are distant,
and which is animated only by Faith and
Hope, will glide by degrees out of the
mind, unless it be invigorated and reim-
pressed by external ordinances, by stated
calls to worship, and the salutary influence of example. [Samuel Johnson: *Life
of Milton*]
12   Dear Mother, dear Mother, the
                    church is cold,
     But the ale-house is healthy and
                    pleasant and warm.
[William Blake: *The Little Vagabond*]
13   If it were not for death and funerals,
I think the institution of the church
would not stand longer. [Thoreau: *Autumn*, November 16, 1861]
14   Gates of hell can never
       'Gainst that Church prevail;
     We have Christ's own promise,
       And that cannot fail.
[Sabine Baring-Gould: *Onward, Christian Soldiers*]

1 The churches must learn humility as well as teach it. [G. B. Shaw: Preface to *Saint Joan*]

2 The fatal theory of the separation of Church and State . . . [Leo XIII: *Libertas Praestantissimum,* 1888]

3 The 11 o'clock hour on Sunday is the most segregated hour in American life. [Bishop James A. Pike, quoted *U. S. News & World Report,* May 16, 1960]

CICERO

4 If I could have known Cicero, and been his friend, and talked with him in his retirement at Tusculum (beautiful Tusculum), I could have died contented. [Dickens: *Dombey and Son* XI]
Mrs. Blimber, who dug up dead languages "like a ghoul."

CIGAR

5 Some sigh for this and that;
My wishes don't go far;
The world may wag at will,
So I have my cigar.
[Thomas Hood: *The Cigar*]

6 A good cigar is as great a comfort to a man as a good cry to a woman. [E. G. Bulwer-Lytton: *Darnley* III.ii.]

7 A woman is only a woman, but a good cigar is a Smoke. [Kipling: *The Betrothed*]

8 What this country needs is a good five-cent cigar. [Thomas Riley Marshall, Vice-President of the United States (1913-1921): after listening to some oratory on what the country needed.]
In 1932 Franklin P. Adams remarked that what the country needed was a good five-cent nickel. The present generation will settle for a good five-cent dime.

CIRCLE

9 Circles are prais'd, not that abound
In largeness, but th' exactly round:
So life we praise, that doth excel
Not in much time, but acting well.
[Edmund Waller: *Long and Short Life*]

10 He drew a circle that shut me out—
Heretic, rebel, a thing to flout.
But Love and I had the wit to win:
We drew a circle that took him in.
[Edwin Markham: *Outwitted*]

CIRCUMSTANCE(S)

11 Men are the sport of circumstances.
[Byron: *Don Juan* V.xvii.]

12 Circumstances alter cases. [T. C. Haliburton: *The Old Judge*]

13 Circumstances alter cases. [Dickens: *Mystery of Edwin Drood* IX]

14 He fixed thee 'mid this dance
Of plastic circumstance.
[Robert Browning: *Rabbi Ben Ezra*]

CITIZEN

15 Paul said, I am a man which am a Jew of Tarsus, a city in Cilicia, a citizen of no mean city. [Acts 21:39]

CITY(IES)

16 Unless the Lord keepeth the city, the watchman waketh but in vain. [Psalms 127:1]
Motto of the city of Edinburgh

17 Tower'd cities please us then,
And the busy hum of men.
[John Milton: *L'Allegro*]

18 God the first garden made, and the first city Cain. [Abraham Cowley: *The Garden*]

19 The Crowd, and Buz, and Murmurings
Of this great Hive, the City.
[Abraham Cowley: *The Wish*]

20 Fly the rank city, shun its turbid air:
Breathe not the chaos of eternal smoke
And volatile corruption.
. . . and tho' the lungs abhor
To drink the dun fuliginous abyss
Did not the acid vigor of the mine,
Roll'd from so many thundring chimneys, tame
The putrid salts that overswarm the sky;
This caustic venom would perhaps corrode
Those tender cells that draw the vital air. . . .
While yet you breathe, away! the rural wilds
Invite.
[Dr. John Armstrong: *The Art of Preserving Health* (1744)]
Aubrey tells us that Bacon would drive in his open coach in the rain "to receive the benefit of irrigation, which he was wont to say was very wholesome because of the nitre in the air."

21 Prepare for death if here at night you

roam,
And sign your will before you sup
from home.
[Samuel Johnson: *London*]

1 Cities humming with a restless crowd.
[William Cowper: *Retirement*]

2 I live not in myself, but I become
Portion of that around me; and to me
High mountains are a feeling, but the
hum
Of human cities torture.
[Byron: *Childe Harold* III.lxxii.]

3 This city now doth, like a garment,
wear
The beauty of the morning.
[Wordsworth: *Composed upon Westminster Bridge*]

4 I have found by experience, that they
who have spent all their lives in cities,
improve their talents, but impair their
virtues; and strengthen their minds, but
weaken their morals. [C. C. Colton: *Lacon*]

5 If you would be known, and not
know, vegetate in a village; if you would
know, and not be known, live in a city.
[C. C. Colton: *Lacon*]

6 The city is recruited from the country. [Emerson: *Manners*]

7 A rose-red city—"half as old as
Time"!
[John William Burgon: *Petra*]

*Petra is a rock city in a deep gorge on
the NE slope of Mt. Hor. Its temples
and dwellings are carved from rose,
crimson and purple limestone. It was a
great commercial city for several centuries, captured by the Moslems in the
7th century and by the Crusaders in the
12th. Its ruins were discovered in 1812.*

*Petra was a prize poem, recited and
published in Oxford in 1845. The phrase
"half as old as Time" is set off with
quotation marks and was probably borrowed from the 1838 revision of Samuel
Rogers's Italy (ii.5).*

*Familiarity with Burgon's line is regarded as a touchstone of academic literary elegance. The knowledge that it
is taken from Rogers offers a splendid
opportunity for one-upmanship, especially the knowledge that it was an addition to the original form of Rogers's
poem. However, even further vistas of
triumph have been opened with the dis-*

*covery that Rogers probably borrowed
the phrase from a satirical poem entitled
Heroic Epistle to Burke, published anonymously in 1791. Therein we are told
that*

*. . . awful grandeur guards the Gothic
hall,*
*And crests and mantles dignify the
wall;*
Ensigns armorial, pedigrees sublime,
*And wax and parchment half as old
as time.*

*This would seem to take the phrase
back to its origin were it not that the
anonymous author states that there is in
his poem "scarcely a single image which
is not extracted from Mr. Burke's celebrated Reflections." No one has yet
found the phrase in Burke, but it may
be lurking somewhere—and Burke may
have borrowed it; he was a widely-read
man!*

8 It is this colossal opportunity to escape from life that brings yokels to the
cities, not mere lust for money. [H. L.
Mencken: *Prejudices: Fourth Series*]

9 All cities are mad: but the madness
is gallant. All cities are beautiful: but the
beauty is grim. [Christopher Morley:
Where the Blue Begins Ch. 6.]

10 As a remedy to life in society, I would
suggest the big city. Nowadays, it is the
only desert within our means. [Albert
Camus: *Notebooks 1935-1942* Ch. III,
p. 173]

CIVILIAN

11 War hath no fury like a noncombatant. [C. E. Montague: *Disenchantment*]

CIVILITIES

12 It was not for me to bandy civilities
with my sovereign. [Samuel Johnson:
in Boswell's *Life* (1767)]

*Johnson, while reading in the royal library, had had a surprise visit from King
George III. In the course of their conversation, the king had paid Johnson a
fine compliment. Later someone asked
him whether he had made any answer
to this. Johnson's answer, given above,
showed, as Boswell said, "a nice and dignified sense of true politeness."*

CIVILIZATION

1 Our laws make law impossible; our liberties destroy all freedom; our property is organized robbery; our morality is an impudent hypocrisy; our wisdom is administered by inexperienced or mal-experienced dupes, our power wielded by cowards and weaklings, and our honor false in all its points. I am an enemy of the existing order for good reasons. [G. B. Shaw: Preface to *Major Barbara*]

2 Civilization is hooped together, brought
Under a rule, under the semblance of peace
By manifold illusion.
[William Butler Yeats: *Supernatural Songs,* "Meru"]

3 Has civilization a motto? Then certainly it must be "Not thy will, O Lord, but ours, be done!" [H. L. Mencken: *Prejudices: Fourth Series*]

4 A concerted effort to remedy the blunders and check the practical joking of God. [H. L. Mencken: *A Book of Burlesques*]

5 Civilizations die from philosophical calm, irony, and the sense of fair play quite as surely as they die of debauchery. [Joseph Wood Krutch: *The Modern Temper* II.iii.]

6 Civilization does not lie in a greater or lesser degree of refinement, but in an awareness shared by a whole people. [Albert Camus: *Notebooks 1935-1942* Ch. I, p. 31]

CIVILIZE

7 I reckon I got to light out for the Territory, because Aunt Sally she's going to adopt me and civilize me and I can't stand it. [Mark Twain: *Huckleberry Finn* (concluding lines)]

CLARET

8 Poor stuff! No, Sir, claret is the liquor for boys; port for men; but he who aspires to be a hero (smiling) must drink brandy. [Samuel Johnson: in Boswell's *Life,* April 7, 1779]

9 Now I like claret . . . For really 'tis so fine—it fills one's mouth with a gushing freshness—then goes down cool and feverless . . . and lies as quiet as it did in the grape; then, it is as fragrant as the Queen Bee, and the more ethereal Part of it mounts into the brain—not assaulting the cerebral apartments like a bully in a bad-house . . . but rather walks like Aladdin about his own enchanted palace so gently that you do not feel his step. [Keats: letter to his brother George, February 18, 1819]

CLARITY

10 Care should be taken, not that the reader may understand, but that he must understand. [Quintilian: *De institutione oratoria*]

11 Everything that can be thought at all can be thought clearly. Everything that can be said can be said clearly. [Ludwig Wittgenstein: *Tractatus Logico-philosophicus*]
   A dissent from the common idea popularly expressed in the words, "I know it but I can't express it."

CLASSICS

12 The praise of ancient authors proceeds not from the reverence of the dead, but from the competition and mutual envy of the living. [Thomas Hobbes: *Leviathan,* "Review and Conclusion"]

13 "Classic." A book which people praise and don't read. [Mark Twain: *Pudd'nhead Wilson's New Calendar*]

14 Every man with a bellyful of the classics is an enemy to the human race. [Henry Miller: *Tropic of Cancer*]

CLAWS

15 I should have been a pair of ragged claws
Scuttling across the floors of silent seas.
[T. S. Eliot: *The Love Song of J. Alfred Prufrock*]

CLAY

16 Imperious Caesar, dead and turn'd to clay,
Might stop a hole to keep the wind away.
[Shakespeare: *Hamlet* V.i.]

CLEANLINESS

17 Cleanliness is, indeed, next to godliness. [John Wesley: *Sermon XCIII,* "On Dress"]

Wesley has the sentence in quotation marks. It has been opined that he was quoting a Hebrew saying. Bacon, in The Advancement of Learning, *Book II, says: "Cleanness of body was ever deemed to proceed from a due reverence to God." But this does not accord with the deliberate maceration and encrustation of the body indulged in by some saints.*

CLEAR

1 That's clear as mud. [R. H. Barham: *The Ingoldsby Legends,* "The Merchant of Venice"]

CLEOPATRA

2 My serpent of old Nile. [Shakespeare: *Antony and Cleopatra* I.v.]

3 Age cannot wither her, nor custom stale
Her infinite variety.
[Shakespeare: *Antony and Cleopatra* II.ii.]

4 If Cleopatra's nose had been shorter, the whole face of the earth would have changed. [Pascal: *Pensées* II]

CLERGY

5 A genius in a reverend gown
Must ever keep its owner down;
'Tis an unnatural conjunction,
And spoils the credit of the function.
[Jonathan Swift: *To Dr. Delany*]
function = *the profession, the action proper to a member of the profession— here, the clergy*

6 A little, round, fat, oily man of God. [James Thomson (1700-1748): *The Castle of Indolence* I.lxix.]

7 [The] merriment of parsons is mighty offensive. [Samuel Johnson: in Boswell's *Life,* March 1781]
Johnson felt strongly that the dignity of the Church required the clergy to live lives apart and never to lose "their distinction in indiscriminate sociality."

8 To a philosophic eye the vices of the clergy are far less dangerous than their virtues. [Edward Gibbon: *The Decline and Fall of the Roman Empire*]

9 As the French say, there are three sexes,—men, women, and clergymen. [Sydney Smith: in Lady Holland's *Mem-*

oir I.ix.]
Lady Holland was Sydney Smith's daughter. She was christened Saba, a name which he made up so that she wouldn't have a commonplace first name with Smith as her last name.

10 His creed no parson ever knew,
For this was still his 'simple plan,'
To have with clergymen to do
As little as a Christian can.
[Sir Francis Doyle: *The Unobtrusive Christian*]

11 A clergyman can hardly ever allow himself to look facts fairly in the face. It is his profession to support one side; it is impossible, therefore, for him to make an unbiased examination of the other. [Samuel Butler (1835-1902): *The Way of All Flesh* XXVI]

12 The clergyman is expected to be a kind of human Sunday. [Samuel Butler (1835-1902): *The Way of All Flesh* XXVI]

13 His helmet was a glance
That spoke of holy gladness;
A saintly smile his lance,
His shield a tear of sadness.
[W. S. Gilbert: *Bab Ballads,* "The Rival Curates"]

14 CLERGYMAN. A man who undertakes the management of our spiritual affairs as a method of bettering his temporal ones. [Ambrose Bierce: *The Devil's Dictionary*]

15 They could understand everything he said, and they began to think he was common. [George Ade: *The Fable of the Preacher who Flew his Kite*]

16 All the same I like Parsons; they think nobly of the Universe, and believe in Souls and Eternal Happiness. And some of them, I am told, believe in Angels— that there are Angels who guide our footsteps, and flit to and fro unseen on errands in the air about us. [Logan Pearsall Smith: *Trivia,* "Parsons"]

17 ARCHBISHOP. A Christian ecclesiastic of a rank superior to that attained by Christ. [H. L. Mencken: *Chrestomathy* 624]

18 Call me *Brother,* if you will;
Call me *Parson*—better still—
Though plain *Mister* fills the bill,
And even *Father* brings no chill
Of hurt or rancor or ill-will.

Preacher, Pastor, Rector, Friend,
Titles almost without end
Never grate and ne'er offend;
A loving ear to all I bend.
But how the man my heart doth rend,
Who blithely calls me *Reverend.*
[Anon.]

This famous little jingle has been in cir-
culation since 1929. Though at different
times ascribed to different clergymen, its
authorship is unknown.

The form of salutation used by Catho-
lics is "Reverend Francis P. Crane,"
though the definite article precedes the
title of a monsignor ("The Very Rever-
end Msgr." or "The Right Rev. Msgr.").
Among Protestants there is a distinction
among the sects. The Calvinists employ
Reverend ("Reverend Calvin," wrote
Bishop Hall, in 1656) and the American
colonists followed this form. The Chap-
lain of the United States Senate is "Rever-
end So-and-So" and commissions for
chaplains in the armed forces designate
the commissioned as "Reverend." Episco-
palians, however, following a later Brit-
ish usage prefer "the Reverend" and have
been known, in lapsed moments, to be
annoyed at its omission.

In the style sheets of some Southern
newspapers, "the Rev." is stipulated for
white clergyman and "Rev." for Negroes
(Time, March 31, 1961, p. 30).

The use of "Reverend" entirely by it-
self ("Mornin', Reverend!") is probably
the galling salutation to which the jingle
refers. Clergymen, for some reason, seem
to find it irritating. Its use is confined
largely to the uneducated, the folksy; but
of such is the kingdom of Heaven.

CLEVER

1 If you can't be clever, be good. [Pa-
lingenius: *Zodiacus Vitae,* "Taurus"]
2 The surest way to be deceived is to
think oneself cleverer than the others.
[La Rochefoucauld: *Maxims*]
3 Be good, sweet maid, and let who can
be clever.
[Charles Kingsley: *A Farewell* (1889
ed.)]

This verse—which became enormously
popular—epitomizes a great deal of Vic-
torian morality, in its assumption that
cleverness and goodness are wholly dif-

ferent things.

There is a touch of pathos in an
emendation it underwent. In earlier ver-
sions Kingsley had written, "Be good,
sweet maid, and let who will be clever."
But twenty-nine years later, after labor-
ing for three decades on his virtuous but
not very scintillating writings, somehow
the idea had gotten through to him that
being clever was not solely a matter of
volition.

4 If all the good people were clever,
And all the clever people were good,
The world would be nicer than ever
We thought that it possibly could.

But somehow, 'tis seldom or never
The two hit it off as they should;
The good are so harsh to the clever,
The clever so rude to the good!
[Elizabeth Wordsworth: *The Clever and*
the Good]

CLIFFS OF DOVER

5 How fearful
And dizzy 'tis to cast one's eyes so low!
The crows and choughs that wing
the midway air
Show scarce so gross as beetles; half
way down
Hangs one that gathers samphire,
dreadful trade!
Methinks he seems no bigger than his
head.
The fishermen that walk upon the
beach
Appear like mice, and yon tall anchoring bark
Diminished to her cock, her cock a
buoy
Almost too small for sight. The murmuring surge
That on the unnumbered idle peb-
bles chafes
Cannot be heard so high.
[Shakespeare: *King Lear* IV.vi.]
samphire = *a succulent apiaceous herb*
of Europe growing in clefts of rock near
the sea; cock = *cockboat.*

Dr. Johnson felt that the samphire-
gatherer broke the terrifying descent and
so weakened the effect of the passage.
Others have asserted that it doubles the
effect, stressing the extent of the fall by
pausing and then continuing. The same

effect is obtained in Paradise Lost *(I.743-6) in Milton's description of Mulciber's fall when angry Jove threw him "sheer o'er the crystal battlements" of Heaven:*

> . . . . *from morn*
> *To noon he fell, from noon to dewy*
> *eve,*
> *A summer's day, and with the setting*
> *sun*
> *Dropt from the zenith, like a falling*
> *star,*
> *On Lemnos, the Aegaean isle.*

1   The cliffs of England stand,
    Glimmering and vast, out in the tranquil bay.
[Matthew Arnold: *Dover Beach*]

CLOCK

2 The capon burns, the pig falls from the spit,
    The clock hath strucken twelve.
[Shakespeare: *The Comedy of Errors* I.ii.]
3 Perfection in a clock does not consist in being fast, but in being on time. [Vauvenargues: *Réflexions*]
4 My grandfather's clock was too large for the shelf.
    So it stood ninety years on the floor.
[H. C. Work: *Grandfather's Clock*]

CLOTHING

5 The woman shall not wear that which pertaineth unto a man, neither shall a man put on a woman's garment; for all that do so are abomination unto the Lord thy God. [Deuteronomy 22:5]
6 Costly thy habit as thy purse can buy,
    But not express'd in fancy; rich, not gaudy;
    For the apparel oft proclaims the man.
[Shakespeare: *Hamlet* I.iii.]
> *Be valyaunt, but not too venturous.*
> *Let thy attyre bee comely, but not costly.*
>   John Lyly: Euphues *(1579)*
7 Set not thy sweet heart on proud array.
[Shakespeare: *King Lear* III.iv.]
8 Thy clothes are all the soul thou hast. [Beaumont and Fletcher: *Honest Man's Fortune* V.iii.]
9 Is not religion a cloak; honesty a pair of shoes worn out in the dirt; self-love a surtout; vanity a shirt; and conscience a pair of breeches, which, though a cover for lewdness as well as nastiness, is easily slipt down for the service of both? [Jonathan Swift: *A Tale of a Tub* II]
> surtout = *literally an "over all," an over-coat or greatcoat*
10 She wears her clothes as if they were thrown on her with a pitchfork. [Jonathan Swift: *Polite Conversation*]
11 I hold that gentleman to be the best dressed whose dress no one observes. [Anthony Trollope: *Thackeray* IX]
12 Beware of all enterprises that require new clothes. [Thoreau: *Walden* I.]
13 My clothes keep my various selves buttoned up together, and enable all these otherwise irreconcilable aggregates of psychological phenomena to pass themselves off as one person. [Logan Pearsall Smith: *More Trivia*, "Reassurance"]

CLOUD(S)

14 There ariseth a little cloud out of the sea, like a man's hand. [I Kings 18:44]
15 Who maketh the clouds his chariot. [Psalms 104:3]
16   Can such things be,
    And overcome us like a summer's cloud,
  Without our special wonder?
[Shakespeare: *Macbeth* III.iv.]
17 Sometimes we see a cloud that's dragonish;
    A vapour sometime like a bear or lion,
    A tower'd citadel, a pendant rock,
    A forked mountain, or blue promontory
  With trees upon 't.
[Shakespeare: *Antony and Cleopatra* IV.xii.]
18   Even with a thought
    The rack dislimns, and makes it indistinct,
  As water is in water.
[Shakespeare: *Antony and Cleopatra* IV.xii.]
19 Was I deceiv'd, or did a sable cloud
    Turn forth her silver lining on the night?
[John Milton: *Comus*]
20   . . . lonely as a cloud
    That floats on high o'er vales and hills.

[Wordsworth: *I Wandered Lonely as a Cloud*]

1 Motionless as a cloud the old Man stood,
That heareth not the loud winds when they call
And moveth all together, if it move at all.

[Wordsworth: *Resolution and Independence*]

2 The clouds that gather round the setting sun
Do take a sober coloring from an eye
That hath kept watch o'er man's mortality.

[Wordsworth: *Intimations of Immortality*]

3 And those thin clouds above, in flakes and bars,
That give away their motion to the stars.

[Coleridge: *Dejection*]

4 I wield the flail of the lashing hail,
And whiten the green plains under,
And then again I dissolve it in rain,
And laugh as I pass in thunder.

[Shelley: *The Cloud*]

5 Wait till the clouds roll by, Jenny,
Wait till the clouds roll by.

[J. T. Wood: *Wait till the Clouds Roll By*]

CLUB

6 A most unclubable man. [Samuel Johnson: referring to Sir John Hawkins]

Quoted in Madame D'Arblay's Diary, I.lxv.

COALS

7 Salt to Dysart, or coals to Newcastle. [Sir James Melville: *Autobiography* I. (1583)]

Newcastle-on-Tyne, the chief port city of England's coal district, famous for its export of coal since the 13th century. To take coals to Newcastle was taking something to the very source of supply, hence absurdly superfluous, a ludicrous waste of effort.

See OWL

COALS OF FIRE

8 If thine enemy be hungry, give him bread to eat; and if he be thirsty, give him water to drink:
For thou shalt heap coals of fire upon his head. [Proverbs 25:21-22]

9 If thine enemy hunger, feed him; if he thirst, give him drink: for in so doing thou shalt heap coals of fire on his head. [Romans 12:20]

COAST

10 The breaking waves dash'd high
On a stern and rock-bound coast,
And the woods, against a stormy sky,
Their giant branches toss'd.

[Felicia Hemans: *The Landing of the Pilgrim Fathers*]

In advertising folders, the coast of Maine is invariably rockbound, without benefit of quotation marks. One of the many dangers of poetry is that it begets clichés.

COCK

11 Before the cock crow twice, thou shalt deny me thrice. [Mark 14:72]

12 The early village cock
Hath twice done salutation to the morn.

[Shakespeare: *Richard III* V.iii.]

13 The cock, that is the trumpet to the morn,
Doth with his lofty and shrill-sounding throat
Awake the god of day.

[Shakespeare: *Hamlet* I.i.]

14 He was like a cock who thought the sun had risen to hear him crow. [George Eliot: *Adam Bede* XVIII]

COCK A DOODLE DOO

15 Cock a doodle doo!
My dame has lost her shoe,
My master's lost his fiddling stick,
And don't know what to do.

[Nursery rhyme]

Many versions. One is definitely dated 1606 and is connected with a child's testimony in a murder case.

The rhyme seems to have been a childish diversion on hearing a cock crow.

COCK ROBIN

16 Who killed Cock Robin?
"I," said the Sparrow,
"With my bow and arrow,
I killed Cock Robin."

[Nursery rhyme]
Earliest known version 1744, and thought by some to refer to the downfall of Sir Robert Walpole. But, though this event may have given it wide popularity, internal evidence suggests a much older date of origin. Some go so far as to relate it to the death of Balder.

COEDUCATION

1 The so-called method of co-education is false in theory and harmful to Christian training. [Pope Pius XI: *Divini illius magistri*, December 31, 1929]

COFFEE

2 For lo! the board with cups and
      spoons is crown'd,
The berries crackle, and the mill
      turns round;
On shining altars of Japan they raise
The silver lamp; the fiery spirits
      blaze:
From silver spouts the grateful liq-
      uors glide,
While China's earth receives the
      smoking tide.
[Alexander Pope: *The Rape of the Lock* III]
grateful = *gratifying*
The passage is meant to be playfully pompous.

3 Coffee, which makes the politician
      wise,
And see through all things with his
      half-shut eyes.
[Alexander Pope: *The Rape of the Lock* III]

COFFEE SPOONS

4 I have measured out my life with cof-
      fee spoons.
[T. S. Eliot: *The Love Song of J. Alfred Prufrock*]

COGITATION

5 Generally youth is like the first cogitations, not so wise as the second. [Francis Bacon: *Youth and Age*]
6 His cogitative faculties immersed
In cogibundity of cogitation.
[Henry Carey: *Chrononhotonthologos* I.i.]

COITION

7 I could be content that we might pro-
create like trees, without conjunction, or that there were any way to perpetuate the world without this trivial and vulgar way of coition; it is the foolishest act a wise man commits in all his life. [Sir Thomas Browne: *Religio Medici* II.ix.]

COLD

8   A man whose blood
Is very snow-broth; one who never
      feels
The wanton stings and motions of the
      sense.
[Shakespeare: *Measure for Measure* I.iv.]
9 As the day lengthens
The cold strengthens.
[John Ray: *English Proverbs* (1670)]
10 And now there came both mist and
      snow,
And it grew wondrous cold:
And ice, mast-high, came floating by,
As green as emerald.
[Coleridge: *The Ancient Mariner* I]
11 St. Agnes' Eve—Ah, bitter chill it
      was!
The owl, for all his feathers, was
      a-cold;
The hare limp'd trembling through
      the frozen grass,
And silent was the flock in woolly
      fold.
[Keats: *The Eve of St. Agnes* (opening lines)]

COLLAPSE

12 You see, of course, if you're not a
      dunce,
How it went to pieces all at once—
All at once, and nothing first—
Just as bubbles do when they burst.
[O. W. Holmes: *The Deacon's Masterpiece*]

COLLEGE

13 A set o' dull conceited hashes
Confuse their brains in college
      classes;
They gang in stirks, and come out
      asses.
[Robert Burns: *Epistle to J. Lapraik*]
stirks = *young bullocks*

COLERIDGE

14 Coleridge, poet and philosopher wrecked in a mist of opium. [Matthew

[Arnold: *Essays in Criticism: Second Series*, "Byron"]

COLOGNE

1 In Köhln, a town of monks and
bones,
And pavements fang'd with murderous stones
And rags and hags, and hideous
wenches;
I counted two and seventy stenches,
All well defined, and several stinks!
Ye Nymphs that reign o'er sewers and
sinks,
The river Rhine, it is well known,
Doth wash your city of Cologne;
But tell me, nymphs, what power divine
Shall henceforth wash the river
Rhine?

[Coleridge: *Cologne*]

COLONIZING

2 A crew of pirates are driven by a storm they know not whither, at length a boy discovers land from the topmast, they go on shore to rob and plunder, they see an harmless people, are entertained with kindness, they give the country a new name . . . they murder two or three dozen of the natives, bring away a couple more by force for a sample. . . . Here commences a new dominion acquired by divine right. Ships are sent with the first opportunity . . . a free license given to all acts of inhumanity and lust, the earth reeking with the blood of its inhabitants: and this execrable crew of butchers employed in so pious an expedition is a *modern colony* sent to convert and civilize an idolatrous and barbarous people. [Jonathan Swift: *Gulliver's Travels* IV. xii.]

COLOSSUS

3 Why, man, he doth bestride the narrow world
Like a Colossus; and we petty men
Walk under his huge legs, and peep
about
To find ourselves dishonourable
graves.
Men at some time are masters of their
fates:
The fault, dear Brutus, is not in our

stars,
But in ourselves, that we are underlings.
[Shakespeare: *Julius Caesar* I.ii.]

COLUMBIA

4 Hail, Columbia! happy land!
Hail, ye heroes! heaven-born band!
Who fought and bled in Freedom's
cause,
Who fought and bled in Freedom's
cause.
[Joseph Hopkinson: *Hail, Columbia*]

COLUMBUS

5 Columbus discovered no isle or key so lonely as himself. [Emerson: *Society and Solitude*]
6 Behind him lay the gray Azores,
Behind the Gates of Hercules;
Before him not the ghost of shores,
Before him only shoreless seas.
[Joaquin Miller: *Columbus*]
7 "Brave admiral, say but one good
word:
What shall we do when hope is
gone?"
The words leapt like a leaping sword:
"Sail on! sail on! sail on! and on!"
[Joaquin Miller: *Columbus*]
8 He gained a world; he gave that
world
Its grandest lesson: "On! sail on!"
[Joaquin Miller: *Columbus*]

COMEDY

9 Comedy is allied to justice. [Aristophanes: *The Acharnians*]
10 The world is a comedy to those who think, a tragedy to those who feel. [Horace Walpole: Letter to Horace Mann, Dec. 31, 1769]
11 Comedy is the clash of character. Eliminate character from comedy and you get farce. [William Butler Yeats: *Dramatis Personae*]
12 Comedy takes place in a world where the mind is always superior to the emotions. [Joseph Wood Krutch: *The Modern Temper* VI.iv.]
13 Comedy is the last refuge of the nonconformist mind. [Gilbert Seldes, in *The New Republic*, Dec. 20, 1954]

COMFORT

14 Thy rod and thy staff they comfort

me. [Psalms 23:4]

1 Be of good comfort, Master Ridley, and play the man. We shall this day light such a candle by God's grace in England, as I trust shall never be put out. [Hugh Latimer, Bishop of Worcester: to Nicholas Ridley, Bishop of London, as—with Thomas Cranmer, Archbishop of Canterbury—they were about to be burned for heresy, at Oxford, October 6, 1555]

2 I beg cold comfort; and you are so strait,
And so ingrateful, you deny me that.
[Shakespeare: *King John* V.vii.]

3 Now I, to comfort him, bid him a' should not think of God; I hoped there was no need to trouble himself with any such thoughts yet. [Shakespeare: *Henry V* II.i.]

4 He receives comfort like cold porridge.
[Shakespeare: *The Tempest* II.i.]

5 It is often a comfort to shift one's position and be bruised in a new place. [Washington Irving: Preface to *Tales of a Traveller*]

6 For thence—a paradox
Which comforts while it mocks—
Shall life succeed in that it seems to fail:
What I aspired to be,
And was not, comforts me:
A brute I might have been, but would not sink i' the scale.
[Robert Browning: *Rabbi Ben Ezra*]

7 We have all sinned and come short of the glory of making ourselves as comfortable as we easily might have done. [Samuel Butler (1835-1902): *The Way of All Flesh*]

8 You canna expect to be baith grand and comfortable. [J. M. Barrie: *The Little Minister* X]

COMFORTERS
9 Miserable comforters are ye all. [Job 16:2]

COMING
10 He onward came; far off his coming shone.
[John Milton: *Paradise Lost* VI.768]

COMMAND
11 Whosoever obeyeth by discretion and not by subjection, corrupteth and abuseth the office of commanding. [Montaigne: *Essays* I.xvi.]

Montaigne is here speaking of military obedience—and states one of those truths that a democratic age doesn't like to face.

12 Whatever is enforced by command is more imputed to him who exacts than to him who performs. [Montaigne: *Essays* III.ix.]

13 Those he commands, move only in command,
Nothing in love.
[Shakespeare: *Macbeth* V.ii.]

14 Whoever can do as he pleases, commands when he entreats.
[Corneille: *Sertorius* IV.ii.]

15 God so commanded, and left that command
Sole daughter of his voice.
[John Milton: *Paradise Lost* IX.652]

COMMANDMENTS
16 Thou shalt have no other gods before me.

Thou shalt not make unto thee any graven image, or any likeness of any thing that is in heaven above, or that is in the earth beneath, or that is in the water under the earth: thou shalt not bow down thyself to them, nor serve them: for I the Lord thy God am a jealous God, visiting the iniquity of the fathers upon the children unto the third and fourth generation of them that hate me; and shewing mercy unto thousands of them that love me, and keep my commandments.

Thou shalt not take the name of the Lord thy God in vain; for the Lord will not hold him guiltless that taketh his name in vain.

Remember the sabbath day, to keep it holy. Six days shalt thou labour, and do all thy work: but the seventh day is the sabbath of the Lord thy God: in it thou shalt not do any work, thou, nor thy son, nor thy daughter, thy manservant, nor thy maidservant, nor thy cattle, nor the stranger that is within thy gates: for in six days the Lord made heaven and earth, the sea, and all that in them is, and rested the seventh day: wherefore the Lord blessed the sabbath day, and hallowed it.

Honour thy father and thy mother: that thy days may be long upon the land which the Lord thy God giveth thee.

Thou shalt not kill.

Thou shalt not commit adultery.

Thou shalt not steal.

Thou shalt not bear false witness against thy neighbour.

Thou shalt not covet thy neighbour's wife, nor his manservant, nor his maidservant, nor his ox, nor his ass, nor any thing that is thy neighbour's. [Exodus 20:3-17]

1 The Eleventh Commandment: Thou shalt not be found out. [George Whyte-Melville: *Holmby House*]

COMMERCE

2 It is naught, it is naught, saith the buyer: but when he is gone his way, then he boasteth. [Proverbs 20:14]

3 But one thing is, ye know it well enow,
Of chapmen, that their money is their plow.
[Chaucer: *The Shipman's Tale*]
chapmen = *merchants*
The word is related to cheapen. *Peddlers were called chapmen in Scotland until quite recently.*

4 The propensity to truck, barter, and exchange . . . is common to all men, and to be found in no other race of animals. [Adam Smith: *The Wealth of Nations* I.ii.]

5 Commerce is the school of cheating. [Vauvenargues: *Réflexions*]

6 Honour sinks where commerce long prevails. [Oliver Goldsmith: *The Traveller*]

7 The greatest meliorator of the world is selfish, huckstering trade. [Emerson: *Society and Solitude,* "Works and Days"]

8 Mercantile morality is really nothing but a refinement of piratical morality. [Nietzsche: *Thus Spake Zarathustra*]

COMMERCIALISM

9 Ill fares the land, to hastening ills a prey,
Where wealth accumulates, and men decay;
Princes and lords may flourish or may fade;
A breath can make them, as a breath has made;
But a bold peasantry, their country's pride,
When once destroy'd, can never be supplied.
[Oliver Goldsmith: *The Deserted Village*]

COMMON

10 As common as a barber's chair. [Stephen Gosson: *Apologie of the Schoole of Abuse* (1579)]
The phrase was as common itself. It was used of Venus and sometimes of loose women.
Sometimes, as in Shakespeare's All's Well that Ends Well *(II.ii.), "that fits all buttocks" is added.*

11 I am not in the roll of common men. [Shakespeare: *I Henry IV* III.i.]

COMMONALTY

12 The common growth of mother-earth
Suffices me—her tears, her mirth,
Her humblest mirth and tears.
[Wordsworth: *Peter Bell*]

COMMONPLACE

13 And fear not lest Existence closing your
Account, and mine, should know the like no more.
The Eternal Saki from that Bowl has poured
Millions of Bubbles like us, and will pour.
[*Rubáiyát of Omar Khayyám* (trans. Edward FitzGerald)]

14 One writes, that "other friends remain,"
That "loss is common to the race"—
And common is the commonplace,
And vacant chaff well meant for grain.
[Tennyson: *In Memoriam VI*]

15 Gone the cry of "Forward, Forward,"
lost within a growing gloom;
Lost, or only heard in silence from the silence of a tomb.
Half the marvels of my morning, triumphs over time and space,
Staled by frequence, shrunk by usage into commonest commonplace!
[Tennyson: *Locksley Hall Sixty Years After*]

COMMON SENSE
1 Common sense is the most widely shared commodity in the world, for every man is convinced that he is well supplied with it. [Descartes: *Discours de la Méthode*]
2 We seldom attribute common sense except to those who agree with us. [La Rochefoucauld: *Maxims*]

COMMUNICATION(S)
3 Evil communications corrupt good manners. [I Corinthians 15:33]
4 A man were better relate himself to a statue or picture than to suffer his thoughts to pass in smother. [Francis Bacon: *Of Friendship*]
relate = *unburden himself, speak out*
in smother = *be repressed, suffocated*
5 There was a man with a tongue of
wood
Who essayed to sing,
And in truth it was lamentable.
But there was one who heard
The clip-clapper of this tongue of
wood
And knew what the man
Wished to sing,
And with that the singer was content.
[Stephen Crane: *There Was a Man*]

COMMUNIST
6 COMMUNIST: an intensely proud person who proposes to enrich the common fund instead of to sponge on it. [G. B. Shaw: *Man and Superman:* "The Revolutionist's Handbook, III"]

COMPANION
7 A pleasant companion reduces the length of the journey. [Publilius Syrus: *Maxims*]

COMPANY
8 Tell me what company you keep, and I'll tell you what you are. [Cervantes: *Don Quixote* II.10.]
9 Company, villainous company, hath
been the spoil of me.
[Shakespeare: *I Henry IV* III. iii.]
10 You should always except the present company. [John O'Keefe: *The London Hermit* I.ii. (1793)]
A saying, usually an interjection, now commonly "present company excepted."

11 A poet could not but be gay,
In such a jocund company.
[Wordsworth: *I Wandered Lonely as a Cloud*]
12 Men who know the same things are not long the best company for each other. [Emerson: *Representative Men*, "Uses of Great Men"]

COMPARISONS: are odious
13 Comparisouns doon offte gret grevaunce. [John Lydgate: *The Fall of Princes* III (1430-38)]
14 Comparison is odious. [Francesco Berni: *Orlando Innamorato* VI.iv.]
15 Comparisons are odious. [John Fortescue: *De Laudibus Legum Angliae* XIX]
16 Comparisons are always odious and ill taken. [Cervantes: *Don Quixote* II.i.]
17 Comparisons are odorous. [Shakespeare: *Much Ado About Nothing* III.v.]
18 Comparisons are odious. [Robert Burton: *Anatomy of Melancholy* III. 3.1.2.]
19 Comparisons are odious, because they are impertinent—making one thing the standard of another which has no relation to it. [William Hazlitt: *Table-Talk* I.ix.]

COMPASSION
20 A certain Samaritan . . . had compassion on him. [Luke 10:33]
Though known today as "the good Samaritan," the Samaritan is nowhere in the Bible so designated. The point of his being a Samaritan is that the Samaritans and the Jews were ancient enemies.

COMPETITION
21 He that seeketh to be eminent amongst able men hath a great task; but that is ever good for the public: but he that plots to be the only figure amongst ciphers is the decay of an whole age. [Francis Bacon: *Of Ambition*]
22 Thou shalt not covet; but tradition
Approves all forms of competition.
[Arthur Hugh Clough: *The Latest Decalogue*]

COMPLACENCY
23 God, I thank thee, that I am not as

other men are. [Luke 18:11]

1 When, as becomes a man who would
prepare
For such an arduous work, I through
myself
Make rigorous inquisition, the report
Is often cheering.
[Wordsworth: *The Prelude* I]

2 Nothing is to me more distasteful
than that entire complacency and satisfaction which beam in the faces of a new-married couple—in that of the lady particularly. [Charles Lamb: *A Bachelor's Complaint*]

COMPLAIN(ING)

3 It is not sufficiently considered how much he assumes who dares to claim the privilege of complaining; for as every man has, in his own opinion, a full share of the miseries of life, he is inclined to consider all clamorous uneasiness as proof of impatience rather than affliction and to ask what merit has this man to show by which he has acquired a right to repine at the distributions of nature. [Samuel Johnson: *The Rambler*, "The Respect Due to Age," No. 50]

4 Those who do not complain are never pitied. [Jane Austen: *Pride and Prejudice*]

5 Never complain and never explain. [Benjamin Disraeli: quoted in John Morley's *Life of Gladstone*]

COMPLEXION

6 To a red man read thy rede,
With a brown man break thy bread,
At a pale man draw thy knife,
From a black man keep thy wife.
[D. Fergusson: *Scottish Proverbs* (1641)]
A very popular proverb that appeared with many variations, this states the temperaments commonly associated with the various humors and complexions. That is, from a florid and sanguine man you may accept advice. The pale man is envious and dangerous. Dark-complexioned men (and women) were thought to be especially amorous.

COMPLIANCE

7 He in a few minutes ravished this fair creature, or at least would have ravished her, if she had not, by a timely compli-ance, prevented him. [Henry Fielding: *Jonathan Wild* III.vii.]

8 As overcompliant as an inexperienced prostitute. [Eric Hodgins: *Episode*, p. 206]

COMPLIMENT

9 'Twas never merry world
Since lowly feigning was called compliment.
[Shakespeare: *Twelfth Night* III.i.]

10 Compliment—a thing often paid by people who pay nothing else. [Horatio Smith: *The Tin Trumpet*]

11 A compliment is something like a kiss through a veil. Pleasure sets her soft seal there, even while hiding herself. [Victor Hugo: *Les Misérables* VIII.i.]

COMPOSING

12 In composing, as a general rule, run your pen through every other word you have written; you have no idea what vigor it will give your style. [Sydney Smith: in Lady Holland's *Memoir* I. xi.]
Thomson's Seasons—*an enormously popular but diffuse and stilted poem—being praised in his company, Samuel Johnson picked up a volume and read a passage from it with sonorous dignity. After the murmurs of applause had subsided, he told the admirers that he had omitted every other line.*

COMPOSURE

13 Charlotte, having seen his body
Borne before her on a shutter,
Like a well-conducted person,
Went on cutting bread and butter.
[W. M. Thackeray: *Sorrows of Werther*]

COMPROMISE

14 All government, indeed every human benefit and enjoyment, every virtue, and every prudent act, is founded on compromise and barter. [Edmund Burke: Speech on Conciliation with America, March 22, 1775]

15 Compromise is never anything but an ignoble truce between the duty of a man and the terror of a coward. [Reginald Wright Kauffman: *The Way of Peace*]

16 The great bourn of all common

sense: compromise. [William Bolitho: *Twelve Against the Gods*, "Mahomet"]

COMPUNCTION
1 No compunctious visitings of nature
Shake my fell purpose.
[Shakespeare: *Macbeth* I.v.]

CONCEALMENT
2　　　　She never told her love,
But let concealment, like a worm i'
　　　　th' bud,
Feed on her damask cheek.
[Shakespeare: *Twelfth Night* II.iv.]
3 If you dissemble sometimes your knowledge of what you are thought to know, you shall be thought another time to know that you know not. [Francis Bacon: *Of Discourse*]

CONCEIT
4 Conceit is to human character what salt is to the ocean; it keeps it sweet and renders it endurable. [O. W. Holmes: *The Autocrat of the Breakfast-Table* I]
5 I've never any pity for conceited people, because I think they carry their comfort about with them. [George Eliot: *The Mill on the Floss* V.iv.]

CONCEPTION
6 The night my father got me
His mind was not on me;
He did not plague his fancy
To muse if I should be
The son you see.
[A. E. Housman: *Last Poems* XIV]

CONCESSIONS
7 The concessions of the weak are the concessions of fear. [Edmund Burke: *Speech on Conciliation with America*, March 22, 1775]

CONCLUSION
8 Let us hear the conclusion of the whole matter. [Ecclesiastes 12:13]
9 This is a short conclusioun.
[Chaucer: *The Knight's Tale*]
10 O most lame and impotent conclusion!
[Shakespeare: *Othello* II.i.]

CONCORD
11 Oh, shame to men! devil with devil damn'd
Firm concord holds, men only disagree
　　Of creatures rational.
[John Milton: *Paradise Lost* II, 496-498]

CONDEMNATION
12 Damn with faint praise, assent with civil leer,
And without sneering, teach the rest to sneer;
Willing to wound, and yet afraid to strike,
Just hint a fault, and hesitate dislike.
[Alexander Pope: *Epistle to Dr. Arbuthnot*]
leer *originally* = *the cheek*
　A leer was a sidelong glance down over the cheek, expressive of slyness or malice. Today it means almost entirely an immodestly suggestive look.
　Pope means one who openly agrees with the speaker but by a sly look conveys his contempt to others who are present.

CONDESCENSION
13 There is nothing more likely to betray a man into absurdity than condescension. [Samuel Johnson: in Boswell's *Life* (1780)]

CONDUCT
14 Conduct is three-fourths of our life and its largest concern. [Matthew Arnold: *Literature and Dogma* I]

CONFESS
15 It is not hard to confess our criminal acts, but our ridiculous and shameful acts. [Jean Jacques Rousseau: *Confessions* I.i.]

CONFESSION
16 The Scripture moveth us, in sundry places to acknowledge and confess our manifold sins and wickedness. [*Book of Common Prayer*, "Morning Prayer"]
17 We have left undone those things which we ought to have done; and we have done those things which we ought not to have done. [*Book of Common Prayer*, "General Confession"]
18 Open confession is good for the soul. [Old Scottish Proverb]
19 He's half absolved who has confessed.

[Matthew Prior: *Alma* II.xxii.]

1 A man should never be ashamed to own he has been in the wrong, which is but saying, in other words, that he is wiser today than he was yesterday. [Jonathan Swift: *Thoughts on Various Subjects*]

2 Most wrong-doing works, on the whole, less mischief than its useless confession. [Edith Wharton: *The Reef* VII]

CONFIDENCE

3 Confidence scarce ever returns to the mind it has quitted. [Publilius Syrus: *Maxims*]

4 Confidence does more to make conversation than wit. [La Rochefoucauld: *Maxims*]

5 The calm confidence of a Christian with four aces. [Attr. Mark Twain]

CONFINEMENT

6 I am cabin'd, cribb'd, confin'd. [Shakespeare: *Macbeth* III.iv.]

CONFLICT

7 The adventurer is within us, and he contests for our favour with the social man we are obliged to be. These two sorts of life are incompatibles; one we hanker after, the other we are obliged to. There is no other conflict so deep and bitter as this. [William Bolitho: Introduction to *Twelve Against the Gods*]

CONFORMITY

8 Do as most do, and men will speak well of thee. [Thomas Fuller (1654-1734): *Gnomologia*]

9 The race of men, while sheep in credulity, are wolves for conformity. [Carl Van Doren: *Why I am an Unbeliever*]

CONFUSION

10 Confusion now hath made his masterpiece! [Shakespeare: *Macbeth* II.iii.]

11 With ruin upon ruin, rout on rout, Confusion worse confounded. [John Milton: *Paradise Lost* II, 996-997]

confounded = *so mixed or mingled that the elements are difficult to distinguish or impossible to separate*

12 And we are here as on a darkling plain

Swept with confused alarms of struggle and flight,

Where ignorant armies clash by night. [Matthew Arnold: *Dover Beach*]

CONGREGATION

13 Where two or three are gathered together in my name, there am I in the midst of them. [Matthew 18:20]

CONGRESS

14 Reader, suppose you were an idiot. And suppose you were a member of Congress. But I repeat myself. [Mark Twain]

This was a favorite of Mark Twain's in his lectures. Legislators have always been the prey of humorists, but Mark seemed to detest members of Congress with a vigor something beyond the call of duty.

CONNUBIALITY

15 I think he's a wictim o' connubiality, as Blue Beard's domestic chaplain said, with a tear of pity, ven he buried him. ["Sam Weller," in Dickens: *The Pickwick Papers* XX]

Many 19th-century British humorists record this interchange of initial v's and w's as a characteristic of cockney speech, but it's puzzling to linguists, especially in that no remnants of it survive. It may have been a sheer convention of condescension on the writers' parts, or one may have copied another and the first may have been misled by an impediment in some individual's speech—or in his own hearing.

CONQUER

16 She Stoops to Conquer. [Oliver Goldsmith: title of play]

CONSCIENCE

17 And al was conscience and tendre herte. [Chaucer: Prologue to *The Canterbury Tales*]

18 Of nice conscience took he no keep. [Chaucer: Prologue to *The Canterbury Tales*]

nice = *finely discriminating*

Chaucer's Shipman was not greatly troubled in his conscience by such moral *trifles as murder, theft and breach of contract. He was not wholly bad, however; he hated heretics.*

1　O coward conscience, how dost thou afflict me!
[Shakespeare: *Richard III* V.iii.]

2　　　　Better be with the dead,
Whom we, to gain our peace, have sent to peace,
Than on the torture of the mind to lie
In restless ecstasy.
[Shakespeare: *Macbeth* III.ii.]

3　A good conscience is a continual feast.
[Robert Burton: *The Anatomy of Melancholy* II]

4　Some make a conscience of spitting in the Church, yet rob the Altar. [George Herbert: *Jacula Prudentum*]

5　There is another man within me that's angry with me.　[Sir Thomas Browne: *Religio Medici* II.vii.]

6　He is one that will not plead that cause, wherein his tongue must be confuted by his conscience. [Thomas Fuller (1608-1661): *The Holy and the Profane State*, "The Good Advocate"]

7　　　Now conscience wakes despair
That slumber'd, wakes the bitter memory
Of what he was, what is, and what must be.
[John Milton: *Paradise Lost* IV.23-25]

8　Why should not Conscience have vacation
As well as other Courts o' the nation?
[Samuel Butler (1612-1680): *Hudibras* II.2.]

9　A brave man risks his life but not his conscience. [Schiller: *Wallenstein's Death* IV.vi.]

CONSCIENCE: cynical and worldly views of

10　Conscience is but a word that cowards use,
Devised at first to keep the strong in awe.
[Shakespeare: *Richard III* V.iii.]

11　Thus conscience does make cowards of us all;
And thus the native hue of resolution
Is sicklied o'er with the pale cast of thought.
And enterprises of great pith and mo-

ment,
With this regard, their currents turn awry,
And lose the name of action.
[Shakespeare: *Hamlet* III.i.]

12　　　　　Their best conscience
Is not to leave 't undone, but keep 't unknown.
[Shakespeare: *Othello* III.iii.]

13　The laws of conscience . . . rise and proceed from custom, every man holding in inward veneration the opinions approved and customs received about him. [Montaigne: *Essays* I.xxii.]

14　Conscience has no more to do with gallantry than it has with politics. [Richard Brinsley Sheridan: *The Duenna* II.iv.]

15　One never does evil so thoroughly and so gaily as when one does it for conscience's sake. [Pascal: *Pensées* II]

16　Conscience is, in most men, an anticipation of the opinion of others. [Sir Henry Taylor: *The Statesman*]

17　What is morality but immemorial custom? Conscience is the chief of conservatives. [Thoreau: *A Week on the Concord and Merrimack Rivers*, "Monday"]

18　Conscience is a thing of fictitious existence, supposed to occupy a seat in the mind. [Jeremy Bentham: *Deontology* I]

19　Conscience and cowardice are really the same things. [Oscar Wilde: *Picture of Dorian Gray* I]

20　Conscience is nothing but other people inside you. [Luigi Pirandello: *Each in His Own Way*]

21　Conscience is the inner voice which warns us that someone may be looking. [H. L. Mencken: *Chrestomathy* 617]

22　Conscience—the accumulated sediment of ancestral faint-heartedness. [H. L. Mencken: in the *Smart Set*, December 1921]

23　There is only one way to achieve happiness on this terrestrial ball,
And that is to have either a clear conscience, or none at all.
[Ogden Nash: *I'm a Stranger Here Myself*, "Inter-Office Memorandum"]

CONSECRATION

24　A picket frozen on duty—
A mother starved for her brood—
Socrates drinking the hemlock,

And Jesus on the rood;
And millions who, humble and name-
                                less,
The straight, hard pathway plod—
Some call it Consecration,
And others call it God.
[W. H. Carruth: *Each in His Own Tongue*]

CONSEQUENCES

1 Logical consequences are the scare-crows of fools and the beacons of wise men. [Thomas Henry Huxley: *Science and Culture,* "Animal Automatism"]
2 In nature there are neither rewards nor punishments—there are conse-quences. [Robert G. Ingersoll: *Some Reasons Why*]

CONSERVATISM

3 A froward retention of custom is as turbulent a thing as an innovation. [Francis Bacon: *Of Innovations*]
   froward = *perverse, refractory, untoward*

CONSERVATIVES

4 The most conservative persons I ever met are college undergraduates. [Wood-row Wilson: in a speech, New York, 1905]
   Almost any college professor would echo the sentiment. The often asserted belief that our colleges are "hotbeds of radical-ism" is a ludicrous fantasy.

CONSIDERATION

5 'Twere to consider too curiously to
                                consider so.
[Shakespeare: *Hamlet* V.i.]
   curiously = *carefully, scrupulously*

CONSISTENCY

6 Nothing that is not a real crime makes a man appear so contemptible and little in the eyes of the world as incon-sistency. [Joseph Addison: *The Specta-tor,* No. 162]
7 A foolish consistency is the hobgoblin of little minds, adored by little statesmen and philosophers and divines. With con-sistency a great soul has simply nothing to do. [Emerson: *Self-Reliance*]

8 Like all weak men he laid an exag-gerated stress on not changing one's mind. [W. Somerset Maugham: *Of Hu-man Bondage* XXXIX]

CONSOLATION

9 Men seyn, "to wrecche is consolacioun
   To have another felawe in his peyne."
[Chaucer: *Troilus and Criseyde* I.708-9]
   Chaucer expresses the same idea in the Canon's Yeoman's Tale (746) where he says that he learned this lore "of a clerk."
10 A common shipwreck is a source of consolation to all. [Erasmus: *Adagia* IV.iii.9]
11 It is cruel to console another for a sorrow a man has not himself experi-enced. [Fernando de Zarate: *La Desgra-cia Venturosa* I]
12 Though nothing can bring back the
                                hour
   Of splendour in the grass, of glory in
                                the flower;
   We will grieve not, rather find
   Strength in what remains behind;
   In the primal sympathy
   Which having been must ever be;
   In the soothing thoughts that spring
   Out of human suffering;
   In the faith that looks through death,
   In years that bring the philosophic
                                mind.
[Wordsworth: *Intimations of Immortal-ity*]
13 It's over, and can't be helped, and that's one consolation, as they always say in Turkey, ven they cuts the wrong man's head off. [Dickens: *The Pickwick Papers* XXIII]

CONSTANCY

14 Since 'tis Nature's law to change,
   Constancy alone is strange.
[John Wilmot, Earl of Rochester: *A Dia-logue* XXXI]
15 Constancy has nothing virtuous in it-self, independently of the pleasure it con-fers. [Shelley: Notes to *Queen Mab*]
16 The fickleness of the women I love is only equalled by the infernal constancy of the women who love me. [G. B. Shaw: *The Philanderer* II]

CONSTANT

1 Constant you are: / But yet a woman. [Shakespeare: *I Henry IV* II.iii.]

CONSTITUTION: of the U.S., Fifth Amendment

2 The Fifth Amendment is an old friend and a good friend. It is one of the great landmarks in man's struggle to be free of tyranny, to be decent and civilized. [William O. Douglas: *An Almanac of Liberty*]

CONSTITUTION: of the U.S., Preamble

3 WE, THE PEOPLE of the United States, in Order to form a more perfect Union, establish Justice, insure domestic Tranquility, provide for the common Defense, promote the general Welfare, and secure the Blessings of Liberty to ourselves and our Posterity, do ordain and establish this Constitution for the United States of America.

CONSUMPTION

4 Conspicuous consumption of valuable goods is a means of reputability to the gentleman of leisure. [Thorstein Veblen: *The Theory of the Leisure Class* IV]

CONTEMPLATION

5 Looks commercing with the skies. [John Milton: *Il Penseroso*]

CONTEMPT

6 Those who are despised usually return the favor. [Phaedrus: *Fables* III.ii.]
7 Contempt putteth an edge upon anger, as much or more than the hurt itself. [Francis Bacon: *Of Anger*]
8 As the air to a bird or the sea to a fish, so is contempt to the contemptible. [William Blake: *Proverbs of Hell*]
9 Contempt is egotism in ill humor. [Coleridge: *Omniana*]
10 One of the disadvantages of expressing contempt [is] that you cannot enjoy at the same time the credit of expressing sympathy. [Henry James: *Portrait of a Lady*]

CONTENT(ED)

11 He is well paid that is well satisfied. [Shakespeare: *The Merchant of Venice* IV.i.]
12 My soul hath her content so absolute, That not another comfort like to this Succeeds in unknown fate. [Shakespeare: *Othello* II.i.]
13 Poor and content is rich, and rich enough. [Shakespeare: *Othello* III.iii.]
14 Shut up / In measureless content. [Shakespeare: *Macbeth* II.i.]
15 Naught's had, all's spent, Where our desire is got without content. [Shakespeare: *Macbeth* III.ii.]
16 'Tis not the food, but the content That makes the Table's merriment. [Robert Herrick: *Content, not Cates*]
17 Who with a little cannot be content, Endures an everlasting punishment. [Robert Herrick: *Poverty and Riches*]
18 Take the goods the gods provide thee. [Dryden: *Alexander's Feast*]
19 I've often wish'd that I had clear For life, six hundred pounds a year; A handsome house to lodge a friend; A river at my garden's end; A terrace walk, and half a rood Of land set out to plant a wood. [Jonathan Swift: *Imitation of Horace* VI.ii.]
20 An elegant sufficiency, content, Retirement, rural quiet, friendship, books, Ease and alternate labor, useful life, Progressive virtue, and approving Heaven. [James Thomson (1700-1748): *The Seasons*, "Spring"]
We can forgive—even envy—the 18th-century gentleman his quiet acceptance of his good fortune, but his continual assurance that he will resign himself with quiet stoicism to a life of luxury is maddening. Thomson says here that all he asks from life is lots of money, privacy, friends, intellectual diversion, freedom from boredom, a flattering sense of being important and slightly holier-than-thou —and a pat on the back from God!

21 Flatter not yourself with contrarieties of pleasure. Of the blessings set before you, make your choice and be content. [Samuel Johnson: *Rasselas* XXIX]
22 Better is a little with content than

much with contention. [Benjamin Franklin: *Poor Richard's Almanack* (1747)]

1 Contented wi' little, and cantie wi' mair.
[Burns: *Contented wi' Little*]
cantie = *delighted, lively;* mair = *more*

2 Nuns fret not at their convent's narrow room,
And hermits are contented with their cells.
[Wordsworth: *Nuns Fret Not*]

3 I'd rather be handsome than homely;
I'd rather be youthful than old;
If I can't have a bushel of silver
I'll do with a barrel of gold.
[James Jeffrey Roche: *Contentment*]

4 That is the land of lost content,
I see it shining plain,
The happy highways where I went
And cannot come again.
[A. E. Housman: *A Shropshire Lad* XL]

CONTENTION

5 Wilfully to strive and obstinately to contest in words are common qualities most apparent in basest minds. [Montaigne: *Essays* I.xxv.]

CONTENTMENT

6 The lines are fallen unto me in pleasant places; yea, I have a goodly heritage. [Psalms 16:6]

7 Here below there is no satisfaction or content, except for brutal or divine minds. [Montaigne: *Essays* III.ix.]

8 The noblest mind the best contentment has.
[Edmund Spenser: *The Faerie Queene* I.i.]

9 For who did ever yet, in honour, wealth,
Or pleasure of the sense, contentment find?
[Sir John Davies: *Nosce Teipsum* XXX.1.]

10 Contentment consisteth not in adding more fuel, but in taking away some fire: not in multiplying of wealth, but in subtracting men's desires. [Thomas Fuller (1608-1661): *The Holy State,* "Of Contentment"]

11 One honest John Tompkins, a hedger and ditcher,
Although he was poor, did not want to be richer;
For all such vain wishes in him were prevented
By a fortunate habit of being contented.
[Jane Taylor: *Contented John*]

12 I have mental joys and mental health,
Mental friends and mental wealth,
I've a wife that I love and that loves me;
I've all but riches bodily.
[William Blake: *Mammon*]

13 Fortune! if thou'll but gie me still
Hale breeks, a bannock, and a gill,
An' rowth o' rhyme to rave at will,
Tak' a' the rest.
[Burns: *Scotch Drink*]
hale breeks = *a good, sound, serviceable pair of pants;* bannock = *an oat cake; a* gill = *of whiskey;* rowth = *plenty*

14 I care not much for gold or land—
Give me a mortgage here and there—
Some good bank-stock, some note of hand,
Or trifling railroad share—
I only ask that Fortune send
A *little* more than I shall spend.
[O. W. Holmes: *Contentment*]

CONTRADICTION

15 Contradiction should awaken Attention, not Passion. [Thomas Fuller (1654-1734): *Gnomologia*]

16 When we risk no contradiction,
It prompts the tongue to deal in fiction.
[John Gay: *Fables* I, "The Elephant and the Bookseller"]

17 People who honestly mean to be true really contradict themselves much more rarely than those who try to be "consistent." [Oliver Wendell Holmes: *The Professor at the Breakfast Table* II]

CONVENTIONALITY

18 It is not difficult to be unconventional in the eyes of the world when your unconventionality is but the convention of your set. [W. Somerset Maugham: *The Moon and Sixpence,* Ch. 14]

CONVERSATION

19 Speech of touch towards others should

be sparingly used; for discourse ought to be as a field, without coming home to any man. [Francis Bacon: *Of Discourse*]
speech of touch towards others = personal remarks, though not necessarily offensive.

To turn a general discussion into a personal matter, whether it be in relation to the speaker or anyone else present, is one of the surest ways to ruin good conversation and is the mark of a booby or a boor.

1   What should we speak of
When we are old as you? when we
            shall hear
The rain and wind beat dark December, how,
In this our pinching cave, shall we
            discourse
The freezing hours away?
[Shakespeare: *Cymbeline* III.iii.]
Dr. Johnson, the great talker, in his edition of Shakespeare paused here to praise the young prince Arviragus for his desire to store up materials for conversation later in life.

2   What things have we seen
Done at the Mermaid! heard words
            that have been
So nimble and so full of subtile flame
As if that every one from whence they
            came
Had meant to put his whole wit in a
            jest,
And resolved to live a fool the rest
Of his dull life.
[Francis Beaumont: *Letter to Ben Jonson*]
Breathes there a man with soul so dead that he does not long to have overheard these feats of wit!

3   A civil guest
Will no more talk all, than eat all the
            feast.
[George Herbert: *The Church-Porch*]

4 With thee conversing I forget all time. [John Milton: *Paradise Lost* IV.639]

5 Confidence does more to make conversation than wit. [La Rochefoucauld: *Maxims*]

6 The reason why so few people are agreeable in conversation is that each is thinking more about what he intends to say than about what others are saying, and we never listen when we are eager to

speak. [La Rochefoucauld: *Maxims*]

7 Conversation, like a salad, should have various ingredients and should be well stirred with salt, oil and vinegar. [Joaquin Setanti: *Centellas*]

8 The wit of conversation consists much less in showing a great deal of it than in bringing it out in others. [La Bruyère: *Les Caractères*]
Repeated by Franklin: Poor Richard's Almanack (1756).

9 Madam, I have not ninepence in ready money, but I can draw for a thousand pounds. [Joseph Addison: quoted in Boswell's *Life of Johnson*, May 7, 1773]
Addison's answer to a lady who complained that he had talked very little in company. The comparison of small talk with petty cash and literary ability with huge sums was, apparently, a metaphor of the times. Addison himself uses it in The Tatler, *No. 30, and it is ascribed to Bishop Wilkins in Burnet's* History of My Own Times *(I.210). Chesterfield in his letters uses it of Lord Bolingbroke (1749).*

10 The feast of reason and the flow of soul. [Alexander Pope: *Second Book of Horace* I]

11 He was scant of news that told his father was hanged. [James Kelly: *Scottish Proverbs* (1721)]
A man is hard up for topics of conversation who must tell of some disgrace he or his family has sustained.

12 The pleasure which men are able to give in conversation holds no stated proportion to their knowledge or their virtue. [Samuel Johnson: *The Rambler* No. 188]

13 He only will please long who, by tempering the acidity of satire with the sugar of civility and allaying the heat of wit with the frigidity of humble chat, can make the true punch of conversation; and, as that punch can be drunk in the greatest quantity which has the largest proportion of water, so that companion will be oftenest welcome whose talk flows out with inoffensive copiousness and unenvied insipidity. [Samuel Johnson: *The Idler* No. 34]

14 There is not, perhaps, among the multitudes of all conditions that swarm upon

the earth a single man who does not believe that he has something extraordinary to relate of himself. [Samuel Johnson: *The Idler* No. 50]

1 Silence propagates itself, and the longer talk has been suspended, the more difficult it is to find anything to say. [Samuel Johnson: *The Adventurer* No. 84]

2 The conversation overflowed and drowned him. [Samuel Johnson: in Boswell's *Life* (1770)]

Johnson's explanation of why a certain gentleman had remained silent throughout an evening of brilliant talk.

3 It is not every man that can carry a *bon mot*. [William Fitzherbert: in Boswell's *Life of Johnson,* April 10, 1775]

4 That is the happiest conversation where there is no competition, no vanity, but a calm quiet interchange of sentiments. [Samuel Johnson: in Boswell's *Life,* April 14, 1775]

Despite the many conversational storms he precipitated and roared through, Johnson preferred peace. In the 89th Rambler he speaks of "that interchange of thoughts which is practised in free and easy conversation; where suspicion is banished by experience and emulation by benevolence; where every man speaks with no other restraint than unwillingness to offend, and hears with no other disposition than desire to be pleased."

5 Questioning is not the mode of conversation among gentlemen. [Samuel Johnson: in Boswell's *Life* (1776)]

6 A man should be careful never to tell tales of himself to his own disadvantage. People may be amused and laugh at the time, but they will be remembered, and brought out against him upon some subsequent occasion. [Samuel Johnson: in Boswell's *Life,* March, 1776]

7 Never speak of a man in his own presence. It is always indelicate, and may be offensive. [Samuel Johnson: in Boswell's *Life,* March, 1776]

8 John Wesley's conversation is good, but he is never at leisure. He is always obliged to go at a certain hour. This is very disagreeable to a man who loves to fold his legs and have out his talk, as I do. [Samuel Johnson: in Boswell's *Life,* March 31, 1778]

9 A man cannot with propriety speak of himself, except as he relates simple facts. [Samuel Johnson: in Boswell's *Life,* April 25, 1778]

10 The happiest conversation is that of which nothing is distinctly remembered, but a general effect of pleasing impression. [Samuel Johnson: in Boswell's *Life* (1781)]

11 But conversation, choose what theme we may,
And chiefly when religion leads the way,
Should flow, like waters after summer show'rs,
Not as if raised by mere mechanic powers.
[William Cowper: *Conversation*]

12 Johnson's conversation was by much too strong for a person accustomed to obsequiousness and flattery; it was *mustard in a young child's mouth.* [Mrs. Piozzi: as quoted in Boswell's *Life of Johnson,* May, 1781]

13 Silence is one great art of conversation. [William Hazlitt: *Characteristics*]

14 The best kind of conversation is that which may be called thinking *aloud.* [William Hazlitt: *Characteristics*]

15 Men of great conversational powers almost universally practise a sort of lively sophistry and exaggeration which deceives for the moment both themselves and their auditors. [Macaulay: *On the Athenian Orators*]

16 You may talk of all subjects save one, namely, your maladies. [Emerson: *Conduct of Life,* "Behavior"]

17 Conversation is an art in which a man has all mankind for his competitors, for it is that which all are practising every day while they live. [Emerson: *Conduct of Life,* "Considerations by the Way"]

18 It requires nothing less than a chivalric feeling to sustain a conversation with a lady. [Thoreau: *Winter,* December 31, 1851]

19 "The time has come," the Walrus said,
"To talk of many things:
Of shoes—and ships—and sealing-wax—
Of cabbages—and kings—
And why the sea is boiling hot—
And whether pigs have wings."
[Lewis Carroll: *Through the Looking-*

Glass, "The Walrus and the Carpenter"]

1 Conversation should touch everything but should concentrate on nothing. [Oscar Wilde: *The Critic as Artist*]

2 A good conversationalist is not one who remembers what was said, but says what someone wants to remember. [John Mason Brown, in *Esquire,* April 1960]

CONVERSION

3 A man who is converted from Protestantism to popery parts with nothing; he is only super-adding to what he already had. But a convert from popery to Protestantism gives up as much of what he has held sacred as anything that he retains. [Samuel Johnson: in Boswell's *Life,* Oct. 26, 1769]

4 You have not converted a man because you have silenced him. [John Morley: *On Compromise*]

CONVICTION(S)

5 Some men are just as firmly convinced of what they think as others are of what they know. [Aristotle: *Nicomachean Ethics* VII]

6 Every man is encompassed by a cloud of comforting convictions, which move with him like flies on a summer day. [Bertrand Russell: *Sceptical Essays*]

7 At eighteen our convictions are hills from which we look; at forty-five they are caves in which we hide. [F. Scott Fitzgerald: *Bernice Bobs Her Hair*]

COOK

8 'Tis an ill cook that cannot lick his own fingers.
[Shakespeare: *Romeo and Juliet* IV.ii.]

9 We may live without poetry, music and art;
We may live without conscience, and live without heart;
We may live without friends; we may live without books;
But civilized man cannot live without cooks.
[E. R. Bulwer-Lytton: *Lucile* II.xix.]

10 Oh, I am a cook and a captain bold
And the mate of the *Nancy* brig,
And a bo'sun tight, *and* a midshipmite,

And the crew of the captain's gig.
[W. S. Gilbert: *Bab Ballads,* "The Yarn of the 'Nancy Bell' "]

These multiple functions were due to his being the final survivor of a cannibal commune.

11 The cook was a good cook, as cooks go; and as cooks go she went. [H. H. Munro ("Saki"): *Reginald*]

COOKING

12 The discovery of a new dish does more for the happiness of the human race than the discovery of a star. [Brillat-Savarin: *Physiologie du Goût,* "Aphorismes du Professeur" IX]

A luckless and impertinent young man once asserted in Dr. Johnson's presence that a good cook was of more value to mankind than all the poets that ever lived. "Sir," said Johnson sternly, "in that opinion you have the support of every dog in town."

COQUETTE

13 The coquets of both sexes are self-lovers, and that is a love no other whatever can dispossess. [John Gay: *The Beggar's Opera* III]

CORD

14 A threefold cord is not quickly broken. [Ecclesiastes 4:12]

CORIOLANUS

15 A broken Coriolanus.
[T. S. Eliot: *The Waste Land* V]

Gaius Marcius Coriolanus was a Roman general of the 5th century B.C. He appears in Shakespeare's Coriolanus *as an uncompromising idealist, the personification of patrician scorn and yet of patrician virtue.*

CORN

16 Where the corn is full of kernels
And the colonels full of corn.
[William James Lampton: *Kentucky*]

CORPORATIONS

17 Corporations cannot commit treason, nor be outlawed, or excommunicated, for they have no souls. [Sir Edward Coke: *Case of Sutton's Hospital* (1612)]

CORPSE
1 He'd make a lovely corpse. [Dickens: *Martin Chuzzlewit* XXV]

CORRECTION
2 Happy is the man whom God correcteth: therefore despise not thou the chastening of the Almighty. [Job 5:17]
3 Better a little chiding than a great deal of heartbreak. [Shakespeare: *The Merry Wives of Windsor* V.iii.]

CORRESPONDENCE
4 Correspondences are like small-clothes before the invention of suspenders; it is impossible to keep them up. [Sydney Smith: letter to Mrs. Crowe, January 31, 1841]

CORROBORATION
5 Merely corroborative detail, intended to give artistic verisimilitude to an otherwise bald and unconvincing narrative. [W. S. Gilbert: *The Mikado* II]

CORRUPTION
6 There is nothing so ill as the corruption of the best. [Bishop Joseph Hall: *Contemplations* IV.ix.]
7 'Tis the most certain sign, the world's accurst
That the best things corrupted are the worst.
[Sir John Denham: *The Progress of Learning*]
8 Corruption, the most infallible symptom of constitutional liberty. [Edward Gibbon: *Decline and Fall of the Roman Empire* XXI]
9 He is a man of splendid abilities, but utterly corrupt. He shines and stinks like rotten mackerel by moonlight. [John Randolph, of Edward Livingston]

CORTEZ
10 Then felt I like some watcher of the skies
When a new planet swims into his ken;
Or like stout Cortez, when with eagle eyes
He stared at the Pacific—and all his men
Looked at each other with a wild sur-

mise—
Silent, upon a peak in Darien.
[Keats: *On First Looking into Chapman's Homer*]

COSMETICS
11 God has given you one face, and you make yourselves another. [Shakespeare: *Hamlet* III.i.]
12 For whom does the blind man's wife paint herself? [Thomas Fuller (1654-1734): *Gnomologia*]
13 For she that paints will doubtless be a whore.
[Ned Ward: *The London Spy*]
> Our tinted ladies have little idea of what interpretation was formerly put on their beautification.
>> Your whores, sir, . . . using painting.
>> Shakespeare: Measure for Measure IV.2.
>> A woman that paints puts up a bill [notice] that she is to let [to be hired].
>> Thomas Fuller (1654-1734): Gnomologia
14 The ladies of St. James's!
They're painted to the eyes;
Their white it stays for ever,
Their red it never dies:
But Phyllida, my Phyllida!
Her color comes and goes;
It trembles to a lily—
It wavers to a rose.
[Austin Dobson: *The Ladies of St. James's*]
15 Most women are not so young as they are painted. [Max Beerbohm: *A Defence of Cosmetics*]

COSMOPOLITAN
16 To be really cosmopolitan, a man must be at home even in his own country. [Thomas Wentworth Higginson: *Short Studies of American Authors*]

COSMOPOLITE
17 I am not an Athenian nor a Greek, but a citizen of the world. [Socrates: in Plutarch: *Of Banishment*]
18 If a man be gracious and courteous to strangers, it shows he is a citizen of the world. [Francis Bacon: *Of Goodness*]
19 That man's the best cosmopolite
Who loves his native country best.
[Tennyson: *Hands All Round*]

COST
1 All good things are cheap: all bad are very dear. [Thoreau: *Journal*, March 3, 1841]

COUGH
2 A convulsion of the lungs vellicated by some sharp serosity. [Samuel Johnson: in the *Dictionary* (1755)]
Definition of cough

COUNSEL
3 Better counsel comes overnight. [Lessing: *Emilia Galotti* IV.iii.]

COUNTENANCE
4 And hadde a wyf that heeld for countenance
A shoppe, and swyved for hir sustenance.
[Chaucer: *The Cook's Tale*]

COUNTING
5 One, two,
Buckle my shoe;
Three, four,
Knock at the door;
Five, six,
Pick up sticks.
. . .
Nineteen, twenty,
My plate's empty.
[Nursery counting rhyme: earliest known printed version in English, 1805; occurs in many other languages.]
Older version of conclusion: Nineteen, twenty, | My belly's empty.

COUNTRY (PATRIOTISM)
6 I only regret that I have but one life to lose for my country. [Nathan Hale: Speech from the gallows, Sept. 22, 1776]
7 Our country: in her intercourse with foreign nations may she always be in the right; but our country, right or wrong! [Stephen Decatur: Toast at a dinner at Norfolk, Va., April 1816]
8 Our country, right or wrong. When right, to be kept right; when wrong, to be put right. [Carl Schurz: Speech in the Senate, Jan. 17, 1872]
9 "My country, right or wrong" is like saying, "My mother, drunk or sober." [G. K. Chesterton: *The Defendant*]
10 What's good for the country is good for General Motors, and vice versa. [Charles E. ("Engine Charlie") Wilson, President of General Motors, *New York Times,* Jan. 23, 1953]
Mr. Wilson had been nominated by President Eisenhower as Secretary of Defense. Senator Richard Russell asked him whether he would be willing, if necessary, to make a decision unfavorable to General Motors.

COURAGE
11 Courage stands halfway between cowardice and rashness, one of which is a lack, the other an excess, of courage. [Plutarch: *De Virtute Morali* VI]
12 If all men were just, there would be no need of courage. [Agesilaus II: in Plutarch's *Life of Agesilaus* XXII.v.]
13 Courage mounteth with occasion. [Shakespeare: *King John* II.i.]
14 Screw your courage to the sticking place.
[Shakespeare: *Macbeth* I.vii.]
The reference is to a peg on a stringed instrument—with the suggestion that Macbeth is, at the moment, unstrung.
15 He either fears his fate too much,
Or his deserts are small,
That dares not put it to the touch,
To gain or lose it all.
[James Graham, Marquis of Montrose: *I'll Never Love Thee More*]
16 None but the brave deserves the fair. [Dryden: *Alexander's Feast*]
17 Courage is a quality so necessary for maintaining virtue that it is always respected, even when it is associated with vice. [Samuel Johnson: in Boswell's *Life*, June 11, 1784]
18 He serves all who dares be true. [Emerson: *The Celestial Love*]
19 Courage, the footstool of the Virtues, upon which they stand. [R. L. Stevenson: *The Great North Road*]
20 As courage and intelligence are the two qualifications best worth a good man's cultivation, so it is the first part of intelligence to recognize our precarious estate in life, and the first part of courage to be not at all abashed before the fact. [R. L. Stevenson: *Aes Triplex*]

1 Captains courageous, whom death could not daunt. [Anon.: *Mary Ambree*]

COURIERS
2 Neither snow, nor rain, nor heat, nor gloom of night stays these couriers from the swift completion of their appointed rounds. [Herodotus: *History* VIII]
> *Herodotus is referring to the couriers of Xerxes. This passage is inscribed on the General Post Office in New York City.*

COURSE
3 I see the better course and I approve of it,
But I follow the worse.
[Ovid: *Metamorphoses* VII]

COURT
4 The two maxims of any great man at court are, always to keep his countenance, and never to keep his word. [Jonathan Swift: *Thoughts on Various Subjects*]

COURTESY
5 I have often seen men prove unmannerly by too much manners and importunate by overmuch courtesy. [Montaigne: *Essays* I.xiii.]
6 Why, what a candy deal of courtesy
This fawning greyhound then did proffer me!
[Shakespeare: *I Henry IV* I.iii.]
> *Dr. Caroline Spurgeon, in her* Shakepeare's Imagery, *calls attention to the recurrence in Shakespeare of metaphors expressing loathing of subservience which combine, as here, dogs and sweets.*

7 Courtesy on one side only lasts not long. [George Herbert: *Jacula Prudentum* (1651)]
8 I have been a most unconscionable time dying, but I hope that you will excuse it. [Charles II, King of England (d. 1685): quoted in Hesketh Pearson: *Merry Monarch*]
9 He was the mildest manner'd man
That ever scuttled ship or cut a throat.
[Byron: *Don Juan* III.xli.]
10 Life is not so short but that there is always time enough for courtesy. [Emerson: *Letters and Social Aims*]

COURTING
11 Remember the old saying, "Faint heart ne'er won fair lady." [Cervantes: *Don Quixote* II.iii.10.]
12 Faint heart never won fair lady. [William Camden: *Remains*]
13 Faint hearts fair ladies never win. [William Elderton: *Britain's Ida* (1569)]
14 Men are April when they woo, December when they wed: maids are May when they are maids, but the sky changes when they are wives. [Shakespeare: *As You Like It* IV.i.]
15 Sweet reluctant amorous delay. [John Milton: *Paradise Lost* IV.311]
16 A man no more believes a woman when she says she has an aversion for him than when she says she'll cry out. [William Wycherley: *The Plain Dealer* II.i.]
17 Courtship [is] to marriage, as a very witty prologue to a very dull play. [William Congreve: *The Old Bachelor* V.x.]
18 They dream in courtship, but in wedlock wake. [Alexander Pope: *The Wife of Bath's Prologue*]
19 My love she's but a lassie yet;
My love she's but a lassie yet;
We'll let her stand a year or twa
She'll no be half sae saucy yet.
[Burns: *My Love She's but a Lassie yet*]
20 And when with envy time transported
Shall think to rob us of our joys,
You'll in your girls again be courted,
And I'll go wooing in my boys.
[Gilbert Cooper: *Winifreda*]
21 Better be courted and jilted
Than never be courted at all.
[Thomas Campbell: *The Jilted Nymph*]

COVENTRY
22 Sent to Coventry.
> *To have been sent to Coventry in the 11th century when Lady Godiva was there might have seemed to most soldiers an interesting assignment. But by the middle of the 17th century, when the phrase acquired its meaning of being "cut off from conversation with," soldiers had a bad time there. The town, apparently, disliked soldiers, and poor wretches who were garrisoned there got a cold reception.*

COVET
23 Thou shalt not covet thy neighbor's house, thou shalt not covet thy neigh-

bor's wife, nor his manservant, nor his maidservant, nor his ox, nor his ass, nor anything that is thy neighbor's. [Exodus 20:17]

COVETOUS
1 A covetous man does nothing well till he dies. [Thomas Wilson: *A Discourse upon Usurye*]

COVETOUSNESS
2 Though ye take from a covetous man all his treasure, he has yet one jewel left; ye cannot bereave him of his covetousness. [John Milton: *Areopagitica*]

COW(S)
3 Till the cows come home. [Jonathan Swift: *Polite Conversation* II (1738)]
> *This meant that by that time the phrase was already hackneyed.*
>
> *It isn't merely that the cows will come in in the evening to be milked; it's as much the straggling, desultory, slow way they do it that suggests* forever.

4 I never saw a purple cow,
  I never hope to see one;
  But I can tell you anyhow
  I'd rather see than be one.
[Gelett Burgess: *The Purple Cow*]
5 The cat is in the parlor, the dog is in the lake;
  The cow is in the hammock—what difference does it make?
[Anon.: *Indifference* (about 1910)]
6 The cow is of the bovine ilk;
  One end is moo, the other milk.
[Ogden Nash: *The Cow*]

COWARD(S)
7 Euer wylle a coward shewe no mercy. [Sir Thomas Malory: *Le Morte d'Arthur* XVIII.xxiv. (1485)]
8 I was a coward on instinct. [Shakespeare: *I Henry IV* II.iv.]
9 Cowards die many times before their deaths;
  The valiant never taste of death but once.
[Shakespeare: *Julius Caesar* II.i.]
10 He was just a coward and that was the worst luck any man could have. [Ernest Hemingway: *For Whom the Bell Tolls* XXX]

COWARDICE
11 Among all cowardices, cowardice of riches is the most. [John Wyclif: *Sermons* (c. 1380)]
12 Cowardice is the mother of cruelty. [Montaigne: *Essays* II.xxvii.]
> *Montaigne says of this saying, "I have often heard it reported."*

13 That which in mean men we entitle patience
  Is pale cold cowardice in noble breasts.
[Shakespeare: *Richard II* I.ii.]
14 For all men would be cowards if they durst. [John Wilmot, Earl of Rochester: *A Satyr Against Mankind*]
15 A coward's fear can make a coward valiant. [Thomas Fuller (1654-1734): *Gnomologia*]
16 Many would be cowards if they had courage enough. [Thomas Fuller (1654-1734): *Gnomologia*]
17 Every recession from temerity is an approach towards cowardice. [Samuel Johnson: *The Rambler* No. 76]
18 It is mutual cowardice that keeps us in peace. Were one-half of mankind brave, and one-half cowards, the brave would be always beating the cowards. Were all brave, they would lead a very uneasy life; all would be continually fighting: but being all cowards, we go on very well. [Samuel Johnson: in Boswell's *Life,* April 28, 1778]
19 He that fights and runs away
  May live to fight another day;
  But he that is in battle slain
  Will never rise to fight again.
[Anon.: in *The Art of Poetry* (1762), probably by Goldsmith]
> *The saying, given in its now-most-quoted form above, goes back to the dawn of history. It was common in Greece and Rome. Erasmus* (Adagia—*1500*) *attributes it to Demosthenes. Samuel Butler, in* Hudibras (*1663-1678*), *has it:*
> > *For those that fly may fight again,*
> > *Which he can never do that's slain.*
> *The 1762 version appeared in a book which it is known Goldsmith revised.*

20 Cowardice is not synonymous with prudence. It often happens that the better part of discretion is valour. [William Hazlitt: *Characteristics*]
21 There are several good protections

against temptations, but the surest is cowardice. [Mark Twain: *Pudd'nhead Wilson's New Calendar*]

1 Many a man has fought because—
He feared to run away.
[Richard Hovey: *The Marriage of Guenevere* IV.iii.]

2 Cowardice, as distinguished from panic, is almost always simply a lack of ability to suspend the functioning of the imagination. [Ernest Hemingway: Introduction to *Men at War*]

COYNESS

3 Had we but world enough, and time,
This coyness, lady, were no crime.
[Andrew Marvell: *To His Coy Mistress*]

CRADLE

4 Rocked in the cradle of the deep,
I lay me down in peace to sleep.
[Emma Willard: *The Cradle of the Deep*]

5 Out of the cradle endlessly rocking,
Out of the mocking-bird's throat, the musical shuttle.
[Walt Whitman: *Leaves of Grass*, "Out of the Cradle Endlessly Rocking"]

CRAFT

6 It is ful hard to halten unespyed
Bifore a crepul, for he can the craft.
[Chaucer: *Troilus and Criseyde* IV]
halten = *limp;* crepul = *cripple;* can the craft = *knows the manner of it*

7 Do not limp before the lame. [Rabelais: *Works* I]

CREATION

8 In the beginning God created the Heaven and the earth. And the earth was without form, and void; and darkness was upon the face of the deep. And the Spirit of God moved upon the face of the waters. And God said, Let there be light; and there was light. [Genesis 1:1]

9 Had I been present at the creation, I would have given some useful hints for the better ordering of the universe. [Attr. Alfonso the Wise (1221-1284)]
It was said of Metternich that he was so conservative that, had he been present at the Creation, he would have begged God to have retained Chaos.

CREDENCE

10 We are inclined to believe those whom we do not know, because they have never deceived us. [Samuel Johnson: *The Idler* No. 8]

CREDO

11 I believe in the incomprehensibility of God. [Balzac: Letter to Madame de Hanska (1837)]

CREDULITY

12 A credulous man is a deceiver. [Francis Bacon: *The Advancement of Learning* I]

13 Your noblest natures are most credulous. [George Chapman: *Revenge of Bussy d'Ambois* IV.i.]

14 That only disadvantage of honest hearts, credulity. [Sir Philip Sidney: *Arcadia* II]

15 He that takes up conclusions on the trust of authors, . . . loses his labour, and does not know anything, but only believeth. [Thomas Hobbes: *Leviathan* I.v.]

16 Men are willing to credit what they wish, and encourage rather those who gratify them with pleasure than those that instruct them with fidelity. [Samuel Johnson: *The Idler* No. 20]

17 The most costly of all follies is to believe passionately in the palpably not true. It is the chief occupation of mankind. [H. L. Mencken: *Chrestomathy* 616]

CRICKET

18 Far from all resort of mirth,
Save the cricket on the hearth.
[John Milton: *Il Penseroso*]
The last line supplied Dickens with the title of one of his most famous Christmas tales (1845).

CRIME

19 He who does not prevent a crime when he can, encourages it. [Seneca: *Troades*]

20 Successful crimes alone are justified. [Dryden: *The Medall*]

21 If you tell me that you had no hand

in your parentage and that it is therefore unjust to lay these things to your charge, I answer that whether your being in a consumption is your fault or no, it is a fault in you, and it is my duty to see that against such faults as this the commonwealth shall be protected. You may say that it is your misfortune to be criminal; I answer that it is your crime to be unfortunate. [Samuel Butler (1835-1902): *Erewhon* XI]

The sentence passed by the Erewhonian judge upon the young man accused of pulmonary consumption. He was an old offender, having been convicted before of bronchitis. His counsel had argued that he was merely simulating consumption in order to defraud an insurance company, but this defense, which would have exculpated him, was broken down by medical evidence.

1 Crime is only the retail department of what, in wholesale, we call penal law. [G. B. Shaw: *Man and Superman,* "The Revolutionist's Handbook: Crime and Punishment"]

CRIMINAL
2 Let me remember, when I find myself inclined to pity a criminal, that there is likewise a pity due to the country. [Matthew Hale: *History of the Pleas of the Crown*]

CRISIS
3 The crisis of yesterday is the joke of tomorrow. [H. G. Wells: *You Can't Be Too Careful*]

CRITIC(S)
4 They who write ill, and they who
     ne'er durst write,
Turn critics out of mere revenge and
     spite.
[Dryden: *Conquest of Granada*]
5 Some are bewilder'd in the maze of
     schools,
And some made coxcombs nature
     meant but fools:
In search of wit these lose their com-
     mon sense,
And then turn critics in their own
     defence:
Each burns alike, who can or cannot
     write,

Or with a rival's or an eunuch's spite.
[Alexander Pope: *An Essay on Criticism* I]
6 Some judge of authors' names, not
     works, and then
Nor praise nor blame the writings,
     but the men.
[Alexander Pope: *An Essay on Criticism* II]
7 There is a certain race of men that either imagine it their duty, or make it their amusement, to hinder the reception of every work of learning or genius, who stand as sentinels in the avenues of fame, and value themselves upon giving Ignorance and Envy the first notice of a prey. [Samuel Johnson: *The Rambler* No. 3]
8 Every good poet includes a critic, but the reverse will not hold. [William Shenstone: *On Writing and Books*]
9 Seek roses in December—ice in June;
Hope constancy in wind, or corn in
     chaff;
Believe a woman or an epitaph,
Or any other thing that's false, before
You trust in critics who themselves
     are sore.
[Byron: *English Bards and Scotch Reviewers*]
10 A wise skepticism is the first attribute of a good critic. [James Russell Lowell: *Among My Books*]
11 The good critic is he who relates the adventures of his soul among masterpieces. [Anatole France: Preface to *The Literary Life*]

CRITICAL
12 I am nothing if not critical. [Shakespeare: *Othello* II.i.]

CRITICISM
13 Criticism is a study by which men grow important and formidable at very small expense. [Samuel Johnson: *The Idler* No. 60]
14 You may scold a carpenter who has made you a bad table, though you cannot make a table. It is not your trade to make tables. [Samuel Johnson: in Boswell's *Life,* June 25, 1763]
15 You do not get a man's most effective criticism until you provoke him. Severe truth is expressed with some bitterness. [Thoreau: *Journal,* March 15, 1854]

1 I am bound by my own definition of criticism: *a disinterested endeavour to learn and propagate the best that is known and thought in the world.* [Matthew Arnold: *Essays in Criticism: First Series* I]
2 People ask you for criticism, but they only want praise. [W. Somerset Maugham: *Of Human Bondage* L]
3 Criticism is the art wherewith a critic tries to guess himself into a share of the artist's fame. [George Jean Nathan: *The House of Satan*]
4 Criticism is never inhibited by ignorance. [Harold Macmillan, quoted *Wall Street Journal*, Aug. 13, 1963]

CROCODILE
5 It is said that dogs drink from the Nile running, lest a crocodile should seize them. [Phaedrus: *Fables* I.xxv.]
The presumed plight of these thirsty hounds afforded many writers a simile.
6   A cruel crafty Crocodile,
Which in false grief hiding his harmful guile,
Doth weep full sore, and sheddeth tender tears.
[Edmund Spenser: *The Faerie Queene* I. xviii.]
7 Your serpent of Egypt is bred now of your mud by the operation of your sun; so is your crocodile. [Shakespeare: *Antony and Cleopatra* II.vii.]
8 How doth the little crocodile
Improve his shining tail,
And pour the waters of the Nile
On every golden scale!

How cheerfully he seems to grin,
How neatly spreads his claws,
And welcomes little fishes in
With gently smiling jaws!
[Lewis Carroll: *Alice's Adventures in Wonderland* II]

CROMWELL
9 Cromwell, damned to everlasting fame. [Alexander Pope: *An Essay on Man* IV]
10 He [Oliver Cromwell] gart kings ken they had a *lith* in their neck. [Alexander Boswell, Lord Auchinleck: quoted in Boswell's *Life of Johnson* (Hill ed. V. 382.n.2.)]
gart kings ken = made kings know; lith

= *joint*
Boswell's father and Dr. Johnson differed violently in politics and did not get on well. Dr. Johnson, enraged at Lord Auchinleck's praise of Cromwell, demanded angrily to know what good Cromwell had ever done—and received the above answer.

CROSS
11 *In hoc signo vinces.* ("Under this sign [the Cross] thou shalt conquer.") [Motto of the Emperor Constantine I]
12 When I survey the wondrous Cross,
On which the Prince of Glory died,
My richest gain I count but loss
And pour contempt on all my pride.
[Isaac Watts: *Hymn*]
13 You shall not press down upon the brow of labor this crown of thorns. You shall not crucify mankind upon a cross of gold. [William Jennings Bryan: in a speech at the National Democratic Convention, Chicago, 1896]

CROSS (ANGRY)
14 She scolded her maid and was as cross as two sticks. [W. M. Thackeray: *The Newcomes* XXXIII]

CROSS-PATCH
15 Cross-patch,
Draw the latch,
Sit by the fire and spin;
Take a cup
And drink it up,
And call your neighbors in.
[Nursery rhyme]
Used as a taunt for a sulky child for at least 200 years.

CROSS-WORD PUZZLES
16 Cross-word puzzles are so called because husbands and wives generally tries to solve them together. [Ring Lardner: *Games for Smart Alecks*]

CROW
17 We'll pluck a crow together. [Shakespeare: *The Comedy of Errors* III.i.]
18 The many-winter'd crow that leads the clanging rookery home. [Tennyson: *Locksley Hall*]

CROWD

1 The crowd is always caught by appearance and the crowd is all there is in the world. [Machiavelli: *The Prince* XVIII]
2 A crowd is not company and faces are but a gallery of pictures and talk but a tinkling cymbal where there is no love. [Francis Bacon: *Of Friendship*]
3 . . . He himself stuck not to call us the many-headed multitude. [Shakespeare: *Coriolanus* II.iii.]
4 The people are a many-headed beast. [Alexander Pope: *Imitations of Horace* I.i.]
5 I live in the crowds of jollity, not so much to enjoy company as to shun myself. [Samuel Johnson: *Rasselas* XVI]
6 Far from the madding crowd's ignoble strife
Their sober wishes never learn'd to stray;
Along the cool sequester'd vale of life
They kept the noiseless tenor of their way.
[Thomas Gray: *Elegy Written in a Country Churchyard*]

CROWN

7 And they clothed him with purple, and platted a crown of thorns, and put it about his head. [Mark 15:17]
8 Then, happy low, lie down!
Uneasy lies the head that wears a crown.
[Shakespeare: *II Henry IV* III.i.]

CRUCIFIXION

9 There is a green hill far away,
Without a city wall,
Where the dear Lord was crucified,
Who died to save us all.
[Cecil Frances Alexander: *There Is a Green Hill*]

CRUELTY

10 Cruelty is fed, not weakened by tears. [Publilius Syrus: *Maxims*]
11 I must be cruel, only to be kind. [Shakespeare: *Hamlet* III.iv.]
12 Come, you spirits
That tend on mortal thoughts! unsex me here,
And fill me from the crown to the toe top full

Of direst cruelty; make thick my blood,
Stop up the access and passage to remorse,
That no compunctious visitings of nature
Shake my fell purpose.
[Shakespeare: *Macbeth* I.v.]
13 Cruelty is more cruel if we defer the pain. [George Herbert: *Jacula Prudentum*]
14 'Tis crueltie to beat a cripple with his own crutches. [Thomas Fuller (1608-1661): *The Holy State*, "Of Jesting"]
15 Scarcely anything awakens attention like a tale of cruelty. The writer of news never fails to tell how the enemy murdered children and ravished virgins. [Samuel Johnson: *The Idler* No. 30]
16 The infliction of cruelty with a good conscience is a delight to moralists. [Bertrand Russell: *Sceptical Essays*]

CRUSADER

17 Many a time hath banish'd Norfolk fought
For Jesus Christ in glorious Christian field,
Streaming the ensign of the Christian cross
Against black pagans, Turks, and Saracens;
And, toil'd with works of war, retir'd himself
To Italy; and there, at Venice, gave
His body to that pleasant country's earth
And his pure soul unto his captain, Christ,
Under whose colors he had fought so long.
[Shakespeare: *Richard II* IV.i.]

CRUST

18 He that keeps nor crust nor crumb,
Weary of all, shall want some.
[Shakespeare: *King Lear* I.iv.]
The crust was the outer part of the loaf, the crumb the soft inner part.

CRY(ING)

19 Sir, there is no crying for shed milk, that which is past cannot be recall'd. [Andrew Yarranton: *England's Improvement* II]

1 Oh! would I were dead now,
Or up in my bed now,
To cover my head now
And have a good cry!
[Thomas Hood: *A Table of Errata*]

CUCKOLD(S)
2 Who hath no wyf, he is no cokewold.
[Chaucer: Prologue to *The Miller's Tale*]
3 This is a great year for cuckolds.
[Rabelais: *Pantagruel* III]
4 He that ears my land spares my team.
. . . If I be his cuckold, he's my drudge.
[Shakespeare: *All's Well that Ends Well*
I.iii.]
5 The cuckold is the last that knows of
it. [William Camden: *Remains* (1636)]

CUCKOO
6 The cuckoo then on every tree,
Mocks married men; for thus sings he,
"Cuckoo!
Cuckoo, cuckoo!" O word of fear,
Unpleasing to a married ear!
[Shakespeare: *Love's Labour's Lost* V.ii.]
7 O blithe New-comer! I have heard,
I hear thee and rejoice.
O Cuckoo! shall I call thee Bird,
Or but a wandering Voice?
[Wordsworth: *To the Cuckoo*]
8 Thrice welcome, darling of the
Spring!
Even yet thou art to me
No bird, but an invisible thing,
A voice, a mystery.
[Wordsworth: *To the Cuckoo*]

CUCUMBER
9 A cucumber should be well sliced and
dressed with pepper and vinegar, and
then thrown out, as good for nothing.
[Samuel Johnson: in Boswell's *Tour to
the Hebrides,* October 5, 1773]
It's an old joke. Johnson called it "a
common saying of physicians."

CULTURE
10 Culture implies all that which gives
the mind possession of its own powers; as
languages to the critic, telescope to the
astronomer. [Emerson: *Letters and Social Aims,* "Progress of Culture"]
11 There is no better motto which it
(culture) can have than these words of
Bishop Wilson, "To make reason and the

will of God prevail." [Matthew Arnold:
Culture and Anarchy I]
12 Culture has one great passion—the
passion for sweetness and light. It has
one even yet greater, the passion for
making them *prevail.* [Matthew Arnold:
Culture and Anarchy I]
13 . . . Culture is, or ought to be, the
study and pursuit of perfection; and . . .
of perfection as pursued by culture,
beauty and intelligence, or, in other
words, sweetness and light, are the main
characters. [Matthew Arnold: *Culture
and Anarchy* II]
14 Culture, the acquainting ourselves
with the best that has been known and
said in the world. [Matthew Arnold:
Preface to *Literature and Dogma*]
15 Culture is on the horns of this dilemma; if profound and noble it must remain rare, if common it must become
mean. [George Santayana: *The Life of
Reason* II]

CUNNING
16 Knowledge that is divorced from justice should be called cunning rather than
wisdom. [Cicero: *De Officiis* I.xix.]
17 We take cunning for a sinister or
crooked wisdom. [Francis Bacon: *Of
Cunning*]
18 Nothing doth more hurt in a state
than that cunning men pass for wise.
[Francis Bacon: *Of Cunning*]
hurt = *harm, damage*
19 There is a great difference between a
cunning man and a wise man, not only
in point of honesty but in point of ability. [Francis Bacon: *Of Cunning*]
20 Time shall unfold what plaited cunning hides;
Who cover faults, at last shame them
derides.
[Shakespeare: *King Lear* I.i.]
21 That crooked wisdom, which is called
craft. [Hobbes: *Leviathan* I.viii.]
22 Every man wishes to be wise, and
they who cannot be wise are almost always cunning. [Samuel Johnson: *The
Idler* No. 92]
23 The whole power of cunning is priva-
tive; to say nothing and to do nothing
is the utmost of its reach. Yet men thus
narrow by nature, and mean by art, are
sometimes able to rise by the miscar-

riages of bravery and the openness of integrity, and by watching failures and snatching opportunities obtain advantages which belong properly to higher characters. [Samuel Johnson: *The Idler* No. 92]

1 Foxes are so cunning
Because they are not strong.
[Emerson: *Orator*]

CUP

2 My cup runneth over. [Psalms 23:5]
3 If it be possible, let this cup pass from me. [Matthew 26:39]
4   Look not thou down but up!
    To uses of a cup,
The festal board, lamp's flash and
        trumpet's peal,
The new wine's foaming flow,
The Master's lips aglow!
Thou, heaven's consummate cup,
    what need'st thou with earth's
        wheel?
[Robert Browning: *Rabbi Ben Ezra*]

CUPID

5 This wimpled, whining, purblind,
        wayward boy,
This senior-junior, giant-dwarf, Dan
        Cupid;
Regent of love-rhymes, lord of
        folded arms,
The anointed sovereign of sighs and
        groans,
Liege of all loiterers and malcontents.
[Shakespeare: *Love's Labour's Lost* III.i.]

CURATE

6 There was a young curate of Salis-
        bury
Whose manners were halisbury-scalis-
        bury.
He went about Hampshire
Without any pampshire
Till his vicar compelled him to walis-
        bury.
[Anon.]
The old name for Salisbury was Sarum. Hampshire is commonly abbreviated to Hants.

CURE

7 It is part of the cure to wish to be cured. [Seneca: *Hippolytus*]
8 Cure the disease and kill the patient. [Francis Bacon: *Of Friendship*]

9 The cure is worse than the disease. [Philip Massinger: *The Bondman* I.i.]
10 The cure for the greatest part of human miseries is not radical, but palliative. [Samuel Johnson: *The Rambler* No. 32]
11 What can't be cured must be endured.
See ENDURE(D)

CURFEW

12 Oft, on a plat of rising ground,
I hear the far-off curfew sound
Over some wide-watered shore,
Swinging slow with sullen roar.
[John Milton: *Il Penseroso*]
13 The curfew tolls the knell of parting
        day,
The lowing herd wind slowly o'er the
        lea,
The ploughman homeward plods his
        weary way,
And leaves the world to darkness and
        to me.
[Thomas Gray: *Elegy Written in a Country Churchyard*]
lea = a tract of open ground, meadow, pasture or arable land
14 Out she swung—far out; the city
        seemed a speck of light below,
There 'twixt heaven and earth sus-
        pended as the bell swung to and
        fro. . . .
Still the maiden clung more firmly,
        and with trembling lips so white,
Said to hush her heart's wild throb-
        bing:
    "Curfew shall not ring to-night."
[Rose Hartwick Thorpe: *Curfew Must Not Ring To-night*]
For the benefit of those who came in late: Basil Underwood is sentenced to die at the ringing of the curfew. Bessie, "with sunny floating hair," to prevent its ringing, clings to the clapper. The ensuing thudding does not, technically, constitute ringing and the execution is delayed. Suddenly no less a person than Oliver Cromwell appears. His eyes are "lit with misty light" and Basil is pardoned. The poem was enormously popular.

CURIOSITY: admirable

15 Desire to know why, and how, curi-

osity, which is a lust of the mind, that by a perseverance of delight in the continued and indefatigable generation of knowledge, exceedeth the short vehemence of any carnal pleasure. [Hobbes: *Leviathan* VI]

1 Curiosity is one of the most permanent and certain characteristics of a vigorous intellect. [Samuel Johnson: *The Rambler* No. 103]

2 Disinterested intellectual curiosity is the life blood of real civilization. [G. M. Trevelyan: Preface to *English Social History*]

CURIOSITY: dangerous and wicked

3 Solicit not thy thoughts with matters hid,
Leave them to God above, him serve and fear.
[John Milton: *Paradise Lost* VIII.160]

4 When we do not know the truth of a thing, it is good that there should exist a common error which determines the mind of man, as, for example, the moon, to which is attributed the change of seasons, the progress of diseases, etc. For the chief malady of man is a restless curiosity about things which he cannot understand; and it is not so bad for him to be in error as to be curious to no purpose. [Pascal: *Pensées*]

5 Curiosity is only vanity. Most frequently we wish not to know, but to talk. We would not take a sea voyage for the sole pleasure of seeing without hope of ever telling. [Pascal: *Pensées*]

6 Where the apple reddens,
Never pry—
Lest we lose our Edens,
Eve and I.
[Robert Browning: *A Woman's Last Word*]

CURIOUS

7 Curiouser and curiouser! [Lewis Carroll: *Alice's Adventures in Wonderland* II]

CURLY LOCKS

8 Curly-locks, Curly-locks,
Wilt thou be mine?
Thou shalt not wash dishes
Nor yet feed the swine,
But sit on a cushion and sew a fine seam,

And feed upon strawberries, sugar and cream.
[Nursery rhyme]
Earliest printed version in 1797.

CURSE(S)(ING)

9 Curse God, and die. [Job 2:9]
Job's wife's advice to him.
The Vulgate has Benedic Deo et morere (*Bless God and die*) and the New American Catholic Edition has "*Bless God and die.*"

10 Let the day perish wherein I was born, and the night in which it was said, there is a man child conceived. [Job 3:3]

11 Why, what an ass am I! This is most brave,
That I, the son of a dear father murder'd,
Prompted to my revenge by heaven and hell,
Must, like a whore, unpack my heart with words,
And fall a-cursing, like a very drab,
A scullion!
[Shakespeare: *Hamlet* II.ii.]
It was not the wickedness of the whore's cursing, but the futility of it, the vulgar meaninglessness of it. Blake, two centuries later, was shocked by "the youthful harlot's curse."

12 Curses, not loud but deep.
[Shakespeare: *Macbeth* V.iii.]

13 You taught me language; and my profit on 't
Is, I know how to curse.
[Shakespeare: *The Tempest* I.ii.]

14 My merry, merry, merry roundelay
Concludes with Cupid's curse,
They that do change old love for new,
Pray gods, they change for worse!
[George Peele: *Cupid's Curse*]

15 An orphan's curse would drag to Hell
A spirit from on high;
But oh! more horrible than that
Is the curse in a dead man's eye.
[Coleridge: *The Ancient Mariner*]

16 Never was heard such a terrible curse!!
But what gave rise
To no little surprise,
Nobody seemed one penny the worse!
[R. H. Barham: *The Jackdaw of Rheims*]

17 She left the web, she left the loom,
She made three paces thro' the room

She saw the water-lily bloom,
She saw the helmet and the plume,
    She look'd down to Camelot.
Out flew the web and floated wide;
The mirror crack'd from side to side;
"The curse is come upon me," cried
    The Lady of Shalott.
[Tennyson: *The Lady of Shalott* III]

CURTAIN LECTURE

1 A curtain lecture is worth all the sermons in the world for teaching the virtues of patience and long-suffering. [Washington Irving: *The Sketch-Book*, "Rip Van Winkle"]

Beds were formerly surrounded by curtains—to insure privacy and to shut out light and the night air, the latter being regarded as unwholesome. A curtain lecture was a reproof given by a wife to her husband in bed.

CURZON

2 My name is George Nathaniel Curzon.
I am a most superior person.
[*The Balliol Masque* (author unknown)]

Lord Curzon was a great statesman, but his chilling reserve, studied hauteur, and even his monocle, made him almost a caricature of the stage English aristocrat.

CUSTOM(S)

3 What times! What customs! (*O tempora, O mores!*) [Cicero: *In Catilinam* I.i.]

4 Certainly, custom is most perfect when it beginneth in young years: this we call education, which is in effect but an early custom. [Francis Bacon: *Of Custom and Education*]

5 The tyrant custom.
[Shakespeare: *Othello* I.iii.]

6 What custom wills, in all things
    should we do 't.
[Shakespeare: *Coriolanus* II.iii.]

7 With customs we live well, but laws undo us. [George Herbert: *Jacula Prudentum*]

8 Custom is the great guide of human life. [David Hume: *Inquiry Concerning Human Understanding* V.i.]

9 Custom reconciles us to everything. [Edmund Burke: *On the Sublime and Beautiful* IV.xviii.]

10 Custom's idiot sway. [William Cowper: *Retirement*]

11 Such is the custom of Branksome
    Hall.
[Sir Walter Scott: *The Lay of the Last
    Minstrel* I.vii.]

12 All men are partially buried in the grave of custom, and of some we see only the crown of the head above ground. [Thoreau: *A Week on the Concord and Merrimack Rivers*, "Monday"]

13 Custom has furnished the only basis which ethics have ever had. [Joseph Wood Krutch: *The Modern Temper* XIII]

CYNIC

14 What is a cynic? A man who knows the price of everything, and the value of nothing. [Oscar Wilde: *Lady Windermere's Fan* III]

15 CYNIC. A blackguard whose faulty vision sees things as they are, not as they ought to be. [Ambrose Bierce: *The Devil's Dictionary*]

16 If to look truth in the face and not resent it when it's unpalatable, and take human nature as you find it, . . . is to be cynical, then I suppose I'm a cynic. [W. Somerset Maugham: *The Back of Beyond*]

CYNICISM

17 Cynicism is intellectual dandyism. [George Meredith: *The Egoist* VII]

18 The temptation shared by all forms of intelligence: cynicism. [Albert Camus: *Notebooks 1935-1942* Ch. II, p. 93.]

D

DAFFODILS

1   Daffodils,
That come before the swallow dares,
                   and take
The winds of March with beauty.
[Shakespeare: *The Winter's Tale* IV.iii.]

2   Fair daffodils, we weep to see
You haste away so soon. . . .
We have short time to stay as you,
We have as short a spring;
As quick a growth to meet decay
As you or anything.
[Robert Herrick: *Daffodils*]

3   When a daffodil I see,
Hanging down his head t'wards me,
Guess I may, what I must be:
First, I shall decline my head;
Secondly, I shall be dead;
Lastly, safely buried.
[Robert Herrick: *Divination by a Daffo-dil*]

4   I wandered lonely as a cloud
    That floats on high o'er vales and
                     hills,
When all at once I saw a crowd,
    A host, of golden daffodils;
Beside the lake, beneath the trees,
Fluttering and dancing in the breeze.
[Wordsworth: *I Wandered Lonely as a Cloud*]

5   Ten thousand saw I at a glance,
Tossing their heads in sprightly dance.
[Wordsworth: *I Wandered Lonely as a Cloud*]

DAGGER

6   Is this a dagger which I see before me,
The handle toward my hand? Come,
                let me clutch thee.
[Shakespeare: *Macbeth* II.i.]

7   I will speak daggers to her, but use
                     none.
[Shakespeare: *Hamlet* III.ii.]

DAISY

8   Of alle the floures in the mede,
Then love I most these floures white
                 and rede,
Swiche as men callen daysies in our
                 toun.

[Chaucer: Prologue to *The Legend of Good Women*]

9   That men by reason well it calle may
The daisie or elles the eye of day,
The emperice, and floure of floures
                 alle.
[Chaucer: *The Legend of Good Women*]
     emperice = *empress*
        Chaucer's etymology is sound: daisy =
     day's eye.

DALHOUSIE

10   And thou Dalhousie, the great God of
                   War,
Lieutenant Colonel to the Earl of
                   Mar.
[Alexander Pope: *The Art of Sinking in Poetry* XI.iii.]
     Pope is quoting from some anonymous poem, as an example of anticlimax.
        The naïveté guarantees the sincerity. To the writer there was, probably, no awareness of anticlimax, the Earl of Mar was so great a personage.

DALLIANCE

11   The primrose path of dalliance.
[Shakespeare: *Hamlet* I.iii.]

DAMNED

12   You'll be damned if you do—And you'll be damned if you don't. [Lorenzo Dow: *Reflections on the Love of God*]
     The quotation is a definition of Calvinism.

13   Gentlemen-rankers out on the spree,
Damned from here to eternity.
[Kipling: *Gentlemen-Rankers*]

DAMP

14   A demd, damp, moist, unpleasant body. [Dickens: *Nicholas Nickleby* XXXIV]
     The reference is to Mantalini.

DAMSEL

15   Have they not divided the prey; to every man a damsel or two? [Judges 5:30]

1 A damsel with a dulcimer
In a vision once I saw.
[Coleridge: *Kubla Khan*]

DAN

2 From Dan even to Beer-sheba. [Judges 20:1]

DANCE(ING)

3 We have piped unto you, and ye have not danced. [Matthew 11:17]

4 In twenty manere coude he trippe
and daunce . . .
And with his legges casten to and fro.
[Chaucer: *The Miller's Tale*]

5 My men, like satyrs grazing on the lawns,
Shall with their goat feet dance an antic hay.
[Christopher Marlowe: *Edward II* I.i.]
antic = *antique;* hay = *a country dance, of a winding or serpentine movement. Apparently, by Marlowe's time (1564-1593), it was regarded as ancient or old-fashioned.*
Aldous Huxley took the title of one of his earliest novels—Antic Hay—*from this passage.*

6 He capers nimbly in a lady's chamber
To the lascivious pleasing of a lute.
[Shakespeare: *Richard III* I.i.]

7 Wherefore are these things hid? . . . Why dost thou not go to church in a galliard and come home in a coranto? My very walk should be a jig. I would not so much as make water but in a sink-a-pace.
[Shakespeare: *Twelfth Night* I.iii.]
galliard = *a quick and lively dance in triple time;* coranto = *a dance with a running, gliding step;* sink-a-pace = cinque-pace = *a lively dance that in some way or figure employed five paces.*
Sir Toby Belch would have his drinking companion, Sir Andrew Aguecheek, woo his niece, the Lady Olivia. Attempting to find some attractions in Sir Andrew, Sir Toby asks him if he can dance and when Sir Andrew replies "Faith, I can cut a caper," Sir Toby eagerly begs him to set so great a talent abroad immediately.
A pun may have been intended.

8 When you do dance, I wish you
A wave o' th' sea, that you might ever do
Nothing but that.

[Shakespeare: *The Winter's Tale* IV.iv.]

9 My dancing days are done.
[Beaumont and Fletcher: *The Scornful Lady* V.iii.]

10 Come and trip it as ye go,
On the light fantastic toe.
[John Milton: *L'Allegro*]

11 And the jocund rebecks sound
To many a youth, and many a maid,
Dancing in the chequered shade.
And young and old come forth to play
On a sunshine holiday.
[John Milton: *L'Allegro*]

12 Her feet beneath her petticoat,
Like little mice, stole in and out,
As if they feared the light;
But oh, she dances such a way!
No sun upon an Easter-day
Is half so fine a sight.
[Sir John Suckling: *A Ballad upon a Wedding*]
There is a very old belief that on Easter Sunday the sun dances in the sky.

13 The poetry of the foot.
[Dryden: *The Rival Ladies* III.i.]

14 They love dancing well that dance barefoot upon thorns. [Thomas Fuller (1654-1734): *Gnomologia*]

15 When a beauteous Nymph decays
We say, she's past her Dancing Days.
[Jonathan Swift: *Stella's Birthday*]

16 All who take part in a waltz or cotillion
Are mounted for hell on the devil's own pillion,
Who, as every true orthodox Christian well knows,
Approaches the heart through the door of the toes.
[James Russell Lowell: *A Fable for Critics*]

17 "Will you walk a little faster?" said a whiting to a snail,
"There's a porpoise close behind us, and he's treading on my tail!
See how eagerly the lobsters and the turtles all advance:
They are waiting on the shingle— will you come and join the dance?"
[Lewis Carroll: *Alice's Adventures in Wonderland*, "The Whiting and the Snail"]

18 It is sweet to dance to violins
When Love and Life are fair:

To dance to flutes, to dance to lutes
Is delicate and rare:
But it is not sweet with nimble feet
To dance upon the air!
[Oscar Wilde: *The Ballad of Reading Gaol* II]

1 O body swayed to music, O brightening glance,
How can we know the dancer from the dance?
[W. B. Yeats: *Among School Children*]

DANGER(S)

2 Danger, the spur of all great minds.
[George Chapman: *Bussy d'Ambois* V.i.]

3 Out of this nettle, danger, we pluck this flower, safety. [Shakespeare: *I Henry IV* II.iii.]

4   You must not think
That we are made of stuff so fat and dull
That we can let our beard be shook with danger
And think it pastime.
[Shakespeare: *Hamlet* IV.vii.]

5 She loved me for the dangers I had pass'd,
And I loved her that she did pity them.
[Shakespeare: *Othello* I.iii.]

6 'Tis true that we are in great danger;
The greater therefore should our courage be.
[Shakespeare: *Henry V* IV.i.]

7 We triumph without glory when we conquer without danger. [Corneille: *Le Cid* II.ii.]

8 Take heed of the wrath of a mighty man, and the tumult of the people; Mad folk in a narrow place; A young wench, a prophetess, and a Latin-bred woman; A person marked, and a Widow thrice married; Foul dirty ways, and long sickness; Wind that comes in at a hole, and a reconciled Enemy; a step-mother. [George Herbert: *Jacula Prudentum*]

9 In worst extremes, and on the perilous edge
    Of battle.
[John Milton: *Paradise Lost* I, 276-277]

10 Dangers bring fears, and fears more dangers bring. [Richard Baxter: *Love Breathing Thanks*]

11 The profession of soldiers and sailors has the dignity of danger. [Samuel Johnson: in Boswell's *Life*, April 10, 1778]

12 Oh pilot, 'tis a fearful night!
There's danger on the deep.
[Thomas Haynes Bayly: *The Pilot*]

13 Confront a child, a puppy, and a kitten with a sudden danger; the child will turn instinctively for assistance, the puppy will grovel in abject submission, the kitten will brace its tiny body for a frantic resistance. [H. H. Munro ("Saki"): *The Achievement of the Cat*]

DANIEL

14 A Daniel come to judgment! yea, a Daniel!
[Shakespeare: *The Merchant of Venice* IV.i.]

DAPPLED THINGS

15 Glory be to God for dappled things.
[Gerald Manley Hopkins: *Pied Beauty*]

DARE(ING)

16 Great daring often conceals great fear.
[Lucan: *Pharsalia* IV.702]

17 I dare do all that may become a man;
Who dares do more is none.
[Shakespeare: *Macbeth* I.vii.]

18 What man dare, I dare.
[Shakespeare: *Macbeth* III.iv.]

DARK(NESS)

19 Finish, good lady; the bright day is done,
And we are for the dark.
[Shakespeare: *Antony and Cleopatra* V.ii.]
The contrast of bright and dark, the touch of alliteration, the rhythm, the conveying of so much pathos and courage in the last eleven monosyllables, make this one of many passages in Shakespeare that leave us musing and breathless.

20   Yet from those flames
No light, but rather darkness visible.
[John Milton: *Paradise Lost* I.62-63]

21 Dark with excessive bright.
[John Milton: *Paradise Lost* III.380]

22 O dark, dark, dark, amid the blaze of noon,
Irrecoverably dark, total eclipse
Without all hope of day.

[John Milton: *Samson Agonistes*]

1 The sun's rim dips; the stars rush out:
At one stride comes the dark.

[Coleridge: *The Ancient Mariner* III]
*In a marginal gloss, later expunged,
Coleridge had at this passage: "No twilight in the Courts of the sun."
    He is alluding to the suddenness with
which darkness succeeds light at the
equator.*

2 Then of the THEE IN ME who
works behind
The Veil, I lifted up my hands to find
A Lamp amid the Darkness; and I
heard,
As from Without— "THE ME
WITHIN THEE BLIND!"

[*Rubáiyát of Omar Khayyám* (trans.
Edward FitzGerald)]

3 When awful darkness and silence
reign
Over the great Gromboolian plain.

[Edward Lear: *The Dong with the Luminous Nose*]

DARLING(S)

4 The wealthy curled darlings of our
nation.

[Shakespeare: *Othello* I.ii.]

5 Better an old man's darling than a
young man's slave. [19th-century saying]
*The idea is very old. In the form "Bet-
ter an old man's darling / Than a young
man's warling" it had appeared in Heywood's collection of proverbs in 1546 and
this had been its common form.
    Warling (an object of contempt, per-
haps "a little thing with which one is at
war") was, apparently, a coined word
used solely in this proverb. The proverb
is definitely an old man's. Young women
have at all times preferred to be war-
lings.*

6 Tenderly bury the fair young dead,
Pausing to drop on his grave a tear;
Carve on the wooden slab at his head,
"Somebody's darling slumbers
here!"

[Marie R. La Coste: *Somebody's Darling*]

DARWIN

7 Darwin was as much of an emancipa-
tor as was Lincoln. [W. G. Sumner:
Conversations]

DAUGHTER(S)

8 My daughter! O my ducats! O my
daughter!

[Shakespeare: *The Merchant of Venice*
II.viii.]

9 Trust not your daughters' minds
By what you see them act.

[Shakespeare: *Othello* I.i.]

10 Daughter am I in my mother's house,
But mistress in my own.

[Kipling: *Our Lady of the Snows*]

DAWN

11 Night's candles are burnt out, and
jocund day
Stands tiptoe on the misty mountain
tops.

[Shakespeare: *Romeo and Juliet* III.v.]

12 The wolves have prey'd; and look, the
gentle day,
Before the wheels of Phoebus, round
about
Dapples the drowsy east with spots of
grey.

[Shakespeare: *Much Ado About Nothing*
V.iii.]

13 But look, the morn, in russet mantle
clad,
Walks o'er the dew of yon high eastward hill.

[Shakespeare: *Hamlet* I.i.]

14 While the still morn went out with
sandals grey.

[John Milton: *Lycidas*]

15 Till morning fair
Came forth with pilgrim steps in amice grey.

[John Milton: *Paradise Regained* IV.
426-427]

16 It is always darkest just before the
day dawneth. [Thomas Fuller: (1608-
1661): *Pisgah Sight*]

17 And like a lobster boil'd, the morn
From black to red began to turn.

[Samuel Butler (1612-1680): *Hudibras*]

18 Brushing with hasty steps the dews
away,
To meet the sun upon the upland
lawn.

[Thomas Gray: *Elegy Written in a
Country Churchyard*]

19 Come into the garden, Maud,
For the black bat, night, has flown,
Come into the garden, Maud,
I am here at the gate alone;

And the woodbine spices are wafted
abroad,
And the musk of the rose is blown.

For a breeze of morning moves,
And the planet of Love is on high,
Beginning to faint in the light that
she loves
On a bed of daffodil sky.
[Tennyson: *Maud* I]
1 O'er night's brim, day boils at last.
[Robert Browning: Introduction to
Pippa Passes]
2 And down the long and silent street
The dawn, with silver-sandalled feet,
Crept like a frightened girl.
[Oscar Wilde: *The Harlot's House*]
3 DAWN. The time when men of rea-
son go to bed. [Ambrose Bierce: *The
Devil's Dictionary*]
4 . . . as cold
And passionate as the dawn.
[William Butler Yeats: *The Fisherman*]

DAY(S)
5 We have seen better days.
[Shakespeare: *As You Like It* II.vii.]
*The expression was a cliché even in
Shakespeare's time. It occurs again in
Timon of Athens IV.ii.*
6 And the gilded car of day
His glowing axle doth allay
In the steep Atlantic stream.
[John Milton: *Comus*]
7 Monday's child is fair of face,
Tuesday's child is full of grace,
Wednesday's child is full of woe,
Thursday's child has far to go,
Friday's child is loving and giving,
Saturday's child works hard for his
living,
And the child that is born on the Sab-
bath day
Is bonny and blithe, and good and
gay.
[Anon.]
*Now included among nursery rhymes.
Although printed versions go back only
to the early 19th century, the rhyme, in
many versions, is unquestionably much
older. All versions agree, however, in as-
cribing favorable traits to the child born
on Sunday.*
8 So here has been dawning
Another blue day.

Think, wilt thou let it
Slip useless away?
[Thomas Carlyle: *Today*]
9 Daughters of Time, the hypocritic
Days,
Muffled and dumb like barefoot der-
vishes,
And marching single in an endless
file,
Bring diadems and fagots in their
hands.
[Emerson: *Days*]
10 But the tender grace of a day that is
dead
Will never come back to me.
[Tennyson: *Break, Break, Break*]
11 When you come to the end of a per-
fect day.
[Carrie Jacobs Bond: *A Perfect Day*]

DAY: day and night
12 Let there be lights in the firmament
of the heaven to divide the day from the
night. [Genesis 1:14]
13 Day unto day uttereth speech, and
night unto night showeth knowledge.
[Psalms 19:2]
14 The night is long that never finds the
day.
[Shakespeare: *Macbeth* IV.iii.]
15 Think in the morning. Act in the
noon. Eat in the evening. Sleep in
the night. [William Blake: *Proverbs of
Hell*]

DAYLIGHT
16 We burn daylight.
[Shakespeare: *The Merry Wives of
Windsor* II.i.]
Also in Romeo and Juliet *I.iv.* Burning
Daylight *was the title of a book by Jack
London.*

DEAD
17 For the living know that they shall
die: but the dead know not anything,
neither have they any more a reward; for
the memory of them is forgotten. [Ec-
clesiastes 9:5]
18 Let the dead bury their dead.
[Matthew 8:22]
19 They rest from their labours. [*Book
of Common Prayer*, "Burial of the
Dead"]
20 I would rather be a slave in the

house of some landless man than king over the dead. [Homer: *Odyssey* XI]

The shade of Achilles, speaking to Odysseus.

1 Of the dead, speak nothing but good. [A proverb recorded as early as the 3rd century A.D. (in Diogenes Laertius). Even today it is often heard in its Latin form: *De mortuis nil nisi bonum.*]

2 But yesterday the word of Caesar might
Have stood against the world; now lies he there,
And none so poor to do him reverence.
[Shakespeare: *Julius Caesar* III.ii.]

3 The graves stood tenantless, and the sheeted dead
Did squeak and gibber in the Roman streets.
[Shakespeare: *Hamlet* I.i.]

4 He is dead and gone, lady,
He is dead and gone.
[Shakespeare: *Hamlet* IV.v.]

O lady, he is dead and gone!
Lady, he's dead and gone!
And at his head a green grass turfe,
And at his heels a stone.

Thomas Percy (ed.): Reliques, "The Friar of Orders Gray"

5 King Pandion, he is dead,
All thy friends are lapp'd in lead.
[Richard Barnfield: *An Ode*]

6 One owes respect to the living; to the dead one owes only the truth. [Voltaire: *Lettres sur Oedipe* I]

7 If we owe regard to the memory of the dead, there is yet more respect to be paid to knowledge, to virtue, and to truth. [Samuel Johnson: *The Rambler* No. 60]

8 Tyrawley and I have been dead these two years; but we don't choose to have it known. [Lord Chesterfield: in Boswell's *Life of Johnson*, April 3, 1773]

9 Each in his narrow cell forever laid,
The rude forefathers of the hamlet sleep.
[Thomas Gray: *Elegy Written in a Country Churchyard*]

10 What fond and wayward thoughts will slide
Into a lover's head!—
"O mercy!" to myself I cried,
"If Lucy should be dead!"
[Wordsworth: *Strange Fits of Passion Have I Known*]

11 Few and short were the prayers we said,
And we spoke not a word of sorrow;
But we steadfastly gazed on the face that was dead,
And we bitterly thought of the morrow.
[Charles Wolfe: *The Burial of Sir John Moore*]

12   All that tread
The globe are but a handful to the tribes
That slumber in its bosom.
[William Cullen Bryant: *Thanatopsis*]
This was much more nearly true in 1817, when the poem was written, than it is today. Among the many effects of the enormous increase in population in the last century is the likelihood that the living may equal the dead in number.

13 Let the dead Past bury its dead.
[Longfellow: *A Psalm of Life*]

14 How fares it with the happy dead?
[Tennyson: *In Memoriam* XLIV]

15 Tread lightly, she is near
Under the snow,
Speak gently, she can hear
The daisies grow.
[Oscar Wilde: *Requiescat*]

16 I shall have more to say when I am dead.
[Edwin Arlington Robinson: *John Brown*]

17 Mistah Kurtz—he dead.
[Joseph Conrad: *Heart of Darkness*]
Used by T. S. Eliot as a motto for his poem The Hollow Men

18 When you're dead, you stay a long time dead. [Ring Lardner: *Zone of Quiet*]

19 Yes, there's something the dead are keeping back.
[Robert Frost: *The Witch of Coös*]

20 There died a myriad,
And of the best, among them,
For an old bitch gone in the teeth,
For a botched civilization.
[Ezra Pound: *E. P. Ode pour l'élection de son sepulchre*]

DEAF(NESS)

21 None is so deaf as who will not hear.
[Thomas Ingeland: *Disobedient Child*]

1 None so deaf as those that will not hear. [Matthew Henry: *Commentaries, Psalm 58*]

2 Deaf, giddy, helpless, left alone,
To all my friends a burden grown;
No more I hear my church's bell
Than if it rang out for my knell;
At thunder now no more I start
Than at the rumbling of a cart;
And what's incredible, alack!
No more I hear a woman's clack.
[Jonathan Swift: *On His Own Deafness*]

DEAR

3 As dear to me as are the ruddy drops
That visit my sad heart.
[Shakespeare: *Julius Caesar* II.i.]

4 You pay a great deal too dear for what's given freely. [Shakespeare: *The Winter's Tale* I.i.]

DEATH: the act of dying

5 As he came forth of his mother's womb, naked shall he return to go as he came, and shall take nothing of his labour, which he may carry away in his hand. [Ecclesiastes 5:15]
Parallel to, and possibly the origin of, the modern "You can't take it with you."

6 Man goeth to his long home, and the mourners go about the streets. [Ecclesiastes 12:5]

7 Or ever the silver cord be loosed, or the golden bowl be broken, or the pitcher be broken at the fountain, or the wheel broken at the cistern. [Ecclesiastes 12:6]

8 How oft when men are at the point
of death
Have they been merry! which their
keepers call
A lightning before death.
[Shakespeare: *Romeo and Juliet* V.iii.]
People who were under spells and were doomed to die, or those doomed by the law to die, were thought to have sudden insights, visions, and fits of irrational high spirits. The Scotch word for this condition was fey, *the word we now use to mean "daft."*

9 . . . death—
The undiscover'd country, from
whose bourne
No traveller returns.
[Shakespeare: *Hamlet* III.i.]

10 We do not die wholly at our deaths: we have mouldered away gradually long before. Death only consigns the last fragment of what we were to the grave. [William Hazlitt: *On the Feeling of Immortality in Youth*]

11 First our pleasures die—and then
Our hopes, and then our fears—and
when
These are dead, the debt is due,
Dust claims dust—and we die too.
[Shelley: *Death*]

12 As the last bell struck, a peculiar sweet smile shone over his face, and he lifted up his head a little, and quickly said, "Adsum!" and fell back. It was the word we used at school, when names were called; and lo, he, whose heart was as that of a little child, had answered to his name, and stood in the presence of The Master. [W. M. Thackeray: *The Newcomes* IX]

13 Because I could not stop for Death,
He kindly stopped for me;
The carriage held but just ourselves
And Immortality.
[Emily Dickinson: *Because I Could Not Stop for Death*]

14 It costs a lot of money to die comfortably. [Samuel Butler (1835-1902): *A Luxurious Death*]

15 To die will be an awfully big adventure. [J. M. Barrie: *Peter Pan* III]

DEATH: brings oblivion

16 For there is no remembrance of the wise more than of the fool for ever; seeing that which now is in the days to come shall all be forgotten. And how dieth the wise man? as the fool. [Ecclesiastes 2:16]

17 For who, to dumb forgetfulness a
prey,
This pleasing anxious being e'er resign'd,
Left the warm precincts of the cheerful day,
Nor cast one longing ling'ring look
behind?
[Thomas Gray: *Elegy Written in a Country Churchyard*]

18 No motion has she now, no force;
She neither hears nor sees;
Rolled round in earth's diurnal
course,

With rocks, and stones, and trees.
[Wordsworth: *A Slumber Did My Spirit Seal*]
> No motion has she now, no force,
> She does not hear or feel;
> Rolled round in earth's diurnal course
> In someone's Oldsmobile.
> > F. Scott Fitzgerald

1 Phlebas the Phoenician, a fortnight dead,
Forgot the cry of gulls, and the deep sea swell.
[T. S. Eliot: *The Waste Land* IV]

DEATH: brings peace

2 And there at Venice gave
His body to that pleasant country's earth,
And his pure soul unto his captain Christ,
Under whose colours he had fought so long.
[Shakespeare: *Richard II* IV.i.]

3 Strew on her roses, roses,
And never a spray of yew.
In quiet she reposes:
Ah! would that I did too!
[Matthew Arnold: *Requiescat*]

4 When I am dead and over me bright April
Shakes out her rain-drenched hair,
Though you should lean above me broken-hearted,
I shall not care.

I shall have peace, as leafy trees are peaceful
When rain bends down the bough;
And I shall be more silent and cold-hearted
Than you are now.
[Sara Teasdale: *I Shall Not Care*]

DEATH: comes to all

5 I am going the way of all the earth. [Joshua 23:14]

6 He has joined the great majority. (*Abiit ad plures*) [A Latin euphemism for dying, used in Petronius and elsewhere.]

7 Brightness falls from the air;
Queens have died young and fair;
Dust hath closed Helen's eye.
[Thomas Nashe: *In Time of Pestilence*]

8 All that lives must die,
Passing through nature to eternity.
[Shakespeare: *Hamlet* I.ii.]

9 The doors of death are ever open.
[Jeremy Taylor: *Contemplation on the State of Man* I.vii.]

10 To every man upon this earth
Death cometh soon or late.
[Macaulay: *Lays of Ancient Rome*, "Horatius"]

11 Every moment dies a man,
Every moment one is born.
[Tennyson: *The Vision of Sin*]

12 For some we loved, the loveliest and the best
That from his Vintage rolling Time hath prest,
Have drunk their Cup a Round or two before,
And one by one crept silently to rest.
[*Rubáiyát of Omar Khayyám* (trans. Edward FitzGerald)]

13 By brooks too broad for leaping
The lightfoot boys are laid;
The rose-lipt girls are sleeping
In fields where roses fade.
[A. E. Housman: *With Rue My Heart is Laden*]

14 Down, down, down into the darkness of the grave,
Gently they go, the beautiful, the tender, the kind;
Quietly they go, the intelligent, the witty, the brave.
I know. But I do not approve. And I am not resigned.
[Edna St. Vincent Millay: *Dirge Without Music*]

15 I had not thought death had undone so many.
[T. S. Eliot: *The Waste Land* I]
This is a translation of Dante's Inferno *III. 56-57.*

16 The goal of all life is death. [Sigmund Freud: quoted *New York Times Magazine*, May 6, 1956]

DEATH: its compensations and rewards

17 He whom the gods love dies young, while he is in health, has his senses and his judgment sound. [Plautus: *Bacchides* IV.vii.]
The first part of the quotation has been variously interpreted. Some interpret it as a consolation for the death of a child.

Some see it as a promise of vitality up to the day of death for the fortunate. The full quotation from Plautus, however, makes it clear that it was intended to mean that it is a misfortune to live on into decay and senility.

1 Death acquits us of all obligations. [Montaigne: *Essays* I.vii.]

2 Death hath this also, that it openeth the gate to good fame, and extinguisheth envy. [Francis Bacon: *Of Death*]

3 He that dies this year is quit for the next. [Shakespeare: *II Henry IV* III.ii.]

4 Death opens the gate of Fame and shuts the gate of Envy after it. [Laurence Sterne: *Tristram Shandy* V.iii.]

5 Death squares all accounts. [Charles Reade: *The Cloister and the Hearth* XCII]

6 Waldo is one of those people who would be enormously improved by death. [H. H. Munro ("Saki"): *The Feast of Nemesis*]

DEATH: the conqueror

7 And though mine arm should conquer twenty worlds,
There's a lean fellow beats all conquerors.
[Thomas Dekker: *Old Fortunatus* I.i.]

8 Like the leaves of the forest when summer is green,
That host with their banners at sunset were seen:
Like the leaves of the forest when Autumn hath blown,
That Host on the morrow lay wither'd and strown.

For the Angel of Death spread his wings on the blast,
And breathed in the face of the foe as he pass'd;
And the eyes of the sleepers wax'd deadly and chill,
And their hearts but once heaved, and for ever grew still!

. . . And the might of the Gentile, unsmote by the sword,
Hath melted like snow in the glance of the Lord!
[Byron: *The Destruction of Sennacherib*]

DEATH: devoutly to be wished

9 Death may be the greatest of all human blessings. [Socrates: in Plato's *Apology*]

10 Lord, now lettest thou thy servant depart in peace. [Luke 2:29]

11 Death is sometimes a punishment, sometimes a gift; to many it has come as a favor. [Seneca: *Hercules Oetaeus*]

12 The stroke of death is as a lover's pinch,
Which hurts, and is desir'd.
[Shakespeare: *Antony and Cleopatra* V.ii.]

13 He is miserable, that dieth not before he desires to die. [Thomas Fuller (1654-1734): *Gnomologia*]

14 Death, kind Nature's signal of retreat. [Samuel Johnson: *The Vanity of Human Wishes*]

15 Now more than ever seems it rich to die,
To cease upon the midnight with no pain,
While thou art pouring forth thy soul abroad
In such an ecstasy!
Still wouldst thou sing, and I have ears in vain—
To thy high requiem become a sod.
[Keats: *Ode to a Nightingale*]

16 Happy men that have the power to die.
[Tennyson: *Tithonus*]

17 Each person is born to one possession which outvalues all the others—his last breath. [Mark Twain: *Pudd'nhead Wilson's Calendar*]

18 Whoever has lived long enough to find out what life is knows how deep a debt of gratitude we owe to Adam, the first great benefactor of our race. He brought death into the world. [Mark Twain: *Pudd'nhead Wilson's Calendar*]

19 From too much love of living,
From hope and fear set free,
We thank with brief thanksgiving
Whatever gods may be
That no life lives for ever;
That dead men rise up never;
That even the weariest river
Winds somewhere safe to sea.
[Swinburne: *The Garden of Proserpine*]

20 There is a great deal to be said

For being dead.
[E. C. Bentley: *Clive*]

DEATH: the end of woe
1 Nobody dies prematurely who dies in misery. [Publilius Syrus: *Maxims*]
2 This world nys but a thurghfare ful
of wo,
And we been pilgrymes, passing to
and fro.
Deeth is an ende of every worldly
score.
[Chaucer: *The Knight's Tale*]
3 Now cracks a noble heart. Good-
night, sweet prince,
And flights of angels sing thee to thy
rest!
[Shakespeare: *Hamlet* V.ii.]
4 We all labour against our own cure, for death is the cure of all diseases. [Sir Thomas Browne: *Religio Medici* II.ix.]
5 The night comes on that knows not
morn,
When I shall cease to be all alone,
To live forgotten, and love forlorn.
[Tennyson: *Mariana in the South*]
6 Her cabin'd, ample spirit,
It flutter'd and fail'd for breath.
To-night it doth inherit
The vasty hall of death.
[Matthew Arnold: *Requiescat*]
7 At the door of life, by the gate of
breath,
There are worse things waiting for
men than death.
[Swinburne: *The Triumph of Time*]

DEATH: an enigma
8 Whence and what art thou, execrable
shape?
[John Milton: *Paradise Lost* II.681]
9 Riddle of destiny, who can show
What thy short visit meant, or know
What thy errand here below?
[Charles Lamb: *On an Infant Dying as soon as Born*]

DEATH: fears and terrors
10 The king of terrors. [Job 18:14]
11 I don't want to die, but I wouldn't care if I were dead. [Cicero: *Tusculan Disputations* I.viii.]
12 The fear of death is more to be dreaded than death. [Publilius Syrus: *Maxims*]

13 Men fear death as children fear to go in the dark; and as that natural fear in children is increased with tales, so is the other. [Francis Bacon: *Of Death*]
14 Ay, but to die, and go we know not
where;
To lie in cold obstruction and to rot;
This sensible warm motion to become
A kneaded clod; and the delighted
spirit
To bathe in fiery floods, or to reside
In thrilling region of thick-ribbed
ice;
To be imprison'd in the viewless
winds,
And blown with restless violence
round about
The pendent world.
[Shakespeare: *Measure for Measure* III.i.]
15 The sense of death is most in appre-
hension.
[Shakespeare: *Measure for Measure* III.i.]
16 The weariest and most loathèd
worldly life
That age, ache, penury, and impris-
onment
Can lay on nature, is a paradise
To what we fear of death.
[Shakespeare: *Measure for Measure* III.i.]
17   Black it stood as night,
Fierce as ten furies, terrible as hell.
[John Milton: *Paradise Lost* II.670-671]
18   I fled, and cry'd out, death!
Hell trembled at the hideous name,
and sigh'd
From all her caves, and back resounded, Death!
[John Milton: *Paradise Lost* II.787-789]
19 Grinned horrible a ghastly smile.
[John Milton: *Paradise Lost* II.846]
20 I am not so much afraid of death, as ashamed thereof; 'tis the very disgrace and ignominy of our natures, that in a moment can so disfigure us that our near-est friends, wife and children stand afraid and start at us. [Sir Thomas Browne: *Religio Medici* I.xl.]
21 He added a new terror to death. [Dr. John Arbuthnot: *alluding to the practice of the rapacious and unscrupulous book-seller, Edmund Curll, of issuing a biogra-phy of any distinguished man as soon as he was dead, paying more heed to sale-ability than to accuracy.*]

1 Those who have endeavoured to teach us to die well, have taught few to die willingly. [Samuel Johnson: in Boswell's *Life,* June 1761]

2 Whatever crazy sorrow saith,
No life that breathes with human breath
Has ever truly longed for death.
[Tennyson: *The Two Voices*]

3 Fear death?—to feel the fog in my throat,
The mist in my face,
When the snows begin, and the blasts denote
I am nearing the place,
The power of the night, the press of the storm,
The post of the foe;
Where he stands, the Arch Fear in a visible form,
Yet the strong man must go.
[Robert Browning: *Prospice*]

4 Death, like life, is an affair of being more frightened than hurt. [Samuel Butler (1835-1902): *Erewhon* XIII]

DEATH: its finality

5 He shall return no more to his house, neither shall his place know him any more. [Job 7:10]

6 Here is my journey's end, here is my butt,
And very sea-mark of my utmost sail.
[Shakespeare: *Othello* V.ii.]

7 His biting is immortal; those that do die of it do seldom or never recover. [Shakespeare: *Antony and Cleopatra* V.ii.]

8 The ancient sage, who did so long maintain
That bodies die, but souls return again,
With all the births and deaths he had in store,
Went out Pythagoras, and came no more.
[Matthew Prior: *Ode to the Memory of Colonel Villiers*]

9 Ah, make the most of what we yet may spend,
Before we too into the Dust descend;
Dust into Dust, and under Dust, to lie,
Sans Wine, sans Song, sans Singer, and—sans End.

[*Rubáiyát of Omar Khayyám* (trans. Edward FitzGerald)]

10 Oh threats of Hell and Hopes of Paradise!
One thing at least is certain—*This* Life flies:
One thing is certain and the rest is Lies;
The Flower that once has blown for ever dies.
[*Rubáiyát of Omar Khayyám* (trans. Edward FitzGerald)]

11 For so the game is ended
That should not have begun.
[A. E. Housman: *Last Poems* XIV]

12 After the first death there is no other. [Dylan Thomas: *A Refusal to Mourn the Death of a Child*]

DEATH: the grisly specter

13 Behold, a pale horse: and his name that sat on him was Death. [Revelation 6:8]

14 Death's a great disguiser.
[Shakespeare: *Measure for Measure* IV.ii.]

15 Death . . . on his pale horse.
[John Milton: *Paradise Lost* X.588]

16 There is a Reaper whose name is Death,
And with his sickle keen,
He reaps the bearded grain at a breath,
And the flowers that grow between.
[Longfellow: *The Reaper and the Flowers*]

17 The Shadow cloak'd from head to foot,
Who keeps the keys of all the creeds.
[Tennyson: *In Memoriam* XXIII]

DEATH: implacable

18 This fell sergeant, death,
Is strict in his arrest.
[Shakespeare: *Hamlet* V.ii.]

19 Death admits no appeals. [Randle Cotgrave: *Dictionary,* "Appeal"]

20 Can storied urn or animated bust
Back to its mansion call the fleeting breath?
Can Honor's voice provoke the silent dust
Or Flatt'ry soothe the dull cold ear of death?
[Thomas Gray: *Elegy Written in a Coun-*

try Churchyard]

1 Death's a debt; his mandamus binds all alike—no bail, no demurrer. [Richard Brinsley Sheridan: *St. Patrick's Day* II.iv.]

2 Pale, beyond porch and portal,
  Crowned with calm leaves, she stands
Who gathers all things mortal
With cold immortal hands.
[Swinburne: *The Garden of Proserpine*]

DEATH: inevitable

3 In the midst of life we are in death. [*Book of Common Prayer,* "Burial of the Dead"]

4 For as we well wot, that a young man may dye soone: so be we very sure that an olde man cannot liue long. [Sir Thomas More: *A Dialogue of Comforte*]

5 The worst is death, and death will have his day.
[Shakespeare: *Richard II* III.ii.]

6 Thou owest God a death.
[Shakespeare: *I Henry IV* V.i.]

7 A man can die but once: we owe God a death.
[Shakespeare: *II Henry IV* III.ii.]

8 Why, what is pomp, rule, reign, but earth and dust?
And, live we how we can, yet die we must.
[Shakespeare: *III Henry VI* V.ii.]

9 By medicine life may be prolong'd, yet death
Will seize the doctor too.
[Shakespeare: *Cymbeline* V.v.]

10 The glories of our blood and state
Are shadows, not substantial things;
There is no armour against fate,
Death lays his icy hand on kings.
  Scepter and crown
  Must tumble down,
And, in the dust, be equal made
With the poor crooked scythe and spade.
[James Shirley: *Contention of Ajax and Ulysses* III]

11 . . . the inevitable hour.
[Thomas Gray: *Elegy Written in a Country Churchyard*]

12 In this world nothing is certain but death and taxes. [Benjamin Franklin: Letter to M. Leroy (1789)]

13 The young may die, but the old must! [Longfellow: *The Cloisters*]

DEATH: the leveller

14 Death reduced to the same condition Alexander the Macedonian and his muleteer. [Marcus Aurelius: *Meditations* VI. xxiv.]

15 O mighty Caesar! dost thou lie so low?
Are all thy conquests, glories, triumphs, spoils,
Shrunk to this little measure?
[Shakespeare: *Julius Caesar* III.i.]

16 Death and dice level all distinction.
[Samuel Foote: *The Minor* I.i.]

17 The incapacity to think of Death the Leveler as applying to *you* is the great psychic protection, I suppose, which permits human aspiration to exist. [Eric Hodgins: *Episode,* p. 190]

DEATH: loneliness

18 I shall go to him, but he shall not return to me. [II Samuel 12:23]

19 What is this world? what asketh men to have?
Now with his love, now in his colde grave
Alone, withouten any compaignye.
[Chaucer: *The Knight's Tale*]

20 We shall die alone.
[Pascal: *Pensées*]
Every man must walk down to the grave alone.   Samuel Johnson

21 Come away, come away, death,
  And in sad cypress let me be laid;
Fly away, fly away, breath:
  I am slain by a fair cruel maid.
My shroud of white, stuck all with yew,
  O! prepare it:
My part of death, no one so true
  Did share it.
[Shakespeare: *Twelfth Night* II.iv.]

22 She, she is dead; she's dead; when thou know'st this,
Thou know'st how dry a cinder this world is.
[Donne: *The First Anniversary*]

23   Then worms shall try
That long preserved virginity,
And your quaint honour turn to dust,
And into ashes all my lust.
The grave's a fine and private place,

But none, I think, do there embrace.
[Andrew Marvell: *To His Coy Mistress*]

1 The sweeping up the heart
And putting love away
We shall not want to use again
Until eternity.
[Emily Dickinson: *Time and Eternity*, XXII.2]
The morning after death.

2 Lovers lying two and two
Ask not whom they sleep beside,
And the bridegroom all night through
Never turns him to the bride.
[A. E. Housman: *A Shropshire Lad* XII]

DEATH: longing for

3 Why died I not from the womb? why did I not give up the ghost when I came out of the belly?

Why did the knees prevent me? or why the breasts that I should suck?

For now I should have lain still and been quiet, I should have slept: then had I been at rest,

With kings and counsellers of the earth, which built desolate places for themselves . . .

Or as an hidden untimely birth I had not been; as infants which never saw the light. [Job 3:11-16]

4 Wherefore is light given to him that is in misery, and life unto the bitter in soul;

Which long for death, but it cometh not; and dig for it more than for hid treasures;

Which rejoice exceedingly, and are glad, when they can find the grave? [Job 3:20-22]

5 I have said to corruption, Thou art my father: to the worm, Thou art my mother, and my sister. [Job 17:14]

6 And on the ground, which is my modres gate,
I knokke with my staf, bothe erly and late,
And seye "Leve moder, leet me in!
Lo, how I vanish, flesh, and blood, and skin!"
[Chaucer: *The Pardoner's Tale*]
leve = *dear*
An old man's staff is the rapper at death's door.
George Herbert: Jacula Prudentum
(1640)

7 Tir'd with all these, for restful death I cry.
[Shakespeare: *Sonnets* LXVI]

8 O amiable, lovely death!
Thou odoriferous stench! sound rottenness!
Arise forth from the couch of lasting night,
Thou hate and terror to prosperity,
And I will kiss thy detestable bones;
And put my eyeballs in thy vaulty brows;
And ring these fingers with thy household worms;
And stop this gap of breath with fulsome dust,
And be a carrion monster like thyself.
[Shakespeare: *King John* III.iv.]

9 Death rock me asleep, abridge my doleful days!
[Shakespeare: *II Henry IV* II.iv.]

10 Vex not his ghost: O, let him pass! he hates him
That would upon the rack of this tough world
Stretch him out longer.
[Shakespeare: *King Lear* V.iii.]

11 I have been half in love with easeful death.
[Keats: *Ode to a Nightingale*]

12 Let us have a quiet hour,
Let us hob-and-nob with Death.
[Tennyson: *The Vision of Sin*]

13 "I saw the Sibyl at Cumae"
(One said) "with mine own eye.
She hung in a cage, and read her rune
To all the passers-by.
Said the boys, 'What wouldst thou, Sibyl?'
She answered, 'I would die.' "
[Dante Gabriel Rossetti: *Fragments*, "The Sibyl"]
Rossetti is translating a passage in Petronius, the same passage that T. S. Eliot uses as an epigraph for The Waste Land.
When bidden by Apollo to choose a gift, the Sibyl had asked for as many years as she had grains of sand in her hand. The gift was granted, but she had forgotten to ask for youth and grew fantastically aged and shrivelled. Trimalchio, in Petronius, says that he has seen her with his own eyes at Cumae, hung in a jar, prophesying, and that when children asked her what she wanted, she

would reply, as here, "I want to die."

1 I have a rendezvous with Death
At some disputed barricade,
When Spring comes back with rustling shade
And apple-blossoms fill the air.
[Alan Seeger: *I Have a Rendezvous with Death*]

DEATH OF KINGS

2 For God's sake, let us sit upon the ground
And tell sad stories of the death of kings:
How some have been deposed, some slain in war,
Some haunted by the ghosts they have deposed;
Some poisoned by their wives, some sleeping killed;
All murdered: for within the hollow crown
That rounds the mortal temples of a king
Keeps Death his court, and there the antic sits,
Scoffing his state and grinning at his pomp;
Allowing him a breath, a little scene,
To monarchize, be feared, and kill with looks,
Infusing him with self and vain conceit
As if this flesh which walls about our life
Were brass impregnable; and humoured thus
Comes at the last, and with a little pin
Bores through his castle-wall, and farewell king!
[Shakespeare: *Richard II* III.ii.]

DEATH: peaceful

3 Thou shalt come to thy grave in a full age, like as a shock of corn cometh in his season. [Job 5:26]
4 The gods conceal from the living how pleasant death is, so that they will continue to live. [Lucan: *Pharsalia* IV.519]
5 Then with no fiery, throbbing pain,
No cold gradations of decay,
Death broke at once the vital chain,
And freed his soul the nearest way.
[Samuel Johnson: *On the Death of Dr. Robert Levet*]

DEATH: proud death

6 O eloquent, just, and mighty Death! whom none could advise, thou hast persuaded; what none hath dared, thou hast done; and whom all the world hath flattered, thou only hast cast out of the world and despised: thou hast drawn together all the far stretchèd greatness, all the pride, cruelty and ambition of man, and covered it all over with these two narrow words, *Hic jacet!* [Sir Walter Raleigh (1552?-1618): *Historie of the World* V.i.]
7 O proud death!
[Shakespeare: *Hamlet* V.ii.]
8 Now boast thee, death, in thy possession lies
A lass unparallel'd.
[Shakespeare: *Antony and Cleopatra* V.ii.]
9 Death, be not proud, though some have called thee
Mighty and dreadful, for thou art not so,
For those whom thou think'st thou dost overthrow
Die not, poor Death, nor yet canst thou kill me.
From rest and sleepe, which but thy pictures bee,
Much pleasure, then from thee much more must flow.
[Donne: *Holy Sonnets*, X]
10 Death is the only thing we haven't succeeded in completely vulgarizing. [Aldous Huxley: *Eyeless in Gaza* XXXI]

DEATH: readiness for

11 I loathe the men who would prolong their lives
By foods and drinks and charms of magic art,
Perverting nature's course to ward off death;
They ought, when they but cumber up the ground,
Get hence and die, and clear the way for youth.
[Euripides: *Suppliants*]
12 Sunset and evening star,
And one clear call for me!
And may there be no moaning of the bar,
When I put out to sea.
[Tennyson: *Crossing the Bar*]

1 I am ready to meet my Maker. Whether my Maker is prepared for the great ordeal of meeting me is another matter. [Winston Churchill: on his 75th birthday]

DEATH: reunion in
2 He first deceased: she for a little tried
To live without him, lik'd it not, and died.
[Sir Henry Wotton: *On the Death of Sir Albert Morton's Wife*]
3 Stay for me there; I will not fail
To meet thee in that hollow vale.
[Henry King: *Exequy on the Death of a Beloved Wife*]
4 It may be we shall touch the Happy Isles,
And see the great Achilles whom we knew.
[Tennyson: *Ulysses*]
5 For tho' from out our bourne of Time and Place
The flood may bear me far,
I hope to see my Pilot face to face
When I have crost the bar.
[Tennyson: *Crossing the Bar*]

DEATH: a sleep
6 He giveth his beloved sleep. [Psalms 127:2]
7 She is not dead, but sleepeth. [Luke 8:52]
8 When once the light of our brief day is extinguished,
There is a night of endless sleep.
[Catullus: *Carmina* V.v.]
9 Duncan is in his grave;
After life's fitful fever he sleeps well.
[Shakespeare: *Macbeth* III.ii.]
10 Unarm, Eros; the long day's task is done
And we must sleep.
[Shakespeare: *Antony and Cleopatra* IV. xiv.]
Eros is Antony's armor-bearer. When Antony demands of him, in fulfillment of an earlier agreement, that he kill him, Eros kills himself.
11 Sleep the sleep that knows not breaking,
Morn of toil, nor night of waking.
[Sir Walter Scott: *The Lady of the Lake* I.xxxi.]
12 The silence of that dreamless sleep

I envy now too much to weep.
[Byron: *And Thou Art Dead*]
13 Death, so called, is a thing which makes men weep,
And yet a third of life is passed in sleep.
[Byron: *Don Juan* XIV.iii.]
14 He lay like a warrior taking his rest,
With his martial cloak around him.
[Charles Wolfe: *The Burial of Sir John Moore*]
15 How wonderful is death, death and his brother sleep!
[Shelley: *Queen Mab* I]
16 Our very hopes belied our fears,
Our fears our hopes belied;
We thought her dying when she slept,
And sleeping when she died.
[Thomas Hood: *The Death-bed*]
17 God's finger touched him, and he slept.
[Tennyson: *In Memoriam* LXXXV]
18 Clay lies still, but blood's a rover;
Breath's a ware that will not keep.
Up, lad: when the journey's over
There'll be time enough to sleep.
[A. E. Housman: *A Shropshire Lad* IV]

DEATH: sudden
19 Those which in times of execution are seen to run to their end and hasten the execution, do it not with resolution but because they will take away time to consider the same; it grieves them not to be dead but to die. [Montaigne: *Essays* II. xiii.]
20 A short death is the chief hap of human life. [Montaigne: *Essays* II.xiii.]
Hap *here seems to mean "felicity."*
21 The slender debt to Nature's quickly paid,
Discharged, perchance, with greater ease than made.
[Francis Quarles: *Emblems* II.xiii.]
22 There is a great difference between going off in warm blood like Romeo, and making one's exit like a frog in a frost. [Keats: Letter to Fanny Brawne, March 1820]

DEATH: triumph over
23 O death, where is thy sting? O grave, where is thy victory? [I Corinthians 15:55]
24 Despise death and you have con-

quered every fear. [Publilius Syrus: *Maxims*]

1 There is no passion in the mind of man so weak, but it mates and masters the fear of death. . . . Revenge triumphs over death; love slights it; honour aspireth to it; grief flieth to it. [Francis Bacon: *Of Death*]

2 He that dies in an earnest pursuit is like one that is wounded in hot blood, who, for the time, scarce feels the hurt; and therefore a mind fixed and bent upon somewhat that is good doth avert the dolors of death. [Francis Bacon: *Of Death*]

3 Thou art not conquer'd; beauty's ensign yet
Is crimson in thy lips, and in thy cheeks,
And death's pale flag is not advancèd there.
[Shakespeare: *Romeo and Juliet* V.iii.]

4   Nothing in his life
Became him like the leaving it; he died
As one that had been studied in his death
To throw away the dearest thing he ow'd,
As 't were a careless trifle.
[Shakespeare: *Macbeth* I.iv.]

5 Thou art slave to Fate, Chance, kings and desperate men
And dost with poison, war, and sickness dwell,
And poppy or charms can make us sleep as well,
And better than thy stroke; why swell'st thou, then?
One short sleep past, we wake eternally,
And death shall be no more; death, thou shalt die.
[Donne: *Holy Sonnets*, X]

6 He lives, he wakes—'tis Death is dead, not he.
[Shelley: *Adonais* XLI]

7 So live, that when thy summons comes to join
The innumerable caravan, which moves
To that mysterious realm, where each shall take
His chamber in the silent halls of death,

Thou go not, like the quarry-slave at night,
Scourged to his dungeon, but, sustained and soothed
By an unfaltering trust, approach thy grave
Like one who wraps the drapery of his couch
About him, and lies down to pleasant dreams.
[William Cullen Bryant: *Thanatopsis*]
The poem was written in 1817, when Bryant was 23. Had he died then, the world would have thought it had lost a great poet. But he lived on.

8 And how can man die better
Than facing fearful odds,
For the ashes of his fathers,
And the temples of his Gods?
[Macaulay: *Lays of Ancient Rome*, "Horatius"]

9 Thou madest Death: and lo, thy foot
Is on the skull which thou hast made.
[Tennyson: Prologue to *In Memoriam*]

10 O death, where is thy sting-a-ling-a-ling,
O Grave, thy victoree?
The bells of Hell go ting-a-ling-a-ling
For you but not for me.
[Anon]
British soldiers' song, popular in 1914-18

DEATH: general and miscellaneous

11 There is death in the pot. [II Kings 4:40]

12 Death is fortunate for the child, bitter to the youth, too late to the old. [Publilius Syrus: *Maxims*]

13 I pray you, Master Lieutenant, see me safe up, and for my coming down let me shift for myself. [Sir Thomas More: as he ascended the scaffold, as reported by his son-in-law, Roper, in his *Life of Sir Thomas More*]
More's brave, ironical jesting at his death was much held against him by his enemies at the time.

14 He who despises his own life may at any time become master of other men's lives. [Montaigne: *Essays* I.xxiii.]
That is, we have no protection against the assassin who is willing to die to carry out the assassination.

1 Our pleasant Willy, ah! is dead of
late:
With whom all joy and jolly merri-
ment
Is also deaded.
[Sir Philip Sidney: *Tears of the Muses*]
2 Nothing can we call our own but
death
And that small model of the barren
earth
Which serves as paste and cover to
our bones.
[Shakespeare: *Richard II* III.ii.]
3 Death hath a thousand doors to let
out life.
I shall find one.
[Philip Massinger: *A Very Woman* V.iv.]
4 The thousand doors that lead to
death.
[Sir Thomas Browne: *Religio Medici*
I.xliv.]
5 His time was come; he ran his race;
We hope he's in a better place.
[Jonathan Swift: *On the Death of Dr.
Swift*]
6 The doctors found, when she was
dead—
Her last disorder mortal.
[Oliver Goldsmith: *Elegy on Mrs. Mary
Blaize*]
7 Death without phrases. [Joseph
Siéyès: on voting for the death penalty
for Louis XVI (1793)]
*The solemnity of the occasion led most
of those who voted to utter some comment with their vote, something rhetorical for posterity. Either Siéyès merely
said "Death," and the reporter added
"without phrases," to mark the fact that
he added nothing to his vote, or Siéyès
himself, perhaps in contempt of his colleagues' grandiloquence, spoke the full
phrase.*
8 His death, which happened in his
berth,
At forty-odd befell;
They went and told the sexton, and
The sexton tolled the bell.
[Thomas Hood: *Faithless Sally Brown*]
9 The mossy marbles rest
On the lips that he has prest
In their bloom;
And the names he loved to hear
Have been carved for many a year
On the tomb.

[O. W. Holmes: *The Last Leaf*]
10 Half a league, half a league,
Half a league onward,
All in the valley of death
Rode the six hundred.
[Tennyson: *The Charge of the Light
Brigade*]
11 He who lives more lives than one
More deaths than one must die.
[Oscar Wilde: *The Ballad of Reading
Gaol*]
12 Death is the mother of beauty.
[Wallace Stevens: *Sunday Morning*]
13 To the fifteenth-century artist a good
death-appeal was as sure a key to popularity as a good sex-appeal is at the present time. [Aldous Huxley: *Beyond the
Mexique Bay*]
14 It's nature's way of telling you to
slow down. [Anonymous witticism, *Newsweek,* April 25, 1960]

DEATHBED UTTERANCES
15 And, behold, this day I am going the
way of all the earth. [Joshua 23:14]
*David, when dying, uses the same phrase
(I Kings 2:1-2). The reference in both
passages is to death. This became changed
in English, by at least the 17th century,
to "the way of all flesh," the phrase
which Samuel Butler (1835-1902) used as
the title of his posthumous novel (1903).
The obsession of Anglo-Saxon morality
with sex has led to the contemporary use
of the expression to allude to sexual impulses.*
16 Woe's me. Methinks I'm turning into
a god. [The Emperor Vespasian, dying:
in Suetonius's *The Deified Vespasian*
XXIII]
*The Roman emperors were deified after
death. Vespasian, a skeptic and a humorist, feeling through some wave of
faintness or of nausea, that his end was
imminent, had his last joke. It must be
rated very high among death-bed utterances.*
17 Even going my journey; they have
greased my boots already. [Attr. Rabelais on his deathbed, after his receiving
extreme unction.]
Quoted in Bacon: Apothegms.
18 I have sent for you that you may see
how a Christian can die. [Joseph Addison: on his deathbed, July 17, 1719, to

his stepson, Lord Warwick]

Addison's improving the occasion in so spectacular a manner was greatly admired throughout the 18th century, but it seems gruesomely priggish to us and, considering the lapses and accidents of dissolution, dangerous.

1 Why, of course, he will forgive me; that's his business. [Heinrich Heine: on his deathbed (1856). A priest had told him that God would forgive him his sins.]

The actual statement: Bien sûr, qu'il me pardonnera; c'est son métier.

A métier is a business or a vocation.

Of this famous bit of gay blasphemy, Freud says: "The joke is intended to mean: 'Certainly he will forgive me; that is what he is here for, and for no other purpose have I engaged him' (just as one retains one's doctor or one's lawyer). Thus, the helpless dying man is still conscious of the fact that he has created God for himself and has clothed Him with power in order to make use of Him as occasion arises. The so-called creature makes himself known as the Creator only a short time before his extinction."—Wit and Its Relation to the Unconscious I.iii.

DEBATE
2 Men only debate and question of the branch, not of the tree. [Montaigne: *Essays* II.xii.]

DEBT(S)
3 If a man ever pays you what he owes you,
You're greatly beholden to him.
[Terence: *Phormio* I.ii.]
4 Debt is the slavery of the free. [Publilius Syrus: *Maxims*]
5 A small debt makes a man your debtor, a large one makes him your enemy. [Seneca: *Ad Lucilium* XIX.xii.]
6 He that dies pays all debts.
[Shakespeare: *The Tempest* III.ii.]
7 Small debts are like small shot; they are rattling on every side, and can scarcely be escaped without a wound; great debts are like cannon, of loud noise but little danger. [Samuel Johnson: Letter to Joseph Simpson]
8 Pay what you owe, and you'll know what is your own. [Benjamin Franklin: *Poor Richard's Almanack* (1739)]

9 A creditor is worse than a master; for a master owns only your person, a creditor owns your dignity, and can belabour that. [Victor Hugo: *Les Misérables* V.ii.]
10 There can be no freedom or beauty about a home life that depends on borrowing and debt. [Henrik Ibsen: *A Doll's House* I]

DEBTORS
11 Creditors have better memories than debtors. [James Howell: *Proverbs*]

DECAY
12 All human things are subject to decay,
And, when fate summons, monarchs must obey.
[Dryden: *Mac Flecknoe*]
13 A general flavor of mild decay,
But nothing local, as one may say.
[O. W. Holmes: *The Deacon's Masterpiece*]
14 The woods decay, the woods decay and fall,
The vapours weep their burthen to the ground,
Man comes and tills the field and lies beneath,
And after many a summer dies the swan.
[Tennyson: *Tithonus*]

DECEMBER
15   When we shall hear
The rain and wind beat dark December, how
In this our pinching cave, shall we discourse
The freezing hours away?
[Shakespeare: *Cymbeline* III.iii.]

DECENCY
16 Immodest words admit of no defence,
For want of decency is want of sense.
[Wentworth Dillon, Earl of Roscommon: *Essay on Translated Verse*]
One is always a little startled to remember that this famous aphorism was written by a courtier and wit during the Restoration (1684).

17 The thin precarious crust of decency is all that separates any civilization, however impressive, from the hells of anarchy or systematic tyranny which lie

in wait beneath the surface. [Aldous Huxley: *Themes and Variations*]

DECEPTION

1 One who deceives will always find those who allow themselves to be deceived. [Machiavelli: *The Prince* XVIII]
2 The deceits of the world, the flesh, and the devil. [*Book of Common Prayer*, "Litany"]
3 Easily doth the world deceive itself in things it desireth or fain would have come to pass. [Montaigne: *Essays* II. xxxvii.]
4 They fool me to the top of my bent. [Shakespeare: *Hamlet* III.ii.]
5 It is a double pleasure to deceive the deceiver. [La Fontaine: *Fables* II.xv.]
6 Oh, what a tangled web we weave
   When first we practice to deceive!
[Sir Walter Scott: *Marmion* VI]
7 You can fool some of the people all of the time, and all of the people some of the time; but you cannot fool all of the people all of the time. [Attr. Lincoln (about 1863), but not to be found in his writings]

DECISION

8 Multitudes, multitudes in the valley of decision. [Joel 3:14]
   Edith Wharton used The Valley of Decision *as a title for one of her novels, 1902.*

DECLINE

9 We have seen the best of our time: machinations, hollowness, treachery, and all ruinous disorders, follow us disquietly to our graves. [Shakespeare: *King Lear* I.ii.]
10 From that full meridian of my glory
    I haste now to my setting: I shall fall
    Like a bright exhalation in the evening,
    And no man see me more.
[Shakespeare: *Henry VIII* III.ii.]

DECREE

11 There went out a decree from Caesar Augustus that all the world should be taxed. [Luke 2:1]

DEED(S)

12 These deeds must not be thought

After these ways; so, it will make us mad.
[Shakespeare: *Macbeth* II.ii.]
13 There shall be done a deed of dreadful note.
[Shakespeare: *Macbeth* III.ii.]
14 A deed without a name.
[Shakespeare: *Macbeth* IV.i.]
15 And now the matchless deed's achiev'd,
    Determined, dared, and done.
[Christopher Smart: *Song to David*]
16 Only where love and need are one,
    And the work is play for mortal stakes,
    Is the deed ever really done
    For Heaven and the future's sakes.
[Robert Frost: *Two Tramps in Mud-Time*]

DEEP

17 He maketh the deep to boil like a pot. [Job 41:31]
18 Deep calleth unto deep. [Psalms 42:7]
19 Before their eyes in sudden view appear
    The secrets of the hoary deep, a dark
    Illimitable Ocean, without bound,
    Without dimension, where length, breadth, and height,
    And time and place are lost; where eldest Night
    And Chaos, ancestors of Nature, hold
    Eternal anarchy, amidst the noise
    Of endless wars, and by confusion stand.
[John Milton: *Paradise Lost* II.890-898]
20 The very deep did rot: O Christ!
    That ever this should be!
[Coleridge: *The Ancient Mariner*]
21 Rocked in the cradle of the deep,
    I lay me down in peace to sleep.
[Emma Willard: *The Cradle of the Deep*]
22 O pilot! 'tis a fearful night,
    There's danger on the deep.
[Thomas Haynes Bayly: *The Pilot*]
23 A life on the ocean wave, a home on the rolling deep.
[Epes Sargent: *A Life on the Ocean Wave*]
24 If this young man expresses himself in terms too deep for me,
    Why, what a very singularly deep

young man this deep young man
must be!
[W. S. Gilbert: *Patience* I]

DEER
1 I was a stricken deer that left the
herd long since.
[William Cowper: *The Task* III]
An echo of Hamlet III.ii.:
Why, let the stricken deer go weep,
The hart ungalled play;
For some must watch [stay awake], while
some must sleep:
So runs the world away.

Cowper had, as a young man, what to-
day would be called a severe nervous
breakdown and spent his life in retire-
ment. He wrote the famous hymn be-
ginning "God moves in a mysterious
way | His wonders to perform" on feel-
ing the approach of one of his attacks of
madness.

Lord David Cecil entitled his biog-
raphy of Cowper The Stricken Deer.

2 A herd-abandoned deer struck by the
hunter's dart.
[Shelley: *Adonais* XXXIII]

DEFEAT
3 How are the mighty fallen! [II Sam-
uel 1:19]
4 Creep into thy narrow bed,
Creep, and let no more be said!
Vain thy onset! all stands fast;
Thou thyself must break at last.
[Matthew Arnold: *The Last Word*]

DEFECT
5 The Chief Defect of Henry King
Was chewing little bits of String.
[Hilaire Belloc: *Henry King*]

DEFENSE
6 Doves will peck in safeguard of their
brood.
[Shakespeare: *III Henry VI* II.ii.]
7 . . . my state
Stands on me to defend, not to de-
bate.
[Shakespeare: *King Lear* V.i.]
The same thought is expressed in
Homer's Iliad XX:
Our business in the field of fight
Is not to question, but to prove our
might.

—*Pope's trans.*
8 What boots it at one gate to make
defence,
And at another to let in the foe?
[John Milton: *Samson Agonistes*]
9 The only fence against the world is a
thorough knowledge of it. [John Locke:
Some Thoughts on Education]
fence = defence
This is the basis of every meaning of
the word fence. *God used formerly to be*
called a fence. *In the sense of a receiver*
of stolen goods, a fence *was the thieves'*
defence against the police.

10 Millions for defense, but not a cent
for tribute. [Attr. Charles Cotesworth
Pinckney, as his answer to Talleyrand's
demand for a bribe to call off attacks on
American shipping (October 1797); actually spoken by Robert G. Harper at a
dinner in Philadelphia in honor of John
Marshall, who had just returned from a
mission to France (1798)]
Pinckney denied that he had made the
famous statement; he said that his an-
swer had been the less rhetorical but
equally effective—with Talleyrand per-
haps more *effective: "Not a penny, not a*
penny."

DEFIANCE
11 By God, 'tis good, and if you like 't,
you may. [Ben Jonson: Epilogue to *Cynthia's Revels*]
Ben had had a stroke and the critics said
that he was done for and that his previous
play showed a marked decline in his
powers. The old lion, wounded but still
dangerous, came roaring out with this
defiance in his next play.

It was customary in the epilogue to
flatter the audience, to state that only
their approval could convey merit, etc.
But Ben was in no mood for the conven-
tional ending.

12 Who durst defy the omnipotent to
arms.
[John Milton: *Paradise Lost* I.49]
13 Come one, come all! this rock shall
fly
From its firm base as soon as I!
[Sir Walter Scott: *The Lady of the Lake*
V.x.]
14 The soul of man, like unextinguished
fire,

Yet burns towards heaven with fierce
reproach, and doubt,
And lamentation, and reluctant
prayer,
Hurling up insurrection, which
might make
Our antique empire insecure, though
built
On eldest faith, and hell's coeval,
fear.
[Shelley: *Prometheus Unbound* III.i.]
Jupiter speaking.

DEFILE
1 Not that which goeth into the mouth
defileth a man; but that which cometh
out of the mouth, this defileth a man.
[Matthew 15:11]

DEFORMITY
2 Whosoever hath anything fixed in his
person that doth induce contempt, hath
also a perpetual spur in himself to rescue and deliver himself from scorn.
[Francis Bacon: *Of Deformity*]
3 Physical deformity calls forth our
charity. But the infinite misfortune of
moral deformity calls forth nothing but
hatred and vengeance. [Clarence Dar-
row]

DEGREE
4   O! when degree is shak'd,
Which is the ladder to all high de-
signs,
The enterprise is sick.
[Shakespeare: *Troilus and Cressida*
I.iii.]
5 Take but degree away, untune that
string,
And, hark! what discord follows.
[Shakespeare: *Troilus and Cressida*
I.iii.]
6 Differing but in degree, of kind the
same.
[John Milton: *Paradise Lost* V.490]

DEJECTION
7 As high as we have mounted in delight,
In our dejection do we sink as low.
[Wordsworth: *Resolution and Independence*]
8 I could lie down like a tired child,

And weep away the life of care.
[Shelley: *Stanzas written in Dejection,
near Naples*]

DELAY
9 Delay is a great procuress.
[Ovid: *The Art of Love* III]
10 It is always those who are ready who
suffer in delays.
[Dante: *The Divine Comedy,* "Inferno"
XXVIII]
11 Sweet reluctant amorous delay.
[John Milton: *Paradise Lost* IV.311]

DELIBERATION
12 The woman that deliberates is lost.
[Joseph Addison: *Cato* IV.i.]

DELICACY
13 If a person has no delicacy, he has
you in his power. [William Hazlitt: *Literary Remains II*]

DELICATELY
14 Agag came unto him delicately. And
Agag said, Surely the bitterness of death
is passed. [I Samuel 15:32]

DELIGHT(S)
15 What more felicitie can fall to creature
Than to enjoy delight with libertie.
[Edmund Spenser: *Muiopotmos*]
16 Violent delights have violent ends.
[Shakespeare: *Romeo and Juliet* II.vi.]
17   His delights
Were dolphin-like; they show'd his
back above
The elements they lived in.
[Shakespeare: *Antony and Cleopatra*
V.ii.]
*These ecstatic lines from Cleopatra's
famed eulogy to her great lover illustrate the alchemy of poetry when we
compare them to the passage in North's
translation of Plutarch on which they
are based: "As the Dolphin shows his
back above the water, so Antony always
rose superior to the pleasures in which
he lived."*

*North simply intended one of the
moral parables then drawn so freely
from what was thought to be natural
history. Shakespeare's lines emerge, like
the creature itself, flashing, vital, irides-*

cent, breathtakingly glorious.

1 They came to the Delectable Mountains. [John Bunyan: *Pilgrim's Progress* I]

2 In truth, he was a strange and wayward wight,
Fond of each gentle and each dreadful scene.
In darkness and in storm he found delight.
[James Beattie: *The Minstrel* I.xxii.]

3 You have delighted us long enough. [Jane Austen: *Pride and Prejudice* XVIII]
Mr. Bennett speaking.

4 Rarely, rarely, comest thou,
Spirit of Delight.
[Shelley: *Rarely, Rarely, Comest Thou*]

5 Not by appointment do we meet delight.
[Gerald Massey: *The Bridegroom of Beauty*]

DELIVERANCE
6 Surely he shall deliver thee from the snare of the fowler, and from the noisome pestilence. [Psalms 91:3]

DELIVERER
7 Many would contentedly suffer the consequences of their own mistakes rather than the insolence of him who triumphs as their deliverer. [Samuel Johnson: *The Rambler* No. 87]

DELUGE
8 After us the deluge. [Attr. variously to Madame de Pompadour and to Louis XV, after the crushing defeat of the French at Rossbach, 1757]
Either may have said it on that occasion, and subsequent events proved the foreboding to be warranted, but the expression itself was proverbial long before 1757.

DELUSION
9 A delusion, a mockery, and a snare. [Lord Denman: *O'Connell vs. The Queen. Clark and Finnelly Reports*]

DEMOCRACY
10 What is democracy?—an aristocracy of blackguards. [Byron: *Diary,* May 1821]

11 The tendency of democracies is, in all things, to mediocrity. [James Fenimore Cooper: *The American Democrat*]

12 Democracy, which means despair of finding any Heroes to govern you, and contented putting up with the want of them. [Thomas Carlyle: *Past and Present* III.xiii.]

13 The world must be made safe for democracy. [Woodrow Wilson: in an address to Congress, April 2, 1917]

14 Christianity can no more escape democracy than democracy can escape socialism. [G. B. Shaw: Preface to *John Bull's Other Island*]

15 Democracy, the last refuge of cheap misgovernment. [G. B. Shaw: *Man and Superman,* "The Revolutionist's Handbook: Democracy"]

16 People who want to understand democracy should spend less time in the library with Aristotle and more time on the buses and in the subway. [Simeon Strunsky: *No Mean City* II]

17 The essential objection to democracy is that, with few exceptions, it imposes degrading acts and attitudes upon the men responsible for the welfare and dignity of the state. [H. L. Mencken: *Notes on Democracy*]

18 The saddest life is that of a political aspirant under democracy. His failure is ignominious and his success is disgraceful. [H. L. Mencken: *Chrestomathy* p. 152]

19 Democracy is the recurrent suspicion that more than half of the people are right more than half of the time. [E. B. White: *World Government and Peace*]

20 I swear to the Lord
I still can't see
Why Democracy means
Everybody but me.
[Langston Hughes: *The Black Man Speaks*]

21 From the time of the Peasants' Rebellion on, all true democratic movements have been branded as anti-religious. [Bergen Evans: *The Natural History of Nonsense* XIX]

22 Democracy is essentially anti-authoritarian—that is, it not only demands the right but imposes the responsibility of thinking for ourselves. [Bergen Evans: *The Natural History of Nonsense* XIX]

1 All the ills of democracy can be cured by more democracy. [Alfred Emmanuel Smith, Speech, June 27, 1933]

DENIAL
2 What thyng we may nat lightly have,
Therafter wol we crie alday and
crave.
[Chaucer: Prologue to *The Wife of Bath's Tale*]
3 For if it be but half-denied,
'Tis half as good as justified.
[Samuel Butler (1612-1680): *Hudibras*]
4 I am the spirit that denies!
[Goethe: *Faust* I (trans. Bayard Taylor)]
Mephistopheles speaking.

DENMARK
5 Something is rotten in the state of
Denmark.
[Shakespeare: *Hamlet* I.iv.]

DEPARTURE
6 And whosoever shall not receive you, nor hear you, when ye depart thence, shake off the dust under your feet, for a testimony against them. [Mark 6:11]
See also Matthew 10:14.
7 Stand not upon the order of your going,
But go at once.
[Shakespeare: *Macbeth* III.iv.]
8 He's gone, and forgot nothing but to say farewell to his creditors. [Benjamin Franklin: *Poor Richard's Almanack* (1733)]

DEPENDENCE
9 Who depends upon another man's ta-
ble often dines late. [John Ray: *English Proverbs* (1678)]

DEPTH(S)
10 Out of the depths have I cried unto thee, O Lord. [Psalms 130:1]
The Latin, in the Vulgate, *which is often quoted, is* De profundis clamavi.
11 Deeper than did ever plummet sound. [Shakespeare: *The Tempest* V.i.]
12 For the Gods approve
The depth, and not the tumult, of the
soul.
[Wordsworth: *Laodamia*]

DERISION
13 All fools have still an itching to de-

ride,
And fain would be upon the laughing
side.
[Alexander Pope: *An Essay on Criticism* I]

DESCRIPTION
14 It beggar'd all description.
[Shakespeare: *Antony and Cleopatra* II.ii.]

DESERT
15 The desert shall rejoice, and blossom as the rose. [Isaiah 35:1]
16 Use every man after his desert, and who should 'scape whipping? [Shakespeare: *Hamlet* II.ii.]

DESERTION
17 Just for a handful of silver he left us,
Just for a riband to stick in his coat.
[Browning: *The Lost Leader* (1845)]
Wordsworth's turning from liberalism to conservatism was the inspiration of Browning's poem. But Wordsworth's change was certainly not motivated by a desire for either wealth or glory. It was the result of a slowly-developed but sincere conviction.

DESIGN
18 It happens very well that Christmas should fall out in the middle of winter. [Joseph Addison: *The Spectator* No. 269]
Sir Roger De Coverley speaking; paralleled by the lady who said that it was too bad that unemployment came during the depression.
19 Many things difficult to design prove easy to performance. [Samuel Johnson: *Rasselas* XIII]
20 O praise the Lord with one consent,
And in this great design
Let Britain and the Colonies
Unanimously jine.
[William Billings: *The New-England Psalm-Singer* (1770)]

DESIRE(S)
21 A short cut to riches is to subtract from our desires. [Petrarch: *Epistolae de Rebus Familiaribus* VII.x.]
22 How lightly is every man enclyned to
his owene desyr.

[Chaucer: *The Tale of Melibeus*]
1 The same desires disturb a gnat and an elephant. [Montaigne: *Essays* II.xii.]
2 The huge army of the world's desires. [Shakespeare: *Love's Labour's Lost* I.i.]
3 Desire hath no rest. [Robert Burton: *The Anatomy of Melancholy* I.2.3.11]
4 He begins to die that quits his desires. [George Herbert: *Outlandish Proverbs*]
5 The desire of the moth for the star,
Of the night for the morrow,
The devotion to something afar
From the sphere of our sorrow.
[Shelley: To——: *One Word Is Too Often Profaned*]
6 . . . vile it were
For some three suns to store and
hoard myself,
And this gray spirit yearning in desire
To follow knowledge like a sinking
star,
Beyond the utmost bound of human
thought.
[Tennyson: *Ulysses*]
7 Ah Love! could you and I with Him
conspire
To grasp this sorry Scheme of Things
entire,
Would not we shatter it to bits—
and then
Re-mould it nearer to the Heart's Desire!
[*Rubáiyát of Omar Khayyám* (trans. Edward FitzGerald)]
8 There are two tragedies in life. One is not to get your heart's desire. The other is to get it. [G. B. Shaw: *Man and Superman* IV]
9 As long as I have a want, I have a reason for living. Satisfaction is death. [G. B. Shaw: *Overruled*]

DESIRE (SEXUAL)
10 I know the nature of women:
When you want to, they don't want
to;
And when you don't want to, they desire exceedingly.
[Terence: *Eunuchus* IV.vii.]
11 Is it not strange that desire should so many years outlive performance? [Shakespeare: *II Henry IV* II.iv.]
12 Why, she would hang on him,

As if increase of appetite had grown
By what it fed on.
[Shakespeare: *Hamlet* I.ii.]
13 Rebellious hell,
If thou canst mutine in a matron's
bones,
To flaming youth let virtue be as
wax,
And melt in her own fire.
[Shakespeare: *Hamlet* III.iv.]
14 Well, I will love, write, sigh, pray, sue and groan. [Shakespeare: *Love's Labour's Lost* III.i.]
15 Desire attained is not desire,
But as the cinders of the fire.
[Sir Walter Raleigh: *A Poesy to Prove Affection is not Love*]
16 Where desire doth bear the sway,
The heart must rule, the head obey.
[Francis Davison (fl. 1602): *Desire's Government*]
17 A dragon among the chambermaids. [Tobias Smollett: *Peregrine Pickle*, Ch. 82]
18 The man's desire is for the woman; but the woman's desire is rarely other than for the desire of the man. [Coleridge: *Table Talk*, July 23, 1827]
This became a fixed tenet in the 19th-century credo of respectability.
19 From the desert I come to thee,
On a stallion shod with fire;
And the winds are left behind
In the speed of my desire.
[Bayard Taylor: *Bedouin Song*]
20 Lads that waste the light in sighing,
In the dark should sigh no more.
[A. E. Housman: *A Shropshire Lad* XI]
21 The warm beast of desire that lies curled up in our loins and stretches itself with a fierce gentleness. [Albert Camus: *Notebooks 1935-1942*, Ch. I, p. 44]

DESOLATION
22 Abomination of desolation. [Matthew 24:15]
23 That isle is now all desolate and bare,
Its dwellings down, its tenants pass'd
away;
None but her own and father's grave
is there,
And nothing outward tells of human
clay;

Ye could not know where lies a thing
so fair,
No stone is there to show, no tongue
to say,
What was; no dirge, except the hollow sea's,
Mourns o'er the beauty of the Cy-
clades.
[Byron: *Don Juan* IV.lxxii.]

1 The blue fly sung in the pane; the
mouse
Behind the mouldering wainscot
shrieked.
[Tennyson: *Mariana*]

2 They say the Lion and the Lizard
keep
The Courts where Jamshyd gloried
and drank deep:
And Bahrám, that great Hunter—
the Wild Ass
Stamps o'er his Head, but cannot
break his Sleep.
[*Rubáiyát of Omar Khayyám* (trans. Edward FitzGerald)]

DESPAIR

3 In the morning thou shalt say, Would
God it were even! and at even thou shalt
say, Would God it were morning! [Deu-
teronomy 28:67]

4 My days are swifter than a weaver's
shuttle, and are spent without hope.
[Job 7:6]

5 Abandon hope, all ye who enter here.
[Dante: *The Divine Comedy,* "Inferno"
III.ix.]
The Italian: Lasciate ogni speranza, voi
ch' entrate. *The phrase as commonly repeated is Cary's translation. Longfellow
translated it: All hope abandon, ye who
enter here.*

6 Grim and comfortless despair.
[Shakespeare: *Comedy of Errors* V.i.]

7 Discomfort guides my tongue
And bids me speak of nothing but
despair.
[Shakespeare: *Richard II* III.ii.]

8 Had I but died an hour before this
chance,
I had liv'd a blessed time; for, from
this instant,
There's nothing serious in mortality;
All is but toys; renown and grace is
dead;
The wine of life is drawn, and the

mere lees
Is left this vault to brag of.
[Shakespeare: *Macbeth* II.iii.]
toys = *trifles*

9 Despair makes the monk. [Robert
Burton: *Anatomy of Melancholy* III.
4.2.3]

10 Shall I, wasting in despair
Die because a woman's fair?
Or make pale my cheeks with care
Cause another's rosy are?
Be she fairer than the day
Or the flowery meads in May,
If she think not well of me,
What care I *how* fair she be?
[George Wither: *The Author's Resolu-
tion*]

11 Vaunting aloud, but racked with
deep despair.
[John Milton: *Paradise Lost* I, 126]

12 So farewell hope, and with hope farewell fear,
Farewell remorse: all good to me is
lost;
Evil be thou my Good.
[John Milton: *Paradise Lost* IV, 108-
110]

13 There was a castle called Doubting
Castle, the owner whereof was Giant Despair. [John Bunyan: *Pilgrim's Progress* I]

14 I can endure my own despair,
But not another's hope.
[William Walsh: *Song*]

15 Black despair succeeds brown study.
[William Congreve: *An Impossible
Thing*]

16 Hollow-ey'd Abstinence, and lean Despair.
[William Cowper: *Hope*]

17 Now a' is done that men can do,
And a' is done in vain.
[Burns: *It Was A' For Our Rightfu'
King*]

18 Sir Ralph the Rover tore his hair;
He curst himself in his despair.
[Robert Southey: *The Inchcape Rock*]

19 There is a very life in our despair,
Vitality of poison—a quick root
Which feeds these deadly branches;
for it were
As nothing did we die; but Life will
suit
Itself to Sorrow's most detested fruit,
Like to the apples on the Dead Sea's

shore,
All ashes to the taste: Did man compute
Existence by enjoyment, and count o'er
Such hours 'gainst years of life—say, would he name threescore?
[Byron: *Childe Harold* III.xxxiv.]

1 I learn'd to love despair.
[Byron: *The Prisoner of Chillon*]

2 Here, where men sit and hear each other groan;
Where palsy shakes a few, sad, last gray hairs,
Where youth grows pale, and specter-thin, and dies;
Where but to think is to be full of sorrow
And leaden-eyed despairs.
[Keats: *Ode to a Nightingale*]

3 A stereotyped but unconscious despair is concealed even under what are called the games and amusements of mankind. [Thoreau: *Walden,* Ch. I: "Economy"]

4 Creep into thy narrow bed,
Creep, and let no more be said!

. . . .

Let the long contention cease!
Geese are swans, and swans are geese,
Let them have it how they will!
Thou art tired; best be still.

. . . .

Let the victors when they come,
When the forts of folly fall,
Find thy body by the wall!
[Matthew Arnold: *The Last Word*]

5 Ah, love, let us be true
To one another! for the world, which seems
To lie before us like a land of dreams,
So various, so beautiful, so new,
Hath really neither joy, nor love, nor light,
Nor certitude, nor peace, nor help for pain;
And we are here as on a darkling plain
Swept with confused alarms of struggle and flight,
Where ignorant armies clash by night.
[Matthew Arnold: *Dover Beach*]

6 Tired of knocking at Preferment's door.
[Matthew Arnold: *The Scholar-Gipsy*]

7 We are getting to the end of visioning
The impossible within this universe,
Such as that better whiles may follow worse,
And that our race may mend by reasoning.
[Thomas Hardy: *We Are Getting to the End*]

DESPERATE MEN

8 Tempt not a desperate man.
[Shakespeare: *Romeo and Juliet* V.iii.]

9 Kings and desperate men.
[John Donne: *Holy Sonnets,* X]

10 Death is the doctor of the desperate.
[Ramon de la Cruz y Cano: *El Marido Sofocado* II]

11 He is dangerous who has nothing to lose.
[Goethe: *Die Natürliche Tochter* I.iii.]

DESPERATION

12   I am one, my liege,
Whom the vile blows and buffets of the world
Have so incens'd that I am reckless what
I do to spite the world.
[Shakespeare: *Macbeth* III.i.]

13 He who cares not for his own, is master of another man's life. [Robert Burton: *The Anatomy of Melancholy* III. 4.2]

14 The mass of men lead lives of quiet desperation. What is called resignation is confirmed desperation. [Thoreau: *Walden* I]

DESPONDENCY

15 Let's talk of graves, of worms, and epitaphs; . . .
Let's choose executors and talk of wills.
[Shakespeare: *Richard II* III.ii.]

16 It is the descent whither the scum and filth that attends conviction for sin doth continually run, and therefore it is called the *Slough of Despond*. [John Bunyan: *The Pilgrim's Progress* I]

DESPOT

17 Every despot must have one disloyal subject to keep him sane. [G. B. Shaw: Preface to *Plays, Pleasant and Unpleasant*]

DESPOTISM

1 Despotism tempered by assassination. [A Russian nobleman: speaking to Count Münster, Hanoverian minister to St. Petersburg, on the assassination of Czar Paul I in 1801]

W. S. Gilbert's description, in Utopia, Limited, *of the government of* Utopia *as a "despotism tempered by dynamite" was a parody.*

2 Kingly conclaves stern and cold
Where blood with guilt is bought and sold.
[Shelley: *Prometheus Unbound* I]

3 Despotism violates the moral frontier, as invasion violates the geographical frontier. [Victor Hugo: *Les Misérables* XIII.iii.]

DESTINY

4 The ancient saying is no heresy:
"Hanging and wiving goes by destiny."
[Shakespeare: *The Merchant of Venice* II.ix.]

The Merchant of Venice was entered in the Stationers' Register in 1598.

The "ancient saying" had appeared in John Heywood's Proverbs *52 years earlier:*

Wedding is destiny,
And hanging likewise.

5 There's a divinity that shapes our ends,
Rough-hew them how we will.
[Shakespeare: *Hamlet* V.ii.]

6 But let determined things to destiny
Hold unbewail'd their way.
[Shakespeare: *Antony and Cleopatra* III.ii.]

7 A consistent man believes in destiny, a capricious man in chance. [Disraeli: *Vivian Grey* VI]

8 My destiny is solitude, and my life is work. [Richard Wagner: Letter to Nathalie Planer, June 20, 1863]

9 DESTINY. A tyrant's authority for crime and a fool's excuse for failure. [Ambrose Bierce: *The Devil's Dictionary*]

DESTRUCTION

10 Wide is the gate, and broad is the way, that leadeth to destruction. [Matthew 7:13]

11 To destroy is still the strongest instinct of our nature. [Max Beerbohm: *Yet Again* (1923), p. 6]

12 The human race has today the means for annihilating itself—either in a fit of complete lunacy, i.e., in a big war, by a brief fit of destruction, or by a careless handling of atomic technology, through a slow process of poisoning and of deterioration in its genetic structure. [Max Born (Nobel Prize in Physics, 1955), in the *Bulletin of the Atomic Scientists*, June, 1957]

DETAIL(S)

13 Our life is frittered away by detail. . . . Simplify, simplify. [Thoreau: *Walden* II]

14 Merely corroborative detail, intended to give artistic verisimilitude to an otherwise bald and unconvincing narrative. [W. S. Gilbert: *The Mikado* II]

DETERMINATION

15 I am in earnest—I will not equivocate—I will not excuse—I will not retreat a single inch and I will be heard. [William Lloyd Garrison: Salutatory of *The Liberator* (1831)]

16 Here I am and here I stay. (*J'y suis, et j'y reste.*) [Attr. Marshal MacMahon, Sebastopol, September 8, 1855]

Marshal MacMahon had taken the Malakof fortress and had been warned to withdraw as the redoubt was said to be mined.

Victor Emmanuel quoted the by-then famous phrase when he occupied Rome in September, 1870.

17 I propose to fight it out on this line if it takes all Summer. [Ulysses S. Grant: in a dispatch to the Secretary of War, Edwin M. Stanton, from before Richmond, May 11, 1864]

DETRACTION

18 Ay, and you had any eye behind you, you might see more detraction at your heels than fortunes before you. [Shakespeare: *Twelfth Night* II.v.]

19 If you don't want the magpies screaming round your head,
Don't climb to the top of the steeple.
[Goethe: *Spruche in Reimen* V.]

DEVIL

1 The Devil as a roaring lion, walketh about, seeking whom he may devour. [I Peter 5:8]

2 For commonly, wheresoever God buildeth a church, the devil will build a chapel just by. [Thomas Becon: *Catechism* (1560)]

3 The Devil was sick;
The Devil a monk would be;
The Devil was well;
The devil a monk was he.
[An old English rhyme that has been traced, in its Latin form, to 1450]
Found in Rabelais' Works IV.xxiv.

4 Talk of the devil and he'll appear. [Erasmus: *Adagia* XVII (1500)]
Proverbial as far back as 1500, the commonest form now heard is "Speak of the devil and he's sure to appear."

5 To give the devil his due. [Cervantes: *Don Quixote* I.iii.3]

6 He needs must go that the devil drives.
[Shakespeare: *All's Well that Ends Well* I.iii.]
A proverb, it had appeared in print at least 40 years earlier. The modern form is: "Needs must when the devil drives."

7 You are one of those that will not serve God if the devil bid you. [Shakespeare: *Othello* I.i.]

8   The spirit that I have seen
May be the devil: and the devil hath power
To assume a pleasing shape.
[Shakespeare: *Hamlet* II.ii.]
Hamlet has to decide whether the ghost is really his father's spirit or whether it is the devil in disguise—whether, that is, he is being incited to revenge or to murder.

9 Whenever God erects a house of prayer
The Devil always builds a chapel there;
And 'twill be found upon examination
The latter has the largest congregation.
[Daniel Defoe: *The True-Born Englishman* I]

10 As if the devil was not so black as he was painted. [Defoe: *History of the Devil* II.vi.]

11 An apology for the Devil—it must be remembered that we have only heard one side of the case. God has written all the books. [Samuel Butler (1835-1902): *Notebooks*]

12 The Devil and me, we don't agree;
I hate him; and he hates me.
[Salvation Army hymn]

DEVOTION

13 Whither thou goest, I will go; and where thou lodgest, I will lodge: thy people shall be my people, and thy God my God. [Ruth I:16]

14 Would I were with him, wheresome'er he is, either in heaven or in hell! [Shakespeare: *Henry V* II.iii.]

15 Complaint is the sincerest part of our devotion. [Jonathan Swift: *Thoughts on Various Subjects*]

16 I never will desert Mr. Micawber. [Dickens: *David Copperfield* XII]

DEW-DROPS

17 Dew-drops are the gems of morning,
But the tears of mournful eve!
[Coleridge: *Youth and Age*]

DEWEY

18 O Dewey was the morning
Upon the first of May
And Dewey was the Admiral
Down in Manila Bay;
And Dewey were the Regent's eyes,
Them orbs of royal blue!
And Dewey feel discouraged?
I Dew not think we Dew.
[Eugene Ware: "Dewey," May 3, 1898]
In the Topeka Daily Capital.

DIALECT

19 Dialect words—those terrible marks of the beast to the truly genteel. [Thomas Hardy: *The Mayor of Casterbridge* XX]

20 Her Negro dialect stories have kept many a drawing room in a state of stoicism. [Ring Lardner: *Dante and . . .*]

DIALOGUE

21 Dialogue in fiction . . . should be reserved for the culminating moments, and regarded as the spray into which the great wave of narrative breaks in curving towards the watcher on the shore.

[Edith Wharton: *The Writing of Fiction*]

DIAMONDS

1 Acres of diamonds. [Russell Herman Conwell (1843-1925): title of a lecture] *The lecture "Acres of Diamonds," with its message that opportunity lies right at our own doorstep, was delivered more than 6,000 times. Conwell (the founder and first President of Temple University, in Philadelphia) kept none of the money gained from these lectures but gave it all away in scholarships. The lecture is said to have produced the money whereby 10,000 young men were able to acquire an education.*

2 Let us not be too particular. It is better to have old second-hand diamonds than none at all. [Mark Twain: *Pudd'nhead Wilson's Calendar*]

DIANA

3 Great is Diana of the Ephesians. [Acts 19:34]

DIARIES

4 It is a strange thing that in sea voyages where there is nothing to be seen but sky and sea, men should make diaries; but in land travel, wherein so much is to be observed, for the most part they omit it. [Francis Bacon: *Of Travel*]

DICE

5 And once or twice to throw the dice
Is a gentlemanly game,
But he does not win who plays with
Sin
In the secret House of Shame.
[Oscar Wilde: *The Ballad of Reading Gaol* III]

6 Entrapt inside a submarine,
With death approaching on the scene,
The crew composed their minds to
dice,
More for the pleasure than the vice.
[Congressman H. C. Canfield: *Elegy on the Loss of the U.S. Submarine S4*]

DICKENS

7 I cannot tell what the dickens his
name is.
[Shakespeare: *The Merry Wives of Windsor* III.ii.]

Mistress Page is trying to call Falstaff's name to mind.

Dickens may have been a euphemism for devil and it may have been a worn-down form of devilkin, *little devil.*

At any rate its use plainly antedates the novelist by several centuries.

DICKINSON, EMILY

8 But Emily hoarded—hoarded—only
giving
Herself to cold, white paper. Starved
and tortured,
She cheated her despair with games
of patience
And fooled herself by winning. Frail
little elf,
The lonely brain-child of a gaunt maturity,
She hung her womanhood upon a
bough
And played ball with the stars—too
long—too long—
The garment of herself hung on a
tree,
Until at last she lost even the desire
To take it down.
[Amy Lowell: *The Sisters*]

DICTATORS

9 Dictators ride to and fro upon tigers which they dare not dismount. [Winston Churchill: *While England Slept* (1936)]

DICTIONARY(IES)

10 A word or a form of speech is not good because it is in the dictionary; it is in the dictionary because it was good before it was put there. [Francesco Maria Zanotti (1692-1777): *Paradossi* XIX]

11 No dictionary of a living tongue ever can be perfect, since while it is hastening to publication, some words are budding and some falling away. [Samuel Johnson: Preface to the *Dictionary* (1755)]

12 Lexicographer: a writer of dictionaries, a harmless drudge. [Samuel Johnson: *Dictionary* (1755)]

13 Dictionaries are like watches; the worst is better than none, and the best cannot be expected to go quite true. [Samuel Johnson: in Mrs. Piozzi's *Anecdotes of the late Samuel Johnson*]

1 The responsibility of a dictionary is to record the language, not set its style. [Philip Gove, Editor-in-Chief of *Webster's Third New International Dictionary*, in a letter to *Life*, November 17, 1961]

DIE
2 The die is cast. (*Iacta alea est*.) [Julius Caesar: as he decided to cross the Rubicon (49 B.C.); quoted by Plutarch in his *Life of Caesar*.]

Plutarch said the phrase was a "proverb frequently in their mouths who enter upon dangerous and bold attempts."

See RUBICON

DIET
3 Beware of sudden change in any great point of diet, and, if necessity enforce it, fit the rest to it. [Francis Bacon: *Of Regimen of Health*]

DIFFER
4 Tho' all things differ, all agree. [Alexander Pope: *Windsor Forest* 16]

DIFFERENCE(S)
5 O, the difference of man and man! [Shakespeare: *King Lear* IV.ii.]
6 We can all perceive the difference between ourselves and our inferiors, but when it comes to a question of the difference between us and our superiors, we fail to appreciate merits of which we have no proper conception. [James Fenimore Cooper: *The American Democrat*]
7 Now, who shall arbitrate?
  Ten men love what I hate,
Shun what I follow, slight what I receive.
[Robert Browning: *Rabbi Ben Ezra* XXII]

DIFFERENCE OF OPINION
8 It is difference of opinion that makes horse races. [Mark Twain: *Pudd'nhead Wilson's Calendar*]

DIFFICULTY
9 The illustration which solves one difficulty by raising another settles nothing. [Horace: *Satires* II.iii.]

DIFFIDENCE
10 No! I am not Prince Hamlet, nor was
        meant to be;
Am an attendant lord, one that will
        do
To swell a progress, start a scene or
        two,
Advise the prince; no doubt, an easy
        tool,
Deferential, glad to be of use,
Politic, cautious, and meticulous;
Full of high sentence, but a bit obtuse;
At times, indeed, almost ridiculous—
Almost, at times, the Fool.
[T. S. Eliot: *The Love Song of J. Alfred Prufrock*]

DIGNITY
11 Where is there dignity unless there is also honesty? [Cicero: *Ad Atticum* VII. xi.]
12 By indignities men come to dignities. [Francis Bacon: *Of Great Place*]
13 The skipping king, he ambled up
        and down
With shallow jesters and rash bavin
        wits,
Soon kindled and soon burnt; carded
        his state;
Mingled his royalty with capering
        fools;
Had his great name profaned with
        their scorns
And gave his countenance, against
        his name,
To laugh at gibing boys and stand
        the push
Of every beardless vain comparative.
[Shakespeare: *I Henry IV* III.ii.]
bavin = *brushwood;* carded = *mixed, adulterated;* comparative = *one who is, or tries to be, clever in making comparisons*
14   My cloud of dignity
  Is held from falling with so weak a
        wind
That it will quickly drop.
[Shakespeare: *II Henry IV* IV.v.]
15 It is terrifying to see how easily, in certain people, all dignity collapses. Yet when you think about it, this is quite normal since they only maintain this dignity by constantly striving against their

own nature. [Albert Camus: *Notebooks 1935-1942*, Ch. III, p. 142]

DILIGENCE

1 With whispering and most guilty diligence. [Shakespeare: *Measure for Measure* IV.i.]
2 That which ordinary men are fit for, I am qualified in; and the best of me is diligence. [Shakespeare: *King Lear* I.iv.]
3 Diligence in a poet is the same as dishonesty in a bookkeeper. There are rafts of bards who are writing too much, too diligently, and too slyly. Few poets are willing to wait out their pregnancy— they prefer to have a premature baby and allow it to incubate after being safely laid in Caslon Old Style. [E. B. White: *One Man's Meat*]

DINING

4 That is to say, if your religion's Roman,
And you at Rome would do as Romans do,
According to the proverb—although no man,
If foreign, is obliged to fast; and you,
If Protestant, or sickly, or a woman,
Would rather dine in sin on a ragout—
Dine, and be d——d! I don't mean to be coarse,
But that's the penalty, to say no worse.
[Byron: *Beppo*]

DINING OUT

5 I maintain that though you would often in the fifteenth century have heard the snobbish Roman say, in a would-be off-hand tone, "I am dining with the Borgias to-night," no Roman ever was able to say, "I dined last night with the Borgias." [Max Beerbohm: *Host and Guests*]

DINNER

6 This was a good dinner enough, to be sure; but it was not a dinner to *ask* a man to. [Samuel Johnson: in Boswell's *Life*, August 5, 1763]

Boswell says that "When invited to dine, even with an intimate friend, he was not pleased if something better than a plain dinner was not prepared for him."

7 That all-softening, overpowering knell,
The tocsin of the soul—the dinner bell.
[Byron: *Don Juan* V.xlix.]
8 Serenely full, the epicure would say, "Fate cannot harm me, I have dined to-day." [Sydney Smith: *A Recipe for Salad*]

DIPLOMACY

9 Diplomacy is to do and say
The nastiest thing in the nicest way.
[Isaac Goldberg: *The Reflex*]
10 Forever poised between a cliché and an indiscretion. [Harold Macmillan, quoted *Newsweek*, April 30, 1956]
11 Diplomacy is the art of fishing tranquilly in troubled waters. [J. Christopher Herold: *Bonaparte in Egypt*, Ch. 1, p. 17]
12 A diplomat is a person who can tell you to go to hell in such a way that you actually look forward to the trip. [Caskie Stinnett: *Out of the Red*]
It was said by one who knew him that Charles II, who was exceedingly gracious and exceedingly immoral, could refuse a request and send the suitor away in a better humor than his father (Charles I, who was moral but stiff and ungracious) sent those away whose wishes he had granted.
13 Protocol, alcohol, and Geritol. [Adlai Stevenson, *listing the main ingredients of the social life of a diplomat* (*Time*, July 24, 1964)]

DIRT

14 An apple, an egg, and a nut,
You may eat after a slut.
[John Ray: *English Proverbs* (1670)]
That is, these things, being protected from the dirt of a sluttish person's hands by a peel and different kinds of shells, may be eaten with impunity. The idea of infection was probably not present; simply that of disgust.
15 You must eat a peck of dirt before you die. [Jonathan Swift: *Polite Conversation* I]

1 This painted child of dirt, that stinks and stings. [Alexander Pope: *Epistle to Dr. Arbuthnot*]

DISADVANTAGE
2 We fight to great disadvantage when we fight with those who have nothing to lose. [Guicciardini: *Storia d'Italia*]

DISAPPOINTMENT
3 Blessed is he who expects nothing, for he shall never be disappointed. [Alexander Pope: Letter to John Gay, October 6, 1727]

DISAPPROBATION
4 No man likes to live under the eye of perpetual disapprobation. [Samuel Johnson: in Boswell's *Life* (1772)]
5 This will never do. [Lord Francis Jeffrey: in *The Edinburgh Review,* November 1814]

DISBELIEF
6 In the affairs of this World, Men are saved, not by Faith, but by the Want of it. [Benjamin Franklin: *Poor Richard's Almanack* (1754)]
7 Infidelity does not consist in believing or in disbelieving: it consists in professing to believe what one does not believe. [Thomas Paine: *Age of Reason* I]
8 That willing suspension of disbelief for the moment, which constitutes poetic faith. [Coleridge: *Biographia Literaria* XIV]
9 I don't believe there's no sich a person! [Dickens: *Martin Chuzzlewit* XLIX]
10 There ain't no such animal. [Caption to a cartoon in *Life,* Nov. 7, 1907]
The sentiment is expressed by a farmer on first seeing a camel.

DISCIPLINE
11 It is better to bind your children to you by a feeling of respect, and by gentleness, than by fear. [Terence: *Adelphi* I.i.]

DISCONTENT(S)
12 Now is the winter of our discontent
Made glorious summer by this sun of York.
[Shakespeare: *Richard III* I.i.]
13 Let thy discontents be thy secrets; if

the world knows them, 'twill despise thee and increase them. [Benjamin Franklin: *Poor Richard's Almanack* (1741)]

DISCORD
14 In times of tumult and discord bad men have most power; mental and moral excellence require peace and quietness. [Tacitus: *Annals* IV.i.]
15 Nay, had I power, I should
Pour the sweet milk of concord into hell,
Uproar the universal peace, confound
All unity on earth.
[Shakespeare: *Macbeth* IV.iii.]

DISCOURSE
16 Some in their discourse desire rather commendation of wit, in being able to hold all arguments, than of judgment, in discerning what is true; as if it were a praise to know what might be said and not what should be thought. [Francis Bacon: *Of Discourse*]
This is the underlying immorality of high-school and college debating teams.

DISCOVERY
17 Then felt I like some watcher of the skies
When a new planet swims into his ken;
Or like stout Cortez when with eagle eyes
He star'd at the Pacific—and all his men
Look'd at each other with a wild surmise—
Silent, upon a peak in Darien.
[Keats: *Sonnet,* "On First Looking into Chapman's Homer"]

DISCRETION
18 Being now come to years of discretion. [*The Book of Common Prayer,* "Confirmation"]
19 At times discretion should be thrown aside,
And with the foolish we should play the fool.
[Menander: *Poloumenoi* II]
20 As a jewel of gold in a swine's snout, so is a fair woman which is without dis-

cretion. [Proverbs 11:22]

1 No discretion is so rare as to know when to be indiscreet. [Jacinto de Herrera: *Duelo de Amor y Amistad* II]

2 Be civil to all; sociable to many; familiar with few; friend to one; enemy to none. [Benjamin Franklin: *Poor Richard's Almanack* (1756)]

DISCRETION: the better part of valor

3 The better part of valour is discretion. [Shakespeare: *I Henry IV* V.iv.]

4 He hath a wisdom that doth guide
his valour
To act in safety.
[Shakespeare: *Macbeth* III.i.]

5 It shew'd discretion, the best part of
valor.
[Beaumont and Fletcher: *A King and No King* IV.iii.]

6 If the better part of valor is discretion, how much more is not discretion the better part of vice? [Samuel Butler (1835-1902): *The Way of All Flesh* LX]

DISDAIN

7 Daff'd the world aside, and bid it
pass.
[Shakespeare: *I Henry IV* IV.i.]

8 My dear Lady Disdain.
[Shakespeare: *Much Ado About Nothing* I.i.]

DISGRACE

9 We should prefer death to disgrace. [Cicero: *De Officiis* I]

10 When in disgrace with fortune and
men's eyes
I all alone beweep my outcast state.
[Shakespeare: *Sonnets* XXIX]

11 If you do not see the honor, I'm sure I feel the disgrace. [Attr. Samuel Johnson: in Mrs. Piozzi's *Anecdotes of the Late Samuel Johnson*]

A certain man had been contradicting Johnson and the host, fearing an outburst, said to Johnson "He's just doing this to be able to say he had the honor of opposing you." The gentleman said angrily, "I see no honor in it." Whereupon Johnson retorted as above.

Boswell, however, doubts that Johnson said what was attributed to him and gives his reasons for doubting it, in Boswell's Life, 1784.

12 To those whose god is honour, disgrace alone is sin. [J. C. and A. W. Hare: *Guesses at Truth*]

DISHES

13 The willow pattern, that we knew
In childhood, with its bridge of blue.
[Longfellow: *Keramos*]

DISHONESTY

14 A man who only does what every one of the society to which he belongs would do, is not a dishonest man. [Samuel Johnson: in Boswell's *Life,* 1784]

DISHONOR

15 His honour rooted in dishonour
stood,
And faith unfaithful kept him falsely
true.
[Tennyson: *Idylls of the King,* "Lancelot and Elaine"]

DISLIKE

16 Nothing is more common than mutual dislike, where mutual approbation is particularly expected. [Samuel Johnson: in a letter to Mrs. Thrale, in Boswell's *Life,* May 1, 1780]

Professor Horatio Hackett Newman, of the University of Chicago, obtained a grant which enabled him, at the time of Chicago's World's Fair in 1933, to bring together a number of identical twins who had been separated at birth and kept apart until maturity. Some of them did not even know they had a twin. In several instances the twins took a dislike to each other. See his Multiple Human Births

DISOBEDIENCE

17 Disobedience in the eyes of any one who has read history is man's original virtue. [Oscar Wilde: *The Soul of Man Under Socialism*]

18 DISOBEDIENCE. The silver lining to the cloud of servitude. [Ambrose Bierce: *The Devil's Dictionary*]

DISORDER

19 A sweet disorder in the dress
Kindles in clothes a wantonness.
[Robert Herrick: *Delight in Disorder*]

20 A winning wave, deserving note,

In the tempestuous petticoat;
A careless shoe-string, in whose tie
I see a wild civility—
Do more bewitch me than when art
Is too precise in every part.
[Robert Herrick: *Delight in Disorder*]

DISSATISFACTION

1 Men would be angels, angels would
be gods. [Alexander Pope: *An Essay on
Man* I]
2 We look before and after,
    And pine for what is not;
Our sincerest laughter
    With some pain is fraught;
Our sweetest songs are those that tell
                of saddest thought.
[Shelley: *To a Skylark* XVIII]

DISSEMBLE(ING)

3 He who dissembles much doesn't
know how to dissemble. [Guillem de
Castro: *El Amor Constante* I]
4 Perhaps it was right to dissemble
                your love,
    But why did you kick me down stairs?
[J. P. Kemble: *The Panel* I.i.]

DISSENSION

5 Alas! how light a cause may move
Dissension between hearts that love!
Hearts that the world in vain had
                tried,
And sorrow but more closely tied;
That stood the storm when waves
                were rough,
Yet in a sunny hour fall off.
[Thomas Moore: *Lalla Rookh*]

DISSIMULATION

6 He who does not know how to dis-
simulate does not know how to live;
for dissimulation is a shield that blunts
every weapon and a weapon that pierces
every shield. [Aretino (1492-1557): *Lo
Ipocrito* I.ii.]
7 Falsehood and dissimulation are certainly to be found at courts; but where
are they not to be found? Cottages have
them, as well as courts, only with worse
manners. [Lord Chesterfield: *Letters,*
May 10, 1748]
8 They say that dissimulation is a crime,
Yet we live by dissimulation.
[Goethe: *Maskenzug*]

DISTANCE

9 If a man makes me keep my distance,
the comfort is he keeps his at the same
time. [Jonathan Swift: *Thoughts on
Various Subjects*]
10 'Tis distance lends enchantment to
the view. [Thomas Campbell: *The Pleasures of Hope* I]

DISTINCTION

11 Distinction without a difference.
[Henry Fielding: *Tom Jones* VI.xiii.]

DIVORCE

12 Divorce is not honorable to women.
[Euripides: *Medea*]
13 Divorces are made in heaven. [Oscar
Wilde: *The Importance of Being Earnest* I]
14 Holy Deadlock. [A. P. Herbert]
*Title of a novel satirizing English divorce
laws.*

DIXIE

15 I wish I was in de land ob cotton,
Old times dar am not forgotten.
Look away, look away,
Look away, Dixie Land.
[Daniel Decatur Emmett: *Dixie* (1859)]
*No one knows for sure why the South is
called Dixie. It certainly seems reason-
able to assume that the Mason and
Dixon Line had something to do with
it, but this can't be proved. Many the-
ories have been advanced. It is interest-
ing that the sentimentalizing of the
South had begun before the Civil War.
Dixie was, at first, a Northern song.*

DO

16 Go, and do thou likewise. [Luke
10:37]
17 Let us do, or die.
[Burns: *Scots Wha Hae*]

DOCTOR(S)

18 A doctor is nothing more than a mental consolation. [Petronius Arbiter: *Satyricon* XLII]
19 Joy and Temperance and Repose
    Slam the door on the doctor's nose.
[Friedrich von Logau: *Die Beste Arznei*
    (trans. Longfellow)]
20 That patient is not like to recover
who makes the doctor his heir. [Thomas

Fuller (1654-1734): *Gnomologia*]

1 Who shall decide when doctors disagree? [Alexander Pope: *Moral Essays* III.i.]

2 "Is there no hope?" the sick man said.
The silent doctor shook his head,
And took his leave with signs of sorrow,
Despairing of his fee tomorrow.
[John Gay: *Fables* I: "The Sick Man and the Angel"]

DOCTOR FELL

3 I do not like thee, Doctor Fell,
The reason why I cannot tell;
But this I know, and know full well,
I do not like thee, Doctor Fell.
[Attr. Thomas Brown (1663-1704): on Dr. John Fell (1625-1686), Dean of Christ Church and Bishop of Oxford.]
Non amo te, Sabidi, nec possum dicere quare; Hoc tantum possum dicere, non amo te. (*I do not love thee, Sabidius, nor can I say why; But this much I can say, I do not love thee.*)
—*Martial (40-102 A.D.): Epigrams I.xxxii.*
The story is that Brown, a student, was in trouble and about to be expelled and that Dr. Fell offered to let him stay on condition of his showing his knowledge of Latin by making an extempore translation of Martial's epigram. DNB (John Fell VI) is of the opinion that Brown, at the best, paraphrased an earlier translation (1661) by Thomas Forde. Chances are the verses were merely attributed to Brown because he had a reputation of being a wag. Fell was not such a simpleton as to invite an insult from an undergraduate and Brown, for all his waggery, was not such a fool as to invite the very expulsion he is supposed to have been attempting to escape.

DOCTRINES

4 What makes all doctrines plain and clear?—
About two hundred pounds a year.
And that which was prov'd true before
Prove false again? Two hundred more.
[Samuel Butler (1612-1680): *Hudibras*]
Two hundred pounds a year would, at the time of the publication of Hudibras *(1663-1678), have represented a good income from a comfortable clerical living. Butler's animadversion is directed against those clergymen who managed, somehow, to hold their livings under Charles I, then under Cromwell and the Puritans, and still under the profligate Charles II.*

DOG: love me, love my dog

5 Love me, love my dog. [Latin proverb]
The meaning is, "If you love me, you will love everything about me, even my dog." It appears as a proverb in most European languages. It is in Heywood's Proverbs (1546) and in Cervantes.

6 He that strikes my dog, would strike me if he durst. [An old Scottish proverb]

7 Whosoever loveth me, loveth my hound. [Sir Thomas More: *Sermon on the Lord's Prayer*]

8 Every time I come to town
The boys keep kickin' my dawg around;
Makes no difference if he is a hound,
They've got to quit kickin' my dawg around.
[Champ Clark's campaign song, 1912]
James Beauchamp Clark (1850-1921), Speaker of the House, 1911-1919, was a prominent candidate for the Democratic Presidential nomination in 1912.

DOG: man's best friend

9 The one absolutely unselfish friend that man can have in this selfish world, the one that never deserts him, the one that never proves ungrateful or treacherous, is his dog. . . . He will kiss the hand that has no food to offer. . . . When all other friends desert, he remains. [George G. Vest: in a speech in the U. S. Senate, 1884]
This flight of dog rhetoric is generally considered to be the origin of the popular "A man's best friend's his dog." Since Homer choked back a sob in his account of old Argus's wagging his aged tail and dropping dead at Odysseus's return, poets and orators have found the dog's devotion a moving theme.

10 He cannot be a gentleman which loveth not a dog. [John Northbrooke: *Against Dicing*]

1 He asks no angel's wing, no seraph's
      fire,
But thinks, admitted to that equal
      sky,
His faithful dog shall bear him com-
      pany.
[Alexander Pope: *An Essay on Man* I]
*The simple-souled canophilic "he" is
"the poor Indian." Pope knew even less,
of course, about Indians than he did
about the fauna of Heaven.*

2 Near this spot are deposited the remains of one who possessed Beauty
without Vanity, Strength without Insolence, Courage without Ferocity, and all
the Virtues of Man, without his Vices.
This Praise, which would be unmeaning
Flattery if inscribed over human ashes, is
but a just tribute to the Memory of Boat-
swain, a Dog. [Byron: Inscription on
the monument of his Newfoundland dog
at Newstead (d. 1808)]
*The monument is a very splendid and
expensive one, a thousand times more
impressive than Byron's own tablet in
the church at Hucknall-Torkard where
he is buried. At one time he had stipulated that he was to be buried with the
dog, but his wishes were not carried out.
Among the differences between dogs and
men which he overlooked is that dogs
are rarely guilty of any such wasteful
and ostentatious follies as the erection of
this monument.*

3 Old dog Tray's ever faithful;
Grief can not drive him away;
He is gentle, he is kind—
I shall never, never find
A better friend than old dog Tray!
[Stephen C. Foster: *Old Dog Tray*]

DOG: unfavorable
4 Is thy servant a dog, that he should
do this great thing? [II Kings 8:13]
5 As a dog returneth to his vomit, so
a fool returneth to his folly. [Proverbs
26:11]
Also II Peter 2:22.
6 Give not that which is holy unto the
dogs. [Matthew 7:6]
7 Beware of dogs. [Philippians 3:2]
8 The dogge waggeth his tayle, not for
you, but for your bread. [Thomas Draxe:
Bibliotheca]
9 Who sleepeth with dogges, shal rise

with fleas. [John Florio: *First Fruites*]
10 He that lies with the dogs, riseth with
fleas. [George Herbert: *Jacula Prudentum*]
11 Like . . . a dog in the manger, he
doth only keep it because it shall do nobody else good, hurting himself and others. [Robert Burton: *Anatomy of Melancholy* I.2.3.12]
*The reference is to Aesop's fable of the
ill-tempered dog in a manger that could
not eat the hay himself but would not
permit the tired ox to eat it.*

DOG: general and favorable
12 A living dog is better than a dead
lion. [Ecclesiastes 9:4]
13 It is not good a sleping hound to
wake. [Chaucer: *Troilus and Criseyde*
III]
14 Keep running after the dog, and he
will never bite you. [Rabelais: *Gargantua* I.v.]
15 Every dog has his day. [Cervantes:
Don Quixote I.iii.6]
16 It is hard to teach an old dog new
tricks. [William Camden: *Remains*]
17 A stick is quickly found to beat a dog
with. [16th-century English proverb]
*It is very easy to find reasons to justify
our dislikes and resentments.*
18 I pray thee let me and my fellow
      have
A haire of the dog that bit us last
      night.
[John Heywood: *Proverbs*]
19 *Celia.* Not a word?
Rosalind. Not one to throw at a dog.
[Shakespeare: *As You Like It* I.iii.]
20 I had rather be a dog, and bay the
      moon,
Than such a Roman.
[Shakespeare: *Julius Caesar* IV.iii.]
21 Let Hercules himself do what he may,
The cat will mew and dog will have
      his day.
[Shakespeare: *Hamlet* V.i.]
22   Mine enemy's dog,
Though he had bit me, should have
      stood that night
Against my fire.
[Shakespeare: *King Lear* IV.vii.]
against = by
23 I do honour the very flea of his dog.
[Ben Jonson: *Every Man in His Hu-*

mour IV.ii.]

1 An old dog will learn no new tricks. [Thomas D'Urfey: *Quixote* I.ii.]

2 I won't keep a dog and bark myself. [Jonathan Swift: *Polite Conversation* I]

3 Your barking curs will seldom bite. [Jonathan Swift: *Traulus* I]

4 Let dogs delight to bark and bite,
  For God hath made them so;
Let bears and lions growl and fight,
  For 'tis their nature, too.

But, children, you should never let
  Such angry passions rise;
Your little hands were never made
  To tear each other's eyes.

[Isaac Watts: *Against Quarrelling and Fighting*]
  The last line of the first stanza is often misquoted "For 'tis their nature to."

5 He that would hang his dog gives out first that he is mad. [John Ray: *English Proverbs* (1670)]
  We always justify our cruelties.

6 Not louder shrieks to pitying heaven
                  are cast,
When husbands or when lap-dogs
                breathe their last.

[Alexander Pope: *The Rape of the Lock* III]

7 I am his Highness' dog at Kew;
  Pray tell me, sir, whose dog are you?

[Alexander Pope: Inscription for the collar of the Prince of Wales's dog]
  The prince had his residence at Kew.
  Dr. Johnson felt that in writing this distich Pope had "relaxed his dignity" more than he should have.

8 The dog, to gain some private ends,
  Went mad and bit the man.

[Oliver Goldsmith: *Elegy on the Death of a Mad Dog*]

9 The man recover'd of the bite,
  The dog it was that died.

[Oliver Goldsmith: *Elegy on the Death of a Mad Dog*]

10 Dogs that bark at a distance, never bite. [Thomas Fuller (1654-1734): *Gnomologia*]

11 Give a dog an ill name and hang him. [George Colman the Elder: *Polly Honeycombe* IV]

12 Every dog is entitled to one bite. [English proverb, not antedating the 18th century]

The commonest modern form is "one bite free." It is often stated as a legal maxim equal to anything asserted in Magna Carta or the Constitution of the United States.

All it means, however, is that a dog's owner is not liable to a person bitten unless it can be shown that the owner was aware of his dog's tendency to bite—and that usually cannot be shown unless the dog had previously bitten someone. A man who posts a notice of a fierce dog, by the way, is not exonerating but inculpating himself; for he can hardly plead ignorance of a fact which he himself had advertised.

13 He has gone to the demnition bow-wows. [Dickens: *Nicholas Nickleby* LXIV]

14 I've got to see a man about a dog. [Dion Boucicault: *Flying Scud* IV.i.]
  In Boucicault's play a character trying to escape the pressure of a lawyer who is accusing him of forgery insists that he can't stay to continue the interview because he has to see a man about a dog. The absurd flimsiness of the excuse tickled the public fancy and the phrase passed into the language. It did not, however, at first have its present meaning—a facetiously "genteel" excuse for going to the toilet. The Elizabethan equivalent was "I'll just look on the hedge." See Shakespeare: Winter's Tale *IV.iv.*

15 If you pick up a starving dog and make him prosperous, he will not bite you. This is the principal difference between a dog and a man. [Mark Twain: *Pudd'nhead Wilson's Calendar*]

16 They say a reasonable number of fleas is good fer a dog—keeps him from broodin' over bein' a dog. [E. N. Westcott: *David Harum*]

17 When a dog bites a man that is not news; but when a man bites a dog that is news. [John B. Bogart, City Editor of the *New York Sun* (about 1880)]
  Often attr. Charles Dana, Editor of the Sun, *but definitely established as by Bogart.*

DOGGEREL

18 This may wel be rym dogerel. [Chaucer: Prologue to *Tale of Meli-*

beus]
doggerel, *prob. from Latin* doga = "*cask stave.*" *Compare the modern terms "barrelhouse" and "beat it out." The Germans have* Stabreim, *or "stave rhyme," for alliterative verse.*

DOGMA
1 Any stigma will do to beat a dogma.
[Philip Guedalla (attr.)]

DOGMATISM
2 It is a peevish infirmity for a man to think himself so firmly grounded that the contrary may not be believed. [Montaigne: *Essays* I.lvi.]
3 Nothing is so firmly believed as that which a man knoweth least. [Montaigne: *Essays* I.xxxi.]

DOING
4 What we have to learn to do, we learn by doing. [Aristotle: *Nicomachean Ethics* II.i.]
5 Whatever is worth doing at all is worth doing well. [Lord Chesterfield: Letter to his son, Oct. 9, 1746]
6 If a thing is worth doing it is worth doing badly. [G. K. Chesterton: *Folly and Female Education*]

DO-IT-YOURSELF
7 If you'd have it done, Go: if not, Send. [Benjamin Franklin: *Poor Richard's Almanack* (1743)]

DOLLAR
8 The almighty dollar. [Washington Irving: *Wolfert's Roost,* "The Creole Village"]
Irving intended almighty *to suggest God, for he added, after* dollar, *"that great object of universal devotion throughout our land."*

DOMESTICITY
9 To suckle fools and chronicle small beer.
[Shakespeare: *Othello* II.i.]
Iago has been making up doggerel rimes about various kinds of women, stressing their wickedness and folly. Desdemona asks him what he would grant a fully virtuous woman would do. And he answers—marry a fool, beget and suckle

foolish children by him, and occupy her life in humdrum keeping of trivial household accounts. Desdemona's exclamation: "O most lame and impotent conclusion" is a double comment.

10 For them no more the blazing hearth shall burn,
Or busy housewife ply her evening care:
No children run to lisp their sire's return,
Or climb his knees the envied kiss to share.
[Thomas Gray: *Elegy Written in a Country Churchyard*]
11 Seldom any prince, however despotic, has so far shaken off all awe of the public eye as to venture upon those freaks of injustice which are sometimes indulged under the secrecy of a private dwelling. [Samuel Johnson: *The Rambler* No. 148]

DOMINANCE
12 No two men can be half an hour together but one will acquire an evident superiority over the other. [Samuel Johnson: in Boswell's *Life* (1776)]

DOMINION
13 God of our fathers, known of old,
Lord of our far-flung battle-line,
Beneath whose awful Hand we hold
Dominion over palm and pine—
Lord God of Hosts, be with us yet,
Lest we forget—lest we forget!
[Kipling: *Recessional*]

DOORNAIL
14 I am ded as dorenail. [Anon.: *William of Palerne* (1350)]
This is the first known use of this comparison and it seems to have been a proverb even then. No one knows why a doornail should be deader than any other inanimate object. It has been conjectured that it was the heavy nail on which the knocker fell and was assumed to be dead because it had been beaten so often. Others have guessed that its deadness may have been suggested by the silence that often greeted knockings— and this is supported by the fact that it was sometimes as dumb as a doornail or as deaf as a doornail or as dour as a

doornail. *But no one knows for sure exactly what it means.*

1 *Falstaff.* What, is the old king dead? *Pistol.* As nail in door.
[Shakespeare: *II Henry IV* V.iii.]

2 Old Marley was as dead as a doornail. [Dickens: *A Christmas Carol*, "Stave One"]

DOORS

3   On a sudden open fly
With impetuous recoil and jarring
        sound
Th' infernal doors, and on their
        hinges grate
Harsh thunder, that the lowest bot-
        tom shook
Of Erebus.
[John Milton: *Paradise Lost* II.879-883]

DOTAGE

4 Dotage is not characteristic of all old men but only of the light-minded. [Cicero: *De Senectute* XI.xxxvi.]

DOTS

5 1 never could make out what those damned dots meant. [Lord Randolph Spencer Churchill: quoted in Winston Churchill, *Lord Randolph Churchill* II.]
The reference is to the decimal mark. Lord Randolph had an aristocratic scorn of such shopkeeper's trivia.

DOUBT(S)

6 To know much is often the cause of doubting more. [Montaigne: *Essays* II. xii.]

7 If a man will begin with certainties, he shall end in doubts; but if he will be content to begin with doubts, he shall end in certainties. [Francis Bacon: *Advancement of Learning* I]

8 Doubtful delay is worse than any
        fever.
[Henry Constable: *Sonnets to Diana*]

9   Our doubts are traitors,
And make us lose the good we oft
        might win,
By fearing to attempt.
[Shakespeare: *Measure for Measure* I.iv.]

10   No hinge nor loop
To hang a doubt on.
[Shakespeare: *Othello* III.iii.]

11 Doubt is not a pleasant condition, but certainty is an absurd one. [Voltaire, Letter to Frederick the Great, April 6, 1767]

12 To doubt is safer than to be secure. [Philip Massinger: *A Very Woman* I.i.]

13 He that knows nothing doubts nothing. [George Herbert: *Jacula Prudentum*]

14 The tepid water of doubt often acts as an emetic to make men vomit their secrets. [Gracián: *Oráculo Manual*]

15 To believe with certainty we must begin with doubting. [Stanislaus (King of Poland): *Maxims*]

16 The first step towards philosophy is incredulity. [Diderot: *Last Conversation*]

17 Doubt, of whatever kind, can be ended by Action alone. [Thomas Carlyle: *Past and Present* III.xi.]

18 There lives more faith in honest
        doubt,
Believe me, than in half the creeds.
[Tennyson: *In Memoriam* XCVI]

19 From doubt to denial is a short step. [Alfred De Musset: *Confession d'un Enfant du Siècle* IV.vi.]

20 All we have gained then by our un-
        belief
Is a life of doubt diversified by faith,
For one of faith diversified by doubt.
[Robert Browning: *Bishop Blougram's Apology*]

21 Irks care the crop-full bird? Frets
        doubt the maw-crammed beast?
[Robert Browning: *Rabbi Ben Ezra*]

22 To doubt would be disloyalty,
   To falter would be sin.
[F. W. Faber: *The Right Must Win*]

23 "I doubt it," said the carpenter,
   And shed a bitter tear.
[Lewis Carroll: *Through the Looking-Glass*, "The Walrus and the Carpenter"]

24 Learning learns but one lesson: doubt! [G. B. Shaw: *The Admirable Bashville* I]

25 An honest man can never surrender an honest doubt. [Walter Malone: *The Agnostic's Creed*]

26 The liberation of the human mind has been best furthered by gay fellows who heaved dead cats into sanctuaries and then went roistering down the high-

ways of the world, proving to all men that doubt, after all, was safe—that the god in the sanctuary was a fraud. One horse-laugh is worth ten thousand syllogisms. [H. L. Mencken: in *The American Mercury*, January 1924]

DOUGHNUT
1 Anyhow, the hole in the doughnut is at least digestible. [H. L. Mencken: *Chrestomathy*, p. 626]

DO UNTO OTHERS
2 Do unto the other feller the way he'd like to do unto you an' do it fust. [E. N. Westcott: *David Harum* XX]

DOVE(S)
3 Oh that I had wings like a dove! [Psalms 55:6]
4 The moan of doves in immemorial
         elms,
 And murmuring of innumerable bees.
[Tennyson: *The Princess* VII]

DOWN
5 He that's down, down with him. [Old English and Scottish Proverb]
6 A man may be down, but he's never out. [Slogan of the Salvation Army]

DRAGONS
7 Dragons in their pleasant palaces. [Isaiah 13:22]

DRAMA
8 The drama's laws, the drama's pa-
        trons give,
 For we that live to please, must
        please to live.
[Samuel Johnson: Prologue, at the Opening of the Theater in Drury Lane]

DREAD
9 Like one that on a lonesome road
 Doth walk in fear and dread,
 And having once turned round, walks
          on,
 And turns no more his head;
 Because he knows a frightful fiend
 Doth close behind him tread.
[Coleridge: *The Ancient Mariner* VI]
10 Weave a circle round him thrice,
 And close your eyes with holy dread,

For he on honey-dew hath fed,
And drunk the milk of Paradise.
[Coleridge: *Kubla Khan*]

DREAM(S)
11 Two gates for ghostly dreams there are: one gateway of honest horn, and one of ivory. Issuing by the ivory gate are dreams of glimmering illusion, fantasies, but those that come through solid polished horn may be borne out, if mortals only know them. [Homer: *Odyssey* XIX (trans. Robert Fitzgerald)]
12 I believe it to be true that dreams are the true interpreters of our inclinations; but there is art required to sort and understand them. [Montaigne: *Essays* III. xiii.]
13   I talk of dreams
 Which are the children of an idle
          brain,
 Begot of nothing but vain fantasy,
 Which is as thin of substance as the
          air
 And more inconstant than the wind.
[Shakespeare: *Romeo and Juliet* I.iv.]
14 Between the acting of a dreadful thing
 And the first motion, all the interim
          is
 Like a phantasma, or a hideous
          dream.
[Shakespeare: *Julius Caesar* II.i.]
15 The eye of man hath not heard, the ear of man hath not seen, man's hand is not able to taste, his tongue to conceive, nor his heart to report, what my dream was. [Shakespeare: *A Midsummer Night's Dream* IV.i.]
16 O God! I could be bounded in a nutshell and count myself a king of infinite space, were it not that I have bad dreams. [Shakespeare: *Hamlet* II.ii.]
17 For in that sleep of death what
        dreams may come!
[Shakespeare: *Hamlet* III.i.]
18   Thou hast nor youth nor age,
 But, as it were, an after-dinner's sleep,
 Dreaming on both.
[Shakespeare: *Measure for Measure* III.i.]
19 The affliction of these terrible dreams
 That shake us nightly.
[Shakespeare: *Macbeth* III.ii.]
20   We are such stuff
 As dreams are made on, and our lit-

tle life
Is rounded with a sleep.
[Shakespeare: *The Tempest* IV.i.]

1 It was the wise Zeno that said, he could collect a man by his dreams. For then the soul, stated in a deep repose, bewrayed her true affections: which, in the busy day, she would rather not show, or not note. . . . The best use we can make of dreams, is observation: and by that, our own correction or encouragement. For 'tis not doubtable, but that the mind is working, in the dullest depth of sleep. [Owen Felltham: *Of Dreams* (c. 1620)]

> Zeno = *Stoic philosopher, c. 300* B.C.; collect = *form a conclusion about;* stated = *settled in safety and quiet;* bewrayed = *revealed;* affections = *shaping influences, emotions, feelings*

2 Such sights as youthful poets dream
On summer eves by haunted stream.
[John Milton: *L'Allegro*]

3 Her face was veiled; yet to my fancied sight
Love, sweetness, goodness, in her person shined
So clear as in no face with more delight.
But, oh! as to embrace me she inclined,
I waked, she fled, and day brought back my night.
[John Milton: *On his Deceased Wife* (1658)]

> Milton married his second wife Katharine Woodcock in 1656 when he was already blind. She died a year later. The pathos of the famous lines lie in the fact that he had never seen her.

4 [Dreams] are mere productions of the brain,
And fools consult interpreters in vain.
[Jonathan Swift: *On Dreams*]

5 In solitude we have our dreams to ourselves, and in company we agree to dream in concert. [Samuel Johnson: *The Idler* No. 32]

6 Wise men dream at night, fools both day and night.
[Melchior de Santa Cruz: *Floresta Española:* I.vi.]

7 Some say that gleams of a remoter world
Visit the soul in sleep.
[Shelley: *Mont Blanc*]

8 I dreamt that I dwelt in marble halls,
With vassals and serfs at my side.
[Alfred Bunn: *The Bohemian Girl* II]

9 If there were dreams to sell,
What would you buy?
Some cost a passing-bell;
Some a light sigh.
[Thomas Lovell Beddoes: *Dream-Pedlary*]

10 Those who dream by day are cognizant of many things which escape those who dream by night. [Edgar Allan Poe: *Eleonora*]

11 All that we see or seem
Is but a dream within a dream.
[Edgar Allan Poe: *A Dream Within a Dream*]

12 And all my days are trances,
And all my nightly dreams
Are where thy grey eye glances,
And where thy footstep gleams—
In what ethereal dances,
By what eternal streams.
[Edgar Allan Poe: *To One in Paradise*]

13 In the world of dreams, I have chosen my part,
To sleep for a season and hear no word
Of true love's truth or of light love's art,
Only the song of a secret bird.
[Swinburne: *A Ballad of Dreamland,* "Envoi"]

14 For each age is a dream that is dying,
Or one that is coming to birth.
[Arthur O'Shaughnessy: *We Are the Music Makers*]

15 There's a long, long trail awinding
Into the land of my dreams,
Where the nightingales are singing
And the white moon beams;
There's a long, long night of waiting
Until my dreams all come true,
Till the day when I'll be going down that
Long, long trail with you.
[Stoddard King: *There's a Long, Long Trail*]

16 I have spread my dreams under your feet;
Tread softly because you tread on my dreams.
[W. B. Yeats: *He Wishes for the Cloths of Heaven*]

DREAMER(S)
1 Behold, this dreamer cometh. [Genesis 37:19]
2 Dreamer of dreams, born out of my
    due time,
Why should I strive to set the
    crooked straight?
[William Morris: *The Earthly Paradise*,
"An Apology"]
3 We are the music makers,
  We are the dreamers of dreams,
Wandering by lone sea-breakers,
  And sitting by desolate streams—
World-losers and world-forsakers,
  On whom the pale moon gleams.
[Arthur O'Shaughnessy: *Ode:* "We Are
the Music-Makers"]

DREAMING
4 If there be, or ever were, one such,
It's past the size of dreaming.
[Shakespeare: *Antony and Cleopatra*
V.ii.]
5 Deep into that darkness peering, long
  I stood there, wondering, fearing,
Doubting, dreaming dreams no mortal ever dared to dream before.
[Edgar Allan Poe: *The Raven*]

DREARY
6 The day is cold, and dark, and dreary;
It rains, and the wind is never weary;
The vine still clings to the mouldering wall,
But at every gust the dead leaves fall,
And the day is dark and dreary.
[Longfellow: *The Rainy Day*]
7 Now dreary dawns the eastern light,
And fall of eve is drear,
And cold the poor man lies at night,
And so goes out the year.
[A. E. Housman: *Last Poems* XXVIII]

DRESSING TABLE
8 Here files of pins extend their shining rows,
Puffs, powders, patches, bibles, billet-doux.
[Alexander Pope: *The Rape of the Lock*
I]
    The confusion on the young lady's dressing table reflects the confusion in her mind.

DRINKER
9 Count not the cups; not therein lies
excess
In wine, but in the nature of the
    drinker.
[Menander: *Fragment*]
10 Under a bad cloak there is often a good drinker. [Cervantes: *Don Quixote* II]
11 BOTTLE-NOSED. Having a nose created in the image of its maker. [Ambrose Bierce: *The Devil's Dictionary*]

DRINKING: delights of
12 So was their jolly whistle well y-wet.
[Chaucer: *The Reeve's Tale*]
13 They drank with unbuttoned bellies.
[Rabelais: *Pantagruel* II.xx.]
14 I cannot eat but little meat,
  My stomach is not good;
But sure I think that I can drink
  With him that wears a hood.
That I go bare, take ye no care,
  I am nothing a-cold:
I stuff my skin so full within
  Of jolly good ale and old.
Back and side go bare, go bare,
  Both foot and hand go cold;
But belly, God send thee good ale
    enough,
  Whether it be new or old.
[*Gammer Gurton's Needle* II.i.]
him that wears a hood = *a monk*
    The authorship of Gammer Gurton's Needle (first acted 1566) is uncertain. When published in 1575, it was said to be "By Mr. S. Mr. of Art" and has been assigned to Bishop Still by some and to William Stevenson by others.

15 If I had a thousand sons, the first human principle I would teach them should be, to forswear thin potations. [Shakespeare: *II Henry IV* IV.iii.]
16 And let me the canakin clink:
  A soldier's a man;
  A life's but a span;
Why then let a soldier drink.
[Shakespeare: *Othello* II.iii.]
17 Nose, nose, jolly red nose,
  And what gave thee that jolly red
    nose?
Nutmeg and ginger, cinnamon and
    cloves,
That's what gave me this jolly red
    nose.
[Song No. 7 in *Deuteromelia* (1609),
prob. by Thomas Ravenscroft. In-

cluded, the same year, in Beaumont and Fletcher's *Knight of the Burning Pestle.*]
In more robust days, usually included in collections of nursery rhymes.

1 If all be true that I do think,
There are five reasons we should drink;
Good wine—a friend—or being dry—
Or lest we should be by and by—
Or any other reason why.
[16th-century Latin epigram (trans. Henry Aldrich)]

2 Inspiring bold John Barleycorn!
What dangers thou canst make us scorn!
Wi' tippenny, we fear nae evil;
Wi' usquebae, we'll face the devil!
[Burns: *Tam o' Shanter*]
tippenny = *twopenny* (*ale*); usquebae = *Gaelic* uisgebeatha = *water of life, Anglicized to* whisky.
The thought is paralleled in the French phrase for brandy, eau de vie, *the Latin* aqua vitae *and the Scandinavian* akvavit.

3 No churchman am I for to rail and to write,
No statesman nor soldier to plot or to fight,
No sly man of business contriving a snare,
For a big-bellied bottle's the whole of my care.
[Burns: *No Churchman am I*]

4 There are two reasons for drinking: one is, when you are thirsty, to cure it; the other, when you are not thirsty, to prevent it. . . . [Thomas Love Peacock: *Melincourt*]

5 The rapturous, wild, and ineffable pleasure
Of drinking at somebody else's expense.
[Henry Sambrooke Leigh: *Stanzas to an Intoxicated Fly*]

6 There was an old hen
She had a wooden leg,
And every damned morning
She laid another egg;
She was the best damned chicken
On the whole damned farm,
And another little drink
Wouldn't do us any harm!
[Anon.]

19th-century drinking song.

7 Fifteen men on a dead man's chest—
Yo-ho-ho and a bottle of rum.
Drink and the Devil had done for the rest—
Yo-ho-ho and a bottle of rum.
[R. L. Stevenson: *Treasure Island*]
Stevenson, in a letter to Sidney Colvin, said that the "seed" of Treasure Island *was a passage in Charles Kingsley's* At Last I. *The passage consists merely of a list of names of islands in the West Indies and a reference to "English buccaneers." One of the islands was "The Dead Man's Chest." This alone would seem to the layman a very small seed but, as Keats's letters show, it would do for a poet.*

8 Candy is dandy
But liquor is quicker.
[Ogden Nash: *Reflection on Ice-Breaking*]

DRINKING: and thinking

9 O God, that men should put an enemy in their mouths to steal away their brains! [Shakespeare: *Othello* II.iii.]

10 A night of good drinking
Is worth a year's thinking.
[Charles Cotton: *Chanson à Boire*]

11 Much drinking, little thinking.
[Jonathan Swift: Letter to Stella, February 26, 1711]

12 Then trust me there's nothing like drinking
So pleasant on this side the grave;
It keeps the unhappy from thinking,
And makes e'en the valiant more brave.
[Charles Dibdin: *Nothing like Grog*]

13 What's drinking?
A mere pause from thinking!
[Byron: *The Deformed Transformed* III.i.]

14 The Grape that can with Logic absolute
The Two-and-Seventy jarring Sects confute:
The sovereign Alchemist that in a trice
Life's leaden metal into Gold transmute.
[*Rubáiyát of Omar Khayyám* (trans. Edward FitzGerald)]

1 Perplexed no more with Human or
Divine,
To-morrow's tangle to the winds re-
sign,
And lose your fingers in the tresses
of
The Cypress-slender Minister of
Wine.
[*Rubáiyát of Omar Khayyám* (trans. Ed-
ward FitzGerald)]

2 Oh, 'tis jesting, dancing, drinking
Spins the heavy world around.
If young hearts were not so clever,
Oh, they would be young for ever:
Think no more; 'tis only thinking
Lays lads underground.
[A. E. Housman: *A Shropshire Lad*
XLIX]

3 Malt does more than Milton can
To justify God's ways to man.
Ale, man, ale's the stuff to drink
For fellows whom it hurts to think:
Look into the pewter pot
To see the world as the world's not.
[A. E. Housman: *A Shropshire Lad*
LXII]

4 Could man be drunk for ever
With liquor, love, or fights,
Lief should I rouse at morning
And lief lie down of nights.

But men at whiles are sober
And think by fits and starts.
And if they think they fasten
Their hands upon their hearts.
[A. E. Housman: *Last Poems* X]

5 Miniver Cheevy, born too late,
Scratched his head and kept on think-
ing;
Miniver coughed and called it fate,
And kept on drinking.
[Edward Arlington Robinson: *Miniver
Cheevy*]

DRINKING: woes and perils

6 In womman vinolent is no defence.
[Chaucer: Prologue to *The Wife of
Bath's Tale*]

7 I have very poor and unhappy brains
for drinking; I could wish courtesy
would invent some other custom of entertainment. [Shakespeare: *Othello* II.
iii.]

8 Every inordinate cup is unblessed
and the ingredient is a devil. [Shake-

speare: *Othello* II.iii.]

9 Drink, sir, is a great provoker of
three things. . . . Marry, sir, nose-paint-
ing, sleep, and urine. Lechery, sir, it provokes and unprovokes: it provokes the
desire, but it takes away the performance. [Shakespeare: *Macbeth* II.iii.]

10 In the flowers that wreathe the sparkling bowl
Fell adders hiss and poisonous ser-
pents roll.
[Matthew Prior: *Solomon* II]

11 See Social-Life and Glee sit down
All joyous and unthinking,
Till, quite transmogrify'd, they're
grown
Debauchery and Drinking.
[Burns: *An Address to the Unco Guid*]

12 First the man takes a drink, then the
drink takes a drink, then the drink
takes the man. [Japanese proverb]

DRINKING: miscellaneous

13 We'll teach you to drink deep ere
you depart.
[Shakespeare: *Hamlet* I.ii.]

14 'Tis evermore the prologue to his
sleep.
He'll watch the horologe a double set
If drink rock not his cradle.
[Shakespeare: *Othello* II.iii.]
*Iago says that drunkenness is now habit-
ual with Cassio, that he'd stay awake
around the clock if he did not stupefy
himself with drink.*

15 Drink to me only with thine eyes,
And I will pledge with mine;
Or leave a kiss but in the cup,
And I'll not look for wine.
[Ben Jonson: *To Celia*]

16 As he brews, so shall he drink. [Ben
Jonson: *Every Man in his Humour* II.i.]

17 Drinking with women is as unnatural
as scolding with 'em. [William Wycherley: *The Country Wife* II]

18 The first glass for myself, the second
for my friends, the third for good humor, and the fourth for mine enemies.
[Joseph Addison: *The Spectator* No.
195]
*Addison states this to be a saying quoted
by Sir William Temple.*

19 And he that will this health deny,
Down among the dead men let him
lie.

[John Dyer: *Song* (1750)]
"Dead men" were empty wine bottles scattered around the floor and under the table. In the 18th century it was considered laudable for men of fashion to drink until they slid unconscious to the floor.

1 A man who has been drinking wine at all freely should never go into a new company. With those who have partaken of wine with him he may be pretty well in unison, but he will probably be offensive, or appear ridiculous, to other people. [Samuel Johnson: in Boswell's *Life,* March 16, 1776]
2 Claret is the liquor for boys; port for men; but he who aspires to be a hero must drink brandy. [Samuel Johnson: in Boswell's *Life,* April 7, 1779]
3 "Mrs. Harris," I says, "leave the bottle on the chimley-piece, and don't ask me to take none, but let me put my lips to it when I am so dispoged." [Dickens: *Martin Chuzzlewit* XIX]
Sairy Gamp speaking.
4 Note in the barracks: "Drink drives out the man and brings out the beast." Which makes men understand why they like it. [Albert Camus: *Notebooks 1935-1942* Ch. II, p. 110]

DRIVEL
5 The ropy drivel of rheumatic brains. [William Gifford: *The Baviad*]

DROP
6 There are people whom one should like very well to drop, but would not wish to be dropped by. [Samuel Johnson: in Boswell's *Life,* March, 1781]

DROWNING
7 'Tis double death to drown in ken of shore.
[Shakespeare: *The Rape of Lucrece*]
8 Lord, Lord! methought, what pain it was to drown:
What dreadful noise of waters in mine ears!
What ugly sights of death within mine eyes!
[Shakespeare: *Richard III* I.iv.]

DRUNK
9 Thou comest home as dronken as a mouse.
[Chaucer: Prologue to *The Wife of Bath's Tale*]
10 Like a glee-man's bitch.
[William Langland: *Piers Plowman* A. V. 197 (1362)]
A glee-man was a singer or minstrel.
Langland is describing the wandering gait of a drunkard. So it would look as though "drunk as a fiddler's bitch" is a venerable comparison.
11 Kings may be blest, but Tam was glorious,
O'er a' the ills o' life victorious.
[Burns: *Tam o' Shanter*]
Tam was drunk.
12 Not drunk is he, who from the floor Can rise alone, and drink some more; But drunk is he, who prostrate lies, Without the power to drink or rise.
[Thomas Love Peacock: *The Misfortunes of Elphin*]

DRUNKARD(S)
13 There are . . . more old drunkards than old physicians. [Rabelais: *Gargantua* I.xli.]
Or maybe they just look older.
14 Lo! the poor toper whose untutor'd sense,
Sees bliss in ale, and can with wine dispense;
Whose head proud fancy never taught to steer,
Beyond the muddy ecstasies of beer.
[George Crabbe: *Inebriety*]
A parody of Pope's famous passage in An Essay on Man, *Epistle I:*
Lo, the poor Indian! whose untutored mind;
Sees God in clouds, or hears him in the wind;
His soul proud science never taught to stray
Far as the solar walk or milky way.
15 If we take habitual drunkards as a class, their heads and their hearts will bear an advantageous comparison with those of any other class. [Abraham Lincoln: in a speech in Springfield, Ill., Feb. 22, 1842]
16 Father, dear father, come home with me now;
The clock in the steeple strikes one. . . .

Our fire has gone out, our house is
all dark,
And mother's been watching since
tea,
With poor brother Benny so sick in
her arms
And no one to help her but me.
[Henry Clay Work: *Father, Dear Father,
Come Home With Me Now*]
*A famous temperance song. A child is
attempting to get her father to leave the
tavern. As the song progresses, the clock
strikes two and then three. Meanwhile
the baby dies and woes continue.*

DRUNKENNESS
1 He injures the absent who quarrels
with a drunken man. [Publilius Syrus:
Maxims]
2 Drunkenness is nothing but voluntary
madness. [Seneca: *Ad Lucilium* LXXX-
III]
3 Dronkennesse is verray sepulture
Of mannes wit and his discrecioun.
[Chaucer: *The Pardoner's Tale*]
4 A man who exposes himself when he
is intoxicated has not the art of getting
drunk; a sober man who happens occasionally to get drunk, readily enough
goes into a new company, which a man
who has been drinking should never do.
Such a man . . . is without skill in in-
ebriation. [Samuel Johnson: in Boswell's
Life, April 24, 1779]
5 Heaven, they say, protects children,
sailors, and drunken men. [Thomas
Hughes: *Tom Brown at Oxford* XII]
6 But I'm not so think as you drunk I
am.
[J. C. Squire: *Ballade of Soporific Absorption*]

DRYDEN
7 Waller was smooth, but Dryden
taught to join
The varying verse, the full resounding line,
The long majestic march, and energy
divine.
[Alexander Pope: *Imitations of Horace*
II.i.]

DUCHESS
8 That's my last Duchess painted on
the wall,

Looking as if she were alive.
[Robert Browning: *My Last Duchess*]

DULCIMER
9 A damsel with a dulcimer
In a vision once I saw:
It was an Abyssinian maid,
And on her dulcimer she played,
Singing of Mount Abora.
[Coleridge: *Kubla Khan*]

DULL
10 I find we are growing serious, and
then we are in great danger of being
dull. [William Congreve: *Old Bachelor*
II.ii.]
11 As Dull as a Dutch commentator.
[Soame Jenyns: *Imitations of Horace*
II.i.]

DULLNESS
12 And duller shouldst thou be than the
fat weed
That rots itself in ease on Lethe
wharf.
[Shakespeare: *Hamlet* I.v.]
13 Dulness is sometimes a good defence
against sharp wits. [La Rochefoucauld:
Maxims]
14 Mature in dulness from his tender
years.
[Dryden: *Mac Flecknoe*]
15 The rest to some faint meaning make
pretence,
But Shadwell never deviates into
sense.
[Dryden: *Mac Flecknoe*]
16 Trust nature, do not labor to be dull.
[Dryden: *Mac Flecknoe*]
17 And lambent dulness played around
his face.
[Dryden: *Mac Flecknoe*]
18 Much was believ'd, but little understood,
And to be dull was construed to be
good.
[Alexander Pope: *Essay on Criticism* III]
19 And gentle Dulness ever loves a joke.
[Alexander Pope: *The Dunciad* II]
20 Why, Sir, Sherry is dull, naturally
dull; but it must have taken him a great
deal of pains to become what we now
see him. Such an excess of stupidity, Sir,
is not in Nature. [Samuel Johnson: about
Dr. Thomas Sheridan, author and lec-

turer, in Boswell's *Life,* July 28, 1763]

1 Dullness is the coming of age of seriousness.

[Oscar Wilde: *Phrases . . . . for the Young*]

2 A dull head among windy spaces.

[T. S. Eliot: *Gerontion*]

DUNCE

3 How much a dunce that has been
sent to roam
Excels a dunce that has been kept at
home!

[William Cowper: *The Progress of Error*]

DUST

4 In the sweat of thy face shalt thou eat bread, till thou return unto the ground; for out of it wast thou taken: for dust thou art, and unto dust shalt thou return. [Genesis 3:19]

5 His enemies shall lick the dust. [Psalms 72:9]

6 We are dust and shadow.
[Horace: *Odes* IV.vii.]
The Latin: Pulvis et umbra sumus.

7 To what base uses we may return, Horatio! Why may not imagination trace the noble dust of Alexander, till he find it stopping a bung-hole? [Shakespeare: *Hamlet* V.i.]

8 And give to dust that is a little gilt
More laud than gilt o'erdusted.
[Shakespeare: *Troilus and Cressida* III. iii.]

9 Fear no more the heat o' the sun,
Nor the furious winter's rages;
Thou thy worldly task hast done,
Home art gone, and ta'en thy
wages.
Golden lads and girls all must,
As chimney-sweepers, come to dust.
[Shakespeare: *Cymbeline* IV.ii.]

10 This quiet Dust was Gentlemen and
Ladies,
And Lads and Girls;
Was laughter and ability and sighing,
And frocks and curls.
[Emily Dickinson: *The Single Hound* LXXIV]

11 There's a peddler deals in dust.
[Robert Underwood Johnson: *Hearth-Song*]

DUTY

12 Let us hear the conclusion of the whole matter: Fear God, and keep his commandments: for this is the whole duty of man. [Ecclesiastes 12:13]

13 I do perceive here a divided duty.
[Shakespeare: *Othello* I.iii.]

14 I ought, therefore I can.
[Attr. Immanuel Kant]

15 England expects every man to do his duty. [Horatio Nelson: signal No. 16 at the beginning of the Battle of Trafalgar, 11:55 A.M., October 21, 1805]

There are several minor variants in the famous signal. Some have it: "expects that every man will do," others: "expects every officer and man."

Nelson originally gave the signal as "Nelson confides that every man will do his duty." Captain Sir Henry Blackwood suggested the happy emendation to "England expects."

The signal was received with mixed feelings. Admiral Cuthbert Collingwood, whose bringing of The Royal Sovereign *into action had just initiated the battle, felt all this fuss was unnecessary. "I wish Nelson would stop signalling," he exclaimed.*

16 Stern Daughter of the Voice of God!
O Duty! if that name thou love
Who art a light to guide, a rod
To check the erring, and reprove;
Thou, who art victory and law
When empty terrors overawe;
From vain temptations dost set free;
And calm'st the weary strife of frail
humanity!

[Wordsworth: *Ode to Duty*]

17 Thou dost preserve the stars from
wrong;
And the most ancient heavens,
through Thee, are fresh and strong.
[Wordsworth: *Ode to Duty*]

18 So nigh is grandeur to our dust,
So near is God to man,
When duty whispers low, Thou must,
The youth replies, I can.
[Emerson: *Voluntaries* III]

*When Duty whispers low, Thou must, /
This erstwhile youth replies, I just can't.*
Ogden Nash: Kind of an Ode to Duty

19 Theirs not to make reply,
Theirs not to reason why,
Theirs but to do or die.

[Tennyson: *The Charge of the Light Brigade*]

1 If . . . England expects every man to do his duty, England is the most sanguine country on the face of the earth, and will find itself continually disappointed. [Dickens: *Martin Chuzzlewit* XLIII]

2 DUTY. That which sternly impels us in the direction of profit, along the line of desire. [Ambrose Bierce: *The Devil's Dictionary*]

3 Duty is what one expects from others. [Oscar Wilde: *A Woman of No Importance* II]

4 When a stupid man is doing something he is ashamed of, he always declares that it is his duty. [G. B. Shaw: *Caesar and Cleopatra* III]

5 That dull, leaden, soul-depressing sensation known as the sense of duty. [O. Henry: *No Story*]

6 O Duty,
Why hast thou not the visage of a sweetie or a cutie?
Why glitter thy spectacles so ominously?
Why art thou clad so abominously?
Why art thou so different from Venus
And why do thou and I have so few interests mutually in common between us?
[Ogden Nash: *Kind of an Ode to Duty*]

DWARF

7 The dwarf sees farther than the giant, when he has the giant's shoulders to mount on. [Coleridge: *The Friend* VIII]

DYING

8 When he was at the last gasp. [II Maccabees 2:32]
And I Maccabees 7:9.

9 I do not wish to die, but care not if I were dead. [Cicero: *Tusculan Disputations* I.viii.]

10 Stay but a little; for my cloud of dignity
Is held from falling with so weak a wind
That it will quickly drop.
[Shakespeare: *II Henry IV* IV.v.]

11 He's in Arthur's bosom, if ever man went to Arthur's bosom. A' made a finer end, and went away an it had been any christom child; a' parted even just between twelve and one, even at the turning o' the tide: for after I saw him fumble with the sheets and play with flowers and smile upon his fingers' ends, I knew there was but one way; for his nose was as sharp as a pen, and a' babbled of green fields. [Shakespeare: *Henry V* II.iii.]

christom child = chrisom child = *a child in its first month, an innocent babe*

This vignette of Falstaff's death is incomparable. Mistress Quickly is moved, breathless, garrulous, tender, superstitious, and eagerly ignorant. "Arthur's bosom" is magnificent.

The folio has "a table of greene fields." The emendation, one of the happiest in all literature, was Theobald's in his edition (1734).

12 I am dying, Egypt, dying. [Shakespeare: *Antony and Cleopatra* IV.xiii.]

13 The long habit of living indisposeth us for dying. [Sir Thomas Browne: *Urn-Burial*, Ch. 5]

14 The soul's dark cottage, batter'd and decay'd,
Lets in new light through chinks that time has made.
Stronger by weakness, wiser men become
As they draw near to their eternal home:
Leaving the old, both worlds at once they view
That stand upon the threshold of the new.
[Edmund Waller: *On the Divine Poems*]

15 Don't cheer, boys, the poor devils are dying. [Captain J. W. Philip, of the battleship *Texas*: at the Battle of Santiago Bay (1898) as the Spanish cruiser *Vizcaya* was driven ashore in flames.]

Spanish losses, in men, were 160 killed, 1800 captured. American losses: 1 man killed, 1 wounded. Cynics later pointed out that our fleet had achieved a score of only 3% hits with major calibre shells.

16 A man's dying is more the survivors' affair than his own. [Thomas Mann: *The Magic Mountain*]

17 Do not go gentle into that good night,

Old age should burn and rave at
close of day;
Rage, rage against the dying of the
light.
[Dylan Thomas: *Do Not Go Gentle into
that Good Night*]

DYING WORDS

1   I am going to seek the great perhaps.
[See Motteux's preface to his translation
of Rabelais]
2   O, but they say the tongues of dying
men
Enforce attention like deep harmony.
[Shakespeare: *Richard II* II.i.]
3   Now I am about to take my last voyage, a great leap in the dark. [Thomas
Hobbes: on his deathbed (1679)]
4   He had been, he said, an unconscionable time dying; but he hoped that they
would excuse it. [Charles II: quoted in
Macaulay's *History of England* I.iv.]

*Charles's apology to his heir and others
in attendance for being such a long time
dying ranks among the more magnificent
statements in the annals of courtesy.*

*A peculiarly parallel remark was made,
when he was dying, by his great enemy,
Oliver Cromwell: "My desire is to make
what haste I can to be gone."*

5   If Mr. Selwyn calls, let him in; if I
am alive I shall be very glad to see him,
and if I am dead he will be very glad to
see me. [Henry Fox: referring to George
Augustus Selwyn]
*Selwyn had a morbid interest in the
dead.*

6   Let us cross the river and rest in the
shade. [Stonewall Jackson]
7   I am bored with it all. [Winston
Churchill. Quoted in *The New York
Times* Feb. 1, 1965, p. 12.]
cf. *"It's all been very interesting." Attr.
Lady Mary Wortley Montagu.*

E

EAGLE

1 He clasps the crag with crookèd hands;
Close to the sun in lonely lands,
Ringed with the azure world, he stands.

The wrinkled sea beneath him crawls;
He watches from his mountain walls,
And like a thunderbolt he falls.
[Tennyson: *The Eagle*]

EAR(S)

2 The ear trieth words, as the mouth tasteth meat. [Job 24:3]

3 Let the ear neither reject anything nor credulously accept anything instantly. [Phaedrus: *Fables* III.10.51]

4 He that hath ears to hear, let him hear. [Mark 4:9]

5 For alle yede out at oon ere
That in that other she dide lere.
[Chaucer: *The Romaunt of the Rose*]
yede = went; lere = learn

This is probably not the origin of "in at one ear and out the other" but simply an indication that it was already proverbial in 1365.

6 And we shal speke of thee some-what, I trowe,
Whan thou art goon, to do thyne eres glow.
[Chaucer: *Troilus and Criseyde* II]
speke = speak; trowe = believe; do = make

The belief that if your ears burn someone is talking about you—particularly, praising you—is very old. Pliny mentions the belief in his Natural History, 1st century A.D.

7 Go shake your ears.
[Shakespeare: *Twelfth Night* II.iii.]
Maria to Malvolio, implying that he is an ass.

8 Give every man thine ear, but few thy voice.
[Shakespeare: *Hamlet* I.iii.]

9 A man may see how this world goes with no eyes.
Look with thine ears.
[Shakespeare: *King Lear* IV.vi.]

10 Take heed what you say. Walls have ears.
[James Shirley: *The Bird in a Cage* I.i.]

11 I was all ear.
[John Milton: *Comus*]

12 More is meant than meets the ear.
[John Milton: *Il Penseroso*]

13 He that hath ears to hear, let him stuff them with cotton. [W. M. Thackeray: *The Virginians* XXXII]

14 I am all ears. [Trollope: *The Belton Estate* XV]

EARLY TO BED

15 Early to bed and early to rise
Will make you miss all the regular guys.

[George Ade: *Early to Bed*]
See also BED

EARNEST

16 If anything is spoken in jest, it is not fair to turn it to earnest. [Plautus: *Amphitruo* III]

17 And eek men shal nat make ernest of game.
[Chaucer: Prologue to *The Miller's Tale*]

18 At seventy-seven it is time to be in earnest. [Samuel Johnson: *Journey to the Western Islands of Scotland*]
Johnson and Boswell had visited an aged minister who had been exceedingly emphatic and dogmatic in asserting his convictions. After they had left him, Boswell commented on the man's dogmatism and Johnson replied as above.

EARTH

19 Give me where to stand and I will move the earth. [Attr. Archimedes of Syracuse (c. 220 B.C.)]
Explaining the principle of the lever, Archimedes is said (in Pliny's Natural

History *VII and elsewhere) to have said that, if he had a lever long enough and a fulcrum strong enough, he could move the world.*

1 The earth is the Lord's, and the fulness thereof; the world, and they that dwell therein. [Psalms 24:1]

2 One generation passeth away, and another generation cometh: but the earth abideth for ever. [Ecclesiastes 1:4]

3 For the earth is the Lord's, and the fulness thereof. [I Corinthians 10:26]

4 The first man is of the earth, earthy. [I Corinthians 15:47]

5   The earth's a thief,
That feeds and breeds by a composture stolen
From general excrement.
[Shakespeare: *Timon of Athens* IV.iii.]

6 Long have I loved what I behold.
The night that calms, the day that cheers;
The common growth of mother-earth
Suffices me.
[Wordsworth: Prologue to *Peter Bell*]

7 Roll on, thou ball, roll on. [It rolls on.]
[W. S. Gilbert: *To the Terrestrial Globe*]

EASE

8 Ease with dignity. (*Otium cum dignitate*)
[Cicero: *Oratio Pro Publio Sextio* XLV]

9 Shall I not take mine ease in mine inn?
[Shakespeare: *I Henry IV* III.iii.]
Falstaff was punning. The earlier meaning of inn was a house or dwelling and there were many references to the delights of taking one's ease therein. By applying the proverbial expression to the Boar's Head tavern, Sir John implies that he has graciously condescended to take up his residence there and that his indignation at having his pocket picked is such as a landholder would feel at such an indignity in his own home.

10 Ignoble ease, and peaceful sloth.
[John Milton: *Paradise Lost* II.226]

11 Whatever he did, was done with so much ease,
In him alone 'twas natural to please.
[Dryden: *Absalom and Achitophel* I]

12 Ease, a neutral state between pain and pleasure. [Samuel Johnson: *The Rambler* No. 85]

13 I could do it as easy as rolling off a log. [Mark Twain: *A Connecticut Yankee in King Arthur's Court*]

14 Anybody who feels at ease in the world today is a fool. [Robert Maynard Hutchins, Address, Jan. 21, 1959]

EAST

15 The East bow'd low before the blast,
In patient, deep disdain;
She let the legions thunder past,
And plunged in thought again.
[Matthew Arnold: *Obermann Once More*]

EAST AND WEST

16 Oh, East is East, and West is West, and never the twain shall meet. [Kipling: *The Ballad of East and West*]

EAT, DRINK AND BE MERRY

17 Then I commended mirth, because a man hath no better thing under the sun, than to eat, than to drink, and to be merry. [Ecclesiastes 8:15; Luke 12:19]

18 Let us eat and drink; for tomorrow we die. [I Corinthians 15:32]
Quoting Isaiah 22:13.

19 Eat thou and drink; to-morrow thou shalt die.
Surely the earth, that's wise being very old,
Needs not our help.
[Dante Gabriel Rossetti: *The House of Life* LXXI]

20 Eat, drink, and be leary. [O. Henry: *The Man Higher Up*]

21 Drink and dance and laugh and lie,
Love, the reeling midnight through,
For tomorrow we shall die!
(But, alas, we never do.)
[Dorothy Parker: *The Flaw in Paganism*]

EATEN

22 He hath eaten me out of house and home.
[Shakespeare: *II Henry IV* II.i.]

EATING

23 The pleasure in eating is not in the costly flavor but in yourself. [Horace: *Satires* II.ii.]

ECCENTRICITY

1 All strangeness and self-particularity in our manners and conditions is to be shunned as an enemy to society and civil conversation. [Montaigne: *Essays*, I.xxv.]
self-particularity = *idiosyncrasy;* conversation = *social intercourse in general*

ECHOES

2 O sweet and far from cliff and scar
The horns of Elfland faintly blowing!
[Tennyson: *The Princess* III]
3 O love, they die in yon rich sky,
They faint on hill or field or river:
Our echoes roll from soul to soul,
And grow for ever and for ever.
[Tennyson: *The Princess* III]
4 The splendour falls on castle walls
And snowy summits old in story:
The long light shakes across the lakes,
And the wild cataract leaps in glory.
Blow, bugle, blow, set the wild echoes flying,
Blow, bugle; answer, echoes, dying, dying, dying.
[Tennyson: *The Princess* III]

ECLIPSE

5 As when the sun . . . from behind the moon,
In dim eclipse, disastrous twilight sheds
On half the nations, and with fear of change
Perplexes monarchs.
[John Milton: *Paradise Lost* I. 594-597]

ECONOMICS

6 The dismal science. [Thomas Carlyle: *Latter-day Pamphlets* I]

ECONOMY

7 It is less dishonorable to abridge petty charges than to stoop to petty gettings. [Francis Bacon: *Of Expense*]
8 Avarice is more opposed to economy than liberality is. [La Rochefoucauld: *Maxims*]
9 Economy is the art of making the most of life. The love of economy is the root of all virtue. [G. B. Shaw: *Maxims for Revolutionists*]
10 Mere parsimony is not economy. . . . Expense, and great expense, may be an essential part of true economy. [Edmund Burke: *Letter to a Noble Lord* (1796)]

ECSTASY

11 It is through the cracks in our brains that ecstasy creeps in. [Logan Pearsall Smith: *Afterthoughts*]

EDEN

12 The voice that breathed o'er Eden. [John Keble: *Holy Matrimony*]
13 Where the apple reddens,
Never pry—
Lest we lose our Edens,
Eve and I.
[Robert Browning: *Bells and Pomegranates,* "A Woman's Last Word"]
14 Eden is that old-fashioned House
We dwell in every day,
Without suspecting our abode
Until we drive away.
[Emily Dickinson: *The Single Hound* CVIII]

EDUCATION

15 The roots of education are bitter, but the fruit is sweet. [Aristotle: *Apothegm*]
16 Only the educated are free. [Epictetus: *Discourses* II.i.]
17 Aristotle was asked how much educated men were superior to the uneducated: "As much," said he, "as the living are to the dead." [Diogenes Laertius: *Aristotle* V.i.]
> Boswell, *in* The Life of Samuel Johnson, *1780, says that Johnson used to quote this passage "with great warmth."*

18 It is not a mind, it is not a body that we erect, but it is a man, and we must not make two parts of him. [Montaigne: *Essays* I.xxv.]
19 The Romans taught their children nothing that was to be learned sitting. [Montaigne: *Essays* II.xxi.]
> *Montaigne attributes this statement to Seneca.*

20 Histories make men wise; poets witty; the mathematics, subtile; natural philosophy, deep; moral, grave; logic and rhetoric, able to contend. . . . Nay, there is no stond or impediment in the wit but may be wrought out by fit studies. [Francis Bacon: *Of Studies*]
> *This is the classical expression of a wide-*

spread belief which, though supported by Plato and Woodrow Wilson, is refuted by common observation. Scientists are no more skeptical, rhetoricians no more articulate, and logicians no more logical than other men. Yet faculties go on basing curricula on the assumption that there is a transfer of aptitude from special to general performance. Consider the millions of life-hours taken from American schoolchildren in the 19th century under the delusion that memorizing increases the power of memory. Ballet dancers are not noticeably more graceful in their common motions than others. Writers seem less fluent in ordinary conversation than many of their associates.

1 Reading maketh a full man, conference a ready man, and writing an exact man. [Francis Bacon: *Of Studies*]

2 He that was only taught by himself had a fool to his master. [Ben Jonson: *Discoveries*]

3 By education most have been misled;
So they believe, because they so were bred.
The priest continues what the nurse began,
And thus the child imposes on the man.
[Dryden: *The Hind and the Panther* III]

4 'Tis education forms the common mind:
Just as the twig is bent the tree's inclined.
[Alexander Pope: *Moral Essays* I]

5 A student may easily exhaust his life in comparing divines and moralists, without any practical regard to morality or religion; he may be learning not to live but to reason. [Samuel Johnson: *The Rambler* No. 87]

6 We talked of the education of children; and I asked him what he thought was best to teach them first. JOHNSON. "Sir, it is no matter what you teach them first, any more than what leg you shall put into your breeches first. Sir, you may stand disputing which is best to put in first, but in the mean time your breech is bare. Sir, while you are considering which of two things you should teach your child first, another boy has learnt

them both." [Samuel Johnson: in Boswell's *Life*, July 26, 1763]

7 Every man who rises above the common level has received two educations: the first from his teachers; the second, more personal and important, from himself. [Edward Gibbon: *Memoirs*]

8 Education makes a people easy to lead, but difficult to drive; easy to govern, but impossible to enslave. [Lord Brougham: in a speech to the House of Commons, 1828]

9 What we must look for here is, first, religious and moral principles; secondly, gentlemanly conduct; thirdly, intellectual ability. [Thomas Arnold: in an address at Rugby, laying down the objectives of a good prep school.]

10 Do not say, the people must be educated, when, after all, you only mean amused, refreshed, soothed, put into good spirits and good humour, or kept from vicious excesses. [John Henry Newman: *The Idea of a University*, Discourse VI]

11 You send your child to the schoolmaster, but 'tis the schoolboys who educate him. You send him to the Latin class, but much of his tuition comes, on his way to school, from the shop-windows. [Emerson: *Conduct of Life*, "Culture"]

12 One of the benefits of a college education is to show the boy its little avail. [Emerson: *Conduct of Life*, "Culture"]

13 Education is the instruction of the intellect in the laws of Nature, under which name I include not merely things and their forces, but men and their ways; and the fashioning of the affections and of the will into an earnest and loving desire to move in harmony with those laws. [T. H. Huxley: *Science and Education* IV]

14 "Reeling and Writhing of course to begin with," the Mock Turtle replied, "and the different branches of Arithmetic—Ambition, Distraction, Uglification, and Derision." [Lewis Carroll: *Alice's Adventures in Wonderland* IX]

15 Education has really only one basic factor, a *sine qua non*—one must want it. [George Edward Woodberry: *John Goffe's Mill*]

16 What we call education and culture is for the most part nothing but the substi-

tution of reading for experience, of literature for life . . . of obsolete fictions for contemporary experience. [G. B. Shaw: *Man and Superman,* "Epistle Dedicatory"]

1 "Whom are you?" said he, for he had been to night school. [George Ade: *Bang! Bang!,* "The Steel Box"]

2 Human history becomes more and more a race between education and catastrophe. [H. G. Wells: *The Outline of History* XV]

3 I find that the three major administrative problems on a campus are sex for the students, athletics for the alumni and parking for the faculty. [Clark Kerr, President of the University of California, quoted in *Time,* Nov. 17, 1958]

EFFEMINACY

4 Amphibious thing! that acting either part,
The trifling head, or the corrupted heart;
Fop at the toilet, flatt'rer at the board,
Now trips a lady, and now struts a Lord.
[Alexander Pope: *Epistle to Dr. Arbuthnot*]
Pope's cruel portrait was based on Lord Hervey, a brilliant but sickly man, lord-in-waiting to George II's queen, and the author of some highly readable Memoirs.

EFFICIENCY

5 Measure not dispatch by the times of sitting, but by the advancement of the business. [Francis Bacon: *Of Dispatch*]

6 To choose time is to save time; and an unseasonable motion is but beating the air. [Francis Bacon: *Of Dispatch*]

EGG(S)

7 Going as if he trod upon eggs. [Robert Burton: *Anatomy of Melancholy* III. 2.3.1]
going = *walking*

8 It is the part of a wise man . . . not even to venture all his eggs in one basket. [Cervantes: *Don Quixote* III.9]

9 An egg will be in three bellies in twenty-four hours. [John Ray: *English Proverbs*]

10 He that would have eggs must endure the cackling of hens. [John Ray: *English Proverbs*]

11 You can't make an omelette without breaking eggs. [Attr. Robespierre, the French Revolutionary leader]
But it seems more probable that it was simply a proverb of which he, in act as well as thought, seems to have been fond.

12 Who can help loving the land that has taught us
Six hundred and eighty-five ways to dress eggs?
[Thomas Moore: *The Fudge Family in Paris,* Letter VIII (1818)]

13 Don't venture all your eggs in one basket. [Samuel Palmer: *Moral Essays on Proverbs*]

14 A hen is only an egg's way of making another egg. [Samuel Butler (1835-1902): *Life and Habit*]
This settles the question of which came first.

15 Put all your eggs in one basket, and —watch the basket. [Mark Twain: *Pudd'nhead Wilson's Calendar*]

16 As innocent as a new-laid egg. [W. S. Gilbert: *Engaged* I]

EGOISM

17 The essence of a self-reliant and autonomous culture is an unshakable egoism. [H. L. Mencken: *Prejudices: Second Series*]

EGOTISM

18 We would rather speak ill of ourselves than not talk of ourselves at all. [La Rochefoucauld: *Maxims*]

19 Though the whole world contradict it, they care not, and as Gregory well notes of such as are vertiginous, they think all turns round and moves. [Robert Burton: *The Anatomy of Melancholy* III.iv.1.3]

20 It is difficult to esteem a man as highly as he wishes to be esteemed. [Vauvenargues: *Réflexions*]

21 No man would, I think, exchange his existence with any other man, however fortunate. We had as lief not be, as not be ourselves. [William Hazlitt: *On the Fear of Death*]
Whether the Walter Mittys, movie mooning and in television trances, wish they

*were someone else—or simply incorpo-
rate the other into themselves—is not
certain.*

1 Every day when he looked into the
glass, and gave the last touch to his consummate toilette, he offered his grateful
thanks to Providence that his family was
not unworthy of him. [Benjamin Disraeli: *Lothair* I]

ELEPHANT(S)

2   Th' unwieldy elephant,
To make them mirth, us'd all his
                        might, and wreath'd
His lithe proboscis.
[John Milton: *Paradise Lost* IV. 345-347]

3   It was six men of Indostan
    To learning much inclined,
Who went to see the Elephant
    (Though all of them were blind);
That each by observation
    Might satisfy his mind.
[J. G. Saxe: *The Blind Men and the
Elephant*]

4 Women and elephants never forget
an injury. [H. H. Munro ("Saki"): *Reginald, "Reginald on Besetting Sins"*]
*Saki merely added ladies to the very old
belief that elephants have a retentive
memory and a vindictive nature. The
ancient Greeks attributed these qualities
to the camel.*

ELEVATION

5 It takes a great deal of elevation of
thought to produce a very little elevation of life. [Emerson: *Journals* IV. p.
441]

EL GRECO

6 Edgar Degas purchased once
  A fine El Greco, which he kept
Against the wall beside his bed
To hang his pants on while he slept.
[Richard Wilbur: *Museum Piece*]

ELISHA

7 The spirit of Elijah doth rest on
Elisha. [II Kings 2:15]

ELIZABETH

8 The spacious times of great Elizabeth.
[Tennyson: *A Dream of Fair Women*]

ELOQUENCE

9 Then words came like a fall of winter

snow.
[Homer: *Iliad* III]
*Priam is describing to Helen a mission
on which Odysseus and Menelaus had
come to Troy. The Trojans were curious
to hear Odysseus, the famous orator. He
seemed to them slow and stiff, even stupid, until he rose to speak.*

10 There would be no eloquence in the
world if we were to speak only with one
person at a time. [Quintilian: *Institutio
Oratoria* I]

11 It is a man's own breast that makes
him eloquent. [Montaigne: *Essays* III.v.]

12 Taffeta phrases, silken terms precise,
  Three-pil'd hyperboles, spruce affec-
                        tation,
Figures pedantical.
[Shakespeare: *Love's Labour's Lost*
V.ii.]

13 Thy paleness moves me more than
                        eloquence.
[Shakespeare: *The Merchant of Venice*
.III.ii.]

14 Profane eloquence is transferred from
the Bar, where it has become obsolete,
to the Pulpit, where it is out of place.
[La Bruyère: *Les Caractères*]

15 A man whose eloquence has power
  To clear the fullest house in half an
                        hour.
[Soame Jenyns: *Imitations of Horace*
II.i.]

16 You'd scarce expect one of my age
To speak in public on the stage;
And if I chance to fall below
Demosthenes or Cicero,
Don't view me with a critic's eye,
But pass my imperfections by.
Large streams from little fountains
                        flow,
Tall oaks from little acorns grow.
[David Everett: *Lines Written for a
School Declamation* (1791)]

ELOQUENT

17 He is an eloquent man who can treat
humble subjects with delicacy, lofty
things impressively, and moderate things
temperately. [Cicero: *De Oratore*]

ELVES

18 Her eyes the glow-worm lend thee,
  The shooting stars attend thee;
    And the elves also,

Whose little eyes glow
Like the sparks of fire, befriend thee.
[Robert Herrick: *The Night Piece: to Julia*]

1 . . . faery elves,
Whose midnight revels by a forest
side
Or fountain, some belated peasant
sees,
Or dreams he sees, while overhead
the Moon
Sits arbitress, and nearer to the Earth
Wheels her pale course; they, on their
mirth and dance
Intent, with jocond music charm his
ear;
At once with joy and fear his heart
rebounds.
[John Milton: *Paradise Lost* I. 781-788]

EMBERS
2 Where glowing embers through the
room
Teach light to counterfeit a gloom.
[John Milton: *Il Penseroso*]

EMBRYO(S)
3 Embryos and idiots, eremites and
friars,
White, black, and gray, with all their
trumpery.
[John Milton: *Paradise Lost* III. 474-
475]
4 . . . every mortal Jack and Jill has
been
The genius of some amniotic mere.
[W. H. Auden: *Lakes*]
*That is, we all began our being in the
amniotic fluid in our mother's womb.*

EMERSON
5 A gap-toothed and hoary ape . . .
coryphaeus or choragus of his Bulgarian
tribe of auto-coprophagous baboons. . . .
[Swinburne: in a letter to Emerson, January 30, 1874]
*The reference is to Emerson himself
who had been quoted as saying certain
uncomplimentary things about Swinburne. Swinburne told Edmund Gosse
that he had written to Emerson in "language of the strictest reserve."*
6 The Codfish Moses. [H. L. Mencken:
Prejudices: Second Series]

EMINENCE
7 To that bad eminence.
[John Milton: *Paradise Lost* II. 6]

EMPEROR
8 He [the Emperor Galba] seemed
greater than a subject while he was a
subject and, by common consent, would
have been judged able to be emperor,
had he never been emperor. [Tacitus:
History I.xlix.]

EMPHASIS
9 Never italicize. [Emerson: *The Superlative*]

EMPIRE
10 His Majesty's dominions, on which
the sun never sets. [John Wilson: *Noctes
Ambrosianae* (1829)]
*Though this phrase is now commonly
associated with the British Empire, it
was originally applied to Spain. Captain
John Smith first claimed it for the English King James I, saying that he saw
no reason why the Spanish soldiers
should brag. Scott, in his* Life of Napoleon *LIX, applies it to the Emperor
Charles V.*
11 Take up the white man's burden—
Send forth the best ye breed—
Go bind your sons to exile
To serve your captives' need.
[Kipling: *The White Man's Burden*]
12 I have not become the King's First
Minister in order to preside over the
liquidation of the British Empire. [Win-
ston Churchill: in a speech at the Mansion House, November 10, 1942]
13 The empires of the future are empires of the mind. [Winston Churchill:
in an address at Harvard University,
1943]

EMPTY(INESS)
14 The empty vessel makes the greatest
sound.
[Shakespeare: *Henry V* IV.iv.]
15 Such as take lodgings in a head
That's to be let unfurnished.
[Samuel Butler (1612-1680): *Hudibras*]
16 Eternal smiles his emptiness betray,
As shallow streams run dimpling all
the way.
[Alexander Pope: *Epistle to Dr. Arbuthnot*]

1 They cannot scare me with their
empty spaces
Between stars—on stars void of hu-
man races.
I have it in me so much nearer home
To scare myself with my own desert
places.
[Robert Frost: *Desert Places*]

EMULATION

2 Men have a foolish manner (both
parents and schoolmasters and servants)
in creating and breeding an emulation
between brothers during childhood,
which many times sorteth to discord
when they are men and disturbeth families. [Francis Bacon: *Of Parents and
Children*]
sorteth = *turns*

3 Envy, to which th' ignoble mind's a
slave,
Is emulation in the learn'd or brave.
[Alexander Pope: *An Essay on Man* II]

END(S)

4 Better is the end of a thing than the
beginning thereof. [Ecclesiastes 7:8]
5 All is well that ends well. [John Heywood: *Proverbs* I.x.]
6 Here is my journey's end, here is my
butt,
And very sea-mark of my utmost sail.
[Shakespeare: *Othello* V.ii.]
7 Unarm, Eros; the long day's task is
done,
And we must sleep.
[Shakespeare: *Antony and Cleopatra* IV.
xii.]
8 Nothing is ended with honour which
does not conclude better than it began.
[Samuel Johnson: *The Rambler* No.
207]
9 Ah, when to the heart of man
Was it ever less than a treason
To go with the drift of things,
To yield with a grace to reason,
And bow and accept the end
Of a love or a season.
[Robert Frost: *Reluctance*]
10 Some say the world will end in fire,
Some say in ice.
From what I've tasted of desire
I hold with those who favor fire.
But if it had to perish twice,

I think I know enough of hate
To say that for destruction ice
Is also great
And would suffice.
[Robert Frost: *Fire and Ice*]
11 This is the way the world ends
Not with a bang but a whimper.
[T. S. Eliot: *The Hollow Men*]
12 The end cannot justify the means, for
the simple and obvious reason that the
means employed determine the nature of
the ends produced. [Aldous Huxley:
Ends and Means I]

ENDURANCE

13 Watch ye, stand fast in the faith, quit
you like men, be strong. [I Corinthians
16:13]
14 Having done what men could, they
suffered what men must. [Edith Hamilton: *The Greek Way* IV]
*The reference is to the Athenians who
sailed away to conquer Sicily and slowly
died, as prisoners, in the quarries of
Syracuse. She is quoting from Thucydides.*

ENDURE(D)

15 It is best to bear what can't be altered.
[Seneca: *Epistolae* CVII]
16 What can't be cured must be endured.
[Rabelais V. 16 (trans. by Peter Mot-
teux)]
*Though this is the first known appear-
ance of the proverb in the exact form
we employ, the thought is as old as
literature.*
What can't be cured must be obscured.
Bergen Evans: The Natural
History of Nonsense *I*
17 What's amiss I'll strive to mend,
And endure what can't be mended.
[Isaac Watts: *Good Resolutions*]
18 They endured. [William Faulkner:
The Sound and the Fury, Appendix]
*Faulkner's tribute to the Negro, through
Dilsey.*

ENEMY(IES)

19 Every man is his own chief enemy.
[Anacharsis (6th century B.C.): in Sto-
baeus's *Florilegium* II (A.D. 5th century)]
20 Hast thou found me, O mine enemy?
[I Kings 21:20]
21 If thine enemy be hungry, give him

bread to eat. [Proverbs 25:21]

1 His enemies shall lick the dust. [Psalms 72:9]

2 A man's enemies are the men of his own house. [Micah 7:6]

3 Love your enemies, bless them that curse you, do good to them that hate you, and pray for them which despitefully use you, and persecute you. [Matthew 5:44]

4 Vengeance is mine; I will repay, saith the Lord.

Therefore if thine enemy hunger, feed him; if he thirst, give him drink: for in so doing thou shalt heap coals of fire on his head. [Romans 12:19-20]

St. Paul is quoting Proverbs 25:21-22.

The coals of fire seems to be a metaphor for the hot shame of the enemy when our superior behavior makes him realize what a dreadful person he is. But many ingrates are remarkably cool.

5 He is his own worst enemy. [Cicero: *Ad Atticum* X.viii.]

Cicero was referring to Julius Caesar. If Caesar was his own worst enemy, it was certainly a large preeminence.

It is said that when this saying was applied in his hearing to someone whom Sir Winston Churchill disliked, he quipped: "Not while I live!"

6 The body of a dead enemy always smells sweet. [Aulus Vitellius: in Suetonius's *Vitellius* X]

Suetonius regarded this as an "abominable saying," but it has at least a certain gruesome honesty, a vital hostility.

7 Every wys man dredeth his enemy. [Chaucer: *The Tale of Melibeus*]

8 My near'st and dearest enemy. [Shakespeare: *I Henry IV* III.ii.]

9 Take heed of a reconciled enemy. [Robert Burton: *The Anatomy of Melancholy* II.3.7]

10 Yet is every man his greatest enemy, and, as it were, his own executioner. [Sir Thomas Browne: *Religio Medici* II.iv.]

11 If you have no enemies, it is a sign fortune has forgot you. [Thomas Fuller (1654-1734): *Gnomologia*]

12 I have never made but one prayer to God, a very short one: "O Lord, make my enemies ridiculous." And God granted it. [Voltaire: Letter to M. Damilaville, May 16, 1767]

A splendid instance of God's helping those who help themselves.

13 There is no little enemy. [Benjamin Franklin: *Poor Richard's Almanack* (1733)]

14 If we could read the secret history of our enemies, we should find in each man's life sorrow and suffering enough to disarm all hostility. [Longfellow: *Driftwood*]

15 For my enemy is dead, a man divine as myself is dead.
[Walt Whitman: *Leaves of Grass,* "Reconciliation"]

16 He hasn't an enemy in the world, and none of his friends like him. [Oscar Wilde: speaking of G. B. Shaw]

Quoted in Shaw's Sixteen Self Sketches.

17 A man cannot be too careful in the choice of his enemies. [Oscar Wilde: *Picture of Dorian Gray* I]

ENGLAND

18 This England never did, nor never shall,
Lie at the proud foot of a conqueror,
But when it first did help to wound itself:
Now these her princes are come home again,
Come the three corners of the world in arms,
And we shall shock them: Nought shall make us rue,
If England to itself do rest but true.
[Shakespeare: *King John* V.vii.]

19 This royal throne of kings, this sceptred isle,
This earth of majesty, this seat of Mars,
This other Eden, demi-paradise,
This fortress built by Nature for herself
Against infection and the hand of war,
This happy breed of men, this little world,
This precious stone set in the silver sea,
Which serves it in the office of a wall
Or as a moat defensive to a house,
Against the envy of less happier lands,
This blessed plot, this earth, this realm, this England,

This nurse, this teeming womb of
    royal kings,
Fear'd by their breed and famous by
    their birth.
[Shakespeare: *Richard II* II.i.]

1 The harlot's cry from street to street
    Shall weave old England's winding-
        sheet,
The winner's shout, the loser's curse,
Dance before dead England's hearse.
[William Blake: *Auguries of Innocence*]

2 Oh, it's a snug little island!
  A right little, tight little island.
[Thomas John Dibdin: *The Snug Little
Island*]
    *There are few things upon which the
    British congratulate themselves more
    warmly than their insularity.*

3 For 'tis a low, newspaper, humdrum,
        lawsuit Country.
[Byron: *Don Juan* XII.lxv.]

4 For England expects—I forbear to
    proceed:
'Tis a maxim tremendous, but trite.
[Lewis Carroll: "The Hunting of the
Snark" IV]

5 All our past acclaims our future:
    Shakespeare's voice and Nelson's
        hand,
Milton's faith and Wordsworth's trust
    in this our chosen and chainless
        land,
Bear us witness: come the world
    against her, England yet shall
        stand.
[Swinburne: *England: An Ode*]

6 And what should they know of Eng-
    land who only England know?
[Kipling: *The English Flag*]

7 If I should die, think only this of me:
  That there's some corner of a for-
      eign field
That is forever England. There shall
    be
In that rich earth a richer dust con-
      cealed;
A dust whom England bore, shaped,
    made aware;
Gave, once, her flowers to love, her
    ways to roam,
A body of England's breathing Eng-
      lish air,
Washed by the rivers, blest by suns
    of home.
[Rupert Brooke: *The Soldier*]

ENGLISH (LANGUAGE)

8 Here will be an old abusing of God's
patience and the king's English. [Shake-
speare: *The Merry Wives of Windsor*
I.iv.]

9 I am biased in favour of boys learning English; and then I would let the
clever ones learn Latin as an honour,
and Greek as a treat. [Winston Churchill: *My Early Life* (1930), "Roving Commission"]

ENGLISH (PEOPLE)

10 The English take their pleasures sadly,
after the fashion of their country. [Duc
De Sully: *Memoirs*]

11 But we, brave Britons, foreign laws
    despised,
And kept unconquered and uncivi-
    lized.
[Alexander Pope: *Essay on Criticism*
III]

12 They are like their own beer: froth
on top, dregs at the bottom, the middle
excellent. [Voltaire: referring to the Brit-
ish]

13 Not only England, but every Englishman is an island. [Novalis: *Fragments*
(1799)]

14 I thank the goodness and the grace
    Which on my birth have smiled,
And made me, in these Christian
    days,
    A happy English child.
[Ann and Jane Taylor: *A Child's Hymn
of Praise*]

15 Of all the nations in the world at
present the English are the stupidest in
speech, the wisest in action. [Thomas
Carlyle: *Past and Present* III.v.]

16 How hard it is to make an Englishman acknowledge that he is happy.
[W. M. Thackeray: *Pendennis* I]

17 He is an Englishman!
    For he himself has said it,
    And it's greatly to his credit,
    That he's an Englishman!
    For he might have been a Rooshian
    A French or Turk or Prooshian,
    Or perhaps Itali-an.
    But in spite of all temptations
    To belong to other nations,
    He remains an Englishman.
[W. S. Gilbert: *H.M.S. Pinafore* I]

18 Mad dogs and Englishmen go out in

the midday sun.
[Noel Coward: *Mad Dogs and English-men*]

ENJOY

1 While you are upon earth, enjoy the good things that are here. [John Selden: *Table Talk*, "Pleasure"]

ENJOYMENT

2 For sleep, health and wealth to be truly enjoyed, they must be interrupted. [Jean Paul Richter: *Flower, Fruit, and Thorn Pieces* VIII]
3 He has spent his life best who has enjoyed it most; God will take care that we do not enjoy it any more than is good for us. [Samuel Butler (1835-1902): *The Way of All Flesh* XIX]
4 There are two things to aim at in life: first, to get what you want; and, after that, to enjoy it. Only the wisest of mankind achieve the second. [Logan Pearsall Smith: *Afterthoughts*]

ENLIGHTENMENT

5 The work of the eighteenth century is sound and good. The Encyclopaedists, Diderot at their head, the physiocratists, Turgot at their head, the philosophers, Voltaire at their head, the utopists, Rousseau at their head: these are four sacred legions. To them the immense advance of humanity towards the light is due. [Victor Hugo: *Les Misérables* VII.iii.]

ENMITY

6 Enmity is anger watching the opportunity for revenge. [Cicero: *Tusculan Disputations* IV.ix.]
7 He that is not with me is against me. [Matthew 12:30]
8 Angry friendship is sometimes as bad as calm enmity. [Edmund Burke: *An Appeal from the New to the Old Whigs*]

ENOUGH

9 Enough is abundance to the wise. [Euripides: *The Phoenissae*]
10 Enough is as good as a feast. [John Heywood: *Proverbs* (1546)]
   The proverb had been around for centuries. In 1420 John Lydgate (Assembly of Gods) *had: As good is enough as a great feast. It is also in George Chapman's* Eastward Ho! *(III.ii.), and elsewhere.*
11 Lord! when you have enough, what need you care
How merrily soever others fare?
[Chaucer: Prologue to *The Wife of Bath's Tale* (Pope's trans.)]
12 Give us enough, but with a sparing hand. [Edmund Waller: *Reflections*]
13 You never know what is enough unless you know what is more than enough. [William Blake: *Proverbs of Hell*]

ENTHUSIASM

14 Nothing great was ever achieved without enthusiasm. [Emerson: *Circles*]
15 Moreover, idealism cannot support itself without enthusiasm, which is a force no less destructive and incalculable than logic; for, like wine, it puts the judgment in a heat. [F. S. Oliver: *The Endless Adventure*]

ENVY

16 He who is not envied is not enviable. [Aeschylus: *Agamemnon*]
17 Wrath is cruel, and anger is outrageous, but who is able to stand before envy? [Proverbs 27:4]
18 Envy is the adversary of the fortunate. [Epictetus: *Encheiridion*]
19 As iron is eaten by rust, so are the envious consumed by envy. [Antisthenes: in Diogenes Laertius VI.i]
20 Envy, like fire, soars upward. [Livy: *Annals* VIII.xxxi.]
21 The greatest harm that you can do unto the envious, is to do well. [John Lyly: *Euphues*]
22 Neither can he, that mindeth but his own business, find much matter for Envy. For Envy is a gadding passion, and walketh the streets, and doth not keep at home. [Francis Bacon: *Of Envy*]
23 Envy is ever joined with the comparing of a man's self; and where there is no comparison, no envy. [Francis Bacon: *Of Envy*]
24 Envy hath no holidays. [Francis Bacon: *The Advancement of Learning* I]
25 I am Envy. I cannot reade, and therefore wish all bookes were burnt. I am leane with seeing others eate. [Christopher Marlowe: *Dr. Faustus* vi.]

1 Every other sin hath some pleasure annexed to it, or will admit of an excuse: envy alone wants both. [Robert Burton: *The Anatomy of Melancholy* I.2.3.7]

2 The envious man dies every time he hears the man he envies praised. [Gracián: *Oráculo Manual* 162]

3 Qui invidet minor est. (*"He who envies, admits his inferiority."*) [Motto of Lord Cadogan]

A good motto for a noble lord. In practice it usually warranted the complete disdain with which the aristocrat, like Voltaire's Magnifico, Pococurante, regarded all men and all things.

4 Envy, to which th' ignoble mind's a
      slave,
Is emulation in the learn'd or brave.
[Alexander Pope: *An Essay on Man* II]

5 Envy will merit as its shade pursue,
But like a shadow proves the sub-
      stance true.
[Alexander Pope: *Essay on Criticism* II]
shade = *shadow*

6 Whoever envies another confesses his superiority. [Samuel Johnson: *The Rambler* No. 183]

7 Envy is mere unmixed and genuine evil; it pursues a hateful end by despicable means and desires not so much its own happiness as another's misery. [Samuel Johnson: *The Rambler* No. 183]

8 Envy is almost the only vice which is practicable at all times and in every place; the only passion which can never lie quiet for want of irritation; its effects therefore are everywhere discoverable and its attempts always to be dreaded. [Samuel Johnson: *The Rambler* No. 183]

9 Envy may act without expense or danger. To spread suspicion, to invent calumnies, to propagate scandal, requires neither labor nor courage. It is easy for the author of a lie, however malignant, to escape detection, and infamy needs very little industry to assist its circulation. [Samuel Johnson: *The Rambler* No. 183]

10 Envy is the most universal passion. [William Hazlitt: *Characteristics*]

11 The dullard's envy of brilliant men is always assuaged by the suspicion that they will come to a bad end. [Max Beerbohm: *Zuleika Dobson* IV]

EPICS

12 At leisure hours in Epic Song he deals,
Writes to the rumbling of his coach's
      wheels.
[Dryden: Prologue to *The Pilgrim*]

The reference is to Sir Richard Blackmore (d.1729), a physician and one of the most voluminous authors that ever lived. Not content with numerous medical treatises and several poetic paraphrases of the Scriptures, he wrote four epics. In the preface to one of these he stated that they had been written in snatches of leisure in his coach as he made his professional calls. Anyone innocent enough to write epics in the brief intervals of another occupation was a natural target for the wits and they poured out their scorn upon him, even publishing an entire volume of ridicule. But he replied and continued until, as Dr. Johnson said, "benevolence was ashamed to favor, and malice was weary of insulting" (Life of Blackmore). And, "being despised as a poet, [he] was in time neglected as a physician."

EPICURUS

13 For he was Epicurus owene sone.
[Chaucer: Prologue to *The Canterbury Tales*]

The reference is to the Franklin who took a frank delight in eating, maintained a well-stocked larder and cellar and even—a remarkable thing, apparently, in the 14th century—kept his table "dormant," or standing, ready to be laid, in his hall.

EPIDEMICS

14 There are epidemics of nobleness as well as epidemics of disease. [J. A. Froude: *Calvinism*]

EPIGRAM

15 Epigram: A platitude with vine-leaves in its hair. [H. L. Mencken: *A Book of Burlesques*]

In Ibsen's Hedda Gabler, "with vine leaves in his hair" is a phrase expressing inspired abandon, the glory and excitement of the artistic and creative life as opposed to the dullness and cold caution of the ordinary humdrum existence. But the phrase acquires bitter, ironic overtones because Eilert Lovborg, the young author to whom it is applied, dies a sordid death, broken and frustrated. Mencken is implying that the brilliance of most epigrams is simply a shining veneer over some dull commonplace.

1 Epigram: a wisecrack that played Carnegie Hall. [Oscar Levant: *Coronet*, Sept., 1958]

EPITAPHS: comment on
2 In lapidary inscriptions a man is not upon oath. [Samuel Johnson: in Boswell's *Life* (1775)]
> lapidary inscriptions = *epitaphs on a tombstone*
> *"Allowance," Johnson added, "must be made for some degree of exaggerated praise." In his* Essay on Epitaphs *he says: "Though a sepulchral inscription is professedly a panegyric, and therefore not confined to historical impartiality, yet it ought always to be written with regard to truth. No man ought to be commended for virtues which he never possessed, but whoever is curious to know his faults must inquire after them in other places."*

3 EPITAPH. An inscription on a tomb, showing that virtues acquired by death have a retroactive effect. [Ambrose Bierce: *The Devil's Dictionary*]

EPITAPHS: famous and curious
4 Stranger, tell the Lacedaemonians that we lie here, obedient to their commands. [Simonides of Ceos: *Fragment*]
> *Epitaph of the 300 Spartans who, under Leonidas, died at the pass of Thermopylae in 480 B.C. One of the noblest and most moving of all epitaphs.*

5 A boy of five years old serene and gay, Unpitying Hades hurried me away. Yet weep not for Callimachus: if few The days I lived, few were my sorrows too.
[Lucian: *Greek Anthology* VII]
6 I live, I don't know how long; I die, I don't know when; I go, I don't know where; I am amazed that I can be so cheerful! [Anon.]
> *Epitaph of Martius of Biberach, 1498; apparently, a folk saying.*

7 Ho, ho, who lies here?

I the good Erle of Devonshere, And Maulde my wife, that was ful deare. We lived together lv. yeare. That we spent, we had: That we gave, we have: That we lefte, we lost.
[Epitaph on Edward Courtenay, Earl of Devon (d.1419) and his Countess: as quoted by Edmund Spenser in *The Shepheardes Calender*, "May."]
> *It has been remarked that the Earl's losses were enormous.*

8 Good frend for Iesus sake forbeare, To digg the dust encloased heare: Blese be ye man yt spares thes stones, And curst be he yt moves my bones. [Shakespeare's epitaph]
9 Underneath this stone doth lie As much beauty as could die; Which in life did harbour give To more virtue than doth live.
[Ben Jonson: *Epitaph on Elizabeth L. H.*]
10 Underneath this sable hearse Lies the subject of all verse: Sidney's sister, Pembroke's mother. Death, ere thou hast slain another Fair and learn'd and good as she, Time shall throw a dart at thee.
[William Browne: *Epitaph on the Countess of Pembroke*]
11 But here's the sunset of a tedious day. These two asleep are; I'll but be undrest, And so to bed. Pray wish us all good rest.
[Robert Herrick: *Epitaph on Sir Edward Giles*]
12 Her name was Margaret Lucas, youngest sister to the Lord Lucas of Colchester, a Noble Familie: for all the brothers were valiant and all the sisters virtuous. [Unknown: Epitaph on Margaret, Duchess of Newcastle, Westminster Abbey]
13 Born in America, in Europe bred, In Africa travelled, in Asia wed, Where long he lived and thrived, in London dead; Much good, some ill he did, so hope all's even, And that his soul through mercy's gone to heaven.
[Anon.]
> *Inscription on the tomb of Eli Yale, in*

Wrexham Churchyard, North Wales.

1 If you would see his monument, look around. [Sir Christopher Wren's epitaph: in St. Paul's Cathedral, London.]
Wren built the cathedral after the Great Fire of 1666 had destroyed the old St. Paul's.
The inscription, written by his son, reads: Si monumentum requiris circumspice.

2 Warm summer sun, shine kindly here;
Warm southern wind, blow softly here;
Green sod above, lie light, lie light—
Good night, dear heart, good night, good night.
[Mark Twain: inscription on the tombstone of his daughter Susy]
The epitaph was changed slightly from Robert Richardson's Requiem.

3 Cast a cold eye
On life, on death.
Horseman, pass by!
[William Butler Yeats: *Under Ben Bulben*]
Yeats's epitaph for himself.

EPITAPHS: mock and literary

4 I was not.
I was.
I am not.
I do not care.
[Epitaph on a common slave in Rome]

5 The waters were his winding sheet,
the sea was made his tomb;
Yet for his fame the ocean sea was
not sufficient room.
[Richard Barnfield: *On the Death of Hawkins*]

6 In this little urne is laid
Prewdence Baldwin (once my maid),
From whose happy spark here let
Spring the purple violet.
[Robert Herrick: *Upon Prue his Maid*]

7 Here she lies a pretty bud,
Lately made of flesh and blood;
Who, as soon fell fast asleep,
As her little eyes did peep.
Give her strewings, but not stir
The earth that lightly covers her.
[Robert Herrick: *Upon a Child that Died*]

8 Here lies my wife: here let her lie!
Now she's at rest, and so am I.
[Dryden: Epitaph for his wife. Attr.]

There was a literary genre of humorous epitaphs.

9 Here lies our Sovereign Lord the King,
Whose word no man relies on.
He never said a foolish thing,
And never did a wise one.
[John Wilmot, Earl of Rochester: Mock epitaph on Charles II]
King Charles answered: "My words are my own; my actions are those of my ministers."

10 Under this stone, Reader, survey
Dead Sir John Vanbrugh's house of clay.
Lie heavy on him, Earth! for he
Laid many heavy loads on thee!
[Abel Evans: Epitaph on Sir John Vanbrugh]
Vanbrugh was a playwright and an architect. His masterpiece is Blenheim Palace, an enormous building.

11 Here lies Lord Coningsby—be civil!
The rest God knows—perhaps the Devil.
[Alexander Pope: *Epitaph on Lord Coningsby*]

12 Here lies Fred,
Who was alive and is dead;
Had it been his father,
I had much rather;
Had it been his brother,
Still better than the other;
Had it been his sister,
No one would have missed her;
Had it been the whole generation,
All the better for the nation;
But since 'tis only Fred,
That was alive and is dead,
Why, there's no more to be said.
[Anon.: Epitaph on Frederick, Prince of Wales (1751)]

13 Here lies David Garrick, describe me who can,
An abridgment of all that was pleasant in man.
[Oliver Goldsmith: *Retaliation*]

14 If there's another world, he lives in bliss;
If there is none, he made the best of this.
[Burns: *Epitaph on Wm. Muir*]

15 Here lies the preacher, judge, and poet, Peter,
Who broke the laws of God, and man,

and metre.

[Lord Francis Jeffrey: *On Peter Robinson*]

1 But Tom's no more—and so no more
of Tom.

[Byron: *Don Juan* XI.xx.]

2 Posterity will ne'er survey
A nobler grave than this:
Here lie the bones of Castlereagh:
Stop, traveller, P——.

[Byron: *Epitaph*]

3 Green be the turf above thee,
Friend of my better days!
None knew thee but to love thee,
Nor named thee but to praise.

[Fitz-Greene Halleck: *On the Death of
Joseph Rodman Drake*]

4 Here lie I, Martin Elginbrodde:
Hae mercy o' my soul, Lord God;
As I wad do, were I Lord God
And ye were Martin Elginbrodde.

[George MacDonald: *David Elginbrod* I]
Ascribed in varied forms to many churchyards but never actually seen.

5 I'm Smith of Stoke, aged sixty-odd,
I've lived without a dame
From youth-time on; and would to
God
My dad had done the same.

[Thomas Hardy: *Epitaph on a Pessimist*]

6 Here lies a most beautiful Lady,
Light of step and heart was she;
I think she was the most beautiful
lady
That ever was in the West Country.

[Walter John De La Mare: *Epitaph*]

7 By and by
God caught his eye.

[David McCord: *Epitaphs*, "The
Waiter"]

8 Here lies the body of Mike O'Day
Who died maintaining his right of
way.
His right was clear, his will was
strong,
But he's just as dead as if he'd been
wrong.

[Author unknown]

9 Don't mourn for me now,
Don't mourn for me never;
I'm going to do nothing
For ever and ever.

[*The Tired Woman's Epitaph* (author
unknown)]

EPITAPHS: self-written

10 Fuller's earth. [Thomas Fuller's
(1608-1661) epitaph for himself.]
An instance of a moribund joke.

*Fuller's earth, a hydrous silicate of
alumina, was used for centuries to clean
cloth.*

11 Here lies the body of Jonathan Swift
. . . where, at last, savage indignation
can no longer lacerate his heart. [Translation of Jonathan Swift's epitaph, which
he wrote himself. It is inscribed over his
grave in St. Patrick's Cathedral, Dublin.]
*The Latin is: . . . ubi saeva indignatio
ulterius cor lacerare nequit.*

12 Life is a jest, and all things show it,
I thought so once, but now I know it.

[John Gay: *My Own Epitaph*]

13 Beneath this stone old Abraham lies;
Nobody laughs and nobody cries.
Where he is gone and how he fares,
Nobody knows, and nobody cares.

[Abraham Newland: *His own epitaph*]

14   The body of
Benjamin Franklin, printer,
(Like the cover of an old book,
Its contents worn out,
And stript of its lettering and gilding)
Lies here, food for worms!
Yet the work itself shall not be lost,
For it will, as he believed, appear
once more
In a new
And more beautiful edition,
Corrected and amended
By its Author!

[Benjamin Franklin: Epitaph for himself]

15 Let there be no inscription upon my
tomb; let no man write my epitaph; no
man can write my epitaph. [Robert
Emmet: Speech on his trial and conviction for high treason, September, 1803]

16 Beneath this sod
A poet lies, or that which once
seemed he—
Oh, lift a thought in prayer for
S.T.C.!
That he, who many a year, with toil
of breath,
Found death in life, may here find
life in death.

[Samuel Taylor Coleridge: Epitaph written for himself (1833)]

1 Here lies one whose name was writ in water. [Inscription, at his own request, on John Keats's tombstone]

2 Under the wide and starry sky,
Dig the grave and let me lie.
Glad did I live and gladly die,
    And I laid me down with a will.
This be the verse you grave for me:
"Here he lies where he longed to be;
Home is the sailor, home from sea,
    And the hunter home from the
                                    hill."
[R. L. Stevenson: *Requiem*]

3 Excuse my dust. [Dorothy Parker: her own epitaph]

4 Here lies a nuisance dedicated to sanity. [David Low, the cartoonist's epitaph for himself, quoted in the *New York Times*, Sept. 29, 1963]

E PLURIBUS UNUM

5 E Pluribus Unum. [Motto of the *Gentleman's Journal* (1692), adopted as the motto for the seal of the United States, 1776]

EQUAL

6 All animals are equal, but some animals are more equal than others. [George Orwell: *Animal Farm* X]

EQUALITARIANISM

7 Your levellers wish to level *down* as far as themselves; but they cannot bear levelling *up* to themselves. [Samuel Johnson: in Boswell's *Life*, July 21, 1763]

EQUALITY

8 Equality is the chief groundwork of equity. [Montaigne: *Essays* I.xix.]

9 We hold these truths to be self-evident, that all men are created equal, that they are endowed by their creator with certain unalienable rights, that among these are Life, Liberty, and the Pursuit of Happiness. [*Declaration of Independence*]

10 One man is as good as another—and a great dale better, as the Irish philosopher said. [W. M. Thackeray: *Roundabout Papers*, "On Ribbons"]

11 The doctrine that all men are, in any sense, or have been, at any time, free and equal, is an utterly baseless fiction. [T.

H. Huxley: *On the Natural Inequality of Man* (1890)]

12 That all men are equal is a proposition to which, at ordinary times, no sane individual has ever given his assent. [Aldous Huxley: *Proper Studies*]

13 We conclude that in the field of public education the doctrine of "separate but equal" has no place. Separate educational facilities are inherently unequal. [Earl Warren, *Brown v. The Board of Education*, May 17, 1954]

EQUANIMITY

14 A man that fortune's buffets and rewards
Hast ta'en with equal thanks.
[Shakespeare: *Hamlet* III.ii.]

EQUESTRIANISM

15 The British upper classes cannot "tolerate the notion that the stable at Bethany was a common peasant farmer's stable instead of a first-rate racing one." [G. B. Shaw: Preface to *The Doctor's Dilemma*]

EQUITY

16 Equity is according to the conscience of him that is Chancellor, and as that is larger or narrower, so is Equity. [John Selden: *Table Talk*, "Equity"]

EQUIVOCATION

17 How absolute the knave is! We must speak by the card, or equivocation will undo us. [Shakespeare: *Hamlet* V.i.]
card = *the circular piece of stiff paper on which the 32 points are marked in the mariner's compass.*
to speak by the card = *to express oneself with nicety, to be exact to a point.*
    Hamlet had asked the gravedigger for what man he was digging a grave. The gravedigger said for no man. For what woman, then? Hamlet asks. For no woman, says the gravedigger in triumph; but for one that was a woman.
    The niggling of the ignorant, in this manner, and their triumphant assumption that they are thereby being precise, is often noted in Shakespeare's plays.

18 And be these juggling fiends no more
                                    believed,
That palter with us in a double sense;

That keep the word of promise to
our ear,
And break it to our hope.
[Shakespeare: *Macbeth* V.vii.]
palter = *to speak evasively, equivocate*

ERASMUS

1 Erasmus, that great injur'd name,
(The glory of the priesthood and the
shame!)
[Alexander Pope: *An Essay on Criticism*
III]
2 Erasmus laid the egg of the Reforma-
tion and Luther hatched it. [R. C.
Trench: *Medieval Church History*
XXVI]

ERR

3 Men are men; they needs must err.
[Euripides: *Hippolytus*]
4 To err is human, to forgive divine.
[Alexander Pope: *An Essay on Criticism*
II]

*The first part of Pope's thought goes
back at least to Seneca's* Humanum est
errare, *and is a proverb in every language.*
To err is human.
　　　　Melchior de Polignac: Anti-Lucre-
　　　　　　　　　　　　　　tius

ERRANDS

5 This is a slight unmeritable man,
Meet to be sent on errands.
[Shakespeare: *Julius Caesar* IV.i.]
*When Johnson and Boswell were visiting
the Duke of Argyle at Inverary, the duke
sent a gentleman to fetch a piece of
marble which he wished to show Johnson. The gentleman brought a wrong
piece and the duke sent him back. Boswell says: "He could not refuse; but, to
avoid any appearance of servility, he
whistled as he walked out of the room,
to show his independency. On my men-
tioning this afterwards to Dr. Johnson,
he said it was a nice trait of character."
(Boswell:* Journal of a Tour to the Hebrides, *October 25, 1773)*

ERROR

6 In law, what plea so tainted and corrupt
But, being season'd with a gracious
voice,

Obscures the show of evil? In religion,
What damned error, but some sober
brow
Will bless it and approve it with a
text?
[Shakespeare: *The Merchant of Venice*
III.ii.]
7 What can we know, or what can we
discern,
When error chokes the windows of
the mind?
[Sir John Davies: *The Vanity of Human
Learning* XV]
8 All men are liable to error; and most
men are, in many points, by passion or
interest, under temptation to it. [John
Locke: *An Essay Concerning Human
Understanding* XX]
9 An error is the more dangerous in
proportion to the degree of truth which
it contains. [Henri Amiel: *Journal,* December 26, 1852]

ESTATE

10 He has a good estate but the right
owner keeps it from him. [John Ray:
English Proverbs (1670)]
*An old joke. Like: "I'd be rich if people
would only pay me what I owe them."*

ETERNAL

11 This was, and is, and yet men shal it
see.
[Chaucer: *Troilus and Criseyde* I]

ETERNITY

12 The created world is but a small
parenthesis in eternity. [Sir Thomas
Browne: *Christian Morals*]
13 I saw Eternity the other night
Like a great ring of pure and endless
light.
All calm, as it was bright;
And round beneath it, Time in hours,
days, years,
Driv'n by the spheres
Like a vast shadow mov'd; in which
the world
And all her train were hurled.
[Henry Vaughan: *The World*]
14 A thousand ages in Thy sight
Are like an evening gone;
Short as the watch that ends the night
Before the rising sun.
[Isaac Watts: Paraphrase of the 90th

Psalm, 4th verse]
AV: For a thousand years in thy sight
are but as yesterday when it is past, and
as a watch in the night.

1 Many an Aeon moulded earth before
   her highest, man, was born,
   Many an Aeon too may pass when
   earth is manless and forlorn.
[Tennyson: *Locksley Hall Sixty Years
After*]

2 Little drops of water, little grains of
   sand,
   Make the mighty ocean and the pleas-
   ant land.
   So the little moments, humble though
   they be,
   Make the mighty ages of eternity.
[Julia A. Fletcher Carney: *Little
Things*]

3 Till the sun grows cold,
   And the stars are old,
   And the leaves of the Judgment Book
   unfold.
[Bayard Taylor: *Bedouin Song*]

4 Many times man lives and dies
   Between his two eternities.
[William Butler Yeats: *Under Ben Bul-
ben*]

ETYMOLOGY

5   Philologists, who chase
   A panting syllable through time and
   space,
   Start it at home, and hunt it in the
   dark,
   To Gaul, to Greece, and into Noah's
   Ark.
[William Cowper: *Retirement*]

6 Examine Language; what, if you except some few primitive elements (of
natural sound), what is it all but Meta-
phors, recognized as such, or no longer
recognized? [Thomas Carlyle: *Sartor
Resartus* I.ii.]

EUNUCHS

7 There are some eunuchs, which were
so born from their mother's womb: and
there are some eunuchs, which were
made eunuchs of men: and there be
eunuchs, which have made themselves
eunuchs for the kingdom of heaven's
sake. [Matthew 19:12]
   *The Skoptsi, a religious sect that flour-
   ished in Russia in the 18th and 19th*

centuries, "made themselves eunuchs for
the kingdom of heaven's sake." The practice has appeared in many places through
the centuries. Tertullian said that "the
kingdom of Heaven is thrown open to all
eunuchs" (De monogamia).

EUREKA

8 *Eureka!* ("I have found it!")
   *The story is that Hieron II, the ruler of
   Syracuse was suspicious that base metal
   had been introduced into his golden
   crown and asked the mathematician
   Archimedes (287-212 B.C.) to decide
   whether it had. Archimedes was at a
   loss—since, apparently, the crown could
   not be melted down—until one day,
   upon his observing the displacement of
   water in his bath by his body, the means
   of testing (by specific gravity) occurred
   to him and in excitement at the discovery he rushed naked through the
   streets joyfully shouting* Eureka!

EUROPE

9 We go to Europe to be Americanized.
[Emerson: *Conduct of Life,* "Culture"]

EUXINE

10 There's not a sea the passenger e'er
                              pukes in,
   Turns up more dangerous breakers
                         than the Euxine.
[Byron: *Don Juan* V.v.]
   *These lines occur at the end of a moving
   description. It is as though Byron sought
   to move the reader and then to scorn
   him for being moved. In his own time
   this was thought to show "the degrada-
   tion of his bold, bad character." We are
   more inclined to see it as an attempt
   to inflict on his reader some of his own
   suffering, perhaps based on his deformity.*

EVANGELISM

11 From Greenland's icy mountains,
   From India's coral strand,
   Where Afric's sunny fountains
   Roll down their golden sand;
   From many an ancient river,
   From many a palmy plain,
   They call us to deliver
   Their land from error's chain.
[Reginald Heber: *Missionary Hymn*]

EVASION

1 He passed by on the other side. [Luke 10:31]

EVEN

2 "Now we are even," quoth Steven, when he gave his wife six blows to one. [Jonathan Swift: Letter to Stella, Jan. 20, 1711]

EVENING

3 Evening, thou that bringest back all that bright morning scattered; thou bringest the sheep, thou bringest the goat, thou bringest the child back to its mother. [Sappho: *Fragment*]

4 Now was the hour that wakens fond
    desire
In men at sea, and melts their
    thoughtful hearts, . . .
And pilgrim, newly on his road, with
    love
Thrills if he hear the vesper bell
    from far
That seems to mourn for the expir-
    ing day.
[Dante: *Purgatorio* VIII.i (translated by Cary)]

5 For though the day be never so longe,
At last the belles ringeth to evensonge.
[Stephen Hawes: *Passetyme of Pleasure* XLII]

6 The gaudy, blabbing, and remorseful
    day
Is crept into the bosom of the sea.
[Shakespeare: *II Henry VI* IV.i.]

7   When the gray-hooded Even,
Like a sad votarist in palmer's weed,
Rose from the hindmost wheels of
    Phoebus' wain.
[John Milton: *Comus*]

8 And the gilded car of day
His glowing axle doth allay
In the steep Atlantic stream.
[John Milton: *Comus*]

9 And now the Sun had stretched out
    all the hills,
And now was dropt into the Western
    bay.
[John Milton: *Lycidas*]

10 Now came still evening on, and twi-
    light gray
Had in her sober livery all things
    clad.
[John Milton: *Paradise Lost* IV. 598-599]

11 Now fades the glimmering landscape
    on the sight,
And all the air a solemn stillness
    holds.
[Thomas Gray: *Elegy Written in a Country Churchyard*]

12 The curfew tolls the knell of parting
    day,
The lowing herd wind slowly o'er
    the lea,
The ploughman homeward plods his
    weary way,
And leaves the world to darkness and
    to me.
[Thomas Gray: *Elegy Written in a Country Churchyard*]

13 It is a beauteous evening, calm and
    free;
The holy time is quiet as a Nun
Breathless with adoration.
[Wordsworth: *It is a Beauteous Evening*]

14   All this long eve, so balmy and se-
    rene,
Have I been gazing on the western
    sky,
And its peculiar tint of yellow green:
And still I gaze—and with how blank
    an eye!
And those thin clouds above, in flakes
    and bars,
That give away their motion to the
    stars;
Those stars, that glide behind them
    or between,
Now sparkling, now bedimmed, but
    always seen:
Yon crescent moon, as fixed as if it
    grew
In its own cloudless, starless lake of
    blue;
I see them all so excellently fair,
I see, not feel, how beautiful they are!
[Coleridge: *Dejection*]

15 It is the hour when from the boughs
The nightingale's high note is heard;
It is the hour when lovers' vows
Seem sweet in every whispered word;
And gentle winds and waters near,
Make music to the lonely ear.
[Byron: *Parisina* I]

16 Oh, Hesperus! thou bringest all good
    things—
Home to the weary, to the hungry

cheer,
To the young bird the parent's brood-
ing wings,
The welcome stall to the o'erlabor'd
steer;
Whate'er of peace about our hearth-
stone clings,
Whate'er our household gods protect
of dear,
Are gather'd round us by thy look of
rest;
Thou bring'st the child, too, to the
mother's breast.
[Byron: *Don Juan* III.cvii.]

1 Soft hour! which wakes the wish and
melts the heart
Of those who sail the seas, on the
first day
When they from their sweet friends
are torn apart;
Or fills with love the pilgrim on his
way
As the far bell of vesper makes him
start,
Seeming to weep the dying day's
decay;
Is this a fancy which our reason
scorns?
Ah, surely nothing dies but something mourns!
[Byron: *Don Juan* III.cviii.]

2 The day is done, and the darkness
Falls from the wings of night,
As a feather is wafted downward
From an eagle in its flight.
[Longfellow: *The Day is Done*]

3 The shades of night were falling fast.
[Longfellow: *Excelsior*]

4 The lights begin to twinkle from the
rocks:
The long day wanes: the slow moon
climbs: the deep
Moans round with many voices.
[Tennyson: *Ulysses*]

5 Now the day is over,
Night is drawing nigh,
Shadows of the evening
Steal across the sky.
[Sabine Baring-Gould: *Now the Day is
Over*]

6 The sun is down and drinks away
From air and land the lees of day.
[A. E. Housman: *Last Poems* I]

7 At the violet hour, when the eyes
and back

Turn upward from the desk, when
the human engine waits
Like a taxi throbbing waiting . . .
At the violet hour, the evening hour
that strives
Homeward, and brings the sailor
home from sea,
The typist home at teatime.
[T. S. Eliot: *The Waste Land* III]

EVENT(S)

8 The event corresponds less to expectations in war than in any other case
whatever. [Livy: *History of Rome* XXX]

9 There is no faith, and no stoicism,
and no philosophy, that a mortal man
can possibly evoke, which will stand the
final test in a real impassioned onset of
Life and Passion upon him. Faith and
philosophy are air, but events are brass.
[Herman Melville: *Pierre*]

EVER

10 For ever and a day.
[Shakespeare: *As You Like It* IV.i.]

EVERYONE

11 Everyone is as God made him, and
often a great deal worse. [Cervantes:
Don Quixote XI.v.]

EVIDENCE

12 Some circumstantial evidence is very
strong, as when you find a trout in the
milk. [Thoreau: *Journal,* Nov. 11, 1854]

EVIL

13 The gods can either take away evil
from the world and will not, or, being
willing to do so cannot; or they neither
can nor will, or lastly, they are both able
and willing. If they have the will to remove evil and cannot, then they are not
omnipotent. If they can, but will not,
then they are not benevolent. If they are
neither able nor willing, then they
are neither omnipotent nor benevolent.
Lastly, if they are both able and willing
to annihilate evil, how does it exist?
[Epicurus: *Aphorisms*]

14 Evil communications corrupt good
manners. [Menander: *Thais,* Fragment;
Euripides: *Fragment*]
  *Quoted by St. Paul, in I Corinthians
  15:33.*

1 Whoever takes it upon himself to establish a commonwealth and prescribe laws must presuppose all men naturally bad, and that they will yield to their innate evil passions as often as they can do so with safety. [Machiavelli: *Discourse on Livy* I]

2 When better choices are not to be had,
We needs must take the seeming best
of bad.
[Samuel Daniel: *The History of the Civile Warres* II.xxiv.]

3 And simple truth miscall'd simplicity,
And captive good attending captain
ill.
[Shakespeare: *Sonnets* LXVI]

4   Foul deeds will rise,
Though all the earth o'erwhelm them,
to men's eyes.
[Shakespeare: *Hamlet* I.ii.]

5 Good and evil, we know, in the field of this world grow up together almost inseparably. [John Milton: *Areopagitica*]

6 Evil, be thou my good.
[John Milton: *Paradise Lost* IV. 110]

7 More safe I sing with mortal voice,
unchang'd
To hoarse or mute, though fall'n on
evil days,
On evil days though fall'n, and evil
tongues,
In darkness, and with dangers compass'd round,
And solitude.
[John Milton: *Paradise Lost* VIII. 24]

8 No man is clever enough to know all the evil he does. [La Rochefoucauld: *Maxims*]

9 . . . my mind is no more shocked at seeing a man a rogue, unjust, or selfish, than at seeing vultures eager for prey, mischievous apes, or fury-lashed wolves. [Molière: *The Misanthrope* I.i.]

10 Men never do evil so completely and cheerfully as when they do it from religious conviction. [Pascal: *Pensées*]

11 Those who do evil to others, hate them. [Vauvenargues: *Réflexions*]

12 There are a thousand hacking at the branches of evil to one who is striking at the root. [Thoreau: *Walden* I]

13 For every evil under the sun,
There is a remedy, or there is none;
If there be one, try and find it,

If there be none, never mind it.
[William C. Hazlitt: *English Proverbs* (1869)]

14 The resolution to avoid an evil is seldom framed till the evil is so far advanced as to make avoidance impossible. [Thomas Hardy: *Far from the Madding Crowd* XVIII]

15 The belief in a supernatural source of evil is not necessary; men alone are quite capable of every wickedness. [Joseph Conrad: *Under Western Eyes* II.iv.]

16 It is a sin to believe evil of others, but it is seldom a mistake. [H. L. Mencken: *A Book of Burlesques*]

17 Evil is unspectacular and always human
And shares our bed and eats at our
own table.
[W. H. Auden: *Herman Melville*]

EVOLUTION

18 Man is descended from a hairy, tailed quadruped, probably arboreal in its habits. [Charles Darwin: *The Descent of Man* XXI]

19 When you were a tadpole and I was
a fish,
In the Paleozoic time,
And side by side on the ebbing tide,
We sprawled through the ooze and
slime, . . .
My heart was rife with the joy of life,
For I loved you even then.
[Langdon Smith: *Evolution*]

20 A fire-mist and a planet—
A crystal and a cell—
A jellyfish and a saurian,
And caves where the cave-men
dwell;
Then a sense of law and beauty,
And a face turned from the clod—
Some call it Evolution,
And others call it God.
[W. H. Carruth: *Each In His Own Tongue*]

21 Nevertheless, it is even harder for the average ape to believe that he has descended from man. [H. L. Mencken: *Chrestomathy* 618]

EXAGGERATION

22 Hyperboles are the peculiar property of young men; they betray a vehement nature. [Aristotle: *Rhetoric* III]

1 The speaking in perpetual hyperbole is comely in nothing but in love. [Francis Bacon: *Of Love*]

2 They draw the long bow better now than ever. [Byron: *Don Juan* XVI.i.]
"Drawing the long bow" has been a term for lying in English since about the time the longbow went out of use as a weapon. The "long" of it may have had something to do with it (as we say "stretching it a little"), but it may simply be that the boasts of the old longbow men exceeded credence. It was certainly a proverb for gross exaggeration by 1678.

3 The report of my death was an exaggeration. [Mark Twain: Cablegram from London to a New York newspaper, June 2, 1897]

EXAMINATION(S)

4 Examinations are formidable even to the best prepared, for the greatest fool may ask more than the wisest man can answer. [C. C. Colton: *Lacon*]

5 In an examination those who do not wish to know ask questions of those who cannot tell. [Sir Walter Raleigh (1861-1922): *Some Thoughts on Examinations*]

EXAMPLE(S)

6 This noble ensample to his sheep he gave,
That first he wrought, and afterward he taughte.
Out of the gospel he tho wordes caughte;
And this figure he added eek thereto,
That if gold ruste, what shall iron do?
For if a preest be foul, on whom we trust,
No wonder is a lewd man to rust.
[Chaucer: Prologue to *The Canterbury Tales*]
lewd man = *layman*
The reference is to the Good Parson, the ideal cleric.

7 Examples draw where precept fails,
And sermons are less read than tales.
[Matthew Prior: *The Turtle and the Sparrow*]

8 A good Example is the best Sermon. [Benjamin Franklin: *Poor Richard's Almanack* (1747)]

9 Setting too Good an Example is a kind of Slander seldom forgiven. [Benjamin Franklin: *Poor Richard's Almanack* (1753)]

10 Example is the school of mankind, and they will learn at no other. [Edmund Burke: *On a Regicide Peace*]

11 Lives of great men all remind us
We can make our lives sublime,
And, departing, leave behind us
Footprints on the sands of time.
[Longfellow: *A Psalm of Life*]
Famous but unfortunate: the sand is a particularly impermanent place to leave a footstep. And then the image conjures up thoughts of Robinson Crusoe and Man Friday.

12 Few things are harder to put up with than the annoyance of a good example. [Mark Twain: *Pudd'nhead Wilson's Calendar*]

EXCELLENCE

13 I assure you I had rather excel others in the knowledge of what is excellent, than in the extent of my power and dominion. [Plutarch: *Lives,* "Alexander"]

14 Still constant in a wondrous excellence.
[Shakespeare: *Sonnets* CV]

15 The choice and master spirits of this age.
[Shakespeare: *Julius Caesar* III.i.]

EXCEPTION

16 The exception proves the rule. [John Wilson: *The Cheats,* "To the Reader" (1664)]
Probably an established saying. Proves here does not mean confirms *but* tests; *that which does not conform to the rule compels us to examine the rule. To speak the phrase—as it is often spoken —as though, by some inevitable paradox, that which fails to confirm of necessity confirms, is to talk nonsense.*

EXCESS

17 Nothing to excess. [Inscription in the Temple of Apollo at Delphi]

18 All actions beyond the ordinary limits are subject to a sinister interpretation. [Montaigne: *Essays* II.ii.]

1 He that is too much in anything, so that he giveth another occasion of satiety, maketh himself cheap. [Francis Bacon: *Of Ceremonies and Respects*]

2 To gild refined gold, to paint the lily,
To throw a perfume on the violet,
To smooth the ice, or add another hue
Unto the rainbow, or with taper-light
To seek the beauteous eye of heaven to garnish,
Is wasteful and ridiculous excess.
[Shakespeare: *King John* IV.ii.]
In the commonly-heard phrase "to gild the lily," the gild has jumped from the first half of the first line to the second half.

3 Why then, can one desire too much of a good thing?
[Shakespeare: *As You Like It* IV.i.]
Already a proverb, since it is also in Cervantes: Don Quixote (1605, 1615) I.i.6.

4 So over violent, or over civil,
That every man with him was God or Devil.
[Dryden: *Absalom and Achitophel* I. 557]

5 The road of excess leads to the palace of wisdom. [William Blake: *Proverbs of Hell*]

EXCHANGE
6 A fair exchange was no robbery. [Smollett: *Roderick Random* XLI]
Smollett was quoting a saying at least a century old.

EXCISE
7 A hateful tax levied upon commodities, and adjudged not by the common judges of property, but wretches hired by those to whom excise is paid. [Samuel Johnson: Definition of *excise* in the *Dictionary* (1755)]
We who pay our enormous taxes with desperate docility are astonished to see how indignant the slightest exaction made our forefathers.
The Commissioners of the Excise were so incensed at Johnson's definition that they sought an opinion of the Attorney General whether it was actionable or no. The Attorney General expressed the opinion that it was actionable but that it would be wise to take no action.

EXCUSE(S)
8 The man that deceiveth his neighbour, and saith, Am not I in sport? [Proverbs 26:19]

9 The ydel man excuseth hym in winter, by cause of the grete cold; and in somer, by enchesoun of the hete. [Chaucer: *Tale of Melibeus*]
enchesoun = *occasion*
Chaucer ascribes the passage to "a versifiour."

10 Give me six lines written by the most honorable of men, and I will find an excuse in them to hang him. [Cardinal Richelieu: *Mirame*]

11 A staff is quickly found to beat a dog. [Shakespeare: *II Henry VI* III.i.]

12 And oftentimes excusing of a fault
Doth make the fault the worse by the excuse.
[Shakespeare: *King John* IV.ii.]

13 He who excuses himself accuses himself. [Gabriel Meurier: *Trésor des Sentences*]

14 Hence with denial vain, and coy excuse.
[John Milton: *Lycidas*]

15 An excuse is a lie guarded.
[Jonathan Swift: *Thoughts on Various Subjects*]

EXECUTION
16 The execution of malefactors is not more for the credit of governors than the death of patients is for the credit of physicians. [Benjamin Whichcote: *Moral and Religious Aphorisms*]

17 They hang us now in Shrewsbury jail:
The whistles blow forlorn,
And trains all night groan on the rail
To men that die at morn.
[A. E. Housman: *A Shropshire Lad* IX]

EXECUTIONER
18 Behold the Lord High Executioner!
A personage of noble rank and title—
A dignified and potent officer,
Whose functions are particularly vital.
[W. S. Gilbert: *The Mikado* I]

EXERCISE
19 For bodily exercise profiteth little.

[I Timothy 4:8]
1 He used for exercise to walk to the alehouse; but he was carried back again. [Samuel Johnson: in Boswell's *Life,* May 24, 1763]

The reference is to Christopher Smart, the author of the poem A Song to David *(1763).*

2 I get my exercise acting as pallbearer to my friends who exercise. [Chauncey Depew: when asked if he took regular exercise]

By this healthful regimen, Mr. Depew lived to be 94.

EXILE

3 And thou shalt prove how salt a savor
     hath
The bread of others, and how hard
     the path
To climb and descend the stranger's
     stairs!
[Dante: *The Divine Comedy,* "Paradise" XVII]
4 The sly-slow hours shall not determinate
The dateless limit of thy dear exile.
[Shakespeare: *Richard II* I.iii.]
5 Some natural tears they dropped, but
     wiped them soon;
The world was all before them,
     where to choose
Their place of rest, and Providence
     their guide.
They, hand in hand, with wandering
     steps and slow,
Through Eden took their solitary way.
[John Milton: *Paradise Lost* XII (concluding lines)]

EXPECTATION

6 There is no greater enemy to those who would please than expectation. [Montaigne: *Essays* III.ix.]

That is, one must not raise too great expectations or whatever is finally done will seem inadequate.

7 For now sits Expectation in the air. [Shakespeare: *Henry V* I. (Chorus)]
8 Blessed is he who expects nothing, for he shall never be disappointed. [Alexander Pope: *Letter to Gay*]

EXPEDIENCE

9 If the chief party, whether it be people, or army, or nobility, which you think most useful and of most consequence to you for the conservation of your dignity, be corrupt, you must follow their humor and indulge them, and in that case honesty and virtue are pernicious. [Machiavelli: *The Prince* XIX]

EXPENDITURE

10 Annual income twenty pounds, annual expenditure nineteen nineteen six, result happiness. Annual income twenty pounds, annual expenditure twenty pounds ought and six, result misery. [Dickens: *David Copperfield* XII]
11 Expenditure rises to meet income. Individual expenditure not only rises to meet income but tends to surpass it. [C. Northcote Parkinson: *The Law and the Profits*]

EXPERIENCE

12 He is happy that can beware by others' harms. [William Camden: *Remains*]
13 I had rather have a fool to make me merry than experience to make me sad. [Shakespeare: *As You Like It* IV.i.]
14 The burnt child dreads the fire. [Ben Jonson: *The Devil Is an Ass*]
15 No man's knowledge here can go beyond experience. [John Locke: *An Essay Concerning Human Understanding* II.i.]
16 To most men, experience is like the stern lights of a ship, which illumine only the track it has passed. [Coleridge: *Table-Talk*]
17 Much have I seen and known; cities of
     men
And manners, climates, councils, governments,
Myself not least, but honour'd of
     them all;
And drunk delight of battle with my
     peers,
Far on the ringing plains of windy
     Troy.
[Tennyson: *Ulysses*]
18 I am a part of all that I have met;
Yet all experience is an arch where-
     thro'
Gleams that untravell'd world, whose
     margin fades
For ever and for ever when I move.
[Tennyson: *Ulysses*]
19 We should be careful to get out of an

experience only the wisdom that is in it—
and stop there; lest we be like the cat that
sits down on a hot stove-lid. She will
never sit down on a hot stove-lid again—
and that is well; but also she will never
sit down on a cold one anymore. [Mark
Twain: *Pudd'nhead Wilson's New Calendar*]
1 Deep experience is never peaceful.
[Henry James: *Madame De Mauves*]
2 Experience is the name everyone
gives to their mistakes. [Oscar Wilde:
Lady Windermere's Fan III]
3 Welcome, O life! I go to encounter
for the millionth time the reality of experience and to forge in the smithy of
my soul the uncreated conscience of my
race. [James Joyce: *A Portrait of the
Artist as a Young Man*]
4 Experience is a fruit tree fruitless,
  Experience is a shoe-tree bootless.
  For sterile wearience and drearience,
  Depend, my boy, upon experience.
[Ogden Nash: *Experience to Let*]

EXPERIENCE: keeps a dear school
5 Experience is the schoolmaster of
fools. [Livy: *History* XX.xxxix.]
6 It is costly wisdom that is bought
by experience. . . . Learning teacheth
more in one year than experience in
twenty. [Roger Ascham: *The Schole-
master*]
7   To wilful men
  The injuries that they themselves
                         procure
  Must be their schoolmasters.
[Shakespeare: *King Lear* II.iv.]
8 Experience teacheth fools, and he is
a great one that will not learn by it.
[Thomas Fuller (1654-1734): *Gnomologia*]
9 Experience keeps a dear school, yet
fools will learn in no other. [Benjamin
Franklin: *Poor Richard's Almanack*
(1743)]
10 A senseless school, where we must
                         give
  Our lives that we may learn to live!
  A dolt is he who memorizes
  Lessons that leave no time for prizes.
[Thomas Hardy: *A Young Man's Epigram on Existence*]
11 Experience is a hard teacher because
she gives the test first, the lesson after-

wards. [Vernon Law: "How to be a
Winner," *This Week*, Aug. 14, 1960]

EXPERT
12 An expert is one who knows more
and more about less and less. [Nicholas
Murray Butler: in a Commencement address, at Columbia University]
13 Expert beyond experience.
[T. S. Eliot: *Whispers of Immortality*]
  Referring to John Donne.

EXPLANATION
14 Many questions are such as the illiterate part of mankind can have neither
interest nor pleasure in discussing, and
which, therefore, it would be a useless
endeavor to level with common minds by
tiresome circumlocutions or laborious
explanations. [Samuel Johnson: *The Idler* No. 70]
15 I wish he would explain his explana-
                         tion.
[Byron: Dedication to *Don Juan*]
16 Explanations explanatory of things
explained. [Abraham Lincoln: *Lincoln-
Douglas Debates*]
17 Shut up, he explained. [Ring Lardner: *The Young Immigrunts* X]

EXPLORATION
18 And through the palpable obscure
                         find out
  His uncouth way.
[John Milton: *Paradise Lost* II.406-407]
  uncouth = *unknown*

EXPRESSION
19 I am of opinion, and Socrates would
have it so, that he who hath a clear and
lively imagination in his mind, may easily produce and utter the same, although it be in Bergamask or Welsh,
and if he be dumb, by signs and tokens.
[Montaigne: *Essays* I.xxv.]
  imagination = *concept, idea;* utter =
  convey, make public; Bergamask = *the
  dialect of Bergamo, a city in Northern
  Italy. Montaigne, it would seem, regarded it as outlandish speech.*
    *This is opposed to the common "I
  know it but I can't express it."*

EXTENUATE
20 Speak of me as I am; nothing extenu-

ate,
Nor set down aught in malice.
[Shakespeare: *Othello* V.ii.]

EXTREME(S)
1 The two extremes appear like man
and wife,
Coupled together for the sake of
strife.
[Charles Churchill: *The Rosciad*]
2 All empty souls tend to extreme opinion.
[William Butler Yeats: *Dramatis Personae*]

EYE(S)
3 If a man put out the eye of another
man, his eye shall be put out. [*The Code
of Hammurabi* (c. 2000 B.C.)]
4 Eye for eye, tooth for tooth, hand for
hand, foot for foot. [Exodus 21:24]
5 Eyes have they, but they see not. They
have ears, but they hear not. [Psalms
115:6]
Also in Psalms 135:16-17.
6 And if thy right eye offend thee,
pluck it out, and cast it from thee: for it
is profitable for thee that one of thy
members should perish, and not that thy
whole body should be cast into hell.
And if thy right hand offend thee,
cut it off. [Matthew 5:29-30]
7 Why beholdest thou the mote that
is in thy brother's eye, but considerest
not the beam that is in thine own eye!
[Matthew 7:3]
8 If thine eye offend thee, pluck it out.
[Matthew 18:9]
9 His eyen twinkled in his heed aright,
As doon the sterres in the frosty
night.
[Chaucer: Prologue to *The Canterbury
Tales*]
eyen = *eyes. This is an old form of the
plural, now lost in standard English except for the single word* oxen, *but kept
in several words in northern dialects in
England, such as* shoon (*shoes*) *and* hosen
(*stockings*).
10 Even in the glasses of thine eyes
I see thy grieved heart.
[Shakespeare: *Richard II* I.iii.]
11 What an eye she has! methinks it
sounds a parley of provocation. [Shake-
speare: *Othello* II.iii.]

12 Thou hast no speculation in those
eyes
Which thou dost glare with!
[Shakespeare: *Macbeth* III.iv.]
13 The eye is bigger than the belly.
[George Herbert: *Jacula Prudentum*]
14 Diseases of the eye are to be cured
with the elbow. [George Herbert: *Jacula Prudentum*]
*The saying has many forms and occurs
in several languages. Since the eye cannot be reached by the elbow, the idea
is: leave your eyes alone; most remedies
merely do further damage. And until
the development of modern surgery and
antisepsis this was probably true. Even
today a large fraction of eye injuries
result from home treatment of minor
ailments.*
*Never rub your eye but with your
elbow.*
Thomas Fuller (1654-1734): Gnomologia
15 With store of ladies, whose bright
eyes
Rain influence, and judge the prize.
[John Milton: *L'Allegro*]
16 The sight of you is good for sore eyes.
[Jonathan Swift: *Polite Conversation*]
The appearance of the expression in
Polite Conversation *is evidence that it
was threadbare and hackneyed by 1738.
It is still in use, forgivable in its homely
exuberance and genuine good nature.*
17 Why has not man a microscopic eye?
For this plain reason, man is not a
fly.
[Alexander Pope: *An Essay on Man* I]
18 That inward eye
Which is the bliss of solitude.
[Wordsworth: *I Wandered Lonely as a
Cloud*]
19 He holds him with his glittering eye.
[Coleridge: *The Ancient Mariner* I]
20 The light that lies
In woman's eyes,
Has been my heart's undoing.

. . .

My only books
Were women's looks,
And folly's all they taught me.
[Thomas Moore: *The Time I've Lost
in Wooing*]
*And in those eyes the love-light lies
And lies—and lies—and lies.*
Anita Owen: Dreamy Eyes

1 With affection beaming in one eye, and calculation shining out of the other. [Dickens: *Martin Chuzzlewit* VIII]

2 He had but one eye, and the popular prejudice runs in favour of two. [Dickens: *Nicholas Nickleby* IV]

3 Those eyes the greenest of things blue, The bluest of things grey.
[Swinburne: *Felise*]

4 Two lovely black eyes,
 Oh! what a surprise!
Only for telling a man he was
 wrong,
 Two lovely black eyes!
[Charles Coborn: *Two Lovely Black Eyes*]

5 The Night has a thousand eyes,
 The Day but one;
 Yet the light of the bright world dies
 With the dying sun.
[F. W. Bourdillon: *The Night Has a Thousand Eyes*]

EYE FOR AN EYE

6 Life shall go for life, eye for eye, tooth for tooth, hand for hand, foot for foot. [Deuteronomy 19:21]
 See also 215:6

EYELESS

7 Eyeless in Gaza, at the mill with
 slaves.
[John Milton: *Samson Agonistes*]

F

FACE(S)

1 Was this the face that launch'd a thousand ships,
And burnt the topless towers of Ilium?
[Christopher Marlowe: *Doctor Faustus* XIV]
Ilium = *Troy*
The reference is to Helen of Troy.

2 God has given you one face, and you make yourselves another.
[Shakespeare: *Hamlet* III.i.]

3 There's no art
To find the mind's construction in the face.
[Shakespeare: *Macbeth* I.iv.]

4 Your face, my thane, is a book where men
May read strange matters. To beguile the time,
Look like the time.
[Shakespeare: *Macbeth* I.v.]

5 I have seen better faces in my time
Than stands on any shoulder that I see
Before me at this instant.
[Shakespeare: *King Lear* II.ii.]

6 It is the common wonder of all men, how among so many millions of faces, there should be none alike. [Sir Thomas Browne: *Religio Medici* II.ii.]

7 Had it any been but she, and that very face,
There had been at least ere this a dozen dozen in her place.
[Sir John Suckling: *A Poem with the Answer*]

8 Sea of upturned faces.
[Sir Walter Scott: *Rob Roy* II.xx.]

9 All, all are gone, the old familiar faces.
[Charles Lamb: *The Old Familiar Faces*]

10 I do not see them here; but after death
God knows I know the faces I shall see,
Each one a murdered self, with low last breath.
[Dante Gabriel Rossetti: *The House of Life* LXXXVI or XL (variant editions)]

11 With chalk in hand the vagabond began
To sketch a face that well might buy the soul of any man.
Then as he placed another lock upon the shapely head,
With a fearful shriek he leaped and fell across the picture—dead!
[Hugh Antoine D'Arcy: *The Face on the Floor*]
Usually called The Face on the Barroom Floor.

12 As a beauty I'm not a great star,
There are others more handsome by far;
But my face I don't mind it
Because I'm behind it—
'Tis the folks out in front that I jar.
[Anthony Euwer: *Limeratomy*]
This limerick delighted Woodrow Wilson.

FACTS

13 When speculation has done its worst, two and two still make four. [Samuel Johnson: *The Idler* No. 36]

14 Facts are stubborn things. [Ebenezer Elliott: *Field Husbandry*]

15 It is as fatal as it is cowardly to blink facts because they are not to our taste. [John Tyndall: *Fragments of Science, Vol. II*, "Science and Man"]

16 Her taste exact
For faultless fact
Amounts to a disease.
[W. S. Gilbert: *The Mikado* II]

17 Facts do not cease to exist because they are ignored. [Aldous Huxley: *A Note on Dogma*]

18 Facts are ventriloquist's dummies. Sitting on a wise man's knee they may be made to utter words of wisdom; elsewhere they say nothing or talk nonsense. [Aldous Huxley: *Time Must Have a Stop*]

19 The civilized man has a moral obligation to be skeptical, to demand the credentials of all statements that claim to

be facts. [Bergen Evans: *The Natural History of Nonsense* XIX]

FAERY

1 The land of faery,
Where nobody gets old and godly and grave,
Where nobody gets old and crafty and wise,
Where nobody gets old and bitter of tongue.
[William Butler Yeats: *The Land of Heart's Desire*]

FAILINGS

2 E'en his failings lean'd to Virtue's side. [Oliver Goldsmith: *The Deserted Village*]

FAILURE(S)

3 He that fails in his endeavours after wealth and power, will not long retain either honesty or courage. [Samuel Johnson: *The Adventurer* No. 99]
4 Of all failures, to fail in a witticism is the worst, and the mishap is the more calamitous in a drawn out and detailed one. [Walter Savage Landor: *Imaginary Conversations*, "Chesterfield and Chatham"]
5 There is the greatest practical benefit in making a few failures early in life. [T. H. Huxley: *On Medical Education*]
6 In the lexicon of youth, which fate reserves
For a bright manhood, there is no such word
As—fail.
[E. G. Bulwer-Lytton: *Richelieu* II.ii.]
Often misquoted as: "In the bright lexicon of youth there is no such word as fail."
As often (see gild the lily) *in popular recollection, an adjective jumps out of place and attaches itself to another noun.*
7 How far high failure overleaps the bounds of low success.
[Sir Lewis Morris: *The Epic of Hades*, "Marsyas"]

FAIN

8 Fain would I, but I dare not; I dare, and yet I may not;
I may, although I care not for pleas-ure when I play not.
[Sir Walter Raleigh (1552?-1615): *Fain Would I*]

FAINT

9 If thou faint in the day of adversity, thy strength is small. [Proverbs 34:10]

FAIR

10 She never yet was foolish that was fair,
For even her folly helped her to an heir.
[Shakespeare: *Othello* II.i.]
11 Fair is foul, and foul is fair.
[Shakespeare: *Macbeth* I.i.]
12 So foul and fair a day I have not seen.
[Shakespeare: *Macbeth* I.iii.]
13 Be she fairer than the day,
Or the flowery meads in May,
If she be not so to me,
What care I how fair she be?
[George Wither: *The Lover's Resolution*]
14 She is not fair to outward view
As many maidens be;
Her loveliness I never knew
Until she smiled on me.
[Hartley Coleridge: *Song*]
15 All's fair in love and war.
[Francis Edward Smedley: *Frank Fairlegh* L (1850)]
This is the first known appearance of this famous phrase in this exact form. However, the idea had been around for several centuries.

> *All stratagems*
> *In love, and that the sharpest war, are lawful.*
> Beaumont and Fletcher: The Lovers' Progress *V.ii.*
> *Advantages are lawful in love and war.*
> Aphra Behn: Emperor of the Moon *I.iii.*
> *Stratagems ever were allow'd of in love and war.*
> Mrs. Centlivre: The Man's Bewitch'd *V.i.*

FAIRIES

16 There are fairies at the bottom of our garden!
[Rose Fyleman: *The Fairies*]

FAIRY TALES

17 Children aren't the only ones who are

fed on fairy tales. [Lessing: *Nathan der Weise* III.vi.]

1 The fairy tales of science.
[Tennyson: *Locksley Hall*]

FAITH

2 If ye have faith as a grain of mustard seed, ye shall say unto this mountain, Remove hence to yonder place; and it shall remove. [Matthew 17:20]
> *Samuel Butler (1835-1902) remarked that faith could certainly move mountains of evidence.*

3 Whosoever shall say unto this mountain, Be thou removed and be thou cast into the sea; and shall not doubt in his heart, but shall believe that those things which he saith shall come to pass; he shall have whatsoever he saith. [Mark 11:23]

4 I have fought a good fight, I have finished my course, I have kept the faith. [II Timothy 4:7]

5 Faith is the substance of things hoped for, the evidence of things not seen. [Hebrews 11:1]

6 Faith without works is dead. [James 2:26]

7 It's no sin to deceive a Christian;
For they themselves hold it a principle,
Faith is not to be held with Heretics.
[Christopher Marlowe: *The Jew of Malta* II.iii.]

8 I had rather believe all the fables in the Legend and the Talmud and the Alcoran than that this universal frame is without a mind. [Francis Bacon: *Of Atheism*]
> *This ringing affirmation of faith must be accepted with considerable coolness by the millions who do believe in the Legends of the Saints, the Talmud and the Koran.*

9 He wears his faith but as the fashion of his hat.
[Shakespeare: *Much Ado About Nothing* I.i.]

10 The faith that looks through death.
[Wordsworth: *Intimations of Immortality*]

11 Let us have faith that right makes might, and in that faith let us to the end dare to do our duty as we understand it. [Abraham Lincoln: Address, at Cooper Union, in New York, February 27, 1860]

12 Faith of our fathers—holy faith,
We will be true to thee till death.
[Frederick William Faber: *Faith of Our Fathers*]
> *If we retained the convictions of our fathers in geography, physics, medicine—and, indeed, in almost any department of human knowledge—we would be in a ludicrous and lamentable plight and utterly unable to function in the modern world.*

FAITH: and doubt

13 In the Affairs of this World Men are saved, not by Faith but by the Want of it. [Benjamin Franklin: *Poor Richard's Almanack* (1754)]

14 If any of the company entertain a doubt of my veracity, I shall only say to such, I pity their want of faith. [Rudolf Erich Raspe: *Travels of Baron Munchausen* VI]

15 Strong Son of God, immortal Love,
Whom we, that have not seen thy face,
By faith, and faith alone, embrace,
Believing where we cannot prove.
[Tennyson: Prologue to *In Memoriam*]

16 We have but faith: we cannot know;
For knowledge is of things we see;
And yet we trust it comes from thee,
A beam in darkness: let it grow.
[Tennyson: Prologue to *In Memoriam*]

17 Faith always implies the disbelief of a lesser fact in favor of a greater. [O. W. Holmes: *The Professor at the Breakfast-Table* V]

18 The sea of faith
Was once, too, at the full, and round earth's shore
Lay like the folds of a bright girdle furl'd.
But now I only hear
Its melancholy, long, withdrawing roar,
Retreating, to the breath
Of the night-wind, down the vast edges drear
And naked shingles of the world.
[Matthew Arnold: *Dover Beach*]

19 Faith may be defined briefly as an illogical belief in the occurrence of the im-

probable. [H. L. Mencken: *Prejudices: Series III*]

1 The most satisfying and ecstatic faith is almost purely agnostic. It trusts absolutely without professing to know at all. [H. L. Mencken: *Damn! A Book of Calumny*]

FAITH: in the impossible

2 *Credo quia impossibile.* ("I believe because it is impossible.") [Tertullian: *De Carne Christi* V]
> *Usual adaptation of* Certum est quia impossibile est. *("It is certain . . .")*

3 To believe only possibilities, is not faith, but mere Philosophy. [Sir Thomas Browne: *Religio Medici* I.xlvi.]

4 Methinks there be not impossibilities enough in Religion for an active faith. [Sir Thomas Browne: *Religio Medici* I.ix.]

FAITHFUL

5 Among the faithless, faithful only he. [John Milton: *Paradise Lost* V.897]
> *The reference is to the Seraph Abdiel who, alone, refused to join the rebel angels.*

6 O come, all ye faithful,
Joyful and triumphant,
O come ye, O come ye to Bethlehem.
[Frederick Oakeley: *O Come, All Ye Faithful*]
> *Trans. from Latin* Adeste Fideles.

FAITHFULNESS

7 If I, by miracle, can be
This live-long minute true to thee,
'Tis all that heaven allows.
[John Wilmot, Earl of Rochester: *Love and Life*]

8 No man worth having is true to his wife, or can be true to his wife, or ever was or ever will be so. [Sir John Vanbrugh: *The Relapse* III.ii.]

9 No, the heart that has truly lov'd never forgets,
But as truly loves on to the close;
As the sunflower turns on her god, when he sets,
The same look which she turn'd when he rose.
[Thomas Moore: *Believe Me, If All Those Endearing Young Charms*]

10 I have been faithful to thee, Cynara,

in my fashion. [Ernest Dowson: *Non Sum Qualis*]

11 It is the secret scandal of Christendom, at least in the Protestant regions, that most men are faithful to their wives. [H. L. Mencken: in *Smart Set*, December 1921]

FALCON

12 A falcon, tow'ring in her pride of place.
[Shakespeare: *Macbeth* II.iv.]
> tow'ring = *hovering at the height of her ascent*
> *Our expression "towering rage" comes from this. It was—when fresh—a good phrase because it suggested that, as the falcon's towering would be followed by her strike, the mounting anger would be followed by a sudden, precipitous, murderous attack on its victim.*

13 I caught this morning morning's minion, kingdom of daylight's dauphin, dapple-dawn-drawn falcon, in his riding
Of the rolling level underneath him steady air, and striding
High there, how he rung upon the rein of a wimpling wing
In his ecstasy!
[Gerard Manley Hopkins: *The Windhover*]

FALL

14 O, what a fall was there, my countrymen!
[Shakespeare: *Julius Caesar* III.ii.]

15 And when he falls, he falls like Lucifer
Never to hope again.
[Shakespeare: *Henry VIII* III.ii.]

16 From morn
To noon he fell, from noon to dewy eve,
A summer's day; and with the setting sun
Dropp'd from the zenith, like a falling star.
[John Milton: *Paradise Lost* I. 742-745]
> *Milton's description of the fall of Mulciber "thrown by angry Jove,/Sheer o'er the crystal battlements" of Heaven doubles, as it were, the enormous declivity of the fall, by that metrical pause half*

way. *It is much like Shakespeare's "Half-*
way down hangs one that gathers sam-
phire, dreadful trade" in his dizzying
gaze down from the top of the cliffs of
Dover in King Lear.

1 Flutt'ring his pinions vain, plumb
                        down he drops.
[John Milton: *Paradise Lost* II.933]
In the sense of marking a true perpen-
dicular, as here, plumb *is correct, though*
very old and, except in the technical
talk of builders, slightly archaic.

2 He that is down can fall no lower.
[Samuel Butler (1612-1680): *Hudibras*
I.]

FALSE

3 Even false becomes true when the
chief says so. [Publilius Syrus: *Maxims*]
4 She was false as water.
[Shakespeare: *Othello* V.ii.]
5   . . . wouldst not play false,
And yet wouldst wrongly win.
[Shakespeare: *Macbeth* I.v.]
6   He seem'd
For dignity compos'd and high ex-
                        ploit:
But all was false and hollow.
[John Milton: *Paradise Lost* II.110]
7 A Hair perhaps divides the False and
                        True.
[*Rubáiyát of Omar Khayyám* (trans. Ed-
ward FitzGerald)]

FALSEHOOD

8 O what a goodly outside falsehood
                        hath!
[Shakespeare: *The Merchant of Venice*
I.iii.]
9 Falsehood playes a larger part in the
                        world than truth.
[Sir Thomas Overbury: *Newes of My
Morning Worke*]

FALSE SECURITY

10 Soul, thou hast much goods laid up
for many years; take thine ease, eat, drink,
and be merry. [Luke 12:19]

FAME: absurdity, impermanence,
      inadequacy, injustice and irony of

11 In the very books in which philosophers bid us scorn fame, they inscribe
their names. [Cicero: *Pro Archia* XI.
xxvi.]

12 Fame is like a river, that beareth up
things light and swollen, and drowns
things weighty and solid. [Francis Bacon:
Of Praise]
13 The evil that men do lives after them;
The good is oft interred with their
                        bones.
[Shakespeare: *Julius Caesar* III.i.]
14 There's hope a great man's memory
              may outlive his life half a year.
[Shakespeare: *Hamlet* III.ii.]
15 Men's evil manners live in brass, their
                        virtues
We write in water.
[Shakespeare: *Henry VIII* IV.ii.]
16 Glories, like glow-wormes, afarre off
                        shine bright,
But lookt to neare, have neither heat
                        nor light.
[John Webster: *The White Devil* V.i.
(1612)]
17 Seldome comes Glorie till a man be
                        dead.
[Robert Herrick: *Glorie*]
18 From fame to infamy is a beaten road.
[Thomas Fuller (1654-1734): *Gnomologia*]
19 All fame is dangerous: Good, bringeth Envy; Bad, Shame. [Thomas Fuller
(1654-1734): *Gnomologia*]
20 Fame goes always with the principals.
[Gracián: *Oráculo Manual* (1647)]
*The acts and sayings of lesser men are
in time ascribed to some great man. Examples are the assigning to Mark Twain
of Sir James Barrie's statement that it's
Heaven for climate and Hell for company, and to Horace Greeley of John
Soule's "Go west, young man."*

21 Herostratus lives that burnt the Temple of Diana; he is almost lost that built
it. [Sir Thomas Browne: *Hydrotaphia*
V (1658)]
*The temple of Artemis (Diana) at Ephe-
sus, on the coast of Asia Minor, was of
great antiquity and one of the wonders
of the ancient world. In 356 B.C. one
Herostratus, to make his name immortal,
burned the temple down.*

*The violently destructive do seem to
have received a disproportionate amount
of fame; one sometimes suspects that
man is innately destructive and these are
his true heroes.*

1 But the fair guerdon when we hope to
find,
And think to burst out into sudden
blaze,
Comes the blind Fury with th' ab-
horred shears
And slits the thin-spun life.
[John Milton: *Lycidas*]

2 If parts allure thee, think how Bacon
shined,
The wisest, brightest, meanest of
mankind:
Or, ravish'd with the whistling of a
name,
See Cromwell, damn'd to everlasting
fame.
[Alexander Pope: *An Essay on Man* IV]
parts = *talents, accomplishments*

*Bacon, the great jurist, essayist and
philosopher, was dismissed from the
highest judicial office in England for
taking bribes. He had, as a young man,
helped to prosecute Essex, his benefactor.*

*In the 18th century, when Pope wrote,
it was assumed that Cromwell would be
eternally execrated. That a statue of him
would be erected before the very gates
of Parliament could not have been imagined.*

3 There have been as great souls unknown to fame as any of the most famous.
[Benjamin Franklin: *Poor Richard's Almanack* (1734)]

4 See nations slowly wise, and meanly
just,
To buried merit raise the tardy bust.
[Samuel Johnson: *Vanity of Human
Wishes*]

5 Those only deserve a monument who
do not need one. [William Hazlitt:
Characteristics]

6 To be remembered after we are dead
is but a poor recompense for being
treated with contempt while we are living. [William Hazlitt: *Characteristics*]

7 Folly loves the martyrdom of fame.
[Byron: *Monody on the Death of Sheridan*]

8 What is the end of Fame? 'tis but to
fill
A certain portion of uncertain paper:
Some liken it to climbing up a hill,
Whose summit, like all hills, is lost in
vapor:
For this men write, speak, preach,
and heroes kill,
And bards burn what they call their
"midnight taper,"
To have, when the original is dust,
A name, a wretched picture, and
worse bust.
[Byron: *Don Juan* I.ccxviii.]

9 Perhaps the most direct way to acquire fame is to affirm, confidently and
persistently, and in every possible way,
that we already have it. [Leopardi: *Pen-
sieri* LX]

10 Popularity?—glory's small change.
[Victor Hugo: *Ruy Blas* III]

11 Fame is not just. She never finely or
discriminatingly praises, but coarsely
hurrahs. [Thoreau: *Summer,* June 4,
1854]

12 It is—last stage of all—
When we are frozen up within, and
quite
The phantom of ourselves,
To hear the world applaud the hol-
low ghost
Which blamed the living man.
[Matthew Arnold: *Growing Old*]

13 Laurel is green for a season, and love
is sweet for a day;
But love grows bitter with treason,
and laurel outlives not May.
[Swinburne: *Hymn to Proserpine*]

14 Fame is a food that dead men eat—
I have no stomach for such meat.
[Austin Dobson: *Fame Is a Food that
Dead Men Eat*]

15 Could any sober man be proud to
hold
A lease of common talk, or die con-
soled
For thinking that on lips of fools to
come
He'll live with Pontius Pilate and
Tom Thumb?
[Robert Bridges: *La Gloire de Voltaire*]

16 The loud impertinence of fame.
[William Watson: *Laleham Churchyard*]

FAME: glory of and desire for

17 Perhaps even our names will some
day be joined with these. [Ovid: *Ars
amatoria* III]

18 It is pleasing to be pointed at with
the finger and to have it said, "There
goes the man." [Persius: *Satires*]

But, of course, seen too often, one is no
longer pointed at:
> Had I so lavish of my presence been,
> So common-hackneyed in the eyes of
> men,
> So stale and cheap to vulgar company,
> Opinion, that did help me to the
> crown,
> Had still kept loyal to possession
> And left me in reputeless banishment,
> A fellow of no mark nor likelihood.
> By being seldom seen, I could not stir
> But, like a comet, I was wond'red at;
> That men would tell their children,
> "This is he!"
> Others would say, "Where? Which is
> Bolingbroke?"

Shakespeare: I Henry IV III.ii.

1 O sacred hunger of ambitious minds.
[Edmund Spenser: The Faerie Queene
V.i.]

2 Though they [philosophers] write
contemptu gloriae, yet as Hieron observes, they will put their names to their
books. [Robert Burton: Anatomy of
Melancholy I.2.3.14]

3 Fame is the spur that the clear spirit
doth raise
(That last infirmity of noble mind)
[John Milton: Lycidas]

Milton, whether consciously or not,
was, in part, quoting John Fletcher: Sir
John van Olden Barnavelt I.i. (1619):
". . . the desire of glory/(That last infirmity of noble minds)." Others had expressed the same thought before either
of them, back to Tacitus, in his History
IV.6., 2nd century A.D.: "The desire of
glory clings to even the best men longer
than any other passion."

4 Fame is no plant that grows on mor-
tal soil,
Nor in the glistering foil
Set off to the world, nor in broad ru-
mor lies,
But lives and spreads aloft by those
pure eyes
And perfect witness of all-judging
Jove;
As he pronounces lastly on each deed,
Of so much fame in heaven expect
thy meed.
[John Milton: Lycidas]

5 By labour and intent study (which I
take to be my portion in this life),
joined with the strong propensity of nature, I might perhaps leave something so
written to after times as they should
not willingly let it die. [John Milton:
The Reason of Church Government II
(Intro.)]

6 Even those who write against fame
wish for the fame of having written well,
and those who read their works desire
the fame of having read them. [Pascal:
Pensées]

7 Every man has a lurking wish to ap-
pear considerable in his native place.
[Samuel Johnson: Letter to Sir Joshua
Reynolds, July 17, 1771]

8 Passion for fame; a passion which is
the instinct of all great souls. [Edmund
Burke: Speech on American Taxation
(1774)]

9 What rage for fame attends both
great and small!
Better be d——n'd than mentioned
not at all.
[John Wolcot ("Peter Pindar"): To the
Royal Academicians IX]

10 Fame is the thirst of youth.
[Byron: Childe Harold III.cxii.]

11 Lives of great men all remind us
We can make our lives sublime,
And, departing, leave behind us
Footprints on the sands of time.
[Longfellow: A Psalm of Life]

FAME: miscellaneous
12 On Fame's eternal bead-roll worthy
to be filed.
[Edmund Spenser: The Faerie Queene
IV.ii.]

13 Not marble, nor the gilded monuments
Of princes, shall outlive this powerful
rhyme.
[Shakespeare: Sonnets LV]

14 Better to leave undone, than by our
deed
Acquire too high a fame, when him
we serve's away.
[Shakespeare: Antony and Cleopatra
III.i.]

15 I'll make thee glorious by my pen,
And famous by my sword.
[James Graham, Marquis of Montrose:
My Dear and Only Love]

Sir Walter Scott, in his Legends of Montrose XV (1819), reversed the adjectives:

I'll make thee famous by my pen,
And glorious by my sword.

1 Fame then was cheap, and the first
comer sped;
And they have kept it since, by being
dead.
[Dryden: Epilogue to *The Conquest of
Granada*]

2 I awoke one morning and found myself famous.
*Byron: his account of the fame that came
with the publishing of the first two
cantos of* Childe Harold, *1812. First published in Thomas Moore:* Memoranda
from Life, *Ch. 14.*

3 Brave men were living before Agamemnon
And since, exceeding valorous and
sage,
A good deal like him too, but quite
the same none;
But then they shone not on the poet's
page.
[Byron: *Don Juan* I.v.]
*Byron is merely putting into his own
verse a passage from Horace (Odes IV.ix.):
"Many heroes lived before Agamemnon;
but all, unwept and unknown, are lost
in eternal night, because they lacked a
sacred poet to sing their glory." This is,
perhaps, the favorite passage in all literature for poets. It has been translated
a score of times. The only difficulty is
that the Agamemnons don't read; they
prefer a publicity release to a poem.*

4 Fame is something which must be
won; honor only something which must
not be lost. [Schopenhauer: *Aphorisms
on the Wisdom of Life*]

5 The final test of fame is to have a
crazy person imagine he is you. [Anon.]

FAMILIAR

6 Be thou familiar, but by no means
vulgar.
[Shakespeare: *Hamlet* I.iii.]
vulgar = *common*

FAMILIARITY

7 Amongst a man's peers a man shall
be sure of familiarity; and therefore it
is good a little to keep state; amongst a
man's inferiors one shall be sure of reverence; and therefore it is good a little

to be familiar. [Francis Bacon: *Of Ceremonies and Respects*]

FAMILIARITY BREEDS CONTEMPT

8 Familiarity breeds contempt. [Pub-
lilius Syrus: *Maxims*]
Mark Twain added, "—and children."

9 I find my familiarity with thee has
bred contempt.
[Cervantes: *Don Quixote* I.iii.6]

10 Though familiarity may not breed
contempt, it takes the edge off admiration. [William Hazlitt: *Characteristics*]

FAMILY(IES)

11 Wife and children are a kind of discipline of humanity. [Francis Bacon: *Of
Marriage and Single Life*]

12 To make a happy fire-side clime
To weans and wife,
That's the true pathos and sublime
Of human life.
[Burns: *To Dr. Blacklock*]
weans = *small children*

13 Mothers of large families, who claim
to common sense,
Will find a Tiger well repay the trouble and expense.
[Hilaire Belloc: *The Tiger*]

FAMINE

14 Famine ends famine. [Ben Jonson:
Explorata, "Amor Nummi"]

FANATIC

15 A fanatic is a man that does what he
thinks th' Lord wud do if He knew th'
facts iv th' case. [Finley Peter Dunne:
Mr. Dooley's Philosophy, "Casual Observations"]

16 A fanatic is one who can't change his
mind and won't change the subject.
[Attr. to Winston Churchill]

FANATICISM

17 Cool was his kitchen, though his
brains were hot.
[Dryden: *Absalom and Achitophel* I.
621]
Description of a parsimonious zealot.

18 This makes the madmen who have
made men mad
By their contagion; Conquerors and
Kings,
Founders of sects and systems, to

whom add
Sophists, Bards, Statesmen, all unquiet
things
Which stir too strongly the soul's secret springs,
And are themselves the fools to those
they fool.
[Byron: *Childe Harold* III.xliii.]
1 Their breath is agitation, and their
life
A storm whereon they ride, to sink
at last,
And yet so nursed and bigoted to
strife,
That should their days, surviving perils past,
Melt to calm twilight, they feel over-
cast
With sorrow and supineness, and so
die;
Even as a flame unfed, which runs to
waste
With its own flickering, or a sword
laid by,
Which eats into itself, and rusts in-
gloriously.
[Byron: *Childe Harold* III.xliv.]
2 Fanaticism consists in redoubling
your efforts when you have forgotten
your aim. [George Santayana: *The Life
of Reason*]

FANCY
3 Tell me where is fancy bred,
Or in the heart or in the head?
[Shakespeare: *The Merchant of Venice*
III.ii.]
4 Chewing the food of sweet and bitter
fancy.
[Shakespeare: *As You Like It* IV.iii.]
5 Whence came this whiffle and whimsy
within the circumference of thy figmen-
titious fancy? [Samuel Fisher: *The Rus-
tick's Alarm* (1660)]
*The "whiffle and whimsy" was that God
had implanted errors in Holy Writ on
purpose to test our faith, to see if we
would believe in spite of evidence and
reason.*
6 All power of fancy over reason is a
degree of insanity. [Samuel Johnson:
Rasselas XLIV]
7 Ever let the fancy roam,
Pleasure never is at home.
[Keats: *Fancy*]

8 Adieu! the fancy cannot cheat so
well
As she is fam'd to do, deceiving elf.
[Keats: *Ode to a Nightingale*]

FANCY-FREE
9 In maiden meditation, fancy free.
[Shakespeare: *A Midsummer Night's
Dream* II.i.]

FAREWELL(S)
10 For ever, brother, hail and farewell.
[Catullus: *Carmina* XCIX]
11 Good night, ladies; good night, sweet
ladies.
[Shakespeare: *Hamlet* IV.v.]
*The mad Ophelia's words are echoed
with powerful effect amid the public-
house chatter at the end of "The Game
of Chess" section of T. S. Eliot's* The
Waste Land.
12   O! now, for ever
Farewell the tranquil mind; farewell
content!
Farewell the plumed troop and the
big wars
That make ambition virtue!
[Shakespeare: *Othello* III.iii.]
*Of this passage John Moore (You Eng-
lish Words, pp. 38-9) says: ". . . it is the
joining up of 'big' and 'wars' which
makes us catch our breath. But we cannot tell why. . . . We only know that if
we substitute 'great' for 'big,' it doesn't
happen."*
*Only recently, in our rapidly expand-
ing world, has ambition been regarded,
in itself, as a virtue. The Elizabethans
regarded it as a very dangerous quality,
useful only in war.*
13 Farewell! a long farewell, to all my
greatness!
[Shakespeare: *Henry VIII* III.ii.]
14 Only a little more
I have to write,
Then I'll give o'er
And bid the world Good-night.
[Robert Herrick: *His Poetrie His Pillar*]
15 Dear, damn'd, distracting town, farewell:
Thy fools no more I'll tease;
This year in peace, ye critics, dwell;
Ye harlots, sleep at ease.
[Alexander Pope: *A Farewell to Lon-
don*]

1 Adieu canals, ducks, rabble! [Voltaire: farewell to Holland (1722)]
Good example of the impossibility of full translation. His actual words: "Adieu, canaux, canards, canaille!" carry in their alliteration a mingled humor and scorn wholly lost in the translation.

2 Ae fond kiss, and then we sever!
Ae farewell, alas, for ever!
Deep in heart-wrung tears I'll pledge thee,
Warring sighs and groans I'll wage thee.
[Burns: *Ae Fond Kiss*]

3 Fare thee well! and if for ever,
Still for ever, fare thee well.
[Byron: *Fare Thee Well*]
Byron has many passages expressing the sadness of farewell. Bert Leston Taylor, in his poem Farewell, *says that "Lord Byron was eternally/Farewelling."*

4 All farewells should be sudden.
[Byron: *Sardanapalus* V.i.]

5 Kathleen mavourneen, the gray dawn is breaking,
The horn of the hunter is heard on the hill,
The lark from her light wing the bright dew is shaking—
Kathleen mavourneen, what, slumbering still?

Oh hast thou forgotten how soon we must sever?
Oh hast thou forgotten this day we must part?
It may be for years and it may be forever;
Oh why art thou silent, thou voice of my heart?
[Louisa Crawford: *Kathleen Mavourneen*]

6 Good-bye, proud world! I'm going home. [Emerson: *Good-Bye*]

7 Fare thee well for I must leave thee,
Do not let this parting grieve thee.
[Anon.: *There is a Tavern in the Town*]

FARMER(S)

8 Our farmers round, well pleased with constant gain,
Like other farmers, flourish and complain.
[George Crabbe: *The Parish Register, I.* "Baptisms"]

9 By the rude bridge that arched the flood,
Their flag to April's breeze unfurled,
Here once the embattled farmers stood,
And fired the shot heard round the world.
[Emerson: *Hymn. Sung at the Completion of the Concord Monument* (July 4, 1837)]

FARMING

10 To plow and to sow, and to reap and to mow,
And to be a farmer's boy.
[Anon.: *The Farmer's Boy*]

FASHION

11 Fashion wears out more apparel than the man.
[Shakespeare: *Much Ado About Nothing* III.iii.]

12 For he that's out of clothes is out of fashion,
And out of fashion is out of countenance,
And out of countenance is out of wit.
[Ben Jonson: *The Staple of News* I.i.]

13 He is only fantastical that is not in fashion. [Robert Burton: *Anatomy of Melancholy* III.2]
fantastical = *outlandish*

14 One had as good be out of the world as out of the fashion.
[Colley Cibber: *Love's Last Shift*]

15 Fashion is gentility running away from vulgarity, and afraid of being overtaken. [William Hazlitt: *Conversations of James Northcote*]

16 Fashion constantly begins and ends in the two things it abhors most—singularity and vulgarity. [William Hazlitt: *On Fashion*]

17 You cannot be both fashionable and first-rate. [Logan Pearsall Smith: *Afterthoughts*]

FAST(ING)

18 Is this a Fast, to keep
The Larder leane? And cleane . . .
Yet still to fill
The platter high with Fish?
[Robert Herrick: *To Keep a True Lent*]

19 Spare fast, that oft with gods doth diet.
[John Milton: *Il Penseroso*]

FAT

1 And ye shall eat the fat of the land. [Genesis 45:18]

2 He was a lord ful fat and in good point. [Chaucer: Prologue to *The Canterbury Tales*]
  in good point, *We today use the French* embonpoint.

3 Fat as a whale, and walkinge as a swan. [Chaucer: *The Summoner's Tale*]

4 Fat paunches have lean pates. [Shakespeare: *Love's Labour's Lost* I.i.]

5 Let me have men about me that are fat,
  Sleek-headed men, and such as sleep o' nights.
[Shakespeare: *Julius Caesar* I.ii.]

6 Fat, fair and forty.
  Variously ascribed to Sir Walter Scott, who used the phrase in St. Ronan's Well *(1823) and again in* Redgauntlet *the following year; to the Prince Regent, who quoted it as a description of the ideal wife; and to John O'Keefe in his* Irish Minnie II. *Chances are it was simply an established phrase. It is heard most often today as "Fair, fat and forty" and, however the adjectives are arranged, remains a pleasing combination.*

7 Who ever hears of fat men heading a riot, or herding together in turbulent mobs? [Washington Irving: *Knickerbocker's History of New York* III.ii.]

8 I find no sweeter fat than sticks to my own bones.
[Walt Whitman: *Leaves of Grass*, "Song of Myself"]

FATALISM

9 That shalbe, shalbe. [John Heywood: *Proverbs*]
  Whether expressed in the Italian Che sera sera *or in any of a dozen English equivalents, from Chaucer down to a popular song of 1962, whether in Euripides' solemn "Of sheer necessity/Must prudent men be bondmen unto fate"* (Iphigenia in Tauris,) *or Marlowe's flippant:*
  What doctrine call you this, Che sara sara.
  What will be, shall be (Dr. Faustus *I.i.,*

written c. 1592); this expression can be both wise and fatuous. Shakespeare seemed to have been amused by it, or probably by the profundity which its users ascribed to themselves, when he had the clown in Twelfth Night (*IV.ii.*) *say: "As the old Hermit of Prague, that never saw pen and ink, very wittily said to a niece of King Gorboduc, 'That that is is.'"*

FATE(S)

10 Things are where things are, and, as fate has willed,
  So shall they be fulfilled.
[Aeschylus: *Agamemnon* 67]
  The translation is Browning's.

11 The gods thought otherwise. [Vergil: *Aeneid* II]
  In the Latin: Dis aliter visum.

12 The fates lead the willing—and drag the unwilling. [Seneca: *Ad Lucilium* CVII]

13 Fate leads him who follows it, and drags him who resists. [Plutarch: *Life of Camillus*]

14 O God! that one might read the book of fate! [Shakespeare: *II Henry IV* III.i.]

15 What fates impose, that men must needs abide;
  It boots not to resist both wind and tide.
[Shakespeare: *III Henry VI* IV.iii.]

16 Men at some time are masters of their fates. [Shakespeare: *Julius Caesar* I.ii.]

17 Let determined things to destiny Hold unbewail'd their way.
[Shakespeare: *Antony and Cleopatra* III.vii.]

18 By time and counsel do the best we can,
  Th' event is never in the power of man.
[Robert Herrick: *Hesperides*: "Event of Things not in our Power."]

19 The glories of our blood and state
  Are shadows, not substantial things;
  There is no armour against fate;
  Death lays his icy hand on kings,
  Sceptre and crown
  Must tumble down,
  And in the dust be equal made

With the poor crooked scythe and
spade.
[James Shirley: *The Contention of Ajax
and Ulysses* III]
1 All human things are subject to decay,
And when fate summons, monarchs
must obey.
[Dryden: *Mac Flecknoe*]
2 Heaven from all creatures hides the
book of fate.
[Alexander Pope: *An Essay on Man* I]
3 Must helpless man, in ignorance se-
date,
Roll darkling down the torrent of his
fate?
[Samuel Johnson: *The Vanity of Hu-
man Wishes*]
4 Every night and every morn
Some to misery are born;
Every morn and every night
Some are born to sweet delight.
[William Blake: *Proverbs*]
5 Let us, then, be up and doing,
With a heart for any fate.
[Longfellow: *A Psalm of Life*]
6 Up from Earth's Center through the
Seventh Gate
I rose, and on the Throne of Saturn
sate,
And many a Knot unraveled by the
Road;
But not the Master-knot of Human
Fate.
[*Rubáiyát of Omar Khayyám* (trans. Ed-
ward FitzGerald)]
7 Destiny has two ways of crushing us—
by refusing our wishes and by fulfilling
them. [Henri Amiel: *Journal*, April 10,
1881]
8 See how the Fates their gifts allot,
For A is happy—B is not.
Yet B is worthy, I dare say,
Of more prosperity than A.
[W. S. Gilbert: *The Mikado* II]
9 It matters not how strait the gate,
How charged with punishments the
scroll,
I am the master of my fate;
I am the captain of my soul.
[W. E. Henley: *Invictus*]
10 'Tis true there's better booze than
brine, but he that drowns must drink it.
[A. E. Housman: *The Oracles*]

FATHER(S)
11 Happy is the child whose father goes
to the devil.
[16th-century proverb]
*That is, happy is the child who, in his
natural rebellion against his father, must
go to the good. It's the opposite of the
common observation that clergymen's
sons often go to the bad.*
*Then there is the further meaning—
happy is the child whose father, being
wicked, may have acquired wealth for
which he goes to Hell but which the
child may virtuously inherit.*
12 It is a wise father that knows his own
child.
[Shakespeare: *The Merchant of Venice*
II.ii.]
13 Had he not resembled
My father as he slept, I had done 't.
[Shakespeare: *Macbeth* II.ii.]
14 Fathers that wear rags
Do make their children blind;
But fathers that bear bags
Shall see their children kind.
[Shakespeare: *King Lear* II.iv.]
15 Fathers should be neither seen nor
heard. That is the only proper basis for
family life. [Oscar Wilde: *An Ideal Husband* III]

FATHER AND SON
16 A wise son maketh a glad father.
[Proverbs 10:1]
17 Wife, the Athenians rule the Greeks,
and I rule the Athenians, and thou me,
and our son thee; let him then use sparingly the authority which makes him,
foolish as he is, the most powerful person
in Greece. [Themistocles: in Plutarch's
Life of Cato VIII]
18 Like father, like son. [William Langland: *Piers Plowman*, Passus II]
19 As a little childe riding behind his
father, sayde simply unto him, Father,
when you are dead, I shal ride in the Saddle. [Stefano Guazzo: *Civile Conversation* III.xliii.]
20 Box about: 'twill come to my father
anon. [Mr. Walter Raleigh: quoted in
Aubrey, *Brief Lives* II]
*Sir Walter Raleigh had taken his scape-
grace son, Mr. Walter, with him to dine
with some great persons, but had warned*

the young man, who had a reputation for indiscretion, to behave himself. At the table the son made a statement that reflected badly on his father. Sir Walter, Aubrey tells us, "being strangely surprised and put out of countenance . . . gives his son a damned blow over the face. His son, rude as he was, would not strike his father, but strikes over the face the gentleman that sat next to him and said 'Box about: 'twill come to my father anon.'"

1 Diogenes struck the father when the son swore.
[Robert Burton: *The Anatomy of Melancholy* III.2.2.5]
2 Greatness of name in the father ofttimes overwhelms the son; they stand too near one another. The shadow kills the growth: so much, that we see the grandchild come more and oftener to be heir of the first. [Ben Jonson: *Timber*]
3 There must always be a struggle between a father and son, while one aims at power and the other at independence. [Samuel Johnson: in Boswell's *Life,* July 14, 1763]
4 A man first quarrels with his father about three-quarters of a year before he is born. It is then he insists on setting up a separate establishment; when this has been once agreed to, the more complete the separation for ever after the better for both. [Samuel Butler (1835-1902): *The Way of All Flesh* LXXIX]

FATHER WILLIAM

5 You are old, Father William, the
                young man cried,
    The few locks which are left you
                are gray;
    You are hale, Father William, a
                hearty old man,
    Now tell me the reason, I pray.
[Robert Southey: *The Old Man's Comforts, and How He Gained Them*]
The Old Man attributes his vigor to having remembered his God in the days of his youth.
  Parodied by Lewis Carroll:
"You are old, Father William," the young man said,
  "And your hair has become very white;
And yet you incessantly stand on your head—

Do you think, at your age, it is right?"
The Old Man says that since he has no brains it can do no harm. (Alice's Adventures in Wonderland *V*)

FATTED CALF

6 And bring hither the fatted calf, and kill it; and let us eat and be merry:
For this my son was dead, and is alive again; he was lost, and is found. [Luke 15:23-24]
Samuel Butler said that one cannot expect the fatted calf to share in the rejoicing at the return of the Prodigal Son.

FAULT(S)

7 Except for being faultless, he has no faults. [Pliny the Younger: *Epistolae* IX. xxvi.]
See ARISTIDES
8 Men's faults do seldom to themselves
                appear.
[Shakespeare: *The Rape of Lucrece*]
9 And oftentimes, excusing of a fault
    Doth make the fault the worse by the
                excuse.
[Shakespeare: *King John* IV.ii.]
10 Condemn the fault, and not the actor
                of it?
[Shakespeare: *Measure for Measure* II.ii.]
11 They say best men are moulded out
                of faults,
    And, for the most, become much
                more the better
    For being a little bad.
[Shakespeare: *Measure for Measure* V.i.]
12 Faults are thick where love is thin.
[James Howell: *Proverbs* (1659)]
i.e., where there is no love, faults are easily perceived and not forgiven.
13 We endeavour to take pride in faults that we do not wish to correct. [La Rochefoucauld: *Maxims*]
14 We confess our little faults only to persuade others that we have no great ones. [La Rochefoucauld: *Maxims*]
15 I like her with all her faults; nay, like her for her faults. [William Congreve: *The Way of the World* I.iii.]
16 We men have many faults;
    Poor women have but two—
    There's nothing good they say,
    There's nothing good they do.
[Anon.: *On Women's Faults*]

FAULT-FINDING

1 Mistrust a subordinate who never finds fault with his superior. [J. C. Collins: *Aphorisms*]

FAVOR(S)

2 To remind a man of the good turns you have done him is very much like a reproach. [Demosthenes: *On the Crown*]
3 Doing a favour for a bad man is quite as dangerous as doing an injury to a good one. [Plautus: *Poenulus* III.iii.]
4 To accept a favor is to sell one's freedom. [Publilius Syrus: *Maxims*]
5 However often a man may receive an obligation from you, one refusal effaces all memory of former favors. [Pliny the Younger: *Epistolae* III.iv.]
6 A favor tardily bestowed is no favor. [Ausonius: *Epigrammata*]
7 You goe about to currey favour. [John Lyly: *Euphues and his England* (1580)]

> The phrase "to curry favor"—to ingratiate oneself for some material advantage —was not invented by Lyly. It was a corruption of an earlier expression to curry favel. Favel or Fauvel was the name of a horse in a 14th-century French satirical poem Roman de Fauvel. In the poem the horse, symbolizing worldly vanity, is soothed and lovingly tended by all classes of society, so that to curry favel was to seek to advance yourself, to ingratiate yourself with the powerful. As the poem became forgotten but the idea of seeking a favor persisted, the corruption of the phrase was almost inevitable.

8 You had better refuse a favour gracefully than to grant it clumsily. [Lord Chesterfield: *Letters*, March 18, 1751]
9 Most people return small Favours, acknowledge middling ones, and repay great ones with Ingratitude. [Benjamin Franklin: *Poor Richard's Almanack* (1751)]
10 He who presumes upon a favor he has conferred, takes it back. [Lessing: *Nathan der Weise* V.viii.]
11 To accept a favor from a friend is to confer one. [J. C. Collins: *Aphorisms*]

FAVORITE

12 A fav'rite has no friend! [Thomas Gray: *On the Death of a Favourite Cat*]

FAWNING

13 Why what a candy deal of courtesy
   This fawning greyhound then did proffer me!
[Shakespeare: *I Henry IV* I.iii.]
14   Sweet words,
   Low-crooked curtsies, and base spaniel fawning.
[Shakespeare: *Julius Caesar* III.i.]
15 No; let the candied tongue lick absurd pomp,
   And crook the pregnant hinges of the knee,
   Where thrift may follow fawning.
[Shakespeare: *Hamlet* III.ii.]

FEAR

16 Thou shalt not be afraid for the terror by night; nor for the arrow that flieth by day. [Psalms 91:5]
17 I was stupefied with fear; my hair stood on end and my voice stuck in my throat. [Vergil: *Aeneid* II.774; III.48]
18 Fear added wings to his feet. [Vergil: *Aeneid* VIII]
19 He must necessarily fear many, whom many fear. [Seneca: *De Ira* II.xi.]

> Also in the Maxims of Publilius Syrus and in the works of many others. The saying is believed to have been coined in reference to Julius Caesar.

20 Without fear and without reproach. *Applied to the knight, Pierre du Terrail, Chevalier de Bayard (1473?-1524), distinguished in the Italian campaigns of Charles VIII, Louis XII and Francis I.*
21 For I am sick and capable of fears,
   Oppress'd with wrongs, and therefore full of fears.
[Shakespeare: *King John* III.i.]
22 Ere we will eat our meal in fear, and sleep
   In the affliction of these terrible dreams
   That shake us nightly.
[Shakespeare: *Macbeth* III.ii.]
23 Cabin'd, cribb'd, confined, bound in
   To saucy doubts and fears.
[Shakespeare: *Macbeth* III.iv.]
24 Fain would I climb, yet fear I to fall.

[Thomas Fuller (1608-1661): *Worthies of England* I.xix.]

Said to be scratched with a diamond on a window pane by Sir Walter Raleigh in Queen Elizabeth's presence. The Queen is supposed to have written under it: "If thy heart fail thee, climb not at all."

1 Fear is one of the passions of human nature, of which it is impossible to divest it. You remember that the Emperor Charles V, when he read upon the tombstone of a Spanish nobleman, "Here lies one who never knew fear," wittily said, "Then he never snuffed a candle with his fingers." [Samuel Johnson: in Boswell's *Life*, October 10, 1769]

2 Early and provident fear is the mother of safety. [Edmund Burke: in a speech (1792)]

3 Fear at my heart, as at a cup,
My life-blood seemed to sip!
[Coleridge: *The Ancient Mariner* III]

4 Like one, that on a lonesome road
Doth walk in fear and dread,
And having once turned round,
             walks on,
And turns no more his head;
Because he knows a frightful fiend
Doth close behind him tread.
[Coleridge: *The Ancient Mariner* VI]

5   Far below
The sea-blooms and the oozy woods
             which wear
The sapless foliage of the ocean,
             know
Thy voice, and suddenly grow gray
             with fear,
And tremble and despoil themselves.
[Shelley: *Ode to the West Wind*]

6 When I have fears that I may cease to
             be
Before my pen has glean'd my teeming brain. . . .
[Keats: *When I Have Fears*]

7 "What are they fear'd on? fools! 'od
             rot 'em!"
Were the last words of Higginbottom.
[Horace Smith: *Rejected Addresses*, "A Tale of Drury Lane"]
A parody of Sir Walter Scott.

8 Deep into that darkness peering, long
      I stood there wondering, fearing,
Doubting, dreaming dreams no mortal ever dared to dream before.
[Edgar Allan Poe: *The Raven*]

9 The one permanent emotion of the inferior man, as of all the simpler mammals, is fear—fear of the unknown, the complex, the inexplicable. [H. L. Mencken: in *The Yale Review*, June 1920]

10 I will show you fear in a handful of
             dust.
[T. S. Eliot: *The Waste Land* I]

FEAR: the burnt child

11 Burnt child fire dredth. [John Heywood: *Proverbs*]

12 The scalded dog fears cold water. [George Herbert: *Jacula Prudentum*]

13 Dogs once scalded, are afraid even of cold water. [Thomas Fuller (1654-1734): *Gnomologia*]

FEAR: the danger of

14 He that fleeth from the fear shall fall into the pit; and he that getteth up out of the pit shall be taken in the snare. [Jeremiah 48:44]

15 In extreme danger fear feels no pity. [Caesar: *De Bello Gallico* VII.xxvi.]

16 Fear makes men believe the worst. [Quintus Rufus: *Alexander the Great* IV.x.]

17 The mere apprehension of an approaching evil has put many into a situation of the utmost danger. [Lucan: *Pharsalia* VII.civ.]

18 There is no passion so contagious as that of fear. [Montaigne: *Essays* I.xlvii.]

19 Our fears do make us traitors. [Shakespeare: *Macbeth* IV.ii.]

20 Foolish fear doubleth danger. [Thomas Fuller (1654-1734): *Gnomologia*]

21 The only thing we have to fear is fear itself. [Franklin Delano Roosevelt: First Inaugural Address, March 4, 1933]

The thing of which I have most fear is fear.   Montaigne: Essays I.xvii.
Nothing is so much to be feared as fear.   Thoreau: Journal, Sept. 7, 1851

FEAR: excessive and overrated

22 We fear things in proportion to our ignorance of them. [Livy: *Histories* XXVIII.xliv.]

23 If evils come not, then our fears are
             vain;

And if they do, fear but augments the
pain.
[Sir Thomas More: *On Fear*]
*The literature of wisdom is crammed
with comments on the folly of fear—a
comment, in itself, on the folly of wisdom.*

1 It is a pity we should so deceive ourselves with our own foolish devices and
apish inventions; as children will be
afeard of their fellow's visage, which
themselves have besmeared and blacked.
[Montaigne: *Essays* II.xii.]

2   Present fears
Are less than horrible imaginings.
[Shakespeare: *Macbeth* I.iii.]

FEAR: and hate
3 Men hesitate less to injure a man who
makes himself loved than to injure one
who makes himself feared, for their love
is held by a chain of obligation which,
because of men's wickedness, is broken
on every occasion for the sake of selfish
profit; but their fear is secured by a
dread of punishment. [Machiavelli: *The
Prince* XVII]

4 In time we hate that which we often
fear.
[Shakespeare: *Antony and Cleopatra*
I.iii.]

5 He that fears you present, will hate
you absent. [Thomas Fuller (1654-
1734): *Gnomologia*]

FEARED
6 It is safer to be despised than to be
feared. [Fernan de Rojas: *La Celestina*
IV]

FEAST
7 Small cheer and great welcome makes
a merry feast.
[Shakespeare: *The Comedy of Errors*
III.i.]

8 The feast of reason and the flow of
the soul.
[Alexander Pope: *Imitations of Horace*
II.i.]

9 The guests are met, the feast is set:
May'st hear the merry din.
[Coleridge: *The Ancient Mariner* I]

FEATHER(S)
10 It hath been an antient custom
among them (Hungarians) that none

should wear a fether but he who had
killed a Turk, to whom onlie yt was lawful to shew the number of his slaine enemys by the number of fethers in his
cappe. [Richard Hansard: *Description
of Hungary, Anno 1599*]

11 Fine feathers make fine birds. [Ber-
nard Mandeville: *The Fable of the Bees*
I.130 (1714)]

12 You might have knocked me down
with a feather. [William Cobbett: *Rural
Rides*]
See also: BIRDS

FEEDING
13 With eager feeding, food doth choke
the feeder.
[Shakespeare: *Richard II* II.i.]

FEELING
14 I cannot love as I have loved,
And yet I know not why;
It is the one great woe of life
To feel all feeling die.
[Philip James Bailey: *Festus*]

15 Real feeling is *always* vulgar. [Wil-
liam Dean Howells: *Letters Home*]

FEET
16 How beautiful upon the mountains
are the feet of him that bringeth good
tidings, that publisheth peace. [Isaiah
52:7]

17 The civilized man has built a coach,
but has lost the use of his feet. [Emer-
son: *Self-Reliance* (1841)]

FEET OF CLAY
18 This image's head was of fine gold,
his breast and his arms of silver, his belly
and his thighs of brass, his legs of iron,
his feet part of iron and part of clay.
[Daniel 2:32-33]
*This is the origin of the phrase "feet of
clay" by which we designate some vulnerable trait or fault in an otherwise
admirable person.*

*Nebuchadnezzar, king of Assyria,
dreamed that he had seen an image,
as described above. A stone struck the
image on its clay feet and it collapsed.
He demanded that his wise men interpret the dream, even though he had forgotten it and couldn't tell them what it
was. This seems unreasonable in a scien-*

tific age, but the king probably argued that if they could interpret *dreams—as they professed to be able to—merely knowing what the dream was should have been comparatively simple. The prophet Daniel—by means of a vision— knew the dream and its significance: the destruction of Assyria. Since the head was of gold, Nebuchadnezzar could be complimented, even though his own destruction was involved. He immediately made Daniel Chief Wise Man.*

FELICITY
1 Absent thee from felicity awhile.
[Shakespeare: *Hamlet* V.ii.]
The felicity *specifically alluded to here is death.*

FELLOW(S)
2 Certain lewd fellows of the baser sort.
[Acts 17:5]
3 A fellow of no mark nor likelihood.
[Shakespeare: *I Henry IV* III.ii.]
4 Hail fellow well met, all dirty and wet;
Find out, if you can, who's master, who's man.
[Jonathan Swift: *My Lady's Lamentation*]

FELLOWMEN
5 Write me as one who loves his fellowmen.
[Leigh Hunt: *Abou Ben Adhem*]

FELLOWSHIP
6 The right hands of fellowship. [Galatians 2:9]
7 In felawschip wel coude she laughe and carpe.
[Chaucer: Prologue to *The Canterbury Tales*]
8 Out upon this half-fac'd fellowship!
[Shakespeare: *I Henry IV* I.iii.]
9 A fellow-feeling makes one wondrous kind. [David Garrick: *Prologue on Quitting the Theatre*]
10 For it's always fair weather
When good fellows get together.
[Richard Hovey: *A Stein Song*]
11 The fountain in the desert,
The cistern in the waste,
The bread we ate in secret,

The cup we spilled in haste.
[Kipling: *The Song of Diego Valdez*]

FELON
12 When a felon's not engaged in his employment,
Or maturing his felonious little plans,
His capacity for innocent enjoyment
Is just as great as any honest man's.
[W. S. Gilbert: *The Pirates of Penzance* II]

FEMALE
13 The female of the species is more deadly than the male.
[Kipling: *The Female of the Species*]

FENCES
14 Love your neighbor, yet pull not down your hedge.
[George Herbert: *Jacula Prudentum*]
15 Good fences make good neighbors.
[Robert Frost: *Mending Wall*]

FERRY
16 A chieftain to the Highlands bound
Cries, "Boatman, do not tarry!
And I'll give thee a silver pound
To row us o'er the ferry."
[Thomas Campbell: *Lord Ullin's Daughter*]

FEVER
17 Poison'd, ill fare! dead, forsook, cast off!
And none of you will bid the winter come
To thrust his icy fingers in my maw,
Nor let my kingdom's rivers take their course
Through my burn'd bosom, nor entreat the North
To make his bleak winds kiss my parched lips
And comfort me with cold.
[Shakespeare: *King John* V.vii.]

FEW
18 Many be called, but few are chosen.
[Matthew 20:16]
19 Never in the field of human conflict was so much owed by so many to so few.
[Winston Churchill: in a speech in the House of Commons, August 20, 1940]

The reference is to the defeat of the **Luftwaffe** *by the Royal Air Force in the Battle of Britain, 1940.*

FICKLENESS

1 Though she were true, when you met
　　　　　　　　　　　　　her,
　And last, till you write your letter,
　　　Yet she,
　　　Will be
False, ere I come, to two, or three.
[Donne: *Song*]

FICTION

2 If this were played upon a stage now, I could condemn it as an improbable fiction. [Shakespeare: *Twelfth Night* III.iv.]
3 It is not easy for the most artful writer to give us an interest in happiness or misery which we think ourselves never likely to feel and with which we have never yet been made acquainted. [Samuel Johnson: *The Rambler* No. 60]

> *Every man can remember with what awful boredom he, as a boy, sat through the brief love passages with which, for some reason, it was thought necessary to interlard the old western movies.*

4 From the time of life when fancy begins to be overruled by reason and corrected by experience, the most artful tale raises little curiosity when it is known to be false. [Samuel Johnson: *The Idler* No. 84]
5 Stranger than fiction.
[Byron: *Don Juan* XIV.ci.]
6 Character in decay is the theme of the great bulk of superior fiction. [H. L. Mencken: *Prejudices*]

FIDDLE

7 He could fiddle all the bugs off a
　　　　　　　　　sweet-potato-vine.
[Stephen Vincent Benét: *The Mountain Whippoorwill*]

FIDDLER

8 When I play on my fiddle in Dooney,
　Folk dance like a wave of the sea.
[William Butler Yeats: *The Fiddler of Dooney*]

FIEND

9 This is the foul fiend Flibbertigibbet.

He begins at curfew, and walks till the first cock. [Shakespeare: *King Lear* III. iv.]
10 Then lies him down the lubber fiend,
　　And stretch'd out all the chimney's
　　　　　　　　　　　　length,
　Basks at the fire his hairy strength.
[John Milton: *L'Allegro*]
　This was "Lob-lie-by-the-fire."

FIERCE

11 The strongest and the fiercest spirit
　That fought in heaven, now fiercer
　　　　　　　　　　　by despair.
[John Milton: *Paradise Lost* II.44]

FIFTH OF NOVEMBER

12 Please to remember
　The fifth of November,
　　The gunpowder treason and plot;
　I see no reason
　Why gunpowder treason
　　Should ever be forgot.
[Anon.]

> *The Gunpowder Plot was a frustrated plan of Guy Fawkes and other Roman Catholic conspirators to blow up the British Houses of Parliament and King James I on November 5, 1605. Its discovery and the punishment of the plotters was celebrated with bonfires and public rejoicing. By a coincidence it was on November 5, eighty-three years later, that the Protestant William of Orange landed in England and took over the throne as the Catholic James II fled. Religious feeling ran high and the old celebration of "Guy Fawkes Day" was revived and has been maintained ever since. It has in England something of the character of our Fourth of July and Halloween.*
>
> *Guy Fawkes is always burned in effigy and children go about begging pennies "for the guy." To stimulate giving they sing various begging songs of which this is one of the most famous.*

FIFTY

13 Ah, what shall I be at fifty
　　Should Nature keep me alive,
　If I find the world so bitter
　　When I am but twenty-five?
[Tennyson: *Maud: A Monodrama* I.vi.]

FIFTY-FOUR FORTY

14 Fifty-four forty, or fight! [Slogan of

the Democratic Party in 1844, sometimes attributed to William Allen in a speech on the Oregon boundary question in the U.S. Senate, 1844.]

It demanded that our western boundary be bounded on the north at 54°40', instead of—as now—at the 49th parallel. The result would have been that Canada would have no access to the Pacific, since the Russian territory came south to 54° 40' and what is now western Canada would have been a part of the USA.

FIGHT: he who fights and runs away

1 He who fled will fight again on another occasion. [Tertullian: *De Fuga in Persecutione* X]

There is no suggestion of humor in Tertullian's sentence.

2 He that fights and runs away
May live to fight another day.
[Anon. (1656)]

This, with the exchange of "who" for "that," is the common modern form of the saying.

The idea, in very close to the same words, goes back to Menander (342?-292 B.C.) and has appeared a hundred times —in Tertullian, Erasmus, Samuel Butler (1612-1680) and in every collection of proverbs and epigrams.

3 For he that fights and runs away
May live to fight another day;
But he who is in battle slain
Can never rise and fight again.
[Oliver Goldsmith: *The Art of Poetry on a New Plan*]

FIGHT ON

4 Saying, Fight on, my merry men all,
And see that none of you be taine;
For rather than men shall say we
were hanged,
Let them report how we were slain.
[Anon.: *The Ballad of Johnnie Armstrong*]
taine = *taken*

5 Said John, Fight on, my merry men
all,
I am a little hurt, but I am not
slain;
I will lay me down for to bleed a
while,
Then I'll rise and fight with you

again.
[Anon.: *The Ballad of Johnnie Armstrong*]
Also in the Ballad of Sir Andrew Barton.

6 I have not yet begun to fight. [John Paul Jones: in answer to a demand for surrender, as his ship the *Bonhomme Richard* was sinking, in his fight with the British *Serapis*, September 23, 1779]

7 'Tis better to have fought and lost,
Than never to have fought at all.
[Arthur Hugh Clough: *Peschiera*]
Surely this depends on the cause.

8 We shall not flag or fail. We shall fight in France, we shall fight on the seas and oceans, we shall fight with growing confidence and growing strength in the air, we shall defend our island, whatever the cost may be, we shall fight on the beaches, we shall fight on the landing grounds, we shall fight in the fields and in the streets, we shall fight in the hills; we shall never surrender. [Winston Churchill: Speech, in the House of Commons, June 4, 1940]

FIGURES

9 Figures won't lie, but liars will figure. [Attr. Charles H. Grosvenor, Representative from Ohio]
Usually: Figures don't lie but liars figure.

FINEST HOUR

10 Let us therefore brace ourselves to our duties, and so bear ourselves that, if the British Empire and its Commonwealth last for a thousand years, men will still say: "'This was their finest hour." [Winston Churchill: Speech, in the House of Commons, June 18, 1940]

FINGER(S)

11 Fingers were made before forks. [Jonathan Swift: *Polite Conversation*]
The appearance of a well-known saying in Swift's Polite Conversation *does not mean that Swift made up the saying; on the contrary, it means that Swift regarded it as a cliché. The date of the* Polite Conversation—*a tissue of moth-eaten phrases, worn-out wisecracks, musty proverbs and threadbare sententiousness —is 1738.*

Forks, by the way, did not come into general use in England much before the time of Queen Elizabeth (d. 1603). They were at first merely bifurcated daggers and until some genius thought of adding a third tine and blunting all three, there were some dreadful accidents with them.

1 The Moving Finger writes; and, hav-
ing writ,
Moves on; nor all your Piety nor Wit
Shall lure it back to cancel half a
Line
Nor all your Tears wash out a Word
of it.
[*Rubáiyát of Omar Khayyám* (trans. Edward FitzGerald)]

FIRE
2 For the Lord thy God is a consuming fire, even a jealous God. [Deuteronomy 4:24]
3 We went through fire and through water. [Psalms 56:12]
4 Can a man take fire in his bosom, and his clothes not be burned? [Proverbs 6:27]
5 A little fire is quickly trodden out;
Which, being suffered, rivers cannot
quench.
[Shakespeare: *III Henry VI* IV.viii.]
6 Where glowing embers through the
room
Teach light to counterfeit a gloom,
Far from all resort of mirth,
Save the cricket on the hearth.
[John Milton: *Il Penseroso*]
7 Some heart once pregnant with celestial fire.
[Thomas Gray: *Elegy Written in a Country Churchyard*]
8 Don't fire until you see the whites of their eyes. [General Israel Putnam: to the American soldiers at the Battle of Bunker Hill (June 17, 1775)]
The famous command is sometimes ascribed to Colonel William Prescott. But it was assigned to Putnam as early as 1849 in Richard Frothingham's History of the Siege of Boston (p. 140, n.).
It was a conventional command. The muzzle loader took considerable time to reload, and during this time the soldiers were helpless and inclined to panic under counterfire (see also: BOLT). One of the problems of a commander was to persuade his nervous men to hold their fire until it could be effective. The fa-

mous request of Lord Charles Hay at Fontenoy (1745) may have been as much cunning as courtesy (see: GUARDS). Prince Charles of Prussia at Jagerndorf, in the same year as Fontenoy, had ordered his men not to fire until they could perceive the whites of the enemies' eyes and Frederick the Great repeated the same order at Prague (1757).

A number of commanders were concerned with directing fire at Bunker Hill. John Stark, with probably a better understanding of his men's marksmanship and courage, cried, "Boys, aim at their waistbands." Such practical advice, though it no doubt accounted for many redcoats, missed posterity.

9 You may fire when you are ready, Gridley. [Admiral George Dewey: addressed to the Captain of Dewey's flagship, at the Battle of Manila Bay, May 1, 1898]
Very fine! Not in the "England expects" tradition nor yet in the "Do you want to live forever, you sons o' bitches" blood-and-guts style. But calm, assured and charmingly considerate. And just a little fuddy-duddy-ish. See also: PRESIDENCY.

FIRMNESS
10 Come one, come all! this rock shall
fly
From its firm base as soon as I.
[Sir Walter Scott: *Lady of the Lake* V]

FIRST
11 Many that are first shall be last; and the last first. [Mark 10:31]

FIRST COME
12 Who-so that first to mille comth, first
grinds.
[Chaucer: Prologue to *The Wife of Bath's Tale*]

FIRST PLACE
13 It is a maxim that those to whom everybody allows the second place have an undoubted title to the first. [Jonathan Swift: *A Tale of a Tub*]

FISH
14 The pleasant'st angling is to see the
fish

Cut with her golden oars the silver
stream,
And greedily devour the treacherous
bait.
[Shakespeare: *Much Ado about Nothing* III.i.]

1 *Third Fisherman.* Master, I marvel
how the fishes live in the sea.
First Fisherman. Why, as men do
aland; the great ones eat up the little
ones. [Shakespeare: *Timon of Athens*
II.i.]

2 We have other fish to fry. [Peter Motteux's rendering of Rabelais's "We have
something else to do here." (*Pantagruel*
V.xii.)]

*Motteux seems to have used a current
phrase. It appears in other works too
near the time of his use of it for him to
have invented it. It sounds like the catch
phrase of some forgotten story or incident.*

3 No man cries stinking fish. [John
Ray: *English Proverbs* (1678)]

*i.e., no peddler hawking fish through the
streets would state that it was rotten,
even if it were. A sort of inverted form
of "Let the buyer beware."*

4 There is as good fish in the sea as
ever came out of it.
[Sir Walter Scott: *Fortunes of Nigel*
XXXV]

5 I never lost a little fish—yes, I am
free to say,
It always was the biggest fish I caught
that got away.
[Eugene Field: *Our Biggest Fish*]

6 Fish say, they have their Stream and
Pond;
But is there anything Beyond?
[Rupert Brooke: *Heaven*]

FISHBALL

7 The waiter he to him doth call,
And gently whispers—"One Fishball."
The waiter roars it through the hall,
The guests they start at "One Fishball."
The guest then says, quite ill at ease,
"A piece of bread, sir, if you please."
The waiter roars it through the hall:
"We don't give bread with one Fishball!"
[George Martin Lane: *One Fishball*
(1855)]

FISHERMAN

8 An excellent angler, and now with
God. [Izaak Walton: *The Compleat Angler* I.iv.]

FISHERS

9 Fishers of men. [Matthew 4:19]

FISHING

10 Best fishing in troubled waters. [Ariosto: *Orlando Furioso* (trans. Sir John
Harington)]

11 I have laid aside business, and gone
a-fishing. [Izaak Walton: *The Compleat
Angler*, "Author's Preface"]

12 We may say of angling as Dr. Boteler
said of strawberries: "Doubtless God
could have made a better berry, but
doubtless God never did"; and so, if I
might be judge, God never did make a
more calm, quiet, innocent recreation
than angling. [Izaak Walton: *The Compleat Angler* I.v.]

13 To fish in troubled waters. [Matthew
Henry: *Commentaries,* Psalm LX]

14 Impaling worms to torture fish.
[George Colman the Younger: *Lady of
the Wreck* II]

15 Angling: incessant expectation, and
perpetual disappointment. [Arthur
Young: *Travels in France* (1787)]

16 And angling, too, that solitary vice,
Whatever Izaak Walton sings or says;
The quaint old cruel coxcomb in his
gullet
Should have a hook and a small trout
to pull it.
[Byron: *Don Juan* XIII.cvi.]

17 A fishing-rod is a stick with a hook at
one end and a fool at the other. [Attr.
Samuel Johnson by William Hazlitt in
Table-Talk, "On Egotism" (1825)]

*But no such observation can be found in
Johnson's own works or in Boswell. And
it doesn't have quite the ring of authenticity. Leigh Hunt had used almost the
same sentence six years before Hazlitt. It
sounds like a joke that was going the
rounds.*

FIT

18 Fitted him to a T. [Samuel Johnson:
in Boswell's *Life* (1784)]

FITS

1 'Twas sad by fits, by starts 'twas wild.
[William Collins: *The Passions* XXVIII]

FITTEST

2 The expression often used by Mr. Herbert Spencer of the Survival of the Fittest is more accurate. [Charles Darwin: *The Origin of Species* III]

Herbert Spencer had used the term, as another wording of Darwin's "natural selection," in Principles of Biology *III.xii.*

Fittest was a word unfortunately adaptable to almost any value that anyone desired to repose in it. It was a long time before the chilling fact emerged that, in this context, it could only mean "fittest to survive."

FITZGERALD

3   F. Scott Fitzgerald
          Hack Writer and Plagiarist
            St. Paul, Minnesota
F. Scott Fitzgerald's letterhead, 1922.

4 Mr. Fitzgerald [F. Scott] is a novelist. Mrs. Fitzgerald is a novelty. [Ring Lardner: *The Other Side*]

FLAG

5 The black flag was set up, which signified there was no mercy to be looked for. [Thomas Nashe: *Christ's Tears over Jerusalem*(1593)]

The displaying of a black flag was formerly an established military procedure to indicate that no quarter would be asked or given. Pirates—notoriously conservative—retained the custom after it had fallen into disuse elsewhere. The skull and crossbones on the "Jolly Roger" was merely a fanciful embellishment; the main thing was the black background.

All that survives of this ancient gruesomeness today is the use of the phrase as the name of a vermin exterminator.

6 Th' imperial ensign, which, full high advanc'd,
Shone like a meteor streaming to the wind.
[John Milton: *Paradise Lost* I.536-537]

7 Oh, say can you see by the dawn's early light,
What so proudly we hailed at the twilight's last gleaming?

Whose broad stripes and bright stars, thro' the perilous fight,
O'er the ramparts we watched were so gallantly streaming?
And the rockets' red glare, the bombs bursting in air,
Gave proof thro' the night that our flag was still there.
Oh, say does that star-spangled banner yet wave
O'er the land of the free and the home of the brave?
[Francis Scott Key: *The Star-Spangled Banner*]

8 When Freedom from her mountain height
Unfurled her standard to the air,
She tore the azure robe of night,
And set the stars of glory there.
She mingled with its gorgeous dyes
The milky baldric of the skies,
And striped its pure celestial white,
With streakings of the morning light.
[Joseph Rodman Drake: *The American Flag*]

9 I name thee Old Glory. [Captain William Driver (1803-1886): on the occasion of hoisting a large American flag which had been presented to him by a band of women.]

The flag is now in the Smithsonian Institution. Old was a common term of honor and endearment when our country was new. Many of the commanders in the Civil War were called "Old" by their men, though many were in their thirties and few beyond their forties: "Old Blue Light" ("Stonewall" Jackson), "Old Fuss and Feathers" (General Winfield Scott), and, especially, "Old Abe."

10 "Shoot, if you must, this old gray head,
But spare your country's flag," she said.
[J. G. Whittier: *Barbara Frietchie*]

FLAME

11 To burn always with this hard, gemlike flame, to maintain this ecstasy, is success in life. [Walter Pater: *The Renaissance* (Conclusion)]

FLATTERY

12 Obsequiousness makes friends; truth

breeds hate. [Terence: *Andria* I.i.]

1 Flatterers are the worst kind of enemies. [Tacitus: *Agricola* XLI]

2 Fair words make fools fain. [Anon.: *Everyman* (about 1530)]

> *That is, fools are easily taken in by flattery and empty promises.*

3 He that speakes me fairer than his
woont was too,
Hath done me harme, or meanes for
to doo.
[George Puttenham: *The Arte of English Poesie*]

4 Too much magnifying of man or matter doth irritate contradiction and procure envy and scorn. [Francis Bacon: *Of Praise*]

> irritate = *arouse by irritation*
>
> *We dislike gross flattery not because it is flattery but because it may border on ridicule and is almost certain to excite ridicule.*

5 Well said: that was laid on with a trowel. [Shakespeare: *As You Like It* I.ii.]

6 But when I tell him he hates flatterers,
He says he does, being then most flattered.
[Shakespeare: *Julius Caesar* II.i.]

7 Why should the poor be flatter'd?
No, let the candied tongue lick absurd pomp,
And crook the pregnant hinges of the knee,
Where thrift may follow fawning.
[Shakespeare: *Hamlet* III.ii.]

8 Lay not that flattering unction to your soul. [Shakespeare: *Hamlet* III.iv.]

9 He would not flatter Neptune for his trident,
Or Jove for 's power to thunder.
[Shakespeare: *Coriolanus* III.i.]

10 We can be stabbed without being flattered, but we're rarely flattered without being stabbed. [Quevedo: *Marco Bruto*]

11 'Tis the most pleasing flattery to like what other men like. [John Selden: *Table Talk*, "Pleasure"]

12 Nothing was too much to be given that a lady might be saved from the disgrace of such a vile performance. [Edmund Waller: in Samuel Johnson's *Life of Waller*]

Waller, a distinguished poet, on hearing some lines from The Hunting of a Stag, *by "the Thrice Noble, Illustrious and Excellent Princess, the Lady Marchioness of Newcastle" (1644), declared that he would give all his own poems to have written these lines. Sample:*

> *Single he was; his horns were all his helps*
> *To guard him from a multitude of whelps,*
> *Besides a company of men were there,*
> *If dogs should fail, to strike him everywhere.*

When taxed with insincerity, Waller replied as above.

13 When we think we hate flattery we only hate the manner of the flatterer. [La Rochefoucauld: *Maxims*]

14 'Tis an old maxim in the schools,
That flattery's the food of fools;
Yet now and then your men of wit
Will condescend to take a bit.
[Jonathan Swift: *Cadenus and Vanessa*]

15 All panegyrics are mingled with an infusion of poppy. [Jonathan Swift: *Thoughts on Various Subjects*]

16 There are, who to my person pay their court:
I cough like Horace, and, tho' lean, am short.
Ammon's great son one shoulder had too high,
Such Ovid's nose, and, "Sir! you have an eye—"
Go on, obliging creatures, make me see
All that disgrac'd my Betters, met in me. . . .
And, when I die, be sure you let me know
Great Homer died three thousand years ago.
[Alexander Pope: *Epistle to Dr. Arbuthnot*]

> Ammon's great son = *Alexander the Great, or Hephaestus;* Ovid's nose = *Publius Ovidius Naso, Roman poet (43 B.C.-18 A.D.); the Naso (= nosy) shows he had a conspicuous nose.*
>
> *Pope was a tiny man with a twisted spine and in delicate health.*

17 One Flatt'rer's worse than all.
Of all mad creatures, if the learn'd are right,

It is the slaver kills, and not the bite.
A fool quite angry is quite innocent:
Alas! 'tis ten times worse when they
repent.
[Alexander Pope: *Epistle to Dr. Arbuthnot*]
innocent = *innoxious, harmless, non-
poisonous*

1 Consider what your flattery is worth
before you bestow it so freely. [Samuel
Johnson: in Boswell's *Life* (1784)]
*The rebuke was administered to Hannah
More who had paid court to the sage "in
the most fulsome strain." Johnson tried
to divert "this indelicate and vain ob-
trusion of compliment" by more polite
means and when they proved futile
spoke as above. The general public's
conception of Johnson as a rude old man
with dirty linen and bad table manners
stems, to a large degree, from Macaulay's
famous essay on Boswell. Hannah More
was Macaulay's aunt. He was fond of
her, and it might well be that this remark whetted the edge of his resentment.*

2 It is simpler and easier to flatter men
than to praise them. [Jean Paul Richter:
Titan Zykel 34]

3 It is no flattery to a prisoner to gild
the jail. [Calderón: *Fortunas de Andromeda y Perseo* II]

4 What really flatters a man is that you
think him worth flattering. [G. B. Shaw:
John Bull's Other Island IV]

FLATTERY: self-flattery

5 The arch flatterer, with whom all the
petty flatterers have intelligence, is a
man's self. [Francis Bacon: *Of Love*]
*Intelligence is used here in the sense in
which we use it in "military intelligence." That is, all who seek advantage
by flattery have secret communication
with our own self-esteem.*

6 If we did not flatter ourselves, the flattery of others would do us no harm. [La
Rochefoucauld: *Maxims*]

7 We should have but little pleasure,
were we never to flatter ourselves. [La
Rochefoucauld: *Maxims*]

8 There is no such Flatterer, as a Man's
self. [Thomas Fuller (1654-1734): *Gnomologia*]

FLEA

9 So, Nat'ralists observe, a Flea
Hath smaller fleas that on him prey;
And these have smaller fleas to bite
'em,
And so proceed *ad infinitum*.
[Jonathan Swift: *On Poetry: A Rhap-
sody* (1733)]
Swift pronounced Flea *as we pronounce*
flay. *There have been many elaborations
and variations on Swift's basic jingle.*

FLESH

10 All flesh is grass, and all the goodli-
ness thereof is as the flower of the field.
[Isaiah 40:6]

11 All flesh is as grass. [I Peter 1:24]

12 The spirit indeed is willing, but the
flesh is weak. [Matthew 26:41]

13 The words expressly are "a pound of
flesh:"
Take then thy bond, take thou thy
pound of flesh.
[Shakespeare: *The Merchant of Venice*
IV.i.]

14 I saw him now going the way of all
flesh.
[John Webster and Thomas Dekker:
Westward Hoe II.ii. (1607)]
I am going the way of all the earth.
Joshua: 23:14
The Way of All Flesh—*title of novel
by Samuel Butler (1903)*

15 I wants to make your flesh creep.
[Dickens: *The Pickwick Papers* VIII]

16 O God! that bread should be so dear,
And flesh and blood so cheap!
[Thomas Hood: *The Song of the Shirt*]

FLIGHT

17 If I take the wings of the morning,
and dwell in the uttermost parts of the
sea. [Psalms 139:9]

18 He who flies from trial confesses his
crime. [Publilius Syrus: *Maxims*]

19 Let us not be dainty of leave-taking,
But shift away.
[Shakespeare: *Macbeth* II.iii.]

20 In love's wars, he who flieth is conqueror. [Thomas Fuller (1654-1734):
Gnomologia]

21 More like a man
Flying from something that he dreads
than one
Who sought the thing he loved.

[Wordsworth: *Tintern Abbey*]
1 To fly from, need not be to hate,
          mankind:
All are not fit with them to stir and
          toil,
Nor is it discontent to keep the mind
Deep in its fountain.
[Byron: *Childe Harold* III.lxix.]
2 I fled Him, down the nights and
          down the days;
I fled Him, down the arches of the
          years;
I fled Him, down the labyrinthine
          ways
Of my own mind; and in the midst
          of tears
I hid from Him, and under running
          laughter.
[Francis Thompson: *The Hound of Heaven*]

FLIRTATION
3 She who trifles with all is less likely
          to fall
  Than she who but trifles with one.
[John Gay: *The Coquette*]
4 Leisured society is full of people who
spend a great part of their lives in flirtation and conceal nothing but the humil-
iating secret that they have never gone
any further. [G. B. Shaw: Preface to
Overruled]

FLOTSAM AND JETSAM
5 Does anybody want any flotsam?
  I've gotsam.
  Does anybody want any jetsam?
  I'll getsam.
[Ogden Nash: *No Doctors Today, Thank You*]

FLOWER(S)
6 When daisies pied and violets blue
    And lady-smocks all silver-white
    And cuckoo-buds of yellow hue
      Do paint the meadows with delight.
[Shakespeare: *Love's Labour's Lost* V.ii.]
7 There's rosemary, that's for remembrance; pray, love, remember: and there
is pansies, that's for thoughts. . . .
There's fennel for you, and columbines:
there's rue for you; and here's some for
me. . . . O, you must wear your rue
with a difference. There's a daisy: I

would give you some violets, but they
withered all when my father died.
[Shakespeare: *Hamlet* IV.v.]
8 Throw hither all your quaint enam-
          ell'd eyes
That on the green turf suck the hon-
          ied showers,
And purple all the ground with ver-
          nal flowers.
Bring the rathe primrose that for-
          saken dies,
The tufted crow-toe, and pale jessa-
          mine,
The white pink, and the pansy freakt
          with jet,
The glowing violet,
The musk-rose, and the well-attir'd
          woodbine,
With cowslips wan that hang the pen-
          sive head,
And every flower that sad embroidery
          wears:
Bid amaranthus all his beauty shed,
And daffadillies fill their cups with
          tears,
To strew the laureate hearse where
          Lycid lies.
[John Milton: *Lycidas*]
9 I've heard them lilting at the ewe
          milking,
Lasses a' lilting, before dawn of
          day;
But now they are moaning, on ilka
          green loaning;
The flowers of the forest are a'
          wede away.
[Jean Elliot: *The Flowers of the Forest* (1763)]
loaning = *right of way, footpath;* wede =
weeded, in the sense of weeded out, plucked up
10 And 'tis my faith that every flower
  Enjoys the air it breathes.
[Wordsworth: *Lines Written in Early Spring*]
11 To me the meanest flower that blows
          can give
Thoughts that do often lie too deep
          for tears.
[Wordsworth: *Intimations of Immortality*]
*It was the total lack of any such percep-
tion that Wordsworth deplored in Peter
Bell, of whom he said:*
  A primrose by a river's brim

A yellow primrose was to him,
And it was nothing more.

Peter Bell XII

1 Here are cool mosses deep,
And thro' the moss the ivies creep,
And in the stream the long-leaved
flowers weep,
And from the craggy ledge the poppy
hangs in sleep.
[Tennyson: *The Lotos-Eaters*]
2 Flower in the crannied wall,
I pluck you out of the crannies,
I hold you here, root and all, in my
hand,
Little flower—but *if* I could understand
What you are, root and all, and all in
all,
I should know what God and man is.
[Tennyson: *Flower in the Crannied
Wall*]
3 The flowers that bloom in the spring,
tra la,
Have nothing to do with the case.
[W. S. Gilbert: *The Mikado* II]
4 "Isn't it odd," I said, as we were
looking at the roses with those ladies, "to
think that flowers are the reproductive
organs of the plants they grow on?" [Lo-
gan Pearsall Smith: *Afterthoughts*]

FLY(IES)
5 It was prettily devised of Aesop,
"The fly sat upon the axle-tree of the
chariot-wheel and said, 'What a dust do
I raise.'" [Francis Bacon: *Of Vainglory*]
6 Busy, curious, thirsty fly,
Drink with me, and drink as I.
[William Oldys: *On a Fly Drinking out
of a Cup of Ale*]
*This little poem, now forgotten, was very
popular in the 18th century, which
lacked our finicky concern with asepsis.
Dr. Johnson translated the poem into
Latin.*
7 This world surely is wide enough to
hold both thee and me. [Laurence
Sterne: *Tristram Shandy* II.xii.]
*Uncle Toby's kindness to the fly that he
shooed out the window was more admired by the sentimental of the 18th
century than by the hygienic of today.*
*Equally famous was a remark of King
James I to a fly that was bothering him:*

*"Have I not three kingdoms, and thou
must needs fly in my eye!"*
8 Shoo fly, don't bother me, I belong to
Company G.
[Billy Reeves: *Shoo Fly, Don't Bother
Me* (1866)]
9 There may be flies on you and me,
But there are no flies on Jesus.
[Salvation Army song (1900)]
*It is hard to believe that vulgarity could
be so blasphemous or blasphemy so vul-
gar.*

FOAM
10 The cruel crawling foam.
[Charles Kingsley: *The Sands of Dee* IV]

FOE(S)
11 I wish my deadly foe no worse
Than want of friends, and empty
purse.
[Nicholas Breton: *A Farewell to Town*]
12 We ne'er see our foes but we wish
them to stay,
They never see us but they wish us
away;
If they run, why, we follow, or run
them ashore,
For if they won't fight us, we cannot
do more.
[David Garrick: *Hearts of Oak*]

FOG
13 This is a London particular. . . . A
fog, miss. [Dickens: *Bleak House* III]
14 The fog comes
on little cat feet.
It sits looking
over the harbor and city
on silent haunches
and then, moves on.
[Carl Sandburg: *Fog*]
15 The yellow fog that rubs its back
upon the window-panes.
[T. S. Eliot: *The Love Song of J. Alfred
Prufrock*]
16 Fog rolled in last night. It came not
on the little cat feet of Carl Sandburg's
phrase, but with the authority of an elephant and with just about the same coloring. [Drew Middleton, in the *New
York Times*, Jan. 30, 1959]
*Mr. Middleton was writing from London
and describing a "pea-souper."*

FOLLY

1 Thou speakest as one of the foolish women speaketh. [Job 2:10]

2   Who builds his house on sands,
Pricks his blind horse across the fallow lands,
Or lets his wife abroad with pilgrims roam,
Deserves a fool's-cap and long ears at home.
[Chaucer: Prologue to *The Wife of Bath's Tale* (trans. Alexander Pope)]

3 To a foolish demur behoveth a foolish answer.
[William Caxton: *Aesop* II]
demur = *caviling objection.*

"*Ask a silly question, you get a silly answer,*" *as Slapsie Maxie Rosenbloom is said to have said when, in answer to a query, someone explained the use of fingerbowls to him.*

4 The chief characteristic of folly is that it mistakes itself for wisdom. [Fray Luis de León: *La Perfecta Casada* XVI]

5 The folly of one man is the fortune of another; for no man prospers so suddenly as by others' errors. [Francis Bacon: *Of Fortune*]

6 He uses his folly like a stalking-horse and under the presentation of that he shoots his wit. [Shakespeare: *As You Like It* V.iv.]

7 A wise man altereth his purpose, but a foole persevereth in his folly. [James Mabbe: *Celestina*]

8 Natural Folly is bad enough; but learned Folly is intolerable. [Thomas Fuller (1654-1734): *Gnomologia*]

9 A fool will ask more questions than the wisest can answer. [Jonathan Swift: *Polite Conversation* II]

10 When lovely woman stoops to folly
And finds too late that men betray,
What charm can soothe her melancholy,
What art can wash her guilt away?
The only art her guilt to cover,
To hide her shame from every eye,
To give repentance to her lover,
And wring his bosom—is to die.
[Oliver Goldsmith: "Song" from *The Vicar of Wakefield* XXIX]
Parodied by T. S. Eliot in The Waste Land *(1922):*
When lovely woman stoops to folly

and

Paces about her room again, alone,
She smoothes her hair with automatic hand,
And puts a record on the gramophone.

11 Where lives the man that has not tried
How mirth can into folly glide,
And folly into sin!
[Sir Walter Scott: *The Bridal of Triermain* I]

12 The ultimate result of shielding men from the effects of folly is to fill the world with fools. [Herbert Spencer: *State Tamperings with Money Banks*]

13 Let the victors, when they come,
When the forts of folly fall,
Find thy body by the wall.
[Matthew Arnold: *The Last Word*]
But ah! which side of the wall?

FOLLY: in praise of

14 It's a good thing to be foolishly gay once in a while. [Horace: *Carmina* IV. xii.]
The Latin is: Dulce est desipere in loco.

15 A fool may eke a wise man often guide.
[Chaucer: *Troilus and Criseyde* I]

16 A little folly is desirable in him that will not be guilty of stupidity. [Montaigne: *Essays* III.ix.]

17 I had rather have a fool to make me merry than experience to make me sad. [Shakespeare: *As You Like It* IV.i.]

18 This fellow is wise enough to play the fool,
And to do that well craves a kind of wit.
[Shakespeare: *Twelfth Night* III.i.]

19 She never yet was foolish that was fair,
For even her folly help'd her to an heir.
[Shakespeare: *Othello* II.i.]
There are many proverbs and passages in literature, from Apuleius (2nd century A.D.*), through Fuller ("She that is born a beauty is half married") down to nursery rhymes ("My face is my fortune, Sir, she said"), that stress the fact that beauty is more helpful toward getting a girl married than a dower.*
Many of the sages, by the way, who make the commonplace observation, feel

that the condition is a peculiarity of their own degenerate times.

1 He who lives without committing any follies is not so wise as he thinks. [La Rochefoucauld: *Maxims*]

2 Play the fool, but at a cheaper rate. [William Cowper: *Retirement*]

3 Thou Greybeard, old Wisdom, mayst boast of thy treasures;
Give me with young Folly to live:
I grant thee thy calm-blooded, time-settled pleasures;
But Folly has raptures to give.
[Burns: *Inscribed on a Tavern Window*]

4 He who hath not a dram of folly in his mixture hath pounds of much worse matter in his composition. [Charles Lamb: *All Fools' Day*]

5 Then, Pallas, take away thine Owl,
And let us have a lark instead.
[Thomas Hood: *To Minerva*]

6 For God's sake give me the young man who has brains enough to make a fool of himself! [R. L. Stevenson: *Crabbed Age and Youth*]

FOOD

7 What is food to one man is bitter poison to others. [Lucretius: *De Rerum Natura IV*]
See MEAT: *One Man's*

8 The food that to him now is as luscious as locusts, shall be to him shortly as bitter as coloquintida. [Shakespeare: *Othello* I.iii.]
locusts = *probably the carob pod;* coloquintida = *the Colocynth, a bitter herb*
It was long believed that these were the "locusts" upon which John the Baptist fed, and luscious *may derive from their association in the biblical narrative with wild honey.*

9 Little Tommy Tucker
Sings for his supper.
[Nursery rhyme: first published version c. 1744]

10 There was an old man of Tobago,
Who lived on rice, gruel, and sago;
Till, much to his bliss,
His physician said this—
To a leg, sir, of mutton you may go.
[John Marshall: in *Anecdotes and Adventures of Fifteen Gentlemen*, c. 1822; possibly by R. S. Sharpe.]

Edward Lear, who in his The Book of Nonsense *(1846) established the limerick as a humorous verse form, states that he was inspired to write his limericks by* The Old Man of Tobago. *Lear, by the way, never used the word* limerick; *its application to this verse form is a minor mystery.*

11 EDIBLE. Good to eat, and wholesome to digest, as a worm to a toad, a toad to a snake, a snake to a pig, a pig to a man, and a man to a worm. [Ambrose Bierce: *The Devil's Dictionary*]

FOOL(S)

12 I have played the fool. [I Samuel 26:21]

13 He that begetteth a fool doeth it to his sorrow. [Proverbs 17:21]

14 Answer not a fool according to his folly, lest thou also be like unto him. [Proverbs 26:4]

15 Answer a fool according to his folly, lest he be wise in his own conceit. [Proverbs 26:5]
To many proverbs there is an anti-proverb, as here. The putting of them one after the other this way was a plain recognition by the author of Proverbs that there is a wisdom in the selection of wisdom.

16 Every fool will be meddling. [Proverbs 20:3]
Meddling is a favorite word of the pious, applied to any unfavorable comment on their particular beliefs. The implication is that anyone who disagrees with them is, plainly, a fool, certified by Holy Writ.

17 For ye suffer fools gladly, seeing ye yourselves are wise. [II Corinthians 11:19]
Now used almost entirely in negative contexts. Not to suffer fools gladly is, today, thought of as the mark of wisdom, even if irritable wisdom.

18 It is impossible to treat quietly and dispute orderly with a fool. [Montaigne: *Essays* III.viii.]

19 Wise men have more to learn of fools than fools of wise men. [Montaigne: *Essays* III.viii.]
Montaigne attributes the thought to "Cato senior."

20 A fool's paradise. [Giles Fletcher: *The Sorcerer of Vain Delights*]

1 There is no fool like an old fool. [John Lyly: *Mother Bombie* IV.ii.]

2 He who makes use of fools has to put up with them. [Cabillo de Aragon: *Las Muñecas de Marcela* I]

3 O! I am Fortune's fool. [Shakespeare: *Romeo and Juliet* III.i.]

4 What fools these mortals be! [Shakespeare: *A Midsummer Night's Dream* III.ii.]

5 These tedious old fools! [Shakespeare: *Hamlet* II.ii.]

6 The triple pillar of the world transform'd
Into a strumpet's fool.
[Shakespeare: *Antony and Cleopatra* I.i.]

7 Fortune, that favors fools. [Ben Jonson: Prologue to *The Alchemist*]

8 Who are a little wise the best fools be. [Donne: *The Triple Fool*]

9 Make not a fool of thyself, to make others merry.
[Robert Burton: *The Anatomy of Melancholy* II.3.7]

10 While the discreet take counsel, the fool doth his business.
[George Herbert: *Jacula Prudentum*]

11 The fool asks much, but he is more fool that grants it.
[George Herbert: *Jacula Prudentum*]

12 A fool and his money is soon parted. [James Howell: *Familiar Letters*, October 20, 1629]

This has been much parodied. One of the best: "A fool and his honey are soon started."

13 For every inch that is not fool is rogue. [Dryden: *Absalom and Achitophel* II.463]

14 A fool always finds a bigger fool to admire him. [Boileau: *L'Art Poétique* I]

This observation is delightfully illustrated in the wonderful scenes in Shakespeare's II Henry IV between Justice Shallow and his cousin Master Silence.

15 Who sendeth a fool upon an errand, must goe himself after. [James Howell: *English Proverbs* (1659)]

16 O fate of fools! officious in contriving;
In executing puzzled, lame and lost.
[William Congreve: *The Mourning Bride* V.i.]

officious = eager, busy, unwantedly helpful; contriving = planning

17 But fools, to talking ever prone,
Are sure to make their follies known.
[John Gay: *Fables* I.xliv.]

18 Fools rush in where angels fear to tread. [Alexander Pope: *An Essay on Criticism* III.lxvi.]

19 Take it for a rule,
No creature smarts so little as a fool.
[Alexander Pope: *Epistle to Dr. Arbuthnot*]

20 Very often, say what you will, a knave is only a fool. [Voltaire: *Le Depositaire* II.vi.]

21 He's a Fool that cannot conceal his Wisdom. [Benjamin Franklin: *Poor Richard's Almanack* (1745)]

22 It is Ill-manners to silence a Fool, and Cruelty to let him go on. [Benjamin Franklin: *Poor Richard's Almanack* (1757)]

23 A fool and his words are soon parted; a man of genius and his money. [William Shenstone: *On Reserve*]

24 Fools, who came to scoff, remain'd to pray. [Oliver Goldsmith: *The Deserted Village*]

25 A rogue is a roundabout fool. [Coleridge: *Table-Talk*, January 4, 1823]

26 I am always afraid of a fool. One cannot be sure that he is not a knave as well. [William Hazlitt: *Characteristics*]

FOOTBALL

27 You base foot-ball player. [Shakespeare: *King Lear* I.iv.]

Philip Stubbes, in his Anatomie of Abuses (1583), described football as "rather a bloody and murdering practise than a felowly sporte or pastime." "For dooth not every one lye in waight for his Adversary," he says, "seeking to overthrowe him . . . though it be uppon hard stones? . . . So that by this meanes, sometimes their necks are broken, sometimes their backs, sometimes their legs, sometimes their armes; sometime one part thrust out of joynt, sometime another; sometime their noses gush out with blood, sometime their eyes start out; and sometimes hurt in one place, sometimes in another. . . . And hereof groweth envie, malice, rancour, choler, hatred, displeasure, enmitie, and what not els: and sometimes fighting, brawling, contention, quarrel picking, mur-

ther, homicide, and great effusion of
blood, as experience dayly teacheth."

FOOTMAN(MEN)

1 If thou hast run with the footmen,
and they have wearied thee, then how
canst thou contend with horses? and if in
the land of peace, wherein thou trusted-
est, they wearied thee, then how wilt thou
do in the swelling of the Jordan? [Jere-
miah 12:5]
2 John Richard William Alexander
Dwyer
Was footman to Justinian Stubbs, Esquire.
[Horace Smith: *Rejected Addresses,*
"The Theatre"]
A parody of Crabbe.

FOOTPRINT(S)

3 One day, about noon, going towards
my boat, I was exceedingly surprised with
the print of a man's naked foot on the
shore. [Daniel Defoe: *Robinson Crusoe*]
4 Lives of great men all remind us
We can make our lives sublime,
And departing, leave behind us
Footprints on the sands of time.
[Longfellow: *A Psalm of Life*]
5 Zuleika, on a desert island, would
have spent most of her time in looking
for a man's foot-print. [Max Beerbohm:
Zuleika Dobson II]

FOP

6 Sir Plume, of amber snuff-box justly
vain,
And the nice conduct of a clouded
cane.
[Alexander Pope: *Rape of the Lock* IV]
nice conduct = *skilful management*
*Amber becomes cloudy in time and
varying degrees of cloudiness are variously prized. The etiquette of the cane
was important in a fop's life.*

FORBEARANCE

7 There is a limit at which forbearance
ceases to be a virtue. [Edmund Burke:
*Observations on a Late State of the Na-
tion*]

FORBIDDEN

8 Forbid us thing, that thing desyren
we.

[Chaucer: Prologue to *The Wife of
Bath's Tale*]
9 To forbid us anything is to make us
have a mind for it. [Montaigne: *Essays*
II.xv.]

FORCE

10 Who overcomes by force hath overcome but half his foe.
[John Milton: *Paradise Lost* I.648]
11 The use of force alone is but temporary. It may subdue for a moment; but
it does not remove the necessity of sub-
duing again: and a nation is not governed, which is perpetually to be conquered. [Edmund Burke: *Second Speech
on Conciliation with America,* "The
Thirteen Resolutions"]
12 Force and right are the governors of
this world; force till right is ready.
[Matthew Arnold: *Essays in Criticism,
First Series* I]
*And when is right ready? And how,
when ready, does it "govern" those who
resist it?*

FOREBODING

13 Against ill chances men are ever
merry;
But heaviness foreruns the good
event.
[Shakespeare: *II Henry IV* IV.ii.]
against = *at the approach of*
14 But in the gross and scope of my opinion,
This bodes some strange eruption to
our state.
[Shakespeare: *Hamlet* I.i.]
15 And what rough beast, its hour come
round at last,
Slouches towards Bethlehem to be
born?
[William Butler Yeats: *The Second Coming*]

FOREGONE CONCLUSION

16 But this denoted a foregone conclusion.
[Shakespeare: *Othello* III.iii.]

FOREIGNERS

17 For any thing I see, foreigners are
fools. [Hugo Meynell: in Boswell's *Life
of Johnson* (1780)]
"Old Meynell," a fox-hunting squire, was

a man of earthy, if limited, intelligence. Johnson quoted him, with amusement but respect, several times. His most famous utterance—given above—must come as close to being a universal sentiment as has ever been uttered.

FORESIGHT
1 He that observeth the wind shall not sow; and he that regardeth the clouds shall not reap. [Ecclesiastes 9:4]

FOREST
2 This is the forest primeval. [Longfellow: *Evangeline*]

FORETHOUGHT
3 Take therefore no thought for the morrow: for the morrow shall take thought for the things of itself. Sufficient unto the day is the evil thereof. [Matthew 6:34]

FOREVER
4 Forever; 'tis a single word!
Our rude forefathers deemed it two:
Can you imagine so absurd
A view?
[Charles Stuart Calverley: *Forever*]

FOREWARNED
5 Forewarned is forearmed; to be prepared is half the victory. [Cervantes: *Don Quixote* II.iv.]

The appearance of a well-known saying in Don Quixote *is not proof that it originated there, even though that appearance might be the first known.*

Part of the wisdom and humor of the great novel is that Sancho Panza speaks eternally in proverbs and repeats himself endlessly. The above, for instance, occurs more than once in the book. So that the appearance of such a saying in Don Quixote *is, rather, evidence that it was already a musty proverb by the time of the book's being written.*

FORGET(TING)
6 If I forget thee, O Jerusalem, let my right hand forget her cunning. [Psalms 137:5]
7 Or that I could forget what I have been,
Or not remember what I must be now.

[Shakespeare: *Richard II* III.iii.]
8 The courtiers who surround him [Louis XVIII] have forgotten nothing and learnt nothing. [Attr. to Maréchal Dumouriez, September, 1795, and attr. to Talleyrand by the Chevalier de Panat: *Letter to Mallet du Pan,* January, 1796.]
9 And we forget because we must
And not because we will.
[Matthew Arnold: *Absence*]
10 I sit beside my lonely fire,
And pray for wisdom yet—
For calmness to remember
Or courage to forget.
[Charles Hamilton Aidé: *Remember or Forget*]

FORGETFULNESS
11   Like a dull actor now,
I have forgot my part, and I am out,
Even to a full disgrace.
[Shakespeare: *Coriolanus* V.iii.]
12 Afflictions induce callosities; miseries are slippery, or fall like snow upon us, which notwithstanding is no unhappy stupidity. To be ignorant of evils to come, and forgetful of evils past, is a merciful provision in nature, whereby we digest the mixture of our few and evil days, and, our delivered sense not relapsing into cutting remembrances, our sorrows are not kept raw by the edge of repetitions. [Sir Thomas Browne: *Of Ambition and Fame*]

stupidity = *stupor, lack of awareness;*
delivered = *liberated, by forgetfulness*

13 For who, to dumb Forgetfulness a prey,
This pleasing anxious being e'er resigned,
Left the warm precincts of the cheerful day,
Nor cast one longing lingering look behind?
[Thomas Gray: *Elegy Written in a Country Churchyard*]
14 When the lamp is shattered
The light in the dust lies dead—
When the cloud is scattered
The rainbow's glory is shed.
When the lute is broken,
Sweet tones are remembered not;
When the lips have spoken,
Loved accents are soon forgot.
[Shelley: *When the Lamp is Shattered*]

1 Better by far that you should forget
and smile
Than that you should remember and
be sad.
[Christina Georgina Rossetti: *Remember*]

2 I remember the way we parted,
The day and the way we met;
You hoped we were both broken-
hearted,
And knew we should both forget.

And the best and the worst of this is
That neither is most to blame,
If you have forgotten my kisses
And I have forgotten your name.
[Swinburne: *An Interlude*]

FORGIVE

3 Father, forgive them; for they know
not what they do. [Luke 23:24]

FORGIVE: and forget

4 Pray you now, forget and forgive.
[Shakespeare: *King Lear* IV.vii.]
Usually rendered forgive and forget.

5 "I can forgive, but I cannot forget,"
is only another way of saying, "I cannot
forgive." [Henry Ward Beecher: *Life
Thoughts*]
*But forgetting is not an act of volition.
It was pulpit sentiments of this kind that
made golf so popular on Sundays.*

FORGIVENESS

6 Until seventy times seven. [Matthew
18:22]

7 The offender never pardons. [George
Herbert: *Jacula Prudentum*]

8 Forgiveness to the injur'd does belong,
But they ne'er pardon who have done
the wrong.
[Dryden: *The Conquest of Granada*
II.i.]

9 O Thou, who Man of baser Earth did
make,
And ev'n with Paradise devise the
snake:
For all the Sin wherewith the Face
of Man
Is blackened—Man's forgiveness give
—and take!
[*Rubáiyát of Omar Khayyám*]
This stanza—81—is not a translation by

*Edward FitzGerald but an interpolation
—a very daring one for mid-19th-century
Victorian England.*

THE FORGOTTEN MAN

10 Who is the Forgotten Man? He is the
clean, quiet, virtuous, domestic citizen,
who pays his debts and his taxes and is
never heard of out of his little circle. . . . The Forgotten Man . . . delv-
ing away in patient industry, supporting
his family, paying his taxes, casting his
vote, supporting the church and the
school. . . . He is the only one for whom
there is no provision in the great scram-
ble and the big divide. Such is the Forgotten Man. He works, he votes, generally
he prays—but his chief business in life is
to pay. [W. G. Sumner: *The Forgotten
Man* (1883)]

11 The forgotten man at the bottom of
the economic pyramid. [Franklin Delano
Roosevelt: in an address over the radio,
1932]
*It is apparent from the two quotations
that Roosevelt borrowed Sumner's famous phrase only to transform its meaning. All they have in common is an
element of self-pity—which accounts for
the phrase's popularity with 99% of the
electorate. Sumner would have been annoyed with Roosevelt's application of
the expression.*
*Alfred E. Smith, who had himself risen
from "the bottom of the economic pyramid," sturdily insisted (The New Outlook, October 1933) that "The forgotten
man is a myth."*

FORLORN

12 Magic casements, opening on the
foam
Of perilous seas, in faery lands forlorn.
[Keats: *Ode to a Nightingale*]

13 But now the old is out of date,
The new is not yet born,
And who can be *alone* elate,
While the world lies forlorn?
[Matthew Arnold: *Obermann Once
More*]

FORM

14   His form had yet not lost

All her original brightness, nor appear'd
Less than archangel ruin'd, and th'
excess
Of glory obscur'd.
[John Milton: *Paradise Lost* I.591-594]
Note Milton's use of her. *His* would
have been ambiguous and its (which we
would use) was not yet fixed in the lan-
guage.

FORMALITY

1 Forms keep fools at a distance. [Sam-
uel Foote: *The Englishman Return'd*
from Paris II (1756)]
   forms = *formality*

FORNICATION

2 Fornication is a lapse from one marriage into many. [Clement of Alexandria: *Stromateis*]
3   Thou hast committed——
Fornication——but that was in another country,
And besides, the wench is dead.
[Christopher Marlowe: *The Jew of Malta*
IV.i.]
4 Sir Henry Blount was called to the
bar for spreading abroad that abominable and dangerous doctrine that it was
far cheaper and safer to lie with common wenches than with ladies of quality.
[John Aubrey: *Brief Lives* I]

FORTITUDE

5 What fortitude the soul contains,
That it can so endure
The accent of a coming foot,
The opening of a door.
[Emily Dickinson: *Elysium Is as Far*]

FORTUNATE

6 Hold him alone truly fortunate who
has ended his life in happy well-being.
[Aeschylus: *Agamemnon*]
7 He who does not consider himself
fortunate is unfortunate. [Samuel Butler (1835-1902): *The Way of All*
Flesh V]

FORTUNE

8   Giftes of fortune,
That passen as a shadwe upon a wal.
[Chaucer: *The Merchant's Tale*]
9 He who owes least to fortune is in the
strongest position. [Machiavelli: *The*
Prince VI]
10 Fortune shows her power when there
is no wise preparation for resisting her.
[Machiavelli: *The Prince* XXV]
11 Fortune is arbiter of half our actions,
but she still leaves the control of the
other half to us. [Machiavelli: *The*
Prince XXV]
12 Every man was not born with a silver
spoon in his mouth.
[Cervantes: *Don Quixote* II.iv.73]
13 To be a well-favoured man is the gift
of fortune; but to write and read comes
by nature. [Shakespeare: *Much Ado*
about Nothing III.iii.]
   well-favored = *handsome*
14 The slings and arrows of outrageous
fortune.
[Shakespeare: *Hamlet* III.i.]
15 Ill Fortune never crushed that man
whom good Fortune deceived not. [Fran-
cis Bacon: *Of Fortune*]
16 No man's fortune can be an end
worthy of his being. [Francis Bacon: *Ad-*
vancement of Learning II]
17 We need greater virtues to sustain
good than evil fortune. [La Rochefoucauld: *Maxims*]
18 If you are too fortunate, you will not
know yourself. If you are too unfortunate,
nobody will know you. [Thomas Fuller
(1654-1734): *Gnomologia*]
19 The power of fortune is confessed
only by the miserable; for the happy impute all their success to prudence and
merit. [Jonathan Swift: *Thoughts on*
Various Subjects]
20 An Englishman who has lost his fortune is said to have died of a broken
heart. [Emerson: *English Traits* X]

FORTUNE: favors the bold and the
foolish

21 Fortune favors the brave. (*Fortis*
fortuna adiuvat) [Terence: *Phormio*]
22 Hap helpeth hardy men alday.
[Chaucer: *The Legend of Good Women,*
   "Lucretia"]
23 Fortune is a young woman, and therefore friendly to the young, who with audacity command her. [Machiavelli: *The*
Prince XXV]
24 Fortune is to be honored and respected and it be but for her daughters,

Confidence and Reputation; for those two Felicity breedeth; the first within a man's self, the latter in others towards him. [Francis Bacon: *Of Fortune*]
    and it be but for = *if only because of*

1   Certainly there be not two more fortunate properties than to have a little of the fool and not too much of the honest. [Francis Bacon: *Of Fortune*]
    fortunate properties = *qualities conducing to good fortune*

2   'Tis a gross error, held in schools,
    That Fortune always favours fools.
[John Gay: *Fables* II.xii.]

FORTUNE: never perfect

3   Will Fortune never come with both
                                hands full,
    But write her fair words still in foulest letters?
    She either gives a stomach and no
                                food;
    Such are the poor, in health; or else
                                a feast
    And takes away the stomach; such are
                                the rich,
    That have abundance, and enjoy it
                                not.
[Shakespeare: *II Henry IV* IV.iv.]

4   Fortune, that arrant whore,
    Ne'er turns the key to the poor.
[Shakespeare: *King Lear* II.iv.]
    That is, never turns the key to open *the door for them.*

5   Dame Fortune is a fickle gipsy,
    And always blind, and often tipsy.
[W. M. Praed: *The Haunted Tree*]

6   Fortune loves to give bedroom slippers to people with wooden legs, and gloves to those who have no hands. [Théophile Gautier: *Mademoiselle de Maupin*]

FORTY

7   Fat, fair and forty were all the toasts
                                of the young men.
[John O'Keefe: *Irish Minnie* II]

8   Fat, fair, and forty.
[Sir Walter Scott: *St. Roman's Well* VII]

9   Every man over forty is a scoundrel.
[G. B. Shaw: *Maxims for Revolutionists*]
    Supported by Bacon's "for the moral part, perhaps youth will have the preeminence, as age hath for the politic" (Youth and Age); *or Thomas Hood's*

"But now 'tis little joy/To know I'm farther off from Heaven / Than when I was a boy" (I Remember, I Remember).

FORWARD

10 Have you come to the Red Sea place
                                in your life,
    Where, in spite of all you can do,
    There is no way out, there is no way
                                back,
    There is no other way but through?
[Annie Johnson Flint: *At the Place of the Sea*]

FOUNDATION

11 The rain descended, and the floods came, and the winds blew, and beat upon that house; and it fell not: for it was founded upon a rock. [Matthew 7:25]

FOUR HUNDRED

12 There are only about four hundred people in New York society. [Ward McAllister; in an interview in the *New York Tribune*, 1888]
    McAllister was a professional party-planner and arbiter of elegance. This remark was the origin of "the four hundred" as a term for exclusiveness.
    It is in reference to this that O'Henry named a collection of his stories about people in New York The Four Million.

FOURTH ESTATE

13 A fourth estate, of able editors, springs up. [Thomas Carlyle: *The French Revolution* II (1837)]

14 Burke said that there were three estates in Parliament; but, in the Reporters' Gallery yonder, there sat a *Fourth Estate* more important far than them all. [Thomas Carlyle: *Heroes and Hero-Worship*, "The Hero as Man of Letters" (1839)]

15 The gallery in which the reporters sit has become a fourth estate of the realm. [Macaulay: *Hallam's Constitutional History* (1828)]
    Carlyle picked up the term and misascribed it to Burke.
    But it had been around quite a while. The Three Estates in France were the Clergy, the Nobles and the Burghers (the Third Estate). Rabelais (1532) had

called lawyers a fourth estate.

Lord Falkland, in Parliament in 1638, had referred to the menace of a fourth estate "which, if not well looked to, will turn us all out of doors." Fielding (1752) had, more justly than any of the others, called the mob "the fourth estate." In contemporary usage, it is a newspaper cliché for the press.

FOXES
1 Take us the foxes, the little foxes, that spoil the vines. [Song of Solomon 2:15]
2 The foxes have holes, and the birds of the air have nests; but the Son of man hath not where to lay his head. [Matthew 8:20]
3 A fox is a wolf who sends flowers. [Ruth Weston, quoted the *New York Post*, Nov. 8, 1955]

FRAGRANCE
4 The breath of flowers is far sweeter in the air (where it comes and goes like the warbling of music) than in the hand. [Francis Bacon: *Of Gardening*]

FRAILTY
5 Frailty, thy name is woman! [Shakespeare: *Hamlet* I.ii.]
6 Wit and woman are two frail things. [Thomas Overbury: *Characters*]

FRANCE
7 France was long a despotism tempered by epigrams. [Thomas Carlyle: *The French Revolution* I]

FRANKNESS
8 Candor and generosity, unless tempered by moderation, lead to ruin. [Tacitus: *History* III.lxxxvi.]
9 He has need of tough ears to hear himself frankly judged. [Montaigne: *Essays* III.xiii.]
10 From your confessor, lawyer and physician,
Hide not your case on no condition.
[Sir John Harington: *Metamorphosis of Ajax*]
11 Plain-dealing is a jewel, and he that useth it shall die a beggar. [Henry Porter: *The Two Angrie Women of Abington*]

12 Ignorance, Madam, pure ignorance. [Samuel Johnson: on being asked how he came, in his *Dictionary*, to define *pastern* as "the knee of a horse"; in Boswell's *Life* (1755)]
13 Always be ready to speak your mind, and a base man will avoid you. [William Blake: *The Marriage of Heaven and Hell*]
14 I reside at Table Mountain, and my name is Truthful James;
I am not up to small deceit, or any sinful games.
[Bret Harte: *The Society upon the Stanislaus*]
15 Every man who says frankly and fully what he thinks is doing a public service. [Leslie Stephen: *The Suppression of Poisonous Opinions*]

FRAUD
16 A pious fraud. [Ovid: *Metamorphoses* IX]
17 Though fraud in other activities be detestable, in the management of war it is laudable and glorious, and he who overcomes an enemy by fraud is as much to be praised as he who does so by force. [Machiavelli: *Discorsi* III]
18 Frost and fraud have always foul ends. [William Camden: *Remains*]

FRAY
19 To the latter end of a fray and the beginning of a feast
Fits a dull fighter and a keen guest.
[Shakespeare: *I Henry IV* IV.ii.]

FREE
20 Paul said, But I was free born. [Acts: 22:28]

FREEDOM
21 It is a strange desire to seek power and to lose liberty; or to seek power over others and to lose power over a man's self. [Francis Bacon: *Of Great Place*]
He had said earlier that men in great place have no freedom of their persons, actions or time.
22 I would not my unhoused free condition
Put into circumscription and confine
For the sea's worth.

[Shakespeare: *Othello* I.ii.]
1 Sufficient to have stood, though free
to fall.
[John Milton: *Paradise Lost* III.99]
2 Man is born free, yet he is every-where in chains. [Jean Jacques Rous-seau: *The Social Contract* I.i.]
3 Those who expect to reap the blessings of freedom must, like men, undergo the fatigue of supporting it. [Thomas Paine: *The American Crisis* IV (September 12, 1777)]
4 Ne'er yet by force was freedom over-come.
[James Thomson (1700-1748): *Liberty* II.494]
5 Me this unchartered freedom tires;
I feel the weight of chance desires:
My hopes no more must change their
name,
I long for a repose that ever is the
same.
[Wordsworth: *Ode to Duty*]
6 Yet, Freedom! yet thy banner, torn,
but flying,
Streams like the thunder-storm
against the wind.
[Byron: *Childe Harold* IV.xcviii.]
7 My very chains and I grew friends,
So much a long communion tends
To make us what we are:—even I
Regain'd my freedom with a sigh.
[Byron: *The Prisoner of Chillon*]
8 When Freedom from her mountain
height
Unfurled her standard to the air,
She tore the azure robe of night
And set the stars of glory there.
[Joseph Rodman Drake: *The American Flag*]
9 But what is Freedom? Rightly under-stood,
A universal license to be good.
[Hartley Coleridge: *Liberty*]
10 Of old sat Freedom on the heights,
The thunders breaking at her feet;
Above her shook the starry lights;
She heard the torrents meet.
[Tennyson: *Of Old Sat Freedom*]
11 In giving freedom to the slave we as-sure freedom to the free—honorable alike in what we give and what we pre-serve. [Abraham Lincoln: *Annual Mes-sage to Congress* (1862)]

12 In the beauty of the lilies Christ was
born across the sea,
With a glory in his bosom that trans-
figures you and me;
As he died to make men holy, let us
die to make men free,
While God is marching on.
[Julia Ward Howe: *The Battle Hymn of the Republic*]
13 Yes, we'll rally round the flag, boys,
we'll rally once again,
Shouting the battle-cry of Freedom,
We will rally from the hill-side, we'll
gather from the plain,
Shouting the battle-cry of Freedom.
[George Frederick Root: *The Battle-Cry of Freedom*]
14 It is by the goodness of God that in our country we have those three un-speakably precious things: freedom of speech, freedom of conscience, and the prudence never to practice either. [Mark Twain: *Pudd'nhead Wilson's Cal-endar*]
15 The first is freedom of speech and expression—everywhere in the world. The second is freedom of every person to worship God in his own way—every-where in the world. The third is free-dom from want . . . everywhere in the world. The fourth is freedom from fear . . . anywhere in the world. [Franklin Delano Roosevelt: *The Four Freedoms* (Address, 1941)]
16 Freedom is the freedom to say that two plus two make four. If that is granted, all else follows. [George Orwell: *1984* VII]
17 While it is true that an inherently free and scrupulous person may be de-stroyed, such an individual can never be enslaved or used as a blind tool. [Al-bert Einstein: *Impact* (UNESCO), 1950]
18 This will remain the land of the free only so long as it is the home of the brave. [Elmer Davis: *But We Were Born Free*]

FREEDOM OF SPEECH

19 Give me the liberty to know, to utter, and to argue freely according to con-science, above all liberties. [John Mil-ton: *Areopagitica*]
20 I disapprove of what you say, but I will defend to the death your right to say it.

Commonly attributed to Voltaire, though actually made up by C. S. Tallentyre (Voltaire in His Letters—1919).

The phrase has enough exaggeration to be striking and enough paradox to seem vaguely witty. And as Voltaire was a champion of freedom of speech, it seems "in keeping."

In reality, however, Voltaire clung to his life with zest and was not prepared to give it up to defend any piece of senseless babble—or anything at all, whether he disapproved or approved. He was a reasonable man, not a martyr. What he actually said in his "Essay on Tolerance," the words that Miss Tallentyre "paraphrased" into the pompous utterance so often attributed to him, was "Think for yourselves and let others enjoy the privilege of doing so too." That is something different.

1 Every man has a right to utter what he thinks truth, and every other man has a right to knock him down for it. [Samuel Johnson: in Boswell's *Life* (1780)]

FREE THOUGHT

2 Certainly there be [those] that delight in giddiness and count it a bondage to fix a belief; affecting free-will in thinking as well as in acting. [Francis Bacon: *Of Truth*]

3 Freedom of speech and freedom of action are meaningless without freedom to think. And there is no freedom of thought without doubt. [Bergen Evans: *The Natural History of Nonsense* XIX]

FREE WILL

4 It is as insignificant to ask whether man's will be free as to ask whether his sleep be swift or his virtue square: liberty is as little applicable to the will as swiftness of motion is to sleep or squareness to virtue. [John Locke: *An Essay Concerning Human Understanding* II. Ch. xxi, "Of Power"]

5 There is no such thing as free will. The mind is induced to wish this or that by some cause, and that cause is determined by another cause, and so on back to infinity. [Spinoza: *Ethics* II]

6 If we grant freedom to man, there is an end to the omniscience of God; for if the Divinity knows how I shall act, I must act so perforce. [Goethe: *Conversations with Eckermann*]

7 To deny the freedom of the will is to make morality impossible. [J. A. Froude: *Calvinism*]

8 Sir, we *know* our will is free, and there's an end on 't. [Samuel Johnson: in Boswell's *Life* (1769)]

The question of the freedom of the will was one with which Boswell loved to pester Johnson. On another occasion Johnson said, "All theory is against the freedom of the will; all experience for it" (Life, April 15, 1778). There really isn't very much more to be said.

9 It may be true that we can act as we choose, but can we choose? Is not our choice determined for us? [J. A. Froude: *Spinoza*]

10 The human will has no more freedom than that of the higher animals, from which it differs only in degree, not in kind. [Ernst Haeckel: *The Riddle of the Universe* VII]

11 Only two possibilities exist: either one must believe in determinism and regard free will as a subjective illusion, or one must become a mystic and regard the discovery of natural laws as a meaningless intellectual game. [Max Born (Nobel Prize in Physics, 1955), in the *Bulletin of the Atomic Scientists*, June 1957]

FRENCH

12 Ful wel she song the service divyne,
Entuned in hir nose ful semely;
And Frensh she spak ful faire and
fetisly
After the scole of Stratford atte Bowe,
For Frensh of Paris was to hir un-
knowe.
[Chaucer: Prologue to *The Canterbury Tales*]

Singing through the nose was regarded as very elegant.

fetisly = elegantly

Stratford atte Bowe was then a village east of London. The Prioress, whom Chaucer is describing, is thought to have been the headmistress of an aristocratic young ladies' finishing school there.

FRENCH LEAVE

13 I felt myself extremely awkward about going away, not choosing, as it was

my first visit, to take French leave. [Madame D'Arblay: *Diary*, Dec. 8, 1782]

> *In eighteenth-century France it was socially permissible to leave a party quietly without taking leave of the hostess or of any of your fellow guests. Possibly because all things French are thought by Anglo-Saxons to be, in some way, slightly wicked, the term for this civilized and merciful custom is used with us to designate surreptitious departures, desertions, abscondings and the like.*

FRENCHMEN

1 Fifty million Frenchmen can't be wrong. [Attr. Texas Guinan (1884-1933): in the *New York World-Telegram*, March 21, 1931]

> *Miss Guinan was a colorful night-club hostess who greeted her patrons with alarming frankness with the cry "Hello, Sucker!" She coined the once-popular phrase "big butter-and-egg man."*
>
> *Although the above is commonly attributed to her, it was an expression among American soldiers in World War I. Its origin is now lost.*
>
> *There weren't fifty million Frenchmen, but alliteration has small regard for the census.*

FREUD

2 One rational voice is dumb: over a grave
The household of Impulse mourns one dearly loved.
Sad is Eros, builder of cities,
And weeping anarchic Aphrodite.
[W. H. Auden: *In Memory of Sigmund Freud* (1940)]

FRIEND(S)

3 A friend is in prosperitie a pleasure, a solace in aduersitie, in grief a comfort, in joy a merry companion, at al times an other I. [John Lyly: *Euphues*]
4 Friends are thieves of time. [Francis Bacon: *The Advancement of Learning* VIII]

> *Bacon adds, "as they are accustomed to say."*

5 To me, fair friend, you never can be old,
For as you were when first your eye I eyed,

Such seems your beauty still.
[Shakespeare: *Sonnets* CIV]
6 A friend i'the court is better than a penny in purse.
[Shakespeare: *II Henry IV* V.i.]

> *Apparently an old saying. Lyly had quoted it 17 years before in Euphues and his England and had added wryly, "but yet I have heard that such a friend cannot be gotten in the court without pence."*

7 My friends were poor, but honest.
[Shakespeare: *All's Well That Ends Well* I.i.]
8 Those friends thou hast, and their adoption tried,
Grapple them unto thy soul with hoops of steel:
But do not dull thy palm with entertainment
Of each new-hatch'd, unfledg'd comrade.
[Shakespeare: *Hamlet* I.iii.]
9 No friend's a friend till he shall prove a friend. [Beaumont and Fletcher: *The Faithful Friends* III.iii.]
10 Old friends are best. King James used to call for his old shoes; they were easiest for his feet. [John Selden: *Table Talk*]
11 It is more shameful to distrust one's friends than to be deceived by them. [La Rochefoucauld: *Maxims*]
12 The wretched have no friends.
[Dryden: *All for Love* III.i.]
13 My guide, philosopher, and friend.
[Alexander Pope: *An Essay on Man* IV]
14 He gave to Mis'ry all he had, a tear,
He gain'd from Heav'n ('twas all he wish'd) a friend.
[Thomas Gray: *Elegy Written in a Country Churchyard*]
15 I like a friend the better for having faults that one can talk about. [William Hazlitt: *The Plain Speaker* I]
16 The only reward of virtue is virtue; the only way to have a friend is to be one. [Emerson: *Friendship*]
17 The ornament of a house is the friends who frequent it. [Emerson: *Domestic Life*]
18 "Wal'r, my boy," replied the Captain, "in the Proverbs of Solomon you will find the following words, 'May we never want a friend in need, nor a bottle to

give him!' When found, make a note of."
[Dickens: *Dombey and Son* XV]

The kindly Cap'n Cuttle, who is fond of quoting but has no great concern with accuracy.

1 The most I can do for my friend is simply to be his friend. [Thoreau: *Journal,* February 7, 1841]

2 What lasting joys the man attend
Who has a polished female friend.
[Cornelius Whurr: *The Female Friend*]

3 The costliness of keeping friends does not lie in what one does for them, but in what one, out of consideration for them, refrains from doing. [Henrik Ibsen]

4 A friend married is a friend lost. [Henrik Ibsen: *Love's Comedy* II]

5 A friend in power is a friend lost. [Henry Adams: *The Education of Henry Adams*]

6 The golden period, when I had not a single friend. [Henry Miller: *Tropic of Cancer*]

7 It is in the thirties that we want friends. In the forties we know they won't save us any more than love did. [F. Scott Fitzgerald: *Note-Books*]

FRIEND(S): and enemies

8 Praise from a friend, or censure from a foe,
Are lost on hearers that our merits know.
[Homer: *Iliad* X (trans. Alexander Pope)]

9 He that is not with me is against me. [Matthew 12:30]

10 For what man that hath freendes through fortune,
Mishap wol make hem enemys, I gesse.
[Chaucer: *The Monk's Tale*]

11 Better to trust an open enemy than a reconciled friend. [Robert Greene: *Planetomachia*]

12 You shall read that we are commanded to forgive our enemies; but you never read that we are commanded to forgive our friends. [Francis Bacon: *Of Revenge*]

Bacon is quoting "Cosmus, Duke of Florence" and regards this as "a desperate saying."

13 Love all, trust a few,
Do wrong to none: be able for thine enemy
Rather in power than use, and keep thy friend
Under thine own life's key: be check'd for silence,
But never tax'd for speech.
[Shakespeare: *All's Well That Ends Well* I.i.]

14 A wise man gets more use from his enemies than a fool from his friends. [Gracián: *Oráculo Manual*]

15 A reconciled Friend is a double Enemy. [Thomas Fuller (1654-1734): *Gnomologia*]

16 I have been gaining enemies by the scores, and friends by the couples, which is against the rules of wisdom, because they say one enemy can do more hurt than ten friends can do good. [Jonathan Swift: *Journal to Stella,* June 30, 1711]

17 To all my foes, dear fortune, send
Thy gifts! but never to my friend;
I tamely can endure the first;
But this with envy makes me burst.
[Jonathan Swift: *On the Death of Dr. Swift*]

18 . . . wise fear, you know,
Forbids the robbing of a foe;
But what, to serve our private ends,
Forbids the cheating of our friends?
[Charles Churchill: *The Ghost* III]

19 Greatly his foes he dreads, but more his friends;
He hurts me most who lavishly commends.
[Charles Churchill: *The Apology*]

20 He who loves his Enemies, hates his Friends;
This is surely not what Jesus intends.
[William Blake: *The Everlasting Gospel* II]

21 He will never have true friends who is afraid of making enemies. [William Hazlitt: *Characteristics*]

22 If you want enemies, excel others; if you want friends, let others excel you. [C. C. Colton: *Lacon*]

23 . . . we should ever conduct ourselves towards our enemy as if he were one day to be our friend. [John Henry Newman: *The Idea of a University,* Discourse VIII]

24 He makes no friend who never made a foe.
[Tennyson: *Idylls of the King,* "Lance-

1 Was it a friend or foe that spread these lies?
Nay, who but infants question in such wise,
'Twas one of my most intimate enemies.
[Dante Gabriel Rossetti: *Fragment*]

2 It takes your enemy and your friend, working together, to hurt you to the heart; the one to slander you and the other to get the news to you. [Mark Twain: *Pudd'nhead Wilson's New Calendar*]

3 Wert thou my enemy, O thou my friend,
How wouldst thou worse, I wonder, than thou dost
Defeat, thwart me?
[Gerard Manley Hopkins: *Thou Art Indeed Just, Lord*]

4 Instead of loving your enemies, treat your friends a little better. [E. W. Howe: *Plain People*]

FRIEND: in need
5 There is a friend that sticketh closer than a brother. [Proverbs 18:24]

6 He that is thy friend indeed,
He will help thee in thy need.
[Richard Barnfield: *Address to the Nightingale*]

7 Think twice before you speak to a friend in need. [Ambrose Bierce: *The Devil's Dictionary*]

8 Whatever the outcome of the appeal, I do not intend to turn my back on Alger Hiss. [Dean Acheson, as quoted in *Time,* Feb. 6, 1950]

FRIEND(S): need of and desire for
9 Those that want friends to open themselves unto are cannibals of their own hearts. [Francis Bacon: *Of Friendship*]
want = *lack*

10 But grant me still a friend in my retreat,
Whom I may whisper, Solitude is sweet.
[William Cowper: *Retirement*]

11 Let me live in my house by the side of the road
And be a friend of man.
[Sam Walter Foss: *The House by the Side of the Road*]

In Homer's *Iliad, Axylus,* son of Teuthranus, had been
    . . . *a friend to human race*
Fast by the road, his ever-open door
Obliged the wealthy, and reliev'd the poor.
(*Alexander Pope's trans.*)

12 It was not foes to conquer,
Nor sweethearts to be kind,
But it was friends to die for
That I would seek and find.
[A. E. Housman: *Last Poems* XXXII]

13 We need new friends; some of us are cannibals who have eaten their old friends up: others must have everrenewed audiences before whom to reenact an ideal version of their lives. [Logan Pearsall Smith: *Afterthoughts*]

FRIEND: a rarity
14 He has no friend who has many friends. [Aristotle: *Eudemian Ethics* VII. xii.]

15 Friends are like melons. Shall I tell you why?
To find one good, you must a hundred try.
[Claude Mermet: *Epigram on Friends*]

16 If you have one true friend, you have more than your share. [Thomas Fuller (1654-1734): *Gnomologia*]

17 There are three faithful friends—an old wife, an old dog, and ready money. [Benjamin Franklin: *Poor Richard's Almanack* (1738)]

18 He cannot be properly chosen for a friend whose kindness is exhaled by its own warmth or frozen by the first blast of slander; he cannot be a useful counselor who will hear no opinion but his own; he will not much invite confidence whose principal maxim is to suspect; nor can the candor and frankness of that man be much esteemed who spreads his arms to humankind and makes every man, without distinction, a denizen of his bosom. [Samuel Johnson: *The Rambler* No. 64]
A friend to all is a friend to none.
Diogenes Laertius: Aristotle *XXI*

19 We walk alone in the world. Friends, such as we desire, are dreams and fables. [Emerson: *Friendship*]

20 One friend in a lifetime is much;

two are many; three are hardly possible. [Henry Adams: *The Education of Henry Adams*]

FRIEND(S): treachery and malice of

1 I was wounded in the house of my friends. [Zechariah 13:6]
2 No friend will approach when wealth is lost. [Ovid: *Tristia* I.ix.]
3 From him whom I trust God defend me, for from him whom I trust not, I will defend myself. [James Howell: *Familiar Letters* II.lxxv.]
4 If men knew what others say of them, there would not be four friends in the world. [Pascal: *Pensées*]
5 Some great misfortune to portend,
   No enemy can match a friend.
[Jonathan Swift: *Verses on the Death of Dr. Swift*]
6 A false Friend and a Shadow attend only while the Sun shines. [Benjamin Franklin: *Poor Richard's Almanack* (1756)]
7 If it is abuse—why one is always sure to hear of it from one damned good-natured friend or other! [Richard Brinsley Sheridan: *The Critic* I.i.]
8 Give me the avowed, the erect, the manly foe,
   Bold I can meet—perhaps may turn his blow!
   But of all plagues, good Heaven, thy wrath can send,
   Save, save, oh save me from the candid friend!
[George Canning: *New Morality*]
9 There is no man so friendless but what he can find a friend sincere enough to tell him disagreeable truths. [E. G. Bulwer-Lytton: *What Will He Do With It?* III.xv.]

FRIENDSHIP

10 Reprove your friends in secret, praise them openly. [Publilius Syrus: *Maxims*]
11 To have a great man for an intimate friend seems pleasant to those who have never experienced it; those who have, fear it. [Horace: *Epistolae* I.xviii.]
12 Greater love hath no man than this, that a man lay down his life for his friends. [John 15:13]
13 Friendship always benefits; love sometimes injures. [Seneca: *Ad Lucil-*

ium XXXV]
14 Friendship is constant in all other things
   Save in the office and affairs of love:
   Therefore all hearts in love use their own tongues;
   Let every eye negotiate for itself
   And trust no agent.
[Shakespeare: *Much Ado About Nothing* II.i.]
15 I decline this over-complaisant kindness, which uses no discrimination. I like to be distinguished; and, to cut the matter short, the friend of all mankind is no friend of mine. [Molière: *The Misanthrope* I.i.]
16 Friendship cannot live with ceremony, nor without civility. [Lord Halifax: *Maxims*]
17 Two friendships in two breasts requires
   The same aversions and desires.
[Jonathan Swift: *Life and Character of Dean Swift*]
18 Who friendship with a knave hath made,
   Is judg'd a partner in the trade.
[John Gay: *The Old Woman and Her Cats*]
19 So many qualities are requisite to the possibility of friendship and so many accidents must concur to its rise and continuance, that the greatest part of mankind content themselves without it and supply its place, as they can, with interest and dependence. [Samuel Johnson: *The Rambler* No. 64]
   as they can = *as best they can;* interest = *self-interest, material advantage or the hope of it*
20 Friendship, compounded of esteem and love, derives from one its tenderness and its permanence from the other. [Samuel Johnson: *The Rambler* No. 64]
21 The man that hails you Tom or Jack,
   And proves by thumps upon your back
      How he esteems your merit,
   Is such a friend, that one had need
   Be very much his friend indeed
      To pardon or to bear it.
[William Cowper: *On Friendship*]
22 Thy friendship oft has made my heart to ache:
   Do be my enemy—for friendship's

sake.
[William Blake: *On Friends and Foes* VI]

1 Friendship is a sheltering tree.
[Coleridge: *Youth and Age*]

2 Friends will be much apart. They will respect more each other's privacy than their communion. [Thoreau: *Journal*, Feb. 22, 1841]

This is a very Thoreauvian conception of friendship.

3 There is an old time toast which is golden for its beauty. "When you ascend the hill of prosperity may you not meet a friend." [Mark Twain: *Pudd'nhead Wilson's New Calendar*]

4 Friendship needs a certain parallelism of life, a community of thought, a rivalry of aim. [Henry Adams: *The Education of Henry Adams* XX]

FRIENDSHIP: fruits and advantages of

5 Friendship makes prosperity brighter, while it lightens adversity by sharing its griefs and anxieties. [Cicero: *De Amicitia* VI]

6 The vulgar herd estimate friendship by its advantages. [Ovid: *Epistolae ex Ponto* II.iii.]

How to Win Friends and Influence People was a very good title for a bad book's purposes.

7 It [friendship] redoubleth joys, and cutteth griefs in halves. [Francis Bacon: *Of Friendship*]

8 No receipt openeth the heart but a true friend, to whom you may impart griefs, joys, fears, hopes, suspicions, counsels, and whatsoever lieth upon the heart to oppress it, in a kind of civil shrift or confession. [Francis Bacon: *Of Friendship*]

receipt = recipe, that particular kind of a recipe which we today call a prescription. The cabalistic sign with which doctors cast an aura of magic over an illegible order for aspirin (℞) is simply an abbreviation of Receipt.

9 A principal fruit of friendship is the ease and discharge of the fulness and swellings of the heart which passions of all kinds do cause and induce. [Francis Bacon: *Of Friendship*]

10 Friendship is seldom lasting but between equals. . . . Benefits which cannot be repaid and obligations which cannot be discharged are not commonly found to increase affection; they excite gratitude indeed and heighten veneration, but commonly take away that easy freedom and familiarity of intercourse without which . . . there cannot be friendship. [Samuel Johnson: *The Rambler* No. 64]

FRIENDSHIP: its hollowness and impermanence

11 A back-friend, a shoulder-clapper.
[Shakespeare: *The Comedy of Errors* IV.ii.]

12 Most friendship is feigning, most loving mere folly.
[Shakespeare: *As You Like It* II.vii.]

13 Thus each extreme to equal danger tends,
Plenty, as well as Want, can sep'rate friends.
[Abraham Cowley: *Davideis* III]

14 If a man does not make new acquaintance as he advances through life, he will soon find himself alone. A man, Sir, should keep his friendship in constant repair. [Samuel Johnson: in Boswell's *Life* (1755)]

15 The great effect of friendship is beneficence, yet by the first act of uncommon kindness it is endangered. [Samuel Johnson: *The Rambler* No. 64]

16 The most fatal disease of friendship is gradual decay, or dislike hourly increased by causes too slender for complaint, and too numerous for removal. [Samuel Johnson: *The Idler* No. 23]

17 The holy passion of Friendship is of so sweet and steady and loyal and enduring a nature that it will last through a whole lifetime, if not asked to lend money. [Mark Twain: *Pudd'nhead Wilson's Calendar*]

18 A man of active and resilient mind outwears his friendships just as certainly as he outwears his love affairs, his politics and his epistemology. [H. L. Mencken: in *Smart Set*, July 1919]

FRIENDSHIP: some unfriendly reflections on

19 There is no friendship between those associated in power; he who rules will

always be impatient of an associate. [Lucan: *Pharsalia* I.xcii.]

1 In the midst of compassion we inwardly feel a kind of bittersweet pricking of malicious delight to see others suffer. [Montaigne: *Essays* III.i.]

La Rochefocauld's maxim that in the misfortunes of our friends we find something pleasing, has shocked many generations—though Montaigne made the same observation a hundred years before and Burke was to repeat it a hundred years later: "We have a degree of delight, and that no small one, in the real misfortunes and pains of others"—Sublime and Beautiful I.xiv. "In all distresses of our friends [wrote Swift]/We first consult our private ends;/While Nature, kindly bent to ease us,/Points out some circumstance to please us."

2 There is little friendship in the world, and least of all between equals. [Francis Bacon: *Of Followers and Friends*]

3 There is flattery in friendship. [Shakespeare: *Henry V* III.vii.]

4 What men call friendship is only a reciprocal conciliation of interests, an exchange of good offices; it is in short simply a form of barter from which self-love always expects to gain something. [La Rouchefoucauld: *Maxims*]

5 Wise Rochefoucauld a Maxim writ,
Made up of Malice, Truth, and Wit.

. . .

He says, "Whenever Fortune sends
Disasters to our Dearest Friends,
Although we outwardly may grieve,
We oft are laughing in our sleeve."
And, as I think upon 't this minute,
I fancy there is something in it.

[Jonathan Swift: *The Life and Character of Dean Swift*]

6 In plain English, when you have made your Fortune by the good Offices of a Friend, you are advised to discard him as soon as you can. [Henry Fielding: *Tom Jones* I.xxiii.]

7 The most generous and disinterested friendship must be resolved at last into the love of ourselves; he therefore whose reputation or dignity inclines us to consider his esteem as a testimonial of desert will always find our hearts open to his endearments. [Samuel Johnson: *The Rambler* No. 166]

8 Most friendships are formed by caprice or by chance—mere confederacies in vice or leagues in folly. [Samuel Johnson: in Boswell's *Life,* May 19, 1784]

9 Our very best friends have a tincture of jealousy even in their friendship. [C. C. Colton: *Lacon*]

10 Never catch at a falling knife or a falling friend. [19th-century proverb]

Many people have been injured by attempting to catch a falling knife. So few have ever tried to catch a falling friend that practically nothing is known of the consequences.

11 When you are down and out something always turns up—and it's usually the noses of your friends. [Orson Welles, quoted in *The New York Times,* April 1, 1962]

FRIGHT

12 I don't know what effect these men will have on the enemy, but, by God, they frighten *me.* [Ascribed—probably apocryphally—to various statesmen and commanders: to the Duke of Wellington, on a draft of troops sent to him in Spain, in 1809; to William Pitt, on being shown a list of English generals to be sent out to fight the colonists, etc.]

FROG(S)

13 It was the saying of Bion that though boys throw stones at frogs in sport, the frogs do not die in sport but in earnest. [Plutarch: *Which are the Most Crafty, Water or Land Animals?*]

14 A frog he would a-wooing go,
 Heigh ho! says Rowley,
A frog he would a-wooing go,
 Whether his mother would let him or
 no.
With a rowley, powley, gammon and
 spinach,
Heigh ho! says Anthony Rowley.

[Nursery rhyme]

In this form, it dates only to the 19th century, but other versions have been traced back to 1580 and 1549.

15 Thus use your frog: put your hook through his mouth and out at his gills, and then with a fine needle and silk sew the upper part of his leg with only one stitch to the arming wire of your hook, or tie the frog's leg above the upper joint to the armed wire; and in so doing use him as though you loved him. [Izaak Walton: *The Compleat Angler* I.viii.]

> *Fishermen are obsessed with the comforting belief that the bait and the fish caught all enter, with a gay and manly gusto, into the "sport."*

1 The frog by nature is both damp and
cold,
Her mouth is large, her belly much
will hold.
[John Bunyan: *A Book for Boys and Girls*]

2 Can I unmoved see thee dying
On a log,
Expiring frog!
[Dickens: *The Pickwick Papers* XV]

3 I don't see no p'ints about that frog that's any better'n any other frog. [Mark Twain: *The Celebrated Jumping Frog*]

4 . . . from the orchised bog
chuckles the ancient and omniscient
frog
his gross venereal hymn. . . .
[Conrad Aiken: *The Return*]

FRONTIER

5 We stand today on the edge of a new frontier—the frontier of the 1960's—a frontier of unknown opportunities and perils—a frontier of unfulfilled hopes and threats. [John F. Kennedy, speech accepting presidential nomination, July 15, 1960]

FROST

6 Frost and fraud have always foul
ends.
[William Camden: *Remains* (1605)]

7 Frost and fraud come to foul ends. [Robert Burton: *The Anatomy of Melancholy* I.2.3.15]

8 The frost performs its secret ministry,
Unhelped by any wind.
[Coleridge: *Frost at Midnight*]

9 When the frost is on the punkin and
the fodder's in the shock.
[James Whitcomb Riley: *When the Frost is on the Punkin*]

FROWN

10 So frown'd the mighty combatants,
that hell
Grew darker at their frown.
[John Milton: *Paradise Lost* II.719]

11 Her very frowns are fairer far,
Than smiles of other maidens are.
[Hartley Coleridge: *She is not Fair*]

FRUGALITY

12 Frugality is a handsome income. [Erasmus: *Familiar Colloquies*]

13 King Stephen was and a worthy peer,
His breeches cost him but a crown;
He held them sixpence all too dear,
With that he called the tailor lown.
[Shakespeare: *Othello* II.iii.]

14 There's husbandry in heaven;
Their candles are all out.
[Shakespeare: *Macbeth* II.i.]

15 Ever a Glutton, at another's Cost,
But in whose Kitchen dwells perpetual Frost.
[*Persius : Satires* IV (trans. Dryden)]

16 Without frugality none can be rich, and with it very few would be poor. [Samuel Johnson: *The Rambler* No. 57]

17 For loss of time,
Although it grieved him sore,
Yet loss of pence, full well he knew,
Would trouble him much more.
[William Cowper: *John Gilpin's Ride*]

18 Though on pleasure she was bent,
She had a frugal mind.
[William Cowper: *John Gilpin's Ride*]

19 Let us be happy and live within our means, even if we have to borrow the money to do it with. [Artemus Ward: *Science and Natural History*]

FRUIT(S)

20 Ye shall know them by their fruits. Do men gather grapes of thorns, or figs of thistles? [Matthew 7:16]

21 The tree is known by his fruit. [Matthew 12:33]

22 The fruit
Of that forbidden tree, whose mortal
taste
Brought death into the world, and all
our woe.
[John Milton: *Paradise Lost* I.]

FRUSTRATION

23 Full little knowest thou that hast not
tried,
What hell it is, in suing long to bide;
To lose good days, that might be better spent;

To waste long nights in pensive discontent;
To speed today, to be put back tomorrow;
To feed on hope, to pine with fear and sorrow. . . .
To fret thy soul with crosses and with cares;
To eat thy heart through comfortless despairs;
To fawn, to crouch, to wait, to ride, to run,
To spend, to give, to want, to be undone.
[Edmund Spenser: *Mother Hubberds Tale*]
speed = *succeed;* want = *to be in want*

1 He that is used to go forward and findeth a stop, falleth out of his own favor and is not the thing he was. [Francis Bacon: *Of Empire*]

2 Never the time and the place
And the loved one all together!
[Robert Browning: *Never the Time and the Place*]

3 . . . the sick fatigue, the languid doubt,
Which much to have tried, in much been baffled, brings.
[Matthew Arnold: *The Scholar-Gipsy*]

FRYING

4 In his owne grece I made hym frye.
[Chaucer: Prologue to *The Wife of Bath's Tale*]

FRYING PAN

5 They lepe lyke a flounder out of the fryenge panne into the fyre. [Sir Thomas More: *A Dyaloge Concerning Heresyes* (1528)]

6 Leape out of the frying pan into the fyre. [John Heywood: *Proverbs*]

7 Leap out of the frying pan into the fire.
[Cervantes: *Don Quixote* I.iii.4]

FUN

8 I've taken my fun where I've found it.
[Kipling: *The Ladies*]

9 No, you never get any fun
Out of the things you haven't done.
[Ogden Nash: *Portrait of the Artist as a Prematurely Old Man*]

FUNERAL

10 Madame has a bad day for her journey. [Louis XV: while watching Mme. de Pompadour's funeral from a window]

11 And when they buried him the little port
Had seldom seen a costlier funeral.
[Tennyson: *Enoch Arden*]
These concluding lines with their unexpected consolation for Enoch's renunciation are often quoted as an instance of bathos and Victorian vulgarity.

12 In the city a funeral is just an interruption of traffic. In the country it is a form of popular entertainment. [George Ade: in *Cosmopolitan,* February 1928]

FUNNY

13 Funny peculiar, or funny ha-ha? [John Hay Beith ("Ian Hay"): *Housemaster* III]

FURTHER

14 Might have gone further and have fared worse. [John Heywood: *Proverbs*]

FURY

15 Think not that anything can surpass
The fury of a woman scorned.
[Francesco Berni: *Orlando Innamorato* IV.xxiii.]

16 No viper has worse venom or keener fangs than a woman enraged because she has been scorned by a man. [Lope de Vega: *La Hermosa Fea* II.iv.]

17 I understand a fury in your words,
But not the words.
[Shakespeare: *Othello* IV.ii.]

18 To be furious is to be frighted out of fear.
[Shakespeare: *Antony and Cleopatra* III.xiii.]

19 Heaven has no rage like love to hatred turned,
Nor Hell a fury like a woman scorned.
[William Congreve: *The Mourning Bride* III.viii. (1697)]
See SCORN

20 War hath no fury like a non-combatant. [C. E. Montague: *Disenchantment* XV]

FUSTEST

21 Git thar fustest with the mostest. [Attr. Confederate General Nathan Bed-

ford Forrest (1821-1877), as a prescription for victory.]

FUTILITY

1 All is vanity and vexation of spirit. [Ecclesiastes 1:14]

2 It is lost labor to play a jig to an old cat. [Thomas Fuller (1654-1734): *Gnomologia*]

Literature is full of amusing similes for futile expenditure of energy. Among them:

to water a post;
to wash an Ethiopian white;
to pound water in a mortar;
to castrate eunuchs;
to plow the sands;
to talk to a stone;
to carry water in a sieve;
to complain to a stepmother;
to muzzle a sheep;
to sing psalms to a dead horse

3 Fair to no purpose, artful to no end,
Young without lovers, old without a
friend;
A Fop their passion, but their prize a
Sot.

[Alexander Pope: *Moral Essays* II]
The reference is to ladies in high society.

4   The toil
Of dropping buckets into empty wells,
And growing old in drawing nothing
up.

[William Cowper: *The Task* III (1785)]
He has spent all his life in letting down empty buckets into empty wells; and he is frittering away his age in trying to draw them up again.

Sydney Smith: in Lady Holland's Memoir I.ix.

5 Most men eddy about
Here and there—eat and drink,
Chatter and love and hate,
Gather and squander, are raised
Aloft, are hurl'd in the dust,
Striving blindly, achieving
Nothing; and then they die.

[Matthew Arnold: *Rugby Chapel*]

FUTURE

6   The never-ending flight
Of future days.

[John Milton: *Paradise Lost* II.221]

7 Heaven from all creatures hides the book of Fate. [Alexander Pope: *An Essay on Man* I.lxxvii.]

8 O blindness to the future! kindly giv'n. [Alexander Pope: *An Essay on Man* I.lxxxv.]

9 The future is purchased by the present. [Samuel Johnson: *The Rambler* No. 178]

10 Keep cool: It will be all one a hundred years hence. [Emerson: *Representative Men:* "Montaigne"]

11 In the sweet by-and-by,
We shall meet on that beautiful shore.

[Ira David Sankey: *Sweet By-and-By*]

12 I have been over into the future and it works. [Lincoln Steffens: *Autobiography* XVIII]

Steffens had accompanied the Bullitt mission to Russia in 1919 and on his return made this comment.

It is usually quoted as: I have seen the future and it works.

13 The Shape of Things to Come. [H. G. Wells: title of a book (1933)]

G

GAIT
1 By her gait one knew the goddess.
[Virgil: *Aeneid* I]

GALILEAN
2 Thou hast conquered, O pale Galilean; the world has grown grey from
thy breath;
We have drunken of things Lethean,
and fed on the fullness of death.
[Swinburne: *Hymn to Proserpine*]

GALLAGHER
3 Let her go, Gallagher!
[William W. Delaney: title of a song
(1887)]

GALLANTRY
4 Conscience has no more to do with
gallantry than it has with politics. [Richard Brinsley Sheridan: *The Duenna* II]
5 I know not if the fault be men's or
theirs;
But one thing's pretty sure; a
woman planted
(Unless at once she plunge for life in
prayers)—
After a decent time must be gallanted.
[Byron: *Don Juan* III.iv.]

GALLEYWEST
6 She grabbed up the basket and
slammed it across the house and knocked
the cat galleywest. [Mark Twain: *Huckleberry Finn* XXXVII (1884)]
*Mark Twain had used the word galleywest in a letter nine years before, so it
was in his vocabulary and, he must have
assumed, that of his correspondent. But,
so far as we know, this was its first appearance in print. It plainly means to
knock into smithereens and seems to
have nothing to do with galley or the
points of the compass. Chances are that
Mark heard it on the river or knew it
as an old family expression. Scholars believe it is a corruption of an English
dialectal* collyweston: *there is, or was, a
place in England called Collyweston; and*

*there was a saying, when things had gone
perversely wrong, "It's all because of
Colly Weston." But no one knows who
or what Colly Weston was.*

GALLOPING
7 I sprang to the stirrup, and Joris,
and he;
I galloped, Dirck galloped, we galloped all three.
[Robert Browning: *How They Brought
the Good News from Ghent to Aix*]
*Once thought to be a splendid example
of onomatopoeia, the echoing of sound
in sense, the passage is too obvious to
please our taste. A real "rocking-horse
meter."*

GAMALIEL
8 Brought up in this city at the feet of
Gamaliel. [Acts 22:3]

GAMBLER
9 Nothing is sacred to a gambler.
[Jacques Saurin: *Beverlei* I.i.]
*Nothing but gambling, that is. An illustration of this was provided by an incident at Will's, the great gambling club
in London, in the eighteenth century. A
passerby dropped to the sidewalk in
front of the club. One of the members
immediately wagered, with odds, that
the man was dead and his wager was accepted by another member. Still other
members sought to render assistance to
the fallen man, but the first man claimed
that this was unethical. The matter was
referred to a committee and by the time
a decision had been reached the gentleman was dead.*

GAMBLING
10 Hazard is very mother of lyings.
And of deceit, and cursed forswearings.
[Chaucer: *The Pardoner's Tale*]
11 Gambling is the child of avarice, but
the parent of prodigality. [C. C. Colton:
Lacon]
12 The gambling known as business

looks with austere disfavor upon the business known as gambling. [Ambrose Bierce: *The Devil's Dictionary*]

GAMING

1 If yet thou love game at so dear a
    rate,
  Learn this, that hath old gamesters
    dearly cost:
Dost lose? rise up: dost win? rise in
    that state.
  Who strive to sit out losing hands
    are lost.
[George Herbert: *The Church-Porch*]

GAMUT

2 She ran the whole gamut of her emotions from A to B. [Attr. Dorothy Parker: speaking of a famous movie actress who was thought, by the less discerning, to have as great a range as the players in *Hamlet*.]

GARDEN

3 God Almighty first planted a garden. And, indeed, it is the purest of human pleasures. [Francis Bacon: *Of Gardens*]
4 Annihilating all that's made
  To a green thought in a green shade.
[Andrew Marvell: *The Garden*]
5 God the first garden made, and the
    first city Cain.
[Abraham Cowley: *The Garden* V]
6 A garden was the primitive prison, till man, with promethean felicity and boldness, luckily sinned himself out of it. [Charles Lamb: Letter to William Wordsworth, January 22, 1830]
7 Come into the garden, Maud,
  For the black bat, night, has flown,
Come into the garden, Maud,
  I am here at the gate alone;
And the woodbine spices are wafted
    abroad,
  And the musk of the rose is blown.
[Tennyson: *Maud: A Monodrama* I.xxii.]
8 A Garden is a lovesome thing, God
    wot!
    Rose plot,
    Fringed pool,
    Ferned grot—
    The veriest school
    Of Peace; and yet the fool
Contends that God is not—
Not God! in Gardens! when the eve

is cool?
  'Tis very sure God walks in mine.
[Thomas Brown: *My Garden*]
9 I know a little garden close
  Set thick with lily and red rose,
  Where I would wander if I might
  From dewy dawn to dewy night,
  And have one with me wandering.
[William Morris: *The Life and Death of Jason* IV]
10 My garden will never make me famous,
  I'm a horticultural ignoramus,
  I can't tell a stringbean from a soybean,
  Or even a girl bean from a boy bean.
[Ogden Nash: *He Digs, He Dug, He Has Dug*]

GARMENT

11 In the tides of Life, in Action's storm,
    A fluctuant wave,
    A shuttle free,
    Birth and the Grave,
    An eternal sea,
    A weaving, flowing
    Life, all-glowing,
  Thus at Time's humming loom 'tis
    my hand prepares
  The garment of Life which the Deity
    wears!
[Goethe: *Faust* I (trans. Bayard Taylor)]
  The song of the Earth Spirit.

GARRICK, DAVID

12 . . . that stroke of death, which has eclipsed the gaiety of nations, and impoverished the public stock of harmless pleasure. [Samuel Johnson: *The Life of Edmund Smith*]
  Johnson was referring to the death of David Garrick.
13 On the stage he was natural, simple,
    affecting;
  'Twas only that when he was off he
    was acting.
[Oliver Goldsmith: *Retaliation*]

GARTER

14 *Honi soit qui mal y pense.* (Evil [lit.: shame] to him who evil thinks) [Motto of the Order of the Garter: originated by King Edward III in 1349.]
  There is a persistent story that the Countess of Salisbury dropped a garter

at a ball and that the gallant king, to still the snickers of ill-bred courtiers and calm the embarrassed lady, picked up the garter, tied it around his own arm, uttered the immortal rebuke in Norman French, and founded the Order of the Garter. He had given his own garter as the signal of battle at Crécy and the motto is more probably believed to be some sort of caution to King Philip of France.

1   I like the Garter; there is no damned merit in it. [Attr. William Lamb, Viscount Melbourne (1779-1848)]

Melbourne's comment is splendidly aristocratic. That we find it amusing shows how completely unaristocratic we are, how completely victorious the ideas of the French Revolution have been. The rewarding of merit is a democratic idea; levelling, utterly destructive of the old social order. "The career open to talents" was one of the most hated doctrines of the French Revolution.

GATE

2   Wide is the gate and broad is the way that leadeth to destruction. [Matthew 7:13]

3   Strait is the gate and narrow is the way which leadeth unto life. [Matthew 7:14]

GATH

4   Tell it not in Gath, publish it not in the streets of Askelon, lest the daughters of the Philistines rejoice. [II Samuel 1:20]

GAUL

5   All Gaul is divided into three parts. [Julius Caesar: *De Bello Gallico* I]

GAUNT

6   Old John of Gaunt, time-honour'd Lancaster. [Shakespeare: *Richard II* I.i.]

John of Gaunt (1340-1399), the 4th son of King Edward III of England, was so called because he was born at Ghent, in Flanders. He was the Duke of Lancaster.

GEM

7   Full many a gem of purest ray serene
The dark unfathomed caves of ocean bear.
Full many a flower is born to blush unseen,
And waste its sweetness on the desert air.
[Thomas Gray: *Elegy Written in a Country Churchyard*]

"There is many a rich stone laid up in the bowels of the earth, many a fair pearl laid up in the bosom of the sea, that never was seen, nor never shall be."
Joseph Hall (Bishop of Norwich): Contemplations *IV*

The Contemplations *were published 1612-1626; the* Elegy *was written in 1750. What innocence of a bygone naive anthropocentrism is in that word* waste!

GENERALITIES

8   . . . it being the nature of the mind of man, to the extreme prejudice of knowledge, to delight in the spacious liberty of generalities, as in a champaign region, and not in the enclosures of particularity. [Francis Bacon: *Advancement of Learning* II]

champaign region = *open country, fields*

9   A man is to guard himself against taking a thing in general. [Samuel Johnson: in Boswell's *Life,* April 3, 1776]

10   Glittering generalities!

The origin of the phrase is not absolutely certain. Rufus Choate (1799-1859) in a letter written in 1856 referred to "the glittering and sounding generalities of natural right" in the Declaration of Independence. But six or seven years earlier "glittering generalities" had been used in a newspaper account of one of Choate's own speeches. The question is: did he then borrow the newspaper's term? or had the newspaper, in its review, used a phrase he had used in his speech? or was the phrase then "in the air" and had each picked it up independently?

GENERALIZATION

11   Men are more apt to be mistaken in their generalizations than in their particular observations. [Machiavelli: *Discourses on Livy* I]

12   Generalization is necessary to the advancement of knowledge; but particularity is indispensable to the creations of

the imagination. [Macaulay: *Milton*]

GENERATION
1 A stubborn and rebellious generation.
[Psalms 78:8]
2 Seldom three descents continue good.
[Dryden: *The Wife of Bath: Her Tale*]

GENEROUS
3 Generous almost to a fault. [T. S.
Arthur: *Ten Nights in a Barroom* II]
A wit has said that we are always gen-
erous to a fault if it is our own.

GENIALITY
4 If ever they were dull or sad,
Their captain danced to them like
mad,
Or told, to make the time pass by,
Droll legends of his infancy.
[W. S. Gilbert: *Bab Ballads*, "Captain
Reece"]

GENIUS
5 There is no great genius without a
touch of madness. [Seneca: *De Tranquil-*
litate Animi XVII.x.]
Seneca says that he is quoting from
Aristotle. The same thought appears in
Plato's Phaedrus *and has been repeated,*
in one form or another, in almost every
European language every generation
since.
6 For that fine madness still he did retain
Which rightly should possess a poet's
brain.
[Michael Drayton: *To Henry Reynolds:*
Of Poets and Poesy]
7 Good God! What a genius I had
when I wrote that book. [Jonathan Swift:
commenting in his later years on *A Tale*
of a Tub]
8 When a true genius appears in the
world, you may know him by this sign,
that the dunces are all in confederacy
against him. [Jonathan Swift: *Thoughts*
on Various Subjects]
9 The true Genius is a mind of large
general powers, accidentally determined
to some particular direction. [Samuel
Johnson: *Life of Cowley*]
10 Genius does what it must, and talent
does what it can.
[E. R. Bulwer-Lytton ("Owen Mere-

dith"): *Last Words*]
Edward Robert, first Earl of Lytton
(1831-1891), son of the novelist Bulwer-
Lytton, was for a part of his life re-
garded as one of the greatest of living
English poets, chiefly for his poem Lucile
(1860). But he is now forgotten, or dimly
remembered only as someone intolerably
verbose and his most famous line, that
given above, is felt to be a self-judgment.
11 Genius, in truth, means little more
than the faculty of perceiving in an un-
habitual way. [William James: *The Prin-*
ciples of Psychology XX]
12 The public is wonderfully tolerant.
It forgives everything except genius. [Os-
car Wilde: *The Critic as Artist*]
13 I have nothing to declare except my
genius. [Oscar Wilde: to the revenue officers, when he landed in America in
January, 1882]

GENIUS: infinite capacity for
taking pains
14 Genius is mainly an affair of energy,
and poetry is mainly an affair of genius;
therefore a nation whose spirit is characterized by energy may well be eminent in
poetry—and we have Shakespeare.
[Matthew Arnold: *Essays in Criticism:*
First Series II]
15 No delusion is greater than the notion that method and industry can make
up for lack of motherwit, either in science or in practical life. [T. H. Huxley: *The Progress of Science*]
16 Genius only means an infinite capacity for taking pains. [Jane Ellice Hopkins: *Work Amongst Working Men*
(1870)]
A great favorite of those who are devoid
of genius; it would be hard to find a
definition less inspired by that which it
defines.
17 Genius is one percent inspiration
and ninety-nine percent perspiration.
[Thomas Alva Edison: in a newspaper
interview]

GENTILITY
18 Gentility is only a more select and artificial kind of vulgarity. [William Hazlitt: *Table-Talk* I.xvi.]

GENTLE
19 The gentle minde by gentle deeds is

knowne.
[Edmund Spenser: *The Faerie Queene*
VI.iii.]

GENTLEMAN(MEN)

1 When Adam dolve, and Eve span,
Who was then the gentleman?
[Attr. Richard Rolle of Hampole (d.
1349); much used as a slogan or war-
cry by the peasants and their leaders
in the Peasants' Rebellion (1381)]
dolve = *delved, dug with a spade*
One would have thought it was Adam.

2 Though he be not gentil born,
Thou mayst well seyn, this is a soth,
That he is gentil, because he doth
As longeth to a gentilman.
[Chaucer: *The Romaunt of the Rose*
(1365)]
*Chaucer's lines are interesting because
they show the beginning of the divergent
definitions and concepts now in the word
gentleman. It used to allude solely to the
gens or family connection, as it still does
—though more in Great Britain than in
the USA. But it acquired the meaning
of designating certain admirable qualities
—and, once in a while, a despised one—
characteristic of the man of aristocratic
birth and upbringing.*

*He was, for instance, more likely to be
gentle than the peasant. A Spanish proverb says that "A gentleman of honor will
wear rags but not patches" (Don Quixote
II.ii.), a concept of pride alien to democratic, middle-class thinking. Clare
Boothe (in Kiss the Boys Good-bye II.ii.)
defines a Southern gentleman as one who
can "shoot like a South Carolinian, ride
like a Virginian, drink like a Kentuckian,
make love like a Georgian, and be proud
of it as an Episcopalian." Others, more
cynical, have defined him as "One who
when his wife staggers in with a load of
firewood opens the door for her."*

(See Semyon Tsarapkin below.)

3 His tribe were God Almighty's gentlemen.
[Dryden: *Absalom and Achitophel* I]

4 Education begins a gentleman, conversation completes him. [Thomas Fuller
(1654-1734): *Gnomologia*]
*Conversation formerly meant all social
intercourse.*

5 It takes three generations to make a
gentleman. [Attr. Sir Robert Peel]

6 It is almost a definition of a gentleman to say he is one who never inflicts
pain. [John Henry, Cardinal Newman:
The Idea of a University]
*A gentleman is one who never hurts any-
one's feelings unintentionally.*
                    *Oliver Herford (1865-1935)
Sometimes attr. Oscar Wilde.*

7 A gentleman must be incapable of a
lie. [Emerson: *Journal*, December 14,
1850]

8 The only infallible rule we know is,
that the man who is always talking about
being a gentleman never is one. [R. S.
Surtees: *Ask Mamma* I]

9 And thus he bore without abuse
      The grand old name of gentleman,
Defamed by every charlatan,
And soiled with all ignoble use.
[Tennyson: *In Memoriam* CXI]

10 For he's one of Nature's Gentlemen.
[William James Linton: *Nature's Gentleman*]

11 The fatal reservation of a gentleman
is that he sacrifices everything to his
honor except his gentility. [G. B. Shaw:
Maxims for Revolutionists]

12 A gentleman is one who never strikes
a woman without provocation. [H. L.
Mencken: *Chrestomathy* 619]

13 A gentleman of our days is one who
has money enough to do what every fool
would do if he could afford it: that is,
consume without producing. [George
Bernard Shaw: *The Quintessence of
Ibsenism*]

14 I am not a gentleman. I am a representative of the Soviet Union. [Semyon
Tsarapkin, speaking in the United Nations, *New York Times,* June 26, 1954]
*Comrade Tsarapkin's remark was not
quite as absurd as it sounded. "Gentleman" in British English (which is the
English that most of the delegates know)
carries the connotation of caste and idleness (or leisure). In America frontier democracy has broadened the term to include any adult white male not, at the
moment of being alluded to, in jail.*

GENTLENESS

15 Throw away thy rod,
Throw away thy wrath:
O my God,

Take the gentle path.
[George Herbert: *Discipline*]

GENTRY

1 What tell you me of gentry? 'tis
nought else . . .
But ancient riches.
[John Webster: *The Devil's Law Case*
I.i.]

GEORGE

2 George the First was always reckoned
Vile, but viler George the Second;
And what mortal ever heard
Any good of George the Third?
When from earth the Fourth descended
God be praised, the Georges ended!
[Walter Savage Landor: *Epigram* (1855)]
The four Georges got a very bad press.
The first two were foreigners and the
Stuarts had all the advantage of a lost
cause. Then the triumph of middle-class,
evangelical morality in the 19th century
made them whipping boys for the wick-
edness of their franker time. But, prin-
cipally, they provoked the wits. George I
didn't speak English. George II an-
nounced bravely that he hated "baint-
ing and boetry." "Farmer George," the
III, regarded much of Shakespeare as
"sad stuff." And George IV, though he
admired Jane Austen and was a friend of
Sir Walter Scott, imprisoned Leigh Hunt
and antagonized the romantics.

3 Let George do it. [Louis XII of
France (1462-1515)]
George = *Georges d'Amboise (1460-1510),*
Cardinal, First Minister of State and
Lieutenant-General of the Army, one of
those incredible Renaissance figures who
seemed able to do everything and to do
it well.
Louis admired the Cardinal and
trusted him, and he was well and faith-
fully served. But perfection is always
slightly annoying and Louis's "Let
George do it" was satirically intended.
In its original form, it was: "Let George
do it; he's the man of the Age."

GEORGE III

4 George the Third
Ought never to have occurred.
One can only wonder

At so grotesque a blunder.
[E. C. Bentley: *George the Third*]

GEORGE IV

5 By God! you never saw such a figure
in your life as he is. Then he speaks and
swears so like old Falstaff, that damn me
if I was not ashamed to walk into a room
with him. [The Duke of Wellington: referring to the Prince Regent, later
George IV, "the first gentleman of Europe."]
6 This Adonis in loveliness was a cor-
pulent man of fifty. [Leigh Hunt: in
The Examiner, March 22, 1812]
For this reference to the Prince Regent,
Hunt was sentenced to two years in
prison.

GEORGIA

7 "Hurrah! hurrah! we bring the Ju-
bilee!
Hurrah! hurrah! the flag that makes
you free!"
So we sang the chorus from Atlanta
to the sea,
As we were marching through
Georgia.
[Henry Clay Work: *Marching Through*
Georgia]

GERMANY

8 The situation in Germany is serious
but not hopeless; the situation in Austria
is hopeless but not serious. [Viennese
proverb]

GETTING AND SPENDING

9 When one told him [Sir Edward
Coke (d.1633)] that his sons would
spend the estate faster than he got it, he
replied, "They cannot take more delight
in spending of it than I did in getting
of it." [John Aubrey: *Brief Lives* I]
10 A man who both spends and saves
money is the happiest man, because he
has both enjoyments. [Samuel Johnson:
in Boswell's *Life*, April 25, 1778]

GETTING INTO

11 Anything is easier to get into than
out of. [Agnes Allen's law]

GETTYSBURG ADDRESS

12 Fourscore and seven years ago our

fathers brought forth on this continent a new nation, conceived in liberty, and dedicated to the proposition that all men are created equal.

Now we are engaged in a great civil war, testing whether that nation, or any nation so conceived and so dedicated, can long endure. We are met on a great battlefield of that war. We have come to dedicate a portion of that field as a final resting-place for those who here gave their lives that that nation might live. It is altogether fitting and proper that we should do this.

But, in a larger sense, we cannot dedicate—we cannot consecrate—we cannot hallow—this ground. The brave men, living and dead, who struggled here, have consecrated it far above our poor power to add or detract. The world will little note nor long remember what we say here, but it can never forget what they did here. It is for us the living, rather, to be dedicated here to the unfinished work which they who fought here have thus far so nobly advanced. It is rather for us to be here dedicated to the great task remaining before us—that from these honored dead we take increased devotion to that cause for which they gave the last full measure of devotion; that we here highly resolve that these dead shall not have died in vain; that this nation, under God, shall have a new birth of freedom; and that government of the people, by the people, for the people, shall not perish from the earth. [Abraham Lincoln: Address at Gettysburg, November 19, 1863]

> There is no clearer illustration of the fact that " 'tis his at last that says it best." The famous phrase "government of the people, by the people, for the people," in slightly different forms, had been knocking about for almost 70 years. John Adams had come close to it in 1798, and John Marshall in 1819 (in the famous McCulloch vs. Maryland decision). In 1830 Daniel Webster had spoken of "the people's government made for the people" (Foote's Resolution). Theodore Parker used the phrases three separate times, coming in 1858 to: "Democracy is self-government, over all the people, for all the people, by all the

> people" (Sermon at Boston, July 4, 1858); and Herndon in his Life of Lincoln states that Lincoln had a copy of this sermon and had marked this passage.

GHOST(S)

1 In the most high and palmy state of Rome,
A little ere the mightiest Julius fell,
The graves stood tenantless and the sheeted dead
Did squeak and gibber in the Roman streets.
[Shakespeare: *Hamlet* I.i.]
2 There needs no ghost, my lord, come from the grave
To tell us this.
[Shakespeare: *Hamlet* I.v.]
3 Hence, horrible shadow!
Unreal mockery, hence!
[Shakespeare: *Macbeth* III.iv.]
4 GHOST. The outward and visible sign of an inward fear. [Ambrose Bierce: *The Devil's Dictionary*]
5 Ghosts were created when the first man woke in the night. [James Matthew Barrie: *The Little Minister* XXII]
6 O lost, and by the wind grieved, ghost, come back again! [Thomas Wolfe: *Look Homeward, Angel* XXXVII *et passim*]

GIANT(S)

7 There were giants in the earth in those days. [Genesis 6:4]
8   O, it is excellent
To have a giant's strength; but it is tyrannous
To use it like a giant.
[Shakespeare: *Measure for Measure* II.ii.]

GIBBON, EDWARD

9 Johnson's style was grand and Gibbon's elegant . . . Johnson marched to kettle-drums and trumpets; Gibbon moved to flutes and hautboys. [George Colman the Younger: *Random Records* I.121]
See also WRITING: the itch to scribble
10 The other, deep and slow, exhausting thought,
And hiving wisdom with each studious year,
In meditation dwelt, with learning wrought,

And shaped his weapon with an edge
severe,
Sapping a solemn creed with solemn
sneer;
The lord of irony—that master spell,
Which stung his foes to wrath, which
grew from fear,
And doom'd him to the zealot's ready
Hell,
Which answers to all doubts so elo-
quently well.
[Byron: *Childe Harold* III.cvii.]
*The reference is to Gibbon, "the lord of
irony," whose* Decline and Fall of the
Roman Empire *contained one of the
most devastating attacks on Christianity
ever published.*

GIFT(S)
1 It is not good to refuse a gift.
[Homer: *Odyssey* XVIII]
2 Every man is a friend to him that
giveth gifts. [Proverbs 19:6]
3 Unwelcome is the gift which is held
long in the hand.
[Seneca: *De Beneficiis* II.i.]
4 I find nothing so dear as that which
is given me. [Montaigne: *Essays* III.ix.]
5 Win her with gifts, if she respect not
words;
Dumb jewels often in their silent
kind
More than quick words do move a
woman's mind.
[Shakespeare: *Two Gentlemen of Verona* III.i.]
6   For, to the noble mind
Rich gifts wax poor when givers
prove unkind.
[Shakespeare: *Hamlet* III.i.]
7 A gift much expected is paid, not
given. [George Herbert: *Jacula Prudentum*]
8 Gifts are scorn'd where givers are
despis'd. [Dryden: *The Hind and the
Panther* III]
9 A blind man will not thank you for a
looking-glass. [Thomas Fuller (1654-
1734): *Gnomologia*]
10 A gift long waited for is sold, not
given. [Thomas Fuller (1654-1734):
Gnomologia]
11 The gifts of an enemy are justly to be
dreaded. [Voltaire: *La Henriade* II]
12 We do not quite forgive a giver. The
hand that feeds us is in some danger of
being bitten. [Emerson: *Gifts*]
13 The Gods themselves cannot recall
their gifts.
[Tennyson: *Tithonus*]
14 God's gifts put man's best dreams to
shame.
[Elizabeth Barrett Browning: *Sonnets
from the Portugese* XXVI]
15 Behold, I do not give lectures or a
little charity,
When I give I give myself.
[Walt Whitman: *Leaves of Grass*, "Song
of Myself" 40]
See also GIVING

GIFT HORSE
16 He always looked a given horse in
the mouth. [Rabelais: *Works* I.xi.]
17 He ne'er consider'd it, as loth
To look a gift-horse in the mouth.
[Samuel Butler (1612-1680): *Hudibras*
I.i.]
See HORSE

GILBERT, W. S.
18 His foe was folly and his weapon wit.
[Anthony Hope Hawkins: Inscription on
Gilbert Memorial, Victoria Embank-
ment, London]

GIOTTO'S O
19 Giotto's O.
*Referred to in many quotations, it is
based on the story that when Pope Bene-
dict XI asked for proof of Giotto's skill
as a painter, Giotto simply took his
brush and with a free sweep drew for
the Pontiff's messenger a perfect circle.
The moral is that only the most assured skill can do the simple-seeming
thing with ease.*

GIRDLE
20 I'll put a girdle round about the
earth
In forty minutes.
[Shakespeare: *A Midsummer Night's
Dream* II.i.]
21 He hath put a girdle 'bout the world,
And sounded all her quicksands.
[John Webster: *The Duchess of Malfi*
III.i.]

GIRL(S)
22 This gallant girle more faire then for-

tunate, and yet more fortunate then faithful. [John Lyly: *Euphues*]

1 One of those little prating girls,
Of whom fond parents tell such tedious stories.
[Dryden: *The Rival Ladies* I.i.]

2 Wretched, un-idea'd girls. [Samuel Johnson: in Boswell's *Life* (1752)]

3 I seek for one as fair and gay,
But find none to remind me;
How blest the hours pass'd away
With the girl I left behind me.
[Anon.: *The Girl I Left Behind Me* (1759)]

4 Auld Nature swears, the lovely dears
Her noblest work she classes, O;
Her 'prentice han' she tried on man,
And then she made the lasses, O!
[Burns: *Green Grow the Rashes*]

5 'Tis true, your budding Miss is very
charming,
But shy and awkward at first coming
out,
So much alarm'd, that she is quite
alarming,
All Giggle, Blush; half Pertness, and
half Pout;
And glancing at *Mamma,* for fear
there's harm in
What you, she, it, or they, may be
about,
The nursery still lisps out in all they
utter—
Besides, they always smell of bread
and butter.
[Byron: *Beppo* XXXIX]

6 There was a little girl
Who had a little curl
Right in the middle of her forehead,
And when she was good
She was very, very good,
But when she was bad she was horrid.
[Longfellow: as recorded in E. W. Longfellow's *Random Memories*]
The little girl was his daughter "Edith with the golden hair" who also appears in The Children's Hour.
The rhyme records, but (alas!) is unable to preserve, the older pronunciation of forehead.

7 Sweet girl-graduates in their golden
hair.
[Tennyson: Prologue to *The Princess*]

8 Three little maids from school are
we,

Pert as a schoolgirl well can be,
Filled to the brim with girlish glee,
Three little maids from school!
[W. S. Gilbert: *The Mikado* I]

9 You may tempt the upper classes
With your villainous demi-tasses,
But Heaven will protect the Working Girl.
[Edgar Smith: *Heaven Will Protect the Working Girl*]

GIVER(S)

10 God loveth a cheerful giver. [II Corinthians 9:7]

11 He that will only Give, and not Receive,
Enslaves the Person whom he would
Relieve.
[Sir Samuel Tuke: *The Adventures of Five Hours* V.iii.]

GIVING

12 He that hath pity upon the poor lendeth unto the Lord. [Proverbs 19:17]

13 When thou doest alms, let not thy left hand know what thy right hand doeth. [Matthew 6:3]

14 It is more blessed to give than to receive. [Acts 20:35]

15 He gives twice that gives quickly. [Publilius Syrus: *Maxims*]
The Latin is Bis dat qui cito dat.
Ben Franklin, after quoting the famous proverb, added drily that he gives twice who gives soon because he will soon be called on to give again (Poor Richard's Almanack, *1752*).

16 Giving requires good sense.
[Ovid: *Amores* I.viii.]

17 Such are not to be liked that give a man a shoulder of mutton and break his head with the spit when they have done. [Thomas Wilson: *The Arte of Rhetorique* (1560)]
That is, they who do a man a favor and then reproach him with it.

18 Defer not charities till death; for certainly, if a man weigh it rightly, he that doth so is rather liberal of another man's than of his own. [Francis Bacon: *Of Riches*]

19 I am not in the giving vein today. [Shakespeare: *Richard III* IV.ii.]

20 The manner of giving is worth more than the gift. [Corneille: *Le Menteur* I.i.]

1 The gift without the giver is bare;
   Who gives himself with his alms feeds
                                    three—
   Himself, his hungering neighbor, and
                                      me.
[James Russell Lowell: *The Vision of
Sir Launfal* II.viii.]

2 You need more tact in the dangerous
art of giving presents than in any other
social action. [William Bolitho: *Twelve
Against the Gods,* "Lola Montez"]

GLADNESS

3 Teach me half the gladness
   That thy brain must know,
   Such harmonious madness
   From my lips would flow,
   The world should listen then, as I am
                            listening now.
[Shelley: *To a Skylark*]

GLANCES

4 For glances beget ogles, ogles sighs,
   Sighs wishes, wishes words, and words
                                  a letter . . .
   And then, God knows what mischief
                               may arise,
   When love links two young people in
                               one fetter,
   Vile assignations, and adulterous beds,
   Elopements, broken vows, and hearts,
                            and heads.
[Byron: *Beppo* XVI]

5 Stolen glances, sweeter for the theft.
[Byron: *Don Juan* I.lxxiv.]

GLASS(ES)

6 We see through a glass, darkly. [I Corinthians 13:12]
   *Today we see through a glass clearly—
   or we did a generation ago, when people could afford to have their windows
   washed. But early glass was—as the
   quotation makes plain—translucent rather than transparent. Chaucer says of
   his Prioress that her eyes "were grey as
   glass."*

7 Thou art thy mother's glass, and she
                              in thee
   Calls back the lovely April of her
                               prime.
[Shakespeare: *Sonnets* III]

8   He was indeed the glass
   Wherein the noble youths did dress
                           themselves.
   He had no legs that practis'd not
                                      his gait;
   And speaking thick (which nature
                        made his blemish)
   Became the accents of the valiant;
   For those that could speak low and
                               tardily
   Would turn their own perfection to
                                   abuse
   To seem like him; so that in speech,
                               in gait,
   In diet, in affections of delight,
   In military rules, humours of blood,
   He was the mark and glass, copy and
                               book,
   That fashion'd others.
[Shakespeare: *II Henry IV* II.iii.]
   speaking thick = *stammering*
      *Lady Percy is speaking of her late hus-
   band, Hotspur.*

9 The glass of fashion, and the mould
                               of form,
   The observed of all observers.
[Shakespeare: *Hamlet* III i.]

10 There was never yet fair woman but
she made mouths in a glass. [Shake-
speare: *King Lear* III.ii.]

11 Men seldom make passes
    At girls who wear glasses.
[Dorothy Parker: *News Item*]

12 A girl who is bespectacled,
    She may not get her nectacled.
[Ogden Nash: Lines written to console
those Ladies distressed by the lines
"Men seldom make Passes," etc.]

GLIBNESS

13 For these fellows of infinite tongue,
that can rhyme themselves into ladies'
favours, they do always reason themselves
out again. [Shakespeare: *Henry V* V.ii.]

GLITTERS

14 Hit is not al gold, that glareth.
[Chaucer: *The Hous of Fame* I]

15 All that glistens is not gold.
[Cervantes: *Don Quixote* II.xxxiii.]

16 All that glisters is not gold.
[Shakespeare: *The Merchant of Venice*
II.vii.]
   *Shakespeare's text makes it plain that
   this was already (1600) a well-known say-
   ing. It had occurred in* Ralph Royster
   Doyster *(1566).*

17 All, as they say, that glitters is not
                                    gold.

[Dryden: *The Hind and the Panther* II]
Dryden seems to have been the first to
use glitters, *the form which one now
most often hears.*

1 Not all that tempts your wandering
eyes
And heedless hearts is lawful prize,
Nor all that glisters gold.
[Thomas Gray: *Ode on the Death of a
Favourite Cat*]
2 All is not gold that glitters. [David
Garrick: Prologue to Oliver Goldsmith's
She Stoops to Conquer]

GLOAMING
3 In the gloaming, O, my darling!
When the lights are dim and low,
And the quiet shadows falling
Softly come and softly go.
[Meta Orred: *In the Gloaming*]

GLORY
4 Arise, shine; for thy light is come,
and the glory of the Lord is risen upon
thee. [Isaiah 60:1]
5 *Sic transit gloria mundi.* ("So passes
away the glory of this world.") [Thomas
à Kempis: *The Imitation of Christ* III.
vi.]
One of the few sayings more often
spoken in Latin than in its English
translation.
6 *Ad majorem Dei gloriam.* ("For the
greater glory of God.") [Motto of the
Society of Jesus]
7 Glory is like a circle in the water,
Which never ceaseth to enlarge itself
Till, by broad spreading it disperse
to nought.
[Shakespeare: *I Henry VI* I.ii.]
8 I have ventured,
Like little wanton boys that swim on
bladders,
This many summers in a sea of glory,
But far beyond my depth.
[Shakespeare: *Henry VIII* III.ii.]
9 To overcome in battle, and subdue
Nations, and bring home spoils with
infinite
Man-slaughter, shall be held the high-
est pitch
Of human glory.
[John Milton: *Paradise Lost* XI.691-694]
10 Stood for his country's glory fast,
And nail'd her colors to the mast!

[Sir Walter Scott: *Marmion*, Introduction to Canto I]
11 One crowded hour of glorious life is
worth an age without a name. [Sir Walter Scott: *Old Mortality* XXXIV]
12 On desperate seas long wont to roam,
Thy hyacinth hair, thy classic face,
Thy Naiad airs have brought me
home
To the glory that was Greece,
And the grandeur that was Rome.
[Edgar Allan Poe: *To Helen*]

GLORY: hollow, and soon fading
13 We go to gain a little patch of
ground,
That hath in it no profit but the
name.
[Shakespeare: *Hamlet* IV.iv.]
14 Like madness is the glory of this life.
[Shakespeare: *Timon of Athens* I.ii.]
15 I have touched the highest point of
all my greatness;
And from that full meridian of my
glory,
I haste now to my setting: I shall fall
Like a bright exhalation in the eve-
ning,
And no man see me more.
[Shakespeare: *Henry VIII* III.ii.]
16 Glories, like glow-worms, afar off
shine bright,
But looked to near, have neither heat
nor light.
[John Webster: *The Duchess of Malfi*
IV.ii.]
17 The road to glory is not strewn with
flowers.
[La Fontaine: *Fables* X.xiv.]
18 The rainbow comes and goes,
And lovely is the rose,
The moon doth with delight
Look round her when the heavens are
bare,
Waters on a starry night
Are beautiful and fair;
The sunshine is a glorious birth:
But yet I know, where'er I go,
That there hath passed away a glory
from the earth.
[Wordsworth: *Intimations of Immortal-
ity*]
19 Some for the Glories of This World;
and some
Sigh for the Prophet's Paradise to

come;
Ah, take the Cash, and let the
Credit go,
Nor heed the rumble of a distant
Drum!
[*Rubáiyát of Omar Khayyám* (trans. Edward FitzGerald)]
1 And early though the laurel grows
It withers quicker than the rose.
[A. E. Housman: *A Shropshire Lad*
XIX]

**GLORY: paths of, lead but to
the grave**
2 Thou shalt confess the vain pursuit
Of human glory yields no fruit
But an untimely grave.
[Thomas Carew: *On the Duke of Buckingham*]
3 The garlands wither on your brow,
Then boast no more your mighty
deeds,
Upon death's purple altar now,
See where the victor-victim bleeds,
Your heads must come,
To the cold tomb;
Only the actions of the just
Smell sweet, and blossom in their
dust.
[James Shirley: *The Contention of Ajax
and Ulysses* III]
4 The paths of glory lead but to the
grave.
[Thomas Gray: *Elegy Written in a Country Churchyard*]

GLOSSING
5 Glosinge is a glorious thing, certeyn,
For lettre sleeth, so as we clerkes seyn.
[Chaucer: *The Summoner's Tale*]
glosinge = *glossing, annotating, explaining—often so as to make the passage
mean whatever the glosser wants it to
mean;* clerkes = *clerics, learned theologians*
The rascally Limitour in the story is
making a jocular and blasphemous reference to II Corinthians 3:6: "For the
letter killeth, but the spirit giveth life."
The letter of the gospel would, indeed,
kill his racket, but by "glosinge" he will
make it support it.

GLOVE(S)
6 See, how she leans her cheek upon

her hand!
O, that I were a glove upon that
hand,
That I might touch that cheek!
[Shakespeare: *Romeo and Juliet* II.ii.]
7 Iron hand in a velvet glove.
[Thomas Carlyle: *Latter-day Pamphlets*
II]
Attr. Charles V.
8 O fat white woman whom nobody
loves,
Why do you walk through the fields
in gloves?
[Frances Cornford: *To a Fat Lady seen
from the Train*]

GLOWWORM
9 The glow-worm shows the matin to
be near,
And 'gins to pale his uneffectual fire.
[Shakespeare: *Hamlet* I.v.]
10 Her eyes the glow-worm lend thee,
The shooting stars attend thee;
And the elves also,
Whose little eyes glow
Like the sparks of fire, befriend thee.
[Robert Herrick: *The Night-Piece, To
Julia*]

GLUTTONY
11 O glotonye, ful of cursednesse,
O cause first of our confusioun,
O original of our dampnacioun!
[Chaucer: *The Pardoner's Tale*]
*Certain straining moralists felt that Eve's
eating of the apple constituted gluttony
and hence made that the first of all sins.*
12 Eat enough and it will make you wise.
[John Lyly: *Midas* IV.iii.]
*Where it is quoted (1592) as "an old
proverb."*
13 He hath eaten me out of house and
home. [Shakespeare: *II Henry IV* II.i.]
*Proverbial by Shakespeare's time. In the
Towneley Plays (c.1400) it appears in the
curious form "out of house and harbour."*
14 Make less thy body hence, and more
thy grace;
Leave gormandizing.
[Shakespeare: *II Henry IV* V.v.]
15 He that eats till he is sick, must fast
till he is well. [Thomas Fuller (1654-
1734): *Gnomologia*]
16 Three good meals a day is bad living.
[Benjamin Franklin: *Poor Richard's Almanack* (1744)]

1 The way to a man's heart is through his stomach. [Sara Payson Parton ("Fanny Fern"): *Willis Parton*]

2 They stuff their bellies with tomorrow's ache.
[Edmund Vance Cooke: *Book of Extenuations: Lazarus*]

3 A gourmet is just a glutton with brains. [Philip W. Haberman, Jr.: "How to be a Calorie Chiseler," *Vogue,* Jan. 15, 1961]

GNATS

4 Then in a wailful choir the small
⠀⠀⠀⠀⠀⠀⠀⠀⠀⠀⠀⠀⠀⠀⠀⠀⠀⠀gnats mourn
Among the river sallows.
[Keats: *To Autumn*]
See STRAIN

GO

5 Whither thou goest, I will go; and where thou lodgest, I will lodge: thy people shall be my people, and thy God my God. [Ruth 1:16]
Ruth is much admired for this saying by those whose god happens to be Naomi's god. But surely affection for your mother-in-law is not, in itself, an admirable reason for changing your religion.

GOBLINS

6 An' all us other children, when the
⠀⠀⠀⠀⠀⠀⠀⠀⠀⠀⠀supper things is done,
We set around the kitchen fire an' has
⠀⠀⠀⠀⠀⠀⠀⠀⠀⠀⠀⠀the mostest fun
A-list'nin' to the witch tales 'at Annie
⠀⠀⠀⠀⠀⠀⠀⠀⠀⠀⠀⠀⠀tells about
An' the gobble-uns 'at gits you
⠀⠀Ef you
⠀⠀⠀⠀Don't
⠀⠀⠀⠀⠀⠀Watch
⠀⠀⠀⠀⠀⠀⠀⠀Out!
[James Whitcomb Riley: *Little Orphant Annie*]

GOD: attempts at definition of

7 I am Alpha and Omega, the beginning and the ending, saith the Lord. [Revelation 1:8]

8 I am Alpha and Omega, the beginning and the end, the first and the last. [Revelation 22:13]

9 There is a God within us. [Ovid: *Fasti* VI.v.]

10 Call it Nature, Fate, Fortune; all these are names of the one and selfsame God. [Seneca: *De Beneficiis* IV.viii.]

11 He clepeth God the firste cause. [John Gower: *Confessio Amantis* III.lxxxvii. (1393)]
clepeth = calleth
Calling God "the first Cause" was a discovery on which the 17th- and 18th-century philosophers prided themselves, but others had been at it long before them.

12 Well, God's a good man.
[Shakespeare: *Much Ado About Nothing* III.v.]
The saying was proverbial and had appeared in print 72 years before Much Ado. *One still hears it.*

13 Father of all! in every age,
⠀In every clime adored,
⠀By saint, by savage, and by sage,
⠀Jehovah, Jove, or Lord!
[Alexander Pope: *The Universal Prayer*]

14 Suppose I had found a watch upon the ground. . . . The mechanism being observed, the inference is inevitable that the watch must have a maker; that there must have existed, at some time and at some place or other, an artificer or artificers who formed it for the purpose which we find it actually to answer. [William Paley: *Natural Theology* I (1802)]
For several generations this puerility passed as one of the deeper profundities.

15 An endless clergyman.
[Tennyson's facetious definition of God]

16 ⠀⠀⠀⠀⠀⠀⠀⠀⠀⠀What I call God,
And fools call Nature.
[Robert Browning: *The Ring and the Book,* "The Pope"]

17 For science, God is simply *the stream of tendency by which all things seek to fulfil the law of their being.* [Matthew Arnold: *Literature and Dogma* I.iv]

18 God . . . a gaseous vertebrate. [Ernst Haeckel: *The Riddle of the Universe* XV]
Haeckel's "paradoxical conception" of the Deity.

19 An honest God's the noblest work of man. [Samuel Butler (1835-1902): *Notebooks*]
Butler's parody of Pope's "An honest man's the noblest work of God" (An Essay on Man IV) had occurred independently of Robert Ingersoll, in Gods I.
Pope's line is perhaps better known

to the common reader from its being quoted in Burns's The Cotter's Saturday Night *XIX.*

1 Has some Vast Imbecility,
　　Mighty to build and blend,
　　But impotent to tend,
　　Framed us in jest, and left us now to
　　　　　　　　　　　hazardry?
　　Or come we of an automation?
　　Unconscious of our pains? . . .
　　Or are we live remains
　　Of Godhead dying downwards, brain
　　　　　　　　and eye now gone?

　　Or is it that some high Plan betides,
　　As yet not understood,
　　Of Evil stormed by Good,
　　We, the Forlorn Hope over which
　　　　　　　Achievement strides?
[Thomas Hardy: *Nature's Questioning*]
2 God is an unutterable sigh in the human heart. [Havelock Ellis: *Impressions and Comments* I]
　　Ellis is quoting "the old German mystic," Jean Paul Richter.
3 God is a verb,
　　Not a noun.
[Richard Buckminster Fuller: *No More Secondhand God*]

GOD: His demise
4 Great Pan is dead. [Plutarch: *Moralia: De Defectu Oracularum.* 17.419C.]
　　And see E. B. Browning: The Dead Pan.
5 But since I was framed in your first
　　　　　　　　　　despair
　　The doing without me has had no
　　　　　　　　　　play
　　In the minds of men when shadows
　　　　　　　　　　scare;
　　And now that I dwindle day by day
　　Beneath the deicide eyes of seers
　　In a light that will not let me stay,
　　And to-morrow the whole of me dis-
　　　　　　　　　　appears,
　　The truth should be told, and the
　　　　　　　　fact be faced
　　That had best been faced in earlier
　　　　　　　　　　years:
　　The fact of life with dependence
　　　　　　　　　placed
　　On the human heart's resource
　　　　　　　　　　alone,
　　In brotherhood bonded close and
　　　　　　　　　graced

With loving-kindness fully blown
And visioned help unsought, un-
　　　　　　　　　　known.
[Thomas Hardy: *A Plaint to Man*]
　　The speaker is God.
6 Whatever may be God's future, we cannot forget His past. [W. H. Mallock: *Is Life Worth Living?*]
7 I sometimes wish that God were back
　　In this dark world and wide;
　　For though some virtues he might
　　　　　　　　　　lack,
　　He had his pleasant side.
[Gamaliel Bradford: *Exit God*]
8 I turned to speak to God
　　About the world's despair;
　　But to make bad matters worse
　　I found God wasn't there.
[Robert Frost: *Not All There*]

GOD: His glory and mystery
9 Surely the Lord is in this place; and I knew it not. [Genesis 28:16]
10 But let not God speak with us, lest we die. [Exodus 20:19]
11 What hath God wrought! [Numbers 23:23]
　　This quotation from the Bible was the first message sent over the telegraph wires by Samuel B. Morse, from Washington to Baltimore, May 24, 1844.
12 And the Lord was with Judah; and he drave out the inhabitants of the mountain; but could not drive out the inhabitants of the valley, because they had chariots of iron. [Judges 1:19]
13 Canst thou by searching find out God? [Job 11:7]
　　The answer in Job *is definitely No. God reveals Himself when and how he chooses, and His ways are not necessarily comprehensible to man.*
14 The heavens declare the glory of God, and the firmament sheweth his handywork. [Psalms 19:1]
15 They that go down to the sea in ships, that do business in great waters; These see the works of the Lord, and his wonders in the deep. [Psalms 107:23-24]
16 The nations are as a drop of a bucket, and are counted as the small dust of the balance: behold, he taketh up the isles as a very little thing. [Isaiah 40:15]
17 No man hath seen God at any time. [John 1:18]

1 Hath God obliged himself not to exceed the bounds of our knowledge? [Montaigne: *Essays* II.xii.]

2 It were better to have no opinion of God at all, than such an opinion as is unworthy of him: for the one is unbelief, the other is contumely. [Francis Bacon: *Of Superstition*]

3   God doth not need
Either man's work or his own gifts; who best
Bear his mild yoke, they serve him best; his state
Is kingly; thousands at his bidding speed,
And post o'er land and ocean without rest.
[John Milton: *On His Blindness*]

4 Dark with excessive bright thy skirts appear.
[John Milton: *Paradise Lost* III.380]
"Bright" in this passage often misquoted as "light."

5 Praise God, from whom all blessings flow!
Praise Him, all creatures here below!
Praise Him above, ye heavenly host!
Praise Father, Son, and Holy Ghost!
[Bishop Thomas Ken: *Morning and Evening Hymn*]

6 God moves in a mysterious way
His wonders to perform;
He plants his footsteps in the sea
And rides upon the storm.
[William Cowper: *Light Shining Out of Darkness*]

7 The world is charged with the grandeur of God. [Gerard Manley Hopkins: *God's Grandeur*]

8 It is the final proof of God's omnipotence that He need not exist in order to save us. [Peter De Vries: *The Mackerel Plaza*]

GOD: His grace and love

9 And the Lord was with Joseph, and he was a prosperous man. [Genesis 39:2]
Tyndale (1530) has: And the Lorde was with Joseph, and he was a luckie felowe; RSV (1952): The Lord was with Joseph, and he became a successful man.
The honors must go to Tyndale.

10 Thou preparest a table before me in the presence of mine enemies: thou anointest my head with oil; my cup runneth over. [Psalms 23:5]

11 Whom the Lord loveth he chasteneth. [Hebrews 12:6]

12 In his will is our peace.
[Dante: *The Divine Comedy*, "Paradiso" III]

13 Batter my heart, three person'd God.
[Donne: *Holy Sonnets* XIV]

14 Lord, I ascribe it to thy grace
And not to chance as others do
That I was born of Christian race
And not a heathen or a Jew.
[Isaac Watts: *Divine Songs for Children*]

15 The angel wrote, and vanished. The next night
It came again, with a great awakening light,
And showed the names of whom the love of God had blessed—
And lo! Ben Adhem's name led all the rest.
[Leigh Hunt: *Abou Ben Adhem*]

16 I know not where His islands lift
Their fronded palms in air;
I only know I cannot drift
Beyond His love and care.
[J. G. Whittier: *The Eternal Goodness*]

17 'Tis heaven alone that is given away,
'Tis only God may be had for the asking.
[James Russell Lowell: *The Vision of Sir Launfal*, Prelude to Part I]

GOD: some irreverent comments on

18 'Twas basely said of Sir W(alter) R(aleigh) to talk of the anagram of Dog. [John Aubrey: *Brief Lives* II]
Aubrey says that, while Sir Walter was not an atheist, "he was a bold man, and would venture at discourse which was unpleasant to the churchmen."

19 If triangles made a god, they would give him three sides. [Montesquieu: *Lettres Persanes* LIX]
See Rupert Brooke's Heaven, *a playful attempt to conceive of the god of fishes.*
Montesquieu describes this thought as "a saying."

20 If God did not exist, it would be necessary to invent him. [Voltaire: *Epître à M. Saurin*, Nov. 10, 1770]
Voltaire was very pleased with this line —as well he might have been! The

thought, however, had been lurking in the human mind since we have any record of its lucubrations.

In the probably spurious Platonic dialogue of Sisyphus (375 B.C.) he is said to have been a wise man who invented God and in Cicero's De Natura Deorum (48 B.C.) is the statement that the immortal gods often seem to have been fabricated for human use.

If God were not a necessary Being of Himself, He might almost seem to be made for the use and benefit of men.
John Tillotson (Archbishop of Canterbury, 1691-1694): Reflections
These two aphorisms, Voltaire's and Tillotson's—so near together in meaning and so far apart in tone—show how differently two men may express the climate of opinion of their age. There is no proof that Voltaire knew Tillotson's statement; the resemblance is wholly coincidental.

1 If God made us in His image, we have certainly returned the compliment. [Voltaire: Le Sottisier XXXII]
2 "There is no God," the wicked saith,
    "And truly it's a blessing,
For what he might have done with us
    It's better only guessing."
[Arthur Hugh Clough: Dipsychus I.v.]
3 Thou shalt have one God only; who
    Would be at the expense of two?
[Arthur Hugh Clough: The Latest Decalogue]
4 Your conduct, gentlemen, has not only grieved Almighty God, but also seriously displeased Me. [Attr. an Oxford Proctor: speaking to some errant undergraduates, in the 19th century]
5 That God should spend His eternity—which might be so much better employed—in spinning countless Solar Systems, and skylarking, like a great child, with tops and teetotums—is not this a serious scandal? I wonder what all our circumgyrating Monotheists really do think of it? [Logan Pearsall Smith: Trivia, "Vertigo"]
6 Father expected a good deal of God. He didn't actually accuse God of inefficiency, but when he prayed his tone was loud and angry, like that of a dissatisfied guest in a carelessly managed hotel. [Clarence Day: God and My Father]

7 If we assume that man actually does resemble God, then we are forced into the impossible theory that God is a coward, an idiot and a bounder. [H. L. Mencken: Prejudices: Third Series]
8 An act of God was defined as something which no reasonable man could have expected. [A. P. Herbert: Uncommon Law]

GOD: our refuge and strength
9 God is our refuge and strength, a very present help in trouble. [Psalms 46:1]
10 If God be for us, who can be against us? [Romans 8:31]
11 A mighty fortress is our God,
    A bulwark never failing.
[Martin Luther: Ein' feste Burg]
The German of the opening lines of this great hymn is:
    Ein' feste Burg ist unser Gott,
    Ein gute Wehr und Waffen
which, translated literally, is:
    An unmovable fortress is our God,
    A good defense and weapon.
Luther's noble hymn echoes David's song of praise to God for having delivered him out of the hand of Saul:
    The Lord is my rock, and my
        fortress, and my deliverer.
                        II Samuel 22:2-3
12 Our God, our help in ages past,
    Our hope for years to come,
    Our shelter from the stormy blast,
    And our eternal home.
[Isaac Watts: Psalms XC]
Lord, thou hast been our dwelling place in all generations.
                        Psalms 90:1
John Wesley changed the opening words to "O God . . ."
13 Our Shield and Defender, the Ancient of Days,
    Pavilioned in splendour, and girded with praise.
[Sir Robert Grant: O Worship the King]
14 Nearer, my God, to Thee,
    Nearer to Thee.
[Sarah Flower Adams: Nearer, My God, to Thee]
15 God of our fathers, known of old,
    Lord of our far-flung battle-line.
[Kipling: Recessional]

GOD: His ubiquity

1 All are but parts of one stupendous
whole,
Whose body Nature is, and God the
soul.
[Alexander Pope: *An Essay on Man* I]

2 A sense sublime
Of something far more deeply inter-
fused,
Whose dwelling is the light of setting
suns,
And the round ocean and the living
air,
And the blue sky, and in the mind of
man.
[Wordsworth: *Tintern Abbey*]

3 God is seen God
In the star, in the stone, in the flesh,
in the soul and the clod.
[Robert Browning: *Saul* XVII]
*This is Wordsworth's "sense sublime of
something far more deeply interfused"
in ragtime.*

GOD: His wrath and justice

4 God is not a man that he should lie.
[Numbers 23:19]

5 But the hand of the Lord was heavy
upon them of Ashdod, and he destroyed
them, and smote them with emerods
[hemorrhoids]. [I Samuel 5:6]

6 Had I but served God as diligently
as I have served the King, he would not
have given me over in my gray hairs.
[Cardinal Wolsey: To Sir William King-
ston]

7 I fear God, yet am not afraid of him.
[Sir Thomas Browne: *Religio Medici*
I.lii.]

8 So spake the Son, and into terror
changed
His countenance, too severe to be beheld,
And full of wrath bent on his enemies.
At once the Four spread out their
starry wings
With dreadful shade contiguous, and
the orbs
Of his fierce chariot rolled, as with
the sound
Of torrent floods, or of a numerous
host.
He on his impious foes right onward
drove

Gloomy as night. Under his burning
wheels
The steadfast Empyrean shook
throughout,
All but the Throne itself of God.
[John Milton: *Paradise Lost* VI.824-834]
Milton's description of the wrath of God.

9 Just are the ways of God,
And justifiable to men.
[John Milton: *Samson Agonistes*]

10 God comes with leaden feet, but
strikes with iron hands. [John Ray: *English Proverbs*]

11 Thou wilt not leave us in the dust:
Thou madest man, he knows not
why,
He thinks he was not made to die;
And thou hast made him: thou art
just.
[Tennyson: Prologue to *In Memoriam*]

GOD: miscellaneous

12 The Lord gave, and the Lord hath
taken away; blessed be the name of the
Lord. [Job 1:21]

13 My God, my God, why hast thou forsaken me? [Matthew 27:46]
A quotation of Psalms 22:1.

14 God is no respecter of persons. [Acts
10:34]

15 Man proposes, but God disposes.
[Thomas à Kempis: *De Imitatione Christi*
I.xix.]

16 Let fools the name of loyalty divide:
Wise men and gods are on the strong-
est side.
[Sir Charles Sedley: *The Death of Marc
Antony* IV.ii.]

17 From this day forward . . . our
school children will daily proclaim . . .
the dedication of our nation and our
people to the Almighty. [Dwight D. Eisenhower, on signing the law that required the inclusion of "under God" in
the pledge of allegiance to the flag, June
14, 1954]
*It seems to have been with the Gettys-
burg Address that "under God" became
a cliché of American political sanctimo-
niousness.*

GODS

18 The issue lies in the laps of the gods.
[Homer: *Iliad* XVII]

19 Ye shall be as gods, knowing good
and evil. [Genesis 3:5]

1 When gods do ill, why should we worship them? [Sophocles: *Philoctetes*]
2 The help of the gods comes slowly, but it is not weak. [Euripides: *Ion*]
3 Alone among the gods, Death loves not gifts. [Aristophanes: *The Frogs*]
The Greeks felt that the god of the underworld was implacable and offered no sacrifices to him.
4 It is expedient there should be gods, and, since it is expedient, let us believe that gods exist. [Ovid: *Ars Amatoria* I]
5 Injury of the gods is the concern of the gods. [Tacitus: *Annals* I.lxxiii.]
That is, let the gods avenge blasphemy and sacrilege. Tacitus is quoting the Emperor Tiberius who was also quoting; so the statement was proverbial.
6 The gods have feet of wool. [Macrobius: *Saturnalia* I.viii.]
The same statement appears in Porphyry's commentaries on Horace, where it is said to be a saying. The idea is that they approach, on their missions of justice, unperceived.
7 Oh senseless man, who cannot possibly make a worm and yet will make Gods by dozens! [Montaigne: *Essays* II.xii.]
8 As flies to wanton boys, are we to the gods;
They kill us for their sport.
[Shakespeare: *King Lear* IV.i.]
9 'Twas only fear first in the world made gods. [Ben Jonson: *Sejanus* II.ii.]
Jonson is repeating a famous statement of Petronius (Fragments 76): Fear first brought gods into the world (1st century A.D.*).*
It is also in Statius: Thebais III; and in Chaucer: Eek drede fond first goddes —Troilus and Criseyde *IV.*
10 When the gods were more manlike, Men were more godlike.
[Schiller: *Die Gotter Griechenlands*]
11 When half-gods go,
The gods arrive.
[Emerson: *Give All to Love*]
12 Live and lie reclined
On the hills like Gods together, careless of mankind.
[Tennyson: *The Lotos-Eaters*]
13 Little Tin Gods on Wheels. [Kipling: *Public Waste*]
14 The Gaseous Vertebrata who own, operate and afflict the universe have

treated me with excessive politeness. [H. L. Mencken: Preface to *Happy Days*]

GOETHE

15 Too fast we live, too much are tried,
Too harass'd, to attain
Wordsworth's sweet calm, or Goethe's wide
And luminous view to gain.
[Matthew Arnold: *Obermann*]

GOLD

16 He who was knotting a halter for his neck, found gold and buried the halter in the treasure's place. But he who had hidden the gold, not finding it, fitted about his neck the halter which he had found. [Ausonius: *Epigrams*]
17 Yet hadde he but litel gold in cofre.
[Chaucer: Prologue to *The Canterbury Tales*]
18 If gold ruste, what shal iren do?
[Chaucer: Prologue to *The Canterbury Tales*]
19 You may buye golde too deare.
[Edmund Spenser: *The Shepheardes Calender*, "August"]
20 Solon said well to Croesus (when in ostentation he showed him his gold), *Sir, if any other come that hath better iron than you, he will be master of all this gold.* [Francis Bacon: *True Greatness of Kingdoms*]
Bacon took the story from Lucian.
21 Saint-seducing gold.
[Shakespeare: *Romeo and Juliet* I.i.]
22 Through tatter'd clothes small vices do appear;
Robes and furr'd gowns hide all.
Plate sin with gold,
And the strong lance of justice hurtless breaks;
Arm it in rags, a pigmy's straw does pierce it.
[Shakespeare: *King Lear* IV.vi.]
23 There's no fence or fortress against an ass laden with gold. [James Howell: *Familiar Letters* I]
24 Gold is the touch-stone whereby to trie men. [Thomas Fuller (1608-1661): *The Holy State*, "The Good Judge"]
25 Gold begets in Brethren hate,
Gold in Families debate;

Gold does Friendship separate,
Gold does Civil Wars create.
These the smallest harms of it!
Gold, alas, does Love beget.
[Abraham Cowley: *Gold*]
1 What female heart can gold despise?
What cat's averse to fish?
[Thomas Gray: *On the Death of a Favourite Cat*]
2 Gold! Gold! Gold! Gold!
Bright and yellow, hard and cold,
Molten, graven, hammer'd, and roll'd;
Heavy to get, and light to hold;
Hoarded, barter'd, bought, and sold,
Stolen, borrow'd, squander'd, doled:
Spurn'd by the young, but hugg'd by
the old
To the very verge of the churchyard
mould;
Price of many a crime untold:
Gold! Gold! Gold! Gold!
Good or bad a thousand-fold!
How widely its agencies vary—
To save—to ruin—to curse—to
bless—
As even its minted coins express,
Now stamp'd with the image of Good
Queen Bess,
And now of a Bloody Mary.
[Thomas Hood: *Miss Kilmansegg: Her Moral*]
3 Cursed be the gold that gilds the
straitened forehead of a fool.
[Tennyson: *Locksley Hall*]
4 Though wisdom cannot be gotten for
gold, still less can it be gotten without
it. [Samuel Butler (1835-1902): *Notebooks*]
5 You shall not press down upon the
brow of labor this crown of thorns; you
shall not crucify mankind upon a cross
of gold. [William Jennings Bryan: in a
speech before the National Democratic
Convention, Chicago, July 10, 1896]
6 Nature's first green is gold,
Her hardest hue to hold.
Her early leaf's a flower;
But only so an hour.
Then leaf subsides to leaf.
So Eden sank to grief,
So dawn goes down to day.
Nothing gold can stay.
[Robert Frost: *Nothing Gold Can Stay*]
7 All is not gold that glitters.
See GLITTERS

GOLDEN AGE
8 The golden age was never the present age. [Thomas Fuller (1654-1734):
Gnomologia]
Also Benjamin Franklin: Poor Richard's
Almanack *(1750).*

GOLDEN RULE
9 Therefore all things whatsoever ye
would that men should do to you, do ye
even so to them. [Matthew 7:12]
10 Do unto the other feller the way he'd
like to do unto you, an' do it fust. [E. N.
Westcott: *David Harum*]

GOLF
11 The golf links lie so near the mill
That almost every day
The laboring children can look out
And see the men at play.
[Sarah Cleghorn: *The Golf Links*]
One of the world's great strokes of irony.
One's first response, before the full impact hits, is to think "How nice for the kiddies!"

GONE
12 The wind passeth over it, and it is
gone; and the place thereof shall know it
no more. [Psalms 103:16]

GOOD
13 All things work together for good to
them that love God. [Romans 8:28]
14 Can one desire too much of a good
thing?
[Shakespeare: *As You Like It* IV.i.]
Probably proverbial, since the same expression is found in Cervantes: Don
Quixote *I. 6.*
15 Good is not good, where better is
expected. [Thomas Fuller (1608-1661):
Church History of Britain XI.3]
16 Better is the enemy of good. [Voltaire: *La Bégueule*]
Where the saying is attributed to "a wise Italian."
17 The greatest good to the greatest
number is the measure of right and
wrong. [Jeremy Bentham: Vol. X of
Works (1830)]
See under HAPPINESS: *miscellaneous
for another version of this famous saying and a tracing of its probable origins.*

1 That is good which commends me to my country, my climate, my means and materials, my associates. [Emerson: *Society and Solitude,* "Works and Days"] *i.e., patriotism, health (or resignation), economy, skill, friendship.*

2 Hold thou the good; define it well;
For fear divine Philosophy
Should push beyond her mark, and be
Procuress to the Lords of Hell.
[Tennyson: *In Memoriam* LIII]

GOOD: and bad

3 Men are not altogether bad or altogether good. [Machiavelli: *Discourses on Livy* I.li.]

4 They say, best men are moulded out of faults;
And, for the most, become much more the better
For being a little bad.
[Shakespeare: *Measure for Measure* V.i.]

5 The world in all doth but two nations bear—
The good, the bad; and these mixed everywhere.
[Andrew Marvell: *The Loyal Scot*]

6 Nothing is good or bad, but by Comparison. [Thomas Fuller (1654-1734): *Gnomologia*]

7 There is so much good in the worst of us,
And so much bad in the best of us,
That it hardly becomes any of us
To talk about the rest of us.
[E. W. Hoch: *Good and Bad*]

8 We are all ready to be savage in some cause. The difference between a good man and a bad one is the choice of the cause. [William James: *Letters* II.xxviii.]

GOOD: doing good

9 Do good to them that hate you. [Matthew 5:44]

10 In this earthly world . . . to do harm
Is often laudable, to do good sometime
Accounted dangerous folly.
[Shakespeare: *Macbeth* IV.ii.]

11 Good actions still must be maintained with good,

As bodies nourished with resembling food.
[Dryden: *Coronation of Charles* II.i.]

12 Do all the good you can,
By all the means you can,
In all the ways you can,
In all the places you can,
At all the times you can,
To all the people you can,
As long as ever you can.
[John Wesley: *John Wesley's Rule*]

13 I expect to pass through the world but once. Any good therefore that I can do, or any kindness that I can show to any fellow creature, let me do it now. Let me not defer it or neglect it, for I shall not pass this way again. [Attr. Stephen Grellet, but not certain]

This saying has been much admired by those who like their altruism out in the open, with none of that furtive don't-let-your-right-hand-know sort of thing. But it has too much the tone of an inter-office moral memo for other tastes.

14 It is not enough to do good; one must do it the right way. [John Morley: *On Compromise*]

GOOD: and evil

15 You are not to do evil that good may come of it. [Latin law maxim]

16 Good does not necessarily succeed evil; another and worse evil may succeed it. [Montaigne: *Essays* III.ix.]

17 Nought so vile that on the earth doth live
But to the earth some special good doth give,
Nor aught so good but strain'd from that fair use
Revolts from true birth, stumbling on abuse.
[Shakespeare: *Romeo and Juliet* II.iii.]

18 There is some soul of goodness in things evil,
Would men observingly distil it out.
[Shakespeare: *King Henry V* IV.i.]

19 The web of our life is of a mingled yarn,
Good and ill together.
[Shakespeare: *All's Well that Ends Well* IV.iii.]

20 Good and evil, we know, in the field of this world grow up together almost inseparably. [John Milton: *Areopagitica*]

1 And out of good still to find means
of evil.
[John Milton: *Paradise Lost* I.165]
2 So farewell hope, and, with hope,
farewell fear,
Farewell remorse; all good to me is
lost.
Evil, be thou my good.
[John Milton: *Paradise Lost* IV.108-110]
3 Knowledge of Good bought dear by
knowing ill.
[John Milton: *Paradise Lost* IV.222]
4 The only admissible moral theory of
Creation is that the Principle of Good
cannot at once and altogether subdue
the powers of evil, either physical or
moral. [John Stuart Mill: *Three Essays
on Religion* (Essay 1, Nature)]
5 Virtue!—to be good and just—
Every heart, when sifted well,
Is a clot of warmer dust,
Mix'd with cunning sparks of hell.
[Tennyson: *The Vision of Sin*]
6 O, yet we trust that somehow good
Will be the final goal of ill.
[Tennyson: *In Memoriam* LIV]
7 Evil saith to good: My brother.
[Swinburne: *Hymn to Proserpine*]

GOOD: the good
8 The good must merit God's peculiar
care:
But who but God can tell us who
they are?
[Alexander Pope: *An Essay on Man* IV]
9 The wicked are always surprised to
find ability in the good. [Vauvenargues:
Réflexions]
10 Be good and you will be lonesome.
[Mark Twain: *Following the Equator*]
11 You Can't Keep a Good Man Down.
[M. F. Carey: title of popular song
(1900)]

GOOD BEHAVIOR
12 Put himself upon his good behavior.
[Byron: *Don Juan* V.xlvii.]
13 A man's ethical behavior should be
based effectually on sympathy, education
and social ties and needs; no religious
basis is necessary. Man would indeed be
in a poor way if he had to be restrained
by fear of punishment and hope of reward after death. [Albert Einstein: "Religion and Science," *New York Times
Magazine,* Nov. 9, 1930]

GOOD BREEDING
14 Good breeding consists in concealing
how much we think of ourselves and how
little we think of the other person.
[Mark Twain: *Notebooks*]

GOOD CHEER
15 It snewed in his hous of mete and
drinke.
[Chaucer: Prologue to *The Canterbury
Tales*]
snewed = snowed
16 Now to the banquet we press;
Now for the eggs and the ham;
Now for the mustard and cress,
Now for the strawberry jam!
[W. S. Gilbert: *The Sorcerer* I]

GOOD INTENTIONS
17 Hell is paved with good intentions.
[Samuel Johnson: in Boswell's *Life,*
April 16, 1775]
*For this and other materials in the pave-
ment of Hell, see* HELL.
18 Of sentences that stir my bile,
Of phrases I detest,
There's one beyond all others vile:
"He did it for the best."
[James Kenneth Stephen: *The Malefac-
tor's Plea*]

GOOD LUCK
19 It is a very bad thing to become accustomed to good luck. [Publilius Syrus:
Maxims]

GOOD MAN(MEN)
20 No evil can happen to a good man,
either in life or after death. [Socrates: in
Plato's *Apology*]
21 There lives not three good men un-
hanged in England, and one of them is
fat and grows old. [Shakespeare: *I
Henry IV* II.iv.]

GOOD MANNERS
22 If a man be gracious and courteous
to strangers, it shows he is a citizen of
the world, and that his heart is no island
cut off from other lands but a continent
that joins to them. [Francis Bacon: *Of*

Goodness and Goodness of Nature]
That is, No civilized man is an island.

GOOD NAME

1 A good name is rather to be chosen than riches. [Proverbs 22:1]
2 I would to God thou and I knew where a commodity of good names were to be bought. [Shakespeare: *I Henry IV* I.ii.]
3 Good name in man and woman, dear
                                    my lord,
Is the immediate jewel of their
                                    souls;
Who steals my purse steals trash; 'tis
                            something, nothing;
'Twas mine, 'tis his, and has been
                            slave to thousands;
But he that filches from me my good
                                    name
Robs me of that which not enriches
                                    him,
And makes me poor indeed.
[Shakespeare: *Othello* III.iii.]

GOODNESS

4 Confidence in the goodness of another is good proof of one's own goodness. [Montaigne: *Essays* I.xl.]
5   Abash'd the devil stood,
And felt how awful goodness is.
[John Milton: *Paradise Lost* IV.846-847]
6 That best portion of a good man's
                                    life,
His little nameless, unremembered
                                    acts
Of kindness and of love.
[Wordsworth: *Tintern Abbey*]
7 Ring in the valiant man and free,
    The larger heart, the kindlier
                                    hand;
Ring out the darkness of the land,
Ring in the Christ that is to be.
[Tennyson: *In Memoriam* CVI]
8 Good, but not religious-good.
[Thomas Hardy: *Under the Greenwood Tree* II]

GOOSE(GEESE)

9 It is a blinde Goose that commeth to the Foxes sermon. [John Lyly: *Euphues and His England*]
10 There is no more pitty to be taken of her then to see a goose goe bare-foote.

[Mateo Alemán: *Guzman de Alfarache* (trans. James Mabbe)]
11 All his geese are swans. [Robert Burton: *The Anatomy of Melancholy,* "Democritus to the Reader"]
    A proverbial phrase applied to one who continually praises everything of his own.
12 What is sauce for the goose is sauce for a gander. [Tom Brown: *New Maxims*]
13 There swims no goose so grey, but
                                    soon or late
    She finds some honest gander for her
                                    mate.
[Chaucer: Prologue, *Wyf of Bath's Tale* (Alexander Pope's version)]
14 The goose is a silly bird—too much for one to eat, and not enough for two. [Charles H. Poole: *Archaic Words*]
15 The wild goose is more cosmopolite than we; he breaks his fast in Canada, takes a luncheon in the Susquehanna, and plumes himself for the night in a Louisiana bayou. [Thoreau: *Journal,* March 21, 1840]

GOSPEL

16 Brown bread and the Gospel is good fare. [Matthew Henry: in *Commentaries,* "Isaiah" XXX (1710)]
    Quoted as "a common saying among the Puritans."

GOSSIP

17 Every man hath in his own life sins enough, in his own mind trouble enough, in his own fortune evils enough, and in performance of his offices failings more than enough to entertain his own inquiry: so that curiosity after the affairs of others cannot be without envy and an evil mind. [Jeremy Taylor: *Holy Living*]
18 What some invent the rest enlarge. [Jonathan Swift: *Journal of a Modern Lady*]
19 At every word a reputation dies. [Alexander Pope: *Rape of the Lock* III]
20 Gossip is vice enjoyed vicariously. [Elbert Hubbard: *Philistine* XIX]
21 LADY SNEER: Sir Peter, you are not going to leave us? SIR PETER: Your ladyship must excuse me, I'm called away by particular business. But I leave my char-

acter behind me. [Richard Brinsley Sheridan: *The School for Scandal* II.ii.]

GOSSIPS

1 It's merry when gossips meet. [Ben Jonson: *The Staple of News*, "Induction"]
2 Gossips are frogs—they drink and talk. [George Herbert: *Jacula Prudentum*]
3 For prying into any human affairs, none are equal to those whom it does not concern. [Victor Hugo: *Les Misérables* V.viii.]
4 Whoever gossips to you will gossip of you. [Spanish proverb]

GOTHAM

5 Three wise men of Gotham
Went to sea in a bowl.
If the bowl had been stronger,
My tale had been longer.
[Nursery rhyme]
Gotham is a town in England. Legend had it that the inhabitants, in order to discourage King John (1167-1216) from establishing a castle and garrison there, pretended to be mad. Some tried to rake the moon's reflection out of a pond. Some tried to drown an eel. Others linked hands around a bush to keep a bird from escaping. For generations wits added to these performances, until there was a whole book of them. One of the most famous, because it got fossilized in a little jingle, was this one of going to sea in a bowl.
Washington Irving called New York Gotham (Salmagundi Papers, 1807) because he thought its inhabitants foolishly wise and wisely foolish.

GOUT

6 Drink wine, and have the gout; drink none, and have the gout. [Thomas Cogan: *The Haven of Health* (1584)]
*From the times of the earliest Greeks on, it has been believed that excessive eating and, particularly, heavy drinking caused gout. Chaucer, Fuller, Cowper and scores of other writers have repeated the common charge. Some few, however, noted that the abstinent also had the gout. Among these was Milton, who lived a life of rigorous self-discipline and asceti-*cism and yet, to his angry anguish and irritable despair, suffered what was commonly regarded as the just punishment of the dissolute.*

GOVERNMENT

7 The four pillars of government are . . . religion, justice, counsel, and treasure. [Francis Bacon: *Of Seditions and Troubles*]
8 All government without the consent of the governed, is the very definition of slavery. [Jonathan Swift: *Drapier's Letters* IV]
9 Government is a contrivance of human wisdom to provide for human wants. [Edmund Burke: *Reflections on the Revolution in France*]
10 The people can never err more than in supposing that by multiplying their representatives beyond a certain limit, they strengthen the barrier against the government of a few. [Alexander Hamilton: *The Federalist* No. 58]
11 Nothing appears more surprising to those who consider human affairs with a philosophical eye, than the easiness with which the many are governed by the few. [David Hume: *First Principles of Government*]
12 Our supreme governors, the mob. [Horace Walpole, Letter to Sir Horace Mann, Sept. 7, 1743]
13 Governments derive their just powers from the consent of the governed. [*The Declaration of Independence*]
14 Of governments, that of the mob is most sanguinary, that of soldiers the most expensive, and that of civilians the most vexatious. [C. C. Colton: *Lacon*]
15 That government is best which governs least. [Thoreau: *Civil Disobedience* (1849)]
Thoreau puts the statement in quotation marks and refers to it as a "motto." It is commonly ascribed to Thomas Jefferson —and does, indeed, reflect one strain of thought in Jefferson's First Inaugural Address. But no one has ever been able to find it in Jefferson's writings.
The idea was certainly in the air— especially in the vicinity of Boston. "The World is governed too much" was the motto of the Boston Globe (1844), and Emerson not only said that he approved

of this motto but expressed the same
sentiment in his Politics (1844): "The
less government we have the better."

1 A government of all the people, by
all the people. [Theodore Parker: in a
speech at Boston, May 29, 1850]
> "Government of the people and for the
> people"—
> > Thomas Cooper: Some Information
> > Respecting America (1795)
> See also GETTYSBURG ADDRESS

2 Government is emphatically a machine: to the discontented a "taxing machine," to the contented a "machine for securing property." [Thomas Carlyle: *Signs of the Times*]

3 In the long run every Government is the exact symbol of its people, with their wisdom and unwisdom. [Thomas Carlyle: *Past and Present* IV.iv.]

4 There is no act more moral between men than that of rule and obedience. [Thomas Carlyle: *On Heroes and Hero-Worship* VI]

5 The divine right of kings may have been a plea for feeble tyrants, but the divine right of government is the keystone of human progress, and without it government sinks into police and a nation into a mob. [Benjamin Disraeli: Preface to *Lothair*]

6 A government of statesmen or of clerks? Of Humbug or of Humdrum? [Benjamin Disraeli: *Coningsby* II.iv.]

7 Though the people support the government, the government should not support the people. [Grover Cleveland: in his veto of the Texas Seed Bill, February 16, 1887]

8 The art of government is the organization of idolatry. [George Bernard Shaw: *Man and Superman: Maxims for Revolutionists*]

GOVERNMENT: overrated

9 Thou little thinkest what a little foolery governs the world. [John Selden: *Table Talk*, "Pope"]

10 Thou dost not know, my son, with how little wisdom the world is governed. [Count Axel Oxenstierna: in a letter to his son (1648)]
> One of the greatest of Sweden's, and Europe's, statesmen, Chancellor under Gustavus Adolphus, director of Sweden's

foreign policy at the height of that country's territorial greatness, guardian of Queen Christina, etc., etc.—few men have been in a better position to know.
> The saying has also been attributed to Pope Julius III (speaking to a monk), and to Conrad von Benningen of Holland.

11 Thousands and tens of thousands flourish in youth and wither in age, without the knowledge of any other than domestic evils, and share the same pleasures and vexations whether their kings are mild or cruel, whether the armies of their country pursue their enemies or retreat before them. [Samuel Johnson: *Rasselas* XXVIII]

12 How small, of all that human hearts
> > > > endure,
> That part which kings or laws can
> > > > cause or cure!
[Samuel Johnson: inserted in Oliver Goldsmith's *The Traveler* (1764)]
> This sentiment was one which Dr. Johnson frequently expressed and may account for the annoyance with which he often met zeal for reform.
> In 1762 he wrote to Baretti, at Milan: "The good or ill success of battles and embassies extends itself to a very small part of domestic life: we all have good and evil, which we feel more sensibly than our petty part of public miscarriage or prosperity."
> This is probably less true today, however, when military conscription, increased taxation and fear of an atomic war concern almost every man.

13 I would not give half a guinea to live under one form of government rather than another. It is of no moment to the happiness of an individual. [Samuel Johnson: in Boswell's *Life*, March 31, 1772]

14 All government, in its essence, is a conspiracy against the superior man. [H. L. Mencken: in *Smart Set*, December 1919]

GRACE: of God

15 An outward and visible sign of an inward and spiritual grace. [*The Book of Common Prayer*, "The Catechism"]

16 There but for the grace of God goes John Bradford. [John Bradford: said to be his comment on seeing some criminals led to execution]

> *Bradford (1510?-1555) was a man of deep piety and it is to be assumed that when he himself was led to the stake—as he was—he did not see that as a withdrawal of the previous grace, but probably as a special added grace.*

1 All is, if I have grace to use it so,
As ever in my great Task-master's eye.
[John Milton: *On His being Arrived to the Age of Twenty-three*]

GRACE: in act
2 He does it with a better grace, but I do it more natural.
[Shakespeare: *Twelfth Night* II.iii.]
3 Buxom, blithe, and debonair.
[John Milton: *L'Allegro*]
buxom = *yielding, graceful*
4 Grace was in all her steps, Heaven in her eye,
In every gesture dignity and love.
[John Milton: *Paradise Lost* VIII.488-489]
5 From vulgar bounds with brave disorder part,
And snatch a grace beyond the reach of art.
[Alexander Pope: *Essay on Criticism* I.152-153]
6 Every man of any education would rather be called a rascal than accused of deficiency in the graces. [Samuel Johnson: in Boswell's *Life*, May 1776]

GRACE: before meat
7 Now good digestion wait on appetite,
And health on both!
[Shakespeare: *Macbeth* III.iv.]
> *This has been called the perfect pagan grace.*
8 Here a little child I stand,
Heaving up my either hand:
Cold as paddocks though they be,
Here I lift them up to thee,
For a benison to fall
On our meat, and on us all.
[Robert Herrick: *Grace for a Child*]
benison = *benediction;* paddocks = *toads*
> *This is the word that makes the whole poem: it's those little hands, cold as toads.*
9 Some hae meat, and canna eat,
And some wad eat that want it;

But we hae meat and we can eat,
And sae the Lord be thankit.
[Burns: *The Selkirk Grace*]

GRADUALNESS
10 The inevitability of gradualness. [Sidney Webb: Presidential Address to the British Labour Party Conference, 1920]

GRAMMAR
11 I am the king of the Romans and above grammar. [The Emperor Sigismund I: at the Council of Constance (1414), when a prelate called his attention to a mistake in grammar in his opening speech.]
> *Grammarians of the past preserved the anecdote to Sigismund's discredit; many modern linguists regard it as rather to his credit.*
12 Do but hear one pronounce *metonymia, metaphor, allegory, etymology* and other such trash-names of Grammar, would you not think they meant some form of a rare and strange language? Yet they are but titles and words that concern your chambermaid's tittle-tattle. [Montaigne: *Essays* I.li.]
13 Our speech hath its infirmities and defects, as all things else have. Most of the occasions of this world's troubles are grammatical. [Montaigne: *Essays* II. xii.]
14 . . . grammar, which rules even kings. [Molière: *Les Femmes Savantes* II.vi. (1672)]
15 The first thing you should attend to is, to speak whatever language you do speak in its greatest purity, and according to the rules of grammar; for we must never offend against grammar. [Lord Chesterfield: *Letters to his Son,* Oct. 17, 1739]
16 It is not the business of grammar, as some critics seem preposterously to imagine, to give law to the fashions which regulate our speech. On the contrary, from its conformity to these, and from that alone, it derives all its authority and value. [George Campbell: *The Philosophy of Rhetoric* (1776)]
17 Heedless of grammar, they all cried, "That's him!" [R. H. Barham: *The Jackdaw of Rheims*]
18 Our modern grammars have done

much more hurt than good. The authors have labored to prove what is obviously absurd, viz., that our language is not made right; and in pursuance of this idea, have tried to make it over again, and persuade the English to speak by Latin rules, or by arbitrary rules of their own. [Noah Webster: Preface to *Dissertations on the English Language* (1789)]

1 When I read some of the rules for speaking and writing the English language correctly, I think—

> Any fool can make a rule
> And every fool will mind it.

[Thoreau: *Journal,* Feb. 3, 1860]

2 For there be women fair as she,
> Whose verbs and nouns do more
> agree.

[Bret Harte: *Mrs. Judge Jenkins*]

3 Prefer geniality to grammar. [H. W. Fowler: *The King's English* II]

4 The grammar has a rule absurd
> Which I would call an outworn
> myth:
> "A preposition is a word
> You mustn't end a sentence with!"

[Berton Braley: *No Rule to Be Afraid Of*]

GRANDFATHER'S CLOCK

5 But it stopped short—never to go
> again—
> When the old man died.

[H. C. Work: *Grandfather's Clock*]

GRANDPARENTS

6 A grandam's name is little less in love
> Than is the doting title of a mother.

[Shakespeare: *Richard III* IV.iv.]

7 Over the river and through the wood,
> To grandfather's house we'll go;
> The horse knows the way
> To carry the sleigh
> Through the white and drifted snow.

[Lydia Maria Child: *Thanksgiving Day*]

8 There are fathers who do not love their children; there is no grandfather who does not adore his grandson. [Victor Hugo: *Les Misérables* V.iii.]

Bacon says it is because he is his enemy's enemy.

9 Every generation revolts against its fathers and makes friends with its grandfathers. [Lewis Mumford: *The Brown Decades*]

GRASS

10 As for man, his days are as grass: as a flower of the field, so he flourisheth. For the wind passeth over it, and it is gone; and the place thereof shall know it no more. [Psalms 103:15]

11 While the grass groweth, the horse starveth. [Thomas Heywood: *Proverbs* (1546)]

The proverb, stressing that planning cannot concentrate wholly on the future, disregarding the present to achieve a distant aim, is alluded to by Hamlet (III.ii.) who speaks only the first words and then breaks it off to comment that "the proverb is something musty."

GRASS ROOTS

12 This party comes from the grass roots. It has grown from the soil of the people's hard necessities. [Albert J. Beveridge (1862-1927): in a speech at the Bull Moose Convention, Chicago, 1912]

Of Senator Beveridge's oratory, Mr. Dooley said, "Ye can waltz to it."

GRATIFICATION

13 The desire accomplished is sweet to the soul. [Proverbs 13:19]

GRATITUDE

14 Down on your knees,
> And thank Heaven, fasting, for a
> good man's love.

[Shakespeare: *As You Like It* III.v.]

15 Thanksgiving for a former, doth invite God to bestow a second benefit. [Robert Herrick: *Thanksgiving*]

16 A grateful mind
> By owing owes not, but still pays, at
> once
> Indebted and discharg'd.

[John Milton: *Paradise Lost* IV. 55-57]

17 Gratitude, in most men, is only a strong and secret hope of greater favors. [La Rochefoucauld: *Maxims*]

18 There are minds so impatient of inferiority that their gratitude is a species of revenge, and they return benefits, not because recompense is a pleasure, but because obligation is a pain. [Samuel Johnson: *The Rambler* No. 87]

19 Gratitude is a fruit of great cultivation; you do not find it among gross people. [Samuel Johnson: in Boswell's

Tour to the Hebrides, Sept. 20, 1773]

1 I've heard of hearts unkind, kind
deeds
With coldness still returning;
Alas! the gratitude of men
Hath oftener left me mourning.
[Wordsworth: *Simon Lee*]
*Wordsworth tells in this poem of per-
forming a trifling task for a poor old
sick man who, in his youth, had been a
vigorous running huntsman. The profuse, trembling gratitude for such a trifle
had moved him to far greater sadness
than any ingratitude could possibly have
done.*

2 Do you like gratitude? I don't. If pity
is akin to love, gratitude is akin to the
other thing. [George Bernard Shaw:
Arms and the Man III]

GRAVE(S)

3 There the wicked cease from trou-
bling; and there the weary be at rest.
[Job 3:17]
*Usually quoted "Where the wicked cease
from troubling, and the weary are at
rest," the form in which it appears in
Gerald Massey's hymn* Jerusalem the
Golden.

4 Whatsoever thy hand findeth to do,
do it with thy might; for there is no work,
nor device, nor knowledge, nor wisdom,
in the grave, whither thou goest. [Ec-
clesiastes 9:10]

5 One foot in the grave. [Montaigne:
Essays II.xxviii.]

6 So be my grave my peace.
[Shakespeare: *King Lear* I.i.]

7 The last inn of all travelers, where
we shall meet worms instead of fleas.
[Sir William Davenant: *The Man's the
Master* I.i.]

8 Thy beauty shall no more be found,
Nor, in thy marble vault, shall sound
My echoing song: then worms shall
try
That long preserved virginity,
And your quaint honor turn to dust,
And into ashes all my lust:
The grave's a fine and private place,
But none, I think, do there embrace.
[Andrew Marvell: *To His Coy Mistress*]

9 How many People daily dig their
own Graves either with their Teeth, their

Tongues, or their Tails. [Oswald Dykes:
English Proverbs (1709)]

10 Beneath those rugged elms, that yew-
tree's shade,
Where heaves the turf in many a
mold'ring heap,
Each in his narrow cell for ever laid,
The rude forefathers of the hamlet
sleep.
[Thomas Gray: *Elegy Written in a
Country Churchyard*]

11 The boast of heraldry, the pomp of
power,
And all that beauty, all that wealth
e'er gave,
Awaits alike the inevitable hour:
The paths of glory lead but to the
grave.
[Thomas Gray: *Elegy Written in a
Country Churchyard*]

12 A violet by a mossy stone
Half hidden from the eye!—
Fair as a star, when only one
Is shining in the sky.
She lived alone, and few could know
When Lucy ceased to be;
But she is in her grave, and, oh,
The difference to me!
[Wordsworth: *She Dwelt Among the
Untrodden Ways*]

13 Perhaps the early grave
Which men weep over may be meant
to save.
[Byron: *Don Juan* IV.xii.]

14 Seek out—less often sought than
found—
A soldier's grave, for thee the best;
Then look around, and choose thy
ground,
And take thy rest.
[Byron: *On This Day I Complete My
Thirty-sixth Year*]

15 Art is long, and Time is fleeting,
And our hearts, though stout and
brave,
Still, like muffled drums, are beating
Funeral marches to the grave.
[Longfellow: *A Psalm of Life*]
*Longfellow may have been echoing a
line from Beaumont and Fletcher's* The
Humorous Lieutenant *(III.v.):*
*Our lives are but our marches to the
grave.*

16 All things have rest, and ripen toward the grave.

[Tennyson: *The Lotus-Eaters,* "Choric Song"]

1 I take the grasses of the grave,
And make them pipes whereon to blow.

[Tennyson: *In Memoriam* XXI]

2 By Nebo's lonely mountain,
On this side Jordan's wave,
In a vale in the land of Moab,
There lies a lonely grave.

[Cecil Frances Alexander: *The Burial of Moses*]

3 And I shall have to bate my price,
For in the grave, they say,
Is neither knowledge nor device
Nor thirteen pence a day.

[A. E. Housman: *Last Poems* V]

bate = *abate*

Thirteen pence a day was the soldier's wage at the time of the Boer War. A dying soldier is speaking. That there is neither knowledge nor device in the grave is stated in Ecclesiastes 9:10.

GRAVEYARD

4 That shabby corner of God's allotment where He lets the nettles grow, and where all unbaptized infants, notorious drunkards, suicides, and others of the conjecturally damned are laid. [Thomas Hardy: *Tess of the D'Urbervilles* XIV]

GRAVITY

5 Is there any thing so assured, so resolute, so disdainful, so contemplative, so serious and so grave as an ass? [Montaigne: *Essays* III.viii.]

resolute = *mind made up, settled, fixed, dogmatic*

6 What doth gravity out of his bed at midnight?

[Shakespeare: *I Henry IV* II.iv.]

7 Gravity is a mysterious carriage of the body invented to cover the defects of the mind. [La Rochefoucauld: *Maxims*]

8 Gravity is of the very essence of imposture. [Anthony Ashley Cooper, Earl of Shaftesbury: *Characteristics*]

9 My boys, let us be grave: here comes a fool. [James Boswell, quoting Dr. Samuel Clarke: in the Dedication to Sir Joshua Reynolds of *The Life of Samuel Johnson, LL.D.*]

Boswell may have taken the saying from a passage in Goldsmith's Life of Nash.

The fool who was approaching was the pompous Beau Nash.

10 He says but little, and that little said
Owes all its weight, like loaded dice, to lead.
His wit invites you by his looks to come,
But when you knock it never is at home.

[William Cowper: *Conversation*]

GRAY HAIR

11 Bring down my gray hairs with sorrow to the grave. [Genesis 42:38]

12 The beauty of old men is the gray head. [Proverbs 20:29]

13 The oldest man he seemed that ever wore grey hairs.

[Wordsworth: *Resolution and Independence*]

14 "Who touches a hair of yon gray head
Dies like a dog! March on!" he said.

[J. G. Whittier: *Barbara Frietchie*]

15 Darling, I am growing old,
Silver threads among the gold
Shine upon my brow today;
Life is fading fast away.

[E. E. Rexford: *Silver Threads Among the Gold*]

GREAT

16 Great and good are seldom the same man. [Thomas Fuller (1654-1734): *Gnomologia*]

GREATEST

17 I would sooner fail than not be among the greatest. [Keats: Letter to James Hessey, October 9, 1818]

GREATNESS

18 And what he greatly thought, he nobly dared. [Homer: *Odyssey* II (trans. Alexander Pope)]

19 Great men are not always wise. [Job 32:9]

20 To have a great man for a friend seems pleasant to those who have never tried it; those who have, fear it. [Horace: *Epistles* I.xviii.]

21 The rising unto place is laborious, and by pains men come to greater pains; and it is sometimes base, and by indignities, men come to dignities. [Francis

Bacon: *Of Great Place*]
1 All rising to great place is by a winding stair. [Francis Bacon: *Of Great Place*]

Bacon has in mind the staircases, then common, that wound in a spiral about a center column. His figure, which is sad and savage, is that you rise in the world only by winding and shifting from side to side as you go up.

2 Men in great place are thrice servants: servants of the sovereign or state, servants of fame, and servants of business; so they have no freedom, neither in their persons, nor in their actions, nor in their times. [Francis Bacon: *Of Great Place*]

3 Certainly great persons had need to borrow other men's opinions to think themselves happy; for if they judge by their own feeling they cannot find it. [Francis Bacon: *Of Great Place*]

4 Upon what meat doth this our Caesar feed,
That he is grown so great?
[Shakespeare: *Julius Caesar* I.ii.]

5 O foolish youth!
Thou seek'st the greatness that will overwhelm thee.
[Shakespeare: *II Henry IV* IV.v.]

6 But be not afraid of greatness: some are born great, some achieve greatness and some have greatness thrust upon 'em. [Shakespeare: *Twelfth Night* II.v.]

7 Rightly to be great
Is not to stir without great argument,
But greatly to find quarrel in a straw,
When honour's at the stake.
[Shakespeare: *Hamlet* IV.iv.]

8 His legs bestrid the ocean; his rear'd arm
Crested the world: his voice was propertied
As all the tuned spheres, and that to friends;
But when he meant to quail and shake the orb,
He was as rattling thunder. For his bounty,
There was no winter in 't; an autumn 'twas
That grew the more by reaping: his delights
Were dolphin-like; they show'd his back above

The elements they lived in: in his livery
Walk'd crowns and crownets; realms and islands were
As plates dropp'd from his pocket.
[Shakespeare: *Antony and Cleopatra* V. ii.]

9 Farewell! a long farewell, to all my greatness!
This is the state of man: to-day he puts forth
The tender leaves of hopes; to-morrow blossoms,
And bears his blushing honours thick upon him;
The third day comes a frost, a killing frost,
And, when he thinks, good easy man, full surely
His greatness is a-ripening, nips his root,
And then he falls, as I do. I have ventured,
Like little wanton boys that swim on bladders,
This many summers in a sea of glory,
But far beyond my depth: my high-blown pride
At length broke under me, and now has left me,
Weary and old with service, to the mercy
Of a rude stream, that must forever hide me.
[Shakespeare: *Henry VIII* III.ii.]

10 Men are we, and must grieve when even the shade
Of that which once was great, is passed away.
[Wordsworth: *On the Extinction of the Venetian Republic* (1802)]

11 No really great man ever thought himself so. [William Hazlitt: *Table Talk*]

12 The world knows nothing of its greatest men. [Henry Taylor: *Philip Van Artevelde* I.v.]

13 There seems to be no interval between greatness and meanness. When the spirit is not master of the world, then it is its dupe. [Emerson: *Heroism*]

14 The heights by great men reached and kept
Were not attained by sudden flight,
But they, while their companions

slept,
Were toiling upward in the night.
[Longfellow: *The Ladder of St. Augustine*]
1 How dreary to be somebody!
[Emily Dickinson: *Poems* I.27]
2 If a great man could make us understand him, we should hang him. [G. B. Shaw: *Maxims for Revolutionists*]

GREECE
3 The isles of Greece, the isles of Greece!
Where burning Sappho loved and
sung,
Where grew the arts of war and
peace,
Where Delos rose and Phoebus
sprung!
Eternal summer gilds them yet,
But all, except their sun, is set.
[Byron: *Don Juan* III.lxxxvi. "The Isles of Greece"]
4 The glory that was Greece
And the grandeur that was Rome.
[Edgar Allan Poe: *To Helen*]

GREEK(S)
5 I fear the Greeks, even when they are
bearing gifts.
[Vergil: *Aeneid* II]
The Latin is: Timeo Danaos et dona ferentes. *Commonly spoken as:* "I fear the Greeks bearing gifts."
6 CASSIUS: Did Cicero say anything?
CASCA: Ay, he spoke Greek. CASSIUS: To what effect? CASCA: Nay, an I tell you that I'll ne'er look you i' the face again: but those that understood him smiled at one another and shook their heads; but, for mine own part, it was Greek to me. [Shakespeare: *Julius Caesar* I.ii.]
"It was Greek to me" was already established as a trope of incomprehensibility. Shakespeare's use of it in this context would be sure-fire for a laugh from the groundlings.
7 When Greeks joyn'd Greeks, then was the tug of war. [Nathaniel Lee: *The Rival Queens* IV.ii. (1677)]
Now commonly: "When Greek meets Greek, then comes the tug-of-war."
8 Of all peoples, the Greeks have best dreamed the dream of life. [Goethe: *Sprüche in Prosa*]

9 Except the blind forces of Nature, nothing moves in this world which is not Greek in its origin. [Sir Henry J. S. Maine: *Rede Lecture* (1875), "Village Communities"]
10 The most un-Greek thing we can do is copy the Greeks. For emphatically they were not copyists. [Alfred North Whitehead: *Adventures of Ideas*]
11 The Greeks Had a Word For It. [Zoë Akins: title of a play (1929)]
The word was hetaera (lit. = companion). It designated a concubine or courtesan, educated and accomplished, who made a more agreeable companion for a man in his leisure hours than the cloistered women of classical Athens.

GREETING
12 If I should meet thee
After long years,
How should I greet thee?—
With silence and tears.
[Byron: *When We Two Parted*]
13 Ships that pass in the night, and
speak each other in passing,
Only a signal shown and a distant
voice in the darkness;
So on the ocean of life, we pass and
speak one another,
Only a look and a voice, then darkness again and a silence.
[Longfellow: *Tales of a Wayside Inn*]

GRENVILLE
14 At Flores in the Azores Sir Richard
Grenville lay.
[Tennyson: *The Revenge*]

GRIEF
15 There is no grief which time does not lessen and soften. [Cicero: *Epistolae* IV.v.]
16 Great grief will not be tould,
And can more easily be thought than
said.
[Edmund Spenser: *The Faerie Queene* I.vii.]
17 Chawing the cud of griefe and inward paine.
[Edmund Spenser: *The Faerie Queene* V.vi.]
18 Light cares speak, when mighty griefs
are dumb.

[Samuel Daniel: *Complaint of Rosamond*]

Light cares speak, the huge are dumb.
        Seneca: Hippolytus
My lighter moods are like to these,
That out of words a comfort win;
But there are other griefs within,
And tears that at their fountain freeze.
        Tennyson: In Memoriam XX
Small griefs find tongues; full casks are
                ever found
To give, if any, yet but little sound.
Deep waters noiseless are; and this we
                know,
That chiding streams betray small depth
                below.
        Robert Herrick: To His Mistress Objecting to Him Neither Toying or Talking

1 I will instruct my sorrows to be
                proud;
For grief is proud, and makes his
                owner stoop.
[Shakespeare: *King John* III.i.]

2 Grief fills the room up of my absent
                child,
Lies in his bed, walks up and down
                with me,
Puts on his pretty looks, repeats his
                words,
Remembers me of all his gracious
                parts,
Stuffs out his vacant garments with
                his form:
Then have I reason to be fond of
                grief.
[Shakespeare: *King John* III.iv.]

3 I am not mad; I would to heaven I
                were!
For then, 'tis like I should forget myself:
O, if I could, what grief should I
                forget!
[Shakespeare: *King John* III.iv.]

4 You may my glories and my state
                depose,
But not my griefs; still am I king of
                those.
[Shakespeare: *Richard II* IV.i.]

5 A plague of sighing and grief! It
blows a man up like a bladder. [Shakespeare: *I Henry IV* II.iv.]

6 Every one can master a grief but he
                that has it.
[Shakespeare: *Much Ado about Nothing*

III.ii.]

7 But I have that within which passeth show;
These but the trappings and the suits
                of woe.
[Shakespeare: *Hamlet* I.ii.]

8   My particular grief
Is of so flood-gate and o'erbearing
                nature
That it engluts and swallows other
                sorrows.
[Shakespeare: *Othello* I.iii.]

9 Give sorrow words; the grief that
                does not speak
Whispers the o'er-fraught heart and
                bids it break.
[Shakespeare: *Macbeth* IV.iii.]

10 Grief is a species of idleness. [Samuel Johnson: *Letters* I]

11   Winter is come and gone,
But grief returns with the revolving
                year.
[Shelley: *Adonais* XVIII]

12 Alas! that all we loved of him should
                be,
But for our grief, as if it had not
                been,
And grief itself be mortal!
[Shelley: *Adonais* XXI]

13 Great grief is a divine and terrible
radiance which transfigures the wretched.
[Victor Hugo: *Les Misérables* V.xiii.]

14 It is the peculiarity of grief to bring
out the childish side of man. [Victor
Hugo: *Les Misérables* III.viii.]

15 From perfect grief there need not be
Wisdom or even memory.
[Dante Gabriel Rossetti: *The Woodspurge*]

GROANING

16 A gronyng horse, and a gronyng wife
Never fail their master.
[John Heywood: *Proverbs* (1546)]
There are a number of sayings in English that point out that a shrewish, complaining woman has virtues that the turtle dove often lacks.

GROWED

17 I 'spect I grow'd. Don't think nobody
ever made me. [Harriet Beecher Stowe:
Uncle Tom's Cabin XX]
*Topsy's artless answer, when asked who
made her, showed her innocence and the*

urgent need of Christian missionaries among the slaves. It showed (the Northerners) that the peculiar institution robbed the Negroes of their souls as well as their bodies.

Little Eva, over whom our grandfathers wept, is now a stock figure of labored comedy. Topsy, who made them laugh and sigh, is forgotten. And Uncle Tom is heard today solely as a term of contempt among the Negroes themselves!

GROWING UP

1 When I am grown to man's estate
I shall be very proud and great,
And tell the other girls and boys
Not to meddle with my toys.
[R. L. Stevenson: *Looking Forward*]

GRUESOME

2 By this time he was cross the ford,
Where in the snaw the chapman
smoor'd;
And past the birks and meikle stane,
Where drunken Charlie brak's neck-
bane;
And thro the whins and by the cairn,
Where hunters fand the murder'd
bairn;
And near the thorn, aboon the well,
Where Mungo's mither hang'd hersel.
[Burns: *Tam o'Shanter*]
snaw = *snow;* chapman = *pedlar;* smoor'd = *smothered;* birks = *birches;* meikle = *large;* whins = *furze;* cairn = *heap of stones;* bairn = *child, baby;* aboon = *above*

GRUNDY, MRS.

3 Be quiet, wull ye. Always ding, dinging Dame Grundy into my ears— What will Mrs. Grundy say? What will Mrs. Grundy think? [Thomas Morton: *Speed the Plow* I.i. (1798)]
Farmer Ashfield's annoyance at his wife because she is eternally concerned about the good or bad opinion of her neighbor, Mrs. Grundy. Mrs. Grundy has become a term for censorious public opinion.

4 And many are afraid of God—
And more of Mrs. Grundy.
[F. Locker-Lampson: *The Jester's Plea*]

GUARD(S)

5 Gentlemen of the French Guard, fire first! [Attr. Lord Charles Hay: at the battle of Fontenoy, April 30, 1745]
The opposing French commander, Comte d'Auteroches, not to be outdone in the amenities of homicide, is supposed to have replied: "Sir, the French Guards never fire first. Please, you fire." Or, "Will the English gentlemen please fire first?"
This exchange must rank high on any list of improbable colloquies.

6 Up, Guards, and at 'em.
Wellington himself questioned the wording of the famous command, granted that he might have said, "Stand up, Guards," just before he gave the command for the decisive charge. See Wellington's letter to J. W. Croker in Croker's Memoirs, p. 544.
That on the return of the remnant, with half the flower of England's chivalry dead upon the field behind them, he raised his hat and said "Thank you," is better attested.

7 The Guard dies, but never surrenders. [Attr. General Pierre Étienne de Cambronne: commanding the Imperial Guard at Waterloo, when called on to surrender.]
General de Cambronne insisted that he said the more succinct "Merde!"
See also WAR: famous utterances.

GUARDIANS

8 But who guards the guardians? (*Quis custodiet ipsos custodes?*) [Juvenal: *Satires* VI]
There have been endless variations on this question, some of the utmost seriousness, some light. A generation ago there was a popular song, "Who takes care of the Caretaker's daughter/When the Caretaker's busy taking care?"

GUEST(S)

9 Withdraw thy foot from in thy neighbour's house; lest he be weary of thee, and so hate thee. [Proverbs 25:17]

10 No guest can stay three continuous days without becoming an annoyance. [Plautus: *Miles Gloriosus* III.iii.]
Plautus lived 254-184 B.C. The message is as old as it is unheeded.

11 Unbidden guests

Are often welcomest when they are
gone.
[Shakespeare: *I Henry VI* II.ii.]
1 A woeful hostess brooks not merry
guests.
[Shakespeare: *The Rape of Lucrece* 1125]
brooks = *enjoys*
2 People are far more sincere and good-
humored at speeding their parting
guests than on meeting them. [Anton
Chekhov: *The Kiss*]

GUIDE
3 Thou wert my guide, philosopher
and friend. [Alexander Pope: *An Essay
on Man,* Epistle IV]

*An echo of "Thou, my companion, my
guide, and mine own familiar friend"—
Book of Common Prayer, "The Psalter,"
Psalm 55:5.*

GUILLOTINE
4 My machine will take off a head in a
twinkling, and the victim will feel nothing but a slight sense of refreshing coolness on the neck. We cannot make too
much haste, gentlemen, to allow the nation to enjoy this advantage. [Dr. Joseph Ignace Guillotin: to the French National Assembly (1789)]

*The guillotine was first urged on demo-
cratic grounds—why should aristocrats
have the exclusive privilege of being be-
headed? And then on humanitarian
grounds—that "refreshing coolness"! At
first called the* louisette, *after Dr. Antoine Louis, the guillotine was resented
by the populace, which felt it was being
cheated of the spectacular contortions of
those who were hanged. However, blood
was soon perceived to be more exciting
than writhing and the new device became exceedingly popular.*

*Neither Dr. Louis nor Dr. Guillotin
invented the machine; they merely improved and advocated the use of a con-
traption which under various names (in
Scotland, "The Maiden") had been used
as a decapitant for at least 300 years.*

*Contrary to legend, both men died
peacefully in their beds. Dr. Guillotin
was imprisoned during the Terror and,
if only because the suitableness of it
would have delighted the mob, must
have had some apprehension of feeling*
*a slight freshness on his own neck. But
he survived and lived until 1814.*

GUILT
5 He who flees from trial confesses his
guilt. [Publilius Syrus: *Maxims*]
6 He who profits by crime is guilty of
it. [Seneca: *Medea*]
7 All go free when multitudes offend.
[Lucan: *Pharsalia* V.cclx.]
8 No man is so exquisitely honest or
upright in living but that ten times in
his life he might not lawfully be hanged.
[Montaigne: *Essays* III.ix.]
9 And then it started like a guilty thing
Upon a fearful summons.
[Shakespeare: *Hamlet* I.i.]
10   Leave her to heaven,
And to those thorns that in her
bosom lodge,
To prick and sting her.
[Shakespeare: *Hamlet* I.v.]
11   I have heard
That guilty creatures sitting at a play
Have by the very cunning of the
scene
Been struck so to the soul that pres-
ently
They have proclaim'd their malefac-
tions.
[Shakespeare: *Hamlet* II.ii.]
presently = *immediately*
12 So full of artless jealousy is guilt,
It spills itself in fearing to be spilt.
[Shakespeare: *Hamlet* IV.v.]
13   Tremble, thou wretch,
That has within thee undivulged
crimes,
Unwhipp'd of justice.
[Shakespeare: *King Lear* III.ii.]
14 Three fatal Sisters wait upon each
sin;
First, Fear and Shame without, then
Guilt within.
[Robert Herrick: *Three Fatal Sisters*]
15 Guilt has very quick ears to an accusation. [Henry Fielding: *Amelia* III.xi.]
16 It is better that ten guilty persons escape than that one innocent suffer. [Wil-
liam Blackstone: *Commentaries on the
Laws of England* IV]

GULF
17 Between us and you there is a great
gulf fixed. [Luke 16:26]

GUNGA DIN

1 You're a better man than I am,
Gunga Din.

[Kipling: *Gunga Din*]

GUNS

2   And but for these vile guns,
He would himself have been a soldier.
[Shakespeare: *I Henry IV* I.iii.]

3 What passing-bells for these who die
as cattle?
Only the monstrous anger of the
guns.
Only the stuttering rifles' rapid rattle
Can patter out their hasty orisons.
[Wilfred Owen: *Anthem for Doomed Youth*]

4 Guns will make us powerful; butter will only make us fat. [Hermann Goering, in radio broadcast, 1936]

GUTS

5 The guts carry the feet, not the feet the guts.
[Cervantes: *Don Quixote* II.xxiv.]

6 The guts uphold the heart. [Thomas Fuller (1654-1734): *Gnomologia*]

H

HABIT
1 Habit is a sort of second nature. [Cicero: *De finibus*]
2 Nothing is stronger than habit. [Ovid: *Ars Amatoria* II]
3 Evil habits are more easily broken than mended. [Quintilian: *Institutio Oratoria* I.iii.]
4 Habit is second nature. [Montaigne: *Essays* III.x.]
5 How use doth breed a habit in a man!
[Shakespeare: *Two Gentlemen of Verona* V.iv.]
6   Refrain tonight,
And that shall lend a kind of easiness
To the next abstinence: the next
          more easy;
For use almost can change the stamp
          of nature.
[Shakespeare: *Hamlet* III.iv.]
7 Habit is the enormous fly-wheel of society, its most precious conservative agent. [William James: *Psychology* I]

HAIL
8 Hail fellow well met. [Jonathan Swift: *My Lady's Lamentation*]

HAIR(S)
9 But the very hairs of your head are all numbered. [Matthew 10:30]
10 If a woman have long hair, it is a glory to her. [I Corinthians 11:15]
11 His hair grows through his hood.
A picturesque 15th-century way of saying that someone is in want.
12 The hair is the finest ornament women have. Of old, virgins used to wear it loose, except when they were in mourning. I like women to let their hair fall down their back; 'tis a most agreeable sight. [Martin Luther: *Table Talk* DCCLI (1569)]
13 Never shake / Thy gory locks at me. [Shakespeare: *Macbeth* III.iv.]
14 Nature herself abhors to see a woman shorn or polled; a woman with cut hair is a filthy spectacle, and much like a monster. [William Prynne: *Histriomastix*]
15 To sport with Amaryllis in the shade

Or with the tangles of Neaera's hair. [John Milton: *Lycidas*]
16 Fair tresses man's imperial race en-
          snare,
And beauty draws us with a single
          hair.
[Alexander Pope: *The Rape of the Lock* II]
One can almost see this line coming to fruition in the womb of time:
    No cord nor cable can so forcibly draw, or hold so fast, as love can do with a twined thread.
        Robert Burton: The Anatomy of Melancholy *(1621)*
One hair of a woman can draw more than a hundred pair of oxen.
        James Howell: Familiar Letters *(1621)*
She knows her man, and when you rant and swear, Can draw you to her with a single hair.
        John Dryden: trans. of Persius, Satire V (1693)
17 Like the bright hair uplifted from the
          head
Of some fierce Maenad.
[Shelley: *Ode to the West Wind*]
18 "Who touches a hair of yon gray
          head
Dies like a dog! March on!" he said.
[J. G. Whittier: *Barbara Frietchie*]

HALF
19 The half was not told me. [I Kings 10:7]

HALF A LOAF
20 Better is half a loaf than no bread. [John Heywood: *Proverbs* (1546)]

HALLUCINATION
21   A false creation,
Proceeding from the heat-oppressed
          brain.
[Shakespeare: *Macbeth* II.i.]
22   Alas! How is 't with you,
That you do bend your eye on va-
          cancy
And with th' incorporal air do hold
          discourse?
[Shakespeare: *Hamlet* III.iv.]

1 As I was going up the stair
I met a man who wasn't there.
He wasn't there again today.
I wish, I wish he'd go away.
[Hughes Mearns: *The Psychoed*]

HAMLET
2 No! I am not Prince Hamlet, nor was
meant to be;
Am an attendant lord, one that will
do
To swell a progress, start a scene or
two,
Advise the prince.
[T. S. Eliot: *The Love Song of J. Alfred
Prufrock*]

HAND(S)
3 His hand will be against every man,
and every man's hand against him. [Genesis 16:12]
*The reference is to Ishmael, the son of
Hagar and Abraham, who with his
mother was banished into the wilderness
by the malevolence of Sarah.*
*Ishmael is believed to have been the
progenitor of the fierce Bedouins.*
4 My times are in thy hand. [Psalms
31:15]
5 Whatsoever thy hand findeth to do,
do it with thy might. [Ecclesiastes 9:10]
*This was the favorite biblical passage of
the elder Clarence Day—the Father of
Life with Father.*
6 Laying on of Hands. [*The Book of
Common Prayer*, "Confirmation"]
7 Living from hand to mouth. [Du
Bartas: *Divine Weekes and Workes*, "Second Week, First Day" IV]
8 All the perfumes of Arabia will not
sweeten this little hand.
[Shakespeare: *Macbeth* V.i.]
9 Help, Hands, for I have no Lands.
[Benjamin Franklin: *Poor Richard's Almanack* (1758)]
10 Hands, that the rod of empire might
have swayed,
Or waked to ecstasy the living lyre.
[Thomas Gray: *Elegy Written in a Country Churchyard*]
11 The hand that rocks the cradle is the
hand that rules the world. [W. R. Wallace: *The Hand That Rules the World*]

12 Pale hands I loved beside the Shali-
mar,
Where are you now? Who lies be-
neath your spell?
. . .
I would have rather felt you round
my throat,
Crushing out life, than waving me
farewell.
[Adela Nicolson ("Laurence Hope"):
Kashmiri Song]

HANDEL
13 Others aver that he to Handel
Is scarcely fit to hold a candle.
[John Byrom: *On the Feud Between
Handel and Bononcini*]
See TWEEDLEDUM

HANDSOME
14 A proper man, as one shall see in a
summer's day.
[Shakespeare: *A Midsummer Night's
Dream* I.ii.]
*proper formerly meant—among other
meanings—handsome. The King James
Version of the Bible (following Tyndale)
says (Hebrews 11:23) that the infant
Moses was "a proper child." The New
English Bible says that he was "a fine
child." The Revised Standard Version
says that he was "beautiful." And when
Desdemona (Othello IV.iii.) says that
"Lodovico is a proper man," Emilia immediately agrees: "A very handsome
man."*
15 Handsome is that handsome does.
[Henry Fielding: *Tom Jones* IV.xii.]
*The saying also appears in John Gay's
Wife of Bath (1713) and Goldsmith's
Vicar of Wakefield (1766).*
*Dekker in The Shoemaker's Holiday
(II.i.) (1600) had: "He is proper that
proper doeth."*
*An earlier version (1580): "Goodly is
he that goodly doth"—where goodly =
handsome.*
Handsome originally meant handy.
16 She was handsome in spite of her ef-
forts to be handsomer. [Ring Lardner:
The Love Nest]

HANG(ING)
17 Hanging and wiving go by destiny.

[Anon.: *The Schoolhouse for Women* (1541)]

1 Hanging was the worst use a man could be put to. [Sir Henry Wotton: *The Disparity Between Buckingham and Essex*]

2 I went out to Charing Cross to see Major General Harrison hanged, drawn, and quartered; which was done there, he looking as cheerful as any man could do in that condition. [Samuel Pepys: *Diary*, Oct. 13, 1660]

3 Clever Tom Clinch, while the rabble
    was bawling,
Rode stately through Holborn to die
    in his calling,
He stopt at the George for a bottle of
    sack,
And promis'd to pay for it when he
    came back.
[Jonathan Swift: *On Tom Clinch Going to be Hanged*]
 The way to the gallows, at Tyburn, lay along Holborn Street.

 A hanging was a public spectacle and the principal was greatly admired if he carried it off with a swagger. Custom permitted him certain trifling perquisites en route and the witticism was probably a stock one. Dr. Johnson thought the show sustained the victim and that private executions were more dreadful.

4 We must all hang together, else we shall all hang separately. [Benjamin Franklin: to John Hancock, on signing the Declaration of Independence, July 4, 1776]

5 It is sweet to dance to violins
 When love and life are fair:
To dance to flutes, to dance to lutes
 Is delicate and rare:
But it is not sweet with nimble feet
 To dance upon the air.
[Oscar Wilde: *The Ballad of Reading Gaol*]

6 For they're hangin' Danny Deever,
 you can hear the Dead March play.
The Regiment's in 'ollow square—
 they're hangin' him today;
They've taken of his buttons off an'
 cut his stripes away.
And they're hangin' Danny Deever in
 the morning.
[Kipling: *Danny Deever*]

HANGOVER

7 A dark brown taste, a burning thirst,
 A head that's ready to split and
    burst. . . .
No time for mirth, no time for laugh-
    ter—
The cold gray dawn of the morning
    after.
[George Ade: *Remorse* (1903)]

HAPPINESS: the achievement of

8 The lines are fallen unto me in pleasant places; yea, I have a goodly heritage. [Psalms 16:6]

9 A man's happiness is to do a man's true work. [Marcus Aurelius: *Meditations* VIII.xxvi.]

10 Let him who would be happy for a day, go to the barber; for a week, marry a wife; for a month, buy him a new horse; for a year, build him a new house; for all his life time, be an honest man. [Thomas Fuller (1608-1661): *Worthies*, "Wales" III]

11 Happy the man whose wish and care
 A few paternal acres bound,
Content to breathe his native air,
 In his own ground.
[Alexander Pope: *Ode on Solitude*]

12 O happiness! our being's end and
    aim!
Good, Pleasure, Ease, Content! what-
    e'er thy name,
That something still which prompts
    th' eternal sigh,
For which we bear to live, or dare to
    die.
[Alexander Pope: *An Essay on Man* IV]

13 We are long before we are convinced that happiness is never to be found; and each believes it possessed by others, to keep alive the hope of obtaining it for himself. [Samuel Johnson: *Rasselas* XVI]

14 The only happiness a brave man ever troubled himself with asking much about was, happiness enough to get his work done. [Thomas Carlyle: *Past and Present* III.iv.]

15 Happiness and Beauty are by-products. [G. B. Shaw: *Maxims for Revolutionists*]

HAPPINESS: definitions

16 Lord of himself, though not of lands;
 And having nothing, yet hath all.

[Sir Henry Wotton: *The Character of a Happy Life*]

1 How happy is he born and taught,
That serveth not another's will;
Whose armour is his honest thought,
And simple truth his utmost skill!

[Sir Henry Wotton: *The Character of a Happy Life*]

2 Happiness . . . is a perpetual possession of being well deceived . . . the serene and peaceful state of being a fool among knaves. [Jonathan Swift: *A Tale of a Tub*, "A Digression Concerning Madness"]

3 Little wealth,
Much health,
And a life by stealth.

[Jonathan Swift: *Journal to Stella*, June 30, 1711]

4 The wise man is happy when he gains his own approbation and the fool when he recommends himself to the applause of those about him. [Joseph Addison: *The Spectator* No. 73]

5 That all who are happy, are equally happy, is not true. A peasant and a philosopher may be equally *satisfied*, but not equally *happy*. Happiness consists in the multiplicity of agreeable consciousness. A peasant has not capacity for having equal happiness with a philosopher. [Samuel Johnson: in Boswell's *Life*, February 1766]

6 If I had no duties, and no reference to futurity, I would spend my life in driving briskly in a post-chaise with a pretty woman. [Samuel Johnson: in Boswell's *Life*, Sept. 19, 1777]

Johnson added, on reflection, that he would be even happier if the pretty woman were intelligent enough to understand his talk.

7 Happiness is no laughing matter. [Richard Whately: *Apothegms*]

8 Wherein lies happiness? In that which becks
Our ready minds to fellowship divine,
A fellowship with essence; till we shine
Full alchemiz'd, and free of space.

[Keats: *Endymion* I]

9 The supreme happiness of life is the conviction that we are loved; loved for ourselves—say rather, loved in spite of ourselves; this conviction the blind have.

[Victor Hugo: *Les Misérables* V.iv.]

10 Happy in the hope of happiness. [Logan Pearsall Smith: *Trivia*, "The Afternoon Post"]

11 Happiness is a wine of the rarest vintage, and seems insipid to a vulgar taste. [Logan Pearsall Smith: *Afterthoughts*]

12 Happiness is probably only a passing accident. For a moment or two the organism is irritated so little that it is not conscious of it; for the duration of that moment it is happy. Thus a hog is always happier than a man, and a bacillus is happier than a hog. [H. L. Mencken: in the *American Mercury*, March 1930]

HAPPINESS: imperfect

13 We must expect of man the latest day,
Nor e'er he die, he's happy, can we say.

[Ovid: *Metamorphoses* III, quoted in Montaigne's *Essays* I. xviii (trans. John Florio)]

14 Happiness is not found in self-contemplation; it is perceived only when it is reflected from another. [Samuel Johnson: *The Idler* No. 41]

15 There comes
For ever something between us and what
We deem our happiness.

[Byron: *Sardanapalus* I]

16 The laws of the cosmos seem to be as little concerned about human felicity as the laws of the United States are concerned about human decency. Whoever set them in motion apparently had something quite different in mind—something that we cannot even guess at. [H. L. Mencken: in the *American Mercury*, March 1930]

HAPPINESS: requisites

17 Whoever does not regard what he has as most ample wealth, is unhappy, though he be master of the world. [Epicurus: *Fragments*]

18 No man is happy unless he believes he is. [Publilius Syrus: *Maxims*]

19 A sound mind in a sound body, is a short but full description of a happy state in this world. He that has these two, has little more to wish for; and he that wants either of them, will be little the better for anything else. [John Locke: *Some Thoughts Concerning Education*]

1 To be happy one must have a good stomach and a bad heart. [Fontenelle: *Dialogues des morts*]

2 Happiness is nothing if it is not known, and very little if it is not envied. [Samuel Johnson: *The Idler* No. 80]

3 It is neither wealth nor splendor, but tranquility and occupation, which give happiness. [Thomas Jefferson: Letter to Mrs. A. S. Marks (1788)]

4   All who joy would win
Must share it,—Happiness was born a
                                   twin.
[Byron: *Don Juan* II.clxxii.]

5 Happiness lies in the consciousness we have of it. [George Sand: *Handsome Lawrence* III]

6 The first requisite for the happiness of the people is the abolition of religion. [Karl Marx: *A Criticism of the Hegelian Philosophy of Right*]

7 Melchisedec was a really happy man. He was without father, without mother and without descent. He was an incarnate bachelor. He was a born orphan. [Samuel Butler (1835-1902): *Notebooks*]

8 The formula for complete happiness is to be very busy with the unimportant. [A. Edward Newton: *This Book-Collecting Game*]

9 A happy life must be to a great extent a quiet life, for it is only in an atmosphere of quiet that true joy can live. [Bertrand Russell: *The Conquest of Happiness*]

HAPPINESS: miscellaneous

10 The majority of men devote the greater part of their lives to making their remaining years unhappy. [La Bruyère: *Les Caractères*]

11 A great obstacle to happiness is to expect too much happiness. [Fontenelle: *Du Bonheur*]

12 With these celestial Wisdom calms
                                   the mind,
And makes the happiness she does
                                   not find.
[Samuel Johnson: *The Vanity of Human Wishes*]
these = faith, hope and patience

13 Still to ourselves in every place consigned,
Our own felicity we make or find.
[Samuel Johnson: lines added to Oliver Goldsmith's *The Traveller* (1763)]

14 I firmly believe, notwithstanding all our complaints, that almost every person upon earth tastes upon the totality more happiness than misery. [Horace Walpole: Letter to the Countess of Upper Ossory, Jan. 19, 1777]

15 The greatest happiness of the greatest number is the foundation of morals and legislation. [Jeremy Bentham: *The Commonplace Book* (1830)]

Bentham attributes the famous sentiment to "Priestley . . . unless it was Beccaria." It is to be found in Beccaria's Trattato dei Delitti e Delle Pene *(1764), in the Introduction. But Bentham seems to have erred in thinking he may have had it from Priestley. It was, rather, from Francis Hutcheson's* Inquiry Concerning Moral Good and Evil *(1720): "That action is best which procures the greatest happiness for the greatest numbers."*

16 The happiest women, like the happiest nations, have no history. [George Eliot: *The Mill on the Floss* VI]

17 What right have we to happiness? [Henrik Ibsen: *Ghosts* I]

18 Behind the door of every contented, happy man there ought to be someone standing with a little hammer and continually reminding him with a knock that there are unhappy people, that however happy he may be, life will sooner or later show him its claws, and trouble will come to him—illness, poverty, losses, and then no one will see or hear him, just as now he neither sees nor hears others. [Anton Chekhov: *Gooseberries*]

19 We have no more right to consume happiness without producing it than to consume wealth without producing it. [G. B. Shaw: *Candida* I]

20 A lifetime of happiness! It would be hell on earth. [G. B. Shaw: *Man and Superman* I]

21 Happy days are here again,
The skies above are clear again.
Let us sing a song of cheer again,
Happy days are here again!
[Jack Yellen: *Happy Days are Here*

Again (in the show *Chasing Rainbows,* 1929)]

It is a confirmation of the more cynical definitions of happiness that this song was wildly popular in 1929 as the bubble of speculation broke and we plunged into the depression. And it is a confirmation of the more pessimistic estimates of the intelligence of the masses that it had a revival as the theme song of F. D. Roosevelt's campaign in 1936, when every sign indicated the imminence of World War II.

HAPPY
1 He is not happy that knoweth not himself happy.
[Richard Taverner: *Proverbs* (1539)]

The observation is ancient. It appears in the Sententiae *of Publilius Syrus (1st century B.C.) and in the* Rambler *No. 150 by Samuel Johnson (1751).*

2 None must be counted happy till his last funeral rites are paid.
[Ovid: *Metamorphoses* III]

Ovid is but one of many of the ancients to make this observation. It was a favorite theme. Aeschylus, in Agamemnon *(928): "Only when a man's life comes to its end in prosperity dare we call him happy." Sophocles: "Of no man judge the destiny, to call it good or evil, till he die" (Trachiniae). Euripides: "Call no mortal blest till thou hast seen his dying day" (Andromache).*

It was, apparently, a proverb. The idea is not that death itself is the crowning blessing, but that a life of happiness may be plunged into sorrow at even the last hour, that while there's life there's danger, and that the ills of life increase in old age.

3 I were but little happy, if I could say how much.
[Shakespeare: *Much Ado About Nothing* II.i.]

4 One is never as happy or as unhappy as one thinks. [La Rochefoucauld: *Maxims*]

5 No man is happy but by comparison. [Thomas Shadwell: *Virtuoso* II]

6 He is happy that knoweth not himself to be otherwise. [Thomas Fuller (1654-1734): *Gnomologia*]

7 The only way to be happy is to shut yourself up in art, and count everything else as nothing. [Gustave Flaubert: Letter to Louise Colet, 1845]

8 The world is so full of a number of things,
I'm sure we should all be as happy as kings.
[R. L. Stevenson: *A Child's Garden of Verses,* "Happy Thought"]

9 There is no duty we so much underrate as the duty of being happy. [R. L. Stevenson: *An Apology for Idlers*]

HARANGUE
10 What is the short meaning of this long harangue? [Schiller: *Die Piccolomini* I.ii (trans. Samuel Taylor Coleridge)]

HARDY, THOMAS
11 Hardy became a sort of village atheist brooding and blaspheming over the village idiot. [G. K. Chesterton: *The Victorian Age in Literature* II]

HARE
12 Hold with the hare and run with the hounds. [Humphrey Robert: *Complaint for Reformation* (1572)]

Already by this date, however, a proverb for duplicity.

HARLOT
13 He was a gentil harlot and a kinde.
[Chaucer: Prologue to *The Canterbury Tales*]

harlot = *rascal*

Chaucer is referring to that alcohol-soaked piece of human flotsam, the stumblebum blackmailer, the Summoner. Harlot is one of many words in English that acquired a worse meaning when applied exclusively to women.

14 For the lips of a strange woman drop as an honeycomb, and her mouth is smoother than oil:
But her end is bitter as wormwood, sharp as a two-edged sword.
Her feet go down to death; her steps take hold on hell. [Proverbs 5:3-5]

15 The harlot's cry from street to street
Shall weave old England's winding-sheet.
[William Blake: *Auguries of Innocence*]

16 But most thro' midnight streets I hear

How the youthful Harlot's curse
Blasts the new born Infant's tear,
And blights with plagues the Mar-
riage hearse.
[William Blake: *London*]

HARM
1 He is not harmless who harms himself. [Joseph Joubert: *Pensées*]

HARMONY
2 Untwisting all the chains that tie
The hidden soul of harmony.
[John Milton: *L'Allegro*]
3 Dust as we are, the immortal spirit
grows
Like harmony in music; there is a
dark
Inscrutable workmanship that recon-
ciles
Discordant elements, makes them
cling together
In one society.
[Wordsworth: *The Prelude* I]

HARP(S)
4 We hanged our harps upon the wil-
lows. [Psalms 137:2]
5 I heard the voice of harpers harping
with their harps. [Revelation 14:2]
6 Harp not on that string.
[Shakespeare: *Richard III* IV.iv.]
7 The harp that once thro' Tara's halls
The soul of music shed,
Now hangs as mute on Tara's walls
As if that soul were fled.
[Thomas Moore: *The Harp that Once*]

HARROW
8 The frog said to the harrow, Cursed
be so many lords. [13th-century saying]
*To the Middle Ages the helplessness of a
frog beneath a harrow typified the peasant under the brutalities and exactions
of the lord. By the 17th century, lords
had become masters.*
*Today a toad under a harrow simply
typifies any man enduring troubles.
Compare Kipling's (Pagett, M.P.):*
*The toad beneath the harrow knows
Exactly where each tooth-point goes,
The butterfly upon the road
Preaches contentment to that toad.*

HART
9 As the hart panteth after the water-

brooks, so panteth my soul after thee.
[Psalms 42:1]

HARVEST
10 The harvest is past, the summer is
ended, and we are not saved. [Jeremiah
8:20]
11 The harvest truly is plenteous, but the
labourers are few. [Matthew 9:37]
12 And thus of all my harvest hope I
have
Nought reaped but a weedye crop of
care.
[Edmund Spenser: *The Shepheardes
Calender,* "December"]

HARVEY, WILLIAM
13 I have heard him [Dr. William Har-
vey] say that after his book of the Circulation of the Blood came out, that he fell
mightily in his practice, and that 'twas
believed by the vulgar that he was crack-
brained. [John Aubrey: *Brief Lives* I]
*It is a chastening reflection, that so im-
portant a medical discovery damaged
the practice of the physician who made
it.*

HASTE: causes trouble
14 For hasty man ne wanteth never care.
[Chaucer: *Troilus and Criseyde* IV]
wanteth = *lacks for*
15 Ther nis no werkman, what-so-ever he
be,
That may bothe werke wel and
hastily.
[Chaucer: *The Merchant's Tale*]
16 Yet, wilful man, he never would fore-
cast
How many mischiefs should ensue his
heedless haste.
[Edmund Spenser: *The Faerie Queene*
I.iii.]
17 Haste comes not alone. [George Herbert: *Jacula Prudentum*]
*That is, excessive or unwise haste almost
always brings some ill in its train.*
18 Good and quickly seldom meet.
[George Herbert: *Outlandish Proverbs*]
19 Haste makes waste, and waste makes
want, and want makes strife between the
goodman and his wife. [John Ray: *English Proverbs*]
20 Raw Haste, half-sister to Delay.
[Tennyson: *Love Thou Thy Land*]

HASTE: make haste slowly

1 Make haste slowly. [Caesar Augustus: quoted in Suetonius, *Divus Augustus* XXV]

The Latin is Festina lente.

Suetonius says this was Augustus's favorite proverb and advice. It was also Erasmus's favorite maxim.

2 He hasteth well that wisely can abide. [Chaucer: *Troilus and Criseyde* I]

3 I knew a wise man that had it for a by-word, when he saw men hasten to a conclusion, *Stay a little, that we may make an end the sooner.* [Francis Bacon: *Of Dispatch*]

In another of his works (Apothegms 76), *Bacon says that the wise man was Sir Amice Pawlet, the grim warden who kept such strict watch over Mary Queen of Scots.*

4 He tires betimes that spurs too fast betimes. [Shakespeare: *Richard II* II.i.]

5 Stay a while, that we may end the sooner. [George Herbert: *Jacula Prudentum*]

6 It's no use making haste; the thing to do is to set out in time. [La Fontaine: *Fables* VI]

HASTE: miscellaneous

7   This sweaty haste
Doth make the night joint-labourer with the day.
[Shakespeare: *Hamlet* I.i.]

8 If it were done when 'tis done, then 'twere well
It were done quickly.
[Shakespeare: *Macbeth* I.vii.]

9 Celerity is never more admired
Than by the negligent.
[Shakespeare: *Antony and Cleopatra* III.vii.]

10 Haste and hurry are very different things. [Lord Chesterfield: *Letters*, August 20, 1749]

11 Though I am always in haste, I am never in a hurry. [John Wesley: *Letters*, December 10, 1777]

12 Three things only are well done in haste: flying from the plague, escaping quarrels, and catching flies. [H. G. Bohn: *Handbook of Proverbs*]

HAT(S)

13 As with my hat upon my head
I walk'd along the Strand,
I there did meet another man
With his hat in his hand.
[Samuel Johnson: in *Johnsonian Miscellanies* II]

Johnson was burlesquing the silly sooth of the ballads.

14 A hat not much the worse for wear. [William Cowper: *History of John Gilpin*]

15 I never saw so many shocking bad hats in my life. [Attr. the Duke of Wellington; upon his seeing the first Reformed Parliament]

HATE

16 Hatred is inveterate anger. [Cicero: *Tusculanae Disputationes* IV]

17 The bitterest hatred is that of near relations. [Tacitus: *History* IV.70]

"A study of 150 murders in Denver since Jan. 1, 1958, indicates that 46 per cent were committed by members of the victim's own family."

AP dispatch in the New York Times, *May 20, 1963.*

18 It is human nature to hate those whom we have injured. [Tactitus: *Agricola* XLII]

19 Unimaginable as hate in Heav'n. [John Milton: *Paradise Lost* VII.54]

20 All men naturally hate each other. [Pascal: *Pensées*]

21 Men hate more steadily than they love; and if I have said something to hurt a man once, I shall not get the better of this by saying many things to please him. [Samuel Johnson: in Boswell's *Life*, September 15, 1777]

22 Short is the road that leads from fear to hate. [Giambattista Casti (1721-1804): *Gli Animali Parlanti* IX.cxi.]

23 National hatred is something peculiar. You will always find it strongest and most violent where there is the lowest degree of culture. [Goethe: *Conversations with Eckermann*, March 14, 1830]

24 Detestation of the high is the involuntary homage of the low. [Dickens: *A Tale of Two Cities* I]

25   . . . to be choked with hate
May well be of all evil chances chief.
[William Butler Yeats: *A Prayer for My Daughter*]

26 The most malicious kind of hatred is

that which is built upon a theological foundation. [George Sarton: *The History of Science and the New Humanism*]

HATE: merits of

1 Hate is gained through good deeds as well as bad ones. [Machiavelli: *The Prince* XIX]
2 What a man hateth, the same thing he takes to heart. [Montaigne: *Essays* I.i.]
3 Now hatred is by far the longest
                   pleasure;
Men love in haste, but they detest at
                   leisure.
[Byron: *Don Juan* XIII.vi.]
4 It does not matter much what a man hates provided he hates something. [Samuel Butler (1835-1902): *Notebooks*]
5 Love, friendship, respect, do not unite people as much as a common hatred for something. [Chekhov: *Notebooks*]
6 We must hate—hatred is the basis of Communism. Children must be taught to hate their parents if they are not Communists. [Lenin: in a speech to the Commissars of Education, Moscow, 1923]

HATER

7 I like a good hater. [Samuel Johnson: in Mrs. Piozzi's *Anecdotes of the late Samuel Johnson* (1786)]
8 Dear Bathurst . . . was a man to my very heart's content: he hated a fool, and he hated a rogue, and hated a *whig;* he was a very good *hater.* [Samuel Johnson: in Mrs. Piozzi's *Anecdotes of the late Samuel Johnson* (1786)]
    The reference is to Dr. Richard Bathurst (d. 1762), Dr. Johnson's dearest friend.

HAVE AND HAVE NOT

9 Unto every one that hath shall be given, and he shall have abundance; but from him that hath not shall be taken away even that which he hath. [Matthew 25:29]
10 He that hath, to him shall be given; and he that hath not, from him shall be taken even that which he hath. [Mark 4:25]
11 There are only two families in the world . . . the Haves and the Havenots. [Cervantes: *Don Quixote* II.xx.]
    The text indicates that the saying was proverbial.
    Ernest Hemingway entitled one of his novels To Have and Have Not *(1937).*
12 Have more than thou showest,
Speak less than thou knowest,
Lend less than thou owest.
[Shakespeare: *King Lear* I.iv.]
13 Them ez hez, gits. [Edward Rowland Sill: *A Baker's Duzzen Uv Wize Sawz*]
14 The' ain't nothin' truer in the Bible 'n that sayin' thet them that has gits. [E. N. Westcott: *David Harum* XXXV]

TO HAVE AND TO HOLD

15 Take, have, and keep are pleasant words. [Thomas Hardy: *The Mayor of Casterbridge* XIV]

HAZARD

16 A hazard of new fortunes.
[Shakespeare: *King John* II.i.]
    Used as the title of a novel by William Dean Howells (1890).
17   I have set my life upon a cast,
And I will stand the hazard of the
                   die.
[Shakespeare: *Richard III* V.iv.]
18   Were it good
To set the exact wealth of all our
                states
All at one cast? to set so rich a main
On the nice hazard of one doubtful
                hour?
[Shakespeare: *I Henry IV* IV.i.]

HAZLITT

19 Though we are mighty fine fellows nowadays, we cannot write like Hazlitt. [R. L. Stevenson: *Virginibus Puerisque,* "Walking Tours"]

HEAD

20 A man indeed ought not to cover his head, forasmuch as he is the image and glory of God: but the woman is the glory of the man. [I Corinthians 11:7]
21 Two heads are better than one. [John Heywood: *Proverbs*]
22 The head is always the dupe of the heart. [La Rochefoucauld: *Maxims*]
23 Off with his head—so much for Buckingham. [Colley Cibber: *Richard III*

IV.iii.]

Cibber seems to have transferred and embellished Shakespeare's III Henry VI *V.v.: "For Somerset, off with his guilty head."*

In the lesson in history which Huck Finn gives Jim (Huckleberry Finn, XXIII, "The Orneriness of Kings") the phrase is transferred to Henry VIII and applied to Nell Gwynn, Jane Shore, Fair Rosamond and Bluebeard's wives. In the process Henry gets confused with William the Conqueror, George III and the Caliph Haroun al Raschid. It's a magnificent passage.

1 'Tis strange how like a very dunce
Man, with his bumps upon his sconce,
Has lived so long, and yet no knowl-
edge he
Has had, till lately, of Phrenology.
[Thomas Hood: *Craniology*]

2 "Talking of axes," said the Duchess, "chop off her head!" [Lewis Carroll: *Alice's Adventures in Wonderland* VI]

3 The Queen turned crimson with fury, and after glaring at her for a moment like a wild beast, began screaming, "Off with her head! Off with—" [Lewis Carroll: *Alice's Adventures in Wonderland* VIII]

HEALING

4 What wound did ever heal but by
degrees?
[Shakespeare: *Othello* II.iii.]

5 It never will get well if you pick it. [H. L. Mencken: in the *American Mercury*, November 1933]

HEALTH

6 To wish to be well is a part of becoming well. [Seneca: *Phaedra*]

7 Tiberius was wont to mock at the arts of physicians, and at those who, after thirty years of age, needed counsel as to what was good or bad for their bodies. [Plutarch: *Morals*, p. 514]

Suetonius (Divus Tiberius LXVIII) says that from the age of 30 on Tiberius enjoyed excellent health: "He took care of it according to his own ideas, without the aid or advice of physicians."

8 A sound mind in a sound body. (*Mens sana in corpore sano*) [Juvenal: *Satires* X]

9 Despise no new accident in your body, but ask opinion of it. [Francis Bacon: *Of Regimen of Health*]

accident = anything which happens, any change

10 It is a safer conclusion to say, *This agreeth not well with me, therefore I will not continue it;* than this, *I find no offence of this, therefore I may use it.* [Francis Bacon: *Of Regimen of Health*]

11 There is a wisdom in this beyond the rules of physic: a man's own observation what he finds good of and what he finds hurt of is the best physic to preserve health. [Francis Bacon: *Of Regimen of Health*]

physic = medicine in general

12 Celsus could never have spoken it as a physician had he not been a wise man withal, when he giveth it for one of the great precepts of health and lasting, that a man do vary and interchange contraries, but with an inclination to the more benign extreme: use fasting and full eating, but rather full eating; watching and sleep, but rather sleep; sitting and exercise, but rather exercise, and the like. [Francis Bacon: *Of Regimen of Health*]

watching = waking

Aulus Cornelius Celsus was a Roman writer of the 1st century A.D. Bacon twists Celsus's words a little; all Celsus says is not to become a slave to a uniform mode of life.

13 I was well; I would be better; I am here. [Anon.]

Epitaph on the tombstone of an Italian health-improver, quoted by Addison in The Spectator No. 25.

14 Health and cheerfulness mutually beget each other. [Joseph Addison: *The Spectator* No. 387]

15 Measure your health by your sympathy with morning and Spring. [Thoreau: *Journal*, February 25, 1859]

16 Objection, evasion, distrust and irony are signs of health. Everything absolute belongs to pathology. [Nietzsche: *Beyond Good and Evil*]

17 It is better to lose health like a spendthrift than to waste it like a miser. [R. L. Stevenson: *Aes Triplex*]

18 Health—silliest word in our language, and one knows so well the popular idea

of health. The English country gentleman galloping after a fox—the unspeakable in full pursuit of the uneatable. [Oscar Wilde: *A Woman of No Importance* I]
1 What is the thing called health? Simply a state in which the individual happens transiently to be perfectly adapted to his environment. Obviously, such states cannot be common, for the environment is in constant flux. [H. L. Mencken: in the *American Mercury*, March 1930]

HEAR
2 Strike, but hear me. [Themistocles: in Plutarch's *Life of Themistocles* II.iii.]
Themistocles's adjuration to one who in an argument threatened to strike him.

HEART: the evil heart
3 For the imagination of man's heart is evil from his youth. [Genesis 8:21]
4 The heart is deceitful above all things, and desperately wicked. [Jeremiah 17:9]
5 For when my outward action doth demonstrate
The native act and figure of my heart
In compliment extern, 'tis not long after
But I will wear my heart upon my sleeve
For daws to peck at. I am not what I am.
[Shakespeare: *Othello* I.i.]
Iago speaking.

HEART: the receptive and joyous heart
6 Create in me a clean heart, O God; and renew a right spirit within me. [Psalms 51:10]
Clene hert make in me, God, and trewe,
And right gaste in mi guttes newe.
Early English Psalter (*about 1300*)
7 A man after his own heart. [I Samuel 13:14]
8 Enough of Science and of Art;
Close up those barren leaves;
Come forth, and bring with you a heart
That watches and receives.
[Wordsworth: *The Tables Turned*]
9 Here's a sigh to those who love me,

And a smile to those who hate;
And whatever sky's above me,
Here's a heart for every fate.
[Byron: in a letter to Thomas Moore, July 10, 1817]
10 The song and the silence in the heart,
That in part are prophecies, and in part
Are longings wild and vain.
[Longfellow: *My Lost Youth*]
11 Art is long. and Time is fleeting,
And our hearts, though stout and brave,
Still, like muffled drums, are beating
Funeral marches to the grave.
[Longfellow: *A Psalm of Life*]
12   She had
A heart—how shall I say?—too soon made glad.
[Robert Browning: *My Last Duchess*]
13 If a good face is a letter of recommendation, a good heart is a letter of credit. [E. G. Bulwer-Lytton: *What Will He Do With It?* II.xi.]
14 My heart is like a singing bird
Whose nest is in a watered shoot;
My heart is like an apple-tree
Whose boughs are bent with thickset fruit.
[Christina Rossetti: *A Birthday*]

HEART: the sad and broken heart
15 A broken and a contrite heart, O God, thou wilt not despise. [Psalms 51:17]
"Still stands Thine ancient sacrifice,
An humble and a contrite heart."
                Kipling: Recessional
16 The heart knoweth his own bitterness; and a stranger doth not intermeddle with his joy. [Proverbs 14:10]
17 Let not your heart be troubled. [John 14:1]
18 A heavy heart bears not a humble tongue.
[Shakespeare: *Love's Labour's Lost* V. ii.]
19 As dear to me as are the ruddy drops
That visit my sad heart.
[Shakespeare: *Julius Caesar* II.i.]
20 I prithee send me back my heart,
Since I cannot have thine:
For if from thine thou wilt not part,
Why then shouldst thou have mine?

[Sir John Suckling: *Song*]

1 They mourn, but smile at length;
and, smiling, mourn;
The tree will wither long before it
fall;
The hull drives on, though mast and
sail be torn;
The roof-tree sinks, but moulders on
the hall
In massy hoariness; the ruined wall
Stands when its wind-worn battlements are gone;
The bars survive the captive they en-
thral;
The day drags through, though
storms keep out the sun;
And thus the heart will break, yet
brokenly live on.

[Byron: *Childe Harold* III.xxxii.]

2 "There are strings," said Mr. Tapper-
tit, ". . . in the human heart that had
better not be wibrated." [Dickens: *Barnaby Rudge* XXII]

3 My heart is a lonely hunter that
hunts on a lonely hill. [William Sharp
("Fiona Macleod"): *The Lonely Hunter*]
*Best known today for its adaptation as
the title of a novel by Carson McCullers,
The Heart is a Lonely Hunter (1940).*

4 When I was one-and-twenty
I heard a wise man say,
"Give crowns and pounds and guin-
eas
But not your heart away;
Give pearls away and rubies
But keep your fancy free."
But I was one-and-twenty,
No use to talk to me.

When I was one-and-twenty
I heard him say again,
"The heart out of the bosom
Was never given in vain;
'Tis paid with sighs a plenty
And sold for endless rue."
And I am two-and-twenty,
And oh, 'tis true, 'tis true.

[A. E. Housman: *A Shropshire Lad*
XIII]

HEART: thought, speech and action

5 Faint heart makes feeble hand. [Eu-
ripides: *Suppliants*]

6 As he thinketh in his heart, so is he.
[Proverbs 23:7]

7 Where your treasure is, there will
your heart be also. [Matthew 6:21]

8 He hath a heart as sound as a bell,
and his tongue is the clapper; for what
his heart thinks his tongue speaks.
[Shakespeare: *Much Ado About Nothing* III.ii.]

9 The heart has its reasons which reason cannot know. [Pascal: *Pensées* IV]

10 If wrong our hearts, our heads are
right in vain. [Edward Young: *Night
Thoughts* VI]

11 Nine times in ten the heart governs
the understanding. [Lord Chesterfield:
Letters to His Son, May 15, 1749]

12 The brave, impetuous heart yields
everywhere to the subtle, contriving
head. [Matthew Arnold: *Empedocles on
Etna*]

13   . . . the heart is slow to learn
What the swift mind beholds at every
turn.

[Edna St. Vincent Millay: *Pity Me Not*]

HEARTACHE

14 My heart aches, and a drowsy numb-
ness pains
My sense, as though of hemlock I had
drunk,
Or emptied some dull opiate to the
drains
One minute past, and Lethe-wards
had sunk.

[Keats: *Ode to a Nightingale*]

HEARTBREAK

15   Never morning wore
To evening, but some heart did break.

[Tennyson: *In Memoriam* VI]
*Tennyson had been reading the Second
Book of the* De rerum natura *of Lucretius. But the Latin writer is much
stronger:*
*Never did night follow day or dawn
follow night but there was heard the
wailing of the newborn mixed with
the shrill lamentations attending
death.*

16 How else but through a broken heart
May Lord Christ enter in?

[Oscar Wilde: *The Ballad of Reading
Gaol*]

HEARTH

17 Where glowing embers through the
room

Teach light to counterfeit a gloom,
Far from all resort of mirth,
Save the cricket on the hearth.
[John Milton: *Il Penseroso*]

HEAT

1 Heat not a furnace for your foe so
hot
That it do singe yourself.
[Shakespeare: *Henry VIII* I.i.]
2 "Heat, ma'am," I said; "it was so
dreadful here, that I found there was
nothing left for it but to take off my
flesh and sit in my bones." [Sydney
Smith: in Lady Holland's *Memoir* I.vii.]

HEATHEN

3 Why do the heathen rage, and the
people imagine a vain thing? [*Psalms*
2:1]
4 What though the spicy breezes
Blow soft o'er Ceylon's isle;
Though every prospect pleases,
And only man is vile:
In vain with lavish kindness
The gifts of God are strown;
The heathen, in his blindness,
Bows down to wood and stone.
[Reginald Heber: *From Greenland's Icy
Mountains* (1819)]

> The 'eathen in 'is blindness bows down
> to wood an' stone;
> 'E don't obey no orders unless they is 'is
> own;
> 'E keeps 'is side-arms awful: 'e leaves 'em
> all about,
> An' then comes up the Regiment an'
> pokes the 'eathen out.
> Rudyard Kipling: The 'Eathen

HEAVEN: descriptions of

5 When they shall rise from the dead,
they neither marry, nor are given in marriage; but are as the angels which are in
heaven. [*Mark* 12:25]
6 In my Father's house are many mansions. [*John* 14:2]

> Mansion, *which now suggests an impos-
> ing or stately residence, the sort of thing
> one would expect in Heaven, originally
> meant simply a dwelling place. The* New
> English Bible *has* "many dwelling-
> places"; *the* Revised Standard, "many
> rooms" (which is disappointing; one
> doesn't want to be a roomer in Heaven).

> There are, by the way, many mansions
> in Hell too. Milton speaks of "her dolor-
> ous mansions" and Dryden of "Th' In-
> fernal Mansions."

7 Heaven lies about us in our infancy.
[Wordsworth: *Intimations of Immortality*]
8 A Persian's heaven is easily made:
'Tis but black eyes and lemonade.
[Thomas Moore: *Intercepted Letters*
VI]
9 Heaven but the Vision of fulfilled
Desire.
[*Rubáiyát of Omar Khayyám* (trans. Edward FitzGerald)]
10 Heaven might be defined as the place
which men avoid. [Thoreau: *Excur-
sions*]
11 Jerusalem the golden, with milk and
honey blest,
Beneath thy contemplation sink heart
and voice opprest.
I know not, oh, I know not, what
joys await us there,
What radiancy of glory, what bliss
beyond compare.
[John Mason Neale: *Jerusalem the
Golden* (trans. from the Latin *Urbs
Syon Aurea*)]
12 In our English popular religion the
common conception of a future state of
bliss is that of . . . a kind of perfected
middle-class home, with labor ended, the
table spread, goodness all around, the
lost ones restored, hymnody incessant.
[Matthew Arnold: *Literature and
Dogma* XII]

HEAVEN: and Hell

13 A thousand tymes have I herd men
telle,
That ther is Joye in heven and
peyne in helle;
And I accorde wel that hit is so;
But natheles, yit wot I wel also,
That ther nis noon dwelling in this
contree,
That either hath in heven or helle
y-be,
Ne may of hit non other weyes witen,
But as he hath herd seyd, or founde
hit writen.
[Chaucer: Prologue to *The Legend of
Good Women*]
wot = *know;* witen = *know*

1 I desire to go to Hell, not to Heaven. In Hell I shall enjoy the company of popes, kings and princes, but in Heaven are only beggars, monks, hermits and apostles. [Machiavelli: On his death-bed]

2 Better to reign in hell than serve in heaven.
[John Milton: *Paradise Lost* I.263]

3 Hell was built on spite, and Heav'n on pride.
[Alexander Pope: *An Essay on Man* III]

4 In hope to merit Heaven by making earth a Hell.
[Byron: *Childe Harold* I.xx.]

5 I sent my Soul through the Invisible
Some letter of that After-life to spell:
And by and by my Soul returned to me,
And answered, "I Myself am Heaven and Hell."
Heaven but the Vision of fulfilled Desire,
And Hell the Shadow from a Soul on fire
Cast on the Darkness into which Ourselves
So late emerged from, shall so soon expire.
[*Rubáiyát of Omar Khayyám* (trans. Edward FitzGerald)]

6 Heaven for climate, hell for company.
[J. M. Barrie: *The Little Minister* III]
In America this came to be attributed to Mark Twain.

7 It took me forty years on earth
To reach this sure conclusion:
There is no Heaven but clarity,
No Hell except confusion.
[Jan Struther: *All Clear*]

HEAVEN: the way to
8 We may not looke at our pleasure to goe to heauen in Fetherbeddes. [Attr. Sir Thomas More]

9 Do not, as some ungracious pastors do,
Show me the steep and thorny way to heaven,
Whiles, like a puff'd and reckless libertine,
Himself the primrose path of dalliance treads,
And recks not his own rede.
[Shakespeare: *Hamlet* I.iii.]

10 I can hardly think there was ever any scared into Heaven; they go the fairest way to Heaven that would serve God without a Hell. [Sir Thomas Browne: *Religio Medici* I.lii.]

HEAVEN: miscellaneous
11 Lay up for yourselves treasures in heaven, where neither moth nor rust doth corrupt and where thieves do not break through nor steal. [Matthew 6:20]

12 I will give unto thee the keys of the kingdom of heaven: and whatsoever thou shalt bind on earth shall be bound in heaven; and whatsoever thou shalt loose on earth shall be loosed in heaven. [Matthew 16:19]

13 There are more things in heaven and earth, Horatio,
Than are dreamt of in your philosophy.
[Shakespeare: *Hamlet* I.v.]

14 A heaven on earth.
[John Milton: *Paradise Lost* IV.208]

15 All this and heaven too. [Matthew Henry: *Life of Philip Henry*]

16 I remember, I remember
The fir-trees dark and high;
I used to think their slender tops
Were close against the sky:
It was a childish ignorance,
But now 'tis little joy
To know I'm farther off from heaven
Than when I was a boy.
[Thomas Hood: *I Remember, I Remember*]

17 Ah, but a man's reach should exceed his grasp,
Or what's a heaven for?
[Robert Browning: *Andrea del Sarto*]

18 And so upon this wise I prayed—
Great Spirit, give to me
A heaven not so large as yours
But large enough for me.
[Emily Dickinson: *A Prayer*]

HEBRIDES
19 Whether beyond the stormy Hebrides,
Where thou perhaps under the whelming tide
Visit'st the bottom of the monstrous world.
[John Milton: *Lycidas*]

20   The Atlantic surge

Pours in among the stormy Hebrides.
[James Thomson (1700-1748): *The Seasons,* "Autumn"]

1 Round the moist marge of each cold
   Hebrid isle.
[William Collins: *Ode on the Popular Superstitions of the Highlands*]

2 A voice so thrilling ne'er was heard
   In spring-time from the Cuckoo bird,
   Breaking the silence of the seas
   Among the farthest Hebrides.
[Wordsworth: *The Solitary Reaper*]

3 From the lone shieling of the misty
                              island
   Mountains divide us, and the waste
                           of seas—
   Yet still the blood is strong, the heart
                       is Highland,
   And we in dreams behold the Heb-
                              rides.
[John Galt: *Canadian Boat Song*]
*Also attr. to John Wilson ("Christopher
North"), Scott, Hogg and D. M. Moir.*

HECUBA

4 What's Hecuba to him or he to Hec-
                              uba,
   That he should weep for her?
[Shakespeare: *Hamlet* II.ii.]

HEEDLESS

5 But how can he expect that others
                           should
   Build for him, sow for him, and at
                        his call
   Love him, who for himself will take
                     no heed at all?
[Wordsworth: *Resolution and Independence*]

HEIGHT

6 Come down, O maid, from yonder
                     mountain height.
   What pleasure lives in height (the
                     shepherd sang)?
[Tennyson: *The Princess* VII]

HEIR(ESS)

7 All heiresses are beautiful.
[Dryden: *King Arthur* I.i.]

8 I, the heir of all the ages, in the fore-
                     most files of time.
[Tennyson: *Locksley Hall*]

HELEN OF TROY

9 Was this the face that launched a
                     thousand ships,
   And burnt the topless towers of Il-
                              ium?
[Christopher Marlowe: *Dr. Faustus* XIV]

HELL: definitions, descriptions
and topography

10 Where their worm dieth not, and the
   fire is not quenched. [Mark 9:44]

11 The descent to hell is easy; the gates
   stand open night and day; but to re-
   climb the slope, and escape to the upper
   air, this is labor. [Vergil: *Aeneid* VI]
   Smooth the descent and easy is the way;
   (The Gates of Hell stand open night and
                              day);
   But to return, and view the cheerful
                              skies,
   In this the task and mighty labour lies.
                     —Dryden's trans.

12   In the throat
   Of Hell, before the very vestibule
   Of opening Orcus, sit Remorse and
                              Grief,
   And pale Disease, and sad Old Age
                         and Fear,
   And Hunger that persuades to crime,
                         and Want:
   Forms terrible to see. Suffering and
                              Death
   Inhabit here, and Death's own
                     brother Sleep;
   And the mind's evil lusts and deadly
                              War,
   Lie at the threshold, and the iron
                              beds
   Of the Eumenides; and Discord wild
   Her viper-locks with bloody fillets
                              bound.
[Vergil: *Aeneid* VI (trans. Cranch)]

13 Hell is full of good meanings and
   wishings. [George Herbert: *Jacula Prudentum*]

14 Hell is paved with infants' skulls.
[Richard Baxter: Sermon at Kidderminster (about 1651)]
   Hazlitt (Table-Talk) says that Baxter
   was almost mobbed by the angry women
   of Kidderminster for making this state-
   ment. A similar story was told of our
   own Jonathan Edwards.

15 A dungeon horrible, on all sides
                              round,
   As one great furnace flam'd; yet from
                     those flames

No light, but rather darkness visible
Serv'd only to discover sights of woe,
Regions of sorrow, doleful shades,
where peace
And rest can never dwell, hope never
comes
That comes to all, but torture with-
out end.
[John Milton: *Paradise Lost* I.61-67]

1   Long is the way
And hard, that out of Hell leads up
to light.
[John Milton: *Paradise Lost* II.432-433]

2   Myself am Hell;
And, in the lowest deep, a lower deep,
Still threat'ning to devour me, opens
wide;
To which the Hell I suffer seems a
Heaven.
[John Milton: *Paradise Lost* IV.75-78]

3 Hell is paved with good intentions.
[Samuel Johnson: in Boswell's *Life*,
April 14, 1775]

*This is the most famous of all the speci-
fications for the pavement of Hell. Johnson didn't invent the expression, but his
wording is the one that has become accepted. Baxter paved it with infants'
skulls, Giles Firmin with the skulls of
scholars, and many had paved it with
good purposes, good desires, and good
intentions.*

4 A perpetual holiday is a good working definition of hell. [G. B. Shaw: *Parents and Children*]

5 Hell is the place where the satisfied
compare disappointments. [Philip Moeller: *Madame Sand* II]

6 The religion of Hell is patriotism,
and the government is an enlightened democracy. [James Branch Cabell: *Jurgen*
XXXVIII]

HELL: miscellaneous

7 The wicked shall be turned into hell,
and all the nations that forget God.
[Psalms 9:17]

8 Hell/Grew darker at their frown.
[John Milton: *Paradise Lost* II.719-720]

9 But wherefore thou alone? Wherefore
with thee
Came not all Hell broke loose?
[John Milton: *Paradise Lost* IV.917-918]
The Archangel Gabriel taunting Satan

*after Ithuriel and Zephon have seized
him in the Garden of Eden.*

*The expression "hell broke loose" an-
tedates* Paradise Lost *almost a century
and must have been fairly common since
it had appeared several times in print.
We must assume, then, that either
Milton had not heard the phrase and
had the bad luck to blunder into it here
or—and more likely—a joking inclusion
of it was his idea of Archangelic sarcasm.*

10 From Hull, Hell and Halifax, Good
Lord, deliver us! [Thomas Fuller (1608-
1661): *Worthies of England*, "Yorkshire"
III]

*Fuller gives the saying as "part of the
beggars' and vagrants' litany."*

*Hell has a bad reputation. Hull had
a severe way with vagrants. Halifax had
two particular deterrents. One was the
belief that by "Halifax Law" a man was
executed first and tried afterwards (also
called "Lydford Law," after Lydford in
Devonshire), and the other was that malefactors at Halifax were decapitated by
a machine much like the guillotine, centuries before the guillotine was known
under that name.*

11 To rest, the cushion and soft dean invite,
Who never mentions hell to ears polite.
[Alexander Pope: *Moral Essays* IV.149]

12 Hell-bent for election. [Campaign
for the Governorship of Maine, 1840]

*Hell-bent is an American expression of
the early 19th century. It meant to be
bent on a course of action so energeti-
cally as to be heedless of all consequences, even of hell itself, and hence
determined to proceed towards a desired
end with reckless fury and speed.*

*The full phrase came into our speech
in the campaign of 1840, when Edward
Kent put up such a vigorous fight for the
governorship of Maine that he was said
to be "Hell-bent for election." He won
and his party, the Whigs, celebrated in a
song:*

*Oh have you heard how old Maine
went?*

*She went hell-bent for Governor
Kent,*

And Tippecanoe and Tyler, too!

HELLENISM AND HEBRAISM

1 The uppermost idea with Hellenism is to see things as they really are; the uppermost idea with Hebraism is conduct and obedience. [Matthew Arnold: *Culture and Anarchy* IV]

HELP

2 'Tis not enough to help the feeble up, But to support him after. [Shakespeare: *Timon of Athens* I.i.]

HELPMATE / HELPMEET

3 And the Lord God said, It is not good that the man should be alone; I will make him an help meet for him. [Genesis 2:18]

> meet = *suitable*
>
> *Wyclif had translated the phrase* an helper like hym *and Coverdale* an helpe, to beare him company. *RSV has* a helper fit for him. *New American Catholic Edition:* a help like unto himself.
>
> *In the 17th century* help *and* meet, *in the King James version, were taken to be one word, and since Adam's fit* helper *turned out to be Eve, his wife, the new compound* helpmeet *was applied to a wife or husband, usually to a wife. In the 18th century* meet *and* mate *were pronounced alike (as they are in Ireland today), and the absurd coinage was soon given a semblance of sense by being spelled* helpmate, *though the older spelling persisted alongside the new one and is still in use today, particularly among those who like to be quaintly learned.*

HEN

4 Higgledy-piggledy, my black hen, She lays eggs for gentlemen; Gentlemen come every day To see what my black hen doth lay. [Nursery rhyme; oldest printed form of this version, 1853]

> *This is, apparently, a Victorian "purification" for nursery use of an older rhyme:* "Little Blue Betty lived in a den,/She sold good ale to gentlemen." *That wasn't all she sold to gentlemen, either.*
>
> *Burns recorded several old Scotch versions, one of which states that* "aye she wagged it wantonly."

5 A hen is only an egg's way of making another egg. [Samuel Butler (1835-1902): *Life and Habit*]

HENPECKED

6 But—Oh! ye lords of ladies intellectual,
Inform us truly, have they not henpeck'd you all?
[Byron: *Don Juan* I.xxii.]

HERD

7 It is the fools and the knaves that make the wheels of the world turn. They are the world; those few who have sense or honesty sneak up and down single, but never go in herds. [George Savile, Marquis of Halifax: *Political, Moral and Miscellaneous Reflections*]

HEREAFTER

8 And rest at last where souls unbodied dwell,
In ever-flow'ring meads of asphodel.
[Homer: *Odyssey* XXIV (Alexander Pope's translation)]

> *Compare Tennyson's* "Resting weary limbs at last on beds of Asphodel." (The Lotos-Eaters)
>
> asphodel = *any of several liliaceous plants;* daffodil *is simply a variant pronunciation of* asphodel.

9 Strange, is it not? that of the myriads who
Before us passed the door of Darkness through,
Not one returns to tell us of the Road,
Which to discover we must travel too.
[*Rubáiyát of Omar Khayyám* (trans. Edward FitzGerald)]

10 Ah Christ, that it were possible
For one short hour to see
The souls we loved, that they might tell us
What and where they be.
[Tennyson: *Maud* II.iv.]

11 Where, on the banks of the forgetful streams,
The pale indifferent ghosts wander, and snatch
The sweeter moments of their broken dreams.
[Robert Bridges: *Elegy On a Lady*]

HEREDITY

12 [The] tenth transmitter of a foolish face.
[Richard Savage: *The Bastard*]

HERESY

1 If forgers and other malefactors are put to death by the secular power, there is much more reason for excommunicating and even putting to death one convicted of heresy. [St. Thomas Aquinas: *Summa Theologicae* II]
2 From all false doctrine, heresy, and schism, Good Lord, deliver us. [*The Book of Common Prayer*, "The Litany"]
3 They that approve a private opinion, call it opinion; but they that dislike it, heresy. [Thomas Hobbes: *Leviathan* Ch. 11]

HERETIC

4 A man may be a heretic in the truth; and if he believe things only because his pastor says so, or the assembly so determines, without knowing other reason, though his belief be true, yet the very truth he holds becomes his heresy. [John Milton: *Areopagitica*]

HERITAGE

5 The lines are fallen unto me in pleasant places; yea, I have a goodly heritage. [Psalms 16:6]

HERO(ES)

6 Mighty men which were of old, men of renown. [Genesis 6:4]
7 Mighty men of valour. [Joshua 6:2]
8 There were brave men before Agamemnon. [Horace: *Odes* IV.ix.]
9 There are heroes in evil as well as in good. [La Rochefoucauld: *Maxims*]
10 Whoe'er excels in what we prize, Appears a hero in our eyes.
[Jonathan Swift: *Cadenus and Vanessa*]
11 See the conquering hero comes!
Sound the trumpets, beat the drums!
[Thomas Morrell: for Handel's oratorios of *Joshua* and *Judas Maccabeus* (1747)]
Also used in later stage versions of Nathaniel Lee's The Rival Queens *II.i.*
12 A light supper, a good night's sleep, and a fine morning have sometimes made a hero of the same man who, by an indigestion, a restless night, and rainy morning would have proved a coward. [Lord Chesterfield: *Letters to his Son*, April 26, 1748]
13 Every hero becomes a bore at last. [Emerson: *Uses of Great Men*]

14 The hero is not fed on sweets, Daily his own heart he eats.
[Emerson: *Heroism*]
15 In the world's broad field of battle, In the bivouac of Life, Be not like dumb, driven cattle! Be a hero in the strife!
[Longfellow: *A Psalm of Life*]
16 Then it's Tommy this, an' Tommy that, an' "Tommy, 'ow's yer soul?" But it's "Thin red line of 'eroes" when the drums begin to roll.
[Kipling: *Tommy*]

HEROD

17 It out-herods Herod.
[Shakespeare: *Hamlet* III.ii.]
Prince Hamlet, lecturing the players on their art, says that it offends him to the soul "to hear a robustious periwig-pated fellow tear a passion to tatters, to very rags, to split the ears of the groundlings" and adds that he "would have such a fellow whipp'd for o'erdoing Termagant. It out-herods Herod."

In the old mystery plays, King Herod was represented as a bellowing, ranting, raging ruffian. He was dear to artless audiences, and successive generations of hams must have worked hard in the role. Termagant was the name the Crusaders gave to an idol or deity which they believed the Mohammedans worshipped. He, too, was introduced into the morality plays to rage and rant. His flowing robes led him to be mistaken for a woman and the word is now applied only to women.

HEROISM

18 Heroism, the Caucasian mountaineers say, is endurance for one moment more. [George Kennan: Letter to Henry Munroe Rogers, July 25, 1921]

HESITATION

19 How long halt ye between two opinions? [I Kings 18:21]

HESPERUS

20 It was the schooner Hesperus, That sailed the wintry sea; And the skipper had taken his little daughter, To bear him company.

[Longfellow: *The Wreck of the Hesperus*]

1 Such was the wreck of the Hesperus,
In the midnight and the snow!
Christ save us all from a death like
this,
On the reef of Norman's Woe!
[Longfellow: *The Wreck of the Hesperus*]

HICKORY DICKORY DOCK

2 Hickory, dickory, dock,
The mouse ran up the clock.
The clock struck one,
The mouse ran down,
Hickory, dickory, dock.
[Nursery rhyme: one of the oldest counting rhymes; earliest printed version, 1744]

HIDING PLACE

3 Thou art my hiding place; thou shalt preserve me from trouble; thou shalt compass me about with songs of deliverance. [Psalms 32:7]
4 Thou art my hiding place and my shield. [Psalms 119:114]
5 And a man shall be as an hiding place from the wind, and a covert from the tempest; as rivers of water in a dry place, as the shadow of a great rock in a weary land. [Isaiah 32:2]

HIGH BIRTH

6 Bishop Warburton is reported to have said that high birth was a thing which he never knew any one disparage except those who had it not, and he never knew any one make a boast of it who had anything else to be proud of. [Richard Whately: Annotation on Bacon's essay *Of Nobility*]

HIGHBROW

7 A highbrow is a person educated beyond his intelligence. [Brander Matthews: Epigram]

HIGHEST

8 We needs must love the highest when we see it.
[Tennyson: *Idylls of the King: Guinevere* 655]

HIGHLAND LASS

9 Behold her, single in the field,
Yon solitary Highland lass!
[Wordsworth: *The Solitary Reaper*]

HIGHLANDS

10 My heart's in the Highlands, my
heart is not here;
My heart's in the Highlands a-chasing the deer;
A-chasing the wild deer, and following the roe—
My heart's in the Highlands wherever I go.
[Burns: *My Heart's in the Highlands*]
11 In the highlands, in the country
places,
Where the old plain men have rosy
faces,
And the young fair maidens
Quiet eyes.
[R. L. Stevenson: *Youth and Love*]

HIGHWAYMAN

12 The wind was a torrent of darkness
among the gusty trees,
The moon was a ghostly galleon
tossed upon cloudy seas,
The road was a ribbon of moonlight
over the purple moor,
And the highwayman came riding,
up to the old inn-door.
[Alfred Noyes: *The Highwayman*]

HILARITY

13 Fan the sinking flame of hilarity with the wing of friendship; and pass the rosy wine. [Dickens: *The Old Curiosity Shop* VII]

HILLS

14 Over the hills and far away.
[John Gay: *The Beggar's Opera* I.i.]
15 So pleas'd at first the tow'ring Alps
we try,
Mount o'er the vales, and seem to
tread the sky;
Th' eternal snows appear already
past,
And the first clouds and mountains
seem the last:
But those attain'd, we tremble to survey
The growing labours of the lengthen'd way;
Th' increasing prospect tires our
wand'ring eyes,

Hills peep o'er hills, and Alps on
Alps arise!
[Alexander Pope: *Essay on Criticism* II]

HINDMOST
1 The devil take the hindmost. [Beaumont and Fletcher: *Bonduca* IV.ii.]
The phrase was proverbial and had appeared in various forms since antiquity.

HINDSIGHT
2 Their hindsight was better than their foresight. [Attr. Henry Ward Beecher]
The idea of wisdom after the event had been expressed by many writers, from Homer (Iliad XVII) on.

HIP
3 He smote them hip and thigh. [Judges 15:8]

HISTORIANS
4 It has been said that though God cannot alter the past, historians can; it is perhaps because they can be useful to Him in this respect that He tolerates their existence. [Samuel Butler (1835-1902): *Erewhon Revisited* XIV]

HISTORY
5 History offers the best training for those who are to take part in public affairs. [Polybius: *Histories* I]
6 Not to know what happened before one was born is to remain a child. [Cicero: *De Oratore* XXXIV]
7 The principal office of history I take to be this: to prevent virtuous actions from being forgotten, and that evil words and deeds should fear an infamous reputation with posterity. [Tacitus: *Annals* III.lxv.]
8 The only good histories are those written by those who had command in the events they describe. [Montaigne: *Essays* II.xxxiii.]
9 We may gather out of history a policy, by the comparison and application of other men's forepassed miseries with our own like errors and ill deservings. [Sir Walter Raleigh: Preface to *History of the World*]
10 We are much beholden to Machiavelli and others, that write what men do, and not what they ought to do. [Francis Bacon: *The Advancement of Learning* II]
11 If an historian were to relate truthfully all the crimes, weaknesses and disorders of mankind, his readers would take his work for satire rather than for history. [Pierre Bayle: *Dictionary*]
12 Anything but history, for history must be false. [Robert Walpole: when asked, as he lay sick, what he wished to have read to him (*Walpoliana*—by his son, Horace Walpole—No. 141)]
13 History can be well written only in a free country. [Voltaire: Letter to Frederick the Great, May 27, 1737]
14 A fair-minded man, when reading history, is occupied almost entirely with refuting it. [Voltaire: *Essai sur les Moeurs* LI]
15 The examples and events of history press upon the mind with the weight of truth; but when they are reposited in the memory they are oftener employed for show than use and rather diversify conversation than regulate life. [Samuel Johnson: *The Idler* No. 84]
16 Great abilities are not requisite for an historian, for in historical composition all the greatest powers of the human mind are quiescent. [Samuel Johnson: in Boswell's *Life,* July 6, 1763]
17 There is but a shallow stream of thought in history. [Samuel Johnson: in Boswell's *Life,* April 19, 1772]
18 All history, so far as it is not supported by contemporary evidence, is romance. [Samuel Johnson: in Boswell's *Tour to the Hebrides,* Nov. 20, 1773]
19 Happy is the nation without a history. [Cesare Beccaria: Introduction to *Treatise of Crimes and of Punishment*]
20 There is the moral of all human tales;
    'Tis but the same rehearsal of the
    past,
    First freedom, and then glory—when
    that fails,
    Wealth, vice, corruption—barbarism
    at last.
[Byron: *Childe Harold* IV.cviii.]
21 History has nothing to record save wars and revolutions: the peaceful years appear only as brief pauses or interludes, scattered here and there. [Schopenhauer: *Parerga and Paralipomena* II]
22 No great man lives in vain. The history of the world is but the biography of

great men. [Thomas Carlyle: *Heroes and Hero-Worship* I]
Carlyle stated this thought several times in the course of this and other of his works.
1 Every student during his academic period ought to get up one bit of history thoroughly from the ultimate sources, in order to convince himself what history is not. [W. G. Sumner: *Folkways*]
2 History—that excited and deceitful old woman! [Guy de Maupassant: *Sur l'Eau. Saint-Tropez, 12 Avril*]
3 Alas! Hegel was right when he said that we learn from history that men never learn anything from history. [G. B. Shaw: Preface to *Heartbreak House*]
4 Read this in the histories:
Newsweek, or Thucydides.
[Daniel G. Hoffman: *In Humbleness*]

HISTORY: definitions
5 History is little else than a picture of human crimes and misfortunes. [Voltaire: *L'Ingénu* X]
6 The history of the great events of the world is little more than a history of crime. [Voltaire: *Essai sur les Moeurs* XXIII]
7 The history of the greatest rulers is often only a recital of mistakes. [Voltaire: *Le Siècle de Louis XIV* XI]
8 On whatever side we regard the history of Europe, we shall preceive it to be a tissue of crimes, follies, and misfortunes. [Oliver Goldsmith: *The Citizen of the World* XLII]
9 History . . . is little more than the register of the crimes, follies and misfortunes of mankind. [Edward Gibbon: *The Decline and Fall of the Roman Empire*]
10 That record of crimes and miseries—history. [Shelley: Letter to Thomas Hookham, Dec. 17, 1812]
11 History a distillation of rumour. [Thomas Carlyle: *History of the French Revolution* I.vii.]
12 The whole history of the species is made up of little except crimes and errors. [Macaulay: *Hallam*]
13 History is bunk. [Attr. Henry Ford]
Mr. Ford denied that he used this actual phrase, though he did not disavow the

sentiment. *It certainly has the support of many eminent historians.*

HIT
14 A hit, a very palpable hit. [Shakespeare: *Hamlet* V.ii.]

HOBBY
15 And now each man bestride his hobby, and dust away his bells to what tune he pleases. [Charles Lamb: *Essays of Elia,* "All Fool's Day"]
16 A hobby a day keeps the doldrums away.
[Phyllis McGinley: *A Pocketful of Wry*]

HOBBY-HORSE
17 So long as a man rides his hobby-horse peaceably and quietly along the king's highway, and neither compels you or me to get up behind him—pray, Sir, what have either you or I to do with it? [Laurence Sterne: *Tristram Shandy* I. vii.]

HOBSON'S CHOICE
18 Where to elect there is but one,
  'Tis Hobson's choice—take that or
                    none.
[Thomas Ward: *England's Reformation* IV]
Tobias or Thomas Hobson (c. 1544-1631) was a carrier at Cambridge who "kept a stable of forty good mounts" but would allow a customer no choice, requiring him to take the horse that stood nearest the stable door or none, "so that every customer was alike well served . . . and every horse ridden with the same justice" (Spectator, No. 512). Hobson's requirement was humane and fair. But it was so opposed to the spirit of the age, in which every gentleman insisted on preferential treatment, that it attracted great attention.
It is one of fame's whimsies that this obscure man should have had a street named after him in Cambridge, a number of the Spectator *devoted to him, been the subject of two poems by Milton, and had his name become a proverb. Few kings have gained as much fame.*

HOG
19 As independent as a hog on ice. [*Cen-*

tury Dictionary: hog² (1889)]

*Listed in the Century as "an ironical
simile" heard in the United States, this
curious term for cocky independence, supreme confidence, has been examined
with great thoroughness by Mr. Charles
Earle Funk in A Hog on Ice and Other
Curious Expressions. His conclusion is
that it is based on the laggard stones in
the game of curling.*

*Readers are referred to his discussion
if only that they may learn how exceedingly difficult it sometimes is to gain
even a rational guess about a phrase's
origin.*

HOLD
1 Hold the fort! I am coming. [Wil-
liam Tecumseh Sherman: signal to General John M. Corse, at the Battle of Al-
latoona, Georgia, Oct. 5, 1864]

*Sometimes: "Hold the fort, for I am
coming."*

*It is agreed that this is not Sherman's
exact message, of which there are several
versions, such as "Hold out. Relief is
coming." The form in which it is now
heard was fixed by P. H. Bliss, who used
it as the title of a hymn in 1870. The
hymn became very popular.*

HOLINESS
2 The lust of the goat is the bounty of
God. [William Blake: *The Marriage of
Heaven and Hell*]
3 Divine am I inside and out, and I
make holy whatever I touch
or am touch'd from;
The scent of these arm-pits, aroma
finer than prayer.
[Walt Whitman: *Leaves of Grass,* "Song
of Myself"]

HOLMES, OLIVER WENDELL
4 Master alike in speech and song
Of fame's great antiseptic—Style,
You with the classic few belong
Who tempered wisdom with a smile.
[James Russell Lowell: *To Oliver Wen-
dell Holmes on His Seventy-fifth Birth-
day*]

HOLY
5 I am holier than thou. [Isaiah 65:5]

HOLY ROMAN EMPIRE
6 This agglomeration which was called
and which still calls itself the Holy Roman Empire is neither holy, nor Roman,
nor an Empire. [Voltaire: *Essai sur les
Moeurs*]

HOME: definitions
7 Home is where the heart is. [Attr. to
Pliny]
8 Home is the girl's prison and the
woman's workhouse. [G. B. Shaw: *Maxims for Revolutionists*]
9 Home is the place where, when you
have to go there,
They have to take you in.
[Robert Frost: *The Death of the Hired
Man*]
10 And this is the way
We start the day
In a corner of Hell called home.
[Louise Cass: *Home*]
11 It takes a heap o' livin' in a house
t' make it home.
[Edgar A. Guest: *Home*]
*Ogden Nash (A Heap o' Livin') says that
it "takes a heap o' payin' " too.*
12 A House is not a Home. [Title of
memoirs by Polly Adler, famous Madam.]

HOME: is best
13 Home is home, though it be ever so
homely. [John Clarke: *Parœmiologia*
(1639)]
14 My house, my house, though thou art
small,
Thou art to me the Escurial.
[George Herbert: *Jacula Prudentum*]
15 'Mid pleasures and palaces though
we may roam,
Be it ever so humble, there's no place
like home;
A charm from the skies seems to hallow us there,
Which sought through the world is
ne'er met with elsewhere.
[John Howard Payne: *Home, Sweet
Home*]
*The song was first sung in the opera
Clari, the Maid of Milan (1823).*
*It would be hard to find any other
four consecutive lines of verse in English
of which the first two are better known
and the last two less known.*
16 Stay, stay at home, my heart, and rest;

Home-keeping hearts are happiest,
For those that wander they know not
where
Are full of trouble and full of care;
To stay at home is best.
[Longfellow: *Song*]

1 Way down upon the Swanee River,
Far, far away,
There's where my heart is turning
ever;
There's where the old folks stay.
All up and down the whole creation,
Sadly I roam,
Still longing for the old plantation,
And for the old folks at home.
[Stephen Foster: *The Old Folks at Home*]

2 East and West, Home is best.
[Charles Haddon Spurgeon: *John Ploughman*]
More often heard as: *East, West, home's best.*

HOME: miscellaneous
3 It is for homely features to keep
home,
They had their name thence.
[John Milton: *Comus*]

4 To be happy at home is the ultimate result of all ambition, the end to which every enterprise and labor tends, and of which every desire prompts the prosecution. [Samuel Johnson: *The Rambler* No. 68]

5 One sweetly solemn thought
Comes to me o'er and o'er;
I am nearer home today
Than I ever have been before.
[Phoebe Cary: *Nearer Home*]

6 Keep the home fires burning,
While your hearts are yearning,
Though your lads are far away
They dream of home.
[Lena Guilbert Ford: *Keep the Home Fires Burning*]

7 Many a man who thinks to found a home discovers that he has merely opened a tavern for his friends. [Norman Douglas: *South Wind*]

8 Home, home on the range,
Where the deer and the antelope
play;
Where seldom is heard a discouraging word,
And the skies are not cloudy all day.

[Dr. Brewster Higley: *Home on the Range* (c. 1873)]
Orig. called The Western Home, *it has many variants and many claims of authorship. The poem echoes other ballads.*

9 We're too unseparate. And going
home
From company means coming to our
senses.
[Robert Frost: *Build Soil—A Political Pastoral*]

HOMECOMING
10 It fell about the Martinmass,
When nights are lang and mirk,
The carline wife's three sons came
hame,
And their hats were o' the birk.

It neither grew in syke nor ditch,
Nor yet in ony sheugh;
But at the gates o' Paradise
That birk grew fair eneugh.
(Anon.: *The Wife of Usher's Well*]
Martinmass = *November 11;* lang = *long;* mirk = *murky;* carline wife = *an old woman, despicable but sinister, probably a witch;* birk = *birch;* sheugh = *furrow, trench, ditch;* syke = *marsh*
Few poems in English convey more passion, menace and bitter mystery than this old ballad. The sons are dead, though the only indication of it is the mysterious birch, and they come home for one night in response to a wild curse of their anguished mother. Kipling's The Sea Wife, *a modern version, is an extraordinary exercise in banalization. The carline wife has become "the weary wife," a sort of gold-star mother, and such of her sons as come home, on furlough one gathers, have been broadened by travel, and come home for her blessing! A masterpiece of inverse alchemy, turning black gold to gilded lead.*

11 Oh dream of joy, is this indeed
The lighthouse top I see?
Is this the hill? is this the kirk?
Is this mine own countree?
[Coleridge: *The Ancient Mariner* VI]

HOMELINESS
12 Over-great homeliness engendereth
dispraising.
[Chaucer: *The Tale of Melibeus*]

HOMEMADE

1 Who hath not met with home-made
bread,
A heavy compound of putty and
lead—
And home-made wines that rack the
head,
And home-made liquors and waters?
Home-made pop that will not foam,
And home-made dishes that drive
one from home—
Home-made by the homely daughters.
[Thomas Hood: *Miss Kilmansegg*]
2 Of all our evils, the worst of the
worst
Is home-made infelicity.
[Thomas Hood: *Miss Kilmansegg*]

HOMER

3 I too am indignant when good
Homer nods, but in a long work it is
permitted to snatch a little sleep. [Horace: *De Arte Poetica*]
*From this passage comes the saying "even
Homer nods."*
4 Seven cities warr'd for Homer, being
dead,
Who, living, had no roof to shroud
his head.
[Thomas Heywood: *Hierarchie of the
Blessed Angels*]
5 Be Homer's works your study and delight;
Read them by day, and meditate by
night.
[Alexander Pope: *Essay on Criticism* I]
6 Seven wealthy towns contend for
Homer dead,
Through which the living Homer
begg'd his bread.
[Thomas Seward: *On Homer* (1738)]
*Seward merely put into a more acceptable rhyme an assertion that had been
repeated since the time of the ancient
Greeks.*
7 Oft of one wide expanse had I been
told
That deep-brow'd Homer ruled as his
demesne;
Yet did I never breathe its pure
serene
Till I heard Chapman speak out loud
and bold:
Then felt I like some watcher of the
skies

When a new planet swims into his
ken;
Or like stout Cortez, when with eagle
eyes
He stared at the Pacific—and all his
men
Look'd at each other with a wild surmise—
Silent, upon a peak in Darien.
[Keats: *On First Looking Into Chapman's Homer*]

HOMES

8 The stately Homes of England!
How beautiful they stand,
Amidst their tall ancestral trees,
O'er all the pleasant land!
[Felicia Hemans: *The Homes of England*]
9 Those comfortably padded lunatic
asylums which are known, euphemistically, as the stately homes of England.
[Virginia Woolf: *The Common Reader*,
"Lady Dorothy Nevill"]

HOMESICK

10 So sick with longing to see if it were
but the smoke of his home spiring up,
that he prays for death. [Homer: *Odyssey* I (trans. T. E. Lawrence)]
he = Odysseus

HONEST

11 I thank God I am as honest as any
man living that is an old man and no
honester than I. [Shakespeare: *Much
Ado About Nothing* III.v.]
12 Ay, sir; to be honest, as this world
goes, is to be one man picked out of ten
thousand. [Shakespeare: *Hamlet* II.ii.]
13 Fools out of favour grudge at knaves
in place,
And men are always honest in disgrace.
[Daniel Defoe: Introduction to *The
True-born Englishman*]

HONESTY

14 Confidence in others' honesty is no
light testimony of one's own integrity.
[Montaigne: *Essays* I.xl.]
15 Honesty is the best policy.
[Cervantes: *Don Quixote* II.xxxiii.]
16 Clear and round dealing is the honor
of a man's nature, and that mixture of

falsehood is like alloy in coin of gold and silver, which may make the metal work the better, but it embaseth it. [Francis Bacon: *Of Truth*]
embaseth = *debases*

1 No legacy is so rich as honesty. [Shakespeare: *All's Well that Ends Well* III.v.]

2 Every man has his fault, and honesty is his. [Shakespeare: *Timon of Athens* III.i.]

3 Though I am not naturally honest, I am so sometimes by chance. [Shakespeare: *The Winter's Tale* IV. iii.]

4 He is only honest who is not discovered. [Susanna Centlivre: *The Artifice* V]

5 An honest man's the noblest work of God. [Alexander Pope: *An Essay on Man* IV]
Quoted by Burns in The Cotter's Saturday Night *and reversed by Robert Ingersoll (late 19th century) to: An honest God is the noblest work of man.*

6 He that resolves to deal with none but honest Men, must leave off dealing. [Thomas Fuller (1654-1734): *Gnomologia*]

7 "Honesty is the best policy," but he who acts on that principle is not an honest man. [Richard Whately: *Thoughts and Apothegms*, "Pious Frauds"]

8 The honest man, though e'er so poor, Is king o' men for a' that. [Burns: *For a' That and a' That*]

9 I am afraid we must make the world honest before we can honestly say to our children that honesty is the best policy. [G. B. Shaw: in a radio address, 1932]

HONESTY: its drawbacks
10 An honest man is always a child. [Martial: *Epigrams* XII.li.]
This is the "natural piety" with which Wordsworth wished his days to be bound each to each.
The Latin word here translated child is tiro *which means a young man just assuming the toga, and by extension a recruit, a beginner. Retained in English, and usually spelled* tyro, *it means a novice and is slightly tinged with contempt.*

11 Honesty is praised and starved. [Juvenal: *Satires* I]

12 Take note, take note, O world, To be direct and honest is not safe. [Shakespeare: *Othello* III.iii.]

13 Mankind's dishonest; if you think it fair, Amongst known cheats, to play upon the square, You'll be undone— Nor can weak truth your reputation save; The knaves will all agree to call you knave. [John Wilmot, Earl of Rochester: *A Satyr Against Mankind*]

14 Honest men Are the soft easy cushions on which knaves Repose and fatten. [Thomas Otway: *Venice Preserved* I.i.]

15 That weary, dejected air which comes from earning a living honestly. [Henry Miller: *Tropic of Cancer*]

HONEY
16 Sweeter also than honey and the honeycomb. [Psalms 19:10]

17 Dear is bought the honey that is licked off the thorn. [The Proverbs of Hendyng]

18 More Flies are taken with a Drop of Honey than a Tun of Vinegar. [Thomas Fuller (1654-1734): *Gnomologia*]

19 One who marries an ill-tempered person attempts to lick honey off a thorn. [William Hone: *Table Book*]

HONOR
20 The man whom the king delighteth to honour. [Esther 6:9]

21 Hath not the potter power over the clay, of the same lump to make one vessel unto honour, and another unto dishonour? [Romans 9:21]

22 There is nothing left to me but honor, and my life, which is saved. [Francis I of France: to his mother after the Battle of Pavia (Feb. 24, 1525), in which he was defeated and captured by the Emperor Charles V]
Usually quoted as "All is lost save honor." Napoleon is said to have quoted this after Waterloo. "Nothing is lost save honor" was Jim Fisk's famous quip when Morgan defeated the notorious Erie ring but paid them off (1869).

Byron had invented the same joke half a century before ("Nothing is lost except our honor"), in his letter to Tom Moore, May 14, 1821.

1 A man is an ill husband of his honor that entereth into any action, the failing wherein may disgrace him more than the carrying of it through can honor him. [Francis Bacon: *Of Honor and Reputation*]

husband = *manager, conserver*

2 By heaven, methinks it were an easy leap,
To pluck bright honor from the pale-faced moon,
Or dive into the bottom of the deep,
Where fathom-line could never touch the ground,
And pluck up drowned honor by the locks.
[Shakespeare: *I Henry IV* I.iii.]

3 Send danger from the east unto the west,
So honor cross it from the north to south.
[Shakespeare: *I Henry IV* I.iii.]

4 For Brutus is an honorable man;
So are they all. all honorable men.
[Shakespeare: *Julius Caesar* III.ii.]

5 But if it be a sin to covet honor,
I am the most offending soul alive.
[Shakespeare: *Henry V* IV.iii.]

6   Rightly to be great
Is not to stir without great argument
But greatly to find quarrel in a straw
When honor's at the stake.
[Shakespeare: *Hamlet* IV.iv.]

argument = *theme, hence justification*

7   Perseverance, dear my lord,
Keeps honor bright. To have done is to hang
Quite out of fashion, like a rusty mail
In monumental mock'ry.
[Shakespeare: *Troilus and Cressida* III. iii.]

perseverance = *continuance in doing, not merely attempting;* mail = *a suit of armor, alluding to the custom of hanging a knight's armor over his tomb*

8 And not a man for being simply man
Hath any honor, but honor for those honors
That are without him, as place, riches, and favor,
Prizes of accident as oft as merit.
[Shakespeare: *Troilus and Cressida* III. iii.]

9 For honor travels in a strait so narrow,
Where one but goes abreast.
[Shakespeare: *Troilus and Cressida* III. iii.]

That is, a man's honor is purely his own responsibility. He can neither be dishonored nor saved from dishonor by the act of another.

10 I could not love thee, dear, so much
Loved I not honor more.
[Richard Lovelace: *To Lucasta: Going to the Wars*]

11 Honour is like a widow, won
With brisk attempt and putting on;
With ent'ring manfully, and urging,
Not slow approaches, like a virgin.
[Samuel Butler (1612-1680): *Hudibras*]

12 The great Point of Honour in Men is Courage, in Women Chastity. [Joseph Addison: *The Spectator* No. 99]

13 Honor rarely leads to wealth. [Jacques Saurin: *Beverlei* II.ii.]

14 The law often allows what honor forbids. [Jacques Saurin: *Spartacus* III.iii.]

15 Honour and shame from no condition rise;
Act well your part: there all the honour lies.
[Alexander Pope: *An Essay on Man* IV]

16 No man can justly aspire to honour, but at the hazard of disgrace. [Samuel Johnson: *The Rambler* No. 83]

17 His honour rooted in dishonour stood,
And faith unfaithful kept him falsely true.
[Tennyson: *Idylls of the King*, "Lancelot and Elaine"]

18 Honour is sometimes found among thieves. [Sir Walter Scott: *Redgauntlet* IX]

This is quite different from the more common—but definitely untrue—assertion that "There is honor among thieves."

19 Honor has come back as a king to earth
And paid his subjects with a royal wage.
[Rupert Brooke: *The Dead*]

20 Honor is simply the morality of superior men. [H. L. Mencken: in *Smart*

Set, October 1919]

1 The difference between a moral man and a man of honor is that the latter regrets a discreditable act, even when it has worked and he has not been caught. [H. L. Mencken: *Chrestomathy* 617]

HONOR: some cynical observations on

2 Honor pricks me on. Yea, but how if honor prick me off when I come on— how then? Can honor set to a leg? no: or an arm? no: or take away the grief of a wound? no. Honor hath no skill in surgery, then? no. What is honour? a word. What is that word honor? Air. A trim reckoning! Who hath it? he that died o' Wednesday. Doth he feel it? no. Doth he hear it? no. It is insensible, then? yea, to the dead. But will it not live with the living? no. Why? detraction will not suffer it. Therefore I'll none of it. Honor is a mere scutcheon. And so ends my catechism. [Shakespeare: *I Henry IV* V.i.]
> scutcheon = *a painted shield, of wood or canvas, hung out in honor of the dead*

3 If he that in the field is slain
Be in the bed of honor lain,
He that is beaten may be said
To lie in Honor's truckle-bed.
[Samuel Butler (1612-1680): *Hudibras*]
> *A truckle-bed was a low bed on castors usually pushed beneath a high or "standing" bed when not in use. It was reserved for servants. To truckle was to sleep in such a bed and hence, by figurative extension, to take a subordinate position, to be subservient.*

4 Honor is but an empty bubble.
[Dryden: *Alexander's Feast*]

5 His designs were strictly honorable, as the saying is; that is, to rob a lady of her fortune by way of marriage. [Henry Fielding: *Tom Jones* XI.iv.]

6 The louder he talked of his honor the faster we counted our spoons. [Emerson: *The Conduct of Life:* "Worship"]

7 But the jingling of the guinea helps the hurt that Honor feels.
[Tennyson: *Locksley Hall*]

HOOK

8 By hook or crook.
> *This phrase first appears in Wyclif's tracts, about 1380 and meant then what*

it means now—"by fair means or foul." *The best guess is that it originated in the early English forest laws governing the rights of the poor to secure firewood. They were not allowed to use axes or saws but were allowed to pull off what they could by hook (a hooked pole, like a shepherd's curved staff) or hack it off by crook (a sickle).*

> *A passage in the Bodmin Register (1525) says that a certain wood was open to the inhabitants of Bodmin "to bear away upon their backs a burden of lop, hook, crook and bag wood." The peasants probably hacked and slashed, with hook and crook, as furiously as they could.*

HOPE: deferred

9 The deadliest of all human woes,
Hope long deferred.
[Statius: *Thebais* II]

10 Hope deferred maketh the heart sick. [Proverbs 13:12]

11 Who against hope believed in hope. [Romans: 4:18]
> *Popularly: Hoping against hope.*

> *It was Abraham who, despite the fact that he was childless to a great age, "against hope believed in hope that he might become the father of many nations; according to that which was spoken" by God.*

12 The sickening pang of hope deferr'd.
[Sir Walter Scott: *Lady of the Lake* III]

13 I hope to see my Pilot face to face
When I have crossed the bar.
[Tennyson: *Crossing the Bar*]

HOPE: definition

14 Hopes are but the dreams of those who are awake. [Pindar: *Fragment*]

15 For hope is but the dream of those that wake. [Matthew Prior: *Solomon on the Vanity of the World* III]

16 Hope is itself a species of happiness, and, perhaps, the chief happiness which this world affords: but, like all other pleasures immoderately enjoyed, the excesses of hope must be expiated by pain; and expectations improperly indulged must end in disappointment. [Samuel Johnson: in Boswell's *Life*, June 8, 1762]

17 Hope is the thing with feathers
That perches in the soul,

And sings the tune without the words,
And never stops at all.
[Emily Dickinson: *Part I, Life* XXXII]

1 Hope is a pathological belief in the occurrence of the impossible. [H. L. Mencken: *Chrestomathy* 617]

HOPE: the delusion of

2 Prisoners of hope. [Zechariah 9:12]

3 This is the state of man: today he
                              puts forth
The tender leaves of hope; tomorrow
                              blossoms,
And bears his blushing honors thick
                            upon him:
The third day comes a frost, a killing
                            frost,
And, when he thinks, good easy man,
                          full surely
His greatness is a-ripening, nips his
                            root,
And then he falls, as I do.
[Shakespeare: *Henry VIII* III.ii.]

4 He that lives in hope dances without music. [George Herbert: *Outlandish Proverbs*]

5 Hope! of all ills that men endure,
The only cheap and universal cure.
[Abraham Cowley: *The Mistress*]

6 Strange cozenage! None would live
                        past years again,
Yet all hope pleasure in what yet re-
                        main;
And from the dregs of life think to
                        receive
What the first sprightly running could
                        not give.
[Dryden: *Aureng-Zebe* IV.i.]

7 Men should do with their hopes as they do with tame fowl, cut their wings that they may not fly over the wall. [Lord Halifax: *Maxims*]

8 Hope springs eternal in the human
                        breast;
Man never is, but always to be blest.
[Alexander Pope: *An Essay on Man*]

9 It is necessary to hope, though hope should always be deluded; for hope itself is happiness, and its frustrations, however frequent, are yet less dreadful than its extinction. [Samuel Johnson: *The Idler* No. 58]

10 Cold hopes swarm like worms within
                      our living clay.
[Shelley: *Adonais* XXXIX]

11 The Worldly Hope men set their
                      Hearts upon
Turns Ashes—or it prospers; and
                      anon,
Like Snow upon the Desert's dusty
                      face
Lighting a little hour or two—is gone.
[*Rubáiyát of Omar Khayyám* (trans. Edward FitzGerald)]

12 Still nursing the unconquerable hope,
Still clutching the inviolable shade.
[Matthew Arnold: *The Scholar-Gipsy*]

HOPE: and despair

13 Our hap is loss, our hope but sad de-
                      spair.
[Shakespeare: *III Henry VI* II.iii.]

14 The miserable have no other medi-
                      cine
But only hope.
[Shakespeare: *Measure for Measure* III.i.]

15 What reinforcement we may gain
                      from hope;
If not, what resolution from despair.
[John Milton: *Paradise Lost* I.190-191]

16 Our final hope / Is flat despair.
[John Milton: *Paradise Lost* II.142-143]

17 I can endure my own despair,
But not another's hope.
[William Walsh: *Of all the Torments*]

18   Worse than despair,
Worse than the bitterness of death, is
                      hope.
[Shelley: *The Cenci* V.iv.]

19 They say Despair has power to kill
With her bleak frown; but I say No;
If life did hang upon her will,
Then Hope had perish'd long ago;
Yet still the twain keep up their "bar-
                      ful strife,"
For Hope Love's leman is, Despair
                      his wife.
[Hartley Coleridge: *Epigram*]

HOPE: and fear

20 Where no hope is left, is left no fear. [John Milton: *Paradise Regained* III. 206]

21 Hope and fear are inseparable. [La Rochefoucauld: *Maxims*]

22 We promise according to our hopes, and perform according to our fears. [La Rochefoucauld: *Maxims*]

23 Fear cannot be without hope nor hope without fear. [Spinoza: *Ethics*,

Definition XIII, Explanation]
1 In such a case they talk in Tropes,
   And, by their Fears express their
                          Hopes.
[Jonathan Swift: *On the Death of Dr.
   Swift*]
2 He has no hope who never had a fear.
[William Cowper: *Truth*]
3   The fear that kills;
   And hope that is unwilling to be fed.
[Wordsworth: *Resolution and Independence*]
4 Hope thou not much, and fear thou
                       not at all.
[Swinburne: *Hope and Fear*]

HOPE: miscellaneous
5 Things which you don't hope happen
more frequently than things which you
do hope. [Plautus: *Mostellaria* I.iii.]
6 While there's life, there's hope. [Cicero: *Ad Atticum* IX.x.]
   The Latin: Dum anima est, spes est *is
   given as "a saying."*
7 Perhaps on the unhappy happier days
                          may wait.
[Vergil: *Aeneid* XII]
8 Hope and patience are two sovereign
remedies for all, the surest reposals, the
softest cushions to lean on in adversity.
[Robert Burton: *Anatomy of Melancholy*
II.3.3]
9 It is always darkest just before the
day dawneth. [Thomas Fuller (1608-
1661): *A Pisgah-sight of Palestine* II]
10 The natural flights of the human
mind are not from pleasure to pleasure,
but from hope to hope. [Samuel Johnson: *The Rambler* No. 2]
11 Those who have much to hope and
nothing to lose will always be dangerous.
[Edmund Burke: in a letter to Charles
James Fox, 1777]
   *The only significant difference between
   political parties is whether they believe
   the solution is to give the desperate less
   to hope or more to lose.*
12 Work without hope draws nectar in a
                          sieve,
   And hope without an object cannot
                          live.
[Coleridge: *Work Without Hope*]
13   To hope till hope creates
   From its own wreck the thing it con-
                      templates.

[Shelley: *Prometheus* IV]
14 Man is, properly speaking, based
upon Hope; he has no other possession
but Hope. [Thomas Carlyle: *Sartor Resartus* II.vii.]
15 And faintly trust the larger hope.
[Tennyson: *In Memoriam* LV]
16 In all the wedding cake, hope is the
sweetest of the plums. [Douglas Jerrold:
The Catspaw]

HORATIUS
17 With weeping and with laughter
      Still is the story told,
   How well Horatius kept the bridge
      In the brave days of old.
[Macaulay: *Lays of Ancient Rome:* "Horatius"]

HORN(S)
18 The horn of the hunter is heard on
                       the hill.
[Louisa Crawford: *Kathleen Mavourneen*]
19 O hark, O hear! how thin and clear,
      And thinner, clearer, farther going!
   O sweet and far from cliff and scar
      The horns of Elfland faintly blowing!
[Tennyson: *The Princess* IV]
20 The sound of horns and motors,
                  which shall bring
   Sweeney to Mrs. Porter in the spring.
[T. S. Eliot: *The Waste Land* III]
   An echo of John Day's The Parliament
   of Bees *(1607):*
      *When of the sudden, listening,
                     you shall hear,
      A noise of horns and hunting,
                     which shall bring
      Actaeon to Diana in the spring,
      Where all shall see her naked
                        skin. . . .*

HORNER, JACK
21 Little Jack Horner
   Sat in a corner,
   Eating a Christmas pie;
   He put in his thumb,
   And pulled out a plum,
   And said, What a good boy am I!
[Nursery rhyme; earliest printed version
1720]
   *This Horner is believed to be one
   Thomas Horner who was dispatched by
   the Abbot of Glastonbury, at the time of*

the dissolution of the Monasteries, to King Henry VIII with a placating gift, a pie. In the pie were the deeds to a number of valuable manors that the Monastery owned. On the journey, Horner is said to have extracted one of the deeds. Certainly, soon after, his family appeared as the owners of one of the manors.

HORROR

1 The time has been my senses would
have cooled
To hear a night-shriek, and my fell of
hair
Would at a dismal treatise rouse and
stir
As life were in't. I have supped full
with horrors;
Direness, familiar to my slaughterous
thoughts,
Cannot once start me.
[Shakespeare: *Macbeth* V.v.]

HORSE

2 Hast thou given the horse strength? Hast thou clothed his neck with thunder? [Job 39:19]
3 He saith among the trumpets, Ha, ha! and he smelleth the battle afar off, the thunder of the captains, and the shouting. [Job 39:25]
4 And I looked, and behold, a pale horse: and his name that sat on him was Death. [Revelation 6:8]
5 No man ought to look a given horse in the mouth. [John Heywood: Proverbs (1546)]

The proverb has been traced back to St. Jerome, 400 A.D. It appears in every European language. The saying is based on the fact that a horse's value depends on its age and its age can be determined by looking at its teeth, so that to look a horse in the mouth is to appraise its value. See GIFT HORSE.

One form of the proverb—the one given here—says that we ought not to attempt to appraise a gift, but to accept it gratefully, and even more gratefully the spirit which prompted the giving. There is a subsidiary saying, however: "Always look a gift horse in the mouth." That is, there are no gifts; all acceptances acknowledge an obligation, so

make sure of what you're getting before you feel grateful or even accept it.

6 A man may well bring a horse to the
water,
But he cannot make him drinke without he will.
[John Heywood: Proverbs (1546)]
7 A horse! a horse! my kingdom for a horse! [Attr. King Richard III of England; at the Battle of Bosworth Field, Aug. 23, 1485]

It appears in Shakespeare's Richard III *V.iv.*

8 Give a man a horse he can ride,
Give a man a boat he can sail;
And his rank and wealth, his strength
and health
On sea nor shore shall fail.
[James Thomson (1834-1882): *Sunday Up the River*]

HORSEMAN

9 Whenever the moon and stars are set,
Whenever the wind is high,
All night long in the dark and wet,
A man goes riding by.
Late in the night when the fires are
out,
Why does he gallop and gallop about?
[R. L. Stevenson: *A Child's Garden of Verses*, "Windy Nights"]

HORSE SENSE

10 Tim was so learned that he could name a horse in nine languages. So ignorant that he bought a cow to ride on. [Benjamin Franklin: *Poor Richard's Almanack*]

HOSPITALITY

11 Alike he thwarts the hospitable end
Who drives the free, or stays the hasty
friend:
True friendship's laws are by this
rule express'd,
Welcome the coming, speed the part-
ing guest.
[Homer: *Odyssey* XV (trans. Alexander Pope)]

Robert Fitzgerald translates the passage:

"I'd think myself or any other host | as ill-mannered for over-friendliness | as for hostility. Measure is best in everything. | To send a guest packing, or cling to

him / when he's in haste—one sin equals the other. / 'Good entertaining ends with no detaining.' "

Pope's line which, because of its smoothness and balance, became immediately a proverb, so pleased him that he used it again in his Imitations of Horace. But he was not content to let felicity alone and spoiled it by a slight change:

Welcome the coming, speed the going guest. Satires *II.ii.*

1 Given to hospitality. [Romans 12:13]
2 Be not forgetful to entertain strangers, for thereby some have entertained angels unawares. [Hebrews 13:2]

Both Abraham and his nephew Lot entertained angels unawares.

HOST
3 Ajax, himself a host. [Homer: *Iliad* III]

HOTEL
4 The great advantage of a hotel is that it's a refuge from home life. [G. B. Shaw: *You Never Can Tell*]

HOT WEATHER
5 What dreadful hot weather we have! It keeps me in a continual state of inelegance. [Jane Austen: Letter to her sister Cassandra, September 18, 1796]

HOUNDS
6 My hounds are bred out of the Spartan kind,
So flewed, so sanded; and their heads are hung
With ears that sweep away the morning dew;
Crook-kneed, and dew-lapped like Thessalian bulls;
Slow in pursuit, but matched in mouth like bells.
[Shakespeare: *A Midsummer Night's Dream* IV.i.]

The Elizabethans prized harmony in a pack of hounds, as well as mere hunting ability. It is to this that the last line refers. It is also to this that Roderigo alludes (Othello II.iii.) when he says: "I do follow here in the chase, not like a hound that hunts, but one that fills up the cry."

7 When the hounds of spring are on winter's traces.
[Swinburne: Chorus from *Atalanta in Calydon*]

HOUR(S)
8 Sad hours seem long.
[Shakespeare: *Romeo and Juliet* I.i.]
9 One crowded hour of glorious life
Is worth an age without a name.
[Sir Walter Scott: *Old Mortality* XXXIV]
See CATHAY

HOUSE(S)
10 Woe unto them that join house to house, that lay field to field, till there be no place! [Isaiah 5:8]

Not intended as a warning to modern subdivision and suburban developers, but the thought is appealing none the less.

11 Set thine house in order. [Isaiah 38:1]
12 Except the Lord build the house, they labour in vain that build it. [Psalms 127:1]

The first three words of this verse were used by Joyce Cary as the title of a novel, 1953.

13 An house not made with hands. [II Corinthians 5:7]
14 Three thinges dryven a man out of his hous; that is to seyn, smoke, dropping of reyn, and wikked wyves. [Chaucer: *The Tale of Melibeus* 15]

Where it is given as an old saying.

15 To "get out of my house" and "what do you want with my wife?" there's no answer. [Cervantes: *Don Quixote* II.43]
16 Houses are built to live in, not to look on; therefore, let use be preferred before uniformity, except where both may be had. [Francis Bacon: *Of Building*]
17 He that builds a fair house upon an ill seat committeth himself to prison. [Francis Bacon: *Of Building*]
18 A plague o' both your houses! [Shakespeare: *Romeo and Juliet* III.i.]
19 He that has a house to put 's head in has a good head-piece. [Shakespeare: *King Lear* III.ii.]
20 A man's house is his castle. [Sir Edward Coke: *Institutes* III (1628-1644)]

Coke has been echoed through the cen-

turies. Emerson (*English Traits: Wealth*): *"The house is a castle which the King cannot enter."* Dryden (*Wild Gallant I.i. —1663*): *"My lodging, as long as I rent it, is my castle."* The redoubtable Mrs. MacStinger, in Dickens's *Dombey and Son IX (1848), "immediately demanded whether an Englishwoman's house was her castle or not."*

Sir William Blackstone, however (Commentaries IV, 1769), is more guarded: "No outward doors of a man's house can in general be broken open to execute any civil process." But that "in general" and limitation to "civil process" are sad restrictions. And, despite baronial illusions of tenants, under practically all leases landlords are entitled to enter to do anything that has to be done to preserve their property or to save themselves from liability. The police may enter for the purpose of making an arrest. Process servers, it is true, may be denied admission.

1 This house is to be let for life or
years;
Her rent is sorrow, and her income
tears.
[Francis Quarles: *Emblems* II]
let = *leased or rented*

2 Whose house is of glass, must not throw stones at another. [George Herbert: *Jacula Prudentum*]

3 Set not your House on fire to be revenged of the Moon. [Thomas Fuller (1654-1734): *Gnomologia*]

4 Old houses mended,
Cost little less than new, before
they're ended.
[Colley Cibber: Prologue to *The Double Gallant*]

5 The man who builds and wants
wherewith to pay,
Provides a home from which to run
away.
[Edward Young: *Love of Fame* I]

6 The poorest man may in his cottage bid defiance to all the force of the Crown. It may be frail, its roof may shake; the wind may blow through it; the storms may enter, the rain may enter, but the King of England cannot enter; all his forces dare not cross the threshold of the ruined tenement! [William Pitt: *Speech, Excise Bill*] See 327:20

7 A man builds a fine house; and now he has a master, and a task for life: he is to furnish, watch, show it, and keep it in repair, the rest of his days. [Emerson: *Works and Days*, "Society and Solitude"]

8 All houses wherein men have lived
and died
Are haunted houses.
[Longfellow: *Haunted Houses*]

9 The first year let your house to your enemy; the second to your friend; the third, live in it yourself. [William C. Hazlitt: *English Proverbs* (1869)]
let = *rent*
The idea is that it takes at least two years after a house is built to make it livable. The first year it will be so much trouble that you will wish your enemy had it. The second it will require many little attentions, such as a friend might supply.

10 Safe upon the solid rock the ugly
houses stand;
Come and see my shining palace built
upon the sand.
[Edna St. Vincent Millay: *A Few Figs from Thistles*, "Second Fig"]

HOUSE DIVIDED

11 If a house be divided against itself, that house cannot stand. [Mark 3:25]

12 "A house divided against itself cannot stand." I believe this government cannot endure permanently half slave and half free. I do not expect the Union to be dissolved—I do not expect the house to fall—but I do expect that it will cease to be divided. [Abraham Lincoln: Speech at the Republican State Convention, Springfield, Illinois, June 16, 1858]

HOUSE OF COMMONS

13 The Commons, faithful to their system, remained in a wise and masterly inactivity. [Sir James Mackintosh: *Vindiciae Gallicae*]

HOUSEWIFE

14 A good housewife is of necessity a humbug. [W. M. Thackeray: *Vanity Fair* I]

HUBBARD, MOTHER

15 Old Mother Hubbard

Went to the cupboard,
To fetch her poor dog a bone;
But when she came there
The cupboard was bare
And so the poor dog had none.
[Sarah Catherine Martin (1805)]
Authorship disputed. One of the rhymes (laughing/coffin, 3rd stanza) suggests much earlier age than early 19th century. Miss Martin may have simply altered or improved an older rhyme. Mother Hubbard was an established figure in English folklore. Edmund Spenser wrote Prosopopoia, *or Mother Hubberd's Tale in 1591.*

HUCKLEBERRY FINN
1 All modern American literature comes from one book by Mark Twain called *Huckleberry Finn.* [Ernest Hemingway: *The Green Hills of Africa* I]

HUMANITARIANISM
2 Hath man no second life?—Pitch this
one high!
Sits there no judge in heaven, our
sins to see?—
More strictly, then, the inward judge
obey!
Was Christ a man like us?—Ah! let us
try
If we then, too, can be such men as
he!
[Matthew Arnold: *Anti-Desperation*]
3 It is easier to love humanity as a whole than to love one's neighbor. [Eric Hoffer, in *New York Times Magazine,* Feb. 15, 1959]

HUMANITY
4 I am a man; and nothing human is foreign to me. (*Homo sum; humani nihil a me alienum puto.*) [Terence: *Heauton-timoroumenos* I.i.]
5 Oh wearisome condition of Human-
ity,
Born under one law, to another
bound;
Vanity begot, and yet forbidden vanity,
Created sick, commanded to be sound.
[Sir Fulke Greville: *The Tragedy of
Mustapha*]
6 The still sad music of humanity.
[Wordsworth: *Tintern Abbey*]

7 There are times when one would like to hang the whole human race, and finish the farce. [Mark Twain: *A Connecticut Yankee in King Arthur's Court*]
8 humanity i love you because
when you're hard up you pawn your
intelligence to buy a drink.
[e. e. cummings: *humanity i love you*]

HUMAN NATURE
9 The race of old men is naturally hasty, choleric and impatient of control. [Euripides: *Andromache*]
10 It is wonderful to see with how little nature will be satisfied. [Montaigne: *Essays* II.xii.]
11 There is in human nature generally more of the fool than of the wise; and therefore those faculties by which the foolish part of men's minds is taken are most potent. [Francis Bacon: *Of Boldness*]
12 Nature is often hidden, sometimes overcome, seldom extinguished. [Francis Bacon: *Of Nature in Men*]
nature = human nature, our natural inclinations
13   Nature her custom holds,
Let shame say what it will.
[Shakespeare: *Hamlet* IV.vii.]
14 One touch of nature makes the whole
world kin.
[Shakespeare: *Troilus and Cressida* III.
iii.]
15 We are all prompted by the same motives, all deceived by the same fallacies, all animated by hope, obstructed by danger, entangled by desire and seduced by pleasure. [Samuel Johnson: *The Rambler* No. 60]
16 On some fond breast the parting soul
relies,
Some pious drops the closing eye requires;
E'en from the tomb the voice of Nature cries,
E'en in our ashes live their wonted
fires.
[Thomas Gray: *Elegy Written in a Country Churchyard*]
17 The duty of man is the same in respect to his own nature as in respect to the nature of all other things, namely not to follow it but to amend it. [John Stuart Mill: *Three Essays on Religion*

(Essay 1: Nature)]

1 There is nothing that can be changed more completely than human nature when the job is taken in hand early enough. [G. B. Shaw: Preface to *On the Rocks*]

2 By what he calls the better part of his nature, man has been betrayed. [Henry Miller: *Tropic of Cancer*]

HUMAN RACE

3 I wish I loved the Human Race;
   I wish I loved its silly face;
   I wish I liked the way it walks;
   I wish I liked the way it talks;
   And when I'm introduced to one
   I wish I thought What Jolly Fun!
[Sir Walter Raleigh (1861-1922): *Wishes of an Elderly Man*]

4 Once apparently the chief concern and masterpiece of the gods, the human race now begins to bear the aspect of an accidental by-product of their vast, inscrutable and probably nonsensical operations. [H. L. Mencken: *Prejudices: Third Series*]

HUMBLE

5 Not only humble but umble, which I look upon to be the comparative, or indeed, superlative degree. [Anthony Trollope: *Doctor Thorne* IV]

As with Dickens's Uriah Heep, the prototype of sinister, groveling humility, the omission of the initial aspirate in hum-ble, making it umble, *was in itself a mark of humility. It was probably a social distinction, the lower classes retaining the older, unaspirated pronunciation. Chaucer's Reeve, also a slightly sinister figure, affected a similar humility by having his hair cut like a peasant's.*

HUMILIATION

6 It is a hard matter for a man to go down into the Valley of Humiliation, and to catch no slip by the way. [John Bunyan: *The Pilgrim's Progress* I]

HUMILITY

7 And of his port as meke as is a mayde. [Chaucer: Prologue to *The Canterbury Tales*]

port = *carriage, manner, deportment*

8 One may be humble out of pride.
[Montaigne: *Essays* II.xvii.]

There is a fine illustration of this in Shakespeare's Antony and Cleopatra *in the scene (II.ii.) in which Antony and Octavius Caesar fiercely reciprocate arrogant courtesies.*

9 Humility is a virtue all men preach, none practise, and yet everybody is content to hear. The master thinks it good doctrine for his servants, the laity for the clergy, and the clergy for the laity. [John Selden: *Table Talk*]

10 To be humble to superiors is duty, to equals courtesy, to inferiors nobleness. [Benjamin Franklin: *Poor Richard's Almanack* (1735)]

11 All censure of a man's self is oblique praise. It is in order to show how much he can spare. [Samuel Johnson: in Boswell's *Life,* April 25, 1778]

12 The Devil did grin, for his darling sin
   Is pride that apes humility.
[Coleridge: *The Devil's Thoughts*]

13 "I'm a very umble person. . . . My mother is likewise a very umble person. We live in a numble abode, Master Copperfield, but have much to be thankful for." [Dickens: *David Copperfield* XVI]

14 You've no idea what a poor opinion I have of myself—and how little I deserve it. [W. S. Gilbert: *Ruddigore* I]

15 The tumult and the shouting dies;
   The Captains and the Kings depart:
   Still stands Thine ancient sacrifice,
   An humble and a contrite heart.
   Lord God of Hosts, be with us yet,
   Lest we forget—lest we forget!
[Kipling: *Recessional*]

HUMOR

16 Humor is odd, grotesque, and wild,
   Only by affectation spoiled;
   'Tis never by invention got;
   Men have it when they know it not.
[Jonathan Swift: *To Mr. Delany*]

invention = *exercise of the invention or imagination, conscious mental effort*
Note rhyming of "wild" and "spoiled." This old pronunciation ("spiled") was heard in rural America up to a generation ago.

17 'Twas the saying of an ancient sage, that humour was the only test of gravity; and gravity, of humour. For a subject which would not bear raillery was suspicious; and a jest which would not bear a serious examination was certainly false wit. [Anthony Ashley Cooper, Third Earl of Shaftesbury: *Characteristicks* V]

1 Raillery is a way of speaking in favor of one's wit at the expense of one's better nature. [Montesquieu: *Pensées Diverses*]

> raillery = *kidding, ribbing, and other forms of sadism thinly disguised as humor*

2 Every man has, some time in his life, an ambition to be a wag. [Samuel Johnson: in Mme. d'Arblay's *Diary* V]

> wag = *a merry fellow, the life of the party*
>
> *In its meaning of a humorist,* wag *is an abbreviation of* waghalter—*that is, one who will end up being hanged or wagging a halter in his death struggles. It seems originally to have been applied to mischievous little boys as a term of endearment and then to older drolls, especially such as kept a youthful impudence.*

3 The humorous thief who drank a pot of beer at the gallows blew off the foam because he had heard it was unhealthy. [Emerson: *Society and Solitude*, "Old Age"]

4 And since, I never dare to write
As funny as I can.
[O. W. Holmes: *The Height of the Ridiculous*]

5 Everything human is pathetic. The secret source of Humor itself is not joy but sorrow. There is no humor in heaven. [Mark Twain: *Pudd'nhead Wilson's New Calendar*]

6 Nothing spoils a romance so much as a sense of humour in the woman. [Oscar Wilde: *A Woman of No Importance* I]

7 If a person desires to be a humorist it is necessary that the people around him shall be at least as wise as he is, otherwise his humor will not be comprehended. [James Stephens: *The Demi-Gods* XXVII]

8 There are men so philosophical that they can see humor in their own toothaches. But there has never lived a man so philosophical that he could see the toothache in his own humor. [H. L. Mencken: *Chrestomathy* 618]

9 Humor is a serious thing. I like to think of it as one of our greatest and earliest national resources which must be preserved at all costs. [James Thurber, on CBS-TV, March 4, 1956]

10 Humor is emotional chaos remembered in tranquillity. [James Thurber, quoted *New York Post*, Feb. 29, 1960]

> *Thurber, of course, was parodying Wordsworth's definition of poetry as "emotion recollected in tranquillity."*

HUMPTY DUMPTY

11 Humpty Dumpty sat on a wall,
Humpty Dumpty had a great fall.
All the king's horses,
And all the king's men,
Couldn't put Humpty together again.
[Nursery rhyme: a riddle, to which the answer was "an egg." Earliest known printed form 1803.]

> *The rhyme seems to be universal in all European languages and Humpty variously known as* Boule-Boule, Thille-Lille, Hillerin-Lillerin, Wirgele-Wargele, *etc.*
>
> *Lewis Carroll used him in* Through the Looking Glass *because he was so well known.*

HUNGER

12 Hunger is the teacher of the arts and the inspirer of invention. [Persius: Prologue to the *Satires*]

13 A hungry people is unreasonable, unjust and unmerciful. [Seneca: *De brevitate vitae* XVIII]

14 Hunger is the best sauce. [Cicero: *De finibus* II]

> *The proverb is universal and has been attributed to Socrates. The Latins had also a saying that hunger is the best cook, as also do the Germans. The French say that hunger is the first course. The proverb appears in John Florio's* Firste Fruites *and in Cervantes:* Don Quixote *II.5., etc., ad infinitum.*

15 I am so sore forhungered that my belly weeneth my throat is cut. [John Palsgrave: *Acolastus* (1540)]

> *Palsgrave was probably quoting, for the jest is redolent of hoary antiquity. Like many jokes whose age must be defined in geologic terms, however, it is still alive. It's very common in rustic American humor where it usually appears as: "I*

*ain't et for so long my belly thinks my
throat is cut." Swift listed it as venerable and in need of retirement in 1738.*

1 They said they were an-hungry;
     sigh'd forth proverbs,
That hunger broke stone walls, that
     dogs must eat,
That meat was made for mouths, that
     the gods sent not
Corn for the rich men only: with
     these shreds
They vented their complainings.
[Shakespeare: *Coriolanus* I.i.]
2 'Tis not the meat, but 'tis the appe-
         tite
Makes eating a delight.
[Sir John Suckling: *Of Thee, Kind Boy*]
3 Hunger is insolent. [Alexander Pope's
trans. of a famous passage in the Seventh
Book of Homer's *Odyssey*]
> *T. E. Lawrence's translation of the en-
> tire passage:*
> *"There is not anything so exigent as a
> man's ravening belly, which will not let
> him alone to feel even so sore a grief as
> this in my heart; but prefers to over-
> whelm his misery with its needs for meat
> and drink, forcibly and shamelessly com-
> pelling him to put its replenishment
> above his soul's agony."*

4 Obliged by hunger and request of
friends. [Alexander Pope: *Epistle to Dr.
Arbuthnot*]
5 An empty stomach is not a good political adviser. [Albert Einstein: *Cosmic
Religion*]
6 No one can worship God or love his
neighbor on an empty stomach. [Wood-
row Wilson, Speech, May 23, 1912]
7 A hungry man is not a free man.
[Adlai Stevenson, Speech, Sept. 6, 1952]

HUNGRY
8 Yond Cassius has a lean and hungry
         look.
[Shakespeare: *Julius Caesar* I.ii.]

HUNTER
9 Nimrod the mighty hunter before the
Lord. [Genesis 10:9]
10 And the hunter home from the hill.
[R. L. Stevenson: *Requiem*]

HUNTING
11 The dusky night rides down the sky

And ushers in the morn:
The hounds all join in glorious cry,
 The huntsman winds his horn;
And a-hunting we will go.
[Henry Fielding: *A-Hunting We Will
Go*]
12 It is very strange, and very melan-
choly, that the paucity of human pleas-
ures should persuade us ever to call
hunting one of them. [Samuel Johnson:
in Mrs. Piozzi's *Anecdotes of the Late
Samuel Johnson*]
> *Johnson added: "The dogs have less sa-
> gacity than I could have prevailed on
> myself to suppose."*

13 The English country gentleman gal-
loping after a fox—the unspeakable in
full pursuit of the uneatable. [Oscar
Wilde: *A Woman of No Importance* I]
14 Hi! handsome hunting man,
 Fire your little gun.
Bang! Now the animal
 Is dead and dumb and done.
Nevermore to peep again, creep
     again, leap again,
Eat or sleep or drink again, oh, what
         fun!
[Walter De La Mare: *Hi!*]

HURRY
15 No man who is in a hurry is quite
civilized. [Will Durant: *The Life of
Greece*]

HURT
16 *Romeo.* Courage, man; the hurt cannot be much.
 Mercutio. No, 'tis not so deep as a
  well, nor so wide as a church door;
  but 'tis enough, 'twill serve.
[Shakespeare: *Romeo and Juliet* III.i.]

HUSBANDS
17   And Jesu Crist us sende
Housbondes meke, yonge, and fresshe
        a-bedde,
And grace t'overbyde hem that we
        wedde.
[Chaucer: *The Wife of Bath's Tale* (con-
clusion)]
> *meke = meek, obedient; t'overbyde = to
> outlive, survive, so that they (their wives)
> can marry again*
> *The Wife's prayer for all women. How
> well the prayer has been answered in*

several particulars we shall—despite Kinsey—never know. But the last item has certainly been granted. Wives now outlive their husbands (statistically) to an unprecedented extent and the condition is increasing.

1 The better the workman, the worse husband. [T. Draxe: *A Treasury of . . . Sententious Proverbs* (1616)]

2 A husband is a plaster which cures all girls' complaints. [Molière: *The Physician in Spite of Himself* II.iii.]

3 Not louder shrieks to pitying heav'n are cast,
When husbands, or when lap-dogs breathe their last.
[Alexander Pope: *The Rape of the Lock* III]

4 The wictim o' connubiality. [Dickens: *The Pickwick Papers* XX]

HUSBANDS AND WIVES

5 Wives, submit yourselves unto your own husbands, as unto the Lord. For the husband is the head of the wife, even as Christ is the head of the church. [Ephesians 5:22-23]

6 Wommen desyren to have sovereyntee
As wel over hir housbond as hir love,
And for to been in maistrie him above.
[Chaucer: *The Wife of Bath's Tale*]
A knight in the tale is given a year and a day—his life to be forfeit if he fails—to answer the question "What is it women most desire?" His answer (supplied by a witch) is above and sufficed to save his life. No one has yet come up with a better one.

7 A good wife maketh a good husband. [John Heywood: *Proverbs*]

8 Serve your husband as your master, and beware of him as a traitor. [Montaigne: *Essays* III.v.]

9 A light wife doth make a heavy husband.
[Shakespeare: *Merchant of Venice* V.i.]

10 Thy husband is thy lord, thy life, thy keeper,
Thy head, thy sovereign: one that cares for thee,
And for thy maintenance commits his body
To painful labor, both by sea and land;
To watch the night in storms, the day in cold,
While thou liest warm at home, secure and safe;
And craves no other tribute at thy hands,
But love, fair looks, and true obedience;
Too little payment for so great a debt.
[Shakespeare: *The Taming of the Shrew* V.ii.]

11 The calmest husbands make the stormiest wives. [Thomas Dekker: *The Honest Whore* Part I. V.i.]
Where it is said to be a proverb carved on cheese trenchers.

12 For nothing lovelier can be found
In woman, than to study household good,
And good works in her husband to promote.
[John Milton: *Paradise Lost* IX.232-234]

13 God's universal law
Gave to the man despotic power
Over his female in due awe.
[John Milton: *Samson Agonistes* 1053]

14 He knows little who will tell his wife all he knows. [Thomas Fuller (1608-1661): *Holy and Profane State*, "The Good Husband"]

15 There are few women so perfect that their husbands do not regret having married them at least once a day. [La Bruyère: *Les Caractères*]

16 For story and experience tell us,
That man grows old and woman jealous;
Both would their little ends secure:
He sighs for freedom, she for power.
His wishes tend abroad to roam,
And hers, to domineer at home.
[Matthew Prior: *Alma* II]

17 A man must ask his wife's leave to thrive. [John Ray: *English Proverbs* (1678)]
That is, no amount of industry, skill and thrift on the husband's part will suffice if the wife is reckless and wasteful.

18 The husband's sullen, dogged, shy,
The wife grows flippant in reply;
He loves command and due restriction,
And she as well likes contradiction.
She never slavishly submits,

She'll have her will, or have her fits;
He his way tugs, she t'other draws;
The man grows jealous, and with
    cause.
[John Gay: *Cupid, Hymen, and Plutus*]
1 Between a man and his wife a husband's infidelity is nothing. The man imposes no bastards upon his wife. [Samuel Johnson: in Boswell's *Life,* October 10, 1779]
2 Ah, gentle dames! it gars me greet
To think how mony counsels sweet,
How mony lengthen'd sage advices,
The husband frae the wife despises!
[Burns: *Tam o' Shanter*]
gars me greet = *makes me cry*
3 A husband and wife ought to continue so long united as they love each other: any law which should bind them to cohabitation for one moment after the decay of their affection would be a most intolerable tyranny, and the most unworthy of toleration. [Shelley: Notes to *Queen Mab*]
4 A manly form at her side she saw,
And joy was duty, and love was law.
[J. G. Whittier: *Maud Muller*]
5 Husband and wife come to look alike at last. [O. W. Holmes: *The Professor at the Breakfast-Table* VII]
6 For him she plays, to him she sings
Of early faith and plighted vows;
She knows but matters of the house,
And he, he knows a thousand things.

Her faith is fixt and cannot move,
She darkly feels him great and wise,
She dwells on him with faithful
    eyes,
"I cannot understand; I love."
[Tennyson: *In Memoriam* XCVII]
In this section of In Memoriam *Tennyson depicts the ideal couple in an evening at home. He, "rapt in matters dark and deep," threading "the labyrinth of the mind," and reading "the secret of the star," while she finds "her bliss" in contemplating "a withered violet" which he had given her years before.*
7 The matter between husband and wife stands much the same as it does between two cocks in the same yard. The conqueror once is generally the conqueror for ever after. The prestige of victory is everything. [Anthony Trollope:

Barchester Towers XVII]
Trollope repeats the observation in XXVI. Barchester Towers *appeared in 1857 and thus antedated by two generations the barnyard studies of the Norwegian ecologist, Schjelderup-Ebbe, which established the phrase "pecking order."*

The scientist (and the novelist) saw that a position in the social hierarchy, once achieved or imposed, is not easily changed and that the struggle for position, which many moralists urge us to scorn, is one of the most serious and important things in life—that a snub accepted relegates one permanently to a position inferior to that of the snubber and that a snub conferred establishes perpetual superiority.

8 There is something so indescribably sweet and satisfying, to a man, in the knowledge that he has forgiven his wife —forgiven her freely, and with all his heart. It seems as if that had made her, as it were, doubly his own; he has given her a new life, so to speak; and she has in a way become both wife and child to him. [Henrik Ibsen: *A Doll's House* III]
9 A man should be taller, older, heavier, uglier, and hoarser than his wife. [E. W. Howe: *Country Town Sayings*]
10 One can always recognize women who trust their husbands. They look so thoroughly unhappy. [Oscar Wilde: *Lady Windermere's Fan* II]
11 There is only one thing for a man to do who is married to a woman who enjoys spending money, and that is to enjoy earning it. [E. W. Howe: *Country Town Sayings*]
12 Every intelligent woman knows instinctively that the highest aspirations of her husband are fundamentally inimical to her, and that their realization is apt to cost her her possession of him. [H. L. Mencken: *Prejudices: Fourth Series*]

HYGIENE
13 Hygiene is the corruption of medicine by morality. [H. L. Mencken: *Prejudices: Third Series*]

HYPERBOLE
14 The speaking in perpetual hyperbole is comely in nothing but love. [Francis Bacon: *Of Love*]

HYPERION

1 So excellent a king; that was, to this,
Hyperion to a satyr.
[Shakespeare: *Hamlet* I.ii.]

HYPNOTISM

2 He holds him with his glittering
eye—
The Wedding-Guest stood still,
And listens like a three years' child:
The mariner hath his will.
[Coleridge: *The Ancient Mariner* I]

HYPOCRISY

3 The smyler with the knyf under the
cloke.
[Chaucer: *The Knight's Tale*]
4 It is of great consequence to disguise
your inclination, and to play the hypocrite well. [Machiavelli: *The Prince* XI]
5 And thus I clothe my naked villainy
With old odd ends stolen out of holy
writ;
And seem a saint, when most I play
the devil.
[Shakespeare: *Richard III* I.iii.]
6 It oft falls out,
To have what we would have, we
speak
Not what we mean.
[Shakespeare: *Measure for Measure*
II.iv.]
7 Away, and mock the time with fairest
show;
False face must hide what the false
heart doth know.
[Shakespeare: *Macbeth* I.vii.]
8 To show an unfelt sorrow is an office
Which the false man does easy.
[Shakespeare: *Macbeth* II.iii.]
9 I want that glib and oily art,
To speak and purpose not.
[Shakespeare: *King Lear* I.i.]
10 A fairer person lost not heav'n; he
seemed
For dignity compos'd and high ex-
ploit:

But all was false and hollow; though
his tongue
Dropt manna, and could make the
worse appear
The better reason, to perplex and
dash
Maturest counsels.
[John Milton: *Paradise Lost* II.110-115]
Belial *is a Hebrew word meaning worthless or lawless one. It is used in the scriptures for the Devil. Milton assigns the
name to the most suavely evil of the
great fallen angels, here described.*
11 For neither man nor angel can discern
Hypocrisy, the only evil that walks
Invisible, except to God alone.
[John Milton: *Paradise Lost* III.682-684]
12 Hypocrisy is the homage which vice
renders to virtue. [La Rochefoucauld:
Maxims]
13 He that speaks me fair and loves me
not,
I'll speak him fair and trust him not.
[John Ray: *English Proverbs*]
14 Hypocrisy at the fashionable end of
the town is very different from hypocrisy
in the city. The modish hypocrite endeavors to appear more vicious than he
really is; the other kind of hypocrite
more virtuous. [Joseph Addison: *The
Spectator* No. 399]

HYPOCRITE(S)

15 No man is a hypocrite in his pleasures. [Samuel Johnson: in Boswell's *Life*
(1783)]
16 We are not hypocrites in our sleep.
[William Hazlitt: *On Dreams*]

HYPOTHESIS

17 The great tragedy of Science—the
slaying of a beautiful hypothesis by an
ugly fact. [T. H. Huxley: *Biogenesis
and Abiogenesis*]
18 An honorable man will not be bul-
lied by a hypothesis. [Bergen Evans:
The Natural History of Nonsense XIX]

I

IBSEN

1   He eliminated the First Act
    He practised economy
        and
    Towards the end of a long and ar-
            duous life
Abolished the soliloquy and the aside
[Bonamy Dobree's suggested epitaph for Ibsen]

ICE

2 And ice, mast-high, came floating by,
   As green as emerald.
[Coleridge: *The Ancient Mariner* I]

ICICLES

3 When icicles hang by the wall.
[Shakespeare: *Love's Labour's Lost* V.ii.]
4   Silent icicles,
   Quietly shining to the quiet moon.
[Coleridge: *Frost at Midnight*]

IDEA(S)

5 It is not in the power of the most exalted wit or enlarged understanding, by
any quickness or variety of thought, to
invent or frame one new simple idea.
[John Locke: *An Essay Concerning Human Understanding* II, Ch. II: "Of Simple Ideas"]
6 That fellow seems to me to possess
but one idea, and that a wrong one.
[Samuel Johnson: in Boswell's *Life* (1770)]
7 It is the idea, the feeling and the love
God means mankind should strive for
           and show forth,
Whatever be the process to that
           end—
And not historic knowledge, logic
           sound,
And metaphysical acumen, sure!
[Robert Browning: *Bishop Blougram's Apology*]
8 Man is not a circle with a single centre; he is an ellipse with two foci. Facts
are one, ideas are the other. [Victor
Hugo: *Les Misérables* VII.i.]
9 The ruling ideas of each age have
ever been the ideas of its ruling class.
[Karl Marx: *Manifesto of the Communist Party* I]

10 The ideas of economists and political
philosophers, both when they are right
and when they are wrong, are more powerful than is commonly understood. Indeed, the world is ruled by little else.
Practical men, who believe themselves
to be quite exempt from any intellectual
influences, are usually the slaves of some
defunct economist. Madmen in authority,
who hear voices in the air, are distilling
their frenzy from some academic scribbler of a few years back. I am sure that
the power of vested interests is vastly ex-
aggerated compared with the gradual
encroachment of ideas. [John Maynard
Keynes: *The General Theory of Employment, Interest, and Money* XXIV]

IDEAL(S)

11 Beauty! I can't endure the thought
that a man of lofty mind and heart begins with the ideal of the Madonna and
ends with the ideal of Sodom. What's
still more awful is that a man with the
ideal of Sodom in his soul does not re-
nounce the ideal of Madonna, and his
heart may be on fire with that ideal, genuinely on fire, just as in his days of youth
and innocence. Yes, man is broad, too
broad, indeed. I'd have him narrower.
[Dostoyevsky: *The Brothers Karamazov* III.iii.]

IDEALIST(S)

12 And therefore does not stoop, nor lie
           in wait
   For wealth, or honours, or for
           worldly state.
[Wordsworth: *Character of the Happy Warrior*]
13 When they come downstairs from
their Ivory Towers, Idealists are apt to
walk straight into the gutter. [Logan
Pearsall Smith: *Afterthoughts*]
14 An idealist is one who, on noticing
that a rose smells better than a cabbage,
concludes that it will also make better
soup. [H. L. Mencken: *Chrestomathy* 617]

IDENTITY

1 There was a little woman,
As I have heard tell,
She went to market
Her eggs for to sell;
She went to market on a market day,
And fell asleep
On the King's highway.
[Nursery rhyme (1775)]

A passing peddler cuts off her petticoats. When she awakes she doubts her own identity and hurries home to see if her little dog will know her. But the little dog "began to bark, | And she began to cry, | Lawk a mercy on me. | This is none of I!"

In a Scottish version (1797) she "got a little drappikie" at the fair and feared her husband: "If Johnnie find me barrel-sick, I'm sure he'll claw my skin." So she lies down to sleep it off. Her uncertainty about who she was has, under these circumstances, been experienced by others.

IDIOM

2 Correct idiom is the foundation of good style. [Aristotle: *Rhetoric* III]

IDIOT

3 The portrait of a blinking idiot. [Shakespeare: *The Merchant of Venice* II.ix.]
4 Him whom you love, your Idiot Boy. [Wordsworth: *The Idiot Boy*]

IDLE

5 As idle as a painted ship
Upon a painted ocean.
[Coleridge: *The Ancient Mariner* II]

IDLENESS

6 By doing nothing, men learn to do evil. [Columella: *De re rustica* XI.i.]
7 The sweetness of idleness. [Tacitus: *Agricola* III]

End of first century, A.D. Possibly the forerunner of the Italian dolce far niente *= the sweetness of doing nothing.*

8 Rushing to and fro, busily employed in idleness. [Phaedrus: *Fables* V.ii.]
9 Idleness, the badge of gentry. [Robert Burton: *The Anatomy of Melancholy* I.ii.2.vi]
10 Of all our faults, the one that we excuse most easily is idleness. [La Rochefoucauld: *Maxims*]
11 The insupportable labour of doing nothing. [Sir Richard Steele: *The Tatler*]
12 For Satan finds some mischief still
For idle hands to do.
[Isaac Watts: *Divine Songs* XX]
still = *always*
13 Certain days set apart by the church to be spent in holy idleness, which is favorable to piety. . . . The safest way of passing such days is to sit and yawn your head off. [Voltaire: *Philosophical Dictionary*]
14 Perhaps man is the only being that can properly be called idle. [Samuel Johnson: *The Idler* No. 1]
15 As peace is the end of war, so to be idle is the ultimate purpose of the busy. [Samuel Johnson: *The Idler* No. 1]
16 Absence of occupation is not rest,
A mind quite vacant is a mind distress'd.
[William Cowper: *Retirement*]
17 How dull it is to pause, to make an end,
To rust unburnish'd, not to shine in use!
As tho' to breathe were life!
[Tennyson: *Ulysses*]
18 I loafe and invite my soul.
[Walt Whitman: *Leaves of Grass,* "Song of Myself" Sec. I.]

IDLER

19 Every man is or hopes to be, an idler. [Samuel Johnson: *The Idler* No. 1]
20 An idler is a watch that wants both hands,
As useless if it goes as if it stands.
[William Cowper: *Retirement*]

IDOLS

21 Four species of idols beset the human mind: idols of the tribe, idols of the den, idols of the market, and idols of the theatre. [Francis Bacon: *Novum Organum* II]

IF

22 Your If is the only peace-maker; much virtue in If.

[Shakespeare: *As You Like It* V.iv.]
1 If you can keep your head when all
about you
Are losing theirs and blaming it on
you. . . .
Yours is the Earth and everything
that's in it.
[Rudyard Kipling: *If—*]

IGNORANCE

2 There is a kind of abecedarian ignorance which precedes learning; another doctoral, following learning—an
ignorance which learning does beget,
even as it spoils the first. [Montaigne:
Essays I.liv.]
3 All the abuses of the world are en-
gendered upon this, that we are taught
to fear to make profession of our ignorance and are bound to accept and allow
all that we cannot refute. [Montaigne:
Essays III.xi.]
4 Art hath an enemy call'd ignorance.
[Ben Jonson: Prologue to *Every Man
Out of His Humour*]
5 The truest characters of ignorance
Are vanity, and pride, and arrogance.
[Samuel Butler (1612-1680): *Miscellaneous Thoughts* 88]
characters = *characteristics*
6 Ignorance, Madam, pure ignorance.
[Samuel Johnson: his answer when
asked by a lady why he had defined *pastern* as "the knee of a horse" in his *Dictionary;* in Boswell's *Life* (1755)]
*Much and justly admired for its down-
right honesty, this celebrated retort must
be judged in its context. The great classical scholar, moralist and wit felt it no
great shame to be a little uncertain of
the anatomy of a horse.*

*Johnson was not always so amiable,
however. To two ladies who had praised
him effusively for omitting indecent
words from the dictionary he said, "I
see you've been looking for them."*
7 Mankind have a great aversion to intellectual labor; even supposing knowledge to be easily attainable, more people would be content to be ignorant
than would take even a little trouble to
acquire it. [Samuel Johnson: in Boswell's *Life*, May 24, 1763]
8 Where ignorance is bliss
'Tis folly to be wise.

[Thomas Gray: *Ode on a Distant Prospect of Eton College*]
9 Ignorance is of a peculiar nature;
once dispelled, it is impossible to rees-
tablish it. It is not originally a thing of
itself, but is only the absence of knowledge; and though man may be kept ignorant, he cannot be made ignorant.
[Thomas Paine: *The Rights of Man* I]
10 There is nothing more frightening
than active ignorance. [Goethe: *Sprüche
in Prosa*]
11 A plowman is not an ignorant man
because he does not know how to read;
if he knows how to plow he is not to be
called an ignorant man. [William Cobbett: *Advice to Young Men* III]
12 Ignorance is degrading only when
found in company with riches. [Scho-
penhauer: *On Books and Reading*]
13 That there should one man die ignorant who had capacity for knowledge,
this I call a tragedy. [Thomas Carlyle:
Sartor Resartus III.iv.]
14 There are many things of which a
wise man might wish to be ignorant.
[Emerson: *Demonology*]
15   Blind and naked Ignorance
Delivers brawling judgments, un-
ashamed,
On all things all day long.
[Tennyson: *Merlin and Vivien*]
16 Ignorance gives one a large range of
probabilities. [George Eliot: *Daniel Deronda* II.xiii.]
17 A man's ignorance is as much his private property and as precious in his own
eyes as his family Bible. [O. W. Holmes:
The Young Practitioner]
18 It is better to know nothing than to
know what ain't so.
[H. W. Shaw ("Josh Billings"): *Proverb*]
19 It may be that the ignorant man,
alone,
Has any chance to mate his life with
life.
[Wallace Stevens: *The Sense of the
Sleight-Of-Hand Man*]

IGNORANT

20 That man must be tremendously ignorant: he answers every question that
is put to him. [Voltaire: *Dictionnaire
Philosophique: Annales*]
21 To be ignorant of one's ignorance is

the malady of the ignorant. [Amos Bronson Alcott: *Table Talk*]
1 Uncultivated minds are not full of wild flowers. Villainous weeds grow in them, and they are the haunt of toads. [Logan Pearsall Smith: *Afterthoughts*]

ILL
2 Things bad begun make strong themselves by ill.
[Shakespeare: *Macbeth* III.ii.]
3 Let well alone, lad, and ill too at times.
[Kingsley: *Water Babies* I]

> "Oh, at home had I but stayed
> 'Prenticed to my father's trade,
> Had I stuck to plane and adze,
> I had not been lost, my lads.
>
> "Then I might have built perhaps
> Gallows-trees for other chaps,
> Never dangled on my own,
> Had I left but ill alone."
>   A. E. Housman: The Carpenter's Son

ILL-FAVORED
4 An ill-favoured thing, sir, but mine own.
[Shakespeare: *As You Like It* V.iv.]

ILL-GOTTEN GAIN
5 That ill-gotten gain never prospers is the trite consolation administered to the easy dupe, when he has been tricked out of his money or estate. [Charles Lamb: *Popular Fallacies*]

ILLICIT
6 The illicit has an added charm. [Tacitus: *Annals* XIII.i.]
7 But on the whole they were a happy pair,
As happy as unlawful love could make them;
The gentleman was fond, the lady fair,
Their chains so slight, 'twas not worth while to break them.
[Byron: *Beppo* LIV]

ILLUSION
8 Doth any man doubt that if there were taken out of men's minds vain opinions, flattering hopes, false valuations, imaginations as one would, and the like, but it would leave the minds of a number of men poor shrunken things, full of melancholy and indisposition, and unpleasing to themselves? [Francis Bacon: *Of Truth*]
    imaginations as one would = *day dreams and what we call rationalizations*

IMAGE
9 Thou shalt not make unto thee any graven image, or any likeness of anything that is in heaven above, or that is in the earth beneath, or that is in the water under the earth. [Exodus 20:4]

IMAGINATION
10 For the imagination of man's heart is evil from his youth. [Genesis 8:21]
11 O, who can hold a fire in his hand
By thinking on the frosty Caucasus?
Or cloy the hungry edge of appetite
By bare imagination of a feast
Or wallow naked in December snow
By thinking on fantastic summer's heat?
O, no! the apprehension of the good
Gives but the greater feeling to the worse.
[Shakespeare: *Richard II* I.iii.]
    fantastic = *fancied*
12 In my mind's eye, Horatio.
[Shakespeare: *Hamlet* I.ii.]
13   My imaginations are as foul
As Vulcan's stithy.
[Shakespeare: *Hamlet* III.ii.]
14 Why do I yield to that suggestion
Whose horrid image doth unfix my hair
And make my seated heart knock at my ribs,
Against the use of nature? Present fears
Are less than horrible imaginings.
[Shakespeare: *Macbeth* I.iii.]
15 Give me an ounce of civet, good apothecary, to sweeten my imagination. [Shakespeare: *King Lear* IV.vi.]
16 Were it not for imagination, Sir, a man would be as happy in the arms of a chambermaid as of a Duchess. [Samuel Johnson: Boswell's *Life,* May 9, 1778]
17 The Right Honorable gentleman is indebted to his memory for his jests, and to his imagination for his facts. [Richard Brinsley Sheridan: *Sheridaniana,*

"Speech in Reply to Mr. Dundas"]
1 The great instrument of moral good is the imagination. [Shelley: *A Defence of Poetry*]
2 We want the creative faculty to imagine that which we know. [Shelley: *A Defence of Poetry*]
> One of the really profound comments on the modern world. Shelley continues:
> "We want the generous impulse to act that which we imagine; we want the poetry of life: our calculations have outrun conception; we have eaten more than we can digest. The cultivation of those sciences which have enlarged the Empire of man over the external world, has, for want of the poetical faculty, proportionately circumscribed those of the internal world; and man, having enslaved the elements, remains himself a slave."

3 What the imagination seizes as beauty must be truth—whether it existed before or not. . . . The imagination may be compared to Adam's dream—he awoke and found it truth. [Keats: Letter to Benjamin Bailey, Nov. 22, 1817]
4 His imagination resembled the wings of an ostrich.
It enabled him to run, though not to soar.
[Macaulay: *On John Dryden*]
5 Imagination is more important than knowledge. [Albert Einstein: *On Science*]

IMITATION
6 Agesilaus, being invited once to hear a man who admirably imitated the nightingale, declined, saying he had heard the nightingale itself. [Plutarch: *Lives,* "Life of Agesilaus"]
7 No man ever yet became great by imitation. [Samuel Johnson: *The Rambler* No. 154]
8 Imitation is the sincerest flattery.
[C. C. Colton: *Lacon*]

IMMORALITY
9 But now I'm going to be immoral; now
I mean to show things really as they are,
Not as they ought to be.
[Byron: *Don Juan* XII.xl.]

> *A good definition. One of the strongest canons of morality is that the current fictions must be respected.*

IMMORTALITY: doubt and fear of
10 As the cloud is consumed and vanisheth away: so he that goeth down to the grave shall come up no more.
He shall return no more to his house, neither shall his place know him any more. [Job 7:9-10]
11 If a man die, shall he live again? [Job 14:14]
12   Who would fardels bear,
To grunt and sweat under a weary life,
But that the dread of something after death,
The undiscover'd country, from whose bourn
No traveler returns, puzzles the will,
And makes us rather bear those ills we have
Than fly to others that we know not of?
[Shakespeare: *Hamlet* III.i.]
13 To desire immortality is to desire the perpetuation of a great mistake. [Schopenhauer: *The World as Will and Idea*]
14 Ah, Christ, that it were possible
For one short hour to see
The souls we loved, that they might tell us
What and where they be.
[Tennyson: *Maud* II]
15 O threats of Hell and Hopes of Paradise!
One thing at least is certain—*This* Life flies,
One thing is certain and the rest is Lies;
The Flower that once has blown for ever dies.
[*Rubáiyát of Omar Khayyám* (trans. Edward FitzGerald)]
16 If a man has sent his teeth and his hair and perhaps two or three limbs to the grave before him, the presumption should be that as he knows nothing further of these when they have once left him, so will he know nothing of the rest of him when it too is dead. The whole may surely be argued from the parts. [Samuel Butler (1835-1902): *Notebooks*]
17 The desire for immortality seems

never to have had a very strong hold upon mankind, and the belief is less widely held than is usually stated. [William Osler: *Science and Immortality* II]

1 The condition of a dead man who doesn't believe that he is dead. [H. L. Mencken]

IMMORTALITY: hope for and affirmation of

2 I believe that our estranged and divided ashes shall unite again; that our separated dust, after so many pilgrimages and transformations into the parts of minerals, plants, animals, elements, shall, at the voice of God, return to their primitive shapes, and join again to make up their primary and predestinate forms. [Sir Thomas Browne: *Religio Medici* I]

3 There is nothing strictly immortal, but immortality; whatever hath no beginning may be confident of no end. [Sir Thomas Browne: *Urn-Burial* V]

4 Weep no more, woeful Shepherds, weep no more,
For Lycidas your sorrow is not dead,
Sunk though he be beneath the watery floor.
So sinks the day-star in the Ocean bed,
And yet anon repairs his drooping head,
And tricks his beams, and with new-spangled Ore,
Flames in the forehead of the morning sky:
So Lycidas sunk low, but mounted high,
Through the dear might of Him that walked the waves
Where, other groves and other streams along,
With Nectar pure his oozy locks he laves,
And hears the unexpressive nuptial Song,
In the blest Kingdoms meek of joy and love.
There entertain him all the Saints above,
In solemn troops, and sweet Societies,
That sing, and singing in their glory move,
And wipe the tears for ever from his eyes.
[John Milton: *Lycidas*]

5 He felt through all his fleshly dress
Bright shoots of everlastingness.
[Henry Vaughn: *Silex Scintillans* I]

6 When I can read my title clear
To mansions in the skies,
I'll bid farewell to every fear,
And wipe my weeping eyes.
[Isaac Watts: *Hymns and Spiritual Songs*]

7 Still seems it strange, that thou shouldst live forever?
Is it less strange, that thou shouldst live at all?
This is a miracle; and that no more.
[Edward Young: *Night Thoughts* VII]

8 Though inland far we be,
Our souls have sight of that immortal sea
Which brought us hither.
[Wordsworth: *Intimations of Immortality*]

9 Immortality is the glorious discovery of Christianity. [William Ellery Channing: *Immortality*]

10 He has out-soared the shadow of our night;
Envy and calumny, and hate and pain,
And that unrest which men miscall delight,
Can touch him not and torture not again;
From the contagion of the world's slow stain,
He is secure, and now can never mourn
A heart grown cold, a head grown gray in vain.
[Shelley: *Adonais*]

11 I am borne darkly, fearfully, afar;
Whilst, burning through the inmost veil of Heaven,
The soul of Adonais, like a star,
Beacons from the abode where the Eternal are.
[Shelley: *Adonais* XL]

12 He lives, he wakes—'tis Death is dead, not he.
[Shelley: *Adonais*]

13 I long to believe in immortality. [Keats: Letter to Fanny Brawne (1818)]

14 Oh, may I join the choir invisible
Of those immortal dead who live again.
[George Eliot: *The Choir Invisible*]

IMMORTALITY: miscellaneous

1   He ne'er is crown'd
With immortality, who fears to fol-
                                      low
Where airy voices lead.
[Keats: *Endymion* II]

2 The blazing evidence of immortality
is our dissatisfaction with any other solution. [Emerson: *Journals*]
*This was also the blazing evidence for
demoniacal possession, phlebotomy, the
four humors and scores of other instances
of ignorance and silliness.*

3 To himself every one is an immortal;
he may know that he is going to die, but
he can never know that he is dead.
[Samuel Butler (1835-1902): *Notebooks*]

4 Humanity will find in itself the
power to live for virtue even without believing in immortality. It will find it in
love for freedom, for equality, for fraternity. [Dostoyevsky: *The Brothers Karamazov* I.ii.]

5 It is futile to assign the place an artist
is likely to take in the future. There are
fashions in immortality. . . . Books and
pictures read differently to different generations. [William Rothenstein: *Men
and Memories* I]

IMPARTIALITY

6 He maketh his sun to rise on the evil
and on the good, and sendeth rain on the
just and on the unjust. [Matthew 5:45]

7 No man's defects sought they to know;
So never made themselves a foe.
No man's good deeds did they com-
                                      mend;
So never rais'd themselves a friend.
[Matthew Prior: *An Epitaph*]

8 Sir Roger told them, with the air of a
man who would not give his judgment
rashly, that much might be said on both
sides. [Joseph Addison: *The Spectator*
No. 122]

9 Alike reserv'd to blame or to com-
                                      mend,
A tim'rous foe, and a suspicious
                                      friend.
[Alexander Pope: *Epistle to Dr. Arbuth-
not*]

IMPATIENCE

10 In the morning thou shalt say, Would
God it were even! and at even thou shalt
say, Would God it were morning! [Deu-
teronomy 28:67]

11   So tedious is this day
As is the night before some festival
To an impatient child that hath new
                                      robes,
And may not wear them.
[Shakespeare: *Romeo and Juliet* III.ii.]

12 Why, what a wasp-stung and impa-
                                 tient fool
Art thou to break into this woman's
                                      mood,
Tying thine ear to no tongue but
                                 thine own.
[Shakespeare: *I Henry IV* I.iii.]

13 Glad of a quarrel, straight I clap the
                                      door,
Sir, let me see your works and you no
                                      more.
[Alexander Pope: *Epistle to Dr. Arbuth-
not*]

14 A populace never rebels from passion
for attack, but from impatience of suffering. [Edmund Burke: *Speech on Conciliation of the American Colonies*]

15 "I have answered three questions,
                      and that is enough,"
Said his father. "Don't give your-
                                 self airs!
Do you think I can listen all day to
                                 such stuff?
Be off, or I'll kick you down-stairs!"
[Lewis Carroll: *Alice's Adventures in
Wonderland* V]

IMPERFECTION

16 Never the time and the place
And the loved one all together!
[Robert Browning: *Never the Time and
the Place*]

IMPETUOSITY

17 He staid not for brake, and he
                      stopp'd not for stone,
He swam the Eske river where ford
                           there was none.
[Sir Walter Scott: *The Lay of the Last
Minstrel,* "Lochinvar"]

IMPIETY

18 IMPIETY. Your irreverence toward my
deity. [Ambrose Bierce: *The Devil's Dictionary*]

IMPOSSIBLE

19 It is certain because it is impossible.

[Tertullian: *De Carne Christi*]
Usually quoted as Credo quia impossible
("I believe because it is impossible").
Attr. St. Augustine, in the form Credo
quia absurdum *("I believe because it is
absurd").*
1 I love those who long for the impossible. [Goethe: *Faust* II.ii.]

IMPOSSIBILITIES
2 Go, and catch a falling star,
Get with child a mandrake root,
Tell me, where all past years are,
Or who cleft the Devil's foot.
[Donne: *Go and Catch a Falling Star*]
*The root of the mandrake, or mandragora, is often bifurcated and was thought
to resemble a man. The root was thought
to produce fertility in women (see: Genesis 30:14-16). Donne is listing a series of
impossibilities.*

IMPROPRIETY
3 Impropriety is the soul of wit.
[W. Somerset Maugham: *The Moon and
Sixpence* IV]

IMPROVEMENT
4 Striving to better, oft we mar what's
well.
[Shakespeare: *King Lear* I.iv.]
5 Mend when thou canst; be better at
thy leisure.
[Shakespeare: *King Lear* II.iv.]
6 Ah Love! could you and I with Him
conspire
To grasp this sorry Scheme of Things
entire,
Would we not shatter it to bits—
and then
Remold it nearer to the Heart's Desire!
[*Rubáiyát of Omar Khayyám* (trans. Edward FitzGerald)]

IMPUDENCE
7 Prompt to assail, and careless of defence,
Invulnerable in his impudence,
He dares the world and, eager of a
name,
He thrusts about and jostles into
fame.
So fond of loud report, that not to
miss
Of being known (his last and utmost
bliss)

He rather would be known for what
he is.
[Dryden: *The Hind and the Panther*]
*Dryden's lines on Bishop Burnet still
serve for the publicity hound. The last
three lines must be among the sharpest
in all satire.*
8 Bold knaves thrive without one grain
of sense,
But good men starve for want of impudence.
[Dryden: *Constantine the Great*]
9 Taylor was an instance of how far
impudence could carry ignorance. [Samuel Johnson: in Boswell's *Life*, April 24,
1779]
*This was the Chevalier John Taylor,
"Ophthalmiater Pontifical, Imperial, and
Royal," as he styled himself. He was a
competent physician but affected enormous learning and omniscience. Before
performing his cures, he made bombastic
orations in what he called "the true Ciceronian, prodigiously difficult." To make
it even more difficult he commenced each
sentence with the genitive case and concluded it with the verb.*
*The story is told of him that, dining
at a tavern in company with some other
gentlemen, he had been so boastful that
one of those present lost all patience and
said, "You have told us everything you
can do. Is there anything you can't do?"
"Yes," replied Taylor cheerfully, "I can't
pay my share of the dinner bill; you'll
have to do it for me."*
10 Ignorance and impudence always go
together; for in proportion as we are unacquainted with other things, must we
feel a want of respect for them. [William Hazlitt: *Manners Make the Man*]

IMPULSE
11 Man's chief merit consists in resisting
the impulses of his nature. [Samuel
Johnson: from "Recollections" by Miss
Reynolds, quoted in *Johnsonian Miscellanies* II]
12 The impulse to create beauty is rather rare in literary men. . . . Far ahead
of it comes the yearning to make money.
And after the yearning to make money
comes the yearning to make a noise.
[H. L. Mencken: *Prejudices: Fifth Series*
189]

INACTION

1 The trenchant blade, Toledo trusty,
  For want of fighting was grown rusty,
  And ate into itself, for lack
  Of somebody to hew and hack.
[Samuel Butler (1612-1680): *Hudibras*]
2 How dull it is to pause, to make an
                                        end,
  To rust unburnish'd, not to shine in
                                        use!
  As tho' to breathe were life! Life
                              piled on life
  Were all too little, and of one to me
  Little remains: but every hour is
                                    saved
  From that eternal silence, something
                                    more,
  A bringer of new things.
[Tennyson: *Ulysses*]
3 And the sin I impute to each frustrate
                                      ghost
  Is—the unlit lamp and the ungirt
                                    loin.
[Robert Browning: *The Statue and the
  Bust*]

INATTENTION

4 With patient inattention hear him
                                  prate.
[George Meredith: *Bellerophon*]

INCENTIVE

5 The mind of man is more cheered
and refreshed by profiting in small things
than by standing at a stay in great.
[Francis Bacon: *Of Empire*]

INCONSISTENCY

6 Who can be wise, amazed, temperate
                              and furious,
  Loyal and neutral, in a moment?
[Shakespeare: *Macbeth* II.iii.]

INCREASE

7 He must increase, but I must decrease.
[John 3:30]
8 I have planted, Apollos watered; but
God gave the increase. [I Corinthians
3:6]
  Apollos = *a learned Jewish scholar*

INCREMENT

9 Unearned increment. [John Stuart
Mill: *Dissertations and Discussions* IV]

INDECISION

10 I am at war 'twixt will and will not.
[Shakespeare: *Measure for Measure* II.ii.]
11 There is no more miserable human
being than one in whom nothing is habitual but indecision. [William James:
Psychology]

INDEPENDENCE

12 Let every vat stand upon its own
bottom. [William   Bullein: *Dialogue
Against the Fever Pestilence* (1564)]
  Tub *is now generally substituted for* vat.
13 If she undervalue me,
   What care I how fair she be?
[Sir   Walter   Raleigh   (1552?-1618):
  Verses to Edmund Spenser]
14 How happy is he born and taught,
   That serveth not another's will;
   Whose armour is his honest thought,
   And simple truth his utmost skill!
[Sir Henry Wotton: *The Character of a
  Happy Life*]
15 The first of earthly blessings, inde-
pendence. [Edward Gibbon: *Autobiog-
raphy*]
16 Let independence be our boast,
   Ever mindful what it cost.
[Joseph Hopkinson: *Hail, Columbia*]
17 His brow is wet with honest sweat
   He earns what'er he can,
   And looks the whole world in the
                                  face,
   For he owes not any man.
[Longfellow: *The Village Blacksmith*]
18 If a man does not keep pace with his
companions, perhaps it is because he
hears a different drummer. Let him step
to the music which he hears, however
measured or far away. [Thoreau: *Walden* XVIII]
19 The strongest man in the world is he
who stands most alone. [Henrik Ibsen:
An Enemy of the People V]

INDEPENDENT

20 To catch Dame Fortune's golden
                                  smile,
   Assiduous wait upon her;
   And gather gear by ev'ry wile
   That's justify'd by honour;
   Not for to hide it in a hedge,
   Nor for a train-attendant,
   But for the glorious privilege

Of being independent.
[Burns: *Epistle to a Young Friend*]

INDEX

1   What act
That roars so loud and thunders in
the index?
[Shakespeare: *Hamlet* III.iv.]

INDIAN(S)

2 Lo, the poor Indian! whose untutor'd
mind
Sees God in clouds, or hears him in
the wind;
His soul proud Science never taught
to stray
Far as the solar walk or milky way;
Yet simple nature to his hope has
giv'n,
Behind the cloud-topt hill, an hum-
bler Heav'n; . . .
To be, contents his natural desire;
He asks no Angel's wing, no Seraph's
fire;
But thinks, admitted to that equal
sky,
His faithful dog shall bear him com-
pany.
[Alexander Pope: *An Essay on Man* I]
3 The only good Indians I ever saw
were dead. [W. T. Sherman: reply to an
Indian at Fort Cobb, who said "Me
good Indian," Jan. 1869]
4 Little Indian, Sioux or Crow,
Little frosty Eskimo,
Little Turk or Japanee,
O! don't you wish that you were me?
[R. L. Stevenson: *A Child's Garden of
Verses*, "Foreign Children"]

INDICTMENT

5 I do not know the method of drawing
up an indictment against a whole people.
[Edmund Burke: *Speech on Conciliation
with America*, March 22, 1775]

INDIFFERENCE

6 He passed by on the other side.
[Luke 10:31]
7 Indifference, clad in wisdom's guise,
All fortitude of mind supplies.
[Jonathan Swift: *On the Death of Dr.
Swift*]

INDIGESTION

8 Indigestion is charged by God with

enforcing morality on the stomach. [Vic-
tor Hugo: *Les Misérables*, III.vii.]

INDISPENSABLE

9 There is no indispensable man.
[Franklin Delano Roosevelt: in a campaign speech, New York, Nov. 3, 1932]
> *Roosevelt was quoting his great prede-
> cessor Woodrow Wilson who in his cam-
> paign in 1912 said:*
> *"There is no indispensable man. The
> government will not collapse and go
> to pieces if any one of the gentlemen
> who are seeking to be entrusted with
> its guidance should be left at home."*
> *Roosevelt's running for office beyond
> the traditional limit of the second term
> and Wilson's passionate determination
> to run the country even though sick and
> partly paralyzed makes it plain that each
> had other men in mind.*
> *The phrase itself is a French proverb:
> "Il n'y a point d'homme nécessaire."*
> *And it can be a boomerang. It was
> almost Wendell Willkie's theme song in
> the 1940 campaign.*

INDIVIDUALISM

10 The American system of rugged individualism. [Herbert Hoover: in a campaign speech, 1928]
> *Hoover popularized the phrase. He in-
> sisted later that he had not invented it,
> that it had been in use for fifty years be-
> fore he employed it.*

INDOMITABLE

11 If the single man plant himself in-
domitably on his instincts, and there
abide, the huge world will come round
to him. [Emerson: *The American
Scholar*]

INDUSTRY

12 I have spent my life laboriously doing nothing. [Hugo Grotius: on his
deathbed]
> *Grotius, Latinized form of Huig de
> Groot, was one of the greatest of Lat-
> inists and jurists. His De Jure Belli et
> Pacis (1625) is generally regarded as the
> foundation of the science of international
> law. By any standards but his own, he
> lived a life of enormous and fruitful in-
> dustry.*

INFAMY

1 Écrasez l'infâme. [Voltaire: subscription to his letters]
Voltaire employed this famous phrase ("crush the infamous thing!") as we employ "Sincerely yours." By l'infâme he did not mean solely and specifically the Church, as has been charged, but all bigotry, intolerance, brutality.

2 A date that will live in infamy. [Franklin Delano Roosevelt: in an address to Congress, December 8, 1941]
The reference is to December 7 and the attack on Pearl Harbor.

INFANT

3   At first, the infant,
Mewling and puking in the nurse's
      arms.
[Shakespeare: As You Like It II.vii.]
This, by the way, is the first (1600) appearance of the verb puke in English. Until mid-nineteenth-century it was a serious word.

4 So runs my dream; but what am I?
An infant crying in the night;
An infant crying for the light,
And with no language but a cry.
[Tennyson: In Memoriam LIV]

INFATUATION

5 It would not grieve him to be hanged, if he might be strangled in her garters. [Robert Burton: The Anatomy of Melancholy III.2.3.1]

INFIDELITY

6 Infidelity has emanated chiefly from the learned. [Emanuel Swedenborg: Heaven and Hell]
This and a number of similar remarks are usually quoted as if the fact stated were a reproach to learning rather than to that which the learned have found incredible. The true reproach to the learned is not their infidelity but the cowardice and self-seeking that leads them to conceal it.

INFINITY

7 It [the universe] is an infinite sphere whose centre is everywhere, its circumference nowhere. [Pascal: Pensées]

8 But how can finite grasp Infinity? [Dryden: Hind and the Panther I]

9 To see a world in a grain of sand,
And a heaven in a wild flower:
Hold infinity in the palm of your
      hand,
And eternity in an hour.
[William Blake: Auguries of Innocence]

10 Where the telescope ends, the microscope begins. Which of the two has the grander view? [Victor Hugo: Les Misérables III.iii.]

INFORMATION

11 Information appears to stew out of me naturally, like the precious otter of roses out of the otter. [Mark Twain: Preface to Roughing It]

INGRATIATION

12 There are few things that we so unwillingly give up, even in advanced age, as the supposition that we have still the power of ingratiating ourselves with the fair sex. [Samuel Johnson: Miscellanies II]

INGRATITUDE

13 Blow, blow, thou winter wind,
Thou art not so unkind
    As man's ingratitude:
Thy tooth is not so keen,
Because thou art not seen,
    Although thy breath be rude.
[Shakespeare: As You Like It II.vii.]

14 Freeze, freeze, thou bitter sky,
That dost not bite so nigh
    As benefits forgot.
[Shakespeare: As You Like It II.vii.]

15 Ingratitude! thou marble-hearted
      fiend,
More hideous, when thou show'st
     thee in a child,
Than the sea-monster!
[Shakespeare: King Lear I.iv.]

16 How sharper than a serpent's tooth
      it is
To have a thankless child!
[Shakespeare: King Lear I.iv.]

17   Filial ingratitude!
Is it not as this mouth should tear
     this hand
For lifting food to 't?
[Shakespeare: King Lear III.iv.]

18 There is much less ingratitude than we think—because there is much less generosity than we imagine. [St. Évremond: Sur les Ingrats III.cxxiv.]

1 One's over-great haste to repay an obligation is a kind of ingratitude. [La Rochefoucauld: *Maxims*]
2 Every time I fill a vacant place I make a hundred malcontents and one ingrate. [Attr. Louis XIV of France (in Voltaire's *Le Siècle de Louis XIV*)]

INHERITANCE
3 Gude grant that thou may aye inherit
Thy mither's person, grace, an' merit,
An' thy poor worthless daddy's spirit,
Without his failins;
'Twill please me mair to see and hear
o't
Than stockit mailins.
[Burns: *The Poet's Welcome to his Love-Begotten Daughter*]
stockit mailins = *well-stocked farms*

INHUMANITY
4 Man is a wolf to man. (*Homo homini lupus.*) [Plautus: *Asinaria* II.iv.]
5 Man's inhumanity to man
Makes countless thousands mourn.
[Burns: *Man Was Made to Mourn*]

INIQUITY
6   I lack iniquity
Sometimes to do me service.
[Shakespeare: *Othello* I.ii.]

INJURY(IES)
7 He who injured you was either stronger or weaker. If he was weaker, spare him; if he was stronger, spare yourself. [Seneca: *De ira* III]
8 It is human nature to hate those we have injured. [Tacitus: *Life of Agricola*]
9 That is no injury which is done with [the injured one's] consent. [Ulpianus: *Corpus Juris Civilis*]
Usually quoted as: Volenti non fit injuria.
10 Injuries should all be done together in order that men may taste their bitterness but a short time and be but little disturbed. Benefits ought to be conferred a little at a time, that their flavor may be tasted better. [Machiavelli: *The Prince* VIII]
11 Sense of injured merit.
[John Milton: *Paradise Lost* I.98]

INJUSTICE
12 No pain equals that of an injury in-

flicted under the pretence of a just punishment. [Lupercio Leonardo de Argensola: *Sonetos* XXVII]
13 No great thing is accomplished without some injustice being done. [Luis de Ulloa: *Porcia y Tancredo* III]

INN
14 Whoe'er has travelled life's dull
round,
Where'er his stages may have been,
May sigh to think he still has found
The warmest welcome, at an inn.
[William Shenstone: *Written at an Inn at Henley*]
15 The incognito of an inn is one of its striking privileges. [William Hazlitt: *On Going a Journey*]

INNISFREE
16 I will arise and go now, and go to Innisfree,
And a small cabin build there, of clay
and wattles made:
Nine bean-rows will I have there, a
hive for the honeybee,
And live alone in the bee-loud
glade.
[William Butler Yeats: *The Lake Isle of Innisfree*]

INNOCENCE
17 A gaudy dress and gentle air,
May slightly touch the heart,
But it's innocence and modesty
That polishes the dart.
[Burns: *My Handsome Nell*]
18 A mind at peace with all below,
A heart whose love is innocent.
[Byron: *She Walks in Beauty*]
19 As innocent as a new-laid egg.
[W. S. Gilbert: *Engaged* I]
20 Of all the forms of innocence, mere ignorance is the least admirable. [Sir Arthur Wing Pinero: *The Second Mrs. Tanqueray* II]

INNOCENT
21 It is better that ten guilty persons escape than that one innocent suffer. [Sir William Blackstone: *Commentaries on the Laws of England* IV]

INNOCUOUS DESUETUDE
22 After an existence of nearly twenty

years of almost innocuous desuetude these laws are brought forth. [Grover Cleveland: *Message,* March 1, 1886]

> Cleveland cheerfully confessed that he had used these sonorities because he thought "they would please the Western taxpayers."

INNOVATION

1 It were good therefore, that men in their innovations would follow the example of time itself, which indeed innovateth greatly, but quietly and by degrees scarce to be perceived. [Francis Bacon: *Of Innovations*]

2 Things unattempted yet in prose or rhyme.
[John Milton: *Paradise Lost* I.16]

INSANITY

3 Were such things here as we do speak about?
Or have we eaten of the insane root
That takes the reason prisoner?
[Shakespeare: *Macbeth* I.iii.]

> The "insane root" was henbane or hemlock. Batman says "if it be eate or dronke it breedeth madnesse . . . it taketh away wit and reason." And Greene, in Never Too Late: "You have gazed against the sun, and so blemished your sight, or else you have eaten of the roots of hemlock, that makes men's eyes conceit unseen objects."

INSATIATE

4 The horseleech hath two daughters, crying, Give, give. [Proverbs 30:15]

5 There are three things that are never satisfied, yea, four things say not, It is enough:
The grave; and the barren womb; the earth that is not filled with water; and the fire that saith not, It is enough.
[Proverbs 30:15-16]

6 Women, Priests, and Poultry have never enough. [Thomas Fuller (1654-1734): *Gnomologia*]

INSECURITY

7 The pillar'd firmament is rottenness, And earth's base built on stubble.
[John Milton: *Arcades*]

INSIGHT

8 In nature's infinite book of secrecy

A little I can read.
[Shakespeare: *Antony and Cleopatra* I.ii.]

9 A moment's insight is sometimes worth a life's experience. [O. W. Holmes: *The Professor at the Breakfast-Table* X]

INSIGNIFICANCE

10 When You and I behind the Veil are passed,
Oh, but the long, long while the World shall last,
Which of our Coming and Departure heeds
As the Sea's self should heed a pebble-cast.
[*Rubáiyát of Omar Khayyám* (trans. Edward FitzGerald)]

INSOLENCE

11 The insolence of office.
[Shakespeare: *Hamlet* III.i.]

12 The sons
Of Belial, flown with insolence and wine.
[John Milton: *Paradise Lost* I.501-502]
flown = *inflated, or, as we would say,* high

13 The insolence of the vulgar is in proportion to their ignorance: they treat everything with contempt which they do not understand. [William Hazlitt: *Characteristics*]

INSTINCT(S)

14 Instinct is a great matter. I was now a coward on instinct. [Shakespeare: *I Henry IV* II.iv.]

15 High instincts before which our mortal nature
Did tremble like a guilty thing surprised.
[Wordsworth: *Intimations of Immortality*]

16 Reas'ning at every step he treads,/ Man yet mistakes his way,/ Whilst meaner things, whom instinct leads,/ Are rarely known to stray. [William Cowper: *The Doves*]

17 Man's natural instinct is never toward what is sound and true; it is toward what is specious and false. [H. L. Mencken: *Prejudices: Third Series*]

INSTITUTION(S)

18 In the infancy of societies, the chiefs

of the state shape its institutions; later the institutions shape the chiefs of state. [Montesquieu: *Grandeur et Décadence des Romains* I]

1 An institution is the lengthened shadow of one man. [Emerson: *Self-Reliance*]

INSTRUMENTS

2 But when to mischief mortals bend their will,
How soon they find fit instruments of ill!
[Alexander Pope: *Rape of the Lock* III]

INSUBSTANTIAL

3 Our revels now are ended. These our actors,
As I foretold you, were all spirits, and
Are melted into air, into thin air;
And, like the baseless fabric of this vision,
The cloud-capp'd towers, the gorgeous palaces,
The solemn temples, the great globe itself,
Yea, all which it inherit, shall dissolve;
And, like this insubstantial pageant faded,
Leave not a rack behind. We are such stuff
As dreams are made on, and our little life
Is rounded with a sleep.
[Shakespeare: *The Tempest* IV.i.]

INSULT(S)

4 If you utter insults you will also hear them. [Plautus: *Pseudolus* IV]
5 Adding insult to injury. [Cicero: *Pro Tullio* XVII]
6 It is often better not to see an insult than to avenge it. [Seneca: *De ira* II. xxii.]
7 You add insult to injury. [Phaedrus: *Fables* V.iii.]
   The fable concerns a bald man who, attempting to kill a fly that had lighted on his head, struck himself a blow on the head. The fly escaped and taunted the man with adding his own insult to the fly's minor injury.
8 An injury is much sooner forgotten than an insult. [Lord Chesterfield: *Letters to His Son,* Oct. 9, 1746]

9 In se'enteen hunder an' forty-nine,
The deil gat stuff to mak a swine,
   An cuist it in a corner;
But by and by he changed his plan,
And made it something like a man,
   An' ca'd it Andrew Turner.
[Burns: *On Andrew Turner*]
   deil = *Devil;* cuist = *threw;* ca'd = *called*

10 The only gracious way to accept an insult is to ignore it; if you can't ignore it, top it; if you can't top it, laugh at it; if you can't laugh at it, it's probably deserved. [Russell Lynes, in *Reader's Digest,* Dec. 1961]

INTEGRITY

11 This above all—to thine own self be true,
And it must follow, as the night the day,
Thou canst not then be false to any man.
[Shakespeare: *Hamlet* I.iii.]
   Be so true to thyself, as thou be not false to others.
      Bacon: Of Wisdom for a Man's Self
12 Integrity without knowledge is weak and useless, and knowledge without integrity is dangerous and dreadful. [Samuel Johnson: *Rasselas* XLI]
13 Neither praise nor money, the two powerful corrupters of mankind, seem to have depraved her. [Samuel Johnson: in Boswell's *Life,* October, 1783]
   The reference is to Mrs. Siddons.
14 Thou hadst *one* aim, *one* business, *one* desire:
Else wert thou long since numbered with the dead.
[Matthew Arnold: *The Scholar-Gipsy*]

INTELLECTUAL

15   . . . amongst us one
Who most has suffered, takes dejectedly
His seat upon the intellectual throne;
And all his store of sad experience he
Lays bare of wretched days;
Tells us his misery's birth and growth and signs,
And how the dying spark of hope was fed,
And how the breast was soothed, and how the head,

And all his hourly varied anodynes.
[Matthew Arnold: *The Scholar-Gipsy*]
1 An intellectual is someone whose mind watches itself. [Albert Camus: *Notebooks 1935-1942* I. p. 28]

INTELLIGENCE
2 Such is the delight of mental superiority that none on whom nature or study have conferred it would purchase the gifts of fortune by its loss. [Samuel Johnson: *The Rambler* No. 150]
3 The voice of the intelligence . . . is drowned out by the roar of fear. It is ignored by the voice of desire. It is contradicted by the voice of shame. It is hissed away by hate, and extinguished by anger. Most of all it is silenced by ignorance. [Karl Menninger, in *The Progressive*, Oct. 1955]

INTELLIGIBLE
4 To be intelligible is to be found out. [Oscar Wilde: *Lady Windermere's Fan* I]

Certainly a great deal of profundity and unintelligibility go together.

INTENT
5 Forget not yet the tried intent
Of such a truth as I have meant;
My great travail so gladly spent
Forget not yet!
[Sir Thomas Wyatt: *Forget Not Yet*]

INTENTIONS
6 For there's nothing we read of in torture's inventions,
Like a well-meaning dunce, with the best of intentions.
[James Russell Lowell: *A Fable for Critics*]
See also HELL

INTERDEPENDENCE
7 All are needed by each one;
Nothing is fair or good alone.
[Emerson: *Each and All*]

INTEREST
8 The case has, in some respects, been not entirely devoid of interest. [Sir Arthur Conan Doyle: *A Case of Identity*]

INTERFERENCE
9 He that finds his knowledge narrow and his arguments weak . . . is pleased that he had the power to interrupt those whom he could not confute, and suspend the decision which he could not guide. [Samuel Johnson: *The Rambler* No. 11]

INTERPRETATION
10 Egad, I think the interpreter is the hardest to be understood of the two. [Richard Brinsley Sheridan: *The Critic* I]
11 A great interpreter of life ought not himself to need interpretation. [John Morley: *Emerson*]
See also EXPLANATION

INTOLERABLE
12 O vile, intolerable, not to be endured!
[Shakespeare: *The Taming of the Shrew* V.ii.]

INTOXICATION
13 Man, being reasonable, must get drunk;
The best of life is but intoxication:
Glory, the grape, love, gold, in these are sunk
The hopes of all men, and of every nation;
Without their sap, how branchless were the trunk
Of life's strange tree, so fruitful on occasion!
[Byron: *Don Juan* II.clxxix.]
See also DRUNK, DRUNKARD(S), DRUNKENNESS

INTRUSIVE
14 Popp'd in between the election and my hopes.
[Shakespeare: *Hamlet* V.ii.]
15 Presume to put in her oar.
[Cervantes: *Don Quixote* II.iii.6]

INTUITION
16 Hence in a season of calm weather
Though inland far we be,
Our souls have sight of that immortal sea
Which brought us hither,
Can in a moment travel thither,
And see the children sport upon the shore,

And hear the mighty waters rolling
evermore.
[Wordsworth: *Intimations of Immortality*]

1 A moment's insight is sometimes worth a life's experience. [O. W. Holmes: *The Professor at the Breakfast-Table* X]

INUNDATION

2 King Christ, this world is all aleak;
and lifepreservers there are none:
and waves which only He may walk
Who dares to call Himself a man.
[e. e. cummings: *Jehovah buried, Satan dead*]

INVENTION(S)

3 God hath made man upright; but they have sought out many inventions. [Ecclesiastes 7:29]
> inventions = *subtle and clever reasonings whereby departure from God's basic creation is justified*

4 Want is the mistress of invention. [Susanna Centlivre: *The Busybody* I]

5 Invention breeds invention. [Emerson: *Society and Solitude,* "Works and Days"]
> See also NECESSITY: the mother of invention

INVITATION

6 Come up and see me some time. [Mae West: *Diamond Lil*]

INVOCATION

7 And chiefly Thou, O Spirit, that dost prefer
Before all temples the upright heart and pure,
Instruct me, for Thou know'st; Thou from the first
Wast present, and, with mighty wings outspread,
Dove-like sat'st brooding on the vast Abyss,
And mad'st it pregnant: what in me is dark
Illumine, what is low raise and support;
That, to the highth of this great argument,
I may assert Eternal Providence,
And justify the ways of God to men.
[John Milton: *Paradise Lost* I.17-26]
> argument = *theme*

Milton did not intend to suggest that a heated difference of opinion might prevail here.

INVULNERABLE

8 I bear a charmed life. [Shakespeare: *Macbeth* V.viii.]

IRELAND

9 Romantic Ireland's dead and gone,
It's with O'Leary in the grave.
[William Butler Yeats: *September 1913*]
> O'Leary = *John O'Leary (d. 1907), one of the Fenian Society's Triumvirate and a personal friend of Yeats*

IRESON

10 Old Floyd Ireson, for his hard heart,
Tarred and feathered and carried in
a cart
By the women of Marblehead!
[J. G. Whittier: *Skipper Ireson's Ride*]
> *Whittier's poem describes an incident which happened in 1808. Floyd Ireson, a Marblehead fishing-boat captain, racing with a full catch to be the first to market and hence to get the top prices, refused to stop to take off some townsmen whose boat was sinking in Chaleur Bay. The men drowned and Ireson was tarred and feathered by the women of Marblehead. Whittier later admitted that Ireson may have been forced to act as he did by a stubborn and cowardly crew.*

IRISH

11 He gave the little Wealth he had
To build a House for Fools and Mad;
And shew'd, by one satiric Touch,
No Nation wanted it so much.
[Jonathan Swift: *On the Death of Dr. Swift*]
> *Swift left his estate to establish a lunatic asylum. He was moved by humanity, but it is typical of him to pretend that it was a sarcastic joke.*

12 The Irish are a fair people; they never speak well of one another. [Samuel Johnson: in Boswell's *Life,* February 1775]
> *Just before this, Johnson, with a plain reflection on the Scotch, had said "The Irish are not in a conspiracy to cheat the world by false representations of the merits of their countrymen."*

1 An Irishman's heart is nothing but his imagination. [G. B. Shaw: *John Bull's Other Island* I]

IRON(S)
2 Hammer the iron when it is glowing hot. [Publilius Syrus: *Maxims*]
Proverbial in the first century B.C., *the thought had achieved its modern form in English or very close to it, by 1546, when it appeared in Heywood's collections of proverbs as "When the iron is hot, strike."*
3 The iron entered into his soul. [*Book of Common Prayer*, "The Psalter" CV.xviii.]
4 Strike the iron whilst it is hot. [Rabelais: *Works* II.xxxi.]
5 He that hath many irons in the fire, some will cool. [John Ray: *English Proverbs* (1670)]

IRON CURTAIN
6 The iron curtain.
Though popularized by Churchill's use of the phrase in his address at Westminster College, Fulton, Missouri, March 5, 1946, Churchill himself had used the phrase earlier in a letter to President Truman (June 4, 1945), and Goebbels had used it four months before that. It has been traced back as far as 1920. The Russians, by the way, use it of us; they speak of us as being "behind the iron curtain," and they may have invented the expression in this sense.

IRONIES
7 Life's Little Ironies. [Thomas Hardy: title of book]

IRRESOLUTION
8 Infirm of purpose! [Shakespeare: *Macbeth* II.ii.]

ISHMAEL
9 And he [Ishmael] will be a wild man; his hand will be against every man, and every man's hand against him. [Genesis 16:12]
10 Call me Ishmael. [Herman Melville: *Moby Dick* I]

ISLAND(S)
11 No man is an Iland, intire of it selfe;

every man is a peece of the Continent, a part of the maine; if a Clod bee washed away by the Sea, Europe is the lesse, as well as if a Promontorie were, as well as if a Mannor of thy friends or of thine owne were; any mans death diminishes me, because I am involved in Mankinde; And therefore never send to know for whom the bell tolls; It tolls for thee. [John Donne: *Devotions Upon Emergent Occasions* XVII]
John Donne's spelling is reproduced because it adds to the charm of this great passage and because it is instructive. Note, for instance, that the possessive apostrophe, that absurd nuisance, had not yet crept into the language. Note that it *does not carry the possessive* s. *Our* its *is a "corruption," and as late as 1825 purists were wringing their hands and prophesying the end of the language if its use continued. So also is our* island. *Donne's* Iland is, *historically, the "correct" spelling. The* s *was inserted in the 16th century by some pedant who knew a little Latin but less English. Donne, who knew both languages, preferred to write in English. We prefer pedantic ignorance.*
12 Many a green isle needs must be
In the deep wide sea of Misery,
Or the mariner, worn and wan,
Never thus could voyage on.
[Shelley: *Lines written amongst the Euganean Hills*]
13 There are no islands any more. [Edna St. Vincent Millay: *There Are No Islands Any More*]

ISOLATION
14 Isolation is the sum-total of wretchedness to man. [Thomas Carlyle: *Past and Present* IV.iv.]

ISRAEL
15 Israel shall be a proverb and a byword among all people. [I Kings 9:7]

ISRAFEL
16 In Heaven a spirit doth dwell
"Whose heart-strings are a lute";
None sing so wildly well

As the angel Israfel.
[Edgar Allan Poe: *Israfel*]

ITALY

1   A man who has not been in Italy is always conscious of an inferiority. [Samuel Johnson: in Boswell's *Life* (1776)]
2   Italy! my Italy!
    Queen Mary's saying serves for me—
    (When fortune's malice
    Lost her—Calais):
    Open my heart, and you will see
    Graved inside of it, "Italy."
[Robert Browning: *Bells and Pomegranates*, "De Gustibus"]
   See CALAIS

ITERATION

3   Thou hast damnable iteration, and art indeed able to corrupt a saint. [Shakespeare: *I Henry IV* I.ii.]

I TOLD YOU SO

4   Of all the horrid, hideous notes of
                woe,
    Sadder than owl-songs or the midnight blast,
    Is that portentous phrase, "I told you
                so."
[Byron: *Don Juan* XIV.i.]

IVORY TOWER

5   Ivory tower.
Tower of ivory *first appeared in the* Song of Solomon *(7:4) where the beloved is told, "Thy neck is as a tower of ivory." In the Litany of Loretto, the Virgin Mary is called "thou Ivory Tower"—in allusion to her immaculate inviolability.*

The modern use of the expression to signify the lofty detachment of pure theorizing probably echoes the litany. It comes from the 19th-century French critic Sainte-Beuve, who in a certain passage (Pensées d'Août: M. Villemain, 1837) praised Victor Hugo as a feudal knight armed for battle, but complained that Alfred de Vigny (a romantic poet who laid great stress on "the inner life") had retreated, before the heat of the day, "into his ivory tower."

J

JABBERWOCK
1 Beware the Jabberwock, my son!
   The jaws that bite, the claws that
                                catch!
   Beware the Jubjub bird, and shun
   The frumious Bandersnatch!
[Lewis Carroll: *Through the Looking-Glass*, "Jabberwocky"]

JACK AND JILL
2 Jack and Jill went up the hill
   To fetch a pail of water;
   Jack fell down and broke his crown,
   And Jill came tumbling after.
[Nursery rhyme: earliest printed form, 1765]
   Great antiquity and profound meaning
   have been claimed—but not established
   —for the rhyme. But the rhyming of
   "water" and "after" show it to be at
   least 300 years old.

JACK ROBINSON
3 Before you could say Jack Robinson.
[Fanny Burney: *Evelina* (1778)]
   Nobody knows why "Jack Robinson" was
   regarded as a name to be pronounced
   with exceptional rapidity. "Jack Smith"
   would seem shorter. The first known ap-
   pearance is in Evelina, but its use there
   implies that it was already a common ex-
   pression.
4 Before a man can say Jack Robinson.
[Dickens: *A Christmas Carol* II]
5 Before you could say Jack Robinson.
[Mark Twain: *Huckleberry Finn* III]

JACKSON, STONEWALL
6 There is Jackson, standing like
a stone wall! [General Bernard Bee
(1823-1861): at the Battle of Bull Run
(in which Bee was later killed), speaking of General Thomas Jonathan Jackson, thereafter known as "Stonewall"
Jackson.]
   See also NICKNAME

JACK SPRAT
7 Jack Sprat could eat no fat,
   His wife could eat no lean,

And so, you see, between them both
   They licked the platter clean.
[Nursery rhyme: known as early as
1639, when it was already a proverb]

JAIL
8 Taken from the county jail
   By a set of curious chances;
   Liberated then on bail,
   On my own recognizances.
[W. S. Gilbert: *The Mikado* I]
9 Write me a letter, write without fail,
   Send it in care of the Birmingham jail.
[Anon.: from a popular song, *Bird in
a Cage, Love*]

JAKES
10 I will tread this unbolted villain into
mortar, and daub the walls of a jakes
with him. [Shakespeare: *King Lear* II.ii.]
   unbolted = unsifted, hence complete,
   unredeemed, unrefined; jakes = privy.
   Elizabethan privies were daubed with
   quicklime.

JAM
11 The rule is, jam to-morrow and jam
yesterday—but never jam to-day. [Lewis
Carroll: *Through the Looking-Glass*
III]

JAMES I
12 King James said to the fly, Have I
three kingdoms and thou must needs fly
into my eye? [John Selden: *Table
Talk*]
   James I of England; his fellow monarch,
   Henri IV of France, called him "the
   wisest fool in Christendom," and the
   epithet stuck.

JAMES, JESSE
13 Oh, the dirty little coward
   That shot Mr. Howard,
   Laid Jesse James in his grave.
[Anon.: 1880's]
   Jesse James, who had been living under
   the name of Thomas Howard, was shot
   by Robert Ford in St. Joseph, Mo., April
   3, 1882.

JAUNDICED

1 All seems infected that th' infected
spy,
As all looks yellow to the jaundic'd
eye.

[Alexander Pope: *Essay on Criticism* II]
*The idea of the famous second line of
Pope's couplet had been expressed many
times before. John Webster, for instance,
in* The White Devil *(I.ii, 1612): "They
that have the yellow Jaundeise, thinke
all objects they looke on to bee yellow."
But Pope's wonderful power of smooth
condensation made it forever his.*

JAWBONE

2 With the jawbone of an ass . . .
have I [Samson] slain a thousand men.
[Judges 15:16]

JEALOUSY

3 Jealousy is cruel as the grave; the
coals thereof are coals of fire. [Song of
Solomon 8:6]

4 O! beware, my lord, of jealousy;
It is the green-ey'd monster which
doth mock
The meat it feeds on.

[Shakespeare: *Othello* III.iii.]
*Scholars have expended much ink on
this passage. Some insist the monster
should have been yellow-ey'd and that
mock should be make. The monster has
been variously identified as a crocodile,
a tiger, a cat, a mouse, and a dragonfly.
Although the general meaning of the
passage is clear, its specific meaning remains uncertain.*

5 That cuckold lives in bliss
Who, certain of his fate, loves not his
wronger;
But, O! what damned minutes tells
he o'er
Who dotes, yet doubts; suspects, yet
soundly loves!

[Shakespeare: *Othello* III.iii.]
*The cuckoo lays its eggs in other birds'
nests, chiefly in the nest of the hedge
sparrow. The cuckold was a man who
had been treated like the hedge sparrow.
It is astonishing how much space the
literature of the past, its plays, poems
and proverbs, gave to this thought. In
part it was a conventional province of
humor, but, making all allowances, our*
ancestors certainly tormented themselves
with it. It was the inevitable obverse of
the double standard and they had it
coming to them.

6 I had rather be a toad,
And live upon the vapour of a dun-
geon,
Than keep a corner in the thing I
love
For others' uses.

[Shakespeare: *Othello* III.iii.]

7 Trifles light as air
Are to the jealous confirmations
strong
As proofs of holy writ.

[Shakespeare: *Othello* III.iii.]
*proofs of holy writ = proofs drawn from
holy writ, not evidence supporting the
veracity of holy writ. In the 17th century,
it would not have entered anyone's mind
that holy writ needed any proof whatsoever.*

8 They are not ever jealous for the
cause,
But jealous for they are jealous.

[Shakespeare: *Othello* III.iv.]

9 One not easily jealous, but, being
wrought,
Perplex'd in the extreme; of one
whose hand,
Like the base Indian, threw a pearl
away
Richer than all his tribe.

[Shakespeare: *Othello* V.ii.]

10 Jealousy is always born with love, but
does not always die with it. [La Rochefoucauld: *Maxims*]

11 There is more self-love than love in
jealousy. [La Rochefoucauld: *Maxims*]

12 Yet he was jealous, though he did not
show it,
For jealousy dislikes the world to
know it.

[Byron: *Don Juan* I.lxv.]

JEANIE

13 I dream of Jeanie with the light
brown hair,
Borne like a vapor on the summer air:
I see her tripping where the bright
streams play,
Happy as the daisies that dance on
her way.

[Stephen Foster: *Jeanie with the Light
Brown Hair* I]

JEHU

1 The driving is like the driving of Jehu, the son of Nimshi; for he driveth furiously. [II Kings 9:20]

JERUSALEM

2 If I forget thee, O Jerusalem, let my right hand forget her cunning. [Psalms 137:5]

3 Jerusalem the golden,
　　With milk and honey blest,
　　Beneath thy contemplation
　　Sink heart and voice oppressed.

[St. Bernard of Cluny: *Hora Novissima: Urbs Syon Aurea* (1145) (trans. John Mason Neale [1858])]

4 I will not cease from mental fight,
　　Nor shall my sword sleep in my
　　　　　　　　　　　　hand,
　　Till we have built Jerusalem
　　In England's green and pleasant
　　　　　　　　　　　　land.

[William Blake: *Milton*]

JEST

5 If anything is spoken in jest, it is not fair to turn it to earnest. [Plautus: *Amphitruo* III.ii.]
　　Chaucer expressed the same thought: "Men shall not make earnest out of game."

6 Full oft in game a sooth I have heard said.
[Chaucer: Prologue to *The Monk's Tale*]
　　Modern form: "Many a true word is spoken in jest."

7 It is better to lose a new jest than an old friend. [Gabriel Harvey: *Works* II]
　　"Better lose a jest than a friend" was a 16th-century proverb.

8 Play with me and hurt me not,
　　Jest with me and shame me not.
[Gabriel Harvey: *Marginalia*]

9 As for jest, there be certain things which ought to be privileged from it; namely, religion, matters of state, great persons, any man's present business of importance and any case that deserveth pity. [Francis Bacon: *Of Discourse*]
　　Today religion, matters of state and great persons are favorite topics of jest. A man's present business of importance may not seem a fit subject of jest to him, but it is likely to seem such to his witty

friends. All agree that any case deserving pity should be exempt from jest, but few agree just what cases deserve pity.

10 And generally, men ought to find the difference between saltness and bitterness. [Francis Bacon: *Of Discourse*]

11 A jest's prosperity lies in the ear
　　Of him that hears it, never in the
　　　　　　　　　　　　tongue
　　Of him that makes it.
[Shakespeare: *Love's Labour's Lost* V.ii.]

12 It would be argument for a week, laughter for a month and a good jest for ever. [Shakespeare: *I Henry IV* II.ii.]
　　argument = *topic of conversation*

13 No, no, they do but jest, poison in jest; no offence i' the world. [Shakespeare: *Hamlet* III.ii.]

14 For things said false and never meant,
　　Do oft prove true by accident.
[Samuel Butler (1612-1680): *Satire Upon the Weakness and Misery of Man* I]

15 Squandering wealth was his peculiar
　　　　　　　　　　　　art;
　　Nothing went unrewarded but desert.
　　Beggar'd by fools, whom still he
　　　　　　　　　　found too late;
　　He had his jest, and they had his es-
　　　　　　　　　　　　tate.
[Dryden: *Absalom and Achitophel* I]

16 Thou canst not joke an enemy into a friend, but thou may'st a friend into an enemy. [Benjamin Franklin: *Poor Richard's Almanack* (1739)]

17 Of all the griefs that harass the distrest,
　　Sure the most bitter is a scornful jest.
[Samuel Johnson: *London*]
　　Poverty has no harder misfortune than this, than that it exposes a man to ridicule.
　　　　　　　　　　Juvenal: *Satire III*

18 Some fiery fop, with new commission
　　　　　　　　　　　　vain,
　　Who sleeps on brambles till he kills
　　　　　　　　　　his man;
　　Some frolic drunkard, reeling from a
　　　　　　　　　　　　feast,
　　Provokes a broil, and stabs you for a
　　　　　　　　　　　　jest.
[Samuel Johnson: *London*]

19 A threadbare jester's threadbare jest.
[Charles Churchill: *The Ghost* IV]

JESTERS

1 Jesters do often prove prophets.
[Shakespeare: *King Lear* V.iii.]

JESUS CHRIST

2 It was the winter wild
While the Heav'n-born child
All meanly wrapt in the rude manger
lies.
[John Milton: *On the Morning of Christ's Nativity*]

3 Joy to the world! the Lord is come;
Let earth receive her King.
Let ev'ry heart prepare Him room,
And heav'n and nature sing.
[Isaac Watts: *Psalm XCVIII*]
Make a joyful noise unto the Lord, all the earth: make a loud noise, and rejoice, and sing praise.   Psalms 98:4

4 Gentle Jesus, meek and mild,
Look upon a little child;
Pity my simplicity,
Suffer me to come to thee.
[Charles Wesley: *Gentle Jesus, Meek and Mild*]

5 Jesus, Lover of my soul,
Let me to Thy bosom fly,
While the nearer waters roll,
While the tempest still is high.
[Charles Wesley: *In Temptation*]

6 All hail the power of Jesus' name!
Let angels prostrate fall;
Bring forth the royal diadem,
To crown Him Lord of all!
[Edward Perronet: *Coronation*]

7 How sweet the name of Jesus sounds
In a believer's ear!
It soothes his sorrows, heals his
wounds,
And drives away his fear.
[John Newton: *How Sweet the Name of Jesus Sounds*]

8 The Son of God goes forth to war,
A kingly crown to gain;
His blood-red banner streams afar!
Who follows in His train?
[Reginald Heber: *The Son of God Goes Forth to War*]

9 If Jesus Christ were to come to-day, people would not even crucify him. They would ask him to dinner, and hear what he had to say, and make fun of it.
[Thomas Carlyle: quoted in D. A. Wilson's *Carlyle at his Zenith*]
As, of course, some did, even with

Carlyle!

10 Strong Son of God, immortal Love,
Whom we, that have not seen thy
face,
By faith, and faith alone, embrace,
Believing where we cannot prove.
[Tennyson: Prologue to *In Memoriam*]

11 Stand up, stand up for Jesus,
Ye soldiers of the cross;
Lift high His royal banner,
It must not suffer loss.
[George Duffield: *Stand Up for Jesus*]

12 Jesus calls us; o'er the tumult
Of our life's wild restless sea.
[Cecil Frances Alexander: *Jesus Calls Us*]

13 Jesus loves me—this I know,
For the Bible tells me so.
[Susan Warner: *The Love of Jesus*]

14 Thou hast conquered, O pale Galilean; the world has grown grey
from Thy breath;
We have drunken of things Lethean,
and fed on the fullness
of death.
[Swinburne: *Hymn to Proserpine*]

15 The Church's one foundation is Jesus
Christ her Lord;
She is His new creation by water and
the Word.
[Samuel John Stone: *The Church's One Foundation*]

JEW(S)

16 For sufferance is the badge of all our
tribe.
[Shakespeare: *The Merchant of Venice.* I.iii.]

17 Hath not a Jew eyes? hath not a Jew hands, organs, dimensions, senses, affections, passions? fed with the same food, hurt with the same weapons, subject to the same diseases, healed by the same means, warmed and cooled by the same Winter and Summer, as a Christian is?
[Shakespeare: *Merchant of Venice* III.i.]

18 How odd
Of God
To choose
The Jews!
[William Norman Ewer: *How Odd*]
In its assumption of naive anti-Semitism —both for itself and for God—this famous little jingle sets in motion volumes of derision of the Christian who worships

a Jewish God and at the same time hates Jews, who professes universal brotherhood while actually disdaining ninetenths of mankind. One of the nicest things about the verse is its faint suggestion of polite, upperclass impatience with God for having such undesirable acquaintances.

Often attr. Hilaire Belloc.

JEWELS

1 These are my jewels. [Attr. Cornelia, the mother of the Gracchi (c. 135 B.C.)]

When a visitor boasted of her jewels, Cornelia embraced her sons and said, "These are my jewels."

JINGO

2 We don't want to fight,
But, by Jingo, if we do,
We've got the ships, we've got the
men,
We've got the money too.

[W. G. Hunt: *We Don't Want to Fight* (1878)]

Hunt's song was popular in England in 1878 when England was thought to be on the verge of war with Russia. The Russophobes became known as Jingoes and noisy war-mongering (which in America, at the approach of the Spanish-American war, borrowed the English song) as jingoism.

"By Jingo," as a euphemism for "By God" or "By Jesus," was borrowed from the jargon of conjurers (17th century). Peter Motteux in his translation of Rabelais (1694) substitutes (IV. lvi.) "by jingo" for "par Dieu." There is a Basque word Jinko or Jainko meaning God, and this may have been borrowed.

JOCULARITY

3 If any cleric or monk speaks jocular words, such as provoke laughter, let him be anathema. [Ordinance, Second Council of Constance (1418)]

4 Miss Corby's role was jocularity: she always entered the conversation with a handspring. [Edith Wharton: *The House of Mirth* I]

JOHNSON, DR. SAMUEL

5 That great Cham of literature, Samuel Johnson. [Tobias Smollett: Letter to

John Wilkes, March 16, 1759, quoted in Boswell's *Life of Johnson*]

See CHAM
See ARGUMENT

6 No, no, it is not a good imitation of Johnson; it has all his pomp without his force; it has all the nodosities of the oak without its strength; it has all the contortions of the Sibyl without the inspiration. [Edmund Burke: in Boswell's *Life of Johnson* (1781)]

The beauty of Burke's comment lies not merely in the clarity of its perception, in opposing Boswell's assertion that a certain book was a good imitation of Johnson's style, but in its couching its point in a good imitation of Johnson. So good an imitation, in fact, that it is often quoted as by Johnson himself, as a particularly good illustration of his style.

JOIE DE VIVRE

7 Here comes Burns
On Rosinante;
She's damn'd poor,
But he's damn'd canty!

[Burns: *On Himself*]

Rosinante = *"formerly a horse," or "formerly a stallion"; poor* = *lean, scrawny; canty* = *cheerful, lively*

Rosinante (or Rozinante or Rocinante) was the name of Don Quixote's horse, a poor thing though he thought it a priceless charger, equal to the Bucephalus of Alexander the Great. Burns may have humorously called his horse after the Don's, or he may have been wryly admitting his own quixotic nature.

JOIN(ED)

8 What therefore God hath joined together, let not man put asunder. [Matthew 19:6]

9 Steal away
The song says. Steal away and stay
away.
Don't join too many gangs. Join few
if any.
Join the United States and join the
family—
But not much in between unless a
college.

[Robert Frost: *Build Soil—A Political Pastoral*]

JOKE

1 A joke's a very serious thing.
[Charles Churchill: *The Ghost* IV]

JOLLITY

2 Haste thee, Nymph, and bring with
thee
Jest, and youthful Jollity,
Quips and Cranks and wanton Wiles,
Nods and Becks and wreathèd Smiles.
[John Milton: *L'Allegro*]

JONAH

3 And he [Jonah] said unto them [the
mariners], take me up and cast me forth
into the sea; so shall the sea be calm
unto you: for I know that for my sake
this great tempest is upon you. [Jonah
1:12]
It is from this incident that "a Jonah"
has come to mean one who brings bad
luck, especially to a ship.
4 Now the Lord had prepared a great
fish to swallow up Jonah. And Jonah was
in the belly of the fish for three days
and three nights. [Jonah 1:17]
But in Matthew 12:40 Christ says the
great fish was a whale.

JONSON, BEN

5 Next these, learn'd Jonson, in this list
I bring,
Who had drunk deep of the Pierian
spring.
[Michael Drayton: *Of Poets and Poesy*]
6 O rare Ben Jonson! [Epitaph on Ben
Jonson's tombstone in Westminster Ab-
bey]
Aubrey (Brief Lives, "Ben Jonson") says
the inscription "was donne at the chardge
of Jack Young (afterwards knighted)
who, walking there when the grave was
covering, gave the fellow eighteen pence
to cutt it."
The overknowing sometimes insist that
the inscription is Orare Ben Jonson
("Pray for Ben Jonson").

JOURNALISM AND JOURNALISTS

7 A news-writer is a man without virtue
who lies at home for his own profit. To
these compositions is required neither
genius nor knowledge, neither industry
nor sprightliness; but contempt of shame
and indifference to truth arc absolutcly

necessary. He who by a long familiarity
with infamy has obtained these qualities
may confidently tell today what he intends to contradict tomorrow; he may
affirm fearlessly what he knows he shall
be obliged to recant, and may write letters from Amsterdam or Dresden to himself. [Samuel Johnson: *The Idler* No.
30]
The first sentence echoes Sir Henry
Wotton's witticism that an ambassador
is a virtuous man sent to lie abroad for
the good of his country.
8 Scarcely anything awakens attention
like a tale of cruelty. The writer of news
never fails to tell how the enemy murdered children and ravished virgins; and
if the scene of action be somewhat distant, scalps half the inhabitants of a
province. [Samuel Johnson: *The Idler*
No. 30]
9 Condemn'd to drudge, the meanest
of the mean,
And furbish falsehoods for a magazine.
[Byron: *English Bards and Scotch Re-*
viewers]
10 The difference between literature
and journalism is that journalism is un-
readable, and literature is not read. [Os-
car Wilde: *The Critic as Artist*]
11 Nameless men and women whose
scandalously low payment is a guarantee
of their ignorance and their servility to
the financial department. [G. B. Shaw:
Common Sense about the War]
12 Newspapers are unable, seemingly, to
discriminate between a bicycle accident
and the collapse of civilization. [G. B.
Shaw: Preface to *Too True to be Good*]
Many editors probably are able to so
discriminate. But the demand of the
circulation department that every day
supply equally exciting headlines and
the fact that—with a few honorable ex-
ceptions—newspapers are run by their
circulation departments, not by their
editors, make any application of the
discrimination impossible. And it is to
this as much as to any one other thing
that we may attribute the utter con-
fusion and puerility of the popular
mind.
13 Has any reader ever found perfect accuracy in the newspaper account of any

event of which he himself had inside knowledge? [E . V. Lucas: *Of Accuracy*]

1 The journalist is partly in the entertainment business and partly in the advertising business. [Claud Cockburn: *In Time of Trouble*]

JOURNEY(S)

2 O mistress mine! where are you roaming?
  O! stay and hear; your true love's coming,
That can sing both high and low.
Trip no further, pretty sweeting;
Journeys end in lovers meeting,
Every wise man's son doth know.
[Shakespeare: *Twelfth Night* II.iii.]

3 Here is my journey's end, here is my butt,
And very sea-mark of my utmost sail.
[Shakespeare: *Othello* V.ii.]

4 One of the pleasantest things in the world is going a journey; but I like to go by myself. [William Hazlitt: *On Going a Journey*]

JOY

5 When the morning stars sang together, and all the sons of God shouted for joy. [Job 38:7]

6 Weeping may endure for a night, but joy cometh in the morning. [Psalms 30:5]

7 For ever the latter end of joy is woe.
God wot that worldly joy is soon ago.
[Chaucer: *The Nun's Priest's Tale*]

8 The most evident token and apparent sign of true wisdom is a constant and unconstrained rejoicing. [Montaigne: *Essays* I.xxv.]
  The translation is Florio's. apparent = visible, clear, not—as it most commonly does today—opposed to reality.

9 I speak of Africa and golden joys.
[Shakespeare: *II Henry IV* V.iii.]

10 With one auspicious and one dropping eye,
With mirth in funeral and with dirge in marriage,
In equal scale weighing delight and dole.
[Shakespeare: *Hamlet* I.ii.]

11 What joy is joy, if Silvia be not by?
[Shakespeare: *The Two Gentlemen of Verona* III.i.]

12 They hear a voice in every wind,
And snatch a fearful joy.
[Thomas Gray: *On a Distant Prospect of Eton College*]

13 Excess of sorrow laughs; excess of joy weeps.
[William Blake: *Proverbs of Hell*]

14 As high as we have mounted in delight
In our dejection do we sink as low.
[Wordsworth: *Resolution and Independence*]

15 Joy in widest commonalty spread.
[Wordsworth: *The Excursion*]

16 And the stern joy which warriors feel
In foemen worthy of their steel.
[Sir Walter Scott: *The Lady of the Lake,* "Coronach"]

17 There's not a joy the world can give like that it takes away,
When the glow of early thought declines in feeling's dull decay;
'Tis not on youth's smooth cheek the blush alone, which fades so fast,
But the tender bloom of heart is gone, ere youth itself be past.
[Byron: *Stanzas for Music*]

18 On with the dance! let joy be unconfined;
No sleep till morn, when Youth and Pleasure meet
To chase the glowing Hours with flying feet.
[Byron: *Childe Harold* III.xxii.]

19 Our sincerest laughter
With some pain is fraught.
[Shelley: *To a Skylark*]

20 Joy, whose hand is ever at his lips,
Bidding adieu.
[Keats: *Ode on Melancholy* III]

21 How terrible is man's estate. There is not one of his joys which does not spring out of some form of ignorance. [Honoré de Balzac: *Eugénie Grandet* I]

22 The year's at the spring
And day's at the morn;
Morning's at seven;
The hillside's dew-pearled;
The lark's on the wing;
The snail's on the thorn:
God's in his heaven—
All's right with the world.
[Robert Browning: *Pippa Passes* I]

23 He chortled in his joy.
[Lewis Carroll: *Through the Looking-*

Glass, "Jabberwocky"]
1 My mirth can laugh and talk, but
cannot sing:
My grief finds harmonies in everything.
[James Thomson (1834–1882): *Two Sonnets* II.xiii.]
2 Comedy is joyous because all assumption of a part, of a personal mask,
whether of the individualized face of
comedy or of the grotesque face of farce,
is a display of energy, and all energy is
joyous. [William Butler Yeats: *Dramatis Personae*]
3 I found more joy in sorrow
Than you could find in joy.
[Sara Teasdale: *The Answer*]
4 Joy is a fruit that Americans eat green.
[Amando Zegri: in *The Golden Book,*
May 1931]

JUDGE(S)

5 Who made thee a prince and a judge
over us? [Exodus 2:14]
6 The judge is condemned when the
criminal is absolved. [Publilius Syrus:
Maxims]
> The selection of this pre-Christian say-
> ing for its motto by the Edinburgh Re-
> view, in 1802, reveals its conception of
> reviewers in relation to writers.

7 When the guilty is acquitted, the
judge is condemned. [Roman legal
maxim]
8 No man should be a judge in his
own case. [Roman legal maxim]
9 Judges ought to be more learned
than witty, more reverend than plausible, and more advised than confident.
[Francis Bacon: *Of Judicature*]
> advised = *deliberate*

10 Judges ought to remember that their
office is *Ius dicere,* and not *Ius dare;* to
interpret law, and not to make law, or
give law. [Francis Bacon: *Of Judicature*]
11 Let them [judges] be lions, but yet
lions under the throne. [Francis Bacon:
Of Judicature]
> Let them, that is, uphold, not make, law.

12 A judge were better a briber than a
respecter of persons, for a corrupt judge
offendeth not so highly as a facile.
[Francis Bacon: *The Advancement of
Learning* I]

13 Judges . . . are picked out from the
most dexterous lawyers, who are grown
old or lazy, and having been biassed all
their lives against truth and equity, are
under such a fatal necessity of favoring
fraud, perjury and oppression, that I
have known several of them refuse a
large bribe from the side where justice
lay, rather than injure the faculty by
doing any thing unbecoming their nature or their office. [Jonathan Swift:
Gulliver's Travels IV.v.]

JUDGMENT(S)

14 Judge not, that ye be not judged.
[Matthew 7:1]
15 There are but few things of which
we may give a sincere judgment: for
there be very few wherein in some sort
or other we do not have a personal or
material concern. Superiority and inferiority, mastery and subjection, are
jointly tied unto a natural kind of envy
and contestation. [Montaigne: *Essays* III.
vii.]
16 Between two hawks, which flies the
higher pitch;
Between two dogs, which hath the
deeper mouth;
Between two blades, which bears the
better temper;
Between two horses, which doth bear
him best;
Between two girls, which hath the
merriest eye;
I have, perhaps, some shallow spirit
of judgment;
But in these nice sharp quillets of
the law,
Good faith, I am no wiser than a
daw.
[Shakespeare: *I Henry VI* II.iv.]
17 Men's judgments are
A parcel of their fortunes, and things
outward
Do draw the inward quality after
them,
To suffer all alike.
[Shakespeare: *Antony and Cleopatra*
III.xiii.]
18 Everyone complains of his memory,
but no one complains of his judgment.
[La Rochefoucauld: *Maxims*]
19 'Tis with our judgments as our
watches, none

Go just alike, yet each believes his
own.
[Alexander Pope: *Essay on Criticism* I]

JUMBLIES

1 Far and few, far and few,
Are the lands where the Jumblies
live.
[Edward Lear: *The Jumblies*]

JUNE

2 And what is so rare as a day in June?
Then, if ever, come perfect days.
[James Russell Lowell: *The Vision of
Sir Launfal* I]
3 Knee-deep in June.
[Alfred Austin: *A Wild Rose*]
4 June is Bustin' Out All Over. [Oscar
Hammerstein II: song from *Carousel*]

JURY

5 The jury, passing on the prisoner's
life,
May in the sworn twelve have a thief
or two
Guiltier than him they try.
[Shakespeare: *Measure for Measure* II.i.]
6 A fox should not be of the jury at a
goose's trial. [Thomas Fuller: (1654-
1734): *Gnomologia*]
7 The hungry judges soon the sentence
sign,
And wretches hang that jurymen may
dine.
[Alexander Pope: *The Rape of the Lock*
III]
*Juries were formerly deprived of seats
and even of food, fire and drinking
water, that they might arrive at a decision the sooner. Criminal trials rarely
ever lasted beyond a day and, more commonly, a few hours. And there can be
little doubt that many an innocent man
was hanged that the jurors might get
home to supper.*
8 The jury system puts a ban upon intelligence and honesty, and a premium
upon ignorance, stupidity and perjury.
[Mark Twain: *Roughing It* XLVIII]

JUSTICE

9   This even-handed justice
Commends the ingredients of our poi-
son'd chalice
To our own lips.

[Shakespeare: *Macbeth* I.vii.]
10   Take physic, pomp;
Expose thyself to feel what wretches
feel,
That thou mayst shake the superflux
to them,
And show the heavens more just.
[Shakespeare: *King Lear* III.iv.]
11 The gods are just, and of our pleasant vices
Make instruments to plague us.
[Shakespeare: *King Lear* V.iii.]
12 Look with thine ears: see how yond
justice rails upon yond simple thief.
Hark, in thine ear: changes places; and,
handy-dandy, which is the justice, which
is the thief. [Shakespeare: *King Lear*
IV.vi.]
*handy-dandy = the game one plays with
little children in which a sweet or something desirable is held in one hand,
with both hands behind the back. The
hands are then brought forward and the
child required to guess in which hand
the thing is.*
*Lear is saying that it's just a guess, a
matter of chance, that distinguishes a
thief from a magistrate.*
13 The usurer hangs the cozener.
[Shakespeare: *King Lear* IV.vi.]
*That is, the big cheat hangs the little
cheat. Or, by wider inference, that which
we call justice is, in G. B. Shaw's phrase,
simply the wholesale division of what in
retail is called crime.*
*There is a Czech proverb: "Big thieves
hang little thieves."*
14 The love of justice in most men is
only the fear of suffering injustice. [La
Rochefoucauld: *Maxims*]
15 Justice without force is powerless;
force without justice is tyrannical. [Pas-
cal: *Pensées*]
16 Eye for eye, tooth for tooth, hand for
hand, foot for foot. [Exodus 21:24]
17 There is a point beyond which even
justice becomes unjust. [Sophocles: *Electra*]
18 Thrice is he arm'd that hath his quarrel just,
And he but naked, though lock'd up
in steel,
Whose conscience with injustice is
corrupted.
[Shakespeare: *II Henry VI* III.ii.]

1
                And then the justice,
In fair round belly with good capon
                                lined,
With eyes severe and beard of formal
                                  cut,
Full of wise saws and modern in-
                            stances.
[Shakespeare: *As You Like It* II.vii.]

2 The law, in its majestic equality, forbids all men to sleep under bridges, to
beg in the streets, and to steal bread—
the rich as well as the poor. [Anatole
France: *Crainquebille*]

3 But how should man be just with
God? [Job 9:2]

4 Only the actions of the just
Smell sweet and blossom in their
                            dust.
[James Shirley: *The Contention of Ajax
and Ulysses* I.iii.]

5 The sweet remembrance of the just
Shall flourish when he sleeps in dust.
[Tate and Brady: *Psalm* 112:6]
  The Authorized Version has: the right-
  eous shall be in everlasting remem-
  brance.

6 Be just before you are generous.
[18th-century proverb]
  Quoted by R. B. Sheridan in The School
  for Scandal *IV.i.*

7 He that buyeth Magistracy, must sell
Justice. [Thomas Fuller (1654–1734):
Gnomologia]

8 Justice is always violent to the party
offending, for every man is innocent in
his own eyes. [Daniel Defoe: *Shortest
Way with Dissenters*]

9 Let justice be done, though the heavens fall. [Lord Mansfield: *Rex* vs. *Wilkes*
(1768)]
  *Lord Mansfield was merely quoting the
  legal maxim:* Fiat justitia et ruant coeli.

10 "Justice" was done, and the President
of the Immortals (in Aeschylean phrase)
had ended his sport with Tess. [Thomas
Hardy: *Tess of the D'Urbervilles* LIX]

11 Justice is too good for some people
and not good enough for the rest. [Nor-
man Douglas: *Good-bye to Western Culture*]

12 Injustice is relatively easy to bear;
what stings is justice. [H. L. Mencken:
Prejudices: Third Series]
  See also LAW

K

KANSAS

1 Kansas had better stop raising corn and begin raising hell. [Attr. Mary Elizabeth Lease]

Mrs. Lease, known as "Mary Yellin' " and "the Kansas Pythoness," was a vigorous lecturer, particularly active in politics with the Populists in 1890.

KEAN, EDMUND

2 To see Kean act was like reading Shakespeare by flashes of lightning. [Coleridge: *Table Talk*]

KEEP

3 As great a craft is keep well as win. [Chaucer: *Troilus and Criseyde* III]

KENTUCKY

4 Weep no more, my lady,
Oh! weep no more today!
We will sing one song for the old Kentucky Home,
For the old Kentucky Home far away.
[Stephen Foster: *My Old Kentucky Home*]

KICK(ING)

5 Jeshurun waxed fat, and kicked. [Deuteronomy 32:15]

6 It is hard for thee to kick against the pricks. [Acts 9:5]

7 When late I attempted your pity to move,
Why seemed you so deaf to my prayers?
Perhaps it was right to dissemble your love,
But—why should you kick me downstairs?
[Anon.: in *The Panel* I.i. (1788)]

The Panel is by John Philip Kemble. The lines are quoted in the play, but Kemble may have written them himself.

KID

8 Thou shalt not seethe a kid in his mother's milk. [Exodus 23:19]

His *does not here necessarily mean a*

male kid. Our word its *is never used in the King James Version of the Bible.*

If repetition marks importance, this is one of the most important commandments in the Bible. It is repeated in Exodus 34:26 and Deuteronomy 14:21: And the Lord said unto Moses, Write thou these words: for after the tenor of these words I have made a covenant with thee and with Israel.

KILL(ING)

9 Thou shalt not kill; but needst not strive
Officiously to keep alive.
[Arthur Hugh Clough: *The Latest Decalogue*]

10 Yet each man kills the thing he loves,
By each let this be heard,
Some do it with a bitter look,
Some with a flattering word,
The coward does it with a kiss,
The brave man with a sword.
[Oscar Wilde: *Ballad of Reading Gaol*]

KIN

11 A little more than kin, and less than kind. [Shakespeare: *Hamlet* I.ii.]

Hamlet's famous aside is much quoted but its exact meaning is much disputed. The general meaning, however, is clear. His stepfather, the usurper Claudius, has just addressed him as "my cousin Hamlet, and my son." Hamlet admits the kinship, states indeed that it is far too close for his liking, but denies any humanity, kindness or natural sympathy which Claudius might claim exists between them.

KINDLED

12 Soon kindled and soon burnt. [Shakespeare: *I Henry IV* III.ii.]

KINDNESS

13 He that lendeth to all that will borowe, sheweth great good will, but lyttle wit. [John Lyly: *Euphues and His England*]

1 The inclination to goodness is imprinted deeply in the nature of man; insomuch that if it issue not towards men it will take unto other living creatures; as is seen in the Turks, a cruel people who nevertheless are kind to beasts and give alms to dogs and birds. [Francis Bacon: *Of Goodness and Goodness of Nature*]

2 Not always actions show the man: we find
Who does a kindness is not therefore kind.
[Alexander Pope: *Moral Essays* I]

3 In misery's darkest cavern known,
His useful care was ever nigh,
Where hopeless anguish pour'd his groan,
And lonely want retir'd to die.
[Samuel Johnson: *On the Death of Mr. Robert Levet*]

4 To cultivate kindness is a valuable part of the business of life. [Samuel Johnson: in Boswell's *Life*, Sept. 21, 1777]

5 A kind and gentle heart he had,
To comfort friends and foes;
The naked every day he clad
When he put on his clothes.
[Oliver Goldsmith: *Elegy on the Death of a Mad Dog*]

6 That best portion of a good man's life—
His little, nameless, unremembered, acts
Of kindness and of love.
[Wordsworth: *Tintern Abbey*]

7 Kind hearts are more than coronets,
And simple faith than Norman blood.
[Tennyson: *Lady Clara Vere de Vere*]

8 One can always be kind to people one cares nothing about. [Oscar Wilde: *The Picture of Dorian Gray*]

9 When kindness has left people, even for a few moments, we become afraid of them, as if their reason had left them. [Willa Cather: *My Mortal Enemy* I.vi.]

10 The cheerful clatter of Sir James Barrie's cans as he went round with the milk of human kindness. [Philip Guedalla: *Some Critics*]

KING(S)

11 Until philosophers are kings, or the kings and princes of this world have the spirit and power of philosophy, and political greatness and wisdom meet in one, and those commoner natures who pursue either to the exclusion of the other are compelled to stand aside, cities [states] will never have rest from their evils—no, nor the human race. [Socrates: in Plato, *The Republic* V (trans. Jowett)]
This is the culminating statement in Plato's Republic.

12 Better is a poor and a wise child than an old and foolish king, who will no more be admonished. [Ecclesiastes 4:13]

13 *Le Roi le veut.* ("The King wills it.") [This is the phrase by which the King of England assents to Acts of Parliament.]
Parliament made it plain, 1649, that he'd better and the Americans made it plain, in 1776, that it didn't really matter.

14 If I had served God as diligently as I have done the king, He would not have given me over in my gray hairs. [Cardinal Wolsey: in Cavendish's *Life of Thomas Wolsey* (1557)]
Cavendish was Wolsey's secretary.

15 I know I have the body of a weak and feeble woman, but I have the heart and stomach of a king, and of a King of England too. [Queen Elizabeth I: speech at Tilbury to the troops, at the approach of the Spanish Armada (1588)]

16 Is it not passing brave to be a king,
And ride in triumph through Persepolis?
[Christopher Marlowe: *Tamburlaine* II.v]

17 It is a miserable state of mind, to have few things to desire and many things to fear: and yet that commonly is the case of Kings. [Francis Bacon: *Of Empire*]

18 Not all the water in the rough rude sea
Can wash the balm off from an anointed king.
[Shakespeare: *Richard II* III.ii.]

19 For God's sake let us sit upon the ground
And tell sad stories of the death of kings!
How some have been depos'd, some slain in war,
Some haunted by the ghosts they have depos'd,
Some poisoned by their wives, some

sleeping kill'd—
All murthered.
[Shakespeare: *Richard II* III.ii.]

murther *and* murder, *as we pronounce
it, are variant pronunciations, like* dem
and them *and* mother *and* mudder. *The
point is that, where usage accepts the* d
*sound, it sounds absolutely "correct";
where it does not, it sounds "low" and
"vulgar" and contemptible.*

1 What must the king do now? Must he
submit?
The king shall do it: Must he be de-
posed?
The king shall be contented: Must he
lose
The name of king? A God's name, let
it go!
I'll give my jewels for a set of beads,
My gorgeous palace for a hermitage,
My gay apparel for an almsman's
gown,
My figured goblets for a dish of wood,
My sceptre for a palmer's walking
staff,
My subjects for a pair of carved
saints,
And my large kingdom for a little
grave,
A little little grave, an obscure grave.
[Shakespeare: *Richard II* III.iii.]

2 You may my glories and my state de-
pose,
But not my griefs; still am I king of
those.
[Shakespeare: *Richard II* IV.i.]

3 There's such divinity doth hedge a
king,
That treason can but peep to what it
would.
[Shakespeare: *Hamlet* IV.v.]

4 Ay, every inch a king.
[Shakespeare: *King Lear* IV.vi.]

5 Had I but served my God with half
the zeal
I served my king, he would not in
mine age
Have left me naked to mine enemies.
[Shakespeare: *Henry VIII* III.ii.]

6 The King of France went up the hill
With forty thousand men;
The King of France came down the
hill,
And ne'er went up again.
[Nursery rhyme: referred to in a letter

dated May 12, 1620]
*The King of France alluded to is prob-
ably Henri IV.*

7 It is atheism and blasphemy to dispute what God can do; so it is presumption and contempt to dispute what a
king can do, or say that a king cannot do
this or that. [James I of England: *Basili-
kon Doron*]

8 A subject and a sovereign are clean
different things. [Charles I of England:
on the scaffold, Jan. 30, 1649]

9 The king can do no wrong. [Sir William Blackstone: *Commentaries* III.17.]

10 The right divine of kings to govern
wrong. [Alexander Pope: *The Dunciad*
IV]

11 God save our gracious king!
Long live our noble king!
God save the king!
[Henry Carey: *God Save the King*]

12 Let us strangle the last king with the
guts of the last priest. [Denis Diderot:
Dithyrambe sur la fête de rois]

13 It little profits that an idle king,
By this still hearth, among these bar-
ren crags,
Matched with an aged wife, I mete
and dole
Unequal laws unto a savage race.
[Tennyson: *Ulysses*]

14 Under kings women govern, but under queens, men. [John Stuart Mill:
The Subjection of Women III]
*Mill quotes the statement as "a bad
joke." But whether bad or a joke, it's an
old saying. Charles II gave it as his answer when a wit asked him why England
was ruled so badly by a man but had
achieved glory under a woman (Elizabeth).*

15 All kings is mostly rapscallions.
[Mark Twain: *Huckleberry Finn* XXIII]

16 He played the King as though under
momentary apprehension that someone
else was about to play the ace. [Eugene
Field's comment: in the Denver *Tribune*
(1880 or thereabouts), on the performance of Creston Clarke in *King Lear*]

KING COLE

17 Old King Cole
Was a merry old soul,
And a merry old soul was he;
He called for his pipe,

And he called for his bowl,
  And he called for his fiddlers three.
[Nursery rhyme]
  In a book published in 1708, the question of King Cole's identity was discussed.
    Some claim him to have been a Celtic king (c. 300) after whom Colchester was named. Some believe he was a wealthy clothier at Reading. Sir Walter Scott thought he was the father of the giant Fyn M'Coule.

KIPLING, RUDYARD

1 When the Rudyards cease from Kipling
  And the Haggards Ride no more.
[James Kenneth Stephen: *Lapsus Calami*, "To R.K."]

KISMET

2 It is he that saith not 'Kismet'; it is he that knows not fate;
  It is Richard, it is Raymond, it is Godfrey at the gate!
[G. K. Chesterton: *Lepanto*]

KISS(ES) (noun)

3 Sweet Helen, make me immortal with a kiss. [Christopher Marlowe: *Dr. Faustus* XIV]
4 Drink to me only with thine eyes,
  And I will pledge with mine;
  Or leave a kiss but in the cup
  And I'll not look for wine.
[Ben Jonson: *To Celia*]
  Drink to me only with your eyes. Take the cup to your lips and fill it with kisses, and give it so to me.
    Philostratus: Letter XXXIII
    (c. 181-250)

5 Were kisses all the joys in bed,
  One woman would another wed.
[Shakespeare: *The Passionate Pilgrim*]
6 Take, O take those lips away,
  That so sweetly were forsworn;
  And those eyes, the break of day,
  Lights that do mislead the morn:
  But my kisses bring again, bring again,
  Seals of love, but sealed in vain, sealed in vain.
[Shakespeare: *Measure for Measure* IV.i.]
7 Give me a kisse, and to that kisse a score;
  Then to that twenty, adde an hundred more;
  A thousand to that hundred; so kisse on,
  To make that thousand up a million;
  Treble that million, and when that is done,
  Let's kisse afresh, as when we first begun.
[Robert Herrick: *To Anthea*]
8 Ae fond kiss! and then we sever!
  Ae farewell, alas, for ever!
[Burns: *Ae Fond Kiss*]
9 I fear thy kisses, gentle maiden,
  Thou needest not fear mine.
[Shelley: To—, *I Fear Thy Kisses*]
10 Oh what lies there are in kisses!
[Heinrich Heine: *In den Küssen, welche Lüge*]
11 Dear as remembered kisses after death.
[Tennyson: *The Princess* IV]
12 A-wastin' Christian kisses on an 'eathen idol's foot. [Kipling: *Mandalay*]
13 The first kiss is stolen by the man; the last is begged by the woman. [H. L. Mencken: *Chrestomathy* 619]

KISS(ING) (verb)

14 Uncouth unkist, said the old famous Poet Chaucer. [Edmund Spenser: *The Shepheardes Calender*, "Letter to Gabriel Harvey"]
  Unknowe, unkist, and lost that is unsought.
    Chaucer: Troilus and Criseyde
    Uncouth, *as the parallel passages show, meant "unknown." The modern meaning reflects the universal dislike of the strange.*
    Chaucer uses couth *to mean "known" ("ferne halwes couthe in sondry landes"); there is an increasing use of it today to mean the opposite of* uncouth, *i.e., to mean suave or polished in manners.*

15 Kiss me, Kate.
[Shakespeare: *The Taming of the Shrew* II.i]
16 This done, he took the bride about the neck
  And kiss'd her lips with such a clamorous smack
  That at the parting, all the church

did echo.
[Shakespeare: *The Taming of the Shrew* III.ii.]

1 Kiss till the cow comes home. [Beaumont and Fletcher: *The Scornful Lady* III.i.]

2 Kissing and bussing differ both in this:
We busse our Wantons, but our Wives we kisse.
[Robert Herrick: *Kissing and Bussing*]

3 You must not kiss and tell. [William Congreve: *Love for Love* II]

4 Kiss me, Hardy. [Horatio Nelson: dying words at Trafalgar]
The 19th century, frozen in an emotionless "good form" found Nelson's words embarrassing. It is—or was—popular in England to insist that, with the admirable stiff upper lip of the playing-field aristocracy, he had actually said "Kismet, Hardy."

But, as Mr. John Moore has pointed out, Kismet, Turkish for "destiny" or "fate," did not arrive in England (via Arabic) until 1849 and Nelson died in 1805. Says Mr. Moore: "There is something Victorian–Nursery–Governessy" about this emendation, "a feminine embarrassment at the thought of a man kissing a man ('which only foreigners do') and an utter lack of appreciation of the heroic atmosphere in which Nelson lived and died."

5 Jenny kissed me when we met,
Jumping from the chair she sat in;
Time, you thief, who love to get
Sweets into your list, put that in.
Say I'm weary, say I'm sad,
Say that health and wealth have missed me;
Say I'm growing old, but add, Jenny kissed me.
[Leigh Hunt: *Jenny Kissed Me*]

6 I love the sex, and sometimes would reverse
The tyrant's wish, "that mankind only had
One neck, which he with one fell stroke might pierce";
My wish is quite as wide, but not so bad,
And much more tender on the whole than fierce;
It being (not *now*, but only while a lad)
That womankind had but one rosy mouth,
To kiss them all at once, from North to South.
[Byron: *Don Juan* VI.xxvii.]
Suetonius, in his life of Caligula XXX, says that the Emperor, angered at the rabble, wished "that the Roman people had but a single neck" so that he could decapitate them all at one stroke. Others have assigned the wish to Nero.

7 You should not take a fellow eight years old
And make him swear to never kiss the girls.
[Robert Browning: *Fra Lippo Lippi*]

8 There is always one who kisses and one who only allows the kiss. [G. B. Shaw: *Man and Superman* I]

KNAVERY
9 Knaves think nothing can be done without knavery. [Thomas Fuller (1654-1734: *Gnomologia*]

KNIGHT
10 He never yet no villany had said
In all his life, unto no manner wight.
He was a very parfit gentle knight.
[Chaucer: Prologue to *The Canterbury Tales*]
villany = *villainy* = *wicked, low, obscene, shameful, abusive language*
Chaucer's knight might have to kill you, in the course of his high calling, but he would do it in a gentlemanly way.

This is the most-quoted passage in all our literature to illustrate that in English, as in all the Germanic languages, multiple negatives do not cancel but reinforce each other.

11 The Knight's bones are dust,
And his good sword rust—
His soul is with the saints, I ... ust.
[Coleridge: *The Knight's Tomb*]

KNOCK
12 Not many sounds in life, and I include all urban and all rural sounds, exceed in interest a knock at the door. [Charles Lamb: *Valentine's Day*]

KNOWLEDGE
13 Shall any teach God knowledge? [Job 21:22]

1 The fear of the Lord is the beginning of knowledge. [Proverbs 1:7]
Also Psalms 111:10; Job 28:28; Proverbs 10:27, 14:26, 15:33, 19:23.

2 Many shall run to and fro, and knowledge shall be increased. [Daniel 12:4]

3 I have taken all knowledge to be my province. [Francis Bacon: in a letter to his uncle, Lord Burleigh, in 1592, seeking employment]
P.S. Bacon did not get the job.

4 Knowledge is power. [Francis Bacon: *De heresibus*]

5 For all knowledge and wonder (which is the seed of knowledge) is an impression of pleasure in itself. [Francis Bacon: *The Advancement of Learning* I]

6 The first and wisest of them all professed
To know this only, that he nothing knew.
[John Milton: *Paradise Regained* IV, 293-294]

7 That observation which is called knowledge of the world will be found much more frequently to make men cunning than good. [Samuel Johnson: *The Rambler* No. 4]

8 All knowledge is of itself of some value. There is nothing so minute or inconsiderable that I would not rather know it than not. [Samuel Johnson: in Boswell's *Life,* April 18, 1775]

9 Knowledge is of two kinds; we know a subject ourselves, or we know where we can find information upon it. [Samuel Johnson: in Boswell's *Life,* April 18, 1775]

10 A man must carry knowledge with him, if he would bring home knowledge. [Samuel Johnson: in Boswell's *Life* (1778)]

11 All that we know is, nothing can be known.
[Byron: *Childe Harold* II.vii.]
Attributed to "Athena's wisest son."

12 An extensive knowledge is needful to thinking people—it takes away the heat and fever; and helps, by widening speculation, to ease the Burden of the Mystery. [Keats: Letter to John Hamilton Reynolds, May 3, 1818]

13 Knowledge is capable of being its own end. [John Henry Newman: *The Idea of a University,* Discourse V]

14 . . . That alone is liberal knowledge, which stands on its own pretensions, which is independent of sequel, expects no complement, refuses to be *informed* . . . by any end, or absorbed into any art, in order duly to present itself to our contemplation. [John Henry Newman: *The Idea of a University,* Discourse V]

15 Knowledge is the antidote to fear. [Emerson: *Courage*]

16 Knowledge is the knowing that we cannot know. [Emerson: *Montaigne*]

17 This gray spirit yearning in desire
To follow knowledge like a sinking star,
Beyond the utmost bound of human thought.
[Tennyson: *Ulysses*]

18 If a little knowledge is dangerous, where is the man who has so much as to be out of danger? [T. H. Huxley: *On Elemental Instruction in Physiology*]

19 It is better to know nothing than to know what ain't so. [Henry Wheeler Shaw ("Josh Billings"): *Encyclopedia of Wit and Wisdom* (1874)]

20 Wonderful little our fathers knew,
Half their remedies cured you dead—
Most of their teaching was quite untrue.
[Kipling: *Our Fathers of Old*]

21 We have learnt that nothing is simple and rational except what we ourselves have invented; that God thinks in terms neither of Euclid nor of Riemann; that science has "explained" nothing; that the more we know the more fantastic the world becomes and the profounder the surrounding darkness. [Aldous Huxley: *Views of Holland*]

KNOWLEDGE: and wisdom

22 In much wisdom is much grief: and he that increaseth knowledge increaseth sorrow. [Ecclesiastes 1:18]

23 No man is the wiser for his learning. [John Selden: *Table Talk,* "Learning"]

24 Knowledge and wisdom, far from being one,
Have ofttimes no connexion. Knowledge dwells
In heads replete with thoughts of other men;

Wisdom in minds attentive to their
own.
[William Cowper: *The Task* VI]
1 Knowledge is proud that he has
learn'd so much;
Wisdom is humble that he knows no
more.
[William Cowper: *The Task* VI]

HAD I ONLY KNOWN
2 Beware of Had I wist. [14th-century
proverb]
Had I wist = *if I had only known!*

KOSCIUSKO
3 Hope, for a season, bade the world
farewell,
And Freedom shriek'd as Kosciusko
fell!
[Thomas Campbell: *Pleasures of Hope* I]
Tadeusz Kosciusko (1746-1817), the great
Polish patriot who assisted the Ameri-
cans in their War of Independence was,
naturally, one of Freedom's heroes and
favorites. And her concern when he fell
in the Battle of Maciejowice, 1794, was
understandable. But he recovered from
his wounds and lived to a good old age.

L

LA BELLE DAME SANS MERCI

1 I saw pale kings and princes too,
  Pale warriors, death-pale were they
                                    all;
  Who cry'd—"La belle Dame sans
                                  merci
  Hath thee in thrall!"
[Keats: *La Belle Dame sans Merci* X]

LABOR

2 What profit hath a man of all his labor which he taketh under the sun?
[Ecclesiastes 1:3]
3 What hath man of all his labor, and
of the vexation of his heart, wherein he
hath labored under the sun? [Ecclesias-
tes 2:22]
4 Labor conquers everything. [Vergil:
Georgics I]
  The Latin is: Labor omnia vincit im-
  probus.
5 Lat Austin have his swink to him re-
                                  served.
[Chaucer: Prologue to *The Canterbury
  Tales*]
  Austin = *St. Augustine;* swink = *toil, hard
  manual labor*
    *St. Augustine had enjoined hard labor
    upon his followers. Chaucer's monk is
    quite willing to leave such work to St.
    Augustine, if he wants it.*
6 The labor we delight in physics pain.
[Shakespeare: *Macbeth* II.iii.]
  physics = *acts as a medicine in relation to*
7 Doth God exact day-labour, light
                                 deny'd,
  I fondly ask.
[John Milton: *On His Blindness*]
  fondly = *foolishly, peevishly, childishly*
8 The friends of humanity cannot but
wish that in all countries the laboring
classes should have a taste for comforts
and enjoyments, and that they should be
stimulated by all legal means in their ex-
ertions to procure them. There cannot
be a better security against a superabun-
dant population. [David Ricardo: *Principles of Political Economy* V]
9 Let us, then, be up and doing,
  With a heart for any fate;

Still achieving, still pursuing,
  Learn to labor and to wait.
[Longfellow: *A Psalm of Life*]
10 Ah, why should life all labour be?
[Tennyson: *The Lotos-Eaters*]
11 Six days shalt thou labor and do all
                             thou art able,
  And on the seventh—holystone the
              decks and scrape the cable.
[R. H. Dana: *Two Years Before the
  Mast* III]
  *Where it is called "the Philadelphia Cate-
  chism."*

12 Labor is prior to, and independent of,
capital. Capital is only the fruit of labor,
and could never have existed if labor
had not first existed. Labor is the superior of capital, and deserves much the
higher consideration. [Abraham Lincoln: Message to Congress, Dec. 3, 1861]

LABORER

13 The laborer is worthy of his hire.
[Luke 10:7]
14 Bowed by the weight of centuries he
                                  leans
  Upon his hoe and gazes on the
                                 ground,
  The emptiness of ages in his face,
  And on his back the burden of the
                                  world.
[Edwin Markham: *The Man With the
  Hoe*]

LADY(IES)

15 If ladies be but young and fair,
  They have the gift to know it.
[Shakespeare: *As You Like It* II.vii.]
16 Look to the lady.
[Shakespeare: *Macbeth* II.iii.]
17 There is scarce a lady of quality in
Great Britain that ever saw the sun rise.
[Richard Steele: *The Tatler,* No. 263]
18 Here lies a most beautiful lady,
  Light of step and heart was she;
  I think she was the most beautiful
                                  lady
  That ever was in the West Country.
[Walter de la Mare: *An Epitaph*]

1　No lady is ever a gentleman. [James Branch Cabell: *Something About Eve*]
2　One man's lady is another man's woman; sometimes, one man's lady is another man's wife. [Russell Lynes: "Is There a Lady in the House?" *Look*, July 22, 1958]

LADYBIRD

3　Ladybird, ladybird,
Fly away home,
Your house is on fire
And your children all gone.
[Nursery rhyme: earliest printed version, 1744]
Ladybird = *Our Lady's bird*
　The rhyme is thought to be of great antiquity. Parallels are found in almost every European language. It is thought that this child's jingle is all that is left of some incantation, charm against witches, or chant to the goddess Freya.

LADY MONDEGREEN

4　Ye Highlands and ye Lowlands,
　Oh where hae ye been?
They hae slain the Earl of Murray
　And laid him on the green.
[Anon: *The Bonny Earl of Murray*]
This verse of the old ballad was, through a childish misunderstanding ("They hae slain the Earl Amurray / And Lady Mondegreen"), the basis of Sylvia Wright's delightful "The Death of Lady Mondegreen." See Miss Wright's Get Away from Me with Those Christmas Gifts.

LAFAYETTE

5　Lafayette, we are here. [Col. Charles E. Stanton: at the tomb of Lafayette, Paris, July 4, 1917]
Attr. General Pershing who, however, was unable to remember saying it.

LAMB(S)

6　But the poor man had nothing, save one little ewe lamb, which he had bought and nourished up . . . and was unto him as a daughter. [II Samuel 12:3]
7　I moorne as doth a lamb after the tete.
[Chaucer: *The Miller's Tale*]
8　The lamb thy riot dooms to bleed today,
Had he thy reason, would he skip and play?
Pleas'd to the last, he crops the flowery food,
And licks the hand just rais'd to shed his blood.
[Alexander Pope: *An Essay on Man* I]
It may be a merciful dispensation of Providence to conceal from sheep the true function of shepherds, but, surely, riot is a strong term for a liking for lamb chops.
9　Like Lambs, you do nothing but suck, and wag your tails. [Thomas Fuller (1654-1734): *Gnomologia*]
10　God tempers the wind to the shorn lamb. [Laurence Sterne: *A Sentimental Journey*, "Maria" (1768)]
The thought was proverbial and had been in print for more than 150 years before Sterne gave it the phrasing that is now quoted. Many quoters assume the phrase is biblical.
11　Little lamb, who made thee?
Dost thou know who made thee?
Gave thee life, and bid thee feed
By the stream and o'er the mead;
Gave thee clothing of delight,
Softest clothing, woolly, bright.
[William Blake: *Songs of Innocence*, "The Lamb"]
12　Young lambs to sell! Young lambs to sell!
If I'd as much money as I could tell,
I never would cry, young lambs to sell.
[Nursery rhyme: earliest printed version c. 1820]
to sell = *for sale, as* to let = *for rent;* tell = *count. Cf. the* teller *in a bank.*
　These were toy lambs sold to children by vendors in the streets.
13　Mary had a little lamb,
　Its fleece was white as snow;
And everywhere that Mary went
　The lamb was sure to go.
[Sarah Josepha Hale: *Poems for Our Children* (containing the famous "Mary's Lamb"), 1830]
One of the few nursery rhymes that can be definitely traced to an author. Other claimants have been advanced, but Mrs. Hale's authorship is now granted by all scholars.

1 We're poor little lambs who've lost
our way, Baa! Baa! Baa!
We're little black sheep who've gone
astray, Baa-aa-aa!
Gentlemen-rankers out on the
spree,
Damned from here to Eternity,
God ha' mercy on such as we, Baa!
Yah! Baa!
[Kipling: *Gentlemen-Rankers*]

LAMENTATION

2 Never night follows day nor day the
night
That there is not heard the sound of
weeping
Mixed with shrill lamentation.
[Lucretius: *De rerum natura* II]
3 Here sighs, plaints, and voices of the
deepest woe resounded through the starless sky. Strange languages, horrid cries,
accents of grief and wrath, voices deep
and hoarse, with hands clenched in despair, made a commotion which whirled
forever through that air of everlasting
gloom, even as sand when whirlwinds
sweep the ground. [Dante: *The Divine
Comedy*, "Inferno" III]
4 Whom universal Nature did lament.
[John Milton: *Lycidas*]
5 He must not float upon his watery
bier
Unwept, and welter to the parching
wind,
Without the meed of some melodious
tear.
[John Milton: *Lycidas*]
6 'Twas when the seas were roaring
With hollow blasts of wind;
A damsel lay deploring,
All on a rock reclin'd.
[John Gay: *The What d'ye Call It* II]
7 Then flash'd the living lightning from
her eyes,
And screams of horror rend th' af-
frighted skies.
Not louder shrieks to pitying Heav'n
are cast,
When husbands, or when lapdogs,
breathe their last;
Or when rich China vessels, fall'n
from high,
In glitt'ring dust and painted frag-
ments lie!

[Alexander Pope: *The Rape of the Lock*
III]
8 A lamentation and an ancient tale of
wrong,
Like a tale of little meaning tho' the
words are strong.
[Tennyson: *The Lotos-Eaters*]

LAMP(S)

9 Thy word is a lamp unto my feet,
and a light unto my path. [Psalms 119:
105]
10 To smell of the lamp.
*Said of some literary effort that shows
the result of uninspired labor. The idea
is that it must have been composed laboriously late in the night when the author was dull with exhaustion and all
sparkle and originality had gone out of
him.*

*Sometimes, earlier, "to smell of the
candle." The expression goes back to
Plutarch (Demosthenes). Modern lighting makes it obscure and one does not
hear it as frequently as one used to.*

11 The lamps are going out all over Europe; we shall not see them lit again in
our lifetime. [Lord Grey of Fallodon:
August 4, 1914]

LAND

12 You may buy land now as cheap as
stinking mackerel.
[Shakespeare: *I Henry IV* II.iv.]
*Falstaff's comment on the economic con-
sequences of the threat of civil war.
Prince Hal takes more of a young man's
view of it: "Why then . . . we shall buy
maidenheads as they buy hobnails, by
the hundreds."*

LANGUAGE(S)

13 God save the king, that is lord of this
language.
[Chaucer: Prologue to *The Astrolabe*]
14 They have been at a great feast of
languages, and stolen the scraps. [Shake-
speare: *Love's Labour's Lost* V.i.]
15 Syllables govern the world. [John Selden: *Table Talk*, "Power"]
16 He that is but able to express
No sense at all in several languages,
Will pass for learneder than he that's
known

To speak the strongest reason in his own.
[Samuel Butler (1612-1680): *Satire Upon the Abuse of Learning*]

1 Our sons their fathers' failing language see.
[Alexander Pope: *An Essay on Criticism* II (1709)]

Every generation has viewed with alarm the "corruption" of the language, not perceiving that "corruption" is growth. There is no surer sign that one is degenerating into age than to become aware that the language is "degenerating."

2 Language is only the instrument of science, and words are but the signs of ideas. [Samuel Johnson: Preface to the *Dictionary*]

science = knowledge in general

3 Academies have been instituted to guard the avenues of their languages, to retain fugitives, and repulse intruders; but their vigilance and activity have hitherto been vain; sounds are too volatile and subtile for legal restraints; to enchain syllables, and to lash the wind, are equally the undertakings of pride, unwilling to measure its desires by its strength. [Samuel Johnson: Preface to the *Dictionary*]

4 That the vulgar [the ordinary people] express their thoughts clearly is far from true, and what perspicuity can be found among them proceeds not from the easiness of their language but the shallowness of their thoughts. [Samuel Johnson: *The Idler* No. 70]

5 Languages are the pedigrees of nations. [Samuel Johnson: in Boswell's *Life*, September 18, 1773]

6 Who does not know another language, does not know his own. [Goethe: *Sprüche in Prosa*]

7 There neither is, nor can be, any essential difference between the language of prose and metrical composition. [Wordsworth: Preface to the *Lyrical Ballads*]

8 Language is fossil poetry. [Emerson: *The Poet*]

9 Use what language you will, you can never say anything but what you are. [Emerson: *Worship*]

10 Language is a city to the building of which every human being brought a stone. [Emerson: *Quotation and Originality*]

11 But, for the unquiet heart and brain
A use in measured language lies;
The sad mechanic exercise,
Like dull narcotics numbing pain.
[Tennyson: *In Memoriam* V]

12 No man fully capable of his own language ever masters another. [G. B. Shaw: *Maxims for Revolutionists*]

13 Perhaps of all the creations of man language is the most astonishing. [Lytton Strachey: *Words and Poetry*]

14 Time that is intolerant
Of the brave and innocent,
And indifferent in a week
To a beautiful physique,
Worships language and forgives
Everyone by whom it lives.
[W. H. Auden: *In Memory of W. B. Yeats*]

LANGUAGE: usage

15 Usage, in which lies the decision, the law and the norm of speech. [Horace: *Ars poetica* LXXI]

16 Ye knowe eek, that in forme of speche is chaunge
With-inne a thousand yeer, and wordes tho
That hadden prys, now wonder nyce and straunge
Us thinketh hem; and yet they spake hem so,
And spedde as wel in love as men now do.
[Chaucer: Proem to *Troilus and Criseyde* II]

tho = then; prys = value, effectiveness; nyce = stupid, senseless. Nice derives, ultimately, from the Latin nescius = not knowing, ignorant.

The last line and a half is a charming perception of the primary function of speech.

17 After a speech is fully fashioned to the common understanding, and accepted by consent of a whole country and nation, it is called a language. [George Puttenham: *The Art of English Poesie* (1589)]

18 For what was the ancient Language, which some men so dote upon, but the ancient Custom? [Ben Jonson: *Discover-*

ies]

1 Custom is the most certain mistress of language, as the public stamp makes the current money. [Ben Jonson: *Grammar*]

2 Every living language, like the perspiring bodies of living creatures, is in perpetual motion and lateration; some words go off, and become obsolete; others are taken in, and by degrees grow into common use; or the same word is inverted to a new sense and notion, which in tract of time makes as observable a change in the air and features of a language as age makes in the lines and mien of a face. [Richard Bentley: *Dissertation upon the Epistles of Phalaris*]

> lateration = *widening; extension.*

3 Write with the learned, pronounce with the vulgar. [Benjamin Franklin: *Poor Richard's Almanack*]

> vulgar = *the common people*
> *This is very good advice, but few of the learned have sufficient humility or good sense to follow it.*

LARK

4 The bisy larke, messager of day. [Chaucer: *The Knight's Tale*]

> *Note Chaucer's "correct" spelling of the word we "misspell" messenger. The "n" no more belongs here, historically, than the "m" in "stromberries" or the "b" in "chimbley."*

5 To rise with the lark. [Nicholas Breton: *Court and Country*]

6 The lark, the herald of the morn. [Shakespeare: *Romeo and Juliet* III.v.]

7 Hark, hark! the lark at heaven's gate sings. [Shakespeare: *Cymbeline* II.iii.]

8 The lark now leaves his watery nest, And climbing, shakes his dewy wings. [Sir William D'Avenant: *Morning Song*]

9 To hear the lark begin his flight, And singing startle the dull Night, From his watch-tower in the skies, Till the dappled dawn doth rise. [John Milton: *L'Allegro*]

10 A skylark wounded on the wing Doth make a cherub cease to sing. [William Blake: *Auguries of Innocence*]

11 Ethereal minstrel, pilgrim of the sky! [Wordsworth: *To a Skylark*]

12 Type of the wise who soar, but never roam:

True to the kindred points of Heaven and Home! [Wordsworth: *To a Skylark*]

13 Hail to thee, blithe spirit!— Bird thou never wert!— That from Heaven, or near it, Pourest thy full heart In profuse strains of unpremeditated art. [Shelley: *To a Skylark*]

14 And drown'd in yonder living blue The lark becomes a sightless song. [Tennyson: *In Memoriam* CXV]

LASSES

15 Green grow the rashes O; Green grow the rashes O, The sweetest hours that e'er I spend, Are spent amang the lasses O! [Burns: *Green Grow the Rashes*]

> rashes = *rushes*

16 Auld Nature swears, the lovely dears Her noblest work she classes, O: Her prentice han' she tried on man, An' then she made the lasses, O. [Burns: *Green Grow the Rashes*]

17 There's nought but care on every hand, In every hour that passes, O: What signifies the life o' man, And 't were na for the lasses, O. [Burns: *Green Grow the Rashes*]

LAST

18 Though last not least. [Edmund Spenser: *Colin Clouts Come Home Again*]

> *This was a saying. It occurs again in Shakespeare's* King Lear *I.i.*

LATE

19 For better than never is late. [Chaucer: *The Canon's Yeoman's Tale*]

20 Five minutes! Zounds! I have been five minutes too late all my lifetime! [Hannah Cowley: *The Belle's Stratagem* I.i.]

LATIN AND GREEK

21 And though thou hadst small Latin and less Greek. [Ben Jonson: *To the Memory of my Beloved, the Author, William Shakespeare*]

22 The Romans would never have found time to conquer the world if they had been obliged first to learn Latin. [Heinrich Heine: *Reisebilder* II]

LAUGH(TER) (noun)

1 The deathless laughter of the blessed gods. [Homer: *Iliad* I; *Odyssey* VIII; and throughout both works]

Plato (Republic III) felt that uninhibited laughter was improper in dignified men, let alone in gods, and that in the properly governed state passages such as the above should be expunged from the classics:

Then persons of worth, even if only mortal men, must not be represented as overcome by laughter, and still less must such a representation of the gods be allowed. (Jowett's trans.)

See Congreve and Chesterfield below.

2 Even in laughter the heart is sorrowful; and the end of mirth is heaviness. [Proverbs 14:13]

3 As the crackling of thorns under a pot, so is the laughter of the fool. [Ecclesiastes 7:6]

4 Than inept laughter nothing is more inept. [Catullus: *Carmina* XXXVII]

5 Delight hath a joy in it either permanent or present; laughter hath only a scornful tickling. [Sir Philip Sidney: *The Defence of Poesy*]

6 Laughter is nothing else but sudden glory arising from some sudden conception of some eminency in ourselves, by comparison with the infirmity of others, or with our own formerly. [Thomas Hobbes: *On Human Nature* IX]

7 Sudden glory is the passion which maketh those grimaces called laughter. [Thomas Hobbes: *Leviathan* I.vi.]

8 He laughs best that laughs last.

The earliest known statement of this proverb is in Sir John Vanbrugh's The Country House II.v. Vanbrugh may have coined it but the thought is so obvious that it was more likely an established expression that simply hadn't yet been printed.

9 There is nothing more unbecoming a man of quality than to laugh; Jesu, 'tis such a vulgar expression of the passion. [William Congreve: *The Double Dealer* I.iv.]

Congreve, in 1694, is ridiculing that affec-

tation of hauteur and disdain which, as late as 1748, Lord Chesterfield urged upon his son.

10 If we may believe our logicians, man is distinguished from all other creatures by the faculty of laughter. [Joseph Addison: *The Spectator* No. 494]

11 Loud laughter is the mirth of the mob, who are only pleased with silly things; for true wit or good sense never excited a laugh since the creation of the world. A man of parts and fashion is therefore only seen to smile, but never heard to laugh. [Lord Chesterfield: *Letters to His Son*, Oct. 19, 1748]

12 There is nothing so illiberal and so ill-bred as audible laughter. I am sure that since I have had the full use of my reason, nobody has ever heard me laugh. [Lord Chesterfield: *Letters to His Son*, Mar. 9, 1748]

13 The loud laugh that spoke the vacant mind. [Oliver Goldsmith: *The Deserted Village*]

14 The landlord's laugh was ready chorus. [Burns: *Tam o' Shanter*]

15 I am convinced that there can be no entire regeneration of mankind until laughter is put down. [Shelley: *To T. J. Hogg*]

16 Laughter is not at all a bad beginning for a friendship, and it is far the best ending for one. [Oscar Wilde: *The Picture of Dorian Gray* I]

LAUGH(ING) (verb)

17 Laugh, if thou art wise. [Martial: *Epigrams* II]

18 We must laugh before we are happy for fear of dying without laughing at all. [La Bruyère: *Les Caractères*]

19 A maid that laughs is half taken. [John Ray: *English Proverbs* (1670)]

Compare a remark of Falstaff's concerning Prince John of Lancaster: "This same young sober-blooded boy doth not love me . . . a man cannot make him laugh."

Shakespeare: II Henry IV IV.iii.

20 We seldom ever laugh without crime. [Thomas Wilson: *Maxims of Piety and of Christianity*]

21 Laugh not too much; the witty man laughs last. [George Herbert: *The*

Church-Porch]

1 Some things are of that nature as to make
One's fancy chuckle, while his heart doth ache.
[John Bunyan: *Pilgrim's Progress*, "The Author's Way of Sending Forth his Second Part of the Pilgrim"]

2 All fools have still an itching to deride,
And fain would be upon the laughing side.
[Alexander Pope: *An Essay on Criticism* I]

3 'Tis not deem'd so great a crime by half
To violate a vestal as to laugh.
[Charles Churchill: *The Rosciad*]

4 Who laughed there? By God, I think it was I myself! [Lessing: *Emilia Galotti* V.vi.]

5 Men show their characters in nothing more clearly than in what they think laughable. [Goethe: *Maxims*]

6 And if I laugh at any mortal thing,
'Tis that I may not weep.
[Byron: *Don Juan* IV.iv.]

> *I hasten to laugh at everything, for fear I will be obliged to cry.*
> Beaumarchais: The Barber of Seville *I.ii.*

7 No man who has once heartily and wholly laughed can be altogether irreclaimably bad. [Thomas Carlyle: *Sartor Resartus* I.iv.]

8 Like the boy who stubbed his toe. He said he was too big to cry and it hurt too bad to laugh. [Abraham Lincoln: in Leslie's *Illustrated Weekly*]

> *Lincoln was so quoted in his comment on the result of the New York elections in which the Democrats had won. The actual words: Lincoln was asked how he felt about the results and answered: "Somewhat like the boy in Kentucky, who stubbed his toe while running to see his sweetheart. The boy said he was too big to cry, and far too badly hurt to laugh."*
> *Adlai Stevenson quoted Lincoln's remark in a statement after losing the election in 1952.*

9 There are those who laugh to show their good teeth; and there are those who cry to show their good hearts. [Joseph Roux: *Pensées*]

10 Laugh and the world laughs with you,
Weep and you weep alone,
For the sad old earth must borrow its mirth,
But has trouble enough of its own.
[Ella Wheeler Wilcox: *Solitude* (1883)]

> *Commonly misquoted as: Cry and you cry alone, For the sad old earth will join in your mirth.*

11 There is so much to laugh at in this vale of tears. [Sudermann: *Es lebe das Leben* I.ii (trans. Edith Wharton)]

LAVENDER

12 Lavender's blue, diddle, diddle,
Lavender's green;
When I am king, diddle, diddle,
You shall be queen.
[Nursery rhyme: earliest appearance as a nursery rhyme, 1805]

> *This song has had a peculiar history. It was known in the 17th century as* The Kind Country Lovers *and was a love song. Whereas the contemporary nursery rhyme has: "Whilst you and I, diddle, diddle, / Keep ourselves warm," the old love song had "keep the bed warm," a wording, by the way, that was retained in the earliest nursery-rhyme form.*
> *In 1948-49 the song suddenly became popular again as a dance tune and was used in a Disney movie. Needless to say, the modern lovers were kept out of bed.*

LAW

13 These, having not the law, are a law unto themselves. [Romans 2:14]

14 The welfare of the people is the chief law. [Cicero: *De legibus* III.iii.]

15 Law hath certain lawful fictions upon which it groundeth the truth of justice. [Montaigne: *Essays* II.xii.]

16 Show me the man and I'll show you the law. [David Ferguson: *Scottish Proverbs* (1641)]

> *That is, the law is what the judge says it is and judges are swayed by personal considerations.*

17 Judges ought above all to remember the Conclusion of the Roman Twelve Tables: *Salus populi suprema lex;* and to know that Lawes, except they be in Order to that End, are but Things Captious, and Oracles not well Inspired. [Francis Bacon: *Of Judicature*]

1 There is no worse torture than the torture of laws. [Francis Bacon: *Of Judicature*]

2 Old father antic the law. [Shakespeare: *I Henry IV* I.ii.]

3 Still you keep o' the windy side of the law. [Shakespeare: *Twelfth Night* III.iv.]

4   The bloody book of law
You shall yourself read in the bitter letter. [Shakespeare: *Othello* I.iii.]
The contemporary phrase is "throw the book at him."

5 Agree, for the law is costly. [William Camden: *Remains*]

6 He that goes to law holds a wolf by the ears. [Robert Burton: *Anatomy of Melancholy*, "Democritus to the Reader"]

7 There is not anything in the world more abused than this sentence, *Salus populi suprema lex esto* [The safety of the people is the supreme law], for we apply it as if we ought to forsake the known law. [John Selden: *Table Talk*, "People"]

8 Equity, in law, is the same that the spirit is in religion: what everyone pleases to make it. [John Selden: *Table Talk*, "Equity"]

9 Ignorance of the law excuses no man; not that all men know the law, but because 'tis an excuse every man will plead, and no man can tell how to confute him. [John Selden: *Table Talk*, "Law"]

10 The law is but words and paper without the hands and swords of men. [James Harrington: *The Commonwealth of Oceana*]

11 In a thousand pounds of law there is not an ounce of love. [John Ray: *English Proverbs* (1670)]

12 Bluster, sputter, question, cavil; but be sure that your argument be intricate enough to confound the court. [William Wycherley: *Plain-Dealer* III.i.]
confound = *utterly confuse*

13 I knew a very wise man who believed that if a man were permitted to make all the ballads, he need not care who should make the laws of a nation. [Andrew Fletcher of Saltoun: Letter to the Marquis of Montrose (1704)]
Often misquoted—with "songs" for "ballads."

Some think the "very wise man" was the Earl of Cromarty, others believe him to have been the jurist-philosopher John Selden.

14 Necessity knows no law; I know some attorneys of the same. [Benjamin Franklin: *Poor Richard's Almanack* (1734)]

15 The law is the last result of human wisdom acting upon human experience for the benefit of the public. [Samuel Johnson: in Mrs. Piozzi's *Anecdotes of the late Samuel Johnson*]

16 How small, of all that human hearts endure,
That part which laws or kings can cause or cure. [Oliver Goldsmith: *The Traveller*]

17 No man e'er felt the halter draw,
With good opinion of the law. [John Trumbull: *M'Fingal* III]

18 And through the heat of conflict keeps the law
In calmness made. [Wordsworth: *Character of the Happy Warrior*]

19 Law and equity are two things which God hath joined, but which man hath put asunder. [C. C. Colton: *Lacon*]

20 "If the law supposes that," said Mr. Bumble, "the law is a ass, a idiot." [Dickens: *Oliver Twist* LI]

21 The prophecies of what the courts will do in fact, and nothing more pretentious, are what I mean by the law. [O. W. Holmes, Jr.: *The Path of the Law*]

22 The laws of God, the laws of man
He may keep that will and can;
Not I: let God and man decree
Laws for themselves and not for me. [A. E. Housman: *Last Poems* XII]

23 We are under a Constitution, but the Constitution is what the judges say it is. [Charles E. Hughes: in a speech at Elmira, N. Y., May 3, 1907]

24 Leave to live by no man's leave, underneath the law. [Kipling: *The Old Issue*]

25 There's never a law of God or man runs north of Fifty-Three. [Kipling: *The Rhyme of the Three Sealers*]

1 I care not who makes th' laws iv a nation if I can get out an injunction. [Finley Peter Dunne: *Mr. Dooley's Philosophy*, "Casual Observations"]

2 If the law is upheld only by government officials, then all law is at an end. [Herbert Hoover: Message to Congress, 1929]

3 It is one thing for the human mind to extract from the phenomena of nature the laws which it has itself put into them; it may be a far harder thing to extract laws over which it has no control. It is even possible that laws which have not their origin in the mind may be irrational, and we can never succeed in formulating them. [Sir Arthur Stanley Eddington: *Space, Time and Gravitation*]

4 Law is merely the expression of the will of the strongest for the time being, and therefore laws have no fixity, but shift from generation to generation. [Brooks Adams: *The Law of Civilization and Decay*]

5 I am the law. [Frank Hague, Mayor of Jersey City, quoted *New York Times*, Nov. 11, 1937]
See also JUSTICE

LAWYER(S)

6 Woe unto you also, ye lawyers! for ye lade men with burdens grievous to be borne, and ye yourselves touch not the burdens with one of your fingers. [Luke: 11:46]

7 The first thing we do, let's kill all the lawyers. [Shakespeare: *II Henry VI* IV.ii.]

8 In all points out of their own trade they were the most ignorant and stupid generation among us, the most despicable in common conversation, avowed enemies to all knowledge and learning, and equally disposed to pervert the general reason of mankind in every other subject of discourse as in that of their own profession. [Jonathan Swift: *Gulliver's Travels* IV.v.]

9 Two attorneys can live in a town where one cannot. [V. S. Lean: *Collectanea* (1902-04)]

10 Three Philadelphia lawyers are a match for the Devil. [Listed by Mencken as a "New England Proverb"]
But Mencken admitted that this particular wording did not antedate 1924. See PHILADELPHIA LAWYER

11 Why does a hearse horse snicker
Hauling a lawyer away?
[Carl Sandburg: *The Lawyers Know Too Much*]

LAZY

12 As lazy as Ludlam's dog, that leaned his head against a wall to bark. [John Ray: *English Proverbs*]
Nothing is known of Ludlam. His dog's lack of energy is paralleled—possibly borrowed—in Thomas Haliburton's "As poor [poorly, feeble] as Job's turkey, that had to lean against the barn to gobble."

13 Lazy people are always wanting to do something. [Vauvenargues: *Réflexions*]

LEADER

14 He led his regiment from behind
(He found it less exciting).
[W. S. Gilbert: *The Gondoliers* I]

LEAR

15 How pleasant to know Mr. Lear!
Who has written such volumes of stuff!
Some think him ill-tempered and queer,
But a few think him pleasant enough.
[Edward Lear: Preface to *Nonsense Songs*]
Cf. T. S. Eliot's: How unpleasant to know Mr. Eliot!

LEARNED

16 More is experienced in one day in the life of a learned man than in the whole lifetime of an ignorant man. [Seneca: *Epistolae* LXXVIII]
Seneca is here quoting Posidonius.

17 All want to be learned, but no one is willing to pay the price. [Juvenal: *Satires* VII]

18 The gretteste clerkes been noght the wysest men.
clerkes = *scholars.*
The statement is given as a saying or proverb.
[Chaucer: *The Reeve's Tale*]

19 The learned pate ducks to the golden fool. [Shakespeare: *Timon of Athens* IV.iii.]

20 Learn'd, without sense, and venerably dull.

[Charles Churchill: *The Rosciad*]

1 Learned men are the cisterns of knowledge, not the fountainheads. [James Northcote: *Table Talk*]

2 It might be argued, that to be a knave is the gift of fortune, but to play the fool to advantage it is necessary to be a learned man. [William Hazlitt: *Table Talk*, "Intellectual Superiority"]

3 The Revelations of Devout and
      Learn'd
Who rose before us, and as Prophets
      burn'd,
Are all but Stories, which, awoke
      from Sleep,
They told their comrades, and to
      Sleep return'd.
[*Rubáiyát of Omar Khayyám* (trans. Edward FitzGerald)] but = *only, merely*

4 A learned man is an idler who kills time by study. [G. B. Shaw: *Maxims for Revolutionists*]

LEARNING: and action

5 What we have to learn to do, we learn by doing. [Aristotle: *Nicomachean Ethics* II.i.]

6 Studies themselves do give forth directions too much at large, except they be bounded in by experience. [Francis Bacon: *Of Studies*]

7 In doing we learn. [George Herbert: *Jacula Prudentum*]

8 No man can with all the wealth in the world buy so much skill as to be a good lutenist; he must go the same way that poor people do, he must learn and take pains: much less can he buy constancy, or chastity, or courage; nay, not so much as the contempt of riches: and by possessing more than we need, we cannot obtain so much power over ourselves as not to require more. [Jeremy Taylor: *Holy Living*]

9 I went to the woods because I wished to live deliberately, to front only the essential facts of life, and see if I could not learn what it had to teach, and not when I came to die, discover that I had not lived. [Thoreau: *Walden* II, "What I Lived For"]

LEARNING: its pains and follies

10 Much learning doth make thee mad. [Acts 26:24]

11 We see man gape after no reputation but learning and when they say such a one is a learned man, they think they have said enough. [Montaigne: *Essays* I.xxv.]
This particular sentiment seems to have been interpolated by John Florio, the translator.

12 To be learned in many errors, as to be ignorant in all things, hath little diversity. [Sir Walter Raleigh (1552?-1618): *History of the World* II.i.]

13 Learning, that cobweb of the brain,
Profane, erroneous, and vain.
[Samuel Butler (1612-1680): *Hudibras*]

14 In Learning let a Nymph delight,
The Pedant gets a Mistress by 't.
[Jonathan Swift: *Cadenus and Vanessa*]

15 So by false learning is good sense
      defac'd;
Some are bewilder'd in the maze of
      schools,
And some made coxcombs Nature
      meant but fools.
[Alexander Pope: *An Essay on Criticism* I]

16 Mark what ills the scholar's life assail,
Toil, envy, want, the patron and the
      gaol.
[Samuel Johnson: *The Vanity of Human Wishes*]
Johnson had first written, "Toil, envy, want, the garret and the gaol." However, he perceived that the garret was merely a special instance of want, and therefore added nothing, whereas the patron introduced a whole new series of the intellectual man's miseries. It was a happy emendation.

17 A student may easily exhaust his life in comparing divines and moralists without any practical regard to morality or religion; he may be learning not to live but to reason . . . while the chief use of his volumes is unthought of, his mind is unaffected, and his life is unreformed. [Samuel Johnson: *The Rambler* No. 87]

18 A set o' dull conceited hashes
Confuse their brains in college classes!
They gang in stirks, and come out
      asses,
  Plain truth to speak;
An' syne they think to climb Parnas
      sus
  By dint o' Greek!

[Burns: *Epistle to John Lapraik*]
hashes = *softies;* stirks = *bull-calves;* syne = *then*

1 With just enough of learning to misquote.
[Byron: *English Bards and Scotch Reviewers*]

2 Vether it's worth goin' through so much to learn so little, as the charity-boy said ven he got to the end of the alphabet, is a matter o' taste. [Dickens: *The Pickwick Papers* XXVII]
For a discussion of Sam Weller's pronunciation, see CONNUBIALITY.

3 With them the seed of Wisdom did
I sow,
And with mine own hand wrought
to make it grow;
And this was all the Harvest that I
reaped—
"I came like Water, and like Wind
I go."
[*Rubáiyát of Omar Khayyám* (trans. Edward FitzGerald)]

LEARNING: and wisdom and virtue
4 Since learned men have appeared, good men have become rare. [Seneca: *Ad Lucilium* XCV]

5 We have need of very little learning to have a good mind. [Montaigne: *Essays* III.xii.]

6 To spend too much time in studies is sloth; to use them too much for ornament is affectation; to make judgment wholly by their rules is the humor of a scholar. [Francis Bacon: *Of Studies*]
humor = *whim, obsession, irrational inclination*

7 There is no great concurrence between learning and wisdom. [Francis Bacon: *Civil Knowledge* IV]

8 No man is the wiser for his learning: it may administer matter to work in, or objects to work upon; but wit and wisdom are born with a man. [John Selden: *Table Talk,* "Learning"]

9 Learning makes a good man better and an ill man worse. [Thomas Fuller (1654-1734): *Gnomologia*]

10 A little learning is a dangerous thing;
Drink deep, or taste not the Pierian
spring.
[Alexander Pope: *An Essay on Criticism* II]

Often misquoted as "a little knowledge."
Pope is echoing a line from Michael Drayton's On Poets and Poesie *(1603):*
... *the learn'd Jonson* ...
Who had drunk deep of the Pierian
spring.
Of Pope's famous line, T. H. Huxley remarked: "If a little knowledge is dangerous, where is the man who has so much as to be out of danger?"
Science and Culture *(1881)*

11 Learning is acquired by reading books; but the much more necessary learning, the knowledge of the world, is only to be acquired by reading men, and studying all the various editions of them. [Lord Chesterfield: *Letters to His Son,* March 16, 1752]

12 Learning makes the wise wiser and the fool more foolish. [John Ray: *English Proverbs* (1670)]

13 One may almost doubt if the wisest man has learned anything of absolute value by living. [Thoreau: *Walden* I, "Economy"]

14 It is only when we forget all our learning that we begin to know. [Thoreau: *Autumn,* October 4, 1859]

LEARNING: miscellaneous
15 Learning is not child's play; we cannot learn without pain. [Aristotle: *Politics* V.v.]

16 The mind is slow in unlearning what it has been long in learning. [Seneca: *Troades* 633]

17 A day of the learned is longer than the life of the ignorant. [Seneca: *Ad Lucilium* LXXVIII]

18 It is impossible for a man to learn what he thinks he already knows. [Epictetus: *Discourses* II]

19 Men learn while they teach. [Seneca: *Ad Lucilium* VII]

20 Who-so that nil be war by othere
men,
By him shul othere men corrected be.
[Chaucer: Prologue to *The Wife of Bath's Tale*]
war = *warned, made wary by the example of*

21 I am too old to learn.
[Shakespeare: *King Lear* II.ii.]

22 A man is never too old to learn.

[Thomas Middleton: *The Mayor of Quinborough* V]

1 The love of money and the love of learning rarely meet. [George Herbert: *Jacula Prudentum*]

2 I have heard Dr. Whistler say that he [Dr. Ralph Kettle, President of Trinity College, Oxford (d. 1643)] scolded the best in Latin of any one that ever he knew. [John Aubrey: *Brief Lives* II]

3 The things which hurt, instruct. [Benjamin Franklin: *Poor Richard's Almanack* (1744)]

4 All licentious passages are left in the decent obscurity of a learned language. [Edward Gibbon: *Autobiography*]
> The reference is to The Decline and Fall of the Roman Empire.

5 Wear your learning, like your watch, in a private pocket; and do not pull it out and strike it, merely to show that you have one. If you are asked what o'clock it is, tell it; but do not proclaim it hourly and unasked, like the watchman. [Lord Chesterfield: *Letters to His Son*, Feb. 22, 1748]
> strike it = *make it strike the hour*

6 'Tis pleasing to be school'd in a
    strange tongue
By female lips and eyes—that is, I
    mean,
When both the teacher and the
    taught are young,
As was the case, at least, where I
    have been;
They smile so when one's right; and
    when one's wrong
They smile still more.
[Byron: *Don Juan* II.clxiv.]

LEAVES

7 Thick as autumnal leaves that strow
    the brooks
In Vallombrosa.
[John Milton: *Paradise Lost* I.302-303]

8 Brown skeletons of leaves that lag
My forest-brook along;
When the ivy-tod is heavy with snow,
And the owlet whoops to the wolf
    below,
That eats the she-wolf's young.
[Coleridge: *The Ancient Mariner* VII]

9 Lisp of leaves and ripple of rain.
[Swinburne: Chorus from *Atalanta in Calydon*]

LECHERY

10   . . . the fyr of lecherye
That is annexed un-to glotonye.
[Chaucer: *The Pardoner's Tale*]

11 And, after wyn, on Venus moste I
    thinke:
For al so siker as cold engendreth
    hayl,
A likerous mouth moste han a liker-
    ous tayl.
In womman vinolent is no defence,
This knowen lechours by experience.
[Chaucer: Prologue to *The Wife of Bath's Tale*]
> wyn = *wine;* siker = *certainly;* likerous (*the first use*) = *greedy, fond of good fare; the second* = *lecherous;* vinolent = *drunk, excited by alcohol*

LEGACY

12 I owe much; I have nothing; I give the rest to the poor. [Rabelais: Last Will (1553)]

13 And all to leave what with his toil he
    won
  To that unfeather'd two-legg'd thing,
    a son.
[Dryden: *Absalom and Achitophel* I]

LEGION

14 My name is Legion: for we are many. [Mark 5:9]
> The answer of the unclean spirit in the man who dwelt among the tombs in the country of the Gadarenes when Christ demanded his name.
>
> The possessed were often possessed with great numbers of spirits at one time and occupied much of their time in designating and classifying them. These particular spirits had a strong attachment to the locality and begged Jesus not to send them out of the country. They suggested that he send them into a herd of swine which was nearby. But the swine were excited by their guests and "ran violently down a steep place into the sea (they were about two thousand), and were choked in the sea."

LEGISLATION

15 One of the greatest delusions in the world is the hope that the evils in this

world are to be cured by legislation. [Thomas B. Reed: in a speech in the House of Representatives, 1886]

LEGISLATOR
1 Ignorance, idleness and vice may be sometimes the only ingredients for qualifying a legislator. [Jonathan Swift: *Gulliver's Travels* II.vi.]

LEISURE
2 The goal of war is peace; of business, leisure. [Aristotle: *Politics* IV]
3 The wisdom of a learned man cometh by opportunity of leisure: and he that hath little business shall become wise. [Ecclesiasticus 38:24]

A piece of wisdom so out of tune with our times that most would regard it as folly. A fine expression of it is in Wordsworth's Expostulation and Reply, *where he insists that we learn in idleness, that there are Powers*

Which of themselves our minds impress;
That we can feed this mind of ours
In a wise passiveness.

Think you, 'mid all this mighty sum
Of things for ever speaking,
That nothing of itself will come,
But we must still be seeking?

4 Leisure with dignity. (*Otium cum dignitate.*) [Cicero: *Pro Sestio* XIV]
Cicero lists this as the thing in life most desirable, after health and modest means.
5 He was never less at leisure than when he was at leisure. [Cicero: *De officiis* III]
6 Leisure is the mother of Philosophy. [Thomas Hobbes: *Leviathan* IV.xlvi.]
7 And add to these retired Leisure,
That in trim gardens takes his pleasure.
[John Milton: *Il Penseroso*]
8 All intellectual improvement arises from leisure. [Samuel Johnson: in Boswell's *Life,* April 13, 1773]
9 A broad margin of leisure is as beautiful in a man's life as in a book. [Thoreau: *Journal,* December 28, 1852]
10 The advantage of leisure is mainly that we may have the power of choosing our own work, not certainly that it confers any privilege of idleness. [John Lubbock (Lord Avebury): *The Pleasures of Life* VI]
11 To be able to fill leisure intelligently is the last product of civilization. [Bertrand Russell: *The Conquest of Happiness*]
12 Generally speaking anybody is more interesting doing nothing than doing anything. [Gertrude Stein: in reference to her opera, *Four Saints in Three Acts*]
13 The office of the leisure class in social evolution is to retard the movement and to conserve what is obsolescent. [Thorstein Veblen: *The Theory of the Leisure Class* VIII]

LENDING
14 Unto a stranger thou mayest lend upon usury; but unto thy brother thou shalt not lend upon usury. [Deuteronomy 23:20]
15 'Tis a godlike thing to lend; to owe is a heroic virtue. [Rabelais: *Works* III.iv.]
16 If you lend money, you make a secret enemy; if you refuse it, an open one. [Voltaire: *Fragments Historiques* XIV]
17 He that has but one Coat, cannot lend it. [Thomas Fuller (1654-1734): *Gnomologia*]

LEOPARD
18 Can the Ethiopian change his skin, or the leopard his spots? [Jeremiah 13:23]

LETHE
19 Far off from these, a slow and silent stream,
Lethe the river of oblivion.
[John Milton: *Paradise Lost* II.582-583]
20 No, no! go not to Lethe.
[Keats: *On Melancholy*]

LETTER(S)
21 Not of the letter, but of the spirit; for the letter killeth, but the spirit giveth life. [II Corinthians 3:6]
In no way is the letter more lethal than in holding a man strictly to the letter of his professed beliefs.
22 The republic of letters. (*La république des lettres*) [Molière: *Le mariage forcé* VI]

1 The republic of letters. [Henry Fielding: *Tom Jones* XIV.i.]

LETTERS (MISSIVES)
2 I have made this letter longer than usual because I lack the time to make it shorter. [Pascal: *Provincial Letters* XVI]
3 A short letter to a distant friend is, in my opinion, an insult like that of a slight bow or cursory salutation—a proof of unwillingness to do much, even where there is a necessity of doing something. [Samuel Johnson: Letter to Joseph Baretti, June 10, 1761]
4 The postman is the agent of impolite surprises. Every week we ought to have an hour for receiving letters—and then go and take a bath. [Nietzsche: *Human All-too-Human* II]
5 I have received no more than one or two letters in my life that were worth the postage. [Thoreau: *Walden* II]
6 "Going to him! Happy letter! Tell him—
Tell him the page I didn't write;
Tell him I only said the syntax,
And left the verb and pronoun out."
[Emily Dickinson: *Poems, Part III, Love* XXIII.i.]

LEVELING
7 Your levellers wish to level down as far as themselves, but they cannot bear levelling up to themselves. [Samuel Johnson: in Boswell's *Life* (1763)]

LEVIATHAN
8 Canst thou draw out leviathan with a hook? [Job 41:1]
9   . . . that sea-beast
Leviathan, which God of all his works
Created hugest that swim the ocean-stream.
[John Milton: *Paradise Lost* I. 200-203]

LEVITY
10 Nothing like a little judicious levity. [R. L. Stevenson and Lloyd Osbourne: *The Wrong Box* VII]

LEWD
11 Certain lewd fellows of the baser sort. [Acts 17:5]

LEXICOGRAPHER
12 Every other author may aspire to praise; the lexicographer can only hope to escape reproach, and even this negative recompense has been yet granted to very few. [Samuel Johnson: Preface to the *Dictionary*]
13 *Lexicographer:* A writer of dictionaries, a harmless drudge. [Samuel Johnson: definition in the *Dictionary*]

LIABILITIES
14 Four be the things I'd been better
                    without:
Love, curiosity, freckles, and doubt.
[Dorothy Parker: *Inventory*]

LIAR(S)
15 I said in my haste, All men are liars. [Psalms 116:11]
16 But Peter said, Ananias . . . thou hast not lied unto men, but unto God.
And Ananias hearing these words fell down, and gave up the ghost. [Acts 5:3-5]
> Ananias sold a piece of land and said that he was giving the full sale price to God; but he had received more than he gave. His wife Sapphira was party to the deception and she too fell down dead.
> Ananias was a common, jocular designation of a liar in 19th-century America.
17 We give no credit to a liar, even when he speaks the truth. [Cicero: *De divinatione* II]
18 A liar ought to have a good memory. [Apuleius: *De Magia* LXIX]
> Apuleius flourished about 155 A.D. Of the statement he says, "I have often heard it said." So it was proverbial then.
> The statement had appeared earlier in Quintilian's De Institutione Oratoria IV and is in Algernon Sidney's Discourses on Government II.xv.
19 A liar is a man who does not know how to deceive. [Vauvenargues: *Réflexions*]
> Because, of course, if he is successful, we do not know that he is a liar.
20 An experienced, industrious, ambitious, and often quite picturesque liar. [Mark Twain: *The Private History of a Campaign That Failed*]

LIBEL
21 The greater the truth, the greater the

libel. [Attr. William Murray, Lord Mansfield: when (1784) he presided over the King's Bench, although he was probably merely quoting an established legal maxim.]
Also attr. Lord Ellenborough.

LIBERAL AND CONSERVATIVE
1 I often think it's comical
    How nature always does contrive
  That every boy and every gal,
    That's born into the world alive,
  Is either a little Liberal,
    Or else a little Conservative!
[W. S. Gilbert: *Iolanthe* II]

LIBERAL EDUCATION
2 Liberal Education makes not the Christian, not the Catholic, but the gentleman. [John Henry Newman: *The Idea of a University*, Discourse V]
3 Liberal Education, viewed in itself, is simply the cultivation of the intellect, as such, and its object is nothing more or less than intellectual excellence. [John Henry Newman: *The Idea of a University*, Discourse V]
4 A liberal education is an artificial education which has not only prepared a man to escape the great evils of disobedience to natural laws, but has trained him to appreciate and to seize upon the rewards, which Nature scatters with as free a hand as her penalties. [T. H. Huxley: *Science and Education* IV]

LIBERALISM
5 The function of Liberalism in the past was that of putting a limit to the powers of kings. The function of true Liberalism in the future will be that of putting a limit to the powers of Parliaments. [Herbert Spencer: *The Man Versus the State*]

LIBERALITY
6 The liberalitie of a poore man is his good will. [John Florio: *Firste Fruites* LXVIII]
7 Liberality should as well have banks as a stream. [Thomas Fuller (1608-1661): *The Holy State and the Profane State*]
8 What is called liberality is most often only the vanity of giving, which we like

better than the thing we give. [La Rochefoucauld: *Maxims*]
9 Liberality consists less in giving much than in giving at the right moment. [La Bruyère: *Les Caractères*]

LIBERATION
10 Freeing oppressed nationalities is perhaps the most dangerous of all philanthropic enterprises. [William Bolitho: *Twelve Against the Gods*, "Napoleon III"]

LIBERTY(IES)
11 Proclaim liberty throughout all the land unto all the inhabitants thereof. [Leviticus 25:10]
  Inscribed on the Liberty Bell, preserved in Independence Hall, Philadelphia.
    Since the bell was cast in 1751, there was something prophetic in placing this inscription on it.
12 Where the spirit of the Lord is, there is Liberty. [II Corinthians 3:17]
13 Few men desire liberty; most men wish only for a just master. [Sallust: *History* IV]
14 Liberties and masters are not easily combined. [Tacitus: *Annals* IV]
15 The mountain nymph, sweet Liberty. [John Milton: *L'Allegro*]
16 For this is not the liberty which we can hope, that no grievance ever should arise in the Commonwealth, that let no man in this world expect; but when complaints are freely heard, deeply considered, and speedily reformed, then is the utmost bound of civil liberty attained that wise men look for. [John Milton: *Areopagitica*]
17 Liberty of conscience is nowadays not only understood to be the liberty of believing what men please, but also of endeavoring to propagate that belief as much as they can. [Jonathan Swift: *Sermon on the Testimony of Conscience*]
18 This is Liberty-hall, gentlemen. You may do just as you please here. [Oliver Goldsmith: *She Stoops to Conquer* II]
19 Liberty, too, must be limited in order to be possessed. [Edmund Burke: *Letter to the Sheriffs of Bristol*]
20 Abstract liberty, like other mere abstractions, is not to be found. [Edmund Burke: *Speech on Conciliation with*

America, March 22, 1775]

1 The people never give up their liberties but under some delusion. [Edmund Burke: in a speech at a county meeting at Buckinghamshire]

2 I know not what course others may take, but as for me, give me liberty, or give me death! [Patrick Henry: in a speech at the Virginia Convention, St. John's Episcopal Church, Richmond, Virginia]

3 The tree of liberty must be refreshed from time to time with the blood of patriots and tyrants. It is its natural manure. [Thomas Jefferson: Letter to W. S. Smith, Nov. 13, 1787]

4 We are not to expect to be translated from despotism to liberty in a featherbed. [Thomas Jefferson: Letter to Lafayette, April 2, 1790]

5 A fig for those by law protected!
    Liberty's a glorious feast!
  Courts for cowards were erected;
    Churches built to please the priest.
[Burns: *The Jolly Beggars*]

6 Two voices are there; one is of the
                                    sea,
  One of the mountains; each a mighty
                                    voice:
  In both from age to age thou didst
                                    rejoice,
  They were thy chosen music, Lib-
                                    erty!
[Wordsworth: *On the Subjugation of Switzerland*]

7 The tree of Liberty only grows when watered by the blood of tyrants. [Bertrand Barère de Vieuzac: in a speech at the National Convention (1792)]

8 Liberty, equality, fraternity. (*Liberté, égalité, fraternité.*) [Motto of the French Republic: usually ascribed to Antoine-François Momoro (1756-94); it was abandoned in 1940]

9 O liberty! what crimes are committed in thy name! [Attr. Madame Roland: as she stood on the scaffold]
  Quoted in Lamartine's Histoire des Girondins.

10 Liberty and Union, now and forever, one and inseparable! [Daniel Webster: in a speech in the Senate, Jan. 26, 1830]

11 Liberty, as a principle, has no application to any state of things anterior to the time when mankind have become capable of being improved by free and equal discussion. [John Stuart Mill: *On Liberty* I]

12 Eternal vigilance is the price of liberty. [Attr. commonly to Thomas Jefferson; but, so far as can be shown, first uttered by Wendell Phillips in a speech before the Massachusetts Antislavery Society, 1852]

13 He takes the strangest liberties—
  But never takes his leave!
[John Godfrey Saxe: *My Familiar*]

14 Give me your tired, your poor,
  Your huddled masses, yearning to
                                breathe free,
  The wretched refuse of your teeming
                                shore.
  Send these, the homeless, tempest
                                tossed, to me:
  I lift my lamp beside the golden door.
[Emma Lazarus: Inscription on Statue of Liberty, New York Harbor]

15 The liberty of thinking and of publishing whatever one likes . . . is the fountain-head of many evils. [Pope Leo XIII: *Immortale Dei,* Nov. 1, 1885]

16 Liberty means responsibility. That is why most men dread it. [G. B. Shaw: *Maxims for Revolutionists*]

17 Liberty does not consist in mere declarations of the rights of man. It consists in the translation of those declarations into definite actions. [Woodrow Wilson: Address, July 4, 1914]

LIBRARY(IES)

18 No place affords a more striking conviction of the vanity of human hopes than a public library. [Samuel Johnson: *The Rambler* No. 106]

19 Meek young men grow up in libraries, believing it their duty to accept the views which Cicero, which Locke, which Bacon, have given; forgetful that Cicero, Locke, and Bacon were only young men in libraries when they wrote these books. [Emerson: *The American Scholar* II]

LICENSE

20 For the Fifth Harry from curb'd license plucks
  The muzzle of restraint, and the wild
                                dog
  Shall flesh his tooth on every inno-
                                cent.

[Shakespeare: *II Henry IV* IV.v.]
1 License they mean when they cry liberty. [John Milton: *On the Same*]

The title refers to a previous sonnet with the most unpoetical title "On the Detraction Which Followed Upon My Writing Certain Treatises."

LIE

2 A mixture of a lie doth ever add pleasure. [Francis Bacon: *Of Truth*]

3 It is not the lie that passeth through the mind, but the lie that sinketh in, and settleth in it, that doth the hurt. [Francis Bacon: *Of Truth*]

4 It often falls out that somewhat is produced of nothing; for lies are sufficient to breed opinion and opinion brings on substance. [Francis Bacon: *Of Vainglory*]

Bacon is alluding to the Latin aphorism that "nothing can come of nothing."

His assertion is one of the mainsprings of advertising, public relations, and the like.

5 These lies are like the father that begets them; gross as a mountain, open, palpable. [Shakespeare: *I Henry IV* II.iv.]

6 He that tells a lie to save his credit, wipes his mouth with his sleeve to spare his napkin. [Sir Thomas Overbury: *Newes from the Lower End of the Table*]

7 The world is naturally averse
To all the truth it sees or hears,
But swallows nonsense and a lie
With greediness and gluttony.
[Samuel Butler (1612-1680): *Hudibras*]

8 He who tells a lie is not sensible of how great a task he undertakes; for he must be forced to invent twenty more to maintain that one. [Alexander Pope: *Thoughts on Various Subjects*]

9 Half the truth is often a great lie. [Benjamin Franklin: *Poor Richard's Almanack* (1758)]

10 A man had rather have a hundred lies told of him than one truth which he does not wish should be told. [Samuel Johnson: in Boswell's *Life*, April 15, 1773]

11 Large offers and sturdy rejections are among the most common topics of falsehood. [Samuel Johnson: *Life of Milton*]

12 Ask me no questions, and I'll tell you no fibs. [Oliver Goldsmith: *She Stoops to Conquer* II]

A fib may be a fable, or it may be something to fob you off.

13 And, after all, what is a lie? 'Tis but
The truth in masquerade; and I defy
Historians, heroes, lawyers, priests, to put
A fact without some leaven of a lie.
[Byron: *Don Juan* XI.xxxvii.]

14 A lie which is half a truth is ever the blackest of lies. [Tennyson: *The Grandmother*]

15 Sin has many tools, but a lie is the handle which fits them all. [O. W. Holmes: *The Autocrat of the Breakfast-Table* VI]

16 One of the most startling differences between a cat and a lie is that a cat has only nine lives. [Mark Twain: *Pudd'nhead Wilson's Calendar*]

17 Merely corroborative detail, intended to give artistic verisimilitude to a bald and unconvincing narrative. [W. S. Gilbert: *The Mikado* II]

18 The cruelest lies are often told in silence. [R. L. Stevenson: *Virginibus Puerisque* I.iv.]

19 Matilda told such Dreadful Lies,
It made one Gasp and Stretch one's Eyes;
Her Aunt, who, from her Earliest Youth,
Had kept a Strict Regard for Truth,
Attempted to Believe Matilda:
The effort very nearly killed her.
[Hilaire Belloc: *Matilda*]

20 The great masses of the people . . . will more easily fall victims to a great lie than to a small one. [Adolf Hitler: *Mein Kampf* I]

21 The two-faced answer or the plain protective lie. [W. H. Auden: *Voltaire at Ferney*]

22 A statesman is an easy man,
He tells his lies by rote;
A journalist makes up his lies
And takes you by the throat;
So stay at home and drink your beer
And let the neighbors vote.
[William Butler Yeats: *The Old Stone Cross*]

LIFE: annoyance, boredom and misery of

1 It is a misery to be born, a pain to live, a trouble to die. [St. Bernard: *De consideratione* III]

2 Life is as tedious as a twice-told tale. [Shakespeare: *King John* III.iv.]

3 No arts; no letters; no society; and which is worst of all, continual fear and danger of violent death; and the life of man, solitary, poor, nasty, brutish, and short. [Thomas Hobbes: *Leviathan* I]
Describing the life of man in the "natural" state.

4 This long disease, my life.
[Alexander Pope: *Epistle to Dr. Arbuthnot*]
In Pope's own case, this was no flight of self-pity but a simple statement of fact. He was a tiny man with a twisted spine, very frail, and afflicted with many ailments. It is astonishing that he lived the 56 years that he did (1688-1744).

5 Human life is everywhere in a state in which much is to be endured, and little to be enjoyed. [Samuel Johnson: *Rasselas* XI]

6 Nothing that lasts too long is very agreeable, not even life. [Vauvenargues: *Réflexions*]

7 All the dreary intercourse of daily life. [Wordsworth: *Tintern Abbey*]

8 My life is one demd horrid grind. [Dickens: *Nicholas Nickleby* II.xxxii.]

9 For most men in a brazen prison live,
Where, in the sun's hot eye,
With heads bent o'er their toil, they languidly
Their lives to some unmeaning task-work give.
[Matthew Arnold: *A Summer Night*]

10 Does the road wind up-hill all the way?
Yes, to the very end.
Will the day's journey take the whole long day?
From morn to night, my friend.
[Christina Rossetti: *Up-hill*]

11 Life is just one damned thing after another. [Attr. Frank Ward O'Malley]

12 The basic fact about human existence is not that it is a tragedy, but that it is a bore. [H. L. Mencken: *Prejudices*]

13 Look at life: the insolence and idleness of the strong, the ignorance and brutishness of the weak, horrible poverty everywhere, overcrowding, degeneration, drunkenness, hypocrisy, lying— Yet in all the houses and on the streets there is peace and quiet; of the fifty thousand people who live in our town there is not one who would cry out, who would vent his indignation aloud. We see the people who go to market, eat by day, sleep by night, who babble nonsense, marry, grow old, good-naturedly drag their dead to the cemetery, but we do not see or hear those who suffer, and what is terrible in life goes on somewhere behind the scenes. Everything is peaceful and quiet and only mute statistics protest. [Anton Chekhov: *Gooseberries*]

LIFE: the art of

14 O God! methinks it were a happy life,
To be no better than a homely swain;
To sit upon a hill, as I do now,
To carve out dials, quaintly, point by point,
Thereby to see the minutes how they run,
How many make the hour full complete;
How many hours bring about the day;
How many days will finish up the year;
How many years a mortal man may live.
[Shakespeare: *III Henry VI* II.v.]

15 The art of life is to know how to enjoy a little and to endure much. [William Hazlitt: *Commonplaces* No. 1]

16 There is no cure for birth and death save to enjoy the interval. [George Santayana: *Soliloquies in England*, "War Shrines"]

LIFE: its brevity and unreality

17 Few and evil have the days of the years of my life been. [Genesis 47:9]

18 We are but of yesterday, and know nothing, because our days upon earth are a shadow. [Job 8:9]

19 Man that is born of woman is of few days, and full of trouble. He cometh forth like a flower, and is cut down; he fleeth also as a shadow, and continueth not. [Job 14:1-2]

1 We spend our years as a tale that is told. [Psalms 90:9]

2 The days of our years are three-score years and ten; and if by reason of strength they be four-score years, yet is their strength labour and sorrow; for it is soon cut off and we fly away. [Psalms 90:10]

3 As for man, his days are as grass: as a flower of the field, so he flourisheth.

For the wind passeth over it, and it is gone; and the place thereof shall know it no more. [Psalms 103:15-16]

4 Man is like to vanity: his days are as a shadow that passeth away. [Psalms 144:4]

5 For what is your life: It is even a vapour, that appeareth for a little time, and then vanisheth away. [James 4:14]

6 Life is short, the art long, opportunity fleeting, experience treacherous, judgment difficult. [Hippocrates: *Aphorisms* I.i.]

7 Nature has given man no better thing than shortness of life. [Pliny the Elder: *Naturalis Historia* VII.li.]

8 The life so short, the craft so long to learn,
Th' assay so hard, so sharp the conquering.
[Chaucer: *The Parlement of Foules*, "Proem"]

9 Like as the waves make towards the pebbled shore,
So do our minutes hasten to their end.
[Shakespeare: *Sonnets* LX]

10 O gentlemen, the time of life is short!
To spend that shortness basely were too long,
If life did ride upon a dial's point,
Still ending at the arrival of an hour.
And if we live, we live to tread on kings;
If die, brave death, when princes die with us!
[Shakespeare: *I Henry IV* V.ii.]

11 Our lives are but our marches to our graves. [John Fletcher: *The Humorous Lieutenant* III.v.]

12 Our Life is nothing but a Winter's day;
Some only break their Fast, and so away:
Others stay to Dinner, and depart full fed:
The deepest Age but Sups, and goes to Bed:
He's most in debt that lingers out the Day:
Who dies betime, has less, and less to pay.
[Francis Quarles: *On the Life of Man*]

13 When all is done, human life is, at the greatest and best, but like a froward child, that must be played with and humoured a little to keep it quiet till it falls asleep, and then the care is over. [Sir William Temple: *Discourse of Poetry*]
froward = *peevish, captious, cross*

14 A little rule, a little sway,
A sunbeam in a winter's day,
Is all the proud and mighty have
Between the cradle and the grave.
[John Dyer: *Grongar Hill*]

15 Well—well; the world must turn upon its axis,
And all mankind turn with it, heads or tails,
And live and die, make love and pay our taxes,
And as the veering wind shifts, shift our sails;
The king commands us, and the doctor quacks us,
The priest instructs us, and so our life exhales,
A little breath, love, wine, ambition, fame,
Fighting, devotion, dust—perhaps a name.
[Byron: *Don Juan* II.iv.]

16 The One remains, the many change and pass;
Heaven's light forever shines, Earth's shadows fly;
Life, like a dome of many-coloured glass,
Stains the white radiance of Eternity,
Until Death tramples it to fragments.
[Shelley: *Adonais* LII]

17 Thus, like a God-created, fire-breathing Spirit-host, we emerge from the Inane; haste stormfully across the astonished Earth; then plunge again into the Inane. [Thomas Carlyle: *Sartor Resartus* III.viii.]

18 Whether at Naishapur or Babylon,
Whether the Cup with sweet or bitter

run,
The Wine of Life keeps oozing drop
by drop,
The Leaves of Life keep falling one
by one.
[*Rubáiyát of Omar Khayyám* (trans.
Edward FitzGerald)]
1 I came like Water, and like Wind I go.
[*Rubáiyát of Omar Khayyám* (trans. Edward FitzGerald)]

LIFE: dear to us
2 All that a man hath will he give for his life. [Job 2:4]
3 For to him that is joined to all the living there is hope: for a living dog is better than a dead lion. [Ecclesiastes 9:4]
4 O, our lives' sweetness!
That we the pain of death would
hourly die
Rather than die at once!
[Shakespeare: *King Lear* V.iii.]
5 It's all been very interesting! [Lady Mary Wortley Montagu: on her death-bed]
6 No life that breathes with human breath
Has ever truly longed for death.
[Tennyson: *The Two Voices*]
7 I will drink / Life to the lees. [Tennyson: *Ulysses*]
8 Nothing could moderate, in the bosom of the great English middle-class, their passionate, absorbing, almost bloodthirsty clinging to life. [Matthew Arnold: Preface to *Essays in Criticism: First Series*]
9 Human existence is always irrational and often painful, but in the last analysis it remains interesting. [H. L. Mencken: in the *Trenton Sunday Times*, April 3, 1927]

LIFE: and death
10 Who knoweth if to die be but to live,
And that called life by mortals be but death?
[Euripides: *Fragment*]
11 In the midst of life we are in death. [*Book of Common Prayer*: Burial of the Dead]
12 The hour which gives us life begins to take it away. [Seneca: *Hercules Furens*]

13 The act of dying is also one of the acts of life. [Marcus Aurelius: *Meditations* VI.ii.]
14 Where life is more terrible than death, it is then the truest valor to dare to live. [Sir Thomas Browne: *Religio Medici* I.xliv.]
15 You purchase pain with all that joy can give,
And die of nothing but a rage to live.
[Alexander Pope: *Moral Essays* II.xcvii.]
16 We are born crying, live complaining, and die disappointed. [Thomas Fuller (1654-1734): *Gnomologia*]
17 Life is a sickness, sleep a palliative, death a cure. [C. J. Weber: *Demokritos* XII]
18 Death is the veil which those who live call life;
They sleep, and it is lifted.
[Shelley: *Prometheus Unbound* III.iii.]
19 But this is human life: the war, the deeds,
The disappointment, the anxiety,
Imagination's struggles, far and nigh,
All human; bearing in themselves this good,
That they are still the air, the subtle food,
To make us feel existence, and to shew
How quiet death is.
[Keats: *Endymion* II]
20 Fill the cup and fill the can:
Have a rouse before the morn:
Every moment dies a man,
Every moment one is born.
[Tennyson: *The Vision of Sin*]
21 Even throughout life, 'tis death that makes life live,
Gives it whatever the significance.
[Robert Browning: *The Ring and the Book*, XI "Guido"]
That the meaning of life is enhanced by the awareness of the presence of death is one of the tenets of Existentialism. Browning's lines remind us that, in the concrete experience of living, poetry shows the way to philosophy.
22 The whole life of some people is a kind of partial death—a long, lingering death-bed, so to speak, of stagnation and nonentity on which death is but the seal, or solemn signing, as the abnegation of all further act and deed on the part

of the signed. [Samuel Butler (1835-1902): *Notebooks*]

1 Alive enough to have strength to die. [Thomas Hardy: *Neutral Tones*]

2 For he who lives more lives than one
More deaths than one must die.
[Oscar Wilde: *The Ballad of Reading Gaol* II.xxxvii.]

3 Cast a cold eye
On life, on death.
Horseman, pass by.
[William Butler Yeats: *Under Ben Bulben*]

LIFE: definitions of

4 The present life of man, O king, seems to me, in comparison of that time which is unknown to us, like to the flight of a sparrow through the room wherein you sit at supper in winter, with your commanders and ministers, and a good fire in the midst, whilst the storms of rain and snow prevail abroad; the sparrow, I say, flying in at one door, and immediately out at another, whilst he is within, is safe from the wintry storm; but after a short space of fair weather, he immediately vanishes out of your sight, into the dark winter from which he had emerged. So this life of man appears for a short space, but of what went before, or what is to follow, we are utterly ignorant. [Bede: *Ecclesiastical History of the English People* (731 A.D.) II.xiii.]

5 Tomorrow, and tomorrow, and tomorrow,
Creeps in this petty pace from day to day,
To the last syllable of recorded time;
And all our yesterdays have lighted fools
The way to dusty death. Out, out, brief candle!
Life's but a walking shadow, a poor player
That struts and frets his hour upon the stage
And then is heard no more: it is a tale
Told by an idiot, full of sound and fury,
Signifying nothing.
[Shakespeare: *Macbeth* V.v.]

6 Life is a pure flame, and we live by an invisible sun within us. [Sir Thomas Browne: *Hydriotaphia,* V]

7 Life is an incurable disease. [Abraham Cowley: *To Dr. Scarborough*]

8 Vain, weak-built isthmus, which dost proudly rise
Up between two Eternities!
[Abraham Cowley: *Life and Fame*]

9 Life is a tragedy wherein we sit as spectators for a while and then act our part in it. [Jonathan Swift: *Thoughts on Various Subjects*]

10 Life is a jest, and all things show it,
I thought so once, and now I know it.
[John Gay: his own epitaph]

Gay wrote these lines in a letter to Pope, in the last year of his life, and stated that he wished them to be put on his tombstone.

They therefore appear, following Pope's epitaph on him, on his monument in Westminster Abbey.

The Dictionary of National Biography sternly condemns them as "flippant" and feels that the monument is "disfigured" by them.

11 Life is a fatal complaint, and an eminently contagious one. [O. W. Holmes: *The Poet at the Breakfast-Table* XII]

12 Life is one long process of getting tired. [Samuel Butler (1835-1902): *Notebooks,* "Life" VII]

13 Life is the art of drawing sufficient conclusions from insufficient premises. [Samuel Butler (1835-1902): *Notebooks,* "Life" IX]

14 Life is a joke that's just begun. [W. S. Gilbert: *The Mikado* I]

15 Life is a long lesson in humility. [James M. Barrie: *The Little Minister* III]

16 Life's a long headache in a noisy street. [John Masefield: *The Widow in the Bye Street*]

LIFE: mysterious and incredible

17 When I consider life, 'tis all a cheat;
Yet, fool'd with hope, men favour the deceit;
Trust on, and think to-morrow will repay:
To-morrow's falser than the former day;
Lies worse, and, while it says, we shall

be blest
With some new joys, cuts off what we
possest.
Strange cozenage! None would live
past years again,
Yet all hope pleasure in what yet re-
main;
And from the dregs of life think to
receive
What the first sprightly running
could not give.
[Dryden: *Aureng-Zebe* IV.i.]
1 Tell me not, in mournful numbers,
Life is but an empty dream!
For the soul is dead that slumbers,
And things are not what they seem.
[Longfellow: *A Psalm of Life*]
2 What are we first? First, animals; and
next
Intelligences at a leap, on whom
Pale lies the distant shadow of the
tomb,
And all that draweth on the tomb for
text.
[George Meredith: *Modern Love* XXX]
3 A great deal of cant is talked about
the mystery of life, as if life were somehow more mysterious than the rest of Nature. . . . Life is neither more nor less
mysterious than is the attraction of the
magnet, the density of a paving-stone, or
the colour of a tie: our presence in the
midst of Nature's achievements does not
affect her estimate of them. She prices all
her wonderful goods at the same value,
like the stock of a sixpence-halfpenny
bazaar, nothing under and nothing over:
she makes them all out of the one stuff,
constructing it with a grain of sand, a
drop of water, a micro-organism, or a
nerve-cell, all with equal ease. [Stephen
Paget: *Confessio Medici*]
4 One's real life is so often the life that
one does not lead. [Oscar Wilde: *Rose-
Leaf and Apple-Leaf*, "Envoi"]
*Dramatized for the 20th century by
James Thurber in* The Secret Life of
Walter Mitty.
5 "But, my dear Sir," I burst out, in the
rudest manner, "think what life is—just
think what really happens! Why people
suddenly swell up and turn dark purple;
they hang themselves on meat hooks;
they are drowned in horse-ponds, are run
over by butchers' carts, and are burnt

alive—cooked like mutton chops!" [Lo-
gan Pearsall Smith: *Trivia*]

LIFE: real and earnest
6 Life is real! Life is earnest!
And the grave is not its goal;
Dust thou art, to dust returnest,
Was not spoken of the soul.
[Longfellow: *A Psalm of Life*]
7 I slept and dreamed that life was
beauty.
I woke—and found that life was duty.
[Ellen Sturgis Hooper: *Beauty and Duty*]
8 I went to the woods because I wished
to live deliberately, to front only the essential facts of life, and see if I could not
learn what it had to teach, and not,
when I came to die, discover that I had
not lived. [Thoreau: *Walden* II ("Where
I Lived, and What I Lived For")]
9 Life isn't all beer and skittles.
[Thomas Hughes: *Tom Brown's School-
days* (1857) I.ii.]
A reference in The Pickwick Papers
*XLI, twenty years before, shows that
"beer and skittles" was proverbial for
the joys of life.*

LIFE: triviality of
10 I do not set my life at a pin's fee.
[Shakespeare: *Hamlet* I.iv.]
11 What trifling coil do we poor mortals
keep;
Wake, eat and drink, evacuate, and
sleep.
[Matthew Prior: *Human Life*]
coil = disturbance, tumult, bustle
12 Behold the child, by Nature's kindly
law,
Pleased with a rattle, tickled with a
straw;
Some livelier plaything gives his
youth delight,
A little louder, but as empty quite:
Scarfs, garters, gold, amuse his riper
stage,
And beads and prayer-books are the
toys of age.
Pleased with this bauble still, as that
before,
Till tired he sleeps, and life's poor
play is o'er.
[Alexander Pope: *An Essay on Man* II]
13 That he was born, it cannot be denied.

He ate, drank, slept, talked politics,
and died.
[John Cunningham: *On an Alderman*]
1 Life is made up of interruptions.
[W. S. Gilbert: *Patience* I]
2 A little work, a little play
To keep us going—and so, good-day!

A little warmth, a little light
Of love's bestowing—and so, good-
night!

A little fun, to match the sorrow
Of each day's growing—and so, good-
morrow!

A little trust that when we die
We reap our sowing! and so—good-
bye!
[George Du Maurier: *Trilby* VIII]
3 For Life I had never cared greatly,
As worth a man's while.
[Thomas Hardy: *For Life I Had Never
Cared Greatly*]

LIFE: miscellaneous
4 Strait is the gate, and narrow is the
way, which leadeth unto life, and few
there be that find it. [Matthew 7:14]
5 Life teaches us to be less severe with
ourselves and others. [Goethe: *Iphige-
nie* IV.iv.]
6 Her lips were red, her looks were free,
Her locks were yellow as gold:
Her skin was as white as leprosy,
The Nightmare Life-in-Death was she,
Who thicks man's blood with cold.
[Coleridge: *The Ancient Mariner* III]
7 As large as life and twice as natural.
[Lewis Carroll: *Through the Looking
Glass* VII]
8 Cats and monkeys, monkeys and cats
—all human life is there. [Henry James:
The Madonna of the Future]
9 To be what we are, and to become
what we are capable of becoming, is the
only end of life. [R. L. Stevenson: *Familiar Studies of Men and Books*]
10 Don't try to live forever. You will
not succeed. [G. B. Shaw: Preface to
The Doctor's Dilemma]
11 The proposition that life is a science
is intellectually indefensible; the proposition that life is an art is pragmatically
impossible. [Joseph Wood Krutch: *The
Modern Temper* VI.iii.]

12 Welcome, O life! I go to encounter
for the millionth time the reality of experience and to forge in the smithy of
my soul the uncreated conscience of my
race. [James Joyce: *Portrait of the Artist as a Young Man* (concluding words)]

LIGHT
13 God said, Let there be light: and
there was light. [Genesis 1:3]
14 Why is light given to a man whose
way is hid, and whom God hath hedged
in? [Job 3:23]
15 Truly the light is sweet, and a pleasant thing it is for the eyes to behold the
sun. [Ecclesiastes 11:7]
16 And the light shineth in the darkness;
and the darkness comprehendeth it not.
[John 1:5]
17 He was a burning and a shining light.
[John 5:35]
18 The first creature of God, in the
works of the days, was the light of the
sense: the last was the light of reason:
and his sabbath work ever since is the il-
lumination of his Spirit. [Francis Bacon:
Of Truth]
19   . . . and by his light
Did all the chivalry of England move
To do brave acts.
[Shakespeare: *II Henry IV* III.ii.]
20 Put out the light, and then put out
the light.
[Shakespeare: *Othello* V.ii.]
21 He's blind with too much light.
[Philip Massinger: *The Great Duke of
Florence* II.i.]
22 When I consider how my light is spent
Ere half my days in this dark world
and wide.
[John Milton: *On His Blindness*]
23 Where there is a great deal of light,
the shadows are deeper. [Goethe: *Götz
von Berlichingen* I.iii.]
24 More light! [Goethe's last words]
25 There was a time when meadow,
grove, and stream,
The earth, and every common sight,
To me did seem
Apparelled in celestial light.
[Wordsworth: *Intimations of Immortality*]
26 The light that never was, on sea or
land,
The consecration, and the Poet's

dream.

[Wordsworth: *Elegiac Stanzas, Suggested by a Picture of Peele Castle in a Storm*]

1 Lead, Kindly Light, amid the encircling gloom,
Lead Thou me on!
The night is dark, and I am far from home—
Lead Thou me on!

[John Henry Newman: *Lead, Kindly Light*]

2 And not by eastern windows only,
When daylight comes, comes in the light;
In front, the sun climbs slow, how slowly,
But westward, look, the land is bright.

[Arthur Hugh Clough: *Say Not the Struggle Naught Availeth*]

3 The pale, cold light of the winter sunset did not beautify—it was like the light of truth itself. [Willa Cather: *My Ántonia* II.vi.]

LIGHT (LEVITY)

4 They made light of it, and went their ways. [Matthew 22:5]

LIGHTNING

5 It is too rash, too unadvised, too sudden;
Too like the lightning, which doth cease to be
Ere one can say it lightens.

[Shakespeare: *Romeo and Juliet* II.ii.]

6 Swift as a shadow, short as any dream,
Brief as the lightning in the collied night,
That, in a spleen, unfolds both heaven and earth,
And ere a man hath power to say, "Behold!"
The jaws of darkness do devour it up:
So quick bright things come to confusion.

[Shakespeare: *A Midsummer Night's Dream* I.i.]
collied = *darkened, black*

LIKELIHOOD

7 A fellow of no mark nor likelihood. [Shakespeare: *I Henry IV* III.ii.]

LIKENESS

8 Likeness causeth liking. [John Clarke: *Paroemiologia*]

LIKING

9 He that doth like is liked. [Ovid: *Metamorphoses* III quoted in Montaigne's *Essays* II.xii (trans. John Florio)]

LILACS

10 When lilacs last in the door-yard bloom'd,
And the great star early droop'd in the western sky in the night,
I mourn'd, and yet shall mourn with ever-returning spring.

[Walt Whitman: *Leaves of Grass,* "When Lilacs Last in the Door-yard Bloom'd"]

11 Lilacs in dooryards
Holding quiet conversations with an early moon;
Lilacs watching a deserted house
Settling sideways into the grass of an old road;
Lilacs, wind-beaten, staggering under a lopsided shock of bloom
Above a cellar dug into a hill.

[Amy Lowell: *Lilacs*]

LILY(IES)

12 Consider the lilies of the field, how they grow; they toil not, neither do they spin:
And yet I say unto you, That even Solomon in all his glory was not arrayed like one of these. [Matthew 6:28-29]

13 Convolvulus . . . carrieth a flower not unlike [the] Lilly . . . for whiteness they resemble one another very much, as if Nature in making this flower were a learning and trying her skill how to frame the Lilly. [Pliny: *Natural History* XXI.x (trans. Holland)]

14 The lilly, lady of the flowring field. [Edmund Spenser: *The Faerie Queene* II.vi.16]

15 Lilies that fester smell far worse than weeds.

[Shakespeare: *Sonnets* XCIV]

16 To gild refined gold, to paint the lily,
To throw a perfume on the violet,
To smooth the ice, or add another hue
Unto the rainbow, or with taper-light

To seek the beauteous eye of heaven
               to garnish,
Is wasteful and ridiculous excess.
[Shakespeare: *King John* IV.ii.]

*Shortened and corrupted in popular use
to "to gild the lily." As often in popular
recollection, an adjective jumps out of
place in a quotation and attaches itself
to another word. Lilies are not golden in
color and hence "to gild" defeats the intent of the original.*

1 Have you seen but a bright lily grow,
    Before rude hands have touch'd it?
  Have you mark'd but the fall o' the
               snow
  Before the soil hath smutch'd it?
  O so white! O so soft! O so sweet is
               she!
[Ben Jonson: *Celebration of Charis*, "Her
Triumph"]

LIMBO

2 Up hither like aerial vapours flew
  Of all things transitory and vain,
               when sin
  With vanity had filled the works of
               men—
  Both all things vain, and all who in
             vain things
  Built their fond hopes. . . .
  Embryos and idiots, eremites and fri-
             ars,
  White, black, and grey, with all their
             trumpery.
[John Milton: *Paradise Lost* III.445-
475]

LIMITATION

3 Art is limitation; the essence of every
picture is the frame. [G. K. Chesterton:
Orthodoxy III]
4 To note an artist's limitations is but
to define his talent. A reporter can write
equally well about everything that is presented to his view, but a creative writer
can do his best only with what lies
within the range and character of his
deepest sympathies. [Willa Cather: *Not
Under Forty*, "Miss Jewett"]

LINCOLN, ABRAHAM

5 I never see that man (Lincoln) without feeling that he is one to become personally attach'd to, for his combination
of purest, heartiest tenderness, and native

western form of manliness. [Walt Whitman: *Specimen Days*, "The Inaugura-
tion, March 4, 1865"]

LINE

6 I propose to fight it out on this line,
if it takes all summer. [Ulysses S. Grant:
dispatch from Spottsylvania Court House,
May 11, 1864]

LINEN

7 Lawn as white as driven snow.
[Shakespeare: *The Winter's Tale* IV.iv.]
8 Send your dirty linen to the laundry!
[Paul Scarron (1610-1660): *Don Japhet
d'Arménie* II.i. (1652)]
  That is, don't wash it here in public.

LION(S)

9 The old lion perisheth for lack of
prey, and the stout lion's whelps are scattered abroad. [Job 4:11]
10 The young lions roar after their prey,
and seek their meat from God. [Psalms
104:21]
11 The slothful man saith, There is a
lion in the way; a lion is in the streets.
[Proverbs 26:13]
12 Do not pluck the beard of a dead
lion. [Martial: *Epigrams* X.xc.]
13 An army of deer commanded by a
lion is more to be feared than an army of
lions commanded by a deer. [Plutarch:
Moralia]
  *Plutarch is quoting Chabrias, an Athen-
  ian general of the 5th century B.C.*
  The saying has been ascribed to others.
14   The blood more stirs
  To rouse a lion than to start a hare.
[Shakespeare: *I Henry IV* I.iii.]
15 God shield us!—a lion among ladies,
is a most dreadful thing; for there is not
a more fearful wild-fowl than your lion
living.
[Shakespeare: *A Midsummer Night's
Dream* III.i.]
16   And dar'st thou then
  To beard the lion in his den,
  The Douglas in his hall?
[Sir Walter Scott: *Marmion* VI.xiv.]

LIP(S)

17 Free of her lips, free of her hips.
[John Ray: *English Proverbs* (1670)]
18 And though hard be the task,

"Keep a stiff upper lip."
[Phoebe Cary: *Keep a Stiff Upper Lip*]

LIQUOR

1 O God, that men should put an enemy in their mouths to steal away their brains!
[Shakespeare: *Othello* II.iii.]

2 Though I look old, yet I am strong
    and lusty;
  For in my youth I never did apply
  Hot and rebellious liquors in my
    blood.
[Shakespeare: *As You Like It* II.iii.]

3 Let schoolmasters puzzle their brain,
  With grammar, and nonsense, and
    learning;
  Good liquor, I stoutly maintain,
  Gives genius a better discerning.
[Oliver Goldsmith: *She Stoops to Conquer* I.i.]

4 You are coming to woo me, but not as
    of yore,
  When I hastened to welcome your
    ring at the door;
  For I trusted that he who stood wait-
    ing me then,
  Was the brightest, the truest, the no-
    blest of men;
  Your lips, on my own, when they
    printed "Farewell,"
  Had never been soiled by the bever-
    age of hell;
  But they come to me now with the
    bacchanal sign,
  And the lips that touch liquor must
    never touch mine.
[George W. Young: *The Lips that Touch Liquor* (1870)]
The ambiguity of the last line was exploited by scofflaws during the Prohibition era.

5 Candy
  Is dandy
  But liquor
  Is quicker.
[Ogden Nash: *Reflections on Ice-Breaking*]
See also CLARET

LIST

6 As some day it may happen that a vic-
    tim must be found,
  I've got a little list—I've got a little
    list,
  Of society offenders who might well
    be under ground,
  And who never would be missed—
    who never would be missed.
[W. S. Gilbert: *The Mikado* I]

LISTEN

7 I know how to listen when clever men are talking. That is the secret of what you call my influence. [Sudermann: *Es Lebe das Leben* I.iv (trans. Edith Wharton)]

LITERARY MEN

8 Literary men are . . . a perpetual priesthood. [Thomas Carlyle: *The State of German Literature*, "Fichte"]

LITERATURE

9 The chief glory of every people arises from its authors. [Samuel Johnson: Preface to the *Dictionary*]

10 For what are the classics but the noblest recorded thoughts of man? They are the only oracles which are not decayed. [Thoreau: *Walden*, III. "Reading"]

11 A great literature is chiefly the product of inquiring minds in revolt against the immovable certainties of the nation. [H. L. Mencken: *Prejudices: Second Series*]

12 Literature is news that stays news. [Ezra Pound: *How to Read*]

13 Great literature is simply language charged with meaning to the utmost possible degree. [Ezra Pound: *How to Read*]

14 That was the chief difference between literature and life. In books, the proportion of exceptional to commonplace people is high; in reality, very low. [Aldous Huxley: *Eyeless in Gaza* XXII]

15 Literature is the orchestration of platitudes. [Thornton Wilder, quoted *Time,* Jan. 12, 1953]
This is not necessarily a derogation; it's the orchestration that counts.

LITTLE

16 Man wants but little here below,
  Nor wants that little long.
[Oliver Goldsmith: *The Vicar of Wakefield* VIII]
Young, in his Night Thoughts *IV had written 24 years before Goldsmith:*
  Man wants but little, nor that little long.

But Goldsmith's version is the one that is always quoted.

There have been several parodies, such as Oliver Wendell Holmes's A Song of Other Days *with its couplet:*
Man wants but little drink below,
But wants that little strong.

1 Every little helps. [John O'Keeffe: *Wild Oats* V.iii.]

2 Little drops of water, little grains of sand,
Make the mighty ocean and the pleasant land.
[Julia A. F. Carney: *Little Things*]

LITTLE BILLEE

3 There was gorging Jack and guzzling Jimmy,
And the youngest he was little Billee.
[W. M. Thackeray: *Little Billee*]

LITTLENESS

4 A little Saint best fits a little Shrine,
A little Prop best fits a little Vine,
As my small Cruse best fits my little Wine.
[Robert Herrick: *A Ternarie of Littles*]

LIVING

5 The land of the living. [Job 28:13]

6 He who postpones the hour of living rightly is like the rustic who waits for the river to run out before he crosses. [Horace: *Epistles* I.ii.]

7 They live badly who always begin to live. [Seneca: *Ad Lucilium* XXIII]
An answer to those who insist on assuring us that "life begins at forty," or some other threshold of senility.

8 While we live, let us live. (*Dum vivimus, vivamus.*) [Medieval Latin proverb]

9 Alas, I have done nothing this day! What? have you not lived? It is not only the fundamental but the noblest of your occupations. [Montaigne: *Essays* III. xiii.]

10 Living from hand to mouth. [Du Bartas: *Divine Weekes and Workes,* "Second Week. First Day. IV."]

11 They do not live but linger. [Robert Burton: *Anatomy of Melancholy* I.2.3. 10.]

12 The long habit of living indisposeth us for dying. [Sir Thomas Browne: *Urn-Burial* V]

13 Teach me to live that I may dread

The grave as little as my bed.
[Bishop Thomas Ken: *Evening Hymn*]

14 Very few men, properly speaking, live at present, but are providing to live another time. [Jonathan Swift: *Thoughts on Various Subjects*]

15 Fix'd like a plant on his peculiar spot,
To draw nutrition, propagate, and rot.
[Alexander Pope: *An Essay on Man* II]

16 Dogs, would you live forever? [Attr. Frederick the Great]
A hearty encouragement, in the Prussian vein, to some soldiers who were discreetly retreating at the Battle of Kolin (1757).

There are variants of the first word. Some have it Rindviehe = *horned beasts = cuckolds.*

In the American army, in World War I, it was "Come on, you sons of bitches! Do you want to live forever?"

The sentence has been ascribed to many warriors. It has the desperate jocularity of combat but is a wonderful anti-enlistment.

17 In order to carry out great enterprises, one must live as if one will never have to die. [Vauvenargues: *Réflexions*]

18 Live dangerously and you live right! [Goethe: *Faust* I.xiv.]

19 Live and let live. [Schiller: *Wallenstein's Camp* VI]

20 Plain living and high thinking are no more. [Wordsworth: *Sonnets Dedicated to Liberty* XIII]

21 We are always getting ready to live, but never living. [Emerson: *Journals,* April 13, 1834]
The thought was frequently expressed in antiquity, especially by Epicurus.

22 Thank Heaven! the crisis,
The danger, is past,
And the lingering illness
Is over at last—
And the fever called 'Living'
Is conquered at last.
[Edgar Allan Poe: *For Annie*]

23 How good is man's life, the mere living! how fit to employ
All the heart and the soul and the senses forever in joy.
[Robert Browning: *Saul*]

24 I did not wish to live what was not life, living is so dear; nor did I wish to

practice resignation, unless it was quite necessary. I wanted to live deep and suck out all the marrow of life, to live so sturdily and Spartanlike as to put to rout all that was not life, to cut a broad swath and shave close, to drive life into a corner, and reduce it to its lowest terms, and, if it proved to be mean, why, then to get the whole and genuine meanness of it, and publish its meanness to the world; or if it were sublime, to know it by experience, and be able to give a true account of it in my next excursion. [Thoreau: *Walden*, II: "Where I Lived and What I Lived For"]

1   To live is like to love—all reason is against it, and all healthy instinct for it. [Samuel Butler (1835-1902): *Notebooks*]

2   From too much love of living,
From hope and fear set free,
We thank with brief thanksgiving
Whatever gods may be
That no life lives forever;
That dead men rise up never;
That even the weariest river
Winds somewhere safe to sea.
[Swinburne: *The Garden of Proserpine*]

3   Is life worth living? It depends on the liver. [A popular improvement, or abridgment, of a joke that appeared in *Punch* in 1877]

4   All say, "How hard it is to die"—a strange complaint from people who have had to live. Pity is for the living, envy for the dead. [Mark Twain: *Pudd'nhead Wilson's Calendar*]

5   Live all you can; it's a mistake not to. [Henry James: *The Ambassadors*]

6   The living are the living
And dead the dead will stay,
And I will sort with comrades
That face the beam of day.
[A. E. Housman: *Last Poems* XIX]

7   The subhuman will to live which is all-sufficient for the animal may be replaced by faith, faith may be replaced by philosophy, and philosophy may attenuate itself until it becomes, like modern metaphysics, a mere game; but each of these developments marks a stage in a progressive enfeeblement of that will to live for the gradual weakening of which it is the function of each to compensate. [Joseph Wood Krutch: *The Modern Temper* VIII]

LIVINGSTONE

8   Dr. Livingstone, I presume?
Henry M. Stanley had been sent by James Gordon Bennett, publisher of the New York Herald *to find Livingstone, who was, presumably, lost in the heart of Africa. On July 2, 1872, Stanley finally found Livingstone and greeted him with the now-famous salutation. The phrase was so formal under the circumstances and so politely restrained, and so superfluous—since it was obviously Livingstone—that it struck the public as comic and passed into general facetious speech.*

LOAD

9   The ass endures the load, but not the overload. [Cervantes: *Don Quixote* II. 71.]

10   All lay the load on the willing horse. [Thomas Fuller (1654-1734): *Gnomologia*]

LOAN

11   What you lend is lost; when you ask for it back, you may find a friend made an enemy by your kindness. [Plautus: *Trinummus* IV.iii.]

12   Seldom comes a loan laughing home. [Fourteenth-century proverb]

13   Loan oft loses both itself and friend. [Shakespeare: *Hamlet* I.iii.]

LOCHINVAR

14   Oh, young Lochinvar is come out of
the West,
Through all the wide Border his
steed was the best.
[Sir Walter Scott: *Marmion* V.xii.]

15   So faithful in love, and so dauntless
in war,
There never was knight like the
young Lochinvar.
[Sir Walter Scott: *Marmion* V.xii.]

LOCKS

16   Thou canst not say I did it; never
shake
Thy gory locks at me.
[Shakespeare: *Macbeth* III.iv.]

LOCK, STOCK AND BARREL

17   Like the highlandman's gun, she wants stock, lock, and barrel, to put her in repair. [Sir Walter Scott: in Lockhart's *Life of Scott* V]

This seems the passage that put "lock, stock and barrel" (as it is now commonly spoken) into general use.

The lock is the mechanism by means of which the charge is exploded. The stock is the wooden or metal piece to which the barrel and the firing mechanism are attached. The barrel is the tube through which the bullet is discharged.

The passage—in Scott—seems to have been an allusion (echoed in a passage in Carlyle) to a standing joke. It is paralleled by Washington's "original" axe, owned by a collector, that had had three new heads and two new handles since the first president's time.

LOCUST

1 That which the palmerworm hath left hath the locust eaten; and that which the locust hath left hath the cankerworm eaten; and that which the cankerworm hath left hath the caterpillar eaten.

Awake, ye drunkards, and weep; and howl, all ye drinkers of wine, because of the new wine, for it is cut off from your mouth. [Joel 1:4-5]

LOGIC

2 He was in logic a great critic,
Profoundly skill'd in analytic;
He could distinguish and divide
A hair 'twixt south and south-west
side.
[Samuel Butler (1612-1680): *Hudibras*]
3 End of the wonderful one-hoss shay.
Logic is logic. That's all I say.
[O. W. Holmes: *The Deacon's Masterpiece*]
In the story of the wonderful one-hoss shay that was built so perfectly that no one part could wear out before another —and hence wore out all at once, "Close by the meet'n'-house on the hill," and left the dazed parson sitting upon a rock, surrounded by a heap of rubbish —Holmes designed a gentle satire on Calvinism.
4 "Contrariwise," continued Tweedledee, "if it was so, it might be; and if it were so, it would be: but as it isn't, it ain't. That's logic." [Lewis Carroll: *Through the Looking-Glass* IV.]

LOINS
5 Gird up now thy loins like a man. [Job 38:3]

LOITERING
6 O what can ail thee, knight at arms,
Alone and palely loitering?
The sedge has withered from the
lake,
And no birds sing!
[Keats: *La Belle Dame sans Merci*]

LONDON
7 When a man is tired of London he is tired of life; for there is in London all that life can afford. [Samuel Johnson: in Boswell's *Life,* Sept. 20, 1777]
8 Oh, London is a fine town,
A very famous city,
Where all the streets are paved with
gold,
And all the maidens pretty.
[George Colman, the Younger: *The Heir-at-Law* II]
9 Earth has not anything to show more
fair:
Dull would be he of soul who could
pass by
A sight so touching in its majesty:
This city now doth, like a garment,
wear
The beauty of the morning; silent,
bare,
Ships, towers, domes, theatres, and
temples lie
Open unto the fields, and to the sky;
All bright and glittering in the smoke-
less air.
[Wordsworth: *Westminster Bridge*]
10 Forget six counties overhung with
smoke,
Forget the snorting steam and piston
stroke,
Forget the spreading of the hideous
town;
Think rather of the pack-horse on the
down,
And dream of London, small, and
white, and clean.
[William Morris: Introduction to *The Earthly Paradise*]

LONDON BRIDGE
11 London Bridge is falling down,
Falling down, falling down,

London Bridge is falling down,
My fair lady.
[Nursery rhyme: earliest known text, c. 1744]

There was a dance "Building London Bridge." Rabelais (1534) lists "the fallen bridges" as a game. Parellel rhymes, songs, games and dances are known in every European language and are of great antiquity. They all have in common the statement that a number of proposed substances will not serve to rebuild the bridge until a "watchman" is set to protect the bridge.

Scholars are agreed that all of this is a reference to the grim custom of immuring a child in the foundations of a bridge to serve as an eternal guardian of the structure. (The skeleton of a child was found embedded in the masonry of the Bridge Gate at Bremen when it was torn down in the 19th century.)

LONELINESS

1 Loneliness is the first thing which God's eye nam'd not good. [John Milton: *Tetrachordon*]
2 I wandered lonely as a cloud. [Wordsworth: *I Wandered Lonely as a Cloud*]
Poem is sometimes called "Daffodils."
3 Alone, alone, all, all alone,
Alone on a wide, wide sea.
[Coleridge: *The Ancient Mariner* IV]
4 So lonely 'twas, that God himself
Scarce seemed there to be.
[Coleridge: *The Ancient Mariner* VII]
5 I feel like one,
Who treads alone
Some banquet-hall deserted,
Whose lights are fled,
Whose garlands dead,
And all but he departed.
[Thomas Moore: *Oft in the Stilly Night*]
6 Jest a-wearyin' fer you—
All the time a-feelin' blue;
Wishin' fer you—wonderin' when
You'll be comin' home again.
[Frank L. Stanton: *Wearyin' for You*]
7 I was lonesomer than Crusoe's goat.
[O. Henry: *The Hiding of Black Bill*]
8 Loneliness . . . is and always has been the central and inevitable experience of every man. [Thomas Wolfe: *You Can't Go Home Again*]
9 People who lead a lonely existence always have something on their minds that they are eager to talk about. [Anton Chekhov: "About Love"]

LONGEST

10 The longest way about is the shortest way home. [George Colman the Elder: *The Spleen* II]

LONGEVITY

11 It is vanity to desire a long life without caring whether it be a good life or not. [Thomas à Kempis: *De Imitatione Christi* I.i.]
12 Two things doth prolong thy lyfe:
A quiet heart and a loving wife.
[Thomas Deloney: *Strange Histories*]
13 To be free minded and cheerfully disposed at hours of meat and sleep and of exercise is one of the best precepts of long lasting. [Francis Bacon: *Of Regimen of Health*]
14 To live long is almost everyone's wish, but to live well is the ambition of a few. [John Hughes: *The Lay Monk*]
15 Enlarge my life with multitude of
days,
In health, in sickness, thus the suppliant prays;
Hides from himself his state, and shuns to know
That life protracted is protracted woe.
[Samuel Johnson: *The Vanity of Human Wishes*]
The days of our years are threescore years and ten; and if by reason of strength they be fourscore years, yet is their strength labour and sorrow.
Psalms 90:10
16 The secret of prolonging life consists in not shortening it. [E. V. Feuchtersleben: *Zur Diätetik der Seele*]
17 The woods decay, the woods decay
and fall,
The vapours weep their burthen to
the ground,
Man comes and tills the field and lies
beneath,
And after many a summer dies the
swan.
[Tennyson: *Tithonus*]

LONGING(S)

18 I have / Immortal longings in me.

[Shakespeare: *Antony and Cleopatra* V.ii.]

1 As pants the hart for cooling streams
When heated in the chase.

[Nahum Tate and Nicholas Brady: *New Version of the Psalms* (1696), *"As Pants the Hart"*]
As the hart panteth after the water brooks, so panteth my soul after thee, O God.

Psalms 42:1

2 We look before and after,
And pine for what is not,
Our sincerest laughter
With some pain is fraught:
Our sweetest songs are those that tell
of saddest thought.

[Shelley: *To a Skylark*]

3 Thou wast all that to me, love,
For which my soul did pine—
A green isle in the sea, love,
A fountain and a shrine.

[Edgar Allan Poe: *To One in Paradise*]

4 O that 'twere possible
After long grief and pain
To find the arms of my true love
Round me once again.

[Tennyson: *Maud* II]

5 My soul to-day is far away
Sailing the Vesuvian Bay.

[Thomas Buchanan Read: *Drifting*]

LOOK

6 O ill-starred wench!
Pale as thy smock! when we shall
meet at compt,
This look of thine will hurt my soul
from heaven,
And fiends will snatch at it.

[Shakespeare: *Othello* V.ii.]

LOOKING BACK

7 He [the angel]said, Escape for thy life; look not behind thee . . .
But his [Lot's] wife looked back from behind him, and she became a pillar of salt. [Genesis 19:17-26]

8 No man, having put his hand to the plough, and looking back, is fit for the kingdom of God. [Luke 9:62]

9 Nor cast one longing, ling'ring look
behind.

[Thomas Gray: *Elegy Written in a Country Churchyard*]

10 Still thou art blest, compared wi' me!
The present only toucheth thee:
But, och! I backward cast my e'e
On prospects drear!
An' forward, though I canna see,
I guess an' fear!

[Robert Burns: *To a Mouse*]

LORD

11 The Lord gave, and the Lord hath taken away; blessed be the name of the Lord. [Job 1:21]

12 Mine eyes have seen the glory of the
coming of the Lord;
He is trampling out the vintage
where the grapes of wrath are stored;
He hath loosed the fateful lightning
of His terrible, swift sword;
His truth is marching on.

[Julia Ward Howe: *Battle Hymn of the Republic*]

THE LORD'S PRAYER

13 Our Father which art in heaven, Hallowed be thy name.
Thy kingdom come. Thy will be done
in earth, as it is in heaven.
Give us this day our daily bread.
And forgive us our debts, as we forgive our debtors.
And lead us not into temptation, but
deliver us from evil:
For thine is the kingdom, and the
power, and the glory, for ever. Amen.

[Matthew 6:9-13 (King James Version)]
Two forms of the prayer appear in the New Testament, the other—briefer and probably older—in Luke 11:2-4. The last verse—called the doxology—does not appear in the oldest and best Greek manuscripts and is omitted from the Revised Standard, the New English Bible, the New American Catholic Edition and, indeed, from almost all modern versions.

LOSS

14 He that is robb'd, not wanting what
is stol'n,
Let him not know 't, and he's not
robb'd at all.

[Shakespeare: *Othello* III.iii.]

15 No man can lose what he never had.
[Izaak Walton: *The Compleat Angler* I.v.]

16 All is lost that is put in a riven dish.

[John Clarke: *Paroemiologia* (1639)]
That is, don't throw good money after bad. Do not attempt to rehabilitate a broken man.

1 But O the heavy change, now thou
art gone,
Now thou art gone, and never must
return!
[John Milton: *Lycidas*]

2 Ay me! Whilst thee the shores, and
sounding seas
Wash far away.
[John Milton: *Lycidas*]

3 Earth felt the wound, and Nature
from her seat
Sighing through all her works gave
signs of woe,
That all was lost.
[John Milton: *Paradise Lost* IX. 782-783]

4 Wealth lost, something lost;
Honor lost, much lost;
Courage lost, all lost.
A form of an old German proverb.

5 She lived unknown, and few could
know
When Lucy ceased to be;
But she is in her grave, and, oh,
The difference to me!
[Wordsworth: *Lucy: She Dwelt Among
the Untrodden Ways*]

6 There was a time when meadow,
grove, and stream,
The earth, and every common sight,
To me did seem
Apparelled in celestial light,
The glory and the freshness of a
dream.
It is not now as it hath been of
yore—
Turn wheresoe'er I may,
By night or day,
The things which I have seen I now
can see no more.
[Wordsworth: *Intimations of Immortality*]

7 Like the dew on the mountain,
Like the foam on the river,
Like the bubble on the fountain,
Thou art gone, and forever!
[Sir Walter Scott: *The Lady of the Lake*
III.xvi.]

8 And the stately ships go on
To their haven under the hill;
But O, for the touch of a vanish'd
hand,

And the sound of a voice that is
still!
[Tennyson: *Break, Break, Break*]

9 That loss is common would not make
My own less bitter, rather more.
Too common!
[Tennyson: *In Memoriam* VI]

10 We shall meet, but we shall miss him,
There will be one vacant chair:
We shall linger to caress him,
When we breathe our evening
prayer.
[Henry Stevenson Washburn: *The Vacant Chair*]

11 We have lost our little Hanner in a
very painful manner.
[Max Adeler: *Little Hanner*]

LOST

12 You are better lost than found. [Clement Robinson: *A Handfull of Pleasant Delites* (1584)]
A common saying in the 16th century, paralleled by the contemporary "Get lost!"

13 "We are lost!" the captain shouted,
As he staggered down the stairs.
[James T. Fields: *Ballad of the Tempest*]

14 "You are all a lost generation." [Attr. Gertrude Stein in conversation.]
So Ernest Hemingway identified the source of the now-famous phrase when, in 1926, he used it as an epigraph in The Sun Also Rises.

In A Moveable Feast (1964), however, he reveals that Miss Stein was not the originator of the phrase, that she had overheard the patron of a garage use it in rebuking a young mechanic who had failed to do a satisfactory repair job on Miss Stein's Model T Ford.

LOTHARIO

15 Is this that Haughty, Gallant, Gay Lothario? [Nicholas Rowe: *The Fair Penitent* V.i. (1703)]
Lothario is a heartless libertine who loves them and leaves them with scornful laughter. He is killed in a duel, but dies thoroughly unrepentant.

LOVABLE

16 To be loved, be lovable.
[Ovid: *De arte amandi* II]

LOVE: at first sight

1 She lovede Right fro the firste sighte.
[Chaucer: *Troilus and Criseyde* II]

2 There is a lady sweet and kind,
Was never face so pleased my mind;
I did but see her passing by,
And yet I love her till I die.
[Barnaby Googe: *There is a Lady Sweet and Kind*]

3 Who ever loved, that loved not at
first sight?
[Christopher Marlowe: *Hero and Leander* I]

Quoted in Shakespeare's As You Like It,
III.v.:

Dead shepherd [Marlowe], now I find
thy saw of might, "Who ever lov'd
that lov'd not at first sight?"

4 No sooner met but they looked; no
sooner looked but they loved; no sooner
loved but they sighed; no sooner sighed
but they asked one another the reason;
no sooner knew the reason but they
sought the remedy. [Shakespeare: *As You
Like It* V.ii.]

5 To see her is to love her, and love
but her for ever,
For Nature made her what she is, and
ne'er made anither!
[Burns: *Bonnie Lesley*]

6 The power of a glance has been so
much abused in love stories, that it has
come to be disbelieved in. Few people
dare now to say that two beings have fallen
in love because they have looked at
each other. Yet it is in this way that love
begins, and in this way only. The rest is
only the rest, and comes afterwards. Nothing
is more real than these great shocks
which two souls give each other in exchanging
this spark. [Victor Hugo: *Les
Misérables* III.vi.]

LOVE: its beginnings

7   My salad days,
When I was green in judgment, cold
in blood.
[Shakespeare: *Antony and Cleopatra*
I.v.]

The expression salad days originated in
this passage. It's a joke of Cleopatra's.
She is praising Antony and insisting she
never had loved Caesar—by whom she
had had a child—so. Her maid, Charmian,
teases her by quoting the enco-

miums she had formerly heaped on
Caesar. Cleopatra says it didn't mean
anything; she had been like a salad, like
the things that make up a salad, green
and cold.

8 Yielded with coy submission, modest
pride,
And sweet, reluctant, amorous delay.
[John Milton: *Paradise Lost* IV. 310-311]

9 What a dear ravishing thing is the beginning
of an Amour! [Mrs. Aphra
Behn: *The Emperor of the Moon* I.i.]

10 At the beginning and at the end of
love the two lovers are embarrassed to
find themselves alone. [La Bruyère: *Les
Caractères*]

11 There's nothing half so sweet in life
As love's young dream.
[Thomas Moore: *Love's Young Dream*]

12 And whispering "I will ne'er consent"—
Consented.
[Byron: *Don Juan* I.cxvii.]

LOVE: is best

13 If thou must love me, let it be for
naught
Except for love's sake only.
[Elizabeth Barrett Browning: *Sonnets
from the Portuguese* XIV]

14 Oh heart! oh blood that freezes, blood
that burns!
Earth's returns
For whole centuries of folly, noise
and sin!
Shut them in,
With their triumphs and their glories
and the rest!
Love is best.
[Robert Browning: *Love among the Ruins*]

LOVE: is blind

15 The swarthy girl is tawny, the
scrawny is a gazelle, the dumb is modest,
she that is half dead with consumption
is slender, and she that is bloated, with
enormous dugs, is Ceres herself. [Lucretius: *De rerum natura* IV.i.]

The infatuated lover is able to view
every deformity of the beloved as an
asset and an adornment. Robert Burton,
in The Anatomy of Melancholy, elaborates
this thought into one of the most

hilariously repulsive passages in all literature—a passage, by the way, which Keats said he would have given his "favorite leg" to have written:

If she be flat-nosed, she is lovely; if hook-nosed, kingly; if dwarfish and little, pretty; if tall, proper and man-like . . . if crooked, wise; if monstrous, comely; her defects are no defects at all, she hath no deformities. Though she be nasty, fulsome, as Sostratus's bitch or Parmeno's sow: thou hadst as lieve have a snake in thy bosom, a toad in thy dish, and callest her witch, devil, hag, with all the filthy names thou canst invent; he admires her, on the other side, she is his Idol, Lady, Mistress Venerilla, Queen, the quintessence of beauty, an Angel, a Star, a Goddess.

1 Love is blind.
[Chaucer: *The Merchant's Tale*]
2 A fool there was and he made his prayer
(Even as you and I!)
To a rag and a bone and a hank of hair
(We called her the woman who did not care)
But the fool he called her his lady fair—
(Even as you and I!)
[Kipling: *The Vampire*]
3 To be in love is merely to be in a state of perpetual anaesthesis—to mistake an ordinary young man for a Greek god or an ordinary young woman for a goddess. [H. L. Mencken: *Prejudices: First Series*]

LOVE: capricious and uncertain
4 I cannot with thee live, nor yet without thee.
[Martial: *Epigrams* XII.xlvii.]
5 When my love swears that she is made of truth,
I do believe her, though I know she lies.
[Shakespeare: *Sonnets* CXXXVIII]
6 Two loves I have, of comfort and despair.
[Shakespeare: *Sonnets* CXLIV]
7 Oh, how this Spring of love resembleth
Th' uncertain glory of an April day,
Which now shows all the beauty of the sun,
And by and by a cloud takes all away.
[Shakespeare: *Two Gentlemen of Verona* I.iii.]
8 How wayward is this foolish love,
That, like a testy babe, will scratch the nurse
And presently, all humbled, kiss the rod.
[Shakespeare: *Two Gentlemen of Verona* I.ii.]
9 How happy could I be with either
Were t'other dear charmer away!
[John Gay: *The Beggar's Opera* II.xiii.]
10 Love's a capricious power: I've known it hold
Out through a fever caused by its own heat,
But be much puzzled by a cough and cold,
And find a quinsy very hard to treat.
[Byron: *Don Juan* II.xxii.]
11 You gave me the key to your heart, my love;
Then why did you make me knock?
"Oh, that was yesterday; saints above,
Last night I changed the lock."
[John Boyle O'Reilly: *Constancy*]
12 The fickleness of the woman I love is only equalled by the infernal constancy of the women who love me. [G. B. Shaw: *The Philanderer*]
13 Oh, when I was in love with you,
Then I was clean and brave,
And miles around the wonder grew
How well did I behave.

And now the fancy passes by,
And nothing will remain,
And miles around they'll say that I
Am quite myself again.
[A. E. Housman: *A Shropshire Lad* XVIII]
14 And if I loved you Wednesday,
Well, what is that to you?
I do not love you Thursday—
So much is true.
[Edna St. Vincent Millay: *Thursday*]

LOVE: constancy in
15 Doubt thou the stars are fire;
Doubt that the sun doth move;
Doubt truth to be a liar;

But never doubt I love.
[Shakespeare: *Hamlet* II.ii.]

1 Out upon it, I have loved
Three whole days together!
And am like to love three more,
If it prove fair weather.
[Sir John Suckling: *A Poem with the Answer*]

2 He who dares love, and for that love
must die,
And, knowing this, dares yet love on,
am I.
[Dryden: *Conquest of Granada: Part Two* IV.iii.]
Parodied by Villiers, Duke of Buckingham, in The Rehearsal *IV.i.*:
He that dares drink, and for
that drink dares die,
And, knowing this, dares yet
drink on, am I.

3 Oh, look in my eyes then, can you
doubt?
—Why, tis a mile from town.
How green the grass is all about!
We might as well sit down.
—Ah, life, what is it but a flower?
Why must true lovers sigh?
Be kind, have pity, my own, my
pretty—
"Good-bye, young man, good-bye."
[A. E. Housman: *A Shropshire Lad* V]

LOVE: and death
4 Love is strong as death; jealousy is
cruel as the grave. [Song of Solomon
8:6]

5 The fearful passage of their death-
mark'd love.
[Shakespeare: Prologue to *Romeo and Juliet*]

6 Men have died from time to time,
and worms have eaten them—but not for
love. [Shakespeare: *As You Like It* IV.i.]

7 O mother, mother, make my bed,
O make it soft and narrow:
My love has died for me to-day,
I'll die for him to-morrow!
[Anon.: *Barbara Allen's Cruelty*]

8 The wind doth blow to-day, my love,
And a few small drops of rain;
I never had but one true love;
In cold grave she was lain.
[Anon.: *The Unquiet Grave*]

9 The night has a thousand eyes,
And the day but one;

Yet the light of the bright world dies,
With the dying sun.

The mind has a thousand eyes,
And the heart but one;
Yet the light of a whole life dies,
When love is done.
[Francis William Bourdillon: *Light*]

10 Yet each man kills the thing he loves,
By each let this be heard,
Some do it with a bitter look,
Some with a flattering word.
The coward does it with a kiss,
The brave man with a sword!
[Oscar Wilde: *The Ballad of Reading Gaol*]

11 The lover of the grave, the lover
That hanged himself for love.
[A. E. Housman: *A Shropshire Lad* XVI]

12 If truth in hearts that perish
Could move the powers on high,
I think the love I bear you
Should make you not to die.
[A. E. Housman: *A Shropshire Lad* XXXIII]

LOVE: definitions of
13 Love is nothing save an insatiate
thirst to enjoy a greedily desired object.
[Montaigne: *Essays* III.v.]

14 Love in young men, for the most part,
is not love but simply sexual desire and
its accomplishment is its end. [Cervantes: *Don Quixote* I.xxiv.]

15 O what a heaven is love! O what a
hell!
[Thomas Dekker: *The Honest Whore* I.i.]

16 My love is of a birth as rare
As 'tis for object strange and high:
It was begotten by Despair
Upon Impossibility.
[Andrew Marvell: *Definition of Love*]

17 Love is love's reward.
[Dryden: *Palamon and Arcite* II]

18 The reduction of the universe to a
single being, the expansion of a single
being even to God, this is love. [Victor
Hugo: *Les Misérables* V.iv.]

19 Love is the business of the idle, but
the idleness of the busy. [E. G. Bulwer-
Lytton: *Rienzi* IV]

20 Love is an egoism of two. [Antoine
de La Sale]

1 The delusion that one woman differs from another. [H. L. Mencken: *A Book of Burlesques*]

2 Love is the idler's occupation, the warrior's relaxation, and the sovereign's ruination. [Napoleon Bonaparte, in *Dictionnaire Napoléon,* ed. Damas Hinard]

LOVE: its delights

3 Come live with me and be my love,
And we will all the pleasures prove,
That valleys, groves, or hills, or fields,
Or woods and steepy mountains
yields.
[Christopher Marlowe: *The Passionate Shepherd to His Love*]

4 Love keeps his revels where there are
but twain.
[Shakespeare: *Venus and Adonis*]

5 For thy sweet love rememb'red such
wealth brings
That then I scorn to change my state
with kings.
[Shakespeare: *Sonnets XXIX*]

6 My bounty is as boundless as the sea,
My love as deep; the more I give to
thee
The more I have, for both are in-
finite.
[Shakespeare: *Romeo and Juliet* II.ii.]

7 Excellent wretch! Perdition catch my
soul,
But I do love thee! and when I love
thee not,
Chaos is come again.
[Shakespeare: *Othello* III.iii.]

8 Eternity was in our lips and eyes,
Bliss in our brows bent.
[Shakespeare: *Antony and Cleopatra* I. iii.]

9   A lover's pinch,
Which hurts, and is desir'd.
[Shakespeare: *Antony and Cleopatra* V. ii.]

10 So let us melt, and make no noise,
No tear-floods, nor sigh-tempests
move,
'Twere profanation of our joys
To tell the laity our love.
[Donne: *A Valediction Forbidding Mourning*]

11 Come live with mee, and bee my love,
And wee will some new pleasures
prove.
[Donne: *The Baite*]

12 For God sake hold your tongue, and
let me love.
[Donne: *The Canonization*]

13 Imparadised in one another's arms.
[John Milton: *Paradise Lost* IV. 506]

14 My heart, which by a secret harmony
Still moves with thine, join'd in con-
nection sweet.
[John Milton: *Paradise Lost* X. 358-359]

15 The pleasure of love is in loving. We are happier in the passion we feel than in that which we excite. [La Rochefoucauld: *Maxims*]

16 Our souls sit close and silently within,
And their own web from their own
entrails spin;
And when eyes meet far off, our
sense is such,
That, spider like, we feel the tender-
est touch.
[Dryden: *Marriage à la Mode* II.i.]
There was a theory that sight resulted from filaments sent out from the eyes.

17 There is more pleasure in loving, than in being beloved. [Thomas Fuller (1654-1734): *Gnomologia*]

18 Serene will be our days and bright,
And happy will our nature be,
When love is an unerring light,
And joy its own security.
[Wordsworth: *Ode to Duty*]

19 Pillow'd upon my fair love's ripening
breast,
To feel for ever its soft fall and swell,
Awake for ever in a sweet unrest,
Still, still to hear her tender-taken
breath,
And so live ever—or else swoon to
death.
[Keats: *Bright Star*]

20 The heart of a poor girl who is both unhappy and in poverty is greedier for love than anything else in the world and the smallest particle of love will make it dilate with joy. [Balzac: *Le Père Goriot*]

21 Two souls with but a single thought,
Two hearts that beat as one.
[Von Munch Bellinghausen: *Ingomar the Barbarian* II]
This famous definition of the "togetherness" of love has been much quoted. More accurate, however, is the adaptation by Philip Barry (1896-1949):
Two minds without a single thought.
You and I, *II*

1 Come, live with me and be my love,
And we will all the pleasures prove
Of peace and plenty, bed and board,
That chance employment may afford.

. . .

Hunger shall make thy modest zone
And cheat fond death of all but bone
—If these delights thy mind may
move,
Then live with me and be my love.
[C. Day Lewis: *Come, Live With Me and Be My Love* (1935)]

LOVE: its departure
2 And desire shall fail. [Ecclesiastes 12:5]
3 You cannot call it love; for at your age
The hey-day in the blood is tame, it's humble,
And waits upon the judgment.
[Shakespeare: *Hamlet* III.iv.]
4 There lives within the very flame of love
A kind of wick or snuff that will abate it.
[Shakespeare: *Hamlet* IV.vii.]
5 Shall I, wasting in despair,
Die because a woman's fair?
Or make pale my cheeks with care
Cause another's rosy are?
Be she fairer than the day,
Or the flow'ry meads in May;
If she be not so to me,
What care I how fair she be?
[George Wither: *Song*]
6 I loved a lass, a fair one,
As fair as e'er was seen;
She was indeed a rare one,
Another Sheba queen:
But, fool as then I was,
I thought she loved me too:
But now, alas! she's left me,
Falero, lero, loo!
[George Wither: *I Loved a Lass*]
7 In love, the one first cured is the one most completely cured. [La Rochefoucauld: *Maxims*]
8 Quit, quit, for shame, this will not move,
This cannot take her.
If of herself she will not love,
Nothing can make her.
The devil take her!

[Sir John Suckling: *Song*]
9 Love has no gift so grateful as his wings.
[Byron: *Childe Harold* I.lxxxii.]
10 'Tis better to have loved and lost,
Than never to have loved at all.
[Tennyson: *In Memoriam* XXVII]
Congreve had expressed the same sentiment in The Way of the World, *Act II:*
. . . 'tis better to be left / Than never to have loved.

Samuel Butler parodied Tennyson's lines:
'Tis better to have loved and lost
Than never to have lost at all.
11 'Tis not love's going hurts my days,
But that it went in little ways.
[Edna St. Vincent Millay: *The Spring and the Fall*]

LOVE: faithful and faithless
12 Those who are faithless know the pleasures of love; it is the faithful who know love's tragedies. [Oscar Wilde: *The Picture of Dorian Gray* I]
13 Will you love me in December as you do in May
Will you love me in the good old fashioned way?
When my hair has all turned gray,
Will you kiss me then and say,
That you love me in December as you do in May?
[James J. Walker: *Will You Love Me in December?*]
Mr. Walker was the whoopee mayor of New York City in the whoopee era of the 1920's.

The answer of the public to the query in his song was "No."

LOVE: its folly
14 Love is not properly nor naturally in season but in the age next unto infancy. [Montaigne: *Essays* III.v.]
Byron and other Great Lovers have reported that the loves of their early adolescence were by far the most passionate and lasting of all they experienced.
15 The stage is more beholding to love than the life of man. [Francis Bacon: *Of Love*]
16 He that preferred Helena, quitted the gifts of Juno and Pallas; for whosoever esteemeth too much of amorous affection

quitteth both riches and wisdom. [Francis Bacon: *Of Love*]

> He = Paris, who gave the golden apple inscribed "for the fairest" to Venus, after she had promised him Helen as his wife. Juno had offered him power and wealth and Pallas (Minerva) had offered him wisdom.
>
> To a modern, one of the most interesting things in the famous story is how bribing the judge was taken completely for granted, even among the gods.

1 Great spirits and great business do keep out this weak passion. [Francis Bacon: *Of Love*]

2 It is impossible to love and be wise. [Francis Bacon: *Of Love*]

> Bacon is paraphrasing Publilius Syrus.

3   To be wise and love
      Exceeds man's might.

[Shakespeare: *Troilus and Cressida* III.ii.]

4 One that loved not wisely but too well.

[Shakespeare: *Othello* V.ii.]

5 I am two fools, I know,
      For loving, and for saying so
      In whining poetry.

[Donne: *The Triple Fool*]

6 No man, at one time, can be wise, and love.

[Robert Herrick: *Hesperides*]

7 There are very few people who, when their love is over, are not ashamed of having been in love. [La Rochefoucauld: *Maxims*]

8 God is Love, I dare say. But what a mischievous Devil Love is. [Samuel Butler (1835-1902): *Notebooks*, "God Is Love"]

LOVE: and hate

9 Better is a dinner of herbs where love is, than a stalled ox and hatred therewith. [Proverbs 15:17]

10 No enmities so bitter prove,
      And sharp, as those which spring of love.

[Propertius: *Elegies* VIII.iii (trans. John Florio)]

11 The wages of scorn'd love is baneful hate. [Beaumont and Fletcher: *The Knight of Malta* I.i.]

12 The self-same thing they will abhor One way, and long another for.

[Samuel Butler (1612-1680): *Hudibras*]

13 If we judge of love by most of its results, it resembles hatred more than friendship. [La Rochefoucauld: *Maxims*]

14 He loves me for little that hates me for naught. [David Ferguson: *Scottish Proverbs* (1641)]

> That is, one who seizes on a slight pretext for dislike could not have had very much liking in the first place.

15 Heav'n has no rage, like love to hatred turn'd,
      Nor Hell a fury like a woman scorn'd.

[William Congreve: *The Mourning Bride* III]

16 And to be wroth with one we love
      Doth work like madness in the brain.

[Coleridge: *Christabel* II]

LOVE: and hope

17 He alone knows love who loves without hope. [Schiller: *Don Carlos* II.viii.]

18 Hope Love's leman is, Despair his wife. [Hartley Coleridge: *Epigram*]

> leman = beloved

19 Where we really love, we often dread more than we desire the solemn moment that exchanges hope for certainty. [Mme. De Staël: *Corinne* VIII.iv.]

LOVE: longings

20 He who is not impatient is not in love. [Aretino: *La Talanta* V.xiii.]

21 Ah! when will this long weary day have end,
      And lende me leave to come unto my love?

[Edmund Spenser: *Epithalamion*]

22 For God sake hold your tongue, and let me love.

[Donne: *The Canonization*]

23 Would I were free from this restraint,
      Or else had hopes to win her:
      Would she could make of me a saint,
      Or I of her a sinner.

[William Congreve: *Pious Selinda*]

24 O that 'twere possible
      After long grief and pain
      To find the arms of my true love
      Round me once again!

[Tennyson: *Maud* IV]

LOVE: and lust

25 Love surfeits not. Lust like a glutton

dies;
Love is all truth, Lust full of forged
lies.
[Shakespeare: *Venus and Adonis*]

1 Love indeed (I may not deny) first united provinces, built cities, and by a perpetual generation makes and preserves mankind; but if it rage it is no more love, but burning lust, a disease, frenzy, madness, hell. . . . It subverts kingdoms, overthrows cities, towns, families; mars, corrupts, and makes a massacre of men; thunder and lightning, wars, fires, plagues, have not done that mischief to mankind, as this burning lust, this brutish passion. [Robert Burton: *Anatomy of Melancholy* III.2.1.2]

2 I was that silly thing that once was
wrought
To practise this thin love;
I climbed from sex to soul, from
soul to thought;
But thinking there to move,
Headlong I rolled from thought to
soul, and then
From soul I lighted at the sex again.
[William Cartwright: *No Platonic Love*]

LOVE: and madness

3 Love is merely a madness; and, I tell you, deserves as well a dark house and whip as madmen do; and the reason why they are not so punished and cured is that the lunacy is so ordinary that the whippers are in love too. [Shakespeare: *As You Like It* III.ii.]

4 This is the very ecstasy of love,
Whose violent property fordoes itself,
And leads the will to desperate undertakings.
[Shakespeare: *Hamlet* II.i.]

5 Love that is not madness is not love.
[Calderón: *El Mayor Monstruo los Zelos* I.v.]

6 Love and pride stock Bedlam.
[Thomas Fuller (1654-1734): *Gnomologia*]

LOVE: and marriage

7 They were as fed horses in the morning: every one neighed after his neighbor's wife. [Jeremiah 5:8]

8 Wommen desyren to have sovereyntee

As well over hir housbond as hir love,
And for to been in maistrie him
above.
[Chaucer: Prologue to *The Wife of Bath's Tale*]

This is the answer to the question that the Knight must answer, at the risk of his life:

What is it that worldly women love most?

And the answer, in brief, is: they want to be the boss in the family.

9 I see no marriages fail sooner, or more troubled, than such as are concluded for beauty's sake, and huddled up for amorous desires. [Montaigne: *Essays* III.v.]

10 Hail, wedded love! mysterious law,
true source
Of human offspring, sole propriety,
In Paradise of all things common
else.
[John Milton: *Paradise Lost* IV. 750-752]

11 Love is often a fruit of marriage.
[Molière: *Sganarelle* I.i.]

12 It is commonly a weak man who marries for love. [Samuel Johnson: in Boswell's *Life,* March 28, 1776]

13 "Come, come," said Tom's father, "at
your time of life,
There's no longer excuse for thus
playing the rake—
It is time you should think, boy, of
taking a wife—"
"Why so it is, father—whose wife
shall I take?"
[Thomas Moore: *A Joke Versified*]

14 'Tis melancholy, and a fearful sign
Of human frailty, folly, also crime,
That love and marriage rarely can
combine,
Although they both are born in the
same clime;
Marriage from love, like vinegar
from wine—
A sad, sour, sober beverage—by time
Is sharpen'd from its high celestial
flavor,
Down to a very homely household-
savor.
[Byron: *Don Juan* III.v.]

15 That moral centaur, man and wife.
[Byron: *Don Juan* V.clviii.]

16 Papas and mammas sometimes ask young men whether their intentions are honorable towards their daughters. I think young men might occasionally ask papas and mammas whether their intentions are honorable before they accept invitations to houses where there are still unmarried daughters. [Samuel Butler (1835-1902): *The Way of All Flesh* IX]

1 One should always be in love. That is the reason one should never marry. [Oscar Wilde: *A Woman of No Importance* III]

2 The most revolutionary invention of the Nineteenth Century was the artificial sterilization of marriage. [G. B. Shaw: *Maxims for Revolutionists*]

3 The psychology of adultery has been falsified by conventional morals, which assume, in monogamous countries, that attraction to one person cannot coexist with a serious affection for another. Everybody knows that this is untrue. [Bertrand Russell: *Marriage and Morals*]

LOVE: of men, and of women

4 Sigh no more, ladies, sigh no more,
  Men were deceivers ever,
  One foot in sea and one on shore;
  To one thing constant never.
[Shakespeare: *Much Ado About Nothing* II.iii.]

5 Much ado there was, God wot,
  He would love, and she would not.
[Nicholas Breton: *Phillida and Corydon*]

6 It is not virtue, wisdom, valour, wit,
  Strength, comeliness of shape, or amplest merit,
  That woman's love can win, or long inherit;
  But what it is, hard is to say,
  Harder to hit.
[John Milton: *Samson Agonistes*]

7 In their first passion, women are in love with their lovers; in all others, they are in love with love. [La Rochefoucauld: *Maxims*]

8 Through all the drama—whether damn'd or not—
  Love gilds the scene, and women guide the plot.
[Richard Brinsley Sheridan: Epilogue to *The Rivals*]

9 Love diminishes the delicacy of women and increases that of men. [Jean Paul Richter: *Titan*]

10 Love is the whole history of a woman's life;
  It is only an episode in man's.
[Mme. De Staël: *De l'influence des passions*]

11 Man's love is of man's life a thing apart,
  'Tis woman's whole existence.
[Byron: *Don Juan* I.cxciv.]

12 In her first passion woman loves her lover,
  In all the others all she loves is love,
  Which grows a habit she can ne'er get over
  And fits her loosely—like an easy glove.
[Byron: *Don Juan* III.iii.]

13 He was her man, but he done her wrong.
[Anon.: *Frankie and Johnny*]

14 Love itself draws on a woman nearly all the bad luck in the world. [Willa Cather: *My Mortal Enemy* III]

15 Find a man of forty who heaves and moans over a woman in the manner of a poet and you will behold either a man who ceased to develop intellectually at twenty-four or thereabout, or a fraud who has his eye on the lands, tenements and hereditaments of the lady's deceased first husband. [H. L. Mencken: *Prejudices: Fourth Series*]

LOVE: nature of

16 Love and dignity cannot share the same abode. [Ovid: *Metamorphoses* II]

17 Love is a credulous thing. (*Credula res amor est.*) [Ovid: *Metamorphoses* VII]

18 Love wol nat ben constreyned by maistrye;
  Whan maistrie comth, the god of love anon
  Beteth hise winges, and farewel! he is gon!
[Chaucer: *The Franklin's Tale*]

19 Love is ever rewarded either with the reciproque or with an inward and secret contempt. [Francis Bacon: *Of Love*]

20 Nuptial love maketh mankind, friendly love perfecteth it, but wanton love corrupteth and imbaseth it. [Francis Bacon: *Of Love*]
  imbaseth = *debases*

21 They do not love that do not show

their love.
[Shakespeare: *The Two Gentlemen of Verona* I.ii.]

1 When love begins to sicken and decay,
It useth an enforcèd ceremony.
There are no tricks in plain and simple faith.
[Shakespeare: *Julius Caesar* IV.ii.]

2 The course of true love never did run smooth.
[Shakespeare: *A Midsummer Night's Dream* I.i.]

3 Love sought is good, but given unsought is better.
[Shakespeare: *Twelfth Night* III.i.]

4 Love's not love
When it is mingled with regards that stand
Aloof from the entire point.
[Shakespeare: *King Lear* I.i.]

5 There's beggary in the love that can be reckon'd.
[Shakespeare: *Antony and Cleopatra* I.i.]

6 Love begets love.
[Robert Herrick: *Hesperides*]

7 It is with true love as it is with ghosts; everyone talks of it, but few have seen it. [La Rochefoucauld: *Maxims*]

8 Love seeketh not itself to please,
Nor for itself hath any care,
But for another gives its ease,
And builds a Heaven in Hell's despair.

Love seeketh only self to please,
To bind another to its delight,
Joys in another's loss of ease,
And builds a Hell in Heaven's despite.
[William Blake: *The Clod and the Pebble*]

9 Love of men cannot be bought by cash-payment; and without love, men cannot endure to be together. [Thomas Carlyle: *Past and Present* IV.iv.]

10 Love is the only game that is not called on account of darkness. [Anon.]

11 A woman can be proud and stiff
When on love intent;
But love has pitched his mansion in
The place of excrement.
[William Butler Yeats: *Crazy Jane Talks with the Bishop*]

LOVE: new love

12 'Tis good to be off wi' the old love
Before you are on wi' the new.
[Richard Edwards: *Damon and Pithias* (1571)]
Often quoted—by Sir Walter Scott (Bride of Lammermoor), among others— as " 'Tis best to be off wi' the old. . . ."

13 'Tis well to be merry and wise,
'Tis well to be honest and true;
'Tis well to be off with the old love
Before you are on with the new.
[Lines used by Maturin: as the motto to *Bertram,* produced at Drury Lane]

14 My merry, merry, merry roundelay
Concludes with Cupid's curse:
They that do change old love for new,
Pray gods, they change for worse!
[George Peele: *Fair and Fair*]

15 Love is of the phoenix kind,
And burns itself with self-made fire,
To breed still new birds in the mind,
From ashes of the old desire.
[Fulke Greville: *The Phoenix Kind*]

16 Love is like linen—often changed, the sweeter. [Phineas Fletcher: *Sicelides* III.v.]

17 Soon or late love is his own avenger.
[Byron: *Don Juan* IV. lxxiii.]

18 And I shall find some girl perhaps,
And a better one than you,
With eyes as wise, but kindlier,
And lips as soft, but true.
And I daresay she will do.
[Rupert Brooke: *The Chilterns*]

LOVE: its permanence

19 Many waters cannot quench love, neither can the floods drown it. [Song of Solomon 8:7]

20 Let me not to the marriage of true minds
Admit impediments. Love is not love
Which alters when it alteration finds.
[Shakespeare: *Sonnets* CXVI]

21 Love's not Time's fool, though rosy lips and cheeks
Within his bending sickle's compass come;
Love alters not with his brief hours and weeks,
But bears it out even to the edge of doom.
[Shakespeare: *Sonnets* CXVI]

22 Oh, no! it is an ever-fixed mark,

That looks on tempests and is never
      shaken.
[Shakespeare: *Sonnets* CXVI]
1 John Anderson my jo, John,
    When we were first acquent,
    Your locks were like the raven,
    Your bonnie brow was brent;
    But now your brow is bald, John,
    Your locks are like the snow;
    But blessings on your frosty pow,
    John Anderson, my jo.

    John Anderson my jo, John,
    We clamb the hill thegither;
    And mony a canty day, John,
    We've had wi' ane anither:
    Now we maun totter down, John,
    And hand in hand we'll go,
    And sleep thegither at the foot,
    John Anderson my jo.
[Burns: *John Anderson My Jo*]
  pow = *poll*, *head*; canty = *gay*, *lively*;
  maun = *must*
2 I love thee, I love but thee,
    With a love that shall not die
    Till the sun grows cold,
    And the stars are old,
    And the leaves of the Judgment Book
        unfold!
[Bayard Taylor: *Bedouin Song*]
3 Yonder a maid and her wight
    Come whispering by:
    War's annals will fade into night
    Ere their story die.
[Thomas Hardy: *In Time of the Breaking of Nations*]
  The title echoes Jeremiah *51:20.*
4 Sing the Lovers' Litany:
    "Love like ours can never die!"
[Kipling: *Lovers' Litany*]

LOVE: and poverty
5 Love lasteth as long as the money endureth. [William Caxton: *The Game and Play of Chess* (1476)]
  Caxton describes the saying as "a common proverb."
6 When poverty comes in at doors, love leaps out at windows. [John Clarke: *Paroemiologia*]
7 It hath beene an old maxime; that as poverty goes in at one doore, love goes out at the other. [Richard Brathwait: *The English Gentlewoman* (1631)]
8 Love is maintain'd by wealth; when

all is spent,
Adversity then breeds the discontent.
[Robert Herrick: *Adversity*]
9 Who marrieth for love without money hath good nights and sorry days. [John Ray: *English Proverbs* (1670)]

LOVE: its power
10 Stay me with flagons, comfort me with apples: for I am sick of love. [Song of Solomon 2:5]
11 Love conquers all things. (*Omnia vincit amor.*) [Vergil: *Eclogues* X.lxix.]
  This was the motto that Chaucer's Prioress had inscribed on the golden brooch that hung from her rosary. She, unquestionably, interpreted it to refer to divine love.
12 Plutarch saith fitly of those who affectionate themselves to monkeys and little dogs, that the loving part which is in us, rather than be idle, will forge a false and frivolous hold. [Montaigne: *Essays* I.iv.]
13 Were beauty under twenty locks kept
        fast,
    Yet love breaks through and picks
        them all at last.
[Shakespeare: *Venus and Adonis*]
14 Steal love's sweet bait from fearful
        hooks.
[Shakespeare: Prologue to *Romeo and Juliet* II]
15 For valor, is not Love a Hercules,
    Still climbing trees in the Hesperides.
[Shakespeare: *Love's Labour's Lost* IV. iii.]
  Among the twelve labors of Hercules was bringing back the golden apples of the Hesperides. In one version of the story, he slew the dragon Ladon that guarded the golden fruit. In another, he persuaded Atlas to fetch the apples, holding up the sky in Atlas's place while he was getting them.
16 O powerful love! that in some respects, makes a beast a man, in some other, a man a beast. [Shakespeare: *The Merry Wives of Windsor* V.v.]
17 Base men being in love have then a nobility in their natures more than is native to them. [Shakespeare: *Othello* II.i.]
18 No cord nor cable can so forcibly draw, or hold so fast, as love can do with

a twined thread. [Robert Burton: *Anatomy of Melancholy* III.2.1.2]

1 The greatest miracle of love is the cure of coquetry. [La Rochefoucauld: *Maxims*]

2 What dire offence from am'rous causes springs.
[Alexander Pope: *The Rape of the Lock* I]

3 Love Laughs at Locksmiths. [George Colman the Younger: title of a comedy]

4 Love rules the court, the camp, the grove,
And men below, and saints above;
For love is heaven, and heaven is love.
[Sir Walter Scott: *The Lay of the Last Minstrel* III.ii.]

5 "La belle dame sans merci
Hath thee in thrall!"
[Keats: *La Belle Dame sans Merci*]

6 Love wakes men, once a lifetime each;
They lift their heavy lids and look;
And, lo, what one sweet page can teach
They read with joy, then shut the book.

And some give thanks, and some blaspheme,
And most forget; but either way,
That, and the child's unheeded dream,
Is all the light of all their day.
[Coventry Patmore: *The Revelation*]

7 Love is a flame to burn out human wills,
Love is a flame to set the will on fire,
Love is a flame to cheat men into mire.
[John Masefield: *The Widow in the Bye Street*]

8 I have found it impossible to carry the heavy burden of responsibility and to discharge my duties as King as I would wish to do without the help and support of the woman I love. [The Duke of Windsor (formerly Edward VIII): in his farewell address]

LOVE: its quarrels and reconciliations
9 Lovers' quarrels are the renewal of love. [Terence: *Andria*]

10 Next to the coming to a good understanding with a new mistress, I love a quarrel with an old one. [Sir George Etherege: *The Man of Mode* I.i.]

11 The difference is wide that the sheets will not decide. [John Ray: *English Proverbs* (1678)]

12 As thro' the land at eve we went,
And plucked the ripened ears,
We fell out, my wife and I;
O we fell out I know not why,
And kissed again with tears.
[Tennyson: *The Princess* II]

LOVE: its regrets
13 Love that comes too late,
Like a remorseful pardon slowly carried.
[Shakespeare: *All's Well That Ends Well* V.iii.]

14 Take, O, take those lips away
That so sweetly were forsworn;
And those eyes, the break of day,
Lights that do mislead the morn;
But my kisses bring again, bring again;
Seals of love, but seal'd in vain, seal'd in vain.
[Shakespeare: *Measure for Measure* IV.i.]

15 "I'm sorry that I spell'd the word;
I hate to go above you,
Because"—the brown eyes lower fell,—
"Because, you see, I love you!"
[J. G. Whittier: *In School Days*]

16 I am shamed thro' all my nature to have loved so slight a thing.
[Tennyson: *Locksley Hall*]

17 His folly has not fellow
Beneath the blue of day
That gives to man or woman
His heart and soul away.
[A. E. Housman: *A Shropshire Lad* XIV]

LOVE: divine and spiritual love
18 Greater love hath no man than this, that a man lay down his life for his friends. [John 15:13]

19 The love that moves the sun and the other stars.
[Dante: *The Divine Comedy*, "Paradiso" XXXIII]

20 Lord, it is my chief complaint,
That my love is weak and faint;
Yet I love thee and adore,
Oh for grace to love thee more!

[William Cowper: *Olney Hymns* XVIII]

1 He prayeth best who loveth best
 All things both great and small;
For the dear God who loveth us,
 He made and loveth all.
[Coleridge: *The Ancient Mariner* VII]

LOVE: its torments and pains
2 In love, ther is but litel reste.
[Chaucer: *Troilus and Criseyde* IV]
3 Love is thing ay ful of bisy drede.
[Chaucer: *Troilus and Criseyde* IV]
4   She never told her love,
But let concealment, like a worm i'
    the bud,
Feed on her damask cheek: she pined
    in thought,
And with a green and yellow melan-
    choly
She sat like patience on a monument,
Smiling at grief.
[Shakespeare: *Twelfth Night* II.iv.]
5 The pangs of dispriz'd love.
[Shakespeare: *Hamlet* III.i.]
6 Whoever loves, if he do not propose
The right true end of love, he's one
    that goes
To sea for nothing but to make him
    sick.
[Donne: *Love's Progress*]
7 Then crown my joys, or cure my pain:
Give me more love, or more disdain.
[Thomas Carew: *Mediocrity in Love Rejected*]
8 Tangl'd in amorous nets.
[John Milton: *Paradise Regained* II. 162]
9 Whom we love best, to them we can
    say least.
[John Ray: *English Proverbs* (1670)]
10 Love reckons hours for months, and
    days for years;
And every little absence is an age.
[Dryden: *Amphitryon* III.i.]
11 Pains of love be sweeter far
Than all other pleasures are.
[Dryden: *Tyrannic Love* IV.i.]
12 Had we never lov'd sae kindly,
Had we never lov'd sae blindly,
Never met—or never parted,
We had ne'er been broken-hearted.
[Burns: *Ae Fond Kiss*]
13 So, we'll go no more a-roving
 So late into the night,
Though the heart be still as loving,
 And the moon be still as bright.

For the sword outwears its sheath,
And the soul wears out the breast,
And the heart must pause to breathe,
And love itself have rest.
[Byron: *So, We'll Go No More A-Roving*]
14   'Tis the pest
Of love, that fairest joys give most
    unrest.
[Keats: *Endymion* II]

LOVE: miscellaneous
15 Oh, what a furious advantage is opportunity! He that should demand of me, what the chief or first part in love is, I would answer, To know how to take fit time; even so the second, and likewise the third. [Montaigne: *Essays* III.v.]
16 Love me little, love me long.
[John Heywood: *Proverbs* (1546)]
17 And all for love, and nothing for reward.
[Edmund Spenser: *The Faerie Queene* II.viii.]
18   The sweetest honey
Is loathsome in his own deliciousness,
And in the taste confounds the appetite:
Therefore, love moderately.
[Shakespeare: *Romeo and Juliet* II.vi.]
19   Down on your knees,
And thank heaven, fasting, for a good
    man's love.
[Shakespeare: *As You Like It* III.v.]
20 I wonder by my troth, what thou,
    and I
Did, till we lov'd?
[Donne: *The Good Morrow*]
21 You say, to me-wards your affection's
    strong;
Pray love me little, so you love me
    long.
[Robert Herrick: *Love me Little, Love me Long*]
22 Love, and a cough, cannot be hid.
[George Herbert: *Jacula Prudentum*]
23 There is no love lost between them.
[17th-century expression]
 Now used solely with the ironic meaning that they hate each other. But formerly it meant that they loved each other, that every bit of love between them was cherished.
24 I could not love thee, dear, so much,
Loved I not honour more.

[Lovelace: *To Lucasta, on Going to the Wars*]
1 For, Lady, you deserve this state,
  Nor would I love at lower rate.
[Andrew Marvell: *To His Coy Mistress*]
2 I sighed as a lover, I obeyed as a son.
[Edward Gibbon: *Autobiography*]
3 The wisest man the warl' e'er saw,
  He dearly lov'd the lasses, O.
[Burns: *Green Grow the Rashes*]
4 One word is too often profaned
    For me to profane it,
  One feeling too falsely disdained
    For thee to disdain it.
[Shelley: *To—, One Word Is Too Often Profaned*]
5 O Love! who bewailest
    The frailty of all things here,
  Why choose you the frailest
    For your cradle, your home, and
                      your bier?
[Shelley: *When the Lamp Is Shattered*]
6 To know her was to love her. [Samuel Rogers: *Jacqueline*]
7 Perhaps they were right in putting love into books. . . . Perhaps it could not live anywhere else. [William Faulkner: *Light in August*]
8 When you love you must either, in your reasoning about that love, start from what is higher, more important than happiness or unhappiness, sin or virtue in their usual meaning, or you must not reason at all. [Anton Chekhov: "About Love"]

LOVER(S)

9 A pair of star-cross'd lovers.
[Shakespeare: Prologue to *Romeo and Juliet*]
10 At lovers' perjuries, they say, Jove
                      laughs.
[Shakespeare: *Romeo and Juliet* II.ii.]
  Lovers' oaths are not subject to penalty.
  Diogenianus: Paroemiae III.xxxvii.
  The courts have held that a young man or a young woman is not under oath in a hammock or a canoe.
11   And then the lover,
  Sighing like furnace, with a woeful
                      ballad
  Made to his mistress' eyebrow.
[Shakespeare: *As You Like It* II.vii.]
12 It was a lover, and his lass,
  With a hey, and a ho, and a hey
  nonino,
  That o'er the green cornfield did
                      pass,
  In Springtime, the only pretty ring
                      time,
  When birds do sing, hey ding a ding,
                      ding;
  Sweet lovers love the Spring.
[Shakespeare: *As You Like It* V.iii.]
13 Journeys end in lovers meeting,
  Every wise man's son doth know.
[Shakespeare: *Twelfth Night* II.iii.]
14 All lovers swear more performance than they are able, and yet reserve an ability that they never perform; vowing more than the perfection of ten, and discharging less than the tenth part of one.
[Shakespeare: *Troilus and Cressida* III.ii.]
15 I long to talk with some old lover's
                      ghost,
  Who died before the god of love was
                      born.
[Donne: *Love's Deity*]
16 The falling out of lovers is the renewing of love. [Robert Burton: *Anatomy of Melancholy* III.2]
17 Why so pale and wan, fond lover,
    Prithee, why so pale?
  Will, when looking well can't move
                      her,
    Looking ill prevail?
    Prithee, why so pale?
[Sir John Suckling: *Song*]
18 The reason why lovers and their mistresses never tire of being together is because they are always talking of themselves. [La Rochefoucauld: *Maxims*]
19 O, I hate a lover that can dare to think he draws a moment's air, independent on the bounty of his mistress. There is not so impudent a thing in Nature, as the saucy look of an assured man, confident of success. [William Congreve: *The Way of the World* IV.v.]
20 A woman rarely discards one lover until she is sure of another. [Royall Tyler: *The Contrast* I.i.]
21 A savage place! as holy and enchanted
  As e'er beneath a waning moon was
                      haunted
  By woman wailing for her demon-
                      lover.

[Coleridge: *Kubla Khan*]
1 He was a lover of the good old school,
  Who still become more constant as
          they cool.
[Byron: *Beppo* XXXIV]
2 I've seen your stormy seas and stormy
          women,
  And pity lovers rather more than
          seamen.
[Byron: *Don Juan* VI.liii.]
3 All mankind love a lover. [Emerson: *Spiritual Laws*]
    All the world loves a lover; but not
    while the love-making is going on.
        Elbert Hubbard (1856-1915): Epigram
4 A lover without indiscretion is no
lover at all. [Thomas Hardy: *The Hand
of Ethelberta* XX]

LUCID
5 Some beams of wit on other souls
          may fall,
  Strike through and make a lucid interval.
[Dryden: *Mac Flecknoe*]

LUCIFER
6 How art thou fallen from heaven, O
Lucifer, son of the morning! [Isaiah 14:
12]

LUCK
7 He forc'd his neck into a noose,
  To show his play at fast and loose;
  And, when he chanc'd t' escape, mistook
  For art and subtlety, his luck.
[Samuel Butler (1612-1680): *Hudibras*]
8 Ill fortune seldom comes alone.
[Dryden: *Cymon and Iphigenia*]
9 Well, Miss, you'll have a sad husband,
you have such good luck at cards. [Jonathan Swift: *Polite Conversation* III]
    This shows that "Lucky in cards, unlucky in love" was proverbial by 1738.
10 Diligence is the mother of good luck.
[Benjamin Franklin: *Poor Richard's Almanack* (1736)]
11 What evil luck soever
  For me remains in store,
  'Tis sure much finer fellows
  Have fared much worse before.
[A. E. Housman: *Last Poems* II]
12 Little is the luck I've had,
  And oh, 'tis comfort small

To think that many another lad
Has had no luck at all.
[A. E. Housman: *Last Poems* XXVIII]
13 "It don't seem fair for us to have all
the luck." "Sure it's fair," I says. "If you
didn't have luck, what would you have?"
[Ring Lardner: *Carmen*]
14 You can take it as understood
  That your luck changes only if it's
          good.
[Ogden Nash: *Roulette Us Be Gay*]
15 Those who mistake their good luck
for their merit are inevitably bound for
disaster. [J. Christopher Herold: *Bonaparte in Egypt,* 11]

LUCUS A NON LUCENDO
16 *Lucus a non lucendo.* [Quintilian:
Institutio Oratoria I.vi.]
    Lucus *is the Latin word for grove.*
    Lucus *was also an old form of* lux, *light.*
    Quintilian here tells of a pedant who
    derived lucus, *grove, from* lucus, *light,*
    on the grounds that it was not light in
    a grove. The lofty absurdity and pompous distortion pleased men's fancies and
    the expression remained for centuries
    as a term of derision for the ignorant
    who strive so laboredly to be learned.
    Curmudgeon, *a word whose origin is*
    unknown, has provided a similar instance in more modern times. When Dr.
    Johnson was preparing his dictionary
    he received a letter suggesting that the
    word was derived from the French coeur
    (heart) and méchant *(evil). Either the*
    letter was unsigned or Johnson lost it
    and forgot who wrote it. The suggestion,
    though unsupported, was interesting and
    Johnson set it down in his dictionary
    (1755) for what it was worth: "a vitious
    manner of pronouncing coeur méchant,
    Fr. an unknown correspondent." In his
    New and Complete Dictionary of the
    English Language (1775), Dr. John Ash,
    cribbing from Johnson but, unfortunately, knowing no French, entered it
    as "from the French coeur *unknown,*
    méchant *correspondent."*

LUCY LOCKET
17 Lucy Locket lost her pocket,
  Kitty Fisher found it;
  Not a penny was there in it,
  Only ribbon round it.

[Nursery rhyme: earliest known version, 1842]
Despite many claims, the identification of the ladies has never been made.

LULLABY

1 Golden slumbers kiss your eyes,
Smiles awake you when you rise
Sleep, pretty wantons, do not cry,
And I will sing a lullaby.
[Thomas Dekker: *Patient Grissill* IV.ii.]

2 Hush, my dear, lie still and slumber!
Holy angels guard thy bed!
Heavenly blessings without number
Gently falling on thy head.
[Isaac Watts: *Cradle Hymn*]

3 Sweet and low, sweet and low,
Wind of the western sea,
Low, low, breathe and blow;
Wind of the western sea!
Over the rolling waters go,
Come from the dying moon, and blow,
Blow him again to me;
While my little one, while my pretty
one sleeps.
[Tennyson: *The Princess* II]

4 Sleep, baby, sleep
Thy Father's watching the sheep,
Thy mother's shaking the dreamland
tree,
And down drops a little dream for
thee.
[Elizabeth Prentiss: *Sleep, Baby, Sleep*]

LUNATIC FRINGE

5 The lunatic fringe in all reform movements. [Theodore Roosevelt: *Autobiography* (1913)]

6 The lunatic fringe wags the underdog.
[H. L. Mencken: *Chrestomathy* 622]

LUNATIC, LOVER, AND POET

7 The lunatic, the lover, and the poet
Are of imagination all compact:
One sees more devils than vast hell
can hold,
That is, the madman: the lover, all
as frantic,
Sees Helen's beauty in a brow of
Egypt:
The poet's eye, in a fine frenzy rolling,
Doth glance from heaven to earth,
from earth to heaven;
And as imagination bodies forth
The forms of things unknown, the
poet's pen
Turns them to shapes, and gives to
airy nothing
A local habitation and a name.
[Shakespeare: *A Midsummer Night's Dream* V.i.]

LUST

8 For men han ever a likerous appetite
On lower things to perform their delight
Than on their wyves, be they never
so faire,
Nor ever so trewe, nor so debonaire.
Flesh is so newfangel, with mischaunce,
That we can in no thing have pleasaunce
That souneth unto virtue any while.
[Chaucer: *The Manciple's Tale*]
likerous = *lecherous;* newfangel = *fond of novelty;* souneth = *tends*
Compare Hamlet *I.v.:*
*So lust, though to a radiant
angel link'd,
Will sate itself in a celestial bed
And prey on garbage.*

9 The expense of spirit in a waste of
shame
Is lust in action; and till action, lust
Is perjured, murderous, bloody, full
of blame,
Savage, extreme, rude, cruel, not to
trust.
[Shakespeare: *Sonnets* CXXIX]

10 Rebellious hell,
If thou canst mutine in a matron's
bones,
To flaming youth let virtue be as
wax,
And melt in her own fire.
[Shakespeare: *Hamlet* III.iv.]

11 As prime as goats, as hot as monkeys,
As salt as wolves in pride.
[Shakespeare: *Othello* III.iii.]
salt = *lustful;* pride = *heat*

12 Behold yond simp'ring dame,
Whose face between her forks presageth snow,
That minces virtue, and does shake
the head
To hear of pleasure's name.
The fitchew nor the soiled horse goes

to't
With a more riotous appetite.
[Shakespeare: *King Lear* IV.vi.]

minces = *counterfeits with a prudish air;*
fitchew = *polecat—thought to have an
insatiable sexual appetite; prostitutes
were called polecats;* soiled = *a stallion
full-fed on green fodder*

1   Thou rascal beadle, hold thy bloody
                                    hand!
Why dost thou lash that whore? Strip
                            thine own back;
Thou hotly lust'st to use her in that
                                    kind
For which thou whipp'st her.
[Shakespeare: *King Lear* IV.vi.]

2   A wanton and lascivious eye
Betrayes the Hearts Adulterie.
[Robert Herrick: *The Eye*]

3   Thunder and lightning, wars, fires,
plagues, have not done that mischief to
mankind as this burning lust, this brutish passion. [Robert Burton: *The Anatomy of Melancholy* III]

4   When lust,
By unchaste looks, loose gestures, and
                                foul talk,
But most by lewd and lavish arts of
                                    sin,
Lets in defilement to the inward parts,
The soul grows clotted by contagion,
Imbodies and imbrutes, till she quite
                                    lose
The divine property of her first be-
                                    ing.
[John Milton: *Comus*]

5   The lust of the goat is the bounty of
                                    God.
[William Blake: *The Marriage of
Heaven and Hell*]

6   For forty years I shunned the lust
        Inherent in my clay:
Death only was so amorous
        I let him have his way.
[Countee Cullen: *Three Epitaphs*, "For
a Virgin Lady"]

LUTHER

7   Then sing, as Martin Luther sang,
As Doctor Martin Luther sang:
"Who loves not wine, woman, and
                                    song,
He is a fool his whole life long."
[W. M. Thackeray: *Adventures of Philip*
VII]

LUXURY(IES)

8   This whole globe of earth must be at
least three times gone round, before one
of our better female Yahoos could get
her breakfast or a cup to put it in. [Jon-
athan Swift: *Gulliver's Travels* IV.vi.]

9   Whoever heard a man of fortune in
England talk of the necessaries of life?
Whether we can afford it or no, we must
have superfluities. [John Gay: *Polly*
I.i.]

10   Men have declaimed against luxury
for two thousand years, in verse and in
prose, and have always loved it. [Vol-
taire: *Philosophical Dictionary*, "Luxury"]

11   No nation was ever hurt by luxury;
for it can reach but to a very few. [Sam-
uel Johnson: in Boswell's *Life*, April 13,
1773]

12   Give us the luxuries of life, and we
will dispense with the necessaries. [John
Lothrop Motley: quoted by Oliver Wendell Holmes: *The Autocrat of the Breakfast-Table* VI]

*The idea had been expressed in Plu-
tarch's* Morals. *Voltaire had said: The
superfluous, a very necessary thing* (Le
Mondain *XXI*).

13   I would sell my bread for marmalade.
[Theophile Gautier: *Caprices et zig-
zags*]

14   Most of the luxuries, and many of
the so-called comforts, of life are not
only not indispensable, but positive hin-
drances to the elevation of mankind.
[Thoreau: *Walden* I. "Economy"]

15   The whole trade in the luxuries of
life is brought into existence and supported by the requirements of women.
[Tolstoy: *The Kreutzer Sonata* IX]

LYING

16   The rulers of the State . . . may be
allowed to lie for the good of the State.
[Plato: *The Republic* III.ii.]

*This is the authorization for propa-
ganda, state control of citizens' thoughts
and other evils of dictatorships.*

17   Never was it given to mortal man
To lie so boldly as we women can.
[Alexander Pope's trans. of a passage in
Chaucer's Prologue to *The Wife of
Bath's Tale*.]

The original has more vigor:

*For half so boldely can ther no man
Swere and lyen as a woman can.*

1 He who hath not a good and ready memory should never meddle with telling lies. [Montaigne: *Essays* I.ix.]
Montaigne prefaces this with "Men say," so it was a proverb or saying even then.

2 Whosoever lies shows that he despises God and fears men. [Montaigne: *Essays* II.xviii.]
Montaigne attributes the saying to "an ancient writer."

3 Whoever believes any thing thinks it a deed of charity to persuade another to believe it. Which, that he may the better do, he does not hesitate to add something of his own invention, so far as seems necessary to remove the resistance and defect which he assumes to be in the other's conception. [Montaigne: *Essays* III.xi.]
Montaigne had just been speaking of the "natural progress" of lying.

4 Who speaks not truly, lies.
[Shakespeare: *King John* IV.iii.]

5 I love to hear him lie.
[Shakespeare: *Love's Labour's Lost* I.i.]

6 Lord, Lord, how this world is given
　　　　　　　　　　　to lying!
[Shakespeare: *I Henry IV* V.iv.]

7 How subject we old men are to this
　　　　　　　　　　　vice of lying!
[Shakespeare: *II Henry IV* III.ii.]

8 'Tis as easy as lying.
[Shakespeare: *Hamlet* III.ii.]

9 Having made one lie, he is fain to make more to maintain it. For an untruth wanting a firm foundation needs many buttresses. [Thomas Fuller (1608-1661): *The Holy State, The Profane State,* "The Lyer"]

10 He never lies but when the holly is green. [David Ferguson: *Scottish Proverbs* (1641)]
Said of one who is an inveterate liar, since holly is an evergreen.

11 Among the calamities of war may be justly numbered the diminution of the love of truth by the falsehoods which interest dictates and credulity encourages. A peace will equally leave the warrior and relater of wars destitute of employment; and I know not whether more is to be dreaded from streets filled with soldiers accustomed to plunder, or from garrets filled with scribblers accustomed to lie. [Samuel Johnson: *The Idler* No. 30]

12 A man who has never looked on Niagara has but a faint idea of a cataract; and he who has not read Barère's Memoirs may be said not to know what it is to lie. [Macaulay: *Mémoires de Bertrand Barère*]

13 The best liar is he who makes the smallest amount of lying go the longest way. [Samuel Butler (1835-1902): *The Way of All Flesh* XXXIX]

14 I do not mind lying, but I hate inaccuracy. [Samuel Butler (1835-1902): *Notebooks,* "Falsehood"]

15 I never lied save to shield a woman or myself. [Ring Lardner: *Ex Parte*]

LYING: and truth

16 If a lie had no more faces but one, as truth hath, we should be in far better terms than we are: For, whatsoever a liar should say, we would take it in a contrary sense. But the opposite of truth hath many shapes and an undefinite field. [Montaigne: *Essays* I.ix.]

17 When my love swears that she is
　　　　　　　　　　made of truth,
I do believe her, though I know she
　　　　　　　　　　　　lies.
[Shakespeare: *Sonnets* CXXXVIII]

18 Half the truth is often a great lie.
[Benjamin Franklin: *Poor Richard's Almanack* (1757)]

19 A truth that's told with bad intent
Beats all the lies you can invent.
[William Blake: *Auguries of Innocence*]

20 Any fool can tell the truth, but it requires a man of some sense to know how to lie well. [Samuel Butler (1835-1902): *Notebooks*]

21 If a man is sufficiently unimaginative to produce evidence in support of a lie, he might just as well speak the truth at once. [Oscar Wilde: *The Decay of Lying*]

22 If you want to be thought a liar, always tell the truth. [Logan Pearsall Smith: *Afterthoughts*]

LYRICS

23 All good lyrics must make sense as a whole yet in details be a little absurd. [Goethe: *Sprüche in Prosa*]

M

MACAULAY

1 Macaulay is well for a while, but one wouldn't *live* under *Niagara*. [Thomas Carlyle: quoted in R. M. Milnes's *Notebook*]

MACDUFF

2   Lay on, Macduff,
And damn'd be him that first cries
                 "Hold, enough!"
[Shakespeare: *Macbeth* V.vii.]

MACHIAVELLI

3 Out of his surname they have coined an epithet for a knave, and out of his Christian name a synonym for the Devil. [Macaulay: *On Machiavelli*]

4 Machiavelli is not an evil genius, nor a demon, nor a cowardly and miserable writer; he is nothing but the fact. And he is not merely the Italian fact, he is the European fact, the fact of the sixteenth century. He seems hideous, and he is so, in presence of the moral idea of the nineteenth. [Victor Hugo: *Les Misérables* I.i.]

MACHINE(S)

5 No machines will increase the possibilities of life. They only increase the possibilities of idleness. [John Ruskin: *Fors Clavigera*, Letter V]

6 One machine can do the work of fifty ordinary men. No machine can do the work of one extraordinary man. [Elbert Hubbard: *The Philistine* XVIII]

MACHINERY

7 Faith in machinery is our besetting danger; often in machinery most absurdly disproportioned to the end which this machinery, if it is to do any good at all, is to serve; but always in machinery, as if it had a value in and for itself. [Matthew Arnold: *Culture and Anarchy* I]

MAD

8 Whom Zeus would destroy, he first makes mad. [Sophocles: *Antigone* (c. 450 B.C.)]
The statement, which may well have been proverbial when Sophocles used it, has passed through its Latin version into almost every European language.

9 Mad were as an hare.
[Chaucer: *The Friar's Tale*]
As mad as a March hare.
      John Heywood: Proverbs (1546)
The wild frolicking of the buck hare in March, its breeding season, has made the creature a trope of giddy recklessness and lunacy for centuries.

10 That he is mad, 'tis true; 'tis true 'tis
                   pity;
   And pity 'tis 'tis true.
[Shakespeare: *Hamlet* II.ii.]

11 Running about like mad. [Henry More: *An Antidote against Atheism* III. vii.]

12 Mad, bad, and dangerous to know. [Lady Caroline Lamb: entry in her diary the day she met Byron]
Byron, with equal justification, could have written the same entry in his diary concerning her.

13 As mad as a hatter.
Though the Mad Hatter is associated in most readers' minds with Alice in Wonderland (1865), *the expression "as mad as a hatter" antedates* Alice *by at least thirty years. Hatters were poisoned by the mercurial compounds formerly used in making hats. Their gait was lurching, their minds confused and their speech often incoherent.*
Weavers, perhaps merely from the confinement and tedium of their work, were often, also, deranged. "Mad as a weaver" was once a common expression. There are many allusions in literature to their being melancholy and singing hymns.

MADMAN(MEN)

14 The worst of madmen is a saint run mad. [Alexander Pope: *Imitations of Horace*, I.vi]

15 Is there no life but these alone?

Madman or slave, must man be one?
[Matthew Arnold: *A Summer Night*]

MADNESS

1 This is very midsummer madness.
[Shakespeare: *Twelfth Night* III.iv.]
2 Though this be madness, yet there is
method in 't.
[Shakespeare: *Hamlet* II.ii.]
3 Now see that noble and most sovereign reason,
Like sweet bells jangled, out of tune
and harsh.
[Shakespeare: *Hamlet* III.i.]
4 I am but mad north-north-west;
when the wind is southerly, I know a
hawk from a handsaw. [Shakespeare:
Hamlet II.ii.]
> *One of the most disputed passages in
> all of Shakespeare.*
> *Hamlet tells Rosenkrantz and Guilden-
> stern—who are hired to spy on him—
> that he is not wholly mad, not mad all
> round the compass. He is still able to
> make some distinctions. Some have
> thought that the distinction between
> a hawk and a handsaw was too obvious
> to serve his purpose and have suggested
> heronshaw, a young heron, the prey of
> a hawk. But his purpose may have been
> merely to mystify Rosenkrantz and Guil-
> denstern and, at the same time, to ex-
> press openly his contempt for them.*

5 Oh! that way madness lies.
[Shakespeare: *King Lear* III.iv.]
6 O matter and impertinency mix'd!
Reason in madness!
[Shakespeare: *King Lear* IV.vi.]
7 The madman who knows that he is
mad is close to sanity. [Ruiz de Alarcón:
La Amistad Castigada II.i.]
8 Man's state implies a necessary curse:
When not himself, he's mad; when
most himself, he's worse.
[Francis Quarles: *Emblems* II.xiv.]
9 Demoniac frenzy, moping melancholy,
And moon-struck madness.
[John Milton: *Paradise Lost* XI. 485-486]
10 One gets into situations in life from
which it is necessary to be a little mad to
extricate oneself successfully. [La Rochefoucauld: *Maxims*]
11 Great wits are sure to madness near
alli'd

And thin partitions do their bounds
divide.
[Dryden: *Absalom and Achitophel* I]
12 There is a pleasure sure,
In being mad, which none but madmen know!
[Dryden: *The Spanish Friar* II.i.]
> *The Spanish Friar appeared in 1681. In
> 1706 George Farquhar used the lines in
> his play* The Recruiting Officer *I.iii.:*
> *And there's a pleasure in being mad,*
> *Which none but madmen know.*

13 Teach me half the gladness
That thy brain must know,
Such harmonious madness
From my lips would flow
The world should listen then—as I
am listening now.
[Shelley: *To a Skylark*]
14 In individuals, insanity is rare, but in
groups, parties, nations and epochs it is
the rule. [Nietzsche: *Beyond Good and
Evil*]
15 There nearly always is method in
madness. It's what drives men mad, being
methodical. [G. K. Chesterton: *The Fad
of the Fisherman*]

MADRIGALS

16 By shallow rivers, to whose falls
Melodious birds sing madrigals.
[Christopher Marlowe: *The Passionate
Shepherd to His Love*]

MAIDENHEADS

17 Tyme . . . wol nat come agayn, with-
outen drede,
Na more than wol Malkins mayden-
hede.
[Chaucer: Prologue to *The Tale of the
Man of Lawe*]
> *with-outen drede = don't worry; Malkin
> = diminutive of Matilda. It was a name
> used formerly, as we now use Moll, for a
> disreputable woman.*

18 Cologne,
A city which presents to the inspector
Eleven thousand maidenheads of
bone,
The greatest number flesh hath ever
known.
[Byron: *Don Juan* X.lxii.]
> *St. Ursula, accompanied by 11,000 noble
> and 60,000 plebeian virgins, encountered
> at Cologne a horde of lecherous and un-*

godly Huns. The noble virgins, to a virgin, preferred death to dishonor and their bones were for many centuries one of the major attractions of the city. Gibbon (Decline and Fall XXVII) points out that "the plebeian sisters have been defrauded of their equal honors" and rejects, with commendable indignation, an allusion in John Trithemius "to the children of these British virgins."

Of the exhibition of the bones there can be no doubt. Whether other anatomical remnants—presumably petrified —were actually displayed or whether this was merely a figment of Byron's presbyterian imagination is uncertain.

MAIDEN(S)

1 Men behove to take heed of maidens: for they be tender of complexion; small, pliant and fair of disposition of body; shamefast, fearful and merry. Touching outward disposition they be well nurtured, demure and soft of speech, and well aware of what they say: and delicate in their apparel. And for a woman is more meeker than a man, she weepeth sooner. And is more envious, and more laughing, and loving, and the malice of the soul is more in a woman than in a man. And she is of feeble kind, and she maketh more lesings, and is more shamefast, and more slow in working and in moving than is a man. [Bartholomaeus Anglicus (fl. 1230-1250): *De proprietatibus rerum* (first printed c. 1470) (trans. John de Trevisa; issued by Wynkyn de Worde in 1495)]

shamefast = *modest;* fearful = *timid;* maketh more lesings = *tells more lies*
For a combination of sophistication and simplicity, it would be hard to match this passage.

2 In maiden meditation, fancy-free. [Shakespeare: *A Midsummer Night's Dream* II.i.]
3 When maidens sue
Men give like gods.
[Shakespeare: *Measure for Measure* I.iv.]
4 Maidens, like moths, are ever caught
by glare.
[Byron: *Childe Harold* I.ix.]

MAIDS

5 "If seven maids with seven mops
Swept it for half a year,

Do you suppose," the Walrus said,
"That they could get it clear?"
"I doubt it," said the Carpenter,
And shed a bitter tear.
[Lewis Carroll: *Through the Looking-Glass,* IV, "The Walrus and the Carpenter"]

MAJESTY

6 Pre-eminence, and all the large effects
That troop with majesty.
[Shakespeare: *King Lear* I.i.]
7 With grave
Aspect he rose, and in his rising
seem'd
A pillar of state; deep on his front
engraven
Deliberation sat, and public care;
And princely counsel in his face yet
shone,
Majestic though in ruin.
[John Milton: *Paradise Lost* II. 300-305]

MAJOR GENERAL

8 I am the very pattern of a modern
major-general.
I've information vegetable, animal
and mineral;
I know the kings of England, and I
quote the fights historical,
From Marathon to Waterloo, in order categorical.
[W. S. Gilbert: *The Pirates of Penzance* I]

MAJORITY

9 The ninety and nine. [Matthew 18: 13]
10 Though the will of the majority is in all cases to prevail, that will, to be rightful, must be reasonable; the minority possess their equal right, which equal laws must protect, and to violate would be oppression. [Thomas Jefferson: *Inaugural Address,* March 4, 1801]
11 A government in which the majority rule in all cases cannot be based on justice, even as far as men understand it. [Thoreau: *Civil Disobedience*]
12 Any man more right than his neighbors constitutes a majority of one. [Thoreau: *Civil Disobedience*]
13 Decision by majorities is as much an expedient as lighting by gas. [W. E. Gladstone: speech in the House of Commons, 1858]

1 A minority may be right; a majority is always wrong. [Henrik Ibsen: *An Enemy of the People* IV]

2 The most dangerous foe to truth and freedom in our midst is the compact majority. Yes, it's the confounded, compact, liberal majority—that, and nothing else. [Henrik Ibsen: *An Enemy of the People* IV]

3 Hain't we got all the fools in town on our side? And ain't that a big enough majority in any town? [Mark Twain: *Adventures of Huckleberry Finn* XXVI]

4 No one can expect a majority to be stirred by motives other than ignoble. [Norman Douglas: *South Wind* X]

5 How a minority,
Reaching majority,
Seizing Authority,
Hates a minority!
[Leonard H. Robbins: *Minorities*]

6 By God, the majority in this country has no rights left that any minority feels bound to respect. [Attr. Colonel Robert McCormick]

MALICE

7 There is such malice in men as to rejoice in misfortunes and from another's woes to draw delight. [Terence: *Andria* IV.i.]

8 Nor set down aught in malice. [Shakespeare: *Othello* V.ii.]

9 Man's life is a warfare against the malice of men. [Gracián: *Oráculo Manual* 13]

10 Malice hath a strong memory. [Thomas Fuller (1608-1661): *A Pisgah-Sight of Palestine* II.iii.]

11 Much malice mingled with a little wit.
[Dryden: *The Hind and the Panther*]

MALICIOUS

12 The malicious have a dark happiness. [Victor Hugo: *Les Misérables* V.ix.]

MALIGNITY

13 Iago's soliloquy—the motive-hunting of a motiveless malignity—how awful it is! [Coleridge: *Notes on Othello*]
This remark of Coleridge's has become a commonplace of Shakespearean criticism. But it is hard to see what stronger motives Iago could have than those he

states: professional and sexual jealousy. He has been displaced in his profession by a man whom he despises, a man the action of the play shows to have been a weakling. Whether or not Othello had "done his office" between his sheets, as he avers, the charge is not as unsupported in the text as Coleridge seemed to think.

MAMMON

14 Ye cannot serve God and mammon. [Matthew 6:24]
mammon is the Greek form of the Aramaic word for riches. Here it means too great a love of wealth, cupidity. Milton personified Mammon as one of the fallen angels and the word is usually capitalized today as if it were a proper name.

15 Make to yourselves friends of the mammon of unrighteousness. [Luke 16:9]
mammon = riches
The very puzzling "moral" of the very puzzling parable of the Unjust Steward.

16 Mammon led them on—
Mammon, the least erected Spirit
that fell
From Heaven.
[John Milton: *Paradise Lost* I. 678-680]

17 How many Altars have been thrown down, and how many Theologies and heavenly Dreams have had their bottoms knocked out of them while He [Mammon] has sat there, a great God, golden and adorned, secure on His ummoved throne? [Logan Pearsall Smith: *Trivia*]

MAN: absurd and vile

18 We are not so full of evil as of emptiness and inanity. We are not so miserable as base and abject. [Montaigne: *Essays* I.i.]

19 God made him, and therefore let him pass for a man.
[Shakespeare: *The Merchant of Venice* I.ii.]

20 When a' was naked, he was, for all the world, like a forked radish with a head fantastically carved. [Shakespeare: *II Henry IV* III.ii.]

21 Though every prospect pleases,
And only man is vile.
[Reginald Heber: *From Greenland's Icy Mountains*]
Poor guilt-ridden man has long pro-

jected his impossible ideals into the brutes and then upbraided himself for being morally inferior to them. But man has no monopoly on "vileness." The stories of chivalry and self-sacrifice among the "lower" animals are fictions.

The most ruthless gangster is considerate and gentle, almost effete, compared to the skua. The basest gigolo maintains some independence, but the male bonellia spends most of his undignified life inside his female, attached to her excretory organs. The mayfly's eggs are liberated only by the rotting of her body —filial ingratitude! Young whelks are born in a sealed capsule, where their only food is one another—sibling rivalry! Divorcees extort alimony—but many female insects eat the male, in the very act of love! Homosexuality and prostitution, Zuckermann tells us, are common among baboons.

1 What is Man? A foolish baby,
   Daily strives, and fights, and frets;
   Demanding all, deserving nothing;
   One small grave is what he gets.
[Thomas Carlyle: *Cui Bono*]
2 All that I care to know is that a man is a human being—that is enough for me; he can't be any worse. [Mark Twain: *Concerning the Jews*]

MAN: brief and weak
3 Man that is born of a woman is of few days, and full of trouble. [Job 14:1]
4 Man that is born of a woman hath but a short time to live, and is full of misery. [*The Book of Common Prayer*, "The Burial of the Dead"]
5 He weaves, and is clothed with derision;
      Sows, and he shall not reap;
   His life is a watch or a vision
      Between a sleep and a sleep.
[Swinburne: *Atalanta in Calydon*]

MAN: definitions
6 Man is a biped without feathers. [Plato: *Politics*]
   That unfeather'd two-legged thing, a son.
      Dryden: Absalom and Achitophel I
   A two-legged animal without feathers.
      Thomas Carlyle: Past and Present I
7 Man is by nature a political animal. [Aristotle: *Politics* I]

8 Man is a reasoning animal. [Seneca: *Ad Lucilium* XLI]
9 Man is a social animal. [Seneca: *De beneficiis* VII.i.]
10 Is man no more than this? Consider him well . . . a poor, bare, forked animal. [Shakespeare: *King Lear* III.iv.]
11 Man is the shuttle, to whose winding
                               quest
   And passage through these looms
   God order'd motion, but ordain'd no
                                rest.
[Henry Vaughan: *Silex Scintillans*, "Man"]
12 Man is but a reed, the most feeble thing in nature, but he is a thinking reed. The entire universe need not arm itself to crush him. A vapor, a drop of water suffices to kill him. But if the universe were to crush him man would still be more noble than that which killed him, because he knows that he dies, and the advantage which the universe has over him: the universe knows nothing of this. [Pascal: *Pensées*]
13 Men are but children of a larger growth.
[Dryden: *All for Love* IV.i.]
14 Man is the only animal that laughs and weeps; for he is the only animal that is struck with the difference between what things are, and what they ought to be. [William Hazlitt: *Lectures on the English Comic Writers* I]
15 Man is a tool-using animal. [Thomas Carlyle: *Sartor Resartus* I]]
16 Man is the only animal that blushes. Or needs to. [Mark Twain: *Pudd'nhead Wilson's New Calendar*]
17 Man is a rational animal who always loses his temper when he is called upon to act in accordance with the dictates of reason. [Oscar Wilde: *The Critic as Artist*]
18 Man is an intelligence in servitude to his organs. [Aldous Huxley: *Themes and Variations*]

MAN: evolution and his animal
                               nature
19 For that which befalleth the sons of men befalleth beasts; even one thing befalleth them: as the one dieth, so dieth the other; yea, they have all one breath; so that a man hath no preeminence

above a beast: for all is vanity.

All go unto one place; all are of the dust, and all turn to dust again.

Who knoweth the spirit of man that goeth upward, and the spirit of the beast that goeth downward to the earth? [Ecclesiastes 3:19-21]

1 Man is of the earth, earthy. [I Corinthians 15:47]

2 When he is best, he is a little worse than a man; and when he is worst, he is little better than a beast. [Shakespeare: *The Merchant of Venice* I.ii.]

3 He [Dr. William Harvey, discoverer of the circulation of the blood] was wont to say that man was but a great mischievous baboon. [John Aubrey: *Brief Lives* I]

4 A spirit free, to choose for my own share,
What sort of flesh and blood I pleas'd to wear,
I'd be a dog, a monkey or a bear,
Or anything, but that vain animal
Who is so proud of being rational.
[John Wilmot, Earl of Rochester: *A Satyr Against Mankind*]

5 We drink without being thirsty and make love at any time; that is all that distinguishes us from other animals. [Beaumarchais: *Le Mariage de Figaro* II.xxi.]

6 Man has never understood how anthropomorphic he is. [Goethe: *Sprüche in Prosa*]

7 Arise and fly
The reeling Faun, the sensual feast;
Move upward, working out the beast,
And let the ape and tiger die.
[Tennyson: *In Memoriam* CXVIII]

8 There was an Ape in the days that were earlier;
Centuries passed, and his hair became curlier;
Centuries more gave a thumb to his wrist—
Then he was Man—and a Positivist.
[Mortimer Collins: *The Positivists*]

MAN: his glory

9 Man is the measure of all things. [Protagoras: in Diogenes Laertius's *Protagoras* IX.li.]

10 There are many wonderful things in nature, but the most wonderful of all is man. [Sophocles: *Antigone*]

11 What a piece of work is man! how noble in reason! how infinite in faculty! in form and moving how express and admirable! in action how like an angel! in apprehension how like a god! the beauty of the world! the paragon of animals! And, yet, to me, what is this quintessence of dust? man delights not me: no, nor woman neither. [Shakespeare: *Hamlet* II.ii.]

12 There is all Africa and her prodigies in us. [Sir Thomas Browne: *Religio Medici* I.xv.]

13 But man is a Noble Animal, splendid in ashes, and pompous in the grave, solemnizing Nativities and Deaths with equal lustre, nor omitting ceremonies of bravery, in the infamy of his nature. [Sir Thomas Browne: *Urn-Burial* V]

14 Glory to Man in the highest! for Man is the master of things.
[Swinburne: *Hymn of Man*]

MAN: his higher nature

15 God created man in his own image, in the image of God created he him; male and female created he them. [Genesis 1:27]

16 Thou hast made him a little lower than the angels. [Psalms 8:5]

17 I held it truth, with him who sings
To one clear harp in divers tones,
That men may rise on stepping-stones
Of their dead selves to higher things.
[Tennyson: *In Memoriam* I]

18 Forward, till you see the highest Human Nature is divine.
Follow Light, and do the Right—for man can half-control his doom—
Till you find the deathless Angel seated in the vacant tomb.
[Tennyson: *Locksley Hall Sixty Years After*]

19 Daily, with souls that cringe and plot, We Sinais climb and know it not.
[James Russell Lowell: *Vision of Sir Launfal*]

MAN: a man's a man

20 Mighty men which were of old, men of renown. [Genesis 6:4]

1 Be strong, and quit yourselves like men. [I Samuel 4:9]

2 A man after his own heart. [I Samuel 13:14]

3 One man is worth a hundred, and a hundred is not worth one. [John Florio: *Firste Fruites*]

4 His life was gentle, and the elements
So mix'd in him that Nature might stand up
And say to all the world, "This was a man!"
[Shakespeare: *Julius Caesar* V.v.]

5 He was a man, take him for all in all,
I shall not look upon his like again.
[Shakespeare: *Hamlet* I.ii.]

6 A combination and a form indeed,
Where every god did seem to set his seal,
To give the world assurance of a man.
[Shakespeare: *Hamlet* III.iv.]

7 'Tis not a year or two shows us a man.
[Shakespeare: *Othello* III.iv.]

8 Think you there was or might be such a man
As this I dreamt of?
[Shakespeare: *Antony and Cleopatra* V. ii.]

9 Man is a name of honour for a king.
[George Chapman: *Bussy d'Ambois* IV.i.]

10 A prince can mak a belted knight,
A marquis, duke, and a' that;
But an honest man's aboon his might,
Guid faith, he maunna fa' that!
[Burns: *For a' That and a' That*]

11 A man's a man for a' that.
[Burns: *For a' That and a' That*]

12 Though I've belted you and flayed you,
By the livin' Gawd that made you,
You're a better man than I am, Gunga Din!
[Kipling: *Gunga Din*]

MAN: the riddle of the world

13 What is man, that thou art mindful of him? and the son of man, that thou visitest him? [Psalms 8:4]

14 Surely, man is a wonderful, vain, diverse and wandering subject. [Montaigne: *Essays* I.i.]

15 They that deny a God destroy man's nobility; for certainly man is of kin to the beasts by his body; and if he be not of kin to God by his spirit, he is a base and ignoble creature. [Francis Bacon: *Of Atheism*]

16 What is a man,
If his chief good and market of his time
Be but to sleep and feed?
[Shakespeare: *Hamlet* IV.iv.]

17 Man, proud man,
Drest in a little brief authority,
Most ignorant of what he's most assur'd,
(His glassy essence), like an angry ape,
Plays such fantastic tricks before high Heaven,
As make the angels weep.
[Shakespeare: *Measure for Measure* II. ii.]

glassy essence = *the essential nature of man, which is like glass in that it reflects the image of others in its own, is fragile and liable to destruction.*

18 Man is man's A, B, C. There's none that can
Read God aright unless he first spell man.
[Francis Quarles: *Hieroglyphics of the Life of Man*]

19 God of our fathers, what is man!
That thou towards him with hand so various—
Or might I say contrarious?—
Temper'st thy providence through his short course.
[John Milton: *Samson Agonistes*]

20 Know then thyself, presume not God to scan;
The proper study of mankind is man.
Placed on this isthmus of a middle state,
A being darkly wise and rudely great:
With too much knowledge for the Sceptic side,
With too much weakness for the Stoic's pride,
He hangs between, in doubt to act or rest;
In doubt to deem himself a God or Beast;
In doubt his mind or body to prefer;
Born but to die, and reas'ning but to err.
[Alexander Pope: *An Essay on Man* II.i.]
scan = *scrutinize*

What a chimera, then, is man! What a novelty! What a monster, what a chaos,

*what a contradiction, what a prodigy!
Judge of all things, feeble worm of the
earth, depositary of truth, a sink of uncertainty and error, the glory and the
shame of the universe.*
          Pascal: Pensées *VIII*
          *Pope echoed the last phrase in his de-
          scription of Erasmus as "The glory of
          the priesthood and its shame."*

1 Before the beginning of years
   There came to the making of man
   Time, with a gift of tears;
   Grief, with a glass that ran;
   Pleasure, with pain for leaven;
   Summer, with flowers that fell;
   Remembrance fallen from heaven,
   And madness risen from hell;
   Strength without hands to smite;
   Love that endures for a breath;
   Night, the shadow of light,
   And life, the shadow of death.
[Swinburne: Chorus to *Atalanta in Caly-
don*]

MAN: a wolf to man
2 There is no animal in the world so
treacherous as man. [Montaigne: *Essays*
II.xii.]
3 I wonder men dare trust themselves
                with men.
[Shakespeare: *Timon of Athens* I.ii.]
4 Man is a wolf to man. [Robert Burton: *Anatomy of Melancholy* I.i.]
   The Latin is Lupus est homo homini.
   Plautus: Asinaria *II.iv. has:* Man is
   no man, but a wolf *(Lupus est homo,
   non homo).*
5 The greatest enemy to man is man,
who, by the devil's instigation, is a wolf,
a devil to himself and others. [Robert
Burton: *Anatomy of Melancholy* I.1.1]
6 Man's inhumanity to man
   Makes countless thousands mourn.
[Burns: *Man was Made to Mourn*]
7 If this belief from heaven be sent,
   If such be Nature's holy plan,
   Have I not reason to lament
   What man has made of man?
[Wordsworth: *Lines Written in Early
Spring*]
8 Man is simply the most formidable of
all the beasts of prey, and, indeed, the
only one that preys systematically on its
own species. [William James: *Remarks
at the Peace Banquet,* Oct. 7, 1904]

MAN: miscellaneous
9 Thou art the man. [II Samuel 12:7]
10 The true science and study of mankind is man. [Pierre Charron: Preface to
De la Sagesse I]
11 Man wants but little, nor that little
                long.
[Edward Young: *Night Thoughts* II]
12 A man has generally the good or ill
qualities which he attributes to mankind.
[William Shenstone: *Of Men and Manners*]
13 Why should a man desire in any way
   To vary from the kindly race of men,
   Or pass beyond the goal of ordinance
   Where all should pause, as is most
              meet for all?
[Tennyson: *Tithonus*]
14 From defending the common man we
pass on to exalting him. . . . Instead of
demanding only that the common man
may be given an opportunity to become
as uncommon as possible, we make his
commonness a virtue and, even in the
case of candidates for high office, we
sometimes praise them for being nearly
indistinguishable from the average man
in the street. [Joseph Wood Krutch: *Is
The Common Man Too Common?*]

MANACLES
15 I wander through each charter'd
                street,
   Near where the charter'd Thames
                does flow,
   And mark in every face I meet
   Marks of weakness, marks of woe.

   In every cry of every Man,
     In every Infant's cry of fear,
   In every voice, in every ban,
     The mind-forg'd manacles I hear.
[William Blake: *London*]

MANDALAY
16 On the road to Mandalay,
   Where the flyin'-fishes play,
   An' the dawn comes up like thunder
   Outer China 'crost the Bay!
[Kipling: *Mandalay*]
17 An' there ain't no buses runnin' from
           the Bank to Mandalay.
[Kipling: *Mandalay*]

MANHATTAN
18 My own Manhattan with spires, and

The sparkling and hurrying tides,
and the ships.
[Walt Whitman: *Leaves of Grass*, "When
Lilacs Last in the Door-yard
Bloom'd"]
1 That enfabled rock, that ship of life,
that swarming million-footed, tower-
masted, and sky-soaring citadel that
bears the magic name of the Island of
Manhattañ. [Thomas Wolfe: *The Web
and the Rock*]
"million-footed Manhattan."
—*Walt Whitman*

MAN-IN-THE-MOON
2 Quoth Pandarus, thou hast a full
great care
Lest that the churl may fall out of the
moon!
[Chaucer: *Troilus and Criseyde* I]
*As an expression of humorous contempt •
for far-fetched and unnecessary fears,
this is very good and our speech is the
poorer for the loss of it.*
*The man-in-the-moon was regarded
as a churl (a peasant) because the markings on the moon's face were seen, by
the medieval eye, as a man with a bundle of faggots on his back.*
3 "What is the news, good neighbor, I
pray?"
"They say a balloon has gone up to
the moon
And won't be back till a week from
today."
[Nursery rhyme: first printed, 1805]

MANKIND
4 How beauteous mankind is! O brave
new world
That has such people in it.
[Shakespeare: *The Tempest* V.i.]
*It is from this passage that Aldous Hux-
ley took the title for his novel of the
world of the future:* Brave New World.
5 The most pernicious race of little
odious vermin that nature ever suffered
to crawl upon the surface of the earth.
[Jonathan Swift: *Gulliver's Travels* II.
vi.]

MANNER
6 A man's natural manner best becomes
him. [Cicero: *De officiis* I]

TO THE MANNER BORN
7 . . . though I am native here
And to the manner born—it is a custom
More honored in the breach than the
observance.
[Shakespeare: *Hamlet* I.iv.]
*Horatio, visiting his old college friend,
Prince Hamlet, is walking with him on
the battlements of the castle of Elsinore
at midnight. Suddenly he hears a flourish of trumpets, a roll of drums and a
discharge of ordnance. He asks what it
means. Hamlet says that Claudius, the
king, is having a drinking party and that
each time his majesty drains a flagon
of wine the feat is hailed with this hulla-
baloo. Horatio asks if this is an old Dan-
ish custom. Hamlet says that it is and
then adds the lines above. Plainly manner = this manner of drinking and celebrating. But the over-knowing insist that
the phrase is to the manor born, that is
to high estate, to the aristocracy. This
is absurd. The text—the original text—
does not support it. And it would be
foolish for a prince—who would have a
score of manors—to insist that he was to
the manor born. Hamlet was born to
the crown and the purple.*

MANNERS
8 Evil communications corrupt good
manners.[I Corinthians 15:33]
9 Maners makyth man. [Motto of William of Wykeham (1324-1404), Bishop
of Winchester, Chancellor of England
and founder of Winchester College at
Winchester and New College at Oxford]
10 As laws are necessary that good manners may be preserved, so good manners
are necessary that laws may be maintained. [Machiavelli: *Discourses on Livy*
I]
11 I have often seen men unmannerly by
too much manners. [Montaigne: *Essays*
I.xiii.]
12 Not only each country, but every city,
yea and every vocation hath its own particular decorum. [Montaigne: *Essays* I.
xiii.]
13 For a man by nothing is so well be-
wrayd
As by his manners.
[Edmund Spenser: *The Faerie Queene*

VI.iii.]
bewrayed = *revealed*

1 If a man be gracious, and courteous to strangers, it shows he is a citizen of the world. [Francis Bacon: *Of Goodness*]

2 Men's evil manners live in brass:
their virtues
We write in water.
[Shakespeare: *Henry VIII* IV.ii.]
It was probably from this passage that Keats took the thought of his famous epitaph.

3 He that has more manners than he ought, is more a fool than he thought. [Thomas D'Urfey: *The Comical History of Don Quixote* II.i.]

4 Let us be very strange and well-bred: Let us be as strange as if we had been married a great while, and as well-bred as if we were not married at all. [William Congreve: *The Way of the World* IV.v.]

5 Everyone thinks himself well-bred. [Anthony Ashley Cooper, Lord Shaftesbury: *Characteristics* I.lxv.]
Support for Lord Shaftesbury's observation is that Samuel Johnson, whom most people considered a paragon of uncouthness, a bear in human form, thought himself "well-bred to a degree of needless scrupulosity."

6 Civility costs nothing and buys everything. [Lady Mary Wortley Montagu: Letter to the Countess of Bute, May 30, 1756]

7 Every man of any education would rather be called a rascal, than accused of deficiency in the *graces*. [Samuel Johnson: in Boswell's *Life*, May 1776]

8 Manners are of more importance than laws. Upon them, in a great measure, the laws depend. [Edmund Burke: *Letters on a Regicide Peace*]

9 The difference is, that in the days of old,
Men made the manners; manners
now make men.
[Byron: *Don Juan* XV.xxvi.]

10 Manners . . . a contrivance of wise men to keep fools at a distance. [Emerson: *Conduct of Life*, "Behavior"]

11 Her manners had not that repose
Which stamps the caste of Vere de Vere.
[Tennyson: *Lady Clara Vere de Vere*]

12 Good breeding consists in concealing how much we think of ourselves and how little we think of the other person. [Mark Twain: *Unpublished Diaries*]

13 The man who bites his bread, or eats
peas with a knife,
I look upon as a lost creature.
[W. S. Gilbert: *Ruddigore* I]
Many an honest citizen who knows, if only from the comic strips, that eating peas with a knife is as déclassé as it is difficult, will bridle on being told that his own comfortable, sensible custom of eating a slice of bread or toast is regarded by some as equally outré.

14 He combines the manners of a Marquis with the morals of a Methodist. [W. S. Gilbert: *Ruddigore* I]

15 The great secret is not having bad manners or good manners or any other particular sort of manners, but having the same manners for all human souls. [George Bernard Shaw: *Pygmalion* V]

MANSIONS

16 In my Father's house are many mansions. [John 14:2]
mansion, historically, means simply a dwelling place. Both Milton and Dryden refer to the "mansions" of hell. The application to the dwelling place of the lord of the manor, which has colored our present feeling about the word, was a specialized application. Still, though it may be more correct, it may be unwise to change the passage, as the Revised Standard has done, to "many rooms" or, as the New English Bible has done, to "many dwelling places." The true believer has been told for centuries there are "mansions" awaiting him and he's not in the mood for semantics.

17 Build thee more stately mansions, O
my soul,
As the swift seasons roll!
Leave thy low-vaulted past!
Let each new temple, nobler than the
last,
Shut thee from heaven with a dome
more vast,
Till thou at length art free,
Leaving thine outgrown shell by life's

unresting sea!
[O. W. Holmes: *The Chambered Nautilus*]

MARATHON

1 The mountains look on Marathon—
And Marathon looks on the sea;
And musing there an hour alone,
I dream'd that Greece might still
be free;
For standing on the Persians' grave,
I could not deem myself a slave.
[Byron: *The Isles of Greece*]

MARCH (MONTH)

2 March comes in like a lion and goes
out like a lamb. [Though this first appears in print in John Fletcher's *A Wife for a Month* II.i. (1624), it was probably an established proverb then.]
3 Like an army defeated
The snow hath retreated,
And now doth fare ill
On the top of the bare hill;
The Ploughboy is whooping—anon
—anon!
There's joy in the mountains;
There's life in the fountains;
Small clouds are sailing,
Blue sky prevailing;
The rain is over and gone.
[Wordsworth: *March*]

MARCHING

4 "Hurrah! hurrah! we bring the Jubilee!
Hurrah! Hurrah! the flag that makes
you free!"
So we sang the chorus from Atlanta
to the sea,
As we were marching through Georgia.
[Henry Clay Work: Chorus, *Marching Through Georgia*]

MARCUS AURELIUS

5 Marcus Aurelius was the ruler of the grandest of empires; and he was one of the best of men. [Matthew Arnold: *Essays in Criticism: First Series* X]

MARE'S NEST

6 He has found a mare's nest. [16th-century figure of speech: alluding to someone who is making a great to-do about something which seems an important discovery to him but is actually silly or nonexistent]

MARGERY DAW

7 See-saw, Margery Daw,
Jennie shall have a new master;
She shall have but a penny a day
Because she can't work any faster!
[Nursery rhyme: earliest known printed version, 1765]
This seems to be an old sawyer's rhyme—two men at either end of a two-handed saw taunting each other. Earlier versions have "Jacky" and "Tommy" unworthy of their hire.
Daw = a sluggard and Margery Daw seems to have been a country term for a slovenly woman. One version of the rhyme went: See-saw, Margery Daw,/ Sold her bed and lay upon straw;/ Was she not a dirty slut/ To sell her bed and lie upon dirt!

MARIGOLD

8 The sun-observing marigold.
[Francis Quarles: *The School of the Heart* XXX.v.]

MARINERS

9 He loves to talk with mariners
That come from a far countree.
[Coleridge: *The Rime of the Ancient Mariner* VII]

MARINES

10 Tell that to the marines—the sailors won't believe it. [Sir Walter Scott: *Redgauntlet* XIII (1824)]
Byron had listed the same statement in The Island (1823) and had referred to it as "an old saying." The marines were originally military police aboard a man-of-war and, of course, disliked and despised by the sailors as ignorant landlubbers. Apparently the mariners amused themselves by playing on the credulousness of the marines.

MARKET

11 If fools went not to market, bad wares would not be sold. [Old Spanish proverb]

MARK HOPKINS

12 A university is a student on one end

of a pine log and Mark Hopkins on the other. [Attr. James Garfield]

Garfield at a Williams College alumni dinner, in New York, 1871, was arguing that funds raised by the alumni should not go for buildings, but to hire a distinguished faculty. Hopkins, a teacher at Williams and for 36 years its president, held the same sentiments. Garfield had studied under Hopkins. His actual words were not quite as in the quotation, but the idea is the same.

MARLOWE

1 Neat Marlowe, bathed in the Thespian springs,
Had in him those brave translunar things
That the first poets had.
[Michael Drayton: *Of Poets and Poesie*]
2 Marlowe's mighty line.
[Ben Jonson: *To the Memory of My Beloved, the Author Mr. William Shakespeare*]
Jonson's verses were prefixed to the First Folio of Shakespeare's plays (1623).

MARRIAGE: definitions

3 Marriage is a covenant which hath nothing free but the entrance. [Montaigne: *Essays* I.xxvii.]
4 Marriage is a desperate thing. [John Selden: *Table Talk,* "Marriage"]
5 Marriage is the only adventure open to the timid. [Voltaire: *Pensées d'un Philosophe*]
6 It's an experiment / Frequently tried. [W. S. Gilbert: *The Gondoliers* II]
7 MARRIAGE. The state or condition of a community consisting of a master, a mistress, and two slaves, making in all, two. [Ambrose Bierce: *The Devil's Dictionary*]

MARRIAGE: delights and compensations

8 Marriage is a staid and serious pleasure . . . and it ought to be a voluptuousness somewhat circumspect and conscientious. [Montaigne: *Essays* I.xxix.]
9 Hail wedded love, mysterious law, true source
Of human offspring, sole propriety
In Paradise of all things common else.
By thee adulterous lust was driv'n

from men
Among the bestial herds to range; by thee,
Founded in reason, loyal, just, and pure,
Relations dear, and all the charities
Of father, son, and brother, first were known.
[John Milton: *Paradise Lost* IV. 750-757]
10 To church in the morning, and there saw a wedding in the church, which I have not seen many a day; and the young people so merry one with another! and strange to see what delight we married people have to see those poor fools decoyed into our condition, every man and woman gazing and smiling at them. [Samuel Pepys: *Diary,* Dec. 25, 1665]
11 Tho' marriage be a lottery in which there are a wondrous many blanks, yet there is one inestimable lot in which the only heaven on earth is written. [John Vanbrugh: *The Provok'd Wife* V.iv.]
12 The boredom of married life is inevitably the death of love whenever love has preceded marriage. Yet, at the same time, as a certain philosopher has pointed out, this boredom soon leads on, with people rich enough not to have to work, to a distaste for every kind of tranquil joy and creates, in all but those women who are cold and hard by nature, a predisposition to love. [Stendhal: *The Red and the Black* I.xxiii.]
13 The voice that breathed o'er Eden,
That earliest wedding-day,
The primal marriage blessing,
It hath not passed away.
[John Keble: *Holy Matrimony*]
14 A married man can do anything he likes if his wife don't mind. A widower can't be too careful. [G. B. Shaw: *Misalliance*]

MARRIAGE: happiness in

15 There may be good, but there are no pleasant marriages. [La Rochefoucauld: *Maxims*]
16 One year of Joy, another of Comfort, the rest of Content, make the married Life happy. [Thomas Fuller (1654-1734): *Gnomologia*]
17 No man is genuinely happy, married, who has to drink worse whiskey than he

used to drink when he was single. [H. L. Mencken: *Prejudices: Fourth Series*]

MARRIAGE: a holy and serious state
1 This is now bone of my bones, and flesh of my flesh. [Genesis 2:23]
2 Therefore shall a man leave his father, and his mother, and shall cleave unto his wife; and they shall be one flesh. [Genesis 2:24]
3 What therefore God hath joined together, let not man put asunder. [Mark 10:9]
4 Those whom God hath joined together let no man put asunder. [*The Book of Common Prayer*, "Solemnization of Matrimony"]
5 To have and to hold from this day forward, for better, for worse, for richer, for poorer, in sickness and in health, to love and to cherish, till death us do part. [*The Book of Common Prayer*, "The Solemnization of Matrimony"]
   This is the man's vow. "To obey" follows "to cherish" in the woman's vow.
   The service used to read "till death us depart," depart meaning "to part asunder." When the old word was forgotten, do was substituted for de to keep the rhythm.
6 More things belong to marriage than four bare legs in a bed. [John Heywood: *Proverbs* (1546)]
7 Marriage is the best state for man in general; and every man is a worse man in proportion as he is unfit for the married state. [Samuel Johnson: in Boswell's *Life*, March 22, 1776]
8 Marriage is a thing you've got to give your whole mind to. [Henrik Ibsen: *The League of Youth* IV]
9 What God hath joined together no man shall ever put asunder: God will take care of that. [G. B. Shaw: *Getting Married*]

MARRIAGE: January and May
10 And trewely, it is an heigh corage
   Of any man, that stapen is in age,
   To take a yong wyf.
[Chaucer: *The Merchant's Tale*]
   stapen = advanced
11 They that marry ancient people, merely in expectation to bury them, hang themselves, in hope that one will

come and cut the halter. [Thomas Fuller (1608-1661): *The Holy State, Profane State* III]
12 What can a young lassie, what shall a
                              young lassie,
   What can a young lassie do wi' an
                              auld man?
[Burns: *What Can a Young Lassie*]
   Burns's answer is that she can torment him to death and then, with his money, find a younger man.
13 An elderly person—a prophet by
                              trade—
   With his quips and tips
   On withered old lips,
   He married a young and a beautiful
                              maid;
   The cunning old blade,
   Though rather decayed,
   He married a beautiful, beautiful
                              maid.
[W. S. Gilbert: *Bab Ballads*, "The Precocious Baby"]

MARRIAGE: and love
14 A good marriage (if any there be) refuses the conditions of love and endeavors to present those of amity. [Montaigne: *Essays* III.v.]
15 Few men have wedded their sweethearts or mistresses but have come home by Weeping Cross and ere long repented their bargain. [Montaigne: *Essays* III.v.]
   "To come home by Weeping Cross" was a proverbial expression meaning "to suffer grievous disappointment or failure." Weeping Cross was a place-name that occurred in several English counties.
16 Let me not to the marriage of true
                              minds
   Admit impediments. Love is not love
   Which alters when it alteration finds.
[Shakespeare: *Sonnets* CXVI]
17 No happiness is like unto it, no love so great as that of man and wife, no such comfort as a sweet wife. [Robert Burton: *Anatomy of Melancholy* III.2.1.2]
18 Love is often a fruit of marriage. [Molière: *Sganarelle* I]
19 Where there's marriage without love, there will be love without marriage. [Benjamin Franklin: *Poor Richard's Almanack* (1734)]

MARRIAGE(S): made in Heaven
1 Marriages are made in Heaven.
[John Lyly: *Euphues and His England*]
2 Matches are made in heaven. [Robert Burton: *Anatomy of Melancholy* III.
2.5.5]
3 Hanging and marriage go by destiny.
[George Farquhar: *The Recruiting Officer* III.ii.]

MARRIAGE: man and wife
4 Tho' marriage makes man and wife
one flesh, it leaves 'em still two fools.
[William Congreve: *The Double Dealer*
II.iii.]
5 I know not which lives more unnatural lives,
Obeying husbands, or commanding
wives.
[Benjamin Franklin: *Poor Richard's Almanack* (1734)]
6 One fool at least in every married
couple. [Henry Fielding: *Amelia* IX.
iv.]
7 That moral centaur, man and wife.
[Byron: *Don Juan* V.clviii.]
*Byron's horrified publisher omitted the
stanza containing this expression and so
it did not appear in the first edition.
But Byron was angry and insisted that
it be restored in all subsequent editions.
Down from the waist they are Centaurs,
Though women all above.
But to the girdle do the gods inherit.*
King Lear *IV.vi. 126-8*
Byron's sin—a major one—was humor.
8 So they were married—to be the
more together—
And found they were never again so
much together,
Divided by the morning tea,
By the evening paper,
By children and tradesmen's bills.
[Louis MacNeice: *Les Sylphides*]

**MARRIAGE: marry in haste, repent
at leisure**
9 Thus grief still treads upon the heels
of pleasure,
Marry'd in haste, we may repent at
leisure.
[William Congreve: *The Old Bachelor*
V.iii.]
10 Such is the common process of mar-

riage. A youth and maiden, meeting by
chance or brought together by artifice,
exchange glances, reciprocate civilities,
go home, and dream of one another.
Having little to divert attention or diversify thought, they find themselves uneasy when they are apart and therefore
conclude that they shall be happy together. They marry and discover what
nothing but voluntary blindness before
had concealed: they wear out life in altercations, and charge nature with cruelty. [Samuel Johnson: *Rasselas* XXIX]
11 He will hold thee, when his passion
shall have spent its novel force,
Something better than his dog, a little
dearer than his horse.
[Tennyson: *Locksley Hall*]
12 Taking numbers into account, I
should think more mental suffering has
been undergone in the streets leading
from St. George's, Hanover Square, than
in the condemned cells of Newgate.
[Samuel Butler (1835-1902): *The Way
of All Flesh* XIII]
*St. George's, Hanover Square, was the
church in London for fashionable marriages. Newgate was London's most
famous prison.*
13 Marry in haste, and repeat at leisure.
[James Branch Cabell: *Jurgen* XXXVIII]

MARRIAGE: the negative view
14 Marriage, to tell the truth, is an evil,
but it is a necessary evil. [Menander:
Fragment]
15 What they do in heaven we are ignorant of; but what they do not we are
told expressly, that they neither marry
nor are given in marriage. [Jonathan
Swift: *Thoughts on Various Subjects*]
*For in the resurrection they neither
marry, nor are given in marriage.*
Matthew 22:30
*For when they shall rise from the dead,
they neither marry, nor are given in
marriage.* Mark 12:25
*They which shall be accounted worthy
to obtain that world, and the resurrection from the dead, neither marry, nor
are given in marriage.* Luke 20:35
16 Every man plays the fool once in his
life, but to marry is playing the fool all
one's life long. [William Congreve:

The Old Bachelor III]

1 It is so far from natural for a man and a woman to live in the state of marriage, that we find all the motives which they have for remaining in that connection, and the restraints which civilized society imposes to prevent separation, are hardly sufficient to keep them together. [Samuel Johnson: in Boswell's *Life* (March 31, 1772)]

2 A system could not well have been devised more studiously hostile to human happiness than marriage. [Shelley: *Notes to Queen Mab*]

3 Don't. [Mr. Punch's advice to young men about to be married (Vol. VIII, 1845); probably by Henry Mayhew]

4 When two people are under the influence of the most violent, most insane, most delusive, and most transient of passions, they are required to swear that they will remain in that excited, abnormal, and exhausting condition continuously until death do them part. [G. B. Shaw: Preface to *Getting Married*]

5 Needless, stupid marriages . . . made out of sheer boredom and idleness. [Anton Chekhov: "The Man in a Shell"]

MARRIAGE: proper time and place

6 The age of eighteen is the best time for women to marry, and the age of thirty-seven, or a little less, for men. [Aristotle: *Politics* VII]

7 For a young man, not yet; for an old man, never. [Diogenes: in Diogenes Laertius's *Diogenes* LIV]

Diogenes's answer when asked what was the proper time to get married.

8 Marry your son when you will; your daughter when you can. [George Herbert: *Jacula Prudentum*]

marry = *marry off*

9 Better wed over the mixon than over the moor. [Thomas Fuller (1608-1661): *Worthies: Cheshire*]

mixon = *compost heap*

The Cheshire proverb which Fuller quotes states that it is better to marry someone who lives near than someone from afar.

Hesiod (about 800 B.C.) had offered the same advice. It seems to be, like much good advice, totally unnecessary, however. When the ardor of matrimony

is upon men, they are too splendidly impatient to go far.

A study made in 1948 revealed that the median distance from home which males of Columbus, Ohio, traversed in search of a mate was 13 blocks. Men over 35 averaged less than 7 blocks. Whether they were decrepit, desperate, cynical or fortunate, the study did not say. A similar study revealed similar eagerness or apathy or plenitude of pulchritude in Duluth.

10 He's a fool that marries at Yule,
For when the corn's to shear the
              bairn's to bear.

[James Kelly: *Scottish Proverbs* (1721)]

corn = *wheat, oats, rye;* bairn = *child*

The custom of June weddings was not based solely on the inevitable consequence of spring courtings or on the desirability of good weather for the honeymoon; the child born of a June wedding would come in March and the mother would be fully recovered and ready for field work before the next harvest.

11 I believe it will be found that those who marry late are best pleased with their children, and those who marry early with their partners. [Samuel Johnson: *Rasselas* XXIX]

MARRIAGE: regrets, dangers and
              woes

12 A young man married is a man
              that's marr'd.

[Shakespeare: *All's Well That Ends Well* II.iii.]

13   O curse of marriage!
That we can call these delicate crea-
              tures ours,
And not their appetites. I had rather
              be a toad,
And live upon the vapour of a dun-
              geon,
Than keep a corner in the thing I
              love
For others' uses.

[Shakespeare: *Othello* III.iii.]

14 Suspicion, Discontent, and Strife,
Come in for Dowrie with a Wife.

[Robert Herrick: *Single Love More Secure*]

15 I fear that in the election of a wife, As in a project of war, to err but

Is to be undone for ever.
[Thomas Middleton: *Anything for a Quiet Life* I.i.]
1 When a couple are newly married, the first month is honeymoon, or smick smack: the second is, hither and thither: the third is thwick thwack: the fourth, the devil take them that brought thee and I together. [John Ray: *English Proverbs* (1670)]
2 To take a wife merely as an agreeable and rational companion will commonly be found to be a grand mistake. [Lord Chesterfield: *Letters to His Son*, October 12, 1765]
3 What can be expected but disappointment and repentance from a choice made in the immaturity of youth, in the ardor of desire, without judgment, without foresight, without inquiry after conformity of opinions, similarity of manners, rectitude of judgment, or purity of sentiment? [Samuel Johnson: *Rasselas* XXIX]
> But how else except under the influence of just such a combination of carelessness, infatuation and delusion would such a choice ever be made? The biological and the social purposes are at variance.

4 I would advise no man to marry who is not likely to propagate understanding. [Samuel Johnson, in Mrs. Piozzi's *Anecdotes of the late Samuel Johnson*]
> The gentleman to whom Johnson returned this answer, when he had asked the sage if he would advise him to get married, was Sir John Lade. He was a foolish young man who had inherited a fortune and insisted on thrusting himself into the conversation. He had badgered Johnson with a number of inane questions and Johnson's patience had run out. Later, however, he tried to make amends.

5 It doesn't much signify whom one marries, for one is sure to find next morning that it was someone else. [Samuel Rogers: *Table Talk*]
6 Don't try to Marry an entire Family or it may work out that way. [George Ade: *The Syndicate Lover*]
7 There's post-operative depression, post-partum depression, post-graduate depression and post-marital depression (sometimes called "the honeymoon"). [Eric Hodgins: *Episode*]
> Mr. Hodgins credits the observation to "a sustaining friend."

MARRIAGE: second marriage
8 A little month, or ere those shoes were old
With which she followed my poor father's body. . . .
She married. O, most wicked speed, to post
With such dexterity to incestuous sheets!
[Shakespeare: *Hamlet* I.ii.]
9 . . . they'll remarry
Ere the worm pierce your winding-sheet, ere the spider
Make a thin curtain for your epitaphs.
[John Webster: *The White Devil* V.vi.]
10 The triumph of hope over experience. [Samuel Johnson: comment on a second marriage; quoted in Boswell's *Life of Johnson*, from notes supplied by the Rev. Dr. Maxwell (1770)]
11 You know, my Friends, with what a brave Carouse
I made a Second Marriage in my house;
Divorced old barren Reason from my Bed,
And took the Daughter of the Vine to Spouse.
[*Rubáiyát of Omar Khayyám* (trans. Edward FitzGerald)]
12 For I'm not so old, and not so plain,
And I'm quite prepared to marry again.
[W. S. Gilbert: *Iolanthe* I]

MARRIAGE: and single life
13 The best works, and of greatest merit for the public, have proceeded from the unmarried or childless men. [Francis Bacon: *Of Marriage and Single Life*]
14 One was never married, and that's his hell; another is, and that's his plague. [Robert Burton: *The Anatomy of Melancholy* I.2.4.7]
15 I would be married, but I'd have no wife,
I would be married to a single life.
[Richard Crashaw: *On Marriage*]

1 [The unmarried] dream away their time without friendship, without fondness, and are driven to rid themselves of the day, for which they have no use, by childish amusements or vicious delights. They act as beings under the constant sense of some known inferiority, that fills their minds with rancor and their tongues with censure. They·are peevish at home and malevolent abroad; and, as the outlaws of human nature, make it their business and their pleasure to disturb that society which debars them from its privileges. [Samuel Johnson: *Rasselas* XXVI]
2 Celibates replace sentiments by habits. [George Moore: *Impressions*]
   See also CELIBACY

MARRIAGE: without love
3 An unwilling woman given to a man in marriage is not his wife but his enemy. [Plautus: *Stichus* I.ii.]
4 Better to sit up all night than to go to bed with a dragon. [Jeremy Taylor: *Holy Living*]
5 I believe marriages would in general be as happy, and often more so, if they were all made by the Lord Chancellor, upon a due consideration of the characters and circumstances, without the parties having any choice in the matter. [Samuel Johnson: in Boswell's *Life*, March 22, 1776]
6 Men marry because they are tired; women because they are curious. Both are disappointed. [Oscar Wilde: *A Woman of No Importance* III]
7 Her beauty was sold for an old man's gold—
   She's a bird in a gilded cage.
[Arthur J. Lamb: *A Bird in a Gilded Cage*]
8 Married women are kept women, and they are beginning to find it out. [Logan Pearsall Smith: *Afterthoughts*]

MARRIAGE: miscellaneous
9 Marriage may be compared to a cage: the birds outside despair to get in and those within despair to get out. [Montaigne: *Essays* III.v.]
10 'Tis safest in matrimony to begin with a little aversion. [Richard Brinsley Sheridan: *The Rivals* I.ii.]

11 Nothing is to me more distasteful than that entire complacency and satisfaction which beam in the countenances of a new-married couple. [Charles Lamb: *The Behaviour of Married People*]
12 All comedies are ended by a marriage. [Byron: *Don Juan* III.ix.]
13 When you're a married man, Samivel, you'll understand a good many things as you don't understand now; but vether it's worth while goin' through so much to learn so little, as the charity boy said ven he got to the end of the alphabet, is a matter o' taste. [Dickens: *Pickwick Papers* XXVII]
14 In married life three is company and two none. [Oscar Wilde: *The Importance of Being Earnest* I]
15 Marriage is popular because it combines the maximum of temptation with the maximum of opportunity. [G. B. Shaw: *Maxims for Revolutionists*]
16 If it were not for the Presents, an Elopement would be preferable. [George Ade: *The General Manager of the Love Affair*]
17 It is better to marry than to burn. [I Corinthians 7:9]
18 If one will not another will; so are all maidens married. [John Heywood: *Proverbs* (1546)]
19 Benedick the married man. [Shakespeare: *Much Ado About Nothing* I.i.]
20 Many a good hanging prevents a bad marriage. [Shakespeare: *Twelfth Night* I.v.]
21 A man may woo where he will, but he will wed where his hap is. [David Ferguson: *Scottish Proverbs* (1641)]
   hap = *chance, opportunity*
      It is in this sense that "marriages are made in heaven."
22 His designs were strictly honorable, as the phrase is; that is, to rob a lady of her fortune by way of marriage. [Henry Fielding: *Tom Jones* XI. iv.]
23 Marriage resembles a pair of shears, so joined that they can not be separated; often moving in opposite directions, yet always punishing anyone who comes between them. [Sydney Smith: in Lady Holland's *Memoir* I.xi.]
24 Remember, it's as easy to marry a rich woman as a poor woman. [W. M. Thackeray: *Pendennis* XXVIII]

1 Reader, I married him. [Charlotte Brontë: *Jane Eyre* XXXVIII]

2 No woman ever married into a family above herself that did not try to make all the mischief she could in it. [William Hazlitt: *Works*, 1930-34. ed. Howe, Vol. XVII]

MARRIED LOVE

3 An old man, like a spider, can never make love without beating his own deathwatch. [C. C. Colton: *Lacon* (1820)]

In some species of spiders, the female devours the male after their mating. This is not invariable, and the allured but terrified male tries in various ways to escape his fate. Some wrap a dead fly elaborately in a piece of leaf and hope to have their way and getaway while she is unwrapping the gift. Others try to catch young females and rope them down helplessly until they mature. Human adolescents don't have all the problems.

4 Romances paint at full length people's wooings,
But only give a bust of marriages:
For no one cares for matrimonial cooings.
[Byron: *Don Juan* III. viii.]
See LOVE: and marriage

MARTLET

5 This guest of summer,
The temple-haunting martlet, does approve,
By his lov'd mansionry, that the heaven's breath
Smells wooingly here; no jutty, frieze,
Buttress, nor coign of vantage, but this bird
Hath made his pendent bed, and procreant cradle:
Where they most breed and haunt, I have observ'd,
The air is delicate.
[Shakespeare: *Macbeth* I.vi.]

MARTYR(S)

6 The blood of the martyrs is the seed of the Church. [Tertullian: *Apologeticus* XXXIX. i.]

7 There's no religion so irrational but can boast its martyrs. [Joseph Glanvill: *The Vanity of Dogmatizing* XIV]

8 I am very fond of truth, but not at all of martyrdom. [Voltaire: Letter to Jean Le Rond d'Alembert, February 1776]

9 He that dies a martyr proves that he is not a knave, but by no means that he is not a fool. [C. C. Colton: *Lacon* I]

10 Martyrdom has always been a proof of the intensity, never of the correctness of a belief. [Arthur Schnitzler: *Buch der Sprüche und Bedenken*]

11 To die for an idea is to place a pretty high price upon conjectures. [Anatole France: *The Revolt of the Angels*]

MARY(S)

12 Yestre'en the queen had four Marys,
This night she'll hae but three:
There was Mary Beaton, and Mary Seaton,
Mary Carmichael, and me.
[Anon: *The Queen's Marys*]

13 I have a passion for the name of "Mary,"
For once it was a magic sound to me,
And still it half calls up the realms of fairy,
Where I beheld what never was to be.
[Byron: *Don Juan* V.iv.]

MASSES

14 . . . more than sixscore thousand persons that cannot discern between their right hand and their left hand; and also much cattle. [Jonah 4:11]

15 The multitude, who require to be led, still hate their leaders. [William Hazlitt: *Characteristics*]

16 It is an easy and vulgar thing to please the mob . . . but to improve them is a work fraught with difficulty, and teeming with danger. [C. C. Colton: *Lacon*]

17 Bow, bow, ye lower middle classes!
Bow, bow, ye tradesmen, bow, ye masses.
[W. S. Gilbert: *Iolanthe* I]

MASTER(S)

18 No man can serve two masters. [Matthew 6:24]

19 We cannot all be masters, nor all masters
Cannot be truly followed.

[Shakespeare: *Othello* I.i.]
1 I believe it will be absolutely necessary that you should prevail on our future masters to learn their letters. [Robert Lowe, Viscount Sherbrooke (1811-1892): speaking in Parliament on the passing of the Reform Bill, extending the franchise, in 1867]
> *Usually quoted as "We must educate our masters," and frequently attr. Disraeli.*

2 It matters not how strait the gate,
  How charged with punishments the
                                    scroll,
  I am the master of my fate:
  I am the captain of my soul.
[W. E. Henley: *Invictus*]

MATE
3 There swims no goose so grey, but
                              soon or late
  She finds some honest gander for her
                                    mate.
[Chaucer: Prologue to *The Wife of Bath's Tale* (trans. Alexander Pope)]
4 One man's mate is another man's passion. [Eugene Healy: *Mr. Sandeman Loses His Life* (1940)]
> *"One man's mate is another man's poison"—a 20th-century Reno-vation.*

MATRIMONY
5 The critical period in matrimony is breakfast-time. [A. P. Herbert: *Uncommon Law*]

MATTER
6 More matter with less art.
[Shakespeare: *Hamlet* II.ii]
7 We stood talking for some time together of Bishop Berkeley's ingenious sophistry to prove the non-existence of matter. . . . I shall never forget the alacrity with which Johnson answered, striking his foot with mighty force against a large stone, till he rebounded from it—"I refute it thus." [James Boswell: in his *Life of Johnson*, Aug. 6, 1763]

MATTER-OF-FACTNESS
8 Talk to him of Jacob's ladder, and he would ask the number of the steps.
[Douglas Jerrold: *A Matter-of-Fact Man*]

MATURITY
9 Such as are of Riper Years. [*The*

Book of Common Prayer, "Public Baptism"]

MAXIM(S)
10 A philosophical Quaker full of mean and thrifty maxims. [Keats: Letter to G. Keats, October 14, 1818]
11 Nothing is so useless as a general maxim. [Macaulay: *Machiavelli*]
12 With a little hoard of maxims preaching down a daughter's heart.
[Tennyson: *Locksley Hall*]

MAY (MONTH)
13 He was as fressh as is the monthe of
                                      May.
[Chaucer: Prologue to *The Canterbury Tales*]
14 Rough winds do shake the darling
                              buds of May.
[Shakespeare: *Sonnets* XVIII]
15 Love, whose month is ever May.
[Shakespeare: *Love's Labour's Lost* IV. iii.]
16 The chestnut casts his flambeaux, and
                              the flowers
  Stream from the hawthorn on the
                              wind away,
  The doors clap to, the pane is blind
                              with showers.
  Pass me the can, lad; there's an end
                              of May.
[A. E. Housman: *Last Poems* IX]
17 May will be fine next year as like as
                                    not:
  Oh, ay, but then we shall be twenty-
                                  four.
[A. E. Housman: *Last Poems* IX]

MAY QUEEN
18 You must wake and call me early, call
                    me early, mother dear;
  Tomorrow 'ill be the happiest time
                    of all the glad New Year—
  Of all the glad New Year, mother, the
                    maddest, merriest day;
  For I'm to be Queen o' the May,
                                  mother,
  I'm to be Queen o' the May.
[Tennyson: *The May Queen*]

MEANDERING
19 Five miles meandering with a mazy
                                    motion.
[Coleridge: *Kubla Khan*]

MEANING

1 Where more is meant than meets the
ear.
[John Milton: *Il Penseroso*]

2 And he, who now to sense, now nonsense leaning,
Means not, but blunders round about
a meaning.
[Alexander Pope: *Epistle to Dr. Arbuthnot*]

3 God and I both knew what it meant
once; now God alone knows. [Friedrich
Klopstock: when asked the meaning of
one of his poems; as quoted in Cesare
Lombroso's *The Man of Genius*]
*Often attr. Robert Browning, when asked
the meaning of* Sordello.

4 "When I use a word," Humpty
Dumpty said, in rather a scornful tone,
"it means just what I choose it to mean
—neither more nor less." [Lewis Carroll: *Through the Looking-Glass* VI]

MEANS

5 How oft the sight of means to do ill
deeds
Make deeds ill done!
[Shakespeare: *King John* IV.ii.]

MEAT

6 Out of the eater came forth meat,
and out of the strong came forth sweetness. [Judges 14:14]

MEAT: one man's

7 What is food to one man may be
sharp poison to others. [Lucretius: *De
rerum natura* IV]

8 One man's meat is another man's
poison. [Oswald Dykes: *English Proverbs* (1709)]
See MATE

MEDDLESOME MATTY

9 One ugly trick has often spoiled
The sweetest and the best;
Matilda, though a pleasant child,
One ugly trick possessed.
[Ann Taylor: *Meddlesome Matty*]
*Note the rhyme: spoiled/ child. Some
would think this an ugly trick of speech.
Others might think the same of Grand-
mamma's habit of taking snuff, though
our grandfathers saw fault only in Ma-
tilda's prying into the snuff box when
Grandmamma was away.*

MEDDLING

10 It is an honour for a man to cease
from strife: but every fool will be meddling. [Proverbs 20:3]

MEDES AND PERSIANS

11 Let it be written among the laws of
the Persians and the Medes, that it be
not altered. [Esther 1:19]

12 According to the law of the Medes
and Persians, which altereth not. [Dan-
iel 6:8]

MEDICINE

13 The arts that promise to keep our
body and mind in good health promise
much, but none perform less what they
promise. [Montaigne: *Essays* III.xiii.]

14 Throw physic to the dogs; I'll none
of it.
[Shakespeare: *Macbeth* V.iii.]
physic = medicines in general

15 Throw out opium, which the Creator
himself seems to prescribe, for we often
see the scarlet poppy growing in the
cornfields, as if it were foreseen that
wherever there is hunger to be fed there
must also be pain to be soothed; throw
out a few specifics which our art did not
discover, and is hardly needed to apply;
throw out wine, which is a food, and
the vapors which produce the miracle of
anesthesia, and I firmly believe that if
the whole *materia medica, as now used,*
could be sunk to the bottom of the sea, it
would be all the better for mankind—
and all the worse for the fishes. [Oliver
Wendell Holmes: *Address to the Massachusetts Medical Society,* May 30, 1860]

16 Medicine, the only profession that
labours incessantly to destroy the reason
for its own existence. [James Bryce: in
an address at a dinner for General W. C.
Gorgas, March 23, 1914.]

MEEK

17 Now the man Moses was very meek,
above all the men which were upon the
face of the earth. [Numbers 12:3]
*A difficult passage, since the statement
—presumably written by Moses himself—doesn't fit the facts within any
known meaning of the word meek.
Moses killed the Egyptian taskmaster,
he destroyed Pharaoh's host, he smashed*

the tablets of the Ten Commandments, he literally forced the golden calf down the throats of its worshippers, he instigated the slaying of 3,000 Israelites as a disciplinary measure, and he smote the rock in Horeb—all of which is hard to reconcile with meekness.

In 1941, speaking before the annual meeting of the Oriental Society, Professor O. R. Sellers, Professor of Old Testament at the Presbyterian Theological Seminary in Chicago, offered a solution. He pointed out that meek *here is a mistranslation of a Hebrew word that would be better rendered as* vexed, bad-tempered, irritable. *The* New Yorker *thought that this might throw light on another puzzling passage: The meek . . . shall inherit the earth.*

1 The meek shall inherit the earth. [Psalms 37:11]
2 Blessed are the meek, for they shall inherit the earth. [Matthew 5:5]
3 And of his port as meke as is a mayde. [Chaucer: Prologue to *The Canterbury Tales*]
4 Let the meek inherit the earth—they have it coming to them. [James Thurber, *Life,* March 14, 1960]

MEEKNESS

5 Meekness takes injuries like pills, not chewing, but swallowing them down. [Sir Thomas Browne: *Christian Morals* III.xii.]

MEETING

6 *First Witch.* When shall we three meet again?
In thunder, lightning, or in rain?
Second Witch. When the hurlyburly's done,
When the battle's lost and won.
[Shakespeare: *Macbeth* I.i.]
7 Stay for me there; I will not fail
To meet thee in that hollow vale.
And think not much of my delay;
I am already on the way,
And follow thee with all the speed
Desire can make, or sorrows breed.
[Henry King: *The Exequy*]
8 If I should meet thee after long years,
How should I greet thee?—
With silence and tears.
[Byron: *When We Two Parted*]

MELANCHOLY

9 I am as melancholy as a gib cat. [Shakespeare: *I Henry IV* I.ii.]
gib = Gilbert
What we call a Tom cat used to be called a Gilbert cat.
10 I can suck melancholy out of a song as a weasel sucks eggs. [Shakespeare: *As You Like It* II.v.]
11 Under the shade of melancholy boughs,
Lose and neglect the creeping hours of time.
[Shakespeare: *As You Like It* II.vii.]
12 My cue is villainous melancholy, with a sigh like Tom o' Bedlam. [Shakespeare: *King Lear* I.ii.]
Tom o' Bedlam—*Bedlam (old pronunciation of Bethlehem) was the hospital in Elizabethan London for the insane. Madness was believed to be caused by demoniac possession and by a sort of willful obstinacy on the part of the possessed. The commonest therapy was whipping and starvation and the patients were usually shackled and given only straw to lie on. No wonder they were villainously melancholy. Those that were thought to be not too dangerous were sometimes allowed to wander forth and beg. These were the Tom o' Bedlams.*
13 Aristotle said . . . melancholy men of all others are most witty. [Robert Burton: *Anatomy of Melancholy* I.3.1.3]
14 If there be a hell upon earth it is to be found in a melancholy man's heart. [Robert Burton: *Anatomy of Melancholy* I.4.1.2]
15 Hence loathèd melancholy,
Of Cerberus and blackest Midnight born.
[John Milton: *L'Allegro*]
16 As melancholy as an unbraced drum. [Susannah Centlivre: *The Wonder* II.i.]
17 And melancholy marked him for her own.
[Thomas Gray: *Elegy Written in a Country Churchyard,* "Epitaph"]
18 As high as we have mounted in delight
In our dejection do we sink as low.
[Wordsworth: *Resolution and Independence*
19 I heard a thousand blended notes,

While in a grove I sat reclined,
In that sweet mood when pleasant
thoughts
Bring sad thoughts to the mind.
[Wordsworth: *Lines Written in Early Spring*]

1 Yet oft-times in his maddest mirthful
mood
Strange pangs would flash along
Childe Harold's brow.
[Byron: *Childe Harold* I.viii.]

2 The melancholy days are come, the
saddest of the year,
Of wailing winds, and naked woods,
and meadows brown and sere.
[William Cullen Bryant: *The Death of the Flowers*]

3 She dwells with Beauty—Beauty that
must die;
And Joy, whose hand is ever at his
lips
Bidding adieu; and aching Pleasure
nigh,
Turning to poison while the bee-
mouth sips.
[Keats: *Ode on Melancholy*]
The antecedent of She *is* Melancholy.

4 There's not a string attuned to mirth
But has its chord in melancholy.
[Thomas Hood: *Ode to Melancholy*]

5 A feeling of sadness and longing
That is not akin to pain,
And resembles sorrow only
As the mist resembles the rain.
[Longfellow: *The Day Is Done*]

6 She only said, "My life is dreary,
He cometh not," she said;
She said, "I am aweary, aweary,
I would that I were dead."
[Tennyson: *Mariana*]

7 The chronic melancholy which is taking hold of the civilized races with the
decline of belief in a beneficent power.
[Thomas Hardy: *Tess of the D'Urbervilles* XVIII]

8 Jest a-wearyin' fer you—
All the time a-feelin' blue.
[Frank L. Stanton: *Wearyin' fer You*]

MELANCHOLY: its pleasures
9 There's naught in this life sweet,
If man were wise to see 't,
But only melancholy;
O sweetest Melancholy!
[John Fletcher: *The Nice Valour* III]

10 All my joys to this are folly,
Naught so sweet as melancholy.
[Robert Burton: *Anatomy of Melan-
choly,* "The Author's Abstract"]

11 These pleasures, Melancholy, give;
And I with thee will choose to live.
[John Milton: *Il Penseroso*]

12 We look before and after,
And sigh for what is not,
Our sincerest laughter
With some pain is fraught:
Our sweetest songs are those that tell
of saddest thought.
[Shelley: *To a Skylark*]

13 Ay, in the very temple of delight
Veiled Melancholy has her sovran
shrine,
Though seen of none save him whose
strenuous tongue
Can burst Joy's grape against his
palate fine;
His soul shall taste the sadness of her
might,
And be among her cloudy trophies
hung.
[Keats: *Ode on Melancholy*]
*Keats took this, the central idea of his
famous ode, from a reference in Burton's* Anatomy of Melancholy, *in which
Burton quotes Macrobius to the effect
that the rites of the goddess of Melancholy (Angerona Dea, the Goddess of
Silence and the Releaser from Secret
Grief) were celebrated in "the Calends
of January . . . in the temple of Vo-
lupia, the Goddess of Pleasure."*

MELODIES
14 Heard melodies are sweet, but those
unheard
Are sweeter; therefore, ye soft pipes,
play on;
Not to the sensual ear, but, more endear'd,
Pipe to the spirit ditties of no
tone.
[Keats: *Ode on a Grecian Urn*]

MELTING POT
15 Here (in America) individuals of all
nations are melted into a new race of
men. [Crèvecoeur: *Letters from an American Farmer* III (1782)]

16 America is God's Crucible, the great
Melting-Pot where all the races of Eu-

rope are melting and re-forming! [Israel Zangwill: *The Melting Pot* I]

MEMORY

1 It is commonly seen by experience that excellent memories do often accompany weak judgments. [Montaigne: *Essays* I.ix.]

2   All these woes shall serve
For sweet discourses in our time to
              come.
[Shakespeare: *Romeo and Juliet* III.v.]

3 Memory, the warder of the brain.
[Shakespeare: *Macbeth* I.vii.]

4 'Tis sweet to thinke on what was
           hard t' endure.
[Robert Herrick: *Satisfaction for Suffering*]

5 Everyone complains of his lack of memory, but nobody of his want of judgment. [La Rochefoucauld: *Maxims*]
Many people seem to think that their humorous insistence on having an extraordinarily poor memory somehow confers a distinction upon them.

6 That which is bitter to endure may be sweet to remember. [Thomas Fuller (1654-1734): *Gnomologia*]

7 The true art of memory is the art of attention. [Samuel Johnson: *The Idler* No. 74]
There is a charming illustration of this in the 4th section of the First book of The Life of Benvenuto Cellini. Cellini tells us that when he was about five his father was, one washday, playing a viol and singing alone "beside a good fire of oak logs" when he espied a salamander among the flames. Perceiving instantly the importance of what he saw, he had his children summoned, pointed the spirit out to them "and gave me a great box on the ears, which caused me to howl and weep. . . . Then he pacified me good-humouredly, and spoke as follows: 'My dear little boy, I am not striking you for any wrong that you have done, but only to make you remember that that lizard which you see in the fire is a salamander, a creature which has never been seen before by anyone of whom we have credible information.' So saying, he kissed me and gave me some pieces of money." Mod-
ern pedagogy would probably support Giovanni Cellini's principle but oppose the particular technique of its application. But, anyway, it worked; Benvenuto did remember the salamander and, indeed, the whole scene, viol, washday and all.

In the middle ages, when literacy among laymen was rare, various practices were carried out to insure memory of certain agreements. On one occasion when a nobleman gave a certain piece of land to a monastery his young son, fully clad, was suddenly thrown into a pond so that he would remember the event and—granted he was fished out and didn't die of pneumonia—at his majority honor the grant.

8 Time whereof the memory of man runneth not to the contrary. [William Blackstone: *Commentaries on the Laws of England* I]

9 What peaceful hours I once enjoy'd!
  How sweet their mem'ry still!
But they have left an aching void,
  The world can never fill.
[William Cowper: *Olney Hymns* I]

10 The Right Honorable gentleman is indebted to his memory for his jests and to his imagination for his facts. [Richard Brinsley Sheridan: Speech in reply to Mr. Dundas]
In Thomas Moore: Life of Sheridan *(1825), Vol. 2, p. 471.*

11 The thought of our past years in me
           doth breed
Perpetual benediction.
[Wordsworth: *Intimations of Immortality*]

12 Oft in the stilly night,
  Ere Slumber's chain has bound me.
Fond Memory brings the light
  Of other days around me;
    The smiles, the tears,
    Of boyhood's years,
  The words of love then spoken;
    The eyes that shone
    Now dimmed and gone.
  The cheerful hearts now broken!
[Thomas Moore: *Oft in the Stilly Night*]

13 Music, when soft voices die,
  Vibrates in the memory;
Odours, when sweet violets sicken,
  Live within the sense they quicken.

Rose leaves, when the rose is dead,
Are heaped for the beloved's bed;
And so thy thoughts, when thou art
gone,
Love itself shall slumber on.
[Shelley: *To* ———: *Music, When Soft
Voices Die*]
1 Four ducks on a pond,
A grass-bank beyond,
A blue sky of spring,
White clouds on the wing:
What a little thing
To remember for years—
To remember with tears!
[William Allingham: *A Memory*]
2 A man's memory may almost become
the art of continually varying and mis-
representing his past, according to his
interests in the present. [George Santa-
yana: *Persons and Places* I]
3 There is not any memory with less
satisfaction in it than the memory of
some temptation we resisted. [James
Branch Cabell: *Jurgen* VII]

MENACE

4 Yes, forsooth, I will hold my tongue;
so your face bids me, though you say
nothing. [Shakespeare: *King Lear* I.iv.]
5 But that two-handed engine at the
door,
Stands ready to smite once, and smite
no more.
[John Milton: *Lycidas*]
6 What if the breath that kindled those
grim fires,
Awaked, should blow them into sev-
enfold rage,
And plunge us in the flames; or from
above
Should intermitted vengeance arm
again
His red right hand to plague us?
[John Milton: *Paradise Lost* II.170-174]
With his red right hand (Rubente dex-
tera). *Horace: Odes I.ii.*

7 Their fatal hands
No second stroke intend.
[John Milton: *Paradise Lost* II.712-713]

MEN AND WOMEN

8 All the pursuits of men are the pursuits of women also, but in all of them a
woman is inferior to a man. [Plato:
The Republic V.v.]
9 A man, though he be gray-haired,
can always get a wife,
But a woman's time is short.
[Aristophanes: *Lysistrata*]
10 One man among a thousand have I
found; but a woman among all those
have I not found. [Ecclesiastes 7:28]
11 There can no man in humblesse him
acquyte
As womman can.
[Chaucer: *The Clerkes Tale* V]
humblesse = *humbleness*
12 The nobility both of England and
Scotland are inferior to brute beasts, for
they do that to women which no male
among the common sort of beasts can be
proved to do to their females; that is,
they reverence them, and quake at their
presence; they obey their commandments,
and that against God. [John Knox: *The
First Blast of the Trumpet Against The
Monstrous Regiment of Women*]
13 When a man dies, the last thing that
moves is his heart; in a woman her
tongue. [George Chapman: *The Wid-
dowes Teares* IV.ii.]
14 [Men] are all but stomachs, and we
all but food;
They eat us hungrily, and when they
are full
They belch us.
[Shakespeare: *Othello* III.iv.]
15 Man is the powder, woman the spark.
[Lope de Vega: *La Dama Melindrosa*
I.xx.]
16 Sigh no more, ladies, sigh no more,
Men were deceivers ever.
[Shakespeare: *Much Ado About Nothing* II.iii.]
17 For contemplation he and valour
formed;
For softness she and sweet attractive
grace,
He for God only, she for God in him.
[John Milton: *Paradise Lost* IV.297-299]
18 Therefore God's universal law
Gave to the man despotic power
Over his female in due awe.
[John Milton: *Samson Agonistes*]
19 I love men, not because they are men,
but because they are not women. [Queen
Christina of Sweden]
20 A man no more believes a woman
when she says she has an aversion for
him than when she says she'll cry out.
[Wycherley: *The Plain Dealer* II.i.]

1 It is because of men that women don't like each other. [La Bruyère: *Les Caractères*]

2 There are more well-pleased old women than old men. [Richard Steele: *The Tatler*]

3 If the heart of a man is depress'd
with cares,
The mist is dispell'd when a woman
appears.
[John Gay: *The Beggar's Opera* II.iii.]

4 In men we various ruling passions
find;
In women two almost divide the kind;
Those only fixed, they first or last
obey,
The love of pleasure, and the love of
sway.
[Alexander Pope: *Moral Essays* Epistle II]

5 Men, some to business, some to pleasure take;
But every woman is at heart a rake:
Men, some to quiet, some to public
strife;
But every lady would be queen for
life.
[Alexander Pope: *Moral Essays:* Epistle II]

6 As the faculty of writing has been chiefly a masculine endowment, the reproach of making the world miserable has always been thrown upon the women. [Samuel Johnson: *The Rambler* No. 18]

Chaucer's Wife of Bath expressed the same sentiment 400 years before, but with more vigor:

For trusteth wel, it is an impossible
That any clerk wol speke good of wyves,
But—if it be of holy seintes lyves,
Ne of noon other womman never the
mo.
Who peyntede the leoun, tel me who?
By God! if wommen had writen stories,
As clerkes han with-inne hir oratories,
They wolde han writen of men more
wickkednesse
Than all the mark of Adam may re-
dresse.

clerk = *cleric (then the only literates); and clerics were celibates;* wyves = *women in general, married and single*

7 Women have often more of what is called good sense than men. They have fewer pretensions; are less implicated in theories; and judge of objects more from their immediate and involuntary impression on the mind, and, therefore, more truly and naturally. They cannot reason wrong; for they do not reason at all. [William Hazlitt: *The Ignorance of the Learned*]

8 As unto the bow the cord is,
So unto the man is woman,
Though she bends him, she obeys him,
Though she draws him, yet she fol-
lows,
Useless each without the other!
[Longfellow: *The Song of Hiawatha* IV.x.]

9 Woman is the lesser man.
[Tennyson: *Locksley Hall*]

Tennyson has some powerful support in this belief: Plato, The Republic *V: "The female sex is in some respects inferior to the male sex, both as regards body and soul."*—Catholic Encyclopaedia, *XV; "As regards the individual nature, woman is defective and misbegotten."—St. Thomas Aquinas:* Summa Theologica, *Question XCII, Article I, Reply Obj. 1.*

10 Man for the field and woman for the
hearth:
Man for the sword, and for the
needle she;
Man with the head, and woman with
the heart;
Man to command, and woman to
obey;
All else confusion.
[Tennyson: *The Princess* V]

11 Man has his will—but woman has her way. [O. W. Holmes: *The Autocrat of the Breakfast-Table* I]

12 'Tis strange what a man may do, and a woman yet think him an angel. [W. M. Thackeray: *Henry Esmond* I. vii.]

13 For men must work, and women must weep. [Charles Kingsley: *The Three Fishers*]

14 I'm not denyin' the women are foolish: God Almighty made 'em to match the men. [George Eliot: *Adam Bede* LIII]

15 I expect that Woman will be the last thing civilized by Man. [George Meredith: *The Ordeal of Richard Feverel* I]

16 Directly domineering ceases in the man, snubbing begins in the woman. [Thomas Hardy: *A Pair of Blue Eyes*

XXVII]

1 Time and circumstance, which enlarge the views of most men, narrow the views of women almost invariably. [Thomas Hardy: *Jude the Obscure* VI]

2 I like men who have a future, and women who have a past. [Oscar Wilde: *The Picture of Dorian Gray* XV]

3 It is a woman's business to get married as soon as possible, and a man's to keep unmarried as long as he can. [G. B. Shaw: *Man and Superman* I]

4 There are such astonishing things to be told about men and women, and hardly a man or a woman to whom one dares to tell them. [Logan Pearsall Smith: *Afterthoughts*]

5 No healthy male is ever actually modest. No healthy male ever really thinks or talks of anything save himself. His conversation is one endless boast—often covert, but always undiluted. . . . Feminine strategy, in the duel of sex, consists almost wholly of an adroit feeding of this vanity. [H. L. Mencken: in *Smart Set*, April 1919]

6 Women do not like timid men. Cats do not like prudent rats. [H. L. Mencken: *Chrestomathy* XXX Sententiae]

7 Women always excel men in that sort of wisdom which comes from experience. To be a woman is in itself a terrible experience. [H. L. Mencken: *Chrestomathy* XXX Sententiae]

8 No matter how happily a woman may be married, it always pleases her to discover that there is a nice man who wishes that she were not. [H. L. Mencken: *Chrestomathy* XXX Sententiae]

9 Men have a much better time of it than women. For one thing, they marry later. For another thing, they die earlier. [H. L. Mencken: *Chrestomathy* XXX Sententiae]

10 At the end of one millennium and nine centuries of Christianity, it remains an unshakable assumption of the law in all Christian countries and of the moral judgment of Christians everywhere that if a man and a woman, entering a room together, close the door behind them, the man will come out sadder and the woman wiser. [H. L. Mencken: *Chrestomathy* XXX Sententiae]

11 Women are wiser than men because

they know less and understand more. [James Stephens: *The Crock of Gold* II]

12 Woman's virtue is man's greatest invention. [Cornelia Otis Skinner: *Paris '90*]

13 Men have more problems than women. In the first place, they have to put up with women. [Françoise Sagan, quoted in the *New York Times*, Oct. 27, 1957]

MENE, MENE

14 MENE, MENE, TEKEL, UPHARSIN. [Daniel 5:25]

As Belshazzar and his lords were desecrating the sacred vessels that Nebuchadnezzar had brought from Jerusalem, there came forth the fingers of a man's hand that "wrote over against the candlestick upon the plaister of the wall of the king's palace" the above words. Though now commonly translated "Thou art weighed in the balance and found wanting" (a slightly changed selection of a part of Daniel's translation), the meaning of the words, despite centuries of scholarly concern, is uncertain.

They are presumably in Aramaic and may mean "numbered, numbered, weighed and divisions." They may also be the names of weights and may mean "A mina, a mina, a shekel and half-shekels." Daniel translated them to mean: "God hath numbered thy kingdom, and finished it. Thou art weighed in the balances, and art found wanting. Thy kingdom is divided, and given to the Medes and Persians." But then Daniel was inspired.

MERCENARIES

15 Their shoulders held the sky suspended;
They stood, and earth's foundations stay;
What God abandoned, these defended,
And saved the sum of things for pay.
[A. E. Housman: *Epitaph on an Army of Mercenaries*]

MERCHANT(S)

16 In vain the state where merchants gild the top.
[John Marston: *What You Will* I]

1 To either India see the merchant fly,
Scared at the spectre of pale Poverty!
See him with pains of body, pangs of
soul,
Burn thro' the Tropics, freeze be-
neath the Pole!
[Alexander Pope: *Imitations of Horace,*
Epistle I]

MERCY
2 The mercy of the Lord is from everlasting to everlasting upon them that
fear Him. [Psalms: 103:17]
3 Who shows mercy to an enemy, denies
it to himself. [Francis Bacon: *The Advancement of Learning,* "Cruelty"]
4 The quality of mercy is not strain'd;
It droppeth as the gentle rain from
heaven
Upon the place beneath: it is twice
blest;
It blesseth him that gives and him
that takes:
'Tis mightiest in the mightiest: it becomes
The throned monarch better than
his crown;
His sceptre shows the force of temporal power,
The attribute to awe and majesty,
Wherein doth sit the dread and fear
of kings;
But mercy is above this sceptred sway;
It is enthroned in the hearts of kings,
It is an attribute to God himself;
And earthly power doth then show
likest God's
When mercy seasons justice.
[Shakespeare: *The Merchant of Venice*
IV.i.]
5 No ceremony that to great ones 'longs,
Not the king's crown, nor the de-
puted sword,
The marshal's truncheon, nor the
judge's robe,
Become them with one half so good a
grace
As mercy does.
[Shakespeare: *Measure for Measure* II.ii.]
6 Between the stirrup and the ground,
I mercy ask'd, I mercy found.
[Samuel Johnson: in Boswell's *Life,*
April 28, 1783]
*Johnson had said that we "are not to
judge determinately of the state in*

*which a man leaves this life. He may
in a moment have repented effectually."
He then quoted (or slightly misquoted)
the famous epitaph from Camden's* Remains *(1623) written for the dissolute
man who was killed by a fall from his
horse:*

My friend, judge not me,
Thou seest I judge not thee;
Betwixt the stirrop and the ground,
Mercy I askt, mercy I found.

*The epitaph, Camden says, was based on
St. Augustine's "The mercy of God [is
to be found] between the bridge and
the stream."*
7 And shut the gates of mercy on mankind.
[Thomas Gray: *Elegy Written in a Country Churchyard*]

MERIT
8 O, if men were to be saved by merit,
what hole in hell were hot enough for
him? [Shakespeare: *I Henry IV* I.ii.]
9 Charms strike the sight, but merit
wins the soul.
[Alexander Pope: *The Rape of the Lock*
V]

MERMAID(S)
10 I'll stop mine ears against the mermaid's song.
[Shakespeare: *The Comedy of Errors*
III.ii.]
11 I have heard the mermaids singing,
each to each.
[T. S. Eliot: *The Love Song of J. Alfred
Prufrock*]

MERMAID TAVERN
12   What things have we seen
Done at the Mermaid! heard words
that have been
So nimble and so full of subtle flame
As if that everyone from whence they
came
Had meant to put his whole wit in a
jest,
And resolved to live a fool the rest
Of his dull life.
[Francis Beaumont: *Letter to Ben Jon-
son*]
*The Mermaid was the gathering place
of the wits in early 17th-century Lon-
don—Ben Jonson, Sir Walter Raleigh,*

Beaumont and Fletcher, John Selden and, most likely, Shakespeare.

1 Souls of poets dead and gone,
  What Elysium have ye known,
  Happy field or mossy cavern,
  Choicer than the Mermaid Tavern?
[Keats: *Lines on the Mermaid Tavern*]

MERRIMENT

2 Is any merry? Let him sing psalms.
[James 5:13]

3 The more the merrier, the fewer the better fare. [John Heywood: *Proverbs (1546)*]
   The proverb had appeared 16 years earlier in John Palsgrave's Lesclarcisse-ment de la Langue Francoyse.

4 How oft when men are at the point
                              of death
  Have they been merry!
[Shakespeare: *Romeo and Juliet* V.iii.]
   The word fey *originally described this condition. In Scotland when someone had a spasm of seemingly irrational merriment, it was customary to say "I hope the body be no fey"—that is, "I hope this does not presage his death."*

5 Come, sing me a bawdy song; make
                            me merry.
[Shakespeare: *I Henry IV* III.iii.]
   He's for a jig or a tale of bawdry, or he sleeps. Hamlet *II.ii.*

6 'Tis merry in hall when beards wag
                               all.
[Shakespeare: *II Henry IV* V.iii.]
   Shakespeare is quoting an old saying which had already appeared in Thomas Tusser's Five Hundred Points of Good Husbandry.

7   As 'tis ever common
  That men are merriest when they are
                          from home.
[Shakespeare: *Henry V* I.ii.]
   from = *away from*

8 There never was a merry world since the fairies left off dancing, and the parson left conjuring. [John Selden: *Table Talk* XCIX]
   conjuring = *exorcising*

9 There is hardly such a thing as being merry, but at another's expense. [Nicholas Rowe: Dedication of *The Fair Penitent*]

10 Nothing is more hopeless than a scheme of merriment. [Samuel Johnson:

The Idler No. 58]
   i.e., it is the essence of merriment that it be spontaneous, unplanned, and free-flowing.

11 A source of innocent merriment!
   Of innocent merriment.
[W. S. Gilbert: *The Mikado* II]

MERRY

12   A merrier man,
   Within the limit of becoming mirth,
   I never spent an hour's talk withal.
[Shakespeare: *Love's Labour's Lost* II.i.]

13 I am not merry; but I do beguile
   The thing I am by seeming otherwise.
[Shakespeare: *Othello* II.i.]

14 A merry heart goes all the day,
   Your sad tires in a mile-a.
[Shakespeare: *The Winter's Tale* IV.iii.]

15 All went merry as a marriage bell.
[Byron: *Childe Harold* III. xxi.]

16 For the good are always the merry,
      Save by an evil chance,
   And the merry love the fiddle,
      And the merry love to dance.
[William Butler Yeats: *The Fiddler of Dooney*]

MESSAGE TO GARCIA

17 It is not book-learning young **men** need, nor instruction about this and that, but a stiffening of the vertebrae which will cause them to be loyal to a trust, to act promptly, concentrate their energies, do a thing—carry a message to Garcia. [Elbert Hubbard: *A Message to Garcia* (1900)]
   In April, 1898, the American military wished certain information from the leader of the insurgent Cuban forces, General Calixto Garcia. There were no lines of communication and Lieutenant Andrew Rowan was dispatched secretly to find the general. He found him, got the wanted information and returned to Washington. The incident would have been forgotten except that it was made the text of a lay sermon by Elbert Hubbard (in The Philistine, March, 1900) and became a catchword. The nation was drunk on the heady wine of Manifest Destiny, and this was one of the hiccups.

METAL
1 Here's metal more attractive.
[Shakespeare: *Hamlet* III.ii.]

METAPHOR
2 The greatest thing in style is to have a command of metaphor. [Aristotle: *Poetics* XXII]
3 A world ends when its metaphor has
died.
[Archibald MacLeish: *Hypocrite Auteur*]
4 One thing that literature would be
greatly the better for
Would be a more restricted employment by authors of simile and
metaphor.
Authors of all races, be they Greeks,
Romans, Teutons or Celts,
Can't seem just to say that anything
is the thing it is but have to go out
of their way to say that it is like
something else.
[Ogden Nash: *Very Like a Whale*]

METAPHYSICS
5 He knew what's what, and that's as
high
As metaphysic wit can fly.
[Samuel Butler (1612-1680): *Hudibras*]
6 When he to whom one speaks does
not understand, and he who speaks himself does not understand, this is metaphysics. [Voltaire]
7 And Coleridge. . . .
Explaining metaphysics to the nation—
I wish he would explain his Explanation.
[Byron: Dedication to *Don Juan*]
8 Metaphysics is the attempt of the
mind to rise above the mind. [Thomas
Carlyle: *Characteristics*]
9 I believe that metaphysicians and
philosophers are, on the whole, the greatest troubles the world has got to deal
with. [John Ruskin: *Modern Painters*]
III.iv.]
10 A metaphysician is a man who goes
into a dark cellar at midnight without a
light looking for a black cat that isn't
there. [Attr. Baron Bowen of Colwood]
*An addition is attr. T. H. Huxley: that
a theologian always found the cat.*
11 Surrendering its pretensions so far as
any ability to establish truths of refer-

ence are concerned and proclaiming itself essentially an art rather than a science, Metaphysics, which promised so
much, thus ends by confirming the very
despair which it set out to combat. [Jo-
seph Wood Krutch: *The Modern Temper* VII.iv.]
12 Metaphysics is almost always an attempt to prove the incredible by an appeal to the unintelligible. [H. L. Menck-
en: *Minority Report: H. L. Mencken's
Notebooks*]

METEOR
13 This hairy meteor did announce
The fall of sceptres and of crowns.
[Samuel Butler (1612-1680): *Hudibras*]
14 Now slides the silent meteor on, and
leaves
A shining furrow, as thy thoughts in
me.
[Tennyson: *The Princess* VII]

METER
15 A needless Alexandrine ends the song,
That, like a wounded snake, drags
its slow length along.
[Alexander Pope: *An Essay on Criticism*
II]
*An alexandrine is an iambic or trochaic
line of 12 syllables, or six feet, with
usually a break at the 6th syllable. It
is so called because of its use in a 12th-
century French metrical romance about
Alexander the Great.*
*The final line of a Spenserian stanza
is an alexandrine—and it was probably
this that led to its being a fashionable
poetical device in the 18th century. Pope
illustrates his meaning in the second of
the two lines given above.*

METHOD
16 There is a certain method in his madness.
[Horace: *Satires* II.iii.]
17 Though this be madness, yet there is
method in 't. [Shakespeare: *Hamlet* II.
ii.]

MEXICO
18 Beyond the Mexique Bay. [Andrew
Marvell: *Bermudas*]
*Used by Aldous Huxley as the title of
a volume of travels in Central America.*

MICHELANGELO

1 In the room the women come and go
Talking of Michelangelo.
[T. S. Eliot: *The Love Song of J. Alfred Prufrock*]

MICROSCOPES

2 Faith is a fine invention
For gentlemen who see;
But microscopes are prudent
In an emergency.
[Emily Dickinson: *Poems, Second Series,* XXX]

MIDDLE AGE

3 In the middle of the road of life
I found myself in a dark wood,
Having strayed from the straight path.
[Dante: *The Divine Comedy,* "Inferno" I.i. (opening lines)]

4 Not so young to love a woman for singing, nor so old to dote on her for anything. I have years on my back forty-eight. [Shakespeare: *King Lear* I.iv.]

5 . . . grim Dante's 'obscure wood,'
That horrid equinox, that hateful section
Of human years that half-way house, that rude
Hut, whence wise travellers drive with circumspection
Life's sad post-horses o'er the dreary frontier
Of age, and looking back to youth, give *one* tear.
[Byron: *Don Juan* X.xxvii.]

6 Of all the barbarous middle ages, that
Which is most barbarous is the middle age
Of man; it is—I really scarce know what;
But when we hover between fool and sage.
[Byron: *Don Juan* XII.i.]

MIDNIGHT

7 We have heard the chimes at midnight, Master Shallow.
[Shakespeare: *II Henry IV* III.ii.]

8 The iron tongue of midnight hath told twelve.
[Shakespeare: *A Midsummer Night's Dream* V.i.]

9 In the dead vast and middle of the night.
[Shakespeare: *Hamlet* I.ii.]

10 Now is the very witching time of night,
When churchyards yawn and hell itself breathes out
Contagion to this world.
[Shakespeare: *Hamlet* III.ii.]
The first line passed into poetry and eventually into common speech as a cliché.
   As in Robert Blair's The Grave *(1743):*
   When it draws near to witching time of night.
   Or Keats's A Prophecy *(1820):*
   'Tis the witching hour of night,
   Orbed is the moon and bright,
   And the stars they glisten, glisten,
   Seeming with bright eyes to listen—
   For what listen they?

11 That hour, o' night's black arch the keystane.
[Burns: *Tam o' Shanter*]

12 Upon the honeyed middle of the night.
[Keats: *The Eve of St. Agnes*]

13 I stood on the bridge at midnight,
As the clocks were striking the hour,
And the moon rose over the city,
Behind the dark church-tower.
[Longfellow: *The Bridge*]

14 Once upon a midnight dreary, while I pondered, weak and weary,
Over many a quaint and curious volume of forgotten lore—
While I nodded, nearly napping, suddenly there came a tapping,
As of some one gently rapping, rapping at my chamber door.
[Edgar Allan Poe: *The Raven*]

15 Upon the middle of the night,
Waking she heard the night-fowl crow.
[Tennyson: *Mariana*]
The name and the mood were taken from Shakespeare's Measure for Measure *(III.i.). This passage echoes IV.i.: "Upon the heavy middle of the night."*

16 The sun was shining on the sea,
Shining with all his might!
He did his very best to make
The billows smooth and bright—
And this was odd, because it was
The middle of the night.
[Lewis Carroll: *Through the Looking-Glass:* "The Walrus and the Carpenter"]

MIGHT

1 Might is right; justice is the interest of the stronger. [Plato: *Republic* I.xii.]

2 Might makes right. [Seneca: *Hercules Furens* 253]

What Seneca says, literally, is that justice lies in arms.

3 Might and right govern everything in the world; might till right is ready. [Joubert: *Pensées* XV.ii.]

Right isn't quite ready yet, but soon will be. See quotation from Clarence Day below.

4 Wider still and wider shall thy
bounds be set;
God who made thee mighty, make
thee mightier yet.
[A. C. Benson: *Song from Pomp and Circumstance* by Elgar]

5 Might and Right are always fighting.
In our youth it seems exciting.
Right is always nearly winning.
Might can hardly keep from grinning.
[Clarence Day: *Might and Right*]

MIGHT HAVE BEEN

6 Hands, that the rod of empire might
have sway'd,
Or wak'd to ecstasy the living lyre.
[Thomas Gray: *Elegy Written in a Country Churchyard*]

7 For of all sad words of tongue or pen,
The saddest are these: "It might have
been."
[J. G. Whittier: *Maud Muller*]

Whittier's pronunciation of been as bĕn is still widespread in America.

8 My name is Might-have-been:
I am also called No-more, Too-late,
Farewell.
[Dante Gabriel Rossetti: *The House of Life* II.xcvii.]

9 If of all words of tongue and pen,
The saddest are, "It might have been,"
More sad are these we daily see:
"It is, but hadn't ought to be."
[Francis Brett Harte: *Mrs. Judge Jenkins*]

MIGHTY

10 How are the mighty fallen. [II Samuel: 1:25]

MILDNESS

11 A soft answer turneth away wrath. [Proverbs 15:1]

12 But I am pigeon-livered, and lack gall
To make oppression bitter.
[Shakespeare: *Hamlet* II.ii.]

13 He was the mildest manner'd man
That ever scuttled ship or cut a
throat.
[Byron: *Don Juan* III.xli.]

MILITARY

14 General John was a soldier tried,
A chief of warlike dons;
A haughty stride and a withering
pride
Were Major-General John's.

A sneer would play on his martial
phiz,
Superior birth to show;
"Pish!" was a favorite word of his,
And he often said "Ho! Ho!"
[W. S. Gilbert: *Bab Ballads*, "General John"]

MILK

15 A land flowing with milk and honey. [Exodus 3:8]

16 It is better to buy a quart of milk by the penny than keep a cow. [James Howell: *Letters* II]

MILKMAID

17 Where are you going, my pretty maid?
I'm going a-milking, sir, she said.
May I go with you, my pretty maid?
You're kindly welcome, sir, she said.
Nursery rhyme: a 19th-century child's version of an old song "Strawberry leaves make maidens fair," which, though the first printed version is 1790, has been traced into the 17th century.

The nursery version, bowdlerized and democratized, ends with a pert snub from the milkmaid to the gentleman who finds her attractive but can't marry her since she has no dowry.

In the old song the social difference between a gentleman and a milkmaid ruled out all thought of marriage in either's mind. The gentleman was more direct, and the young lady's attitude is summed up in "You're kindly welcome, sir, she said."

MILK OF HUMAN KINDNESS

18   Yet do I fear thy nature:

It is too full o' the milk of human
kindness
To catch the nearest way.
[Shakespeare: *Macbeth* I.v.]

MILL(ER)

1 More water glideth by the mill
Than wots the miller of.
[Shakespeare: *Titus Andronicus* II.i.]
2 The miller sees not all the water that
goeth by his mill. [Robert Burton: *Anatomy of Melancholy* III.3.4.1.]
3 There was a jolly miller once
Lived on the river Dee;
He work'd, and sung, from morn till
night,
No lark more blythe than he.
And this the burden of his song,
For ever us'd to be,
"I care for nobody, not I,
If no one cares for me."
[Commonly attr. to Isaac Bickerstaffe, in
whose opera, *Love in a Village*, it appeared in 1762 and was a great hit. It
was probably, however, an old song inserted into the opera or, at best,
adapted.]
*The first modern mechanics—necessary
to the social order, yet dependent solely
on their own skill, and free from the restrictions of feudalism or of the guilds
or the church organizations—millers
were proverbially independent. Chaucer's certainly was. There was a popular
ballad that represented Henry VIII as
envious of the Miller of Dee.*

MILLS OF THE GODS

4 God's mill grinds slow, but sure.
[George Herbert: *Jacula Prudentum*]
5 Though the mills of God grind slowly,
yet they grind exceeding small.
[Longfellow: *Retribution*]

MILLSTONE

6 Whoso shall offend one of these little ones which believe in me, it were better that a millstone were hanged about
his neck, and that he were drowned in
the depth of the sea. [Matthew 18:6]
7 It were better for him that a millstone were hanged about his neck, and
he cast into the sea, than that he should
offend one of these little ones. [Luke
17:2]

MILTON, JOHN

8 Three poets in three distant ages
born,
Greece, Italy, and England did adorn.
The first in loftiness of thought surpass'd,
The next in majesty, in both the last:
The force of nature could no farther
go;
To make the third she join'd the
former two.
[Dryden: *Lines under the Portrait of
Milton*]
The reference is to Homer, Vergil, Milton.
9 Some mute, inglorious Milton here
may rest.
[Thomas Gray: *Elegy Written in a Country Churchyard*]
*There are no mute, inglorious Miltons,
save in the hallucinations of poets. The
one sound test of a Milton is that he
functions as a Milton.*
H. L. Mencken: Prejudices: Third
Series *(1922)*
10 Milton! thou shouldst be living at
this hour:
England hath need of thee.
[Wordsworth: *London* (1802)]
11 Thy soul was like a star and dwelt
apart.
[Wordsworth: *London* (1802)]
12 The character of Milton was peculiarly distinguished by loftiness of
spirit: that of Dante by intensity of feeling. [Macaulay: *Milton*]
13 Of all the poets who have introduced
into their works the agency of supernatural beings, Milton has succeeded
best. [Macaulay: *Milton*]
14 O mighty-mouth'd inventor of harmonies,
O skill'd to sing of Time or Eternity,
God-gifted organ-voice of England,
Milton, a name to resound for ages.
[Tennyson: *Milton*]
15 And malt does more than Milton can
To justify God's ways to man.
[A. E. Housman: *A Shropshire Lad*
LXII]

MINCING

16 The daughters of Zion . . . walk with
stretched forth necks and wanton eyes,

walking and mincing as they go, and making a tinkling with their feet. [Isaiah 3:16]

MIND

1 My mind to me a kingdom is,
   Such perfect joy therein I find
As far exceeds all earthly bliss
   That God or nature hath assigned.
[Edward Dyer: *My Mind to Me a Kingdom Is*]
2 I had rather believe all the fables in the Legend and the Talmud and the Alcoran, than that this universal frame is without a mind. [Francis Bacon: *Of Atheism*]
3 There is one radical distinction between different minds . . . that some minds are stronger and apter to mark the differences of things, others to mark their resemblances. [Francis Bacon: *Novum Organum* I]
4 O! what a noble mind is here o'erthrown.
[Shakespeare: *Hamlet* III.i.]
5 Canst thou not minister to a mind diseased,
   Pluck from the memory a rooted sorrow,
   Raze out the written troubles of the brain,
   And with some sweet oblivious antidote
   Cleanse the stuff'd bosom of that perilous stuff
Which weighs upon the heart?
[Shakespeare: *Macbeth* V.iii.]
6 When the mind's free, the body's delicate.
[Shakespeare: *King Lear* III.iv.]
   That is, when the mind is free from strain or worry we are aware of minor physical discomforts, but when we are suffering some fear or anguish or fired with some excitement, quite serious physical afflictions often go unnoticed.
7 The mind is its own place, and in itself
Can make a heaven of Hell, a hell of Heaven.
[John Milton: *Paradise Lost* I.254-255]
8 The mind, that ocean where each kind
Does straight its own resemblance find;

Yet it creates, transcending these,
Far other worlds, and other seas,
Annihilating all that's made
To a green thought in a green shade.
[Andrew Marvell: *The Garden*]
9 Riches, Fame, and Pleasure. With these three the mind is so engrossed that it can hardly think of any other good. [Spinoza: *On the Improvement of the Understanding* I.iii.]
10 Such is the delight of mental superiority, that none on whom nature or study have conferred it, would purchase the gifts of fortune by its loss. [Samuel Johnson: *The Rambler* No. 150]
11 Nor less I deem that there are Powers
   Which of themselves our minds impress;
   That we can feed this mind of ours
   In a wise passiveness.
[Wordsworth: *Expostulation and Reply*]
12 What is mind? No matter. What is matter? Never mind. [Thomas Hewitt Key: epigram in *Punch* (1855)]
13 No, what it [my mind] is really most like is a spider's web, insecurely hung on leaves and twigs, quivering in every wind, and sprinkled with dewdrops and dead flies. And at its geometric centre, pondering for ever the Problem of Existence, sits motionless and spider-like the uncanny Soul. [Logan Pearsall Smith: *Trivia,* "The Spider"]
14 An improper mind is a perpetual feast. [Logan Pearsall Smith: *Afterthoughts*]

MIND AND BODY

15 The mind grows and decays with the body. [Lucretius: *De rerum natura* III]
16 Diseases of the mind impair the powers of the body.
[Ovid: *Tristium* III.viii.]
17 A sound mind in a sound body. (*Mens sana in corpore sano*) [Juvenal: *Satires* X.]
   Much used—in the Latin form—as an inscription on college gymnasiums.
18 A sound mind in a sound body, is a short but full description of a happy state in this world. [John Locke: *Some Thoughts on Education* I]
19   We are not ourselves
   When nature, being oppress'd, com-

mands the mind
To suffer with the body.
[Shakespeare: *King Lear* II.iv.]
1 There is an unseemly exposure of the mind, as well as of the body. [William Hazlitt: *Sketches and Essays*]
2   Reason kens he herits in
A haunted house.
[Robert Bridges: *Low Barometer*]

MINE OWN
3 Is it not lawful for me to do what I will with mine own? [Matthew: 20:15]
4 An ill-favoured thing, sir, but mine own.
[Shakespeare: *As You Like It* V.iv.]

MINIVER CHEEVY
5 Miniver Cheevy, born too late,
Scratched his head and kept on thinking:
Miniver coughed, and called it fate,
And kept on drinking.
[Edwin Arlington Robinson: *Miniver Cheevy*]

MINORITY
6 Every new opinion, at its starting, is precisely in a minority of one. [Thomas Carlyle: *On Heroes and Hero-Worship* II]
7 If all mankind minus one, were of one opinion, and only one person were of the contrary opinion, mankind would be no more justified in silencing that one person, than he, if he had the power, would be justified in silencing mankind. [John Stuart Mill: *On Liberty* II]
See also MAJORITY

MINSTREL
8 The way was long, the wind was cold,
The minstrel was infirm and old:
His withered cheek, and tresses gray,
Seem'd to have known a better day.
[Sir Walter Scott: *The Lay of the Last Minstrel*]
9 The minstrel boy to the war is gone,
In the ranks of death you'll find him;
His father's sword he has girded on,
And his wild harp slung behind him.
[Thomas Moore: *The Minstrel Boy*]
10 A wandering minstrel I—

A thing of shreds and patches,
Of ballads, songs and snatches,
And dreamy lullaby.
[W. S. Gilbert: *The Mikado* I]
An echo of Shakespeare's "A king of shreds and patches" (Hamlet III.iv).

MIRACLE(S)
11 Miracles are according to the ignorance wherein we are by nature, and not according to nature's essence. [Montaigne: *Essays* I.xxii.]
12 How many things do we name miraculous and against Nature? Each man and every nation doth it according to the measure of his ignorance. [Montaigne: *Essays* II.xii.]
13 Mysteries are not necessarily miracles. [Goethe: *Sprüche in Prosa*]
14 To me every hour of the light and dark is a miracle,
Every cubic inch of space is a miracle.
[Walt Whitman: *Leaves of Grass,* "Miracles"]
15 It is almost impossible to exaggerate the proneness of the human mind to take miracles as evidence, and to seek for miracles as evidence. [Matthew Arnold: *Literature and Dogma* V]
16 A miracle drug is any drug that will do what the label says it will do. [Eric Hodgins: *Episode*]

MIRROR(S)
17 To hold as 'twere the mirror up to nature.
[Shakespeare: *Hamlet* III.ii.]
18 All mirrors are magical mirrors; never can we see our faces in them. [Logan Pearsall Smith: *Afterthoughts*]

MIRTH
19   A merrier man,
Within the limit of becoming mirth,
I never spent an hour's talk withal.
[Shakespeare: *Love's Labour's Lost* II.i.]
20 Very tragical mirth.
[Shakespeare: *A Midsummer Night's Dream* V.i.]
21 You have displaced the mirth, broke the good meeting,
With most admired disorder.
[Shakespeare: *Macbeth* III.iv.]
admired = to-be-wondered-at

1 I love such mirth as does not make friends ashamed to look upon one another next morning. [Izaak Walton: *The Compleat Angler* I.v.]

2 Mirth should always be accidental. It should naturally arise out of the occasion, and the occasion seldom be laid for it. [Richard Steele: *The Spectator* No. 196]

3 Dance and Provençal song and sunburnt mirth!
[Keats: *Ode to a Nightingale*]

MISCHIEF

4 This is Miching Malicho: it means mischief.
[Shakespeare: *Hamlet* III.ii.]
mischief = *a stronger word then than now, meant serious trouble;* miching = *probably means truant;* malicho = *usually changed to* mallecho *to make it nearer to the Spanish* malhecho *("misdeed")*
But *the Spanish word was not used in English. The emendation is conjectural. And the passage remains tantalizingly obscure.*

5 For Satan finds some mischief still For idle hands to do.
[Isaac Watts: *Divine Songs* XX]
still = *continually*

6 He had a head to contrive, a tongue to persuade, and a hand to execute any mischief. [Edward Hyde, Earl of Clarendon: *History of the Rebellion* III.vii. (1702)]

7 Whether it be the heart to conceive, the understanding to direct, or the hand to execute. [Junius: *Letter 37* (March 19, 1770)]

8 In every deed of mischief he [Andronicus] had a heart to resolve, a head to contrive, and a hand to execute. [Edward Gibbon: *Decline and Fall of the Roman Empire* XLVIII.]
Chapter 48 of the Decline and Fall *first appeared in vol. V of that work, in 1788.*
Gibbon, who is usually credited with the sentence, would appear to be echoing Junius rather than Clarendon.
Clarendon, whose sentence is superior to either of its echoes, was referring to John Hampden. Mischief *was a much stronger word then than now and meant trouble, injury, an act of malice.*

It is interesting to find Hampden so described for, with the ultimate triumph of the Puritan cause, he was to become a symbol of forthright courage and uncompromising idealism ("Some village Hampden that with dauntless breast/ The little tyrant of his fields withstood"—*Gray's Elegy [1750]).*

MISER

9 A ful gret fool is he, ywis, That bothe riche and nygard is.
[Chaucer: *The Romaunt of the Rose*]

10 He was such a covetous miser that he would have flayed a louse to save the skin of it. [John Florio: *Second Frutes* (1591)]
This may have been proverbial. It appeared soon after in several collections of proverbs, with the addition that he would sell the tallow. Some later wit transferred the idea to skinning a flint and skinflint *came into being.*

11 A youthful miser's a monstrosity.
[Voltaire: *L'Enfant Prodigue* I.iv.]

MISERY(IES)

12 Twins ev'n from birth are Misery and Man.
[Homer: *Odyssey* VII (trans. Pope)]

13 The comfort derived from the misery of others is slight. [Cicero: *Epistolae* VI.iii.]

14 In misery it is great comfort to have a companion. [John Lyly: *Euphues*]

15 Nothing almost sees miracles But misery.
[Shakespeare: *King Lear* II.ii.]
i.e., only the desperately wretched, whose sole hope is in the miraculous, see miracles.

16 To have a stomach and lack meat, to have meat and lack a stomach, to lie in bed and cannot rest, are great miseries.
[William Camden: *Remains*]

17 Misery loves company. [John Ray: *English Proverbs* (1670)]

18 The cure for the greatest part of human miseries is not radical but palliative. [Samuel Johnson: *The Rambler* No. 32]

19 But misery still delights to trace Its semblance in another's case.
[William Cowper: *The Castaway*]

20 Many a green isle needs must be In the deep wide sea of Misery.

[Shelley: *Lines written among the Euganean Hills*]

1 A still small voice spake unto me,
"Thou art so full of misery,
Were it not better not to be?"

[Tennyson: *The Two Voices*]

2   Never morning wore
To evening, but some heart did
          break.

[Tennyson: *In Memoriam* VI]

3 If misery loves company, misery has company enough. [Thoreau: *Journal,* September 1, 1851]

4   . . . the turbid ebb and flow
Of human misery.

[Matthew Arnold: *Dover Beach*]

5 Yonder, lightening other loads,
The seasons range the country roads,
But here in London streets I ken
No such helpmates, only men;
And these are not in plight to bear,
If they would, another's care.
They have enough as 'tis: I see
In many an eye that measures me
The mortal sickness of a mind
Too unhappy to be kind.
Undone with misery, all they can
Is to hate their fellow man;
And till they drop they needs must
          still
Look at you and wish you ill.

[A. E. Housman: *A Shropshire Lad* XLI]

6 There are indeed specific human virtues, but they are those necessary to existence, like patience and courage. Supported on these indispensable habits, mankind always carries an indefinite load of misery and vice. [George Santayana: *Reason in Religion*]

MISFORTUNE(S)

7 If we were all to bring our misfortunes into a common store, so that each person should receive an equal share in the distribution, the majority would be glad to take up their own and depart. [Socrates: in Plutarch's *Moralia*]

8 In the midst of compassion, we feel within us a kind of bitter-sweet pricking of malicious delight in the misfortunes of others. [Montaigne: *Essays* III.i.]

9 Solon said, that should a man heape up in one masse all evils, together, there is none, that would not rather chuse to carry back with him such evils as he alreadie hath, then come to a lawfull division with other men of that chaos of evils and take his allotted share of them. [Montaigne: *Essays* III.ix. (trans. John Florio)]

10 Misfortunes seldom come singly. [Cervantes: *Don Quixote* I.iii.6]

11 "For all that let me tell thee, brother Panza," said Don Quixote, "that there is no recollection which time does not put an end to, and no pain which death does not remove."

"And what greater misfortune can there be," replied Panza, "than the one that waits for time to put an end to it and death to remove it?" [Cervantes: *Don Quixote* II.15.]

12 I never knew any man in my life who could not bear another's misfortunes perfectly like a Christian.[Alexander Pope: *Thoughts on Various Subjects*]

13 One misfortune never comes alone. [Henry Fielding: *Jonathan Wild* I.viii.]

14 If a man *talks* of his misfortunes, there is something in them that is not disagreeable to him; for when there is nothing but pure misery, there never is any recourse to the mention of it. [Samuel Johnson: in Boswell's *Life* (1780)]

In Rasselas *II, the prince perceives that one who is recounting his miseries is receiving solace from the narration of them—"from consciousness of the delicacy with which he felt and the eloquence with which he bewailed them."*

Johnson himself later in life, rereading his somber essays in the Rambler, *exclaimed with delight that he had "warbled out his groans with uncommon elegance."*

15 I am convinced that we have a degree of delight, and that no small one, in the real misfortunes and pains of others. [Edmund Burke: *On the Sublime and Beautiful* I.xiv.]

16 Most of our misfortunes are more supportable than the comments of our friends upon them. [C. C. Colton: *Lacon* I]

See also FRIEND(S)

MISOGYNIST

17 *Misogynist*—A man who hates women as much as women hate one another.

[H. L. Mencken: *Chrestomathy* XXX *Sententiae*]

1 Wicked women bother one. Good women bore one. That is the only difference between them. [Oscar Wilde: *Lady Windermere's Fan* III]

Oscar Wilde cannot be accepted as a reliable judge of the attractions of women.

MISSOURI

2 I come from a state that raises corn and cotton and cockleburs and Democrats, and frothy eloquence neither convinces nor satisfies me. I am from Missouri. You have got to show me. [Congressman Willard D. Vandiver (1854-1932): in a speech at a naval dinner in Philadelphia in 1899]

MISTAKEN

3 I beseech you, in the bowels of Christ, think it possible you may be mistaken. [Oliver Cromwell: *Letter to the General Assembly of the Church of Scotland,* August 3, 1650]

A month later, to the day, at the Battle of Dunbar, he showed them that they were.

MISTAKES

4 In war there is no room for two mistakes. [Lamachus, an Athenian general: in Plutarch's *Moralia*]

MISTRESS(ES)

5 O mistress mine, where are you roaming?

[Shakespeare: *Twelfth Night* II.iii.]

6 No, I will only have mistresses.

George II of England, in response to the urging of his queen, on her deathbed, that he remarry. To his remark—spoken amid sobs—she replied: "My God, that won't prevent you!"

The scene was recorded by Lord Hervey, one of the Queen's gentlemen-in-waiting. The royal couple spoke in French.

MISTRUST

7 He that speaks me fair and loves me not, I'll speak him fair and trust him not. [T. Draxe: *A Treasury of . . . Sententious Proverbs* (1616)]

8 I'll trust him no further than I can fling him. [John Ray: *English Proverbs* (1670)]

MITTENS

9 He killed the noble Mudjokivis.
Of the skin he made him mittens,
Made them with the fur side inside
Made them with the skin side outside.
He, to get the warm side inside,
Put the inside skin side outside.
He, to get the cold side outside,
Put the warm side fur side inside.
That's why he put the fur side inside,
Why he put the skin side outside,
Why he turned them inside outside.

[George A. Strong: *The Song of Milkanwatha*]

Longfellow tells us that Hiawatha had mittens, "Magic mittens made of deerskin," but does not give us the details of their manufacture. The parodist has caught very well Longfellow's rhythm and his hypnotic repetitive involution of the obvious that, somehow, gives Hiawatha its charm and aboriginal flavor. In Longfellow's poem Mudjekeewis was Hiawatha's father.

MITTY

10 Then, with that faint fleeting smile playing about his lips, he faced the firing squad; erect and motionless, proud and disdainful, Walter Mitty, the undefeated, inscrutable to the last. [James Thurber: *My World and Welcome to It,* "The Secret Life of Walter Mitty"]

MIZPAH

11 The Lord watch between me and thee, when we are absent one from another. [Genesis 31:49]

The heap of stones or cairn which Jacob and his father-in-law Laban erected to mark their covenant was called Mizpah ("watchtower") and the invocation to the Lord to watch between them, spoken by Laban, is often called "the Mizpah benediction." It might equally well, however, be called the Mizpah malediction, for there was no love lost between them and the invocation was more of a warning than a blessing.

MOBLED

12 The mobled queen. [Shakespeare: *Hamlet* II.ii.]

mobled = with the head muffled or wrapped

MODERATION

1 There is a proper measure in all things, certain limits beyond which and short of which right is not to be found. [Horace: *Satires* I.i.106]
2 A wise man will use moderation
Even in things of commendation.
[Juvenal: *Satires* VI]
> Trans. John Florio, in Montaigne's Essays II.xxviii.

3 You will go most safely in the middle. [Ovid: *Metamorphoses* II]
4 Mesure is medicine. [William Langland: *Piers Plowman*]
> mesure = measure = moderation
> There was also a saying that "The merry mean is best"—merry meaning "happy."

5 All actions beyond the ordinary limits are subject to some sinister interpretation. [Montaigne: *Essays* II.ii.]
6 Fear and dull disposition, lukewarmness and sloth, are not seldom wont to cloak themselves under the affected name of moderation. [John Milton: *An Apology for Smectymnuus*]
7 Moderation is the languor and laziness of the soul, as ambition is its activity and ardor. [La Rochefoucauld: *Maxims*]
8 Men have made a virtue of moderation to limit the ambition of the great, and to console people of mediocrity for their want of fortune and of merit. [La Rochefoucauld: *Maxims*]
9 The moderation of fortunate people comes from the calm which good fortune gives to their tempers. [La Rochefoucauld: *Maxims*]
10 This only grant me, that my means may lie
Too low for envy, for contempt too high.
[Abraham Cowley: *The Vote*]
11 Good sense avoids all extremes, and requires us to be soberly rational. [Molière: *The Misanthrope* I.i.]
12 He knows to live who keeps the middle state. [Alexander Pope: *Imitations of Horace*, "Satires" II.2.]
13 By God, Mr. Chairman, I stand astonished at my own moderation! [Robert, Lord Clive (1725-1774): statement during a Parliamentary investigation (1773) of his reputed plunderings in India]
14 There is moderation even in excess. [Disraeli: *Vivian Grey* VI.i.]
15 Moderation is a fatal thing. Nothing succeeds like excess. [Oscar Wilde: *A Woman of No Importance* III]

MODERN

16 The modern town-dweller has no God and no Devil; he lives without awe, without admiration, without fear. [William Ralph Inge: *Our Present Discontents*]
> And most people, in civilized countries, now live in cities. Curiously, the town-dweller used to regard the bumpkin as irreligious. A heathen is simply one who dwells on a heath, and pagan is probably derived from a word for village. What this meant was that the old religions lingered on in the country, while the towns (urbane and civil) espoused the new religions.

MODERN LIFE

17 This strange disease of modern life,
With its sick hurry, its divided aims.
[Matthew Arnold: *The Scholar-Gipsy*]
18 Too fast we live, too much are tried,
Too harass'd to attain
Wordsworth's sweet calm, or Goethe's wide
And luminous view to gain.
[Matthew Arnold: *Stanzas in Memory of the Author of "Obermann"*]

MODESTY

19 Modesty is of no use to a beggar. [Homer: *Odyssey* XVII]
20 Modesty . . . is a kind of fear of disrepute. [Aristotle: *Nicomachean Ethics* IV.ix.]
> Therefore, he says, it cannot be considered as a virtue.

21 It is difficult for a rich person to be modest, or a modest person rich. [Epictetus: *Enchiridion*]
22 A woman who goes to bed with a man ought to lay aside her modesty with her skirt and put it on again with her petticoat. [Montaigne: *Essays* I.xxi.]
> Montaigne attributes the saying to "the daughter-in-law of Pythagoras."

23 Have you no modesty, no maiden

shame?
[Shakespeare: *A Midsummer Night's Dream* III.ii.]

1 Women commend a modest man, but like him not. [Thomas Fuller (1654-1734): *Gnomologia*]

2 A modesty in delivering our sentiments leaves us a liberty of changing them without blushing. [Thomas Wilson: *Maxims of Piety* (1707)]

MOHAMMED AND THE MOUNTAIN

3 Nay, you shall see a bold fellow many times do Mahomet's miracle. Mahomet made the people believe that he would call a hill to him, and from the top of it offer up his prayers for the observers of his law. The people assembled: Mahomet called the hill to come to him again and again; and when the hill stood still, he was never a whit abashed, but said, "If the hill will not come to Mahomet, Mahomet will go to the hill."
[Francis Bacon: *Of Boldness*]

Bacon speaks as though the story were well known, but it cannot be traced beyond this passage—in the 1612 edition of the Essays. *In modern use, "hill" has been changed to "mountain," probably for the force of the alliteration. And it is usually merely a reference: "If the mountain won't come to Mohammed, Mohammed will go to the mountain."*

In the Middle Ages "Mahound" was thought to be a demon, worshiped as a god by his misguided followers. Later he was regarded as an impostor and the success of his teachings attributed to his boldness and impudence—of which this anecdote was a specimen.

MOHICANS

4 The Last of the Mohicans. [James Fenimore Cooper: title of novel]
The last of the Mohicans was Uncas, the son of Chingachgook.

MOLE

5 If you would keep your soul
From spotted sight or sound,
Live like the velvet mole;
Go burrow underground.

And there hold intercourse
With roots of trees and stones,
With rivers at their source,
And disembodied bones.
[Elinor Wylie: *The Eagle and the Mole*]

MOLOCH

6 First Moloch, horrid King, besmear'd with blood.
[John Milton: *Paradise Lost* I.392]
Molech or Moloch [Heb. = king], a Canaanitish god of fire to whom children were offered in sacrifice. Both Solomon and Ahaz were said to have introduced his worship. "The cult was heathenish in the eyes of the prophetic party. But the people at large seem to have regarded the Melech as a manifestation of Jehovah."—A New Standard Bible Dictionary.

MOMENT

7 When thus I hail the Moment flying:
"Ah, still delay—thou art so fair!"
Then bind me in thy bonds undying,
My final ruin then declare!
[Goethe: *Faust* I.iv.]

8 The psychological moment.
This phrase came into English in 1870 when it was so translated from "Das psychologische Moment" of the Neue Preussische Zeitung *of December 16, in an article discussing the psychological considerations that impelled or restrained the bombardment of Paris, then under siege. The German Moment ("momentum") was mistaken for the English moment, and the phrase was adopted as meaning "the propitious minute."*

MONARCH

9 I am monarch of all I survey,
My right there is none to dispute:
From the center all round to the sea
I am lord of the fowl and the brute.
[William Cowper: *Verses Supposed to Have Been Written by Alexander Selkirk*]

MONEY: its delights

10 A heavy purse makes a light heart.
[16th-century English proverb]

11 Let all the learn'd say what they can,
'Tis ready money makes the man;
Commands respect where'er we go,
And gives a grace to all we do.
[William Somerville: *Ready Money*]

1 There are few ways in which a man can be more innocently employed than in getting money. [Samuel Johnson: in Boswell's *Life*, March 27, 1775]

Johnson made it clear, however, in many places that while he admired innocence, he did not admire the mere making of money. "The sons and daughters of alleys" as he loftily described the commercial world, might be innocent but they were not admirable.

2 A man who both spends and saves money is the happiest man, because he has both enjoyments. [Samuel Johnson: in Boswell's *Life*, April 25, 1778]

3 Ready money is Aladdin's lamp. [Byron: *Don Juan* XII.xii.]

4 As I sat at the café, I said to myself,
They may talk as they please about
what they call pelf,
They may sneer as they like about
eating and drinking,
But help it I cannot, I cannot help
thinking
How pleasant it is to have money,
heigh-ho!
How pleasant it is to have money!
[Arthur Hugh Clough: *Spectator Ab Extra*]

5 Moreover, dangerous human proclivities can be canalised into comparatively harmless channels by the existence of opportunities for money-making and private wealth, which, if they cannot be satisfied in this way, may find their outlet in cruelty, the reckless pursuit of personal power and authority, and other forms of self-aggrandisement. It is better that a man should tyrannize over his bank balance than over his fellow-citizens; and whilst the former is sometimes denounced as being but a means to the latter, sometimes at least it is an alternative. [John Maynard Keynes: *The General Theory of Employment, Interest, and Money* XXIV]

MONEY: filthy lucre

6 Not greedy of filthy lucre. [I Timothy 3:3]

7 Money without honor is a disease. [Balzac: *Eugénie Grandet* IV]

8 And they covenanted with him for thirty pieces of silver. [Matthew 26:15]

MONEY: the lack of it

9 Nothing stings more sharply than the loss of money. [Livy: *History* XXX. xliv.]

10 A son can bear with equanimity the loss of his father, but the loss of his inheritance may drive him to despair. [Machiavelli: *The Prince* XVII]

11 There is commonly less money, less wisdom, and less good faith, than men do account upon. [Francis Bacon: *The Advancement of Learning* II]

12 Who in his pocket hath no money,
In his mouth he must have honey.
[Rowland Watkins: *Flamma Sine Fumo*]

13 Alas! how deeply painful is all payment! . . .
They hate a murderer much less than
a claimant. . . .
Kill a man's family, and he may
brook it—
But keep your hands out of his
breeches' pocket.
[Byron: *Don Juan* X.lxxix.]

14 It has been said that the love of money is the root of all evil. The want of money is so quite as truly. [Samuel Butler (1835-1902): *Erewhon* XX]

15 Lack of money is the root of all evil. [G. B. Shaw: *Maxims for Revolutionists*]

16 Certainly there are lots of things in
life that money won't buy,
but it's very funny—
Have you ever tried to buy them without money?
[Ogden Nash: *The Terrible People*]

MONEY: its limitations

17 Money doesn't change your birth. [Horace: *Epodes* IV.5.]

18 Money is like muck, not good except it be spread. [Francis Bacon: *Of Seditions and Troubles*]
muck = *manure*

19 The love of money and the love of learning rarely meet. [George Herbert: *Jacula Prudentum*]

20 If your riches are yours, why don't you take them with you to t'other world? [Benjamin Franklin: *Poor Richard's Almanack* (1751)]

21 The fact is, in my opinion, that we often buy money very much too dear. [W. M. Thackeray: *Barry Lyndon* XIII]

1 Money is like the reputation for ability—more easily made than kept. [Samuel Butler (1835-1902): *The Way of All Flesh* XIX]

2 There's no pocket in a shroud. [John Alexander Joyce: *There's No Pocket in a Shroud*]

3 You Can't Take It With You. [Moss Hart and George Kaufman: title of a play (1936)]

4 Money is like manure. If you spread it around, it does a lot of good. But if you pile it up in one place, it stinks like hell. [Clint Murchison, Jr., quoted in *Time*, June 16, 1961]

MONEY: and love

5 No woman is worth money that will take money. [John Vanbrugh: *The Relapse* II]

6 Money is the sinews of love, as of war. [George Farquhar: *Love and a Bottle* II.i.]

7 But I knaw'd a Quaäker feller as
    often 'as towd me this:
"Doänt thou marry for munny, but
    goä wheer munny is!"
[Tennyson: *Northern Farmer: New Style*]

8 I think I could be a good woman if I had five thousand a year. [W. M. Thackeray: (Becky Sharp) *Vanity Fair* II.1]

MONEY: the love of

9 The love of money is the mother of all evil. [Phocylides (6th century B.C.): *Sententiae*]

10 For the love of money is the root of all evil: which while some coveted after, they have erred from the faith, and pierced themselves through with many sorrows. [I Timothy 6:10]

11 [The rich] are indeed rather possessed by their money than possessors. [Robert Burton: *Anatomy of Melancholy* I.2.3.12.]

12 Were it not that they are loath to lay out money on a rope, they would be hanged forthwith, and sometimes die to save charges. [Robert Burton: *Anatomy of Melancholy* I.2.3.12]

13 They may be false who languish and
             complain,
But they who sigh for money never
             feign.
[Mary Wortley Montagu: Letter to James Steuart, November 27, 1759]

MONEY: its power

14 Wine maketh merry: but money answereth all things. [Ecclesiastes 10:19]

15 Money, the sinews of war. [Cicero: *Philippics* V.ii.]

16 Alle thinges obeyen to moneye. [Chaucer: *The Tale of Melibeus*]

17 When in the box the money rings,
The soul from Purgatory springs.
The common version:
    Sobald das Geld in Kasten klingt,
    Die Seele aus dem Fegfeuer springt
is, apparently, based on the rhyme that Hans Sachs ascribed to Johann Tetzel, the Dominican monk appointed (1517) by Archbishop Albert of Mainz to sell indulgences. His zeal in getting money aroused Luther to publish his 95 theses at Wittenberg (1517).
Sachs's lines occur in Die Wittenbergisch Nachtigall *("The Wittenberg Nightingale"), 1523.*
    Legt ein gebt euwer hilff und stewr
    Und lösst die seel auss dem Fegfewr
    Bald der guldin im Kasten klinget
    Die Seel sich auff gen hymel schwinget.
    "Repose in prayer your help and
             guide
    And free the soul from Purgatory.
    As soon as your coins clink in the
             box
    The soul springs up towards
             heaven."

18 Wilt thou lend me thy mare to ride
             but a mile?
No, she's lame, going over a stile;
But if thou wilt her to me spare,
Thou shalt have money for thy mare.
Ho ho, say you so!
Money shall make my mare to go.
[Mss. addition to *The Second Part of Musicks Melodie* (1609), in the British Museum. Quoted by Iona and Peter Opie, *The Oxford Dictionary of Nursery Rhymes.*]
The rhyme became a nursery rhyme and the last line, usually as "Money makes the mare go," became a proverb.

19 It is pretty to see what money will do. [Samuel Pepys: *Diary*, March 21, 1667]

20 They say that knowledge is power. I

used to think so, but I now know that they meant money. . . . Every guinea is a philosopher's stone. . . . Cash is virtue. [Byron: Letter to Douglas Kinnaird]

1 Whoso has sixpence is sovereign (to the length of sixpence) over all men; commands cooks to feed him, philosophers to teach him, kings to mount guard over him—to the length of sixpence. [Thomas Carlyle: *Sartor Resartus* I]

2 Cash payment has become the sole nexus of man to man. [Thomas Carlyle: *Chartism*]

3 The jingling of the guinea helps the hurt that honor feels.
[Tennyson: *Locksley Hall*]

4 Money is indeed the most important thing in the world; and all sound and successful personal and national morality should have this fact for its basis. [G. B. Shaw: Preface to *The Irrational Knot*]

5 The seven deadly sins. . . . Food, clothing, firing, rent, taxes, respectability and children. Nothing can lift those seven millstones from man's neck but money; and the spirit cannot soar until the millstones are lifted. [G. B. Shaw: *Major Barbara* III]

6 There are few sorrows, however poignant, in which a good income is of no avail. [Logan Pearsall Smith: *Afterthoughts*]

7 It's a kind of spiritual snobbery that makes people think they can be happy without money. [Albert Camus: *Notebooks 1935-1942* II]

8 Money is like a sixth sense—and you can't make use of the other five without it. [Somerset Maugham: in the *N. Y. Times Magazine,* Oct. 18, 1958]

MONEY: put money in thy purse
9 Get money by fair means if you can; if not, get money. [Horace: *Epistles* I]

10 Nothing comes amiss, so money comes withal.
[Shakespeare: *The Taming of the Shrew* I.ii.]

11 Put money in thy purse.
[Shakespeare: *Othello* I.iii.]

12 The rule, Get money, still get money, boy;
No matter by what means.
[Ben Jonson: *Every Man in His Humour* II.iii.]

13 Put not your trust in money, but put your money in trust. [O. W. Holmes: *The Autocrat of the Breakfast-Table* II]

14 The gospel left behind by Jay Gould is doing giant work in our days. Its message is 'Get money. Get it quickly. Get it in abundance. Get it dishonestly, if you can, honestly, if you must.' [Mark Twain: in *Mark Twain in Eruption,* by Bernard de Voto]

Mark's error lies in "in our days" and the naive assumption that Jay Gould invented cupidity. But see above the quotation from Horace, who lived in the first century B.C.

MONEY: miscellaneous
15 That man is admired above all men, who is not influenced by money. [Cicero: *De officiis* II.xi.]

16 Money has no smell. [Vespasian: in Suetonius's *The Deified Vespasian* XXIII]

Among the revenue-raising devices which the Emperor Vespasian instituted was a tax on public urinals. His son Titus felt this was unseemly and reproached his father for it. Vespasian—a great joker—held a piece of money from the first payment to his son's nose and asked him if it smelled.

The Parisians call the urinals along the boulevards "vespasiennes."

17 What is worth in anything
But so much money as 'twill bring?
[Samuel Butler (1612-1680): *Hudibras*]

18 Some people's money is merited,
And other people's is inherited.
[Ogden Nash: *The Terrible People*]

19 If Karl, instead of writing a lot about Capital, made a lot of Capital, it would have been much better. [Karl Marx's mother, quoted in Alan Valentine's *Fathers to Sons*]

MONKEY(S)
20 I believe that our Heavenly Father invented man because he was disappointed in the monkey. [Mark Twain: in *Mark Twain in Eruption* by Bernard de Voto]

21 Monkeys . . . very sensibly refrain from speech, lest they should be set to earn their livings. [Kenneth Grahame: *The Golden Age*]

MONOGAMY

1 Monogamy . . . forces the high contracting parties into an intimacy that is too persistent and unmitigated; they are in contact at too many points, and too steadily. By and by all the mystery of the relation is gone, and they stand in the unsexed position of brother and sister. [H. L. Mencken: in *Smart Set,* December 1921]

MONOTHEISM

2 Thou shalt have one God only; who
 Would be at the expense of two?
[Arthur Hugh Clough: *The Latest Decalogue*]

MONROE DOCTRINE

3 The American continents . . . are henceforth not to be considered as subjects for future colonization by any European powers. [James Monroe: *Message to Congress* (1823)]
4 I called the New World into existence to redress the balance of the Old. [George Canning: in a speech in the House of Commons (1826)]

MONSTER(S)

5 Those which we call monsters are not so with God. [Montaigne: *Essays* II. XXX.]
6   By heaven, he echoes me,
 As if there were some monster in his
 thought
 Too hideous to be shown.
[Shakespeare: *Othello* III.iii.]
7 Gorgons and Hydras, and Chimaeras
 dire.
[John Milton: *Paradise Lost* II.628]

MONTREAL

8 "The Discobolus is out here because
 he is vulgar—
He has neither vest nor pants with
 which to cover his limbs:
I, sir, am a person of the most respectable connections—
My brother-in-law is haberdasher to
 Mr. Spurgeon."
O God! O Montreal!
[Samuel Butler (1835-1902): *A Psalm of Montreal*]
 Butler had visited the museum in Montreal and found the Discobolus hidden away because it was "rather vulgar."
 Mrs. Trollope relates that in Philadelphia ladies and gentlemen were not allowed to view antique statuary in mixed groups.
 See also PRUDERY

MONUMENT(S)

9 I would rather have men ask, after I am dead, why I have no monument than ask why I have one. [Attr. Marcus Porcius Cato the Elder (234-149 B.C.)]
10 Death comes even to monuments and to the names engraved on them. [Ausonius: *Epitaphs* No. 32]
 See also OZYMANDIAS
11 Not marble nor the gilded monuments
 Of princes shall outlive this pow'rful
 rhyme.
[Shakespeare: *Sonnets* LV]
12 A forted residence 'gainst the tooth
 of time
 And razure of oblivion.
[Shakespeare: *Measure for Measure* V.i.]

MOOD

13 That blessed mood,
 In which the burthen of the mystery,
 In which the heavy and the weary
 weight
 Of all this unintelligible world,
 Is lightened.
[Wordsworth: *Tintern Abbey*]

MOON

14 He made his friends believe the moon to be made of green cheese. [Erasmus: *Adagia* (1500)]
 A proverb, apparently, even then; quoted also by John Frith (1503-1533), A Pistle to the Christen Reader.
15 Late late yestreen I saw the new
 moone,
 Wi the auld moóne in hir arme,
 And I feir, I feir, my deir master,
 That we will cum to harme.
[Anon: *Sir Patrick Spens*]
16 With how sad steps, O moon, thou
 climb'st the skies!
 How silently, and with how wan a

face!
[Sir Philip Sidney: *Astrophel and Stella*, Sonnet XXXI]

1 Eager Wolves bark at ye Moone, though they cannot reach it. [John Lyly: *Euphues and His England*]

2 O, swear not by the moon, the inconstant moon,
That monthly changes in her circled orb,
Lest that thy love prove likewise variable.
[Shakespeare: *Romeo and Juliet* II.ii.]

3 Let us be Diana's foresters, gentlemen of the shade, minions of the moon.
[Shakespeare: *I Henry IV* I.ii.]
These are euphemisms—here—for robbers, footpads, night prowlers.

4 How slow / This old moon wanes!
[Shakespeare: *A Midsummer Night's Dream* I.i.]

5 Doth the moon care for the barking of a dog? [Robert Burton: *Anatomy of Melancholy* II.3.7]

6   I walk unseen
On the dry smooth-shaven green,
To behold the wandering Moon
Riding near her highest noon,
Like one that had been led astray
Through the heav'n's wide pathless way;
And oft, as if her head she bow'd,
Stooping through a fleecy cloud.
[John Milton: *Il Penseroso*]

7   The Moon,
Rising in clouded majesty, at length
Apparent Queen, unveil'd her peerless light,
And o'er the dark her silver mantle threw.
[John Milton: *Paradise Lost* IV.606-609]

8 Till clomb above the eastern bar
The hornèd moon, with one bright star
Within the nether tip.
[Coleridge: *The Ancient Mariner* III]

9 The moving moon went up the sky,
And nowhere did abide;
Softly she was going up,
And a star or two beside.
[Coleridge: *The Ancient Mariner* IV]

10 That orbed maiden with white fire laden,
Whom mortals call the moon.
[Shelley: *The Cloud*]

11 But tenderly above the sea
Hangs, white and calm, the hunter's moon.
[J. G. Whittier: *The Eve of Election*]

12 The moon was a ghostly galleon tossed upon cloudy seas.
[Alfred Noyes: *The Highwayman*]

13 And then one night, low above the trees, we saw the great, amorous, unabashed face of the full Moon. It was an exhibition that made me blush, feel that I had no right to be there. "After all these millions of years, she ought to be ashamed of herself!" I cried. [Logan Pearsall Smith: *Trivia*]

MOONLIGHT

14 How sweet the moonlight sleeps upon this bank!
[Shakespeare: *The Merchant of Venice* V.i.]

15 Ill met by moonlight, proud Titania.
[Shakespeare: *A Midsummer Night's Dream* II.i.]

MOORE, TOM

16 My boat is on the shore,
And my bark is on the sea:
But, before I go, Tom Moore,
Here's a double health to thee.
[Byron: *To Thomas Moore*]

MORAL

17 A moral expression at the close of a lewd play is much like a pious expression in the mouth of a dying man. . . . The doctor comes too late for the disease and the antidote is much too weak for the poison. [Jeremy Collier: *The Immorality of the English Stage*]

18 "Tut, tut, child," said the Duchess. "Everything's got a moral if only you can find it." [Lewis Carroll: *Alice's Adventures in Wonderland* IX]

MORALITY

19 We know no spectacle so ridiculous as the British public in one of its periodical fits of morality. [Macaulay: *Moore's Life of Lord Byron*]

20 The foundation of morality is to have done, once and for all, with lying.
[T. H. Huxley: *Science and Morals*]

21 Veracity is the heart of morality.
[T. H. Huxley: *Universities Actual and*

Ideal]
1 The foundations of morality are like all other foundations: if you dig too much about them, the superstructure will come tumbling down. [Samuel Butler (1835-1902): *Notebooks*]
2 Morality was made for man, not man for morality. [Israel Zangwill: *Children of the Ghetto*]
3 Moral indignation is jealousy with a halo. [H. G. Wells: *The Wife of Sir Isaac Harman* IX]
4 . . . a moral truth is a hollow tooth
Which must be propped with gold.
[Edgar Lee Masters: *Sexsmith the Dentist*]
5 To be a moral man is to obey the traditional maxims of your community without hesitation or discussion. Hence, ethics, which is reasoning out an explanation of morality, is—I will not say immoral, that would be going too far—composed of the very substance of immorality. [Charles S. Peirce: *Collected Papers* I]
6 No known race is so little human as not to suppose a moral order so innately desirable as to have an inevitable existence. It is man's most fundamental myth. [Joseph Wood Krutch: *The Modern Temper* I]
7 What is morality in any given time or place? It is what the majority then and there happen to like and immorality is what they dislike. [Alfred North Whitehead: *Dialogues* (Recorded by Lucien Price)]
8 What is moral is what you feel good after and what is immoral is what you feel bad after. [Ernest Hemingway: *Death in the Afternoon*]
9 It is a moral and political axiom that any dishonorable act, if performed by oneself, is less immoral than if performed by someone else, who would be less well-intentioned in his dishonesty. [J. Christopher Herold: *Bonaparte in Egypt* I]

MORALS AND MANNERS

10 They teach the morals of a whore, and the manners of a dancing master. [Samuel Johnson: in Boswell's *Life* (1754)]

Johnson was referring to Chesterfield's Letters to His Son.

MORE

11 Please, sir, I want some more. [Dickens: *Oliver Twist* II]

MORNING

12 The wings of the morning. [Psalms 139:9]
13 Full many a glorious morning have I seen
Flatter the mountain tops with sovereign eye,
Kissing with golden face the meadows green,
Gilding pale streams with heavenly alchemy.
[Shakespeare: *Sonnets* XXXIII]
14 The grey-eyed morn smiles on the frowning night,
Chequering the eastern clouds with streaks of light.
[Shakespeare: *Romeo and Juliet* II.iii.]
15 *King Henry.* How bloodily the sun begins to peer
Above yon busky hill! The day looks pale
At his distemp'rature.
Prince of Wales. The southern wind
Doth play the trumpet to his purposes
And by his hollow whistling in the leaves
Foretells a tempest and a blust'ring day.
[Shakespeare: *I Henry IV* V.i.]
16 A red morn, that ever yet betoken'd
Wrack to the seaman, tempest to the field.
[Shakespeare: *The Taming of the Shrew* V.ii.]
17 But, look, the morn, in russet mantle clad,
Walks o'er the dew of yon high eastward hill.
[Shakespeare: *Hamlet* I.i.]
18 The glow-worm shows the matin to be near,
And 'gins to pale his uneffectual fire.
[Shakespeare: *Hamlet* I.v.]
19 While the cock with lively din
Scatters the rear of darkness thin,
And to the stack, or the barn door,
Stoutly struts his dames before,

Oft list'ning how the hounds and
horn
Cheerly rouse the slumb'ring morn.
[John Milton: *L'Allegro*]
1 Under the opening eyelids of the
morn.
[John Milton: *Lycidas*]
2 While the still morn went out with
sandals grey.
[John Milton: *Lycidas*]
3 Sweet is the breath of morn, her ris-
ing sweet,
With charm of earliest birds.
[John Milton: *Paradise Lost* IV. 641-642]
4 Morn,
Wak'd by the circling hours, with
rosy hand
Unbarr'd the gates of light.
[John Milton: *Paradise Lost* VI. 2-4]
5 And like a lobster boiled, the morn
From black to red began to turn.
[Samuel Butler (1612-1680): *Hudibras*]
6 The breezy call of incense-breathing
Morn.
[Thomas Gray: *Elegy Written in a
Country Churchyard*]
7 There was a roaring in the wind all
night;
The rain came heavily and fell in
floods;
But now the sun is rising calm and
bright;
The birds are singing in the distant
woods;
Over his own sweet voice the Stock-
dove broods;
The Jay makes answer as the Mag-
pie chatters;
And all the air is filled with pleas-
ant noise of waters.
[Wordsworth: *Resolution and Independence*]
8 Each matin bell, the Baron saith,
Knells us back to a world of death.
[Coleridge: *Christabel* II]
9 Never glad confident morning again.
[Robert Browning: *The Lost Leader*]
10 Round the cape of a sudden came
the sea,
And the sun looked over the mountain's rim:
And straight was a path of gold for
him,
And the need of a world of men for
me.

[Robert Browning: *Parting at Morn-
ing*]
11 Yonder see the morning blink:
The sun is up, and up must I,
To wash and dress and eat and drink
And look at things and talk and
think
And work, and God knows why.
[A. E. Housman: *Last Poems* XI]
12 The candles burn their sockets,
The blinds let through the day,
The young man feels his pockets
And wonders what's to pay.
[A. E. Housman: *Last Poems* XXI]
13 The diamond tears adorning
Thy low mound on the lea,
Those are the tears of morning,
That weeps, but not for thee.
[A. E. Housman: *Last Poems* XXVII]

MORON
14 I don't know what a moron is,
And I don't give a damn.
I'm thankful that I am not one—
My God! perhaps I am.
[Henry Pratt Fairchild: in *Harper's,*
May 1932]

MORTALITY
15 Nature has given to man nothing of
more value than shortness of life. [Pliny
the Elder: *Natural History* VII.v.]
16 Had I but died an hour before this
chance,
I had liv'd a blessed time; for, from
this instant,
There's nothing serious in mortality.
[Shakespeare: *Macbeth* II.iii.]
17 All men think all men mortal but
themselves.
[Edward Young: *Night Thoughts* I]
18 The clouds that gather round the
setting sun
Do take a sober coloring from an eye
That hath kept watch o'er man's
mortality.
[Wordsworth: *Intimations of Immortality*]
19 Mortality
Weighs heavily on me like unwilling
sleep.
[Keats: *On Seeing the Elgin Marbles*]

MORTAL(S)
20 Lord, what fools these mortals be!

[Shakespeare: *A Midsummer Night's Dream* III.ii.]

1 Oh, why should the spirit of mortal
be proud?
Like a fast-flitting meteor, a fast-
flying cloud,
A flash of the lightning, a break of
the wave,
He passes from life to his rest in the
grave.

[William Knox: *Mortality*]

MOTE(S)

2 And why beholdest thou the mote
that is in thy brother's eye, but considerest not the beam that is in thine own
eye? [Matthew 7:3]

3 As thick and numberless
As the gay motes that people the sunbeams.

[John Milton: *Il Penseroso*]
As thick as motes in the sun-beame.
—*Chaucer:* The Wife of Bath's Tale

MOTH(S)

4 All the yarn she spun in Ulysses' absence did but fill Ithaca full of moths.
[Shakespeare: *Coriolanus* I.iii.]

5 The desire of the moth for the star,
Of the night for the morrow,
The devotion to something afar
From the sphere of our sorrow.

[Shelley: *To ———. One Word is Too
Often Profaned*]

6 Not a moth with vain desire
Is shrivel'd in a fruitless fire,
Or but subserves another's gain.

[Tennyson: *In Memoriam* LIV]

MOTHER

7 Her children arise up and call her
blessed. [Proverbs 31:28]

8 Can a woman forget her sucking
child, that she should not have compassion on the son of her womb? [Isaiah
49:15]

9 He that wipes the child's nose kisses
the mother's cheek. [George Herbert:
Jacula Prudentum (1651)]
*That is, interest in a child, particularly
when shown by a man, is usually a courting of the mother.*

10 Mothers soften their children with
kisses and imperfect noises, with the pap
and breast-milk of soft endearments;
they rescue them from tutors, and snatch
them from discipline, they desire to keep
them fat and warm, and their feet dry,
and their bellies full, and then the children govern, and cry, and prove fools
and troublesome. [Jeremy Taylor: *Holy
Dying* III]

11 A light-heel'd mother makes a heavy-
heel'd daughter. Because she doth all the
work herself, and her daughter the mean
while sitting idle, contracts a habit of
sloth. [John Ray: *English Proverbs*
(1670)]

12 Every one can keep House better
than her Mother, till she trieth.
[Thomas Fuller (1654-1734): *Gnomologia*]

13 Where yet was ever found a mother,
Who'd give her booby for another?

[John Gay: *The Mother, the Nurse, and
the Fairy* III]

14 A mother is a mother still,
The holiest thing alive.

[Coleridge: *The Three Graves*]

15 Who ran to help me when I fell,
And would some pretty story tell,
Or kiss the place to make it well?
My Mother.

[Ann Taylor: *My Mother*]

16 Youth fades; love droops, the leaves
of friendship fall;
A mother's secret hope outlives them
all.

[O. W. Holmes: *A Mother's Secret*]

17 Mother is the name for God in the
lips and hearts of children. [W. M.
Thackeray: *Vanity Fair*]

18 That best academy, a mother's knee.
[James Russell Lowell: *The Cathedral*]

19 For the hand that rocks the cradle
Is the hand that rules the world.

[William Ross Wallace: *What Rules the
World*]

20 What is Home without a Mother?
[Alice Hawthorne: Title of poem]

21 She's somebody's mother, boys, you
know,
For all she's aged and poor and slow.

[Mary Dow Brine: *Somebody's Mother*]

22 Ah, lucky girls who grow up in the
shelter of a mother's love—a mother
who knows how to contrive opportunities without conceding favors, how to
take advantage of propinquity without
allowing appetite to be dulled by habit.

[Edith Wharton: *The House of Mirth* I]

1 If I were hanged on the highest hill,
    Mother o' mine, O mother o' mine!
    I know whose love would follow me
        still,
    Mother o' mine, O mother o' mine!
[Kipling: *Mother o' Mine*]

2 Sure I love the dear silver that shines
        in your hair,
    And the brow that's all furrowed, and
        wrinkled with care.
    I kiss the dear fingers, so toilworn for
        me,
    Oh, God bless you and keep you,
        Mother Machree.
[Rida Johnson Young: *Mother Machree*]

3 I want a girl just like the girl that married dear old dad. [William Dillon: popular song (1911)]
One of the naïver expressions of the Oedipus complex.

4 The obese multipara in her greasy kimono. [H. L. Mencken: *Prejudices: First Series*]

5 The florists are everywhere the most ardent of matriolaters. [Aldous Huxley: *Jesting Pilate,* "America"]

6 Megaloid momworship has got completely out of hand. [Philip Wylie: *Generation of Vipers* XI]

MOTION

7 Jack Whirler, whose business keeps him in perpetual motion and whose motion always eludes his business; who is always to do what he never does, who cannot stand still because he is wanted in another place, and who is wanted in many places because he stays in none. [Samuel Johnson: *The Idler* No. 19]
What Sinclair Lewis was to describe as "a hustler."

MOTIVE(S)

8 We would often be ashamed of our finest actions if the world understood all the motives which produced them. [La Rochefoucauld: *Maxims*]

9 There are countless actions which appear ridiculous, whose hidden motives are very wise and weighty. [La Rochefoucauld: *Maxims*]

10 If I fling half a crown to a beggar with intention to break his head, and he picks it up and buys victuals with it, the physical effect is good; but, with respect to me, the action is very wrong. [Samuel Johnson: in Boswell's *Life,* May 24, 1763]

11 What makes life dreary is the want of motive. [George Eliot: *Daniel Deronda* VIII.lxv.]

MOUNTAINS

12 They came to the Delectable Mountains.
[John Bunyan: *The Pilgrim's Progress* I]

MOURNING

13 No longer mourn for me when I am
        dead
    Than you shall hear the surly sullen
        bell
    Give warning to the world that I am
        fled.
[Shakespeare: *Sonnets* LXXI]

14 By fairy hands their knell is rung;
    By forms unseen their dirge is sung.
    There Honour comes, a pilgrim grey,
    To bless the turf that wraps their
        clay,
    And Freedom shall awhile repair,
    To dwell a weeping hermit there!
[William Collins: *Ode Written in the Year 1746*]

15   . . . Nature's law
    That man was made to mourn.
[Burns: *Man was Made to Mourn*]

16 Ah, surely nothing dies but something mourns.
[Byron: *Don Juan* III.cviii.]

17 I weep for Adonais—he is dead!
    Oh, weep for Adonais! though our
        tears
    Thaw not the frost which binds so
        dear a head!
[Shelley: *Adonais* I]

18 Come not, when I am dead,
    To drop thy foolish tears upon my
        grave,
    To trample round my fallen head,
    And vex the unhappy dust thou
        wouldst not save.
    There let the wind sweep and the
        plover cry;
    But thou, go by.
[Tennyson: *Come Not, When I Am Dead*]

19 When I am dead, my dearest,
    Sing no sad songs for me.
[Christina Rossetti: *Song*]

1 With rue my heart is laden
    For golden friends I had,
    For many a rose-lipt maiden
    And many a lightfoot lad.

By brooks too broad for leaping
    The lightfoot boys are laid;
    The rose-lipt girls are sleeping
    In fields where roses fade.
[A. E. Housman: *A Shropshire Lad* LIV]

MOUSE (MICE)

2 The mountains were in labor; a ridiculous mouse was born.
[Horace: *Ars poetica*]
3 I holde a mouses herte nat worth a leek
    That hath but oon hole for to sterte to.
[Chaucer: Prologue to *The Wife of Bath's Tale*]
4 Playing the mouse in absence of the cat.
[Shakespeare: *Henry V* I.ii.]
5 Pour not Water on a drowning Mouse. [Thomas Fuller (1654-1734): *Gnomologia*]
6 I doubt na, whyles, but thou may thieve;
    What then? poor beastie, thou maun live!

A daimen icker in a thrave
    'S a sma' request:
    I'll get a blessin' wi' the lave,
    And never miss 't!
[Burns: *To a Mouse*]
    whyles = *at times;* maun = *must;* daimen icker = *an occasional ear of wheat;* thrave = *two shocks*

7 When a building is about to fall down, all the mice desert it. [Pliny the Elder: *Natural History* VIII.]
8 Three blind mice, see how they run!
    They all ran after the farmer's wife.
    She cut off their tails with the carving knife,
    Did ever you see such a sight in your life,
    As three blind mice?
[An Elizabethan round, first recorded in 1609]
    Now a nursery rhyme but not regarded as one, apparently, until the middle of the 19th century.

9 Mice and rats and such small deer
    Have been Tom's food for seven long year.
[Shakespeare: *King Lear* III.iv.]
    deer = *animals*
    The Anglo-Saxon word for animals in general was deor. *That the unspecialized meaning survived into Elizabethan English, in this passage, is due to the fact that the speaker in the play is quoting an old poem in which the word is imbedded.*

MOUSETRAP

10 If a man write a better book, preach a better sermon, or make a better mousetrap than his neighbor, though he build his house in the woods, the world will make a beaten path to his door. [Commonly attr. Emerson, though not to be found in his works, and commonly given in the form: "If a man make a better mouse-trap, the world will beat a path to his door."]
    The statement was first attributed to Emerson by Mrs. Sarah Yule, who stated that he had used it in a lecture which he gave at either San Francisco or Oakland in 1871. Scholars accept it as authentic—something that occurred to Emerson as he was speaking—despite the fact that he did not write it down. We do know that in his essay Common Fame *(1855) he has a passage that is strikingly similar: "If a man has good corn, or wood, or boards, or pigs, to sell, or can make better chairs or knives, crucibles, or church organs, than anybody else, you will find a broad, hard-beaten road to his house, though it be in the woods."*

11 There is a danger when the better mousetrap is better at catching people than at catching mice. [Charles Eames: quoted in *Time*, May 3, 1963]

MOUTH(S)

12 Out of thine own mouth will I judge thee. [Luke 19:22]
13 Blind mouths! that scarce themselves know how to hold
    A sheep hook, or have learned aught else the least
    That to the faithful Herdman's art belongs!
[John Milton: *Lycidas*]

MOVE

1 But it does move! (*E pur si muove*) [Attr. Galileo Galilei; after he had recanted his assertion that the earth moved round the sun]

The earliest the phrase can be dated is 1761, 128 years after the recantation.

MOVING

2 Three removes are as bad as a fire. [Benjamin Franklin: *Poor Richard's Almanack* (1736)]

MUCKRAKER(S)

3 [There] was a man who could look no way but downwards, with a muckrake in his hand. [John Bunyan: *Pilgrim's Progress* II (1684)]

It was this passage that Theodore Roosevelt had in mind when he coined the word muckrakers to describe the journalists who were busy exposing corruptions in our cities and businesses. Roosevelt, at the Gridiron Club dinner in Washington, in 1906, said that the muckrakers were valuable "but only if they know when to stop raking the muck." TR loved bold attack in careful moderation.

MUFFET

4 Little Miss Muffet
Sat on a tuffet,
  Eating her curds and whey:
There came a big spider
Who sat down beside her
  And frightened Miss Muffet away.
[Anon.: earliest known date, 1805]

There was a famous entomologist, Dr. Thomas Muffet (d.1604), whose specialty was arachnology and some think the verse may allude to a contretemps in the Muffet household. The more scholarly see it as a parallel to other rhymes connected with the old cushion dance, a mating and marriage dance. The young lady sits demure and expectant—and something horrible may happen.

MULE

5 Father and mother he does not resemble, sons and daughters he will never have; vindictive and patient (it is a known fact that he will labor ten years willingly and patiently for you, for the privilege of kicking you once); solitary but without pride, self-sufficient but without vanity; his voice is his own derision. Outcast and pariah, he has neither friend, wife, mistress, or sweetheart; celibate, he is unscarred . . . he is not assaulted by temptations nor flagellated by dreams nor assuaged by vision; faith, hope and charity are not his. Misanthropic, he labors six days without reward for one creature whom he hates, bound with chains to another whom he despises, and spends the seventh day kicking or being kicked by his fellows . . . meek, his inheritance is cooked away from him along with his soul in a glue factory. Ugly, untiring and perverse, he can be moved neither by reason, flattery, nor promise of reward; he performs his humble monotonous duties without complaint, and his meed is blows. Alive he is haled through the world, an object of general derision; unwept, unhonored and unsung, he bleaches his awkward bones among rusting cans and broken crockery and worn-out automobile tires on lonely hillsides while his flesh soars unawares against the blue in craws of buzzards. [William Faulkner: *Sartoris*]

MUMMY

6 The Egyptian mummies, which Cambyses or time hath spared, avarice now consumeth. Mummy is become merchandise, Mizraim cures wounds, and Pharaoh is sold for balsams. [Sir Thomas Browne: *Of Ambition and Fame*]

Mizraim—son of Noah's son Ham, eponymous ancestor of the Hamitic peoples of lower Egypt.

Cambyses II, King of Persia (529-522 B.C.), conquered Egypt and sacked many tombs. Powdered mummy was, for centuries, esteemed as a medicine and there was a considerable trade, carried on by "men wondrous audacious and covetous," in imitation mummy—hanged criminals merely salted and browned in an oven. Paré, the great French physician, said that the only effect on the patient of eating mummy, that he could see, was "vomiting and stink of the mouth."

MURDER

7 Mordre wol out, certeyn, it wol nat

faille.
[Chaucer: *The Prioress's Tale*]
Also in The Nun's Priest's Tale. *It was firmly believed that a murderer would be exposed, by supernatural means if necessary.*

1   Murder most foul.
[Shakespeare: *Hamlet* I.v.]
2   Thus was I, sleeping, by a brother's hand
Of life, of crown, of queen, at once dispatch'd:
Cut off even in the blossoms of my sin,
Unhousel'd, disappointed, unaneled,
No reckoning made, but sent to my account
With all my imperfections on my head.
[Shakespeare: *Hamlet* I.v.]
unhousel'd = *not having received the Eucharist;* unaneled = *not having received extreme unction;* disappointed = *lacking the proper appointments, hence not fitted out, unprepared*
    This special meaning of disappointed, *now obsolete, illustrates the pitfalls that await the unwary reader who attempts, unguided, to read the literature of a former age. To a modern, the ghost's complaint of being "disappointed" seems a ludicrous understatement.*

3   For murder, though it have no tongue, will speak
With most miraculous organ.
[Shakespeare: *Hamlet* II.ii.]
4   Carcasses bleed at the sight of the murderer. [Robert Burton: *Anatomy of Melancholy* I.1.2.5]
5   If once a man indulges himself in murder, very soon he comes to think little of robbing; and from robbing he next comes to drinking and Sabbath-breaking, and from that to incivility and procrastination. [Thomas De Quincey: *On Murder Considered as One of the Fine Arts*]

MUSEUMS
6   Museums—cemeteries of the arts.
[Alphonse de Lamartine: *Voyage en Orient. Athenes*]

MUSIC: descriptions of
7   Untwisting all the chains that tie

The hidden soul of harmony.
[John Milton: *L'Allegro*]
8   And ever, against eating cares,
Lap me in soft Lydian airs,
Married to immortal verse,
Such as the meeting soul may pierce,
In notes with many a winding bout
Of linkèd sweetness long drawn out.
[John Milton: *L'Allegro*]
Lydian music was melting and voluptuous, in contrast with Dorian, which was solemn and martial. Eating cares bothers us a little now, since eating in this sense ("What's eating you?") is now slang, though a word once applied only to animals, fretting, has maintained a dignity.

9   Sonorous metal blowing martial sounds.
[John Milton: *Paradise Lost* I.540]
10   Music, the greatest good that mortals know,
And all of heaven we have below.
[Joseph Addison: *Song for St. Cecilia's Day*]
11   Where through the long-drawn aisle and fretted vault
The pealing anthem swells the note of praise.
[Thomas Gray: *Elegy Written in a Country Churchyard*]
12   The silver, snarling trumpets 'gan to chide.
[Keats: *The Eve of St. Agnes*]
13   Seated one day at the organ,
I was weary and ill at ease,
And my fingers wandered idly
Over the noisy keys.

I do not know what I was playing,
Or what I was dreaming then;
But I struck one chord of music,
Like the sound of a great Amen.
[Adelaide Anne Procter: *A Lost Chord*]
First line of 2nd stanza better known in form in which it was set to music by Sir Arthur Sullivan—as The Lost Chord—: *I know not what I was playing.*

14   The banjos rattled, and the tambourines
Jing-jing-jingled in the hands of Queens!
[Vachel Lindsay: *General Booth Enters Heaven*]
15   The hackneyed melancholy of street

music; a music which sounds like the actual voice of the human Heart, singing the lost joys, the regrets, the loveless lives of the people who blacken the pavements, or jolt along on the busses. [Logan Pearsall Smith: *Trivia*, "The Organ of Life"]

1 There are only two kinds of music; German music and bad music. [H. L. Mencken: quoted in *The Man Mencken* by Isaac Goldberg (1925)]

2 It will be generally admitted that Beethoven's Fifth Symphony is the most sublime noise that has ever penetrated into the ear of man. [E. M. Forster: *Howards End* V]

3 That which penetrates the ear with facility and quits the memory with difficulty. [Sir Thomas Beecham (defining good music), quoted in the *New York Times*, March 9, 1961]

MUSIC: its power

4 Where griping griefs the heart would wound
And doleful dumps the mind oppress,
There music with her silver sound
With speed is wont to send redress.
[Richard Edwards: *A Song to the Lute*]
Shakespeare uses a version of this song in Romeo and Juliet *IV.v. (1595).*

5 Is it not strange that sheep's guts should hale souls out of men's bodies? [Shakespeare: *Much Ado About Nothing* II.iii.]

6 This music crept by me upon the waters,
Allaying both their fury, and my passion,
With its sweet air.
[Shakespeare: *The Tempest* I.ii.]

7 Sweet compulsion doth in music lie. [John Milton: *Arcades*]

8 Such strains as would have won the ear
Of Pluto, to have quite set free
His half-regain'd Eurydice.
[John Milton: *L'Allegro*]

9 Or bid the soul of Orpheus sing
Such notes as, warbled to the string,
Drew iron tears down Pluto's cheek,
And made Hell grant what Love did seek.
[John Milton: *Il Penseroso*]

Orpheus went down to Hell to beg Pluto to allow his dead wife, Eurydice, to return to life and, moved by the power of his music, Pluto assented.
That Pluto wept iron tears is Milton's poetic addition to the legend.

10 There let the pealing organ blow,
To the full voiced quire below,
In service high, and anthems clear,
As may with sweetness, through mine ear,
Dissolve me into ecstasies,
And bring all Heaven before mine eyes.
[John Milton: *Il Penseroso*]

11 Strains that might create a soul
Under the ribs of Death.
[John Milton: *Comus*]

12 Music and women I cannot but give way to, whatever my business is. [Samuel Pepys: *Diary*, March 9, 1666]

13 Music hath charms to soothe a savage breast,
To soften rocks, or bend a knotted oak.
[William Congreve: *The Mourning Bride* I.i.]
Often spoken as "the savage beast" and sometimes, even, so written.

14 All the delusive seduction of martial music. [Mme. d'Arblay (Fanny Burney): *Diary*, April 24, 1802]

15 And music lifted up the listening spirit
Until it walked, exempt from mortal care,
Godlike, o'er the clear billows of sweet sound.
[Shelley: *Prometheus Unbound* II.iv.]

16 And the night shall be filled with music
And the cares, that infest the day,
Shall fold their tents, like the Arabs,
And as silently steal away.
[Longfellow: *The Day Is Done*]

17 There is sweet music here that softer falls
Than petals from blown roses on the grass, . . .
Music that gentlier on the spirit lies,
Than tired eyelids upon tired eyes;
Music that brings sweet sleep down from the blissful skies.
[Tennyson: *The Lotos-Eaters*]

18 We are the music-makers,

And we are the dreamers of dreams,
Wandering by lone sea-breakers,
And sitting by desolate streams;
World-losers and world-forsakers,
On whom the pale moon gleams:
Yet we are the movers and shakers
Of the world for ever, it seems.
[Arthur O'Shaughnessy: *Ode, "The Music-Makers"*]

1 There is no music in Nature, neither melody or harmony. Music is the creation of man. [Hugh R. Haweis: *Music and Morals* I.i.]

2 Sweet sounds, oh, beautiful music, do not cease!
Reject me not into the world again.
With you alone is excellence and peace,
Mankind made plausible, his purpose plain.
[Edna St. Vincent Millay: *On Hearing a Symphony of Beethoven*]

MUSIC: miscellaneous

3 So discord oft in music makes the sweet lay.
[Edmund Spenser: *The Faerie Queene* III.ii.]

4 I perceive you delight not in music.
[Shakespeare: *The Two Gentlemen of Verona* IV.ii.]

5 How sour sweet music is
When time is broke and no proportion kept!
So is it in the music of men's lives.
[Shakespeare: *Richard II* V.v.]

6 One whom the music of his own vain tongue
Doth ravish like enchanting harmony.
[Shakespeare: *Love's Labour's Lost* I.i.]

7 The man that hath no music in himself,
Nor is not moved with concord of sweet sounds,
Is fit for treasons, stratagems and spoils.
[Shakespeare: *The Merchant of Venice* V.i.]

8 If music be the food of love, play on;
Give me excess of it, that, surfeiting,
The appetite may sicken, and so die.
[Shakespeare: *Twelfth Night* I.i.]

9 The isle is full of noises,
Sounds and sweet airs, that give delight, and hurt not.
Sometimes a thousand twangling instruments
Will hum about mine ears; and sometimes voices,
That, if I then had wak'd after long sleep,
Will make me sleep again.
[Shakespeare: *The Tempest* III.ii.]

10 Nothing is capable of being well set to music that is not nonsense. [Joseph Addison: *The Spectator* No. 18]

11 Music resembles poetry; in each
Are nameless graces which no methods teach,
And which a master-hand alone can reach.
[Alexander Pope: *An Essay on Criticism*]

12 Some to church repair,
Not for the doctrine, but the music there.
[Alexander Pope: *An Essay on Criticism*]

13 There's sure no passion in the human soul, but finds its food in music. [George Lillo: *Fatal Curiosity*]

14 The Most High has a decided taste for vocal music, provided it be lugubrious and gloomy enough. [Voltaire: *Philosophical Dictionary*]

15 The music in my heart I bore,
Long after it was heard no more.
[Wordsworth: *The Solitary Reaper*]

16 Music, when soft voices die,
Vibrates in the memory—
Odors, when sweet violets sicken,
Live within the sense they quicken.
[Shelley: *To——: Music, When Soft Voices Die*]

17 Was it a vision, or a waking dream?
Fled is that music:—do I wake or sleep?
[Keats: *Ode to a Nightingale*]

18 See to their desks Apollo's sons repair,
Swift rides the rosin o'er the horse's hair!
In unison their various tones to tune,
Murmurs the oboe, growls the hoarse bassoon;
In soft vibration sighs the whispering lute,
Tang goes the harpsichord, too-too the flute,

Brays the loud trumpet, squeaks the
    fiddle sharp,
Winds the French-horn, and twangs
    the tingling harp;
Till, like great Jove, the leader, figur-
    ing in,
Attunes to order the chaotic din.
[Horace and James Smith: *Rejected Ad-
dresses*, "The Theatre"]

1 And music pours on mortals
    Her magnificent disdain.
[Emerson: *The Sphinx*]
*Emerson assumed a reciprocation; he
confessed (Journals, 1861) that he had
no ear for music though it served, at
concerts, "to soothe the lunatics and
keep them amused."*

2 Wagner's music is better than it
sounds. [Attr. Mark Twain, Bill Nye
and other American popular humorists]

3 Hell is full of musical amateurs. Music is the brandy of the damned. [G. B.
Shaw: *Man and Superman* III]

4 He knew music was Good, but it
didn't sound right. [George Ade: *Fable
of the Married Girl Who Ran the Eating Station for the Luminaries*]

5 Even before the music begins there
is that bored look on people's faces. A
polite form of self-imposed torture, the
concert. [Henry Miller: *Tropic of Cancer*]

MUST

6 Well, if we must we must. [Sheri-
dan: *The Critic* II.ii.]

MUTABILITY

7 What is this world? what asketh men
    to have?
Now with his love, now in his colde
    grave
Allone, with-outen any companye.
[Chaucer: *The Knight's Tale*]

MUTE

8 Why so dull and mute, young sinner?
    Prythee, why so mute?
Will, when speaking well can't win
    her,
    Saying nothing do 't?
    Prythee, why so mute?
[Sir John Suckling: *Encouragements to
a Lover*]

MYRTLES

9   Once more,

Ye myrtles brown, with ivy never
    sere,
I come to pluck your berries harsh
    and crude,
And with forc'd fingers rude,
Shatter your leaves before the mellow-
    ing year.
[John Milton: *Lycidas*]

MYSELF

10 I celebrate myself and sing myself.
[Walt Whitman: *Leaves of Grass*, "Song
of Myself"]

11 I dote on myself, there is that lot of
    me and all so luscious.
[Walt Whitman: *Leaves of Grass*, "Song
of Myself"]

12 I find no sweeter fat than sticks to
    my own bones.
[Walt Whitman: *Leaves of Grass*, "Song
of Myself"]

13 Now and then, at the sight of my
name on a visiting card, or of my face
photographed in a group among other
faces, or when I see a letter addressed in
my hand, or catch the sound of my own
voice, I grow shy in the presence of a
mysterious Person who is myself, is
known by my name, and who apparently
does exist. Can it be possible that I am as
real as anyone? [Logan Pearsall Smith:
Trivia, "At the Bank"]

14 The warm, familiar sense of my own
existence, with all its exasperation, all
its charm. [Logan Pearsall Smith: *More
Trivia*, "The Rescue"]

MYSTERY(IES)

15 There be three things which are too
wonderful for me, yea, four which I
know not: The way of an eagle in the
air; the way of a serpent upon a rock;
the way of a ship in the midst of the
sea; and the way of a man with a maid.
[Proverbs 30:18-19]

16 You would pluck out the heart of my
    mystery.
[Shakespeare: *Hamlet* III.ii.]

17 What song the Syrens sang, or what
name Achilles assumed when he hid himself among women, though puzzling
questions, are not beyond all conjecture.
[Sir Thomas Browne: *Urn-Burial* V]
"His (Tiberius') special aim was a

knowledge of mythology, which he car-
ried to a silly and laughable extreme;
for he used to test even the grammarians
. . . by questions something like this:
'Who was Hecuba's mother?' 'What
was the name of Achilles among the
maidens?' 'What were the Sirens in the
habit of singing?' "

> *Suetonius:* Tiberius *LXX*

1 Mystery is the wisdom of blockheads.
[Horace Walpole: Letter to Horace
Mann, Jan. 2, 1761]

2 There was the Door to which I found
no Key;
There was the Veil through which I
might not see:
Some little talk awhile of ME AND
THEE
There was—and then no more of
THEE AND ME.
[*Rubáiyát of Omar Khayyám* (trans. Ed-
ward FitzGerald)]

N

NAGGING

1 A continual dropping in a very rainy day and a contentious woman are alike. [Proverbs 27:15]
2 My lord shall never rest;
I'll watch him tame, and talk him out of patience:
His bed shall seem a school, his board a shrift.
[Shakespeare: *Othello* III.iii.]

NAIL(S)

3 Hit the nail on the head. [Beaumont and Fletcher: *Love's Cure* II.i.]
4 For want of a nail the shoe is lost, for want of a shoe the horse is lost, for want of a horse the rider is lost. [George Herbert: *Jacula Prudentum* (1651)]
5 A little neglect may breed mischief: for want of a nail the shoe was lost; for want of a shoe the horse was lost; and for want of a horse the rider was lost. [Benjamin Franklin: *Poor Richard's Almanack* (1757)]
6 Each finger nail a crimson petal, seen
Through a pale garnishing of nicotine.
[Robert Hillyer: *A Letter to the Editor*]

NAKED(NESS)

7 Naked came I out of my mother's womb, and naked shall I return thither. [Job 1:21]
8 As he came forth of his mother's womb, naked shall he return to go as he came. [Ecclesiastes 5:15]
9 There syr launcelot toke the fayrest lady by the hand, and she was naked as a nedel. [Sir Thomas Malory: *Le Morte d'Arthur* XI.i.]
10 Nakedness is uncomely, as well in mind as body. [Francis Bacon: *Of Simulation and Dissimulation*]
11 There is an unseemly exposure of the mind, as well as of the body. [William Hazlitt: *Sketches*]
12 For me, the naked and the nude
(By lexicographers construed
As synonyms that should express
The same deficiency of dress
Or shelter) stand as wide apart
As love from lies, or truth from art.
[Robert Graves: *The Naked and the Nude*]

NAMBY-PAMBY

13 Let the verse the subject fit,
Little subject, little wit.
Namby-Pamby is your guide.
[Henry Carey: *Namby-Pamby* (1729)]
Ambrose Philips, Henry Carey and Alexander Pope all wrote pastorals. The public preferred the insipid verses of Philips whom Carey dubbed Namby Pamby. Pope picked up Philips's nickname and used it in The Dunciad *(1733). It struck the popular fancy and stays in our speech long after Carey, Philips, pastorals and even* The Dunciad *have mercifully been forgotten. For a very minor poet, Carey has gained quite a bit of fame: he invented Namby-Pamby and he wrote* Sally in Our Alley *and, it is believed,* God Save the King.

NAME(S)

14 A good name is better than precious ointment. [Ecclesiastes 7:1]
15 A good name is rather to be chosen than great riches. [Proverbs 22:1]
16 My name is Legion: for we are many. [Mark 5:9]
17 A bold bad man! that dared to call by name
Great Gorgon, prince of darkness and dead night.
[Edmund Spenser: *The Faerie Queene* I.i.37]
The names of deities are indissolubly connected with the beings they designate. The name of YHWH is still shrouded in unspeakable mystery.
The Devil's name was in some ways even more dreadful, for if it were pronounced he might appear. Satan simply means "the adversary." Devil, like god, is a generic term. Fiend = "the enemy." Lucifer was—presumably—the name Satan held in Heaven before his fall. But

what was his actual name? Lactantius, in the 4th century, said it was Demogorgon—*the most dreaded name of all dreadful names ("the dreaded name of Demogorgon"—Milton,* Paradise Lost, *II.956)—but since Lactantius lived to pronounce the word, he may have been misinformed. The name has been applied to assorted demons and spooks.*

1 What's in a name? that which we call
a rose
By any other name would smell as
sweet.
[Shakespeare: *Romeo and Juliet* II.ii.]

2 Fools' names, like fools' faces,
Are often seen in public places.
[Thomas Fuller (1654-1734): *Gnomologia*]

3 Good name in man and woman, dear
my lord,
Is the immediate jewel of their souls:
Who steals my purse steals trash; 'tis
something, nothing;
'Twas mine, 'tis his, and has been
slave to thousands;
But he that filches from me my good
name
Robs me of that which not enriches
him,
And makes me poor indeed.
[Shakespeare: *Othello* III.iii.]

4 I hate the man who builds his name
On ruins of another's fame.
[John Gay: *The Poet and the Rose*]

5 He left a name at which the world
grew pale,
To point a moral, or adorn a tale.
[Samuel Johnson: *The Vanity of Human Wishes*]
The reference is to Charles XII of Sweden who after a military career of unparalleled brilliance was defeated, sank into obscurity, was killed in a minor engagement and is remembered now only by historians and moralists.

6 The Glory and the Nothing of a
Name.
[Byron: *Churchill's Grave*]

NAPOLEON

7 God was bored by him. [Victor Hugo: *Les Châtiments*]

8 Napoleon . . . mighty somnambulist of a vanished dream. [Victor Hugo: *Les Misérables*. I.xiii.]

NARCOTICS

9 Not poppy, nor mandragora,
Nor all the drowsy syrups of the
world
Shall ever medicine thee to that sweet
sleep
Which thou ow'dst yesterday.
[Shakespeare: *Othello* III.iii.]

10 Two great European narcotics, alcohol and Christianity. [Nietzsche: *The Twilight of the Idols,* "Things the Germans Lack"]

NARRATIVE

11 Whoso shal telle a tale after a man,
He moot reherce as ny as evere he
can
Everich a word, if it be in his charge,
Al speke he never so rudeliche and
large,
Or ellis he moot telle his tale untrewe,
Or feyne thing, or finde wordes new.
[Chaucer: Prologue to *The Canterbury Tales*]

NATIVITY

12 *Glendower.* At my nativity
The front of heaven was full of fiery
shapes,
Of burning cressets; and at my birth
The frame and huge foundation of
the earth
Shak'd like a coward.

Hotspur. Why, so it would have done
at the same season, if your mother's cat
had but kittened. [Shakespeare: *I Henry IV* III.i.]

NATURAL

13 What is natural is never disgraceful.
[Euripides: *Fragments*]

NATURAL SELECTION

14 I have called this principle, by which each slight variation, if useful, is preserved, by the term Natural Selection. [Charles Darwin: *The Origin of Species* III]

NATURE: and art

15 Those things are better which are perfected by nature than those which are finished by art. [Cicero: *De natura deorum* II]

16 Nature's above art in that respect.

[Shakespeare: *King Lear* IV.vi.]
1 All nature is but art, unknown to thee.

[Alexander Pope: *An Essay on Man* I]
2 Nature I loved, and next to nature, art.

[W. S. Landor: *The Last Fruit of an Old Tree*]

NATURE: and God

3 Nature is the art of God.

[Dante: *De Monarchia* I]
4 Nature, the vicaire of th' almighty Lorde.

[Chaucer: *The Parlement of Foules*]
vicaire = *vicar* = the earthly representative of God

5 All things are artificial, for nature is the art of God.

[Sir Thomas Browne: *Religio Medici* I. xvi.]
6 All are but parts of one stupendous whole,
   Whose body Nature is, and God the soul.

[Alexander Pope: *An Essay on Man* Epistle I]
7 Slave to no sect, who takes no private road,
   But looks thro' Nature up to Nature's God.

[Alexander Pope: *An Essay on Man* Epistle IV]
8 The pride of the peacock is the glory of God.
   The lust of the goat is the bounty of God.
   The wrath of the lion is the wisdom of God.
   The nakedness of woman is the work of God.

[William Blake: *The Marriage of Heaven and Hell*, "Proverbs of Hell"]
9 And what if all of animated nature
   Be but organic harps diversely fram'd,
   That tremble into thought, as o'er them sweeps,
   Plastic and vast, one intellectual breeze,
   At once the soul of each, and God of all?

[Coleridge: *The Eolian Harp*]
10 Are God and Nature then at strife,
    That Nature lends such evil dreams?

[Tennyson: *In Memoriam* LV]

NATURE: the great teacher

11 And this our life, exempt from public haunt,
    Finds tongues in trees, books in the running brooks,
    Sermons in stones, and good in everything.

[Shakespeare: *As You Like It* II.i.]
12 One impulse from a vernal wood
    May teach you more of man,
    Of moral evil and of good,
    Than all the sages can.

[Wordsworth: *The Tables Turned*]
13 And hark! how blithe the throstle sings!
    He, too, is no mean preacher:
    Come forth into the light of things,
    Let Nature be your teacher.

[Wordsworth: *The Tables Turned*]
14 Sweet is the lore which Nature brings;
    Our meddling intellect
    Misshapes the beauteous forms of things:
    We murder to dissect.

[Wordsworth: *The Tables Turned*]
15 The stars of midnight shall be dear
    To her; and she shall lean her ear
    In many a secret place
    Where rivulets dance their wayward round,
    And beauty born of murmuring sound
    Shall pass into her face.

[Wordsworth: *Three Years She Grew*]
16 Love had he found in huts where poor men lie;
    His daily teachers had been woods and rills,
    The silence that is in the starry sky,
    The sleep that is among the lonely hills.

[Wordsworth: *Song at the Feast of Brougham Castle*]
17 For what has made the sage or poet write
    But the fair paradise of Nature's light?

[Keats: *I Stood Tip-toe*]
18 To him who in the love of nature holds
    Communion with her visible forms,

she speaks
A various language; for his gayer
hours
She has a voice of gladness, and a
smile
And eloquence of beauty, and she
glides
Into his darker musings, with a mild
And healing sympathy that steals
away
Their sharpness, ere he is aware.
[William Cullen Bryant: *Thanatopsis*]
1 The chess-board is the world, the
pieces are the phenomena of the universe, the rules of the game are what we
call the laws of Nature. The player on
the other side is hidden from us. We
know that his play is always fair, just,
and patient. But also we know, to our
cost, that he never overlooks a mistake,
or makes the smallest allowance for ignorance. [T. H. Huxley: *A Liberal Education*]

> *Huxley is really merely substituting
> "Nature" for "God" here. That is, the
> fault of the analogy is its assumption of
> "rules," "laws," "fair," "just," and "pa-
> tient." Nature has often changed the
> rules of the game in mid-play (as she
> has done with hundreds of extinct
> species) without even bothering to in-
> form them that the "rules" had been
> changed.*

**NATURE: wise, eternal, mysterious,
cruel**

2 Nothing which we can imagine
about Nature is incredible. [Pliny the
Elder: *Natural History* XI.ii.]
3 We call that against nature which
cometh against custom. But there is
nothing, whatsoever it be, that is not
according to nature. [Montaigne: *Essays* II.xxx.]

> *Montaigne is supported by Goethe's:
> "The unnatural, that too is natural."*

4 Let us permit nature to have her
way: she understands her business better
than we do. [Montaigne: *Essays* III.
xiii.]
5 In nature's infinite book of secrecy
A little I can read.
[Shakespeare: *Antony and Cleopatra* I.
ii.]
6 There are no grotesques in nature.

[Sir Thomas Browne: *Religio Medici*
I.xv.]
7 Let dogs delight to bark and bite,
For God hath made them so;
Let bears and lions growl and fight,
For 'tis their nature, too.
[Isaac Watts: *Divine Songs* XVI]
8 O Lady! we receive but what we give
And in our life alone does Nature
live.
[Coleridge: *Dejection: An Ode* IV]
9 For men may come and men may go,
But I go on forever.
[Tennyson: *The Brook*]
10 So careful of the type she seems,
So careless of the single life.
[Tennyson: *In Memoriam* LV]
11 Nature, red in tooth and claw.
[Tennyson: *In Memoriam* LVI]
12 Nature, with equal mind,
Sees all her sons at play;
Sees man control the wind,
The wind sweep man away;
Allows the proudly-riding and the
foundering bark.
[Matthew Arnold: *Empedocles on Etna*]
13 Nature, heartless, witless nature.
[A. E. Housman: *Tell Me Not Here*]
14 To those who study her, Nature reveals herself as extraordinarily fertile
and ingenious in devising *means*, but
she has no *ends* which the human mind
has been able to discover or comprehend. [Joseph Wood Krutch: *The Modern Temper* II.iii.]

NATURE: miscellaneous

15 Never does nature say one thing and
wisdom another. [Juvenal: *Satires* XIV]
> *Quoted by Edmund Burke in* Letters on
> a Regicide Peace *III, and sometimes
> attributed to Burke.*

16 Tak any brid, and put it in a cage,
And do al thyn entente and thy
corage
To fostre it tendrely with mete and
drinke,
Of alle deyntees that thou canst
bithinke,
And keep it al-so clenly as thou
may;
Al-though his cage of gold be never so
gay,
Yet hath this brid, by twenty thousand fold,

Lever in a forest, that is rude and cold,
Gon ete wormes and swich wrecched-
nesse.
[Chaucer: *The Manciple's Tale*]
corage = *heart, good will*
1 Nature is not governed except by
obeying her. [Francis Bacon: *The Advancement of Learning*]
2 The prodigality of nature.
[Shakespeare: *Richard III* I.i.]
3 See one promontory (said Socrates
of old), one mountain, one sea, one
river, and see all. [Robert Burton: *Anatomy of Melancholy* I.2.4.7]
4 Whom universal Nature did lament.
[John Milton: *Lycidas*]
5   The sounding cataract
Haunted me like a passion: the tall
                                    rock,
The mountain, and the deep and
                          gloomy wood,
Their colours and their forms, were
                          then to me
An appetite.
[Wordsworth: *Tintern Abbey*]
6 Nature never did betray the heart
                   that loved her.
[Wordsworth: *Tintern Abbey*]
7 Nature's old felicities.
[Wordsworth: *The Trossachs*]
8 I love not man the less, but nature
                              more.
[Byron: *Childe Harold* IV.clxxviii]
9 Nature, like us, is sometimes caught
Without her diadem.
[Emily Dickinson: *Poems, Part II, Na-
ture*, LXXX.viii.]

NAUGHTY

10 How far that little candle throws his
                              beams!
So shines a good deed in a naughty
                              world.
[Shakespeare: *The Merchant of Venice*
V.i.]
naughty *in Elizabethan English was a
much stronger condemnation than it
now is. It was weakened by being applied almost exclusively to children and
came to mean impishly disobedient. But
a vicious ox was formerly "a naughty
beast" and a house of prostitution a
"naughty house." When Regan, in* King
Lear, *helps her husband mutilate the
aged Gloster, brutally blinding him, he*

calls her *"naughty lady," a reproach that
under the circumstances seems almost
ludicrous to us.*

NAVEL

11 The man without a Navel yet lives
in me. [Sir Thomas Browne: *Religio
Medici* II.x.]
*The question of whether or not Adam
had a navel exercised theologians centuries ago and keeps humorists employed
today. The ascription unto Adam, Sir
Thomas Browne wrote, of "that tortuos-
ity or complicated nodosity we usually
call the Navel" was a mistake, notwithstanding "the authentick draughts of
Angelo and others," in that such an
ascription implied that "the Creator affected superfluities or ordained parts
without use or office."*

NAVY

12 When I was a lad I served a term
As office boy to an Attorney's firm.
I cleaned the windows and I swept
                          the floor
And I polished up the handle of the
                          big front door.
I polished up that handle so care-
                              fullee
That now I am the Ruler of the
                          Queen's Navee!
[W. S. Gilbert: *H.M.S. Pinafore* I]
13 Now landsmen all, whoever you may
                              be,
If you want to rise to the top of the
                              tree,
If your soul isn't fettered to an office
                              stool,
Be careful to be guided by this
                          golden rule—
Stick close to your desks and *never go
                              to sea*,
And you all may be the Rulers of
                      the Queen's Navee!
[W. S. Gilbert: *H.M.S. Pinafore* I]

NAZARETH

14 Can there any good thing come out
of Nazareth? [John 1:46]

NEAR

15 So near and yet so far. [Martial:
Epigrams I. lxxxvi.]
16 He seems so near and yet so far.
[Tennyson: *In Memoriam* XCVII]

NEARER

1 Nearer, my God, to Thee—
  Nearer to Thee—
  E'en though it be a cross
  That raiseth me;
  Still all my song shall be
  Nearer, my God, to Thee,
  Nearer to Thee!

[Sarah Flower Adams: *Nearer, my God, to Thee!*]

NEAT

2 Neat but not gaudy, will true critics please. [Samuel Wesley: *An Epistle to a Friend concerning Poetry*]

The reference is to literary style.

NECESSITY: knows no law

3 Necessity knows no law. [Publilius Syrus: *Maxims*]
4 Necessity has no law. [Langland: *Piers Plowman* XIV.xlv.]
5 Nede hath no lawe. [John Gower: *Confessio Amantis* IV]
6 Necessity is mightier than the law. [Goethe: *Faust* II.i.]

NECESSITY: making a virtue of

7 Thus maketh vertue of necessitee. [Chaucer: *Troilus and Criseyde* IV]

One of the first appearances of this much-quoted phrase in English. It appears in most European languages, back at least as far as the Institutio Oratoria *(I.viii.) of Quintilian (1st century A.D.)*

8 Thanne is it wysdom, as thynketh me,
  To maken vertu of necessite.
[Chaucer: *The Knight's Tale*]
9 Making a virtue of necessity. [Benvenuto Cellini: *Life* I.lxvii.]
10   Are you content
  To make a virtue of necessity?
[Shakespeare: *The Two Gentlemen of Verona* IV.i.]
11 There is no virtue like necessity. [Shakespeare: *Richard II* I.iii.]

NECESSITY: the mother of invention

12 Necessity is a violent school-mistress and teacheth strange lessons. [Montaigne: *Essays* I.xlvii.]
13 He that stands upon a slippery place
  Makes nice of no vile hold to stay
                him up.

[Shakespeare: *King John* III.iv.]
  makes nice of no vile hold = *is not over-scrupulous about the cleanliness of whatever he can hang on to*

14 The art of our necessities is strange,
  That can make vile things precious.
[Shakespeare: *King Lear* III.ii.]
15 Necessity is the mother of invention.
[Richard Franck: *Northern Memoirs* (1658)]

Franck's work is the earliest in which this common saying has been found, but that doesn't mean that he invented it. The idea had found expressions in many forms from almost the beginning of history. Aeschylus (B.C. 470) had said that necessity was stronger than art. Rabelais said that necessity "devises all manner of shifts." Ascham (1545) had seen it as the "mother of eloquence." Franck's phrase was picked up, or re-coined, by Wycherley (1672). That it was already a proverb is suggested by the fact that Swift, in Gulliver *IV puts it in quotation marks.*

Invention here plainly meant "trickery," "shifts," "stratagems." The modern speaker of English usually uses it as if it meant some mechanical contrivance. Thus Francis Beeding says smugly (1938) that a basic difference between Spaniards and English is illustrated by the fact that Spaniards proverbially refer to necessity as the enemy of chastity, while the English see it as the mother of invention. That is, we assume that "invention" is, somehow, virtuous. The Spaniards see a danger where we see an opportunity.

NECESSITY: needs must

16 He must needes go that the dyvell dryveth. [in *Johan the Husbande, Tyb His Wyfe and Syr Jhan the Priest.* Anon.]
17 Needs must when the Devil drives. [Rabelais: *Works* IV.lvii.]
18 What you cannot as you would achieve,
  You must perforce accomplish as you may.
[Shakespeare: *Titus Andronicus* II.i.]
19 Well, God's a good man; an two men ride of a horse, one must ride behind. [Shakespeare: *Much Ado about Nothing* III.v.]

1   Cheer your heart!
Be you not troubled with the time,
          which drives
O'er your content these strong neces-
          sities;
But let determin'd things to destiny
Hold unbewail'd their way.
[Shakespeare: *Antony and Cleopatra*
III.vi.]
2 Necessity delivers us from the em-
barrassment of choice. [Vauvenargues:
Réflexions]
3 A world I did not wish to enter
Took me and poised me on my cen-
          ter,
Made me grimace, and foot, and
          prance,
As cats on hot bricks have to dance
Strange jigs to keep them from the
          floor,
Till they sink down and feel no more.
[Thomas Hardy: *A Necessitarian's Epi-
taph*]

NECESSITY: supreme
4 But who can turne the stream of des-
          tinee,
Or break the chayne of strong neces-
          sitee,
Which fast is tyde to Jove's eternall
          seat?
[Edmund Spenser: *The Faerie Queene*
I.v.]
5 Nature must obey necessity.
[Shakespeare: *Julius Caesar* IV.iii.]
6 I find no hint throughout the Uni-
          verse
Of good or ill, of blessing or of
          curse;
I find alone Necessity Supreme.
[James Thomson (1834-1882): *The City
of Dreadful Night* XIV]

NECESSITY: the tyrant's plea
7 Necessity, the tyrant's plea.
[John Milton: *Paradise Lost* IV.393]
8 Necessity is the plea for every in-
fringement of human freedom. It is the
argument of tyrants; it is the creed of
slaves. [William Pitt: in a speech in the
House of Commons, November 18, 1783]

NECESSITY: miscellaneous
9 Dire necessity. [Horace: *Odes* III.
xxiv.]

10 Why is it necessary that you should
live? [Tertullian: *De Idolatria* V]
11 A wise man will see to it that his
acts always seem voluntary and not done
by compulsion, however much he may be
compelled by necessity. [Machiavelli:
Discourses on Livy I]
12 If it be bad to live in necessity, at
least there is no necessity to live in
necessity. [Montaigne: *Essays* I.xl. (trans.
John Florio)]
    That is, one can always commit suicide.
13   I am sworn brother, sweet,
To grim Necessity, and he and I
Will keep a league till death.
[Shakespeare: *Richard II* V.i.]
14 Necessity's sharp pinch.
[Shakespeare: *King Lear* II.iv.]
15 I do not see the necessity! [Count
d'Argenson (1696-1764), one of the ministers of Louis XV: in reply to the Abbé
Desfontaines, who had defended his publication of a scurrilous libel by saying
"A man must live!"]
16 Necessity never made a good bargain.
[Benjamin Franklin: *Poor Richard's Almanack* (1735)]

NECK
17 O that the Roman people had but
one neck! [Caligula: in Suetonius's
Gaius Caligula XXX]
    *The populace had angered the emperor
by applauding a faction which he opposed. He regretted that he could not
have them all killed with one stroke.*

    *For the sweep of its malice, Caligula's
wish is exceeded only by Ibsen's regret
that he had not been able to torpedo the
Ark.*

NECK VERSE
18 Touch not mine anointed ones, and
do my prophets no harm. [I Chronicles
16:22]
    *This was the so-called "neck verse"
which, read in court, proved the reader
—by virtue of his being able to read—
entitled to "benefit of clergy."*

    *Originally a privilege granted to
clergymen arraigned for felony, it exempted them from trial by a secular
court, and since the Ecclesiastical courts
did not give the death penalty, it saved
the accused's life. He was branded on
the hand and could not claim the privi-*

lege a second time. In 1691 the privilege was extended, in England, to women. It was abolished in 1827.

Ben Jonson claimed benefit of clergy to escape the death penalty for killing a man in a duel.

NEED(S)
1 He who buys what he doesn't need, sells what he does need. [Alemán: *Guzmán de Alfarache* II.iii.]
2 O, reason not the need! Our basest beggars
Are in the poorest thing superfluous.
Allow not nature more than nature needs,
Man's life is cheap as beast's.
[Shakespeare: *King Lear* II.iv.]
3 As much need on't, as he hath of the pip. [John Ray: *English Proverbs* (1670)]
There are many humorous folk similes for the totally unneeded. The current one is: "He needs that like he needs a hole in the head."
Older: "as much need of it as a toad of side pockets."
"He needs that as much as he needs water in his shoes."
". . . as a bull needs religion."
4 From each according to his abilities, to each according to his needs. [Karl Marx: *Critique of the Gotha Programme*]

NEEDFUL
5 And Jesus answered and said unto her, Martha, Martha, thou art careful and troubled about many things:
But one thing is needful; and Mary hath chosen that good part, which shall not be taken away from her. [Luke 10:41-42]

NEEDLE
6 As well look for a needle in a bottle of hay. [Cervantes: *Don Quixote* II.iii. 10.]
This is the old form of the saying now heard as "a needle in a haystack." Bottle is the diminutive of the archaic botte, bundle. Chaucer speaks of something being "nat worth a Botel hey" and Robert Greene (1592): "He gropeth in the dark to find a needle in a bottle of hay." A

bottle-horse was a horse that carried bundles, what was later called a "pack-horse."

NEGATIVE(S)
7 If your four negatives make your two affirmatives, why then, the worse for my friends and the better for my foes. [Shakespeare: *Twelfth Night* V.i. (1599)]
The idea was coming in among the pedants. Gabriel Harvey had affirmed in 1593 that two negatives make an affirmative and Sir John Harington had repeated the affirmation in 1596. By Fuller's time (1647) it was asserted as axiomatic.

NEGLECT
8 A wise and salutary neglect. [Edmund Burke: *On Conciliation with America*]
Burke's wisdom found an echo in the admirable slogan with which Prime Minister Macmillan campaigned for the Chancellorship of Oxford University in 1961: "He will not interfere!"

NEGOTIATING
9 To use too many circumstances ere one come to the matter is wearisome; to use none at all is blunt. [Francis Bacon: *Of Discourse*]
circumstances=*introductory observations*

NEGOTIATION
10 It is better to sound a person with whom one deals afar off than to fall upon the point at first, except you mean to surprise him by some short question. [Francis Bacon: *Of Negotiating*]

NEGRO
11 My mother bore me in the southern wild,
And I am black, but O my soul is white!
[William Blake: *The Little Black Boy*]

NEIGHBOR
12 Thou shalt love thy neighbour as thyself. [Leviticus 19:18]
13 Love your neighbor, yet pull not down your hedge. [George Herbert: *Jacula Prudentum* (1640)]

An earlier form of Robert Frost's: "Good fences make good neighbors."

NELL GWYNN
1 Pretty, witty Nell. [Samuel Pepys: *Diary*, April 3, 1665]
A comment on Nell Gwynn. Pepys, though an industrious and honest public servant and something of a puritan, was fascinated by the wicked goings-on at court.

2 Let not poor Nelly starve. [Charles II: on his deathbed, to his brother and successor, James]
Nelly = *Nell Gwynn, Charles's mistress*

NET
3 Surely in vain the net is spread in the sight of the bird. [Proverbs 1:17]

NETWORK
4 NETWORK. Any thing reticulated or decussated, at equal distances, with interstices between the intersections. [Samuel Johnson: the *Dictionary*]
Of all Johnson's definitions, this excited most ridicule. But the obvious is not easy to define; of necessity, the simplest must be defined in terms less simple. This remains one of the best definitions of network *we have.*

NEVERMORE
5 With outstretch'd hoe I slew him at the door,
And taught him NEVER TO COME THERE NO MORE.
[William Cowper: *The Colubriad*]
6 No more—no more—Oh! never more on me
The freshness of the heart can fall like dew.
[Byron: *Don Juan* I.ccxiv.]
7 Quoth the Raven, "Nevermore."
[Edgar Allan Poe: *The Raven*]
8 Startled at the stillness broken by reply so aptly spoken,
"Doubtless," said I, "what it utters is its only stock and store
Caught from some unhappy master whom unmerciful Disaster
Followed fast and followed faster till his songs one burden bore— . . .
Of 'Never—nevermore.' "
[Edgar Allan Poe: *The Raven*]

NEW
9 There is no new thing under the sun. [Ecclesiastes I.ix.]
10 There is nothing new except what has been forgotten.
Attr. Mlle. Bertin, Marie Antoinette's milliner, about 1785.

NEW DEAL
11 A New Deal for Everyone. [David Lloyd George, campaign slogan, 1919]
12 I pledge you, I pledge myself, to a new deal for the American people. [Franklin Delano Roosevelt, nomination acceptance speech, July 2, 1932]
Despite the similarity, FDR was not following Lloyd George but evoking the memory of his cousin Theodore Roosevelt who in his 1904 campaign had promised to "see to it that every man has a square deal."

NEWS
13 How beautiful upon the mountains are the feet of him that bringeth good tidings. [Isaiah 52:7]
14 There's villainous news abroad.
[Shakespeare: *I Henry IV* II.iv.]
15 The first bringer of unwelcome news
Hath but a losing office, and his tongue
Sounds ever after as a sullen bell,
Remember'd tolling a departing friend.
[Shakespeare: *II Henry IV* I.i.]
16 Tidings do I bring, and lucky joys,
And golden times, and happy news of price.
[Shakespeare: *II Henry IV* V.iii.]
17 The nature of bad news infects the teller.
[Shakespeare: *Antony and Cleopatra* I.ii.]
18 Be it true or false, so it be news.
[Ben Jonson: *News from the New World*]
19 For evil news rides post, while good news baits.
[John Milton: *Samson Agonistes*]
baits = *stops for rest and refreshment, and hence travels slowly*
20 News, the manna of a day.
[Matthew Green: *The Spleen*]
21 Don't expect news, for I know no more than a newspaper. [Horace Wal-

pole: Letter to George Montagu, November 3, 1746]

1 No news is good news. [George Colman the Elder: *The Spleen* I]

2 All the news that's fit to print. [Motto of the *New York Times*, adopted 1896]

3 When a dog bites a man that is not news, but when a man bites a dog that is news.
> *Attr. Charles A. Dana, editor of the* New York Sun, *1882, but probably by John B. Bogart, city editor of the* Sun.

NEWSPAPER(S)

4 Thou god of our idolatry, the Press. [William Cowper: *The Progress of Error*]

5 Were it left to me to decide whether we should have a government without newspapers, or newspapers without a government, I should not hesitate a moment to prefer the latter. [Thomas Jefferson: Letter to Colonel Edward Carrington, January 16, 1787]

6 The man who never looks into a newspaper is better informed than he who reads them, inasmuch as he who knows nothing is nearer the truth than he whose mind is filled with falsehoods and errors. [Thomas Jefferson: *Writings* XI]

7 Newspapers always excite curiosity. No one ever lays one down without a feeling of disappointment. [Charles Lamb: *Detached Thoughts on Books and Reading*]

8 Blessed are they who never read a newspaper, for they shall see Nature, and, through her, God. [Thoreau: *Essays and Other Writings*]

9 I have been reading the morning paper. I do it every morning—well knowing that I shall find in it the usual depravities and basenesses and hypocrisies and cruelties that make up civilization, and cause me to put in the rest of the day pleading for the damnation of the human race. [Mark Twain: Letter to W. D. Howells (1899)]

10 He had been kicked in the Head by a Mule when young and believed everything he read in the Sunday Papers. [George Ade: *The Slim Girl*]

11 A newspaper is a device for making

the ignorant more ignorant and the crazy crazier. [H. L. Mencken: *Chrestomathy* 625]

NEWSWRITERS

12 In a time of war the nation is always of one mind, eager to hear something good of themselves, and ill of the enemy. At this time the task of news-writers is easy; they have nothing to do but to tell that the battle is expected, and afterwards that a battle has been fought, in which we and our friends, whether conquering or conquered, did all, and our enemies did nothing. [Samuel Johnson: *The Idler* No. 30]

NEWTON, SIR ISAAC

13 To myself I seem to have been only like a boy playing on the sea-shore, and diverting myself in now and then finding a smoother pebble or a prettier shell than ordinary, whilst the great ocean of truth lay all undiscovered before me. [Sir Isaac Newton: quoted in Brewster's *Memoirs of Newton* II.xxvii.]

14 Nature and Nature's laws lay hid in night:
> God said, *Let Newton be!* and all was light.

[Alexander Pope: *Epigram on Sir Isaac Newton*]
> *It did not last: the Devil howling "Ho!*
> *Let Einstein be!" restored the status quo.*
> J. C. Squire (1884-1958):
> *Answer to Pope's Epitaph*
> *for Sir Isaac Newton*

15   Newton, childlike sage!
Sagacious reader of the works of God.

[William Cowper: *The Task,* III, "The Garden"]

16   Where the statue stood
Of Newton with his prism and silent face,
The marble index of a mind forever
Voyaging through strange seas of thought, alone.

[Wordsworth: *The Prelude* III]
> *The reference is to the statue of Newton in the antechapel of Trinity College, Cambridge.*

17 When Newton saw an apple fall, he found . . .
A mode of proving that the earth

turn'd round
In a most natural whirl, called "grav-
itation";
And thus is the sole mortal who could
grapple,
Since Adam, with a fall or with an
apple.
[Byron: *Don Juan* X.i.]

NEW YEAR
1 Ring out, wild bells, to the wild sky,
The flying cloud, the frosty light:
The year is dying in the night;
Ring out, wild bells, and let him die.
[Tennyson: *In Memoriam* CVI]
2 Ring out the old, ring in the new,
Ring, happy bells, across the snow;
The year is going, let him go;
Ring out the false, ring in the true.
[Tennyson: *In Memoriam* CVI]
3 Full knee-deep lies the winter snow,
And the winter winds are wearily
sighing:
Toll ye the church-bell sad and slow,
And tread softly and speak low,
For the old year lies a-dying.
[Tennyson: *The Death of the Old Year*]

NEW YORK
4 East Side, West Side, all around the
town,
The tots sang "Ring-a-rosie," "London Bridge is falling down;"
Boys and girls together, me and Ma-
mie O'Rourke,
Tripped the light fantastic on the
sidewalks of New York.
[James Blake: *The Sidewalks of New
York*]

NICE
5 A nice man is a man of nasty ideas.
[Jonathan Swift: *Thoughts on Various
Subjects*]

NICKNAME
6 Of all eloquence a nickname is the
most concise; of all arguments the most
unanswerable. [William Hazlitt: *On
Nicknames*]
7 A nickname is the heaviest stone that
the devil can throw at a man. [William
Hazlitt: *On Nicknames*]
*Not invariably. Some men owe most, if
not all, of their fame to their nickname.*

*Thus Richard I of England is now
known as "The Lion-Hearted" and is
thought of as a paragon of valor. But in
his own time he was known as Richard-
Yea-and-Nay, because no one trusted his
word, and surely the whole popular concept of him would have been different
had this sobriquet stuck. Before General
Bee referred to General Thomas Jackson
as "standing like a stone wall," General
Jackson was known as "The Professor"
or "Old Blue Light" and it is hard to
believe that he would have attained the
fame that he has under either of these
designations.*

NIGGER
8 "We blowed out a cylinder head."
"Good gracious! anybody hurt?"
"No'm. Killed a nigger."
"Well, it's lucky; because sometimes
people do get hurt." [Colloquy between
Huck Finn and Aunt Sally Phelps, in
Mark Twain's *Huckleberry Finn* XXXII]

NIGHT
9 Watchman, what of the night? [Isai-
ah 21:11]
10 The night cometh when no man can
work. [John 9:4]
11 Night has a thousand eyes.
[John Lyly: *The Maydes Metamorphosis* III.i.]
12 How sweet the moonlight sleeps upon
this bank!
Here we will sit and let the sounds
of music
Creep in our ears: soft stillness and
the night
Become the touches of sweet harmony.
Sit, Jessica. Look how the floor of
heaven
Is thick inlaid with patines of bright
gold:
There's not the smallest orb which
thou behold'st
But in his motion like an angel sings,
Still quiring to the young-eyed cheru-
bins.
[Shakespeare: *The Merchant of Venice*
V.i.]
13 Now o'er the one half-world
Nature seems dead.
[Shakespeare: *Macbeth* II.i.]

1 I must become a borrower of the
                                night.
For a dark hour or twain.
[Shakespeare: *Macbeth* III.i.]
2   Come, seeling night,
Scarf up the tender eye of pitiful
                                day.
[Shakespeare: *Macbeth* III.ii.]
    seeling = *closing*
    Seeling *was a process in falconry in
    which the eyes of the hawk were closed
    by stitching up the eyelids with a thread
    tied behind the head.*

3 Alack, the night comes on, and the
                            bleak winds
Do sorely ruffle.
[Shakespeare: *King Lear* II.iv.]
4   Things that love night
Love not such nights as these. The
                            wrathful skies
Gallow the very wanderers of the
                                dark
And make them keep their caves.
[Shakespeare: *King Lear* III.ii.]
    gallow = *terrify*

5 What hath night to do with sleep?
[John Milton: *Comus*]
6 Sable-vested Night, eldest of things.
[John Milton: *Paradise Lost* II.962]
7   All but the wakeful nightingale;
She all night long her amorous des-
                            cant sung;
Silence was pleas'd: now glow'd the
                            firmament
With living sapphires; Hesperus, that
                            led
The starry host, rode brightest, till
                            the moon,
Rising in clouded majesty, at length
Apparent queen, unveil'd her peer-
                            less light,
And o'er the dark her silver mantle
                            threw.
[John Milton: *Paradise Lost* IV.602-609]
8 The ploughman homeward plods his
                            weary way,
And leaves the world to darkness and
                            to me.
[Thomas Gray: *Elegy Written in a Coun-
try Churchyard*]
9 The sun's rim dips; the stars rush out:
At one stride comes the dark.
[Coleridge: *The Ancient Mariner* III]
10 I pass like night from land to land;
I have strange power of speech.

[Coleridge: *The Ancient Mariner* VII]
11 The night / Shows stars and women
                        in a better light.
[Byron: *Don Juan* II.clii.]
12 Swiftly walk o'er the western wave,
Spirit of Night!
[Shelley: *To Night*]
13 I arise from dreams of thee
In the first sweet sleep of night,
When the winds are breathing low,
And the stars are shining bright.
[Shelley: *The Indian Serenade*]
14 The day is done, and the darkness
Falls from the wings of Night,
As a feather is wafted downward
From an eagle in his flight.
[Longfellow: *The Day Is Done*]
15 The calm, majestic presence of the
                                Night.
[Longfellow: *Hymn to the Night*]
16 Now lies the Earth all Danaë to the
                                stars.
[Tennyson: *The Princess* VII]
17 Now sleeps the crimson petal, now
                            the white;
Nor waves the cypress in the palace
                            walk:
Nor winks the gold fin in the por-
                            phyry font:
The fire-fly wakens; waken thou with
                            me.
[Tennyson: *The Princess* VII]
18 The huge and thoughtful night.
[Walt Whitman: *Leaves of Grass,*
"When Lilacs Last in the Door-yard
Bloom'd"]
19 Night with her train of stars
And her great gift of sleep.
[W. E. Henley: *Margaritae Sorori*]
20 I have been one acquainted with the
                                night.
[Robert Frost: *Acquainted With the
Night*]
21 The prehuman dignity of night.
[Robinson Jeffers: *Black-out*]
22 Over the dark mountain, over the
                            dark pinewood,
Down the long dark valley along the
                            shrunken river,
Returns the splendor without rays,
                            the shining shadow,
Peace-bringer, the matrix of all shin-
                            ing and quieter of shining.
[Robinson Jeffers: *Night*]
23 In a real dark night of the soul it is

always three o'clock in the morning. [F. Scott Fitzgerald: *The Crack-up*]

NIGHTINGALE
1 Sweet bird that shunn'st the noise of folly,
Most musical, most melancholy!
[John Milton: *Il Penseroso*]
2 Satiate the hungry dark with melody.
[Shelley: *The Woodman and the Nightingale*]
3 Thou wast not born for death, immortal bird!
No hungry generations tread thee down.
[Keats: *To a Nightingale*]
4 Last night the nightingale woke me,
Last night, when all was still.
It sang in the golden moonlight,
From out of the woodland hill.
[Christian Winther: *Sehnsucht* (trans. Theophile Narzials [1850-1920]: *Last Night*)]

NIGHTINGALE, FLORENCE
5 A Lady with a Lamp shall stand
In the great history of the land,
A noble type of good,
Heroic womanhood.
[Longfellow: *Santa Filomena*]
The reference is to Florence Nightingale.

NIGHTMARE
6 Saint Withold footed thrice the 'old;
He met the nightmare, and her nine fold;
Bid her alight
And her troth plight,
And aroint thee, witch, aroint thee.
[Shakespeare: *King Lear* III.iv.]
'old = wold = an open tract of high country; fold can mean times, like twofold and manifold, and suggests, and may mean, foals
The jingle, spoken by Edgar in his disguise as Mad Tom, is a charm against the nightmare. It is of great interest in that it shows the old mare, demon, getting mixed up with mare, horse. Furthermore, except for the last line, the poem is a limerick. Yet limericks were not known until 200 years later.
7 Her lips were red, her looks were free,
Her locks were yellow as gold:
Her skin was white as leprosy,

The Night-mare Life-in-Death was she,
Who thicks man's blood with cold.
[Coleridge: *The Ancient Mariner* III]

NO
8 I like the sayers of No better than the sayers of Yes. [Emerson: *Journals*]

NOBILITY
9 And what he greatly thought, he nobly dared.
[Homer: *Odyssey* II]
10 It becomes noblemen to do nothing well.
[George Chapman: *The Gentleman Usher* I.i.]
11 Thou art the ruins of the noblest man
That ever lived in the tide of times.
[Shakespeare: *Julius Caesar* III.i.]
12 Nothing is here for tears, nothing to wail
Or knock the breast; no weakness, no contempt,
Dispraise, or blame; nothing but well and fair,
And what may quiet us in a death so noble.
[John Milton: *Samson Agonistes*]
13 Nobility is nothing but ancient riches. [John Ray: *English Proverbs* (1670)]
14 A Spanish nobleman with more names than shirts. [Oliver Goldsmith: *Citizen of the World,* Letter CXX]
15 There is
One great society alone on earth:
The noble Living, and the noble Dead.
[Wordsworth: *The Prelude* X]
16 Real nobility is based on scorn, courage, and profound indifference. [Albert Camus: *Notebooks 1935-1942* III]

NOBODY
17 I'm nobody! Who are you?
Are you nobody, too?
Then there's a pair of us—don't tell!
They'd banish us, you know.
[Emily Dickinson: *Poems, Part I, Life,* XXVII.1]

NOD
18 A nod's as good as a wink to a blind horse.
[Frederick Marryat: *Peter Simple* LI]

NOISE

1 A noisy man is always in the right.
[William Cowper: *Conversation*]
2 King Borria Bungalee Boo
 Was a man-eating African swell;
 His sigh was a hullaballoo,
 His whisper a horrible yell—
 A horrible, horrible yell.
[W. S. Gilbert: *Bab Ballads,* "King Borria Bungalee Boo"]

NONCONFORMIST

3 Whoso would be a man must be a nonconformist. [Emerson: *Self-Reliance*]

NONEXISTENTS

4 He that seeketh after these thinges, looseth his tyme: A fatte hogge among Iewes, truth among hypocrites, faith in a flaterer, sobernesse in a drunkard, mony with a prodigal, wisedome in a foole, great riches in a scoolmaister, silence in a woman, vertue in euyll company. [John Florio: *Firste Fruites* XXIV]

NONSENSE

5 No one is exempt from talking nonsense; the misfortune is to do it solemnly. [Montaigne: *Essays* III.i.]
6   Sometimes he angers me
With telling me of the moldwarp and
     the ant,
Of the dreamer Merlin and his proph-
     ecies,
And of a dragon and a finless fish,
A clip-wing'd griffin and a moulten
     raven,
A couching lion and a ramping cat,
And such a deal of skimble-skamble
     stuff
As puts me from my faith.
[Shakespeare: *I Henry IV* III.i.]

NOON

7 The huge drowse and cricketing stitch of noon. [Thomas Wolfe: *Of Time and the River*]

NORMALCY

8 Back to normalcy. [Warren G. Harding (1865-1923): slogan (1920)]
 Lured by alliteration and the spirit of the war-weary electorate, Harding, speaking in Boston in 1920, had declared that what America then needed was "not heroics but healing; not nostrums but normalcy; not revolution but restoration . . . not surgery but serenity."
 The wits assumed that normalcy *was an error for* normality *and made* normalcy *a term of derision. But the ignorance was theirs, not Harding's; it's a perfectly legitimate synonym for* normality *and had been in use seventy years before Harding employed it.*

NOSE

9 Plain as a nose in a man's face. [Rabelais: *Works,* The Author's Prologue to the Fifth Book]
10 As clear and as manifest as the nose in a man's face. [Robert Burton: *Anatomy of Melancholy* III.3.4.1]
11 Made them pay for it most unconscionably and through the nose. [Andrew Marvell: *The Rehearsal Transpos'd* I (1672)]
 All this does is show us that the expression "to pay through the nose" (= to pay reluctantly and exorbitantly) was in use by 1672. The origin is obscure. It probably came from thieves' cant. It is known that "rhino" was, at this time, a slang word for money and there may be a pun on Greek rhines, *the nostrils. Or it may merely mean that the money will gush out as freely and as painfully as blood from a bloodied nose.*
12 He that has a great Nose thinks every body is speaking of it. [Thomas Fuller (1654-1734): *Gnomologia*]
13 If the nose of Cleopatra had been a little shorter the whole face of the world would have been changed. [Pascal: *Pensées* VI]

NO SOAP

14 So she went into the garden to cut a cabbage leaf to make an apple pie; and, at the same time, a great she-bear coming up the street pops its head into the shop—"What! no soap?" So he died; and she very imprudently married the barber; and there were present the Picninnies, and the Joblillies, and the Garyulies, and the Grand Panjandrum himself, with the little round button at top. [Samuel Foote (1755)]
 A famous actor, Charles Macklin,

boasted that he could repeat anything after hearing it once and Samuel Foote, the comic actor, made up this nonsense to test him. According to an article in The Quarterly Review, *in Sept. 1854, Macklin failed the test. The farrago, apparently, passed into some schoolbooks as a mnemonic exercise and one still hears fragments of it. ("No soap" has become fixed in American slang.) It had appeared in Maria Edgeworth's* Harry and Lucy Concluded *(1825) and the* Harry and Lucy *stories were not only widely read by themselves but were plundered by the School Readers.*

NOSTALGIA

1 . . . old, unhappy, far-off things
  And battles long ago.
[Wordsworth: *The Solitary Reaper*]
2 I am homesick for my mountains—
  My heroic mother hills—
And the longing that is on me
  No solace ever stills.
[Bliss Carman: *The Cry of the Hill-born*]
3 Backward, turn backward, O Time
        in your flight;
  Make me a child again just for to-
        night.
[Elizabeth Akers Allen: *Rock Me to Sleep*]
4 I wandered today to the hill, Maggie,
    To watch the scene below,
  The creek and the old rusty mill,
        Maggie,
    As we used to, long ago.
[George Washington Johnson: *When You and I Were Young, Maggie*]

NOTE(S)

5 A chiel's amang you takin' notes,
  And faith he'll prent it.
[Burns: *On the Late Captain Grose's Peregrinations thro' Scotland* I (1793)]
  chiel = *chap, fellow, guy*
  Francis Grose (d. 1791) was an antiquary and draughtsman. He wrote A Classical Dictionary of the Vulgar Tongue *(1785), a valuable work.*
6 When found, make a note of. [Dickens: *Dombey and Son* XV (*et passim*)]

NOTHING

7 He knew nothing, except—that he

knew nothing. [Diogenes Laertius: *Socrates*]
8 As for me, all I know is that I know nothing. [Socrates: in Plato's *Phaedrus*]
9 Nothing can be created out of nothing. [Lucretius: *De rerum natura* I]
10 Nothing can come out of nothing any more than a thing can go back to nothing. [Marcus Aurelius Antoninus: *Meditations* IV.iv.]
  So also Persius (A.D. *34-62*): Satıres *III; Diogenes Laertius (c.* A.D. *200*): Diogenes of Apollonia; *Shakespeare:* King Lear, *I.i.: "Nothing can come of nothing" and I.iv.: "Nothing can be made out of nothing."*
11 Thou hast seen nothing yet.
[Cervantes: *Don Quixote* I.III.11.]
12 Did nothing in particular,
  And did it very well.
[W. S. Gilbert: *Iolanthe* II]
13 Nothing to do but work,
    Nothing to eat but food,
  Nothing to wear but clothes
      To keep one from going nude.
[Benjamin Franklin King: *The Pessimist*]

NOVEL(S)

14 Novels (receipts to make a whore).
[Matthew Green: *The Spleen*]
  receipts = *recipes*
    This estimation of the effect of novels was widely held by the rigidly righteous until quite recently and even yet has not completely disappeared.
15 A novel is a mirror carried along a main road. [Stendhal: *The Red and the Black* LXIX]
16 The phantasmagorical world of novels and of opium. [Matthew Arnold: *Literature and Dogma* II]

NOVELTY

17 One generation passeth away, and another generation cometh: but the earth abideth for ever:
  The sun also ariseth, and the sun goeth down, and hasteth to his place where he arose.
  The wind goeth toward the south, and turneth about unto the north; it whirleth about continually, and the wind returneth again according to his circuits.

All the rivers run into the sea; yet the sea is not full; unto the place from whence the rivers come, thither they return again. . . .

The thing that hath been it is that which shall be; and that which is done is that which shall be done: and there is no new thing under the sun. [Ecclesiastes 1: 4-7,9]

1 Men love . . . newfangledness. [Chaucer: *The Squire's Tale*]

2 He that will not apply new remedies must expect new evils. [Francis Bacon: *Of Innovations*]

3 . . . all with one consent praise new-
born gauds,
Though they are made and moulded
of things past,
And give to dust that is a little gilt
More laud than gilt o'erdusted.
[Shakespeare: *Troilus and Cressida* III. iii.]

4 New opinions are always suspected, and usually opposed, without any other reason but because they are not already common. [John Locke: *An Essay Concerning Human Understanding*, "Dedicatory Epistle"]

5 Be not the first by whom the new are
tried,
Nor yet the last to lay the old aside.
[Alexander Pope: *An Essay on Criticism* II]

6 When I was a young man, being anxious to distinguish myself, I was perpetually starting new propositions. But I soon gave this over; for I found that generally what was new was false. [Samuel Johnson: in Boswell's *Life* (1779)]

NOVEMBER

7 When chill November's surly blast

Made fields and forests bare.
[Burns: *Man Was Made to Mourn*]

8 No warmth, no cheerfulness, no
healthful ease,
No comfortable feel in any mem-
ber—
No shade, no shine, no butterflies, no
bees,
No fruits, no flowers, no leaves, no
birds,—
November!
[Thomas Hood: *No!*]

9 The desolate, deserted trees,
The faded earth, the heavy sky,
The beauties she so truly sees,
She thinks I have no eye for these,
And vexes me for reason why.

Not yesterday I learned to know
The love of bare November days
Before the coming of the snow;
But it were vain to tell her so,
And they are better for her praise.
[Robert Frost: *My November Guest*]

NOWHERE

10 He is nowhere who is everywhere. [Seneca: *Epistolae* II.ii.]
Samuel Johnson drew an amusing portrait of such a one in Jack Whirler, in The Idler *No. 19 (1758).*
See MOTION

NURSE

11 The nurse sleeps sweetly, hir'd to
watch the sick,
Whom, snoring, she disturbs.
[William Cowper: *The Task*, I. "The Sofa"]

O

OATH(S)
1 It is great sin to swear unto a sin,
But greater sin to keep a sinful oath.
[Shakespeare: *II Henry VI* V.i.]
2 A good mouth-filling oath.
[Shakespeare: *I Henry IV* III.i.]
3 Oaths are straws, men's faiths are wafer-cakes,
And hold-fast is the only dog.
[Shakespeare: *Henry V* II.iii.]
4 A terrible oath, with a swaggering accent sharply twanged off, gives manhood more approbation than ever proof itself would have earned him. [Shakespeare: *Twelfth Night* III.iv.]
5 Oathes are Crutches, upon which Lyes go.
[Thomas Dekker: *The Seven Deadly Sinnes of London* II.xxi.]
6 Oaths are but words, and words but wind. [Samuel Butler (1612-1680): *Hudibras*]
7 Oaths are the fossils of piety. [George Santayana: *Interpretations of Poetry*]

OATS
8 OATS. A grain which in England is generally given to horses, but in Scotland supports the people. [Samuel Johnson: *Dictionary* (1755)]
"Very true," said Lord Elibank, when the definition was first called to his attention, "and where will you find such men and such horses?"

OBEDIENCE
9 Obedience is much more seen in little things than in great. [Thomas Fuller (1654-1734): *Gnomologia*]
10 The boy stood on the burning deck,
Whence all but him had fled.
[Felicia Dorothea Hemans: *Casabianca*]
No poem was so respected in the 19th century and so ridiculed in the 20th as this one.

It commemorates the death of the child Giacomo Jocante, whose father, Captain Louis Casabianca, commanded the ill-fated French warship, L'Orient,
which caught fire and blew up at the Battle of Abukir Bay (1798).

All that is known for sure is that the Captain and his nine- or ten-year-old son were on the ship when the action began and were never seen after the explosion. It was Napoleon, in his report of the battle, which he labored to present, somehow, as not a disaster but a glorious performance by the French—especially since the defeat was in large measure his own fault—who first told the story of the child's obedience unto death. And Napoleon could have had no direct knowledge of the event.

There are a dozen parodies ("The boy stood on the burning deck / Eating peanuts by the peck"; ". . . till all but he had fled / And when his legs were burnt right off / He stood upon his head").

At heart they are sound. We are shocked at the idea of a father taking his child aboard a man-of-war when action was expected. Samuel Butler speaks for the 20th century when he says (The Way of All Flesh, XXIX) that the moral of the poem is "that young people cannot begin too soon to exercise discretion in the obedience they pay to their papa and mamma."

11 Theirs not to make reply,
Theirs not to reason why,
Theirs but to do and die:
Into the valley of Death
Rode the six hundred.
[Tennyson: *The Charge of the Light Brigade*]
Lord Cardigan who—under protest—led the famous charge had strong opinions about the famous poem. "If you see Tennyson," he said to a friend who was returning to England, "ask him how he came to write all that rot about Balaclava?"

OBJECTIVE
12 No wind makes for him that hath no intended port to sail unto. [Montaigne: *Essays* II.i.]

OBLIGATION

1 What fear and danger hath once forced me to will and consent unto, I am bound to will and perform, being out of danger and fear. [Montaigne: *Essays* III.i.]

Montaigne's position is certainly the moral one. Dr. Johnson agreed with him. Machiavelli did not. Most men would agree with Montaigne in word and Machiavelli in deed.

Is a man, for example, morally obligated to pay a sum he had agreed to pay kidnappers if, by chance, he manages to get his child back unharmed before the ransom was paid? Most men would insist that he was not. But, then, most men are amoral.

2 In . . . the book of Egoism, it is written, Possession without obligation to the object possessed approaches felicity. [George Meredith: *The Egoist* XIV]
3 Never in the field of human conflict was so much owed by so many to so few. [Sir Winston Churchill: Tribute to the Royal Air Force, August 20, 1940]

OBLIGING

4 So obliging that he ne'er obliged. [Alexander Pope: *Epistle to Dr. Arbuthnot*]

OBLIVION

5 Time hath, my lord, a wallet at his back,
Wherein he puts alms for oblivion.
[Shakespeare: *Troilus and Cressida* III. iii.]
6 But the iniquity of oblivion blindly scattereth her poppy, and deals with the memory of men without distinction to merit of perpetuity. . . . Who knows whether the best of men be known, or whether there be not more remarkable persons forgot than any that stand remembered in the known account of time? [Sir Thomas Browne: *Urn-Burial* V]
7 Darkness and light divide the course of time, and oblivion shares with memory a great part even of our living beings; we slightly remember our felicities, and the smartest strokes of affliction leave but short smart upon us. Sense endureth no extremities, and sorrows destroy us or themselves. [Sir Thomas

Browne: *Urn-Burial* V]
8 Forget thyself to marble.
[John Milton: *Il Penseroso*]
9 Far off from these, a slow and silent stream,
Lethe, the River of Oblivion, rolls
Her wat'ry labyrinth, whereof who drinks
Forthwith his former state and being forgets.
[John Milton: *Paradise Lost* II. 582-585]
10 The world forgetting, by the world forgot.
[Alexander Pope: *Eloisa to Abelard*]
11 Thetis baptized her mortal son in Styx;
A mortal mother would on Lethe fix.
[Byron: *Don Juan* IV.iv.]
12 The dust and silence of the upper shelf.
[Macaulay: *Milton*]
13 The heart asks pleasure first;
And then, excuse from pain;
And then, those little anodynes
That deaden suffering;

And then, to go to sleep;
And then, if it should be
The will of its Inquisitor,
The liberty to die.
[Emily Dickinson: *The Heart Asks Pleasure First*]
14 All my life, as down an abyss without a bottom, I have been pouring van-loads of information into that vacancy of oblivion I call my mind. [Logan Pearsall Smith: *Afterthoughts*]
15 Treadmill to Oblivion. [Fred Allen: title of his autobiographical reminiscences]

OBSCENITY

16 I know that the wiser sort of men will consider, and I wish that the ignorant sort would learn, how it is not the baseness or homeliness, whether of words or matters, that makes them foul and obscene, but their base minds, filthy conceits, or lewd intents that handle them. [Sir John Harington: *The Metamorphosis of Ajax*]

occupy was a dirty word in Elizabethan usage. The Restoration wits made mother and sister grossly indecent. In our times fairy has plunged from nursery inno-

cence to utmost lewdness. And so on, and so on.

1 As a book-worm I have got so used to lewd and lascivious books that I no longer notice them. The most virtuous lady novelists write things that would have made a bartender blush two decades ago. If I open a new novel and find nothing about copulation in it, I suspect at once that it is simply a reprint of some forgotten novel of 1885, with a new name. When I began reviewing I used to send my review copies, after I had sweated through them, to the Y.M.C.A. By 1920 I was sending all discarded novels to a medical college. [H. L. Mencken: *Prejudices: Fifth Series* (1926)]

2 Obscenity is whatever happens to shock some elderly and ignorant magistrate. [Bertrand Russell: *Look,* Feb. 23, 1954]

OBSCURITY

3 Whatsoever people direful fate oppresses, the greatness of the chief men places them in danger, but the lowly escape notice in easy safety. [Phaedrus: *Fables* III.v.]

> *Let hist'ry tell where rival kings command,*
> *And dubious title shakes the madded land,*
> *When statutes glean the refuse of the sword,*
> *How much more safe the vassal than the lord;*
> *Low skulks the hind beneath the rage of power,*
> *And leaves the wealthy traitor in the Tower.*
> Samuel Johnson: The Vanity of Human Wishes

4 Unknowe, unkist, and lost that is unsought. [Chaucer: *Troilus and Criseyde* I]
unknowe = *unknown*

5 Not to know me argues yourselves unknown. [John Milton: *Paradise Lost* IV. 830]

6 For night being the universal mother of things, wise philosophers hold all writings to be fruitful in the proportion as they are dark. [Jonathan Swift: *A Tale of a Tub,* "A Farther Digression"]

7 Thus let me live, unseen, unknown;

Thus unlamented let me die,
Steal from the world, and not a stone
Tell where I lie.
[Alexander Pope: *Ode on Solitude*]

8 Far from the madding crowd's ignoble strife,
Their sober wishes never learned to stray;
Along the cool, sequestered vale of life
They kept the noiseless tenor of their way.
[Thomas Gray: *Elegy Written in a Country Churchyard*]

9 But the truth is, that no man is much regarded by the rest of the world. He that considers how little he dwells upon the condition of others, will learn how little the attention of others is attracted by himself. [Samuel Johnson: *The Rambler* No. 159]

10 Cowley said it engagingly: *Bene qui latuit, bene vixit:* he lives well, that has lain well hidden. The pleasantest condition of life is in incognito. [Louise Imogen Guiney: "Patrius on the Delights of an Incognito"]

> *One reason why Cowley said it so engagingly is that he was quoting Ovid (Tristia III.4.i.25).*

See STEALTH

OBSERVATION

11 *Armado.* How hast thou purchased this experience?
Moth. By my penny of observation.
[Shakespeare: *Love's Labour's Lost* III.i.]

12 To observations which ourselves we make,
We grow more partial for th' observer's sake.
[Alexander Pope: *Moral Essays:* "Epistle I. To Lord Cobham"]

13 Let observation with extensive view,
Survey mankind from China to Peru.
[Samuel Johnson: *The Vanity of Human Wishes* (1749)]

> *The opening lines of the famous poem.*
> *Goldsmith parodied them:*
> *Let observation with observant view,*
> *Observe mankind from China to Peru.*
> *Tennyson said they were the equivalent of saying: Let observation with extended observation observe extensively.*

1 It was six men of Indostan
    To learning much inclined,
Who went to see the Elephant
    (Though all of them were blind),
That each by observation
    Might satisfy his mind.
[J. G. Saxe: *The Blind Men and the Elephant*]
2 Innocent and infinite are the pleasures of observation. [Henry James: *The Middle Years*]
3 You can observe a lot just by watchin'. [Yogi Berra, quoted in Eric Hodgins's *Episode*]
    Mr. Hodgins, quite properly, calls this "a great utterance."

OBSERVER
4 The observ'd of all observers. [Shakespeare: *Hamlet* III.i.]

OBSESSION
5 That fellow seems to me to possess but one idea, and that is a wrong one. [Samuel Johnson: in Boswell's *Life* (1770)]

OBSTINACY
6 Obstinacy is the sister of constancy. [Montaigne: *Essays* II.xxxii.]
7 Obstinacy and heat of opinion are the surest proof of stupidity. Is there anything so assured, resolved, disdainful, contemplative, solemn, and serious, as an ass? [Montaigne: *Essays* III.viii.]
8   But out, affection!
All bond and privilege of nature,
                                break!
Let it be virtuous to be obstinate.
[Shakespeare: *Coriolanus* V.iii.]
9 His own opinion was his law. [Shakespeare: *Henry VIII* IV.ii.]
    The reference is to Cardinal Wolsey, "a man of an unbounded stomach" (i.e., haughtiness).
10 Stiff in opinions, always in the wrong. [Dryden: *Absalom and Achitophel* I. 547]
11 Obstinacy in a bad Cause is but constancy in a good. [Sir Thomas Browne: *Religio Medici* I.xxiv.]
12 He can never be good that is not obstinate. [Bishop Thomas Wilson (1663-1755): *Maxims of Piety*]
13 For fools are stubborn in their way,
    As coins are harden'd by th' allay;

And obstinacy's ne'er so stiff
As when 'tis in a wrong belief.
[Samuel Butler (1612-1680): *Hudibras*]
14 The obstinate Man does not hold Opinions; they hold him. [Samuel Butler (1612-1680): *Remains* II]
15 Swine, women, and bees cannot be turned. [John Ray: *English Proverbs* (1670)]
16 Those who never retract their opinions love themselves more than they love truth. [Joseph Joubert: *Pensées*]
17 Here I am—and here I stay! [Marshal MacMahon: in the trenches before the Malakoff, in the Crimean War, September 8, 1855]
    "J'y suis, j'y reste."

OBVIOUS
18 It requires a very unusual mind to undertake the analysis of the obvious. [Alfred North Whitehead: *Science and the Modern World*]

OCCUPATION
19 Othello's occupation's gone! [Shakespeare: *Othello* III.iii.]

OCEAN
20 That great fishpond. [Thomas Dekker: *The Honest Whore* I.ii. (1604)]
    "The big pond" was a common facetious term for the Atlantic during and for some time after World War I.
21 Old ocean's gray and melancholy
                                waste.
[William Cullen Bryant: *Thanatopsis*]
22 Old ocean rolls a lengthened wave to
                                the shore,
Down whose green back the short-
                                lived foam, all hoar,
Bursts gradual, with a wayward in-
                                dolence.
[Keats: *Endymion* II]
23 A life on the ocean wave,
    A home on the rolling deep,
Where the scattered waters rave,
    And the winds their revels keep!
[Epes Sargent: *A Life on the Ocean Wave*]
24 "We are lost!" the captain shouted,
    As he staggered down the stairs.

But his little daughter whispered,
    As she took his icy hand,
"Isn't God upon the ocean,

Just the same as on the land?"
[James T. Fields: *The Captain's Daughter* (1849)]

Sometimes called by its more formal title, The Ballad of the Tempest, *this poem was included in* The McGuffey Readers *and was a great favorite. But* The Wreck of the Hesperus *was also included, just to insure a moral balance.*

1 Eternal Father! strong to save,
Whose arm hath bound the restless
wave,
Who bidd'st the mighty ocean deep
Its own appointed limits keep:
O, hear us when we cry to Thee
For those in peril on the sea!
[William Whiting: *Eternal Father, Strong to Save*]

2 There's never a wave of all her waves
But marks our English dead.
[Kipling: *A Song of the English*]

OCTOBER
3 The skies they were ashen and sober;
The leaves they were crispèd and
sere—
The leaves they were withering
and sere;
It was night in the lonesome October
Of my most immemorial year.
[Edgar Allan Poe: *Ulalume*]

ODDITIES
4 Any well-established village in New England or the northern Middle West could afford a town drunkard, a town atheist, and a few Democrats. [Denis Brogan: *The American Character*]

ODYSSEY
5 They hear like Ocean on a western
beach
The surge and thunder of the Odyssey.
[Andrew Lang: *The Odyssey*]

OFF AGIN
6 Off agin, on agin,
Gone agin, Finnigin.
[Strickland W. Gillilan: *Finnigin to Flannigan*]

Finnigin, the section boss, wrote "Full minny a tajus, blunderin' wurrd" in his labored accounts, to Superintendent Flannigan, of derailments and rerailments. Flannigan told Finnigin to "Make

'em brief," and the next time there was an accident Finnigin spent the whole night "Bilin' down 's repoort" to the above.*

OFFEND(ING)
7 Men are more ready to offend one who desires to be beloved than one who wishes to be feared. [Machiavelli: *The Prince* XVII]

8 The very head and front of my offend-
ing
Hath this extent, no more.
[Shakespeare: *Othello* I.iii.]

OFFENSE
9 O! my offence is rank, it smells to
heaven.
[Shakespeare: *Hamlet* III.iii.]

10 All's not offence that indiscretion
finds
And dotage terms so.
[Shakespeare: *King Lear* II.iv.]

11 There are offences given and offences not given but taken. [Izaak Walton: Preface to *The Compleat Angler*]

OFFICE
12 The insolence of office.
[Shakespeare: *Hamlet* III.i.]

13 Every time I fill a vacant place I make a hundred malcontents and one ingrate. [Attr. Louis XIV: in Voltaire's *Siècle de Louis XIV*]

14 A man who has no office to go to—I don't care who he is—is a trial of which you can have no conception. [G. B. Shaw: *The Irrational Knot* XVIII]

OFFICIAL
15 And with the best will, no one can
Be an official and a man.
[Henrik Ibsen: *Brand*]

OFFICIOUS
16 Abra was ready ere I called her name;
And, though I called another, Abra
came.
[Matthew Prior: *Solomon* II]

17 Officious, innocent, sincere,
Of every friendless name the friend.
[Samuel Johnson: *On the Death of Mr. Robert Levet*]

So much vanity is interfused into most helpfulness that officious which form-

erly, as here, meant sincerely and usefully helpful, has come to mean intrusively meddlesome.

Levet had worked as a waiter in a coffee house in Paris much frequented by physicians and had picked up a smattering of medical lore. He established himself as an amateur physician and, according to Johnson, did a great deal of good among the miserable, poverty-stricken wretches who could not afford proper medical treatment.

Most of Levet's patients could not pay him anything. But they would offer him gin (then very cheap) and his pride, demanding some payment, compelled him to accept it. Johnson said that Levet was the only man he knew who was consistently drunk "on principle."

OIL

1 Oil on troubled waters.
The common use is metaphorical. It has been known since the beginning of time, apparently, that oil spread on stormy waters lessened the fury of the waves. Pliny (in Holland's translation) said that "it dulceth and allayeth the unpleasant nature thereof." Plutarch said it was because the winds slipping on the oil "have no force nor cause any waves." The Venerable Bede (Ecclesiastical History III) records the use of holy oil, furnished by Bishop Aidan, and attributes the effect to supernatural powers.

2 Whence is thy learning? Hath thy toil
O'er books consum'd the midnight oil?
[John Gay: *The Shepherd and the Philosopher*]

3 My temples throb, my pulses boil,
I'm sick of Song, and Ode, and Ballad—
So, Thyrsis, take the Midnight Oil,
And pour it on a lobster salad.
[Thomas Hood: *To Minerva*]

4 I forget the punishment for compassing the death of the Heir Apparent. . . . Something lingering, with boiling oil in it, I fancy. [W. S. Gilbert: *The Mikado* II]

OINTMENT

5 Dead flies cause the ointment of the apothecary to send forth a stinking savour; so doth a little folly him that is in reputation for wisdom and honour. [Ecclesiastes 10:1]
This verse is the basis for the common expression a fly in the ointment.

O.K.

6 O. K.
Possibly the most universally used expression in the world today. In the U. S. alone it is probably uttered close to a billion times a day, perhaps more frequently. Its origin is uncertain. Some say it is the Choctaw Indian okeh, "it is so." Others trace it to the initial letters of "Oll Korrect," a humorous illiteracy variously ascribed to Andrew Jackson, John Jacob Astor and Obadiah Kelly, a railway clerk. There was an O. K. Club, formed in 1840 by partisans of Martin Van Buren and so named because Van Buren, born at Kinderhook, N. Y., was known as Old Kinderhook. But the club may have been so named to explain the expression which, we know, was used on the Stock Exchange before that.

OLD

7 To me, fair friend, you never can be old.
[Shakespeare: *Sonnets* CIV]

8 Is not old wine wholesomest, old pippins toothsomest? Does not old wood burn brightest, old linen wash whitest? Old soldiers, sweethearts, are surest, and old lovers are soundest. [John Webster: *Westward Hoe* II.ii.]

9 Old friends are best. King James us'd to call for his old shoes, they were easiest for his Feet. [John Selden: *Table Talk*, "Friends"]

10 I love everything that's old: old friends, old times, old manners, old books, old wines. [Oliver Goldsmith: *She Stoops to Conquer* I]

11 Ring out the old, ring in the new,
Ring, happy bells, across the snow;
The year is going, let him go;
Ring out the false, ring in the true.
[Tennyson: *In Memoriam* CVI]

12 The old order changeth, yielding place to new.
[Tennyson: *The Passing of Arthur*]

OLD BLACK JOE
1 I'm coming, I'm coming, for my head
          is bending low;
  I hear those gentle voices calling,
          "Old Black Joe."
[Stephen Foster: *Old Black Joe*]

OLD KENTUCKY HOME
2 The sun shines bright in the old Ken-
          tucky home;
  'Tis summer, the darkies are gay;
  The corn-top's ripe, and the mead-
          ow's in the bloom,
  While the birds make music all the
          day.
[Stephen Foster: *My Old Kentucky Home*]

OMENS
3 Lamentings heard i' the air; strange
          screams of death,
  And prophesying with accents ter-
          rible
  Of dire combustion and confused
          events
  New hatch'd to the woeful time. The
          obscure bird
  Clamour'd the livelong night: some
          say, the earth
  Was feverous and did shake.
[Shakespeare: *Macbeth* II.iii.]
4 This day black omens threat the
          brightest fair,
  That e'er deserv'd a watchful spirit's
          care.
[Alexander Pope: *The Rape of the Lock* II]

OMISSION
5 We have left undone those things
which we ought to have done; and we
have done those things which we ought
not to have done. [*Book of Common
Prayer,* "General Confession"]

ONCE
6 Nothing can be grievous that is but
once. [Montaigne: *Essays* I.xix.]
7 ONCE. Enough. [Ambrose Bierce:
The Devil's Dictionary]

ONE
8 All for one, one for all. [Alexandre
Dumas: *The Three Musketeers* IX]

ONE-HOSS SHAY
9 Have you heard of the wonderful one-
          hoss shay,
  That was built in such a logical way
  It ran a hundred years to a day?
[O. W. Holmes: *The Deacon's Master-
piece*]

ONION
10 Let onion atoms lurk within the bowl
  And, half suspected, animate the
          whole.
[Sydney Smith: *Recipe for Salad Dressing*]

ONOMATOPOEIA
11 Soft is the strain when zephyr gently
          blows,
  And the smooth stream in smoother
          numbers flows;
  But when loud surges lash the sound-
          ing shore,
  The hoarse, rough verse should like
          the torrent roar.
  When Ajax strives some rock's vast
          weight to throw,
  The line too labors, and the words
          move slow:
  Not so when swift Camilla scours the
          plain,
  Flies o'er th' unbending corn, and
          skims along the main.
[Alexander Pope: *An Essay on Criticism* II]
    *Pope had said that "the sound must
    seem an echo to the sense" and in this,
    the immediately-ensuing passage, dem-
    onstrated his own theory.*

OPEN MIND
12 An unsophisticated Unitarian with
an open-work mind. [George Ade: *Forty
Fables*]

OPINION(S)
13 So many men, so many opinions.
[Terence: *Phormio* II.iv.]
14 A plague of opinion! a man may wear
it on both sides, like a leather jerkin.
[Shakespeare: *Troilus and Cressida* III.
iii.]
    *It is interesting that reversible coats
    have been in use so long.*
15   I have bought
  Golden opinions from all sorts of

people.
[Shakespeare: *Macbeth* I.vii.]

1 Opinion is something wherein I go about to give reasons why all the world should think as I think. [John Selden: *Table Talk*]

2 Where we desire to be informed 'tis good to contest with men above ourselves; but to confirm and establish our opinions, 'tis best to argue with judgments below our own, that the frequent spoils and victories over their reasons may settle in ourselves an esteem and confirmed opinion of our own. [Sir Thomas Browne: *Religio Medici* I.vi.]

3 Opinion in good men is but knowledge in the making. [John Milton: *Areopagitica*]

4 He that complies against his will,
  Is of his own opinion still.
[Samuel Butler (1612-1680): *Hudibras*]
  Often misquoted as "A man convinced against his will | Is of the same opinion still."

  But, of course, a man can't be convinced against his will. Many an honest man has been convinced, by irrefutable evidence, against his deepest wish to believe otherwise. But that is not what is meant by either Butler's distich or its popular perversion.

5 Some praise at morning what they
      blame at night,
  But always think the last opinion
      right.
[Alexander Pope: *An Essay on Criticism* II]

6 When any opinion leads to absurdity, it is certainly false; but it is not certain that an opinion is false because it is of dangerous consequence. [David Hume: *An Enquiry Concerning Human Understanding* III]

7 As force is always on the side of the governed, the governors have nothing to support them but opinion. It is, therefore, on opinion only that government is founded; and this maxim extends to the most despotic and most military governments, as well as to the most free and the most popular. [David Hume: *Essays, Moral and Political* I]

8 Where an opinion is general, it is usually correct. [Jane Austen: *Mansfield Park* XI]

9 Men get opinions as boys learn to
      spell,
  By reiteration chiefly.
[Elizabeth Barrett Browning: *Aurora Leigh* VI.vi.]

10 Opinion is ultimately determined by the feelings, and not by the intellect. [Herbert Spencer: *Social Statics* III. xxx.]

11 The public buys its opinions as it buys its meat or takes in its milk, on the principle that it is cheaper to do this than to keep a cow. So it is, but the milk is more likely to be watered. [Samuel Butler (1835-1902): *Notebooks*]

12 The more unpopular an opinion is, the more necessary is it that the holder should be somewhat punctilious in his observance of conventionalities generally. [Samuel Butler (1835-1902): *Notebooks*, "The Art of Propagating Opinion"]

OPPORTUNITY

13 Opportunity has hair in front but is bald behind. [Attr. Aesop]
  The meaning is made clear in Rabelais's Gargantua I:
  Opportunity hath all her hair on her forehead; when she is past, you may not recall her. She hath no tuft whereby you can lay hold on her, for she is bald on the hinder part of her head, and never returneth again.

14 He that wyl nat whan he may,
  He shal nat whan he wyl.
[Robert Manning of Brunne: *Handlyng Synne*]

15 Opportunity is whoredom's Bawd. [William Camden: *Remains*]

16 Occasion turneth a bald Noddle, after she hath presented her locks in front, and no hold taken. [Francis Bacon: *Of Delays*]

17 A wise man will make more opportunities than he finds. [Francis Bacon: *Of Ceremonies and Respects*]

18 We must take the current when it
      serves,
  Or lose our ventures.
[Shakespeare: *Julius Caesar* IV.iii.]

19 Who seeks, and will not take when
      once 'tis offer'd,
  Shall never find it more.
[Shakespeare: *Antony and Cleopatra* II.

vii.]

1 He that will not when he may,
When he will he shall have nay.
[Robert Burton: in *Anatomy of Melancholy* III.2.5.5]
One of the oldest of English proverbs, going back to the 10th century.

2 Time's ancient bawd, Opportunity.
[William Rowley: *All's Lost by Lust* I]

3 The opportunity for doing mischief is found a hundred times a day, and of doing good once in a year. [Voltaire: *Zadig*]

4 He that would not when he might,
He shall not when he wolda.
[Thomas Percy: *Reliques*, "The Baffled Knight"]

5 No great man ever complains of want of opportunity. [Emerson: *Journals* V]

6 OPPORTUNITY. A favorable occasion for grasping a disappointment. [Ambrose Bierce: *The Devil's Dictionary*]

7 Wealth in modern societies is distributed according to opportunity; and while opportunity depends partly upon talent and energy, it depends still more upon birth, social position, access to education and inherited wealth; in a word, upon property. [Richard H. Tawney: *The Acquisitive Society*]

OPPOSITION

8 Many a man's strength is in opposition; and when that faileth, he groweth out of use. [Francis Bacon: *Of Faction*]

9 His Majesty's Opposition. [John Cam Hobhouse (Baron Broughton)]
Hobhouse tells us, in his Recollections of a Long Life, *that he invented the phrase and that Canning complimented him on it. As well he might. It is felicitous in itself (sometimes strengthened now to "His Majesty's Loyal Opposition") and is a fine illustration of the interaction of language and history.*

The phrase could have been coined only in 19th-century England and it at once defined and shaped parliamentarianism.

OPTIMISM

10 All is for the best in the best of possible worlds. (*Tout est pour le mieux dans le meilleur des mondes possibles.*)
[Voltaire: *Candide* XXX]

11 Something will turn up. [Benjamin Disraeli: *Popanilla* VII (1827)]
Disraeli cites the saying as "the national motto of England."

Note that Disraeli's book was published 22 years before Dickens's David Copperfield *(1849-1850) appeared. In* Copperfield *one of the outstanding characters is Mr. Micawber whose whole philosophy of life was based on this "motto," and it is with Micawber that most people associate it.*

12 Optimism is a kind of heart stimulant —the digitalis of failure. [Elbert Hubbard: *A Thousand and One Epigrams*]

13 Optimism is the content of small men in high places. [F. Scott Fitzgerald: *The Crack-up*]

OPTIMIST

14 A pessimist is a man who thinks all women are bad. An optimist is a man who hopes they are. [Chauncey Depew: after-dinner speech]

15 Two men look out through the same bars:
One sees the mud, and one the stars.
[Frederick Langbridge: *Pessimist and Optimist*]

16 An optimist is a guy that has never had much experience. [Don(ald) Marquis: *archy and mehitabel*]

17 'Twixt the optimist and pessimist
The difference is droll:
The optimist sees the doughnut
But the pessimist sees the hole.
[McLandburgh Wilson: *Optimist and Pessimist*]

18 The optimist proclaims that we live in the best of all possible worlds; and the pessimist fears this is true. [James Branch Cabell: *The Silver Stallion* XXVI]

ORACLE(S)

19 I am Sir Oracle,
And when I ope my lips, let no dog bark!
[Shakespeare: *The Merchant of Venice* I.i.]

20 The oracles are dumb,
No voice or hideous hum
Runs through the arched roof in words deceiving.
Apollo from his shrine
Can no more divine,

With hollow shriek the steep of Del-
phos leaving.
No nightly trance or breathèd spell,
Inspires the pale-eyed priest from the
prophetic cell.
[John Milton: *On the Morning of Christ's
Nativity*]
*There was a belief that at the birth of
Christ the ancient oracles were silenced.*
See PAN

1 A vehement assertor of uncontroverted truth. [Samuel Johnson: *The
Idler* No. 78]
2 And mute's the midland navel-stone
beside the singing fountain,
And echoes list to silence now where
gods told lies of old.
[A. E. Housman: *The Oracles*]

ORDER

3 Set thine house in order. [II Kings
20:1; Isaiah 38:1]
4 There is no course of life so weak
and sottish as that which is managed by
order, method, and discipline. [Mon-
taigne: *Essays* III]
5 The heavens themselves, the planets
and this centre
Observe degree, priority and place,
Insisture, course, proportion, season,
form,
Office and custom, in all line of order.
[Shakespeare: *Troilus and Cressida* I.
iii.]
insisture — steady motion onward

6 Order the beauty even of Beauty is.
[Thomas Traherne: quoted by Edith
Wharton as the motto for her *The
Writing of Fiction*]
7 Order is Heav'n's first law. [Alexan-
der Pope: *An Essay on Man* IV]
8 Beauty from order springs.
[William King: *The Art of Cookery*
(1708)]
9 Good order is the foundation of all
good things. [Edmund Burke: *Reflections on the Revolution in France*]
10 The old order changeth, yielding
place to new,
And God fulfils himself in many ways,
Lest one good custom should corrupt
the world.
[Tennyson: *The Passing of Arthur*]
11 A place for everything, and every-

thing in its place. [Samuel Smiles:
Thrift V]
12 Have a place for everything and keep
the thing somewhere else. This is not ad-
vice, it is merely custom. [Mark Twain:
Diaries]
13 Order is a lovely thing;
On disarray it lays its wing,
Teaching simplicity to sing.
It has a meek and lowly grace,
Quiet as a nun's face.
[Anna Hempstead Branch: *The Monk
in the Kitchen*]

ORGIES

14 I am for those who believe in loose
delights—
I share the midnight orgies of young
men;
I dance with the dancers, and drink
with the drinkers.
[Walt Whitman: *Leaves of Grass,* "Native Moments"]
15 I say orgies, not because it's the common term, because it ain't—obsequies
bein' the common term—but because
orgies is the right term. . . . Orgies is
better, because it means the thing you're
after more exact. It's a word that's made
up out'n the Greek *orgo,* outside, open,
abroad; and the Hebrew *jeesum,* to plant,
cover up. So, you see, funeral orgies is
an open er public funeral. ["The King":
in Mark Twain's *Huckleberry Finn,*
XXV]
*If anyone thinks that, even in a chapter
entitled "All Full of Tears and Flap-
doodle," the king's etymology is outrageous, let him consult the entry* LUCUS
A NON LUCENDO.

16 The natural rhythm of human life is
routine punctuated by orgies. [Aldous
Huxley: *Beyond the Mexique Bay*]

ORIGINALITY

17 For I fear I have nothing original in
me—
Excepting Original Sin.
[Thomas Campbell: *To a Young Lady,
Who Asked Me to Write Something
Original for Her Album*]
18 He has left off reading altogether, to
the great improvement of his originality.
[Charles Lamb: *Detached Thoughts on
Books and Reading*]

1 All good things which exist are the fruits of originality. [John Stuart Mill: *Liberty* III]

2 Originality does not consist in saying what no one has ever said before, but in saying exactly what you think yourself. [J. F. Stephen: *Horae Sabbaticae*]

ORPHAN

3 He reminds me of the man who murdered both his parents, and then, when sentence was about to be pronounced, pleaded for mercy on the grounds that he was an orphan. [Attr. Abraham Lincoln]

4 Little Orphant Annie's come to our house to stay,
An' wash the cups an' saucers up, an' brush the crumbs away,
An' shoo the chickens off the porch, an' dust the hearth, an' sweep,
An' make the fire, an' bake the bread, an' earn her board-an'-keep.
[James Whitcomb Riley: *Little Orphant Annie*]

5 You better mind yer parents, an' yer teachers fond and dear,
An' churish them 'at loves you, an' dry the orphant's tear,
An' help the pore an' needy ones 'at clusters all about,
Er the Gobble-uns'll git you
Ef you
Don't
Watch
Out!
[James Whitcomb Riley: *Little Orphant Annie*]

ORTHODOX

6 Such as do build their faith upon
The holy text of pike and gun
. . .
And prove their doctrine orthodox
By apostolic blows and knocks.
[Samuel Butler (1612-1680): *Hudibras*]

ORTHODOXY

7 Orthodoxy is my doxy—heterodoxy is another man's doxy. [William Warburton (Bishop of Gloucester) (1698-1779)]

This famous definition is quoted by Joseph Priestley in his Memoirs *I. The story is that during a debate in the House of Lords on the Test Laws, Lord Sandwich whispered to Warburton that he had often heard* orthodoxy *and* heterodoxy *but wasn't sure what they meant and Warburton whispered back the above definition.*

Warburton's joke was based on the two words doxy:

doxy[1] = *a slang term for a beggar's wench, prob. from archaic Dutch* docke, *doll.*

doxy[2] = *the "doxy" of* orthodoxy, doxology, *etc., is from Greek* doxa, *glory.*

A very learned joke, but a very good one—Warburton's finest hour.

OSSA

8 To pile Ossa on Pelion, and to roll wooded Olympus upon Ossa. [Vergil: *Georgics* I]

It was Otus and Ephialtes, the juvenile delinquents of the Greek gods, who piled Ossa on Pelion and then Olympus on Ossa in an attempt to scale heaven and attack Juno. They had formerly, out of sheer exuberance, imprisoned Ares, the god of war, in a bronze jar for thirteen months. Zeus was not amused and destroyed them.

OSTENTATION

9 They that are glorious must needs be factious; for all bravery stands upon comparisons. [Francis Bacon: *Of Vainglory*]

glorious = *ostentatious, boastful;* bravery = *showing off*

OURSELVES

10 Why do you laugh? Change but the name, and the story is told of you. [Horace: *Satires* I.i.]

This is the "De te fabula" of Browning's The Statue and the Bust.

11 O wad some Pow'r the giftie gie us
To see oursels as others see us!
It wad frae mony a blunder free us,
And foolish notion:
What airs in dress an' gait wad lea'e us,
And ev'n devotion!
[Burns: *To a Louse*]

OUT

12 It is easier to stay out than to get out.

[Mark Twain: *Pudd'nhead Wilson's New Calendar*]
1 The best way out is always through. [Robert Frost: *A Servant to Servants*]

OUTLAW
2 The wandering outlaw of his own dark mind. [Byron: *Childe Harold* III.iii.]

OUTSPOKEN
3 His nature is too noble for the world:
He would not flatter Neptune for his trident,
Or Jove for 's power to thunder. His heart's his mouth:
What his breast forges, that his tongue must vent.
[Shakespeare: *Coriolanus* III.i.]

OWE
4 I owe much; I have nothing; the rest I leave to the poor. [Rabelais: his will]

OWL
5 Like sending Owls to Athens, as the proverb is. [Diogenes Laertius: *Lives of Eminent Philosophers*, "Plato" **XXXII** (c. A.D. 200-250)]
   The owl, sacred to Athena, was apparently protected and hence plentiful in Athens; to send any more there would be like sending "coals to Newcastle."
   Aristophanes' (c. 448-c. 380 B.C.) Birds, 301, had alluded to this proverb.

6 Then nightly sings the staring owl:
'Tu-who!
Tu-whit, tu-who!' a merry note,
While greasy Joan doth keel the pot.
[Shakespeare: *Love's Labour's Lost* V.ii.]
   keel = *to cool by stirring or skimming*

7 I heard the owl scream and the crickets cry.
[Shakespeare: *Macbeth* II.ii.]

8 The moping owl does to the moon complain.
[Thomas Gray: *Elegy Written in a Country Churchyard*]

9 While Anna's peers and early playmates tread,
In freedom, mountain-turf and river's marge;
Or float with music on the festal barge;
Rein the proud steed, or through the dance are led;
Her doom it is to press a weary bed—
Till oft her guardian Angel, to some charge
More urgent called, will stretch his wings at large,
And friends too rarely prop the languid head.
Yet, helped by Genius—untired comforter,
The presence even of a stuffed Owl for her
Can cheat the time; sending her fancy out
To ivied castles and to moonlight skies,
Though he can neither stir a plume, nor shout;
Nor veil, with restless film, his staring eyes.
[Wordsworth: *Sonnet*]
   In a note Wordsworth states that the subject was related to him by a Miss Jewsbury who, long confined by sickness, had derived pleasure from "the inanimate object on which this sonnet turns." Some connoisseurs of bathos regard this as an unrivaled masterpiece of banality, though the same poet's sonnet on the umbrella may challenge the preeminence.

10 Alone and warming his five wits,
The white owl in the belfry sits.
[Tennyson: *The Owl*]

11 The Owl and the Pussy-cat went to sea
In a beautiful pea-green boat,
They took some honey, and plenty of money,
Wrapped up in a five-pound note.
The Owl looked up to the stars above,
And sang to a small guitar,
"O lovely Pussy! O Pussy, my love,
What a beautiful Pussy you are,
   You are,
   You are,
What a beautiful Pussy you are!"
[Edward Lear: *The Owl and the Pussy-Cat*]

OX(EN)
12 Thou shalt not muzzle the ox when

he treadeth out the corn. [Deuteronomy 25:4]
1 As an ox goeth to the slaughter. [Proverbs 7:22]
2 And we shall feed like oxen at a stall. The better cherish'd, still the nearer death. [Shakespeare: *I Henry IV* V.ii.]
3 Who drives fat oxen should himself be fat. [Samuel Johnson: in Boswell's *Life* (1784)]

Boswell says that Johnson was present when a tragedy was read, in which occurred the line:
Who rules o'er freemen should himself be free.
The company admired this line, but Johnson scoffed at such talk by making up the line given above.
The play was Henry Brooke's The Earl of Essex and the line of rodomontade which the company admired is in Act I. "Liberty" and "freedom" were vogue words in the 18th century, especially among the upper classes, who tolerated very little of either.

4 The years like great black oxen tread the world,
And God the herdsman goads them on behind,
And I am broken by their passing feet.
[William Butler Yeats: *The Countess Cathleen* IV]

OXFORD
5 There was a clerk of Oxenford also That unto logick hadde long y-go. [Chaucer: Prologue to *The Canterbury Tales*]
6 Home of lost causes, and forsaken beliefs, and unpopular names, and impossible loyalties! [Matthew Arnold: Preface to *Essays in Criticism*]
7 I saw the spires of Oxford As I was passing by,
The gray spires of Oxford Against a pearl-gray sky.
[Winifred Mary Letts: *The Spires of Oxford*]

OYSTER(S)
8 It is unseasonable and unwholesome in all months that have not an R in their name to eat an oyster. [Henry Buttes:

Dyet's Dry Dinner (1599)]
Before the development of refrigerated transportation this ancient belief may have had some basis in the fact that the months without an r are summer months when sea food that had to be shipped inland was particularly likely to spoil. Then, the summer is the spawning season of oysters and during that season they often taste flat. But—says the U. S. Govt.—there is nothing poisonous per se about them.

9 The world's mine oyster, Which I with sword will open. [Shakespeare: *The Merry Wives of Windsor* II.ii.]
10 TRANIO: He . . . in countenance somewhat doth resemble you.
BIONDELLO: As much as an apple doth an oyster. [Shakespeare: *The Taming of the Shrew* IV.ii.]
The comparison, for something that did not resemble something else, was a cliché by Shakespeare's time. Sir Thomas More had used it more than sixty years before.
11 A man may as well open an oyster without a knife, as a lawyer's mouth without a fee. [Barten Holyday: *Technogamia* II.5]
12 He was a very valiant man who first adventured on eating of oysters. [Thomas Fuller (1608-1661): *Worthies of England*]
Attr. King James I.
In 1738, in his Polite Conversation, *Swift listed it as a cliché.*
13 They say oysters are a cruel meat, because we eat them alive; then they are an uncharitable meat, for we leave nothing to the poor; and they are an ungodly meat, because we never say grace. [Jonathan Swift: *Polite Conversation* II]
Swift's upper-class conversationalists were mouthing the moldy wit of their grandsires. In 1611 Tarlton's Jests, a collection of threadbare quips and whimsies, had included:
"Oysters are ungodly, because they are eaten without grace; uncharitable, because they leave nought but shells; and unprofitable, because they swim in wine."
14 An oyster may be crossed in love. [Richard Brinsley Sheridan: *The Critic* III.i.]

"An oyster may be crossed in love," and
why?
Because he mopeth idly in his shell,
And heaves a lonely subterraqueous sigh,
Much as a monk may do within his cell.
     Byron: Don Juan *XIV.lxxxi.*

In some species of oysters the sexes are
separate and in others they are united
in one individual. This must lead to
frustrations and complications of so re-
markable a nature that human beings,
considering the difficulties they have with
a comparatively simple system, should
charitably refrain from comment.

1 Oysters are amatory food.
[Byron: *Don Juan* II.clxx.]

Our fathers drew up page-long lists of
foods that were thought to be aphrodis-
iac. The power was ascribed to so many
articles of diet that one suspects that,
virile but undernourished, all they
needed was a meal. Oysters ranked high
on every list.

2 Nor brighter was his eye, nor moister,
Than a too-long-opened oyster.
[Browning: *The Pied Piper* IV]

3 Secret and self-contained, and solitary as an oyster. [Dickens: *A Christmas
Carol*]

4 "A loaf of bread," the Walrus said,
  "Is what we chiefly need:
Pepper and vinegar besides
  Are very good indeed—
Now, if you're ready, Oysters dear,
  We can begin to feed."

"But not on us!" the Oysters cried,
  Turning a little blue.
"After such kindness, that would be
  A dismal thing to do!"
"The night is fine," the Walrus said,
  "Do you admire the view?"
[Lewis Carroll: *Through the Looking-
Glass* Ch. 4]

OZYMANDIAS

5 My name is Ozymandias, king of
               kings:
Look on my works, ye Mighty, and
               despair!
[Shelley: *Ozymandias*]

P

PA
1 Ma! Ma! Where's my Pa?
Gone to the White House, ha, ha, ha!
Adapted from H. R. Monroe's more dignified Ma! Ma! Where's My Pa? *by the Democrats in the campaign of 1884. It was alleged that Cleveland had had an illegitimate child by Maria Halpin, of Buffalo. Cleveland did not deny the possibility and his frankness gained him more than the attack lost him. His own side followed his lead and countered with:* Hurrah for Maria, / Hurrah for the kid, / I voted for Grover / And am damn glad I did.

PAGAN
2   Great God! I'd rather be
A Pagan suckled in a creed outworn;
So might I, standing on this pleasant
                            lea,
Have glimpses that would make me
                        less forlorn;
Have sight of Proteus rising from the
                            sea,
Or hear old Triton blow his wreathèd
                            horn.
[Wordsworth: *The World Is Too Much
With Us*]
*Good Lord! I'd rather be
Quite unacquainted with the A.B.C.
Than write such hopeless rubbish as thy
                            worst.*
James Stephen (1859-1892): To R. K.
                (i.e., To Rudyard Kipling)

PAIN
3 A mighty pain to love it is,
And 'tis a pain that pain to miss.
[Abraham Cowley: *From Anacreon* VII,
"Gold"]
4 Those who do not feel pain seldom
think that it is felt. [Samuel Johnson:
The Rambler No. 48]
5 The mind is seldom quickened to
very vigorous operations but by pain, or
the dread of pain. We do not disturb
ourselves with the detection of fallacies
which do us no harm. [Samuel Johnson:
The Idler No. 18]

6 Pain has an element of blank;
It cannot recollect
When it began, or if there were
A day when it was not.

It has no future but itself,
Its infinite realms contain
Its past, enlightened to perceive
New periods of pain.
[Emily Dickinson: *Pain Has an Element
of Blank*]
7 Nothing begins and nothing ends
That is not paid with moan;
For we are born in other's pain,
And perish in our own.
[Francis Thompson: *Daisy*]

PAINTING
8 One is never tired of painting, because you have to set down, not what you knew already, but what you have just discovered. There is a continual creation out of nothing going on. [William Hazlitt: *The Pleasure of Painting*]
9 I have seen, and heard, much of cockney impudence before now; but never expected to hear a coxcomb ask two hundred guineas for flinging a pot of paint in the public's face. [John Ruskin: *On Whistler*]
10 It does not matter how badly you paint, so long as you don't paint badly like other people. [George Moore: *Confessions of a Young Man* VII]

PAN
11 Great Pan is dead. [Plutarch: *Why the Oracles Cease to Give Answers*]
In Isis and Osiris, *Plutarch tells of a ship, filled with passengers, which was driven by the tides near to the Ionian island of Paxos. Suddenly a loud voice was heard calling unto one Thanus, telling him "the great god Pan is dead." Plutarch lived from* A.D. *46 to 120.*
Legend later placed this happening at the hour at which Christ died on the cross.
12 And that dismal cry rose slowly
And sank slowly through the air,

Full of spirit's melancholy
And eternity's despair!
And they heard the words it said—
Pan is dead! great Pan is dead!
Pan, Pan is dead!
[Elizabeth Barrett Browning: *The Dead Pan*]

PANTHEISM

1 He is made one with Nature: there is
    heard
His voice in all her music, from the
    moan
Of thunder to the song of night's
    sweet bird.
[Shelley: *Adonais* XLII]

PANTS

2 The things named "pants" in certain
    documents,
A word not made for gentlemen, but
    "gents."
[O. W. Holmes: *A Rhymed Lesson*]

PAPACY

3 The Papacy is not other than the
Ghost of the deceased Roman Empire,
sitting crowned upon the grave thereof.
[Thomas Hobbes: *Leviathan* IV.xlvii.]

PAPERWORK

4 The man whose life is devoted to
paperwork has lost the initiative. He is
dealing with things that are brought to
his notice, having ceased to notice anything for himself. He has been essentially
defeated by his job. [C. Northcote Parkinson: *In-Laws and Outlaws* IX]

PARADISE

5 Today shalt thou be with me in para-
dise. [Luke 23:43]
6 They looking back, all th' eastern
    side beheld
Of Paradise, so late their happy seat,
Wav'd over by that flaming brand,
    the Gate
With dreadful faces throng'd and
    fiery arms.
Some natural tears they dropped, but
    wiped them soon;
The world was all before them, where
    to choose
Their place of rest, and Providence
    their guide:

They hand in hand with wandering
    steps and slow
Through Eden took their solitary
    way.
[John Milton: *Paradise Lost* XII. 641-
649]
7 A Book of Verses underneath the
    Bough,
A Jug of Wine, a Loaf of Bread—and
    Thou
Beside me singing in the Wilder-
    ness—
Oh, Wilderness were Paradise enow!
[*Rubáiyát of Omar Khayyám* (trans. Ed-
ward FitzGerald)]

PARADISE LOST

8 The majesty which through thy work
    doth reign
Draws the devout, deterring the pro-
    fane.
And things divine thou treat'st of in
    such state
As them preserves, and thee, inviolate.
[Andrew Marvell: *On Paradise Lost*]
Prefixed to the Second Edition.

PARADISE OF FOOLS

9 Into a Limbo large and broad, since
    call'd
The Paradise of Fools, to few un-
    known.
[John Milton: *Paradise Lost* III. 495-
496]
The Limbus fatuorum *of the medieval
theologians, between heaven and hell
where Dante placed "the praiseless and
the blameless dead." Here Milton, in
agreement with many theologians, placed
"embryos and idiots" and, on his own,
added "eremites and friars."*
See LIMBO

PARADOXES

10 These are old fond paradoxes to
make fools laugh i' the alehouse. [Shake-
speare: *Othello* II.i.]

PARDON

11 Now may the good God pardon all
    good men!
[Elizabeth Barrett Browning: *Aurora
Leigh* IV]

PARENTS

12 Honour thy father and thy mother;

that thy days may be long upon the land which the Lord thy God giveth thee. [Exodus 20:12]

1 The joys of parents are secret, and so are their griefs and fears. [Francis Bacon: *Of Parents and Children*]

2 I wish either my father or my mother, or indeed both of them, as they were in duty both equally bound to it, had minded what they were about when they begot me. [Laurence Sterne: *Tristram Shandy* I.i. (opening sentence)]

3 Honor thy parents; that is, all
From whom advancement may befall.
[Arthur Hugh Clough: *The Latest Decalogue*]

4 There are orphanages for children who have lost their parents—oh! why, why, why, are there no harbors of refuge for grown men who have not yet lost them? [Samuel Butler (1835-1902): *The Way of All Flesh* LXVIII]

PARENTS: and children

5 Friendship is nourished by communication which by reason of the disparity in age cannot be found in them [parents and children] and would offend the duties of nature. For all the secret thoughts of parents cannot be communicated unto children, lest it engender an unseemly familiarity, and the admonitions and corrections which parents must use cannot be reciprocated from children to parents. [Montaigne: *Essays* I.xxvii.]

6 An unpractised observer expects the love of parents and children to be constant and equal; but this kindness seldom continues beyond the years of infancy: in a short time the children become rivals to their parents; benefits are allayed by reproaches, and gratitude debased by envy. [Samuel Johnson: *Rasselas* XXVI]

7 I tell you there's a wall ten feet thick and ten miles high between parent and child. [G. B. Shaw: *Misalliance*]

8 Oh, what a tangled web do parents weave
When they think that their children are naïve.
[Ogden Nash: *What Makes the Sky Blue?*]

PARIS

9 Paris is well worth a mass. [Henry IV of France: *Caquets de l'Accouchée*]

10 Paris is a veritable ocean. Take as many soundings in it as you will, you will never know its depth. [Balzac: *Père Goriot*]

11 Good Americans when they die go to Paris. [Thomas Appleton: quoted in O. W. Holmes's *The Autocrat of the Breakfast-Table* VI]

12 When good Americans die they go to Paris. [Oscar Wilde: *The Portrait of Dorian Gray* III]

13 Old, crumbling walls and the pleasant sound of water running in the urinals. [Henry Miller: *Tropic of Cancer*]

PARKINSON'S LAW

14 Work expands so as to fill the time available for its completion. [C. Northcote Parkinson: *Parkinson's Law* I]
This is Parkinson's First Law. Parkinson's Second Law is: *Expenditure rises to meet income* (The Law and the Profits *I*). Parkinson's Third Law: *Expansion means complexity, and complexity, decay. Or: the more complex, the sooner dead* (In-Laws and Outlaws *XII*).

PARLIAMENTS

15 England is the mother of parliaments. [John Bright: in a speech in Birmingham, England, Jan. 18, 1865]

PARNASSUS

16 One top of Parnassus was sacred to Bacchus, the other to Apollo. [Jonathan Swift: *Thoughts on Various Subjects*]

17 An' syne they think to climb Parnassus
By dint o' Greek!
[Robert Burns: *Epistle to John Lapraik*]

PARSON

18 A little, round, fat, oily man of God. [James Thomson (1700-1748): *The Castle of Indolence* I.lxix.]

PARTING

19 The glory is departed from Israel: for the ark of God is taken. [I Samuel 4:22]

20 In farewells we heat above ordinary our affections to the things we forego. [Montaigne: *Essays* III.v.]

1 Since there's no help, come let us kiss
and part,
Nay, I have done: you get no more of
me,
And I am glad, yea glad with all my
heart,
That thus so clearly, I myself can free.
Shake hands for ever, cancel all our
vows,
And when we meet at any time again,
Be it not seen in either of our brows,
That we one jot of former love re-
tain;
Now at the last gasp of love's latest
breath,
When, his pulse failing, passion
speechless lies,
When faith is kneeling by his bed of
death,
And innocence is closing up his eyes,
Now if thou wouldst, when all have
given him over,
From death to life thou might'st him
yet recover.
[Michael Drayton: *Sonnet*]
2 Parting is such sweet sorrow.
[Shakespeare: *Romeo and Juliet* II.ii.]
3 Let us not be dainty of leave-taking,
But shift away.
[Shakespeare: *Macbeth* II.iii.]
4 When I died last, and dear, I die
As often as from thee I go.
[Donne: *The Legacy*]
5 But dearest friends, alas! must part.
[Gay: *The Hare and Many Friends*]
6 When we two parted
In silence and tears,
Half broken-hearted
To sever for years,
Pale grew thy cheek and cold,
Colder thy kiss;
Truly that hour foretold
Sorrow to this!
[Byron: *When We Two Parted*]
7 Maid of Athens, ere we part,
Give, oh give me back my heart!
[Byron: *Maid of Athens*]
8 Ah! then and there was hurrying to
and fro,
And gathering tears, and tremblings
of distress,
And cheeks all pale, which but an
hour ago
Blush'd at the praise of their own
loveliness;

And there were sudden partings, such
as press
The life from out young hearts, and
choking sighs
Which ne'er might be repeated; who
could guess
If ever more should meet those mu-
tual eyes,
Since upon night so sweet such aw-
ful morn could rise!
[Byron: *Childe Harold* III.xxiv.]
9 In every parting there is an image of
death. [George Eliot: *Amos Barton* X]
10 God be with you, till we meet again,
By His counsels guide, uphold you,
With His sheep securely fold you:
God be with you, till we meet again.
[Jeremiah Eames Rankin: *Hymn*]
11 Parting is all we know of heaven,
And all we need of hell.
[Emily Dickinson: *Poems, Part I, Life*
XCVI]
12 I will not let thee go.
I hold thee by too many bands:
Thou sayest farewell, and lo!
I have thee by the hands,
And will not let thee go.
[Robert Bridges: *I Will Not Let Thee
Go*]
13 My man, from sky to sky's so far,
We never crossed before;
Such leagues apart the world's ends
are,
We're like to meet no more;

What thoughts at heart have you and
I
We cannot stop to tell;
But dead or living, drunk or dry,
Soldier, I wish you well.
[A. E. Housman: *A Shropshire Lad*
XXII]
14 The rain, it streams on stone and hil-
lock,
The boot clings to the clay.
Since all is done that's due and right
Let's home, and now, my lad, good-
night,
For I must turn away.
[A. E. Housman: *Last Poems* XVIII]

PARTY
15 I always voted at my party's call,
And I never thought of thinking for
myself at all.

[W. S. Gilbert: *H.M.S. Pinafore* I]
1 How can one conceive of a one-party system in a country that has over two hundred varieties of cheeses? [Charles de Gaulle, quoted in the *New York Times Magazine,* June 29, 1958]

PASS(ING)
2 He passed by on the other side. [Luke 10:31]
3 Ships that pass in the night, and
        speak each other in passing,
Only a signal shown and a distant
        voice in the darkness;
So on the ocean of life, we pass and
        speak one another,
Only a look and a voice, then dark-
        ness again and a silence.
[Longfellow: *Tales of a Wayside Inn,* "The Theologian's Tale: Elizabeth IV"]

PASSION(S)
4   Most wretched man,
That to affections does the bridle
        lend!
In their beginning they are weak and
        wan,
But soone through suff'rance growe
        to fearful end.
[Edmund Spenser: *The Faerie Queene* II.iv.]
5 One passion doth expel another.
[George Chapman: *Monsieur d'Olive* V]
6   Give me that man
That is not passion's slave, and I will
        wear him
In my heart's core, ay, in my heart of
        heart,
As I do thee.
[Shakespeare: *Hamlet* III.ii.]
7 The sea's my mind, which calm would
        be
Were it from winds (my passions)
        free.
[Sir John Suckling: *Love's World*]
8 If we resist our passions it is more from their weakness than from our strength. [La Rochefoucauld: *Maxims*]
9 All subsists by elemental strife;
And passions are the elements of life.
[Alexander Pope: *An Essay on Man* I]
10 As fruits ungrateful to the planter's
        care,
On savage stocks inserted, learn to
        bear,

The surest Virtues thus from Passions
        shoot,
Wild Nature's vigour working at the
        root.
[Alexander Pope: *An Essay on Man* II]
11 What reason weaves, by passion is un-
        done.
[Alexander Pope: *An Essay on Man* II]
12 Strange fits of passion have I known:
    And I will dare to tell,
But in the lover's ear alone,
    What once to me befell.
[Wordsworth: *Strange Fits of Passion*]
13   Passion in a lover's glorious,
But in a husband is pronounced ux-
        orious.
[Byron: *Don Juan* III.vi.]
14 All breathing human passion far
        above,
That leaves a heart high-sorrowful
        and cloyed,
A burning forehead and a parching
        tongue.
[Keats: *Ode on a Grecian Urn*]
15   In tragic life, God wot,
No villain need be! Passions spin the
        plot:
We are betrayed by what is false
        within.
[George Meredith: *Modern Love* XLIII]
16 The natural man has only two primal passions, to get and to beget. [Sir William Osler: *Science and Immortality* II]
17 There is always something ridiculous about the passions of people whom one has ceased to love. [Oscar Wilde: *The Picture of Dorian Gray*]
18 They are not long, the weeping and
        the laughter,
    Love and desire and hate:
    I think they have no portion in us
        after
    We pass the gate.
[Ernest Dowson: *Vitae Summa Brevis*]
19 Mortal lovers must not try to remain at the first step: for lasting passion is the dream of a harlot and from it we wake in despair. [C. S. Lewis: *The Pilgrim's Regress*]

PAST: and future
20 What's past is prologue.
[Shakespeare: *The Tempest* II.i.]
21 You can never plan the future by the

past. [Edmund Burke: *Letter to a Member of the National Assembly*]

1 A man he seems of cheerful yesterdays
And confident tomorrows.
[Wordsworth: *The Excursion* VII]

2 We are tomorrow's past. [Mary Webb: *Precious Bane*]

PAST: and present

3 Ask counsel . . . of the ancient time what is best, and of the latter time what is fittest. [Francis Bacon: *Of Great Place*]

4 Past and to come, seems best; things present, worse.
[Shakespeare: *II Henry IV* I.iii.]

5 To Antiquity it self I think nothing due. For if we will reverence Age, the Present is the Oldest. [Thomas Hobbes: *Leviathan* (Conclusion)]

6 Praise they that will Times past, I joy to see
My selfe now live: *this age best pleaseth me.*
[Robert Herrick: *The Present Time Best Pleaseth*]

7 There was a time when meadow, grove, and stream,
The earth, and every common sight,
To me did seem
Apparelled in celestial light,
The glory and the freshness of a dream.
It is not now as it hath been of yore—
Turn wheresoe'er I may,
By night or day,
The things which I have seen I now can see no more.
[Wordsworth: *Intimations of Immortality*]

8 The Present is the living sum-total of the whole Past. [Thomas Carlyle: *Characteristics*]

9 We fret ourselves to reform life, in order that posterity may be happy, and posterity will say as usual: "In the past it used to be better, the present is worse than the past." [Anton Chekhov: *Notebooks*]

THE PAST: irrevocable

10 Though nothing can bring back the hour
Of splendour in the grass, of glory in the flower.

[Wordsworth: *Intimations of Immortality*]

11 But the tender grace of a day that is dead
Will never come back to me.
[Tennyson: *Break, Break, Break*]

12 [Odin] of all powers the mightiest far art thou,
Lord over men on Earth, and Gods in Heaven;
Yet even from thee thyself hath been withheld
One thing: to undo what thou thyself hast rul'd.
[Matthew Arnold: *Balder Dead*, "Funeral"]

13 Gone with the wind. [Ernest Dowson: *Non Sum Qualis Eram Bonae Sub Regno Cynarae*]

THE PAST: sadness of, longing for

14 Old, unhappy, far-off things,
And battles long ago.
[Wordsworth: *The Solitary Reaper*]

15 Men are we, and must grieve when even the shade
Of that which once was great is passed away.
[Wordsworth: *On the Extinction of the Venetian Republic*]

16 The rainbow comes and goes,
And lovely is the rose,
The moon doth with delight
Look round her when the heavens are bare,
Waters on a starry night
Are beautiful and fair;
The sunshine is a glorious birth;
But yet I know, where'er I go,
That there hath past away a glory from the earth.
[Wordsworth: *Intimations of Immortality*]

17 For now I see the true old times are dead,
When every morning brought a noble chance,
And every chance brought out a noble knight.
[Tennyson: *Morte d'Arthur*]

18 So sad, so strange, the days that are no more.
[Tennyson: *The Princess* IV]

19 There is no time like the old time, when you and I were young. [O. W.

Holmes: *No Time Like the Old Time*]
1 The world broke in two in 1922 or
thereabouts, and all that went before
belongs with yesterday's seven thousand
years. [Willa Cather: Prefatory note to
Not Under Forty]
2 Into my heart an air that kills
  From yon far country blows:
  What are those blue remembered
                        hills,
  What spires, what farms are those?

  That is the land of lost content,
  I see it shining plain,
  The happy highways where I went
  And cannot come again.
[A. E. Housman: *A Shropshire Lad* XL]

THE PAST: miscellaneous
3 Say not thou, What is the cause that
the former days were better than these?
for thou dost not inquire wisely concerning this. [Ecclesiastes 7:10]
4 God has no power over the past,
except to cover it with oblivion. [Pliny
the Elder: *Natural History* II.v.]
5 Where are the snows of yesteryear?
(*Où sont les neiges d'antan?*) [François
Villon: *Ballade des dames du temps
jadis*]
6 Ye, fare wel al the snow of ferne
                       yere!
[Chaucer: *Troilus and Criseyde* V]
7 The dark backward and abysm of
                       time.
[Shakespeare: *The Tempest* I.ii.]
8 The "good old times"—all times,
             when old, are good.
[Byron: *The Age of Bronze* I]
9 The world is weary of the past,
  Oh, might it die or rest at last!
[Shelley: Final Chorus from *Hellas*]
10 Let the dead Past bury its dead!
[Longfellow: *A Psalm of Life*]
11 Th' past always looks bebther thin
it was. It's only pleasant because it
isn't here. [Finley Peter Dunne ("Mr.
Dooley"): *A Family Union*]
12 Those who cannot remember the past
are condemned to repeat it. [George Santayana: *Life of Reason* I, "Reason in
Common Sense"]
13 There is always something rather absurd about the past. [Max Beerbohm:
1880]

PATIENCE
14 In your patience possess ye your souls.
[Luke 21:19]
15 Let us run with patience the race
that is set before us. [Hebrews 12:1]
16 Ye have heard of the patience of Job.
[James 5:11]
17 Extreme patience or long-sufferance,
if it once come to be dissolved, produc-
eth most bitter and excessive revenges.
[Montaigne: *Essays* III.v.]
18 Though patience be a tired mare,
             yet she will plod.
[Shakespeare: *Henry V* II.i.]
19 She sat, like patience on a monument,
  Smiling at grief.
[Shakespeare: *Twelfth Night* II.iv.]
20 PANDARUS. He that will have a cake
out of the wheat must tarry the grinding.
  TROILUS. Have I not tarried?
  PANDARUS. Ay, the grinding; but you
must tarry the bolting.
  TROILUS. Have I not tarried?
  PANDARUS. Ay, the bolting; but you
must tarry the leavening.
  TROILUS. Still have I tarried?
  PANDARUS. Ay, to the leavening; but
here's yet in the word 'hereafter' the
kneading, the making of the cake, the
heating of the oven, and the baking;
nay, you must stay the cooling too, or
you may chance to burn your lips.
[Shakespeare: *Troilus and Cressida* I.i.]
21 How poor are they that have not pa-
             tience!
[Shakespeare: *Othello* II.iii.]
22   But, for true need—
  You heavens, give me that patience,
            patience I need!
[Shakespeare: *King Lear* II.iv.]
23 Patience, the beggar's virtue.
[Philip Massinger: *A New Way to Pay
Old Debts* V.i.]
24 When I consider how my light is
             spent
  Ere half my days in this dark world
            and wide,
  And that one Talent which is death
            to hide
  Lodged with me useless, though my
           soul more bent
  To serve therewith my Maker, and
           present
  My true account, lest He returning

chide,
"Doth God exact day-labor, light
denied?"
I fondly ask. But Patience, to pre-
vent
That murmur, soon replies, "God
doth not need
Either man's work or his own gifts.
Who best
Bear his mild yoke, they serve him
best. His state
Is kingly: thousands at his bidding
speed,
And post o'er land and ocean with-
out rest;
They also serve who only stand and
wait."
[John Milton: *On His Blindness*]
1 Arm the obdur'd breast
With stubborn patience as with triple
steel.
[John Milton: *Paradise Lost* II.568-569]
2 Beware the fury of a patient man.
[Dryden: *Absalom and Achitophel* I]
3 Possess your soul with patience.
[Dryden: *The Hind and the Panther*
III]
4 Patience, sov'reign o'er transmuted
ill. [Samuel Johnson: *The Vanity of
Human Wishes*]
5 There is a point when patience ceases
to be a virtue. [Thomas Morton: *Speed
the Plough* IV.iii.]
6 Everything comes if a man will only
wait. [Benjamin Disraeli: *Tancred* IV]
7 Learn to labor and to wait.
[Longfellow: *A Psalm of Life*]
8 All things come round to him who
will but wait. [Longfellow: *Tales of a
Wayside Inn*, "The Student's Tale"]
9 Sad patience, too near neighbor to
despair. [Matthew Arnold: *The Scholar-
Gipsy*]
10 Patience, that blending of moral
courage with physical timidity. [Thomas
Hardy: *Tess of the D'Urbervilles*]

PATRIOT(ISM)

11 A glorious death is his
Who for his country falls.
[Homer: *Iliad* XV]
12 It is sweet and proper to die for the
fatherland. (*Dulce et decorum est pro
patria mori*) [Horace: *Odes* III.ii.]
One of the most famous of all quota-

*tions, repeated in a hundred variations
in all languages of Europe through the
centuries but with marked less frequency
since universal military conscription has
given writers a much larger likelihood of
enjoying this particular sweet than they
used to have.*
*"They wrote in the old days that it is
sweet and fitting to die for one's country. But in modern war there is nothing
sweet nor fitting in your dying. You will
die like a dog for no good reason."*
Ernest Hemingway (1899-1961): Notes
on the Next War
13 Who is here so vile that will not
love his country?
[Shakespeare: *Julius Caesar* III.ii.]
14 A Patriot's all-atoning name. [Dry-
den: *Absalom and Achitophel* I]
15 What pity is it
That we can die but once to serve
our country!
[Joseph Addison: *Cato* IV]
16 Patriotism is the last refuge of a
scoundrel. [Samuel Johnson: in Boswell's *Life*, April 7, 1775]
*Probably the most-quoted of all John-
son's aphorisms, it is an animadversion
not on patriotism but on scoundrels
who, in Dryden's phrase, usurp a patriot's all-atoning name.*
17 I only regret that I have but one life
to lose for my country. [Nathan Hale:
his last words, Sept. 22, 1776]
Quoted in Stewart's Life of Capt. Nathan
Hale *VII.*
18 Breathes there the man, with soul so
dead,
Who never to himself hath said,
This is my own, my native land!
Whose heart hath ne'er within him
burn'd
As home his footsteps he hath turn'd,
From wandering on a foreign strand!
If such there breathe, go, mark him
well;
For him no minstrel raptures swell;
High though his titles, proud his
name;
Boundless his wealth as wish can
claim—
Despite those titles, power, and pelf,
The wretch, concentred all in self,
Living, shall forfeit fair renown,
And, doubly dying, shall go down

To the vile dust, from whence he
sprung,
Unwept, unhonour'd, and unsung.
[Sir Walter Scott: *The Lay of the Last
Minstrel* VI]

1 Then conquer we must, for our cause
it is just,
And this be our motto: "In God is
our trust!"
And the star-spangled banner in tri-
umph shall wave,
O'er the land of the free, and the
home of the brave!
[Francis Scott Key: *The Star-Spangled
Banner*]

2 Though I love my country, I do not
love my countrymen. [Byron: Letter,
April 22, 1823]

3 And how can man die better
Than facing fearful odds,
For the ashes of his fathers
And the temples of his gods?
[Macaulay: *Lays of Ancient Rome: Ho-
ratius* XXVII]

4 That man's the best Cosmopolite
Who loves his native country best.
[Tennyson: *Hands All Round*]

5 My country, 'tis of thee,
Sweet land of liberty,
Of thee I sing.
[Samuel Francis Smith: *America*]

6 The Beautiful, the Sacred—
Which, in all climes, men that have
hearts adore
By the great title of their mother
country!
[E. G. Bulwer-Lytton: *Richelieu* IV.ii.]

7 Patriotism is a kind of religion; it is
the egg from which wars are hatched.
[Guy de Maupassant: *My Uncle Sosthe-
nes*]

8 That pernicious sentiment, "Our
country, right or wrong." [James Russell Lowell: *The Biglow Papers* I.iii.]

9 Let not Avarice quench the fire,
That Patriotism should inspire;
With general voice exclaim: "Away
All sordid thoughts of greater pay."
[*Chambers' Journal*, October 1854]
*An innocent appeal by a thrifty civilian
to the British troops during the Crimean
War—urging them to die for him but
not to raise his taxes.*

10 You'll never have a quiet world till
you knock the patriotism out of the human race. [G. B. Shaw: *O'Flaherty,
V.C.*]

11 Originality and initiative are what I
ask for my country. [Robert Frost: *The
Figure a Poem Makes*]

12 Died some, pro patria
non "dulce" non "et decor" . . .
walked eye-deep in hell
believing in old men's lies.
[Ezra Pound: *Hugh Selwyn Mauberley*
IV]

13 One of the great attractions of patriotism—it fulfills our worst wishes. In
the person of our nation we are able,
vicariously, to bully and cheat. Bully
and cheat, what's more, with a feeling
that we are profoundly virtuous. [Al-
dous Huxley: *Eyeless in Gaza* XVII]

14 Everybody likes to hear about a man
laying down his life for his country, but
nobody wants to hear about a country
giving her shirt for her planet. [E. B.
White: *World Government and Peace*]

15 Ask not what your country can do
for you; ask what you can do for your
country. [John F. Kennedy: *Inaugural
Address*, 1961]

PATRON

16 Is not a Patron, my Lord, one who
looks with unconcern on a man struggling for life in the water, and, when he
has reached ground, encumbers him with
help? [Samuel Johnson: Letter to the
Earl of Chesterfield, Feb. 7, 1755]
*When Johnson, unknown and impover-
ished, had undertaken to compile his
Dictionary of the English Language,
Lord Chesterfield had made condescending overtures but had offered no significant help. When, after seven years of
labor, the book was about to appear,
Chesterfield had written two short articles praising it. In his famous letter,
Johnson indignantly rejected these belated offers of patronage and, as is sometimes said, "broke the back of patronage"
as a system. He was not a patronizable
man, anyway. In his Vanity of Human
Wishes he had listed "Toil, envy, want,
the patron and the jail" as ills that assail the scholar's life. And in the Dictionary he defined a patron as "a wretch
who supports with insolence and is paid
with flattery."*

1 No fav'ring patrons have I got,
But just enough to boil the pot.
[William Combe: *The Tour of Dr. Syntax* XXIII.xviii.]

PATTERNS

2 Christ! what are patterns for?
[Amy Lowell: *Patterns*]

PAUPER

3 Rattle his bones over the stones;
He's only a pauper, whom nobody
owns!
[Thomas Noel: *Rhymes and Roundelays*, "The Pauper's Drive"]

PAYMENT

4 Pay beforehand was never well
served. [16th-century proverb]
5 Always those that dance must pay the
music.
[John Taylor ("the Water Poet"): *Taylor's Feast*]
6 I warrant you, if he danced till
doomsday, he thought I was to pay the
piper. [William Congreve: *Love for Love* II.v]

PEACE

7 Had Zimri peace, who slew his master? [II Kings 9:31]
8 It is better to dwell in a corner of
the housetop, than with a brawling
woman in a wide house. [Proverbs
21:9]
9 It is better to dwell in the wilderness
than with a contentious and an angry
woman. [Proverbs 21:19]
10 They shall beat their swords into
plowshares, and their spears into pruning-hooks; nation shall not lift up sword
against nation, neither shall they learn
war any more. [Isaiah 2:4]
11 The wolf also shall dwell with the
lamb, and the leopard shall lie down
with the kid; and the calf and the young
lion and the fatling together; and a little
child shall lead them. [Isaiah 11:6]
12 There is no peace, saith the Lord,
unto the wicked. [Isaiah 48:22]
13 How beautiful upon the mountains
are the feet of him that bringeth good
tidings, that publisheth peace. [Isaiah
52:7]
14 Saying, Peace, peace; when there is

no peace. [Jeremiah 6:14]
15 Think not that I am come to send
peace on earth: I came not to send peace,
but a sword. [Matthew 10:34]
16 Glory to God in the highest, and on
earth peace, good will toward men.
[Luke 2:14]
17 The peace of God, which passeth all
understanding. [Philippians 4:7]
18 Give peace in our time, O Lord.
[*Book of Common Prayer,* "The Lord
Be with You"]
19 Where they make a desert, they call
it peace. [Tacitus: *Agricola* XXX]
20 In His will is our peace. [Dante:
The Divine Comedy, "Paradiso" III]
21 The most disadvantageous peace is
better than the most just war. [Erasmus:
Adagia]
22 Anything for a quiet life. [Thomas
Heywood: *The Captives* III.iii.]
23 Certainly, it is heaven upon earth, to
have a man's mind move in charity, rest
in providence, and turn upon the poles
of truth. [Francis Bacon: *Of Truth*]
24 No war, or battle's sound
Was heard the world around.
The idle spear and shield were high
up hung.
[John Milton: *On the Morning of
Christ's Nativity*]
25 Hence with denial vain and coy excuse:
So may some gentle Muse
With lucky words favour my destined
urn,
And as he passes turn,
And bid fair peace be to my sable
shroud.
[John Milton: *Lycidas*]
26 His servants He, with new acquist
Of true experience from this great
event,
With peace and consolation hath
dismissed,
And calm of mind, all passion spent.
[John Milton: *Samson Agonistes* (concluding lines)]
27 Peace hath her victories
No less renowned than war.
[John Milton: *To the Lord General
Cromwell*]
*Fame may be won in peace as well as in
war.*

Sallust: Catiline *III.i.*

1 Along the cool sequestered vale of
life,
They kept the noiseless tenor of their
way.
[Thomas Gray: *Elegy Written in a Country Churchyard*]

2 When the voices of children are
heard on the green
And laughing is heard on the hill,
My heart is at rest within my breast
And everything else is still.
[William Blake: *Nurse's Song*]

3 He makes a solitude and calls it
—peace!
[Byron: *The Bride of Abydos* II.xx.]

4 Peace at any price. (*La paix à tout prix*) [Alphonse de Lamartine: *Méditations poétiques*]

5 He has outsoared the shadow of our
night;
Envy and calumny and hate and
pain,
And that unrest which men miscall
delight
Can touch him not and torture not
again;
From the contagion of the world's
slow stain
He is secure, and now can never
mourn
A heart grown cold, a head grown
gray in vain.
[Shelley: *Adonais* XL]

6 Far off the noises of the world retreat;
The loud vociferations of the street
Become an undistinguishable roar.
[Longfellow: *Introductory Sonnets to The Divina Commedia* I]

7 Here are cool mosses deep,
And thro' the moss the ivies creep,
And in the stream the long-leaved
flowers weep,
And from the craggy ledge the poppy
hangs in sleep.
[Tennyson: *The Lotos-Eaters*]

8 Till the war-drum throbbed no
longer, and the battle-flags were furled
In the Parliament of man, the Federation of the world.
[Tennyson: *Locksley Hall*]

9 And thou from earth are gone
Long since, and in some quiet
churchyard laid;
Some country nook, where o'er thy
unknown grave
Tall grasses and white flowering
nettles wave—
Under a dark red-fruited yew-tree's
shade.
[Matthew Arnold: *The Scholar-Gipsy*]

10 "Peace upon earth!" was said. We
sing it
And pay a million priests to bring it.
After two thousand years of mass
We've got as far as poison-gas.
[Thomas Hardy: *Christmas: 1924*]

11 It must be a peace without victory.
[Woodrow Wilson: in an address to the Senate, January 22, 1917]

12 I believe it is peace for our time . . .
peace with honor. [Neville Chamberlain: in his speech on returning to England from Munich, October 1938]

PEACOCK

13 It is the foulness of the peacock's
feet which abates his pride and stoops
his gloating-eyed tail. [Montaigne: *Essays* III.v.]

It was formerly believed that the peacock was given ugly feet as a check on the pride which his gorgeous plumage would inspire, and it was believed that he was so ashamed of his feet that if he chanced to see them while displaying, he would let his train fall out of sheer humiliation and chagrin. The fact is that a peacock must keep his head erect in order to advance his train (which, by the way, is not his tail), so that when his head is lowered, the train of necessity falls. But the ascription of this to wounded vanity is folk morality.

PEARL

14 One pearl of great price. [Matthew 13:46]

15 One not easily jealous, but, being
wrought,
Perplex'd in the extreme; of one
whose hand,
Like the base Indian, threw a pearl
away
Richer than all his tribe.
[Shakespeare: *Othello* V.ii.]

PEARLS BEFORE SWINE

16 Give not that which is holy unto the

dogs, neither cast ye your pearls before swine. [Matthew 7:6]

1 Neither give thou Aesop's cock a gem, who would be better pleased and happier if he had a barley-corn. [Francis Bacon: *Of Goodness and Goodness of Nature*]

PEASANT

2 Bowed by the weight of centuries he leans
　Upon his hoe and gazes on the ground,
The emptiness of ages in his face,
And on his back the burden of the world.

[Edwin Markham: *The Man with the Hoe*]

PEASE PORRIDGE

3 Pease porridge hot,
Pease porridge cold,
Pease porridge in the pot
Nine days old.

Some like it hot,
Some like it cold,
Some like it in the pot,
Nine days old.

[Children's handwarming clapping rhyme: earliest known version, 1797, but probably much older]
　pease = *pea*
　Pease *is the old singular; pea was made up later because the final sibilant was mistaken for the sign of the plural.*

PEDANTRY

4 We commonly say of some compositions that they smell of the oil and of the lamp, by reason of a certain harshness and rudeness which long-plodding labor imprints in them that be much elaborated. [Montaigne: *Essays* I.x.]

5 The boastful blockhead ignorantly read,
　With loads of learned lumber in his head.

[Alexander Pope: *An Essay on Criticism* III]

6 Pedantry is the unseasonable ostentation of learning. [Samuel Johnson: *The Rambler* No. 173]

7 With various readings stored his empty skull,

Learn'd without sense, and venerably dull.

[Charles Churchill: *The Rosciad*]
　various = *variant*

8 It is the vice of scholars to suppose that there is no knowledge in the world but that of books. [William Hazlitt: *The Complete Works of William Hazlitt*, London, 1930-34, vol. XVII, p.100]

PEDESTRIAN

9 A pedestrian . . . is a man who has two cars—one being driven by his wife, the other by one of his children. [Robert Bradbury, a citizen of Liverpool, England, as quoted in the *New York Times*, Sept. 5, 1962]

PEEL, JOHN

10 D'ye ken John Peel with his coat so gay?
D'ye ken John Peel at the break of day?
D'ye ken John Peel when he's far far away
　With his hounds and his horn in the morning?
'Twas the sound of his horn brought me from my bed,
And the cry of the hounds he has oft-times led;
For Peel's view-halloo would awaken the dead,
Or the fox from his lair in the morning.

[John Woodcock Graves: *John Peel*]
　Sometimes listed as anonymous; Graves probably rewrote an old hunting song.

PEERS

11 The House of Peers, throughout the war,
　Did nothing in particular
　And did it very well.

[W. S. Gilbert: *Iolanthe* II]

PEEVISHNESS

12 It is not easy to imagine a more unhappy condition than that of dependence on a peevish man. [Samuel Johnson: *The Rambler* No. 112]

PELICAN(S)

13 Ploffskin, Pluffskin, Pelican jee!
　We think no Birds so happy as we!

Plumpskin, Ploshkin, Pelican jill!
We think so then, and we thought so
still.
[Edward Lear: *The Pelican Chorus*]

1 A wonderful bird is the pelican!
His beak holds more than his belican.
He can take in his beak
Enough food for a week,
But I'm darned if I know how the
helican.
[Dixon L. Merritt: *The Pelican*]
*Said to be one of Woodrow Wilson's fa-
vorite poems.*

PEN
2 The pen of a ready writer. [Psalms
45:1]

PEN: and sword
3 Let none presume to tell me that
the pen is preferable to the sword. [Cer-
vantes: *Don Quixote* I.iv.10]
4 How much more cruel the pen may
be than the sword. [Robert Burton:
The Anatomy of Melancholy I.2.4.4.]
5 Caesar had perished from the world
of men
Had not his sword been rescued by
his pen.
[Henry Vaughan: *Sir Thomas Bodley's
Library*]
6 Beneath the rule of men entirely
great,
The pen is mightier than the sword.
[E. G. Bulwer-Lytton: *Richelieu* II.ii.]
*Bulwer-Lytton was simply quoting an
established thought. Saint-Simon (1702)
had alluded to pen and sword. Rosencrantz, in Hamlet (II.ii.), says that "many
wearing rapiers are afraid of goose-
quills," etc.*
7 "For the Pen," said the Vicar; and in
the sententious pause which followed I
felt that I would offer all the gold of
Peru to avert or postpone the solemn,
inevitable, and yet, as it seemed to me,
perfectly appalling statement that "the
Pen is mightier than the Sword." [Logan
Pearsall Smith: *Trivia*, "In Church"]

PENANCE
8   When the scourge
Inexorably, and the torturing hour
Calls us to penance.
[John Milton: *Paradise Lost* II.90-92]

9 Quoth he, "The man hath penance
done,
And penance more will do."
[Coleridge: *The Ancient Mariner* V]

PENNY(IES)
10 "A penny saved is a penny got"—
Firm to this scoundrel maxim keepeth he.
[James Thomson (1700-1748): *The Castle of Indolence* I.1.]
11 All our lives we are putting pennies—
our most Golden Pennies—into penny-
in-the-slot machines that are empty. [Lo-
gan Pearsall Smith: *Afterthoughts*]

PENSION
12 PENSION. An allowance made to anyone without an equivalent. In England
it is generally understood to mean pay
given to a state hireling for treason to
his country. [Samuel Johnson: in the
Dictionary]
*This definition proved slightly embar-
rassing when, seven years later, he himself was given a pension.*
13 It ought to be quite as natural and
straightforward a matter for a laborer
to take his pension from his parish, because he has deserved well of his parish,
as for a man in higher rank to take his
pension from his country, because he has
deserved well of his country. [John
Ruskin: Preface to *Unto This Last*]
*It is interesting that what seemed a wild
vision in 1860 is, a hundred years later,
taken for granted. It is only by such
markings that we can perceive the rapidity of social change.*

PENSIONER
14 A kept patriot. [H. L. Mencken: *A
Book of Burlesques*]

PEOPLE(S)
15 The voice of the people is the voice
of God. [Hesiod: *Works and Days*]
*This is the origin, in all its forms, of the
phrase sometimes shortened to* vox pop.
*"The voice of the people needs a whole
art of harmonic transcription to be understood."*
William Bolitho: Twelve Against the
Gods, *"Woodrow Wilson" (1929)*
16 Let my people go. [Exodus 7:16]

1 No doubt but ye are the people, and wisdom shall die with you. [Job 12:2]

2 O stormy peple! unsad and ever untrewe!
Ay undiscreet and chaunging as a vane,
Delyting ever in rumbel that is newe,
For lyk the mone ay wexe ye and wane.
[Chaucer: *The Clerk's Tale*]
unsad = *light*
Sad *meant heavy, a meaning retained in the term "sad iron." And cakes are said to be "sad" when they fall in the oven.*

3 That great enemy of reason, virtue, and religion, the Multitude, that numerous piece of monstrosity. [Sir Thomas Browne: *Religio Medici* II.i.]

4 For the People . . . I must tell you that their Liberty and Freedom consists in having the Government of those Laws, by which their Life and their Goods may be most their own; 'tis not for having share in Government, that is nothing pertaining to 'em. A Subject and a Sovereign are clean different things. [Charles I: speech on the scaffold, Jan. 30, 1649]
Since the People at that very moment held the headsman's axe poised over his head, this was, in a way, a noble utterance. It supports Andrew Marvell's description of the event:
He nothing common did, or mean,
Upon that memorable scene.
Note also, in a speech of this solemnity, the use of clean *("entirely," "clearly"), now regarded as a vulgarism.*

5 The people are a many-headed beast. [Alexander Pope: *Imitations of Horace*, Epistle I]

6 Who will not sing *God save the King!*
Shall hang as high's the steeple;
But while we sing *God save the King!*
We'll not forget the people!
[Burns: *Does Haughty Gaul Invasion Threat?*]

7 Peoples and governments never have learned anything from history. [Hegel: *Philosophy of History*]

8 There is not a more mean, stupid, dastardly, pitiful, selfish, spiteful, envious, ungrateful animal than the Public. It is the greatest of cowards, for it is afraid of itself. [William Hazlitt: *Table-Talk, "On Living to Oneself"*]

9 All great Peoples are conservative; slow to believe in novelties; patient of much error in actualities. [Thomas Carlyle: *Past and Present* III.v.]

10 People who like this sort of thing will find this the sort of thing they like. [Abraham Lincoln: passing judgment on a book. (Quoted by G. W. E. Russell in *Collections and Recollections*)]
A nice example of a humorous evasion.

11 Why should there not be a patient confidence in the ultimate justice of the people? Is there any better or equal hope in the world? [Abraham Lincoln: Inaugural Address, March 4, 1861]

12 You can fool some of the people all of the time, and all of the people some of the time, but you can't fool all of the people all of the time. [Attr. Abraham Lincoln, but not until 1904 in A. K. McClure's *Lincoln's Yarns and Stories;* also attr. Phineas T. Barnum]
The thought—that there are limitations to deceptions, with varying juxtapositions of the one and the many—has been expressed since the time of Pliny the Younger in the first century A.D.

13 The great unwashed. [Attr. Lord Brougham (d. 1868)]
This famous sneering appellation for the masses was coined sometime towards the middle of the 19th century, when the upper classes were beginning to take great pride in bathing and the growth of industrial slums was making it impossible for the poor to have even the sanitary minimum of cleanliness.
Dr. Johnson, one of the Unwashed Great, was able to assert, a century earlier, that he hated immersion and had no love for clean linen.

14 The people people have for friends
Your common sense appall,
But the people people marry
Are the queerest folk of all.
[Charlotte Gilman: *Queer People*]

15 About the only thing we have left that actually discriminates in favor o' the plain people is the stork. [Kin Hubbard: *Sayings*]

16 No art can conquer the people alone —the people are conquered by an ideal of life upheld by authority. [William Butler Yeats: *Dramatis Personae*]

1 The people will stand for anything. What they can't stand for, they'll fall for. [Ross Winne (1882-1960)]
The author of this comment on the United States presidential nominating conventions of 1952, who with his wife Gertrude was an early pioneer settler in Florida's Everglades, was a hunter, fisherman, and a farmer. He was also a Federal Wildlife Conservation Officer, Deputy Sheriff of Palm Beach County, and, of course, a politician.

PERCEPTION
2 Some have been beaten till they know
What wood a cudgel's of by th' blow;
Some kick'd until they can feel
whether
A shoe be Spanish or neat's leather.
[Samuel Butler (1612-1680): *Hudibras*]
3 All the mighty world
Of eye, and ear,—both what they
half create,
And what perceive.
[Wordsworth: *Tintern Abbey*]
4 It is a flaw
In happiness, to see beyond our
bourn—
It forces us in summer skies to
mourn,
It spoils the singing of the Nightingale.
[Keats: *Epistle to John Hamilton Reynolds*]

PERDITION
5 Him the Almighty Power
Hurled headlong flaming from th'
ethereal sky
With hideous ruin and combustion
down
To bottomless perdition, there to
dwell
In adamantine chains and penal fire
Who durst defy th' Omnipotent to
arms.
[John Milton: *Paradise Lost* I.44-49]

PERFECTION
6 Whoever thinks a faultless piece to
see
Thinks what ne'er was, nor is, nor
e'er shall be.
[Alexander Pope: *An Essay on Criticism* II]

7 The very pink of perfection. [Oliver Goldsmith: *She Stoops to Conquer* I]
8 . . . the way to perfection is through a series of disgusts. [Walter Pater: *The Renaissance*, "Leonardo da Vinci"]

PERFUME(S)
9 A woman smells well when she smells of nothing. [Plautus: *Mostellaria*]
10 He does not smell well, who always smells well. [Martial: *Epigrams* II.xii.]
That is, one who uses perfume consistently must be concealing some unpleasant odor.

11 To smell sweet is to stink. [Montaigne: *Essays* I.lv.]
Montaigne means that it is best not to smell at all. Casanova—who has a right to be heard on the subject—declared that he liked the smell of the sweat of the women he loved.

12 All the perfumes of Arabia will not sweeten this little hand. [Shakespeare: *Macbeth* V.i.]
13 So perfumed that
The winds were love-sick.
[Shakespeare: *Antony and Cleopatra* II.ii.]
14 Still to be neat, still to be drest,
As you were going to a feast;
Still to be powder'd, still perfum'd:
Lady, it is to be presum'd,
Though art's hid causes are not
found,
All is not sweet, all is not sound.
[Ben Jonson: *Epicoene, or The Silent Woman* I.i.]
still = always
15 Sabean odors from the spicy shore
Of Araby the blest.
[John Milton: *Paradise Lost* IV.162-163]
16 A woman smells best when she hath no perfume at all. [Robert Burton: *The Anatomy of Melancholy* III]
Havelock Ellis thought that there must be a definite difference in the sense of smell of men and women; otherwise he did not think women would wear the amount of perfume that many of them do.

PERHAPS
17 I am going to seek the great perhaps. [Rabelais: his last words, according to Motteux]

PERILS
1 Perils commonly ask to be paid in pleasures. [Francis Bacon: *Of Love*]
It is for this reason, says Bacon, that "martial men are given to love."
2 Great perils have this beauty, that they bring to light the fraternity of strangers. [Victor Hugo: *Les Misérables* XII.iv.]

PERISH
3 Perish that thought!
[Colley Cibber: *Richard III* V]

PERJURY
4 Each man swore to do his best
To damn and perjure all the rest.
[Samuel Butler (1612-1680): *Hudibras*]

PERMISSION
5 *Nihil obstat.* ("Nothing hinders.")
[A formula of the Roman Catholic Church used on title pages signifying the *imprimatur* ("let it be printed") of the official censor, whose name follows.]

PERPLEXITY
6 I can neither live with you nor without you. [Martial: *Epigrams* XII.xlvii.]
7 To laugh, were want of goodness and of grace,
And to be grave, exceeds all Pow'r of face.
[Alexander Pope: *Epistle to Dr. Arbuthnot*]

PERSECUTION
8 Saul, Saul, why persecutest thou me?
[Acts 9:4]

PERSEVERANCE
9 For a just man falleth seven times and riseth up again. [Proverbs 24:16]
10 God is with those who persevere. [*The Koran* VIII]
11 Take not the first refusal ill:
Tho' now she won't, anon she will.
[Thomas D'Urfey: *A Song*]
12 Great works are performed not by strength but by perseverance. [Samuel Johnson: *Rasselas* XIII]
13 'Tis known by the name of perseverance in a good cause—and of obstinacy in a bad one. [Laurence Sterne: *Tristram Shandy* I.xvii.]

14 The heights by great men reached and kept
Were not attained by sudden flight,
But they, while their companions slept,
Were toiling upward in the night.
[Longfellow: *The Ladder of Saint Augustine*]
15 Never say die. [Dickens: *The Pickwick Papers* II]
16 I propose to fight it out on this line if it takes all summer. [Ulysses S. Grant: dispatch from Spottsylvania Court House, May 11, 1864]
17 PERSEVERANCE. A lowly virtue whereby mediocrity achieves an inglorious success. [Ambrose Bierce: *The Devil's Dictionary*]

PERSONS
18 There is no respect of persons with God. [Romans 2:11]

PESSIMISM
19 Say not, the struggle naught availeth,
The labour and the wounds are vain,
The enemy faints not, nor faileth,
And as things have been they remain.
[Arthur Hugh Clough: *Say Not the Struggle Naught Availeth*]
20 Pessimism, when you get used to it, is just as agreeable as optimism. [Arnold Bennett: *Things That Have Interested Me*, "The Slump in Pessimism"]

PESSIMIST
21 I'm Smith of Stoke, aged sixty-odd,
I've lived without a dame
From youth-time on; and would to God
My dad had done the same.
[Thomas Hardy: *Epitaph on a Pessimist*]
I never married, and I wish my father never had.
       Anon.: Greek Anthology *VII*
See OPTIMIST

PETAR
22 For 'tis the sport to have the enginer
Hoist with his own petar.
[Shakespeare: *Hamlet* III.iv.]

petar = petard = *bomb, or mine;* enginer
= engineer = *sapper.*

The sycophants, Rosencrantz and
Guildenstern, feigning friendship to
Hamlet, are actually part of a conspiracy to have him killed. They are to accompany him to England, bearing secret
letters in which the King of Denmark
asks the King of England to have Hamlet
executed immediately. Hamlet plans to
get hold of the letters and so change the
wording that Rosencrantz and Guildenstern will be designated as the ones to be
executed. In telling his mother of his
plans he admits that it would be "knavery," but adds that it is "sport to have
the enginer (the sapper) hoist (i.e.,
blown up, hoisted into the air by the
explosion) with his own petard."

PETTICOAT

1 To fifty chosen sylphs, of special note,
   We trust th' important charge, the
   petticoat;
   Oft have we known that sev'n-fold
   fence to fail,
   Tho' stiff with hoops, and arm'd with
   ribs of whale.
[Alexander Pope: *The Rape of the Lock*
II]
2 I for one venerate a petticoat—
   A garment of a mystical sublimity,
   No matter whether russet, silk, or
   dimity.
[Byron: *Don Juan* XIV.xxvi.]

PHANTOM

3 She was a phantom of delight
   When first she gleamed upon my
   sight;
   A lovely apparition, sent
   To be a moment's ornament.
[Wordsworth: *She Was a Phantom of
Delight*]
   *The germ of this poem was four lines
   composed as part of the famous lines on
   the Highland Lass.*

PHILADELPHIA LAWYER

4 It would take a Philadelphia lawyer
to get you out of that.
   *The astuteness of a Philadelphia lawyer
   was proverbial in America before 1788.
   "That would puzzle a dozen Philadelphia lawyers" was described in 1803 as*

"a Yankee phrase." Some think it refers
to the famous defense in 1735 of John
Peter Zenger by Andrew Hamilton, an
aged Philadelphia lawyer. And it may
be. Some think it a compliment to Ben
Franklin. Some think it merely reflects
the fact that Philadelphia was our greatest city in colonial times and that most
Americans were farmers. So that it may
merely have meant "a big-city lawyer,"
as we today might say "a Wall Street
lawyer."

PHILANDERING

5 Nothing plays a smaller part in philandering than love. [La Rochefoucauld:
Maxims]
6 That which he gave and they received as love was only a careless distribution of superfluous time. [Samuel
Johnson: *Rasselas* XXXIX]

PHILANTHROPY

7 Philanthropy is almost the only virtue which is sufficiently appreciated by
mankind. [Thoreau: *Walden* I]
8 Then why should I sit in the scorner's
   seat,
   Or hurl the cynic's ban?
   Let me live in my house by the side
   of the road,
   And be a friend to man.
[Sam Walter Foss: *House by the Side of
the Road*]
   *Axylus, the son of Teuthras, was a man
   of wealth and dear to his fellow men,
   for his house was by the side of the road,
   and he welcomed all who passed by.*
   —*Homer:* Iliad *VI*
   *Only a cynic would now live by the
   side of a road, and he would not need a
   house, but a hospital. He wouldn't live
   long, either; the number of those killed
   every year while befriending the injured
   is large.*

PHILISTINES

9 The Philistines be upon thee, Samson. [Judges 16:9]
10 The people who believe most that
our greatness and welfare are proved by
our being very rich, and who most give
their lives and thoughts to becoming
rich, are just the very people whom we
call the Philistines. [Matthew Arnold:

Culture and Anarchy (1869)]

The use of philistine to designate someone lacking in, and often scornful of or hostile to, art and culture is derived from this passage by Matthew Arnold.

The Philistines in the Old Testament are the chief enemies of the Jews, God's Chosen People, and in this common use of philistine *there is an implication (which does much to explain much philistinism) that the cultured regard themselves as God's Chosen.*

Arnold probably took the term from German. It had passed into German in this sense—Philister—in the universities where it was used of a townsman in contrast to a gownsman. In 1693, for instance, the text of a funeral sermon of a student killed in a town-and-gown riot at Jena was Judges 16:9: "The Philistines be upon thee, Samson."

PHILISTINISM

1 The hostility of comfortable, self-satisfied people towards any serious effort. [Willa Cather: *The Song of the Lark* IV.iv.]
That is, intellectual or artistic effort.

PHILOSOPHER(S)

2 The troubles of states will not end . . . until philosophers become kings, or until . . . kings and rulers really and truly become philosophers. [Plato: *The Republic* V.xviii]
3 There is nothing so absurd but some philosopher has said it. [Cicero: *De divinatione* II]
4 For hym was levere have at his beddes heed
Twenty bookes, clad in blak or reed,
Of Aristotle and his philosophie,
Than robes riche, or fithele, or gay sautrie,
But al be that he was a philosophre,
Yet hadde he but litel gold in cofre.
[Chaucer: Prologue to *The Canterbury Tales*]
The alchemists in Chaucer's day called themselves "philosophers." One of their great aims was to find the "Philosopher's stone" which had the power to transmute base metals into gold. The lines refer to the Clerk of Oxford, who was a philosopher in our sense, yet just as poor

as most alchemists.

5 For there was never yet philosopher
That could endure the toothache patiently.
[Shakespeare: *Much Ado About Nothing* V.i.]
6 For every why he had a wherefore.
[Samuel Butler (1612-1680): *Hudibras*]
7 I have tried in my time to be a philosopher; but, I don't know how, cheerfulness was always breaking in. [Oliver Edwards: in Boswell's *Life of Johnson*, April 17, 1778]
April 17 was Good Friday. On returning from Church in Boswell's company, Dr. Johnson had been accosted by Edwards, an old school-fellow, who, among other things, said that Dr. Johnson was a philosopher and then added this famous, innocent remark.

Hume was once told by a wine merchant that he, the merchant, had taken it into his head to be a philosopher but had "tired of it most confoundedly." Hume asked him what books he had read during his philosophic period. "Nay, sir, I read no books," was the answer; "but I used to sit you whole forenoons a-yawning and poking the fire."

8 The true philosophical temperament may, we think, be described in four words: much hope, little faith. [Macaulay: *Francis Bacon*]
9 A blind man in a dark room looking for a black cat which isn't there. [Attr. to Lord Bowen and others, as a definition of a philosopher]
Some versions say "a black hat."

Some later wit added that the difference between a philosopher and a theologian is that the theologian always finds the cat.

PHILOSOPHIC

10   Is this the nature
Whom passion could not shake?
whose solid virtue
The shot of accident, nor dart of chance,
Could neither graze nor pierce?
[Shakespeare: *Othello* IV.i.]

PHILOSOPHY

11 Philosophy is the cultivation of the mental faculties; it roots out vices and

prepares the mind to receive proper seed.
[Cicero: *Tusculanae disputationes* II]
1 Philosophy is no other thing than
for a man to prepare himself to death.
[Montaigne: *Essays* I.xix (trans. John
Florio)]
The saying is attributed to Cicero.
2 And, truly, Philosophy is nothing else
but a sophisticated poetry. [Montaigne:
Essays II.xii.]
sophisticated = adulterated
3 Adversity's sweet milk—philosophy.
[Shakespeare: *Romeo and Juliet* III.iii.]
4 Hast any philosophy in thee, shepherd?
[Shakespeare: *As You Like It* III.ii.]
5 There is something in this more than
natural, if philosophy could find it out.
[Shakespeare: *Hamlet* II.ii.]
6 How charming is divine Philosophy!
Not harsh and crabbed, as dull fools
suppose,
But musical as is Apollo's lute,
And a perpetual feast of nectar'd
sweets,
Where no crude surfeit reigns.
[John Milton: *Comus*]
7 Others apart sat on a hill retir'd,
In thoughts more elevate, and rea-
soned high
Of providence, foreknowledge, will
and fate,
Fixed fate, free will, foreknowledge
absolute;
And found no end, in wand'ring
mazes lost.
[John Milton: *Paradise Lost* II.557-561]
8 Philosophy triumphs easily over past
evils and future evils; but present evils
triumph over it. [La Rochefoucauld:
Maxims]
9 This same philosophy is a good horse
in the stable, but an arrant jade on a
journey. [Oliver Goldsmith: *The Good-
Natured Man* I]
10 Undoubtedly the study of the more
abstruse regions of philosophy . . . always seems to have included an element
not very much removed from a sort of
insanity. [John Keble: *Lectures on Poetry* No. 34]
11 Do not all charms fly
At the mere touch of cold philosophy?
[Keats: *Lamia* II]
12 Philosophy will clip an Angel's wings,

Conquer all mysteries by rule and
line,
Empty the haunted air, and gnomed
mine—
Unweave a rainbow. . . .
[Keats: *Lamia* II]
13 . . . the aim of the Platonic philosophy was to exalt man into a god. The
aim of the Baconian philosophy was to
provide man with what he requires
while he continues to be man. [Macau-
lay: *Francis Bacon*]
14 Hold thou the good: define it well:
For fear divine Philosophy
Should push beyond her mark, and
be
Procuress to the Lords of Hell.
[Tennyson: *In Memoriam* LIII]
15 All philosophies, if you ride them
home, are nonsense. [Samuel Butler
(1835-1902): *Notebooks*]
16 PHILOSOPHY. A route of many roads
leading from nowhere to nothing. [Am-
brose Bierce: *The Devil's Dictionary*]
17 Most philosophical treatises show the
human cerebrum loaded far beyond its
Plimsoll mark. [H. L. Mencken: *Prejudices: Fourth Series*]

PHOEBES
18 One had to be versed in country
things
Not to believe the phoebes wept.
[Robert Frost: *The Need of Being
Versed in Country Things*]
*Frost is referring to the "murmur" of
phoebes nesting in the ruins of a burned-
out farmhouse. The* not *turns pathos to
profundity.*

PHOENIX
19 By incest, murder, suicide
Survives the sacred purple bird
Himself his father, son and bride
And his own Word.
[Howard Nemerov: *The Phoenix*]

PHYSICIAN(S)
20 Asa . . . was diseased in his feet,
until his disease was exceedingly great:
yet in his disease he sought not to the
Lord, but to the physicians. And Asa
slept with his fathers. [II Chronicles
16:12-13]
21 They that be whole need not a

physician. [Matthew 9:12]

1 Physician, heal thyself. [Luke 4:23]
Where it is called "this proverb."

2 How ill the doctor fares, if none fare ill but he. [Philemon the Younger: *Fragment*]

3 The competent physician, before he attempts to give medicine to his patient, makes himself acquainted not only with the disease which he wishes to cure, but also with the habits and constitution of the sick man. [Cicero: *De oratore* II]

4 Tiberius Caesar was wont to say, That a man, being once above threescore years of age, deserveth to be mocked and derided if he put forth his hand unto the Physician for to have his pulse felt. [Plutarch: *Morals*]

5 He used to ridicule those who after the age of thirty consulted a physician as to what was good or bad for their bodies. [Tacitus: *Annals* VI.xlvi.]
he = *the emperor Tiberius*
Tiberius felt that by thirty a man ought to know more about his own body than anyone could tell him.

6 A physician is only a consoler of the mind. [Petronius Arbiter: *Satyricon*]

7 Where there are three physicians, there are two atheists. [Latin proverb]
Though it accords ill with the present conservatism and ultra-respectability of the medical profession, physicians were for millennia proverbially atheists. Chaucer remarks drily of his Doctour of Phisyk that although he was a mighty learned man "His studie was but litel on the bible." Of course the physician was the priest's one learned rival in the community and the healing art was bound up with sorcery, magic and other evil. The disappearance of the proverb— which lingered well towards the end of the 19th century—may be due to the physician's finally superseding the priest in popular awe.

8 A physician gets no pleasure out of the health of his friends. [Montaigne: *Essays* I]

9 I do not greatly condemn them [physicians] for seeking to profit by our foolishness. [Montaigne: *Essays* II.xxxvii.]

10 Physicians are some of them so pleasing and conformable to the humor of the patient as they press not the true cure of the disease; and some other are so regular in proceeding according to art for the disease as they respect not sufficiently the condition of the patient. Take one of a middle temper; or, if it may not be found in one man, combine two of either sort; and forget not to call as well the best acquainted with your body as the best reputed of for his faculty. [Francis Bacon: *Of Regimen of Health*]
humor = *whim;* faculty = *skill*

11 I observe the Phisician with the same diligence as hee the disease. [Donne: *Devotions* VI]
Hygiene: Or How to Diagnose Your Doctor—a course in the Colleges of Unreason, in Samuel Butler's novel Erewhon *(1872).*

12 Of all odors he likes best the smell of urine, and holds Vespasian's rule, that no gain is unsavory. [Bishop John Earle: *Microcosmographie,* "Phisitian"]
*The Roman Emperor Vespasian (*A.D. *70-79) levied a tax on urinals. When his son, Titus, protested that this was unseemly, Vespasian answered that money had no smell.*
Physicians formerly attached ludicrous importance to examining the patient's urine. "Piss prophets," Robert Burton called them in The Anatomy of Melancholy.

13 That patient is not likely to recover who makes the Doctor his heir. [Thomas Fuller (1654-1734): *Gnomologia*]
Used also by Benjamin Franklin in Poor Richard's Almanack, *and by others before him, back to Publilius Syrus in the first century* B.C.

14 Every man is a fool or a physician at forty. [Thomas Fuller (1654-1734): *Gnomologia*]

15 Cur'd yesterday of my disease,
I died last night of my physician.
[Matthew Prior: *The Remedy Worse Than the Disease*]

16 The best doctors in the world are Doctor Diet, Doctor Quiet, and Doctor Merryman. [Jonathan Swift: *Polite Conversation* II (1738)]
The saying was worn threadbare by 1738, or it would not have appeared in Polite Conversation.

They were sometimes called "The Three Salernitan Doctors," since they were connected with a regimen of health popularly associated with the great medical school at Salerno in Italy. References to them appear in English as early as Bullein's Government of Health *(1558). They are repeatedly mentioned in Robert Burton's* Anatomy of Melancholy *(1621).*

1 He'd rather choose that I should die
　　Than his prediction prove a lie.
[Jonathan Swift: *On the Death of Dr. Swift*]

Since they have abandoned blood-letting and the terrible cathartics they used to prescribe, physicians are no longer able to prognosticate death with the certainty they once enjoyed. In consequence, they rarely foretell their patients' deaths anymore and have lost a little respect because of it.

2 Removed from kind Arbuthnot's aid,
　　Who knows his art, but not the trade.
[Alexander Pope: *In Sickness*]

Dr. John Arbuthnot was Pope's friend and physician. Pope's line is one of the most graceful compliments ever paid a doctor of medicine.

3 Ev'n Radcliffe's Doctors travel first
　　　　　　to France,
　　Nor dare to practise till they've
　　　　　learn'd to dance.
[Alexander Pope: *Imitations of Horace* Epistle I, Book II, 1:183.]

Dr. John Radcliffe (1650-1714), a wealthy physician, endowed two medical traveling fellowships at Oxford. Then as now, apparently, social accomplishments were indispensable to success in the practice of medicine. Today it might be golf instead of dancing.

4 A physician in a great city seems to be the mere plaything of fortune; his degree of reputation is, for the most part, totally casual: they that employ him know not his excellence; they that reject him know not his deficience. [Samuel Johnson: *Life of Akenside*]

5 The doctors found, when she was
　　　　　　　　dead—
　　Her last disorder mortal.
[Oliver Goldsmith: *Elegy on Mrs. Mary Blaize*]

6 I had rather follow you to your grave than see you owe your life to any but a regular-bred physician. [Richard Brinsley Sheridan: *St. Patrick's Day* II. iv.]

7 "What sort of a doctor is he?"
"Well, I don't know much about his ability; but he's got a very good bedside manner." [*Punch*, March 15, 1884]

8 One doctor makes work for another. [V. S. Lean: *Collectanea* IV.lxxiii.]

9 PHYSICIAN. One upon whom we set our hopes when ill, and our dogs when well. [Ambrose Bierce: *The Devil's Dictionary*]

10 APOTHECARY. The Physician's accomplice. [Ambrose Bierce: *The Devil's Dictionary*]

Chaucer, 500 years earlier, had remarked that physician and apothecary "made each other for to win" and that their friendship "was not new to begin."

PIANIST

11 Please do not shoot the pianist. He is doing his best.

Adjuration to the patrons in a saloon in Leadville, Colorado. Oscar Wilde was enchanted by it; it seemed to him to express the finer spirit of America.

See Oscar Wilde's Impressions of America, *"Leadville."*

PICKING

12 To keep my hands from picking and stealing. [*Book of Common Prayer*, "Catechism"]

13 Children and Chickens must be always picking. [Thomas Fuller (1654-1734): *Gnomologia*]

PICKWICKIAN

14 He had used the word in its Pickwickian sense . . . he had merely considered him a humbug in a Pickwickian point of view. [Dickens: *The Pickwick Papers* I]

When Mr. Pickwick referred to certain of Mr. Blotton's actions as "vile and calumnious," and Mr. Blotton referred to Mr. Pickwick as "a humbug," the chairman of the distinguished club felt it imperative to demand whether these opprobrious terms were to be received in their commonly understood senses. It appeared that they were not, that the disputants held each other in the highest esteem, and that the terms were used solely in their "Pickwickian sense."

PICTURE
1   Look here, upon this picture, and on this.
[Shakespeare: *Hamlet* III.iv.]

PIE
2   He has an oar in every man's boat, and a finger in every pie. [Cervantes: *Don Quixote* II.22]

PIED PIPER
3   At Hammel in Saxony, on the 20th of June, 1484, the Devil, in the likeness of a pied piper, carried away 130 children, that were never after seen. [Robert Burton: *The Anatomy of Melancholy* Part I. Sec.II.i.ii.]

PIETY
4   One that feared God, and eschewed evil. [Job 1:1]
5   No piety can delay the wrinkles. [Horace: *Carmina* II]
6   Ignorance is the mother of true piety. [Henry Cole, Dean of St. Paul's: in a famous disputation at Westminster, March 31, 1559]
   The statement was uttered in high and solemn seriousness. On this one point, it is possible for the religious and the skeptical to agree.
7   Thou villain, thou art full of piety. [Shakespeare: *Much Ado About Nothing* IV.ii.]
8   Thou liest in Abraham's bosom all the year,
   And worship'st at the Temple's inner shrine,
   God being with thee when we know it not.
[Wordsworth: *It Is a Beauteous Evening*]
9   The child is father of the man;
   And I could wish my days to be
   Bound each to each by natural piety.
[Wordsworth: *My Heart Leaps Up*]

PIG(S)
10   Though ye love not to buy a pig in the poke. [John Heywood: *Proverbs* (1546)]

poke = *sack, bag*
   Montaigne has "a cat in a poke," which Florio translated "pig." Several European languages have the phrase, but they all have "cat" instead of "pig."
   The idea is: Don't buy anything you have not been allowed to examine.
11   As pigs are said to see the wind.
[Samuel Butler (1612-1680): *Hudibras*]
   That pigs can see the wind was a very old belief. It may have been due to the unperceived fact that pigs have a much more acute sense of hearing than human beings have and hence would show awarenesses that would seem very mysterious.

PIGEONS
12   Pigeons in the grass alas. [Gertrude Stein: *Four Saints in Three Acts*]

PILGRIMS
13   The Pilgrims landed, worthy men,
   And saved from wreck on raging seas,
   They fell upon their knees, and then
   Upon the Aborigines.
[Arthur Guiterman: *The Pilgrim's Thanksgiving*]

PILGRIM'S PROGRESS
14   Some said, John, print it; others said, Not so;
   Some said, It might do good; others said, No.
[John Bunyan: *The Pilgrim's Progress*, "The Author's Apology for His Book"]

PILLAR
15   The Lord went before them by day in a pillar of a cloud, to lead them the way; and by night in a pillar of fire. [Exodus 13:21]
16   From pillar to post.
   The expression was in existence in the early 15th century and was listed as proverbial by 1546.
   It probably alludes to the pillory and the whipping post and still retains the idea of being harried and driven.
   Parishes were formerly required to care for their own indigent and one of the functions of the parish beadle was to whip vagabonds out of the parish so that they could not be accounted resi-

dents and hence a legitimate charge. Anthony Wood (1632-1695) tells of the unseemly dragging of a dying pauper back and forth across two parish boundaries in Oxford, each determined that the other should pay for the funeral when it was necessary.

PILOT
1 For tho' from out our bourne of
Time and Place
The flood may bear me far,
I hope to see my Pilot face to face
When I have crossed the bar.
[Tennyson: *Crossing the Bar*]

PINE
2 Weary se'nnights nine times nine
Shall he dwindle, peak and pine.
[Shakespeare: *Macbeth* I.iii.]

PIONEERS
3 Conquering, holding, daring, venturing as we go the unknown ways,
Pioneers! O pioneers!
[Walt Whitman: *Leaves of Grass*, "Pioneers! O Pioneers"]

PIOUS
4 *Pithecanthropus biblicus.* [H. L. Mencken: *Prejudices: Sixth Series*]

PIRACY
5 PIRACY. Commerce without its folly-swaddles, just as God made it. [Ambrose Bierce: *The Devil's Dictionary*]

PIT
6 Whoso diggeth a pit shall fall therein. [Proverbs 26:27]
Also in Ecclesiastes *10:8.*

PITCH
7 He that toucheth pitch shall be defiled therewith. [Ecclesiasticus 13:1]

PITCHER
8 The pot so long to the water goeth,
That home it cometh at the last y-
broke.
[Thomas Hoccleve: *De regimine principum*]
9 If the pitcher strikes the stone or the stone strikes the pitcher, it is equally bad for the pitcher. [Cervantes: *Don Quixote* II.xliii. (and elsewhere)]

PITIFUL
10 'Twas pitiful, 'twas wondrous pitiful. [Shakespeare: *Othello* I.iii.]
11 A pitiful surgeon makes a dangerous
sore.
[John Marston: *The Malcontent* IV]

PITY
12 For pitee renneth sone in gentil herte. [Chaucer: *The Knight's Tale*]
renneth = *runs*
13 Pity ever healeth envy. [Francis Bacon: *Of Envy*]
14 But yet the pity of it, Iago! O! Iago, the pity of it, Iago! [Shakespeare: *Othello* IV.i.]
15 Of all paths that lead to a woman's
love
Pity's the straightest.
[Beaumont and Fletcher: *The Knight of Malta* I.i.]
16 He that pities another remembers himself. [George Herbert: *Jacula Prudentum*]
17 Pity is a perception of our own misfortunes in those of others. [La Rochefoucauld: *Maxims*]
18 To pity the unhappy is not contrary to selfish desire; on the other hand, we are glad of the occasion to thus testify friendship, and attract to ourselves the reputation of tenderness, without giving anything. [Pascal: *Pensées*]
19 Can you pretend to love
And have no pity? Love and that are
twins.
[Dryden: *Don Sebastian* III.i.]
20 Pity, though it is the most gentle and the least mischievous of all our passions, is yet as much a frailty of our nature as anger, pride or fear. The weakest minds have generally the greatest share of it. [Bernard de Mandeville: *An Inquiry into the Origin of Moral Virtue* (1728)]
21 Pity is not natural to man. Children are always cruel. Savages are always cruel. Pity is acquired and improved by the cultivation of reason. [Samuel Johnson: in Boswell's *Life*, July 20, 1763]
22 Pity! the scavenger of misery. [G. B. Shaw: *Major Barbara* III]
23 One of those sudden shocks of pity

that sometimes decentralize a life. [Edith Wharton: *The House of Mirth* I.xiv.]

1 Piety to mankind must be three-fourths pity. [George Santayana: *Reason in Religion*]

PLACE(S)
2 One cannot be in two places at once. [17th-century proverb]

It depends on what sort of a life one has led. Saints, it is said, are capable of being in two places at once. The theological term is bilocation.

3 A place for everything, and everything in its place. [Samuel Smiles: *Thrift* V]

PLACE: position
4 Preserve the right of thy place, but stir not questions of jurisdiction; and rather assume thy right in silence and *de facto* than voice it with claims and challenges. [Francis Bacon: *Of Great Place*]

PLAGIARISM
5 They lard their lean books with the fat of others' works. [Robert Burton: *Anatomy of Melancholy,* "Democritus to the Reader"]

PLAGIARY
6 Whatever has been well said by anyone is mine. [Seneca: *Epistolae* XVI.vii.]
7 Amongst so many borrowed things, I am glad if I can steal one, disguising and altering it for some new service. [Montaigne: *Essays* III.xii.]
8 Truth and reason are common to all and no more belong to him that spoke them heretofore than unto him that shall speak them hereafter. [Montaigne: *Essays* I.xxv.]
9 I am but a gatherer and disposer of other men's stuff. [Sir Henry Wotton: Preface to *The Elements of Architecture*]
10 We can say nothing but what hath been said. . . . Our poets steal from Homer. . . . Our storydressers do as much; he that comes last is commonly best. [Robert Burton: *Anatomy of Melancholy,* "Democritus to the Reader"]
11 Borrowing, if it be not bettered by the borrower, is accounted plagiary.

[John Milton: *Iconoclastes* XXIII]
12 Next, o'er his books his eyes began to
roll,
In pleasing memory of all he stole.
[Alexander Pope: *The Dunciad* I]
13 Steal! And egad, serve your best thoughts as gypsies do stolen children, disfigure them to make 'em pass for their own. [Richard Brinsley Sheridan: *The Critic* I.i.]
14 All that can be said is, that two people happened to hit on the same thought —and Shakespeare made use of it first, that's all. [Richard Brinsley Sheridan: *The Critic* III.i.]
15 It has come to be practically a sort of rule in literature, that a man, having once shown himself capable of original writing, is entitled thenceforth to steal from the writings of others at discretion. [Emerson: *Shakespeare*]
16 Though old the thought and oft ex-
prest,
'Tis his at last who says it best.
[James Russell Lowell: *For an Autograph*]
17 You will, Oscar, you will. [James McNeill Whistler: when, after one of his witticisms, Oscar Wilde had remarked, "I wish I had said that."]

Quoted in L. C. Ingleby's Oscar Wilde.
18 When 'Omer smote 'is bloomin' lyre,
He'd 'eard men sing by land an'
sea;
An' what he thought 'e might require,
'E went an' took—the same as me!
[Kipling: *When 'Omer Smote 'is Bloomin' Lyre*]
19 Immature artists imitate. Mature artists steal. [Lionel Trilling, in *Esquire,* September, 1962]

PLAGUE
20 A plague o' both your houses. [Shakespeare: *Romeo and Juliet* III.i.]

PLAIN SPEAKING
21 An honest tale speeds best being
plainly told.
[Shakespeare: *Richard III* IV.iv.]
22 I will a round unvarnish'd tale deliver.
[Shakespeare: *Othello* I.iii.]

PLAN

1 It's a bad plan that can't be changed. [Publilius Syrus: *Maxims*]
2 You can never plan the future by the past. [Edmund Burke: *Letter to a member of the National Assembly*]

PLANETS

3 The planets in their stations list'ning stood. [John Milton: *Paradise Lost* VII 563]

PLATITUDE(S)

4 Tom Steady was a vehement assertor of uncontroverted truth; and by keeping himself out of the reach of contradiction had acquired all the confidence which the consciousness of irresistible abilities could have given. [Samuel Johnson: *The Idler* No. 78]
5 Thou say'st an undisputed thing
   In such a solemn way.
[O. W. Holmes: *To an Insect*]
6 I am not fond of uttering platitudes
   In stained-glass attitudes.
[W. S. Gilbert: *Patience* I]
7 Nothing produces such an effect as a good platitude. [Oscar Wilde: *An Ideal Husband* I]
8 To stroke a platitude until it purrs like an epigram. [Don(ald) Marquis: *The Sun Dial*]

PLAY (vb.). *See* WORK

PLAY(S)

9 For what man that is entered in a
                                        pley,
   He nedes must unto the pleye assente.
[Chaucer: Prologue to *The Clerk's Tale*]
10 Play out the play.
[Shakespeare: *I Henry IV* II.iv.]
11   The play's the thing
   Wherein I'll catch the conscience of
                                    the king.
[Shakespeare: *Hamlet* II.ii.]
12 Popular Stage-plays are sinful, heathenish, lewd, ungodly Spectacles, and most pernicious Corruptions; condemned in all ages, as intolerable Mischiefs to Churches, to Republics, to the manners, minds and souls of men. [William Prynne: *Histriomastix* (1632)]
13 In other things the knowing artist
                                        may

Judge better than the people; but a
                                        play,
(Made for delight, and for no other
                                        use)
If you approve it not, has no excuse.
[Edmund Waller: Prologue to *The Maid's Tragedy*]
14 A play ought to be a just and lively image of human nature, representing its passions and humors, and the changes of fortune to which it is subject, for the delight and instruction of mankind. [Dryden: *Of Dramatic Poesy*]
15 There is a mode in plays as well as clothes. [Dryden: Prologue to *The Rival Ladies*]
16 In play there are two pleasures for
                              your choosing—
   The one is winning, and the other
                                    losing.
[Byron: *Don Juan* XIV.xii.]

PLEASING

17 It is hard to please everyone. (*Durum est omnibus placere.*) [Latin proverb]
18 The excessive desire of pleasing goes along almost always with the apprehension of not being liked. [Thomas Fuller (1608-1661): *Introductio ad Prudentiam* II]
19 He who is pleased with nobody is much more unhappy than he with whom nobody is pleased. [La Rochefoucauld: *Maxims*]
20 Whate'er he did was done with so
                                   much ease,
   In him alone, 'twas natural to please.
[Dryden: *Absalom and Achitophel* I]
21 And sure he must have more than
                               mortal Skill,
   Who pleases any one against his Will.
[William Congreve: Epilogue to *The Way of the World*]
22 He more had pleas'd us, had he
                              pleas'd us less.
[Joseph Addison: *English Poets*]
   The reference is to Abraham Cowley, a poet known now only to scholars but in the 18th century considered almost the equal of Milton.
23 That which is good only because it pleases cannot be pronounced good until it has been found to please. [Samuel Johnson: *Life of Dryden*]
24 The art of pleasing is the art of de-

ceiving. [Vauvenargues: *Réflexions*]

1 And if you mean to profit, learn to please. [Charles Churchill: *Gotham* II]

2 We not only wish to be pleased, but to be pleased in that particular way in which we have been accustomed to be pleased. [Wordsworth: Preface to *The Lyrical Ballads*]

3 The art of pleasing consists in being pleased. [William Hazlitt: *The Round Table,* "On Manners"]

PLEASURE

4 There is nothing better for a man, than that he should eat and drink, and that he should make his soul enjoy good in his labor. [Ecclesiastes 11:24]

5 I know not how to conceive the good, apart from the pleasures of taste, sexual pleasures, the pleasures of sound, and the pleasures of beautiful form. [Diogenes Laertius: *Epicurus* X.vi.]

6 Of all the pleasures we know, the pursuit of them is pleasant. [Montaigne: *Essays* I.xix.]

7 Pleasure is one of the chiefest kinds of profit. [Montaigne: *Essays* III.i.]

8 No pleasure is fully delightsome without communication; and no delight absolute, except imparted. [Montaigne: *Essays* III.ix.]

9 Sleepe after toyle, port after stormie
     seas,
  Ease after warre, death after life,
          does greatly please.
[Edmund Spenser: *The Faerie Queene* I.ix.]

10 The English take their pleasures sadly, after the fashion of their country. [Duc de Sully: *Memoirs*]

11 Pleasure and action make the hours
          seem short.
[Shakespeare: *Othello* II.iii.]

12 Pleasures are all alike, simply considered in themselves. He that takes pleasure to hear sermons enjoys himself as much as he that hears plays. [John Selden: *Table Talk,* "Pleasure"]

13 Now that the fields are dank, and
          ways are mire,
  Where shall we sometimes meet, and
          by the fire
  Help waste a sullen day? . . .
  What neat repast shall feast us, light
          and choice,

Of Attic taste, with wine, whence we
          may rise
  To hear the lute well touched, or
          artful voice
  Warble immortal notes and Tuscan
          air?
[John Milton: *To Mr. Lawrence* (1656)]
A wonderfully restrained sensuality.

14 Let us roll all our strength and all
  Our sweetness up into one ball,
  And tear our pleasures with rough
          strife
  Through the iron gates of life.
[Andrew Marvell: *To His Coy Mistress*]
coy = *shy, hesitant, reluctant*

15 It is true, heaven forbids certain pleasures, but one manages to compromise. [Molière: *Tartuffe* IV.v.]

16 I will not make a toil of a pleasure, quoth the good man, when he buried his wife. [Old Scottish proverb]

17 The most delicious pleasure is to cause that of other people. [La Bruyère: *Les Caractères*]

18 When our pleasures have exhausted us, we think that we have exhausted pleasure. [Vauvenargues: *Réflexions*]

19 Men seldom give pleasure where they are not pleased themselves. [Samuel Johnson: *The Rambler* No. 74]

20 He who endeavors to please must appear pleased. [Samuel Johnson: *The Rambler* No. 152]

21 The greatest part of human gratifications approach nearly to vice. [Samuel Johnson: *The Rambler* No. 160]

22 The public pleasures of far the greater part of mankind are counterfeit. [Samuel Johnson: *The Idler* No. 18]

23 Pleasure is very seldom found where it is sought. [Samuel Johnson: *The Idler* No. 58]

24 Having now nobody to please, I am little pleased. [Samuel Johnson: *Diary in France,* October 17, 1775]

25 No man is a hypocrite in his pleasures. [Samuel Johnson: in Boswell's *Life* (1784)]

26 A life of pleasure is the most unpleasant thing in the world. [Oliver Goldsmith: *The Citizen of the World*]

27 But pleasures are like poppies
          spread—
  You seize the flow'r, its bloom is shed;

Or like the snow falls in the river—
A moment white, then melts for ever;
Or like the borealis race,
That flit ere you can point their
place;
Or like the rainbow's lovely form
Evanishing amid the storm.
[Burns: *Tam o' Shanter*]
1 The last pleasure in life is the sense
of discharging our duty. [William Hazlitt: *Characteristics*]
2 On with the dance! Let joy be unconfined.
[Byron: *Childe Harold* III.xxii.]
3 Pleasure's a sin, and sometimes sin's a
pleasure.
[Byron: *Don Juan* I.cxxxiii.]
4 Though sages may pour out their
wisdom's treasure,
There is no sterner moralist than
Pleasure.
[Byron: *Don Juan* III.lxv.]
5 Talking of pleasure, this moment I
was writing with one hand, and with the
other holding to my mouth a nectarine.
Good God, how fine! It went down soft,
pulpy, slushy, oozy—all its delicious
embonpoint melted down my throat
like a large beatified strawberry. [John
Keats: letter to his friend Dilke, from
Winchester, August or September, 1819]
6 Love not Pleasure; love God. This
is the EVERLASTING YEA. [Thomas
Carlyle: *Sartor Resartus* II.ix.]
7 Life would be very pleasant if it
were not for its enjoyments. [R. S. Surtees: *Mr. Jorrocks in Paris* XXXII]
8 Life would be tolerable were it not
for its amusements. [Sir George Cornewall Lewis (1806-1863): quoted by Lord
Grey of Fallodon in *Twenty-Five
Years*]
9 The true pleasure of life is to live
with your inferiors. [W. M. Thackeray:
The Newcomes IX]
10 They dined on mince, with slices of
quince,
Which they ate with a runcible
spoon,
And hand in hand, on the edge of
the sand,
They danced by the light of the
moon.
[Edward Lear: *The Owl and the Pussy-Cat*]

11 The horrible pleasure of pleasing inferior people. [Arthur Hugh Clough:
Amours de Voyage XI]
12 Simple pleasures are the last refuge
of the complex. [Oscar Wilde: *Aphorisms* No. 35]
13 A life of pleasure requires an aristocratic setting to make it interesting.
[George Santayana: *Life of Reason* II
"Reason in Society," Ch.5]
14 All the things I really like to do are
either immoral, illegal or fattening. [Alexander Woollcott]
15 Speed provides the one genuinely
modern pleasure. [Aldous Huxley: *Music at Night*, "Wanted, a New Pleasure"]
16 Surely a King who loves pleasure is
less dangerous than one who loves glory?
[Nancy Mitford: *The Water Beetle* 105]

PLEASURE: and pain
17 There is no such thing as pure pleasure; some anxiety always goes with it.
[Ovid: *Metamorphoses* VII]
18 Pleasure is the absence of pain. [Cicero: *De finibus* II.ii.]
This definition fails to distinguish pleasure from insensibility. Perhaps "a release from tension" would be a better definition.

Cicero's word is voluptas *and, certainly, there is a voluptuousness in the first cessation of such pains as those caused by tight shoes or by hard labor.*
19 Pleasure is nothing else but the intermission of pain. [John Selden: *Table Talk*, "Pleasure"]
So defined, also, by Epicurus (300 B.C.), in his maxims.
20 The honest man takes pains, and
then enjoys pleasures; the knave takes
pleasure, and then suffers pain. [Benjamin Franklin: *Poor Richard's Almanack*]
21 I can sympathize with people's pains,
but not with their pleasures. There is
something curiously boring about somebody else's happiness. [Aldous Huxley:
Limbo, "Cynthia"]

PLEASURE-DOME
22 In Xanadu did Kubla Khan
A stately pleasure-dome decree:
Where Alph, the sacred river, ran

Through caverns measureless to man
Down to a sunless sea.
So twice five miles of fertile ground
With walls and towers were girdled
round.
[Coleridge: *Kubla Khan*]

PLENTY
1 Here is God's plenty.
[Dryden: Preface to the *Fables* (1700)]
The reference is to Chaucer's Canterbury
Tales.

PLODDERS
2 Small have continual plodders ever
won
Save base authority from others'
books.
[Shakespeare: *Love's Labour's Lost* I.i.]

PLOT
3 What the devil does the plot signify,
except to bring in fine things? [George
Villiers, Duke of Buckingham: *The Rehearsal* III.i.]
4 Ay, now the plot thickens. [George
Villiers, Duke of Buckingham: *The Rehearsal* III.ii.]

PLOW(S)
5 I have, God woot, a large feeld to ere,
And wayke been the oxen in my
plough.
[Chaucer: *The Knight's Tale*]
ere = *plow*
6 And Jesus said unto him, No man,
having put his hand to the plough, and
looking back, is fit for the kingdom of
God. [Luke 9:62]
7 He that by the plow would thrive
Himself must either hold or drive.
[Benjamin Franklin: *Poor Richard's Almanack*]

POBBLE
8 The Pobble who has no toes
Had once as many as we;
When they said, "Some day you may
lose them all,"
He replied, "Fish fiddle-de-dee!"
And his Aunt Jobiska made him
drink
Lavender water tinged with pink,
For she said, "The World in general
knows

There's nothing so good for a Pob-
ble's toes!"
[Edward Lear: *The Pobble Who Has
No Toes*]

POCKET
9 POCKET. The cradle of motive and
the grave of conscience. [Ambrose
Bierce: *The Devil's Dictionary*]

POE
10 There comes Poe, with his raven, like
Barnaby Rudge,
Three fifths of him genius and two
fifths sheer fudge.
[James Russell Lowell: *A Fable for Critics*]

POEM
11 It is easier to write a mediocre poem
than to understand a good one. [Mon-
taigne: *Essays* I]
12 It begins in delight and ends in wisdom. [Robert Frost: *The Figure a Poem
Makes*]
Frost is referring to a good poem.
13 A poem should be equal to:
Not true.
. . .
A poem should not mean
But be.
[Archibald MacLeish: *Ars Poetica*]
14 If the poem can be improved by its
author's explanations, it never should
have been published. [Archibald Mac-
Leish: *Poems* (author's note)]

POET: less favorable views
15 The irritable tribe of poets. [Horace:
Epistles II.ii.]
16 Those who err follow the steps of the
poets . . . they rove as bereft of their
senses. [*The Koran XXVI*]
17 Poets lose half the praise they should
have got,
Could it be known what they discreetly blot.
[Edmund Waller: *Upon Roscommon's
Translation of Horace, De Arte Poetica*]
18 George Wither was taken prisoner,
and was in danger of his life, having
written severely against the king. Sir
John Denham went to the king, and desired his majesty not to hang him, for

that whilst G. W. lived he should not be the worst poet in England. [John Aubrey: *Brief Lives* I]

> *Wither and Denham were minor 17th-century poets.*

1 What poet would not grieve to see
His brother write as well as he?
But rather than they should excel,
Would wish his rivals all in Hell?
[Jonathan Swift: *On the Death of Dr. Swift*]

2 A maudlin poetess.
[Alexander Pope: *Epistle to Dr. Arbuthnot*]

3 While pensive poets painful vigils keep,
Sleepless themselves to give their readers sleep.
[Alexander Pope: *The Dunciad* I.xciii.]

4 Buffoons and poets are near related
And willingly seek each other out.
[Goethe: *Epigramme* XLVIII]

> *This is not wholly a slur; both are deeply interested in the associations in words.*

5 One that would peep and botanize
Upon his mother's grave.
[Wordsworth: *A Poet's Epitaph*]

6 Poets and painters, as all artists know,
May shoot a little with a lengthened bow.
[Byron: *Hints from Horace*]

7 His strain display'd some feeling—
right or wrong;
And feeling, in a poet, is the source
Of others' feeling; but they are such liars,
And take all colours—like the hands of dyers.
[Byron: *Don Juan* III.lxxxvii.]

8 A man all poesy and bussem.
[W. S. Gilbert: *Bab Ballads,* "John and Freddy"]

9 A poet can survive everything but a misprint. [Oscar Wilde: *The Children of the Poets*]

10 The modest cough of a minor poet.
[G. B. Shaw: *The Dark Lady of the Sonnets*]

11 A taste for drawing-rooms has spoiled more poets than ever did a taste for gutters. [Thomas Beer: *The Mauve Decade*]

POET: to madness near allied

12 Democritus maintains that there can be no great poet without a spice of madness. [Cicero: *De divinatione* I]

13 A settled and reposed man doth in vain knock at Poesie's gate. [Montaigne: *Essays* II.ii.]

> *Montaigne attributes the thought to Plato.*

14 The poet's eye, in a fine frenzy rolling,
Doth glance from heaven to earth,
from earth to heaven.
[Shakespeare: *A Midsummer Night's Dream* V.i.]

15 All poets are mad. [Robert Burton: *Anatomy of Melancholy,* "Democritus to the Reader"]

16 The Dog-star rages! nay 'tis past a doubt,
All Bedlam, or Parnassus, is let out:
Fire in each eye, and papers in each hand,
They rave, recite, and madden round the land.
[Alexander Pope: *Epistle to Dr. Arbuthnot*]

17 By our own spirits are we deified:
We Poets in our youth begin in gladness;
But thereof come in the end despondency and madness.
[Wordsworth: *Resolution and Independence*]

18 Perhaps no person can be a poet, or can even enjoy poetry, without a certain unsoundness of mind. [Macaulay: *Milton*]

POET: his power

19 Poets were the first teachers of mankind. [Horace: *Ars poetica*]

20 True poets are the guardians of the state. [Wentworth Dillon: *Essay on Translated Verse*]

21 Poets alone are permitted to tell the real truth. [Horace Walpole: Letter to Mary Coke, Feb. 12, 1761]

22 The poet is the rock of defense for human nature. [Wordsworth: Preface to *The Lyrical Ballads*]

23 Poets are the hierophants of an unapprehended inspiration; the mirrors of the gigantic shadows which futurity casts upon the present; the words which express what they understand not; the trumpets which sing to battle, and feel

not what they inspire; the influence which is moved not, but moves. [Shelley: *A Defence of Poetry*]

hierophants = *interpreters of sacred mysteries*

1 Poets are the unacknowledged legislators of the world. [Shelley: *A Defence of Poetry*]

2 Like a poet hidden
   In the light of thought,
Singing hymns unbidden,
   Till the world is wrought
To sympathy with hopes and fears it
           heeded not.
[Shelley: *To a Skylark*]

3 The poet and the dreamer are distinct,
Diverse, sheer opposite, antipodes.
The one pours out a balm upon the
           world,
The other vexes it.
[Keats: *The Fall of Hyperion* I]

POET: his sensitivity, ecstasy and pains

4 Had in him those brave translunary
           things
That the first poets had.
[Michael Drayton: *Of Poets and Poesy* (1627)]

Drayton was referring to Christopher Marlowe.

5 Alas! What boots it with uncessant
           care
To tend the homely, slighted Shepherd's trade,
And strictly meditate the thankless
           Muse?
[John Milton: *Lycidas*]

6 A poet soaring in the high region of his fancies with his garland and singing robes about him. [John Milton: *Reason of Church Government* II.i.]

7 There is a pleasure in poetic pains
Which only poets know.
[William Cowper: *The Task* II]

8 I am nae poet, in a sense,
But just a rhymer, like, by chance,
An' hae to learning nae pretence,
   Yet what the matter?
Whene'er my Muse does on me
           glance,
   I jingle at her.
[Burns: *Epistle to John Lapraik*]

9 A poet is a man speaking to men, endowed with more lively sensibility, more enthusiasm and tenderness, who has a greater knowledge of human nature, and a more comprehensive soul than are supposed to be common among mankind; a man pleased with his own passions and volitions, and who rejoices more than other men in the spirit of life that is in him. [Wordsworth: Preface to *The Lyrical Ballads*]

10 The poet is chiefly distinguished from other men by a greater promptness to think and feel without immediate external excitement, and a greater power in expressing such thoughts and feelings as are produced in him in that manner. [Wordsworth: Preface to *The Lyrical Ballads*]

11 Poems of value were never produced but by a man who, being possessed of more than usual organic sensibility, had also thought long and deeply. [Wordsworth: Preface to *The Lyrical Ballads*]

12 A poet could not but be gay,
   In such a jocund company.
[Wordsworth: *I Wandered Lonely as a Cloud*]

13 Mighty Poets in their misery dead.
[Wordsworth: *Resolution and Independence*]

14 A poet is great, first, in proportion to the strength of his passion, and then, that strength being granted, in proportion to his government of it. [John Ruskin: *Modern Painters* III.iv.12]

15 Ah! Two desires toss about
   The poet's feverish blood.
One drives him to the world without,
   And one to solitude.
[Matthew Arnold: *Stanzas in Memory of the Author of "Obermann"*]

16 Such, poets, is your bride, the Muse!
           young, gay,
Radiant, adorn'd outside; a hidden
           ground
Of thought and of austerity within.
[Matthew Arnold: *Austerity of Poetry*]

POET: miscellaneous

17 Every man is a poet when he is in love. [Plato: *Symposium*]

18 Many brave men lived before Agamemnon, but all unwept and unknown they sleep in endless night, for they had no poets to sound their praises. [Hor-

ace: *Carmina* IV]

1 A poet is born, not made. [Florus: *De qualitate vitae*]

2 The impossibility of any man's being a good poet without first being a good man. [Ben Jonson: Dedication to *Volpone*]

3 He knew himself to sing, and build the lofty rhyme.
[John Milton: *Lycidas*]

4 A Poet is the most unpoetical of any thing in existence, because he has no Identity—he is continually in for and filling some other Body. [Keats: Letter to Richard Woodhouse, October 27, 1818]

5 We are all poets when we read a poem well. [Thomas Carlyle: *On Heroes and Hero-Worship,* Lecture III]

6 He who, in an enlightened and literary society, aspires to be a great poet must first become a little child, he must take to pieces the whole web of his mind. [Macaulay: *Milton*]

7 The poet in a golden clime was born,
With golden stars above;

Dower'd with the hate of hate, the scorn of scorn,

The love of love.

[Tennyson: *The Poet*]

POETRY: attempts at definition

8 Jigging veins of rhyming mother wits. [Christopher Marlowe: Prologue to *Tamburlaine*]

9 Poetry is the spontaneous overflow of powerful feelings; it takes its origin from emotion recollected in tranquillity. [Wordsworth: Preface to *The Lyrical Ballads*]

> There have been many attempts to define poetry. Most poets think very well of it, though some seem a little uncertain. Carl Sandburg, for instance, says that poetry is "a spot about half-way between where you listen and where you wonder what it was you heard."
>
> There have been some very unpoetical definitions. Isaac Barrow called poetry "a kind of ingenious nonsense" and Jeremy Bentham said that the difference between prose and poetry is that in prose all lines in a paragraph except the last one go clear out to the margin.

10 Poetry is the breath and finer spirit of all knowledge; it is the impassioned expression which is in the countenance of all science. [Wordsworth: Preface to *The Lyrical Ballads*]

11 Wisdom married to immortal verse. [Wordsworth: *The Excursion* VII]

12 Poetry is the record of the best and happiest moments of the happiest and best minds. [Shelley: *A Defence of Poetry*]

13 A poem is the very image of life expressed in its eternal truth. [Shelley: *A Defence of Poetry*]

14 [Poetry] is the suggestion, by the imagination, of noble grounds for the noble emotions. [John Ruskin: *Modern Painters* III.iv.l.]

15 Poetry is at bottom a criticism of life. [Matthew Arnold: *Essays in Criticism: Second Series* "Wordsworth"]

16 Let us understand by poetry all literary production which attains the power of giving pleasure by its form, as distinct from its matter. [Walter Pater: *The Renaissance*]

17 Poetry is simply the most beautiful, impressive and widely effective mode of saying things, and hence its importance. [Matthew Arnold: *Heinrich Heine*]

18 Poetry is the opening and closing of a door, leaving those who look through to guess about what is seen during a moment. [Carl Sandburg: *Ten Definitions of Poetry*]

19 Poetry is a comforting piece of fiction set to more or less lascivious music. [H. L. Mencken: *Prejudices: Third Series*]

POETRY: and prose

20 What a poor appearance the tales of poets make when stripped of the colours which music puts upon them, and recited in simple prose. [Plato: *The Republic* X 601B]

21 It is not poetry, but prose run mad.
[Alexander Pope: *Epistle to Dr. Arbuthnot*]

22 There neither is nor can be any essential difference between the language of prose and metrical composition. [Wordsworth: Preface to *The Lyrical Ballads*]

23 Poetry sheds no tears "such as angels weep," but natural and human tears:

she can boast of no celestial ichor that distinguishes her vital juices from those of prose; the same human blood circulates through the veins of them both. [Wordsworth: Preface to *The Lyrical Ballads*]

1 Prose—words in their best order; poetry—the best words in their best order. [Coleridge: *Table-Talk,* July 12, 1827]

2 Didactic poetry is my abhorrence; nothing can be equally well expressed in prose that is not tedious and supererogatory in verse. [Shelley: Preface to *Prometheus Unbound*]

3 Science is for those who learn; poetry, for those who know. [Joseph Roux: *Meditations of a Parish Priest*]

POETRY: rhyme

4 I was promised on a time
To have reason for my rhyme;
From that time unto this season,
I received nor rhyme nor reason.
[Edmund Spenser: *Lines on His Promised Pension*]

There is a story that Queen Elizabeth ordered Lord Burghley to pay Spenser a hundred pounds for a poem in her praise and that when Burghley objected that this was too much "for a song," she said "Then give him what is reason." Then, when Burghley made no payment at all, the poet wrote these lines to him.

But the story is probably apocryphal, for John Skelton, who died 23 years before Spenser was born, had written, in his Against Garnesche:

For reson can I non fynde
Nor good ryme in your mater.

So the expression was proverbial and the story probably merely an attempt to explain its origin.

The phrase also occurs in the anonymous French Maistre Pierre Pathelin, composed about 1470.

5 The troublesome and modern bondage of Rhyming.
[John Milton: Preface to *Paradise Lost*]

6 Rhyme being no necessary adjunct or true ornament of poem or good verse, in longer works especially, but the invention of a barbarous age, to set off wretched matter with lame meter. [John Milton: Preface to *Paradise Lost*]

7 For rhyme the rudder is of verses,
With which, like ships, they steer
their courses.
[Samuel Butler (1612-1680): *Hudibras* I. i.]

8 But those that write in rhyme still
make
The one verse for the other's sake;
For one for sense and one for rhyme,
I think's sufficient at one time.
[Samuel Butler (1612-1680): *Hudibras* II. i.]

9 Till barbarous nations, and more
barbarous times,
Debased the majesty of verse to
rhymes.
[Dryden: *To the Earl of Roscommon*]

POETRY: rhythm

10 The bitter but wholesome iambic.
[Sir Philip Sidney: *Apologie for Poetrie* II]

11 The proud full sail of his great verse.
[Shakespeare: *Sonnets* LXXXVI]

12 The elegancy, facility, and golden
cadence of poesy.
[Shakespeare: *Love's Labour's Lost* IV. ii.]

13 I had rather hear a brazen canstick
turn'd,
Or a dry wheel grate on the axle-tree;
And that would set my teeth nothing
on edge,
Nothing so much as mincing poetry;
'Tis like the forc'd gait of a shuffling
nag.
[Shakespeare: *I Henry IV* III.i.]

14 Lap me in soft Lydian airs,
Married to immortal verse,
Such as the meeting soul may pierce,
In notes, with many a winding bout
Of linkéd sweetness long drawn out.
[John Milton: *L'Allegro*]

15 These equal syllables alone require,
Tho' oft the ear the open vowels tire,
While expletives their feeble aid do
join,
And ten low words oft creep in one
dull line.
[Alexander Pope: *An Essay on Criticism* II]

16 The fatal facility of the octosyllabic verse. [Byron: Preface to *The Corsair*]

17 The rise
And long roll of the Hexameter.

[Tennyson: *Lucretius*]
1 Writing free verse is like playing tennis with the net down. [Robert Frost: in an address, May 17, 1935]
2 VERS LIBRE: A device for making poetry easier to write and harder to read. [H. L. Mencken: *A Book of Burlesques*]

POETRY: suggests more than it states
3 Poetry gives most pleasure when only generally and not perfectly understood. [Coleridge: *Notebooks*]
4 We hate poetry that has a palpable design upon us—and if we do not agree, seems to put its hand in its breeches pocket. Poetry should be grand and unobtrusive, a thing which enters into one's soul, and does not startle or amaze it with itself, but with its subject. [Keats: Letter to J. H. Reynolds, Feb. 3, 1818]
5 Like a piece of ice on a hot stove the poem must ride on its own melting. [Robert Frost: Preface to *Collected Works*]
6 Poetry has nothing to do with the intellect: it is, in fact, a violent and irreconcilable enemy to the intellect. Its purpose is not to establish facts, but to evade and deny them. [H. L. Mencken: *Prejudices: Sixth Series* (1927)]
7 There should always be an enigma in poetry. [Jules Huret: *Enquête sur L'évolution littéraire*]
8 A poet dares be just so clear and no clearer; he approaches lucid ground warily, like a mariner who is determined not to scrape his bottom on anything solid. A poet's pleasure is to withhold a little of his meaning, to intensify by mystification. He unzips the veil from beauty, but does not remove it. A poet utterly clear is a trifle glaring. [E. B. White: *One Man's Meat*]

POETRY: its uses
9 Poetry is finer and more philosophical than history; for poetry expresses the universal, and history only the particular. [Aristotle: *Poetics* IX]
10 O divine and mighty power of poetry, thou rescuest all things from the grasp of death, and biddest the mortal hero live to all time. [Lucan: *Pharsalia* IX]

11 And as imagination bodies forth
The forms of things unknown, the poet's pen
Turns them to shapes and gives to airy nothing
A local habitation and a name.
[Shakespeare: *A Midsummer Night's Dream* V.i.]
12 A verse may find him who a sermon flies,
And turn delight into a sacrifice.
[George Herbert: *The Church Porch*]
13 Delight is the chief if not the only end of poesy: instruction can be admitted but in the second place, for poetry only instructs as it delights. [Dryden: *An Essay of Dramatic Poesy*]
14 Poetry cannot be translated; and, therefore, it is the poets that preserve the languages. [Samuel Johnson: in Boswell's *Life* (1776)]
15 The principal object proposed in these poems was to choose incidents and situations from common life and to relate or describe them throughout, as far as was possible, in a selection of language really used by men and, at the same time, to throw over them a certain coloring of imagination whereby ordinary things should be presented to the mind in an unusual aspect; and . . . above all, to make these incidents and situations interesting by tracing in them . . . the primary laws of our nature. [Wordsworth: Preface to *The Lyrical Ballads*]
16 . . . the great end
Of poesy . . . should be a friend
To soothe the cares, and lift the thoughts of man.
[Keats: *Sleep and Poetry*]
17 Poetry does not consist in saying everything, but in making one dream everything. [Sainte-Beuve: *Causeries du Lundi,* "Raphael"]
18 But, for the unquiet heart and brain,
A use in measured language lies;
The sad mechanic exercise,
Like dull narcotics, numbing pain.
[Tennyson: *In Memoriam* V]
19 The noble and profound application of ideas to life is the most essential part of poetic greatness. [Matthew Arnold: *Essays in Criticism: Second Series,* "Wordsworth"]

POETRY: miscellaneous

1 It is indignation that leads to the writing of poetry. [Juvenal: *Satires* I]

2 But since the world with writing is possest,
I'll versify in spite; and do my best
To make as much waste-paper as the rest.
[Juvenal: *Satires* I (trans. Dryden)]

3 And strictly meditate the thankless Muse.
[John Milton: *Lycidas*]

4 He touch'd the tender stops of various quills,
With eager thought warbling his Doric lay.
[John Milton: *Lycidas*]

5 Poetry . . . simple, sensuous, and passionate. [John Milton: *Tractate of Education*]

6 The first happiness of the poet's imagination is properly invention, or finding of the thought; the second is fancy, or the variation, deriving or molding of that thought as the judgment represents it proper to the subject; the third is elocution, or the art of clothing and adorning that thought so found and varied, in apt, significant and sounding words. [Dryden: *Annus Mirabilis*]

7 There's no second-rate in poetry. [John Oldham: *An Ode on St. Cecilia's Day*]

8 Made poetry a mere mechanic art. [William Cowper: *Table Talk*]
The reference is to Alexander Pope.

9 Poetry and Truth. [Goethe: title of his autobiography]
The German is Dichtung und Wahrheit.

10 The moving accident is not my trade;
To freeze the blood I have no ready arts:
'Tis my delight, alone in summer shade,
To pipe a simple song for thinking hearts.
[Wordsworth: *Hart-leap Well* II]

11 Nothing so difficult as a beginning
In poesy, unless perhaps the end.
[Byron: *Don Juan* IV.i.]

12 Most wretched men
Are cradled into poetry by wrong;
They learn in suffering what they teach in song.
[Shelley: *Julian and Maddalo*]

13 I consider poetry very subordinate to moral and political science. [Shelley: Letter to Thomas L. Peacock, 1819]

14 Much have I travelled in the realms of gold,
And many goodly states and kingdoms seen;
Round many western islands have I been
Which bards in fealty to Apollo hold.
[Keats: *On First Looking into Chapman's Homer*]

15 Away! away! for I will fly to thee,
Not charioted by Bacchus and his pards,
But on the viewless wings of poesy.
[Keats: *Ode to a Nightingale*]

16 The poetry of earth is never dead. [Keats: *On the Grasshopper and the Cricket*]

17 If poetry comes not as naturally as the leaves to a tree, it had better not come at all. [Keats: Letter to John Taylor, Feb. 27, 1818]

18 Poetry should surprise by a fine excess, and not by singularity; it should strike the reader as a wording of his own highest thoughts, and appear almost a remembrance. [Keats: Letter to John Taylor, February 27, 1818]
This is so typically "romantic" that the last place one would look for a parallel, almost a pre-statement of it, would be in the writings of Dr. Samuel Johnson. But there it is:
The essence of poetry is invention; such invention as, by producing something unexpected, surprises and delights. Life of Waller

19 I do but sing because I must,
And pipe but as the linnets sing.
[Tennyson: *In Memoriam* XXI]

20 I love the old melodious lays
Which softly melt the ages through,
The songs of Spenser's golden days,
Arcadian Sidney's silver phrase,
Sprinkling our noon of time with freshest morning dew.
[J. G. Whittier: *Proem*]

21 I hold that a long poem does not exist. I maintain that the phrase, "a long poem" is simply a flat contradiction in terms. [Edgar Allan Poe: *The Poetic Principle*]

1 The works of the great poets have never yet been read by mankind, for only great poets can read them. . . . [Thoreau: *Walden* III "Reading"]
2 I sound my barbaric yawp over the roofs of the world. [Walt Whitman: *Leaves of Grass*, "Song of Myself"]
3 A poetry of revolt against moral ideas is a poetry of revolt against life; a poetry of indifference towards moral ideas is a poetry of indifference towards life. [Matthew Arnold: *Essays in Criticism: Second Series*, "Wordsworth"]
4 In poetry, as a criticism of life under the conditions fixed for such a criticism by the laws of poetic truth and poetic beauty, the spirit of our race will find . . . as time goes on and as other hopes fail, its consolation and stay. [Matthew Arnold: *Essays in Criticism: Second Series*, "The Study of Poetry"]
5 Indeed there can be no more useful help for discovering what poetry belongs to the class of the truly excellent, and can therefore do us most good, than to have always in one's mind lines and expressions of the great masters, and to apply them as a touchstone to other poetry. [Matthew Arnold: *Essays in Criticism: Second Series*, "The Study of Poetry"]
6 . . . the grand style arises in poetry, *when a noble nature, poetically gifted, treats with simplicity or with severity a serious subject.* [Matthew Arnold: *On Translating Homer: Last Words*]
7 And while the great and wise decay, And all their trophies pass away,
Some sudden thought, some careless rhyme,
Still floats above the wrecks of Time. [W. E. H. Lecky: *On an Old Song*]
8 Its [poetry's] essential character lies in its bold flouting of what every reflective adult knows to be the truth. [H. L. Mencken: in *Smart Set*, June 1920]

POINT
9 Not to put too fine a point upon it. [Dickens: *Bleak House* XXXII]
10 I know no point to which she sticks; She begs the simplest questions. [Alfred Cochrane: *Upon Lesbia Arguing*]

POINT OF VIEW
11 The least change in our point of view gives the whole world a pictorial air. A man who seldom rides needs only to get into a coach and traverse his own town, to turn the street into a puppet-show. [Emerson: *Nature*]
12 Two men look out through the same bars:
One sees the mud, and one the stars. [Frederick Langbridge: *Pessimist and Optimist*]

POISON
13 In poison there is physic. [Shakespeare: *II Henry IV* I.i.]
14 Alcohol, hashish, prussic acid, strychnine, are weak dilutions: the surest poison is time. [Emerson: *Society and Solitude*, "Old Age"]

POLICEMAN
15 A policeman's lot is not a happy one. [W. S. Gilbert: *The Pirates of Penzance* II]

POLITENESS
16 Politeness and good-breeding are absolutely necessary to adorn any, or all other good qualities or talents. . . . The scholar, without good-breeding, is a pedant; the philosopher, a cynic; the soldier, a brute; and every man disagreeable. [Lord Chesterfield: *Letters to His Son*, October 9, 1747]
17 Politeness is fictitious benevolence. [Samuel Johnson: in Boswell's *Tour to the Hebrides*, August 21, 1773]
18 Aristocratic drawing-rooms are pleasant to refer to after one has left them, but that is all; mere politeness is worth nothing save on first acquaintance. [Stendhal: *The Red and the Black* II. xi.]
19 There is an old story of a punctiliously polite Greek, who, while performing the funeral of an infant daughter, felt bound to make his excuses to the spectators for "bringing out such a ridiculously small corpse to so large a crowd." [Thomas Anstey Guthrie ("F.

Anstey") (1856-1934): Preface to *Vice Versa, or a Lesson to Fathers*]

1 If we treat people too long with that pretended liking called politeness, we shall find it hard not to like them in the end. [Logan Pearsall Smith: *Afterthoughts*]

POLITICAL ASPIRANT

2 The saddest life is that of a political aspirant under democracy. His failure is ignominious and his success is disgraceful. [H. L. Mencken: in the *Baltimore Evening Sun*, Dec. 9, 1929]

3 I do not choose to run. [Calvin Coolidge, statement to the press, August 2, 1927]

> *Coolidge's statement certainly lacked the force of General Sherman's "If nominated I will not run; if elected, I will not serve" (1884). These were not Sherman's exact words, but the public preferred this form as expressing the refusal more vigorously.*
>
> *Coolidge's wording left the possibility that he might be persuaded to accept a draft, but if he was being coy, he overdid it; there was no draft. These famous words were very popular on jalopies in the days when it was fashionable among collegiate wits to decorate their cars with humorous inscriptions.*

POLITICIAN(S)

4 A politician . . . one that would circumvent God.
[Shakespeare: *Hamlet* V.i.]

5   Get thee glass eyes;
And, like a scurvy politician, seem
To see the things thou dost not.
[Shakespeare: *King Lear* IV.vi.]

6 For politicians neither love nor hate.
[Dryden: *Absalom and Achitophel* I]

7 In friendship false, implacable in hate,
Resolv'd to ruin or to rule the state.
[Dryden: *Absalom and Achitophel* I]

8 He gave it for his opinion, "that whoever could make two ears of corn, or two blades of grass, to grow upon a spot of ground where only one grew before, would deserve better of mankind, and do more essential service to his country, than the whole race of politicians put together." [Jonathan Swift:

Gulliver's Travels II]

9 An honest politician is one who, when he is bought, will stay bought. [Attr. Simon Cameron, Republican Boss of Pennsylvania (1860)]

10 The proper memory for a politician is one that knows what to remember and what to forget. [John, Viscount Morley: *Recollections* II]

11 Idealism is the noble toga that political gentlemen drape over their will to power. [Aldous Huxley: *New York Herald Tribune*, Nov. 24, 1963]

POLITICS

12 The good of man must be the end of the science of politics. [Aristotle: *The Nicomachean Ethics* I.ii.]

13 Politics and philosophy are alike. Socrates neither set out benches for his students, nor sat on a platform, nor set hours for his lectures. He was philosophizing all the time—while he was joking, while he was drinking, while he was soldiering, whenever he met you on the street, and at the end when he was in prison and drinking the poison. He was the first to show that all your life, all the time, in everything you do, whatever you are doing, is the time for philosophy. And so also it is of politics. [Plutarch: *Old Men in Public Affairs*]

14 The greatest virtue in a prince is to know his friends. [Martial: *Epigrams* VIII.xv.]

15 Politics, as the word is commonly understood, are nothing but corruptions. [Jonathan Swift: *Thoughts on Various Subjects*]

16 All political parties die at last of swallowing their own lies. [John Arbuthnot: *Epigram* (1735)]

17 In politics there is no honour. [Benjamin Disraeli: *Vivian Gray* IV.i.]

18 The word *right* should be excluded from political language, as the word *cause* from the language of philosophy. Both are theological and metaphysical conceptions; and the former is as immoral and subversive as the latter is unmeaning and sophistical. [Auguste Comte: *Catéchisme positiviste*]

19 The results of political changes are hardly ever those which their friends hope or their foes fear. [T. H. Huxley:

Government]
1 Politics makes strange bedfellows. [Charles Dudley Warner: *My Summer in a Garden*]
2 If the conscience of an honest man lays down stern rules, so also does the art of politics. At a juncture where no accommodation is possible between the two, the politician may be faced by these alternatives: "Shall I break the rules of my art in order to save my private honour? or shall I break the rules of my conscience in order to fulfil my public trust?" [F. S. Oliver: *The Endless Adventure*]
3 POLITICS. The conduct of public affairs for private advantage. [Ambrose Bierce: *The Devil's Dictionary*]
4 Politics consists wholly of a succession of unintelligent crazes, many of them so idiotic that they exist only as battle-cries and shibboleths and are not reducible to logical statement at all. [H. L. Mencken: *Prejudices: Third Series*]
5 The whole aim of practical politics is to keep the populace alarmed (and hence clamorous to be led to safety) by an endless series of hobgoblins. [H. L. Mencken: *In Defense of Women*]
6 You cannot adopt politics as a profession and remain honest. [Louis McHenry Howe, address, Jan. 17, 1933]
> *Howe was secretary to President Franklin D. Roosevelt.*

7 What is politics but persuading the public to vote for this and support that and endure these for the promise of those? [Gilbert Highet: "The Art of Persuasion," *Vogue,* Jan., 1951]
8 Politics are too serious a matter to be left to the politicians. [Charles De Gaulle, in a letter quoted by Clement Attlee in his *Twilight of Empire* (1962)]
> *De Gaulle was extending Clemenceau's dictum that war was too important to be entrusted to generals.*

POLYGAMY

9 Polygamy may well be held in dread, Not only as a sin, but as a bore. [Byron: *Don Juan* VI.xii.]
10 There was an old party of Lyme, Who married three wives at one time. When asked, "Why the third?"

He replied, "One's absurd, And bigamy, sir, is a crime!" [William Cosmo Monkhouse: *Limerick*]

POMP

11 Pomp and circumstance. [Shakespeare: *Othello* III.iii.]
12 Lo, all our pomp of yesterday Is one with Nineveh and Tyre! [Kipling: *Recessional* (1897)]
> *Nineveh was the last capital of the Assyrian Empire. Tyre was a seaport of Phoenicia. They are both mentioned in the Bible and, together, serve as symbols of great power now departed.*

POMPADOUR

13 Madame has a bad day for her journey. [Louis XV of France (1715-74): as, from his window, he watched the funeral cortege of Mme. de Pompadour]
> *One of the most pathetic of historical utterances. Fed on spicy historical fiction, the modern reader assumes that kings of old lived in open profligacy. But that was rarely the case. Royal mistresses were either concealed completely or attached to the court as ladies-in-waiting, and the most elaborate mummery was gone through to preserve the fiction of their status. Voltaire got into serious trouble for even mentioning Louis XV and Mme. de Pompadour in the same poem. Etiquette did not permit Louis to attend Mme. de Pompadour's funeral.*

POOR

14 Grind the faces of the poor. [Isaiah 3:15]
15 He that hath pity upon the poor lendeth unto the Lord. [Proverbs 19:17]
16 For ye have the poor always with you. [Matthew 26:11]
17 For the poor always ye have with you. [John 12:8]
18 Poor and content is rich and rich enough,
But riches fineless is as poor as winter
To him that ever fears he shall be poor.
[Shakespeare: *Romeo and Juliet* V.i.]
fineless = *limitless, boundless*
19 Poor but honest. [Shakespeare: *All's Well That Ends Well* I.iii.]

1 There is none poor but such as God hates. [James Howell: *Proverbs* (1659)]

> *Here the meaning is: There is no real poverty so long as piety secures the love of God.*

2 The short and simple annals of the poor.
[Thomas Gray: *Elegy Written in a Country Churchyard*]

3 Nobody has occasion for pride but the poor; everywhere else it is a sign of folly. [Thomas Gray: Letter to Thomas Warton, October 18, 1753]

4 The murmuring poor, who will not fast in peace.
[George Crabbe: *The Newspaper*]

5 A poor man stinks, and God hates him. [Willa Cather: *My Mortal Enemy* II]

> *The sentence is spoken by John Driscoll, threatening to cut off his daughter Myra if she marries a penniless man whom Driscoll detests. Driscoll's statement is a perversion of a very old proverb: He is poor indeed whom God hates (Thomas Fuller [1654-1734]: Gnomologia [1732]. It is recorded a century before even that in English, and is known in French back to 1550. The meaning was that God's displeasure would outweigh all earthly gain. There was a companion saying: He is rich indeed whom God loves.*

POORHOUSE

6 Over the hill to the poor-house I'm trudgin' my weary way.
[Will Carleton: *Over the Hill to the Poor-house*]

POOR RELATION(S)

7 Like some poor nigh-related guest,
That may not rudely be dismissed,
Yet hath outstayed his welcome while,
And tells the jest without the smile.
[Coleridge: *Youth and Age*]

8 A poor relation is the most irrelevant thing in nature. [Charles Lamb: *Poor Relations*]

9 A poor relation is an odious approximation—a preposterous shadow, lengthening in the noontide of your prosperity—an unwelcome remembrancer—a rebuke to your rising—a stain in your blood, a blot on your 'scutcheon—a rent in your garment—a death's head at your banquet—a lion in your path—a frog in your chamber—a fly in your ointment—a mote in your eye—a triumph to your enemy—an apology to your friends—the one thing not needful—the hail in harvest—the ounce of sour in a pound of sweet. [Charles Lamb: *Poor Relations*]

10 He calleth you by your Christian name, to imply that his other is the same with your own. He is too familiar by half, yet you wish he had less diffidence. With half the familiarity, he might pass for a casual dependent; with more boldness, he would be in no danger of being taken for what he is. [Charles Lamb: *Poor Relations*]

POPE

11 POPE ELOPES
[Attr. Dorothy Parker]

> *Said to be Miss Parker's prize-winning entry in an Algonquin Round-Table contest for the most sensational conceivable headline. Another wit, not content with perfection, felt the addition of WITH MARIE STOPES would be an improvement.*

POPE, ALEXANDER, AND DRYDEN, JOHN

12 In Pope I cannot read a line,
But with a sigh I wish it mine;
When he can in one couplet fix
More sense than I can do in six,
It gives me such a jealous fit,
I cry, "Pox take him and his wit!"
[Jonathan Swift: *On the Death of Dr. Swift*]

13 I told him that Voltaire . . . had distinguished Pope and Dryden thus:— "Pope drives a handsome chariot, with a couple of neat trim nags; Dryden a coach and six stately horses." JOHNSON, "Why, Sir, the truth is, they both drive coaches and six; but Dryden's horses are either galloping or stumbling: Pope's go at a steady even trot." [Boswell's *Life*, February, 1766]

> *In his Life of Pope Johnson says: "The style of Dryden is capricious and varied, that of Pope is cautious and uniform; Dryden obeys the motions of his own mind, Pope constrains his mind to his own rules of composition. Dryden is*

sometimes vehement and rapid; Pope is always smooth, uniform, and gentle."

1 We are to regard Dryden as the puissant and glorious founder, Pope as the splendid high priest, of our age of prose and reason, of our excellent and indispensable eighteenth-century. [Matthew Arnold: *Essays in Criticism: Second Series,* "The Study of Poetry"]

POPPIES

2 But pleasures are like poppies spread—
You seize the flow'r, its bloom is shed.
[Burns: *Tam o' Shanter*]

3 In Flanders fields the poppies blow
Between the crosses, row on row.
[John McCrae: *In Flanders Fields*]

POPULACE

4 The mutable, rank-scented many.
[Shakespeare: *Coriolanus* III.i.]

5 You common cry of curs! whose breath I hate.
[Shakespeare: *Coriolanus* III.iii.]

6 This common body,
Like to a vagabond flag upon the stream,
Goes to and back, lackeying the varying tide,
To rot itself with motion.
[Shakespeare: *Antony and Cleopatra* I. iv.]

flag = *rush;* lackeying = *following closely, like a lackey*

The image is based on a tidal river. Shakespeare spent most of his life in close contact with two tidal rivers, the Avon and the Thames, and the idea that rivers flowed two different ways every day seems to have been taken for granted in his unconscious mind.

7 The inertia, the indifference, the insubordination and instinctive hostility of the mass of mankind. [H. G. Wells: *The Research Magnificent*]

POPULARITY

8 Enfeoff'd himself to popularity.
[Shakespeare: *I Henry IV* III.ii.]

9 A habitation giddy and unsure
Hath he that buildeth on the vulgar heart.
[Shakespeare: *II Henry IV* I.iii.]

vulgar = *common*

10 Popularity is a crime from the moment it is sought; it is only a virtue when men have it whether they will or not. [George Savile (Marquis of Halifax): *Miscellaneous Reflections*]

11 I have heard you mentioned as a man whom everybody likes. I think life has little more to give. [Samuel Johnson: to James Boswell, in a letter, July 3, 1778]

12 The love of popularity is the love of being beloved. [William Shenstone: *Of Men and Manners*]

POPULATION

13 Population, when unchecked, increases in a geometrical ratio. Subsistence only increases in an arithmetical ratio. [T. R. Malthus: *The Principle of Population* I]

14 If government knew how, I should like to see it check, not multiply the population. [Emerson: *The Conduct of Life* VII]

PORPOISE

15 "Will you walk a little faster?" said a whiting to a snail,
"There's a porpoise close behind us, and he's treading on my tail."
[Lewis Carroll: *Alice's Adventures in Wonderland* X]

POSSIBILITIES

16 It is a most mortifying reflection for a man to consider what he has done, compared to what he might have done. [Samuel Johnson: in Boswell's *Life* (1770)]

POSTERITY

17 Posterity gives every man his true value. [Tacitus: *Annals* IV]

Certainly many an inflated reputation has shrunk after the great one's death but since the reputation of many men has changed again and again in the course of time, who shall decide what moment constitutes posterity? The 18th century saw Cromwell, for instance, as a villain; the 20th sees him more as a hero. The Middle Ages revered Vergil, in part, as a necromancer. Richard III, time's chiefest villain, is now in the process of being deodorized. Posterity is merely a later present and, like all presents, sets its own values—and all are subject to change.

1 The care of Posterity is most in them that have no Posterity. [Francis Bacon: *Of Parents and Children*]

2 We are always doing, says he, something for posterity, but I would fain see Posterity do something for us. [Joseph Addison: *The Spectator* No. 583 (1712)] he = *is described as "an old fellow of a college."*

The drollery has been much repeated and various wits are credited with it, especially Sir Boyle Roche, in a speech in the Irish Parliament in 1780. But Addison's is the earliest known statement of it, and it has an Addisonian flavor.

3 What has posterity done for us? [John Trumbull: *McFingal* II]

4 Posterity is just around the corner. [Kaufman and Ryskind: *Of Thee I Sing* II.iii.(1931)]

POSTSCRIPT

5 I knew one that when he wrote a letter he would put that which was most material in the postscript, as if it had been a by-matter. [Francis Bacon: *Of Cunning*]

6 A woman seldom writes her mind but in her postscript. [Richard Steele: *The Spectator* No. 79]

POTENTIALITY

7 Perhaps in this neglected spot is laid
Some heart once pregnant with celestial fire;
Hands, that the rod of empire might have swayed,
Or waked to ecstasy the living lyre.
[Thomas Gray: *Elegy Written in a Country Churchyard*]

POUND OF FLESH

8 The pound of flesh.
[Shakespeare: *The Merchant of Venice* IV.i.]

POVERTY: its advantages

9 A pore man, that bereth no richesse on him by the weye, may boldely singe biforn theves. [Chaucer: *Boethius* II.v.]

The observation was made in antiquity by Juvenal and Seneca, and repeated by assorted philosophers since. The well-to-do have always stressed this as one of the advantages of poverty, but no poor man has ever derived comfort from the reflection that he couldn't be robbed.

10 Poverty in youth, when it succeeds, is so far magnificent that it turns the whole will towards effort, and the whole soul towards aspiration. Poverty strips the material life entirely bare, and makes it hideous; thence arise inexpressible yearnings towards the ideal life. [Victor Hugo: *Les Misérables* V.iii.]

11 Poverty keeps together more homes than it breaks up. [H. H. Munro ("Saki"): *The Chronicles of Clovis*, "Esmé"]

POVERTY: some definitions

12 It is not the man who has little, but he who desires more, that is poor. [Seneca: *Ad Lucilium*]

13 Poverty is the Muse's patrimony. [Robert Burton: *Anatomy of Melancholy* I.2.3.15]

14 There is no man so poor but what he can afford to keep one dog. And I have seen them so poor that they could afford to keep three. [Josh Billings: *On Poverty*]

15 Poverty is the strenuous life—without brass bands, or uniforms. [William James: *The Varieties of Religious Experience* XIV]

This isn't quite what Theodore Roosevelt meant by "the strenuous life" but he would have had a better mind if it had been.

16 Poverty is the openmouthed relentless hell which yawns beneath civilized society. [Henry George: *Progress and Poverty* IX]

POVERTY: its miseries

17 They do not easily rise whose abilities are repressed by poverty at home. [Juvenal: *Satires* III]

Samuel Johnson's London *(1738), an imitation of this satire, renders this line:* SLOW RISES WORTH, BY POVERTY DEPREST. *Johnson felt the sentiment so strongly that he put the entire line in capitals.*

18 If thou be poure, thy brother hateth thee,

And alle thy freendes fleen fro thee, alas!
[Chaucer: Prologue to *The Man of Law's Tale*]

1 Right so as by richesses ther comen manye goodes, right so by poverte come ther manye harmes and yveles. [Chaucer: *The Tale of Melibeus*]

2 The devil dances in an empty pocket. [15th-century proverb]
That is, the poor are always subject to temptation.

3 There is no virtue that poverty destroyeth not. [John Florio: *Firste Fruites* XXXII]

4 Poverty is no vice, but an inconvenience. [John Florio: *Second Fruites* CV]

5 All crimes are safe but hated poverty. This, only this, the rigid law pursues. [Samuel Johnson: *London*]

6 In the prospect of poverty there is nothing but gloom and melancholy; the mind and body suffer together; its miseries bring no alleviations; it is a state in which every virtue is obscured, and in which no conduct can avoid reproach; a state in which cheerfulness is insensibility, and dejection sullenness, of which the hardships are without honor, and the labors without reward. [Samuel Johnson: *The Rambler* No. 53]

7 Kindness is generally reciprocal; we are desirous of pleasing others because we receive pleasure from them; but by what means can the man please whose attention is engrossed by his distresses and who has no leisure to be officious; whose will is restrained by his necessities and who has no power to confer benefits; whose temper is perhaps vitiated by misery, and whose understanding is impeded by ignorance? [Samuel Johnson: *The Rambler* No. 166]
officious = helpful

8 Poverty is a great enemy to human happiness; it certainly destroys liberty, and it makes some virtues impracticable, and others extremely difficult. [Samuel Johnson: in Boswell's *Life*, Dec. 7, 1782]

9 All the arguments which are brought to represent poverty as no evil show it to be evidently a great evil. You never find people laboring to convince you that you may live very happily with a plentiful fortune. [Samuel Johnson: in Boswell's *Life*, July 20, 1763]

10 Chill Penury repressed their noble rage,
And froze the genial current of the soul.
[Thomas Gray: *Elegy Written in a Country Churchyard*]

11 To be poor and independent is very nearly an impossibility. [William Cobbett: *Advice to Young Men*, "To a Young Man"]

12 Rattle his bones over the stones;
He's only a pauper whom nobody owns!
[Thomas Noel: *The Pauper's Drive*]

13 Poverty is a soft pedal upon all branches of human activity, not excepting the spiritual. [H. L. Mencken: *A Book of Prefaces* IV]

POVERTY: its shame

14 The poor man's wisdom is despised, and his words are not heard. [Ecclesiastes 9:16]

15 The shame and avoidance of poverty. [Horace: *Epistles* I.xviii.]

16 Cheerless poverty has no harder trial than this, that it makes men the subject of ridicule. [Juvenal: *Satires* III]
Samuel Johnson, whose poem London *(1738) was an imitation of this satire of Juvenal's, enlarges this passage:*
Of all the griefs that harass the Distrest,
Sure the most bitter is a scornful Jest;
Fate never wounds more deep the gen'rous Heart
Than when a Blockhead's Insult points the Dart.

17 Poverty is not a shame, but the being ashamed of it is. [Thomas Fuller (1654-1734): *Gnomologia*]

18 It is the fate of those who toil at the lower employments of life to be rather driven by the fear of evil than attracted by the prospect of good; to be exposed to censure without hope of praise; to be disgraced by miscarriage, or punished for neglect, where success would have been without applause, and diligence without reward. [Samuel Johnson: Preface to the *Dictionary*]

1 A poor man has no honour. [Samuel Johnson: in Boswell's *Life,* Sept. 22, 1777]

2 It's no disgrace t' be poor, but it might as well be. [Frank McKinney (Kin) Hubbard: *Abe Martin's Sayings and Sketches*]

POVERTY: miscellaneous

3 As poor as Job.
Job was a proverb for poverty as early as 1300. "As poor as Job's turkey" was an American 18th or 19th-century improvement. Turkeys were scavengers and Job's turkey would have had few leftovers. Poor in the American proverb carried also the meaning of "scrawny," "sickly," "emaciated," "feeble."

4 My poverty, but not my will, consents. [Shakespeare: *Romeo and Juliet* V.i.]

5 I can get no remedy against this consumption of the purse: borrowing only lingers and lingers it out, but the disease is incurable. [Shakespeare: *II Henry IV* I.ii.]

6 Poor naked wretches, wheresoe'er
  you are,
That bide the pelting of this pitiless
  storm,
How shall your houseless heads and
  unfed sides,
Your looped and windowed ragged-
  ness, defend you
From seasons such as these?
[Shakespeare: *King Lear* III.iv.]

7 Poverty has, in large cities, very different appearances: it is often concealed in splendor, and often in extravagance. [Samuel Johnson: *Rasselas* XXV]

8 Let not Ambition mock their useful
  toil,
Their homely joys, and destiny obscure;
Nor Grandeur hear with a disdainful
  smile
The short and simple annals of the
  poor.
[Thomas Gray: *Elegy Written in a Country Churchyard*]

9 A man may tak a neibor's part,
Yet hae nae cash to spare him.
[Burns: *Epistle to a Young Friend*]

10 O God! that bread should be so dear,
And flesh and blood so cheap!
[Thomas Hood: *The Song of the Shirt*]

11 I see one-third of a nation ill-housed, ill-clad, ill-nourished. [Franklin Delano Roosevelt: *Second Inaugural Address,* January 20, 1937]
  . . . that the majority of the people of England are destitute and miserable, ill-clothed, ill-fed, ill-educated.
  —*Shelley:* A Philosophical View of Reform *XI*

POWDER

12 Trust in God and keep your powder dry. [Oliver Cromwell: to his troops as they were about to cross a stream to attack the enemy]
  The popular version is that given above. Older versions varied but were a little longer: "Put your trust in God, my boys . . ." and ". . . but mind to keep your powder dry." The combination of piety and practicality tickled the fancy of a nation of shopkeepers. Some say the famous words were spoken at the Battle of Edgehill (Oct. 23, 1642), but nothing about the saying is absolutely certain.

POWER

13 Power is more retained by wary measures than by daring counsels. [Tacitus: *Annals* XI]

14 Nothing is so weak and unstable as a reputation for power not based on force. [Tacitus: *Annals* XIX]

15 He who makes another powerful ruins himself, for he makes the other so either by shrewdness or force, and both of these qualities are feared by the one who becomes powerful. [Machiavelli: *The Prince* III]

16 It is a strange desire, to seek power, and to lose liberty; or to seek power over others, and to lose power over a man's self. [Francis Bacon: *Of Great Place*]

17 It is a miserable state of mind to have few things to desire, and many things to fear. [Francis Bacon: *Of Empire*]

18 Power, like lightning, injures before its warning. [Calderón: *Gustos y Disgustos son no mas que Imaginacion* I.xvii.]

19 Power is always gradually stealing away from the many to the few, because the few are more vigilant and consistent.

[Samuel Johnson: *The Adventurer* No. 45]

1 I am more and more convinced that man is a dangerous creature; and that power, whether vested in many or a few, is ever grasping, and like the grave, cries "Give, give!" [Abigail Adams, letter to John Adams, Nov. 27, 1775]

2 To know the pains of power, we must go to those who have it; to know its pleasures, we must go to those who are seeking it: the pains of power are real, its pleasures imaginary. [C. C. Colton: *Lacon*]

3 The awful shadow of some unseen Power
Floats, tho' unseen, amongst us.
[Shelley: *Hymn to Intellectual Beauty*]

4 Self-reverence, self-knowledge, self-control,
These three alone lead life to sovereign power.
[Tennyson: *Oenone*]

5 The only prize much cared for by the powerful is power. The prize of the general is not a bigger tent, but command. [O. W. Holmes, Jr.: *Law and the Court*]

6 Admiral Pip directly went
To the Lord at the head of the Government,
Who made him, by a stroke of the quill,
Baron de Pippe, of Pippetonneville.
[W. S. Gilbert: *Bab Ballads,* "The Three Kings of Chickeraboo"]

7 Wherever I found a living creature, there I found the will to power. [Nietzsche: *Thus Spake Zarathustra*]

POWER: corrupts

8 The lust for power, for dominating others, inflames the heart more than any other passion. [Tacitus: *Annals* XV. liii.]

9 Every wand or staff of empire is curved at the top. [Francis Bacon: *De Sapientia Veterum,* "Pan, sive Natura"]
From the shepherd's crook to the bishop's crozier.

10 Then everything includes itself in power,
Power into will, will into appetite;
And appetite, an universal wolf,
So doubly seconded with will and power,

Must make perforce an universal prey,
And last eat up himself.
[Shakespeare: *Troilus and Cressida* I.iii.]

11 Unlimited power is apt to corrupt the minds of those who possess it. [William Pitt (Earl of Chatham): in a speech, House of Lords, January 9, 1770]

12 Power gradually extirpates from the mind every humane and gentle virtue. [Edmund Burke: *A Vindication of Natural Society*]

13 It is impossible to reign innocently. [Antoine Saint-Just: the opening words of his speech on the sentencing of Louis XVI to death (1793)]
The "archangel of the Revolution," Saint-Just, as President of the Convention, took over, with Robespierre, the reign of France. A year later, he was adjudged not to have done so innocently and was guillotined.

14 Power, like a desolating pestilence,
Pollutes whate'er it touches.
[Shelley: *Queen Mab* III]

15 Power tends to corrupt; absolute power corrupts absolutely. [Lord Acton (John Emerich Dalberg): in a letter to Bishop Mandell Creighton (1887)]

POWERFUL

16 They who are in highest places, and have the most power, have the least liberty, because they are most observed. [John Tillotson: *Reflections*]

PRACTICE

17 If a man that is not perfect be ever in practice, he shall as well practice his errors as his abilities and induce one habit of both; and there is no means to help this but by seasonable intermissions. [Francis Bacon: *Of Nature in Men*]

PRACTICE WHAT YOU PREACH

18 We must practise what we preach. [Sir Roger L'Estrange: *Seneca's Morals* II (1680)]
The idea is ancient and universal. The most common modern form is: Practice what you preach.

19 That we should practise what we preach is generally admitted; but anyone who preaches what he and his hearers

practise must incur the gravest moral disapprobation. [Logan Pearsall Smith: *Afterthoughts*]

PRAIRIE
1 The immeasurable yearning of all flat lands. [Willa Cather: *The Song of the Lark* II.v.]

PRAISE
2 Praise from a friend, or censure from a foe,
Are lost on hearers that our merits know.
[Homer: *Iliad* (trans. Alexander Pope)]
3 Let another man praise thee, and not thine own mouth. [Proverbs 27:2]
4 Let us now praise famous men, and our fathers that begat us. [Ecclesiasticus 44:1]
5 O all ye Green Things upon the Earth, bless ye the Lord: praise him, and magnify him for ever. [*The Book of Common Prayer*, "Morning Prayer"]
6 We are all excited by the love of praise, and it is the noblest spirits that feel it most. [Cicero: *Pro Archia*]
7 And Queens hereafter shall be glad to live
Upon the alms of thy superfluous praise.
[Michael Drayton: *Sonnets* VI, "Idea"]
8 Praises, of whose taste the wise are fond.
[Shakespeare: *Richard II* II.i.]
9 If all the world
Should in a pet of temp'rance, feed on pulse,
Drink the clear stream, and nothing wear but frieze,
Th' All-giver would be unthank'd, would be unprais'd.
[John Milton: *Comus*]
10 We participate, in a sense, in noble deeds when we praise them sincerely. [La Rochefoucauld: *Maxims*]
11 O, let our voice His praise exalt
Till it arrive at Heaven's vault,
Which thence (perhaps) rebounding may
Echo beyond the Mexique bay!
[Andrew Marvell: *Bermudas*]
12 Praise God, from whom all blessings flow,
Praise Him, all creatures here below.

[Bishop Thomas Ken: *Morning and Evening Hymn*]
13 Praise makes good men better and bad men worse. [Thomas Fuller (1654-1734): *Gnomologia*]
14 He is not good himself, who speaks well of every body alike. [Thomas Fuller (1654-1734): *Gnomologia*]
15 Ye monsters of the bubbling deep,
Your Maker's praises spout;
Up from the sands ye codlings peep,
And wag your tails about.
[Cotton Mather: *Hymn*]
16 Praising all alike is praising none. [John Gay: *Epistles* I]
17 Be thou the first true merit to befriend,
His praise is lost who stays till all commend.
[Alexander Pope: *An Essay on Criticism* II]
18 The highest panegyric . . . that private virtue can receive is the praise of servants. [Samuel Johnson: *The Rambler* No. 68]
19 I would rather praise it than read it. [Samuel Johnson: *Life of Congreve*]
Johnson was alluding to a novel Congreve wrote as a young man—Incognita, or Love and Duty Reconciled. He had not read the book—and had no intention of reading it—but had read praise of it by others.
20 It is a certain sign of mediocrity always to praise moderately. [Vauvenargues: *Réflexions*]
21 Good people all, with one accord,
Lament for Madame Blaize,
Who never wanted a good word—
From those who spoke her praise.
[Oliver Goldsmith: *Elegy on Mrs. Mary Blaize*]
22 Among the smaller duties of life I hardly know any one more important than that of not praising where praise is not due. [Sydney Smith: *Sketches of Moral Philosophy* IX]

PRAISE: faint and excessive
23 Good men hate those who praise them, if they praise them too much. [Euripides: *Iphigenia in Aulis*]
24 It is as great a spite to be praised in the wrong place, and by a wrong person, as can be done to a noble nature. [Ben

Jonson: *Explorata*]
1 Of whom to be dispraised were no small praise.
[John Milton: *Paradise Regained* III.56]
2 He that praiseth publickly, will slander privately. [Thomas Fuller (1654-1734): *Gnomologia*]
3 Faint Praise is Disparagement. [Thomas Fuller (1654-1734): *Gnomologia*]
4 Damn with faint praise, assent with civil leer,
And without sneering, teach the rest to sneer;
Willing to wound, and yet afraid to strike,
Just hint a fault, and hesitate dislike;
Alike reserv'd to blame, or to commend,
A tim'rous foe, and a suspicious friend.
[Alexander Pope: *Epistle to Dr. Arbuthnot*]
5 Praise is like ambergris: a little whiff of it, and by snatches, is very agreeable; but when a man holds a whole lump of it to your nose, it is a stink, and strikes you down. [Alexander Pope: *Thoughts on Various Subjects*]
6 Of praise a mere glutton, he swallow'd what came,
And the puff of a dunce, he mistook it for fame;
Till his relish grown callous, almost to disease,
Who pepper'd the highest was surest to please.
[Oliver Goldsmith: *Retaliation*]
The reference is to Garrick.
7 The praise of a fool is more harmful than his blame. [Florian: *Fables* IV]
8 Praises of the unworthy are felt by ardent minds as robberies of the deserving. [Coleridge: *Biographia Literaria* III]
9 Praise to the face
Is open disgrace.
[V. S. Lean: *Collectanea* (1902-04)]

PRAISE: reciprocal
10 I will praise any man that will praise me.
[Shakespeare: *Antony and Cleopatra* II.vi.]

11 He who discommendeth others obliquely commendeth himself. [Sir Thomas Browne: *Christian Morals* I. xxxiv.]
12 Our heartiest praise is usually reserved for our admirers. [La Rochefoucauld: *Maxims*]
13 It would seldom be a bad bargain to disclaim all praise on condition of receiving no blame. [La Rochefoucauld: *Maxims*]
14 The refusal of praise is a wish to be praised twice. [La Rochefoucauld: *Maxims*]
15 Usually we praise only to be praised. [La Rochefoucauld: *Maxims*]
16 Fondly we think we honor merit then,
When we but praise ourselves in other men.
[Alexander Pope: *An Essay on Criticism* II]

PRAY
17 Nay, that's past praying for.
[Shakespeare: *I Henry IV* II.iv.]
18 At church with meek and unaffected grace,
His looks adorn'd the venerable place;
Truth from his lips prevail'd with double sway,
And fools, who came to scoff, remain'd to pray.
[Oliver Goldsmith: *The Deserted Village*]

PRAYER(S)
19 When thou prayest, thou shalt not be as the hypocrites are: for they love to pray standing in the synagogues and in the corners of the streets, that they may be seen of men. . . . But thou, when thou prayest, enter into thy closet, and when thou hast shut thy door, pray to thy Father which is in secret; and thy Father which seeth in secret shall reward thee openly. [Matthew 6:5-6]
20 The effectual fervent prayer of a righteous man availeth much. [James 5:16]
21 Our prayers should be for a sound mind in a healthy body. [Juvenal: *Satires* X.]
The Latin: Orandum est ut sit mens

sana in corpore sano.

1 The first petition that we are to make to Almighty God is for a good conscience, the next for health of mind, and then of body. [Seneca: *Epistles* XIV]

2 Who-so wal preye, he moot faste and be clene,
And fatte his soule and make his body lene.
[Chaucer: *The Summoner's Tale*]

3 His worst fault is, that he is given to prayer; he is something peevish that way. [Shakespeare: *Merry Wives of Windsor* I.iv.]

4 Bow, stubborn knees! and heart with strings of steel
Be soft as sinews of the new-born babe.
[Shakespeare: *Hamlet* III.iii.]

5 My words fly up, my thoughts remain below:
Words without thoughts never to heaven go.
[Shakespeare: *Hamlet* III.iii.]

6 We, ignorant of ourselves,
Beg often our own harms, which the wise powers
Deny us for our good; so find we profit
By losing of our prayers.
[Shakespeare: *Antony and Cleopatra* II.i.]

7 Now I am past all comforts here, but prayers.
[Shakespeare: *Henry VIII* IV.ii.]

8 In Prayer the Lips ne'er act the winning part
Without the sweet concurrence of the Heart.
[Robert Herrick: *The Heart*]

9 He that will learn to pray, let him go to sea. [George Herbert: *Jacula Prudentum*]
A modern equivalent would be: He that would learn to pray, let him be in a small plane in heavy turbulence.

10 What in me is dark,
Illumine; what is low, raise and support;
That to the height of this great argument
I may assert Eternal Providence,
And justify the ways of God to men.
[John Milton: *Paradise Lost* I.22-26]

11 If by prayer

Incessant I could hope to change the will
Of him who all things can, I would not cease
To weary him with my assiduous cries.
[John Milton: *Paradise Lost* XI. 307-310]

12 Ejaculations are short prayers darted up to God on emergent occasions. [Thomas Fuller (1608-1661): *Good Thoughts in Bad Times*]

13 Pray, madam, let this farce be played. The Archbishop will act it very well. You may bid him be as short as he will. It will do the Queen no hurt, no more than any good; and it will satisfy all the wise and good fools, who will call us all atheists if we don't pretend to be as great fools as they are. [Sir Robert Walpole, Prime Minister: speaking to the Princess Emily, concerning a request that the Archbishop of Canterbury pray for the dying Queen Caroline, consort of King George II]
The report—which is revealing of the coarseness (and honesty) of the Court in the early 18th century—is by Lord Hervey, who was present. It is in Hervey's Memoirs.

14 Gentle Jesus, meek and mild,
Look upon a little child,
Pity my simplicity,
Suffer me to come to Thee.
[Charles Wesley: *Gentle Jesus*]

15 "What is good for a bootless bene?"
With these dark words begins my Tale;
And their meaning is, whence can comfort spring
When Prayer is of no avail?
[Wordsworth: *Force of Prayer*]

16 He prayeth best who loveth best
All things both great and small;
For the dear God who loveth us,
He made and loveth all.
[Coleridge: *The Ancient Mariner* VII]

17 Kneeling in prayer, and not ashamed to pray,
The tumult of the time disconsolate
To inarticulate murmurs dies away,
While the eternal ages watch and wait.
[Longfellow: *Divina Commedia. Prefatory Sonnets*]

1 More things are wrought by prayer
Than this world dreams of.
[Tennyson: *Morte d'Arthur*]
2 Battering the gates of heaven with
storms of prayer.
[Tennyson: *St. Simeon Stylites*]
3 Every prayer reduces itself to this:
"Great God, grant that twice two be not
four." [Ivan Turgeniev: *Prayer*]
4 Who rises from Prayer a better man,
his prayer is answered. [George Meredith: *The Ordeal of Richard Feverel* XII]
5 You can't pray a lie—I found that
out. [Mark Twain: *Huckleberry Finn* XXXI]
6 Onc't there was a little boy wouldn't
say his pray'rs—
An' when he went to bed at night,
away up stairs,
His mammy heerd him holler, an' his
daddy heerd him bawl,
An' when they turn't the kivvers
down, he wasn't there at all!
An' they seeked him in the rafter-
room, an' cubby-hole, an' press,
An' seeked him up the chimbly-flue,
an' ever'wheres, I guess;
But all they ever found was thist his
pants an' roundabout!
An' the Gobble-uns'll git you
Ef you
Don't
Watch
Out!
[James Whitcomb Riley: *Little Orphant Annie*]
7 When the gods wish to punish us
they answer our prayers. [Oscar Wilde:
An Ideal Husband II]
8 Common people do not pray; they
only beg. [G. B. Shaw: *Misalliance*]

PREACHING

9 I told him that I had been that morning at a meeting of the people called
Quakers, where I had heard a woman
preach. JOHNSON. "Sir, a woman's
preaching is like a dog's walking on his
hinder legs. It is not done well; but you
are surprised to find it done at all."
[Samuel Johnson: in Boswell's *Life*, July
31, 1763]
  *There is an apocryphal story of John-
  son's wife coming upon him kissing the
  maid and saying "I am surprised!" and
  his answering "No, madam, I am surprised; you are astonished."
    Those who use the story to illustrate,
  as they assume, the "correct" use of
  surprise might bear this, one of the
  most famous of his authentic sayings,
  in mind.*
10 Hear how he clears the points o'
Faith
Wi' rattlin' an' thumpin'!
Now meekly calm, now wild in
wrath,
He's stampin', an' he's jumpin'!
[Burns: *The Holy Fair*]
  Holy Fair = *revival meeting*
11 Preaching has become a by-word for
long and dull conversation of any kind;
and whoever wishes to imply, in any
piece of writing, the absence of everything agreeable and inviting, calls it a
sermon. [Sydney Smith: in Lady Holland's *Memoir* I.3.]
12 Preach not because you have to say
something, but because you have something to say. [Richard Whately: *Apothegms*]

PRECEDENCE

13 An two men ride of a horse, one must
ride behind.
[Shakespeare: *Much Ado About Noth-
ing* III.v.]
14 The king himself has followed her—
When she has walked before.
[Oliver Goldsmith: *Elegy on Mrs. Mary
Blaize*]
15 Lead the way, and we'll precede.
[Mrs. Malaprop: in Richard Brinsley
Sheridan's *The Rivals* V.i.]

PRECEDENCY

16 Sir, there is no settling the point of
precedency between a louse and a flea.
[Samuel Johnson: in Boswell's *Life*
(1783)]
  *A Mr. Morgann had asked Dr. Johnson
  whether he reckoned "Derrick or Smart
  the best poet?"
    Merely as men, by the way, Dr. John-
  son thought well of both of them.*

PRECEDENT

17 It is a maxim among lawyers that
whatever hath been done before may

legally be done again: and therefore they take special care to record all the decisions formerly made against common justice and the general reason of mankind. These, under the name of *precedents,* they produce as authorities to justify the most iniquitous opinions; and the judges never fail of directing accordingly. [Jonathan Swift: *Gulliver's Travels* IV.v.]

PRECEPT
1 For precept must be upon precept, precept upon precept; line upon line, line upon line; here a little, and there a little. [Isaiah 28:10]

PRECISION
2 Exactitude is the sublimity of the stupid. [Attr. Fontenelle, who disclaimed it]

PRECOCITY
3 So wise so young, they say, do never live long.
[Shakespeare: *Richard III* III.i.]
That precocious children die young is a strong conviction of the parents of unprecocious children. Keats, Shelley, Chatterton, Schubert and Mozart are often cited as proof. But Keats died of tuberculosis, Shelley of drowning, Chatterton by suicide, Schubert of typhoid or typhus and Mozart of typhus or typhoid, or—as he believed—of poisoning. None of these causes indicates an inherent frailty.

Most men of genius have displayed their superiority early and have enjoyed vigorous health and lived longer than the average of their contemporaries. See the results of an examination of the life span of more than two thousand musicians, philosophers and poets, by Chester Alexander, in School and Society, *April 15, 1944.*

4 Mature in dulness from his tender years.
[Dryden: *Mac Flecknoe*]
5 As yet a child, nor yet a fool to fame, I lisp'd in numbers, for the numbers came.
[Alexander Pope: *Epistle to Dr. Arbuthnot*]
6 You forget the great Lipsius, quoth Yorick, who composed a work the day he was born;—they should have wiped it up, said my uncle Toby, and said no more about it. [Laurence Sterne: *Tristram Shandy* VI.ii.]
7 He early determined to marry and wive,
For better or worse
With his elderly nurse—
Which the poor little boy didn't live to contrive:
His health didn't thrive—
No longer alive,
He died an enfeebled old dotard at five!
[W. S. Gilbert: *Bab Ballads,* "The Precocious Baby"]

PREGNANCY
8 Long-tongued wives go long with bairn. [John Ray: *English Proverbs* (1670)]
bairn = *child*
That is, an over-talkative woman will announce her pregnancy as soon as she knows of it.

PREGNANT
9 Great with child, and longing . . . for stewed prunes.
[Shakespeare: *Measure for Measure* II.i.]
Such importance was formerly attached to a pregnant woman's longings that "longing" was a euphemism for "pregnant." It was believed that if these longings were balked the child might be imperfect—a belief which many a wily wife exploited. In many places pregnant women were allowed to pilfer certain foods, in the public interest. The longing for fruits and vegetables out of season was in itself regarded as a proof of pregnancy. In Webster's The Duchess of Malfi *the Duchess's frantic eagerness for apricots proved to her suspicious brothers that she was with child. Joanna Southcot, a prophetess who in 1814 claimed to be gravid with the second coming of Christ, supported her claim by eating vast amounts of asparagus. Stewed prunes were thought to be aphrodisiac and were served as a sort of free lunch in Elizabethan brothels.*

PREJUDICE
10 Prejudice is the reasoning of the

stupid. [Voltaire: *Sur la Loi Naturelle* IV]

1 Passion and prejudice govern the world; only under the name of reason. [John Wesley: Letter to Joseph Benson (1770)]

2 Prejudice is never easy unless it can pass itself off for reason. [William Hazlitt: *On Prejudice*]

3 Without the aid of prejudice and custom, I should not be able to find my way across the room. [William Hazlitt: *Sketches and Essays*]

4 Prejudices are the props of civilization. [André Gide: *The Counterfeiters* I.ii.]

PREPOSITION
5 This is an impertinence up with which I will not put. [Attr. Sir Winston Churchill]
> Said to be a marginal note of Churchill's at a point in one of his wartime speeches at which some zealous subordinate had altered a sentence because it ended in a preposition.

PRESBYTERIAN
6 For his religion, it was fit
To match his learning and his wit;
'Twas Presbyterian true blue;
For he was of that stubborn crew
Of errant saints, whom all men grant
To be the true Church Militant;
Such as do build their faith upon
The holy text of pike and gun;
Decide all controversies by
Infallible artillery;
And prove their doctrine orthodox
By Apostolic blows and knocks.
[Samuel Butler (1612-1680): *Hudibras*]

PRESENT
7 Trust no Future, howe'er pleasant!
Let the dead Past bury its dead!
Act—act in the living Present!
Heart within, and God o'erhead!
[Longfellow: *A Psalm of Life*]

8 The now, the here, through which all future plunges to the past. [James Joyce: *Ulysses* II]

PRESIDENCY
9 I am convinced that the office of the President is not such a very difficult one to fill, his duties being mainly to execute the laws of Congress. Should I be chosen for this exalted position I would execute the laws of Congress as faithfully as I have always executed the orders of my superiors. [Admiral George Dewey: announcing his candidacy for the office of President of United States, April 3, 1900]
> How it must have grieved Congress that the Constitution did not allow them to elect him at once by acclamation!

PRESS
10 The tenth Muse, who now governs the periodical press. [Anthony Trollope: *Doctor Thorne* IV]

PREVENT
11 Prevent us, O Lord, in all our doings. [*The Book of Common Prayer* "Collects after the Offertory"]
> prevent = go before

PREVENTION
12 How far more easy it is not to enter than to get forth. [Montaigne: *Essays* III.x.]
> This may be regarded as an early form of Agnes Allen's Law: Anything is easier to get into than out of.

13 He that cannot shut the door against them, shall never expel them being entered. [Montaigne: *Essays* III.x.]
> That is, if you can't keep 'em out, you'll hardly put 'em out.

PREY
14 Have they not divided the prey; to every man a damsel or two? [Judges 5:30]

PRICE
15 The real price of everything is the toil and trouble of acquiring it. [Adam Smith: *Wealth of Nations* I]

PRIDE
16 Pride goeth before destruction, and a haughty spirit before a fall. [Proverbs 16:18]

17 When Adam dalfe and Eve spane
To spire of thou may spede,
Whare was then the pride of man,
That now merres his meed?

[Richard Rolle of Hampole: *Early English Text Society Reprints* No. 26]

1 Pryde, the general root of all harmes; for of this root springen . . . Ire, Envye, Accidie or Sloth, Avarice, Glotonye and Lecherye. [Chaucer: *The Parson's Tale*]

2 Three thinges displease God and man, A poore man proude, a riche man a lyer, and an olde man in loue. [John Florio: *Firste Fruites* XXIII]

3 Small things make base men proud. [Shakespeare: *II Henry VI* IV.i.]

4 My pride fell with my fortunes. [Shakespeare: *As You Like It* I.ii.]

5   Pride hath no other glass
To show itself but pride; for supple knees
Feed arrogance and are the proud man's fees.
[Shakespeare: *Troilus and Cressida* III. iii.]
supple knees = *quickly bending in homage.*

6 'Tis pride that pulls the country down.
[Shakespeare: *Othello* II.iii.]

7 Prouder than rustling in unpaid-for silk.
[Shakespeare: *Cymbeline* III.iii.]

8 They are proud in humility, proud in that they are not proud. [Robert Burton: *Anatomy of Melancholy* I.2.3.14]

9 If we had no pride we should not complain of that of others. [La Rochefoucauld: *Maxims*]

10 Likeness begets Love; yet proud Men hate one another. [Thomas Fuller (1654-1734): *Gnomologia*]

11 Of all the causes which conspire to blind
Man's erring judgment, and misguide the mind,
What the weak head with strongest bias rules,
Is pride, the never-failing vice of fools.
[Alexander Pope: *An Essay on Criticism* II]

12 Beauty that shocks you, parts that none will trust,
Wit that can creep, and pride that licks the dust.
[Alexander Pope: *Epistle to Dr. Arbuthnot*]

13 Pride is undoubtedly the original of anger; but . . . a passionate man, upon the review of his day, will have very few gratifications to offer to his pride, when he has considered how his outrages were caused, why they were borne, and in what they are likely to end at last. [Samuel Johnson: *The Rambler* No. 11]

14 Pride is unwilling to believe the necessity of assigning any other reason than her own will; and would rather maintain the most equitable claims by violence and penalties than descend from the dignity of command to dispute and expostulation. [Samuel Johnson: *The Rambler* No. 114]

> Browning has caught this in his *My Last Duchess, where the haughty duke says:*
>> *Even had you skill*
> *In speech—(which I have* not)—*to make your will*
> *Quite clear to such a one, and say,*
>> *"Just this*
> *Or that in you disgusts me . . ."—*
>> *and if she let*
> *Herself be lessoned so, nor plainly set*
> *Her wits to yours, forsooth, and made excuse,*
> *— E'en then would be some stooping;*
>> *and I choose*
> *Never to stoop.*
>
> *"Damn you," roared the 4th duke of Queensberry ("Old Q."—1724-1810) to a lackey who, on answering a summons, had asked what his Grace wanted, "I am not obliged to tell you what I want!"*

15 Pride is seldom delicate: it will please itself with very mean advantages. [Samuel Johnson: *Rasselas* IX]
mean = *low, petty, vulgar*

16 Pride in their port, defiance in their eye,
I see the lords of humankind pass by.
[Oliver Goldsmith: *The Traveler*]

17 He was so proud that should he meet
The Twelve Apostles in the street,
He'd turn his nose up at them all
And shove his Saviour from the wall.
[Charles Churchill: *The Duellist* III]
> *The reference is said to be to William Warburton, Bishop of Gloucester.*
>
> *When there were no sidewalks to the narrow, traffic-jammed city streets and slops were emptied from the overhanging upper stories, the safest and most salubrious place to walk was close to the*

wall. This became the position of precedence and a refusal to "give the wall" or an instance of "taking the wall" was one of the commonest causes of violence in 18th-century London.

1 He saw a cottage with a double
                 coach-house,
  A cottage of gentility;
And the Devil did grin, for his dar-
                 ling sin
  Is pride that apes humility.
[Coleridge: *The Devil's Thoughts*]
The verse is sometimes assigned to Southey, who rewrote and enlarged it as The Devil's Walk. *It ran through many printings and revisions and was much imitated.*

2 Oh! Why should the spirit of mortal
                 be proud?
Like a swift-fleeting meteor, a fast-
                 flying cloud,
A flash of the lightning, a break of
                 the wave,
Man passes from life to his rest in
                 the grave.
[William Knox: *Oh! Why Should the Spirit of Mortal be Proud?*]

3 "You're wounded!" "Nay," the sol-
                 dier's pride
  Touched to the quick, he said:
"I'm killed, Sire!" And his chief be-
                 side,
  Smiling the boy fell dead.
[Robert Browning: *Incident of the French Camp*]

4 Though pride is not a virtue, it is the parent of many virtues. [J. C. Collins: *Aphorisms*]

5 That odious strain of plebeian pride which plumes itself upon not having risen above its sources. [Willa Cather: *The Troll Garden,* "The Marriage of Phaedra"]

PRIEST

6 Wel oghte a preest ensample for to
                 yive
By his clennesse how that his sheep
                 sholde lyve.
[Chaucer: Prologue to *The Canterbury Tales*]

7 New Presbyter is but Old Priest writ
                 large.
[John Milton: *On the New Forcers of Conscience*]

8 The priest promotes war, and the
                 soldier peace.
[William Blake: *Gnomic Verses* No. 3]

9 Nay I may ask, is not every true reformer, by the nature of him, a priest first of all? He appeals to Heaven's invisible justice against earth's visible force; knows that it, the invisible, is strong and alone strong. He is a believer in the divine truth of things; a seer, seeing through the shows of things; a worshipper, in one way or the other, of the divine truth of things; a priest, that is. [Thomas Carlyle: *On Heroes and Hero-Worship* IV]

10 Those trees in whose grim shadow
    The ghastly priest doth reign,
    The priest who slew the slayer,
    And shall himself be slain.
[Macaulay: *The Battle of Lake Regillus* X]
The priesthood of the shrine of **Diana** *at Aricia in the Alban hills (*Diana Nemorensis = "Diana of the grove"*) was by custom given to a runaway slave after he had plucked a branch from a certain tree in the grove and killed in a single combat the priest who previously occupied the office.*
  Compare Aeneid VI.136 et seq.; and, for the significance, see Sir James Frazer's The Golden Bough.

PRIMITIVE

11 People so primitive that they did not know how to get Money except by Working for it. [George Ade: *Fable of the Cut-Up who Came very Near Losing his Ticket*]

PRIMROSE

12 A primrose by a river's brim,
  A yellow primrose was to him,
  And it was nothing more.
[Wordsworth: *Peter Bell* I.xii.]

PRIMROSE PATH

13 The primrose way to the everlasting
                 bonfire.
[Shakespeare: *Macbeth* II.iii.]

14   But, good my brother,
  Do not as some ungracious pastors
                 do,
Show me the steep and thorny way to
                 heaven,

Whiles, like a puff'd and reckless
    libertine,
Himself the primrose path of dalli-
    ance treads
And recks not his own rede.
[Shakespeare: *Hamlet* I.iii.]
  recks = *heeds;* rede = *advice*

PRINCE(S)

1 Who made thee a prince and a judge
over us? [Exodus 2:14]
2 Put not your trust in princes.
[Psalms 146:3]
3 Vain pomp and glory of this world, I
    hate ye:
I feel my heart new opened. O! how
    wretched
Is that poor man that hangs on
    princes' favours!
There is, betwixt that smile we
    would aspire to,
That sweet aspect of princes, and
    their ruin,
More pangs and fears than wars or
    women have—
And when he falls, he falls like Luci-
    fer,
Never to hope again.
[Shakespeare: *Henry VIII* III.ii.]
4 Princes, like Beautys, from their
    youth
Are strangers to the voice of truth.
[John Gay: *Fables* I]

PRINCIPLE(S)

5 There is nothing so bad or so good
that you will not find Englishmen doing
it; but you will never find an Englishman in the wrong. He does everything
on principle. He fights you on patriotic
principles; he robs you on business
principles; he enslaves you on imperial
principles. [G. B. Shaw: *The Man of
Destiny*]
6 It is often easier to fight for principles than to live up to them. [Adlai
Stevenson: in a speech, at New York
City, August 27, 1952]

PRINT(ING)

7 He who first shortened the labor of
Copyists by device of *Movable Types*
was disbanding hired Armies and cash-
iering most Kings and Senates, and cre-

ating a whole new Democratic world:
he had invented the Art of printing.
[Thomas Carlyle: *Sartor Resartus* I.v.]
  *He was also, of course, instituting con-
  script armies, Führers, Duces, Commissars, and the like.*
8 "Gracious heavens!" he cries out,
leaping up and catching hold of his
hair, "what's this? Print!" [Dickens:
Somebody's Luggage III]

PRISON(S)

9 Now my soul's palace is become a
    prison.
[Shakespeare: *III Henry VI* II.i.]
10 Stone walls do not a prison make,
    Nor iron bars a cage;
Minds innocent and quiet take
    That for an hermitage.
[Richard Lovelace: *To Althea: From
Prison*]
11 Prisons are built with stones of law,
brothels with bricks of religion. [Wil-
liam Blake: *The Marriage of Heaven
and Hell*]
12 I know not whether Laws be right,
    Or whether Laws be wrong;
All that we know who be in gaol
    Is that the wall is strong;
And that each day is like a year,
    A year whose days are long.
[Oscar Wilde: *The Ballad of Reading
Gaol*]
13 The vilest deeds like poison-weeds
    Bloom well in prison-air:
It is only what is good in Man
    That wastes and withers there:
Pale Anguish keeps the heavy gate
    And the Warder is Despair.
[Oscar Wilde: *The Ballad of Reading
Gaol*]

PRIVACY

14 Give me, kind Heaven, a private
    station,
A mind serene for contemplation.
[John Gay: *Fables* II]
15 A privacy of glorious light is thine.
[Wordsworth: *To a Skylark*]
16 I might have been a gold-fish in a
glass bowl for all the privacy I got.
[H. H. Munro ("Saki"): *Reginald* I]
17 The personal life of every individual
is based on secrecy, and perhaps it is

partly for that reason that civilized man is so nervously anxious that personal privacy should be respected. [Anton Chekhov: *The Lady with the Dog*]

1 A man has a right to pass through this world, if he wills, without having his picture published, his business enterprises discussed, his successful experiments written up for the benefit of others, or his eccentricities commented upon, whether in handbills, circulars, catalogues, newspapers or periodicals. [Judge Alton B. Parker, *Decision, Robertson v. Rochester Folding Box Co.,* 1901]

2 The general look of an elderly fallen angel traveling incognito. [Peter Quennell: *The Sign of the Fish*]
Mr. Quennell is describing André Gide.

PRIVILEGED
3 The Privileged and the People form Two Nations. [Benjamin Disraeli: *Sybil* III.ii.]

PROBABILITY
4 Lest men suspect your tale untrue,
Keep probability in view.
[John Gay: *The Painter Who Pleased Nobody*]

5 The laws of probability, so true in general, so fallacious in particular. [Edward Gibbon: *Autobiography*]
Gibbon went on to say that the laws of probability allowed him about fifteen years more of life, but he provided a striking illustration of his own dictum. On January 15, 1794, he said he thought himself "good for ten, twelve, or perhaps twenty years" more of life. He was taken ill that night and died at a quarter to one the following afternoon.

PROCRASTINATION
6 Procrastination is the thief of time. [Edward Young: *Night Thoughts* I (1742)]
Oscar Wilde said (Picture of Dorian Gray III) that punctuality was the thief of time — i.e., nothing like being on time for wasting your time, since everyone else is always late — and most of what is done in meetings is only a waste of time.

7 Never do today what you can do tomorrow. Something may occur to make you regret your premature action. [Aaron Burr, in Parton's *Life of Aaron Burr*]

8 With Earth's first Clay They did the Last Man knead,
And there of the Last Harvest sowed the Seed:
And the first Morning of Creation wrote
What the Last Dawn of Reckoning shall read.
[*Rubáiyát of Omar Khayyám* (trans. Edward FitzGerald)]

9 Procrastination is the art of keeping up with yesterday. [Don(ald) Marquis: *certain maxims of archy*]

PRODIGAL
10 I will arise and go to my father, and will say unto him, Father, I have sinned against heaven, and before thee, And am no more worthy to be called thy son: make me as one of thy hired servants. [Luke 15:18-19]

11 The Prodigal generally does more Injustice than the Covetous. [Benjamin Franklin: *Poor Richard's Almanack* (1732)]

PRODIGY
12 A man does not wonder at what he sees frequently, even though he is ignorant of the reason for its happening. But if anything happens which he has not seen before, he calls it a prodigy. [Cicero: *De divinatione* II.xxii.]

PROFANITY
13 Bad language or abuse
I never, never use,
Whatever the emergency;
Though "Bother it" I may
Occasionally say,
I never never use a big, big D.
[W. S. Gilbert: *H.M.S. Pinafore* I]

14 In certain trying circumstances, urgent circumstances, desperate circumstances, profanity furnishes a relief denied even to prayer. [Mark Twain: *Pudd'nhead Wilson's Calendar*]

15 Well, why does God have a swearword for a name? [Samuel Montgomery (aged 5): when reproved for swearing]

PROFESSION(S)

1 The utmost expectation that experience can warrant is that they [members of the same profession] should forbear open hostilities and secret machinations and when the whole fraternity is attacked be able to unite against a common foe. [Samuel Johnson: *The Rambler* No. 64]
2 Divers professions and many vocations subsist and are grounded only upon public abuses and popular errors. [Montaigne: *Essays* II.xxxvii.]
3 In time a profession is like marriage, we cease to note anything but its inconveniences. [Balzac: *Cousin Pons* XVIII]
4 All professions are conspiracies against the laity. [G. B. Shaw: Preface to *The Doctor's Dilemma*]

PROFESSORS

5 College professors in one-building universities on the prairie, still hoping, at the age of sixty, to get their whimsical essays into the *Atlantic Monthly*. [H. L. Mencken: in *Smart Set*, November 1921]

PROFIT

6 What is a man profited, if he shall gain the whole world, and lose his own soul? [Matthew 16:26]
7 Who profits from this? (*Cui bono?*) [Cicero: *Pro Milone* XII.xxxii.]
   Together with cherchez la femme (*"look for the woman in the case"*), *this is one of the great principles of criminal investigation.*
8 No man profiteth but by the loss of others. [Montaigne: *Essays* I.xxi.]
9 Unearned increment. [John Stuart Mill: *Dissertations and Discussions* IV]

PROFUNDITY

10 Where I am not understood, it shall be concluded that something very useful and profound is couched underneath. [Jonathan Swift: Preface to *The Tale of a Tub*]
11 If this young man expresses himself
      in terms too deep for me,
   Why, what a very singularly deep
      young man this deep young
         man must be!
[W. S. Gilbert: *Patience* I]
12 Any profound view of the world is

mysticism. [Albert Schweitzer: *Out of My Life and Thought*]

PROGENY

13 A progeny of learning. [Mrs. Malaprop: in Richard Brinsley Sheridan's *The Rivals* I.ii.]

PROGRESS

14 Would you realize what Revolution is, call it Progress; and would you realize what Progress is, call it Tomorrow. [Victor Hugo: *Les Misérables* I.xvii.]
15 Not enjoyment, and not sorrow,
      Is our destined end or way;
   But to act, that each to-morrow
      Find us farther than to-day.
[Longfellow: *A Psalm of Life*]
16 "A slow sort of country!" said the Queen. "Now, here, you see, it takes all the running you can do, to keep in the same place. If you want to get somewhere else, you must run at least twice as fast as that!" [Lewis Carroll: *Through the Looking-Glass* II]
17 All progress is based upon a universal innate desire on the part of every organism to live beyond its income. [Samuel Butler (1835-1902): *Notebooks*]
18 All the modern inconveniences. [Mark Twain: *Life on the Mississippi* III]
19 It is through disobedience that progress has been made. [Oscar Wilde: *The Soul of Man Under Socialism*]
20 The reasonable man adapts himself to the world: the unreasonable one persists in trying to adapt the world to himself. Therefore all progress depends on the unreasonable man. [G. B. Shaw: *Maxims for Revolutionists*]
21 The cry was for vacant freedom and indeterminate progress: *Vorwärts! Avanti! Onward! Full speed ahead!*, without asking whether directly before you was a bottomless pit. [George Santayana: Epilogue in *My Host the World*]
22 All progress has resulted from people who took unpopular positions. [Adlai Stevenson, speech, March 22, 1954]

PROHIBITION

23 A great social and economic experiment, noble in motive and far-reaching in purpose. [Herbert Hoover: in a let-

ter to Senator Borah, in 1928]
The reference is to Prohibition.
1 All I kin git out o' the Wickersham position on prohibition is that the distinguished jurist seems to feel that if we'd let 'em have it the problem o' keepin' 'em from gittin' it would be greatly simplified. [Frank McKinney ("Kin") Hubbard: *Abe Martin's Broadcast* 125]

PROLOGUE
2 It is a foolish thing to make a long prologue, and to be short in the story itself. [II Maccabees 2:32]

PROMISE(S)
3 And be these juggling fiends no more believ'd,
That palter with us in a double sense;
That keep the word of promise to our ear,
And break it to our hope.
[Shakespeare: *Macbeth* V.viii.]
4 We promise according to our hopes, and perform according to our fears. [La Rochefoucauld: *Maxims*]
5 Promises don't fill the belly. [C. H. Spurgeon: *Ploughman's Pictures*]

PROOF
6 The proof of the pudding is in the eating [A proverb, it appears in *Don Quixote* (1605-1615), in Addison's *Spectator* (No. 567), and many other places]
7 We must never assume that which is incapable of proof. [G. H. Lewes: *The Physiology of Common Life* XIII]

PROPAGANDA
8 Among the calamities of war may be justly numbered the diminution of the love of truth by the falsehoods which interest dictates and credulity encourages. A peace will equally leave the warrior and relater of wars destitute of employment; and I know not whether more is to be dreaded from streets filled with soldiers accustomed to plunder or from garrets filled with scribblers accustomed to lie. [Samuel Johnson: *The Idler* No. 30]
O happy age, in which peace and war could be distinguished in this respect!
9 The Marine Corps is the Navy's po-

lice force and as long as I am President that is what it will remain. They have a propaganda machine that is almost equal to Stalin's. [Harry S. Truman, quoted in *Time*, Sept. 18, 1950]
Mr. Truman's comparison was unfortunate. The validity of his basic statement was immediately demonstrated, however, by a furor which led him to apologize.

PROPER
10 As proper men as ever trod upon neat's leather.
[Shakespeare: *Julius Caesar* I.i.]
In Elizabethan English proper had the additional meaning of handsome.
Neat's leather was what we today commonly mean by the general designation of leather, leather from cattle of the genus Bos. Leather of split horsehide, which we call cordovan, was then called Spanish leather.

PROPERTY
11 The great and chief end of men . . . putting themselves under government, is the preservation of their property. [John Locke: *Treatises on Government*]
12 Doesn't thou 'ear my 'erse's legs, as they canters awaäy?
Proputty, proputty, proputty—that's what I 'ears 'em saäy.
[Tennyson: *Northern Farmer, New Style*]
13 The highest law gives a thing to him who can use it. [Thoreau: *Journal*, Nov. 9, 1852]
14 Property is theft. [Proudhon: *Principle of Right* I]
Fifty years before Proudhon's famous dictum, Brissot had said: Exclusive property is a theft in nature.
15 Property is desirable, is a positive good in the world. [Abraham Lincoln: *Message to Congress*, Dec. 3, 1861]
16 The rights and interests of the laboring man will be protected and cared for —not by the labor agitators, but by the Christian gentlemen to whom God has given control of the property rights of the country and upon the successful management of which so much depends. [George F. Baer, Letter to W. F. Clark, Wilkes-Barre, Pa., April 1, 1902]
Despite the date, Mr. Baer was in ear-

nest. As a railroad magnate, he was himself one of those very appointees of God and therefore knew whereof he spake.

PROPHECY

1 When a prophet speaketh in the name of the Lord, if the thing follow not, nor come to pass, that is the thing which the Lord hath not spoken, but the prophet hath spoken it presumptuously: thou shalt not be afraid of him. [Deuteronomy 18:22]

2   The prophetic soul
Of the wide world, dreaming on
       things to come.
[Shakespeare: *Sonnets* CVII]

3 If you can look into the seeds of
       time,
And say which grain will grow and
       which will not,
Speak then to me.
[Shakespeare: *Macbeth* I.iii.]

4 Oh, blindness to the future! kindly
       giv'n,
That each may fill the circle mark'd
       by heaven.
[Alexander Pope: *An Essay on Man* I]

5 Matrons, who toss the cup, and see
The grounds of fate in grounds of
       tea.
[Charles Churchill: *The Ghost* I]

6 Drive my dead thoughts over the
       universe,
Like withered leaves, to quicken a
       new birth!
And, by the incantation of this verse,
Scatter, as from an unextinguished
       hearth
Ashes and sparks, my words among
       mankind!
Be through my lips to unawakened
       Earth
The trumpet of a prophecy!
[Shelley: *Ode to the West Wind*]

7 Ancestral voices prophesying war.
[Coleridge: *Kubla Khan*]

8 Perhaps some day—say 1938, their centenary—they might be allowed to return . . . and perhaps then, for the first time since man began his education among the carnivores, they would find a world that sensitive and timid natures could regard without a shudder. [Henry Adams: *The Education of Henry Adams* (last words in the book)]

they = *Adams and two of his friends*

An illustration of the danger of prophecy. It would be hard to find a time when sensitive and timid natures had more reason to shudder than in 1938. It would be safer to move the date up at least two millennia.

PROPHET(S)

9 The best of seers is he who guesses well. [Euripides: *Fragment*]

10 Is Saul also among the prophets? [I Samuel 10:12]

The amazement which the passage tells us seized "those who knew him aforetime" when Saul "prophesied among" the company of prophets that met him by the way is confusing to the common reader who thinks of prophesying merely as foretelling the future. But such foretelling was only a part of the response of being moved by a spirit. Much of it was what we call having a fit, or raving. Thus a little later, when an evil spirit from God came upon Saul, he "prophesied in the midst of the house"—and his prophesying consisted of an attempt to kill David. RSV translates it "raved within his house." See I Samuel 10:5, II Kings 3:15, 19:24, 18:10 and 9:11, for evidence that prophesying was a state of religious ecstasy which was likely to pass into convulsions and dangerous frenzy. The prophets that Saul met on the hill were probably whirling dervishes and his excited joining in their gyrations may have been what alarmed his attendants and friends.

11 And God said to Jonah, Doest thou well to be angry for the gourd? And he said, I do well to be angry, even unto death. [Jonah 4:9]

12 Beware of false prophets, which come to you in sheep's clothing, but inwardly they are ravening wolves. [Matthew 7:15]

13 A prophet is not without honour, save in his own country, and in his own house. [Matthew 13:57]

14 A prophet is not without honour, but in his own country, and among his own kin, and in his own house. [Mark 6:4]

15 The voice of one crying in the wilderness. [John 1:23]

1 I wonder that a soothsayer doesn't laugh whenever he sees another soothsayer. [Cicero: *De divinatione* II.xxiv.]
Cicero attributes the remark to Cato.

2 All armed prophets succeed and unarmed prophets come to ruin. [Machiavelli: *The Prince* VI]

PROPOSAL

3 Afraid he would . . . pop the question, which he had not the courage to put. [Samuel Richardson: *Sir Charles Grandison*]
Probably more proposals of marriage are popped than put.

PROPOSES

4 Man proposes but God disposes. [Thomas à Kempis: *Imitation of Christ* I.xix.]

PROSE

5 For more than forty years I have been talking prose without knowing it. [Molière: *Le Bourgeois Gentilhomme* II.iv.]

PROSPECT

6 The noblest prospect which a Scotchman ever sees is the highroad that leads him to England. [Samuel Johnson: in Boswell's *Life* (1763)]

7 Cheered with the prospect of a
brighter day.
[Wordsworth: the last line in his sequence of 14 sonnets *opposing* the abolition of the death penalty]

8 What though the spicy breezes
Blow soft o'er Ceylon's isle;
Though every prospect pleases,
And only man is vile.
[Reginald Heber: *From Greenland's Icy Mountains*]

9 Take a mere beggar-woman, lazy, ragged, filthy, and not over-scrupulous of truth,—but if she is chaste, and sober, and cheerful and goes to her religious duties—she will, in the eyes of the Church, have a prospect of heaven. [John Henry Newman: *Anglican Difficulties* VIII]

PROSPERITY

10 A state that is prosperous always honors the gods. [Aeschylus: *The Seven Against Thebes*]

11 In human life there is nothing which prospers to the end. [Euripides: *Suppliants*]

12 So long as a man enjoys prosperity, he cares not whether he is beloved. [Lucan: *Pharsalia* VII]

13 No man may alwey han prosperitee. [Chaucer: *The Clerk's Tale*]

14 Prosperity is the blessing of the Old Testament; adversity is the blessing of the New; which carrieth the greater benediction. [Francis Bacon: *Of Adversity*]

15 Prosperity doth best discover vice; but adversity doth best discover virtue. [Francis Bacon: *Of Adversity*]

16 Prosperity is not without many fears and distastes; and adversity is not without comforts and hopes. [Francis Bacon: *Of Adversity*]

17 The vertue of prosperity is temperance; the vertue of adversity is fortitude: which in morals is the more heroicall vertue. [Francis Bacon: *Of Adversity*]

18 And you shall find the greatest enemy
A man can have is his prosperity.
[Samuel Daniel: *Philotas*]

19 Prosperity doth bewitch men, seeming clear;
As seas do laugh, show white, when rocks are near.
[John Webster: *The White Devil* V.vi.]

20 Adversity is easier borne, than Prosperity forgot. [Thomas Fuller (1654-1734): *Gnomologia*]

21 Prosperity is just around the corner. [Herbert Hoover: *Sixty Days Proclamation,* March 1931]

22 Industrialism is the systematic exploitation of wasting assets . . . progress is merely an acceleration in the rate of that exploitation. Such prosperity as we have known up to the present is the consequence of rapidly spending the planet's irreplaceable capital. [Aldous Huxley: *Themes and Variations*]

PROSTITUTE

23 'Tis the strumpet's plague
To beguile many, and be beguil'd by one.
[Shakespeare: *Othello* IV.i.]

24 The prostitute draggles her shawl, her bonnet bobs on her tipsy and pimpled neck;

The crowd laugh at her blackguard
oaths, the men jeer and wink to each
other;
(Miserable! I do not laugh at your
oaths, nor jeer you.)
[Walt Whitman: *Leaves of Grass,* "Song
of Myself"]

PROTECTION

1 Governments exist to protect the
rights of minorities. The loved and the
rich need no protection—they have
many friends and few enemies. [Wendell Phillips: in a speech, December 21,
1860]

PROTEST

2 The lady doth protest too much, methinks.
[Shakespeare: *Hamlet* III.ii.]

PROTESTANTISM

3 All Protestantism, even the most cold
and passive, is a sort of dissent. But the
religion most prevalent in our northern
colonies is a refinement on the principle
of resistance; it is the dissidence of dissent, and the Protestantism of the Protestant religion. [Edmund Burke: *Speech
on Conciliation with America*]
4 The true force of Protestantism was
its signal return to the individual conscience—to the method of Jesus.
[Matthew Arnold: Preface to *God and
the Bible*]

PROUD

5   That title of respect
Which the proud soul ne'er pays but
to the proud.
[Shakespeare: *I Henry IV* I.iii.]
6 The proud hate pride—in others.
[Benjamin Franklin: *Poor Richard's Almanack*]
7 The truly proud man knows neither
superiors nor inferiors. The first he does
not admit of: the last he does not concern himself about. [William Hazlitt:
Characteristics]
8 There is such a thing as a man being
too proud to fight. [Woodrow Wilson:
in a speech at Philadelphia, May 10,
1915]
    Oswald Garrison Villard—in Fighting
Years, *1939—says that he made up this
phrase.*

PROVE

9 Prove all things; hold fast that which
is good. [I Thessalonians 1:21]

PROVERBS

10 And thou shalt become an astonishment, a proverb, and a byword, among
all nations. [Deuteronomy 28:37]
11 A proverb and a byword among all
people. [I Kings 9:7]
12 As Love and I late harbour'd in one
inn,
With proverbs thus each other entertain:
tertain:
"In love there is no lack," thus I begin;
gin;
"Fair words make fools," replieth he
again;
"Who spares to speak doth spare to
speed," quoth I;
"As well," saith he, "too forward as
too slow;"
"Fortune assists the boldest," I reply;
ply;
"A hasty man," quoth he, "ne'er
wanted woe;"
"Labour is light where love," quoth
I, "doth pay;"
Saith he, "Light burden's heavy, if
far borne;"
Quoth I, "The main lost, cast the
by away;"
"Y'have spun a fair thread," he replies in scorn.
plies in scorn.
And having thus awhile each other
thwarted
Fools as we met, so fools again we
parted.
[Michael Drayton: *Proverbs*]
13 This formal fool speaks naught but
proverbs. [Henry Porter: *The Two Angrie Women of Abingdon*]
14 Proverb'd with a grandsire phrase.
[Shakespeare: *Romeo and Juliet* I.iv.]
15 Patch grief with proverbs.
[Shakespeare: *Much Ado about Nothing* V.i.]
16 The proverb is something musty.
[Shakespeare: *Hamlet* III.ii.]
17 Proverbs may not improperly be
called the philosophy of the common
people. [James Howell: *Proverbs*]
18 A proverb is much matter decocted
into few words. [Thomas Fuller (1608-
1661): *Worthies of England* II]

1 Proverbial expressions and trite sayings are the flowers of the rhetoric of a vulgar man. . . . A man of fashion never has recourse to proverbs and vulgar aphorisms. [Lord Chesterfield: *Letters to His Son,* September 27, 1749]

2 The wise make proverbs and fools repeat them. [Isaac D'Israeli: *Curiosities of Literature* II.i.]

3 A proverb is no proverb to you till life has illustrated it. [Keats: *Letter to George and Georgiana Keats,* Feb. 14-May 3, 1819]

4 Nothing is so useless as a general maxim. [Macaulay: *Machiavelli*]

5 A proverb is one man's wit and all men's wisdom. [Attr. Lord John Russell (1792-1878): quoted in *Memoirs of Mackintosh* II]

6 Proverbs are the sanctuary of the intuitions. [Emerson: *Compensation*]

7 With a little hoard of maxims preaching down a daughter's heart.
[Tennyson: *Locksley Hall*]

8 As it will be in the future, it was at the birth of Man—
There are only four things certain since Social Progress began—
That the Dog returns to his Vomit and the Sow returns to her Mire,
And the burnt Fool's bandaged finger goes wobbling back to the Fire.
[Kipling: *The Gods of the Copybook Headings*]
The fourth thing is that, whatever happens, someone will have a trite maxim to explain it.

9 Proverbs may be called the literature of the illiterate. [Frederick S. Cozzens: *Sayings*]

PROVIDENCE

10 I have been young, and now am old; yet have I not seen the righteous forsaken, nor his seed begging bread. [Psalms 37:25]

11 Take therefore no thought for the morrow: for the morrow shall take thought for the things of itself. [Matthew 6:34]

12 God sends the cold according to the coat. [Montaigne: *Essays* III.vi.]
The saying was apparently proverbial. And see quotation from Sterne under LAMB.

13 What in me is dark
Illumine, what is low raise and support;
That to the height of this great argument
I may assert Eternal Providence,
And justify the ways of God to men.
[John Milton: *Paradise Lost* I.22-26]

14 If you leap into a well, Providence is not bound to fetch you out. [Thomas Fuller (1654-1734): *Gnomologia*]

PRUDE

15 . . . twenty, as everyone well knows, is not an age to play the prude. [Molière: *The Misanthrope* III.v.]

PRUDENCE

16 He that observeth the wind shall not sow; and he that regardeth the clouds shall not reap. [Ecclesiastes 11:4]

17 It is not good a sleping hound to wake.
[Chaucer: *Troilus and Criseyde* III]

18 Prudence consists in the power to recognize the nature of disadvantages and to take the less disagreeable as good. [Machiavelli: *The Prince* XXI]

19 Too much taking heed is loss. [George Herbert: *Jacula Prudentum*]

20 Neither trust, nor contend, nor lay wagers, nor lend,
And you'll have peace to your lives end.
[Benjamin Franklin: *Poor Richard's Almanack* (1749)]

21 Nature sets her gifts on the right hand and on the left . . . we cannot seize both, but by too much prudence may pass between them at too great a distance to reach either. [Samuel Johnson: *Rasselas* XXIX]

22 Prudence operates on life in the same manner as rules on composition: it produces vigilance rather than elevation, rather prevents loss than procures advantage; and often escapes miscarriages, but seldom reaches either power or honor. . . . Prudence keeps life safe, but does not often make it happy. [Samuel Johnson: *The Idler* No. 57]
Chekhov in his notebooks tells of a man who obsessively drilled into his children the wisdom of wearing overshoes. They

*wore overshoes all their lives but, none
the less, they weren't happy.*

1 Aristotle is praised for naming fortitude first of the cardinal virtues, as that without which no other virtue can steadily be practiced; but he might, with equal propriety, have placed prudence and justice before it, since without prudence fortitude is mad; without justice, it is mischievous. [Samuel Johnson: *Life of Pope*]

mischievous = *dangerous*
Aristotle: Nicomachean Ethics *III.vi.*

2 Prudence is a rich, ugly old maid, courted by Incapacity. [William Blake: *Proverbs of Hell*]

PRUDERY

3 The peculiarity of prudery is to multiply sentinels, in proportion as the fortress is less threatened. [Victor Hugo: *Les Misérables* II.viii.]

4 The perfect hostess will see to it that the works of male and female authors be properly separated on her book shelves. Their proximity, unless they happen to be married, should not be tolerated. [Lady Gough: *Etiquette* (1863)]

See MONTREAL

PRUNES AND PRISMS

5 Papa, potatoes, poultry, prunes, and prism, are all very good words for the lips: especially prunes and prism. [Dickens: *Little Dorrit* II.v.]

P's AND Q's

6 You must mind your P's and Q's with him, I can tell you. [Hannah Cowley: *Who's the Dupe?* I.i.]

Mrs. Cowley was employing a very old phrase. Mind means "be careful of." Beyond that all is conjecture. Some say it means that you are to watch your p(int)s *and* q(uart)s *at the alehouse. Some say it's advice from a French dancing master urging his pupils to be careful of their* p(ied)s [feet] *and their* q(ueue)s [pigtails]. *Some say it's advice from sailors' wives to their husbands to be careful not to get the tar from their queues onto their peajackets. Most think it is simply a warning from a schoolmaster to his scholars to make a proper distinction in writing between the* p's

and q's. *And this may be, though the oldest quotation that contains the expression seems to support the peajacket interpretation.*

PUBLIC

7 About things on which the public thinks long it commonly attains to think right. [Samuel Johnson: *The Life of Addison*]

8 The public has neither shame nor gratitude. [William Hazlitt: *Characteristics*]

9 The Public be damned! [William H. Vanderbilt]

Vanderbilt's famous snort was a retort to a reporter for the Chicago Daily News, *Clarence Dresser, October 8, 1882. Dresser had asked whether the public should not be consulted about luxury trains.*

Though long advanced as an illustration of the brutal arrogance of the Robber Barons, there is, in this age of oleaginous public-relations' smarming of every utterance of the great, something refreshing about it.

PUBLICITY

10 That fierce light which beats upon a throne
And blackens every blot.
[Tennyson: Dedication of *Idylls of the King*]

11 The price of justice is eternal publicity. [Arnold Bennett: *Things That Have Interested Me*]

PUBLIC OPINION

12 When the people have no other tyrant, their own public opinion becomes one. [E. G. Bulwer-Lytton: *Ernest Maltravers* VI.v.]

13 Public opinion is no more than this.
What people think that other people think.
[Alfred Austen: *Prince Lucifer* VI.ii.]

14 Public opinion, a vulgar, impertinent, anonymous tyrant who deliberately makes life unpleasant for anyone who is not content to be the average man. [William Ralph Inge: *Our Present Discontents*]

15 Public opinion's always in advance of the Law. [John Galsworthy: *Windows* I]

PUBLIC SCHOOLS

1 Public schools are the nurseries of all vice and immorality. [Henry Fielding: *Joseph Andrews* III.v.]

PUBLISHING

2 I account the use that a man should seek of the publishing of his own writings before his death, to be but an untimely anticipation of that which is proper to follow a man, and. not to go along with him. [Francis Bacon: *Epistle Dedicatory* to *An Advertisement Touching a Holy War*]

3 I sit with sad civility, I read
 With honest anguish, and an aching
  head;
 And drop at last, but in unwilling
  ears,
 This saving counsel, "Keep your
  piece nine years."
[Alexander Pope: *Epistle to Dr. Arbuthnot*]
 sad = *sober*

> *Pope himself never showed a reluctance to print, holding—even boasting of—something close to the record for early publication.*

See also WRITING: labor and patience

4 Publishing a volume of verse is like dropping a rose-petal down the Grand Canyon and waiting for the echo. [Don(ald) Marquis: *The Sun Dial*]

PUFF

5 Puffing is of various sorts: the principal are, the puff direct—the puff preliminary—the puff collateral—the puff collusive, and the puff oblique, or puff by implication. [Richard Brinsley Sheridan: *The Critic* I.ii.]

PULL

6 A long pull, and a strong pull, and a pull all together. [Dickens: *David Copperfield* XXX]

PULPIT

7 Pulpit, drum ecclesiastic.
[Samuel Butler (1612-1680): *Hudibras*]

PULSE

8 There are worse occupations in this world than feeling a woman's pulse. [Laurence Sterne: *A Sentimental Journey* I]

PUN(NING)

9 And torture one poor word ten thousand ways.
[Dryden: *Mac Flecknoe*]

10 The seeds of punning are in the minds of all men, and though they may be subdued by reason, reflection, and good sense, they will be very apt to shoot up in the greatest genius. [Joseph Addison: *The Spectator* No. 61]

11 A quibble, poor and barren as it is, gave him [Shakespeare] such delight that he was content to purchase it by the sacrifice of reason, propriety and truth. A quibble was to him the fatal Cleopatra for which he lost the world and was content to lose it. [Samuel Johnson: Preface to his edition of Shakespeare (1765)]
 quibble = *pun*

12 A pun is a noble thing per se. It fills the mind; it is as perfect as a sonnet; better. [Charles Lamb: Letter to Coleridge]

13 Punning is a low species of wit. [Noah Webster]

> *Often quoted as "the lowest form of wit." But punning is often an instrument of wit and even by themselves puns often surprise us with that "fine excess" which Keats saw as the essence of poetry. Certainly some very witty men—Charles Lamb, Thomas Hood, and, above all, Shakespeare—have been addicted to punning.*

PUNCTUALITY

14 Punctuality is the politeness of kings. [Louis XVIII: in *Souvenirs de J. Lafitte* I]

15 Punctuality is the thief of time. [Oscar Wilde: *The Picture of Dorian Gray* III]

PUNISHMENT

16 My punishment is greater than I can bear. [Genesis 4:13]

17 We withdraw our wrath from the man who admits that he is justly punished. [Aristotle: *Rhetoric* II]

> *i.e., if our victim will flatter our vanity, we will abate our cruelty.*

18 If the frost chance to nip the vines about my village, my priest doth immediately argue that the wrath of God

hangs over our head and threateneth all mankind—and judgeth that the Pip is already fallen upon the Cannibals. [Montaigne: *Essays* I.xxv.]

1   I'll rack thee with old cramps,
    Fill all thy bones with aches, make
           thee roar.
[Shakespeare: *The Tempest* I.ii.]
2 Many without punishment, but none without sin. [John Ray: *English Proverbs* (1670)]
3 The rod produces an effect which terminates in itself. A child is afraid of being whipped, and gets his task, and there's an end on 't; whereas, by exciting emulation and comparisons of superiority, you lay the foundation of lasting mischief; you make brothers and sisters hate each other. [Samuel Johnson: in Boswell's *Life* (1717-1725)]
4 To equal robbery with murder is to reduce murder to robbery, to confound in common minds the gradations of iniquity, and incite the commission of a greater crime to prevent the detection of a less. [Samuel Johnson: *The Rambler* No. 114]
   Johnson's remark was part of a protest against hanging a man for theft.
5 Whenever the offence inspires less horror than the punishment, the rigour of penal law is obliged to give way to the common feelings of mankind. [Edward Gibbon: *The Decline and Fall of the Roman Empire* XIV]
6 The fear of punishment may be necessary to the suppression of vice; but it also suspends the finer motives to virtue. [William Hazlitt: *Characteristics*]
7   My object all sublime
   I shall achieve in time—
   To make the punishment fit the
             crime.
[W. S. Gilbert: *The Mikado* II]
8 No more fiendish punishment could be devised, were such a thing physically possible, than that one should be turned loose in society and remain absolutely unnoticed by all the members thereof. [William James: *The Principles of Psychology* XII]
9 If you strike a child, take care that you strike it in anger, even at the risk of maiming it for life. A blow in cold blood neither can nor should be forgiven.

[G. B. Shaw: *Maxims for Revolutionists*]

PURE
10 Blessed are the pure in heart: for they shall see God. [Matthew 5:8]
11 Unto the pure all things are pure. [Titus 1:15]
12 The purest soul that e'er was sent
   Into a clayey tenement.
[Thomas Carew: *Epitaph on the Lady Mary Villiers*]
13 The stream is always purer at its source. [Pascal: *Lettres Provinciales* IV]
14 Oh do not thou too fondly brood . . .
   On any earthly hope, however pure!
[Wordsworth: *Elegiac Verses*]
15 Soft as the memory of buried love,
   Pure as the prayer which childhood
             wafts above.
[Byron: *The Bride of Abydos* I.vi.]
16 Blest are the pure in heart,
   For they shall see our God.
[John Keble: *The Christian Year: The Purification*]
   Keble's "our" was not intended as an emendation of Matthew 5:8; it is simply an expression of innocent monotheism.
17 She's as pure as the lily in the dell. [Harry Lauder: *I Love a Lassie*]

PURGE
18 I'll purge, and leave sack, and live
             cleanly.
[Shakespeare: *I Henry IV* V.iv.]

PURITAN(S)
19 But one puritan among them, and
      he sings psalms to hornpipes.
[Shakespeare: *The Winter's Tale* IV. iii.]
   Shakespeare had a deep aversion to puritans and dogs.
20 A formal Puritan,
   A solemn and unsexual man.
[Shelley: *Peter Bell the Third* VI]
21 The Puritan hated bear-baiting, not because it gave pain to the bear, but because it gave pleasure to the spectators. [Macaulay: *History of England* I.ii. (1849)]
   An echo of a passage in Hume's History of England *(1754), I.lxii.*
   Even bear-baiting was esteemed heathenish and unchristian: the sport of it, not the inhumanity, gave offense.

1 He is the Puritan under whose tall
hat
Evil is nested like an ugly toad,
And in his eye he holds the basilisk,
And in his weathered hand the
knotted goad;
Brimstone is on his tongue, for he
will risk
Hellfire to pleasure; sin is his abode,
A barn and Bible his best habitat.
[Karl Shapiro: *The Puritan*]

PURITANISM
2 Puritanism restricted natural pleasures; it substituted the Jeremiad for the
Paean. [Samuel Butler: (1835-1902): *The
Way of All Flesh* V]

PURITY
3 Wearing the white flower of a blameless life.
[Tennyson: Dedication of *Idylls of the
King*]
The reference is to Prince Albert.
4 My strength is as the strength of ten,
Because my heart is pure.
[Tennyson: *Sir Galahad*]
5 Feed the budding rose of boyhood
with the drainage of your sewer;
Send the drain into the fountain,
lest the stream should issue pure.
Set the maiden fancies wallowing in
the troughs of Zolaism—
Forward, forward, ay and backward,
downward too into the abysm.
[Tennyson: *Locksley Hall Sixty Years
After*]

PURPLE COW
6 I never saw a Purple Cow,
I never hope to see one;
But I can tell you, anyhow,
I'd rather see than be one.
[Gelett Burgess: *The Purple Cow*
(1895)]
*This is one of those rare rhymes that
almost instantaneously became a craze.
The popularity of the jingle was too
much for even the author's patience.
Five years later he wrote:*
Ah, yes, I wrote the "Purple Cow"—
I'm sorry, now, I wrote it!
But I can tell you, anyhow,
I'll kill you if you quote it.

PURPOSE
7 Infirm of purpose.
[Shakespeare: *Macbeth* II.ii.]
8 We shall express our darker purpose.
[Shakespeare: *King Lear* I.i.]
9 The mind is enlarged and elevated
by mere purposes, though they end as
they begin by airy contemplation. [Samuel Johnson: Letter to Hester Thrale,
November 29, 1782]
10 Yet I doubt not thro' the ages one
increasing purpose runs,
And the thoughts of men are widen'd
with the process of the suns.
[Tennyson: *Locksley Hall*]

PURSE
11 The master-organ, soul's-seat, and
true pineal gland of the body social.
[Thomas Carlyle: *Sartor Resartus* I]

PURSUIT
12 I heard among the solitary hills
Low breathings coming after me, and
sounds
Of undistinguishable motion, steps
Almost as silent as the turf they
trod.
[Wordsworth: *The Prelude* I]
13 Like one that on a lonesome road
Doth walk in fear and dread,
And having once turned round walks
on,
And turns no more his head;
Because he knows a frightful fiend
Doth close behind him tread.
[Coleridge: *The Ancient Mariner* V]

PYRAMID(S)
14 Soldiers, forty centuries look down
upon you. [Napoleon I: pointing to the
Pyramids, just before the Battle of the
Pyramids, July 2, 1797]
*Or, at least, that's what Napoleon said
he did and said.*
*Christopher Herold (Bonaparte in
Egypt) is inclined to doubt it, however.
He points out that Napoleon's soldiers
were spread over several square miles
and that the pyramids were ten miles
away. Furthermore he suspects that at
this point the common French soldier
was still "puzzled as to what the Pyramids were." Napoleon may have spoken*

the words to some of his officers.

The forty centuries were still looking down, the following spring, when Napoleon sneaked back to France and left the army to disaster.

1   Who shall doubt "the secret hid
    Under Egypt's pyramid"
    Was that the contractor did
    Cheops out of several millions?
[Kipling: *A General Summary*]

Q

QUALITY
1 Come, give us a taste of your quality.
[Shakespeare: *Hamlet* II.ii.]

QUARREL(S) (noun)
2 　　　　　　　　　Beware
Of entrance to a quarrel; but being
　　　　　　　　　　　in,
Bear 't that th 'opposed may beware
　　　　　　　　　　of thee.
[Shakespeare: *Hamlet* I.iii.]
3 Quarrels would not last long if the
fault was only on one side. [La Rochefoucauld: *Maxims*]
4 The quarrel is a very pretty quarrel
as it stands; we should only spoil it by
trying to explain it. [Richard Brinsley
Sheridan: *The Rivals* IV.iii.]
5 For souls in growth, great quarrels
are great emancipations. [Logan Pearsall
Smith: *Afterthoughts*]
6 　　　　　If you'll patch a quarrel,
As matter whole you have not to
　　　　　　　　make it with.
[Shakespeare: *Antony and Cleopatra*
II.ii.]

QUARREL(ING) (verb)
7 In quarreling the truth is always lost.
[Publilius Syrus: *Maxims*]
8 Why, thou wilt quarrel with a man
that hath a hair more or a hair less in
his beard than thou hast. Thou wilt
quarrel with a man cracking nuts, having no other reason but because thou
hast hazel eyes. . . . Thou hast quarreled with a man for coughing in the
street, because he hath wakened thy
dog that hath lain asleep in the sun.
[Shakespeare: *Romeo and Juliet* III.i.]
9 O sir, we quarrel in print, by the
book, as you have books for good manners. I will name you the degrees. The
first, the Retort Courteous; the second,
the quip Modest; the third, the Reply
Churlish; the fourth, the Reproof Valiant; the fifth, The Countercheck Quarrelsome; the sixth, the Lie with Circumstance; the seventh, the Lie Direct. All
these you may avoid but the Lie Direct,
and you may avoid that too, with an
If. [Shakespeare: *As You Like It* V.iv.]
　*avoid = evade the responsibility of, talk
　your way out of, explain away*
　　*Touchstone is delineating the degrees
　of contention for those that "quarrel in
　print, by the book." All good manners
　came from France; so, good quarreling.*
10 Quarreling dogs come halting home.
[James Kelly: *Scottish Proverbs* (1721)]
　halting = limping

QUEER
11 As queer as Dick's hatband.
　*There are many variations of the
　saying. Dick, it is generally agreed,
　was Richard Cromwell, "Tumbledown
　Dick," who succeeded his father as Pro-
　tector of England, but for only a brief
　period, and then fled to the continent
　where, against all reasonable expecta-
　tion, he lived to a great old age. The
　hatband may have been the crown.*
12 All the world is queer save thee and
me, and even thou art a little queer.
[Robert Owen: on separating from his
business partner, William Allen,
(1828)]

QUESTION(S)
13 Protagoras asserted that there were
two sides to every question, exactly opposite to each other. [Diogenes Laertius: *Protagoras*]
　*In popular logic, this is advanced as
　a warrant for every statement being the
　warranty for its opposite. In many ques-
　tions, there are not two sides; and in
　many others, there may be a score of
　valid shades of opinion.*
14 Ask me no questions, and I'll tell
you no fibs. [Oliver Goldsmith: *She
Stoops to Conquer* III]
15 A question not to be asked is a question not to be answered. [Robert
Southey: *The Doctor* XII]
16 Any question can be made immater-
ial by subsuming all its answers under a
common head. Imagine what college

ball-games and races would be if the teams were to forget the absolute distinctness of Harvard from Yale and think of both as One in the higher genus College. [William James: *Principles of Psychology* II]

1   I keep six honest serving-men
      (They taught me all I knew):
    Their names are What and Why and
                              When
    And How and Where and Who.
[Kipling: *The Serving-men*]

QUESTIONING

2   Those obstinate questionings
    Of sense and outward things,
    Fallings from us, vanishings;
    Blank misgivings of a Creature
    Moving about in worlds not realized.
[Wordsworth: *Intimations of Immortality*]

QUIET

3   The good and the wise lead quiet lives. [Euripides: *Ion*]
4   A quiet heart is a continual feast. [Proverbs 15:15]
    The quotation is from Coverdale's version (1535).
    The King James Version *(1611): He that is of a merry heart hath a continual feast.*
    Revised Standard Version (1952): A cheerful heart has a continual feast.
5   Better is an handful with quietness, than both the hands full with travail and vexation of spirit. [Ecclesiastes 4:6]
6   All the glory I pretend in my life is that I have lived quietly. [Montaigne: *Essays* II.xvi.]
7   Anything for a quiet life. [Thomas Heywood: *Captives* III.iii.]
8   But quiet to quick bosoms is a hell,
      And *there* hath been thy [Napo-

leon's] bane; there is a fire
And motion of the soul which will
                         not dwell
In its own narrow being, but aspire
Beyond the fitting medium of desire;
And, but once kindled, quenchless
                         evermore,
Preys upon high adventure, nor can
                         tire
Of aught but rest; a fever at the
                         core,
Fatal to him who bears, to all who
                         ever bore.
[Byron: *Childe Harold* III.xlii.]

9   The holy time is quiet as a Nun
    Breathless with adoration.
[Wordsworth: *It is a Beauteous Evening*]

10 Here at the quiet limit of the world.
[Tennyson: *Tithonus*]

11 All quiet along the Potomac tonight.
[Ethel L. Beers: *The Picket Guard*]

12 All Quiet on the Western Front.
[Erich Maria Remarque: title of a novel (1929)]
    One of the great realistic novels based on World War I, the title is taken from the communiqué of the German army when there was nothing to report: Im Westen, nichts neues. *The ironic use of the phrase as the novel's title is paralleled by "All Quiet Along the Potomac."*

QUOTATION

13 Some for renown, on scraps of learning dote,
    And think they grow immortal as
                         they quote.
[Edward Young: *Love of Fame*]

14 Next to the originator of a good sentence is the first quoter of it. [Emerson: *Letters and Social Aims: Quotation and Originality*]

R

RACE

1 The race is not to the swift, nor the battle to the strong. [Ecclesiastes 9:11]

RACING

2 I come down dah wid my hat caved in,
Doodah! doodah!
I go back home wid a pocket full of tin,
Oh! doodah day!
Gwine to run all night!
Gwine to run all day!
I'll bet my money on de bobtail nag—
Somebody bet on de bay.
[Stephen Foster: *Camptown Races*]

RADICAL

3 I never dared be radical when young
For fear it would make me conservative when old.
[Robert Frost: *Precaution*]
4 A radical is a man with both feet firmly planted in the air. [F. D. Roosevelt: in a radio speech, Oct. 26, 1939]

RAILLERY

5 Raillery is a mode of speaking in favor of one's wit at the expense of one's better nature. [Montesquieu: *Pensées Diverses*]
Raillery today is commonly called "kidding" or "ribbing." Under the cowardly pretense of pleasantry, it is usually sadistic.

RAILROADS

6 Railroads . . . are positively the greatest blessing that the ages have wrought out for us. They give us wings; they annihilate the toil and dust of pilgrimage; they spiritualize travel! [Nathaniel Hawthorne: *The House of Seven Gables* XVII]
7 We do not ride on the railroad; it rides upon us. [Thoreau: *Walden* II]

RAIN

8 Hath the rain a father? or who hath begotten the drops of dew? [Job 38:28]
9 He maketh his sun to rise on the evil and on the good, and sendeth rain on the just and on the unjust. [Matthew 5:45]
10 Lord, this is an huge rayn!
This were a weder for to slepen inne!
[Chaucer: *Troilus and Criseyde* III]
11 Fools have the wit to keep themselves out of the rain. [Henry Buttes: *Dyets Drie Dinner* IV]
12 When that I was and a tiny little boy,
With hey, ho, the wind and the rain,
A foolish thing was but a toy,
For the rain it raineth every day.
[Shakespeare: *Twelfth Night* V.i.]
He that has a little tiny wit—
With hey, ho, the wind and the rain—
Must make content with his fortunes fit,
Though the rain it raineth every day.
Shakespeare: King Lear III.ii.
13 While rocking winds are piping loud,
Or usher'd with a shower still,
When the gust hath blown his fill,
Ending on the rustling leaves,
With minute drops from off the eaves.
[John Milton: *Il Penseroso*]
14 The thirsty earth soaks up the rain,
And drinks, and gapes, for drink again.
[Abraham Cowley: *Anacreon*, II. "Drinking"]
15 Sir John will go, though he were sure it would rain cats and dogs. [Jonathan Swift: *Polite Conversation* II (1738)]
The appearance of a phrase in Swift's A Complete Collection of Genteel and Ingenious Conversations does not mean that it originated there, but that by 1738 it was already threadbare.
At their conception many such phrases were felicitous. Whoever first thought of "raining cats and dogs," with its suggestion of snarling and yelping tumult heard in the rush and splatter of a downpour, had something in the violence of his exaggeration that corresponded enough with the violence it described to catch and hold the fancy for centuries of all who have used the language.

1 The tucked-up sempstress walks with
hasty strides,
While streams run down her oil'd
umbrella's sides.
[Jonathan Swift: *Description of a City
Shower*]
2 It never rains but it pours. [Thomas
Gray: Letter to Dr. Wharton, February
2, 1771]
3 There was a roaring in the wind all
night;
The rain came heavily and fell in
floods.
[Wordsworth: *Resolution and Independence*]
4 For after all, the best thing one can
do
When it is raining, is to let it rain.
[Longfellow: *Tales of a Wayside Inn*]
5 Into each life some rain must fall,
Some days must be dark and dreary.
[Longfellow: *The Rainy Day*]
6 Thro' scudding drifts the rainy Hy-
ades
Vext the dim sea.
[Tennyson: *Ulysses*]
7 The rain it raineth on the just
And also on the unjust fella;
But chiefly on the just, because
The unjust steals the just's um-
brella.
[Charles Bowen: *Umbrella*]
8 It is not raining rain to me,
It's raining violets.
[Robert Loveman: *April Rain*]
9 Cleanness and rapture—excellence
made plain—
The storming, thrashing arrows of
the rain!
[Stephen Vincent Benét: *Rain After a
Vaudeville Show*]

RAINBOW
10 My heart leaps up when I behold
A rainbow in the sky:
So was it when my life began;
So is it now I am a man;
So be it when I shall grow old,
Or let me die!
The Child is father of the Man;
And I could wish my days to be
Bound each to each by natural piety.
[Wordsworth: *My Heart Leaps Up*]
piety = *filial devotion*

RAKE
11 . . . don't girls like a rake better
than a milksop? [W. M. Thackeray:
Vanity Fair XIII]

RANCOR
12 'Tis not my speeches that you do mis-
like,
But 'tis my presence that doth trouble ye.
Rancour will out.
[Shakespeare: *II Henry VI* I.i.]

RANDOM
13 Oh, many a shaft at random sent
Finds mark the archer little meant!
And many a word, at random spoken,
May soothe or wound a heart that's
broken!
[Sir Walter Scott: *The Lord of the Isles*
V.xviii.]

RANT(ING)
14 Tear a passion to tatters, to very rags,
to split the ears of the groundlings.
[Shakespeare: *Hamlet* III.ii.]
15 Nay, an thou'lt mouth,
I'll rant as well as thou.
[Shakespeare: *Hamlet* V.i.]
16 Some write a narrative of wars, and
feats
Of heroes little known, and call the
rant
An history: describe the man, of
whom
His own coevals took but little note,
And paint his person, character and
views,
As they had known him from his
mother's womb.
[William Cowper: *The Task* III]
as = *as if*

RARENESS
17 Thus did I keep my person fresh and
new,
My presence, like a robe pontifical,
Ne'er seen but wond'red at, show'd
like a feast
And won by rareness such solemnity.
[Shakespeare: *I Henry IV* III.ii.]

RARITIES
18 These eyght thynges are rare times
seene, A fayre mayden without a lover, a
great Faire without theeves, an old usurer without money, a young man with-

out joy, an old barn without Mice, a scald head without Lice, an old goate without a beard, a sleepyng man with learnyng sapience. [John Florio: *Firste Fruites* 18]

scald = *scabby*

RASHNESS

1 Rashness brings success to few, misfortune to many. [Phaedrus: *Fables* V. iv.]

2 Rashness is not always fortunate. [Livy: *Annals* XXVIII.xlii.]

An excellent saying to hold in reserve to admonish those who listened to us when we said, "Fortune favors the brave," or "Audacity, always audacity."

3 For, though I am not splenitive and rash,

Yet have I something in me dangerous.

[Shakespeare: *Hamlet* V.i.]

4 None are rash when they are not seen by anybody. [Stanislas Leszcynski: *Oeuvres du Philosophe Bienfaisant* (1763)]

RAT(S)

5 I begin to smell a rat. [Cervantes: *Don Quixote* I.iv. 10.]

6 It is the wisdom of rats that will be sure to leave a house somewhat before it fall. [Francis Bacon: *Of Wisdom for a Man's Self*]

7 How now! a rat? Dead, for a ducat, dead!

[Shakespeare: *Hamlet* III.iv.]

8 A rotten carcass of a butt, . . . the very rats

Instinctively have quit it.

[Shakespeare: *The Tempest* I.ii.]

9 Now, Muse, let's sing of rats. [James Grainger: *The Sugar Cane*]

Grainger submitted his mss. to Samuel Johnson and others, who dissuaded him from including this particular invocation in the printed version. Originally it had been mice.

The poetic fault was not—as Boswell conceived it—that of introducing rats into poetry. Shakespeare had mentioned them and T. S. Eliot was to mention them again. It was, rather, the selection of such a thoroughly unpoetical subject as the manufacture and distribution of cane sugar and, in this particular pas-

sage, a sort of clapping the muse on the back.

10 Mr. Speaker, I smell a rat; I see him forming in the air and darkening the sky; but I'll nip him in the bud. [Attr. Sir Boyle Roche]

11 Rats!

They fought the dogs and killed the cats,

And bit the babies in the cradles,

And ate the cheeses out of the vats,

And licked the soup from the cooks' own ladles,

Split open the kegs of salted sprats,

Made nests inside men's Sunday hats,

And even spoiled the women's chats

By drowning their speaking

With shrieking and squeaking

In fifty different sharps and flats.

[Robert Browning: *The Pied Piper of Hamelin*]

RAVENS

12 The eye that mocketh at his father, and despiseth to obey his mother, the ravens of the valley shall pick it out, and the young eagles shall eat it. [Proverbs 30:17]

13 O, it comes o'er my memory,

As doth the raven o'er the infected house,

Boding to all.

[Shakespeare: *Othello* IV.i.]

14 And the Raven, never flitting, still is sitting, still is sitting

On the pallid bust of Pallas just above my chamber door;

And his eyes have all the seeming of a demon's that is dreaming,

And the lamplight o'er him streaming throws his shadow on the floor;

And my soul from out that shadow that lies floating on the floor,

Shall be lifted—nevermore!

[Edgar Allan Poe: *The Raven*]

READ(ING)

15 Read, mark, learn, and inwardly digest. [*Book of Common Prayer*, "Collect for the Second Sunday in Advent"]

16 That day we read no more. [Dante: *Inferno* V]

17 Read not to contradict and confute, nor yet to believe and take for granted, nor to find talk and discourse, but to weigh and consider. [Francis Bacon: *Of*

Studies]

1 If I had spent as much time in reading as other men of learning, I should have been as ignorant as they. [Thomas Hobbes quoted in Isaac D'Israeli's *Curiosities of Literature* ii.179]

2   Who reads
Incessantly, and to his reading brings
                              not
A spirit and judgment equal or superior,
(And what he brings what needs he
                     elsewhere seek?)
Uncertain and unsettled still remains,
Deep-versed in books and shallow in
                              himself.
[John Milton: *Paradise Regained* IV. 322-327]

3 Reading furnishes our mind only with materials of knowledge; it is thinking makes what we read ours. [John Locke: *An Essay Concerning Human Understanding*]

4 Thanks to my friends for their care
                     in my breeding,
Who taught me betimes to love work-
                     ing and reading.
[Isaac Watts: *The Sluggard*]

5 Let blockheads read what blockheads wrote. [Lord Chesterfield: *Letters to His Son,* November 1, 1750]

6 A man ought to read just as inclination leads him; for what he reads as a task will do him little good. [Samuel Johnson: in Boswell's *Life,* July 14, 1763]

7 He that runs may read. [William Cowper: *Tirocinium* (1785)]

This is the classic example of a misquotation so firmly established that the original seems an error. Cowper was not the first misquoter; he had merely accepted the long-distorted version.

In Habakkuk 2:2 the Lord instructed the prophet Habakkuk to Write the vision, and make it plain upon tables, that he may run that readeth it. *Whether the running would be out of fear or out of zeal is not made certain. What is certain, though, is that the passage has been misread and misquoted for centuries. It was commonly assumed that the injunction was to write so plainly that even a running man could read it. Bacon (Advancement of Learning) so construed it: "Write it in such text and Capital*

letters, that, as the Prophet saith, He that runneth may read it." Keble made the misreading the basis of one of his hymns: "There is a book, who runs may read/ Which heavenly truth imparts."

8 He has left off reading altogether, to the great improvement of his originality. [Charles Lamb: *Detached Thoughts on Books and Reading*]

9 The art of reading is to skip judiciously. [Philip G. Hamerton (1834-1894): *Intellectual Life* IV.iv.]

Mr. Hamerton is not alone. Mr. Norman Lewis, in How to Get More out of Your Reading *states that "up to 75%" of the time normally spent in reading a book can be saved by "expert skipping."*

Expert skipping is not the same thing as skipping by an expert and one suspects that Mr. Hamerton and Mr. Lewis have confused the two. It is true that someone deeply read in a special subject can sometimes form an opinion of a new book on that subject by merely turning a few leaves and reading here and there. And this tentative opinion may prove to be a sound one, one that a careful reading will corroborate. But the expert probably turned to one or two crucial passages to judge the extent of the new author's knowledge or the bent of his attitudes. A single word is often enough to reveal a point of view and a whole set of values behind that point of view, and the expert knows that, given those values and that point of view, this or that interpretation must follow. But only the expert is equipped to make such judgments—and he can do so not because he skips but because he has read thoroughly.

10 All that wearies profoundly is to be condemned for reading. The mind profits little by what is termed heavy reading. [Lafcadio Hearn: *Reading*]

11 People say that life is the thing, but I prefer reading. [Logan Pearsall Smith: *Afterthoughts*]

12 Then I thought of reading—the nice and subtle happiness of reading . . . this joy not dulled by Age, this polite and unpunishable vice, this selfish, serene, life-long intoxication. [Logan Pearsall Smith: *Trivia,* "Consolation"]

13 Education . . . has produced a vast

population able to read but unable to distinguish what is worth reading. [G. M. Trevelyan: *English Social History* XVIII]

1 I'm quite illiterate, but I read a lot. [J. D. Salinger: *The Catcher in the Rye*]

READER

2 There is an implied contract between author and reader. [Wordsworth: Preface to *Lyrical Ballads*]

READINESS

3 If it be now, 'tis not to come; if it be not to come, it will be now; if it be not now, yet it will come: the readiness is all. [Shakespeare: *Hamlet* V.ii.]

4 It warn't no use to worry; there warn't nothing to do but just hold still, and try and be ready to stand from under when the lightning struck. [Mark Twain: *Huckleberry Finn* XXXII]

REALISM

5 There is such a difference between the way men live and the way they ought to live, that anybody who abandons what is for what ought to be will learn something that will ruin rather than preserve him. [Machiavelli: *The Prince* XV]

6 We are much beholden to Machiavelli and others, that write what men do, and not what they ought to do. [Francis Bacon: *The Advancement of Learning* II]

7 As accidental as my life may be, or as that random humour is, which governs it, I know nothing, after all, so real or substantial as myself. [Lord Shaftesbury: *Characteristics* II.353]
   accidental = *solely a matter of subjective sensation*

8 They got into a hackney coach,
   And trotted down the street.
   I saw them go: one horse was blind,
   The tails of both hung down behind,
   Their shoes were on their feet.
[Horace and James Smith: *The Baby's Debut*]
   From Rejected Addresses, *one of the most brilliant collection of parodies ever penned. The Baby's Debut is a parody of Wordsworth's "silly sooth" vein.*

9 To think that two and two are four
   And neither five nor three
   The heart of man has long been sore
   And long 'tis like to be.
[A. E. Housman: *Last Poems* XXXV]

10 Is not realism, more than it is anything else, an attitude of mind on the part of the writer toward his material, a vague indication of the sympathy and candor with which he accepts, rather than chooses, his theme? [Willa Cather: *Not Under Forty*, "The Novel Démeublé"]

REALITY

11 The dragon's wing, the magic ring,
   I shall not covet for my dower,
   If I along that lowly way
   With sympathetic heart may stray,
   And with a soul of power.

   These given, what more need I desire
   To stir, to soothe, or elevate?
   What nobler marvels than the mind
   May in life's daily prospect find,
   May find or there create?
[Wordsworth: Prologue to *Peter Bell*]

12 Here, where men sit and hear each
                        other groan;
   Where palsy shakes a few, sad, last
                        gray hairs,
   Where youth grows pale, and specter-
                        thin, and dies;
   Where but to think is to be full of
                        sorrow
   And leaden-eyed despairs;
   Where Beauty cannot keep her lus-
                        trous eyes,
   Or new Love pine at them beyond to-
                        morrow.
[Keats: *Ode to a Nightingale*]

13 Ah! poor real life, which I love. Can I make others share the delight I feel in thy foolish and insipid face? [W. D. Howells: *Their Wedding Journey*]

14 But each for the joy of working, and
                each in his separate star
   Shall draw the Thing as he sees It for
                the God of Things as They are.
[Kipling: *When Earth's Last Picture is Painted*]

15 I awoke this morning out of dreams into what we call Reality, into the daylight, the furniture of my familiar bedroom—in fact into the well-known, often-

discussed, but, to my mind, as yet un-explained Universe. [Logan Pearsall Smith: *Trivia,* "Today"]

1   Human kind
Cannot bear very much reality.
[T. S. Eliot: *Burnt Norton*]

2   Chaos is the score upon which reality is written. [Henry Miller: *Tropic of Cancer*]

3   The monstrous thing is not that men have created roses out of this dung heap, but that, for some reason or other, they should *want* roses. For some reason or other man looks for the miracle, and to accomplish it he will wade through blood. He will debauch himself with ideas, he will reduce himself to a shadow if for only one second of his life he can close his eyes to the hideousness of reality. [Henry Miller: *Tropic of Cancer*]

4   The horror no less than the charm of real life consists precisely in the recurrent actualization of the inconceivable. [Aldous Huxley: *Themes and Variations*]

5   Melancholy and remorse form the deep leaden keel which enables us to sail into the wind of reality; we run aground sooner than the flat-bottomed pleasure-lovers, but we venture out in weather that would sink them. [Cyril Connolly: *The Unquiet Grave*]

REASON (noun)

6   To make the worse appear the better reason. [Aristotle: *Rhetoric* II]

It was one of the charges brought against Socrates, that he "made the worse appear the better reason." Milton's Belial had a tongue that "Dropt manna, and could make the worse appear/ The better reason." The phrase is one of the bywords of the unreasonable; for reason could not continue to consider as the "worse" that which had been shown to be "the better reason."

7   I have no other but a woman's reason:
I think him so, because I think him so.
[Shakespeare: *The Two Gentlemen of Verona* I.ii.]

8   His reasons are as two grains of wheat hid in two bushels of chaff; you shall seek all day ere you find them, and when you have them, they are not worth the search. [Shakespeare: *The Merchant of Venice* I.i.]

9   Reason panders will.
[Shakespeare: *Hamlet* III.iv.]

10   Sure, he that made us with such large
discourse,
Looking before and after, gave us
not
That capability and god-like reason
To fust in us unused.
[Shakespeare: *Hamlet* IV.iv.]

11   As reason is a Rebel unto Faith, so Passion unto Reason. [Sir Thomas Browne: *Religio Medici* I.xix.]

12   Those that differ upon reason may come together by reason. [Benjamin Whichcote: *Moral Aphorisms*]

13   The heart has its reasons, which reason cannot know. [Pascal: *Pensées*]

14   Reason, an ignis fatuus of the mind. [John Wilmot, Earl of Rochester: *A Satyr Against Mankind*]

15   The feast of reason and the flow of soul. [Alexander Pope: *The First Satire of the Second Book of Horace*]

16   It's common for men to give pretended Reasons instead of one real one. [Benjamin Franklin: *Poor Richard's Almanack* (1745)]

17   Wretched would be the pair above all names of wretchedness who should be doomed to adjust by reason, every morning, all the minute detail of a domestic day. [Samuel Johnson: *Rasselas* XXIX]

18   This picklock Reason is still a-fum-
bling at the wards,
bragging to unlock the door of stern
Reality.
[Robert Bridges: *The Testament of Beauty* I]

19   The man who listens to Reason is lost; Reason enslaves all whose minds are not strong enough to master her. [G. B. Shaw: *Maxims for Revolutionists*]

20   But is this struggle for a healthy mind in a maggoty world really after all worth it? Are there not soporific dreams and sweet deliriums more soothing than Reason? [Logan Pearsall Smith: *Trivia,* "Microbes"]

REASON (verb)

21   I desire to reason with God. [Job

13:3]
1 Come now, and let us reason together.
[Isaiah 1:18]
2 Who reasons wisely is not therefore
wise;
His pride in reasoning, not in acting,
lies.
[Alexander Pope: *Moral Essays* I]

REBELLION
3 Rebellion lay in his way, and he
found it.
[Shakespeare: *I Henry IV* V.i.]
4 A little rebellion . . . is a medicine
necessary for the sound health of government. [Thomas Jefferson: Letter to
James Madison (1787)]
5 When the government violates the
people's rights insurrection is, for the
people and for each portion of the people, the most sacred of rights and the
most indispensable of duties. [Lafayette:
in a speech to the French Constituent Assembly, February 20, 1790]
6 The laws of God, the laws of man,
He may keep that will and can;
Not I: let God and man decree
Laws for themselves and not for me;
And if my ways are not as theirs
Let them mind their own affairs.
[A. E. Housman: *Last Poems* XII]
7 We for a certainty are not the first
Have sat in taverns while the tempest
hurled
Their hopeful plans to emptiness,
and cursed
Whatever brute and blackguard
made the world.
[A. E. Housman: *Last Poems* IX]

REBUFF
8 Then, welcome each rebuff
That turns earth's smoothness
rough,
Each sting that bids nor sit nor stand
but go!
Be our joys three-parts pain!
Strive, and hold cheap the strain;
Learn, nor account the pang; dare,
never grudge the throe!
[Robert Browning: *Rabbi Ben Ezra*]

RECEPTIVITY
9 Enough of Science and of Art;
Close up those barren leaves;

Come forth, and bring with you a
heart
That watches and receives.
[Wordsworth: *The Tables Turned*]

RECIPROCITY
10 Life cannot subsist in society but by
reciprocal concessions. [Samuel Johnson: Letter to Boswell (1766)]

RECKLESSNESS
11 Over-daring is as great a vice as over-
fearing. [Ben Jonson: *The New Inn*
IV.iii.]

RECOLLECTION
12 How dear to this heart are the scenes
of my childhood,
When fond recollection presents
them to view!
[Samuel Woodworth: *The Old Oaken
Bucket*]

RECTITUDE
13 A soul conscious of its own rectitude.
[Vergil: *Aeneid* I]
*This is often, no doubt, a comfort to the
possessor; but it is, equally often, a trial
to others.*

REED
14 Lo, thou trustest in the staff of this
broken reed, on Egypt; whereon if a
man lean, it will go into his hand, and
pierce it. [Isaiah 36:6]
15 A bruised reed shall he not break,
and the smoking flax shall he not quench.
[Isaiah 42:3]

REELING
16 "I only took the regular course," said
the Mock Turtle. "Reeling and Writhing, of course, to begin with, and then
the different branches of Arithmetic—
Ambition, Distraction, Uglification, and
Derision." [Lewis Carroll: *Alice's Adventures in Wonderland* IX]

REFORM
17 At thirty, man suspects himself a fool;
Knows it at forty, and reforms his
plan;
At fifty chides his infamous delay,
Pushes his prudent purpose of re-
solve;
In all the magnanimity of thought

Resolves, and re-resolves; then dies
the same.
[Edward Young: *Night Thoughts* I.
xviii.]
1 Bring me my bow of burning gold!
Bring me my arrows of desire!
Bring me my spear! O clouds, unfold!
Bring me my chariot of fire!

I will not cease from mental fight,
Nor shall my sword sleep in my hand,
Till we have built Jerusalem
In England's green and pleasant land.
[William Blake: Preface to *Milton*]
2 Every reform is only a mask under
cover of which a more terrible reform,
which dares not yet name itself, advances.
[Emerson: *Journals* VII]
3 The only way a woman can ever reform a man is by boring him so completely that he loses all possible interest
in life. [Oscar Wilde: *The Picture of
Dorian Gray*]
4 The utopium of the people. [Prof.
Arthur Case: commenting on vague
promises of the welfare state]

REFUGE
5 And a man shall be as an hiding place
from the wind, and a covert from the
tempest; as rivers of water in a dry place,
as the shadow of a great rock in a weary
land. [Isaiah 32:2]

REFUSAL
6 It is kindness to refuse immediately
what you intend to deny. [Publilius Syrus: *Maxims*]
7 He who refuses nothing will soon
have nothing to refuse. [Martial: *Epigrams* XII.lxxix.]
8 But yet she listen'd—'tis enough—
Who listens once will listen twice;
Her heart, be sure, is not of ice,
And one refusal no rebuff.
[Byron: *Mazeppa*]
9 There is something wanting in the
man who does not hate himself whenever
he is constrained to say no. [R. L. Stevenson: *Familiar Studies of Men and
Books* IV]

REGRET
10 　　　　What 'twas weak to do

'Tis weaker to lament, once being
done.
[Shelley: *The Cenci* V.iii.]
11 O last regret, regret can die!
[Tennyson: *In Memoriam* LXIV]
12 Familiar as an old mistake,
And futile as regret.
[Edwin Arlington Robinson: *Bewick Fin-
zer*]

REIGN
13 Better to reign in Hell than serve in
Heaven.
[John Milton: *Paradise Lost* I. 263]

REJECTION
14 I hoed and trenched and weeded,
And took the flowers to fair:
I brought them home unheeded;
The hue was not the wear.
[A. E. Housman: *A Shropshire Lad*
LXIII]

REJOICE
15 It is sad to rejoice alone. [Lessing:
Minna von Barnhelm II.iii.]

RELATIONS
16 At best, the renewal of broken relations is a nervous matter. [Henry
Brooks Adams: *The Education of Henry
Adams* XVI]
17 Really, universally, relations stop nowhere, and the exquisite problem of the
artist is eternally but to draw, by a geometry of his own, the circle within
which they shall happily appear to do so.
[Henry James: *Roderick Hudson*]

RELATIVES
18 Nature ordains friendship with relatives, but it is never very stable. [Cic-
ero: *De amicitia*]
19 And so do his sisters and his cousins
and his aunts.
[W. S. Gilbert: *H.M.S. Pinafore* I]
20 One would be in less danger
From the wiles of the stranger
If one's own kin and kith
Were more fun to be with.
[Ogden Nash: *Family Court*]

RELATIVISM
21 To the modern spirit nothing is, or
can be rightly known, except relatively

and under conditions. [Walter Pater: *Appreciations,* "Coleridge"]

RELATIVITY

1 There was a young lady named Bright,
Who could travel much faster than light.
She started one day
In the relative way
And came back on the previous night. [Anonymous]

RELIEF

2 For this relief, much thanks. [Shakespeare: *Hamlet* I.i.]

RELIGION

3 Every one's true worship was that which he found in use in the place where he chanced to be. [Montaigne: *Essays* II.xii.]

4 Religion is knight-errantry. [Cervantes: *Don Quixote* II.8.]

5 A little philosophy inclineth men's minds to atheism; but depth in philosophy bringeth men's minds about to religion. [Francis Bacon: *Of Atheism*]

6 Religion can bear no jesting. [George Herbert: *Jacula Prudentum*]

7 The religion of one seems madness unto another. [Sir Thomas Browne: *Urn-Burial* II]

8 Ignorance is the mother of devotion. [Jeremy Taylor: *To a Person Newly Converted to the Church of England*]

To a modern this would seem to be an attack on religion. But it was spoken in simple sincerity by a deeply religious man and expresses an idea long held by many of religion's warmest supporters.

9 Possibly if a true estimate were made of the morality and religions of the world, we should find that the far greater part of mankind received even those opinions and ceremonies they would die for, rather from the fashions of their countries and the constant practice of those about them than from any conviction of their reasons. [John Locke: *On Education*]

10 In matters of religion, it is very easy to deceive a man, and very hard to undeceive him. [Bayle: *Dictionary*]

11 Religion is the best armor, but the worst cloak. [Thomas Fuller: (1654-1734) *Gnomologia*]

12 It matters not what religion an ill man is of. [Thomas Fuller: (1654-1734) *Gnomologia*]
ill = *evil*

13 What religion is he of? Why, he is an Anythingarian. [Jonathan Swift: *Polite Conversation*]

14 Our religion is in a book; we have an order of men whose duty it is to teach it; we have one day in the week set apart for it, and this is in general pretty well observed: yet ask the first ten gross men you meet, and hear what they have to tell of their religion. [Samuel Johnson: in Boswell's *Life,* April 26, 1776]

15 A man who has never had religion before, no more grows religious when he is sick, than a man who has never learnt figures can count, when he has need of calculation. [Samuel Johnson: in Boswell's *Life,* April 28, 1783]

16 The various modes of worship, which prevailed in the Roman world, were all considered by the people as equally true; by the philosopher, as equally false; and by the magistrate, as equally useful. [Edward Gibbon: *Decline and Fall of the Roman Empire* II]

17 Congress shall make no law respecting an establishment of religion, or prohibiting the free exercise thereof. [*Constitution of the United States:* First Amendment, December 15, 1791]

18 No religious test shall ever be required as a qualification to any office or public trust under the United States. [*Constitution of the United States:* Article VI.iii. (1787)]

19 A God-intoxicated man. [Novalis: said of Spinoza]

20 Things have come to a pretty pass when religion is allowed to invade the sphere of private life. [Attr. William Lamb, Lord Melbourne]

21 The essence of Religion is the idea of a Moral Governor, and a particular Providence. [John Henry Newman: *The Tamworth Reading-Room*]

22 We are for religion against the religions. [Victor Hugo: *Les Misérables* VII. viii.]

A typically romantic utterance. In the popular credo there is no tenet more

*sacred than that there is something
called religion apart from all particular
religions.*

1 Even in religious fervor there is a
touch of animal heat.
[Walt Whitman: *Democratic Vistas*]
2 Religion is . . . morality touched by
emotion. [Matthew Arnold: *Literature
and Dogma* I]
3 The strongest part of our religion today is its unconscious poetry. [Matthew
Arnold: *Essays in Criticism: Second
Series,* "The Study of Poetry"]
4 God is for men and religion for
women. [Joseph Conrad: *Nostromo* IV]
5 The virtues of enterprise, diligence,
and thrift are the indispensable foundation of any complex and vigorous civilization. It was Puritanism which, by
investing them with a supernatural sanc-
tion, turned them from an unsocial eccentricity into a habit, and a religion.
[R. H. Tawney: *Religion and the Rise
of Capitalism*]
6 Fish say, they have their Stream and
Pond;
But is there anything Beyond? . . .
One may not doubt that, somehow,
good
Shall come of Water and of Mud;
And, sure, the reverent eye must see
A Purpose in Liquidity.
[Rupert Brooke: *Heaven*]
7 Mythology, religion, and philosophy
. . . are alike in that each has as its
function the interpretation of experience in terms which have human value.
[Joseph Wood Krutch: *The Modern
Temper* I]
8 The world of poetry, mythology, and
religion represents the world as a man
would like to have it, while science represents the world as he gradually comes
to discover it. [Joseph Wood Krutch:
The Modern Temper I]
9 A refusal to come to an unjustified
conclusion is an element of an honest
man's religion. [Bergen Evans: *The Natural History of Nonsense* XIX]

RELIGION: negative comments
10 To what great evils has religion
been able to impel men! [Lucretius: *De
rerum natura* I]
11 It was fear that first brought gods

into the world. [Petronius Arbiter: *Satyricon*]
12 I count religion but a childish toy,
And hold there is no sin but ignorance.
[Christopher Marlowe: *The Jew of
Malta* I.xiv.]
*Although, for safety's sake, Marlowe
placed the utterance of such daring Renaissance thoughts in the mouth of a
villain, there is good reason to believe
they may have echoed his own. At the
time of his death, the Council was inves-
tigating certain "horrible and damnable
opinions uttered by Christopher Marly."*
13 Fear of power invisible, feigned by
the mind or imagined from tales publicly allowed, [is] religion; not allowed,
superstition. [Thomas Hobbes: *Leviathan* I]
14 Men never do evil so completely and
cheerfully as when they do it from religious conviction. [Pascal: *Pensées*]
15 We have just enough religion to
make us hate, but not enough to make us
love one another. [Jonathan Swift:
Thoughts on Various Subjects]
16 The truths of religion are never so
well understood as by those who have
lost the power of reasoning. [Voltaire:
Philosophical Dictionary]
17 Every sect is a moral check on its
neighbor. Competition is as wholesome
in religion as in commerce. [Walter Savage Landor: *Imaginary Conversations,*
"Martin and Jack"]
18 There's nought, no doubt, so much
the spirit calms
As rum and true religion.
[Byron: *Don Juan* II. xxxiv.]
19 Religion is the sigh of the oppressed
creature, the feelings of a heartless world,
just as it is the spirit of unspiritual conditions. It is the opium of the people.
[Karl Marx: *Introduction to a Critique
of the Hegelian Philosophy of Right*
(1844)]
20 Where it is a duty to worship the sun,
it is pretty sure to be a crime to examine
the laws of heat. [John Morley: *Voltaire*]
21 RELIGION. A daughter of Hope and
Fear, explaining to Ignorance the nature
of the Unknowable. [Ambrose Bierce:
The Devil's Dictionary]

1 Religion is a monumental chapter in the history of human egotism. [William James: *The Varieties of Religious Experience* XX]

2 The Revelations of Devout and
        Learned
Who rose before us, and as Prophets
        burned,
Are all but Stories, which, awoke
        from Sleep,
They told their comrades, and to
        Sleep returned.
[*Rubáiyát of Omar Khayyám* (trans. Edward FitzGerald)]

3 At present there is not a single credible established religion in the world. [G. B. Shaw: Preface to *Major Barbara*]

4 Religion is comparable to a childhood neurosis. [Sigmund Freud: *The Future of an Illusion* p. 92]

5 To sum up:
1) The cosmos is a gigantic fly-wheel making 10,000 revolutions a minute.
2) Man is a sick fly taking a dizzy ride on it.
3) Religion is the theory that the wheel was designed and set spinning to give him the ride. [H. L. Mencken: in *Smart Set,* December 1920]

6 Religions, like castles, sunsets and women, never reach their maximum of beauty until they are touched by decay. [H. L. Mencken: in *Smart Set,* March 1920]

7 The Jews fastened their religion upon the Western world, not because it was more reasonable than the religions of their contemporaries—as a matter of fact, it was vastly less reasonable than many of them—but because it was far more poetical. [H. L. Mencken: in *American Mercury,* January 1924]

8 The most curious social convention of the great age in which we live is the one to the effect that religious opinions should be respected. [H. L. Mencken: in *American Mercury,* March 1930]

9 Religion, like poetry, is simply a concerted effort to deny the most obvious realities. [H. L. Mencken: *Prejudices: Third Series*]

10 What mean and cruel things men do for the love of God. [Somerset Maugham: *A Writer's Notebook*]

11 The infantile cowardice of our time which demands an external pattern, a non-human authority. . . . [Archibald MacLeish: quoted in *Time,* Dec. 22, 1958]

REMEDY(IES)

12 Extreme remedies are very appropriate for extreme diseases. [Hippocrates: *Aphorisms*]

13 Some remedies are worse than the disease. [Publilius Syrus: *Maxims*]

14 The remedy is worse than the disease. [Francis Bacon: *Of Seditions*]

15 Our remedies oft in ourselves do lie,
Which we ascribe to heaven.
[Shakespeare: *All's Well that Ends Well* I.i.]

16   Diseases desperate grown
By desperate appliance are relieved,
Or not at all.
[Shakespeare: *Hamlet* IV.iii.]

17   Things without all remedy
Should be without regard; what's
        done is done.
[Shakespeare: *Macbeth* III.ii.]

REMEMBERING HAPPIER THINGS

18 For in all adversity of fortune the worst sort of misery is to have been happy. [Boethius: *The Consolation of Philosophy* II.iv.]
Boethius d. 524

19 For of fortunes sharp adversitee
The worste kynde of infortune is this,
A man to han ben in prosperitee,
And it remembren, whan it passed is.
[Chaucer: *Troilus and Criseyde* III]

20 The memory of happier days causes a feeling of solitude in those who have lost them. [Montemayor: *Diana* VI]

21 Sorrow's crown of sorrow is remembering happier things.
[Tennyson: *Locksley Hall* (1842)]
Tennyson merely put into its now-most-commonly-quoted form one of the oldest of ideas. Dante, in the Inferno *V had said that "There is no greater pain than to recall a happy time in wretchedness."*

REMEMBRANCE

22 Sweet is the remembrance of troubles when you are in safety. [Euripides: Fragment: *Andromeda*]

23 If I do not remember thee, let my tongue cleave to the roof of my mouth. [Psalms 137:6]

1 Perhaps someday even this will be pleasant to remember.
[Vergil: *Aeneid* I]
  The Latin: Forsan et haec olim meminisse iuvabit.

2 But, lord Crist! whan that it remembreth me
Upon my yowthe, and on my jolitee,
It tikleth me aboute myn herte rote.
Unto this day it dooth myn herte bote
That I have had my world as in my tyme.
[Chaucer: Prologue to *The Wife of Bath's Tale*]
  bote = *good*

3 When to the sessions of sweet silent thought
I summon up remembrance of things past,
I sigh the lack of many a thing I sought,
And with old woes new wail my dear times' waste:
Then can I drown an eye, unused to flow,
For precious friends hid in death's dateless night,
And weep afresh love's long since cancelled woe,
And moan the expense of many a vanished sight.
[Shakespeare: *Sonnets* XXX]

4 There's rosemary, that's for remembrance. [Shakespeare: *Hamlet* IV.v.]

5 Pray, love, remember: and there is pansies, that's for thoughts. [Shakespeare: *Hamlet* IV.v.]
  Pansy *comes from the French* pensée, *"a thought."*

6 How sharp the point of this remembrance is!
[Shakespeare: *The Tempest* V.i.]

7 'Tis sweet to thinke on what was hard t'endure.
[Robert Herrick: *Satisfaction for Suffering*]

8 That which is bitter to endure may be sweet to remember. [Thomas Fuller: (1654-1734) *Gnomologia*]

9 No traces left of all the busy scene,
But that remembrance says: The things have been.
[Samuel Boyse: *The Deity*]

10 O joy! that in our embers
Is something that doth live,
That nature yet remembers
What was so fugitive!
[Wordsworth: *Intimations of Immortality*]

11 I remember, I remember
The house where I was born,
The little window where the sun
Came peeping in at morn.
[Thomas Hood: *I Remember, I Remember*]

12 I shall remember while the light lives yet,
And in the night-time I shall not forget.
[Swinburne: *Erotion*]

REMORSE

13 Leave her to heaven
And to those thorns that in her bosom lodge,
To prick and sting her.
[Shakespeare: *Hamlet* I.v.]

14 Farewell, remorse! All good to me is lost;
Evil, be thou my Good.
[John Milton: *Paradise Lost* IV.109-110]

15 Remorse, the fatal egg by Pleasure laid. [William Cowper: *The Progress of Error*]

16 Remorse is pride's *ersatz* for repentance. [Aldous Huxley: *Time Must Have a Stop* XXX]

17 One man's remorse is another's reminiscence. [Ogden Nash: *A Clean Conscience Never Relaxes*]

18 There are some people who are very resourceful
At being remorseful.
[Ogden Nash: *Hearts of Gold*]

REMOTENESS

19 Plac'd far amid the melancholy main.
[James Thomson (1700-1748): *The Castle of Indolence* I.xxx.]

20 Breaking the silence of the seas
Among the farthest Hebrides.
[Wordsworth: *The Solitary Reaper*]

REMUNERATION

21 Remuneration! O! that's the Latin word for three farthings.
[Shakespeare: *Love's Labour's Lost* III.i.]

RENDEZVOUS
1 And I to my pledged word am true,
    I shall not fail that rendezvous.
[Alan Seeger: *I Have a Rendezvous with Death*]

RENEWAL
2 For out of olde feldes, as men seith,
    Cometh al this newe corn fro yeer to yeer.
[Chaucer: *Parlement of Foules*]
3 The world's great age begins anew,
    The golden years return,
    The earth doth like a snake renew
    Her winter weeds outworn.
[Shelley: Final Chorus from *Hellas*]
    weeds = *garment*

RENUNCIATION
4 I'll give my jewels for a set of beads,
    My gorgeous palace for a hermitage . . .
    And my large kingdom for a little grave,
    A little little grave, an obscure grave.
[Shakespeare: *Richard II* III.iii.]

REPENT
5 I abhor myself, and repent in dust and ashes. [Job 42:6]
6 Well, I'll repent, and that suddenly, while I am in some liking; I shall be out of heart shortly, and then I shall have no strength to repent. [Shakespeare: *I Henry IV* III.iii.]
7 If one good deed in all my life I did, I do repent it from my very soul.
[Shakespeare: *Timon of Athens* V.iii.]
8 If my wind were but long enough to say my prayers,
    I would repent.
[Shakespeare: *The Merry Wives of Windsor* IV.v.]
9 We as often repent the good we have done as the ill. [William Hazlitt: *Characteristics*]

REPENTANCE
10 Joy shall be in heaven over one sinner that repenteth, more than over ninety and nine just persons, which need no repentance. [Luke 15:7]
11 Our repentance is not so much sorrow for the ill we have done, as fear of the ill that may happen to us in consequence. [La Rochefoucauld: *Maxims*]
12 Repentance is the virtue of weak minds.
[Dryden: *The Indian Emperor* III.i.]
13 There's no repentance in the grave.
[Isaac Watts: *Solemn Thoughts of God and Death*]
14 Come, fill the Cup, and in the fire of Spring
    Your Winter-garment of Repentance fling:
    The Bird of Time has but a little way
    To flutter—and the Bird is on the Wing.
[*Rubáiyát of Omar Khayyám* (trans. Edward FitzGerald)]
15 Indeed, indeed, Repentance oft before
    I swore—but was I sober when I swore?
[*Rubáiyát of Omar Khayyám* (trans. Edward FitzGerald)]

REPLACEMENT
16 When I am dead, you'll find it hard, says he,
    To ever find another man like me.
    What makes you think, as I suppose you do,
    I'll ever want another man like you?
[Eugene F. Ware: *He and She*]

REPOSE
17 Our foster-nurse of nature is repose.
[Shakespeare: *King Lear* IV.iv.]

REPREHENSION
18 It is easier to reprehend than to correct. [Livy: *Histories* XXX.xxx.]

REPROOF
19 Fear not the anger of the wise to raise;
    Those best can bear reproof who merit praise.
[Alexander Pope: *An Essay on Criticism* III]

REPUTATION
20 Woe unto you, when all men shall speak well of you! [Luke 6:26]
21 How many worthy men have we seen

survive their own reputation? [Montaigne: *Essays* II.xvi.]

1 Seeking the bubble reputation
Even in the cannon's mouth.
[Shakespeare: *As You Like It* II.vii.]

2 Reputation, reputation, reputation! Oh! I have lost my reputation. I have lost the immortal part of myself, and what remains is bestial. [Shakespeare: *Othello* II.iii.]

3 Reputation is an idle and most false imposition; oft got without merit, and lost without deserving. [Shakespeare: *Othello* II.iii.]

4 He that hath the name to be an early riser may sleep till noon. [James Howell: *Proverbs* (1659)]

5 No man was ever written out of reputation but by himself. [Richard Bentley, in Monk: *Life of Bentley* I. ch. 6]

6 Convey a libel in a frown,
And wink a reputation down.
[Jonathan Swift: *Journal of a Modern Lady*]

7 At every word a reputation dies.
[Alexander Pope: *The Rape of the Lock* III]

8 A man may write himself out of reputation when nobody else can do it. [Thomas Paine: *The Rights of Man* II (1791)]

9 Reputation has one advantage: it allows us to have confidence in ourselves and to declare our thoughts frankly. [Alfred de Vigny: *Journal d'un Poète*]

10 Be it true or false, what is said about men often has as much influence upon their lives, and especially upon their destinies, as what they do. [Victor Hugo: *Les Misérables* I]

11 How many people live on the reputation of the reputation they might have made! [O. W. Holmes: *The Autocrat of the Breakfast-Table* III]

12 Perhaps the most valuable of all human possessions, next to an aloof and sniffish air, is the reputation of being well-to-do. [H. L. Mencken: in *Smart Set,* May 1920]

13 The easiest way to get a reputation is to go outside the fold, shout around for a few years as a violent atheist or a dangerous radical, and then crawl back to the shelter. [F. Scott Fitzgerald: *Notebooks*]

RESEARCH

14 He made an instrument to know
If the moon shine at full or no.
[Samuel Butler (1612-1680): *Hudibras*]

15 He had been eight years upon a project for extracting sunbeams out of cucumbers, which were to be put in phials hermetically sealed, and let out to warm the air in raw, inclement summers. [Jonathan Swift: *Gulliver's Travels* III.v.]

16 [The] gloom of uninspired research. [Wordsworth: *The Excursion* IV (1814)]

RESENTMENT

17 To ruminate upon evils, to make critical notes upon injuries, and be too acute in their apprehension, is to add unto our own tortures, to feather the arrows of our enemies, and to resolve to sleep no more. [Sir Thomas Browne: *Christian Morals* III.xii.]

18 Nursing her wrath to keep it warm. [Burns: *Tam O'Shanter*]

19 The patient search and vigil long
Of him who treasures up a wrong.
[Byron: *Mazeppa* X]

RESIGNATION

20 Indifference, clad in Wisdom's guise,
All fortitude of mind supplies:
For how can stony bowels melt
In those who never pity felt!
When we are lash'd, they kiss the rod,
Resigning to the will of God.
[Jonathan Swift: *Verses on the Death of Dr. Swift*]
Kiss the rod: *schoolchildren were formerly required, after punishment, to kiss the rod with which they had been beaten, as a mark of submission. Our fathers, in this as in so much else mistaking themselves for God, greatly prized a broken and a contrite heart.*

21 I sighed as a lover, I obeyed as a son. [Edward Gibbon: *Autobiography*]
When his father ordered him to break off his engagement.

22 I strove with none; for none was
worth my strife.
Nature I loved and, next to nature,
art;
I warmed both hands before the fire
of life;
It sinks, and I am ready to depart.
[W. S. Landor: *The Last Fruit of an*

Old Tree]
1 What is called resignation is confirmed desperation. [Thoreau: *Walden* I]

RESOLUTE
2 Be bloody, bold, and resolute; laugh to scorn
The power of man, for none of woman born
Shall harm Macbeth.
[Shakespeare: *Macbeth* IV.i.]

RESOLUTION
3 The very firstlings of my heart shall be
The firstlings of my hand.
[Shakespeare: *Macbeth* IV.i.]
4 Now who will stand on either hand,
And keep the bridge with me?
[Macaulay: *Lays of Ancient Rome*, "Horatius"]
5 Let us, then, be up and doing,
With a heart for any fate;
Still achieving, still pursuing,
Learn to labour and to wait.
[Longfellow: *A Psalm of Life*]
6 Tho' much is taken, much abides; and tho'
We are not now that strength which in old days
Moved earth and heaven, that which we are, we are:
One equal temper of heroic hearts,
Made weak by time and fate, but strong in will
To strive, to seek, to find, and not to yield.
[Tennyson: *Ulysses*]
7 My purpose holds
To sail beyond the sunset, and the baths
Of all the western stars, until I die.
It may be that the gulfs will wash us down;
It may be we shall touch the Happy Isles,
And see the great Achilles, whom we knew.
[Tennyson: *Ulysses*]

RESOLVE
8 His way once chose, he forward thrust outright,
Nor stepped aside for dangers or delight.

[Abraham Cowley: *Davideis* IV.361]
9 There is no such thing in man's nature as a settled and full resolve either for good or evil, except at the very moment of execution. [Nathaniel Hawthorne: *Twice-Told Tales*, "Fancy's Show Box"]

RESPECT
10 There is no respect of persons with God. [Romans 11:11]
11 Is there no respect of place, persons, nor time in you?
[Shakespeare: *Twelfth Night* II.iii.]
12 Nothing is more despicable than respect based on fear. [Albert Camus: *Notebooks 1935-1942* III.153]

RESPECTABLE
13 Respectable means rich, and decent means poor. I should die if I heard my family called decent. [Thomas Love Peacock: *Crotchet Castle* III]
14 The more things a man is ashamed of, the more respectable he is. [G. B. Shaw: *Man and Superman* I]

REST
15 Come unto me, all ye that labour and are heavy laden, and I will give you rest. [Matthew 11:28]
16 Swich is this world; who-so it can biholde,
In eche estat is litel hertes reste;
God leve us for to take it for the beste!
[Chaucer: *Troilus and Criseyde* V]
17 All things have rest, and ripen toward the grave
In silence; ripen, fall and cease.
[Tennyson: *The Lotos-Eaters*]
18 Surely, surely, slumber is more sweet than toil, the shore
Than labour in the deep mid-ocean, wind and wave and oar;
Oh rest ye, brother mariners, we will not wander more.
[Tennyson: *The Lotos-Eaters*]
19 When Earth's last picture is painted and the tubes are twisted and dried,
When the oldest colours have faded, and the youngest critic has died,
We shall rest, and, faith, we shall need it—lie down for an aeon or two,
Till the Master of All Good Work-

men shall put us to work anew.
[Kipling: *When Earth's Last Picture Is Painted*]

RESTLESSNESS

1 In the morning thou shalt say, Would God it were even! and at even thou shalt say, Would God it were morning! [Deuteronomy 28:67]
2 When I lie down, I say, When shall I arise, and the night be gone? and I am full of tossings to and fro unto the dawning of the day. [Job 7:4]
3   Better be with the dead . . .
    Than on the torture of the mind to lie
  In restless ecstasy.
[Shakespeare: *Macbeth* III.ii.]
4 So when a raging fever burns,
    We shift from side to side by turns;
    And 'tis a poor relief we gain
    To change the place, but keep the pain.
[Isaac Watts: *Hymns and Spiritual Songs*]

RESTRAINT

5 You praise the firm restraint with which they write—
  I'm with you there, of course:
  They use the snaffle and the curb all right,
  But where's the bloody horse?
[Roy Campbell: *On Some South African Novelists*]

RESURRECTION

6 Behold a man raised up by Christ!
[Tennyson: *In Memoriam* XXXI]

RETICENCE

7 Tell it not in Gath, publish it not in the streets of Askelon; lest the daughters of the Philistines rejoice, lest the daughters of the uncircumcised triumph. [II Samuel 1:20]
8 Do you wish people to speak well of you? Then do not speak at all yourself. [Pascal: *Pensées*]
9 Tar-baby ain't sayin' nuthin', en Brer Fox, he lay low. [Joel Chandler Harris: *Uncle Remus*]

RETIREMENT

10 His helmet now shall make a hive for bees;
  And lovers' sonnets turned to holy psalms,
  A man-at-arms must now serve on his knees,
  And feed on prayers, which are Age his alms.
[George Peele: *A Farewell to Arms*]
  It was from this, one of the most beautiful of the Elizabethan lyrics, that Ernest Hemingway took the title of his great novel.
11 Far from the madding crowd's ignoble strife.
[Thomas Gray: *Elegy Written in a Country Churchyard*]
  madding (often misquoted as maddening) can mean either to act as if mad or to drive mad.

RETREAT

12 A good retreat is worth more than a foolish abiding. [William Caxton: *Jason* 23]
13 Let us make an honorable retreat. [Shakespeare: *As You Like It* III.ii.]
14 In all the trade of war no feat
  Is nobler than a brave retreat.
[Samuel Butler (1612-1680): *Hudibras*]
15 Our wearisome pedantic art of war,
  By which we prove retreat may be success.
[Robert Browning: *Luria* I.]

RETURN

16 When weather-beaten I come back; my hand
  Perhaps with rude oars torn, or sunbeams tann'd . . .
  My body a sack of bones, broken within,
  And powder's blue stains scatter'd on my skin.
[John Donne: *Elegies* V]
17 I shall return. [General Douglas MacArthur: on leaving Bataan Peninsula for Australia, 1942]

REUNION

18 O that 't were possible
  After long grief and pain
  To find the arms of my true love
  Round me once again!
[Tennyson: *Maud* II]

REVELRY

1 Let's have one other gaudy night.
[Shakespeare: *Antony and Cleopatra* III.xiii.]
gaudy *here is not disparaging. It means luxurious, brilliantly showy, fine, praiseworthy.*

2 Midnight shout and revelry,
Tipsy dance and jollity.
[John Milton: *Comus*]

3 There was a sound of revelry by
night,
And Belgium's capital had gather'd
then
Her Beauty and her Chivalry, and
bright
The lamps shone o'er fair women
and brave men;
A thousand hearts beat happily; and
when
Music arose with its voluptuous swell,
Soft eyes look'd love to eyes which
spake again,
And all went merry as a marriage
bell.
[Byron: *Childe Harold* III.xxi.]

REVENGE

4 Revenge is the poor delight of little
minds. [Juvenal: *Satires* XIII]

5 Revenge is a kind of wild justice,
which the more man's nature runs to,
the more ought law to weed it out: for
as for the first wrong, it doth but offend
the law, but the revenge of that wrong
putteth the law out of office. [Francis
Bacon: *Of Revenge*]

6 A man that studieth revenge keeps
his own wounds green. [Francis Bacon:
Of Revenge]

7 The most tolerable sort of revenge is
for those wrongs which there is no law
to remedy; but then, let a man take heed
the revenge be such as there is no law to
punish, else a man's enemy is still beforehand, and it is two for one. [Francis
Bacon: *Of Revenge*]

8 Vengeance is in my heart, death in
my hand,
Blood and revenge are hammering in
my head.
[Shakespeare: *Titus Andronicus* II.iii.]

9 Like to the Pontic sea,
Whose icy current and compulsive
course

Ne'er feels retiring ebb, but keeps
due on
To the Propontic and the Hellespont,
Even so my bloody thoughts, with
violent pace,
Shall ne'er look back, ne'er ebb to
humble love,
Till that a capable and wide revenge
Swallow them up.
[Shakespeare: *Othello* III.iii.]

10 Had all his hairs been lives, my great
revenge
Had stomach for them all.
[Shakespeare: *Othello* V.ii.]

11 I will have such revenges on you both
That all the world shall——I will do
such things,
What they are, yet I know not; but
they shall be
The terrors of the earth.
[Shakespeare: *King Lear* II.iv.]

12 O revenge, how sweet thou art! [Ben
Jonson: *The Silent Woman* IV.v.]

13 Too many there be to whom a dead
enemy smells well, and who find musk
and amber in revenge. [Sir Thomas
Browne: *Christian Morals* III.xii.]

14 Women do most delight in Revenge.
[Sir Thomas Browne: *Christian Morals*
III.xii.]

15 Which if not victory is yet revenge.
[John Milton: *Paradise Lost* II.105]

16 Revenge, at first though sweet,
Bitter ere long back on itself recoils.
[John Milton: *Paradise Lost* IX.171-172]

17 Revenge is sweet. [Thomas Southerne: *Sir Antony Love* IV.iii.]

18 A man who receives a buffet in the
dark may be allowed to be vexed; but it
is an odd kind of revenge to go cuffs in
broad day with the first he meets with
and lay the last night's injury at his door.
[Jonathan Swift: *A Tale of a Tub,* "An
Apology"]

19 Revenge is profitable, gratitude is expensive. [Edward Gibbon: *The Decline
and Fall of the Roman Empire* II]

20 Sweet is revenge—especially to
women.
[Byron: *Don Juan* I.cxxiv.]

REVERE, PAUL

21 Listen, my children, and you shall
hear,
Of the midnight ride of Paul Revere,

On the eighteenth of April, in Sev-
enty-five;
Hardly a man is now alive
Who remembers that famous day and
year.
[Longfellow: *Tales of a Wayside Inn,*
"Paul Revere's Ride"]

1 One if by land, and two if by sea;
And I on the opposite shore will be,
Ready to ride and spread the alarm
Through every Middlesex village and
farm.
[Longfellow: *Tales of a Wayside Inn,*
"Paul Revere's Ride"]

REVOLUTION

2 Every revolution is the consequence
of one revolution and the beginning
of another. [Chateaubriand: *Revolutions
Anciennes* I.i.]

3 Who stops revolutions half-way? The
bourgeoisie. [Victor Hugo: *Les Misérables* I.ii.]

4 The French Revolution had its reasons. Its wrath will be pardoned by the
future; its result is a better world.
From its most terrible blows comes a
caress for the human race. [Victor Hugo:
Les Misérables I.x.]

5 The French Revolution, which is
nothing more nor less than the ideal
armed with the sword, started to its feet,
and by the very movement, closed the
door of evil and opened the door of
good. [Victor Hugo: *Les Misérables* iii.]
iii.]

6 A revolution is not cut off square. It
has always some necessary undulations
before returning to the condition of
peace, like a mountain on descending
towards the plain. [Victor Hugo: *Les
Misérables* X.ii.]

7 This country, with its institutions,
belongs to the people who inhabit it.
Whenever they shall grow weary of the
existing government they can exercise
their constitutional right of amending it,
or their revolutionary right to dismem-
ber or overthrow it. [Abraham Lincoln:
Inaugural Address (1861)]

8 Revolutions have never lightened the
burden of tyranny: they have only shifted
it to another shoulder. [G. B. Shaw:
Preface to *The Revolutionist's Handbook*]

9 I bid you to a one-man revolution—
The only revolution that is coming.
[Robert Frost: *Build Soil—A Political
Pastoral*]

10 Revolution is delightful in the preliminary stages. So long as it's a question
of getting rid of the people at the top.
[Aldous Huxley: *Eyeless in Gaza* XXII]

11 Revolutions are apt to take their
color from the regime they overthrow.
[Richard H. Tawney: *The Acquisitive
Society*]

12 The export of revolution is nonsense.
Every country makes its own revolution
if it wants to, and if it does not want to,
there will be no revolution. [Joseph
Stalin, interview, 1936]

REVULSION

13 But wither'd beldams, auld and droll,
Rigwoodie hags wad spean a foal,
Louping and flinging on a crummock,
I wonder didna turn thy stomach.
[Burns: *Tam o'Shanter*]
beldams = *old women;* rigwoodie = *sap-
less;* spean = *wean;* louping = *leaping;*
crummock = *crutch*

REWARD(S)

14 Letters be for students, richesse for
the carefull, the world for the presump-
tuous, paradise for the devoute. [John
Florio: *Firste Fruites*]

15 See how the World its Veterans re-
wards!
A Youth of Frolics, an old Age of
Cards;
Fair to no purpose, artful to no end,
Young without Lovers, old without a
Friend;
A Fop their Passion, but their Prize
a Sot;
Alive ridiculous, and dead forgot.
[Alexander Pope: *Moral Essays* II]

16 The reward of a thing well done is to
have done it. [Emerson: *New England
Reformers*]
Emerson is quoting Seneca: Ad Lucilium
LXXI.

17 Something attempted, something
done,
Has earned a night's repose.
[Longfellow: *The Village Blacksmith*]

RHETORIC

18 For all a rhetorician's rules

Teach nothing but to name his tools.
[Samuel Butler (1612-1680): *Hudibras*]

1 For rhetoric, he could not ope
His mouth, but out there flew a trope.
[Samuel Butler (1612-1680): *Hudibras*]

2 Flowers of rhetoric, in sermons and serious discourses, are like the blue and red flowers in corn, pleasing to them who come only for amusement, but prejudicial to him who would reap profit. [Jonathan Swift: *Thoughts on Various Subjects*]

3 His speech was a fine sample, on the whole,
Of rhetoric, which the learn'd call rigmarole.
[Byron: *Don Juan* I.clxxiv.]

4 A sophistical rhetorician, inebriated with the exuberance of his own verbosity. [Benjamin Disraeli: in a speech, London, 1878]
The reference is to Gladstone.

RHINE

5 The castled crag of Drachenfels
Frowns o'er the wide and winding Rhine,
Whose breast of waters broadly swells
Between the banks which bear the vine;
And hills all rich with blossom'd trees,
And fields which promise corn and wine,
And scatter'd cities crowning these,
Whose far white walls along them shine.
[Byron: *Childe Harold* III.lv.]

RHODES, CECIL

6 I admire him [Cecil Rhodes], I frankly confess it; and when his time comes I shall buy a piece of the rope for a keepsake. [Mark Twain: *Following the Equator*]

RHYME NOR REASON (See under POETRY)

RICH: and content

7 The sleep of a laboring man is sweet, whether he eat little or much, but the abundance of the rich will not suffer him to sleep. [Ecclesiastes 5:12]

8 Poor and content is rich and rich enough,

But riches fineless is as poor as winter
To him that ever fears he shall be poor.
[Shakespeare: *Othello* III.iii.]
fineless = *boundless, indefinite, unlimited*
The fine we pay for a traffic violation is the same word; it marks the end or termination of the charge.

9 He that needs five thousand pound to live,
Is full as poor as he that needs but five.
[George Herbert: *The Church Porch* 18]

10 I am indeed rich, since my income is superior to my expense, and my expense is equal to my wishes. [Edward Gibbon: *Memoirs*]

11 A man is rich in proportion to the number of things which he can afford to let alone. [Thoreau: *Walden* II]

12 That man is the richest whose pleasures are the cheapest. [Thoreau: *Journal*, March 11, 1856]

RICH: dangers of being

13 He that maketh haste to be rich shall not be innocent. [Proverbs 28:20]

14 It is easier for a camel to go through the eye of a needle, than for a rich man to enter into the kingdom of God. [Mark 10:25]

15 He that will be rich before night, may be hanged before noon. [Sir Roger L'Estrange: *Aesop's Fables*]

16 It is the wretchedness of being rich that you have to live with rich people. [Logan Pearsall Smith: *Afterthoughts*]

RICH: and poor

17 For any city [state], however small, is in fact divided into two, one the city [state] of the poor, the other of the rich; these are at war with one another. [Plato: *The Republic* IV]

18   Small aid is wealth
For daily gladness; once a man be done
With hunger, rich and poor are all as one.
[Euripides: *Electra*]

19 It is the nature of the poor to hate and envy men of property. [Plautus:

Captivi III]

1 Then I began to think, that it is very true which is commonly said, that the one-half of the world knoweth not how the other half liveth. [Rabelais: *Works* II.xxxii.]

2 Well, whiles I am a beggar, I will rail,
And say there is no sin, but to be rich;
And, being rich, my virtue then shall be,
To say there is no vice, but beggary.
[Shakespeare: *King John* II.i.]

3 One half the world knows not how the other half lives. [George Herbert: *Jacula Prudentum*]

4 The right time to dine—for a rich man, when he is hungry; for a poor man, when he has something to eat. [Velez de Guevara: *Sobremesa* I]

An aged handy man was asked by a benevolent employer what size shoes he wore. "I wear any size," he answered, "but tens fit."

5 The rich follow Wealth, and the Poor the Rich. [Thomas Fuller (1654-1734): *Gnomologia*]

6 Benefits which are received as gifts from wealth are exacted as debts from indigence; and he that in a high station is celebrated for superfluous goodness would in a meaner condition have barely been confessed to have done his duty. [Samuel Johnson: *The Rambler* No. 166]

7 Laws grind the poor, and rich men rule the law. [Oliver Goldsmith: *The Traveler*]

8 "And wherefore do the poor complain?"
The rich man asked of me—
"Come walk abroad with me," I said,
"And I will answer thee."
[Robert Southey: *The Complaints of the Poor*]

9 The setting sun is reflected from the windows of the almshouse as brightly as from the rich man's abode. [Thoreau: *Walden* XVIII]

This must be one of the clammiest crumbs of comfort ever offered the indigent.

10 The rich and the poor—the have-nots and the haves. [E. R. Bulwer-Lytton: *Athens*]

11 The rich man in his castle,
The poor man at his gate,
God made them, high or lowly,
And ordered their estate.
[Cecil Frances Alexander: *All Things Bright and Beautiful* (1849)]

That the rich should have uttered such sentiments is understandable. But we are puzzled by the docility with which many of the poor accepted them. One of the most dreadful things about the Titanic disaster, to a modern, is the calmness with which the steerage passengers accepted class distinction in filling the life boats. See Walter Lord's A Night to Remember.

In 1963 Mrs. Alexander's famous hymn was officially removed from the Anglican hymnal, God's ordering, apparently, being open to question. The poor man at the castle gate today is waiting impatiently with the price of admission which the rich man is eager to earn by serving as a guide.

12 Avarice hoards itself poor; charity gives itself rich. [German proverb: quoted by R. C. Trench in *On the Lessons in Proverbs* (1853)]

13 It's the same the whole world over,
Isn't it a bleeding shame!
It's the rich what lives in clover;
It's the poor what gets the blame!
[Anonymous]

14 God must love the poor, said Lincoln, or he wouldn't have made so many of them. He must love the rich, or he wouldn't divide so much *mazuma* among so few of them. [H. L. Mencken: *Chrestomathy*]

RICH: miscellaneous

15 The rich have many consolations. [Plato: *The Republic* I]

16 He who wishes to become rich wishes to become so speedily. [Juvenal: *Satires* XIV]

17 Perhaps you will say a man is not young; I answer, he is rich; he is not gentle, handsome, witty, brave, good-humored, but he is rich, rich, rich, rich— that one word contradicts everything you say against him. [Henry Fielding: *The Miser* III]

1   Let me smile with the wise, and feed with the rich. [Samuel Johnson: in Boswell's *Life*, Oct. 6, 1769]

Mrs. Thrale had just praised a line from Garrick's song in Florizel and Perdita:*

I'd smile with the simple, and feed with the poor.

"Nay, my dear lady," said Johnson, "this will never do. Poor David! Smile with the simple! What folly is that! And who would feed with the poor that can help it?" Garrick was "not a little irritated" at the sally.

2   I am rich beyond the dreams of avarice. [Edward Moore: *The Gamester* II.ii.]

This passage is known to most people through Dr. Johnson's use of it. When the sale of Thrale's brewery was going forward, Johnson, one of Thrale's executors, bustled briskly about. On being asked what he estimated the value of the property to be, he answered: "We are not here to sell a parcel of boilers and vats, but the potentiality of growing rich beyond the dreams of avarice."

3   To be thought rich is as good as to be rich. [W. M. Thackeray: *The Virginians* II]

RICHARDSON, SAMUEL

4   If you were to read Richardson for the story your impatience would be so much fretted that you would hang yourself. You must read him for the sentiment. [Samuel Johnson: in Boswell's *Life*, April 6, 1772]

5   Richardson . . . could not be contented to sail quietly down the stream of his reputation, without longing to taste the froth from every stroke of the oar. [Samuel Johnson: *Johnsonian Miscellanies* I]

The reference is to Samuel Richardson (1689-1761), the novelist. Johnson laughingly told Mrs. Thrale that Richardson "died merely for want of change among his flatterers: he perished for want of more, like a man obliged to breathe the same air till it is exhausted."

RICHELIEU

6   If there be a God, the Cardinal de Richelieu will have much to answer for. If there be none, why he lived a successful life. [Pope Urban VIII: on learning of the death of Cardinal Richelieu, (quoted in Hilaire Belloc's *Richelieu*)]

The remark, with slight variations, is given in many lives of Richelieu.

RICHES

7   Riches certainly make themselves wings; they fly away as an eagle toward heaven. [Proverbs 23:5]

8   Infinite riches in a little room. [Christopher Marlowe: *The Jew of Malta* I.i.]

9   He may love riches that wanteth them, as much as he that hath them. [Richard Baxter: *Christian Ethics*]

   wanteth = *lacks*

10   The embarrassment of riches. [Voltaire: *Le Droit du Seigneur* II.vi.]

11   His best companions, innocence and
                                     health;

   And his best riches, ignorance of
                                     wealth.

[Oliver Goldsmith: *The Deserted Village*]

12   Riches have wings, and grandeur is a
                                     dream.

[William Cowper: *The Task* III]

13   Riches are chiefly good because they give us time. [Charles Lamb: Letter to Bernard Barton, October 9, 1822]

14   For all you can hold in your cold
                                 dead hand

   Is what you have given away.

[Joaquin Miller: *Peter Cooper*]

15   The simple piety that has the earnest worship of and respect for riches as the first article of its creed. [F. Scott Fitzgerald: *The Diamond as Big as the Ritz*]

RICHES: the baggage of virtue

16   He that trusteth in his riches shall fall. [Proverbs 24:28]

17   Virtue, glory, honor, all things human and divine, are slaves to riches. [Horace: *Satires* II]

18   I cannot call riches better than the baggage of virtue; the Roman word is better, *impedimenta;* for as the baggage is to any army, so is riches to virtue; it cannot be spared nor left behind, but it hindereth the march; yea and the care of it sometimes loseth or disturbeth the victory. [Francis Bacon: *Of Riches*]

Note Bacon's use of riches *as a singular.*

It is not a true plural, being an anglicization of the French richesse, *wealth.*

1 The ways to enrich are many, and most of them foul. [Francis Bacon: *Of Riches*]

2 There are some foolish rich covetous men that take a pride in having no children, because they may be thought the richer. [Francis Bacon: *Of Marriage and Single Life*]

3 There is paine in getting, care in keeping, and griefe in losing riches. [Thomas Draxe: *Bibliotheca*]

4   Let none admire
That riches grow in hell: that soil may best
Deserve the precious bane.
[John Milton: *Paradise Lost* I.690-692]
admire = *wonder at*
   Precious Bane was taken by Mary Webb, in 1924, as the title of a novel.

5 Riches have made more covetous Men, than Covetousness hath made rich Men. [Thomas Fuller (1654-1734): *Gnomologia*]

6 Since all the riches of this world
May be gifts from the devil and earthly kings,
I should suspect that I worshipped the devil
If I thanked my God for worldly things.
[William Blake: *Riches*]

RIDDLE OF THE SPHINX

7 The riddle of the Sphinx.
The Sphinx was a monster with a woman's head and bust on a lion's body. She lay in the road where it wound round a cliff on the way to Thebes and propounded her riddle to all who passed by. Those who could not answer it she destroyed. In the story of Oedipus her riddle was: What is it that walks on four legs in the morning, on two at noon, on three in the evening? Oedipus solved the riddle: it was man, who crawled as a child, stood erect in manhood and leaned on a staff in his old age. The Sphinx hurled herself over the cliff when he gave the proper answer and he—to his woe—was made King of Thebes and given the queen, Jocasta, to wife.
   Shelley, in the Final Chorus from

Hellas, *prophesies man's ultimate triumph:*
   Although a subtler sphinx renew
   Riddles of death Thebes never knew.

RIDICULE

8 Man learns more readily and remembers more willingly what excites his ridicule than what deserves his esteem and respect. [Horace: *Epistles* II]

9 Ridicule dishonors more than dishonor. [La Rochefoucauld: *Maxims*]

10 A man who has the gift of ridicule is apt to find fault with any thing that gives him an opportunity of exerting his beloved talent. [Joseph Addison: *The Spectator* No. 291]

11 Mockery is often indigence of wit. [La Bruyère: *Les Caractères* Ch. 5]

12 [Ridicule] often checks what is absurd, and fully as often smothers that which is noble. [Sir Walter Scott: *Quentin Durward* Ch. 24]

RIFT

13 It is the little rift within the lute,
That by and by will make the music mute,
And ever widening slowly silence all.
[Tennyson: *Merlin and Vivien*]

RIGHT

14 *Dieu et mon droit.* ("God and my own right.") [Motto of the royal arms of England: adopted by Richard I (The Lion-hearted) at the battle of Gisors (1198), as an assertion that he was not a vassal of France but was royal by God's grace and his own right.]

15 He that will do right in gross must needs do wrong by retail. [Montaigne: *Essays* III.xiii.]
   Montaigne says this is an "ancient opinion." The issue is, surely, in the word needs. *Must one of necessity do wrong in little things to do right in great ones? Is it even permissible?*

16 Right now is wrong, and wrong that was is right,
As all things else in time are changed quite.
[Edmund Spenser: Prologue to *The Faerie Queene* V]

17 All nature is but art, unknown to

thee;
All chance, direction, which thou
canst not see;
All discord, harmony not understood;
All partial evil, universal good;
And spite of pride, in erring reason's
spite,
One truth is clear, Whatever is, is
right.
[Alexander Pope: *An Essay on Man* I]
1 A fool must now and then be right,
by chance. [William Cowper: *Conversation*]
2 I would rather be right than be
President. [Henry Clay: in a speech in
the United States Senate (1850)]
*No man ever wanted more to be President than Clay. He ran three times for
the presidency and was defeated.*
3 Divine *right*, take it on the great
scale, is found to mean divine *might*
withal! [Thomas Carlyle: *Heroes and
Hero Worship* VI]
4 Let us have faith that right makes
might, and in that faith let us to the end
dare to do our duty as we understand it.
[Abraham Lincoln: in an address at
Cooper Union, N.Y., Feb. 27, 1860]
5 Because right is right, to follow right
Were wisdom in the scorn of consequence.
[Tennyson: *Oenone*]
6 God's in his heaven—
All's right with the world!
[Robert Browning: *Pippa Passes* I]
7 Always do right. This will gratify
some people, and astonish the rest.
[Mark Twain: *To the Young People's
Society, Greenpoint Presbyterian Church,
Brooklyn*]
8 I am right, and you are right,
And all is right as right can be.
[W. S. Gilbert: *The Mikado* I]
9 Oh, don't the days seem lank and
long,
When all goes right and nothing goes
wrong?
And isn't your life extremely flat
With nothing whatever to grumble
at?
[W. S. Gilbert: *Princess Ida* III]
10 The need to be right—the sign of a
vulgar mind. [Albert Camus: *Notebooks
1935-1942* I]

11 The bitterness of being right. [Albert Camus: *Notebooks 1935-1942* III]

RIGHTEOUS

12 Who ever perished, being innocent?
or where were the righteous cut off?
[Job 4:7]
*These words of Eliphaz the Temanite
are much quoted to strengthen the virtuous. But they beg the question, since
they assume that all who perish or are
cut off are neither innocent nor righteous. Furthermore in 42:7, God's wrath
was kindled against Eliphaz, "for ye have
not spoken of me the thing that is right."*
13 Is it any pleasure to the Almighty,
that thou art righteous? [Job 22:3]
14 I have been young, and now am old;
yet have I not seen the righteous forsaken, nor his seed begging bread.
[Psalms 37:25]
15 The righteous shall flourish like the
palm tree: he shall grow like a cedar in
Lebanon. [Psalms 92:12]
16 Be not righteous overmuch. [Ecclesiastes 7:16]

RIGHTEOUSNESS

17 Blessed is the man that walketh not
in the counsel of the ungodly, nor standeth in the way of sinners, nor sitteth in
the seat of the scornful. [Psalms 1:1]
18 Righteousness exalteth a nation.
[Proverbs 14:34]
19 Ye high, exalted, virtuous Dames,
Tied up in godly laces,
Before ye gie poor Frailty names,
Suppose a change o' cases;
A dear lov'd lad, convenience snug,
A treacherous inclination—
But, let me whisper i' your lug,
Ye're aiblins nae temptation.
[Burns: *Address to the Unco Guid*]
unco guid = *uncommonly virtuous;* gie
= *give;* lug = *ear;* aiblins = *perhaps*

RIGHTS

20 A sort of institution and digest of
anarchy, called the Rights of Man. [Edmund Burke: *Reflections on the Revolution in France*]
21 Among the natural rights of the colonists are these: First a right to life,
secondly to liberty, thirdly to property.
[Samuel Adams: *Statement of the Rights*

of the Colonists, November 20, 1772]

1 We hold these truths to be self-evident—that all men are created equal; that they are endowed by their Creator with certain unalienable rights; that among these are life, liberty and the pursuit of happiness. [Thomas Jefferson: *The Declaration of Independence*, July 4, 1776]

2 A generation may bind itself as long as its majority continues in life; when that has disappeared, another majority is in its place, holds all the rights and powers their predecessors once held, and may change their laws and institutions to suit themselves. Nothing then is unchangeable but the inherent and unalienable rights of man. [Thomas Jefferson: Letter to Major John Cartwright (1824)]

> But what "inherent and unalienable" rights are there which a majority cannot, by amending the Constitution, abrogate?

3 There is no such thing as "natural rights"; there are only adjustments of conflicting claims. [Aldous Huxley: *Music at Night*, "Notes on Liberty"]

RILEY

4 Is that Mr. Riley, can anyone tell?
Is that Mr. Riley that owns the hotel?
Well, if that's Mr. Riley, they speak
of so highly,
Upon me soul, Riley, you're doin'
quite well.
[Pat Rooney: *Is That You, Mr. Riley?*]

> Professor Spaeth (A History of Popular Music in America, N.Y., Random House, 1948, p. 277) says that the authorship is "beyond dispute." The "basic authorship," that is; for Rooney's song was the origin of a cycle in which the affluent Hibernian was variously Reilly and O'Reilly, though the first name remained Terence.
>
> The singer is merely dreaming of what he will do when he strikes it rich. The famous chorus—above—is his pleasing imagination of the excited cries of the crowd as he strolls up Broadway.
>
> The sinister, saturnine Bolingbroke, in Shakespeare's I Henry IV (III.ii.) perceived—though he pretended to scorn—the eager curiosity of the crowd as a sign of greatness:

> By being seldom seen, I could not
> stir
> But, like a comet, I was wondered
> at;
> That men would tell their children,
> "This is he!"
> Others would say, "Where? Which
> is Bolingbroke?"

RIOT

5 Wasted his substance with riotous living. [Luke 15:13]

6 Our sovereign Lord the King chargeth and commandeth all persons being assembled immediately to disperse themselves, and peaceably to depart to their habitations. [*Act for Preventing Tumults and Riotous Assemblies* (1714)]

> The Riot Act of 1714 empowered a Justice, Sheriff, Mayor, or other person in authority to read a proclamation beginning with the above words. After the reading of the proclamation (or the hindering of its reading), continued assembly constituted a felony. The reading of this proclamation (not the act itself) thus constituted a serious procedure, and usually served to quell most tumults and disperse most unlawful assemblies, for felony was punishable by death.

RIPENESS

7 And so, from hour to hour, we ripe
and ripe,
And then, from hour to hour, we rot
and rot.
[Shakespeare: *As You Like It* II.vii.]

8 Men must endure
Their going hence, even as their coming hither:
Ripeness is all.
[Shakespeare: *King Lear* V.ii.]

RISE AND FALL

9 For the lives, not only of men, but of Commonwealths, and the whole World, run not upon an Helix that still enlargeth; but on a Circle, where arriving to their Meridian, they decline in obscurity, and fall under the Horizon again. [Sir Thomas Browne: *Religio Medici* I.xvii.]

> still = continually

RISING

1 Pompey bade Sylla recollect that more worshipped the rising than the setting sun. [Plutarch: *Life of Pompey*]

2 He doth like the ape, that the higher he climbs the more he shows his ars. [Francis Bacon: *Promus*]

The saying, derogatory to those who are rising in the world, appears in many languages. It is not likely that Bacon invented it.

3 The rising unto place is laborious, and by pains men come to greater pains; and it is sometimes base; and by indignities, men come to dignities. [Francis Bacon: *Of Vainglory*]

4 Men rather honour the sun rising than the sun going down. [George Chapman: *Alphonsus* I.i.]

5 Scorning the base degrees
By which he did ascend.
[Shakespeare: *Julius Caesar* II.i.]

6 There are three methods by which a man may rise to be chief minister: the first is by knowing how with prudence to dispose of a wife, a daughter, or a sister; the second, by betraying or undermining his predecessor; and the third by a furious zeal in public assemblies against corruptions. [Jonathan Swift: *Gulliver's Travels* IV.vi.]

7 And hate for arts that caused himself to rise. [Alexander Pope: *Epistle to Dr. Arbuthnot*]

8 I held it truth, with him who sings
To one clear harp in divers tones,
That men may rise on stepping-stones
Of their dead selves to higher things.
[Tennyson: *In Memoriam* I]

THE RISING MAN

9 Love ends with hope, the sinking statesman's door
Pours in the morning worshipper no more;
For growing names the weekly scribbler lies,
To growing wealth the dedicator flies.
[Samuel Johnson: *The Vanity of Human Wishes*]

10 How many "coming men" has one known? Where on earth do they all go to? [Sir Arthur Wing Pinero: *The Notorious Mrs. Ebbsmith*]

RISK

11 Be wary of the man who urges an action in which he himself incurs no risk. [Joaquin Setanti: *Centellas*]

RIVALRY

12 In ev'ry age and clime we see
Two of a trade can ne'er agree.
[John Gay: *The Rat-catcher and the Cats*]

RIVER

13 The river glideth at his own sweet will.
[Wordsworth: *Composed upon Westminster Bridge*]

14 He told me . . . he would sell me down river. [Harriet Beecher Stowe: *Uncle Tom's Cabin* III]

A slave in the border states, employed chiefly around the house or in ordinary farm work, regarded being sold to one of the cotton plantations in the deep South as little better than a sentence of death.

15 Let us cross the river and rest in the shade. ["Stonewall" Jackson: dying words (May 10, 1863)]

Quoted—slightly differently—by Stephen Vincent Benét in John Brown's Body *(1928) and used—again the wording slightly different—by Ernest Hemingway as the title of one of his last novels.*

16 Yes, we'll gather at the river,
The beautiful, the beautiful river,
Gather with the saints at the river
That flows from the throne of God.
[Robert Lowry: *Shall We Gather at the River?*]

17 Dark brown is the river,
Golden is the sand,
It flows along for ever,
With trees on either hand.
[R. L. Stevenson: *A Child's Garden of Verses*]

ROADS

18 Two roads diverged in a wood, and I—
I took the one less traveled by,
And that has made all the difference.
[Robert Frost: *The Road Not Taken*]

ROAR

19 I will roar you as gently as any sucking dove; I will roar you, as 'twere any nightingale. [Shakespeare: *A Midsummer Night's Dream* I.ii.]

ROAST BEEF

1 When mighty roast beef was the Englishman's food
It ennobled our hearts and enriched
our blood—
Our soldiers were brave and our courtiers were good.
Oh! the roast beef of England,
And Old England's roast beef.
[Henry Fielding: *Grub Street Opera*
III.ii.]
*Though the masses of Englishmen can at
no time have had much roast beef, it is
popular to assume that it is plentiful and
sentimental to assume that it was once
more so and that times were better when
it was. (See Hogarth's drawing "Calais
Gate.") It was well known that the enfeebled French ate frogs' legs.*

ROBBERY

2 He that is robb'd, not wanting what
is stolen,
Let him not know't and he's not
robb'd at all.
[Shakespeare: *Othello* III.iii.]
The loss which is unknown is no loss.
Publilius Syrus: Maxims

ROBBING PETER

3 He robbeth Peter to pay Paul. [John
Florio: *Firste Fruites* (1578)]
*Florio was simply using a proverbial say-
ing that had been in use for more than a
century. In France there had been a saying "to strip Peter to clothe Paul" and
there are other variations. It is sometimes asserted that the expression derives from the refusal of Dean Williams
to take from the lands of St. Peter's at
Westminster Abbey to give to the maintenance of St. Paul's Cathedral. So stated
by Fuller in Church-History of Britain
XI (1655), and others. But the expression
had been long in use and counterparts
existed in other European languages. Alliteration probably had more to do with
it than any historical event.*

4 Give not Saint Peter so much, to
leave Saint Paul nothing. [George Herbert: *Jacula Prudentum*]

ROBE

5 Now does he feel his title
Hang loose about him, like a giant's
robe
Upon a dwarfish thief.
[Shakespeare: *Macbeth* V.ii.]

ROBESPIERRE

6 The seagreen Incorruptible.
[Thomas Carlyle: *The French Revolution* II]
*Carlyle's famous epithet for Robespierre
was based on the revolutionary leader's
pallor and his uncompromising fanaticism.*

ROBIN

7 Who killed Cock Robin?
*Anon. nursery rhyme. Earliest known
recording: 1744. May refer to fall of Sir
Robert Walpole (1742) but probably very
much older. May allude to Balder.*

ROBIN OSTLER

8 This house is turned upside down
since Robin Ostler died. [Shakespeare:
I Henry IV II.i.]

ROBINSON CRUSOE

9 There exists one book, which, to my
taste, furnishes the happiest treatise of
natural education. What then is this
marvellous book? Is it Aristotle? Is it
Pliny, is it Buffon? No—it is *Robinson
Crusoe*. [Jean Jacques Rousseau: *Émile*
III]

ROCK

10 Rock of Ages, cleft for me,
Let me hide myself in Thee!
[Augustus Montague Toplady: *Rock of
Ages* (1776)]
*The thought of the great hymn seems to
have been borrowed from Daniel Brevint
(1679).*

11 Come one, come all! this rock shall
fly
From its firm base as soon as I.
[Sir Walter Scott: *Lady of the Lake* V.x.]

ROD

12 Spare the rod and spoil the child.
[One of the oldest of English proverbs,
going back to the year A.D. 1000]
*It is borrowed from the Latin. The senti-
ment is widespread in many languages.*

1 He that spareth his rod hateth his son: but he that loveth him chasteneth him betimes. [Proverbs 13:24]
This is the nearest the Bible comes to "Spare the rod and spoil the child."

2 He that will not use the rod on his child, his child shall be used as a rod on him. [Thomas Fuller (1608-1661): *The Good Parent*]

RODERICK
3 Where, where was Roderick then?
One blast upon his bugle horn
Were worth a thousand men!
[Sir Walter Scott: *The Lady of the Lake* VI.xviii.]

ROGUE
4 What a frosty-spirited rogue is this! [Shakespeare: *I Henry IV* II.iii.]

5 A more praeternotorious rogue than himself. [John Fletcher: *Fair Maid of the Inn* IV]

ROLAND
6 To give one a Roland for an Oliver. [John Ray: *English Proverbs* (1670)]
Proverbial for more than a century before, meaning, as Ray adds, "a quid pro quo, to be even with one." Roland and Oliver were two of Charlemagne's Paladins, evenly matched in strength and prowess.

ROMAN(S)
7 I am a Roman citizen. (*Civis Romanus sum.*) [Cicero: *In Verrem* VI. lvii.]
In impeaching Gaius Verres, the cruel and rapacious propraetor in Sicily (73-71 B.C.), Cicero told of Publius Gavius who when beaten with rods in the forum at Messina made no groan or outcry, but with dignity said only, "I am a Roman citizen"—and, therefore, not to be so treated.

8 It is not the custom of the Roman people to make any conditions with an enemy under arms. [Caesar: *De bello Gallico* V.xli.]

9 Friends, Romans, countrymen, lend me your ears;
I come to bury Caesar, not to praise him.
The evil that men do lives after them,
The good is oft interred with their bones.
[Shakespeare: *Julius Caesar* III.ii.]

10 This was the noblest Roman of them all.
[Shakespeare: *Julius Caesar* V.v.]

11 The gale, it plies the saplings double,
It blows so hard, 'twill soon be gone:
To-day the Roman and his trouble
Are ashes under Uricon.
[A. E. Housman: *A Shropshire Lad* XXXI]

ROMANCE
12 Alas! they were so young, so beautiful,
So lonely, loving, helpless, and the hour
Was that in which the heart is always full,
And, having o'er itself no further power,
Prompts deeds eternity cannot annul.
[Byron: *Don Juan* II.cxcii.]

13 When I behold, upon the night's starr'd face,
Huge cloudy symbols of a high romance.
[Keats: *When I Have Fears*]

14 Nothing spoils a romance so much as a sense of humour in the woman. [Oscar Wilde: *A Woman of No Importance* I]

15 When one is in love, one always begins by deceiving oneself, and one always ends by deceiving others. That is what the world calls a romance. [Oscar Wilde: *The Picture of Dorian Gray* IV]

ROMAN HOLIDAY
16 Butcher'd to make a Roman holiday. [Byron: *Childe Harold* IV.cxli.]
Said of the dying gladiator.

ROMANTIC SPIRIT
17 The essential elements . . . of the romantic spirit are curiosity and the love of beauty. [Walter Pater: *Appreciations,* "Postscript"]

ROME
18 He [Caesar Augustus] found Rome brick and left it marble. [Suetonius: *Divus Augustus* II.xxviii.]

19 When I am at Rome I fast as the Romans do; when I am at Milan I do

not fast. So likewise you, whatever church you come to, observe the custom of the place. [St. Ambrose (337-397 A.D.): *Advice to St. Augustine on Sabbath Keeping*]

1 Diverse pathes leden diverse folk the righte way to Rome. [Chaucer: Prologue to *Astrolabe*]

2 When they are at Rome, they do there as they see done. [Robert Burton: *The Anatomy of Melancholy* III.4.2.1]

3 All roads lead to Rome. [Voltaire: Letter to Mme. de Fontaine, Sept. 23, 1750]

4 The Goth, the Christian, Time, War, Flood, and Fire,
Have dealt upon the seven-hill'd city's pride;
She saw her glories star by star expire,
And up the steep barbarian monarchs ride,
Where the car climb'd the Capitol.
[Byron: *Childe Harold* IV.lxxx.]

5 The Niobe of nations! there she stands
Childless and crownless, in her voiceless woe.
[Byron: *Childe Harold* IV.lxxix.]
Niobe, the mother of 12 children, taunted the goddess Latona because she had only 2. The goddess had her two, Apollo and Diana, kill Niobe's twelve. Niobe, the personification of maternal sorrow, changed to a stone from which water flowed. Cf.: "like Niobe, all tears" (Hamlet I.ii.).

6 Go thou to Rome—at once the Paradise,
The grave, the city, and the wilderness.
[Shelley: *Adonais*]

7 The grandeur that was Rome. [Edgar Allan Poe: *To Helen*]

8 It is fiddling while Rome is burning. [Charles Kingsley: *Westward Ho!* X]
Kingsley was using a proverbial phrase. That Nero fiddled while Rome burned goes back to at least George Daniel's Trinarchodia (1649). Some say that he played the lute or lyre. Suetonius, in Nero XXXVIII, says that he set the city on fire and then "exulting in the beauty of the flames" sang the "Sack of Ilium" in a stage costume. Tacitus says that Nero was 50 miles away, hurried back

and did what he could to control the fire and assist its victims.

So villainous is Nero in our minds that we are startled to learn that the Romans revered his memory and the Greeks honored him, for a century after his death, as a great patron of literature and art. He was thought to be immortal and it was believed he would return in time of need as a savior.

ROMEO

9 O Romeo, Romeo! wherefore art thou Romeo?
[Shakespeare: *Romeo and Juliet* II.ii.]

ROOM

10 I had as lief have their room as their company. [Robert Greene: *Farewell to Folly* (1591)]
A common Elizabethan expression of contempt, still heard in England.

11 A smoke-filled room. [Harry M. Daugherty (1920): in Mark Sullivan's *Our Times* VI.xxxvii.]
Daugherty, Warren G. Harding's campaign manager, predicted that his man would be selected—as he was—not on the floor of the convention, but in "a smoke-filled room in some hotel" at two in the morning, after the convention had become deadlocked over other candidates.

ROOTS

12 Beauty, strength, youth, are flowers but fading seen;
Duty, faith, love, are roots, and ever green.
[George Peele: *A Farewell to Arms*]

ROPE(S)

13 The captain, who "knew the ropes," took the steering oar. [Richard Henry Dana: *Two Years Before the Mast* IX (1840)]
This passage is adduced as evidence that the phrase "knew the ropes" is nautical in origin. But it seems, rather, to prove that it is not, since Dana carefully encloses it in quotation marks to suggest that he knew he was using it out of its proper meaning. The oldest known uses of the expression refer to the racetrack, the ropes being the reins and those who

knew *them being the most successful
jockeys.*

ROPE OF SAND
1   For he a rope of sand could twist
As tough as learned Sorbonist.
[Samuel Butler (1612-1680): *Hudibras*]

ROSARY
2   The hours I spent with thee, dear
heart,
Are as a string of pearls to me;
I count them over, every one apart,
My rosary, my rosary.
[Robert Cameron Rogers: *My Rosary*]

ROSE(S)
3   The desert shall rejoice and blossom
as the rose. [Isaiah 35:1]
4   I am the rose of Sharon, and the lily
of the valleys. [Song of Solomon 2:1]
5   When the rose dies, the thorn is left
behind. [Ovid: *Ars amatoria* II.cxvi.]
6   That which we call a rose
By any other name would smell as
sweet.
[Shakespeare: *Romeo and Juliet* II.ii.]
7   But ne'er the rose without the thorn.
[Robert Herrick: *The Rose*]
8   He repents in thorns, that sleeps in
beds of roses. [Francis Quarles: *Emblems*
I.vii.]
9   Ask no more where Jove bestows,
When June is past, the fading rose;
For in your beauty's orient deep
These flowers, as in their causes sleep.
[Thomas Carew: *To Celia*]
10   When we desire to confine our words,
we commonly say they are spoken under
the rose. [Sir Thomas Browne: *Pseu-
doxia Epidemica* V.xxii.]
*The term "under the rose" or in its
Latin form, sub rosa, as an expression
meaning "in secrecy," came into use in
English about the time of the early
Tudors. There was a story that Cupid
had bribed Harpocrates, the god of
silence, with a rose to conceal the doings
of Venus. Banqueting halls sometimes
had a rose carved in the ceiling to signify that whatever was spoken under the
influence of wine or within the license
and protection of hospitality was to be
regarded as confidential.*
11   Go, lovely rose!

Tell her that wastes her time and me
That now she knows,
When I resemble her to thee,
How sweet and fair she seems to be.
[Edmund Waller: *Go, Lovely Rose*]
*"But most of all I envy the octogenarian
poet who joined three words—
'Go, lovely Rose'—
so happily together, that he left his
name to float down through Time on
the wings of a phrase and a flower."*
Logan Pearsall Smith: Afterthoughts
12   Die of a rose in aromatic pain. [Alex-
ander Pope: *An Essay on Man* I (1733)]
*Insisting that "whatever is, is right,"
Pope says that had man more sensitive
perceptions than he has, he might not be
able to bear them, that he might "Die of
a rose, etc."*
*There seems to be an echo here of a
couplet from Anne Finch, Lady Win-
chilsea's The Spleen (1701):*
*Now the Jonquille o'ercomes the
feeble brain;*
We faint beneath the aromatic pain.
13   Red as a rose is she.
[Coleridge: *The Ancient Mariner* I]
14   'Tis the last rose of summer,
Left blooming alone;
All her lovely companions
Are faded and gone.
[Thomas Moore: *The Last Rose of Summer*]
15   You may break, you may shatter the
vase, if you will,
But the scent of the roses will hang
round it still.
[Thomas Moore: *Farewell!*]
16   And mid-May's eldest child,
The coming musk-rose, full of dewy
wine,
The murmurous haunt of flies on
summer eves.
[Keats: *Ode to a Nightingale*]
17   As though a rose should shut, and be
a bud again.
[Keats: *The Eve of St. Agnes* XXVII]
18   I sometimes think that never blows
so red
The Rose as where some buried Caesar bled;
That every Hyacinth the Garden
wears
Dropt in her Lap from some once
lovely Head.

[*Rubáiyát of Omar Khayyám* (trans. Edward FitzGerald)]
1 Sweetest li'l feller, everybody knows;
Dunno what to call him, but he's
mighty lak' a rose.
[Frank L. Stanton: *Mighty Lak' a Rose*]
2 Rose is a rose is a rose is a rose. [Gertrude Stein: *Sacred Emily*]

ROSE AYLMER
3 Ah, what avails the sceptered race,
Ah, what the form divine!
What every virtue, every grace!
Rose Aylmer, all were thine.
Rose Aylmer, whom these wakeful
eyes
May weep, but never see,
A night of memories and of sighs
I consecrate to thee.
[Walter Savage Landor: *Rose Aylmer*
(1806)]
*Rose Aylmer, an early love of Landor's,
had died in India in 1800.*

ROSEBUDS
4 Let us crown ourselves with rosebuds
before they be withered. [The Apocrypha. Wisdom of Solomon 2:8]

ROTTEN
5 Something is rotten in the state of
Denmark.
[Shakespeare: *Hamlet* I.iv.]

ROUGHNESS
6 Roughness is a needless cause of discontent: severity breedeth fear, but
roughness breedeth hate. [Francis Bacon: *Of Great Place*]

ROUSSEAU
7   . . . wild Rousseau,
The apostle of affliction, he who
threw
Enchantment over passion, and from
woe
Wrung overwhelming eloquence.
[Byron: *Childe Harold* III.lxxvii.]

ROW (verb)
8 And all the way, to guide their chime,
With falling oars they kept the time.
[Andrew Marvell: *Bermudas*]
9 Row, brothers, row, the stream runs
fast,

The rapids are near, and the daylight's past.
[Thomas Moore: *A Canadian Boat-song*]

ROYAL ROAD
10 There is no royal road to geometry.
[Euclid: to Ptolemy I, when the monarch asked if there were not some easier
ways of mastering geometry than learning it]

RUBICON
11 Crossing the Rubicon.
*The Rubicon was a small stream which
in ancient Italy formed the boundary
between Italy and Cisalpine Gaul. Julius
Caesar had been given command of the
Gallic legions but he had no military authority in Italy itself and when, in 49
B.C., he crossed the Rubicon, he knew
that by so doing he had started a civil
war.*
*Plutarch tells us (Life of Caesar) that,
when he came to the fateful stream, he
communed with himself for a long time
in silence, "computing how many calamities his passing that river would bring
upon mankind." But finally "with a sort
of passion . . . uttering the phrase with
which men usually prelude their plunge
into desperate and daring fortunes, 'Let
the die be cast,' he hastened to cross the
river."*
*Suetonius (The Deified Julius, XXXII)
says that a wondrous apparition appeared
as Caesar stood in doubt and, "sounding
the war-note," led the way across, so that
Caesar merely took "the course which
the signs of the gods pointed out," an
interpretation of which the deified Julius
would have warmly approved.*

RUDENESS
12 This rudeness is a sauce to his good
wit,
Which gives men stomach to digest
his words
With better appetite.
[Shakespeare: *Julius Caesar* I.ii.]
13 Incivility is not a Vice of the Soul,
but the effect of several Vices: of Vanity,
Ignorance of Duty, Laziness, Stupidity,
Distraction, Contempt of others, and
Jealousy. [La Bruyère: *Les Caractères*]
distraction = *absent mindedness*

1 For conversation well endu'd,
    She calls it witty to be rude;
    And, placing raillery in railing,
    Will tell aloud your greatest failing.
[Jonathan Swift: *The Furniture of a Woman's Mind*]

RUE

2 You must wear your rue with a difference.
[Shakespeare: *Hamlet* IV.v.]

RUGGED INDIVIDUALISM

3 The American system of rugged individualism. [Herbert Hoover: in a speech, in New York, Oct. 22, 1928]

RUIN(S)

4 Thou art the ruins of the noblest man
    That ever lived in the tide of times.
[Shakespeare: *Julius Caesar* III.i.]
5 Stern ruin's ploughshare drives elate
    Full on thy bloom.
[Burns: *To a Mountain Daisy*]
6 There's a fascination frantic
    In a ruin that's romantic;
    Do you think you are sufficiently decayed?
[W. S. Gilbert: *The Mikado* II]
7 "And whence such fair garments, such prosperi-ty?"
    "O! didn't you know I'd been ruined?" said she.
[Thomas Hardy: *The Ruined Maid*]

RULE

8 He shall rule them with a rod of iron.
[Revelation 2:27]
9 The desire to rule is more vehement than all the passions. [Tacitus: *Annals* XV.liii.]
10 He ruleth all the roste. [John Skelton (1460?-1529): *Why Come Ye nat to Courte?*]
    In America today the phrase is plainly "rule the roost," and the idea would be explained as exercising the sort of dominance that a cock holds in the henhouse —with, perhaps, an amused implication that the authority being exercised is a petty one.
    But in England—back to the 14th century—it was "rule the roast" ["He that ruleth the rost in the kitchen"—Thomas Heywood, History of Women *(1624)].*
    Yet other than the obvious meaning of being master of the house, no exact meaning can be assigned. The American meaning may have, by a pun, infused a meaning into a phrase that time had emptied.

11 In friendship false, implacable in hate,
    Resolved to ruin or to rule the state.
[Dryden: *Absalom and Achitophel* I]
    The reference is to Anthony Ashley Cooper, First Earl of Shaftesbury (1621-1683), Chancellor, fomenter of the Popish plot and a supporter of the Duke of Monmouth. Dryden says of him:
    Of these the rebel the false Achitophel was first;
    A name to all succeeding ages curst;
    For close designs and crooked counsels fit;
    Sagacious, bold, and turbulent of wit;
    Restless, unfix'd in principles and place;
    In power unpleased, impatient in disgrace.
    AV (II Samuel 15) gives the name as Ahitophel. Achitophel is the form in the Vulgate and in Coverdale's version.

RULER(S)

12 A prudent ruler cannot and should not observe faith [i.e., keep his word] when such observance is to his disadvantage. [Machiavelli: *The Prince* XVIII]
13 The first method for estimating the intelligence of a ruler is to look at the men he has around him. [Machiavelli: *The Prince* XXII]
14 And they that rule in England,
    In stately conclave met,
    Alas, alas for England
    They have no graves as yet.
[G. K. Chesterton: *Elegy in a Country Churchyard*]

RUM

15 We are Republicans and don't propose to leave our party and identify ourselves with the party whose antecedents are rum, Romanism, and rebellion. [Samuel Dickinson Burchard: in a speech in New York, Oct. 29, 1884]

Indignation and alliteration have often combined with explosive violence, but rarely with more disastrous consequences than in this utterance of the Reverend Mr. Burchard's. James G. Blaine later said that this phrase cost him the election to the presidency.

RUMOR

1 In times of calamity any rumor is believed. [Publilius Syrus: *Maxims*]
2 Rumour doth double, like the voice
                              and echo,
The numbers of the fear'd.
[Shakespeare: *II Henry IV* III.i.]
3 Foul whisperings are abroad.
[Shakespeare: *Macbeth* V.i.]

RUSSIA

4 Whenever you are unhappy . . . go to Russia. Anyone who has come to understand that country well will find himself content to live anywhere else. [Marquis de Custine: *Russia in 1839*]
5 Russia is a riddle wrapped in a mystery inside an enigma. [Sir Winston Churchill: in a broadcast, Oct. 1, 1939]

RUSSIAN

6 Scratch a Russian, and you will wound a Tartar. [Joseph de Maistre: *Soirées de Saint Petersbourg*]
   Attr. also to Napoleon and the Prince de Ligne.

RUST

7 How dull it is to pause, to make an
                                  end,
To rust unburnish'd, not to shine in
                                  use.
[Tennyson: *Ulysses*]

RUSTICS

8 What hempen homespuns have we
                          swaggering here?
[Shakespeare: *A Midsummer Night's Dream* III.i.]
9 All country people hate each other. They have so little comfort that they envy their neighbours the smallest pleasure or advantage. [William Hazlitt: *The Round Table* II]

RUTH

10 The voice I hear this passing night
                                  was heard
In ancient days by emperor and
                                  clown:
Perhaps the self-same song that found
                                  a path
Through the sad heart of Ruth,
                      when, sick for home,
She stood in tears amid the alien
                                  corn.
[Keats: *Ode to a Nightingale*]
   We are so used to Keats's lines that Thomas Hood's treatment of the same topic startles us:
      Thus she stood among the stooks,
      Praising God with sweetest looks.
                              —Ruth
   How anyone could write that after Keats's lines were in existence will remain a mystery.

RUTHLESSNESS

11 Men should be either caressed or exterminated, because they can avenge light injuries but not severe ones. The damage done to a man should be such that there is no fear of revenge. [Machiavelli: *The Prince* III]

S

SABBATH

1 God blessed the seventh day, and sanctified it: because that in it he had rested from all his work which God created and made. [Genesis 2:3]

2 For in six days the Lord made heaven and earth, the sea, and all that in them is, and rested the seventh day: wherefore the Lord blessed the sabbath day, and hallowed it. [Exodus 20:11]

3 Ye shall kindle no fire throughout your habitations upon the sabbath day. [Exodus 35:3]

It is this injunction that has led to the employment of the shabbas goy, a non-Jew who tends the fire, turns on and extinguishes lights and performs other services on the Sabbath which the Jews are forbidden to perform.

It is hard to see how even this is permitted in the face of the explicitness of Exodus 20:10:

". . . nor thy manservant, nor thy maidservant . . . nor the stranger that is within thy gates."

4 The sabbath was made for man, and not man for the sabbath. [Mark 2:27]

5 And never broke the Sabbath, but for gain. [Dryden: *Absalom and Achitophel* I]

6 Six days shalt thou labor and do all
    that thou art able,
And on the seventh—holystone the
    decks and scrape the cable.
[Richard Henry Dana: *Two Years Before The Mast* (1840)]

7 It is a common proverb of the people, that when we cross the Mississippi, we "travel beyond the Sabbath." [Timothy Flint: *Recollections*]

Compare with later assertions by some of Kipling's characters that "there ain't no Ten Commandments" east of Suez and "There's never a law of God or man / Runs north of Fifty-three."

8 I do not love the Sabbath
    The soapsuds and the starch,
The troops of solemn people
    Who to Salvation march.

[Robert Graves: *The Boy Out of Church*]

SACRAMENT

9 He was the word that spake it,
He took the bread and brake it;
And what that word did make it,
I do believe and take it.
[Donne: *On the Sacrament*]

SACRIFICE

10 Upon such sacrifices, my Cordelia,
The gods themselves throw incense.
[Shakespeare: *King Lear* V.iii.]

11 The tumult and the shouting dies;
    The Captains and the Kings depart:
Still stands Thine ancient sacrifice,
    An humble and a contrite heart.
[Kipling: *Recessional*]

The sacrifices of God are a broken spirit: a broken and a contrite heart, O God, thou wilt not despise.

Psalms 51:17

SACRILEGE

12 Let the gods avenge themselves.

A Roman legal maxim relating to blasphemy, far more intelligent—and pious —than most modern statutes.

SADDER

13 A sadder and a wiser man,
He rose the morrow morn.
[Coleridge: *The Ancient Mariner* VII]

SAFETY

14 Who can hope to be safe?
[Horace: *Odes* II.xiii.13]

15 The only safety for the conquered is to expect no safety. [Vergil: *Aeneid* II]

16 The desire for safety stands against every great and noble enterprise. [Tacitus: *Annals* XV]

17 Out of this nettle, danger, we pluck
    this flower, safety.
[Shakespeare: *I Henry IV* II.iii.]

18 In skating over thin ice our safety is in our speed. [Emerson: *Essays, First Series:* "Prudence"]

SAILING

1 A wet sheet and a flowing sea,
   A wind that follows fast,
   And fills the white and rustling sail,
   And bends the gallant mast.
[Allan Cunningham: *A Wet Sheet and a Flowing Sea*]
   sheet = *a rope or chain fastened to a lower aftercorner of a sail.*

SAILORS

2 They that go down to the sea in ships, that do business in great waters. [Psalms 107:23]
3 They'll tell thee sailors, when away, In every port a mistress find.
[John Gay: *Sweet William's Farewell*]
4 Sailors get money like horses and spend it like asses. [Tobias Smollett: *Peregrine Pickle* II (1751)]
   It is quoted as "an old saying."

SAINT(S)

5 Would I were free from this restraint, Or else had hopes to win her:
   Would she could make of me a saint, Or I of her a sinner.
[William Congreve: *Pious Selinda*]
6 The worst of madmen is a saint run mad. [Alexander Pope: *Imitations of Horace*, I.vi]
7 The sight of hell-torments will exalt the happiness of the saints for ever.
[Jonathan Edwards: *The Eternity of Hell-torments*]
8 But of all prides, since Lucifer's attaint,
   The proudest swells a self-elected saint.
[Thomas Hood: *Ode to Rae Wilson*]
9 Why, all the Saints and Sages who discussed
   Of the Two Worlds so wisely—they are thrust
   Like foolish Prophets forth; their Words to Scorn
   Are scattered, and their Mouths are stopped with Dust.
[*Rubáiyát of Omar Khayyám* (trans. Edward FitzGerald)]
10 I don't believe in God, but I do believe in His saints. [Edith Wharton: quoted in Lubbock's *Portrait of Edith Wharton*]

SALAD

11 According to the Spanish proverb, four persons are wanted to make a good salad: a spendthrift for oil, a miser for vinegar, a counsellor for salt, and a madman to stir all up. [Abraham Hayward: *The Art of Dining*]

SALLY

12 Of all the girls that are so smart
   There's none like pretty Sally.
   She is the darling of my heart
   And she lives in our alley.
[Henry Carey: *Sally in Our Alley*]
   smart = *trim, neat;* alley = *a narrow street or lane, usually wide enough for foot passengers only; not necessarily the dirty, degraded place of residence the term now suggests.*
   Carey, a very minor poet, managed to secure more immortality than many a better man, for he is commonly believed to have written God Save the King.

SALT

13 With a grain of salt.
   The expression goes back to Pliny's Natural History XXIII (A.D. 77) *where it appears as "a grain of salt being added"* (addito salis grano). *Mithridates, it will be remembered, fearing to be poisoned, inured himself to poison by taking minimal doses. Pliny says that when Pompey seized Mithridates's palace he found the prescription for Mithridates's famous antidote against poison, the last line of which read:* to be taken fasting, plus a grain of salt. *Just how the phrase became a formula of skepticism is uncertain. Maybe the doubt of Mithridates's diet helped; maybe the idea is that salt makes food palatable and hence will help something "hard to swallow" to "go down."*
14 Ye are the salt of the earth: but if the salt have lost his savour, wherewith shall it be salted? [Matthew 5:13]

SALUTATION

15 *Ave, Caesar, morituri te salutant.* ("Hail, Caesar, the to-be-dying salute thee.")
   The cry of the gladiators as they entered the arena—usually rendered "Hail, Caesar, we who are about to die salute thee"

—one of our most dreadful mementos of antiquity, is invested with gloomy and terrifying grandeur.

One of the earliest incidents from which our knowledge of the phrase is drawn, however, is ludicrous. Suetonius (Life of Claudius, *XXI*) tells us that the Emperor Claudius was a great maker of feeble jokes, a wag. On one occasion he had arranged a mock sea battle on Lake Fucinus. When the gladiators shouted the usual greeting, Claudius quipped "Or not"—meaning, apparently, that some of them might die and some might not—that gladiators, that is, often talked with more ferocity than they fought. But the gladiators threw down their arms, insisting that the imperial "Or not" constituted a complete pardon for all of them and hence they needn't fight at all. Claudius was furious, jumped from his throne and ran along the edge of the lake "with his ridiculous tottering gait [he was knock-kneed]" and with threats and bribes finally persuaded them to put on some sort of a show.

In this instance, by the way, the gladiators did not shout "Ave" but "Have." Latin, like English, had uncertainties with its initial aspirates.

SALVATION
1 Work out your own salvation. [Philippians 2:12]
2 There is no salvation outside the church. [St. Augustine: *De Bapt.* IV.xvii.]
See also St. Cyprian's Epistles *IV.4.lxii.18.* The Latin is Salus extra ecclesiam non est.

SAMSON
3
   Samson hath quit himself
Like Samson, and heroically hath finish'd
A life heroic.
[John Milton: *Samson Agonistes*]

SAND(S)
4 How small are grains of sand! Yet if enough are placed in a ship they sink it. [St. Augustine: *Confessions*]
5 With sweating brows I have long ploughed the sands.
[Robert Greene: *Never Too Late* (1590)]

The comparison of the profitless labor of poets and scholars to plowing the sands of the seashore, goes back to the Latin and Greek poets. Juvenal, for instance (Satires *VII*): "We plow the shore and sow the sand." And Odysseus tried to prove himself mad (and therefore exempt from going to the Trojan war) by plowing the sands.
6 The highway where the slow wheel
               pours the sand.
[Robert Frost: *Into My Own*]

SANE
7 Clothed and in his right mind. [Luke 8:35]
The madman of the Gadarenes, after the unclean spirits had been driven from him by Christ.
8 Who then is sane? [Horace: *Satires* II]

SANITY
9 Sanity is a madness put to good uses. [George Santayana: *Little Essays*]

SANTA CLAUS
10 He had a broad face and a little
                round belly,
That shook, when he laughed, like a
                bowlful of jelly.
[Clement C. Moore: *A Visit from St. Nicholas*]
11 Yes, Virginia, there is a Santa Claus. . . . Not believe in Santa Claus? You might as well not believe in fairies. . . . No Santa Claus! Thank God, he lives, and he lives forever. [Francis Church (1839-1906): Editorial, *Is There a Santa Claus?* in the *New York Sun*, Sept. 21, 1897 (in answer to a letter of inquiry from Miss Virginia O'Hanlon asking if there really was a Santa Claus)]
William McKinley had just defeated Bryan and the Populists. The Supreme Court had ruled the Income Tax unconstitutional. The Trusts were unbusted. Unskilled labor was getting $1 a day. Manifest Destiny was holding out enticing hunks of the White Man's lucrative burden while the British taxpayer policed the world. How could any solid, well-to-do person not believe in Santa Claus! Virginia ought to have been spanked!
12 No sane local official who has hung

up an empty stocking over the municipal fireplace is going to shoot Santa Claus just before a hard Christmas. [Alfred E. Smith: in a press interview in New York, Nov. 30, 1933 (commenting on the New Deal)]

1 That's where I reckon Santa Claus comes in—
To be our parents' pseudonymity
In Christmas giving, so they can escape
The thanks and let him catch it as a scapegoat.
[Robert Frost: *From Plane to Plane*]

SARCASM

2 Sarcasm I now see to be, in general, the language of the devil. [Thomas Carlyle: *Sartor Resartus* II.iv.]
3 Blows are sarcasms turned stupid. [George Eliot: *Felix Holt* II.xxx.]
Sarcasms were sometimes called "dry blows."

SATAN

4 How art thou fallen from heaven, O Lucifer, son of the morning! [Isaiah 14: 12]
5 Get thee behind me, Satan. [Mark 8:33]
In Mark and in Luke 4:8, Christ speaks these words to Satan. In Matthew 16:23, he speaks them to Peter.
6 The prince of darkness is a gentleman. [Shakespeare: *King Lear* III.iv.]
Perhaps in deference to his former status as an archangel, perhaps merely the peasant's envious assumption that all the high-born were wicked, as wicked as he would be if he had their power and opportunities. But, for whatever reason, the Devil was always thought of as a gentleman. In the old Morality Plays he always spoke Norman French and in fairly recent times was usually depicted as wearing an opera cape, white tie and silk topper. One cannot conceive of the Devil in a dinner jacket!
7   . . . the Arch-Enemy
And thence in Heaven call'd Satan.
[John Milton: *Paradise Lost* I.81-82]
The word satan occurs many times in the Old Testament, but this is obscured from the modern reader by its being usually translated as adversary *when applied to*

a human adversary. In only three instances is it used to denote an evil spirit, "the adversary of God and man" (Zechariah 3:1; I Chronicles 21:1; Job 2:1 et passim).

8 High on a throne of royal state, which far
Outshone the wealth of Ormus and of Ind,
Or where the gorgeous East with richest hand
Showers on her kings barbaric pearl and gold,
Satan exalted sat, by merit rais'd
To that bad eminence.
[John Milton: *Paradise Lost* II.1-6]
9 Incens'd with indignation Satan stood
Unterrified, and like a comet burn'd.
[John Milton: *Paradise Lost* II.707-708]
10 A winnock-bunker in the east,
There sat auld Nick, in shape o' beast;
A towzie tyke, black, grim and large.
[Burns: *Tam o'Shanter*]
towzie = rough, shaggy; tyke = a vagrant dog

SATIETY

11 Satiety begets disgust. [Montaigne: *Essays* II.xv.]

SATIRE

12 Certainly he that hath a satirical vein, as he maketh others afraid of his wit, so he had need to be afraid of others' memory. [Francis Bacon: *Of Discourse*]
Ben Franklin expressed the same thought in a more homely fashion when he said (Poor Richard's Almanack [1742]) that he was always surprised that those who were clever enough to write satires were foolish enough to publish them.
13 Men are satirical more from vanity than from malice. [La Rochefoucauld: *Maxims*]
14 I wear my pen as others do their Sword.
To each affronting sot I meet, the word
Is *Satisfaction:* straight to thrusts I go,
And pointed satire runs him through and through.
[John Oldham: *Satire Upon a Printer*]
15 Satire is a sort of glass wherein beholders do generally discover everybody's face but their own, which is the chief

reason for that kind reception it meets with in the world. [Jonathan Swift: Preface to *The Battle of the Books*]

1 Satire should, like a polished razor keen,
Wound with a touch that's scarcely felt or seen.
[Lady Mary Wortley Montagu: *To the Imitator of the First Satire of Horace* II]

SATISFACTION

2 He is well paid that is well satisfied. [Shakespeare: *The Merchant of Venice* IV.i.]

SATURN

3 Deep in the shady sadness of a vale
Far sunken from the healthy breath of morn,
Far from the fiery noon, and eve's one star,
Sat gray-haired Saturn, quiet as a stone.
[Keats: *Hyperion* I]

SAUL

4 Saul hath slain his thousands, and David his ten thousands. [I Samuel 18:7]

SAVAGE(S)

5 Ere the base laws of servitude began,
When wild in woods the noble savage ran.
[Dryden: *The Conquest of Granada* I.i.]
6 I will take some savage woman, she shall rear my dusky race,
Iron-jointed, supple-sinew'd, they shall dive, and they shall run,
Catch the wild goat by the hair, and hurl their lances in the sun;
Whistle back the parrot's call, and leap the rainbows of the brooks,
Not with blinded eyesight poring over miserable books.
[Tennyson: *Locksley Hall*]
7 Savages are the most conservative of human beings. [A. H. Sayce: *Introduction to the Science of Language* I]
8 Your new-caught, sullen peoples,
Half-devil and half-child.
[Kipling: *The White Man's Burden*]
9 A savage is simply a human organism that has not received enough news from the human race. [John Ciardi: *The Saturday Review*, Jan. 31, 1959]

SCANDAL

10 Greatest scandal waits on greatest state.
[Shakespeare: *The Rape of Lucrece*]
11 We in the world's wide mouth
Live scandalized and foully spoken of.
[Shakespeare: *I Henry IV* I.iii.]
12 Love and scandal are the best sweeteners of tea. [Henry Fielding: *Love in Several Masques* IV.ii.]
13 Every whisper of infamy is industriously circulated, every hint of suspicion eagerly improved, and every failure of conduct joyfully published by those whose interest it is that the eye and voice of the public should be employed on any rather than on themselves. [Samuel Johnson: *The Rambler* No. 76]
14 Aspersion is the babbler's trade,
To listen is to lend him aid.
[William Cowper: *Friendship*]
15 Dead scandals form good subjects for dissection.
[Byron: *Don Juan* I.xxxi.]
16 Scandal is gossip made tedious by morality. [Oscar Wilde: *Lady Windermere's Fan* III]
17 How awful to reflect that what people say of us is true. [Logan Pearsall Smith: *Afterthoughts*]

SCAPEGOAT

18 The goat . . . shall . . . go for a scapegoat into the wilderness. [Leviticus 16:9-10]

One of the most puzzling passages in the Bible. As part of the ritual for the Day of Atonement, the high priest was required to bring two goats before the altar of the tabernacle. By lot one was selected for Jehovah. The other was "for Azazel," presumably a demon that lived in the wilderness. The high priest transferred the sins of the people to this goat and allowed it to escape and go to Azazel.

In 1525 William Tyndale translated this: "To let him go for a scapegoat into the wilderness." We would say escapegoat. *The Authorized Version adopted Tyndale's translation. RSV (1952) merely has "that it may be sent away into the wilderness to Azazel." The New American Catholic edition calls it "the emissary goat" and ignores Azazel. So we owe the word* scapegoat *to William Tyndale's pronunciation of* escape *and his interpretation of the Azazel problem.*

SCARCITY

1 And having looked to government for bread, on the very first scarcity they will turn and bite the hand that fed them. [Edmund Burke: *Thoughts and Details on Scarcity*]

SCARS

2 He jests at scars that never felt a wound. [Shakespeare: *Romeo and Juliet* II.ii.]

SCHEMES

3 But, Mousie, thou art no thy lane,
In proving foresight may be vain:
The best laid schemes o' mice an' men
    Gang aft a-gley,
An' lea'e us nought but grief an' pain
    For promis'd joy.
Still thou art blest compar'd wi' me!
The present only toucheth thee:
But oh! I backward cast my e'e
    On prospects drear!
An' forward tho' I canna see,
    I guess an' fear!
[Burns: *To a Mouse*]
no thy lane = *not alone;* gang aft agley = *go off the planned line*

SCHOLAR(S)

4 A mere scholar, a mere ass. [Robert Burton: *Anatomy of Melancholy* I.ii.3. 15]
5 Deign on the passing world to turn thine eyes,
And pause awhile from letters to be wise;
There mark what ills the scholar's life assail,
Toil, envy, want, the patron, and the gaol.
See nations, slowly wise and meanly just,
To buried merit raise the tardy bust.
[Samuel Johnson: *The Vanity of Human Wishes*]
6 To talk in public, to think in solitude, to read and to hear, to inquire and answer inquiries, is the business of a scholar. [Samuel Johnson: *Rasselas* VIII]
7 Harris is a sound sullen scholar.

[Samuel Johnson: in Boswell's *Life*, April 7, 1778]
The reference is to James Harris (1709-1780), the author of Hermes, *or a Philosophical Inquiry Concerning Universal Grammar. In the word* sullen *Johnson, himself a scholar, showed a fine feeling for a scholar's single-mindedness, his solitary, unsociable, uncompromising life.*
8 A diller, a dollar,
A ten o'clock scholar,
What makes you come so soon?
You used to come at ten o'clock,
But now you come at noon.
[Nursery rhyme: first printed version, 1784]
diller *and* dollar *may mean to suggest* dilly-dally; noon *was originally nine o'clock and there may be some playful reference to that.*
9 A mere scholar, who knows nothing but books, must be ignorant even of them. [William Hazlitt: *The Ignorance of the Learned*]
10 The world's great men have not commonly been great scholars, nor its great scholars great men. [O. W. Holmes: *The Autocrat of the Breakfast-Table* VI]
11 Scholars are wont to sell their birthright for a mess of learning. [Thoreau: *A Week on the Concord and Merrimack Rivers*, "Sunday"]
12 Scholars . . . an unmannered species. [George Meredith: *The Egoist* XIX]

SCHOOL(S)

13 Like th' affected fool . . . who hates whate'er he read at school. [Alexander Pope: *Imitation of Horace*, "Epistles" II.i.]
14 There is now less flogging in our great schools than formerly, but then less is learned there; so that what the boys get at one end they lose at the other. [Samuel Johnson: in Boswell's *Life* (1775)]
15 But to go to school in a summer morn,
Oh, it drives all joy away!
Under a cruel eye outworn,
The little ones spend the day—
In sighing and dismay.
[William Blake: *The Schoolboy*]
16 Torture in a public school is as much licensed as the knout in Russia. [W. M.

Thackeray: *Vanity Fair* V]
1 There is nothing on earth intended for innocent people so horrible as a school. To begin with, it is a prison. But it is in some respects more cruel than a prison. In a prison, for instance, you are not forced to read books written by the warders and the governor. [G. B. Shaw: *Parents and Children*]

SCHOOLBOY

2 And then the whining schoolboy, with his satchel
And shining morning face, creeping like a snail
Unwillingly to school.
[Shakespeare: *As You Like It* II.vii.]
3 Every school-boy knows it. [Jeremy Taylor: *On the Real Presence* (1654)]
4 How haughtily he cocks his nose
To tell what every schoolboy knows.
[Jonathan Swift: *The Country Life*]
5 Every schoolboy knows who imprisoned Montezuma and who strangled Atahualpa. [Macaulay: *Historical Essays,* "Lord Clive"]

> *There are few things that every schoolboy would be less likely to know. Still "every schoolboy knows" has long been a cliché with which to intimidate cowering adults. The phrase is usually attr. Macaulay and, indeed, he was fond of it ("What schoolboy of fourteen is ignorant of this remarkable circumstance?"—Literary Essays, "Sir William Temple"), but it is much older.*

SCIENCE

6 For oute of olde feldys, as men sey,
Comyth al this newe corn from yere to yere;
And out of olde bokis, in good fey,
Comyth al this newe science that men lere.
[Chaucer: *The Parlement of Foules*]
7 Science appears but what in truth she is,
Not as our glory and our absolute boast,
But as a succedaneum, and a prop
To our infirmity. . . .
. . . that false secondary power
By which we multiply distinctions, then
Deem that our puny boundaries are

things
That we perceive, and not that we have made.
[Wordsworth: *The Prelude* II]
8 Science moves, but slowly, slowly, creeping on from point to point.
[Tennyson: *Locksley Hall*]
9 Hast thou not dragged Diana from her car,
And driven the Hamadryad from the wood . . .
The Elfin from the green grass, and from me
The summer dream beneath the tamarind tree?
[Edgar Allan Poe: *Sonnet,* "To Science"]
10 Science is organized knowledge. [Herbert Spencer: *Education* II]
11 Science is nothing but trained and organized common sense. [T. H. Huxley: *The Method of Zadig*]
12 What is called science today consists of a haphazard heap of information, united by nothing. [Tolstoy: *What is Religion?*]
13 Science is nothing but developed perception, interpreted intent, common sense rounded out and minutely articulated. [George Santayana: *The Life of Reason:* "Reason in Science" V]
14 True science teaches, above all, to doubt, and to be ignorant. [Miguel de Unamuno: *The Tragic Sense of Life*]
15 The wallpaper with which the men of science have covered the world of reality is falling to tatters. [Henry Miller: *Tropic of Cancer*]
16 In science, the total absorption of the individual event in the generalization is the goal; on the other hand, the humanities are concerned rather with providing for the special meaning of the individual event within an appropriate general system. [Moody E. Prior: *Science and the Humanities* (1962)]

SCIENTIFIC SPIRIT

17 One that would peep and botanize
Upon his mother's grave.
[Wordsworth: *A Poet's Epitaph*]

SCOLD

18 She will scold the Devil out of a

haunted House. [Thomas Fuller (1654-1734): *Gnomologia*]

SCORN

1 Disdain and scorn ride sparkling in
her eyes.
[Shakespeare: *Much Ado About Nothing*
III.i.]
2 But, alas! to make me
A fixed figure for the time of scorn
To point his slow unmoving finger at!
[Shakespeare: *Othello* IV.ii.]
3 He hears
On all sides, from innumerable
tongues,
A dismal universal hiss, the sound
Of public scorn.
[John Milton: *Paradise Lost* X.506-509]
4 Heav'n has no rage like love to ha-
tred turn'd,
Nor hell a fury like a woman scorn'd.
[William Congreve: *The Mourning Bride*
III.viii. (1697)]

*Congreve's famous line seems a sort of
rhymed echo of a passage in a play
which had appeared only the year before, Colley Cibber's* Love's Last Shift
IV.i:

*We shall find no fiend in hell can
match the fury of a disappointed
woman—scorned, slighted, dismissed
without a parting pang.*

5 We scorn many things in order not to
scorn ourselves. [Vauvenargues: *Réflexions*]
6 I, too late,
Under her solemn fillet saw the scorn.
[Emerson: *Days*]
7 Godolphin Horne was nobly born;
He held the human race in scorn.
[Hilaire Belloc: *Godolphin Horne*]

SCOTCHMAN

8 Much may be made of a Scotchman
if he be caught young. [Samuel Johnson: in Boswell's *Life* (1772)]
9 A Scotchman must be a very sturdy
moralist who does not love Scotland better than truth. [Samuel Johnson: *A Journey to the Western Isles of Scotland*]

*It was the clannishness of the Scots and
their disregard of accuracy when it came
to Scotland or brother Scots that was the
basis of Johnson's animus against them.*

*Some of his best friends, however, were
Scots.*

SCOTLAND

10 Oh, ye'll tak' the high road an' I'll
tak' the low road,
An' I'll be in Scotland afore ye.
[Anon.: *Loch Lomond*]
11 O Caledonia! stern and wild,
Meet nurse for a poetic child!
Land of brown heath and shaggy
wood;
Land of the mountain and the flood!
[Sir Walter Scott: *The Lay of the Last
Minstrel* VI.ii.]
12 A land of meanness, sophistry, and
mist.
[Byron: *The Curse of Minerva*]

*It must be remembered that Byron was
half-Scottish.*

SCOTS

13 Scots, wha hae wi' Wallace bled,
Scots, wham Bruce has aften led,
Welcome to your gory bed,
Or to victorie.
[Robert Burns: *Scots Wha Hae*]

*Wallace = Sir William Wallace, 1272?-
1305, a leader of the Scots against England. After many victories defeated and
executed. Bruce = Robert I, King of Scotland, freed Scotland from English over-
lordship at Battle of Bannockburn (1314).
Burns's poem is an assumed address of
Bruce to his soldiers before the Battle of
Bannockburn.*

*One of the most famous legends of
Bruce concerns his being encouraged,
when at the low ebb in his fortunes and
after repeated failure, by the tenacity of
a spider in anchoring a filament for her
web.*

SCOUNDREL

14 Every man over forty is a scoundrel.
[G. B. Shaw: *Maxims for Revolutionists*]

SCRATCHING

15 Scratching . . . begins with Pleasure,
and ends with Pain. [Thomas Fuller
(1654-1734): *Gnomologia*]

SCRIPTURE(S)

16 Search the scriptures. [John 5:39]
John Selden, in his Table Talk, "Scrip-

ture," says that "these two words (Scrutamini scripturas) *have undone the world.*"

undone = *ruined*

1 The devil can cite Scripture for his purpose.
[Shakespeare: *The Merchant of Venice* I.iii.]
This is literally so. Every word that Satan spoke to Christ at the Temptation is quoted from the Old Testament.

SCRUPLE(S)

2 Some craven scruple
Of thinking too precisely on the event.
[Shakespeare: *Hamlet* IV.iv.]
event = *outcome, consequences*

3 He could raise scruples dark and nice,
And after solve 'em in a trice;
As if Divinity had catch'd
The itch, on purpose to be scratch'd.
[Samuel Butler (1612-1680): *Hudibras*]

SCYLLA AND CHARYBDIS

4 On this side lay Scylla, while on that Charybdis in her terrible whirlpool was sucking down the sea. [Homer: *Odyssey* XII (T. E. Lawrence's trans.)]
Scylla was a loathsome and dangerous monster, inhabiting an inaccessible cave in an unscalable rock; Charybdis was a fatal whirlpool. The two names have come to stand for dreadful alternatives between which a man must make a choice. Odysseus, warned by Circe that not even Poseidon's power could save him from Charybdis, chose to suffer at the hands of Scylla.

SEA

5 They that go down to the sea in ships, that do business in great waters; These see the works of the Lord, and his wonders in the deep. [Psalms 107:23-24]

6 All the rivers run into the sea, yet the sea is not full. [Ecclesiastes 1:7]

7 For all, that here on earth we dreadful hold,
Be but as bugs to fearen babes withal,
Compared to the creatures in the seas entrall.
[Edmund Spenser: *The Faerie Queene* II.xii.25.]
bugs = *bugaboos;* fearen = *frighten;* entrall = *interior.*

8 The always wind-obeying deep.
[Shakespeare: *The Comedy of Errors* I.i.]

9 Now would I give a thousand furlongs of sea for an acre of barren ground.
[Shakespeare: *The Tempest* I.i.]

10 Full fathom five thy father lies;
Of his bones are coral made;
Those are pearls that were his eyes:
Nothing of him that doth fade
But doth suffer a sea-change
Into something rich and strange.
[Shakespeare: *The Tempest* I.ii.]

11 You gentlemen of England
That live at home at ease,
Ah! little do you think upon
The dangers of the seas.
[Martyn Parker: *Song*]

12 Have sight of Proteus rising from the sea,
Or hear old Triton blow his wreathèd horn.
[Wordsworth: *The World Is Too Much With Us*]

13 The fair breeze blew, the white foam flew,
The furrow followed free;
We were the first that ever burst
Into that silent sea.
[Coleridge: *The Ancient Mariner* II]

14 Roll on, thou deep and dark blue ocean—roll!
Ten thousand fleets sweep over thee in vain;
Man marks the earth with ruin—his control
Stops with the shore.
[Byron: *Childe Harold* IV.clxxix.]

15 No doubt he would have been much more pathetic,
But the sea acted as a strong emetic.
[Byron: *Don Juan* II.xxi.]

16 It keeps eternal whisperings around
Desolate shores, and with its mighty swell
Gluts twice ten thousand caverns.
[Keats: *On the Sea*]

17 Old ocean's gray and melancholy waste.
[William Cullen Bryant: *Thanatopsis*]

18 Oh, Pilot! 'tis a fearful night, there's danger on the deep.
[Thomas Haynes Bayly: *The Pilot*]

19 A baby was sleeping, its mother was weeping,
For her husband was far on the wild-

raging sea.
[Samuel Lover: *The Angel's Whisper*]

1 I remember the black wharves and
the slips,
And the sea-tides tossing free;
And Spanish sailors with bearded
lips,
And the beauty and mystery of the
ships,
And the magic of the sea.
[Longfellow: *My Lost Youth*]

2 The white cold heavy-plunging foam
Whirl'd by the wind.
[Tennyson: *A Dream of Fair Women*]

3 A life on the ocean wave!
A home on the rolling deep;
Where the scattered waters rave,
And the winds their revels keep!
[Epes Sargent: *Life on the Ocean Wave*]

4 The unplumb'd, salt, estranging sea.
[Matthew Arnold: *To Marguerite*]

5 I will go back to the great sweet
mother,
Mother and lover of men, the sea.
[Swinburne: *The Triumph of Time*]

6 The widow-making unchilding unfa-
thering deeps.
[Gerard Manley Hopkins: *The Wreck of
the Deutschland*]

7 . . . the murderous innocence of the
sea.
[William Butler Yeats: *A Prayer for My
Daughter*]

8 I must down to the seas again, to the
lonely sea and the sky,
And all I ask is a tall ship and a star
to steer her by,
And the wheel's kick and the wind's
song and the white sail's shaking,
And a grey mist on the sea's face and
a grey dawn breaking.
[John Masefield: *Sea-Fever*]

9 The dragon-green, the luminous, the
dark, the serpent-haunted sea. [James El-
roy Flecker: *The Gates of Damascus*,
"West Gate"]

SEAL
10 Set me as a seal upon thine heart, as a
seal upon thine arm: for love is strong as
death; jealousy is cruel as the grave.
[Song of Solomon 8:6]

SEASON(S)
11 While the earth remaineth, seed-time

and harvest, and cold and heat, and summer and winter, and day and night shall
not cease. [Genesis 8:22]

12 To every thing there is a season, and a
time to every purpose under the heaven:
A time to be born, and a time to die; a
time to plant, and a time to pluck up
that which is planted;
A time to kill, and a time to heal; a time
to break down, and a time to build up;
A time to weep, and a time to laugh; a
time to mourn, and a time to dance;
A time to cast away stones, and a time to
gather stones together; a time to embrace,
and a time to refrain from embracing;
A time to get, and a time to lose; a time
to keep, and a time to cast away;
A time to rend, and a time to sew; a time
to keep silence, and a time to speak;
A time to love, and a time to hate; a time
of war, and a time of peace.
[Ecclesiastes 3:1-8]

SECOND PLACE
13 It is a maxim, that those to whom everybody allows the second place have an
undoubted title to the first. [Jonathan
Swift: Dedication of *The Tale of a Tub*]

SECRECY
14 Stolen waters are sweet, and bread
eaten in secret is pleasant. [Proverbs 9:
17]

15 To be perfectly secret, one must be so
by nature, not by obligation. [Mon-
taigne: *Essays* III.v.]

16 There be many wise men, that have
secret hearts, and transparent countenances. [Francis Bacon: *Of Cunning*]

17 The best composition and temperature is to have openness in fame and
opinion; secrecy in habit; dissimulation
in seasonable use; and a power to feign
if there be no remedy. [Francis Bacon:
Of Simulation and Dissimulation]
temperature = *temperament*

18 The secret man heareth many confessions; for who will open himself to a
blab or a babbler? [Francis Bacon: *Of
Simulation and Dissimulation*]

19 Two may keep counsel, putting one
away. [Shakespeare: *Romeo and Juliet*
II.iv.]
There it is quoted as a proverb.
*It occurs again, in a slightly different
form, in* Titus Andronicus *IV.ii.*

1   I well believe
Thou wilt not utter what thou dost
                   not know,
And so far will I trust thee.
[Shakespeare: *I Henry IV* II.iii.]
2 There is no secrecy comparable to
celerity. [Francis Bacon: *Of Delays*]
3 Mum's the word. [Thomas Brown: *A
Walk Round the London Coffee Houses*
III.iii. (1704)]
> *The phrase was approaching this, its
> present form, for 200 years before: "Mum
> is counsel" (1540); "No more words but
> mum" (1568); "Seal up your lips, and
> give no words but mum" (Shakespeare:
> II Henry VI I.ii. (1590).*

SECRET(S)
4 If you do not want another to tell
your secrets, you must not tell them yourself. [Seneca: *Phaedra*]
5 Sooner will men hold fire in their
mouths than keep a secret. [Petronius:
Fragments]
6 If you would know secrets, look for
them in grief or pleasure. [George Herbert: *Jacula Prudentum*]
> *i.e., look for them to be disclosed.*

7 When a secret is revealed, it is the
fault of the man who confided it. [La
Bruyère: *Les Caractères*]
8 Three may keep a secret if two of
them are dead. [Benjamin Franklin:
Poor Richard's Almanack (1735)]
9 If you would keep your secret from
an enemy, tell it not to a friend. [Ben-
jamin Franklin: *Poor Richard's Almanack* (1741)]
10 The vanity of being known to be entrusted with a secret is generally one of
the chief motives to disclose it. [Samuel
Johnson: *The Rambler* No. 13]
11 As every one is pleased with imagin-
ing that he knows something not yet commonly divulged, secret history easily
gains credit; but it is for the most part
believed only while it circulates in whispers, and when once it is openly told is
openly confuted. [Samuel Johnson: *The
Rambler* No. 114]
12 None are so fond of secrets as those
who do not mean to keep them. [C. C.
Colton: *Lacon*]
13 A secret's safe

'Twixt you, me, and the gate-post!
[Robert Browning: *The Inn Album* II]
14 Some secrets may the poet tell,
   For the world loves new ways;
To tell too deep ones is not well—
   It knows not what he says.
[Matthew Arnold: *Stanzas in Memory of
the Author of "Obermann"*]

SECTS
15 Petulant capricious sects,
   The maggots of corrupted texts.
[Samuel Butler (1612-1680): *Hudibras*]

SECURE
16 He that's secure is not safe. [Benja-
min Franklin: *Poor Richard's Almanack*
(1748)]

SECURITY
17 It is much more secure to be feared
than to be loved. [Machiavelli: *The
Prince* XVII]
18 Only those means of security are good,
are certain, are lasting, that depend on
yourself and your own vigor. [Machia-
velli: *The Prince* XXIV]
19 Distrust and caution are the parents
of security. [Benjamin Franklin: *Poor
Richard's Almanack* (1733)]

SEDUCTION
20 If a man entice a maid that is not betrothed, and lie with her, he shall surely
endow her to be his wife. [Exodus 22:
16]

SEEING
21 Seeing is believing. [Farquhar: *The
Recruiting Officer* IV.iii. (1706)]
> *A proverb since at least the 2nd century
> B.C. it appears in Plautus:* Truculentus
> II.vi.

22 Worth seeing? yes; but not worth going to see. [Samuel Johnson: in Boswell's *Life*, October 12, 1779]
> *Johnson was referring to the Giant's
> Causeway, thousands of basaltic columns
> of volcanic origin extending for three
> miles along the north coast of County
> Antrim in Northern Ireland. Boswell
> had mentioned the Causeway as an in-
> ducement to get Johnson to make a
> journey to Ireland with him.*

SEEK(ING)

1 Seek, and ye shall find. [Matthew 7:7]

2 Think you mid all this mighty sum
Of things for ever speaking,
That nothing of itself will come,
But we must still be seeking?
[Wordsworth: *Expostulation and Reply*]
still = *continually*

SEEMING

3 Things are not always what they seem. [Phaedrus: *Fables* IV.ii.]

4 Things are seldom what they seem.
Skim milk masquerades as cream.
[W. S. Gilbert: *H.M.S. Pinafore* II]

SEER

5 Like some bold seër in a trance,
Seeing all his own mischance—
With a glassy countenance
Did she look to Camelot.
[Tennyson: *The Lady of Shalott* IV]

SELF-CONFIDENCE

6 The confidence which we have in ourselves engenders the greatest part of that we have in others. [La Rochefoucauld: *Maxims*]

7 Self-confidence is the first requisite to great undertakings. [Samuel Johnson: *Life of Pope*]

8 Trust thyself: every heart vibrates to that iron string. [Emerson: *Self-Reliance*]

SELF-CONTROL

9 He that is slow to anger is better than the mighty; and he that ruleth his spirit than he that taketh a city. [Proverbs 16:32]

10 I pray you, school yourself. [Shakespeare: *Macbeth* IV.ii.]

11 And mistress of herself, tho' China fall.
[Alexander Pope: *Moral Essays* II]

12 Reader, attend! whether thy soul
Soars fancy's flights beyond the pole,
Or darkling grubs this earthly hole
In low pursuit;
Know prudent cautious self-control
Is wisdom's root.
[Burns: *A Bard's Epitaph*]

13 Charlotte, having seen his body
Borne before her on a shutter,
Like a well-conducted person,
Went on cutting bread and butter.
[W. M. Thackeray: *Sorrows of Werther*]

SELF-DEFENSE

14 Self-preservation is the first law of nature. [Samuel Butler (1612-1680): *Remains* II.xxvii. (1675)]

15 Self-preservation, Nature's first great law. [Andrew Marvell: *Hodge's Vision*]

16 Self-defense is nature's eldest law. [Dryden: *Absalom and Achitophel* I]

17 If a madman were to come into this room with a stick in his hand no doubt we should pity the state of his mind, but our primary consideration would be to take care of ourselves. We should knock him down first, and pity him afterward. [Samuel Johnson: in Boswell's *Life*, April 3, 1776]

18 . . . the sole end for which mankind are warranted, individually or collectively, in interfering with the liberty of action of any of their number, is self-protection. [John Stuart Mill: *On Liberty* I]

SELF-ESTEEM

19 The coward regards himself as cautious; the miser, as thrifty. [Publilius Syrus: *Maxims*]

20 It is a poor center of a man's actions, himself. [Francis Bacon: *Of Wisdom for a Man's Self*]

21 He that is giddy thinks the world turns round.
[Shakespeare: *The Taming of the Shrew* V.ii.]

22 Oft-times nothing profits more
Than self-esteem, grounded on just and right
Well manag'd.
[John Milton: *Paradise Lost* VIII.571-573]

23 They hug themselves and reason thus:
It is not yet so bad with us.
[Jonathan Swift: *Verses on the Death of Dr. Swift*]

24 A man's true merit 'tis not hard to find;
But each man's secret standard in his mind,
That Casting-weight pride adds to

emptiness,
This, who can gratify? for who can
guess?
[Alexander Pope: *Epistle to Dr. Arbuthnot*]
Casting-weight = *the weight that turns
the scale*

1 It is easy for every man, whatever be
his character with others, to find reasons
for esteeming himself. [Samuel Johnson:
The Rambler No. 79]

2 High though his titles, proud his
name,
Boundless his wealth as wish can
claim—
Despite those titles, power, and pelf,
The wretch, concentred all in self,
Living, shall forfeit fair renown,
And, doubly dying, shall go down
To the vile dust from whence he
sprung,
Unwept, unhonoured, and unsung.
[Sir Walter Scott: *Lay of the Last Min-
strel* VI.i.]

3 We talk little, if we do not talk about
ourselves. [William Hazlitt: *Characteristics*]

4 I, painting from myself and to myself,
Know what I do, am unmoved by
men's blame
Or their praise either.
[Robert Browning: *Andrea del Sarto*]

5 He is a poor creature who does not believe himself to be better than the whole
world else. No matter how ill we may be,
or how low we may have fallen, we would
not change identity with any other person. Hence our self-conceit sustains and
always must sustain us till death takes us
and our conceit together so that we need
no more sustaining. [Samuel Butler
(1835-1902): *Notebooks*]

6 We reproach people for talking about
themselves; but it is the subject they treat
best. [Anatole France: *La Vie Littéraire*]

7 Every new adjustment is a crisis in
self-esteem. [Eric Hoffer: *The Ordeal of
Change*]

SELF-IMPROVEMENT

8 He that teaches himself has a fool for
his master. [17th-century proverb]

9 "I must really improve my mind," I
tell myself, and once more begin to patch
and repair that crazy structure. So I toil

and toil on at the vain task of edification,
though the wind tears off the tiles, the
floors give way, the ceilings fall, strange
birds build untidy nests in the rafters,
and owls hoot and laugh in the tumbling
chimneys. [Logan Pearsall Smith: *Trivia*,
"Edification"]

SELF-INTEREST

10 Self-interest is the enemy of all true
affection. [Tacitus: *History* I]

11 As far as the stars are from the earth,
and as different as fire is from water, so
much do self-interest and integrity differ.
[Lucan: *Pharsalia* VIII.lxv.]

12 It is not from the benevolence of the
butcher, the brewer, or the baker that
we expect our dinner, but from their regard to their own interest. [Adam Smith:
The Wealth of Nations II]

SELF-KNOWLEDGE

13 Know thyself. [Inscribed on the temple at Delphi (according to Plato's *Protagoras*) as one of the world's fundamental pieces of wisdom.]

14 A man is least known to himself. [Cic-
ero: *De oratore* III]

15 Thales was asked what was most difficult to man; he answered: "To know
one's self." [Diogenes Laertius: *Lives of
the Philosophers*]

16 Where I seek myself, I find not myself:
and I find myself more by chance than by
the search of mine own judgment. [Mon-
taigne: *Essays* I.x.]

17 We are all framed of flaps and patches
and of so shapeless and diverse a con-
texture that every piece and every moment playeth his part. And there is as
much difference found between us and
ourselves as there is between ourselves
and others. [Montaigne: *Essays* II.i.]

18 No man knows himself to be covetous
or niggardly. [Montaigne: *Essays* II.
xxv.]
*That is, the covetous man sees himself
as "alert," "enterprising," "on the ball,"
"out to get his," "able to take care of
himself." The niggardly man sees himself as "thrifty," "economical," "practical."*

19 We that acquaint ourselves with every
zone
And pass both tropics and behold
the poles,

When we come home are to ourselves
unknown,
And unacquainted still with our
own souls.
[John Davies: *Nosce Teipsum*]

1 It is as easy to deceive oneself without perceiving it as it is difficult to deceive others without their perceiving it. [La Rochefoucauld: *Maxims*]

2 More skilful in self-knowledge, even
more pure,
As tempted more; more able to en-
dure,
As more exposed to suffering and dis-
tress;
Thence also, more alive to tenderness.
[Wordsworth: *Character of the Happy Warrior*]

3 Of four things every man has more than he knows: sins, debts, years, and foes. [Archbishop Trench: *Lessons in Proverbs*]

4 Resolve to be thyself; and know that
he
Who finds himself, loses his misery!
[Matthew Arnold: *Self-Dependence*]

5 The tragedy of a man who has found himself out. [J. M. Barrie: *What Every Woman Knows* IV]

6 Who in the world am I? Ah, that's the great puzzle! [Lewis Carroll: *Alice's Adventures in Wonderland* II]

7 To know oneself, one should assert oneself. [Albert Camus: *Notebooks 1935-1942*]

SELF-LOVE

8 All men love themselves. [Plautus: *Captivi* III]

9 At the kinges court, my brother,
Ech man for him-self, ther is non
other.
[Chaucer: *The Knight's Tale*]

10 It is the nature of extreme self-lovers, as they will set an house on fire, and it were but to roast their eggs. [Francis Bacon: *Of Wisdom for a Man's Self*]

11 Why should I be angry with a Man, for loving himself better than me? [Francis Bacon: *Of Revenge*]

12 Self-love, my liege, is not so vile a sin
As self-neglecting.
[Shakespeare: *Henry V* II.iv.]

13 O villainous! I have looked upon the world for four times seven years; and since I could distinguish betwixt a benefit and an injury, I never found man that knew how to love himself. [Shakespeare: *Othello* I.iii.]

14 Every man for himself, the devil for all. [Robert Burton: *Anatomy of Melancholy* III.1.]

15 There is no passion wherein self-love reigns so powerfully as in love, and one is always more ready to sacrifice the peace of the loved one than one's own. [La Rochefoucauld: *Maxims*]

16 How few
Know their own good, or knowing it,
pursue.
[Juvenal: *Satires* X (trans. Dryden)]

17 He that falls in love with himself will have no rivals. [Benjamin Franklin: *Poor Richard's Almanack* (1739)]

18 He that considers how little he dwells upon the condition of others, will learn how little the attention of others is attracted by himself. [Samuel Johnson: *The Rambler* No. 159]

19 There is no crevice so small or intricate at which our self-love will not contrive to creep in. [William Hazlitt: *Traveling Abroad*]

20 To love oneself is the beginning of a lifelong romance. [Oscar Wilde: *An Ideal Husband* III]

SELF-PITY

21 I am a lone lorn creetur and everythink goes contrairy with me. [Dickens: *David Copperfield* III]
Mrs. Gummidge's "creetur" was the English pronunciation of what in the United States was pronounced "critter."

22 I never saw a wild thing
Sorry for itself.
[D. H. Lawrence: *Self-Pity*]

23 Oh the years we waste and the tears
we waste,
And the work of our head and
hand,
Belong to the woman who did not
know
(And now we know that she never
could know)
And did not understand.
[Kipling: *The Vampire*]

SELF-PRAISE

24 He who discommendeth others

obliquely commendeth himself. [Sir Thomas Browne: *Christian Morals* I. xxxiv.]

1 One would rather speak evil of himself than not speak of himself at all. [La Rochefoucauld: *Maxims*]

2 All censure of a man's self is oblique praise. . . . It has all the invidiousness of self-praise, and all the reproach of falsehood. [Samuel Johnson: in Boswell's *Life,* April 25, 1778]

3 If you wish in this world to advance
Your merits you're bound to enhance;
You must stir it and stump it,
And blow your own trumpet,
Or, trust me, you haven't a chance.
[W. S. Gilbert: *Ruddigore* I]

SELF-RELIANCE

4 Heaven ne'er helps the men who will not act. [Sophocles: *Fragment*]

5 The gods help him who helps himself. [Euripides: *Fragment* (c. 425 B.C.)]
Apparently a proverb, even then.

6 I have heard said, eke times twice
twelve,
"He is a fool that will forget himselve."
[Chaucer: *Troilus and Criseyde* V.xcvii.]

7 Help, hands, for I have no lands. [16th-century proverb]

8 God helps those who help themselves. [Algernon Sidney: *Discourse Concerning Government* II]

9 This above all—to thine own self be
true,
And it must follow, as the night the
day,
Thou canst not then be false to any
man.
[Shakespeare: *Hamlet* I.iii.]

10 If you will only help yourself, God will help you. [Mathurin Regnier: *Satires* XIII]
The same sentiment is expressed by La Fontaine, in the Fables *VI: "Help thyself and heaven will help thee."*

11 Every tub must stand on its own bottom. [Charles Macklin: *The Man of the World* I.ii.]
The saying was already a proverb. John Bunyan had used it in its older form: Every fat [vat] must stand upon his own bottom. (Pilgrim's Progress I.)

12 If you want a thing done, go; if not, send. [Benjamin Franklin: *Poor Richard's Almanack* (1758)]

13 Great God, I ask thee for no meaner
pelf
Than that I may not disappoint myself.
[Thoreau: *My Prayer*]

14 Go far; come near;
You still must be
The center of your own small mystery.
[Walter de la Mare: *Go Far; Come Near*]

15 My heart has grown rich with the
passing of years,
I have less need now than when I
was young
To share myself with every comer,
Or shape my thoughts into words
with my tongue.

. . .

Let them think I love them more than
I do,
Let them think I care, though I go
alone,
If it lifts their pride, what is it to me,
Who am self-complete as a flower
or a stone?
[Sara Teasdale: *The Solitary*]

SELF-REPROACH

16 God defend me from myself. [Montaigne: *Essays* III.xiii.]
Montaigne describes this as "that Spanish saying," and adds that it pleases him in every way.

17 Desiring this man's art, and that
man's scope,
With what I most enjoy contented
least;
Yet in these thoughts myself almost
despising.
[Shakespeare: *Sonnets* XXIX]

18 Alas, 'tis true I have gone here and
there,
And made myself a motley to the view,
Gor'd mine own thoughts, sold cheap
what is most dear,
Made old offences of affections new.
[Shakespeare: *Sonnets* CX]
motley = a fool; from the fact that fools wore motley, a cloth of variegated colors.

19 O, what a rogue and peasant slave am
I!
[Shakespeare: *Hamlet* II.ii.]

1 Too liberal self-accusations are generally but so many traps for acquittal with applause.[Samuel Richardson: *Pamela* I.i.]

2 A man should be careful never to tell tales of himself to his own disadvantage. People may be amused and laugh at the time, but they will be remembered and brought against him upon some subsequent occasion. [Samuel Johnson: in Boswell's *Life*, March 25, 1776]

3 All censure of a man's self is oblique praise. It is in order to show how much he can spare. [Samuel Johnson: in Boswell's *Life* (April 25, 1778)]

4 There is a luxury in self-dispraise;
  And inward self-disparagement affords
       To meditative spleen a grateful feast.
[Wordsworth: *The Excursion* IV]

5 Self-contempt, bitterer to drink than blood.
[Shelley: *Prometheus Unbound* II]

6 I can never be satisfied with anyone who would be blockhead enough to have me. [Abraham Lincoln: Letter to Mrs. O. H. Browning, April 1, 1838]
  Lincoln was writing in the spirit of the date. The modern version is Groucho Marx's refusal of an invitation to join a club on the ground that he didn't want to belong to a club that was willing to have such people as himself in it.

SELF-RESPECT

7 Self-respect—The secure feeling that no one, as yet, is suspicious. [H. L. Mencken: *Chrestomathy* 618]

8 I have to live with myself, and so
  I want to be fit for myself to know;
  I want to be able as days go by,
  Always to look myself straight in the eye.
  I don't want to stand with the setting sun
  And hate myself for the things I've done.
[Edgar A. Guest: *Myself*]
  It's difficult to look oneself in the eye without using a mirror, and a mirror reverses the image.

SELF-SACRIFICE

9 No person . . . shall be compelled in any criminal case to be a witness against himself. [*Constitution of the United States,* Amendment V: adopted December 15, 1791]

10 It is a far, far better thing that I do, than I have ever done. [Dickens: *A Tale of Two Cities* III.xv.]
  Sidney Carton does not actually speak these words on the scaffold. Dickens merely says that had Carton been able to express his last thoughts they might have been something like this.

11 Self-denial is not a virtue; it is only the effect of prudence on rascality. [G. B. Shaw: *Maxims for Revolutionists*]

12 Self-sacrifice enables us to sacrifice other people without blushing. [G. B. Shaw: *Maxims for Revolutionists*]

SELLING

13 The having anything to sell is what
  Is the disgrace in man or state or nation.
[Robert Frost: *New Hampshire*]
  Frost attributes the statement to "a lady from the South."

SENILITY

14   Last scene of all,
  That ends this strange eventful history,
  Is second childishness and mere oblivion,
  Sans teeth, sans eyes, sans taste, sans everything.
[Shakespeare: *As You Like It* II.vii.]

15 In life's last scene what prodigies surprise,
  Fears of the brave, and follies of the wise!
  From Marlborough's eyes the streams of dotage flow,
  And Swift expires a driveller and a show.
[Samuel Johnson: *The Vanity of Human Wishes*]
  The Duke of Marlborough died in 1722, aged 72. Five years before his death, he had two strokes, which impaired his speech and weakened his faculties and compelled him to live in semiretirement. Johnson, who came up to London in 1737, could have known many who had seen the Duke in his last years.
  Swift died in 1745, aged 78, only 4 years before Johnson wrote these lines.

Swift had been in a decline for several years before his death. It is said that his servants exhibited him for money.

SENSATION(S)
1 Of all smells, bread; of all tastes, salt.
[George Herbert: *Jacula Prudentum*]
2   Sensations sweet,
   Felt in the blood, and felt along the
                         heart.
[Wordsworth: *Tintern Abbey*]
3 O for a life of sensations rather than
                    of thoughts!
[Keats: *Letter to Benjamin Bailey*, November 22, 1817]

SENSIBLE
4 Men of sense are really all of one religion. But men of sense never tell what it is. [Anthony Ashley Cooper (Earl of Shaftesbury): *Characteristics*]
5 "As for that," said Waldershare, "sensible men are all of the same religion." "And pray, what is that?" inquired the prince. "Sensible men never tell." [Benjamin Disraeli: *Endymion* LXXXI]
   Disraeli evidently borrowed the remark of Lord Shaftesbury's. The religion alluded to was most probably deism.

SENSITIVITY
6 The hand of little employment hath the daintier sense. [Shakespeare: *Hamlet* V.i.]

SENTENCE
7 A sentence should read as if its author, had he held a plough instead of a pen, could have drawn a furrow deep and straight to the end. [Thoreau: *A Week on the Concord and Merrimac Rivers*, "Sunday"]

SENTIMENTALITY
8 The sentimental people fiddle harmonics on the string of sensualism. [George Meredith: *Diana of the Crossways* I]

SENTIMENTS
9 Them's my sentiments. [W. M. Thackeray: *Vanity Fair* I.xxi.]

SEPULCHRE
10 Ye are like unto whited sepulchres, which indeed appear beautiful outward, but are within full of dead men's bones, and of all uncleanness. [Matthew 23:27]

SERAGLIO
11 If I kept a seraglio the ladies would all wear linen gowns, or cotton—I mean stuffs made of vegetable substances. I would have no silk: you cannot tell when it is clean. [Samuel Johnson: in Boswell's *Tour of the Hebrides*, Sept. 17, 1773]

SERENITY
12 Now fades the glimmering landscape
                     on the sight,
  And all the air a solemn stillness
                       holds,
  Save where the beetle wheels his
                  droning flight,
  And drowsy tinklings lull the distant
                       folds.
[Thomas Gray: *Elegy Written in a Country Churchyard*]
13 Serene will be our days and bright,
   And happy will our nature be,
  When love is an unerring light,
   And joy its own security.
[Wordsworth: *Ode to Duty*]
14 Mrs. Bennett was restored to her usual querulous serenity. [Jane Austen: *Pride and Prejudice* XLII]
15 And the night shall be filled with
                       music,
  And the cares that infest the day
  Shall fold their tents like the Arabs
  And as silently steal away.
[Longfellow: *The Day is Done*]

SERIOUS
16 Setting raillery aside, let us be serious. [Horace: *Satires* I.i.]
   The modern equivalent—"But seriously . . ."—is our first intimation, often, that anything humorous had been intended in the previous remarks.

SERMONS
17 And this our life, exempt from public
                       haunt,
  Finds tongues in trees, books in the
                running brooks,
  Sermons in stones, and good in everything.
[Shakespeare: *As You Like It* II.i.]

SERPENT

1 Because thou hast done this, thou art cursed above all cattle, and above every beast of the field; upon thy belly shalt thou go, and dust shalt thou eat all the days of thy life. [Genesis 3:14]

2 What, wouldst thou have a serpent sting thee twice?
[Shakespeare: *The Merchant of Venice* IV.i.]

3 Look like the innocent flower,
But be the serpent under 't.
[Shakespeare: *Macbeth* I.v.]

4 The infernal serpent; he it was, whose guile,
Stirr'd up with envy and revenge, deceived
The mother of mankind.
[John Milton: *Paradise Lost* I.34-36]

5 The serpent, subtlest beast of all the field.
[John Milton: *Paradise Lost* VII.495]
Milton is echoing Genesis 3:1.

SERVANT(S)

6 Hewers of wood and drawers of water [Joshua 9:21]

7 He that is greatest among you shall be your servant. [Matthew 23:11]

8 Well done, thou good and faithful servant. [Matthew 25:21]

9 O good old man, how well in thee appears
The constant service of the antique world,
When service sweat for duty, not for meed!
Thou art not for the fashion of these times,
Where none will sweat but for promotion.
[Shakespeare: *As You Like It* II.iii.]

10 Choose none for thy servant who have served thy betters. [George Herbert: *Jacula Prudentum* (1651)]

11 More knowledge may be gained of a man's real character by a short conversation with one of his servants than from a formal and studied narrative, begun with his pedigree and ended with his funeral. [Samuel Johnson: *The Rambler* No. 60]

SERVE

12 That sir which serves and seeks for gain,
And follows but for form,
Will pack when it begins to rain,
And leave thee in the storm.
[Shakespeare: *King Lear* II.iv.]

13 They also serve who only stand and wait.
[John Milton: *On His Blindness*]

SERVICE

14 'Tis mad idolatry
To make the service greater than the god.
[Shakespeare: *Troilus and Cressida* II. ii.]

15 All service is the same with God.
[Robert Browning: *Pippa Passes* IV]

SESAME

16 Open, Sesame.
The magic password by which Ali Baba, in The Arabian Nights, *gains admission to the treasure cave.*
It has come to be used of a shibboleth, password, sign, status symbol or whatever gains a desired admittance.

SETTING OUT TO SEA

17 The ship was cheered, the harbour cleared,
Merrily did we drop
Below the kirk, below the hill,
Below the lighthouse top.
[Coleridge: *The Ancient Mariner* I]
John Livingston Lowes, in The Road to Xanadu, *points out that these lines view the ship from the shore—a reflection of the fact that, at the time of writing his great sea poem, Coleridge had never been to sea.*

SEVEN

18 Still
The little maid would have her will,
And said, "Nay, we are seven!"
[Wordsworth: *We Are Seven*]

SEVEN AGES OF MAN

19 All the world's a stage,
And all the men and women merely players.
They have their exits and their entrances;
And one man in his time plays many parts,

His acts being seven ages. At first the
infant,
Mewling and puking in the nurse's
arms.
And then the whining school-boy,
with his satchel
And shining morning face, creeping
like a snail
Unwillingly to school. And then the
lover,
Sighing like furnace, with a woeful
ballad
Made to his mistress' eyebrow. Then
a soldier,
Full of strange oaths, and bearded
like the pard;
Jealous in honour, sudden and quick
in quarrel,
Seeking the bubble reputation
Even in the cannon's mouth. And
then the justice,
In fair round belly with good capon
lined,
With eyes severe and beard of formal
cut,
Full of wise saws and modern in-
stances;
And so he plays his part. The sixth
age shifts
Into the lean and slipper'd pantaloon,
With spectacles on nose and pouch on
side;
His youthful hose, well saved, a
world too wide
For his shrunk shank; and his big
manly voice
Turning again toward childish treble,
pipes
And whistles in his sound. Last scene
of all,
That ends this strange eventful his-
tory,
Is second childishness, and mere obliv-
ion,
Sans teeth, sans eyes, sans taste, sans
everything.
[Shakespeare: *As You Like It* II.vii.]

SEX

1 There is no greater nor keener pleasure than that of bodily love—and none
which is more irrational. [Plato: *The
Republic* III.403]
2 When we will, they won't; when we
don't want to, they [women] want to exceedingly. [Terence: *Eunuchus* IV.vi.]
3 'Tis the Devil inspires this evanescent
ardor, in order to divert the parties from
prayer. [Martin Luther: *Table-talk*
DCCXXXII]
*Luther's explanation of marriages which
commence with excessive amorous ardor
and end soon after in disgust.*
4 The lustful longing which allures us
to women seeks but to expel that pain
which an earnest and burning desire doth
possess us with, and desireth but to allay
it thereby to come to rest and be exempted from this fever. [Montaigne:
Essays II.xii.]
5 It is a common proverb in Italy that
he knows not the perfect pleasure of
Venus that hath not lain with a limping
woman. [Montaigne: *Essays* III.xi.]
6 Morality in sexual relations, when it
is free from superstition, consists essentially of respect for the other person, and
unwillingness to use that person solely as
a means of personal gratification, without regard to his or her desires. [Ber-
trand Russell: *Marriage and Morals* XI]
7 I doubt that the lives of normal men,
taking one with another, are much colored or conditioned, directly or indi-
rectly by purely sexual considerations.
[H. L. Mencken: *Prejudices: Fifth Series*]
8 All this humorless document [the Kinsey Report] really proves is: (*a*) that all
men lie when they are asked about their
adventures in amour, and (*b*) that peda-
gogues are singularly naive and credulous creatures. [H. L. Mencken: *Chrestomathy*]
9 Breathes there a man with hide so
tough
Who says two sexes aren't enough?
[Samuel Hoffenstein: *The Sexes*]
10 Woman, observing that her mate
went out of his way to make himself entertaining, rightly surmised that sex
had something to do with it. From that
she logically concluded that sex was rec-
reational rather than procreational.
(The small hardy band of girls who
failed to get this point were responsible
for the popularity of women's field
hockey.) [James Thurber and E. B.
White: *Is Sex Necessary?* IV]

SHADOW(S)

1 Himself a shadow, hunting shadows.
[Homer: *Odyssey* XI.574]
Odysseus in the underworld sees the spirit of the hunter Orion forever pursuing the spirits of the game he had killed when alive.

2 Shall the shadow go forward ten degrees, or go back ten degrees?

And Hezekiah answered, It is a light thing for the shadow to go down ten degrees: nay, but let the shadow return backward ten degrees. [II Kings 20:9-10]

3 Our days on the earth are as a shadow. [I Chronicles 29:15]

4 As the shadow of a great rock in a weary land. [Isaiah 32:2]

5   Hence, horrible shadow!
Unreal mockery, hence!
[Shakespeare: *Macbeth* III.iv.]

6 Come like shadows, so depart!
[Shakespeare: *Macbeth* IV.i.]

7 When the sun sets, shadows, that
         showed at noon
But small, appear most long and terrible.
[Nathaniel Lee: *Oedipus* IV.i.]

8 Coming events cast their shadows
         before.
[Thomas Campbell: *Lochiel's Warning*]

9 The only safe and rational procedure for him who does not cast a shadow is to stay out of the sun. [Chamisso: *Peter Schlemihl* III]
It was widely believed that the Devil cast no shadow. The idea, then, is that if you have some mysterious and sinister secret it is advisable not to draw attention to yourself but to court obscurity.

10 The awful shadow of some unseen
         Power
Floats, though unseen, amongst us.
[Shelley: *Hymn to Intellectual Beauty*]

11 That shadow my likeness that goes
         to and fro
seeking a livelihood, chattering,
         chaffering,
How often I find myself standing
        and looking at it where it flits,
How often I question and doubt
        whether that is really me.
[Walt Whitman: *That Shadow My Likeness*]

12 We are no other than a moving row

Of Magic Shadow-shapes that come
        and go.
[*Rubáiyát of Omar Khayyám* (trans. Edward FitzGerald)]

SHAKESPEARE

13 His mind and hand went together, and what he thought he uttered with that easiness that we have scarce received from him a blot in his papers. [John Heminge and Henry Condell: in their preface to the First Folio (1623) of Shakespeare's plays]
blot = correction
Heminge and Condell were two players in Shakespeare's company to whom he entrusted his manuscripts. Ben Jonson, commenting on this, and saying that the players "had often mentioned it as an honor," said "would he had blotted a thousand" for he felt that Shakespeare, his friend, "most faulted" by the lack of careful revision. Ben Jonson: Discoveries *(c. 1635)*

14 Renowned Spenser, lie a thought
        more nigh
To learned Chaucer, and rare Beaumont lie
A little nearer Spenser, to make room
For Shakespeare in your threefold,
        fourfold tomb.
[William Basse: *On Shakespeare* (1616)]

15 He was not of an age, but for all time. [Ben Jonson: *To the Memory of My Beloved . . . Wm. Shakespeare* (1623)]

16 Sweet swan of Avon. [Ben Jonson: *To the Memory of My Beloved . . . Wm. Shakespeare* (1623)]

17 I loved the man, and do honor his memory, on this side idolatry, as much as any. [Ben Jonson: *Discoveries*]

18 Many were the wit combats betwixt him and Ben Jonson, which two I behold like a Spanish great galleon and an English man-of-war. Master Jonson, like the former, was built far higher in learning—solid, but slow in his performances; Shakespeare, with the English man-of-war, lesser in bulk but lighter in sailing, could turn with all tides, tack about, and take advantage of all winds by the quickness of his wit and invention. [Thomas Fuller (1608-1661): *Worthies of England*]

1 What needs my Shakespeare for his
honoured bones,
The labour of an age in pilèd stones?
Or that his hallowed relics should be
hid
Under a star-ypointing pyramid?
Dear son of Memory, great heir of
Fame,
What need'st thou such weak witness
of thy name?
Thou, in our wonder and astonishment
Hast built thyself a livelong monument.
[John Milton: *On Shakespeare*]
2 Or sweetest Shakespeare, fancy's child,
Warble his native wood-notes wild.
[John Milton: *L'Allegro*]
3 But Shakespeare's magic could not
copied be;
Within that circle none durst walk
but he.
[Dryden: Prologue to his version of
Shakespeare's *The Tempest*]
4 He (Shakespeare) was the man who
of all modern, and perhaps ancient poets,
had the largest and most comprehensive
soul. [Dryden: *Essay of Dramatic Poesy*]
5 Was there ever such stuff as a great
part of Shakespeare? Only one must not
say so! [George III: to Fanny Burney
quoted in *The Diary of Madame D'Arblay* II (1842)]
6 The stream of Time, which is continually washing the dissoluble fabrics
of other poets, passes without injury by
the adamant of Shakespeare. [Samuel
Johnson: *Preface to Shakespeare*]
7 It must be at last confessed that, as
we owe everything to him [Shakespeare],
he owes something to us; that, if much
of our praise is paid by perception and
judgement, much is likewise given by custom and veneration. We fix our eyes
upon his graces and turn them from his
deformities, and endure in him what we
should in another loathe or despise.
[Samuel Johnson: *Preface to Shakespeare*]
8 Shakespeare never had six lines together without a fault. [Samuel Johnson: in Boswell's *Life*, Oct. 19, 1769]
9 Our myriad-minded Shakespeare.
[Coleridge: *Biographia Literaria* xv]
10 If we wish to know the force of hu-

man genius, we should read Shakespeare.
If we wish to see the insignificance of
human learning, we may study his com-
mentators. [William Hazlitt: *On the
Ignorance of the Learned*]
11 Shakespeare led a life of Allegory:
his works are the comments on it. [Keats:
Letter to George and Georgiana Keats,
February 14, 1819]
12 Others abide our question. Thou art
free.
We ask and ask: Thou smilest and art
still,
Out-topping knowledge.
[Matthew Arnold: *Shakespeare*]

SHALOTT, LADY OF

13 But who hath seen her wave her
hand?
Or at the casement seen her stand?
Or is she known in all the land,
The Lady of Shalott?
[Tennyson: *The Lady of Shalott* I]
14 She left the web, she left the loom,
She made three paces thro' the room,
She saw the water-lily bloom,
She saw the helmet and the plume,
She looked down to Camelot.
[Tennyson: *The Lady of Shalott* III]

SHAME

15 Of all kinds of shame, the worst,
surely, is being ashamed of frugality or
poverty. [Livy: *History* XXXIV]
16 Where the heart is past hope, the face
is past shame. [16th-century proverb]
17 Where the mind is past hope, the
heart is past shame. [John Lyly: *Euphues*]
18 There is no vice that doth so cover a
man with shame as to be found false and
perfidious. [Francis Bacon: *Of Truth*]
19 The expense of spirit in a waste of
shame.
[Shakespeare: *Sonnets* CXXIX]
20 Must I hold a candle to my shames?
[Shakespeare: *The Merchant of Venice*
II.vi.]
21 Makest thou this shame thy pastime?
[Shakespeare: *King Lear* II.iv.]
22 Love taught him shame; and shame,
with love at strife,
Soon taught the sweet civilities of
life.

[Dryden: *Cymon and Iphigenia*]

1 I never wonder to see men wicked, but I often wonder to see them not ashamed. [Jonathan Swift: *Thoughts on Various Subjects*]

2 While shame keeps its watch, virtue is not wholly extinguished in the heart. [Edmund Burke: *Reflections on the Revolution in France*]

3 When people are ashamed they hold aloof, above all from those nearest to them. [Anton Chekhov: *The Name-Day Party*]

4 We live in an atmosphere of shame. We are ashamed of everything that is real about us; ashamed of ourselves, of our relatives, of our incomes, of our accents, of our opinions, of our experience, just as we are ashamed of our naked skins. [G. B. Shaw: *Man and Superman* I]

SHAPE

5 Whence and what art thou, execrable shape?
[John Milton: *Paradise Lost* II.681]

6 When that strange shape drove suddenly
Betwixt us and the Sun.
[Coleridge: *The Ancient Mariner* III]

SHARING

7 What's mine is yours, and what is yours is mine.
[Shakespeare: *Measure for Measure* V.i.]

SHARK

8 When the sands are all dry, he is gay as a lark,
And will talk in contemptuous tones of the Shark:
But, when the tide rises and sharks are around,
His voice has a timid and tremulous sound.
[Lewis Carroll: *Alice's Adventures in Wonderland* X]

SHAVING

9 Of a thousand shavers, two do not shave so much alike as not to be distinguished. [Samuel Johnson: in Boswell's *Life*, Sept. 19, 1777]

10 Men for their sins
Have shaving too entail'd upon their chins—
A daily plague, which in the aggregate
May average on the whole with parturition.
[Byron: *Don Juan* XIV.xxiii-xxiv.]

SHAW, G. B.

11 He [G. B. Shaw] hasn't an enemy in the world, and none of his friends like him. [Oscar Wilde: on Shaw]

12 Sherard Blaw, the dramatist who had discovered himself, and who had given so ungrudgingly of his discovery to the world. [H. H. Munro ("Saki") *The Unbearable Bassington*]

SHE

13 Whoe'er she be
That not impossible she
That shall command my heart and me.
[Richard Crashaw: *Wishes to his Supposed Mistress*]

SHEEP

14 And before him shall be gathered all nations: and he shall separate them one from another, as a shepherd divideth his sheep from the goats. [Matthew 25:32]

SHELL

15   I have seen
A curious child, who dwelt upon a tract
Of inland ground, applying to his ear
The convolutions of a smooth-lipped shell;
To which, in silence hushed, his very soul
Listened intensely; and his countenance soon
Brightened with joy; for from within were heard
Murmurings, whereby the monitor expressed
Mysterious union with its native sea.
[Wordsworth: *The Excursion* IV]
Wordsworth expresses here a common folk belief, that the murmuring one hears when one applies a convoluted shell to the ear is the sound of the sea whence the shell came. Science, more prosaically, says that it is simply the sound of our own pulse magnified.

SHELLEY

1 Shelley I saw once. His voice was the most obnoxious squeak I ever was tormented with. [Charles Lamb: *Letter to Bernard Barton*, Oct. 9, 1822]

2 The author of *Prometheus Unbound* . . . has a fire in his eye, a fever in his blood, a maggot in his brain, a hectic flutter in his speech. . . . [William Hazlitt: *On Paradox and Commonplace*]

3 And did you once see Shelley plain,
And did he stop and speak to you,
And did you speak to him again?
How strange it seems and new!
[Robert Browning: *Memorabilia* I]
And did you once find Browning plain?
And did he really seem quite clear?
And did you read the book again?
How strange it seems and queer.
—*Charles W. Stubbs*

4 A beautiful and ineffectual angel beating in the void his luminous wings in vain. [Matthew Arnold: *Shelley*]

SHEPHERD(S)

5 The Lord is my shepherd; I shall not want.
He maketh me to lie down in green pastures: he leadeth me beside the still waters.
He restoreth my soul: he leadeth me in the paths of righteousness for his name's sake.
Yea, though I walk through the valley of the shadow of death, I will fear no evil: for thou art with me; thy rod and thy staff they comfort me.
Thou preparest a table before me in the presence of mine enemies: thou anointest my head with oil; my cup runneth over.
Surely goodness and mercy shall follow me all the days of my life: and I will dwell in the house of the Lord for ever.
[Psalms 23]
comfort = *support*

6 The good shepherd giveth his life for the sheep. [John 10:11]

7 Every shepherd tells his tale
Under the hawthorn in the vale.
[John Milton: *L'Allegro*]
tells his tale = *counts his tally of sheep*

8 While shepherds watch'd their flocks
by night,
All seated on the ground,
The Angel of the Lord came down,
And glory shone around.
"Fear not," said he, for mighty dread
Had seized their troubled mind;
"Glad tidings of great joy I bring
To you and all mankind."
[Nicholas Brady: *While Shepherds Watched*]

9 The King of love my Shepherd is
Whose goodness faileth never;
I nothing lack if I am His,
And He is mine for ever.
[Sir H. W. Baker: paraphrase of the twenty-third Psalm]

10 From the point of view of the individual lambs, rams and ewes, there is no such thing as a *good* shepherd. [Aldous Huxley: *Themes and Variations*]

SHERIDAN, GENERAL PHILIP

11 And Sheridan twenty miles away.
[T. B. Read: *Sheridan's Ride*]

SHERRY

12 A good sherris-sack hath a two-fold operation in it. It ascends me into the brain; dries me there all the foolish and dull and crudy vapours which environ it; makes it apprehensive, quick, forgetive, full of nimble fiery and delectable shapes; which, deliver'd o'er to the voice, the tongue, which is the birth, becomes excellent wit. The second property of your excellent sherris is, the warming of the blood; which, before cold and settled, left the liver white and pale, which is the badge of pusillanimity and cowardice: but the sherris warms it and makes it course from the inwards to the parts extreme. It illumineth the face, which, as a beacon, gives warning to all the rest of this little kingdom, man, to arm; and then the vital commoners and inland petty spirits muster me all to their captain, the heart, who, great and puffed up with this retinue, doth any deed of courage; and this valour comes of sherris. So that skill in the weapon is nothing without sack, for that sets it a-work; and learning, a mere hoard of gold kept by a devil till sack commences it and sets it in act and use. [Shakespeare: *II Henry IV* IV.iii.]
sherry *derives from* sherris, *which derives from the town of Xeres.*

sack = sec = *dry, so that* sherris-sack = *dry sherry.*

SHIBBOLETH

1 The Gileadites took the passages of Jordan before the Ephraimites: and it was so, that when those Ephraimites which were escaped said, Let me go over; that the men of Gilead said unto him, Art thou an Ephraimite? If he said, Nay; Then said they unto him, Say now Shibboleth: and he said Sibboleth: for he could not frame to pronounce it right. Then they took him, and slew him at the passages of Jordan: and there fell at the time of the Ephraimites forty and two thousand. [Judges 12: 5-6]

From this passage comes our use of shibboleth to mean a peculiarity of pronunciation, or a habit or mode of dress, which distinguishes a particular class or set of persons. The grim scene at the passages of the Jordan has been repeated in history. In 1282 the Sicilians slew a French garrison, using a local pronunciation as the distinguishing test. In 1381 an English mob hunted down Flemings and killed them when they gave the Flemish, rather than the English, pronunciation of "bread and cheese."

SHIELD

2 Come back either with your shield or upon it. [Plutarch: *Apothegms,* "The Spartan Mother to her Son"]

i.e., undefeated or dead.

SHIP(S)

3 His heart was encompassed in oak and triple brass who first committed a fragile bark to the raging sea. [Horace: *Odes* II.ix.]

The Latin for triple brass—aes triplex— is sometimes used by itself. It was the title of one of Robert Louis Stevenson's best known essays.

4 What is a ship but a prison? [Robert Burton: *The Anatomy of Melancholy* II.3.4]

5 A great ship asks deep waters. [George Herbert: *Jacula Prudentum*]

That is, great abilities usually require great opportunities. But for the Civil War, for example, who would ever have guessed that Grant was an extraordinary man?

6 No man will be a sailor who has contrivance enough to get himself into a jail; for being in a ship is being in a jail, with the chance of being drowned. . . . A man in a jail has more room, better food, and commonly better company. [Samuel Johnson: in Boswell's *Life,* March 16, 1759]

7 Don't give up the ship! [Capt. James Mugford, of the schooner Franklin: during a British attack in Boston Harbor, May 19, 1776]

Captain Mugford died in the engagement. The same words were attributed to Captain James Lawrence, commander of the American frigate Chesapeake, *who was killed in an engagement with the British* Shannon, *June 1, 1813. By this time, the words had achieved a glory and served as the signal at the masthead of Commodore Perry's flagship, the* Lawrence, *at the battle of Lake Erie, September 10, 1813.*

8 She starts—she moves—she seems to feel
The thrill of life along her keel!
[Longfellow: *The Building of the Ship*]

9 Ships that pass in the night, and speak each other in passing.
[Longfellow: *The Theologian's Tale*]

10 A capital ship for an ocean trip
Was the "Walloping Window-blind."
No gale that blew dismayed her crew
Or troubled the Captain's mind.
The man at the wheel was taught to feel
Contempt for the wildest blow,
And it often appeared, when the weather had cleared,
That he'd been in his bunk below.
[Charles Carryl: *A Nautical Ballad*]

11 There's something wrong with our bloody ships to-day, Chatfield. [Vice-Admiral Sir David Beatty: during the Battle of Jutland, 1916 (as quoted in Sir Winston Churchill's *The World Crisis*]

Not quite Nelson's prose style, but candid. Something was wrong with more than the bloody ships. It was from Beatty's own flagship, Lion, *that at 9:30 p.m., May 31, was flashed the signal: "Please give me challenge and reply now in force as they have been lost." The* Princess Royal *obligingly gave the de-*

sired information. The Germans intercepted it and used it with telling effect. See Jutland, *by* Capt. Donald Macintyre.

1 The Liner she's a lady, an' she never
looks nor 'eeds—
The Man-o'-War's 'er 'usband, an' 'e
gives 'er all she needs;
But, oh, the little cargo-boats, that
sail the wet seas roun',
They're just the same as you an' me
a-plyin' up an' down!
[Rudyard Kipling: *The Liner She's a Lady*]

2 A ship is always referred to as a "she" because it costs so much to keep her in paint. [Admiral Chester Nimitz, quoted, the *New York Times*, May 24, 1959]

> Even a man-of-war takes the feminine pronoun. There have been many explanations. One: "Because you can see her (r)udder."

SHOE(S)

3 Put off thy shoes from off thy feet, for the place whereon thou standest is holy ground. [Exodus 3:5]

4 Whose shoe's latchet I am not worthy to unloose. [John 1:27]

5 None of you can tell where it pinches me. [Anon.: in Plutarch's *Life of Aemilius Paulus*]

> Plutarch tells of an unnamed Roman who was divorced from his wife, to the amazement of his friends who could see no fault in her. The man handed them one of his shoes, a new and well-made shoe, and asked them if they could tell him where it pinched.
>
> Plutarch adds: "Certain it is, that great and open faults have often led to no separation; while mere petty repeated annoyances, arising from unpleasantness or incongruity of character, have been the occasion of such estrangement as to make it impossible for man and wife to live together."
>
> The expression became proverbial. Justinius, in Chaucer's The Merchant's Tale says that his neighbors all think he has an ideal wife—
>
> But I wot best wher wringeth me my sho.

6 While the leg warmeth the boot harmeth. [John Heywood: *English Proverbs* (1546)]

> Many a pair of boots has been ruined by warming the feet before the fire.
>
> This was the original sin of Little Polly Flinders.

7 Who is worse shod than the shoemaker's wife? [John Heywood: *Proverbs* (1546)]

8 Him that makes shoes goes barefoot himself. [Robert Burton: *The Anatomy of Melancholy*, "Democritus to the Reader"]

SHOP

9 Keep thy shop, and thy shop will keep thee. [Chapman, Marston and Ben Jonson: *Eastward Ho* I]

SHOPKEEPERS

10 To found a great empire for the sole purpose of raising up a people of customers may at first sight appear a project fit only for a nation of shopkeepers. It is, however, a project altogether unfit for a nation of shopkeepers; but extremely fit for a nation whose Government is influenced by shopkeepers. [Adam Smith: *Wealth of Nations* II.iv.7. (1776)]

> The phrase "a nation of shopkeepers" was picked up and applied contemptuously to the English by Napoleon. The English accepted it with pride.

SHORE

11 And thou art long, and lank, and
brown,
As is the ribbed sea-sand.
[Coleridge: *The Ancient Mariner* IV]

12 The myriad shriek of wheeling ocean-
fowl,
The league-long roller thundering on
the reef.
[Tennyson: *Enoch Arden*]

13 Still bent to make some port he
knows not where,
Still standing for some false impossible shore.
[Matthew Arnold: *A Summer Night*]

14 "If seven maids with seven mops
Swept it for half a year,
Do you suppose," the Walrus said,
"That they could get it clear?"
"I doubt it," said the Carpenter,
And shed a bitter tear.
[Lewis Carroll: *Through the Looking-*

Glass IV, "The Walrus and the Carpenter"]

SHOUT

1 The universal host up sent
A shout that tore Hell's concave,
and beyond,
Frighted the reign of Chaos and old
Night.
[John Milton: *Paradise Lost* I.541-543]

SHREW

2 It is better to marry a shrew than a
sheep. [16th-century proverb]
*Whether the malignant, ferocious little
blood-sucking carnivore is named after
a similar aspect of human nature (a*
shrew *used to mean a cursed, actively
wicked man, and then came to be restricted to a scolding woman), or whether
shrewishness in human nature is named
after the animal, is uncertain.*
*There is an amusing 17th-century
poem that amplifies the proverb and
says that whoso marries a scold is in
for a merry life—*
*For when she's in her fits
He may cherish his wits.*
3 Cursed be the man, the poorest
wretch in life,
The crouching vassal to the tyrant
wife,
Who has no will but by her high
permission;
Who has not sixpence but in her possession;
Who must to her his dear friend's
secret tell;
Who dreads a curtain lecture worse
than hell.
Were such the wife had fallen to my
part,
I'd break her spirit or I'd break her
heart.
[Burns: *The Henpecked Husband*]
*Burns had trials in his hard life, but a
domineering wife wasn't one of them.
Jean Armour was patient and very, very
understanding. "Rob could hae done
wi' two wives," she once remarked about
his philanderings.*
4 Every man can rule a shrew save he
that hath her. [William C. Hazlitt: *English Proverbs* (1869)]

SHROUD

5 A lady that was drowned at sea and
had a wave for her winding sheet.
[George Villiers, Duke of Buckingham:
The Rehearsal]
*The year before (1670) Dryden had used
the same figure (The Conquest of Granada). Both are echoing Richard Barnfield's lines* On the Death of Hawkins
("*The waters were his winding sheet*")
(1595).

SHUDDER

6 *Horresco referens.* ("I shudder at the
very mention of it.") [Vergil: *Aeneid* II]

SHYNESS

7 Shy and unready men are great be-
trayers of secrets; for there are few
wants more urgent for the moment than
the want of something to say. [Henry
Taylor: *The Statesman*]

SICKNESS

8 Philosophers apply the term sickness
to all disturbances of the soul, and they
say that no foolish person is free from
such sickness; sufferers from disease are
not sound, and the souls of all unwise
persons are sick. [Cicero: *Tusculanarum
Disputationum* III.iv.9]
9 Infirmity doth still neglect all office
Whereto our health is bound.
[Shakespeare: *King Lear* II.iv.]
10 Sickness is the mother of modesty,
putteth us in mind of our mortality; and
when we are in the full career of worldly
pomp and jollity, she pulleth us by the
ear, and maketh us know ourselves.
[Robert Burton: *The Anatomy of Melancholy* II.3.2]
11　　　　　　　All maladies
Of ghastly spasm, or racking torture,
qualms
Of heart-sick agony, all feverous
kinds,
Convulsions, epilepsies, fierce ca-
tarrhs,
Intestine stone and ulcer, colic pangs,
Daemonic phrenzy, moping melancholy,
And moon-struck madness, pining
atrophy,
Marasmus, and wide-wasting pestilence,

Dropsies and asthmas, and joint-racking rheums.
[John Milton: *Paradise Lost* XI.480]
marasmus = *consumption, wasting away*
1 I reckon being ill as one of the great pleasures of life, provided one is not too ill and is not obliged to work till one is better. [Samuel Butler (1835-1902): *The Way of All Flesh* LXXX]
2 When there is someone in a family who has long been ill, and hopelessly ill, there come terrible moments when all those close to him timidly, secretly, at the bottom of their hearts wish for his death. [Anton Chekhov: "Peasants"]

SIDNEY [HILLMAN]
3 Clear everything with Sidney. [Attr. Franklin D. Roosevelt: speaking to Robert Hannegan, Chairman of the Democratic National Committee, at Chicago, during Democratic National Convention, 1944]
Sidney = *Sidney Hillman, head of the Political Action Committee of the Congress of Industrial Organizations;* everything—*some claim the remark applied solely to the choice of the Vice-President, others that it meant what it says.*
Whether Roosevelt made the statement or not, the Republicans strengthened his hold over the labor vote by their exploitation of it.

SIEVE
4 They went to sea in a sieve, they did;
  In a sieve they went to sea;
  In spite of all their friends could say,
  On a winter's morn, on a stormy day,
  In a sieve they went to sea.
[Edward Lear: *The Jumblies*]

SIGH(ING)
5 A plague of sighing and grief! it blows a man up like a bladder. [Shakespeare: *I Henry IV* II.iv.]
6 With a sigh like Tom o' Bedlam. [Shakespeare: *King Lear* I.ii.]
7 Sighs are the natural language of the heart. [Thomas Shadwell: *Psyche* III]
8 The passing tribute of a sigh.
[Thomas Gray: *Elegy Written in a Country Churchyard*]
9 Had sighed to many, though he loved
  but one.

[Byron: *Childe Harold* I.v.]
10 On earth there's little worth a sigh,
  And nothing worth a tear!
[Adam Lindsay Gordon: *To My Sister*]
11 When he is here, I sigh with pleasure—
  When he is gone, I sigh with grief.
[W. S. Gilbert: *The Sorcerer* I]

SIGHT(S)
12 The sense of sight is the keenest of all our senses. [Cicero: *De oratore*]
13 Far from eye, far from heart. [Hendying: *Proverbs* (c. 1320)]
14 And for to see, and eke for to be
  seen.
[Chaucer: Prologue to *The Wife of Bath's Tale*]
15 And when a man is out of sight, quickly also is he out of mind. [Thomas à Kempis: *The Imitation of Christ* I. xxiii. (1424)]
This seems to be the origin of "Out of sight, out of mind," but there is the possibility that à Kempis was merely expanding slightly an already-established phrase.
16 Out of syght, out of mynd. [Barnabe Googe: *Eglogs*]
17 Foure things hurt the sight of al menne, that is, Teares, smoke, wynde, and the woorst of al, to see his friend unluckie and his enimies happy. [John Florio: *Firste Fruites* XXIII]
18 A ship under sail, a man in complete armour, and a woman with a big belly, are the three handsomest sights in the world. [James Howell: *Proverbs* (1659)]
19 The sight of you is good for sore eyes. [Jonathan Swift: *Polite Conversation* I (1738)]
Swift did not invent the phrase. Indeed, its appearance in Polite Conversation *simply means that it was corny and wornout as long ago as 1738.*
20 The Spanish fleet thou canst not see
  —because
  —It is not yet in sight!
[Richard Brinsley Sheridan: *The Critic* II.ii.]
21 Earth has not anything to show more
  fair:
  Dull would he be of soul who
  could pass by
  A sight so touching in its majesty.

[Wordsworth: *Composed Upon Westminster Bridge*]
1 A sight to dream of, not to tell! [Coleridge: *Christabel* I]

SIGN(S)
2 The signs of the times. [Matthew 16:3]
3 An outward and visible sign of an inward and spiritual grace. [*The Book of Common Prayer,* "The Catechism"]
4   At my nativity
The front of heaven was full of fiery
           shapes,
Of burning cressets; and at my birth
The frame and huge foundation of
           the earth
Shaked like a coward.
[Shakespeare: *I Henry IV* III.i.]
5 I have always looked upon it as a high point of indiscretion in monster-mongers, and other retailers of strange sights, to hang out a fair large picture over the door, drawn after the life, with a most eloquent description underneath. This hath saved me many a three-pence; for my curiosity was fully satisfied, and I never offered to go in, though often invited by the urging and attending orator. [Jonathan Swift: *A Tale of a Tub* V]

SILENCE
6 The rest is silence.
[Shakespeare: *Hamlet* V.ii.]
7 My gracious silence, hail!
[Shakespeare: *Coriolanus* II.i.]
8 I'll speak to thee in silence.
[Shakespeare: *Cymbeline* V.iv.]
9 It is never so difficult to speak as when we are ashamed of our silence. [La Rochefoucauld: *Maxims*]
10 An horrid stillness first invades the
           ear,
And in that silence we the tempest
           fear.
[Dryden: *Astraea Redux*]
11 Silence is the wit of fools. [La Bruyère: *Les Caractères*]
12 Silence gives consent. [Oliver Goldsmith: *The Good-natured Man* II]
    Goldsmith simply put into the form in which it is now most often spoken an idea that had been expressed in much the same words since antiquity. It ap-

pears in Plutarch (Life of Aristides), *in Euripides* (Iphigenia at Aulis), *in Ovid, and elsewhere.*
13 Breaking the silence of the seas
Among the farthest Hebrides.
[Wordsworth: *The Solitary Reaper*]
14 Our noisy years seem moments in the
           being
Of the eternal silence.
[Wordsworth: *Intimations of Immortality*]
15 The silence that is in the starry sky,
The sleep that is among the lonely
           hills.
[Wordsworth: *Song at the Feast of Brougham Castle*]
16 The silence of a friend commonly amounts to treachery. [William Hazlitt: *Characteristics*]
17 Thou foster-child of Silence and slow
           Time.
[Keats: *Ode on a Grecian Urn*]
18   And then there crept
A little noiseless noise among the
           leaves,
Born of the very sigh that silence
           heaves.
[Keats: *I Stood Tip-toe upon a Little Hill*]
19 Noiseless as fear in a wide wilder-
           ness.
[Keats: *The Eve of St. Agnes*]
20 But the silence was unbroken, and
           the stillness gave no token,
And the only word there spoken was
           the whispered word, "Lenore!"—
Merely this and nothing more.
[Edgar Allan Poe: *The Raven*]
21 It was exactly the silence ensuing on the retreat of a servant. [Henry James: *The Story In It*]

SILENCE: its eloquence
22 There is no reply so sharp as silent contempt. [Montaigne: *Essays* II.xxxi.]
23 Silence in love betrays more woe
Than words, though ne'er so witty.
[Sir Walter Raleigh (1552-1618): *The Silent Lover*]
24 The silence often of pure innocence
Persuades when speaking fails.
[Shakespeare: *The Winter's Tale* II.ii.]
25 There is an eloquent silence: it serves sometimes to approve, sometimes to condemn; there is a mocking silence;

there is a respectful silence. [La Rochefoucauld: *Réflexions Diverses* IV]
1 Silence is one great art of conversation. [William Hazlitt: *Characteristics*]
2 Silence may be as variously shaded as speech. [Edith Wharton: *The Reef* XVII]

SILENCE: is golden
3 Even a fool, when he holdeth his peace, is counted wise. [Proverbs 17:28]
4 To use silence in time and place passeth all well speaking. [Stefano Guazzo: *Civile Conversation* II]
5   Be check'd for silence,
But never tax'd for speech.
[Shakespeare: *All's Well That Ends Well* I.i.]
6 Speech is silvern, Silence is golden. [Thomas Carlyle: *Sartor Resartus* III. iii.]
> *Carlyle is translating a "Swiss inscription." The proverb is common in German and has, indeed, been traced back to the Babylonian Talmud.*

7 Silence is deep as Eternity; speech is shallow as Time. [Thomas Carlyle: *Sir Walter Scott*]
> *This is the sort of bellowing pseudoprofundity that earns a man the awe of one generation and the contempt of the next.*

8 Silence is the eternal duty of man. [Thomas Carlyle: Inaugural Address as Lord Rector of Edinburgh University]
9 Blessed is the man who, having nothing to say, abstains from giving us wordy evidence of the fact. [George Eliot: *The Impressions of Theophrastus Such* IV]
10 Speech is silver; silence is golden. [James Russell Lowell: Introduction to *The Biglow Papers*]
11 The whole of the golden Gospel of Silence is now effectively compressed into thirty-five volumes. [John Morley: *Critical Miscellanies,* "Carlyle"]
> *Lord Morley was alluding to the verbosity with which Carlyle, all his life, had promulgated the value of silence.*

SILENT
12 The world would be happier if men had the same capacity to be silent that they have to speak. [Spinoza: *Ethics* II]

13 When this poor, lisping, stammering
tongue
Lies silent in the grave.
[William Cowper: *Olney Hymns* XV]
14 Is it a party in a parlor?
Cramm'd just as they on earth were
cramm'd—
Some sipping punch, some sipping
tea,
But as you by their faces see,
All silent and all damn'd!
[Wordsworth: *Peter Bell*]
> *In the 1819 ed. Omitted after that.*

15 We were the first that ever burst
Into that silent sea.
[Coleridge: *The Ancient Mariner* II]
16 What, silent still? and silent all?
[Byron: *The Isles of Greece*]
17 Silent upon a peak in Darien.
[Keats: *On First Looking into Chapman's Homer*]

SILK
18 When as in silks my Julia goes,
Then, then (methinks) how sweetly
flows
That liquefaction of her clothes.
[Robert Herrick: *Upon Julia's Clothes*]

SILK PURSE
19 You can't make a silk purse out of a sow's ear. [Jonathan Swift: *Polite Conversation*]
> *The appearance of the expression in Polite Conversation means that it was hackneyed by 1738. Yet no earlier version of this exact form is known. Earlier it had appeared as a satin purse (1659) and a cheverill purse (1611)—both of them plainly proverbial by those dates.*

SILVER AND GOLD
20 He that loveth silver shall not be satisfied with silver, nor he that loveth abundance with increase. [Ecclesiastes 5:10]
21 Silver and gold have I none; but such as I have give I thee. [Acts 3:6]

SIMILE(S)
22 Similes should be sparingly used in prose, for they are at bottom poetical. [Aristotle: *Rhetoric* III]
23 Thou hast the most unsavoury similes. [Shakespeare: *I Henry IV* I.ii.]
24 A simile, to be perfect, must both il-

lustrate and ennoble the subject; must show it to the understanding in a clearer view, and display it to the fancy with greater dignity; but either of these qualities may be sufficient to recommend it. [Samuel Johnson: *Life of Pope*]

SIMON PURE
1 The real Simon Pure. [Susanna Centlivre: *A Bold Stroke for a Wife* V.i.]
Simon Pure, in the play, was a Quaker. His bride-to-be, an heiress, was stolen by Col. Feignwell, who impersonated him.

SIMPLICITY
2 Give me a look, give me a face,
That makes simplicity a grace;
Robes loosely flowing, hair as free:
Such sweet neglect more taketh me
Than all th' adulteries of art;
They strike mine eyes, but not my
heart.
[Ben Jonson: *Epicoene, or The Silent Woman* I.i.]
adulteries = *adulterations, sophistications*
3 Affected simplicity is a subtle form of imposture. [La Rochefoucauld: *Maxims*]
4 The moving accident is not my trade;
To freeze the blood I have no
ready arts:
'Tis my delight, alone in summer
shade,
To pipe a simple song for thinking
hearts.
[Wordsworth: *Hart-Leap Well*]
5 There is a simplicity of cunning no less than a simplicity of innocence. [Dickens: *Martin Chuzzlewit* XI]

SIMPLIFY
6 Simplify, simplify. [Thoreau: *Walden* II]
The essence of Thoreau's social message.

SIMULATION
7 That simulation which aids truth cannot be regarded as a lie. [Petrarch: *Epistolae de Rebus Familiaribus* XXII.v.]
Unfortunately many of the most dangerous lies ever told were thought, by those disseminating them, to be assisting some larger truth.

SIN(S)
8 Be sure your sin will find you out.

[Numbers 32:23]
9 I was shapen in iniquity; and in sin did my mother conceive me. [Psalms 51:5]
10 He that is without sin among you, let him first cast a stone. [John 8:7]
11 The wages of sin is death. [Romans 6:23]
12 The pomps and vanity of this wicked world, and all the sinful lusts of the flesh. [*Book of Common Prayer*, "The Catechism"]
13 We have left undone those things
which we ought to have done;
And we have done those things which
we ought not to have done.
[*Book of Common Prayer*, "A General Confession"]
14 Other men's sins are before our eyes; our own are behind our back. [Seneca: *De ira* II]
15 Forsaketh sin, ere sin you forsake. [Chaucer: *The Physician's Tale*]
16 We estimate vices and weigh sins not according to their nature, but according to our advantage and self-interest. [Montaigne: *Essays* II.v.]
17 Commit the oldest sins the newest
kind of ways.
[Shakespeare: *II Henry IV* IV.v.]
18   Nymph, in thy orisons
Be all my sins remembered.
[Shakespeare: *Hamlet* III.i.]
19 Some rise by sin, and some by virtue
fall.
[Shakespeare: *Measure for Measure* II.i.]
20   I am a man
More sinn'd against than sinning.
[Shakespeare: *King Lear* III.ii.]
21   Plate sin with gold,
And the strong lance of justice hurtless breaks;
Arm it in rags, a pigmy's straw does
pierce it.
[Shakespeare: *King Lear* IV.vi.]
22 Few love to hear the sins they love
to act.
[Shakespeare: *Pericles* I.i.]
23 The longer thread of life we spin,
The more occasion still to sin.
[Robert Herrick: *Long Life*]
24 Of Man's first disobedience, and the
fruit
Of that forbidden tree whose mortal
taste

Brought death into the world, and all
our woe.
[John Milton: *Paradise Lost* I.1-3]

1 Compound for sins they are inclined
to
By damning those they have no mind
to.
[Samuel Butler (1612-1680): *Hudibras*
I.i.]

2 He passed a cottage with a double
coach-house,
A cottage of gentility!
And he owned with a grin
That his favorite sin
Is pride that apes humility.
[Robert Southey: *The Devil's Walk*]
The enormous summer palaces built by
great American financiers at Newport
and elsewhere sixty and seventy years
ago were invariably called "cottages."

3 The Catholic Church holds that it
were better for sun and moon to drop
from heaven, for the earth to fail, and
for all the many millions who are upon
it to die of starvation in extremest
agony, as far as temporal affliction goes,
than that one soul, I will not say, should
be lost, but should commit one single
venial sin, should tell one wilful untruth, . . . or steal one poor farthing
without excuse. [John Henry (Cardinal)
Newman: *Lectures on Anglican Difficulties,* Lecture VIII]

4 Oh Thou, who didst with pitfall and
with gin
Beset the Road I was to wander in,
Thou wilt not with Predestined
Evil round
Enmesh, and then impute my Fall to
Sin!
[*Rubáiyát of Omar Khayyám* (trans. Ed-
ward FitzGerald)]
gin = *trap or snare*
Omar would not have regarded the
other gin, had he known it, as a snare.

5 The sin I impute to each frustrate
ghost
Is—the unlit lamp and the ungirt
loin.
[Robert Browning: *The Statue and the
Bust*]

6 Pride, covetousness, lust, anger, gluttony, envy and sloth, are the seven capital sins. [*A Catechism of Christian Doctrine for General Use* (1866)]

7 "Oh, holy father," Alice said,
" 'twould grieve you, would it not?
To discover that I was a most dis-
reputable lot!
Of all unhappy sinners, I'm the most
unhappy one!"
The padre said, "Whatever have you
been and gone and done?"
[W. S. Gilbert: *Bab Ballads,* "Gentle
Alice Brown"]

8 "I have helped mamma to steal a
little kiddy from its dad,
I've assisted dear papa in cutting up
a little lad.
I've planned a little burglary and
forged a little check,
And slain a little baby for the coral
on its neck!"
The worthy pastor heaved a sigh, and
dropped a silent tear—
And said, "You mustn't judge your-
self too heavily, my dear—
It's wrong to murder babies, little
corals for to fleece;
But sins like these one expiates at
half-a-crown apiece."
[W. S. Gilbert: *Bab Ballads,* "Gentle
Alice Brown"]

9 The seven deadly sins . . . food,
clothing, firing, rent, taxes, respectability
and children. [G. B. Shaw: *Major Barbara* III]

10 The sin they do by two and two they
must pay for one by one. [Kipling: *Tom-
linson*]

SINCERITY

11 Love of talking about ourselves and
displaying our faults in the light in
which we wish them to be seen is the
chief element in our sincerity. [La
Rochefoucauld: *Maxims*]

12 A little sincerity is a dangerous thing,
and a great deal of it is absolutely fatal.
[Oscar Wilde: *The Critic as Artist*]

13 It is dangerous to be sincere unless
you are also stupid. [G. B. Shaw: *Maxims for Revolutionists*]

SING(ING)

14 Singest with vois memorial in the
shade.
[Chaucer: Proem to *Anelida and Arcite*]

15 Warble, child; make passionate my
sense of hearing.

[Shakespeare: *Love's Labour's Lost* III.i.]

1 She will sing the savageness out of a bear.
[Shakespeare: *Othello* IV.i.]

2 I sing of brooks, of blossoms, birds, and bowers:
Of April, May, of June, and July flowers.
I sing of maypoles, hock-carts, wassails, wakes,
Of bridegrooms, brides, and of their bridal cakes.
I write of youth, of love, and have access
By these, to sing of cleanly-wantonness.
[Robert Herrick: *Hesperides*, "The Argument of his Book"]

3   He knew
Himself to sing, and build the lofty rhyme.
[John Milton: *Lycidas*]

4 That which is not worth speaking, they can sing. [Beaumarchais: *Le Barbier de Seville* I.i.]
Rendered into English by G. B. Shaw as:
"What's too silly to be said can be sung."

5 Swans sing before they die—'twere no bad thing
Should certain persons die before they sing.
[Coleridge: *On a Bad Singer*]

6 I do but sing because I must,
And pipe but as the linnets sing.
[Tennyson: *In Memoriam* XXI]
Tennyson is echoing Goethe's:
I sing but as the bird does sing
That in the silence dwelleth.
          —Der Sänger

SINGLE LIFE

7 Single blessedness.
[Shakespeare: *A Midsummer Night's Dream* I.i.]

8 A man accustomed to hear only the echo of his own sentiments soon bars all the common avenues of delight and has no part in the general gratifications of mankind. [Samuel Johnson: *The Rambler*, No. 112]

9 They that have grown old in a single state are generally found to be morose, fretful, and captious; tenacious of their own practices and maxims; soon offended by contradiction or negligence; and impatient of any association but with those that will watch their nod, and submit themselves to unlimited authority. Such is the effect of having lived without the necessity of consulting any inclination but their own. [Samuel Johnson: *The Rambler* No. 112]

SINK(ING)

10 Or sink or swim.
[Shakespeare: *I Henry IV* I.iii.]

11 I have a kind of alacrity in sinking.
[Shakespeare: *The Merry Wives of Windsor* III.v.]

SINNER

12 God be merciful to me a sinner.
[Luke 18:13]

SISTER(S)

13 We have a little sister, and she hath no breasts. [Song of Solomon 8:8]

14 When you get to a man in the case,
They're like as a row of pins—
For the Colonel's Lady an' Judy O'Grady
Are sisters under their skins!
[Kipling: *The Ladies*]

SKATING

15   All shod with steel
We hissed along the polished ice, in games
Confederate.
[Wordsworth: *The Prelude* I]

SKELETON

16 They have a skeleton in their closet.
[W. M. Thackeray: *The Newcomes* LV]

SKEPTICISM

17 The first step towards philosophy is incredulity. [Diderot: *Last Conversation*]

18 In the last analysis all tyranny rests on fraud, on getting someone to accept false assumptions, and any man who for one moment abandons or suspends the questioning spirit has for that moment betrayed humanity. [Bergen Evans: *The Natural History of Nonsense* XIX]

SKILL

19 But it needs Heaven-sent moments for this skill! [Matthew Arnold: *The Scholar-Gipsy*]

1 The achieve of, the mastery of the
thing!
[Gerard Manley Hopkins: *The Windhover*]

SKIN
2 My skin hangs about me like an old
lady's loose gown! I am withered like an
old apple-john. [Shakespeare: *I Henry
IV* III.iii.]
apple-john = *a late apple, which shrinks
when it ripens*

SKIN OF MY TEETH
3 I am escaped with the skin of my
teeth. [Job 19:20]
*Job, lamenting the evil plight into which
he has fallen, says (in the King James
Version) "my bone cleaveth to my skin
and to my flesh, and I am escaped with
the skin of my teeth." In popular usage
this is often "by the skin of my teeth"
and it means "by the narrowest conceiv-
able margin of safety."*
*What the biblical passage means is
much disputed. The* Revised Standard
Version *has "by the skin of my teeth."
The* New American Catholic *edition has
"nothing but lips are left about my
teeth." Some scholars say that this means
that his teeth had fallen out. Some say
it means that he was so lean he could
gnaw his own bones. Some say it's a reference to Nasmyth's membrane, a cuta-
neous covering of the teeth of a foetus.*
The Interpreter's Bible *sums the matter up precisely: "No certain interpretation seems to be possible."*

SKULL
4 He came to ask what he had found,
That was so large, and smooth, and
round.
[Robert Southey: *The Battle of Blenheim*]
5 Look on its broken arch, its ruin'd
wall,
Its chambers desolate, and portals
foul:
Yet this [a skull] was once Ambition's
airy hall,
The dome of Thought, the palace of
the Soul.
[Byron: *Childe Harold* II.vi.]

SKY
6 But suppose, as some folks say, the
sky should fall? [Terence: *Heautonti-
morumenos* IV.iii. (trans. George Colman)]
7 And that inverted Bowl they call the
Sky,
Whereunder crawling coop'd we live
and die,
Lift not your hands to It for help
—for it
As impotently moves as you or I.
[*Rubáiyát of Omar Khayyám* (trans. Edward FitzGerald)]
8 Elsewhere the sky is the roof of the
world; but here the earth was the floor
of the sky. [Willa Cather: *Death Comes
for the Archbishop* VII.iv.]

SKYLARK
9 Ethereal minstrel! pilgrim of the sky!
[Wordsworth: *To a Skylark*]
10 Type of the wise who soar, but never
roam;
True to the kindred points of Heaven
and Home!
[Wordsworth: *To a Skylark*]
11 And singing still dost soar, and soaring ever singest.
[Shelley: *To a Skylark*]

SLANDER
12 I will be hang'd, if some eternal vil-
lain,
Some busy and insinuating rogue,
Some cogging cozening slave, to get
some office,
Have not devis'd this slander.
[Shakespeare: *Othello* IV.ii.]
13 'Tis slander,
Whose edge is sharper than the sword,
whose tongue
Outvenoms all the worms of Nile.
[Shakespeare: *Cymbeline* III.iv.]

SLAUGHTER
14 He smote them hip and thigh with a
great slaughter. [Judges 15:8]
15 As an ox goeth to the slaughter.
[Proverbs 7:22]

SLAVE(S)
16 So many slaves, so many enemies.
[Seneca: *Epistolae* XLVII]

Here the expression is said to be proverbial.

1 Slaves of drink and thralls of sleep.
[Shakespeare: *Macbeth* III.vi.]

2 If you put a chain around the neck of a slave, the other end fastens itself around your own. [Emerson: *Compensation*]

SLAVERY

3 My paramount object in this struggle is to save the Union, and is not either to save or to destroy slavery. If I could save the Union without freeing any slave, I would do it; and if I could do it by freeing all the slaves, I would do it; and if I could save it by freeing some and leaving others alone, I would also do that. [Abraham Lincoln: Letter to Horace Greeley, Aug. 22, 1862]

SLEEP

4 The vigorous are no better than the lazy during one half of life, for all men are alike when asleep. [Aristotle: *Eudemian Ethics* II.i.]

5 He giveth his beloved sleep. [Psalms 127:2]

6 I will not give sleep to mine eyes, or slumber to mine eyelids. [Psalms 132:4]

7 Yet a little sleep, a little slumber, a little folding of the hands to sleep:
So shall thy poverty come as one that travelleth, and thy want as an armed man. [Proverbs 6:10-11]

8 To bed, to bed,
Says Sleepy-head;
Let's tarry a while, says Slow.
Put on the pot,
Says Greedy-gut,
We'll sup before we go.
[Nursery rhyme: earliest printed version, 1784]
 In most modern collections Greedy-gut is regarded as coarse and replaced by: Put on the pan,/ Says Greedy Nan.

9 Blest be the man who first invented sleep—a cloak to cover all human imaginings, food to satisfy hunger, water to quench thirst, fire to warm cold air, cold to temper heat, and, lastly, a coin to buy whatever we need. [Cervantes: *Don Quixote* II.68]
 food—*the Spaniards have a proverb: "He who sleeps, eats."*

10 He sleeps well who knows not that he sleeps ill. [Publilius Syrus: *Maxims*]
 Quoted by Francis Bacon in Ornamenta Rationalia.

11   O sleep, O gentle sleep!
Nature's soft nurse, how have I
      frighted thee,
That thou no more wilt weigh my
      eyelids down
And steep my senses in forgetfulness?
Why rather, sleep, liest thou in smoky
      cribs,
Upon uneasy pallets stretching thee,
And hush'd with buzzing night-flies
      to thy slumber,
Than in the perfum'd chambers of
      the great,
Under the canopies of costly state,
And lull'd with sound of sweetest
      melody?
[Shakespeare: *II Henry IV* III.i.]

12   Not poppy, nor mandragora,
Nor all the drowsy syrups of the
      world,
Shall ever medicine thee to that sweet
      sleep
Which thou ow'dst yesterday.
[Shakespeare: *Othello* III.iii.]
 ow'dst = *ownest*

13   . . . the innocent sleep.
Sleep that knits up the ravell'd sleave
      of care,
The death of each day's life, sore
      labor's bath,
Balm of hurt minds, great nature's
      second course,
Chief nourisher in life's feast.
[Shakespeare: *Macbeth* II.ii.]
 sleave = *a tangled skein of yarn;* second course = *the second course in an Elizabethan meal was the main course.*

14 I have not slept one wink.
[Shakespeare: *Cymbeline* III.iv.]

15   Weariness
Can snore upon the flint, when resty
      sloth
Finds the down pillow hard.
[Shakespeare: *Cymbeline* III.vi.]
 resty = *sluggish, indolent*

16 One hour's sleep before midnight is worth three after. [George Herbert: *Jacula Prudentum*]

17 To keep our eyes open longer were but to act our antipodes. The huntsmen are up in America, and they are already past their first sleep in Persia. But who can be drowsy at that hour which freed us from everlasting sleep? or have slumbering thoughts at that time, when sleep itself must end, and, as some conjecture, all shall awake again? [Sir Thomas Browne: *The Garden of Cyrus*]

1 I shall sleep like a top. [Sir William Davenant: *The Rivals* III]

Some believe that top *in this phrase is the French* taupe, *mole; but there is no need to go so far afield. The seeming motionlessness of a spinning top and its soft humming well suggest sleep. And tops were very common. Many parishes kept a top for the use of parishioners— the earliest hint of the Welfare State! There is a reference to one of these tops in* Twelfth Night *I.iii.*

2 He hath slept well that remembers not that he hath slept ill. [Thomas Fuller (1654-1734): *Gnomologia*]

3 'Tis the voice of the sluggard, I heard him complain,
"You have waked me too soon, I must slumber again";
As the door on its hinges, so he on his bed,
Turns his sides, and his shoulders, and his heavy head.
[Isaac Watts: *The Sluggard*]

As the door turneth upon his hinges, so doth the slothful upon his bed. Prov- erbs 26:14.

4 Distrust yourself, and sleep before you fight. [Dr. John Armstrong: *The Art of Preserving Health* IV (1744)]

One of the best prescriptions for preserving health yet known.

5 The winds come to me from the fields of sleep.
[Wordsworth: *Intimations of Immortality*]

6 Come, blessed barrier between day and day,
Dear mother of fresh thoughts and joyous health!
[Wordsworth: *To Sleep*]

7 Oh sleep! it is a gentle thing,
Beloved from pole to pole.
[Coleridge: *The Ancient Mariner* V]

8 Sleep, which will not be commanded. [Byron: *Marino Faliero* IV]

9 Our life is two-fold: Sleep hath its own world,

A boundary between the things misnamed
Death and existence: Sleep hath its own world,
And a wide realm of wild reality.
[Byron: *The Dream*]

10 Stars of the summer night!
Far in yon azure deeps
Hide, hide your golden light!
She sleeps! my lady sleeps!
[Longfellow: *The Spanish Student*]

11 Let's contend no more, Love,
Strive nor weep:
All be as before, Love,
—Only sleep!
[Robert Browning: *A Woman's Last Word*]

12 "God bless the man who first invented sleep!"
So Sancho Panza said and so say I;
And bless him, also, that he didn't keep
His great discovery to himself, nor try
To make it—as the lucky fellow might—
A close monopoly by patent-right.
[J. G. Saxe: *Early Rising*]

13 Over my slumber your loving watch keep—
Rock me to sleep, mother; rock me to sleep.
[Elizabeth Akers Allen: *Rock Me to Sleep, Mother*]

14 I am tired of tears and laughter,
And men that laugh and weep
Of what may come hereafter
For men that sow to reap:
I am weary of days and hours,
Blown buds of barren flowers,
Desires and dreams and powers,
And everything but sleep.
[Swinburne: *The Garden of Proserpine*]

15 Sleep lay upon the wilderness, it lay across the faces of nations, it lay like silence on the hearts of sleeping men; and low upon lowlands and high upon hills, flowed gently sleep, smooth-sliding sleep—sleep—sleep. [Thomas Wolfe: *Of Time and the River*]

SLEEP: and death

16 Sleep, the brother of death. [Hesiod: *Theogony* (8th century B.C.)]

The thought probably antedated Hesiod.

We find it in Homer (Iliad XVI) and in Vergil (Aeneid VI), and it's been echoed and repeated by a hundred poets since.

1 Now I lay me down to sleep,
I pray the Lord my soul to keep;
If I should die before I wake,
I pray the Lord my soul to take.
This prayer has been traced back to A.D. 1160. The form in which it is most commonly known appeared in The New England Primer *in 1784. A variant had appeared there earlier.*

2 Sleepe after toyle, port after stormie seas,
Ease after warre, death after life does greatly please.
[Edmund Spenser: *The Faerie Queene* I.ix.]

3 To die—to sleep—
No more; and by a sleep to say we end
The heartache, and the thousand natural shocks
That flesh is heir to. 'Tis a consummation
Devoutly to be wish'd. To die—to sleep.
To sleep—perchance to dream: ay, there's the rub!
For in that sleep of death what dreams may come
When we have shuffled off this mortal coil,
Must give us pause.
[Shakespeare: *Hamlet* III.i.]

4 The sleeping and the dead
Are but as pictures; 'tis the eye of childhood
That fears a painted devil.
[Shakespeare: *Macbeth* II.ii.]

5 Downy sleep, death's counterfeit.
[Shakespeare: *Macbeth* II.iii.]

6 After life's fitful fever he sleeps well.
[Shakespeare: *Macbeth* III.ii.]

7 Unarm, Eros; the long day's task is done,
And we must sleep.
[Shakespeare: *Antony and Cleopatra* IV.xii.]

8 Death, so called, is a thing which makes men weep,
And yet a third of life is passed in sleep.
[Byron: *Don Juan* XIV.iii.]

9 Sleep is the interest we have to pay on the capital which is called in at death; and the higher the rate of interest and the more regularly it is paid, the further the date of redemption is postponed. [Schopenhauer: *Our Relation to Ourselves*]

SLEEVE

10 We had no time for make-believe
So early each began
To wear his liver on his sleeve,
To snarl, and be an angry man.
[Roy Campbell: *Poets in Africa*]
Iago says that he will not wear his heart upon his sleeve, for daws to peck at. The heart was a symbol of courage, of deep, inner emotion and hence of one's sincerest self. The liver was a symbol of cowardice and irritation.

SLEIGH

11 Jingle, bells! jingle, bells!
Jingle all the way!
Oh, what fun it is to ride
In a one-horse open sleigh!
[John Pierpont: *Jingle, Bells*]
Pierpont was J. P. Morgan's grandfather. As late as 1915 Harper's Encyclopaedia of U.S. History *stated that "his best-known poem is* Warren's Address *at Bunker Hill."*

SLIGHT

12 Away, slight man!
[Shakespeare: *Julius Caesar* IV.iii.]

SLIP

13 A Slip of the Foot you may soon recover,
But a Slip of the Tongue you may never get over.
[Benjamin Franklin: *Poor Richard's Almanack* (1747)]

14 There's many a slip 'twixt the cup and the lip. [R. B. Barham: *The Ingoldsby Legends* (1840)]
Although the form in which the saying is now heard dates back only to 1840, the idea is very old. Aulus Gellius (Noctes Atticae XIII—2nd century A.D.) says that "Many things come between the mouth and the morsel" but adds that he had so heard. So it was proverbial then. By 1539 Richard Taverner, in his collection of Proverbs, gave it as "Many things fall between the cup and the mouth." Robert Greene (Perimedes—

1588): "Oft times many things fall out between the cup and the lip"; Burton, in The Anatomy of Melancholy *II.2.3. (1621): "Many things happen between the cup and the lip." Barham's version with its jingle shapes the saying to lighter, gayer use—and it is in such moods that it is now most frequently employed.*

SLOTH

1 The slothful man saith, There is a lion in the way; a lion is in the streets. [Proverbs 26:13]
2 They go but faintly to work, as they say, with one buttock. [Montaigne: *Essays* III.v.]

Montaigne lived from 1533 to 1592. This section of his Essais *was published in 1588 and translated into English by John Florio in 1603.*

The expression above is a curious anticipation of its modern American slang equivalent: half-ass'd.

3   Thus Belial with words clothed in
                        reason's garb
        Counselled ignoble ease and peaceful sloth
        Not peace.
[John Milton: *Paradise Lost* II.226-228]

SLOW

4 But I am slow of speech, and of a slow tongue. [Exodus 4:10   ]

SLUGGARD

5 As vinegar to the teeth, and as smoke to the eyes, so is the sluggard to them that send him. [Proverbs 10:26]
6 He . . . hoped to catch larks if ever the heavens should fall. [Rabelais: *Works* I.xi.]
7 Plough deep while sluggards sleep;
    And you shall have Corn to sell and
                        to keep.
[Benjamin Franklin: *Poor Richard's Almanack* (1756)]

SMELL

8 The rankest compound of villainous smell that ever offended nostril. [Shakespeare: *The Merry Wives of Windsor* III.v.]

SMILE(S)

9 Seldom he smiles, and smiles in such

                        a sort
As if he mock'd himself, and scorn'd
                        his spirit
That could be moved to smile at anything.
[Shakespeare: *Julius Caesar* I.ii.]
10 One may smile, and smile, and be a
                        villain.
[Shakespeare: *Hamlet* I.v.]
11 The robb'd that smiles, steals something from the thief.
[Shakespeare: *Othello* I.iii.]
12 There's daggers in men's smiles.
[Shakespeare: *Macbeth* II.iii.]
13 Eternal smiles his emptiness betray,
    As shallow streams run dimpling all
                        the way.
[Alexander Pope: *Epistle to Dr. Arbuthnot*]
14 With a smile on her lips, and a tear
                        in her eye.
[Sir Walter Scott: *The Lay of the Last Minstrel*, "Lochinvar"]
15   Oh, sir, she smiled, no doubt,
        Whene'er I passed her; but who
                        passed without
        Much the same smile?
[Robert Browning: *My Last Duchess*]
16 But he smiled, as he sat by the table,
    With the smile that was childlike and
                        bland.
[Bret Harte: *Plain Language from Truthful James*]
17 He smiled a kind of sickly smile and
                        curled up on the floor,
    And the subsequent proceedings interested him no more.
[Bret Harte: *The Society Upon the Stanislaus*]
18 'Tis easy enough to be pleasant,
        When life flows along like a song;
    But the man worth while is the one
                        who will smile
        When everything goes dead wrong.
[Ella Wheeler Wilcox: *Worth While*]
19 The pathetic forced smile of people who do not respect themselves. [Anton Chekhov: *The Letter*]
20 "When you call me that, *smile!*"
[Owen Wister: *The Virginian* II]
    "*that*" = "*son of a bitch*"
21 What's the use of worrying?
        It never was worth while,
    So, pack up your troubles in your
                        old kit-bag,

And smile, smile, smile.
[George Asaf ("George Powell"): *Pack Up Your Troubles in Your Old Kitbag*]

SMILER
1 The smyler with the knyf under the cloke.
[Chaucer: *The Knight's Tale*]

SMOKE(ING)
2 There can no great smoke arise, but there must be some fire, no great report without great suspicion. [John Lyly: *Euphues* (1579)]
A proverb that goes back to antiquity. Plautus says (Curculio I.i.) that Fire is near Smoke.
The modern version, which differs significantly from Lyly's statement, is "Where there's smoke, there's fire."
It is one of the vilest of proverbs, since it says, in effect, that all suspicions are warranted.
3 Smoking is a shocking thing—blowing smoke out of our mouths into other people's mouths, eyes and noses, and having the same thing done to us. [Samuel Johnson: in Boswell's *Tour of the Hebrides*, Aug. 19, 1773]
4 I smoke like a furnace.
[W. S. Gilbert: *Trial by Jury*]
See CIGAR, TOBACCO

SMOOTH
5 Smooth as monumental alabaster.
[Shakespeare: *Othello* V.ii.]
6 What cannot a neat knave with a smooth tale
Make a woman believe?
[John Webster: *The Duchess of Malfi* I]
7 Men, like bullets, go farthest when they're smooth. [Jean Paul Richter: *Titan*]

SMUGNESS
8 Think, what right have you to be scornful, whose virtue is a deficiency of temptation, whose success may be a chance, whose rank may be an ancestor's accident, whose prosperity is very likely a satire? [W. M. Thackeray: *Vanity Fair* LVII]

SNAIL
9 Sage snail, within thine own self curled,
Instruct me softly to make haste,
Whilst these my feet go slowly fast.
[Richard Lovelace: *The Snail*]

SNAKE
10 Now the serpent was more subtil than any beast of the field which the Lord God had made. [Genesis 3:1]
subtil = *crafty, artful, sly, cunning*
11 A snake lurks in the grass. [Vergil: *Eclogues* III]
12 Lyk to the nadder in bosom sly untrewe.
[Chaucer: *The Merchant's Tale*]
nadder = *what we today, as a result of false division, miscall a(n) adder*
All references to a snake in one's bosom—and they are plentiful in every European language—go back to Aesop's story of the peasant who, finding a snake half dead with cold and warming it in his bosom, was fatally bitten, or "stung," for his kindness. This is the classic parable of ingratitude.
13 Who sees the lurking serpent steps aside.
[Shakespeare: *The Rape of Lucrece*]
14 We have scotch'd the snake, not kill'd it:
She'll close and be herself, whilst our poor malice
Remains in danger of her former tooth.
[Shakespeare: *Macbeth* III.ii.]
15 Man spurns the worm, but pauses ere he wake
The slumbering venom of the folded snake.
[Byron: *The Corsair* I.xi.]

SNARK
16 For the snark was a Boojum, you see.
[Lewis Carroll: *The Hunting of the Snark*, Fit VIII]

SNEER(ING)
17 Damn with faint praise, assent with civil leer,
And without sneering, teach the rest to sneer.
[Alexander Pope: *Epistle to Dr. Arbuthnot*]

1 Who can refute a sneer? [William Paley: *Moral Philosophy* II]
2 I can't help it. I was born sneering. [W. S. Gilbert: *The Mikado* I]

SNEEZE(ING)
3 Will you demand of me, whence this custom ariseth, to bless and say God help to those that sneeze? We produce three sorts of wind: that issuing from below is too undecent; that from the mouth implieth some reproach of gourmandise; the third is sneezing; and because it cometh from the head, and is without imputation, we thus kindly entertain it. Smile not at this sublety; it is (as some say) Aristotle's. [Montaigne: *Essays* III.vi.]
4 Not to be sneezed at. [George Colman the Younger: *The Heir-at-Law* II.i (1797)]
5 Speak roughly to your little boy,
　And beat him when he sneezes:
He only does it to annoy,
　Because he knows it teases.
[Lewis Carroll: *Alice's Adventures in Wonderland* VI]

SNOB
6 He who meanly admires a mean thing is a Snob—perhaps that is a safe definition of the character. [W. M. Thackeray: *Book of Snobs* II]
7 The word Snob belongs to the sour-grape vocabulary. [Logan Pearsall Smith: *Afterthoughts*]

SNORING
8 There ain't no way to find out why a snorer can't hear himself snore. [Mark Twain: *Tom Sawyer Abroad* X]

SNOW
9 Like an army defeated
The snow hath retreated.
[Wordsworth: *Written in March*]
10 Announced by all the trumpets of the sky,
Arrives the snow, and, driving o'er the fields,
Seems nowhere to alight: the whited air
Hides hills and woods, the river, and the heaven,
And veils the farm-house at the garden's end.

The sled and traveller stopped, the courier's feet
Delayed, all friends shut out, the housemates sit
Around the radiant fireplace, enclosed
In a tumultuous privacy of storm.
[Emerson: *The Snow-Storm*]
11 No cloud above, no earth below—
A universe of sky and snow.
[J. G. Whittier: *Snow-Bound*]

SNUG
12 Away from the world and its toils and its cares,
I've a snug little kingdom up four pairs of stairs.
[W. M. Thackeray: *The Cane-bottom'd Chair*]

SOCIABILITY
13 Ez soshubble ez a baskit er kittens. [Joel Chandler Harris: *Uncle Remus* III]
Harris's stories do not deserve the complete oblivion into which they have fallen. But, in part, he himself is to blame. He was convinced that the speech of Negroes was comic and even when it was exactly the same as that of educated whites (sociable pronounced soshubble and basket, baskit), he insisted by a condescending spelling on making it seem ludicrous. And the result is not that people die a-laughing, but that they don't read him. And that's too bad. "Sociable as a basket of kittens" is a good, humorous simile but the modern reader is not willing to work on a pointless cryptogram.

SOCIALISM
14 For socialism is not merely the labour question, it is before all things the atheistic question, the question of the form taken by atheism today, the question of the tower of Babel built without God, not to mount to Heaven from earth but to set up Heaven on earth. [Dostoyevsky: *The Brothers Karamazov* I.i.5]
15 We shall now proceed to construct the Socialist order. [V. I. Lenin (Vladimir Ilyich Ulanov), Address, Congress of the Soviets, Nov. 8, 1917]
16 Socialism is nothing but the capitalism of the lower classes. [Oswald Spen-

gler: *The Hour of Decision*]
1 I am a firm believer in socialism and I know that the quicker you have monopoly in this country the quicker you will have socialism. [Charles P. Steinmetz, in *The Congressional Record,* January 27, 1949]

SOCIALIST
2 The socialist who is a Christian is more to be dreaded than a socialist who is an atheist. [Dostoyevsky: *The Brothers Karamazov* I.ii.5.]

SOCIETY
3 Man seeketh in society comfort, use, and protection. [Francis Bacon: *The Advancement of Learning* II]
4   Society is no comfort
To one not sociable.
[Shakespeare: *Cymbeline* IV.ii.]
5 Men would not live long in society were they not the dupes of one another. [La Rochefoucauld: *Maxims*]
6   All
The dreary intercourse of daily life.
[Wordsworth: *Tintern Abbey*]
7 Society is now one polish'd horde,
Form'd of two mighty tribes, the bores and bored.
[Byron: *Don Juan* XIII.xcv.]
8 Such is SOCIETY, the vital articulation of many individuals into a new collective individual. [Thomas Carlyle: *Characteristics*]
9 What men call social virtue, good fellowship, is commonly but the virtue of pigs in a litter, which lie close together to keep each other warm. [Thoreau: *Journal,* Oct. 23, 1852]
10 To get into the best society nowadays, one has either to feed people, amuse people, or shock people. [Oscar Wilde: *A Woman of No Importance* III]
11 There are only two classes in good society in England: the equestrian classes and the neurotic classes. [G. B. Shaw: *Heartbreak House*]
> *Since the Scythian cavalry destroyed the legions, Europe's nobility have been horsemen. Consider the implications of chivalry, chevalier, cavalier, caballero, Marshall, Ritter, etc. See also* EQUESTRIANISM
12 There are only about four hundred

people in New York society. [Ward McAllister: in an interview with Charles H. Crandall in the *New York Tribune,* 1888]

SOCRATES
13 Socrates acted wickedly, and is criminally curious in searching into things under the earth, and in the heavens, and in making the worse appear the better cause, and in teaching these same things to others. [Charge against Socrates: as stated in his *Apology* (399 B.C.)]
14 Socrates . . .
Whom, well inspir'd, the oracle pronounced
Wisest of men.
[John Milton: *Paradise Regained* IV. 274-276]

SOCRATIC
15 The Socratic manner is not a game at which two can play. [Max Beerbohm: *Zuleika Dobson* XV]

SODA WATER
16 O the moon shone bright on Mrs. Porter
And on her daughter
They wash their feet in soda water.
[T. S. Eliot: *The Waste Land* III]
> *Eliot says that this is a ballad known in Australia—and he insists that the water is not carbonated, but merely has had* $NaHCO_3$ *added.*

SOLDIER(S)
17 It is easier to find false witnesses against the civilian than anyone willing to speak the truth against the interest and honor of the soldier. [Juvenal: *Satires* XVI]
18 I maintain, contrary to the general opinion, that the sinews of war are not gold, but good soldiers; for gold alone will not procure good soldiers, but good soldiers will always procure gold. [Machiavelli: *Discourses on Livy* X]
19 Soldiers ought more to fear their general than their enemy. [Montaigne: *Essays* III.xii.]
> *Montaigne calls it an "ancient precept." Norman Mailer makes much of this idea in* The Naked and the Dead.
20 The painful warrior famoused for fight,
After a thousand victories once foiled,

Is from the book of honour razed
quite,
And all the rest forgot for which he
toiled.
[Shakespeare: *Sonnets* XXV]

1   He made me mad
To see him shine so brisk and smell
so sweet
And talk so like a waiting-gentle-
woman
Of guns, and drums, and wounds—
God save the mark!—
And telling me the sovereign'st thing
on earth
Was parmaceti for an inward bruise;
And that it was great pity, so it was,
This villainous saltpetre should be
digged
Out of the bowels of the harmless
earth,
Which many a good tall fellow had
destroyed
So cowardly; and but for these vile
guns,
He would himself have been a soldier.
[Shakespeare: *I Henry IV* I.iii.]

2 Food for powder, food for powder;
they'll fill a pit as well as better: tush,
man, mortal men, mortal men. [Shake-
speare: *I Henry IV* IV.ii.]

3   Then a soldier,
Full of strange oaths and bearded
like the pard,
Jealous in honor, sudden and quick
in quarrel,
Seeking the bubble reputation
Even in the cannon's mouth.
[Shakespeare: *As You Like It* II.vii.]
pard = *leopard—i.e., having because of
youth an as-yet slight beard; strange
oaths = until very recent times men
prided themselves on particular and
picturesque oaths. Colorful, even shocking, profanity was part of a soldier's
swagger, an indication of his recklessness.*

4   Mere prattle, without practice,
Is all his soldiership.
[Shakespeare: *Othello* I.i.]

5 The man commands like a full soldier.
[Shakespeare: *Othello* II.i.]

6 He is a soldier fit to stand by Caesar
And give direction.
[Shakespeare: *Othello* II.iii.]

7   'Tis the soldiers' life
To have their balmy slumbers waked
with strife.
[Shakespeare: *Othello* II.iii.]

8 A soldier's a man;
O, man's life's but a span,
Why then, let a soldier drink.
[Shakespeare: *Othello* II.iii.]

9 You stink of brandy and tobacco,
most soldier-like.
[William Congreve: *The Old Bachelor*
III]

10 A soldier is a Yahoo hired to kill in
cold blood as many of his own species,
who have never offended him, as possibly he can. [Jonathan Swift: *Gulliver's
Travels* IV.v.]

11 Every man thinks meanly of himself
for not having been a soldier. [Sam-
uel Johnson: in Boswell's *Life,* April 10,
1778]

12 The first virtue in a soldier is endurance of fatigue; courage is only the
second virtue. [Napoleon Bonaparte:
quoted in Thiers's *Histoire du Consulat
et de l'Empire* I]

13 Every French soldier carries a marshal's baton in his knapsack. [Attr. Napoleon Bonaparte]

14 The scum of the earth—the mere
scum of the earth. [Duke of Wellington:
his opinion of the army, as quoted in
Stanhope's *Notes of Conversations with
the Duke of Wellington*]

15 Soldier, rest! thy warfare o'er,
Sleep the sleep that knows not
breaking,
Dream of battled fields no more,
Days of danger, nights of waking.
[Sir Walter Scott: *The Lady of the
Lake* I.xxxi.]

16 No useless coffin enclosed his breast,
Not in sheet or in shroud we wound
him;
But he lay like a warrior taking his
rest
With his martial cloak around him.
[Charles Wolfe: *The Burial of Sir John
Moore at Corunna*]

17 Ben Battle was a soldier bold,
And used to war's alarms;
But a cannon-ball took off his legs,
So he laid down his arms.
[Thomas Hood: *Faithless Nellie Gray*]

1 Nothing will mix and amalgamate more easily than an old priest and an old soldier. In reality, they are the same kind of man. One has devoted himself to his country upon earth, the other to his country in heaven; there is no other difference. [Victor Hugo: *Les Misérables* III.ii.]

2 A soldier of the Legion lay dying in Algiers;
There was lack of woman's nursing, there was dearth of woman's tears.
[Caroline Norton: *Bingen on the Rhine*]

3 . . . the soldier's trade, verily and essentially, is not slaying, but being slain. [John Ruskin: *Unto This Last* I]

4 A certain amount of stupidity is necessary to make a good soldier. [Florence Nightingale: letter to Sydney Herbert, January 1855, from Scutari]

5 I am the very pattern of a modern major-general.
I've information vegetable, animal and mineral;
I know the kings of England, and I quote the fights historical,
From Marathon to Waterloo, in order categorical.
[W. S. Gilbert: *The Pirates of Penzance* I]

6 The soldier's is the trade:
In any wind or weather
He steals the heart of maid
And man together.
[A. E. Housman: *Last Poems* VII]

7 Oh, it's Tommy this, an' Tommy that, an' "Tommy, wait outside";
But it's "Special train for Atkins" when the trooper's on the tide.
[Kipling: *Tommy*]

8 A soldier is an anachronism. [George Bernard Shaw: *The Devil's Disciple* III]

9 I did not raise my boy to be a soldier. [Alfred Bryan: title of song]

10 Old soldiers never die;
They simply fade away.
[Anon.: British army song, 1914-1918]

11 Soldiers who wish to be a hero
Are practically zero;
But those who wish to be civilians,
Jesus, they run into the millions.
[Anon.: quoted by Norman Rosten in *The Big Road*]

SOLEMNITY

12 Thou say'st an undisputed thing
In such a solemn way.
[O. W. Holmes: *To an Insect*]

SOLITARY

13 She dwelt among the untrodden ways
Beside the springs of Dove,
A maid whom there were none to praise
And very few to love.
[Wordsworth: *She Dwelt Among the Untrodden Ways*]

SOLITUDE

14 It is not good that the man should be alone. [Genesis 2:18]

15 I have trodden the winepress alone. [Isaiah 63:3]

16 Whoever is delighted in solitude is either a wild beast or a god. [Francis Bacon: *Of Friendship*]
Bacon, who says that it would have been hard "to have put more truth and untruth together in few words," is paraphrasing Aristotle's Politics *I.ii.*

17 A man, alone, is either a saint or a devil. [Robert Burton: *The Anatomy of Melancholy* I.2.2.6]

18 Be not solitary, be not idle. [Robert Burton: *Anatomy of Melancholy* (the end)]
Burton's final, summarizing advice for the avoidance of melancholy.
Samuel Johnson, who was himself inclined to melancholia, and who said that Burton's Anatomy of Melancholy *"was the only book that ever took him out of bed two hours sooner than he wished to rise," "modified" Burton's prescription in a letter to Boswell (October 27, 1779), thus: If you are idle, be not solitary; if you are solitary, be not idle.*

19 By all means use sometimes to be alone. [George Herbert: *The Church Porch*]
use = *make it a custom to be*

20 Who can enjoy alone?
[John Milton: *Paradise Lost* VIII.365]

21 Thus let me live, unseen, unknown,
Thus unlamented let me die;
Steal from the world, and not a stone
Tell where I lie.
[Alexander Pope: *Ode on Solitude*]

22 The happiest of all lives is a busy

solitude. [Voltaire: letter to Frederick the Great (1751)]

1 She that has no one to love or trust has little to hope. She wants the radical principle of happiness. [Samuel Johnson: *Rasselas* XXXV]
wants = *lacks;* radical = *basic*

2 Solitude excludes pleasure, and does not always secure peace. [Samuel Johnson: letter to Mrs. Aston, Nov. 17, 1767]

3 Oh for a lodge in some vast wilderness,
Some boundless contiguity of shade.
[William Cowper: *The Timepiece*]

4 I was never less alone than while by myself. [Edward Gibbon: *Memoirs* I]

5 I praise the Frenchman, his remark was shrewd—
"How sweet, how passing sweet is solitude!"
But grant me still a friend in my retreat,
Whom I may whisper—Solitude is sweet.
[William Cowper: *Retirement*]
The Frenchman was La Bruyère.

6 O solitude! where are the charms
That sages have seen in thy face?
[William Cowper: *Verses Supposed to be Written by Alexander Selkirk*]

7 Never less alone than when alone.
[Samuel Rogers: *Human Life*]

8 That inward eye
Which is the bliss of solitude.
[Wordsworth: *I Wandered Lonely as a Cloud*]

9 The self-sufficing power of Solitude.
[Wordsworth: *The Prelude* II]

10 There is a pleasure in the pathless woods,
There is a rapture on the lonely shore,
There is society, where none intrudes,
By the deep Sea, and music in its roar.
[Byron: *Childe Harold* IV.clxxviii.]

11 Now the New Year reviving old Desires,
The thoughtful Soul to Solitude retires.
[*Rubáiyát of Omar Khayyám* (trans. Edward FitzGerald)]

12 I never found the companion that was so companionable as solitude. [Thoreau: *Walden* V]

13 SOLITUDE: A good place to visit, but a poor place to stay. [Josh Billings: *Comical Lexicon*]

14 Yes: in the sea of life enisl'd,
With echoing straits between us thrown,
Dotting the shoreless watery wild,
We mortal millions live alone.
[Matthew Arnold: *To Marguerite*]

15 Solitude, a luxury of the rich. [Albert Camus: *Notebooks 1935-1942*]

SOMEBODY

16 In short, whoever you may be,
To this conclusion you'll agree,
When everyone is somebodee,
Then no one's anybody!
[W. S. Gilbert: *The Gondoliers* II]

SON(S)

17 My son Absalom, would God I had died for thee! O Absalom, my son, my son! [II Samuel 18:33]

18 Unto us a child is born, unto us a son is given. [Isaiah 9:6]

19 This is my beloved Son, in whom I am well pleased. [Matthew: 3:17]

20 Put forth their sons to seek preferment out:
Some to the wars, to try their fortune there;
Some to discover islands far away;
Some to the studious universities.
[Shakespeare: *The Two Gentlemen of Verona* I.iii.]

21 O Lord! my boy, my Arthur, my fair son!
My life, my joy, my food, my all the world!
My widow-comfort, and my sorrows' cure!
[Shakespeare: *King John* III.iv.]

22 And all to leave what with his toil he won
To that unfeather'd two-legg'd thing, a son.
[Dryden: *Absalom and Achitophel* I]

23 This is my son, mine own Telemachus. [Tennyson: *Ulysses*]

24 Get you the sons your fathers got,
And God will save the Queen.
[A. E. Housman: *A Shropshire Lad* I]

SONG(S)

25 The morning stars sang together, and

all the sons of God shouted for joy. [Job 38:7]

1 How shall we sing the Lord's song in a strange land? [Psalms 137:4]

2 He could songes make and well indite. [Chaucer: Prologue to *The Canterbury Tales*]

3 Sweete Themmes! runne softly, till I end my Song.
[Edmund Spenser: *Prothalamion* (refrain)]

4 Fierce wars and faithful loves shall moralize my song. [Edmund Spenser: Introduction to *The Faerie Queene*]

5 I never heard the old song of Percy and Douglas that I found not my heart moved more than with a trumpet. [Sir Philip Sidney: *Defence of Poesy*]

6 Come, sing me a bawdy song; make me merry.
[Shakespeare: *I Henry IV* III.iii.]

7 The spinsters and the knitters in the sun
And the free maids that weave their thread with bones
Do use to chant it.
[Shakespeare: *Twelfth Night* II.iv.]

8 I had rather than forty shillings I had my *Book of Songs and Sonnets* here. [Shakespeare: *The Merry Wives of Windsor* I.i.]

9 Soft words, with nothing in them, make a song.
[Edmund Waller: *To Mr. Creech*]

10 He touch'd the tender stops of various quills,
With eager thought warbling his Doric lay.
[John Milton: *Lycidas*]

11   Their lean and flashy songs
Grate on their scrannel pipes of wretched straw.
[John Milton: *Lycidas*]

12   Still govern thou my song,
Urania, and fit audience find, though few.
[John Milton: *Paradise Lost* VII.30-31]

13 He did not see any reason why the devil should have all the good tunes. [E. W. Broome: *Rev. Rowland Hill* VII]

14 Behold her, single in the field,
Yon solitary Highland Lass!
Reaping and singing by herself;
Stop here, or gently pass!
[Wordsworth: *The Solitary Reaper*]

15 O listen! for the Vale profound
Is overflowing with the sound.
[Wordsworth: *The Solitary Reaper*]

16 No Nightingale did every chaunt
More welcome notes to weary bands
Of travellers in some shady haunt,
Among Arabian sands.

A voice so thrilling ne'er was heard
In spring-time from the Cuckoo-bird,
Breaking the silence of the seas
Among the farthest Hebrides.
[Wordsworth: *The Solitary Reaper*]

17 Our sweetest songs are those which tell of saddest thought.
[Shelley: *To a Skylark*]

18 On the wings of song.
[Heinrich Heine: *Lyrical Intermezzo*]

19 Short swallow-flights of song, that dip
Their wings in tears, and skim away.
[Tennyson: *In Memoriam* XLVIII]

20 Bring the good old bugle, boys! we'll sing another song—
Sing it with a spirit that will start the world along—
Sing it as we used to sing it, fifty thousand strong,
While we were marching through Georgia.
[Henry Clay Work: *Marching Through Georgia*]

21 Let us go hence, my songs; she will not hear.
[Swinburne: *A Leave-taking*]

22 I cannot sing the old songs
I sang long years ago,
For heart and voice would fail me,
And foolish tears would flow.
[Charlotte Alington Barnard: *I Cannot Sing the Old Songs*]
  Yet though I'm filled with music,
  As choirs of summer birds,
  "I cannot sing the old songs"—
  I do not know the words.
  Robert J. Burdette: Songs Without Words

23 One man with a dream, at pleasure,
Shall go forth and conquer a crown;
And three with a new song's measure
Can trample an empire down.
[Arthur O'Shaughnessy: *Ode*]

SONNET

24 Scorn not the sonnet; Critic, you

have frowned,
Mindless of its just honors; with this
key
Shakespeare unlocked his heart.
[Wordsworth: *Scorn Not the Sonnet*]
1 . . . in his hand
The thing became a trumpet; whence
he blew
Soul-animating strains—alas, too few!
[Wordsworth: *Scorn Not the Sonnet*]
his = *Milton's;* thing = *the sonnet form*
2 A sonnet is a moment's monument—
Memorial from the Soul's eternity
To one dead deathless hour.
[Dante Gabriel Rossetti: *The House of
Life,* "The Sonnet"]

SON OF A BITCH
3 The son and heir of a mongrel bitch.
[Shakespeare: *King Lear* II.ii.]

SOPHISTRY
4 His tongue
Dropt manna, and could make the
worse appear
The better reason.
[John Milton: *Paradise Lost* II.112-114]
*It is Belial who shares the accusation
brought against Socrates.*

SOPHOCLES
5 . . . whose even-balanc'd soul,
From first youth tested up to extreme
old age,
Business could not make dull, nor
passion wild:
Who saw life steadily and saw it
whole:
The mellow glory of the Attic stage;
Singer of sweet Colonus, and its child.
[Matthew Arnold: *To a Friend*]

SOPHONISBA
6 Oh! Sophonisba! Sophonisba! Oh!
[James Thomson (1700-1748): *Sophonisba* III.ii.]
*Taste is a very strange thing. This line
from Thomson's play was greatly admired for what was felt, apparently, to
be its simple poignancy—until one
night in the theater, immediately after
its utterance, some wag shouted "Oh!
Jemmy Thomson! Jemmy Thomson!
Oh!" and the mirage dissolved in laughter.*

SORROW(S)
7 In sorrow thou shalt bring forth children. [Genesis 3:16]
8 Ye shall bring down my gray hairs
with sorrow to the grave. [Genesis 44:
29]
*The phrase may have been proverbial.
Jacob had expressed it in almost the
same words two chapters earlier.*
9 Is it nothing to you, all ye that pass
by? behold, and see if there be any sorrow like unto my sorrow. [Lamentations
1:12]
10 It is good to grow wise by sorrow.
[Aeschylus: *Eumenides*]
11 I will instruct my sorrows to be
proud.
[Shakespeare: *King John* III.i.]
12 But I have that within which passeth
show;
These, but the trappings and the suits
of woe.
[Shakespeare: *Hamlet* I.ii.]
13 More in sorrow than in anger.
[Shakespeare: *Hamlet* I.ii.]
14 When sorrows come, they come not
single spies,
But in battalions.
[Shakespeare: *Hamlet* IV.v.]
15 For sorrow ends not when it seemeth
done.
[Shakespeare *Richard II* I.ii.]
16 One woe doth tread upon another's
heel,
So fast they follow.
[Shakespeare: *Hamlet* IV.vii.]
17 Down, thou climbing sorrow.
[Shakespeare: *King Lear* II.iv.]
18 Bad is the trade that must play fool
to sorrow.
[Shakespeare: *King Lear* IV.i.]
19 Give sorrow words; the grief that
does not speak
Whispers the o'er-fraught heart and
bids it break.
[Shakespeare: *Macbeth* IV.iii.]
20 Sorrows are like thunderclouds. Far
off they look black, but directly over us
merely gray. [Jean Paul Richter: *Hesperus*]
21 Some natural sorrow, loss, or pain,
That has been, and may be again.
[Wordsworth: *The Solitary Reaper*]
22 When I was young, I said to Sorrow,
"Come and I will play with thee!"

He is near me now all day,
And at night returns to say,
"I will come again to-morrow—
I will come and stay with thee."
[Aubrey de Vere: *When I Was Young I
Said to Sorrow*]
1 This is my last message to you: in
sorrow seek happiness. [Dostoyevsky:
The Brothers Karamazov I.ii.7]
2 The day goes by like a shadow o'er
the heart,
With sorrow, where all was delight.
[Stephen C. Foster: *My Old Kentucky
Home*]
3 For oh, the sons we get
Are still the sons of men.
The sumless tale of sorrow
Is all unrolled in vain.
[A. E. Housman: *Last Poems* XXXIV]
4 Tears of eternity and sorrow,
Not mine, but man's.
[A. E. Housman: *More Poems*, "They
Say My Verse is Sad"]

SOUL
5 What is a man profited, if he shall
gain the whole world, and lose his own
soul? [Matthew 16:26]
6 O fleeting soul of mine, my body's
friend and guest, whither goest thou,
pale, fearful, and pensive one? Why
laugh not as of old? [Hadrian: *Ad ani-
mam*]
  One of the most famous of all quotations. The Latin is:
    Animula, vagula, blandula
    Hospes comesque corporis!
    Quae nunc abibis in loca,
    Pallidula, frigida nudula
    Nec ut soles dabis joca?
  Alexander Pope answered the pagan
  fears and sadness with his The Dying
  Christian to His Soul—wherein the certainty of immortality made a "bliss of
  dying." With the passing of this certainty, the melancholy of antiquity re-
  turns.
  Byron's rendition:
  Ah! gentle, fleeting, wav'ring sprite,
  Friend and associate of this clay!
  To what unknown region borne,
  Wilt thou now wing thy distant
flight?
  No more, with wonted humor gay,
  But pallid, cheerless, and forlorn.

7   The prophetic soul
Of the wide world, dreaming on
things to come.
[Shakespeare: *Sonnets* CVII]
8 Every subject's duty is the king's; but
every subject's soul is his own. [Shake-
speare: *Henry V* IV.i.]
9 Thinkest thou I'll endanger my soul
gratis?
[Shakespeare: *The Merry Wives of
Windsor* II.ii.]
10 A fiery soul, which, working out its
way,
Fretted the pigmy body to decay,
And o'er-informed the tenement of
clay.
[Dryden: *Absalom and Achitophel* I.]
  informed = *formed from within, imparted a vital quality to*
    The reference is to Anthony Ashley
    Cooper, Earl of Shaftesbury. Dryden felt
    that the man's spirit, what today would
    be called his "drive," was too strong for
    his body.
11 My soul, the seas are rough, and thou
a stranger
In these false coasts: O keep aloof;
there's danger;
Cast forth thy plummet; see, a rock
appears;
Thy ship wants sea-room; make it
with thy tears.
[Francis Quarles: *Emblems* III.11]
  plummet = *a sounding-lead;* aloof = *to
  the windward;* sea-room, *here* = *sufficient
  depth of water to be maneuverable*
12 Here lies buried the soul of the licentiate, Pedro Garcias. [Le Sage: Preface to *Gil Blas*]
  Excavation showed the licentiate's soul
  to consist of his savings.
13 Awake, my soul! stretch every nerve,
And press with vigour on;
A heavenly race demands thy zeal,
And an immortal crown.
[Philip Doddridge: *Zeal and Vigour in
the Christian Race*]
  nerve = *sinew*
14 A charge to keep I have,
A God to glorify:
A never-dying soul to save,
And fit it for the sky.
[Charles Wesley: *Christian Fidelity*]
15 The gods approve the depth, and not
the tumult, of the soul.

[Wordsworth: *Laodamia*]
1   For the sword outwears its sheath,
And the soul wears out the breast.
[Byron: *So We'll Go No More a-Roving*]
2   A man's soul may be buried and perish under a dungheap or in a furrow of the field, just as well as under a pile of money. [Nathaniel Hawthorne: *Journals,* June 1, 1841]
3   Dust thou art, to dust returnest,
Was not spoken of the soul.
[Longfellow: *A Psalm of Life*]
4   Why, if the Soul can fling the Dust aside,
And naked on the Air of Heaven ride,
Wer't not a Shame—wer't not a Shame for him
In this clay carcass crippled to abide?
[*Rubáiyát of Omar Khayyám* (trans. Edward FitzGerald)]
5   For as this appalling ocean surrounds the verdant land, so in the soul of man there lies one insular Tahiti, full of peace and joy, but encompassed by all the horrors of the half-known life. [Herman Melville: *Moby Dick* LVIII]
6   I am that which began;
Out of me the years roll;
Out of me God and man;
I am equal and whole;
God changes, and man, and the form of them bodily; I am the soul.
[Swinburne: *Hertha*]
7   My mind is incapable of conceiving such a thing as a soul. I may be in error, and man may have a soul; but I simply do not believe it. [Thomas A. Edison: *Do We Live Again?*]
8   Out of the night that covers me,
Black as the pit from pole to pole,
I thank whatever gods may be
For my unconquerable soul.
[W. E. Henley: *Invictus*]

SOULFUL
9   A most intense young man,
A soulful-eyed young man,
An ultra-poetical, super-aesthetical,
Out-of-the-way young man!
[W. S. Gilbert: *Patience* II]

SOUND
10   Hark! from the tombs a doleful sound.

[Isaac Watts: *Hymns* II]
11   Sound is more than sense. [Logan Pearsall Smith: *Afterthoughts*]

SOUP
12   Soup of the evening, beautiful soup!
[Lewis Carroll: *Alice's Adventures in Wonderland* X]

SOURCE
13   Our life runs down in sending up the clock.
The brook runs down in sending up our life.
The sun runs down in sending up the brook.
And there is something sending up the sun.
It is this backward motion toward the source,
Against the stream, that most we see ourselves in:
The tribute of the current to the source.
It is from this in nature we are from.
It is most us.
[Robert Frost: *West-Running Brook*]

SOUR GRAPES
14   The fathers have eaten sour grapes, and the children's teeth are set on edge. [Ezekiel: 18:2]
In Ezekiel the saying is called a proverb (it occurs also in Jeremiah 31:29), and the Lord God assures Ezekiel that "ye shall not have occasion any more to use this proverb in Israel." That is (apparently) men will henceforth be held accountable only for their own sins; retribution will not be visited "unto the third and fourth generation."
15   Sour grapes! [Aesop's fables]
The statement of the fox in the fable that the grapes which he could not reach were sour is alluded to today to indicate that some belittling remark is, at bottom, an expression of envy. La Fontaine, however, regarded the attitude of the fox as admirable and felt that scorn for the unattainable was better than complaining.

THE SOUTH
16   Alas for the South: her books have grown fewer—
She never was much given to literature.

[J. Gordon Coogler: *Purely Original Verse*]

SOUTHERNERS
1 The palavery kind of Southerners; all that slushy gush on the surface, and no sensibilities whatever—a race without consonants and without delicacy. [Willa Cather: *My Mortal Enemy* II.i.]
Willa Cather was a Virginian.

SOVEREIGNTY
2 Every succeeding scientific discovery makes greater nonsense of old-time conceptions of sovereignty. [Sir Anthony Eden: in a speech, in the House of Commons, Nov. 22, 1945]

SOWING AND REAPING
3 Whatsoever a man soweth, that shall he also reap. [Galatians 6:7]

SPADE
4 A loose, plain, rude writer, I call a spade a spade. [Robert Burton: *The Anatomy of Melancholy*, "Democritus to the Reader" (1621)]
The saying goes back to a story which Plutarch tells of Philip of Macedon, the father of Alexander the Great. Certain ambassadors whom Philip did not trust complained to him that they had been called traitors by some of his entourage. Philip said they must excuse his followers; the Macedonians were notorious clods who hadn't any more sense than to call a tub a tub. The substitution of spade for tub was the doing of Erasmus in his relation of the incident in his Adagia (1500).

There have been a number of objects whose simple designation has been proverbial, among different nations, for plain speaking. The Greeks said "to call a fig a fig" (in some way, now forgotten, a fig was indecent) and, as above, "a tub a tub." The phrase as now used—to call a spade a spade—is a contradiction of what it asserts. No one objects to calling a spade a spade; it is coarser and less inoffensive things that are glossed over with euphemisms.

SPAIN
5 Oh, lovely Spain! renown'd romantic land!

[Byron: *Childe Harold* I.xxxv.]

SPARROWS
6 Are not two sparrows sold for a farthing? and one of them shall not fall on the ground without your Father. [Matthew 10:29]
7 Lecherous as a sparwe.
[Chaucer: Prologue to *The Canterbury Tales*]

SPARTANS
8 Earth! render back from out thy breast
A remnant of our Spartan dead!
Of the three hundred grant but three,
To make a new Thermopylae!
[Byron: *The Isles of Greece*]

SPEAK(ING)
9 Nature has given man one tongue and two ears, that we may hear twice as much as we speak. [Epictetus: *Fragments*]
10 No man pleases by silence; many please by speaking briefly. [Ausonius: *Epistolae* XXV.xliv.]
11 Speak, Lord; for thy servant heareth. [I Samuel 3:9]
12 Let him now speak, or else hereafter for ever hold his peace. [*The Book of Common Prayer*, "Solemnization of Matrimony"]
13 There's language in her eye, her cheek, her lip,
Nay, her foot speaks; her wanton spirits look out
At every joint and motive of her body.
[Shakespeare: *Troilus and Cressida* IV.v.]
14 He speaks plain cannon fire, and smoke and bounce.
[Shakespeare: *King John* II.i.]
15 Thou but offend'st thy lungs to speak so loud.
[Shakespeare: *The Merchant of Venice* IV.i.]
16 She sits tormenting every guest,
Nor gives her tongue one moment's rest,
In phrases batter'd, stale, and trite,
Which modern ladies call polite.
[Jonathan Swift: *The Journal of a Modern Lady*]
17 "Why don't you speak for yourself,

John?" [Longfellow: *The Courtship of Miles Standish* III]

1 So all who hide too well away
  Must speak and tell us where they are.
[Robert Frost: *Revelation*]

SPECTACLE
2 As many more crowd round the door,
  To see them going to see it.
[Thomas Hood: *Miss Kilmansegg: Her Fancy Ball*]

SPECTATOR
3 The spectator ofttimes sees more than the gamester. [James Howell: *Familiar Letters* I]

SPECULATE
4 There are two times in a man's life when he should not speculate: when he can't afford it, and when he can. [Mark Twain: *Pudd'nhead Wilson's New Calendar*]

SPEECH(ES)
5 The speeches of one that is desperate, which are as wind. [Job 6:26]
6 Thy speech bewrayeth thee. [Matthew 26:73]
7 Let your speech be alway with grace, seasoned with salt. [Colossians 4:6]
8 Somewhat he lipsed, for his wantownesse,
  To make his English swete up-on his tonge.
[Chaucer: Prologue to *The Canterbury Tales*]
  wantownesse = *effeminacy, foppish affectation*
    Note lipsed, *the word that we now pronounce* lisped.
9 I love a natural, simple and unaffected speech, written as it is spoken and such upon the paper as it is in the mouth, a pithy, sinewy, full, strong, compendious and material speech. [Montaigne: *Essays* I.xxv.]
10 Discretion of speech is more than eloquence. [Francis Bacon: *Of Discourse*]
11 Liberty of speech inviteth and provoketh liberty to be used again, and so bringeth much to a man's knowledge. [Francis Bacon: *The Advancement of Learning* II]
  again = *in return*
12 That which we are capable of feeling,

we are capable of saying. [Cervantes: *Novelas Ejemplares,* "El Amante Liberal"]
13 I will speak in a monstrous little voice. [Shakespeare: *A Midsummer Night's Dream* I.ii.]
14 There was speech in their dumbness, language in their very gesture. [Shakespeare: *The Winter's Tale* V.ii.]
15 I do not much dislike the matter, but The manner of his speech. [Shakespeare: *Antony and Cleopatra* II.ii.]
16   Rude am I in my speech,
  And little bless'd with the soft phrase of peace.
[Shakespeare: *Othello* I.iii.]
17   Mend your speech a little,
  Lest it may mar your fortunes.
[Shakespeare: *King Lear* I.i.]
18 Language most shews a man: Speak, that I may see thee. [Ben Jonson: *Explorata,* "Oratio Imago Animi"]
19 The greatest things gain by being expressed simply; they are spoiled by emphasis. But one must say trifling things nobly, because they are supported solely by expression, tone and manner. [La Bruyère: *Les Caractères* II.82]
20 Little said is soonest mended. [George Wither: *The Shepherd's Hunting*]
21 Speech was given to the ordinary sort of man whereby to communicate their mind; but to wise men, whereby to conceal it. [Robert South: *Sermon* (1676)]
  The sentiment has been expressed by many others—among them Edward Young: Love of Fame *II;* Goldsmith: The Bee *No. 3 (1759). The best known is* Voltaire: Le Chapon et la Poularde, Dialogue XIV *(1766):*
    Men use thought only to justify their wrongdoings and speech only to conceal their thoughts.
22 When the heart is afire, some sparks will fly out of the mouth. [Thomas Fuller (1654-1734): *Gnomologia*]
23 His speech was a fine sample, on the whole,
  Of rhetoric, which the learn'd call "rigmarole."
[Byron: *Don Juan* I.clxxiv]
  It is interesting that Byron in 1818 (and Washington Irving, in 1809) considered

rigmarole *a learned word. Boswell, in 1791, had called it "vulgar." Prior to 1600 it had been "Ragman roll" and had disappeared from print for 150 years. It combines the name of a statute of 1233 (establishing a court of special claims) with an old game and a nickname for the devil. But how all this came to mean rambling nonsense is anybody's guess.*

1 That the vulgar express their thoughts clearly is far from true, and what perspicuity can be found among them proceeds not from the easiness of their language but the shallowness of their thoughts. [Samuel Johnson: *The Idler* No. 70]
the vulgar = *the common people*

2 That's easier said than done. [David Garrick: *Neck or Nothing*]
The thought is very old. It is expressed in Livy's History *XXXI.*

3 You have only, when before your glass, to keep pronouncing to yourself mimini-pimini—the lips cannot fail of taking their *plie*. [John Burgoyne: *The Heiress* III.ii]

4 The true use of speech is not so much to express our wants as to conceal them. [Oliver Goldsmith: *The Bee*]

5 He mouths a sentence as curs mouth a bone. [Charles Churchill: *The Rosciad*]

6 Don't quote Latin; say what you have to say, and then sit down. [Duke of Wellington: Advice to a new Member of Parliament.]

7 Choice word and measured phrase, above the reach
Of ordinary men.
[Wordsworth: *Resolution and Independence*]

8 I pass, like night, from land to land;
I have strange power of speech.
[Coleridge: *The Ancient Mariner*]

9 Congress shall make no law . . . abridging the freedom of speech or of the press. [*Constitution of the United States,* Amendment I]

10 He gave man speech, and speech created thought,
Which is the measure of the universe.
[Shelley: *Prometheus Unbound* II.iv.]
He = *Prometheus* = *the spirit of man in revolt against the inhuman cosmos*

11 The music that can deepest reach,

And cure all ill, is cordial speech.
[Emerson: *Conduct of Life,* "Considerations by the Way"]
Cordial *has a double meaning here: 1) warm, friendly; 2) medicinal.*

12 The flowering moments of the mind
Drop half their petals in our speech.
[Oliver Wendell Holmes: *To My Readers* XI]

13 Before a man speaks it is always safe to assume that he is a fool. After he speaks, it is seldom necessary to assume it. [H. L. Mencken: *Chrestomathy*]

14 Bright vocabularies are transient as
rainbows.
Speech requires blood and air to
make it.
Before the word comes off the end of
the tongue,
While the diaphragms of flesh negotiate the word,
In the moment of doom when the
word forms,
It is born alive, registering an imprint—
Afterward it is a mummy, a dry fact,
done and gone.
The warning holds yet: Speak now or
forever hold your peace.
Ecce Homo had meanings: Behold
the man! Look at him!
Dying he lives and speaks!
[Carl Sandburg: *Precious Moments*]

SPEED

15 I'll put a girdle round about the
earth in forty minutes.
[Shakespeare: *A Midsummer Night's Dream* II.i.]
Ariel's record still holds, but it is threatened. It is almost frightening to think that a flight of reality is now nearly equal to the wildest flight of fancy three hundred years ago.

SPELLING

16 As our alphabet now stands, the bad spelling, or what is called so, is generally the best, as conforming to the sound of the letters and of the words. [Benjamin Franklin: letter to Mrs. Jane Mecom, July 4, 1786]

17 "I'm sorry that I spelt the word:

I hate to go above you,
Because,"—the brown eyes lower
fell—
"Because, you see, I love you!"
[J. G. Whittier: *In School Days*]
1 They spell it Vinci and pronounce it
Vinchy; foreigners always spell better
than they pronounce. [Mark Twain:
The Innocents Abroad XIX]

SPENS, SIR PATRICK
2 Half-owre, half-owre to Aberdour,
'Tis fifty fadom deep,
And there lies guid Sir Patrick Spens
Wi' the Scots lords at his feet.
[Anon.: *Sir Patrick Spens*]

SPENSER, EDMUND
3 The palfrey pace and the glittering
grace
Of Spenser's magical song.
[Robert Buchanan: *Cloudland*]

SPHERICAL
4 His body is perfectly spherical,
He weareth a runcible hat.
[Edward Lear: Preface to *Nonsense
Songs*]

SPIDER(S)
5 The spider taketh hold with her
hands, and is in kings' palaces. [Proverbs 30:28]
6 The spider's touch, how exquisitely
fine!
Feels at each thread, and lives along
the line.
[Alexander Pope: *An Essay on Man* I]
7 There webs were spread of more than
common size,
And half-starved spiders prey'd on
half-starved flies.
[Charles Churchill: *The Prophecy of
Famine*]
8 "Will you walk into my parlour?"
Said a spider to a fly;
" 'Tis the prettiest little parlour
That ever you did spy."
[Mary Howitt: *The Spider and the Fly*]

SPIRIT(S)
9 Then a spirit passed before my face;
the hair of my flesh stood up. [Job 4:
15]
10 A wounded spirit who can bear?

[Proverbs 18:14]
11 The spirits of just men made perfect.
[Hebrews 12:23]
12 *Glendower.* I can call spirits from the
vasty deep.
Hotspur. Why, so can I, or so can any
man;
But will they come when you do call
for them?
[Shakespeare: *I Henry IV* III.i.]
13 The choice and master spirits of this
age.
[Shakespeare: *Julius Caesar* III.i.]
14 Calling shapes, and beck'ning shadows dire,
And airy tongues that syllable men's
names
On sands and shores and desert wildernesses.
[John Milton: *Comus*]
15 Spirits, when they please,
Can either sex assume, or both.
[John Milton: *Paradise Lost* I.423-424]
16 Millions of spiritual creatures walk
the earth
Unseen, both when we wake, and
when we sleep.
[John Milton: *Paradise Lost* IV.677-678]
17 Spirits . . .
Cannot but by annihilating die;
Nor in their liquid texture mortal
wound
Receive, no more than can the fluid
air.
[John Milton: *Paradise Lost* VI.344]
18 Unnumbered spirits round thee fly,
The light militia of the lower sky.
[Alexander Pope: *The Rape of the
Lock* I]
the light militia—*Pope wished to distinguish his supernatural beings, taken
with mocking intent from the mythology
of the Rosicrucians, from the awe-inspiring angelic warriors of Milton's* Paradise Lost.

19 A sense sublime
Of something far more deeply interfused,
Whose dwelling is the light of setting
suns,
And the round ocean and the living
air,
And the blue sky, and in the mind of
man;
A motion and a spirit, that impels

All thinking things, all objects of all
thought,
And rolls through all things.
[Wordsworth: *Tintern Abbey*]
1 A slumber did my spirit seal;
I had no human fears:
She seemed a thing that could not
feel
The touch of earthly years.

No motion has she now, no force;
She neither hears nor sees;
Rolled round in earth's diurnal
course,
With rocks, and stones, and trees.
[Wordsworth: *A Slumber Did My Spirit
Seal*]
2 Hail to thee, blithe spirit!
Bird thou never wert,
That from heaven, or near it,
Pourest thy full heart
In profuse strains of unpremeditated art.
[Shelley: *To a Skylark*]
Poured forth his unpremeditated strain.
—*James Thomson:* The Castle of Indolence *LXVIII (1748).*
See Thomas Hardy's Shelley's Skylark
(1902).
3 Be thou, Spirit fierce,
My spirit! Be thou me, impetuous
one!
[Shelley: *Ode to the West Wind*]
4 A pard-like spirit, beautiful and swift.
[Shelley: *Adonais*]
pard = *leopard*

SPLIT INFINITIVE
5 The English-speaking world may be
divided into (1) those who neither know
nor care what a split infinitive is; (2)
those who do not know, but care very
much; (3) those who know & condemn;
(4) those who know & approve; & (5)
those who know and distinguish. Those
who neither know nor care are the vast
majority, & are a happy folk, to be envied by most of the minority classes.
[H. W. Fowler: *Modern English Usage*]

SPOILS
6 To the victor belong the spoils of
the enemy. [William L. Marcy: in a
speech in the Senate, Jan. 21, 1832]

SPORT
7 If all the year were playing holidays,
To sport would be as tedious as to
work.
[Shakespeare: *I Henry IV* I.ii.]
8 The sport of kings. [William Somerville: *The Chase*]
9 The sports, to which with boyish glee
I sprang erewhile, attract no more;
Although I am but sixty-three
Or four.
[Charles Stuart Calverley: *Changed*]
10 I hate all sports as rabidly as a person who likes sports hates common sense.
[H. L. Mencken: *Heathen Days*]

SPOT
11 Out, damned spot! out, I say!
[Shakespeare: *Macbeth* V.i.]

SPRING
12 For lo, the winter is past, the rain is
over and gone;
The flowers appear on the earth; the
time of the singing of birds is come, and
the voice of the turtle is heard in our
land. [Song of Solomon 2:11-12]
turtle = *dove*
13 One swallow does not make a Spring.
[Aristotle: *Nicomachean Ethics* I (c.
340 B.C.)]
*The saying may have been proverbial
in Aristotle's time. It has been echoed
through literature and was listed as an
English proverb by John Heywood, in
1546.*
See SWALLOW
14 In spring time, the only pretty ring
time,
When birds do sing, hey ding a ding,
ding:
Sweet lovers love the spring.
[Shakespeare: *As You Like It* V.iii.]
15 When daffodils begin to peer,
With heigh! the doxy over the dale,
Why, then comes in the sweet o' the
year;
For the red blood reigns in the
winter's pale.
[Shakespeare: *Winter's Tale* IV.iii.]
doxy = *sweetheart, but in an equivocal
sense*
16 In those vernal seasons of the year,
when the air is calm and pleasant, it
were an injury and sullenness against

Nature not to go out and see her riches, and partake in her rejoicing with heaven and earth. [John Milton: *Of Education*]

1 When things were as fine as could possibly be
I thought 'twas the spring; but also it was she.
[John Byrom: *A Pastoral*]

2 Spring hangs her infant blossoms on the trees,
Rock'd in the cradle of the western breeze.
[William Cowper: *Tirocinium*]

3 In days when daisies deck the ground,
And blackbirds whistle clear,
With honest joy our hearts will bound
To see the coming year.
[Burns: *Epistle to Davie*]

4 And the spring comes slowly up this way.
[Coleridge: *Christabel*]

5 O Wind,
If Winter comes, can Spring be far behind?
[Shelley: *Ode to the West Wind*]

6 Now fades the last long streak of snow,
Now burgeons every maze of quick
About the flowering squares, and thick
By ashen roots the violets blow.
[Tennyson: *In Memoriam* CXV]

7 In the spring a young man's fancy lightly turns to thoughts of love.
[Tennyson: *Locksley Hall*]

8 The year's at the spring
And day's at the morn;
Morning's at seven;
The hill-side's dew-pearled;
The lark's on the wing;
The snail's on the thorn;
God's in his heaven—
All's right with the world!
[Robert Browning: *Pippa Passes*, "Morning"]

9 The flowers that bloom in the Spring, tra la,
Have nothing to do with the case.
[W. S. Gilbert: *The Mikado* II]

10 When the hounds of spring are on winter's traces,
The mother of months in meadow or plain

Fills the shadows and windy places
With lisp of leaves and ripple of rain.
[Swinburne: Chorus of *Atalanta in Calydon*]

11 I'm going out to clean the pasture spring;
I'll only stop to rake the leaves away
(And wait to watch the water clear, I may):
I shan't be gone long.—You come too.
[Robert Frost: *The Pasture*]

SQUARE PEGS

12 If you choose to represent the various parts in life by holes upon a table, of different shapes—some circular, some triangular, some square, some oblong—and the persons acting these parts by bits of wood of similar shapes, we shall generally find that the triangular person has got into the square hole, the oblong into the triangular, and a square person has squeezed himself into the round hole.
[Sydney Smith: *Lectures on Moral Philosophy* (1804)]
This seems to be the origin of the expression "a square peg in a round hole." The idea has been attributed to Bishop Berkeley (1685-1753), but no supporting passage has been found in Berkeley's writings.

STAFF

13 Thy rod and thy staff they comfort me.
[Psalms 23:4]
comfort = *support*

14 I'll break my staff,
Bury it certain fathoms in the earth,
And, deeper than did ever plummet sound
I'll drown my book.
[Shakespeare: *The Tempest* V.i.]

STAG

15 The stag at eve had drunk his fill,
Where danced the moon on Monan's rill,
And deep his midnight lair had made
In lone Glenartney's hazel shade.
[Sir Walter Scott: *The Lady of the Lake* I.i.]
An American parody goes:
The stag at eve had drunk his fill,

*But midnight found him drinking
still.*

STAKE

1 They have tied me to a stake; I can-
not fly,
But bear-like I must fight the course.
[Shakespeare: *Macbeth* V.vii.]

*The figure is from bear-baiting. A bear
was chained to a stake in a pit and attacked by savage dogs. Shakespeare, almost alone among the Elizabethans,
seemed to have had sympathy for the
bear. The figure occurs again in* King
Lear (III.vii.) *where the aged Gloucester,
bound and fiercely interrogated, says, "I
am tied to th' stake, and I must stand
the course."*

STALE

2 How weary, stale, flat and unprofit-
able
Seem to me all the uses of this world!
[Shakespeare: *Hamlet* I.ii.]

STAND

3 Here I stand! I can't do anything else.
God help me! Amen. [Martin Luther:
before the Diet of Worms, April 18,
1521]

The German: Hier stehe ich! Ich kann
nicht anders. Gott helfe mir! Amen.

STANDARD

4 Let us raise a standard to which the
wise and honest can repair. [George
Washington: at the Constitutional Convention, 1787]

STAR(S)

5 The stars in their courses fought
against Sisera. [Judges 5:20]
6 The morning stars sang together, and
all the sons of God shouted for joy.
[Job 38:7]
7 Canst thou bind the sweet influences
of Pleiades, or loose the bands of Orion?
[Job 38:31]
8 Canst thou guide Arcturus with his
sons? [Job 38:32]
9 He that strives to touch a star,
Oft stumbles at a straw.
[Edmund Spenser: *The Shepheardes Calender*]
10 These earthly godfathers of heaven's

lights,
That give a name to every fixed star,
Have no more profit of their shining
nights
Than those that walk and wot not
what they are.
[Shakespeare: *Love's Labour's Lost* I.i.]
11 Look how the floor of heaven
Is thick inlaid with patines of bright
gold.
[Shakespeare: *The Merchant of Venice*
V.i.]
12 Two stars keep not their motion in
one sphere.
[Shakespeare: *I Henry IV* V.ii.]
13 The fault, dear Brutus, is not in our
stars,
But in ourselves, that we are under-
lings.
[Shakespeare: *Julius Caesar* I.ii.]
14 There's husbandry in Heaven;
Their candles are all out.
[Shakespeare: *Macbeth* II.i.]
husbandry = *economy*
15 The stars above us govern our condi-
tions.
[Shakespeare: *King Lear* IV.iii.]
16 Let not the dark thee cumber:
What though the moon does slum-
ber?
The stars of the night
Will lend thee their light
Like tapers clear without number.
[Robert Herrick: *The Night-Piece, to
Julia*]
17 The starry cope of Heav'n.
[John Milton: *Paradise Lost* IV.992-993]
18 And made the stars,
And set them in the firmament of
Heav'n
T' illuminate the earth, and rule the
day
In their vicissitude, and rule the
night.
[John Milton: *Paradise Lost* VII.348-351]
19 Th' evening star, Love's harbinger.
[John Milton: *Paradise Lost* XI.588]
20 Thus some, who have the stars sur-
vey'd,
Are ignorantly led
To think those glorious lamps were
made
To light Tom Fool to bed.
[Nicholas Rowe: *On a Fine Woman
Who Had a Dull Husband*]

1   The number is certainly the cause. The apparent disorder augments the grandeur, for the appearance of care is highly contrary to our idea of magnificence. Besides, the stars lie in such apparent confusion, as makes it impossible on ordinary occasions to reckon them. This gives them the advantage of a sort of infinity. [Edmund Burke: *On the Sublime and the Beautiful*]

2   Fair as a star, when only one
Is shining in the sky.
[Wordsworth: *She Dwelt Among the Untrodden Ways*]

3   Continuous as the stars that shine
And twinkle on the milky way.
[Wordsworth: *I Wandered Lonely as a Cloud*]

4   Twinkle, twinkle, little star,
How I wonder what you are!
Up above the world so high,
Like a diamond in the sky.
[Anne and Jane Taylor: *The Star* (1806)]
Much parodied; the most famous parody, the Mad Hatter's:
Twinkle, twinkle, little bat!
How I wonder what you're at!
Up above the world you fly,
Like a tea-tray in the sky.
—Alice's Adventures in Wonderland VII, Lewis Carroll.

5   Bright Star! would I were steadfast as thou art!
[Keats: *Bright Star* (last sonnet)]

6   Hitch your wagon to a star. [Emerson: *Civilization*]
Now used merely to suggest the stimulus of an unattainable ideal, the joining of the homely and the divine, when Emerson coined the phrase he had in mind, in addition, a more practical interpretation. Everything good in man, he said, depends on what is higher. We can succeed only if we borrow "the aid of the elements." Thus the carpenter and the mason can accomplish their ends only if they work with the force of gravity. So mills on the seashore that are driven by the tides "engage the assistance of the moon, like a hired hand." So it is wisdom for a man in his labor to "hitch his wagon to a star and see his chore done by the gods themselves."

7   "The stars," she whispers, "blindly run;
A web is wov'n across the sky;
From our waste places comes a cry,
And murmurs from the dying sun."
[Tennyson: *In Memoriam* III.v.]

8   Many a night I saw the Pleiads, rising thro' the mellow shade,
Glitter like a swarm of fireflies tangled in a silver braid.
[Tennyson: *Locksley Hall*]

9   Great Orion sloping slowly to the west.
[Tennyson: *Locksley Hall*]

10   Now lies the Earth all Danaë to the stars,
And all thy heart lies open unto me.
[Tennyson: Song from *The Princess* VII]

11   While the stars that oversprinkle
All the heavens, seem to twinkle
With a crystalline delight.
[Edgar Allan Poe: *The Bells*]

12   A star looks down at me,
And says: "Here I and you
Stand, each in our degree.
What do you mean to do—
Mean to do?"
I say: "For all I know,
Wait, and let Time go by,
Till my change come."—"Just so,"
The star says: "So mean I:—
So mean I."
[Thomas Hardy: *Waiting Both*]

13   Behind the western bars
The shrouded day retreats,
And unperceived the stars
Steal to their sovran seats.
[Robert Bridges: *The Clouds Have Left the Sky*]

STARGAZING

14   A man gazing on the stars is proverbially at the mercy of the puddles on the road. [Alexander Smith: *Dreamthorp*, "Men of Letters"]

STAR-SPANGLED BANNER

15   Then conquer we must, for our cause it is just,
And this be our motto: "In God is our trust."
And the star-spangled banner in triumph shall wave
O'er the land of the free and the home of the brave.

[Francis Scott Key: *The Star-Spangled
Banner*]
> *Written 1814, and printed in* The Balti-
> more Patriot *September 20; declared the
> National Anthem by Congress in 1931.*

STATE

1 The safety of the State is the highest
law. [Justinian: *Twelve Tables*]
> *The Latin of this, the greatest of the
> legal maxims, is:* Salus populi suprema
> lex.
> *It is a common plea of tyrants.*

2 In the youth of a state arms do flourish; in the middle age of a state, learning; and then both of them together for
a time; in the declining age of a state,
mechanical arts and merchandise. [Fran-
cis Bacon: *Of Vicissitude of Things*]

3 Cares of state.
[Shakespeare: *King Lear* I.i.]

4 That state of life unto which it shall
please God to call me. [*Book of Common Prayer*, Catechism]

5 I am the State! (*L'état, c'est moi!*)
[Attr. Louis XIV of France]
> *The story—as given by J. A. Dulaure:*
> History of Paris *(1863)—is that Louis
> uttered the famous phrase at the age of
> 17, interrupting the President of the
> French Parliament. But while he no
> doubt longed to say it, it is unlikely that
> he did. Not in public.*
> *He was far from being the absolute
> ruler he would have liked to be. At the
> height of his power he could not even
> get* Tartuffe *played openly. Then the
> phrase expresses his arrogance and self-
> esteem too neatly; it has more style than
> one expects from a king and reflects too
> neatly the age of enlightenment's idea of
> the Grand Monarch. It was probably
> made by Voltaire.*
> *In 1766, speaking to the Paris Parlia-
> ment, his successor, Louis XV, said:
> "Sovereignty lies in me alone. The leg-
> islative power is mine unconditionally
> and indivisibly. The public order ema-
> nates from me, and I am its supreme
> guardian. My people is one with me."
> Twenty-seven years later the people reg-
> istered a dramatic dissent.*

6 The State and the family are for ever
at war. [George Moore: *The Bending
of the Bough* I]

STATESMAN

7 A ginooine statesman should be on
his guard,
Ef he *must hev* beliefs, not to b'lieve
'em tu hard.
[James Russell Lowell: *The Biglow
Papers* II.v.]

8 A statesman is a politician who's
been dead ten or fifteen years. [Harry S.
Truman, quoted in the *New York World-
Telegram & Sun*, April 12, 1958]

STATUTES

9 Wherefore I gave them also statutes
that were not good and judgments
whereby they should not live. [Ezekiel
20:25]
> *Aside from the startling information that
> Jehovah deliberately gave the Israelites
> false commandments and then punished
> them for obeying them, the passage al-
> ludes, apparently, to the worship of Mo-
> lech or Moloch (II Kings 21:6; II Chron-
> icles 33) whose worship seems to have
> blended for a while with that of Jeho-
> vah.*
> *In the* King James Version, *God told
> Ezekiel that He gave the Israelites false
> statutes "that I might make them des-
> olate." The* Revised Standard *helpfully
> has this read "that I might horrify
> them." Whether it had the desired ef-
> fect on the Israelites is uncertain, but
> it certainly has on the modern reader.*

STEAL(ING)

10 Thou shalt not steal. [Exodus 20:15]

11 My duty towards my Neighbour is
. . . to keep my hands from picking and
stealing. [*Book of Common Prayer*, "Catechism"]

STEALTH

12 Stolen waters are sweet, and bread
eaten in secret is pleasant. [Proverbs
9:17]

13 Little wealth,
Much health,
And a life by stealth.
[Jonathan Swift: *Journal to Stella*, June
30, 1711]

STEAM

14 Soon shall thy arm, unconquer'd
steam! afar

Drag the slow barge, or drive the
rapid car;
Or on wide-waving wings expanded
bear
The flying chariot through the field
of air.
[Erasmus Darwin: *The Botanic Garden*
I.i.]

*Erasmus Darwin (1731-1802) was a minor
poet, an enthusiast and a prophet. Among
other things he foretold much that his
famous grandson was later to verify in
the realm of organic evolution.*

*To a modern the interesting thing
about his prophecy concerning steam
power (1791) is not that he was partly
right—but how brief the reign of steam
as motive power has been!*

STEIN

1 There's a wonderful family called
Stein,
There's Gert and there's Epp and
there's Ein;
Gert's poems are bunk,
Epp's statues are junk,
And no one can understand Ein.
[Anonymous]

*Of limericks, this might be called "The
Philistine's Favorite."*

STEP

2 They Were All Out of Step but Jim.
[Irving Berlin: title of song]

STEPMOTHERS

3 Stepmothers hate their stepchildren.
[Euripides: *Ion* (about 420 B.C.)]

*The death of women in childbirth, for-
merly very common, made the stepmother
much more common than she is today.
She appears in literature as a sinister
figure. This may reflect reality but, at
least in part, it probably reflects fantasy,
offering the resentful child an object for
the hatred which he, and especially she,
dared not release against the true
mother.*

STERILITY

4 A sterile wife makes you dear to a
happy friend. [Juvenal: *Satires* V.cxl.]

*Because it raises his hopes of inheriting
your property.*

5 Birds build—but not I build; no, but

strain,
Time's eunuch, and not breed one
work that wakes.
Mine, O thou lord of life, send my
roots rain.
[Gerard Manley Hopkins: *Thou Art Indeed Just, Lord*]

6 What are the roots that clutch, what
branches grow
Out of this stony rubbish?
[T. S. Eliot: *The Waste Land* I]

STICKS

7 Sticks Nix Hicks Pix

Famous headline in Variety, *intended to
convey the "show-biz" news that small
towns and rural areas had shown, as indicated by box office receipts, a dislike
for moving pictures dealing with rustic
characters and themes.*

*The headline is attr. Sime Silverman
(1873-1933), founder and editor of* Variety.

STIFF UPPER LIP

8 Keep a stiff upper lip.

*The common jocular expression for
maintaining dignity and courage in
trying circumstances, now commonly
thought to be a Briticism, seems to have
originated in America. It was in print as
early as 1833. Among the early uses of
the phrase is an adjuration to Uncle
Tom, in* Uncle Tom's Cabin, *to keep a
stiff upper lip.*

9 Providence requires three things of
us before it will help us—a stout heart, a
strong arm, and a stiff upper lip. [Sam
Slick: *Wise Saws* XIII]

*"Sam Slick" was the pseudonym of
Thomas Chandler Haliburton (1796-
1865), Canadian jurist and humorist.*

STILLNESS

10 The river glideth at his own sweet
will:
Dear God! the very houses seem
asleep;
And all that mighty heart is lying
still!
[Wordsworth: *Composed upon Westminster Bridge*]

11 No stir of air was there,
Not so much life as on a summer's
day

Robs not one light seed from the
feather'd grass,
But where the dead leaf fell, there
did it rest.
[Keats: *Hyperion* I]

STILL WATERS
1 He leadeth me beside the still waters.
[Psalms 23:2]
2 Smooth runs the water where the
brook is deep.
[Shakespeare: *II Henry VI* III.i.]
> That "Still waters run deep" has been
> a proverb from antiquity. It is one of
> many sayings that project into nature
> certain assumptions about human be-
> ings, and then find in the assumed "nat-
> ural" situation sanction for the human.
> Actually, neither human beings nor
> streams are necessarily deep because they
> are silent.

STIMULATION(S)
3 The human mind is capable of being
excited without the application of gross
and violent stimulants . . . and one being is elevated above another in proportion as he possesses this capability.
[Wordsworth: Preface to *Lyrical Ballads*
(1800)]
4 A multitude of causes, unknown to
former times, are now acting with a combined force to blunt the discriminating
powers of the mind, and, unfitting it for
all voluntary exertion, to reduce it to a
state of almost savage torpor. Chief
among the causes of this is the increasing
accumulation of men in cities, where the
uniformity of their occupation causes a
craving for extraordinary incident. This
outrageous thirst for stimulation is gratified by the press. [Wordsworth: Preface
to *Lyrical Ballads* (1800)]

STINK
5 'Tis noted as the nature of a sink,
Ever the more it is stirred, the more
to stink.
[Sir John Harington: *The Metamorphosis of Ajax*]

STOICISM
6 I could not exactly play the Stoic
with a woman who had scrambled eight
hundred miles to unphilosophize me.
[Byron: letter to Augusta Leigh, Sept.
8, 1816]
7 Heroic, stoic Cato, the sententious,
Who lent his lady to his friend Hor-
tensius.
[Byron: *Don Juan* VI.vii.]
8 Her dialect stories have kept many a
drawing room in a state of stoicism.
[Ring Lardner: *A Few Parodies:* "Dante
and. . . ."]

STOMACH
9 An army marches on its stomach.
[Attr. Napoleon Bonaparte]

STONE
10 The stone which the builders refused
is become the head stone of the corner.
[Psalms 118:22]
11 Turn every stone.
> Now usually "Leave no stone unturned."
> Originally the answer of the Delphian
> oracle to Polycrates when he asked how
> to find a treasure which Mardonius, one
> of Xerxes' generals, had buried on the
> field of Plataea.
12 The stone that is rolling can gather
no moss.
Who often removeth is sure of loss.
[Thomas Tusser: *Five Hundred Points
of Good Husbandry*]
13 As a huge stone is sometimes seen to
lie
Couched on the bald top of an eminence.
[Wordsworth: *Resolution and Independence*]

STOOLS
14 But it is said and ever shall,
Between two stools lieth the fall.
[John Gower: Prologue to *Confessio
Amantis*]
15 Betweene two stooles my taile goes
to the ground. [John Heywood: *Proverbs* (1546)]
> The more common modern form: "To
> fall between two stools."

STORK
16 The bird of war is not the eagle but
the stork. [Attr. Charles F. Potter (1931)]

STORM
17 A fuller blast ne'er shook our battlements.

[Shakespeare: *Othello* II.i.]
1 The chidden billow seems to pelt the
clouds;
The wind-shak'd surge, with high and
monstrous mane,
Seems to cast water on the burning
Bear
And quench the guards of th' ever-
fixed Pole.
I never did like molestation view
On the enchafed flood.
[Shakespeare: *Othello* II.i.]

2 Blow, winds, and crack your cheeks!
rage! blow!
You cataracts and hurricanoes, spout
Till you have drench'd our steeples,
drown'd the cocks!
[Shakespeare: *King Lear* III.ii.]
cocks = *the weathercocks on top of the
steeples*

3   The wrathful skies
Gallow the very wanderers of the
dark,
And make them keep their caves.
[Shakespeare: *King Lear* III.ii.]

4   Since I was man,
Such sheets of fire, such bursts of
horrid thunder,
Such groans of roaring wind and
rain, I never
Remember to have heard.
[Shakespeare: *King Lear* III.ii.]

5 All friends shut out, the housemates
sit
Around the radiant fireplace, en-
closed
In a tumultuous privacy of storm.
[Emerson: *The Snow-Storm*]

6 A strong nor'wester's blowing, Bill;
Hark! don't ye hear it roar, now?
Lord help 'em, how I pities them
Unhappy folks on shore now!
[Charles Dibdin: *The Sailor's Consola-
tion*]

7 The breaking waves dashed high
On a stern and rock-bound coast,
And the woods, against a stormy sky,
Their giant branches tossed.
[Felicia Hemans: *The Landing of the
Pilgrim Fathers*]

STORY

8 A story, in which native humour
reigns,
Is often useful, always entertains;

A graver fact, enlisted on your side,
May furnish illustration, well applied;
But sedentary weavers of long tales
Give me the fidgets, and my patience
fails.
[William Cowper: *Conversation*]

STOUTNESS

9 I see no objection to stoutness, in
moderation.
[W. S. Gilbert: *Iolanthe* I]

STOWE, HARRIET BEECHER

10 A blatant Bassarid of Boston, a rampant Maenad of Massachusetts. [Swin-
burne: *Under the Microscope*]
*The Maenads and the Bassarids were
female votaries of Dionysus who in wild
frenzy, excited by wine and the god,
roamed the hills celebrating their rites.*
*Americans are a little startled to find
Harriet Beecher Stowe so described, but
Swinburne, always a victim of alliteration's artful lure and not a little proud
of his powers of invective, had been
aroused by Mrs. Stowe's articles in the*
Atlantic Monthly *about Lord Byron's
private life. In the Chorus from Atalanta he refers to Pan and the satyrs as
filling with delight "The Maenad and
the Bassarid."*

STRAIGHT

11 The street which is called Straight.
[Acts 9:11]

STRAIN (verb)

12 Ye blind guides, which strain at a
gnat, and swallow a camel. [Matthew
23:24]
*The passage is often used with the as-
sumption that "strain at" here means to
make a great effort to swallow, to choke
over, as it were, to retch with revulsion
in the effort. Actually, however, the word
strain here has the meaning: to filter.
The passage means "Hypocrites! . . .
who strain the liquor if they find a gnat
in it and yet swallow a camel when it
suits them to do so." The* Revised Standard Version *gives the proper meaning by
having it read* which strain out a gnat.
The King James Version, *given above,
is not, as has been claimed, however, a
mistranslation; it was an adoption of a*

reading already (1611) current, which even then had proved misleading.

STRAIN

1 That strain again! it had a dying fall:
O, it came o'er my ear like the sweet
sound
That breathes upon a bank of violets,
Stealing and giving odor!
[Shakespeare: *Twelfth Night* I.i.]
It has been suggested that sound is a misprint for south (i.e., the south wind).
2 But would you sing, and rival Orpheus' strain,
The wond'ring forests soon should dance again.
[Alexander Pope: *Pastorals*, "Summer"]

STRANGE

3 'Twas strange, 'twas passing strange;
'Twas pitiful, 'twas wondrous pitiful.
[Shakespeare: *Othello* I.iii.]

STRANGER(S)

4 Everyone is ready to speak evil of a stranger. [Aeschylus: *The Suppliants*]
5 I have been a stranger in a strange land. [Exodus 2:22]
6 I was a stranger, and ye took me in. [Matthew 25:35]
7 I do desire we may be better strangers.
[Shakespeare: *As You Like It* III.ii.]
8 And how am I to face the odds
Of man's bedevilment and God's?
I, a stranger and afraid
In a world I never made.
[A .E. Housman: *Last Poems* XII]

STRAW

9 Take a straw and throw it up into the air, you may see by that which way the wind is. [John Selden: *Table Talk*]
10 The last straw breaks the camel's back. [John Ray: *English Proverbs* (1670)]
There are many proverbs that warn us that a sequence of trifles can produce a catastrophe—a catastrophe which will be commonly attributed to the last trifle.
Seneca said that it was not the last outflowing drop that emptied the vessel but all the drops that had flowed out before. The Spanish have a saying that the rope breaks at last by the weakest pull. Thomas Fuller (1654-1734) said that it is always the superfluous added drop

that is blamed for the running over of the cup. There was formerly an English proverb that it was the last feather that broke the horse's back.

STRAWBERRY

11 As Dr. Boteler said of strawberries: "Doubtless God could have made a better berry, but doubtless God never did." [Izaak Walton: *The Compleat Angler* I.v.]

STREAM(S)

12 Gilding pale streams with heavenly alchemy.
[Shakespeare: *Sonnets* XXXIII]
13 Liquid lapse of murmuring streams.
[John Milton: *Paradise Lost* VIII.263]
14 A mighty stream of tendency.
[William Hazlitt: *Why Distant Objects Please*]
Hazlitt was echoing Wordsworth (The Excursion IX.87). Emerson and Matthew Arnold also used the phrase.
15 The stream is brightest at its spring.
[John Greenleaf Whittier: *Amy Wentworth* II]
The metaphor had been used by Pascal and Metastasio.

STRENGTH

16 They go from strength to strength.
[Psalms 84:7]
17 What is strength without a double share
Of wisdom? vast, unwieldy, burdensome,
Proudly secure, yet liable to fall
By weakest subtleties, not made to rule,
But to subserve where wisdom bears command.
[John Milton: *Samson Agonistes*]

STRENUOUS

18 I wish to preach, not the doctrine of ignoble ease, but the doctrine of the strenuous life. [Theodore Roosevelt: in a speech in Chicago, April 10, 1899]

STRIFE

19 Let there be no strife, I pray thee, between me and thee . . . for we be brethren. [Genesis 13:8]
20 To strive with an equal is dangerous; with a superior, mad; with an inferior,

degrading. [Seneca: *De ira*]

1 So when two dogs are fighting in the
streets,
When a third dog one of the two
dogs meets:
With angry teeth he bites him to
the bone,
And this dog smarts for what that
dog has done.
[Henry Fielding: *Tom Thumb* I.v.]

STRIKE

2 There is no right to strike against the
public safety by anybody, anywhere, any-
time. [Calvin Coolidge: letter to Samuel Gompers, September 1919, referring
to the strike of the Boston, Mass. police
force]

STRIVINGS

3 I am a parcel of vain strivings tied
By a chance bond together.
[Thoreau: *Sic Vita*]

STRONG

4 Be strong, and quit yourselves like
men. [I Samuel 4:9]

5 Strong is the lion—like a coal
His eyeball—like a bastion's mole
His chest against the foes:
Strong the gier-eagle on his sail;
Strong against tide the enormous
whale
Emerges as he goes.
[Christopher Smart: *A Song to David*]

STRUCK

6 I was struck all of a heap.
[Richard Brinsley Sheridan: *The Duenna*
II.ii.]

STRUGGLE

7 Man tends to increase at a greater
rate than his means of subsistence; consequently he is occasionally subjected to
a severe struggle for existence. [Charles
Darwin: *The Descent of Man* XXI]

8 Say not the struggle nought availeth.
[A. H. Clough: *Say Not The Struggle
Nought Availeth*]

STUBBORN

9 A stiffnecked people. [Exodus 33:3]

10 A stubborn and rebellious generation. [Psalms 78:8]

STUDY(IES)

11 Much study is a weariness of the flesh.
[Ecclesiastes 12:12]

12 What sholde he studie, and make
himselven wood,
Upon a book in cloistre alwey to
poure,
Or swinken with his handes, and la-
boure,
As Austin bit? How shal the world
be served?
Lat Austin have his swink to him
reserved.
[Chaucer: Prologue to *The Canterbury
Tales*]
wood = *mad, crazy;* swink = *labor, toil;*
Austin = *St. Augustine, the founder of
the monastic order of which the Monk,
to whom these lines ironically refer, was
a member;* bit = *bid, commanded*

13 As plants are suffocated and drowned
with too much moisture, and lamps with
too much oil, so is the active part of the
understanding with too much study.
[Montaigne: *Essays* I.xxv.]

14 The good that should come of study
is to prove better, wiser, and honester.
[Montaigne: *Essays* I.xxv.]

15 To spend too much time in studies
is sloth. [Francis Bacon: *Of Studies*]

16 Reading maketh a full man, conference a ready man and writing an exact
man. [Francis Bacon: *Of Studies*]

17 Histories make men wise; poets, witty;
the mathematics, subtile; natural philosophy, deep; moral, grave; logic and rhetoric, able to contend. [Francis Bacon:
Of Studies]

18 With unwearied fingers drawing out
The lines of life, from living knowl-
edge hid.
[Spenser: *The Faerie Queene* IV.ii.48]

19 Balk logic with acquaintance that you
have,
And practice rhetoric in your com-
mon talk;
Music and poesy use to quicken you;
The mathematics and the metaphysics
Fall to them as you find your stomach
serves you;
No profit grows where is no pleasure
ta'en;
In brief, sir, study what you most
affect.
[Shakespeare: *Taming of the Shrew* I.i.]

1 Studies . . . teach not their own use; but that is a wisdom without them and above them, won by observation. [Francis Bacon: *Of Studies*]
without = *outside of*

2 Crafty men contemn studies, simple men admire them, and wise men use them. [Francis Bacon: *Of Studies*]
contemn = *despise, scorn, treat as of small value*

3 Studies serve for delight, for ornament, and for ability. Their chief use for delight is in privateness and retiring; for ornament is in discourse; and for ability is in the judgment and disposition of business. [Francis Bacon: *Of Studies*]

4 Study is like the heaven's glorious
sun,
That will not be deep-search'd
with saucy looks;
Small have continual plodders ever
won,
Save base authority from others'
books.
[Shakespeare: *Love's Labour's Lost* I.i.]

5 The quiet and still air of delightful studies. [John Milton: *Reason of Church Government* II, Introduction to Chap. 1]

6 Hiving wisdom with each studious
year.
[Byron: *Childe Harold* III.cvii.]

7 The studious class are their own victims; they are thin and pale, their feet are cold, their heads are hot . . . pallor, squalor, hunger, and egotism. [Emerson: *Representative Men*, "Montaigne"]

STUMBLE

8 A Stumble may prevent a Fall. [Thomas Fuller (1654-1734): *Gnomologia*]

STUPIDITY

9 More than sixscore thousand persons that cannot discern between their right hand and their left hand; and also much cattle. [Jonah 4:11]

10 The rest to some faint meaning make
pretense,
But Shadwell never deviates into
sense.
Some beams of wit on other souls
may fall,
Strike through and make a lucid interval.
But Shadwell's genuine night admits
no ray,
His rising fogs prevail upon the day.
[Dryden: *Mac Flecknoe*]

11 Why, Sir, Sherry [Thomas Sheridan] is dull, naturally dull; but it must have taken a great deal of pains to become what we now see him. Such an excess of stupidity, Sir, is not in Nature. [Samuel Johnson: in Boswell's *Life*, July 28, 1763]

12 Against stupidity the gods themselves fight in vain. [Schiller: *Die Jungfrau von Orleans* III.vi.]
Nietzsche, in The Antichrist, *said that it was against boredom that they strove in vain.*

13 With Stupidity and Sound Digestion man may front much. [Thomas **Carlyle**: *Sartor Resartus* II.vii.]

14 Whenever a man does a thoroughly stupid thing, it is always from the noblest motives. [Oscar Wilde: *Picture of Dorian Gray* VI]

STYLE

15 A good style must, first of all, be clear. It must not be mean or above the dignity of the subject. It must be appropriate. [Aristotle: *Rhetoric* III]

16 Often a purple patch or two is stuck on a serious work to give it a touch of color. [Horace: *Ars Poetica* XIV]

17 Style has no fixed laws; it is changed by the usage of the people, never the same for any length of time. [Seneca: *Ad Lucilium* CXIV]

18 Base is the style and matter mean
withall.
[Edmund Spenser: *Mother Hubberds Tale*]

19 The chief virtue of a style is perspicuity, and nothing so vicious in it as to need an interpreter. Words borrowed of antiquity do lend a kind of majesty to style, and are not without their delight sometimes. For they have the authority of years, and out of their intermission do win themselves a kind of grace-like newness. But the eldest of the present, and newest of the past language, is the best. [Ben Jonson: *Discoveries*]

20 A strict and succinct style is that, where you can take away nothing with-

out loss, and that loss to be manifest.
[Ben Jonson: *Explorata*, "Consuetudo"]
1 That must be very fine; I don't understand it in the least! [Molière: *Le Médecin Malgré Lui* II.iv.]
That is not good language that all understand not.
—*George Herbert*: Jacula Prudentum
2 Style! style! why, all writers will tell you that it is the very thing which can least of all be changed. A man's style is nearly as much a part of him as his physiognomy, his figure, the throbbing of his pulse—in short, as any part of his being which is at least subjected to the action of the will. [Fénelon: *Dialogues sur l'Eloquence*]
3 Some by old words to fame have
made pretence,
Ancients in phrase, mere moderns in
their sense;
Such labour'd nothings, in so strange
a style,
Amaze the unlearn'd, and make the
learned smile.
[Alexander Pope: *An Essay on Criticism* II]
4 A vile conceit in pompous words expressed
Is like a clown in regal purple
dressed.
[Alexander Pope: *An Essay on Criticism* II]
vile conceit = an idea of little worth, a commonplace observation; clown = a country lout
5 All styles are good, except the tiresome. [Voltaire: Preface to *L'Enfant Prodigue*]
6 The style is the man. [Buffon: *Discourse*]
7 Read over your compositions, and where ever you meet with a passage which you think is particularly fine, strike it out. [Samuel Johnson: in Boswell's *Life*, April 30, 1773]
Johnson was quoting "an old tutor of a college." The quip is still a staple of criticism at Oxford.
8 I own I like not Johnson's turgid
style,
That gives an inch the importance
of a mile,
Casts of manure a wagon-load around
To raise a simple daisy from the

ground.
[John Wolcot ("Peter Pindar"): *On Dr. Samuel Johnson*]
Johnson's style, by the way, was better suited to his purposes than Wolcot's to his.
9 An author can have nothing truly his own but his style. [Isaac D'Israeli: *Literary Miscellanies*, "Style"]
10 No style is good that is not fit to be spoken or read aloud with effect. [William Hazlitt: *The Conversation of Authors*]
11 Take care of the sense and the sounds will take care of themselves. [Lewis Carroll: *Alice's Adventures in Wonderland* IX]
12 . . . the chief stimulus of good style is to possess a full, rich, complex matter to grapple with. [Walter Pater: *Appreciations*, "Style"]
13 And the Devil said to Simon Legree: "I like your style, so wicked and free." [Vachel Lindsay: *A Negro Sermon*]
See also BATHOS

SUBDUED
14   My nature is subdu'd
To what it works in, like the dyer's
hand.
[Shakespeare: *Sonnets* CXI]

SUBLIME AND RIDICULOUS
15 The sublime and the ridiculous are often so nearly related that it is difficult to class them separately. One step above the sublime makes the ridiculous, and one step above the ridiculous makes the sublime again. [Thomas Paine: *The Age of Reason* II]
Sometimes attributed Napoleon after his return from Russia, 1812. The idea could well have been thought of by many people at different times, but Paine's writings were well known in France.

SUBLIMITY
16 Sublimity is Hebrew by birth. [Coleridge: *Table-Talk*, July 25, 1832]

SUBMISSION
17   Away! take heed;
I will abroad.
Call in thy death's-head there, tie up
thy fears;

He that forbears
To suit and serve his need
Deserves his load.
But as I rav'd and grew more fierce
and wild
At every word,
Methought I heard one calling,
"Child";
And I replied, "My Lord."
[George Herbert: *The Collar*]
1 Subjection, but requir'd with gentle
sway,
And by her yielded, by him best re-
ceiv'd,
Yielded with coy submission, modest
pride,
And sweet reluctant, amorous delay.
[John Milton: *Paradise Lost* IV.308-311]

SUBWAY
2 The subway yawns the quickest promise home.
[Hart Crane: *The Tunnel*]

SUCCESS: definitions
3 Success depends on three things: who
says it, what he says, how he says it; and
of these three things, what he says is the
least important. [John Morley: *Recollections* II]
4 To burn always with this hard, gemlike flame, to maintain this ecstasy, is
success in life. [Walter Pater: *The Renaissance*, "Conclusion"]
5 So our self-feeling in this world depends entirely on what we *back* ourselves
to be and do. It is determined by the
ratio of our actualities to our supposed
potentialities; a fraction of which our
pretensions are the denominator and
the numerator our success: thus,

$$\text{Self esteem} = \frac{\text{Success}}{\text{Pretensions}}$$

such a fraction may be increased as well
by diminishing the denominator as by
increasing the numerator. [William
James: *Principles of Psychology*]
6 How can they say my life isn't a
success? Have I not for more than sixty
years got enough to eat and escaped being eaten? [Logan Pearsall Smith: *Afterthoughts*]
7 There is only one success—to be able
to spend your life in your own way.

[Christopher Morley: *Where the Blue
Begins*]
8 Success is that old ABC—ability,
breaks and courage. [Charles Luckman:
quoted in the *New York Mirror*, Sept. 19,
1955]

SUCCESS: how to achieve
9 Success or failure lies in conformity
to the times. [Machiavelli: *Discourses on
Livy* III.ix.]
10 Have more than thou showest,
Speak less than thou knowest,
Lend less than thou owest,
Ride more than thou goest,
Learn more than thou trowest,
Set less than thou throwest;
Leave thy drink and thy whore,
And keep in-a-door,
And thou shalt have more
Than two tens to a score.
[Shakespeare: *King Lear* I.iv.]
11 There are only two ways of getting on
in the world: by one's own industry, or
by the weaknesses of others. [La Bruyère: *Les Caractères*]
12 I have always observed that to succeed in the world one should seem a
fool, but be wise. [Montesquieu: *Pensées Diverses*]
13 Be commonplace and creeping, and
you will be a success. [Beaumarchais: *Le
Barbier de Séville* III]
14 He owed his success to the art of
uniting suppleness to others with confidence in himself. [Fanny Burney: *Cecilia* I]

SUCCESS: miscellaneous
15 But, Lord, to see what success do,
whether with or without reason, and
making a man seem wise. [Samuel Pepys:
Diary, August 15, 1666]
16 'Tis not in mortals to command success,
But we'll do more, Sempronius; we'll
deserve it.
[Joseph Addison: *Cato* I.ii.]
*Thought by the 18th century to be one
of the greatest of human utterances, and
much quoted. To our own times—dubious alike of success and deserving—it
seems labored and stilted.*

17 Success has ruined many a man.
[Benjamin Franklin: *Poor Richard's Al-*

manack (1752)]

1 If Fortune wishes to make a man estimable, she gives him virtue; if she wishes to make him esteemed, she gives him success. [Joubert: *Pensées*]

2 Nothing succeeds like success. [Alexandre Dumas, père: *Ange Pitou* I.vii.]

3 How is it that we so seldom hear of the death of a very successful public man without private satisfaction? We are generally glad. I suppose it is because successful men are generally humbugs. [Samuel Butler (1835-1902): *Notebooks*]

4 The theory seems to be that so long as a man is a failure he is one of God's chillun, but that as soon as he has any luck he owes it to the Devil. [H. L. Mencken: *Chrestomathy*]

5 Success—"the bitch-goddess, Success," in William James's phrase—demands strange sacrifices from those who worship her. [Aldous Huxley: *Proper Studies*]

6 The compensation of very early success is a conviction that life is a romantic matter. In the best sense one stays young. [F. Scott Fitzgerald: *The Crack-up*]

7 The toughest thing about success is that you've got to keep on being a success. Talent is only a starting point in this business. [Irving Berlin, in *Theatre Arts*, Feb., 1958]

SUCCOR

8 Throw out the life-line, throw out
    the life-line,
Someone is sinking today.
[Edward Smith Ufford: *Throw Out the Life-line*]

SUCKER

9 A sucker is born every minute. [Attr. P. T. Barnum]
 Said to be Barnum's answer to one who told him that his trickery was apparent to everyone who entered his museum and that they would not come back.

SUEZ

10 Ship me somewheres east of Suez,
  where the best is like the worst,
Where there aren't no Ten Commandments an' a man can raise a thirst.
[Kipling: *Mandalay*]

SUFFERANCE

11 Sufferance is the badge of all our
       tribe.
[Shakespeare: *The Merchant of Venice* I.iii.]

SUFFERING

12 By suffering comes wisdom. [Aeschylus: *Agamemnon*]

13 He that can say how he doth fry
In pettie-gentle flames doth lie.
[Montaigne: *Essays* I.ii.]
 Montaigne is quoting a sonnet of Petrarch's. The translation is John Florio's.
 Shakespeare expresses the same thought in Lear (*IV.i.*):
     The worst is not
 So long as we can say "This is the
       worst."

14 It is not true that suffering ennobles the character; happiness does that sometimes, but suffering, for the most part, makes men petty and vindictive. [W. S. Maugham: *The Moon and Sixpence* XVII]

SUFFICIENT

15 Sufficient unto the day is the evil thereof. [Matthew 7:34]

SUICIDE(S)

16 Many hold that we should not desert from the world's garrison without the express command of him who has placed us there. [Montaigne: *Essays* II.iii.]

17 Some of his Gutts were cut in two
And mangled in such sort,
That he himself could never doe
But had some helper for't.
Eight hours or more this man did
       live,
 In grievous woe and pain,
What sustinance they did him give,
 Came straight way forth again.
 The Devil's Cruelty to Mankind, Being a True Relation of the Life and Death of George Gibbs, a Sawyer by his Trade, who being many times tempted by the Divill to destroy himselfe, did on Friday, being the 7 of March 1663, most cruelly Ripp up his own Belly, and pull'd out his Bowells and Guts, and cut them in pieces: to the Amazement of all the Beholders, the sorrow of his friends, and the great grief of his Wife, being not

long married: and both young People.
Quoted in Hyder Rollins's *The Pack
of Autolycus*

1 O! that this too too solid flesh would
melt,
Thaw and resolve itself into a dew;
Or that the Everlasting had not fix'd
His canon 'gainst self-slaughter! O
God! O God!
How weary, stale, flat, and unprofi-
table
Seem to me all the uses of this world.
[Shakespeare: *Hamlet* I.ii.]

2 To be, or not to be—that is the ques-
tion:
Whether 'tis nobler in the mind to
suffer
The slings and arrows of outrageous
fortune
Or to take arms against a sea of
troubles,
And by opposing end them.
[Shakespeare: *Hamlet* III.i.]

3 For who would bear the whips and
scorns of time,
The oppressor's wrong, the proud
man's contumely,
The pangs of dispriz'd love, the law's
delay,
The insolence of office, and the spurns
That patient merit of the unworthy
takes,
When he himself might his quietus
make
With a bare bodkin?
[Shakespeare: *Hamlet* III.i.]
bare = *mere;* bodkin = *a long needle*
*Dr. Johnson pointed out that with the
exception of "dispriz'd love" these are
not evils to which a prince is likely to
be exposed.*

4 A farmer that hang'd himself on th'
expectation of plenty.
[Shakespeare: *Macbeth* II.iii.]
*The farmer had bought up grain, antici-
pating a bad season and a dearth that
would raise prices.*
*The likelihood of a good season, with
a bountiful crop, which would lower
prices and mean his ruin, drove him to
suicide.*
*It is something like the spectacular
losses that our own Stock Exchange has
occasionally experienced at a rumor of
peace.*

5 Let's do it after the high Roman
fashion,
And make death proud to take us.
[Shakespeare: *Antony and Cleopatra* IV.
xv.]

6   And it is great
To do that thing that ends all other
deeds,
Which shackles accidents and bolts
up change,
Which sleeps, and never palates more
the dung,
The beggar's nurse and Caesar's.
[Shakespeare: *Antony and Cleopatra* V.
ii.]

7   Against self-slaughter
There is a prohibition so divine
That cravens my weak hand.
[Shakespeare: *Cymbeline* III.iv.]

8 9 Men in 10 are suicides. [Benjamin
Franklin: *Poor Richard's Almanack*
(1749)]

9 She drank prussic acid without any
water,
And died like a Duke-and-a-Duchess's
daughter.
[Richard Harris Barham: *The Ingoldsby
Legends,* "The Tragedy"]

10 One more unfortunate
Weary of breath,
Rashly importunate,
Gone to her death.
[Thomas Hood: *The Bridge of Sighs*]
importunate = *urgent, insistent, not stay-
ing to deliberate*

11 The assumption of the veil or the
frock is a suicide reimbursed by an eternity. [Victor Hugo: *Les Misérables* VII.
vii.]

12 I take it that no man is educated
who has never dallied with the thought
of suicide. [William James: *Letters* II.
xxxix.]

13 The thought of suicide is a great consolation: by means of it one gets successfully through many a bad night. [Fried-
rich Nietzsche: *Beyond Good and Evil*
IV.iii.]

14 These are the thoughts I often think
As I stand gazing down
In act upon the cressy brink
To strip and dive and drown;
But in the golden-sanded brooks
And azure meres I spy

A silly lad that longs and looks
And wishes he were I.
[A. E. Housman: *A Shropshire Lad* XX]
1 Suicide is a belated acquiescence in the opinion of one's wife's relatives.
[H. L. Mencken: *Chrestomathy*]
2 Guns aren't lawful;
  Nooses give;
  Gas smells awful;
  You might as well live.
[Dorothy Parker: *Résumé*]

SUIT
3 Full little knowest thou that hast not
                                    tried,
  What hell it is in suing long to bide:
  To loose good dayes, that might be
                              better spent;
  To waste long nights in pensive dis-
                                  content;
  To speed to-day, to be put back to-
                                  morrow;
  To feed on hope, to pine with feare
                              and sorrow.
[Edmund Spenser: *Mother Hubberds Tale*]

SUMMER
4 Sumer is icumen in.
  Lhude sing cuccu!
  Groweth sed, and bloweth med,
  And springeth the wude nu—
  Sing cuccu!
[Anon.: *Cuckoo Song* (c. 1250)]
  Winter is icummen in,
  Lhude sing Goddamm.
  Raineth drop and staineth slop,
  And how the wind doth ramm!
          Sing: Goddamm.
          —Ezra Pound: Ancient Music
5 Rough winds do shake the darling
                          buds of May,
  And summer's lease hath all too short
                              a date.
[Shakespeare: *Sonnets* XVIII]
6 All the live murmur of a summer's day. [Matthew Arnold: *The Scholar-Gipsy*]

SUM OF THINGS
7 Think you, 'mid all this mighty sum
    Of things forever speaking,
  That nothing of itself will come,
    But we must still be seeking?

[Wordsworth: *Expostulation and Reply*]
  still = *always, ceaselessly*

SUN
8 The sun also ariseth, and the sun goeth down, and hasteth to his place where he arose. [Ecclesiastes 1:5]
9 Truly the light is sweet, and a pleasant thing it is for the eyes to behold the sun. [Ecclesiastes 11:7]
10 The sun also shines on the wicked. [Seneca: *De beneficiis* III]
11 Right against the Eastern gate,
  Where the great Sun begins his state.
[John Milton: *L'Allegro*]
12 I 'gin to be aweary of the sun.
[Shakespeare: *Macbeth* V.v.]
13 For Lycidas your sorrow is not dead,
  Sunk though he be beneath the
                          watery floor;
  So sinks the day-star in the ocean
                              bed,
  And yet anon repairs his drooping
                              head,
  And tricks his beams, and with new-
                          spangled ore
  Flames in the forehead of the morn-
                              ing sky.
[John Milton: *Lycidas*]
14 Nor dim nor red, like God's own
                              head,
  The glorious sun uprist.
[Coleridge: *The Ancient Mariner* II]
15 All in a hot and copper sky,
  The bloody sun, at noon,
  Right up above the mast did stand,
  No bigger than the moon.
[Coleridge: *The Ancient Mariner* II]
16 Not till the sun excludes you do I
                          exclude you.
[Walt Whitman: *Leaves of Grass*, "To a Common Prostitute"]
17 Is it so small a thing
  To have enjoy'd the sun?
[Matthew Arnold: *Empedocles on Etna* I.ii.]
18 The night has a thousand eyes,
    And the day but one;
  Yet the light of the bright world dies,
    With the dying sun.
[Francis William Bourdillon: *Light*]

SUNDAY
19 Day of all the week the best,

Emblem of eternal rest.
[John Newton: *Saturday Evening*]

SUNDIAL

1 *Horas non numero nisi serenas* is the motto of a sun-dial near Venice. There is a softness and harmony in the words and in the thought unparalleled. Of all conceits it is surely the most classical. "I count only the hours that are serene." [William Hazlitt: *On a Sun-Dial*]

SUNFLOWER

2 As the sun-flower turns on her god
when he sets,
The same look which she turned
when he rose.
[Thomas Moore: *Believe Me if all Those Endearing Young Charms*]

SUNRISE

3 It is true, I never assisted the sun materially in his rising; but, doubt not, it was of the last importance only to be present at it. [Thoreau: *Walden* I]

SUNSET

4 Men shut their doors against a setting sun.
[Shakespeare: *Timon of Athens* I.ii.]
5 Behold him setting in his western
skies,
The shadows lengthening as the vapours rise.
[Dryden: *Absalom and Achitophel* I]
6 Whose dwelling is the light of setting suns.
[Wordsworth: *Tintern Abbey*]
7 That hour of the day when, face to face, the rising moon beholds the set-ting sun. [Longfellow: *Hyperion* II.x.]
8 To sail beyond the sunset, and the
baths
Of all the western stars, until I die.
[Tennyson: *Ulysses*]
9 Cold upon the dead volcano sleeps
the gleam of dying day.
[Tennyson: *Locksley Hall Sixty Years After*]
10 There are sunsets who whisper a
good-by.
It is a short dusk and a way for stars.
Prairie and sea rim they go level and
even,
And the sleep is easy.

There are sunsets who dance good-by.
They fling scarves half to the arc,
To the arc then and over the arc.
Ribbons at the ears, sashes at the
hips,
Dancing, dancing good-by. And here
sleep
Tosses a little with dreams.
[Carl Sandburg: *Sunsets*]

SUNSHINE

11 Make hay while the sun shines. [While the proverb first appeared in English in a collection of proverbs published in 1546, its appearance in almost every European language suggests that it is of great antiquity.]
12 Wait till the sun shines, Nellie,
When the clouds go drifting by.
[Andrew B. Sterling: *Wait Till the Sun Shines, Nellie* (1905)]

SUPERFLUOUS

13 The superfluous, a very necessary thing. [Voltaire: *Le Mondain* 21]
14 As superfluous as a Gideon Bible in the Ritz. [F. Scott Fitzgerald: *The Crack-Up*]

SUPERIORITY

15 No two men can be half an hour together but one shall acquire an evident superiority over the other. [Samuel Johnson: in Boswell's *Life* (1776)]
16 Nothing costs us so much as an acknowledgment of superiority, which is always forced from us; and nothing is such relief as any pretense or opportunity afforded us for shaking off the uneasy obligation. [William Hazlitt: *The Ruling Passion*]

SUPERIOR PEOPLE

17 High people are the best. Take a hundred ladies of quality, you'll find them better wives, better mothers, more willing to sacrifice their own pleasures to their children, than a hundred other women. [Samuel Johnson: in Boswell's *Life*, May 14, 1778]

SUPERLATIVE

18 It is not enough for the knight of romance that you agree that his lady is a very nice girl—if you do not admit

that she is the best that God ever made or will make, you must fight. There is in all men a demand for the superlative, so much so that the poor devil who has no other way of reaching it attains it by getting drunk. It seems to me that this demand is at the bottom of the philosopher's effort to prove that truth is absolute and of the jurist's search for criteria of universal validity which he collects under the head of natural law. [O. W. Holmes, Jr.: *Collected Legal Papers*]

SUPERNUMERARY

1 No! I am not Prince Hamlet, nor was meant to be;
Am an attendant lord, one that will do
To swell a progress, start a scene or two.
[T. S. Eliot: *The Love Song of J. Alfred Prufrock*]

SUPERSTITION

2 Superstition is a senseless fear of God. [Cicero: *De natura deorum* I]
3 Superstition is the reproach of the Deity. [Francis Bacon: *Of Superstition*]
4 As it addeth deformity to an ape to be so like a man, so the similitude of superstition to religion makes it the more deformed. [Francis Bacon: *Of Superstition*]

Bacon could only have intended the antecedent of the second it to be superstition, not religion.

5 There is a superstition in avoiding superstition. [Francis Bacon: *Of Superstition*]

There is an anti-superstition society that meets on Friday-the-thirteenths, seats thirteen at a table, ritualistically breaks a mirror, spills salt, etc. Presumably, were one of these defiances omitted, the membership might feel uneasy.

6 Such is the way of all superstition, whether in astrology, dreams, omens, divine judgments, or the like; wherein men, having a delight in such vanities, mark the events where they are fulfilled, but where they fail, though this happen much oftener, neglect and pass them by. [Francis Bacon: *Novum Organum* I]

vanities = follies, emptinesses

7 Superstition is godless religion, devout impiety. [Joseph Hall: *Of the Superstitious*]
8 Sickness and sorrows come and go, but a superstitious soul hath no rest. [Robert Burton: *Anatomy of Melancholy* III.4.1.3.]
9 Superstition is the religion of feeble minds. [Edmund Burke: *Reflections on the Revolution in France*]

SUPPORT

10 'Tis not enough to help the feeble up, But to support him after.
[Shakespeare: *Timon of Athens* I.i.]

SUPREME COURT

11 No matther whether th' constitution follows th' flag or not, th' supreme coort follows th' iliction returns. [Finley Peter Dunne: *Mr. Dooley's Opinions*, "The Supreme Court's Decisions"]

SURETY

12 He that is surety for a stranger shall smart for it: and he that hateth suretiship is sure. [Proverbs 11:15]
13 A person who can't pay, gets another person who can't pay, to guarantee that he can pay. [Dickens: *Little Dorrit* I. xxiii.]

SURF

14 Now the great winds shoreward blow;
Now the salt tides seaward flow;
Now the wild white horses play,
Champ and chafe and toss in the spray.
[Matthew Arnold: *The Forsaken Merman*]

SURFEIT

15 They are as sick that surfeit with too much, as they that starve with nothing. [Shakespeare: *The Merchant of Venice* I.ii.]
16 As a surfeit of the sweetest things
The deepest loathing to the stomach brings.
[Shakespeare: *A Midsummer Night's Dream* II.ii.]

SURGEON

17 In a good surgeon, a hawk's eye: a lion's heart: and a lady's hand. [Leonard Wright: *Display of Dutie*]

SURMISE

1 So to interpose a little ease,
Let our frail thoughts dally with
false surmise.
[John Milton: *Lycidas*]

SURRENDER

2 No terms except an unconditional
and immediate surrender can be accepted. I propose to move immediately
upon your works. [Ulysses S. Grant: to
General S. B. Buckner, Fort Donelson,
February 16, 1862]
3 The awful daring of a moment's surrender
Which an age of prudence can never
retract.
[T. S. Eliot: *The Waste Land* V]

SURVIVAL

4 I have survived! [Answer of Siéyès:
when someone asked him, after the Reign
of Terror, what he had done]
*He was really a master of survival. He
survived the Terror, the Directorate, the
Consulate, the Empire, the Restoration
and the July Revolution, to die peaceably in his bed, an elderly gentleman of
88.*

5 A unanimous chorus of praise is not
an assurance of survival [for an author].
[André Gide: *Pretexts*]
6 Victory at all costs, victory in spite
of all terror, victory however long and
hard the road may be; for without
victory there is no survival. [Winston
Churchill: Speech, May 13, 1940]
See also FITTEST

SURVIVORS

7 Friends who set forth at our side,
Falter, are lost in the storm.
We, we only, are left!
[Matthew Arnold: *Rugby Chapel*]

SUSANNA

8 O, Susanna! O, don't you cry for me,
I've come from Alabama, wid my
banjo on my knee.
[Stephen Foster: *O, Susanna* (Chorus)]

SUSPENSE

9 Suspense in news is torture.
[John Milton: *Samson Agonistes*]

SUSPICION(S)

10 Caesar's wife should be above suspicion. [Julius Caesar: in Plutarch's
Lives X.vi.]
*Caesar divorced his wife Pompeia be-
cause she had merely been a bystander
at an act of sacrilege committed by the
ruffian Clodius. When asked by the
prosecutor at Clodius's trial why he had
done so if, as he claimed, he believed her
innocent, Caesar answered as above.*

*It would not be excessively cynical to
assume that he was looking for a moral
road to convenience, as have so many
dictators since his day.*

11 Suspicions amongst thoughts are like
bats amongst birds, they ever fly by
twilight. [Francis Bacon: *Of Suspicion*]
12 Nothing makes a man suspect much,
more than to know little. [Francis Bacon: *Of Suspicion*]
13 Suspicions that the mind, of itself,
gathers, are but buzzes; but suspicions
that are artificially nourished and put
into men's heads by the tales and whisperings of others, have stings. [Francis
Bacon: *Of Suspicion*]
14 Bid suspicion double-lock the door.
[Shakespeare: *Venus and Adonis*]
15 He makes a false wife that suspects a
true. [Nathaniel Field: *Amends for Ladies* I.i.]
16 Distrust is the Mother of Safety, but
must keep out of Sight. [Thomas Fuller
(1654-1734): *Gnomologia*]
17 Suspicion may be no fault, but showing it may be a great one. [Thomas
Fuller (1654-1734): *Gnomologia*]
18 Suspicion is no less an enemy to virtue than to happiness. [Samuel Johnson:
The Rambler No. 79]

SWALLOW.

19 One swallow maketh not summer.
[John Heywood: *Proverbs* (1546)]
*The proverb goes back to antiquity and
is alluded to in the plays of Aristophanes.
It derives from a fable of Aesop's (though,
of course, it is equally likely that Aesop
made up the fable to illuminate an established proverb) that tells of the young
spendthrift who seeing a swallow towards the end of winter assumed that
spring had come and sold his cloak to*

get money for summer festivities, only to
have the frost return.

SWAN(S)

1 And now this pale swan in her watery
nest
Begins the sad dirge of her certain
ending.
[Shakespeare: *The Rape of Lucrece*]

2 All the water in the ocean
Can never turn the swan's black legs
to white,
Although she lave them hourly in
the flood.
[Shakespeare: *Titus Andronicus* IV.ii.]

3 As I have seen a swan
With bootless labour swim against
the tide
And spend her strength with over-
matching waves.
[Shakespeare: *III Henry VI* I.iv.]

4 I am the cygnet to this pale faint
swan,
Who chants a doleful hymn to his
own death;
And, from the organ-pipe of frailty,
sings
His soul and body to their lasting
rest.
[Shakespeare: *King John* V.vii.]
cygnet = *a young swan*

5 The swan's down-feather,
That stands upon the swell at full of
tide,
And neither way inclines.
[Shakespeare: *Antony and Cleopatra*
III.ii.]

6 Such as ne'er saw swans
May think crows beautiful.
[Massinger: *Great Duke of Florence* III]

7 The cock swan holdeth himself to one
female only, and for this cause nature
hath conferred on him a gift before all
others; that is, to die so joyfully, that
he sings sweetly when he dies. (Sir Edward Coke: Decision, *The Case of Swans*,
1600]

8 The swan, with arched neck
Between her white wings mantling
proudly, rows
Her state with oary feet.
[John Milton: *Paradise Lost* VII.438-440]

9 Thus on Meander's flowery margin
lies
Th' expiring swan, and as he sings

he dies.
[Alexander Pope: *The Rape of the Lock*
V]
*It was believed for centuries that the
swan, normally mute, sang melodiously
just before death. The idea had appealed
strongly to poets who may have seen in
it the comforting assurance that a rival's
success might presage his death and ultimate hope even for themselves.*

10 Let . . .
The swan on still St. Mary's lake
Float double, swan and shadow!
[Wordsworth: *Yarrow Unvisited*]

11 The woods decay, the woods decay
and fall,
The vapours weep their burthen to
the ground,
Man comes and tills the field and lies
beneath,
And after many a summer dies the
swan.
[Tennyson: *Tithonus*]
*Swans were thought to live to a very
great age. But the poetry of the line
rests on its sibilant alliteration that gives
it a moving splendor like the motion of
a swan. All of the grace, the dignity, the
beauty and the thick-coming poetical
associations of the word* swan *add to the
effect. Aldous Huxley, who borrowed
part of the line for the title of one of his
own books, observed that the line loses
everything if "duck" is substituted for
"swan."*

12 Like some full-breasted swan
That, fluting a wild carol ere her
death,
Ruffles her pure cold plume, and
takes the flood
With swarthy webs.
[Tennyson: *The Passing of Arthur*]

SWAP

13 It is not best to swap horses while
crossing the river. [Abraham Lincoln:
reply to delegation from National Union
League, June 9, 1864]

SWEARING

14 Hir gretteste ooth was but by sëynt
Loy. [Chaucer: Prologue to *The Canter-
bury Tales*]
*Chaucer is describing the Nun, the
Prioress. In any present-day description*

of a nun one would hardly feel called on to comment on the reserve and delicacy of her swearing—for Saint Loy (St. Eligius) was a very gentle saint.

But in Chaucer's day everybody swore. In fact, inquisitors' manuals listed not swearing as an indication of heresy! Distinguished people had their personal oaths, as popular musicians today on radio and TV have a theme song with which they identify themselves. William the Conqueror swore "by the Splendor of God." King John swore "by God's teeth," Henry I "by God's death," Edward I in a splendid and mystical oath of "before God and the Swans." Queen Elizabeth, out of filial piety, used her father's oath—"by God's body." Henry VI did not swear. He was an exceedingly meek man and under intolerable pressure would say "Forsoothe and forsoothe." But he was a lunatic.

1 Great swering is a thing abhominable,
  And false swering is yet more reprevable.
[Chaucer: *The Pardoner's Tale*]

2 When I swear after my own fashion, it is only by God, the directest of all oaths. [Montaigne: *Essays* III.v.]

3 Swear me, Kate, like a lady as thou art,
  A good mouth-filling oath, and leave "in sooth,"
  And such protest of pepper-gingerbread
  To velvet-guards and Sunday-citizens.
[Shakespeare: *I Henry IV* III.i.]
Hotspur, a feudal noble, objects (humorously) to his wife, Lady Percy, swearing like a London middle-class citizen. The citizens were largely puritans and objected strongly to swearing—or at least to the old-fashioned oaths. They had their substitute oaths—"in sooth," "as true as day," and so on—which, as he says, are just as much oaths, really, but offer very feeble security. The modern equivalents are "gosh," "darn," "Gee!" and the like.

"Velvet-guards" refers to velvet trimmings or facings, a "simpering fashion" which was popular with the citizens in their Sunday-go-to-meeting clothes. An aristocrat would have scorned the idea

of special attire for Sunday.

4 When a gentleman is disposed to swear, it is not for any standers-by to curtail his oaths. [Shakespeare: *Cymbeline* II.i.]

5 A footman may swear, but he cannot swear like a lord. He can swear as often, but can he swear with equal delicacy, propriety and judgment? [Jonathan Swift: Introduction to *Polite Conversation*]

6 Damn braces. Bless relaxes. [William Blake: *Proverbs of Hell*]

7 If you swear till you are black in the face, I shan't believe you. [Fanny Burney: *Evelina* II.xxiii.]

8 But the Deacon swore (as Deacons do,
  With an "I dew vum," or an "I tell yeou.")
[O. W. Holmes: *The Deacon's Masterpiece*]

9 Though "Bother it" I may
  Occasionally say,
  I never never use a big, big D.
[W. S. Gilbert: *H.M.S. Pinafore* I]

10 Stealthily, like a parson's damn. [Thomas Hardy: *The Hand of Ethelberta* XXVI]

11 Take not God's name in vain; select
  A time when it will have effect.
[Ambrose Bierce: *The Devil's Dictionary*]

SWEAR-WORD

12 A swear-word in a rustic slum
  A simple swear-word is to some,
  To Masefield something more.
[Max Beerbohm: *Fifty Caricatures* (1913)]
Max's lines served as a caption to a cartoon. He is probably alluding to such lines as those in Masefield's The Everlasting Mercy:
  "I'm climber Joe who climbed the spire!"
  "You're bloody Joe, the bloody liar!"
He is parodying a famous passage from Wordsworth's Peter Bell, in which Wordsworth says of the insensitive Peter:
  A primrose by a river's brim
  A yellow primrose was to him,
  And it was nothing more.

SWEAT

13 In the sweat of thy face shalt thou

eat bread. [Genesis 3:19]

1 A cold sweat bedewed all my limbs.
[Vergil: *Aeneid* III]

2   Falstaff sweats to death,
And lards the lean earth as he walks
along.
[Shakespeare: *I Henry IV* II.ii.]

SWEET(NESS)

3 Sweeter also than honey and the
honeycomb. [Psalms: 19:10]

4 Sweet things quickly bring satiety.
[Macrobius: *Saturnalia* VII.vii.]

5 Take the sweet with the sour. [John
Heywood: *Proverbs* (1546)]

6 Sweet is the rose, but grows upon a
briar;
Sweet is the juniper, but sharp his
bough;
Sweet is the eglantine, but pricketh
near;
Sweet is the firbloom, but his
branches rough;
Sweet is the cypress, but his rind is
tough;
Sweet is the nut, but bitter is his pill;
Sweet is the broom-flower, but yet
sour enough;
And sweet is moly, but his root is ill.
So every sweet with sour is tempered
still.
[Edmund Spenser: *Amoretti* XXVI]

7 Sweets grown common lose their dear
delight.
[Shakespeare: *Sonnets* CII]
This thought recurs often enough in
Shakespeare's plays to suggest that it
had some personal value to him beyond
its immediate use in the speech and ac-
tion in which he employs it.

8 The sweets we wish for turn to
loathed sours
Even in the moment that we call
them ours.
[Shakespeare: *The Rape of Lucrece*]

9 Things sweet to taste prove in digestion sour.
[Shakespeare: *Richard II* I.iii.]

10 Speak sweetly, man, although thy
looks be sour.
[Shakespeare: *Richard II* III.ii.]

11   The sweetest honey
Is loathsome in his own deliciousness
And in the taste confounds the appe-
tite.
[Shakespeare: *Romeo and Juliet* II.vi.]

12 They surfeited with honey and began
To loathe the taste of sweetness,
whereof a little
More than a little is by much too
much.
[Shakespeare: *I Henry IV* III.ii.]

13 A surfeit of the sweetest things
The deepest loathing to the stomach
brings.
[Shakespeare: *A Midsummer Night's*
Dream II.ii.]

14 The bitter past, more welcome is the
sweet.
[Shakespeare: *All's Well That Ends Well*
V.iii.]

15 Sweets to the sweet: farewell.
[Shakespeare: *Hamlet* V.i.]

16 The two noblest things, which are
sweetness and light. [Jonathan Swift:
Preface to *The Battle of the Books*]

17 The sweetest thing that ever grew
Beside a human door!
[Wordsworth: *Lucy Gray*]

18 The little sweet doth kill much bitterness.
[Keats: *Isabella, or The Pot of Basil*]

19 Ah that such sweet things should be
fleet,
Such fleet things sweet!
[Swinburne: *Félise*]

SWORD

20 All they that take the sword shall
perish with the sword. [Matthew 26:52]

21 Men are as the time is: to be tender-
minded
Does not become a sword.
[Shakespeare: *King Lear* V.iii.]

22 I have seen the day, with my good
biting falchion
I would have made them skip.
[Shakespeare: *King Lear* V.iii.]

23 The arbitrement of swords.
[Shakespeare: *Cymbeline* I.iv.]

24 One sword keeps another in the
sheath. [George Herbert: *Jacula Pruden-*
tum]

25   High in front advanced,
The brandished sword of God be-
fore them blazed,
Fierce as a comet.
[John Milton: *Paradise Lost* XII.632-634]

1 My good blade carves the casques of
men,
My tough lance thrusteth sure.
[Tennyson: *Sir Galahad*]

SWORN
2 My tongue hath sworn, but not my
mind. [Euripides: *Hippolytus*]

SYLVIA
3 Who is Sylvia? what is she?
That all our swains commend her?
Holy, fair, and wise is she;
The heavens such grace did lend
her.
[Shakespeare: *The Two Gentlemen of
Verona* IV.ii.]

SYMBOL
4 In a Symbol there is concealment and
yet revelation: here therefore, by Silence
and by Speech acting together, comes a
double significance. [Thomas Carlyle:
Sartor Resartus III.iii.]

SYMPATHY
5 Our sympathy is cold to the relation
of distant misery. [Edward Gibbon: *The
Decline and Fall of the Roman Empire*
XLIX]

SYSTEM(S)
6 The most ingenious method of becoming foolish is by a system. [Anthony
Ashley Cooper, Earl of Shaftesbury]
7 Our little systems have their day;
They have their day and cease to
be:
They are but broken lights of thee,
And thou, O Lord, art more than
they.
[Tennyson: *In Memoriam* I]

T

TACITURNITY
1 He that hath knowledge spareth his words. [Proverbs 17:9]
2 Blessed is the man who, having nothing to say, abstains from giving us wordy evidence of the fact. [George Eliot: *Theophrastus Such* IV]

TACT
3 'Tis ill talking of halters in the house of a man that was hanged. [Cervantes: *Don Quixote* I.iii.2]
4 Mention not a halter in the house of him that was hanged. [George Herbert: *Jacula Prudentum* (1640)]
   The proverb was old by Herbert's time. It is found in almost every European language. The Babylonian Talmud *has a stronger version, stating that if there has been a hanging in the family, do not say in that house, "Hang up this fish."*

TADPOLE
5 When you were a tadpole and I was a fish in the Palaeozoic time
   And side by side in the sluggish tide, we sprawled in the ooze and slime.
[Langdon Smith: *Evolution*]

TAKEN
6 One shall be taken, and the other left. [Matthew 24:40]

TALE(S)
7 We spend our years as a tale that is told. [Psalms 90:9]
8 This is a long preamble of a tale. [Chaucer: Prologue to *The Wife of Bath's Tale*]
9 For though myself be a ful vicious man,
   A moral tale yet I yow telle can.
[Chaucer: Prologue to *The Pardoner's Tale*]
10 A tale which holdeth children from play, and old men from the chimney corner. [Sir Philip Sidney: *Apologie for Poetrie*]
11 As tedious as a twice-told tale. [Shakespeare: *King John* III.iv.]
12 An honest tale speeds best being plainly told. [Shakespeare: *Richard III* IV.iv.]
13 Thereby hangs a tale. [Shakespeare: *The Taming of the Shrew* IV.i.]
14 I could a tale unfold whose lightest word
   Would harrow up thy soul.
[Shakespeare: *Hamlet* I.v.]
15 I will a round unvarnished tale deliver
   Of my whole course of love.
[Shakespeare: *Othello* I.iii.]
16 Mar a curious tale in telling it. [Shakespeare: *King Lear* I.iv.]
17 A sad tale's best for winter. [Shakespeare: *The Winter's Tale* II.i.]
18 A tale should be judicious, clear, succinct;
   The language plain, and incidents well link'd;
   Tell not as new what every body knows;
   And, new or old, still hasten to a close.
[William Cowper: *Conversation*]
19 O reader! had you in your mind
   Such stores as silent thought can bring,
   O gentle Reader! you would find
   A tale in every thing.
[Wordsworth: *Simon Lee*]
20 'Tis hard to venture where our betters fail,
   Or lend fresh interest to a twice-told tale.
[Byron: *Hints from Horace*]
21 Tell me the tales that to me were so dear,
   Long, long ago, long, long ago.
[Thomas Haynes Bayly: *Long, Long Ago*]

TALEBEARER
22 Where no wood is, there the fire goeth out: so where there is no talebearer, the strife ceaseth. [Proverbs 26:20]
23 He that repeateth a matter separateth very friends. [Proverbs 17:9]

Very *here means "true," as in "this is the very Christ"* (*John 7:26*).

TALENT(S)

1 Unto one he gave five talents, to another two, and to another one; to every man according to his several ability. [Matthew 25:15]
several = *individual*
> *A talent was a weight of silver or gold, hence a sum of money. The modern meaning of talent, a high degree of skill or ability, derives from the parable of the talents.*

2 It's a great talent to be able to conceal one's talents. [La Rochefoucauld: *Maxims*]

3 That one talent which is death to hide.
[John Milton: *On His Blindness*]

4 And sure the Eternal Master found
The single talent well employed.
[Samuel Johnson: *On the Death of Mr. Levett*]
See OFFICIOUS

5 Genius must have talent as its complement and implement. [Coleridge: *Table Talk*]

6 Every natural power exhilarates; a true talent delights the possessor first. [Emerson: *The Scholar*]

7 In this world people have to pay an extortionate price for any exceptional gift whatever. [Willa Cather: *The Old Beauty and Others* IV]

8 There is no substitute for talent. Industry and all the virtues are of no avail. [Aldous Huxley: *Point Counter Point* XIII]

9 I think this is the most extraordinary collection of talent, of human knowledge, that has ever been gathered together at the White House—with the possible exception of when Thomas Jefferson dined alone. [John F. Kennedy, at a dinner in the White House for the American Nobel Prize winners, April 29, 1962]
> *Conspicuously absent from this remarkable gathering was William Faulkner who was at Richmond, Virginia. Faulkner said that sixty miles was a very long distance to go for a meal.*

TALK(ING)

10 Talkative people say many things in company which they deplore when alone. [Antonio de Guevara: *Marco Aurelio y Faustina* II]

11 The honorablest part of talk is to give the occasion; and again to moderate and pass to somewhat else; for then a man leads the dance. [Francis **Bacon**: *Of Discourse*]

12 Your fair discourse hath been as sugar,
Making the hard way sweet and delectable.
[Shakespeare: *Richard II* II.iii.]

13 A gentleman, nurse, that loves to hear himself talk, and will speak more in a minute than he will stand to in a month. [Shakespeare: *Romeo and Juliet* II.iv.]

14 A good old man, sir; he will be talking.
[Shakespeare: *Much Ado About Nothing* III.v.]

15 Talk thy tongue weary: speak.
[Shakespeare: *Cymbeline* III.iv.]

16 Talking is a disease of age. [Ben Jonson: *Explorata*, "Homeri Ulysses"]
> *The volubility of the aged, their last substitute for every other form of calling attention to themselves, has often been noted. Pope speaks of "narrative old age," and Goldsmith of "talking age."*

17 It would talk; Lord, how it talked!
[Beaumont and Fletcher: *The Scornful Lady* IV.i.]

18 We know well enough that we should not talk of our wives, but we seem not to know that we should talk still less of ourselves. [La Rochefoucauld: *Maxims*]

19 Then he will talk—good gods! how he will talk!
[Nathaniel Lee: *The Rival Queens, or, The Death of Alexander the Great* I.iii.]

20 He was not an agreeable companion, for he always talked for fame. A man who does so never can be pleasing. The man who talks to unburden his mind is the man to delight you. [Samuel Johnson: in Boswell's *Life*, April 7, 1778]

21 So much they talked, so very little said.
[Charles Churchill: *The Rosciad*]

22 We talk little, if we do not talk about ourselves. [William Hazlitt: *Characteristics*]

1 An American cannot converse, but he can discuss, and his talk falls into a dissertation. He speaks to you as if he was addressing a meeting. [Alexis de Tocqueville: *Democracy in America* I.xiv.]
> *Queen Victoria complained that Mr. Gladstone addressed her in the same manner.*

2 The man that often speaks, but never talks.
[O. W. Holmes: *The Banker's Secret*]

3 Talking is like playing on the harp; there is as much in laying the hands on the strings to stop their vibration as in twanging them to bring out their music. [Oliver Wendell Holmes: *The Autocrat of the Breakfast Table* I]

4 All natural talk is a festival of ostentation; . . . each accepts and fans the vanity of the other. [Robert Louis Stevenson: *Memories and Portraits*, "Talk and Talkers"]

5 Though I'm anything but clever,
I could talk like that for ever.
[W. S. Gilbert: *H. M. S. Pinafore* II]

6 A gossip is one who talks to you about others; a bore is one who talks to you about himself; a brilliant conversationalist is one who talks to you about yourself. [Lisa Kirk, quoted in the *New York Journal-American,* March 9, 1954]

7 The four-letter word for psychotherapy is Talk. [Eric Hodgins: *Episode*]

TALKER

8 The most fluent talkers or most plausible reasoners are not always the justest thinkers. [William Hazlitt: *On Prejudice*]

9 A good talker, even more than a good orator, implies a good audience. [Leslie Stephen: *Life of Samuel Johnson* III]

TAR-BABY

10 Tar-Baby ain't sayin' nuthin', en Brer Fox, he lay low. [Joel Chandler Harris: *Uncle Remus* II]

TARDY

11 Five minutes! Zounds! I have been five minutes too late all my life-time! [Hannah Cowley: *The Belle's Stratagem* I.i.]

TARN

12 It was down by the dank tarn of
Auber,
In the ghoul-haunted woodland of
Weir.
[Edgar Allan Poe: *Ulalume*]

TARTNESS

13 The tartness of his face sours ripe grapes.
[Shakespeare: *Coriolanus* V.iv.]

TASTE

14 There is no disputing about taste. (*De gustibus non est disputandum.*) [Latin proverb]

15 Every man as he loveth, quoth the good man when he kissed the cow. [John Heywood: *Proverbs* (1546)]

16 At table, I prefer the witty before the grave; in bed, beauty before goodness; and in common discourse, eloquence, whether or no there be sincerity. [Montaigne: *Essays* I]

17 The distasted impute wallowishness unto wine; the healthy, good taste: and the thirsty, briskness, relish and delicacy. [Montaigne: *Essays* II.xii.]
> *wallowishness = insipidity, also nauseousness from being oversweet*

18 There is such a thing as a general revolution which changes the taste of men as it changes the fortunes of the world. [La Rochefoucauld: *Maxims*]

19 Every one as they like, as the woman said when she kissed her cow. [An interpolation of what was, apparently, a proverbial saying in England and Scotland, into his translation of Rabelais (V.xxix.) by Peter Motteux (1693)]
> *In 1738 Swift included it in his* Polite Conversation, *which indicates it was already worn out.*

20 You had no taste when you married me. [Richard Brinsley Sheridan: *The School for Scandal* I.ii.]

21 Every great and original writer, in proportion as he is great and original, must himself create the taste by which he is to be relished. [Wordsworth: Preface to *Lyrical Ballads*]

22 Now, who shall arbitrate?
Ten men love what I hate,
Shun what I follow, slight what I receive.

[Robert Browning: *Rabbi Ben Ezra*]
1 Taste is the only morality. . . . Tell me what you like, and I'll tell you what you are. [John Ruskin: *The Crown of Wild Olive* II]
2 You can't get high aestnetic tastes, like trousers, ready made. [W. S. Gilbert: *Patience* II]
3 A man of great common sense and good taste, meaning thereby a man without originality or moral courage. [G. B. Shaw: Notes to *Caesar and Cleopatra*.]

TAVERN(S)
4 He knew the tavernes wel in every toun.
[Chaucer: Prologue to *The Canterbury Tales*]
5 There is nothing which has been contrived by man by which so much happiness is produced as by a good tavern or inn. [Samuel Johnson: in Boswell's *Life,* March 21, 1776]
6 I have heard him assert, that a tavern chair was the throne of human felicity. [Samuel Johnson: in Sir John Hawkins' *Life of Johnson*]
7 There is a tavern in the town,
And there my true love sits him down,
And drinks his wine 'mid laughter free,
And never, never thinks of me.
Fare thee well, for I must leave thee,
Do not let this parting grieve thee,
And remember that the best of friends must part.
Adieu, adieu, kind friends, adieu, adieu,
I can no longer stay with you.
I'll hang my harp on a weeping willow-tree,
And may the world go well with thee.
[Anon.: *There is a Tavern in the Town*]

TAXATION
8 The art of taxation consists in so plucking the goose as to obtain the largest amount of feathers with the least possible amount of hissing. [Attr. J. B. Colbert (1619-1683), Louis XIV's Controller-General of Finance]

By modern standards, the taxes were onerous and the hissing was warranted, if only because almost all who had money —the Church and the Nobles—were exempted from taxation. Montaigne (Essays I.xv.) says that the Lord of Franget, being convicted of cowardice and dereliction of his military duty, was degraded of all nobility and he and his heirs "declared villains and clowns, taxable and incapable to bear arms." To be compelled to pay taxes when others did not pay them and at the same time to be despised for paying them would seem to justify a certain amount of hissing. In 1789, of course, the hissing rose to a scream.
9 Taxation without representation is tyranny. [Attr. James Otis: in an argument before the Superior Court of Massachusetts, 1761]
The exact words that Otis used are unknown. The phrase, on the authority of John Adams, first appeared fifty years later in Tudor's Life of James Otis.
The famous sentiment was carried a step further by an indignant Massachusetts matron who protested an increase in her real-estate tax by picketing with a banner that read "Taxation without permission is tyranny."

TAXED
10 There went out a decree from Caesar Augustus that all the world should be taxed. [Luke 2:1]

TAX(ES)
11 What reason is there that he which laboreth much, and, sparing the fruits of his labor, consumeth little, should be more charged than he that, living idly, getteth little and spendeth all he gets, seeing the one hath no more protection from the commonwealth than the other? [Thomas Hobbes: *Leviathan* II]
12 As certain as death and taxes. [Daniel Defoe: *History of the Devil* II.vi.]
13 In constitutional states liberty is compensation for the heavy taxation; in despotic states the equivalent of liberty is light taxes. [Montesquieu: *The Spirit of the Laws* XIII]
14 In this world nothing is certain but

death and taxes. [Benjamin Franklin: letter to M. Leroy, 1789]

1 When plunder bears the name of impost, fortitude is intimidated and wisdom confounded: resistance shrinks from an alliance with rebellion, and the villain remains secure in the robes of the magistrate. [Samuel Johnson: *The Rambler* No. 148]

2 The power to tax involves the power to destroy. [Chief Justice John Marshall: Decision in *McCulloch vs. Maryland,* March 6, 1819]

3 Taxes are what we pay for civilized society. [O. W. Holmes, Jr.: *Compañia de Tabacos v. Collector, 275 U. S. 87, 100*]

4 There is one difference between a tax collector and a taxidermist—the taxidermist leaves the hide. [Mortimer Caplan, Director of the Bureau of Internal Revenue, *Time,* Feb. 1, 1963]

TEA

5 Tea! thou soft, thou sober, sage, and venerable liquid.
[Colley Cibber: *The Lady's Last Stake* I.i.]

6 The cups that cheer but not inebriate.

[William Cowper: *The Task* IV]
Cowper is referring to tea. However, he seems to be echoing a comment of Bishop George Berkeley's (1685-1753), in his Siris, *on Tarwater, a liquid "of a nature so mild and benign . . . as to warm without heating, to cheer but not inebriate."*

7 Free yourselves from the slavery of tea and coffee and other slopkettle. [William Cobbett: *Advice to Young Men* I]

TEACH(ING)

8 Most commonly the authority of them that teach hinders them that would learn. [Cicero: *De natura deorum,* quoted in Montaigne's *Essays* I.xxv. (trans. John Florio)]

9 While we teach, we learn. [Seneca: *Epistolae* VII.viii.]

10 I can easier teach twenty what were good to be done, than be one of the twenty to follow my own teaching. [Shakespeare: *The Merchant of Venice* I.ii.]

11 The vanity of teaching often tempteth a man to forget he is a blockhead. [George Savile, Marquis of Halifax, *Maxims*]

12 There taught us how to live; and
(O, too high
The price for knowledge!) taught us how to die.
[Thomas Tickell: *On the Death of Mr. Addison*]

13 Let such teach others who themselves excel,
And censure freely who have written well.
[Alexander Pope: *An Essay on Criticism* I]

14 Men must be taught as if you taught them not,
And things unknown proposed as things forgot.
[Alexander Pope: *An Essay on Criticism* III]

15 Delightful task! to rear the tender thought,
To teach the young idea how to shoot.
[James Thomson (1700-1748): *The Seasons,* "Spring"]

16 It is not often that any man can have so much knowledge of another as is necessary to make instruction useful. [Samuel Johnson: *The Rambler* No. 87]

17 There is no other method of teaching that of which anyone is ignorant but by means of something already known. [Samuel Johnson: *The Idler* No. 34]

18 Nobody can be taught faster than he can learn. . . . Every man that has ever undertaken to instruct others can tell what slow advances he has been able to make, and how much patience it requires to recall vagrant inattention, to stimulate sluggish indifference, and to rectify absurd misapprehension. [Samuel Johnson: *Life of Milton*]

19 One impulse from a vernal wood
May teach you more of man,
Of moral evil and of good,
Than all the sages can.
[Wordsworth: *The Tables Turned*]

20 Everybody who is incapable of learning has taken to teaching. [Oscar Wilde: *The Decay of Lying*]

21 Nothing that is worth knowing can

be taught. [Oscar Wilde: *The Critic as Artist*]

TEACHER

1 Brought up in this city at the feet of Gamaliel. [Acts 22:3]

2 Gladly wolde he lerne, and gladly teche.
[Chaucer: Prologue to *The Canterbury Tales*]
> The reference is to the unworldly Clerk of Oxenford "That un-to logik hadde longe y-go."

3 Whoe'er excels in what we prize,
Appears a hero in our eyes;
Each girl, when pleased with what is taught,
Will have the teacher in her thought.

. . . .

A blockhead with melodious voice,
In boarding-schools may have his choice.
[Jonathan Swift: *Cadenus and Vanessa*]

4 Charming women can true converts make,
We love the precepts for the teacher's sake.
[George Farquhar: *A Constant Couple* V.iii.]

5 Full well they laughed, with counterfeited glee,
At all his jokes, for many a joke had he;
Full well the busy whisper, circling round,
Convey'd the dismal tidings when he frown'd.
[Oliver Goldsmith: *The Deserted Village*]

6 We are not quite at our ease in the presence of a schoolmaster because we are conscious that he is not quite at his ease in ours. He is awkward, and out of place, in the society of his equals. He comes like Gulliver from among his little people, and he cannot fit the stature of his understanding to yours. [Charles Lamb: *The Old and the New Schoolmaster*]

7 The true teacher defends his pupils against his own personal influence. [A. Bronson Alcott: *Orphic Sayings*]
> This is one of the great pedagogic principles, though not one teacher out of

fifty has the dimmest awareness of it.

8 A teacher affects eternity; he can never tell where his influence stops. [Henry Adams: *The Education of Henry Adams*]

9 He who can, does. He who cannot, teaches. [G. B. Shaw: *Maxims for Revolutionists* (1903)]
> The common inference from this much-quoted statement, that the teacher is a sort of failure in the world of action, greatly comforts anti-intellectuals. But almost to a man successful men of action (all of whom think they could be teachers if they chose to turn aside to it) have proved failures as teachers.

10 The best teacher, until one comes to adult pupils, is not the one who knows most, but the one who is most capable of reducing knowledge to that simple compound of the obvious and the wonderful which slips into the infantile comprehension. A man of high intelligence, perhaps, may accomplish the thing by a conscious intellectual feat. But it is vastly easier to the man (or woman) whose habits of mind are naturally on the plane of a child's. The best teacher of children, in brief, is one who is essentially childlike. [H. L. Mencken: in the *New York Evening Mail*, Jan. 23, 1918]

11 The truth is that the average schoolmaster, on all the lower levels, is and always must be . . . next door to an idiot, for how can one imagine an intelligent man engaging in so puerile an avocation? [H. L. Mencken: in the *New York Evening Mail*, Jan. 23, 1918]

12 It is the mission of the pedagogue, not to make his pupils think, but to make them think *right,* and the more nearly his own mind pulsates with the great ebbs and flows of popular delusion and emotion, the more admirably he performs his function. He may be an ass, but that is surely no demerit in a man paid to make asses of his customers. [H. L. Mencken: in the Baltimore *Evening Sun*, March 12, 1923]

TEAR(S)

13 A time to weep and a time to laugh. [Ecclesiastes 3:4]

14 Hence these tears. (*Hinc illae la-*

crimae) [Terence: *Andria*]

1 With mine own tears I wash away my
balm,
With mine own hands I give away my
crown.
[Shakespeare: *Richard II* IV.i.]

2 If you have tears, prepare to shed
them now.
[Shakespeare: *Julius Caesar* III.ii.]

3 All my mother came into mine eyes
And gave me up to tears.
[Shakespeare: *Henry V* IV.vi.]

4 Like Niobe, all tears.
[Shakespeare: *Hamlet* I.ii.]

5 If that the earth could teem with
woman's tears,
Each drop she falls would prove a
crocodile.
[Shakespeare: *Othello* IV.i.]
*The reference is to the popular belief
that crocodiles wept to attract the helpful and tender-hearted whom they then
devoured.*

6 One, whose subdu'd eyes,
Albeit unused to the melting mood,
Drop tears as fast as the Arabian trees
Their medicinal gum.
[Shakespeare: *Othello* V.ii.]

7 Let not women's weapons, water-
drops,
Stain my man's cheeks!
[Shakespeare: *King Lear* II.iv.]

8 The tears live in an onion that
should water this sorrow.
[Shakespeare: *Antony and Cleopatra* I.
ii.]
*That is, it's not a genuine sorrow and
hence does not deserve genuine tears.*

9 Thou knowst how drie a Cinder this
world is,
And learn'st thus much by our Anat-
omy,
That 'tis in vaine to dew, or mollifie
It with thy teares, or sweat, or blood.
[Donne: *First Anniversary*]
See also BLOOD

10 He must not float upon his watery
bier
Unwept, and welter to the parching
wind,
Without the meed of some melodious
tear.
[John Milton: *Lycidas*]

11 Thrice he assay'd, and thrice, in spite
of scorn,

Tears, such as angels weep, burst
forth.
[John Milton: *Paradise Lost* I.619-620]

12 Nothing is here for tears, nothing to
wail
Or knock the breast.
[John Milton: *Samson Agonistes*]

13 When the big lip and wat'ry eye
Tell me the rising storm is nigh.
[Matthew Prior: *The Lady's Looking
Glass*]

14 Yet tears to human suffering are due.
[Wordsworth: *Laodamia*]

15 None are so desolate but something
dear,
Dearer than self, possesses or possess'd
A thought, and claims the homage of
a tear.
[Byron: *Childe Harold* II.xxiv.]

16 What lost a world, and bade a hero
fly?
The timid tear in Cleopatra's eye.
[Byron: *The Corsair* II.xv.]

17 Her tears fell with the dews at even;
Her tears fell ere the dews were dried.
[Tennyson: *Mariana*]

18 Why wilt thou ever scare me with
thy tears?
[Tennyson: *Tithonus*]

19 Tears, idle tears, I know not what
they mean,
Tears from the depths of some divine despair.
[Tennyson: *The Princess* IV]

20 "I weep for you," the Walrus said:
"I deeply sympathize."
With sobs and tears he sorted out
Those of the largest size,
Holding his pocket-handkerchief
Before his streaming eyes.
[Lewis Carroll: *Through the Looking-
Glass* IV, "The Walrus and the Car-
penter"]

21 In any really good subject one has
only to probe deep enough to come to
tears. [Edith Wharton: *The Writing of
Fiction*]

TEDIOUS

22 Life is as tedious as a twice-told tale
Vexing the dull ear of a drowsy man.
[Shakespeare: *King John* III.iv.]
*Alexander Pope's use of the first of these
two famous lines in his translation of*

Homer (*"What so tedious as a twice-told tale?"*—Odyssey *XII*) illustrates the difficulties of attributing a quotation. The casual reader coming on it in Pope would assume that it was either his or Homer's; whereas it is Shakespeare's.

Fitzgerald translates the passage: *"I do not hold with the tiresome repetition of a story."* T. E. Shaw has: *"It goes against my grain to repeat a tale already plainly told."* W. H. D. Rouse has: *"No one cares for a twice-told tale."*

1 O, he is as tedious as a tired horse, a railing wife;
Worse than a smoky house.
[Shakespeare: *I Henry IV* III.i.]

TELEOLOGY
2 Neither malt nor Milton can
Explain to God the ways of Man.
[Daniel G. Hoffman: *In Humbleness*]
An elaboration of A. E. Housman's:
Malt does more than Milton can
To justify God's ways to man.
—A Shropshire Lad LXII

TELEVISION
3 Chewing gum for the eyes. [John Mason Brown, in an interview with James B. Simpson, July 28, 1955 (quoted by Mr. Simpson in his *Contemporary Quotations*).]

TELLING
4 I am not arguing with you—I am telling you. [Whistler: *The Gentle Art of Making Enemies*]

TEMPER
5 A hot temper leaps o'er a cold decree. [Shakespeare: *The Merchant of Venice* I.ii.]
6 It's my rule never to lose me temper till it would be detrimental to keep it. [Sean O'Casey: *The Plough and the Stars*]

TEMPERAMENTS
7 To a red man read thy rede,
With a brown man break thy bread,
At a pale man draw thy knife,
From a black man keep thy wife.
[Robert Tofte: *Blazon of Jealousy* (1615)]
The red, or sanguine, man was thought

to be wise; hence you could ask his advice concerning your "rede," riddle, or problem. The brown man was peaceful, reliable: you could trust him. The pale man, the melancholy man, was envious and dangerous. The black man, the swarthy brunet, was lustful.

TEMPERANCE
8 Temperance is the noblest gift of the gods. [Euripides: *Medea*]
9 Temperance is the moderating of one's desires in obedience to reason. [Cicero: *De finibus* II]
10 *Auream mediocritatem.* ("the golden mean") [Horace: *Odes* II.x.]
11 Temperance is the greatest of all the virtues. [Plutarch: *Moralia*]
12 Tho' deep yet clear, tho' gentle yet not dull;
Strong without rage, without o'er-flowing full.
[Sir John Denham: *Cooper's Hill*]

TEMPERATE
13 We become temperate by abstaining from indulgence, and we are the better able to abstain from indulgence after we have become temperate. [Aristotle: *The Nicomachean Ethics* II]

TEMPEST
14 A tempest in a teapot. [Cicero: *De legibus* III.xvi.]
The Latin is fluctus in simpulo. *A simpulum was a small ladle used in sacrifices.*
A literal translation would be "a billow in a basin."
15 'Tis a fearful thing in winter
To be shattered in the blast,
And to hear the rattling trumpet
Thunder, "Cut away the mast!"
[James Thomas Fields: *Ballad of the Tempest*]

TEMPTATION
16 The woman whom thou gavest to be with me, she gave me of the tree, and I did eat. [Genesis 3:12]
Often—and not insignificantly—quoted as "the woman thou gavest me."
17 Lead us not into temptation. [Matthew 6:13]
18 Watch ye and pray, lest ye enter into temptation. The spirit truly is ready, but

the flesh is weak. [Mark 14:38]

1 Tempt not a desperate man.
[Shakespeare: *Romeo and Juliet* V.iii.]

2 We love to overlook the boundaries which we do not wish to pass. [Samuel Johnson: *The Rambler* No. 114]

3 Few can review the days of their youth without recollecting temptations which shame rather than virtue enabled them to resist. [Samuel Johnson: *The Rambler* No. 159]

4 There are several good protections against temptation, but the surest is cowardice. [Mark Twain: *Pudd'nhead Wilson's New Calendar*]

5 Do you really think that it is weakness that yields to temptation? I tell you that there are terrible temptations which it requires strength, strength and courage, to yield to. [Oscar Wilde: *An Ideal Husband* II]

6 I can resist everything except temptation. [Oscar Wilde: *Lady Windermere's Fan* I]

7 The only way to get rid of a temptation is to yield to it. [Oscar Wilde: *The Picture of Dorian Gray* II]

8 Never resist temptation: prove all things: hold fast that which is good. [G. B. Shaw: *Maxims for Revolutionists*]

9 The last temptation is the greatest treason:
To do the right deed for the wrong reason.
[T. S. Eliot: *Murder in the Cathedral* I]

TEMPTING FATE

10 Who-so that buildeth his hous al of salwes,
And priketh his blinde hors over the falwes,
And suffreth his wyf to go seken halwes,
Is worthy to been hanged on the galwes.
[Chaucer: Prologue to *The Wife of Bath's Tale*]
salwes = *willow, willow withes;* priketh = *spurs;* falwes = *fallow ground;* go seken halwes = *make pilgrimages to far-off shrines;* galwes = *gallows*

TENACITY

11 For Witherington my heart was woe

That ever he slain should be:
For when both his legs were hewn in two
Yet he kneel'd and fought on his knee.
[Anon.: *Chevy Chase* II.i.]

TENDER-HEARTEDNESS

12 Billy, in one of his nice new sashes,
Fell in the fire and was burnt to ashes:
Now, although the room grows chilly,
I haven't the heart to poke poor Billy.
[Harry J. C. Graham: *Tender-Heartedness*]

TENDERNESS

13 Tenderness is the repose of passion.
[Joseph Joubert: *Pensées*]

TENNYSON

14 The bower we shrined to Tennyson,
Gentlemen,
Is roof-wrecked; damps there drip upon
Sagged seats, the creeper-nails are rust,
The spider is sole denizen:
Even she who voiced those rhymes is dust,
Gentlemen!
[Thomas Hardy: *An Ancient to Ancients*]

TENTING

15 We're tenting tonight on the old camp-ground,
Give us a song to cheer
Our weary hearts, a song of home
And friends we love so dear.
[Walter Kittredge: *Tenting on the Old Camp-ground*]

TERRIBLE

16 Terrible as an army with banners.
[Song of Solomon: 6:4-10]

TERROR

17 I could a tale unfold whose lightest word
Would harrow up thy soul, freeze thy young blood,
Make thy two eyes, like stars, start from their spheres,
Thy knotted and combined locks to part

And each particular hair to stand on
end,
Like quills upon the fretful porpen-
tine.
[Shakespeare: *Hamlet* I.v.]
*Hamlet's father's ghost is speaking to
Hamlet. That which would have such an
effect upon the prince is a description
of Purgatory—which, however, the ghost
is forbidden to divulge.*

    porpentine = *porcupine. This was
Shakespeare's regular spelling of the
word. He used it eight times. Few animals have had as much difficulty achieving a name in English as* Erethizon dor-
satum. *Among the variants were:* porken-
pik, porc de spyne, portepyne, porkpen,
porcupig *and* portpen.

1   I will do such things—
What they are yet I know not; but
they shall be
The terrors of the earth!
[Shakespeare: *King Lear* II.iv.]
A line from Sandys' translation of Ovid's
Metamorphoses *(appearing some ten
years after* King Lear) *seems an echo
of this passage:*
   *The deed I intend is great,
   But what, as yet, I know not.*

2 Her lips were red, her looks were free,
Her locks were yellow as gold:
Her skin was white as leprosy,
The Night-mare LIFE-IN-DEATH
              was she,
Who thicks man's blood with cold.
[Coleridge: *The Ancient Mariner* III]
3 I wants to make your flesh creep.
[Dickens: *The Pickwick Papers* VIII]

TEXAS
4 If I owned Hell and Texas, I'd rent
out Texas and live in Hell. [P. H. Sheridan: in a speech at Fort Clark, Texas
(1855)]

TEXT
5 There's a great text in Galatians,
   Once you trip on it, entails
   Twenty-nine distinct damnations,
   One sure, if another fails.
[Robert Browning: *Soliloquy of the
Spanish Cloister*]

THANKS
6 God, I thank thee, that I am not as
other men are. [Luke 18:11]
7 Thanks, the exchequer of the poor.
[Shakespeare: *Richard II* II.iii.]
8 Beggar that I am, I am even poor
             in thanks.
[Shakespeare: *Hamlet* II.ii.]

THANK YOU
9 Thank you for nothing. [Cervantes:
Don Quixote I.iii.1]

THE THEATER
10 As in a theatre, the eyes of men,
   After a well-graced actor leaves the
            stage,
   Are idly bent on him that enters next,
   Thinking his prattle to be tedious.
[Shakespeare: *Richard II* V.ii.]
11 Then to the well-trod stage anon,
   If Jonson's learned sock be on,
   Or sweetest Shakespeare, Fancy's
            child,
   Warble his native wood-notes wild.
[John Milton: *L'Allegro*]
sock = Latin soccus, *the light shoe, reach-
ing only to the ankle, worn by the comic
actors of Greece and Rome; hence a
trope of comedy itself. Tragedians wore
the buskin, reaching to the knee.*

12 It hath evermore been the notorious
badge of prostituted Strumpets and the
lewdest Harlots, to ramble abroad to
plays, to Playhouses; whither no honest,
chaste or sober Girls or Women, but only
branded Whores and infamous Adulter-
esses, did usually resort in ancient times.
[William Prynne: *Histrio-Mastix*]
*Unhappily for Prynne, Queen Henrietta
Maria had taken part in the performance
of a play at Court, and these lines were
construed as an aspersion on her Majesty.
He was sentenced (1634) to be branded,
have his ears cut off, heavily fined and
imprisoned for life. He bore his punishment with defiant courage and was released from prison, after eight years, by
the Long Parliament. Some compensation was made him for his sufferings.*

13 *Whereas* . . . the distracted state of
England . . . call(s) for all possible
means to appease and avert the wrath
of God . . . it is thought fit and ordered
by the Lords and Commons in this
Parliament assembled, that . . . public
stage-plays shall cease and be forborne.

[Ordinance of Parliament, September 2, 1642]

This Ordinance marked the end of the great Elizabethan and Jacobean theater. When plays were again permitted, under Charles II, in 1660, the theater was almost exclusively the plaything of the Court and the upper classes. In many respects it did not recover its vigor and popularity until the late 19th and early 20th century.

THEFT

1   O, theft most base,
That we have stol'n what we do
                              fear to keep!
[Shakespeare: *Troilus and Cressida* II. ii.]

THEOLOGIAN

2   He could raise scruples dark and nice,
And after solve 'em in a trice;
As if Divinity had catched
The itch, on purpose to be scratched.
[Samuel Butler (1612-1680): *Hudibras*]

THEOLOGY

3   The study of theology, as it stands in Christian churches, is the study of nothing; it is founded on nothing; it rests on no principles; it proceeds by no authorities; it has no data; it can demonstrate nothing; and it admits of no conclusion. [Thomas Paine: *The Age of Reason*]
4   Men are better than their theology. Their daily life gives it the lie. [Emerson: *Compensation*]
5   An effort to explain the unknowable by putting it into terms of the not worth knowing. [H. L. Mencken: *A Book of Burlesques*]

THEORY(IES)

6   The bookish theoric.
[Shakespeare: *Othello* I.i.]
7   "Let us work without theorizing," said Martin; " 'tis the only way to make life endurable." [Voltaire: *Candide* XXX]
8   Gray are all theories,
And green alone Life's golden tree.
[Goethe: *Faust* I.iv.]
9   A favorite theory is a possession for life. [William Hazlitt: *Characteristics*]
10   Throw theory into the fire; it only

spoils life. [Mikhail A. Bakunin: letters to his sisters, Nov. 4, 1842]
None the less, few men have done more theorizing than Bakunin or been the cause of more theorizing in others. He was active in founding the First International and was highly influential in the thought of Lenin. He is thought to have been the original of Prince Stavrogin in Dostoyevsky's The Possessed.

THEY

11   Have you heard of the terrible family They,
And the dreadful venomous things
                              They say?
[Ella Wheeler Wilcox: *They Say*]

THICK

12   Thurgh thikke and thurgh thenne.
[Chaucer: *The Reves Tale* 146]
Probably a proverbial shortening of "through thicket and thin wood."
13   As thick as three in a bed. [Sir Walter Scott: Introduction to *The Monastery*]

THIEF(VES)

14   Save a thief from the gallows and he will cut your throat. [William Camden: *Remains*]
15   A plague upon it when thieves cannot be true one to another!
[Shakespeare: *I Henry IV* II.ii.]
16   All men love to appropriate the belongings of others. It is a universal desire; only the manner of doing it differs. [Alain René Lesage: *Gil Blas* I.v.]
17   In this world, the big thief condemns the little thief. [Quevedo: *La Hora de Todos y la Fortuna con Seso* XXVIII]
The same thought is expressed by Shakespeare in King Lear *(IV.vi.), where Lear says that "the usurer hangs the cozener."*
18   Always set a thief to catch a thief; the greatest deer-stealers make the best park-keepers. [Thomas Fuller (1608-1661): *Church History of Britain* IV.iii.]
19   Set a thief to catch a thief. [Sir Robert Howard: *The Committee* I]
Referred to as "an old saying."

THINGS

20   How many things there are here that

I do not want! [Socrates: in Diogenes Laertius's *Socrates,* on seeing the display of the market place]

1 Things are in the saddle,
And ride mankind.

[Emerson: *Ode to W. H. Channing*]

THINK(ING)

2 In military affairs, "I didn't think of it" is a disgraceful phrase. [Scipio Africanus in *Valerius Maximus* VII.ii.]

3 To think is to live. [Cicero: *Tusculan Disputations* V]

4 There is nothing either good or bad,
but thinking makes it so.

[Shakespeare: *Hamlet* II.ii.]

5 You do unbend your noble strength,
to think
So brainsickly of things.

[Shakespeare: *Macbeth* II.ii.]

6 I think, but dare not speak.

[Shakespeare: *Macbeth* V.i.]

7 I think; therefore I am. (*Cogito, ergo sum*) [Descartes: *Discourse on Method*]
"*I think I think; therefore, I think I am.*"
—*Ambrose Bierce:* The Devil's Dictionary *(1906)*

8 Why should I disparage my parts by thinking what to say? None but dull rogues think. [William Congreve: *The Double-Dealer* IV.ii.]

9 Plain living and high thinking are no more. [Wordsworth: *Poems Dedicated to National Independence* I]

10 . . Man Thinking; him Nature solicits with all her placid, all her monitory pictures; him the past instructs; him the future invites. [Emerson: *The American Scholar*]

11 We think so because other people all
think so,
Or because—or because—after all we
do think so,
Or because we were told so, and
think we must think so,
Or because we once thought so, and
think we still think so,
Or because having thought so, we
think we *will* think so.

[Henry Sidgwick: *Memoir* II]

12 Freud regards dreaming as fiction that helps us to sleep; thinking we may regard as fiction that helps us to live. Man lives by imagination. [Havelock Ellis:

The Dance of Life]

13 "I am inclined to think—" said I [Dr. Watson]. "I should do so," Sherlock Holmes remarked, impatiently. [A. Conan Doyle: *The Valley of Fear*]

14 Oh, 'tis jesting, dancing, drinking
Spins the heavy world around.
If young hearts were not so clever,
Oh, they would be young for ever:
Think no more; 'tis only thinking
Lays lads underground.

[A. E. Housman: *A Shropshire Lad* XLIX]

15 But men at whiles are sober
And think by fits and starts,
And if they think they fasten
Their hands upon their hearts.

[A. E. Housman: *Last Poems* X]

16 As soon as you can say what you think and not what some other person has thought for you, you are on the way to being a remarkable man. [Sir James M. Barrie: *Tommy and Grizel*]

17 If you make people think they're thinking, they'll love you. If you really make them think, they'll hate you. [Don-(ald) Marquis: *The Sun Dial*]

18 This very remarkable man
Commends a most practical plan:
You can do what you want
If you don't think you can't,
So don't think you can't think you
can.

[Charles Inge: *On Monsieur Coué*]

19 The action of thinking may incidentally have other results; it may serve to amuse us, for example, and among *dilettanti* it is not rare to find those who have so perverted thought to the purposes of pleasure that it seems to vex them to think that the questions upon which they delight to exercise it may ever get finally settled; and a positive discovery which takes a favorite subject out of the arena of literary debate is met with ill-concealed dislike. [Charles S. Peirce: *How to Make Our Ideas Clear*]
See THOUGHT

THINKERS

20 Let me have men about me that are
fat;
Sleek-headed men, and such as sleep
o'nights.

Yond Cassius has a lean and hungry
       look;
He thinks too much: such men are
       dangerous.
[Shakespeare: *Julius Caesar* I.ii.]

THIRST
1 The thirst that from the soul doth
       rise,
 Doth ask a drink divine;
But might I of Jove's nectar sup,
 I would not change for thine.
[Ben Jonson: *To Celia*]
2 I drank at every vine.
 The last was like the first.
I came upon no wine
 So wonderful as thirst.
[Edna St. Vincent Millay: *Feast*]

THIRTEEN
3 A baker's dozen. [Rabelais: *Works*
V.xxii.]
*The best explanation of "a baker's
dozen" for 13 is that retailers were formerly privileged by law to receive a 13th
loaf free every time they bought a dozen,
the extra loaf to be their profit. The
13th loaf was sometimes called "in
bread" or "vantage bread."*

 *It is also claimed that the term de-
rives from the baker's custom of throwing in an extra loaf with every dozen to
cover any possible shortage of weight.
But this is not as well supported by quotations as the other explanation.*

THIRTY
4   No man,
Till thirty, should perceive there's a
       plain woman.
[Byron: *Don Juan* XIII.iii.]

THIRTY-FIVE
5 Ladies, stock and tend your hive,
 Trifle not at thirty-five;
For howe'er we boast and strive,
 Life declines from thirty-five;
He that ever hopes to thrive
 Must begin by thirty-five.
[Samuel Johnson: to Hester Thrale on
 her thirty-fifth birthday (1776)]

THIRTY-THREE
6 Through life's road, so dim and dirty,
 I have dragged to three and thirty:

What have these years left to me?
Nothing, except thirty-three.
[Byron: *Diary*, Jan. 22, 1821]

THOREAU
7 This Concord Pan. [A. Bronson Alcott: *Thoreau*]
8 The bachelor of thought and Nature.
[Emerson: *Thoreau*]
9 I love Henry, but I cannot like him.
[Emerson: *Lectures and Biographical
Sketches,* "Thoreau"]
*Emerson is quoting a friend of Thoreau's
who added that he would as soon think
of taking the arm of an elm-tree as
Thoreau's arm.*

 *One is reminded of Oscar Wilde's
statement that George Bernard Shaw had
no enemies and his friends didn't like
him.*

THORN(S)
10 They shall be as thorns in your sides.
[Judges 2:3]
11 A thorn in the flesh. [II Corinthians
12:7]
12 I fall upon the thorns of life;
 I bleed.
[Shelley: *Ode to the West Wind*]

THOU
13 Thou viper—for I *thou* thee, thou
traitor! [Sir Edward Coke to Sir Walter
Raleigh, on Raleigh's indictment for
high treason, Nov. 17, 1603 (from *The
Life of Sir Walter Raleigh,* 1677)]
*Although Raleigh was not executed until
1618 and the* Life *not published until
almost 60 years after that, it alleges that
the evidence was "exactly and faithfully
taken." Linguists are particularly interested in this passage because it shows
that the second person singular, at least
under these circumstances, was deliberately insulting. Raleigh answered: "It
becometh not a man of quality and virtue to call me so."*

THOUGHT(S)
14 What he greatly thought, he nobly
dared. [Homer: *Odyssey* II (trans. Pope)]
15 Which of you by taking thought can
add one cubit unto his stature? [Mat-
thew 6:27]
*The cubit was the measure of a man's
arm from the elbow to the end of the*

middle finger. The ancient Hebrew cubit was about 17½ inches; the Roman cubit was about 21 inches.
See also: Luke 12:25.

1 High erected thoughts seated in the heart of courtesy.
[Sir Philip Sidney: *The Arcadia* I.ii.]

2 But thought's the slave of life, and life time's fool.
[Shakespeare: *I Henry IV* V.iv.]

3 Thou hid'st a thousand daggers in thy thoughts,
Which thou hast whetted on thy stony heart.
[Shakespeare: *II Henry IV* IV.v.]

4 Give thy thoughts no tongue,
Nor any unproportion'd thought his act.
[Shakespeare: *Hamlet* I.iii.]

5 And thus the native hue of resolution
Is sicklied o'er with the pale cast of thought.
[Shakespeare: *Hamlet* III.i.]

6 On the sudden
A Roman thought hath struck him.
[Shakespeare: *Antony and Cleopatra* I.ii.]

7 I do begin to have bloody thoughts.
[Shakespeare: *The Tempest* IV.i.]

8 For who would lose,
Though full of pain, this intellectual being,
Those thoughts that wander through eternity,
To perish rather, swallowed up and lost
In the wide womb of uncreated night,
Devoid of sense and motion?
[John Milton: *Paradise Lost* II.146-151]

9 His thoughts were low;
To vice industrious, but to nobler deeds
Timorous and slothful.
[John Milton: *Paradise Lost* II.115-117]

10 There is no less wit nor invention in applying rightly a thought one finds in a book than in being the first author of that thought. [Pierre Bayle: *Works* II]

11 A penny for your thought. [Jonathan Swift: Introduction to *Polite Conversation*]

12 Perish that thought! [Colley Cibber: *Richard III* V]
Cibber's play is an adaptation of Shakespeare's Richard III. This much-quoted

phrase does not, however, occur in Shakespeare.

13 Great thoughts come from the heart.
[Vauvenargues: *Réflexions*]

14 When a thought is too weak to be expressed simply, it is a proof that it should be rejected. [Vauvenargues: *Réflexions*]

15 In that sweet mood when pleasant thoughts
Bring sad thoughts to the mind.
[Wordsworth: *Lines Written in Early Spring*]

16 O Reader! had you in your mind
Such stores as silent thought can bring,
O gentle Reader! you would find
A tale in every thing.
[Wordsworth: *Simon Lee*]

17 My brain
Worked with a dim and undetermined sense
Of unknown modes of being.
[Wordsworth: *The Prelude* I.xxxix.]

18 The cud of bitter thoughts.
[Robert Southey: *Oliver Newman* VII]

19 The blight of life—the demon Thought.
[Byron: *Childe Harold* I.lxxxiv.]

20 I will war, at least in words (and should
My chance so happen—deeds) with all who war
With thought.
[Byron: *Don Juan* IX.xxiv.]

21 Strange thoughts beget strange deeds.
[Shelley: *The Cenci* IV]

22 He gave man speech, and speech created thought,
Which is the measure of the universe;
And Science struck the thrones of earth and heaven,
Which shook, but fell not; and the harmonious mind
Poured itself forth in all-prophetic song;
And music lifted up the listening spirit
Until it walked, exempt from mortal care,
Godlike, o'er the clear billows of sweet sound.
[Shelley: *Prometheus Unbound* II.iv.]

23 In fact, it is as difficult to appropriate the thoughts of others as it is to invent.

[Emerson: *Quotation and Originality*]
1 Break, break, break,
 On thy cold gray stones, O Sea!
 And I would that my tongue could
utter
 The thoughts that arise in me.
[Tennyson: *Break, Break, Break*]
2 Stung by the splendor of a sudden
thought.
[Robert Browning: *A Death in the Desert*]
3 The deep well of unconscious cerebration. [Henry James: Preface to *The American*]
4 And too often, among the thoughts in the loveliest heads, we come on nests of woolly caterpillars. [Logan Pearsall Smith: *Trivia,* "The Quest"]
5 What impossible company we keep in the kind thoughts of those who think kindly of us! [Logan Pearsall Smith: *Afterthoughts*]
6 Thought is not free if the profession of certain opinions makes it impossible to earn a living. [Bertrand Russell: *Sceptical Essays*]
7 For masterpieces are not single and solitary births; they are the outcome of many years' thinking in common, of thinking by the body of the people, so that the experience of the mass is behind a single voice. [Virginia Woolf: *A Room of One's Own*]
8 But the soul and meaning of thought, abstracted from the other elements which accompany it, though it may be voluntarily thwarted, can never be made to direct itself toward anything but the production of belief. Thought in action has for its only possible motive the attainment of thought at rest; and whatever does not refer to belief is no part of the thought itself. [Charles S. Peirce: *How to Make Our Ideas Clear*]

THOUGHTS: second thoughts
9 Among mortals second thoughts are the wisest. [Euripides: *Hippolytus*]
10 The thoughts that come often unsought, and, as it were, drop into the mind, are commonly the most valuable of any we have. [John Locke: Letter to Samuel Bold (1699)]
11 Men's first thoughts in this matter are generally better than their second; their

natural notions better than those refin'd by study, or consultation with casuists. [Anthony Ashley Cooper, Earl of Shaftesbury: *Characteristics*]
12 Second thoughts oftentimes are the very worst of all thoughts. First and third very often coincide. Indeed, second thoughts are too frequently formed by the love of novelty, of showing penetration, of distinguishing ourselves from the mob, and have consequently less of simplicity, and more of affectation. [William Shenstone: *Of Men and Manners*]
13 First thoughts are best, being those of generous impulse; whereas Second Thoughts are those of Selfish Prudence. [Edward FitzGerald: *Polonius: Second Thoughts*]
 See THINK(ING)

THREAT(S)
14 He threatens many who injures one. [Publilius Syrus: *Maxims*]
15 Threatened folks live long. [Henry Porter: *The Two Angrie Women of Abingdon* IV.iii.]
16 He who does not fear death does not fear threats. [Corneille: *Le Cid* II.i.]
17 Nor think thou with wind
 Of aery threats to awe whom yet
 with deeds
 Thou canst not.
[John Milton: *Paradise Lost* VI.282-284]
18 The proverb says that threatened men live long. [Dickens: *Edwin Drood* XIV]

THRESHING
19 When his wheat crop failed, he threshed the straw at a dead loss, to demonstrate how little grain there was, and thus prove his case against Providence. [Willa Cather: *O Pioneers!* I.iv.]

THRIFT
20 Thrift, thrift, Horatio! the funeral
 baked meats
 Did coldly furnish forth the marriage
 tables.
[Shakespeare: *Hamlet* I.ii.]
21 Die to save charges. [Robert Burton: *The Anatomy of Melancholy* I.2.3. 12]
 charges = *expenses*
22 Did wisely from expensive sins refrain,

And never broke the Sabbath, but for
gain.
[Dryden: *Absalom and Achitophel* I]

1 Thrift is the Philosopher's Stone.
[Thomas Fuller (1654-1734): *Gnomologia*]

> The Philosopher's Stone was supposed
> to transmute base metals into gold.

2 A penny sav'd 's a penny got. [William Somerville: *The Sweet-Scented Miser* (1727)]

> Somerville was merely quoting a maxim,
> a maxim that in our commercial times
> is esteemed even if not always heeded.
> But see James Thomson below.

3 "A penny saved is a penny got"—
Firm to this scoundrel maxim keepeth he.
[James Thomson (1700-1748): *The Castle of Indolence* I.L]

> To hear his favorite aphorism so described must have startled Ben Franklin.

4 It was said of old Sarah, Duchess of Marlborough, that she never puts dots over her i's, to save ink. [Horace Walpole: letter to Sir Horace Mann, Oct. 4, 1785]

THRONE

5 That fierce light which beats upon a
throne,
And blackens every blot.
[Tennyson: Dedication of *Idylls of the King*]

THRUSH

6 That's the wise thrush: he sings each
song twice over
Lest you should think he never could
recapture
The first fine careless rapture!
[Robert Browning: *Home-thoughts from Abroad*]

7 O thrush, your song is passing sweet,
But never a song that you have
sung
Is half so sweet as thrushes sang
When my dear love and I were
young.
[William Morris: *Other Days*]

THULE

8 Ultima Thule.
[Vergil: *Georgics* I.xxx.]

> = farthest Thule, the northernmost part

of the habitable world.

> Some think Norway was meant; some
> Iceland; some Mainland, the largest of
> the Shetland Islands.

THUMBS

9 They win applause by slaying with a turn of the thumb. [Juvenal: *Satires* III]

> They = the nouveau riche who courted
> popularity by giving gladiatorial shows.
> Apparently the patron gave the sign but
> was influenced, in giving it, by the mood
> of the spectators, and—then as now—the
> mob liked blood.
>
> Dryden translates the line (1.68):
> With thumbs bent back, they popularly kill.
>
> It is not certain just what was done
> with the thumb in this famous gesture,
> but it is certain that the modern American assumption that "thumbs up" was
> favorable, "thumbs down" unfavorable, is
> wrong. From passages in Horace, Juvenal, Prudentius and others, it is plain
> that the thumb was turned some way
> (verso pollice and converso pollice) and
> that its being up was unfavorable. The
> evidence suggests that the thumb was
> turned up and back and possibly rotated in the unfavorable verdict and
> folded down into the fist for the favorable. But this is not absolutely certain.
> The American interpretation is very
> new. Throughout the 19th century,
> "thumbs up" was in England an expression of disapprobation.

THUNDER

10 The deep, dread-bolted thunder.
[Shakespeare: *King Lear* IV.vii.]

> Until very recently—from antiquity—it
> was believed that the damage was done
> by the thunder, that physical objects
> called thunderbolts were hurled against
> those things which were struck. They
> were sometimes called thunderstones
> and, since they were believed in, were
> frequently found—for faith can produce
> as well as remove mountains of evidence.
> Lightning was thought to be either the
> glow of the hot thunderbolts, or a
> "vaunt-courier" or messenger, riding
> ahead to announce the coming of the
> bolt.

1 The dread rattling thunder.
[Shakespeare: *The Tempest* V.i.]
2   The thunder,
Wing'd with red lightning and im-
                         petuous rage,
Perhaps hath spent his shafts, and
                            ceases now
To bellow through the vast and
                      boundless deep.
[John Milton: *Paradise Lost* I.174-177]
3 Their rising all at once was as the
                              sound
Of thunder heard remote.
[John Milton: *Paradise Lost* II.476-477]
4 They will not let my play run, but
                 yet they steal my thunder!
[John Dennis: in the *Biographia Bri-
tannica* (1747-66)]

*Dennis, an irascible man, had devised a
special sort of mechanical thunder for
his play* Appius and Virginia *(1709). The
play failed, but a few nights later the
thunder was used in a production of*
Macbeth. *Dennis was in the audience
and, hearing his own thunder made use
of, rose in a violent passion and exclaimed, "See how the rascals use me!
They will not let my play run, but yet
they steal my thunder."*

5 From peak to peak the rattling crags
                              among
Leaps the live thunder!
[Byron: *Childe Harold* III.xcii.]
6 Dry sterile thunder without rain.
[T. S. Eliot: *The Waste Land* V]

THUS

7 Why is this thus? What is the reason
of this thusness? [Artemus Ward: *Artemus Ward's Lecture*]

TICKETS

8 Conductor, when you receive a fare,
Punch in the presence of the passen-
                              jare.
A blue trip slip for an eight-cent fare,
A buff trip slip for a six-cent fare,
A pink trip slip for a five-cent fare,
Punch in the presence of the passen-
                              jare.
Punch, brother, punch with care.
[Noah Brooks]

*The jingle was inspired by a directive to
conductors posted in the New York
horsecars. The thing became a mania.*

*Mark Twain has left an amusing ac-
count of its vogue in* Literary Nightmare
(1876).

TICKLE

9 Nothing tickles that doesn't pinch.
[Montaigne: *Essays* III.xii.]

TIDE

10 Hoist up sail while gale doth last,
Tide and wind stay no man's pleas-
                              ure.
[Robert Southwell: *St. Peter's Com-
plaint*]
11 There is a tide in the affairs of men,
Which, taken at the flood, leads on to
                              fortune;
Omitted, all the voyage of their life
Is bound in shallows and in miseries.
[Shakespeare: *Julius Caesar* IV.iii.]
12 A' parted even just between twelve
and one, even at the turning o' the tide.
[Shakespeare: *Henry V* II.iii.]

*That dying men "go out with the tide"
has been believed, and probably still is,
wherever men are familiar with tides.
Pliny, no timid skeptic, said (Natural
History II) that no animal dies except
as the tide goes out. Sir John Falstaff
went that way, as Mistress Quickly assures us in the above lines, and 300
years later the "calling of the sea" took
Enoch Arden. And the "willin'" Barkis,
too. "People can't die along the coast,"
Mr. Peggoty informed David Copperfield, "except when the tide's pretty nigh
out. They can't be born unless it's pretty
nigh in—not properly born till flood.
He's a-going out with the tide. . . . If
he lives till it turns, he'll hold his own
till past the flood, and go out with the
next tide."*

(Dickens: David Copperfield XXX.)

13 There is a tide in the affairs of
                              women
Which, taken at the flood, leads—
                     God knows where.
[Byron: *Don Juan* VI.ii.]
14 Truly there is a tide in the affairs of
men, but there is no gulf-stream setting
forever in one direction. [James Russell
Lowell: *New England Two Centuries
Ago*]
15 Now the great winds shoreward blow;
Now the salt tides seaward flow;
Now the wild white horses play,

Champ and chafe and toss in the
spray.
[Matthew Arnold: *The Forsaken Merman*]
1 The western tide crept up along the
sand,
And o'er and o'er the sand,
And round and round the sand,
As far as eye could see.
The rolling mist came down and hid
the land:
And never home came she.
[Charles Kingsley: *The Sands of Dee*]
2 The tide turns at low water as well
as at high. [Havelock Ellis: *Impressions
and Comments* I]
3 The great tide that treads the shifting shore.
[Edna St. Vincent Millay: *The Harp-Weaver,* Sonnet 6]

TIDYING UP
4 The sweeping up the heart,
And putting love away
We shall not want to use again
Until eternity.
[Emily Dickinson: *Poems, Part IV, Time
and Eternity* XXII.2]

TIE
5 Blest be the tie that binds
Our hearts in Jesus' love.
[John Fawcett: *Blest Be the Tie That
Binds*]

TIGER
6 O tiger's heart wrapp'd in a woman's
hide!
[Shakespeare: *III Henry VI* I.iv.]
*This line, which occurs in a long passage
of glorious fustian that tears a passion
to tatters moved young Shakespeare's envious competitors to ribald scorn. "Tyger's hart wrapt in a Player's hide!"
scoffed the pamphleteer Robert Greene
in A Groats-Worth of Wit Bought with
a Million of Repentance (1592). Little
did the luckless pamphleteer know that
this jibe would be the most famous thing
he ever wrote, merely because it fixes
some dates in the career of the despised
"Shake-scene" who dared to suppose that
he was "as well able to bombast out a
blanke verse as the best of you."*
7 Tiger! Tiger! burning bright
In the forests of the night,

What immortal hand or eye
Could frame thy fearful symmetry?
[William Blake: *The Tiger*]
8 When the stars threw down their
spears,
And water'd heaven with their tears,
Did he smile his work to see?
Did he who made the Lamb make
thee?
[William Blake: *The Tiger*]

TIGHT
9 She was tight as the paper on the
wall. [Mignon Eberhart: *Escape the
Night*]

TIME: and action
10 Go to my love, where she is careless
laid
Yet in her winter's bower, not well
awake;
Tell her the joyous time will not be
staid,
Unless she do him by the forelock
take.
[Edmund Spenser: *Amoretti* (Sonnet
70)]
11 Time is the measure of business, as
money is of wares. [Francis Bacon: *Of
Dispatch*]
12 The time is out of joint; O cursed
spite,
That ever I was born to set it right!
[Shakespeare: *Hamlet* I.v.]
13 Every time
Serves for the matter that is then
born in't.
[Shakespeare: *Antony and Cleopatra* II.
ii.]
14 What may be done at any time will
be done at no time. [Old Scottish proverb]
15 Time is money. [Benjamin Franklin:
Advice to a Young Tradesman]

TIME: brings change
16 Time is the greatest innovator.
[Francis Bacon: *Of Innovations*]
17 Time is like a fashionable host
That slightly shakes his parting guest
by the hand,
And with his arms outstretch'd, as he
would fly,
Grasps in the comer: welcome ever
smiles,
And farewell goes out sighing.

[Shakespeare: *Troilus and Cressida* III. iii.]

1 There's a new foot on the floor, my friend,
And a new face at the door, my friend,
A new face at the door.
[Tennyson: *The Death of the Old Year*]

2 Time turns the old days to derision,
Our loves into corpses or wives;
And marriage and death and division
Make barren our lives.
[Swinburne: *Dolores*]

TIME: brings our own end

3 So minutes, hours, days, months, and years,
Pass'd over to the end they were created,
Would bring white hairs unto a quiet grave.
Ah, what a life were this! how sweet! how lovely!
[Shakespeare: *III Henry VI* II.v.]

4 How soon hath Time, the subtle thief of youth,
Stol'n on his wing my three-and-twentieth year.
[John Milton: *On His Having Arrived at the Age of Twenty-three*]

5 Time, like an ever-rolling stream,
Bears all its sons away;
They fly forgotten, as a dream
Dies at the opening day.
[Isaac Watts: *O God, Our Help in Ages Past*]

6 Everything presses on—whilst thou art twisting that lock, see, it grows grey!
[Laurence Sterne: *Tristram Shandy* IX viii.]

7 As we advance in life, we acquire a keener sense of the value of time. Nothing else, indeed, seems of any consequence; and we become misers in this respect. [William Hazlitt: *The Feeling of Immortality in Youth*]

8 Let us alone. Time driveth onward fast,
And in a little while our lips are dumb,
Let us alone. What is it that will last?
All things are taken from us, and become
Portions and parcels of the dreadful past.
Let us alone.
[Tennyson: *The Lotos-Eaters*]

9 Time: that which man is always trying to kill, but which ends in killing him. [Herbert Spencer: *Definitions*]

10 Anno domini—that's the most fatal complaint of all in the end. [James Hilton: *Good-bye, Mr. Chips* I]

TIME: the destroyer

11 Time that devours all things. [Ovid: *Metamorphoses* XV]
The Titan Kronos, in Greek mythology, the father of the gods, devoured his own children.

12 The wreckful siege of battering days.
[Shakespeare: *Sonnets* LXV]

13 Cormorant devouring Time.
[Shakespeare: *Love's Labour's Lost* I.i.]

14 Beauty, wit,
High birth, vigour of bone, desert in service,
Love, friendship, charity, are subjects all
To envious and calumniating time.
[Shakespeare: *Troilus and Cressida* III. iii.]

15 There is no antidote against the Opium of time . . . the iniquity of oblivion blindly scattereth her poppy, and deals with the memory of men without distinction to merit of perpetuity. [Sir Thomas Browne: *Urn-Burial* V]

16 Ever eating, never cloying,
All-devouring, all-destroying,
Never finding full repast,
Till I eat the world at last.
[Jonathan Swift: *On Time*]

17 Time, a maniac scattering dust.
[Tennyson: *In Memoriam* L]

TIME: and eternity

18 Time is. . . . Time was. . . . Time is past.
[Robert Greene: *Friar Bacon and Friar Bongay*, "The Brazen Head" XI]

19 But thought's the slave of life, and life time's fool;
And time, that takes survey of all the world,
Must have a stop.
[Shakespeare: *I Henry IV* V.iv.]

20 The dark backward and abysm of time.

[Shakespeare: *The Tempest* I.ii.]

1 The night of time far surpasseth the day, and who knows when was the Equinox? [Sir Thomas Browne: *Urn-Burial* V]

2 But at my back I always hear
  Time's winged chariot hurrying near;
  And yonder all before us lie
  Deserts of vast eternity.

[Andrew Marvell: *To His Coy Mistress*]

3 Time whereof the memory of man runneth not to the contrary. [Sir William Blackstone. *Commentaries* I]

4 What's time? Leave Now for dogs and
                                    apes:
  Man has Forever.

[Robert Browning: *A Grammarian's Funeral*]

5 Time goes, you say? Ah no!
  Alas, Time stays, *we* go.

[Austin Dobson: *The Paradox of Time*]

6 The years to come seemed waste of
                                  breath,
  A waste of breath the years behind.

[William Butler Yeats: *An Irish Airman Foresees His Death*]

7 God stands winding His lonely horn,
  And time and the world are ever in
                                  flight;
  And love is less kind than the grey
                                  twilight,
  And hope is less clear than the dew of
                                the morn.

[William Butler Yeats: *Into the Twilight*]

TIME: flies

8 My days are swifter than a weaver's shuttle. [Job 7:6]

9 A thousand years in thy sight are but as yesterday when it is past, and as a watch in the night. [Psalms 90:4]

10 Times flies. [Ovid: Fasti VI.v.]
  Ovid's phrase is Tempora labuntur, *though it is more commonly given as* Tempus fugit.

11 The noiseless foot of time steals
                              swiftly by,
  And, ere we dream of manhood, age
                                is nigh!

[Juvenal: *Satires* IX (trans. William Gifford)]

12 For though we sleep or wake, or roam
                                  or ride,
  Ay fleets the time, it will no man
                                  abide.

[Chaucer: *The Clerk's Tale*]

13 Thirty days hath September,
  April, June, and November;
  All the rest have thirty-one,
  Excepting February alone,
  And that has twenty-eight days clear
  And twenty-nine in each leap year.

[Richard Grafton: *Abridgment of the Chronicles of England*]
  There are several Elizabethan variations and it is doubtful if Grafton made it up. Although the most famous of all rhyming aids to memory in our language, it often fails because it can't be remembered—or the reciter is confused by the different versions he has heard. After all, there are only 12 months, and there are 28 words in the reminder!

14 Like as the waves make towards the
                              pebbled shore,
  So do our minutes hasten to their
                                    end.

[Shakespeare: *Sonnets* LX]

15 I hate all times, because all times do
                                    fly
  So fast away, and may not stayèd be.

[Edmund Spenser: *Daphnaida*]

16 Old Time the clock-setter, that bald
                              sexton Time.

[Shakespeare: *King John* III.i.]

17 The inaudible and noiseless foot of
                                    Time.

[Shakespeare: *All's Well That Ends Well* V.iii.]

18   Come what come may,
  Time and the hour runs through the
                              roughest day.

[Shakespeare: *Macbeth* I.iii.]

19 A thousand ages in Thy sight
  Are like an evening gone;
  Short as the watch that ends the
                                  night
  Before the rising sun.

[Isaac Watts: *Psalms* XC]

20 How swift the shuttle flies, that weaves thy shroud! [Edward Young: *Night Thoughts* IV]

21 Nae man can tether time or tide.

[Burns: *Tam o' Shanter*]
  The proverb has many forms, most of them alliterative: Time nor tide tarrieth no man (1592); Time and tide for no man stay (1727).

Tide *means time (Whitsuntide, Easter-tide, whate'er betide); from the beginning men were impressed by the regularity of the tides.*

1 Time rolls his ceaseless course.
[Sir Walter Scott: *The Lady of the Lake* III.i.]

2 Ah! the clock is always slow;
It is later than you think.
[Robert W. Service: *It Is Later Than You Think*]

3 HURRY UP PLEASE ITS TIME.
[T. S. Eliot: *The Waste Land* II]
The warning of closing time in the British pubs, used ironically by Eliot for its accepted meaning and, at the same time, as a menacing warning of the passage of time.

TIME: reveals, consoles, revenges

4 Time shall unfold what plaited cunning hides.
[Shakespeare: *King Lear* I.i.]
plaited = *twisted, involved, hidden under many plies*
This statement is one of the commonest reflections on time in all of Shakespeare's plays.

5 And thus the whirligig of time brings in his revenges.
[Shakespeare: *Twelfth Night* V.i.]

6 Consider, Sir, how insignificant this will appear a twelve-month hence. [Samuel Johnson: in Boswell's *Life* (1763)]
Boswell had planned a dinner but had quarreled with his landlord and been asked to change his lodgings. He was overcome with chagrin at having to change the place of the entertainment to a tavern. Johnson's robust consolation has a wide application.

7 Time passes, Time the consoler, Time the anodyne.
[W. M. Thackeray: *Pleasures of Being a Fogy*]

8 Time is a test of trouble,
But not a remedy.
If such it prove, it proves too
There was no malady.
[Emily Dickinson: *Poems, Part IV, Time and Eternity* LXVIII.2]

TIME: the waste of

9 For time y-lost may not recovered be.
[Chaucer: *Troilus and Criseyde* IV]

10 Who hath time, and tarrieth for time,
loseth time.
[John Florio: *First Fruites* 19]

11 The clock upbraids me with the waste of time.
[Shakespeare: *Twelfth Night* III.i.]

12 Those who make the worst use of their time most complain of its shortness.
[La Bruyère: *Les Caractères*]

TIME: miscellaneous

13 Time which is the author of authors.
[Francis Bacon: *The Advancement of Learning* I]

14 That old bald cheater, Time. [Ben Jonson: *The Poetaster* I.l.]

15 Time and I against any two. [John Arbuthnot: postscript to *History of John Bull* (1712)]
Arbuthnot is quoting a Spanish proverb.

16 He [Time] keeps all his customers
still in arrears
By lending them minutes and charging them years.
[O. W. Holmes: *Our Banker*]

17 Time, so complain'd of,
Who to no one man
Shows partiality,
Brings round to all men
Some undimm'd hours.
[Matthew Arnold: *Consolation*]

18 Backward, turn backward, O Time,
in your flight,
Make me a child again just for tonight.
[Elizabeth Akers Allen: *Rock Me to Sleep, Mother*]

TIMEPIECE

19 An ancient timepiece says to all—
"Forever—never!
Never—forever!"
[Longfellow: *The Old Clock on the Stairs*]

TIMES

20 Can ye not discern the signs of the times? [Matthew 16:3]

21 These are the times that try men's souls. [Thomas Paine: *The American Crisis* I]

TIMIDITY

22 He who begs timidly invites a refusal. [Seneca: *Hippolytus*]

The thought—that a timid request encourages a refusal—has echoed through the literature of all subsequent ages. See the quotation in Robert Herrick, following.

1 Nothing is well done, which is doubtfully and fearfully done. [Stefano Guazzo: *Civil Conversation* III.lxxxii.]

2　　　　What thou wouldst highly,
That wouldst thou holily; wouldst
　　　　　　　not play false,
And yet wouldst wrongly win.
[Shakespeare: *Macbeth* I.v.]

3 Letting "I dare not" wait upon "I
　　　　　　　would,"
Like the poor cat i' the adage.
[Shakespeare: *Macbeth* I.vii.]

The cat in the adage, to which Lady Macbeth scornfully compares her hesitant spouse, wanted fish but was afraid to wet her paws.

More than 200 years before, Chaucer had alluded to the same proverb:

For ye be lyk the sweynte cat,
That wolde have fish; but wostow
　　what?
He wolde no-thing wete his clowes.
　　　　—The Hous of Fame III.693

sweynte = *tired, lazy;* wostow what? = *do you know what?;* clowes = *claws, paws*

4 Who fears to ask doth teach to be
　　　　　　　deny'd.
[Robert Herrick: *Hesperides*]

5 He either fears his fate too much,
　Or his deserts are small,
That dares not put it to the touch
　To gain or lose it all.
[James Graham, Marquis of Montrose: *My Dear and Only Love*]

6 Willing to wound, and yet afraid to
　　　　　　　strike,
Just hint a fault, and hesitate dislike.
[Alexander Pope: *Epistle to Dr. Arbuthnot*]

7 Timidity in power is always tyrannical. [Giambattista Casti: *Gli Animali Parlanti* XV]

8 Shall I part my hair behind? Do I
　　　　dare to eat a peach?
I shall wear white flannel trousers,
　　　　and walk upon the beach.
I have heard the mermaids singing,
　　　　each to each.
[T. S. Eliot: *The Love Song of J. Alfred Prufrock*]

9 I have measured out my life with coffee spoons. [T. S. Eliot: *The Love Song of J. Alfred Prufrock*]

TIPPERARY

10 It's a long way to Tipperary, it's a
　　　　long way to go.
[The opening line of a song written by Harry Williams and Jack Judge in 1908. It became a sort of campaign song of the British troops in the first years of World War I.]

Tipperary is a county and a town in S. Eire.

TIRED

11 Tir'd with all these, for restful death
　　　　　　　I cry.
[Shakespeare: *Sonnets* LXVI]

TITLE(S)

12 It is ful faire to been y-clept *"ma
　　　　　　　dame."*
[Chaucer: Prologue to *The Canterbury Tales*]

13 It is not titles that honor men, but men that honor titles. [Machiavelli: *Discourses on Livy* III]

14 There was one [a letter] also for me from Mr. Blackburne; who with his own hand superscribes it to S.P., Esq., of which God knows I was not a little proud. [Samuel Pepys: *Diary*, March 25, 1660]

Pepys had the endearing obverse of the pride that apes humility; he took such eager and innocent delight in minor honors.

15 And in soft sounds, "Your Grace"
　　　　　　　salutes their ear.
[Alexander Pope: *The Rape of the Lock* I.86]

16 The rank is but the guinea stamp. [Burns: *For a' that and a' that*]

TOAST

17 I never had a piece of toast
　　Particularly long and wide
But fell upon the sanded floor,
　　And always on the buttered side.
[James Payn: *Poem* (1884)]

TOBACCO: against

18 A custom loathsome to the eye, hateful to the nose, harmful to the brain, dangerous to the lungs, and in the black,

stinking fume thereof nearest resembling the horrible Stygian smoke of the pit that is bottomless. [James I of England: *A Counterblaste to Tobacco*]

1 Herein is not only a great vanity, but a great contempt of God's good gifts, that the sweetness of man's breath, being a good gift of God, should be wilfully corrupted by this stinking smoke. [James I of England: *A Counterblaste to Tobacco*]

2 Tobacco is . . . rather taken of many for wantonness when they have nothing else to do than of any absolute or necessary use. [Edmund Gardiner: *The Trial of Tobacco* (1610)]
wantonness = foppish affectation

3 Odds me, I marvel what pleasure or felicity they have in taking this roguish tobacco! it's good for nothing but to choke a man, and fill him full of smoke and embers. [Ben Jonson: *Every Man in His Humour* III.ii.]

4 Pernicious weed! whose scent the fair
    annoys,
  Unfriendly to society's chief joys,
  Thy worst effect is banishing for
    hours
  The sex whose presence civilizes ours.
[William Cowper: *Conversation*]
One wonders whether Cowper would have regarded having the ladies smoke too as a happy solution.

5 The Indian weed now withered quite;
  Green at morn, cut down at night;
  Shows thy decay: all flesh is hay:
  Thus think, then drink Tobacco.
[Attr. Robert Wisdom: *A Religious Use of Tobacco*]
Perhaps because of the idea of sucking the smoke in, tobacco was formerly said to be drunk.

6 Tobacco had nowhere been forbidden in the Bible, but then it had not yet been discovered. . . . St. Paul would almost certainly have condemned tobacco if he had known of its existence. . . . It was possible [though] that God knew Paul would have forbidden smoking, and had purposely arranged the discovery of tobacco for a period at which Paul should no longer be living. This might seem rather hard on Paul, considering all he had done for Christianity, but it would be made up to him in other ways. [Samuel Butler (1835-1902): *The Way of All Flesh* L]

TOBACCO: for

7 Divine Tobacco.
[Edmund Spenser: *The Faerie Queene* III.v.]

8 Tobacco, divine, rare, superexcellent tobacco, which goes far beyond all the panaceas, potable gold and philosopher's stones, a sovereign remedy to all diseases. [Robert Burton: *Anatomy of Melancholy* II.4.2.2.]

9 He [Sir Walter Raleigh] took a pipe of tobacco a little before he went to the scaffold, which some formal persons were scandalized at, but I think 'twas well done and properly done, to settle his spirits. [John Aubrey: *Brief Lives* II]
formal = prim, puritanical

10 Tobacco is the delight of Dutchmen, as it diffuses a torpor and pleasing stupefaction. [Edmund Burke: Introduction to *The Sublime and Beautiful*]

11 Tobacco has been my evening comfort and my morning curse for these five years. [Charles Lamb: letter to Wordsworth (1805)]

12 For thy sake, tobacco, I
  Would do anything but die.
[Charles Lamb: *A Farewell to Tobacco*]

13 Sublime tobacco! which from east to
    west,
  Cheers the tar's labor or the Turk-
    man's rest;
  Which on the Moslem's ottoman di-
    vides
  His hours, and rivals opium and his
    brides;
  Magnificent in Stamboul, but less
    grand,
  Though not less loved, in Wapping
    or the Strand.
[Byron: *The Island* II]

14 Divine in hookas, glorious in a pipe
  When tipp'd with amber, mellow,
    rich, and ripe;
  Like other charmers, wooing the ca-
    ress
  More dazzlingly when daring in full
    dress;
  Yet thy true lovers more admire by
    far
  Thy naked beauties—give me a cigar!
[Byron: *The Island* II]

1 Some sigh for this and that,
My wishes don't go far,
The world may wag at will,
So I have my cigar.
[Thomas Hood: *The Cigar*]
2 A lone man's companion, a bachelor's friend, a hungry man's food, a sad man's cordial, a wakeful man's sleep, and a chilly man's fire . . . there's no herb like unto it under the canopy of heaven. [Charles Kingsley: *Westward Ho!* VII]
3 A woman is only a woman, but a good cigar is a smoke. [Kipling: *The Betrothed*]
4 Tobacco is a dirty weed. I like it.
It satisfies no normal need. I like it.
It makes you thin, it makes you lean,
It takes the hair right off your bean.
It's the worst darn stuff I've ever seen. I like it.
[Graham Lee Hemminger: *Tobacco*]
See CIGAR, SMOKE(ING)

TOES
5 It's a fact the whole world knows,
That Pobbles are happier without their toes.
[Edward Lear: *The Pobble Who Has No Toes*]

TOIL
6 We have toiled all the night and have taken nothing. [Luke 5:5]
The choosing of this verse as a text for the sermon he preached the day after his wedding was one of Laurence Sterne's first public demonstrations of the peculiar nature of his genius.

TOLERANCE: general and favorable
7 Differing from a man in doctrine was no reason why you should pull his house about his ears. [Samuel Johnson: in Boswell's *Tour to the Hebrides*, August 19, 1773]
8 Toleration is good for all or it is good for none. [Edmund Burke: in a speech (1773)]
9 Then gently scan your brother man,
Still gentler sister woman;
Though they may gang a kennin wrang,
To step aside is human.
One point must still be greatly dark,
The moving why they do it;

And just as lamely can ye mark
How far perhaps they rue it.
[Burns: *Address to the Unco Guid, or the Rigidly Righteous*]
10 The first thing to learn in intercourse with others is non-interference with their own peculiar ways of being happy, provided those ways do not assume to interfere by violence with ours. [William James: *Talks to Teachers on Psychology*]
11 Mrs. Bart . . . had no tolerance for scenes which were not of her own making. [Edith Wharton: *The House of Mirth* I.iii.]
12 Though all society is founded on intolerance, all improvement is founded on tolerance. [G. B. Shaw: Preface to *Saint Joan*]
13 It is easy to be tolerant when you do not care. [Clement F. Rogers: *Verify Your Reference*]

TOLERATION: an evil
14 He that is willing to tolerate any religion, or discrepant way of religion, besides his own, either doubts of his own, or is not sincere in it. [Nathaniel Ward: *The Simple Cobbler of Aggawam*]
15 It is not lawful for the State . . . to hold in equal favor different kinds of religion. . . . The equal toleration of all religions . . . is the same thing as atheism. [Leo XIII: *Immortale Dei,* Nov. 1, 1885]
16 Nothing is more logical than persecution. Religious tolerance is a kind of infidelity. [Ambrose Bierce: *Collected Works* VIII]

TOMBS
17 Kings for such a tomb would wish to die.
[John Milton: *On Shakespeare*]
18 Hark! from the tombs a doleful sound.
[Isaac Watts: *Hymns and Spiritual Songs* II]

TOMORROW
19 Boast not thyself of to-morrow; for thou knowest not what a day may bring forth. [Proverbs 27:1]
20 Take therefore no thought for the morrow: for the morrow shall take

thought for the things of itself. Sufficient unto the day is the evil thereof. [Matthew 6:34]

1 The goodness that thou mayest do this day, do it; and . . . delay it not till tomorrow. [Chaucer: *The Tale of Melibeus*]

2 Today for thee and tomorrow for me. [Cervantes: *Don Quixote* II.LXVI]

3 To-morrow, and to-morrow, and to-morrow,
Creeps in this petty pace from day to day
To the last syllable of recorded time,
And all our yesterdays have lighted fools
The way to dusty death.
[Shakespeare: *Macbeth* V.v.]

4 Tomorrow to fresh woods, and pastures new.
[John Milton: *Lycidas*]

5 Never put off till tomorrow what you can do today.
[Lord Chesterfield: *Letters to His Son,* Dec. 26, 1749]
Chesterfield attributes the saying to De-Witt, but it was probably much older. It appeared in Franklin's Poor Richard's Almanack *and the wits have labored on many variations of it.*

6 To-morrow never yet
On any human being rose or set.
[William Marsden: *What Is Time?*]

7 Tomorrow, tomorrow, not to-day,
Lazy people always say.
[German proverb]

8 Tomorrow never comes. [George Colman the Younger: *Man and Wife* III]

9 A man he seems of cheerful yesterdays
And confident to-morrows.
[Wordsworth: *The Excursion* VII]

TONE

10 Susceptible persons are more affected by a change of tone than by unexpected words. [George Eliot: *Adam Bede* XXVII]

TONGUE

11 Keep thy tongue from evil, and thy lips from speaking guile. [Psalms 34:13]

12 The stroke of the tongue breaketh the bones.
Many have fallen by the edge of the sword:
But not so many as have fallen by the tongue.
[Ecclesiasticus 28:17]
Far better known is the anti-proverb, expressed in the childish jingle:
Sticks and stones will break my bones
But calling will not hurt me.

13 The first virtue, son, if thou wilt learn,
Is to restrain and keep well thy tongue.
[Chaucer: *The Manciple's Tale*]

14 O, that my tongue were in the thunder's mouth!
Then with a passion would I shake the world.
[Shakespeare: *King John* III.iv.]

15 My tongue will tell the anger of my heart:
Or else my heart concealing it will break.
[Shakespeare: *The Taming of the Shrew* IV.iii.]

16 For these fellows of infinite tongue, that can rhyme themselves into ladies' favours, they do always reason themselves out again. [Shakespeare: *Henry V* V.ii.]

17 A still-soliciting eye, and such a tongue
As I am glad I have not.
[Shakespeare: *King Lear* I.i.]

18 Yes, forsooth, I will hold my tongue; so your face bids me, though you say nothing. [Shakespeare: *King Lear* I.iv.]

19 You play the spaniel,
And think with wagging of your tongue to win me.
[Shakespeare: *Henry VIII* V.iii.]

20 A fluent tongue is the only thing a mother don't like her daughter to resemble her in. [Richard Brinsley Sheridan: *St. Patrick's Day* I.ii.]

21 A sharp tongue is the only edge tool that grows keener with constant use. [Washington Irving: *Rip Van Winkle*]

TOO LATE

22 Too late, too late! ye cannot enter now.
[Tennyson: *Guinevere*]

1 While we send for the napkin the
soup gets cold,
While the bonnet is trimming the
face grows old,
When we've matched our buttons the
pattern is sold,
And everything comes too late—too
late.

[Fitzhugh Ludlow: *Too Late*]

TOOLS
2 It is ill jesting with edged tools.
[Robert Greene: *Pandosto* IV]
3 An ill workman quarrels with his
tools. [John Ray: *English Proverbs*
(1670)]
4 Man is a tool-using animal. Nowhere
do you find him without tools; without
tools he is nothing, with tools he is all.
[Thomas Carlyle: *Sartor Resartus* I]
5 Men have become the tools of their
tools. [Thoreau: *Walden* I]

TOOTH (TEETH)
6 For there was never yet philosopher
That could endure the toothache patiently.
[Shakespeare: *Much Ado About Nothing* V.i.]
7 Every tooth in a man's head is more
valuable to him than a diamond. [Cer-
vantes: *Don Quixote* I.iii.4]
8 The best of friends fall out, and so
His teeth had done some years ago.
[Thomas Hood: *A True Story*]
9 Nature, red in tooth and claw.
[Tennyson: *In Memoriam* LVI]
10 The man with the toothache thinks
everyone happy whose teeth are sound.
[G. B. Shaw: *Maxims for Revolutionists*]

TOPICS
11 Sir, you have but two topics, yourself
and me, and I am sick of both. [Samuel
Johnson: in Boswell's *Life* (1776)]
Boswell's Life of Johnson *was to a considerable extent a created biography.
Boswell was always dinging questions
at Johnson in order to get a quotable
answer for his notes—and sometimes, as
here, Johnson turned on him.*
*Notice, however, Johnson's subtle cour-
tesy of including himself among the
causes of his irritation.*

TORMENTS
12 Three thinges dryven a man out of
his hous; that is to seyn, smoke, dropping of reyn, and wikked wyves. [Chau-
cer: *The Tale of Melibeus*]

TORPEDOES
13 Damn the torpedoes! Captain Drayton, go ahead! Jouett, full speed!
[David G. Farragut: at Mobile Bay,
August 5, 1864]
*torpedoes = what we now call mines
Fortunately for Farragut, the Confederate torpedoes proved to be defective;
otherwise this might have had to be
listed under "famous last words."*

TOUCH
14 Touch me not. [John 20:17]
The Vulgate: Noli me tangere.
15 Touch not; taste not; handle not.
[Colossians 2:21]

TOWNS
16 Cain was the first builder of towns.
[Rabelais: *Works* V.xxxv.]

TOWN AND COUNTRY
17 God made the country, and man
made the town.
[William Cowper: *The Task* I]
18 To one who has been long in city
pent,
'Tis very sweet to look into the fair
And open face of heaven—to breathe
a prayer
Full in the smile of the blue firmament.
[Keats: *Sonnet*]

TOYS
19 When I am grown to man's estate
I shall be very proud and great,
And tell the other girls and boys
Not to meddle with my toys.
[R. L. Stevenson: *A Child's Garden of
Verses*, "Looking Forward"]
20 The little toy dog is covered with
dust,
But sturdy and staunch he stands;
And the little toy soldier is red with
rust,
And his musket moulds in his
hands.
Time was when the little toy dog was
new,
And the soldier was passing fair;

And that was the time when our Little Boy Blue
Kissed them and put them there.
[Eugene Field: *Little Boy Blue*]

TRADE

1 Let me have no lying; it becomes none but tradesmen. [Shakespeare: *The Winter's Tale* IV.iii.]
2 A merchant may, perhaps, be a man of an enlarged mind, but there is nothing in trade connected with an enlarged mind. [Samuel Johnson: in Boswell's *Tour to the Hebrides,* Oct. 18, 1773]
3 Trade could not be managed by those who manage it if it had much difficulty. [Samuel Johnson: letter to Hester Thrale, Nov. 16, 1779]

TRAGEDY

4 A tragedy, then, is the imitation of an action that is serious and also, as having magnitude, complete in itself; in language with pleasurable accessories, each kind brought in separately in the parts of the work; in a dramatic, not in a narrative form; with incidents arousing pity and fear, wherewith to accomplish its catharsis of such emotions. [Aristotle: *Poetics*]
5 All tragedies are finish'd by a death,
All comedies are ended by a marriage;
The future states of both are left to faith.
[Byron: *Don Juan* II.ix.]
6 Let me here remind you that the essence of dramatic tragedy is not unhappiness. It resides in the solemnity of the remorseless working of things. This inevitableness of Destiny can only be illustrated in terms of human life by incidents which in fact involve unhappiness. For it is only by them that the futility of escape can be made evident in the drama. This remorseless inevitableness is what pervades scientific thought. The laws of physics are the decrees of Fate. [Alfred N. Whitehead: *Science and the Modern World* I]
7 The temper of mind that sees tragedy in life has not for its opposite the temper that sees joy. The opposite pole to the tragic view of life is the sordid view. [Edith Hamilton: *The Greek Way to Western Civilization*]
8 Commonplace people dislike tragedy, because they dare not suffer and cannot exult. The truth and rapture of man are holy things, not lightly to be scorned. [John Masefield: *The Tragedy of Nan*]

TRAINING

9 Train up a child in the way he should go, and when he is old he will not depart from it. [Proverbs 22:6]

TRANQUILLITY

10 Now of all the benefits of virtue the contempt of death is the chiefest, a means to furnish our life with an easeful tranquillity and give us a pure and amiable taste of it, without which every other voluptuousness is extinguished. [Montaigne: *Essays* I.xix.]

TRANSGRESSOR(S)

11 The way of transgressors is hard. [Proverbs 13:15]
Usually spoken in the singular: The way of the transgressor is hard.

TRANSLATION(S)

12 Translators, traitors.
An Italian proverb that, recognizing that no translation can be exact, says that all translations to some extent betray the reader by misrepresenting the original.
13 Poesy is of so subtle a spirit, that in pouring out of one Language into another, it will all evaporate. [Sir John Denham: Preface to *The Destruction of Troy* (1636)]
14 Nor ought a genius less than his that writ
Attempt translation.
[Sir John Denham: *To Sir Richard Fanshawe*]
Dryden, himself a great translator, said that of the two languages, it is more important for the translator to know the language into which he is translating.
15 He is Translation's thief that addeth more,
As much as he that taketh from the store
Of the first author.
[Andrew Marvell: *To Dr. Witty*]
16 It is impossible to translate poetry.

Can you translate music? [Voltaire: letter to Mme. de Deffand, May 19, 1754]

1 Many a missionary has fixed his own misunderstanding of a primitive language as law eternal in the process of reducing it to writing. There is much in the social habits of a people which is dispersed and distorted by the mere act of making inquiries about it. [Norbert Wiener: *Cybernetics* p.190]

2 I have always said that the best translations—the "Rubaiyat," for example—are those that depart most widely from the originals—that is, if the translator is himself a good poet. [Edmund Wilson: in *The New Yorker,* June 2, 1962]

TRAPEZE

3 He'd fly through the air with the greatest of ease,
This daring young man on the flying trapeze;
His movements were graceful, all girls he could please,
And my love he purloined her away!
[George Leybourne: *The Man on the Flying Trapeze*]

TRAVEL: delights and rewards of

4 Crowns in my purse I have and goods at home,
And so am come abroad to see the world.
[Shakespeare: *The Taming of the Shrew* I.ii.]

5 The use of traveling is to regulate imagination by reality, and, instead of thinking how things may be, to see them as they are. [Samuel Johnson: in Mrs. Piozzi's *Anecdotes of the late Samuel Johnson*]

6 I should like to spend the whole of my life in traveling abroad, if I could anywhere borrow another life to spend afterwards at home. [William Hazlitt: *On Going a Journey*]

7 The soul of a journey is liberty, perfect liberty, to think, feel, do just as one pleases. We go a journey chiefly to be free of all impediments and of all inconveniences; to leave ourselves behind, much more to get rid of others. [William Hazlitt: *On Going a Journey*]

8 Done with indoor complaints, libraries, querulous criticisms,

Strong and content I travel the open road.
[Walt Whitman: *Song of the Open Road*]

9 The proud exultancy of voyages. [Thomas Wolfe: *Of Time and the River*]

TRAVEL: illusions, hardships and futility of

10 Fell among thieves. [Luke 10:30]

11 They change their sky, not their mind, who cross the sea. A busy idleness possesses us; we seek a happy life with ships and carriages: the object of our search is present with us. [Horace: *Epistolae* I.xi.]

12 Everywhere is nowhere. When a person spends all his time in foreign travel, he ends by having many acquaintances, but no friends. [Seneca: *Ad Lucilium* II]

13 He that travelleth into a country before he hath some entrance into the language goeth to school and not to travel. [Francis Bacon: *Of Travel*]

14 Ay, now am I in Arden: the more fool I; when I was at home, I was in a better place: but travellers must be content. [Shakespeare: *As You Like It* II. iv.]

15 Dr. Stubbins was one of his cronies; he was a jolly fat Dr. . . . As Dr. Corbet [Bishop of Oxford—d. 1635] and he were riding in Lob-lane, in wet weather, ('tis an extraordinary deep dirty lane) the coach fell; and Dr. Corbet said that Dr. Stubbins was up to the elbows in mud, he was up to the elbows in Stubbins. [John Aubrey: *Brief Lives* I]

16 All the pleasure that is received [in traveling] ends in an opportunity of splendid falsehood, in the power of gaining notice by the display of beauties which the eye was weary of beholding, and a history of happy moments, of which, in reality, the most happy was the last. [Samuel Johnson: *The Idler* No. 50]

17 He traveled here, he traveled there—
But not the value of a hair
Was heart or head the better.
[Wordsworth: *Peter Bell* I]

18 There's not a sea the passenger e'er pukes in,
Turns up more dangerous breakers

than the Euxine. [Byron: *Don Juan* V.v.]

1 The soul is no traveller; the wise man stays at home. . . . Travelling is a fool's paradise. [Emerson: *Self-Reliance*]

2 It is not worth while to go round the world to count the cats in Zanzibar. [Thoreau: *Walden* (Conclusion)]

3 How many there are who seem to have travelled for the purpose of getting up their rancour against all that is opposed to their notions. [Charles B. Fairbanks: *My Unknown Chum*, "The Philosophy of Foreign Travel"]

4 To travel hopefully is a better thing than to arrive. [R. L. Stevenson: *El Dorado*]

5 Those find, who most delight to roam
　　'Mid castles of remotest Spain,
　That there's, thank Heaven, no
　　　　　　place like home;
　So they set out upon their travels
　　　　　　again.
[Aldous Huxley: *Ninth Philosopher's Song*]

TRAVEL: miscellaneous

6 A man should know something of his own country, too, before he goes abroad. [Laurence Sterne: *Tristram Shandy* VII.ii.]

7 How much a dunce that has been
　　　　　　sent to roam
　Excels a dunce that has been kept at
　　　　　　home.
[William Cowper: *The Progress of Error*]

8 Always roaming with a hungry heart. [Tennyson: *Ulysses*]

9 They sailed away, for a year and a
　　　　　　day,
　To the land where the Bong-tree
　　　　　　grows;
　And there in a wood a Piggy-wig
　　　　　　stood
　With a ring at the end of his nose.
[Edward Lear: *The Owl and the Pussy-Cat*]

10 I have travelled a good deal in Concord. [Thoreau: *Walden* I]

11 I travel not to go anywhere, but to go. [R. L. Stevenson: *Travels with a Donkey*]

TRAVELER

12 If you will be a traveller, have always the eyes of a falcon, the ears of an ass, the face of an ape, the mouth of a hog, the shoulder of a camel, the legs of a stag, and see that you never want two bags very full, that is one of patience and another of money. [John Florio: *Second Fruites* xciii.]

13 Farewell, Monsieur Traveller: look you lisp and wear strange suits, disable all the benefits of your own country, be out of love with your nativity, and almost chide God for making you that countenance you are, or I will scarce think you have swam in a gondola. [Shakespeare: *As You Like It* IV.i.]

14 Now spurs the lated traveler apace
　To gain the timely inn.
[Shakespeare: *Macbeth* III.iii.]

15 Never any weary traveller complained that he came too soon to his journey's end. [Thomas Fuller (1608-1661): *Good Thoughts in Bad Times*]

16 The man who goes alone can start today; but he who travels with another must wait till that other is ready. [Thoreau: *Walden* I]

TREACHERY

17 And forthwith he [Judas] came to Jesus, and said, Hail, Master; and kissed him. [Matthew 26:49]

18 Et tu, Brute!
[Shakespeare: *Julius Caesar* III.i.]
Suetonius and Plutarch say that Caesar believed Brutus to be his son.

19 　　　　　　We are at the stake,
　And bay'd about with many enemies;
　And some that smile have in their
　　　　　　hearts, I fear,
　Millions of mischiefs.
[Shakespeare: *Julius Caesar* IV.i.]

20 Those uncatalogued faint treacheries which vanity makes young people commit. [Willa Cather: *Lucy Gayheart* I.ii.]

21 Fifth Column. [General Emilio Mola]
In 1936 General Mola was leading four columns to attack Madrid. He told reporters, and (by radio) the defenders of the city, that he had a fifth column of sympathizers within the city, who were only waiting for his attack to join him. The phrase was helped into English by Hemingway's use of it, in 1938, as the title for a melodrama. Hemingway sympathized with the defenders of Ma-

drid; so to him the fifth columnists were enemies. To Mola, they were friends.

TREASON

1 Treason doth never prosper: what's the reason?
Why, if it prosper, none dare call it treason.
[Sir John Harington: *Alcilia*]
2 The strength of fifth columns resides not so much in their numbers as in the vague fear and panic they inspire: nothing serves the purpose of traitors better than do shouts of "Treason!" Conversely, nothing is more convenient to those who do not care to fight than to claim that they have been betrayed. [J. Christopher Herold: *Bonaparte in Egypt*]

TREASURE(S)

3 Lay not up for yourselves treasures upon earth, where moth and rust doth corrupt, and where thieves break through and steal. [Matthew 6:19]
4 Where your treasure is, there will your heart be also. [Matthew 6:21]
5 The unsunn'd heaps of miser's treasure.
[John Milton: *Comus*]

TREE(S)

6 Spreading himself like a green bay tree. [Psalms 37:35]
7 If the tree fall toward the south, or toward the north, in the place where the tree falleth, there it shall be. [Ecclesiastes 11:3]
8 The tree is known by his fruit. [Matthew 12:33]
9 The sailing Pine, the Cedar proud and tall,
The vine-prop Elm, the Poplar never dry,
The builder Oake, sole king of forrests all,
The Aspen good for staves, the Cypress funeral.
The Laurel, meed of mighty Conquerors
And Poets sage, the Fir that weepeth still,
The Willow worn of forlorn Paramours,
The Yew obedient to the bender's will,

The Birch for shafts, the Sallow for the mill,
The Mirrh sweet bleeding in the bitter wound,
The warlike Beech, the Ash for nothing ill,
The fruitful Olive, and the Platane round,
The carver Holm, the Maple seldom inward sound.
[Edmund Spenser: *The Faerie Queene* I.i.8-9]
10 Under the greenwood tree
Who loves to lie with me.
[Shakespeare: *As You Like It* II.v.]
Although the next two lines of the song:
And turn his merry note
Unto the sweet bird's throat
make it clear that only the most innocent actions were contemplated, the Reverend Mr. Plumtre, who "expurgated and improved" Shakespeare's songs for his friend, Dr. Bowdler's edition, "designed for reading in the family circle" (1818), thought it better to alter the lines to read:
Under the greenwood tree,
Who loves to work with me.
See: *"O western wind, when wilt thou blow?" under* WIND.
11 It is not growing like a tree
In bulk, doth make man better be;
Or standing long an oak, three hundred year,
To fall a log at last, dry, bald, and sere:
A lily of a day
Is fairer far in May,
Although it fall and die that night;
It was the plant and flower of light.
In small proportions we just beauties see;
And in short measures life may perfect be.
[Ben Jonson: *To the Immortal Memory of Sir H. Morison*]
12 Generations pass while some trees stand, and old families last not three oaks. [Sir Thomas Browne: *Urn-Burial* V.vi.]
13 She gave me of the tree, and I did eat.
[John Milton: *Paradise Lost* X.143]
Quoting Genesis 3:12.
14 The tree is no sooner down, but ev-

ery one runs for his Hatchet. [Thomas Fuller (1654-1734): *Gnomologia*]

Forest laws were very strict. The country folk had certain rights to dead wood but were not allowed to fell a tree.

1 There is a Yew-tree, pride of Lorton
              Vale,
Which to this day stands single, in
              the midst
Of its own darkness, as it stood of
              yore.

[Wordsworth: *Yew-Trees*]

2 The tree will wither long before it
              fall.

[Byron: *Childe Harold* III.xxxii.]

3 In a drear-nighted December,
   Too happy, happy tree,
Thy branches ne'er remember
   Their green felicity.

[Keats: *Stanzas*]

4 Woodman, spare that tree!
Touch not a single bough!
In youth it sheltered me,
And I'll protect it now.

[George Pope Morris: *Woodman, Spare that Tree* (1830)]

Oh leave this barren spot to me!
Spare, woodman, spare the beechen
              tree!
Thomas Campbell: The Beech-Tree's
              Petition

5 Little we fear
Weather without,
Sheltered about
The Mahogany Tree.

[W. M. Thackeray: *The Mahogany Tree*]

Mahogany Tree = *the dining table*

6 Loveliest of trees, the cherry now
  Is hung with bloom along the bough,
And stands about the woodland ride
Wearing white for Eastertide.

[A. E. Housman: *A Shropshire Lad* II]

7 I like trees because they seem more resigned to the way they have to live than other things do. [Willa Cather: *O Pioneers!*]

8 I think that I shall never see
A poem lovely as a tree . . .
Poems are made by fools like me,
But only God can make a tree.

[Joyce Kilmer: *Trees*]

A few years ago, the Allegheny County Commissioners had to cut down two-thirds of the trees surrounding the Joyce Kilmer Memorial at South Park because the trees obscured the memorial and prevented visitors from reading the famous lines.

9 I think that I shall never see
A billboard lovely as a tree.
Indeed, unless the billboards fall
I'll never see a tree at all.

[Ogden Nash: *Song of the Open Road*]

TRELAWNY

10 Trelawny he's in keep and hold,
   Trelawny he may die;
But here's twenty thousand Cornish
              bold
Will know the reason why!

[Robert Hawker: *Song of the Western Men* (1825)]

Hawker's song was based on a song sung in 1688 when Bishop Sir Jonathan Trelawny was one of the Seven Bishops imprisoned by King James II and tried later on the charge of seditious libel (and acquitted—June 30, 1688). It is believed, however, that the 1688 song was first raised in 1628 when Sir John Trelawny, first Baronet, had been committed by Parliament to the Tower for opposing the election to Parliament from Cornwall of Sir John Eliot.

TRIBUTE

11 Yet ev'n these bones from insult to
              protect
Some frail memorial still erected nigh,
With uncouth rhymes and shapeless
              sculpture deck'd,
Implores the passing tribute of a sigh.

[Thomas Gray: *Elegy Written in a Country Churchyard*]

TRICK(S)

12 I know a trick worth two of that. [Shakespeare: *I Henry IV* II.i.]

13 If I be served such another trick, I'll have my brains ta'en out and buttered, and give them to a dog for a new-year's gift. [Shakespeare: *The Merry Wives of Windsor* III.v.]

14 All tricks are either knavish or childish. [Samuel Johnson: in a letter to James Boswell, September 9, 1779, quoted in Boswell's *Life*]

TRIFLE(S)

1 Small matters win great commendation. [Francis Bacon: *Of Ceremonies*]

2 Trifles, light as air.
[Shakespeare: *Othello* III.iii.]

3 A snapper-up of unconsidered trifles.
[Shakespeare: *The Winter's Tale* IV.iii.]

4 Those who concern themselves too much with little things usually become incapable of great ones. [La Rochefoucauld: *Maxims*]

5 At every trifle scorn to take offence;
   That always shows great pride or little sense.
[Alexander Pope: *An Essay on Criticism* II]

6 What dire offence from am'rous causes springs,
   What mighty contests rise from trivial things.
[Alexander Pope: *The Rape of the Lock* I]

7 Pretty! in amber to observe the forms
   Of hairs, or straws, or dirt, or grubs, or worms!
   The things, we know, are neither rich nor rare,
   But wonder how the devil they got there.
[Alexander Pope: *Prologue to the Satires*]

8 The main of life is composed of small incidents and petty occurrences; of wishes for objects not remote, and grief for disappointments of no fatal consequence; of insect vexations which sting us and fly away, impertinences which buzz a while about us, and are heard no more; of meteorous pleasures which dance before us and are dissipated; of compliments which glide off the soul like other music, and are forgotten by him that gave and him that received them.
[Samuel Johnson: *The Rambler* No. 68]

9 There is nothing too little for so little a creature as man. It is by studying little things that we attain the great art of having as little misery and as much happiness as possible. [Samuel Johnson: in Boswell's *Life*, July 14, 1763]

   A little thing comforts us because a little thing afflicts us.

                    Pascal: Pensées

10 Little things are great to little man.
[Oliver Goldsmith: *The Traveller*]

TRINITY

11 For there are three that bear record in heaven, the Father, the Word, and the Holy Ghost: and these three are one. [I John 5:7]

   This verse, long regarded as one of the bulwarks of the belief in the Trinity, appears in contemporary versions in various forms.

   RSV: There are three witnesses, the Spirit, the water, and the blood; and these three agree. New English Bible: *For there are three witnesses, the Spirit, the water, and the blood, and these three are in agreement.*

12 A solemn, unsmiling, sanctimonious old iceberg that looked like he was waiting for a vacancy in the Trinity. [Mark Twain: *Letter from New York to the Alta Californian* (San Francisco), June 6, 1867]

   Appropriated by Mencken and applied by him to Woodrow Wilson, saying that the President's advisers had nominated him for the first vacancy in the Trinity.

TRITON

13 Triton blowing loud his wreathèd horn.
[Edmund Spenser: *Colin Clout's Come Home Again*]
   And hear old Triton blow his wreathèd horn.
   —Wordsworth: The World is too Much with Us

14 Hear you this Triton of the minnows? mark you
   His absolute "shall"?
[Shakespeare: *Coriolanus* III.i.]

TRIUMPH

15 For me, with Roman pride, above
   The conquest, do the triumph love:
   Nor think a perfect victory gained,
   Unless they through the streets their captive lead enchained.
[Abraham Cowley: *Dialogue*]

16 Say, shall my little bark attendant sail,
   Pursue the triumph, and partake the gale?
[Alexander Pope: *An Essay on Man* IV]

17 Hail to the Chief who in triumph advances!

[Sir Walter Scott: *The Lady of the Lake* II.xix.]
1 Not in the clamor of the crowded street,
Not in the shouts and plaudits of the throng,
But in ourselves, are triumph and defeat.
[Longfellow: *The Poets*]

TROUBLE(S)
2 This I know—if all men should take their troubles to market to barter with their neighbors, not one when he had seen the troubles of other men but would be glad to carry his own home again. [Herodotus: *History* VII]
3 Of our troubles we must seek some other cause than God. [Plato: *The Republic* II.xix.]
4 For my sighing cometh before I eat, and my roarings are poured out like the waters.
For the thing which I greatly feared is come upon me, and that which I was afraid of is come unto me.
I was not in safety, neither had I rest, neither was I quiet; yet trouble came. [Job 3:24-26]
5 Man is born unto trouble, as the sparks fly upward. [Job 5:7]
6 Man that is born of a woman is of few days, and full of trouble. [Job 14:1]
7 It is pleasant to recall past troubles. [Cicero: *De finibus* II]
8 Double, double, toil and trouble;
Fire burn and cauldron bubble.
[Shakespeare: *Macbeth* IV.i.]
9 The world is full of care, much like unto a bubble,
Women and care, and care and women, and women and care and trouble.
[Nathaniel Ward: *The Simple Cobbler of Aggawam*]
10 Better never trouble Trouble
Until Trouble troubles you;
For you only make your trouble
Double-trouble when you do.
[David Keppel: *Trouble*]
11 The troubles of our proud and angry dust
Are from eternity, and shall not fail.
[A. E. Housman: *Last Poems* IX]
12 The only incurable troubles of the

rich are the troubles that money can't cure,
Which is a kind of trouble that is even more troublesome if you are poor.
[Ogden Nash: *The Terrible People*]

TROWEL
13 Well said: that was laid on with a trowel.
[Shakespeare: *As You Like It* I.ii.]
A felicitous metaphor that almost at once, apparently, passed into the language. There is a sort of sloppy plethora about mortar as it is laid on with a trowel that is particularly applicable to flattery. And it serves to bind. Great structures are held together by it. And so on.

TRUE
14 A thing is not necessarily true because a man dies for it. [Oscar Wilde: *Portrait of Mr. W. H.*]

TRUMPET(S)
15 If the trumpet give an uncertain sound, who shall prepare himself to the battle? [I Corinthians 14:8]
16 Where the bright Seraphim in burning row
Their loud up-lifted angel trumpets blow.
[John Milton: *At a Solemn Music*]
17 Sonorous metal blowing martial sounds.
[John Milton: *Paradise Lost* I.540]
18 So he passed over, and all the trumpets sounded for him on the other side.
[John Bunyan: *The Pilgrim's Progress* II]
19 The silver, snarling trumpets 'gan to chide.
[Keats: *The Eve of St. Agnes*]

TRUST
20 Though he slay me, yet will I trust in him. [Job 13:15]
21 Thus saith the Lord: Cursed be the man that trusteth in man. [Jeremiah 17:5]
22 Trust, like the soul, never returns, once it is gone. [Publilius Syrus: *Maxims*]
23 The greatest trust between man and

man is the trust of giving counsel. [Francis Bacon: *Of Counsel*]

1 He's mad that trusts in the tameness of a wolf, a horse's health, a boy's love, or a whore's oath. [Shakespeare: *King Lear* III.vi.]

2 Grant I may never prove so fond
To trust a man on his oath or bond,
Or a harlot for her weeping,
Or a dog that seems a-sleeping,
Or a keeper with my freedom,
Or my friends if I should need 'em.
[Shakespeare: *Timon of Athens* I.ii.]
fond = *foolish*

3 Trust him no further than you can throw him. [Thomas Fuller (1654-1734): *Gnomologia*]

4 Never trust the man who hath reason to suspect that you know he hath injured you. [Henry Fielding: *Jonathan Wild* III.iv.]

5 It is better to suffer wrong than to do it, and happier to be sometimes cheated than not to trust. [Samuel Johnson: *The Rambler* No. 79]

6 It is better never to trust anybody. [Henrik Ibsen: *An Enemy of the People* II]

TRUTH

7 Pilate saith unto him, What is truth? [John 18:38]

8 What is truth? said jesting Pilate; and would not stay for an answer. [Francis Bacon: *Of Truth*]
jesting = *scoffing*
Bacon, a jesting sceptic, saw Pilate's question as jesting scepticism. Lancelot Andrewes, a philosophic but busy prelate, saw it as one of those philosophic inquiries which, unfortunately, are pushed aside by the press of business. Pilate asked his question, he said [Sermons: Of the Resurrection (1613)], "And then some other matter took him in the head, and so up he rose and went his way before he had his answer."

9 Truth is always strange—
Stranger than fiction.
[Byron: *Don Juan* XIV.ci]
Mark Twain said: "Truth is stranger than fiction—to some people; but I am measurably familiar with it." (Pudd'nhead Wilson's New Calendar.)

10 Geometry deceives; the hurricane

alone is true. [Victor Hugo: *Les Misérables* I.v.]

11 History warns us that it is the customary fate of new truths to begin as heresies and to end as superstitions. [T. H. Huxley: *The Coming of Age of "The Origin of Species"*]

12 Truth, in matters of religion, is simply the opinion that has survived. [Oscar Wilde: *The Critic as Artist*]

13 If I knew what *was* true, I'd probably be willing to sweat and strive for it, and maybe even to die for it to the tune of bugle-blasts. But so far I have not found it. [H. L. Mencken: *In Defense of Women* XVIII]

14 There are no whole truths: all truths are half-truths. [Alfred North Whitehead: *Dialogues: Recorded by Lucien Price*]

TRUTH: dangers and difficulties of telling

15 It is a common saying: *Veritas odium parit:* Truth purchaseth hatred. [Thomas Wilson: *Discourse Upon Usury* (1572)]
The idea is very old, being found in Ausonius (4th century A.D.) and much repeated. Burton uses it in The Anatomy of Melancholy, and wildly translates it as "Verjuice and oatmeal is good for a parrot."

16 Truth itself hath not the privilege to be employed at all times and in every kind: be her use never so noble, it hath its circumscriptions and limits. [Montaigne: *Essays* III]

17 Truth begetteth hatred; Virtue, envy; Familiarity, contempt. [Gabriel Harvey: *Works* I]

18 Truth's a dog must to kennel; he must be whipped out, when Lady the brach may stand by the fire and stink. [Shakespeare: *King Lear* I.iv.]

19 Follow not truth too near the heels, lest it dash out thy teeth. [George Herbert: *Jacula Prudentum*]

20 Beware of telling an improbable truth. [Thomas Fuller (1608-1661): *Introductio ad Prudentiam* II]

21 Truth never comes into the world but like a bastard, to the ignominy of him that brought her forth. [John Milton: *Areopagitica*]

1 Hard are the ways of truth, and
rough to walk.
[John Milton: *Paradise Regained* I.478]
2 Truth does not do so much good in
the world as its appearances do evil. [La
Rochefoucauld: *Maxims*]
3 The beauty of truth, as of a picture,
is not acknowledg'd but at a distance.
[Joseph Glanvill: *The Vanity of Dogmatizing* XV]
4 A man that should call everything by
its right name, would hardly pass the
streets without being knocked down as a
common enemy. [Lord Halifax: *Maxims*]
5 Blunt truths more mischief than nice
falsehoods do.
[Alexander Pope: *An Essay on Criticism*
III]
  mischief = *harm, injury;* nice = *carefully
  discriminated, delicate*
6 An honest man speaks truth, though
it may give offence; a vain man, in order
that it may. [William Hazlitt: *Characteristics*]
7 God offers to every mind its choice
between truth and repose. Take which
you please—you can never have both.
[Emerson: *Intellect*]
8 A lively, disinterested, persistent liking for truth is extraordinarily rare. Action and faith enslave thought, both of
them in order not to be troubled or inconvenienced by reflection, criticism and
doubt. [Henri Amiel: *Journal,* Jan. 22,
1874]
9 The ill-timed truth we might have
kept—
Who knows how sharp it pierced
and stung?
The word we had not sense to say—
Who knows how grandly it had
rung?
[Edward Rowland Sill: *The Fool's
Prayer*]
10 If one tells the truth, one is sure,
sooner or later, to be found out. [Oscar
Wilde: *Phrases and Philosophies for the
Use of the Young*]
11 Truth telling is not compatible with
the defence of the realm. [G. B. Shaw:
Preface to *Heartbreak House*]
12 All the durable truths that have
come into the world within historic
times have been opposed as bitterly as if
they were so many waves of smallpox,
and every individual who has welcomed
and advocated them, absolutely without
exception, has been denounced and punished as an enemy of the race. [H. L.
Mencken: in *Smart Set,* June 1920]
13 The smallest atom of truth represents some man's bitter toil and agony;
for every ponderable chunk of it there is
a brave truth-seeker's grave upon some
lonely ash-dump and a soul roasting in
Hell. [H. L. Mencken: *Prejudices: Third
Series*]

TRUTH: and lies
14 Truth may perhaps come to the price
of a pearl that showeth best by day, but
it will not rise to the price of a diamond
or carbuncle that showeth best in varied
lights. [Francis Bacon: *Of Truth*]
15 Between falsehood and useless truth
there is little difference. As gold which
he cannot spend will make no man rich,
so knowledge which he cannot apply
will make no man wise. [Samuel Johnson: *The Idler* No. 84]
16 A truth that's told with bad intent
Beats all the lies you can invent.
[William Blake: *Auguries of Innocence*]
17 Any fool can tell the truth, but it requires a man of some sense to know how
to lie well. [Samuel Butler (1835-1902):
Notebooks]

TRUTH: our obligation to
18 Flee fro the prees, and dwelle with
sothfastnesse.
[Chaucer: *Truth* I]
  prees = *press, throng, mob, herd;* sothfastnesse = truth
19 When truth or virtue an affront endures,
Th' affront is mine, my friend, and
should be yours. [Alexander Pope: *Epilogue to the Satires,* Dialogue II]
20 If we owe regard to the memory of
the dead, there is yet more respect to be
paid to knowledge, to virtue, and to
truth. [Samuel Johnson: *The Rambler*
No. 60]
21 I deny the lawfulness of telling a lie
to a sick man, for fear of alarming him.
You have no business with consequences;

you are to tell the truth. [Samuel Johnson: in Boswell's *Life,* June 13, 1784]

TRUTH: will prevail

1 If you will be persuaded by me, pay little attention to Socrates, but much more to the truth; and if I appear to you to say anything true, assent to it; but if not, oppose me with all your might, taking good care that in my zeal I do not deceive both myself and you. [Socrates: in Plato's *Phaedo*]

2 Who ever knew truth put to the worse in a free and open encounter? [John Milton: *Areopagitica*]

3 For truth has such a face and such a
                                    mien,
As to be lov'd needs only to be seen.
[Dryden: *The Hind and the Panther* I]

4 Truth, crushed to earth, shall rise
                                    again;
The eternal years of God are hers;
But Error, wounded, writhes in pain,
And dies among his worshippers.
[William Cullen Bryant: *The Battle-Field*]

5 The dictum that truth always triumphs over persecution, is one of those pleasant falsehoods which men repeat one after another till they pass into commonplaces, but which all experience refutes. [John Stuart Mill: *On Liberty*]

6 It is a piece of idle sentimentality that truth, merely as truth, has any inherent power denied to error, of prevailing. . . . The real advantage which truth has consists in this, that when an opinion is true it may be extinguished once, twice, or many times, but in the course of ages there will generally be found persons to rediscover it, until some one of its reappearances falls on a time when from favorable circumstances it escapes persecution until it has made such head as to withstand all subsequent attempts to suppress it. [John Stuart Mill: *On Liberty*]

7 The truth is great, and shall prevail
When none cares whether it prevail
                                    or not.
[Coventry Patmore: *Magna Est Veritas*]

TRUTH: miscellaneous

8 The language of truth is simple. [Seneca: *Ad Lucilium* XLIX]
A common thought, expressed also by

Ammianus Marcellinus, Annals, *XIV.x.*

9 There is a common saying amongst us: Say the truth and shame the Devil. [Hugh Latimer: *Sermon* (1552)]
Tell truth and shame the Devil
        —Shakespeare: I Henry IV *III.i.*

10 I speak truth, not so much as I would, but as much as I dare; and I dare a little the more as I grow older. [Montaigne: *Of Repentance*]

11 Forget not yet the tried intent
Of such a truth as I have meant,
My great travail so gladly spent
        Forget not yet.
[Sir Thomas Wyatt: *Forget Not Yet*]

12 Children and fools speak true. [John Lyly: *Endymion* II]

13 Democritus said, "That truth did lie in profound pits, and when it was got, it needed much refining." [Francis Bacon: *Apothegms*]

14 It is a pleasure to stand upon the shore, and to see ships tossed upon the sea: a pleasure to stand in the window of a castle, and to see a battle and the adventures thereof below: but no pleasure is comparable to the standing upon the vantage ground of truth, and to see the errors, and wanderings, and mists and tempests, in the vale below. [Francis Bacon: *Of Truth*]
Bacon is paraphrasing Lucretius: De rerum natura *II.*

15 For fools and mad men tell commonly truth. [Robert Burton: *The Anatomy of Melancholy* II.3.8]

16 Nobody has a right to put another under such a difficulty that he must either hurt the person by telling the truth or hurt himself by telling what is not true. [Samuel Johnson: in Boswell's *Life,* April 25, 1778]

17 And in the light of truth thy Bond-
                                    man let me live!
[Wordsworth: *Ode to Duty*]

18 The greatest friend of truth is Time, her greatest enemy is Prejudice, and her constant companion is Humility. [C. C. Colton: *Lacon*]

19 It is one thing to wish to have truth on our side, and another to wish sincerely to be on the side of truth. [Richard Whately: *On the Love of Truth*]

20 Truth is not always in a well. In fact, as regards the more important knowl-

edge, I do believe that she is invariably superficial. [Edgar Allan Poe: *The Murders in the Rue Morgue*]

1 Truth is tough. It will not break, like a bubble, at a touch; nay, you may kick it about all day, like a foot-ball, and it will be round and full at evening. [O. W. Holmes: *The Professor at the Breakfast-Table*]

2 It takes two to speak the truth—one to speak, and another to hear. [Thoreau: *A Week on the Concord and Merrimack Rivers,* "Wednesday"]

3 Truth forever on the scaffold, Wrong forever on the throne. [James Russell Lowell: *The Present Crisis*]

4 Truth is said to lie at the bottom of a well, for the very reason, perhaps, that whoever looks down in search of her sees his own image at the bottom. [James Russell Lowell: *Democracy*]

5 Speaking truth is like writing fair, and only comes by practice. [John Ruskin: *The Seven Lamps of Architecture* II.i.]

6 What everybody echoes as true today, may turn out to be falsehood tomorrow, mere smoke of opinion. [Thoreau: *Walden* Ch. I]

7 Truth is as old as God,
His twin identity—
And will endure as long as He,
A co-eternity,
And perish on the day
That He is borne away
From mansion of the universe,
A lifeless Deity.
[Emily Dickinson: *Truth Is as Old as God*]

8 When in doubt tell the truth. [Mark Twain: *Pudd'nhead Wilson's New Calendar*]

9 All great truths begin as blasphemies. [G. B. Shaw: *Annajanska*]

10 My way of joking is to tell the truth. [G. B. Shaw: *John Bull's Other Island* II]

11 It is always the best policy to speak the truth, unless of course you are an exceptionally good liar. [Jerome K. Jerome: *The Idler,* February 1892]

12 When you have eliminated the impossible, whatever remains, however improbable, must be the truth. [Sir Arthur Conan Doyle: *The Sign of Four* VI]

13 How awful to reflect that what people say of us is true! [Logan Pearsall Smith: *Afterthoughts*]

14 For truth there is no deadline. [Heywood Broun: in *The Nation,* Dec. 30, 1939]

15 A man is always a prey to his truths. Once he has admitted them, he cannot free himself from them. [Albert Camus: *The Myth of Sisyphus*]

16 I never give them hell. I just tell the truth, and they think it is hell. [Harry S Truman: in *Look,* April 3, 1956]

TRY

17 'Tis a lesson you should heed,
Try, try again.
If at first you don't succeed,
Try, try again.
[William Edward Hickson: *Try and Try Again*]

TUMULT

18 The tumult and the shouting dies;
The captains and the kings depart.
[Kipling: *Recessional*]

TUNE(S)

19 There was an old man and he had an old cow,
But he had no fodder to give her,
So he took up his fiddle, and played her a tune,
Consider, good cow, consider;
This isn't the time for the grass to grow;
Consider, good cow, consider.
[See *Notes and Queries* Sec. II. vol. 2, p. 309.]

The tune the old cow died of *is used today as a humorous expression of distaste or boredom. It is usually felt that the tune in the saying was so dreary that even a cow died from hearing it too often.*

Formerly, however, the saying referred not to boredom but to irritation at being given good advice or a sound explanation when what you needed was help. The story, which goes back at least 250 years, concerns a man (sometimes called Jack Whaley) who had nothing to feed his cow. He explained to her—even with a musical accompaniment—that it was not the growing season, there was no fodder, and he begged her to be considerate, to be reasonable. But, despite this appeal, musically couched, the old cow was not considerate and selfishly died of hunger.

1 Why should the Devil have all the good tunes? [Attr. Rowland Hill]
Hill (1744-1833) was a popular, though irregular, preacher. He saw no reason why Sunday School songs, and the like, should not be set to popular tunes, though many of his contemporaries were shocked by the suggestion.

TURK
2 Out-paramoured the Turk.
[Shakespeare: *King Lear* III.iv.]

TURN
3 One good turn deserves another.
[Beaumont and Fletcher: *The Little French Lawyer* III.ii.]

TURNING
4 It's a long lane that has no turning.
[Samuel Richardson: *Clarissa Harlowe* IV]
The saying was proverbial. It also appears in Samuel Foote's A Trip to Calais.

TURNIP
5 If the man who turnips cries,
Cry not when his father dies,
'Tis a proof that he had rather
Have a turnip than his father.
[Samuel Johnson: paraphrase of Lope de Vega, in *Johnsonian Miscellanies*]
6 There's no getting blood out of a turnip. [Frederick Marryat: *Japhet* IV]
Usually heard as "You can't get blood out of a turnip," meaning there is a limit to exactions.

TWEEDLEDUM AND TWEEDLEDEE
7 Tweedledum and Tweedledee
Agreed to have a battle,
For Tweedledum said Tweedledee
Had spoiled his nice new rattle.
[Lewis Carroll: *Through the Looking-Glass* IV]
A parody on the famous lines of John Byrom (1725) On the Feud Between Handel and Bononcini:
Some say, compared to Bononcini,
That Mynheer Handel's but a ninny;

Others aver that he to Handel
Is scarcely fit to hold a candle.
Strange all this difference should be
'Twixt Tweedledum and Tweedledee.
The two musicians had become symbols of a political division. George I supported Handel, and the Prince of Wales, who was at odds with his father, supported Bononcini. Society split and there was a great to-do between the factions.

TWENTY-THREE, SKIDDOO
8 Twenty-three, skiddoo!
Skiddoo may be a humorous development of skedaddle=to decamp, to retire hastily—which appeared in American colloquial speech soon after the Civil War.
An editorial in the Louisville Times *(May 9, 1929) quotes Frank Parker Stockbridge to the effect that the humorous use of twenty-three, with skiddoo added, apparently just for good measure, dates back to The Only Way, a dramatization of Dickens's Tale of Two Cities performed in New York in 1899. In the last act an old woman counted the victims of the guillotine and Sydney Carton was 23. Like other instances of overwrought horror, this struck the public as funny and became a catchword. It may be. In the use of the phrase there was usually a humorous menace: "Get out of here, fast, or. . . ."*

TWIG
9 'Tis education forms the common mind:
Just as the twig is bent the tree's inclined.
[Alexander Pope: *Moral Essays* I]

TWILIGHT
10 Light thickens; and the crow
Makes wing to the rooky wood:
Good things of day begin to droop and drowse,
Whiles night's black agents to their preys do rouse.
[Shakespeare: *Macbeth* III.ii.]
This great passage, heightened by the menace of three lines immediately following in the next scene: "The west yet glimmers with some streaks of day: /

Now spurs the lated traveler apace | To gain the timely inn," constitutes one of the great mood passages of the plays.

1 When twilight dews are falling soft
Upon the rosy sea, love,
I watch the star, whose beam so oft
Has lighted me to thee, love.
[Thomas Moore: *When Twilight Dews*]

TWINKLING
2 In the twinkling of an eye.
[I Corinthians 15:52]

TWO AND TWO
3 When speculation has done its worst, two and two still make four. [Samuel Johnson: *The Idler* No. 36]
4 To think that two and two are four,
And neither five nor three,
The heart of man has long been sore,
And long is like to be.
[A. E. Housman: *When First My Way to Fair I Took*]

TYPES
5 How many human types have fallen out of fashion! Where can we find the Black Sheep, the Angel Child, and the Permanent Invalid on her sofa? Into what suburb or sad limbo have departed the deaf Old Lady with her cap and laces, the Seducer, the Fop, the Aesthete and the Fallen Daughter? [Logan Pearsall Smith: *Afterthoughts*]

TYRANNY
6 I have sworn upon the altar of God, eternal hostility against every form of tyranny over the mind of man. [Thomas Jefferson: Letter to Dr. Benjamin Rush, September 23, 1800]
7 Think'st thou there is no tyranny but that

Of blood and chains? The despotism of vice—
The weakness and the wickedness of luxury—
The negligence—the apathy—the evils
Of sensual sloth—produce ten thousand tyrants,
Whose delegated cruelty surpasses
The worst acts of one energetic master,
However harsh and hard in his own bearing.
[Byron: *Sardanapalus* I.ii.]
8 Protection . . . against the tyranny of the magistrate is not enough: there needs protection also against the tyranny of the prevailing opinion and feeling. [John Stuart Mill: *On Liberty* I]
9 *Sic semper tyrannis.* ("Thus always to tyrants") [Motto of the State of Virginia]
Best known to most Americans as John Wilkes Booth's exultant cry as he leaped from Lincoln's box, after the assassination, down onto the stage. It is said that Matthew Arnold felt that the use of Latin on this occasion offered a ray of hope in the United States' otherwise bleak cultural outlook.

TYRANTS
10 Tyrants commonly cut off the stairs by which they climb unto their thrones. [Thomas Fuller (1608-1661): *Worthies of England* XXIII]
11 All men would be tyrants if they could. [Daniel Defoe: *The Kentish Petition* (Addenda)]
There are few minds to which tyranny is not delightful.
    —Samuel Johnson: Letters *II*
12 Tyrants seldom want pretexts. [Edmund Burke: Letter to a member of the National Assembly]

U

UGLY

1 I cannot tell by what logic we call a toad, a bear, or an elephant ugly; they being created in those outward shapes and figures which best express the actions of their inward forms; and having passed that general visitation of God, who saw that all that He had made was good. [Sir Thomas Browne: *Religio Medici* I]

2 She is most splendidly, gallantly ugly. [William Wycherley: *The Plain Dealer* II.i.]

UNAWARENESS

3 Surely the Lord is in this place; and I knew it not. [Genesis 28:16]

UNBOWED

4 In the fell clutch of circumstance,
    I have not winced nor cried aloud:
Under the bludgeonings of chance
    My head is bloody, but unbowed.
[W. E. Henley: *Invictus*]

UNCLE SAM

5 Uncle Sam.
The earliest known use of Uncle Sam for the United States was in an editorial in the Troy (N.Y.) Post, *September 7, 1813. By 1815 the expression was known as "a cant term in the army for the United States." There is the belief that the original Uncle Sam was Samuel Wilson, of Troy, an army contractor.*

UNCONQUERABLE

6 What though the field be lost?
All is not lost—th' unconquerable
                                    will
And study of revenge, immortal hate,
And courage never to submit or yield.
[John Milton: *Paradise Lost* I.105-108]

UNCONSCIOUS

7 The uttered part of a man's life, let us always repeat, bears to the unuttered, unconscious part a small unknown proportion. He himself never knows it, much less do others. [Thomas Carlyle: *Sir Walter Scott*]

8 The deep well of unconscious cerebration. [Henry James: *The American*]

UNCTION

9 Lay not that flattering unction to
                        your soul.
[Shakespeare: *Hamlet* III.iv.]

UNDERLINGS

10 The fault, dear Brutus, is not in our
                                    stars,
    But in ourselves, that we are under-
                                    lings.
[Shakespeare: *Julius Caesar* I.ii.]

UNDERSTAND

11 I have made it my earnest concern not to laugh at, nor to deplore nor to detest, but to understand, the actions of human beings. [Spinoza: *Tractatus Politicus* I.iv.]

12 What a man doesn't understand, he doesn't have. [Goethe: *Sprüche in Prosa*]

UNDERSTANDING

13 Get wisdom: and with all thy getting get understanding. [Proverbs 4:7]

14 I shall light a candle of understanding in thine heart, which shall not be put out. [II Esdras 14:25]

15 The improvement of the understanding is for two ends: first, for our own increase of knowledge; secondly, to enable us to deliver and make out that knowledge to others. [Locke: *Thoughts Concerning Reading and Study:* App. B]

16 Chew the cud of understanding. [William Congreve: *Love for Love* I.i.]

17 Each might his sev'ral province well
                                command,
    Would all but stoop to what they
                                understand.
[Pope: *Essay on Criticism* I.66]

18 To understand everything makes one very indulgent. [Madame de Staël: *Corinne* XVIII.v.]
This seems to be the basis of "To understand all is to forgive all," which is often attr. Madame de Staël, but not to be found in her works.

1 It is not granted to the fortunate to understand the sorrow of others. [A. V. Platen: *Der Mädchen Friedenslieder* (Schluss)]

2 The healthy understanding, we should say, is not the logical, argumentative, but the intuitive; for the end of understanding is not to prove and find reasons, but to know and believe. [Thomas Carlyle: *Characteristics*]

UNEDUCATED
3 All uneducated people are hypocrites. [William Hazlitt: *Table-talk*, "On the Knowledge of Character"]

UNFAITHFUL
4   If I do prove her haggard,
Though that her jesses were my dear
                  heart-strings,
I'd whistle her off and let her down
                  the wind,
To prey at fortune.
[Shakespeare: *Othello* III.iii.]
haggard = *untamable. It is a term from falconry.*

5 O faithless world, and thy most faith-
                  less part,
   A woman's heart!
The true shop of variety, where sits
   Nothing but fits
And fevers of desire, and pangs of
                  love,
   Which toys remove.
[Sir Henry Wotton: *The World*]
toys = *gaudy but worthless trifles*

UNFULFILLMENT
6 Some village Hampden, that, with
                  dauntless breast
The little tyrant of his fields with-
                  stood,
Some mute inglorious Milton here
                  may rest,
Some Cromwell guiltless of his coun-
                  try's blood.
[Thomas Gray: *Elegy Written in a Country Churchyard*]

UNHAPPINESS
7 No unhappiness is equal to that of anticipating unhappiness. [Calderón: *El Mayor Monstruo los Zelos* I.i.]
8 Men who are unhappy, like men who sleep badly, are always proud of the fact. [Bertrand Russell: *The Conquest of Happiness* I]

UNIFORM
9 The uniform 'e wore
   Was nothin' much before,
   An' rather less than 'arf o' that be'ind.
[Kipling: *Gunga Din*]

UNIMPORTANCE
10 Keep cool: it will be all one a hundred years hence. [Emerson: *Montaigne, or, The Skeptic*]

UNION
11 When bad men combine, the good must associate, else they will fall, one by one, an unpitied sacrifice in a contemptible struggle. [Edmund Burke: *Thoughts on the Cause of the Present Discontents*]
12 Sail on, O Ship of State!
   Sail on, O Union, strong and great!
   Humanity with all its fears,
   With all the hopes of future years,
   Is hanging breathless on thy fate!
[Longfellow: *The Building of the Ship*]

UNIQUE
13 Nature made him, and then broke the mold. [Ariosto: *Orlando Furioso* X]

UNITED STATES
14 *Q.* If you find so much that is unworthy of reverence in the United States, then why do you live here?
   A. Why do men go to zoos? [H. L. Mencken: in *The American Mercury*, September 1924]

UNITY
15 Behold, how good and how pleasant it is for brethren to dwell together in unity! [Psalms 133:1]
16 All are but parts of one stupendous
                  whole,
   Whose body nature is, and God the
                  soul.
[Alexander Pope: *An Essay on Man* I]
17 All for one; one for all. [Alexandre Dumas, père: *The Three Musketeers* IX]
18 I am a part of all that I have met. [Tennyson: *Ulysses*]
19 Till the war drum throbbed no longer
                  and the battle flags were furled
In the Parliament of Man, the Federation of the world.
[Tennyson: *Locksley Hall*]

UNIVERSE
1 The universe is one of God's thoughts.
[Schiller: *Philosophische Briefe,* "Theosophie des Julius"]
2 Taken as a whole, the universe is absurd. [W. S. Landor: *Literary Studies* I]
3 The Universe is but one vast Symbol of God. [Thomas Carlyle: *Sartor Resartus* III.iii.]
4 . . . —listen: there's a hell
of a good universe next door; let's go.
 [e. e. cummings: *Pity This Busy Monster, Manunkind*]
 An excellent motto for the space age.

UNIVERSITY
5 The true university of these days is a collection of books. [Thomas Carlyle: *Heroes and Hero-Worship* V]
6 A University is, according to the usual designation, an Alma Mater, knowing her children one by one, not a foundry, or a mint, or a treadmill. [John Henry Newman: *The Idea of a University,* Discourse VI]
7 The medieval university looked backwards; it professed to be a storehouse of old knowledge. . . . The modern university looks forward, and is a factory of new knowledge. [T. H. Huxley: letter to E. Ray Lankester, April 11, 1892]

UNKINDNESS
8 This was the most unkindest cut of all.
[Shakespeare: *Julius Caesar* III.ii.]
9 Sharp-tooth'd unkindness.
[Shakespeare: *King Lear* II.iv.]

UNKNOWN
10 Everything unknown is magnified. [Tacitus: *Agricola* XXX]
11 Not to know me argues yourselves unknown.
[John Milton: *Paradise Lost* IV.830]

UNMARRIED
12 Unmarried men are best friends, best masters, best servants; but not always best subjects, for they are light to run away, and almost all fugitives are of that condition. [Francis Bacon: *Of Marriage and Single Life*]
 light = *unencumbered, or apt*
13 Certainly the best works, and of greatest merit for the public, have proceeded from the unmarried or childless men, which both in affection and means have married and endowed the public. [Francis Bacon: *Of Marriage and Single Life*]
 Bacon stated the thought in another of his essays—Of Parents and Children: "The noblest works and foundations have proceeded from childless men."
14 The most ordinary cause of a single life is liberty, especially in certain self-pleasing and humorous minds, which are so sensible of every restraint as they will go near to think their girdles and garters to be bonds and shackles. [Francis Bacon: *Of Marriage and Single Life*]
 humorous = *crotchety, whimsical, eccentric;* sensible = *sensitive*
15 Single blessedness.
[Shakespeare: *A Midsummer Night's Dream* I.i.]
16 Lord of yourself, uncumbered with a wife.
[John Dryden: *Epistle to John Driden*]
17 I wish I was single again,
 With money to jingle again!
[Anon.: *I Married a Wife* (19th century)]
18 Who travels alone, without lover or friend,
 But travels from nothing to nought at the end.
[Ella Wheeler Wilcox: *Reply to Kipling*]
 See 19:1

UNNATURAL
19 Nothing is unnatural that is not physically impossible. [Richard Brinsley Sheridan: *The Critic* II.i.]
 "The unnatural—that too is natural."
 —*Goethe*

UNPARTICULAR
20 A nice unparticular man. [Thomas Hardy: *Far From the Madding Crowd*]

UNWEPT
21 Unwept, unhonored, and unsung. [Sir Walter Scott: *The Lay of the Last Minstrel* VI]

UNWORTHY
22 Whose shoe's latchet I am not worthy to unloose. [John 1:27]

UP-HILL
23 Does the road wind up-hill all the way?

Yes, to the very end.
[Christina Georgina Rossetti: *Up-Hill*]

UPLIFTING
1 In uplifting, get underneath. [George Ade: *Fables in Slang*, "The Good Fairy" (1900)]

URGENCY
2 But at my back I always hear
Time's winged chariot hurrying near;
And yonder all before us lie
Deserts of vast eternity.
[Andrew Marvell: *To His Coy Mistress*]

USAGE
3 Those that will combat use and custom by the strict rules of grammar do but jest. [Montaigne: *Essays* III.v.]
4 The meaning of a word in general use is determined, not by pundits, still less by official action of any kind, but by the people. It is the duty of the professional linguist to find out, by investigation, what the usage of the people is, in this particular matter, and to record his findings. [Kemp Malone: *On Defining Mahogany*]

USE
5 How use doth breed a habit in a man. [Shakespeare: *The Two Gentlemen of Verona* V.iv.]

USELESS
6 Sensible people regard nothing as useless. [La Fontaine: *Fables* V.19]
Of course, every half-crazed accumulator of refuse, who lives among old bottles, stacked newspapers, and the like, regards himself as eminently sensible.

UTILITY
7 I regard utility as the ultimate appeal on all ethical questions; but it must be utility in the largest sense, grounded on the permanent interests of man as a progressive being. [John Stuart Mill: *On Liberty* I]

UTOPIA
8 To arrest a downward movement is the utmost to which a Utopia can aspire, since Utopias seldom begin to be written in any society until after its members have lost the expectation and ambition of making further progress and have been cowed by adversity into being content if they can succeed in holding the ground which has been won for them by their fathers. [Arnold J. Toynbee: *A Study of History* (Vol. III)]

UTTERANCE
9 That large utterance of the early
Gods!
[Keats: *Hyperion* I.li.]

V

VACUUM
1 Nature abhors a vacuum. (*Natura abhorret vacuum*.) [Latin proverb]

VALET
2 Many a man has been a wonder to the world, whose wife and valet have seen nothing in him that was even remarkable. Few men have been admired by their servants. [Montaigne: *Essays* III. ii.]

3 No man is a hero to his valet. [Mme. de Cornuel: (about 1670) see *Lettres de Mlle. Aissé*, Aug. 13, 1728]

This famous saying has been attributed to the Duc de Condé (d. 1686). But whoever originated it, it quickly caught on and became so established that further epigrams grew from it. La Bruyère, in Les Caractères, *felt that it illustrated the fact that greatness was an illusion, that men are only men, and that a public role cannot be sustained in domestic privacy. Carlyle, who believed in heroes, felt that the blame for nonrecognition must fall on the "mean valet-soul" (The Hero as Man of Letters). Goethe agreed: "A hero can be recognized only by a hero." (Sprüche in Prosa, III.204)*

VALLEY
4 Yea, though I walk through the valley of the shadow of death, I will fear no evil: for thou art with me; thy rod and thy staff they comfort me. [Psalms 23:4]

VALOR
5 When valor preys on reason, it eats the sword it fights with. [Shakespeare: *Antony and Cleopatra* III. xiii.]

6   No thought of flight,
None of retreat, no unbecoming deed
That argued fear; each on himself relied,
As only in his arm the moment lay
Of victory.
[John Milton: *Paradise Lost* VI.236-240]

7 Valour that parleys is near yielding.

[George Herbert: *Jacula Prudentum*]

8 My valour is certainly going!—it is sneaking off!—I feel it oozing out, as it were, at the palms of my hands. [Richard Brinsley Sheridan: *The Rivals* V. iii.]

VALUE
9 The value of a thing is the amount of laboring or work that its possession will save the possessor. [Henry George: *The Science of Political Economy*]

VANITY(IES)
10 Vanity of vanities, saith the Preacher, vanity of vanities; all is vanity.

What profit hath a man of all his labor which he taketh under the sun?

One generation passeth away, and another generation cometh: but the earth abideth for ever.

The sun also ariseth, and the sun goeth down, and hasteth to his place where he arose.

The wind goeth toward the south, and turneth about unto the north: it whirleth about continually, and the wind returneth again according to his circuits.

All the rivers run into the sea: yet the sea is not full; unto the place from whence the rivers come, thither they return again.

All things are full of labor; man cannot utter it: the eye is not satisfied with seeing, nor the ear filled with hearing.

The thing that hath been, it is that which shall be; and that which is done is that which shall be done: and there is no new thing under the sun. [Ecclesiastes I: 2-9]

vanity = empty, futile, worthless

11 I have seen all the works that are done under the sun; and behold, all is vanity and vexation of spirit. [Ecclesiastes 1:14]

12 The pomps and vanity of this wicked world. [*Book of Common Prayer*, "Catechism"]

13 What makes the vanity of other people insupportable is that it wounds our

own. [La Rochefoucauld: *Maxims*]

1 Vanity, like murder, will out. [Hannah Cowley: *The Belle's Stratagem* I.iv.]

2 Life without vanity is almost impossible. [Leo Tolstoy: *The Kreutzer Sonata* XXIII]

3 One will rarely err if extreme actions be ascribed to vanity, ordinary actions to habit, and mean actions to fear. [Nietzsche: *Human, All Too Human*]

4 Cruelty was the vice of the ancient, vanity is that of the modern world. Vanity is the last disease. [George Moore: *Mummer-Worship*]

5 Peacock Vanities, great, crested Cockatoos of Glory, gay Infatuations and painted Daydreams;—what a pity it is all the Blue Birds of impossible Paradises have such beaks and sharp claws, that one really has to keep them shut up in their not too-cleanly cages! [Logan Pearsall Smith: *More Trivia*, "The Aviary"]

6 Vanity is so intimately associated with our spiritual identity that whatever hurts it, above all if it came from it, is more painful in the memory than serious sin. [William Butler Yeats: *Dramatis Personae*]

7 Vanity, vanity, all is vanity
That's any fun at all for humanity.
[Ogden Nash: *Ha! Original Sin!*]

VANITY FAIR

8 When they were got out of the wilderness, they presently saw a town before them, and the name of that town is Vanity; and at the town there is a fair kept, called Vanity Fair. At this fair are all such merchandise sold, as houses, lands, trades, places, honors, preferments, titles, countries, kingdoms, lusts, pleasures and delights of all sorts, as whores, bawds, wives, husbands, children, masters, servants, lives, blood, bodies, souls, silver, gold, pearls, precious stones, and what not. [John Bunyan: *Pilgrim's Progress* I]

9 It beareth the name of Vanity Fair, because the town where 'tis kept is lighter than vanity. [John Bunyan: *Pilgrim's Progress* I]

10 There is great quantity of eating and drinking, making love and jilting, laughing and the contrary, smoking, cheating, fighting, dancing and fiddling; there are bullies pushing about, bucks ogling the women, knaves picking pockets. . . . Yes, this is Vanity Fair; not a moral place certainly; nor a merry one, though very noisy. [W. M. Thackeray: *Vanity Fair*, "Before the Curtain"]

VANQUISHED

11 Woe to the vanquished! (*Vae victis!*) [Livy: *Histories* V]

The story is that when the Gauls, under Brennus, captured Rome in 390 B.C., the Romans were compelled to ransom the city. As the ransom was being weighed, the Romans complained of false weights; whereupon Brennus flung his sword into the scales, to add even more to what they had to pay, and cried "Woe to the vanquished!" Perhaps the story was dear to the Romans because it justified their own victorious exactions.

12 The vanquished never yet spake well of the conqueror. [Samuel Daniel: *A Defence of Rhyme*]

VARIETY

13 No pleasure lasts long unless there is variety in it. [Publilius Syrus: *Maxims*]

14 Age cannot wither her, nor custom stale
Her infinite variety; other women cloy
The appetites they feed, but she makes hungry
Where most she satisfies.
[Shakespeare: *Antony and Cleopatra* II ii.]

15 Variety's the very spice of life. [William Cowper: *The Task* II]

Usually: "Variety is the spice of life."
Christopher Morley said that spice *is the plural of* spouse.

16 They are the weakest-minded and the hardest-hearted men, that most love variety and change. [John Ruskin: *Modern Painters* II.vi.7.]

VENGEANCE

17 Vengeance is mine; I will repay, saith the Lord. [Romans 12:19]

18 Heat not a furnace for your foe so hot
That it do singe yourself.
[Shakespeare: *Henry VIII* I.i.]

1 Revenge, that thirsty dropsy of our
souls,
Which makes us covet that which
hurts us most.
[Philip Massinger: *A Very Woman* IV.ii.]
2 There's small revenge in words, but
words may be greatly revenged. [Benjamin Franklin: *Poor Richard's Almanack*,
1735]
3 Now vengeance has a brood of eggs,
But Patience must be hen.
[George Meredith: *Archduchess Anne*
XII]

VENICE
4 In Venice they do let heaven see the
pranks
They dare not show their husbands;
their best conscience
Is not to leave't undone, but to keep't
unknown.
[Shakespeare: *Othello* III.iii.]
5 Once did She hold the gorgeous east
in fee
And was the safeguard of the
west. . . .
Venice, the eldest Child of Liberty.
She was a maiden City, bright and
free;
No guile seduced, no force could
violate;
And when she took unto herself a
Mate,
She must espouse the everlasting Sea.
[Wordsworth: *On the Extinction of the
Venetian Republic*]
6 In Venice Tasso's echoes are no more,
And silent rows the songless gondolier;
Her palaces are crumbling to the
shore,
And music meets not always now the
ear:
Those days are gone, but Beauty still
is here:
States fall, arts fade, but Nature doth
not die,
Nor yet forget how Venice once was
dear.
[Byron: *Childe Harold* IV.iii.]
7 I stood in Venice, on the Bridge of
Sighs;
A palace and a prison on each hand;
I saw from out the wave her structure
rise

As from the stroke of the enchanter's
wand.
A thousand years their cloudy wings
expand
Around me, and a dying glory smiles
O'er the far times, when many a subject land
Look'd to the winged Lion's marble
piles,
Where Venice sat in state, throned
on her hundred isles.
[Byron: *Childe Harold* IV.i.]

VENI, VIDI, VICI
8 Veni, vidi, vici.
*The famous statement ("I came, I saw,
I conquered") was written by Caesar in
a letter announcing his victory over
Pharnaces at Zela, in Pontus, in 47 B.C.*
*As a publicist, Caesar was, plainly,
very pleased with the message. Suetonius
(Life of Caesar XXXVII) tells us that
when he had ended the wars Caesar celebrated five triumphs, four in a single
month. And that "In his Pontic triumph
he displayed among the show pieces of
the procession an inscription of but
three words, 'I came, I saw, I conquered,'
not indicating the events of the war, as
the others did, but the speed with which
it was finished."*
*It is not often in history that the vanity of the author and the vanity of the
conqueror must strive for precedence.*
9 Caesar's thrasonical brag of "I came,
saw, and overcame."
[Shakespeare: *As You Like It* V.ii.]
thrasonical = *bragging*
Thraso was a boastful soldier in Terence's Eunuchus.
10 *Peccavi.* [Sir Charles Napier: dispatch
after winning a battle at Hyderabad, in
India, 1843]
Peccavi = *I have sinned*
*The conquest of Hyderabad gave Sir
Charles control of the Indian province
of Sind or Sindh. So that* Peccavi = *I
have Sindh.*
*Caesar has much to answer for in military dispatches. This one is too clever by
half. One has to know Roman history,
Latin grammar, Indian geography and
military humor to understand it. However, it affords explainers a pleasant
quarter of an hour.*

VENUS

1 The children of Mercurie and of Venus
Been in hir wirking ful contrarious.
[Chaucer: Prologue to *The Wife of Bath's Tale*]

Mercurie was the god of commerce, of knowledge and science. This anticipates one of the themes of D. H. Lawrence's Lady Chatterley's Lover.

2 Venus smiles not in a house of tears. [Shakespeare: *Romeo and Juliet* IV.i.]

3 Venus, a notorious strumpet, as common as a barber's chair. [Robert Burton: *The Anatomy of Melancholy* I.4.1]

4 The foulest, the vilest, the obscenest picture the world possesses—Titian's Venus. It isn't that she is naked and stretched out on a bed—no, it is the attitude of one of her arms and hand. . . . Without any question it was painted for a bagnio and was probably refused because it was a trifle too strong. [Mark Twain: *A Tramp Abroad*]

VERACITY

5 He commended one of the Dukes of Devonshire for "a dogged veracity." [Samuel Johnson: in Boswell's *Life,* April 1, 1779]

This was William, third Duke (d. 1755). On another occasion (Sept. 22, 1777) Johnson said of him:

"He was not a man of superior abilities, but he was a man strictly faithful to his word. If, for instance, he had promised you an acorn, and none had grown that year in his woods, he would not have contented himself with that excuse; he would have sent to Denmark for it."

VERBOSITY

6 He draweth out the thread of his verbosity finer than the staple of his argument. [Shakespeare: *Love's Labour's Lost* V.i.]

Richard Porson in a letter to George Travis (1789) used this line without quotation marks—assuming that Travis would recognize it. But subsequent compilers did not and the sentence is sometimes ascribed to Porson.

7 In general those who nothing have to say

Contrive to spend the longest time in doing it.
[James Russell Lowell: *An Oriental Apologue*]

VERDICT

8 The *a priori* opinion of that juror who smokes the worst cigars. [H. L. Mencken: *A Book of Burlesques*]

VERGIL

9 Mantua bore me; Calabria captivated me; Naples now holds me. I sang of pastures, of country things, and of the leaders of war. [Vergil's epitaph: as given in Claudius Donatus's *Life of Vergil*]

Vergil was born in Mantua, wrote his eclogues of life in Calabria and was buried at Parthenope, where Naples now stands.

VERSATILITY

10 A man so various, that he seem'd to be
Not one, but all mankind's epitome;
Stiff in opinions, always in the wrong,
Was everything by starts, and nothing long;
But, in the course of one revolving moon,
Was chymist, fiddler, statesman, and buffoon.
[Dryden: *Absalom and Achitophel* I]

The reference is to George Villiers, second duke of Buckingham who made "the whole body of vice his study."

VERSE

11 Mad Verse, Sad Verse, Glad Verse and Bad Verse.
[Title of a book by John Taylor, the Water Poet (1644)]

After serving long in Elizabeth's navy, Taylor (1580-1653) became a London waterman—one who lived by rowing passengers on the Thames. An energetic eccentric, one of the gay oddities of the human race, he prided himself on his titles—of which here are a few: A Kicksey Winsey; or a Lerry Come-Twang (1619); A Very Merry Wherry-Ferry-Voyage; Yorke for My Money (1622); A Bawd, a vertuous Bawd, a modest Bawd (1635); A most Horrible, Terrible, Tollerable, Termagant Satyre (1635).

1 Cursed be the verse, how well soe'er
it flow,
That tends to make one worthy man
my foe.
[Alexander Pope: *Epistle to Dr. Arbuthnot*]

VESTAL

2 How happy is the blameless vestal's
lot!
The world forgetting, by the world
forgot.
[Alexander Pope: *Eloisa to Abelard*]

VICAR OF BRAY

3 In good King Charles's golden days,
When loyalty no harm meant,
A zealous high-churchman was I,
And so I got preferment. . . .
And this is law that I'll maintain
Unto my dying day, sir,
That whatsoever king shall reign,
Still I'll be Vicar of Bray, sir.
[Anon.: *The Vicar of Bray* (about
1700)]

*With King Charles I a strong high-churchman, Cromwell an Independent,
Charles II secretly a Catholic but publicly a fairly tolerant Church-of-Englandman, James II openly a Catholic,
quarreling with the Establishment, William III personally a deist but functioning as Head of the Church of England
and Anne deeply religious and Head of
the Church—and all of this in less than
50 years—a Vicar who wished to hang on
to his livings had to be pretty adroit.
Fuller, in his* Worthies of Berkshire
*(1662), identifies the famous Vicar as
Symon Symonds who under the shifting
Tudors was twice Protestant and twice
Catholic. The echo of "Simony" in the
name, however, makes one suspicious.*

VICE(S)

4 We bear with those vices we are accustomed to; we reprove new ones. [Publilius Syrus: *Maxims*]
5 What were once vices are now the
manners of the day. [Seneca: *Ad Lucilium* XXXIX]
6 No one ever reached the worst of a
vice at one leap. [Juvenal: *Satires* II]
7 I hate him that my vices telleth me.
[Chaucer: Prologue to *The Wife of
Bath's Tale*]
8 The mother of vices. [John Lydgate:
The Fall of Princes II (c.1440)]
9 There is no vice so simple but assumes
Some mark of virtue on his outward
parts.
[Shakespeare: *The Merchant of Venice*
III.ii.]
10 The gods are just, and of our pleasant vices
Make instruments to plague us.
[Shakespeare: *King Lear* V.iii.]
11 Vice may be had at all prices. [Sir
Thomas Browne: *Christian Morals* II]
12 He that can apprehend and consider
vice with all her baits and seeming
pleasures, and yet abstain, and yet distinguish, and yet prefer that which is
truly better, he is the true wayfaring
Christian. [John Milton: *Areopagitica*]
13 We are often saved from exclusive
addiction to a single vice by the possession of others. [La Rochefoucauld: *Maxims*]
14 When our vices leave us, we flatter
ourselves with the idea that we have
left them. [La Rochefoucauld: *Maxims*]
15 I prefer an accommodating vice to an
obstinate virtue. [Molière: *Amphitryon*
I.iv.]
16 Vice is a monster of so frightful mien
As to be hated needs but to be seen;
Yet seen too oft, familiar with her
face,
We first endure, then pity, then embrace.
[Alexander Pope: *An Essay on Man* II]
(1732)]
*"Vice is a creature of such heejous mien
. . . that th' more ye see it th' better
ye like it."*
Finley Peter Dunne: Mr. Dooley's
Opinions, *"The Crusade Against Vice"*
(1900)
17 The greatest part of human gratifications approach nearly to vice. [Samuel
Johnson: *Rambler* No. 160]
18 The world can ill spare any vice
which has obtained long and largely
among civilized people. [Samuel Butler
(1835-1902): *Notebooks*]
19 Vice is waste of life. Poverty, obedience, and celibacy are the canonical

vices. [G. B. Shaw: *Maxims for Revolutionists*]

VICISSITUDES
1 A man used to vicissitudes is not easily dejected. [Samuel Johnson: *Rasselas* (1759)]

VICTORY
2 Another such victory and we are ruined. [Pyrrhus, King of Epirus: in Plutarch's *Pyrrhus*]
In 280 B.C. Pyrrhus defeated the Romans at Asculum but at a cost so severe that when congratulated on the victory, Pyrrhus spoke as above. Hence our term "a pyrrhic victory," meaning a victory that has cost the victor more than the vanquished.

3 Victory is by nature insolent and haughty. [Cicero: *Pro Marcello*]
4 Who ever asks whether the enemy were defeated by strategy or valor? [Vergil: *Aeneid* II]
5 The better man may win, but he will be the worse for his victory. [Seneca: *Epistolae* XIV.xiii.]
6 They preferred victory to peace. [Tacitus: *History* III.ix.]
The "unconditional surrender" psychology.

7 There are some defeats more triumphant than victories. [Montaigne: *Essays* I.xxxii.]
8 Nothing can seem foul to those that win.
[Shakespeare: *I Henry IV* V.i.]
9 All the gods go with you! upon your sword
Sit laurel victory! and smooth success
Be strew'd before your feet!
[Shakespeare: *Antony and Cleopatra* I.iii.]
10   Peace hath her victories
No less renowned than War.
[John Milton: *To the Lord General Cromwell*]
11   Who overcomes
By force, hath overcome but half his foe.
[John Milton: *Paradise Lost* I. 648-649]
12 But what good came of it at last?
Quoth little Peterkin,
Why, that I cannot tell, said he,
But 'twas a famous victory.

[Robert Southey: *The Battle of Blenheim*]
13 To suffer woes which hope thinks infinite;
To forgive wrongs darker than death or night;
To defy power, which seems omnipotent;
To love, and bear; to hope till hope creates
From its own wreck the thing it contemplates;
Neither to change, nor falter, nor repent;
This, like thy glory, Titan, is to be
Good, great and joyous, beautiful and free;
This is alone life, joy, empire, and victory.
[Shelley: *Prometheus Unbound* IV]
14 God how the dead men
Grin by the wall,
Watching the fun
Of the Victory Ball.
[Alfred Noyes: *A Victory Dance*]
15 In war there is no substitute for victory. [Douglas MacArthur, address to Congress, April 19, 1951]

VIGILANCE
16 The condition upon which God has given liberty to man is eternal vigilance. [John Philpot Curran: Speech upon the Right of Election, July 10, 1790]

VILE
17 Wisdom and goodness to the vile seem vile;
Filths savour but themselves.
[Shakespeare: *King Lear* IV.ii.]

VILLAGE
18 Sweet Auburn! loveliest village of the plain,
Where health and plenty cheer'd the labouring swain,
Where smiling spring its earliest visit paid,
And parting summer's lingering blooms delay'd.
[Oliver Goldsmith: *The Deserted Village*]

VILLAIN
19 Wronged shall he live, insulted o'er,

oppressed,
Who dares be less a villain than the
rest.
[John Wilmot, Earl of Rochester: *A
Satyr Against Mankind*]

1 And therefore, since I cannot prove a
lover . . .
I am determined to prove a villain.
[Shakespeare: *Richard III* I.i.]

2 O villain, villain, smiling, damnèd
villain!
[Shakespeare: *Hamlet* I.v.]

3 Bloody, bawdy villain!
Remorseless, treacherous, lecherous,
kindless villain!
[Shakespeare: *Hamlet* II.ii.]

4 The villain still pursued her.
[Milton Nobles: *The Phoenix* I.iii.]

VILLAINY

5 Barring that natural expression of
villainy which we all have, the man
looked honest enough. [Mark Twain: *A
Mysterious Visit*]

VINDICATION

6 Laugh where we must, be candid
where we can;
But vindicate the ways of God to
man.
[Alexander Pope: *An Essay on Man* I]

VINE

7 They shall sit every man under his
vine and under his fig-tree. [Micah 4:4]

8 I can see him already—with vine
leaves in his hair—flushed and fearless.
[Henrik Ibsen: *Hedda Gabler* II (1890)]
*The reference is to Eilert Lövborg, an
author of promise who has turned from
dissipation to significant achievement,
from which he falls to a sordid death.
The vine leaves—symbols of a pagan vitality lacking in the dull lives of the
other townsmen—alludes to the adorn-
ments of the excited followers of Dionysus.*

VINTAGE

9 Eggs of an hour, bread of a day, wine
of a year, a friend of thirty years. [Old
Italian proverb]

VIRGINITY

10 There never was virgin got till vir-
ginity was first lost.
[Shakespeare: *All's Well That Ends Well*
I.i.]

11 Some say no evil thing that walks by
night,
In fog or fire, by lake or moorish fen,
Blue meagre hag, or stubborn unlaid
ghost,
That breaks his magic chains at cur-
few time,
No goblin, or swart faery of the mine,
Hath hurtful power o'er true virgin-
ity.
[John Milton: *Comus*]

VIRGINNY

12 Carry me back to old Virginny,
There's where the cotton and the
corn and taters grow;
There's where the birds warble sweet
in the springtime,
There's where this old darky's heart
am long'd to go.
[James A. Bland: *Carry Me Back to Old
Virginny*]

VIRGINS

13 Where the virgins are soft as the roses
they twine,
And all save the spirit of man is
divine.
[Byron: *The Bride of Abydos* I.i.]

VIRTUE: its nature

14 Virtue is a kind of health, beauty and
good habit of the soul. [Plato: *The Republic* IV]

15 Whatsoever things are true, whatsoever things are honest, whatsoever things
are just, whatsoever things are pure,
whatsoever things are lovely, whatsoever
things are of good report: if there be any
virtue, and if there be any praise, think
on these things. [Philippians 4:8]

16 Virtue consists in fleeing vice. [Hor-
ace: *Epistles* I]

17 Virtue is like precious odours—most
fragrant when they are incensed, or
crushed. [Francis Bacon: *Of Adversity*]

18 Virtue is like a rich stone, best set
plain. [Francis Bacon: *Of Beauty*]

19 So our virtues
Lie in the interpretation of the time.
[Shakespeare: *Coriolanus* IV.vii.]

20 Good company and good discourse

are the very sinews of virtue. [Izaak Walton: *The Compleat Angler* I.li.]

1 I cannot praise a fugitive and cloistered virtue, unexercised and unbreathed, that never sallies out and sees her adversary, but slinks out of the race, where that immortal garland is to be run for, not without dust and heat. [John Milton: *Areopagitica*]

2 We need greater virtues to sustain good fortune than bad. [La Rochefoucauld: *Maxims*]

3 Virtue would not go so far if vanity did not keep it company. [La Rochefoucauld: *Maxims*]

4 Virtue is everywhere that which is thought praiseworthy; and nothing else but that which has the allowance of public esteem is called virtue. [John Locke: *An Essay Concerning Human Understanding* II]

5 Virtue debases itself in justifying itself. [Voltaire: *Œdipe* I.iv.]

6 The virtue which requires to be ever guarded is scarcely worth the sentinel. [Oliver Goldsmith: *The Vicar of Wakefield* V]

7 Virtue and pleasure are not, in fact, so nearly allied in this life as some eloquent writers have laboured to prove. [Mary Wollstonecraft: *A Vindication of the Rights of Woman* IV]

8 Rare virtues are like rare plants or animals, things that have not been able to hold their own in the world. A virtue to be serviceable must, like gold, be alloyed with some commoner but more durable metal. [Samuel Butler (1835-1902): *The Way of All Flesh* XIX]

9 What is virtue but the Trade Unionism of the married. [G. B. Shaw: *Man and Superman* III]

VIRTUE: its rewards and penalties

10 Of all the benefits that virtue confers upon us, the contempt of death is one of the greatest. [Montaigne: *Essays* I.xix.]

11 Virtue is its own reward. [Dryden: *The Assignation* III.i.]

> Dryden was simply repeating a hackneyed aphorism. Almost every moral writer of antiquity felt called on to voice this lofty sentiment—Cicero, Seneca, Ovid, Philo, Claudian and, of course, our own moralists, Carlyle and Emerson.

> There are very few anti-statements. Sir Thomas Browne (Religio Medici *I* (1643) felt it to be "but a cold principle," unable to maintain us in "a settled way of goodness." Vauvenargues (Réflexions (1746)) felt it made virtue not a human but a supernatural quality. But these are rare voices, that and the popular but cynical: Virtue is its own and only reward.

12 Know then this truth (enough for man to know),
"Virtue alone is happiness below."
[Alexander Pope: *An Essay on Man* IV]

13 Virtue is the compensation to the poor for the want of riches. [Horace Walpole: letter to Hannah More, Sept. 22, 1788]

14 Be good and you will be lonesome. [Mark Twain: *Following the Equator*]

VIRTUE: and vice

15 Virtue is a mean state between two vices, the one of excess and the other of deficiency. [Aristotle: *The Nicomachean Ethics* II]

16 Vices creep into our hearts under the name of virtues. [Seneca: *Ad Lucilium*]

17 Virtue itself turns vice, being misapplied.
[Shakespeare: *Romeo and Juliet* II.iii.]

18 Our virtues would be proud if our faults whipped them not; and our crimes would despair if they were not cherished by our virtues. [Shakespeare: *All's Well That Ends Well* IV.iii.]

19 For in the fatness of these pursy times
Virtue itself of vice must pardon beg.
[Shakespeare: *Hamlet* III.iv.]

20 Some rise by sin, and some by virtue fall.
[Shakespeare: *Measure for Measure* II.i.]

21 He redeemed his vices with his virtues. There was ever more in him to be praised than to be pardoned. [Ben Jonson: *Discoveries*]

22 In social life, we please more often by our vices than our virtues. [La Rochefoucauld: *Maxims*]

23 Our virtues are most frequently but vices in disguise. [La Rochefoucauld: *Maxims*]

24 Virtue in distress, and vice in triumph
Make atheists of mankind.

[Dryden: *Cleomenes* IV.i.]
1 'Tis the first virtue vices to abhor.
[Alexander Pope: *Imitations of Horace,* Epistle I]

> The cardinal moral principle among the Unco Guid. *It often absorbs so much of their energy that they have none left over with which to sin, had they a mind to. The mere abhorrence of vice is not a virtue at all.*

2 So much are the modes of excellence settled by time and place, that men may be heard boasting in one street of that which they would anxiously conceal in another. [Samuel Johnson: *The Rambler* No. 201]
3 If he does really think there is no distinction between virtue and vice, why, Sir, when he leaves our houses let us count our spoons. [Samuel Johnson: in Boswell's *Life,* July 9, 1763]
4 Virtue, enlightened, can be as calculating as vice. [Balzac: *Eugénie Grandet* III]
5 Change in a trice
The lilies and languors of virtue
For the raptures and roses of vice.
[Swinburne: *Dolores*]

VIRTUE: miscellaneous
6 Virtue is persecuted more by the wicked than it is loved by the good. [Cervantes: *Don Quixote* I.47]
7 As in nature things move violently to their place, and calmly in their place, so virtue in ambition is violent, in authority settled and calm. [Francis Bacon: *Of Great Place*]
8 Assume a virtue, if you have it not. [Shakespeare: *Hamlet* III.iv.]
9 Besides, this Duncan
Hath borne his faculties so meek, hath been
So clear in his great office, that his virtues
Will plead like angels, trumpet-tongued against
The deep damnation of his taking-off;
And pity, like a naked new-born babe,
Striding the blast, or heaven's cherubim, horsed
Upon the sightless couriers of the air,
Shall blow the horrid deed in every eye,

That tears shall drown the wind.
[Shakespeare: *Macbeth* I.vii.]
10 There is no road or ready way to virtue. [Sir Thomas Browne: *Religio Medici* I.lv.]
11 Virtue could see to do what virtue would
By her own radiant light, though sun and moon
Were in the flat sea sunk.
[John Milton: *Comus*]
12 Love Virtue, she alone is free;
She can teach ye how to climb
Higher than the spheary chime:
Or, if Virtue feeble were,
Heaven itself would stoop to her.
[John Milton: *Comus* (concluding lines)]
spheary chime = *the spheres and their famed music*
13 And e'en his failings leaned to Virtue's side.
[Oliver Goldsmith: *The Deserted Village*]
14 And he by no uncommon lot
Was famed for virtues he had not.
[William Cowper: *To the Rev. William Bull*]
15 I think I could be a good woman if I had five thousand a year. [W. M. Thackeray: *Vanity Fair* II.I]
16 Virtue has always been conceived of as victorious resistance to one's vital desire. [James Branch Cabell: *Beyond Life* 114]
> cf. Ella Wheeler Wilcox: *"And the life that is worth the honor of earth/ Is the one that resists desire."* (Worth While)

VIRTUOUS
17 Who shall ascend into the hill of the Lord? or who shall stand in his holy place?
He that hath clean hands, and a pure heart; who hath not lifted up his soul unto vanity, nor sworn deceitfully. [Psalms 24:1-2]
18 Many wish not so much to be virtuous, as to seem to be. [Cicero: *De Amicitia* XXVI]
19 The more virtuous any man is, the less easily does he suspect others to be vicious. [Cicero: *Ad Fratrem* I]
20 When men grow virtuous in their old age, they only make a sacrifice to God of the devil's leavings. [Alexander Pope:

Thoughts on Various Subjects]

1 The wicked are wicked, no doubt, and they go astray and they fall, and they come by their deserts; but who can tell the mischief which the very virtuous do? [W. M. Thackeray: *The Newcomes* I.xx.]

2 Be virtuous and you will be eccentric. [Mark Twain: *Mental Photographs*]

VISION

3 Where there is no vision, the people perish. [Proverbs 29:18]

4 Is this a vision? is this a dream? do I sleep?
[Shakespeare: *Merry Wives of Windsor* III.v.]

5 Our revels now are ended. These our actors,
As I foretold you, were all spirits and
Are melted into air, into thin air:
And, like the baseless fabric of this vision,
The cloud-capp'd towers, the gorgeous palaces,
The solemn temples, the great globe itself,
Yea, all which it inherit, shall dissolve
And, like this insubstantial pageant faded,
Leave not a rack behind.
[Shakespeare: *The Tempest* IV.i.]

6 Where the great Vision of the guarded mount
Looks toward Namancos and Bayona's hold.
[John Milton: *Lycidas*]

7 The youth who daily farther from the east
Must travel, still is Nature's priest,
And by the vision splendid
Is on his way attended;
At last the man perceives it die away,
And fade into the light of common day.
[Wordsworth: *Intimations of Immortality* IV]

8 Whither is fled the visionary gleam?
Where is it now, the glory and the dream?
[Wordsworth: *Intimations of Immortality* IV]

9 Hence in a season of calm weather

Though inland far we be,
Our souls have sight of that immortal sea
Which brought us hither,
Can in a moment travel thither,
And see the children sport upon the shore,
And hear the mighty waters rolling evermore.
[Wordsworth: *Intimations of Immortality* IX]

10 Was it a vision, or a waking dream?
Fled is that music:—do I wake or sleep?
[Keats: *Ode to a Nightingale*]

11 Do I sleep? do I dream?
Do I wonder and doubt?
Are things what they seem?
Or is visions about?
[Bret Harte: *Further Language from Truthful James*]

12 Ah splendid Vision, golden time,
An end of hunger, cold, and crime,
An end of rent, an end of rank,
An end of balance at the bank!
[Andrew Lang: *The New Millennium*]

VISIT

13 A great place to visit, but I wouldn't want to live there! [Hoary cliché of timid travelers.]

Just how hoary is illustrated by a passage from Montaigne: Essays III.i:

"*Isocrates used to say that people liked Athens the way men like the ladies they serve for love. Everyone loved to come and wander around and pass his time there; no one loved it enough to marry it, that is to say, to reside and settle there.*"

Montaigne does not furnish the exact reference. Isocrates, a great Athenian orator, lived from 436 to 338 B.C.

VISITOR(S)

14 Those that come to see me do me honor; and those that stay away, do me a-favor. [Louis Morin, French physician and botanist: in Samuel Johnson's *Life of Morin*]

Johnson's Life is largely a translation of an éloge by Fontenelle.

15 Fish and visitors smell in three days. [Benjamin Franklin: *Poor Richard's Almanack*]

16 "'T is some visitor," I muttered,

"tapping at my chamber door—
Only this and nothing more."
[Edgar Allan Poe: *The Raven*]

VITALITY

1 Sae rantingly, sae wantonly,
Sae dauntingly gaed he;
He played a spring and danced it
round,
Below the gallows tree.
[Burns: *MacPherson's Farewell*]
*MacPherson was an outlaw who was
executed in 1700. The night before his
death he wrote a gay song.*

VOCATION

2 'Tis my vocation, Hal; 'tis no sin for
a man to labour in his vocation. [Shakespeare: *I Henry IV* I.ii.]

VOICE(S)

3 The voice of the people is the voice
of God.
[Hesiod: *Works and Days*]
4 The voice is Jacob's voice, but the
hands are the hands of Esau. [Genesis
27:22]
5 But the Lord was not in the wind:
and after the wind an earthquake; but
the Lord was not in the earthquake:
And after the earthquake a fire; but
the Lord was not in the fire: and after
the fire a still small voice. [I Kings 19:
11-12]
6 The voice of one crying in the wilderness. [Mark 1:3]
*See Matthew 3:3; Luke 3:4; John 1:23;
and Isaiah 40:3: The voice of him that
crieth in the wilderness.*
7 I will aggravate my voice so that I
will roar you as gently as any sucking
dove; I will roar you as 't were any nightingale. [Shakespeare: *A Midsummer
Night's Dream* I.ii.]
8 Her voice was ever soft,
Gentle and low, an excellent thing in
woman.
[Shakespeare: *King Lear* V.iii.]
9 His voice was propertied
As all the tuned spheres.
[Shakespeare: *Antony and Cleopatra* V.
ii.]
propertied = *endowed with qualities*
10 The melting voice through mazes
running,
Untwisting all the chains that tie

The hidden soul of harmony.
[John Milton: *L'Allegro*]
11 The angel ended, and in Adam's ear
So charming left his voice that he a
while
Thought him still speaking.
[John Milton: *Paradise Lost* VIII.1-3]
12 Lord, in the morning thou shalt hear
My voice ascending high.
[Isaac Watts: *Psalms V*]
*My voice shalt thou hear in the morning, O Lord; in the morning will I direct
my prayer unto thee, and will look up.
—Psalms 5:3*
13 Ancestral voices prophesying war!
[Coleridge: *Kubla Khan*]
14 Like music on the waters
Is thy sweet voice to me.
[Byron: *Stanzas for Music*]
15 The devil hath not, in all his quiver's
choice,
An arrow for the heart like a sweet
voice.
[Byron: *Don Juan* XV.xiii.]
16 The voice that breathed o'er Eden,
That earliest wedding day.
[John Keble: *Holy Matrimony*]
17 But O for the touch of a vanish'd
hand,
And the sound of a voice that is still!
[Tennyson: *Break, Break, Break*]
18 A still small voice spake unto me.
[Tennyson: *The Two Voices*]
19 What's more enchanting than the
voice of young people when you can't
hear what they say? [Logan Pearsall
Smith: *Afterthoughts*]
20 All the intelligence and talent in the
world can't make a singer. The voice is a
wild thing. It can't be bred in captivity.
[Willa Cather: *The Song of the Lark*
II.vi.]

VOLTAIRE

21 The Scripture was his jest-book.
[William Cowper: *Truth*]
22 Thou art so witty, profligate and thin,
At once we think thee Satan, Death,
and Sin.
[Arthur Young: *Epigram on Voltaire*]
23 The one was fire and fickleness, a
child
Most mutable in wishes, but in mind
A wit as various—gay, grave, sage, or
wild—

Historian, bard, philosopher, combined;
He multiplied himself among mankind,
The Proteus of their talents: But his
own
Breathed most in ridicule—which, as
the wind,
Blew where it listed, laying all things
prone—
Now to o'erthrow a fool, and now to
shake a throne.
[Byron: *Childe Harold's Pilgrimage* III.
cvi.]

VOLUPTUOUSNESS

1 Voluptuousness is a quality little ambitious. It holds itself rich enough of itself without any access of reputation and
is pleased with obscurity. [Montaigne:
Essays III.v.]

VOW(S)

2 Better is it that thou shouldest not
vow, than that thou shouldest vow and
not pay. [Ecclesiastes 5:5]
3 When the blood burns, how prodigal
the soul
Lends the tongue vows.
[Shakespeare: *Hamlet* I.iii.]
4 He who breaks a resolution is a weakling;
He who makes one is a fool.
[Frederick Lawrence Knowles: *A Cheerful Year Book*]

VULGAR

5 A thing is not vulgar merely because
it is common. [William Hazlitt: *On Vulgarity*]
*But there is no surer mark of vulgarity
than thinking it is.*

W

WABASH

1 Oh the moonlight's fair to-night
along the Wabash,
From the fields there comes the
breath of new-mown hay;
Thro' the sycamores the candle lights
are gleaming,
On the banks of the Wabash far
away.
[Paul Dresser: *On the Banks of the Wabash*]
Paul Dresser was Theodore Dreiser's older brother. Theodore may have written the last two lines of this verse.

WAG

2 I never yet knew a wag who was not a dunce. [Jonathan Swift: *Thoughts on Various Subjects*]
wag = a card, a humorist, a great kidder, a practical joker
The word is a shortening of waghalter—that is, one who will end up on the gallows, wagging a noose or halter in his death struggles. The word was first applied as a term of abusive endearment to mischievous boys and then extended to merry fellows who kept a youthful impudence and juvenile sense of humor.

WAGER(S)

3 Fools for arguments use wagers. [Samuel Butler (1612-1680): *Hudibras*]
4 Most men (till by losing rendered
sager)
Will back their own opinions by a
wager.
[Byron: *Beppo*]

WAILING

5 A savage place! as holy and enchanted
As e'er beneath a waning moon was
haunted
By woman wailing for her demon-lover!
[Coleridge: *Kubla Khan*]

WAITING

6 They also serve who only stand and
wait.
[John Milton: *On His Blindness*]

7 But we like sentries are oblig'd to
stand
In starless nights, and wait th' appointed hour.
[Dryden: *Don Sebastian* II.i.]
8 Learn to labor and to wait.
[Longfellow: *A Psalm of Life*]
9 Ah, "All things come to those who
wait."
They come, but often come too late.
[Lady Mary M. Currie: *Tout Vient à Qui Sait Attendre* (1890)]
10 Long for me the rick will wait,
And long will wait the fold,
And long will stand the empty plate,
And dinner will be cold.
[A. E. Housman: *A Shropshire Lad* VIII]

WAKE

11 This ae nighte, this ae nighte,
Every nighte and alle,
Fire and sleet and candle-lighte,
And Christ receive thy saule.
[*A Lyke-wake Dirge* (author unknown)]
Lyke-wake = *a watch or sitting up with a body*

WALKING

12 It is good walking when one hath his horse in hand. [John Lyly: *Endymion* IV.ii (1591)]
This was proverbial. The idea is that it is very pleasant to endure a few mild "hardships" when you don't have to, to hold a humble job if you have a fortune or, as here, to go afoot when it is in your power to ride whenever you want to.

WALL(S)

13 These are Sparta's walls. [Agesilaus, King of Sparta: in Plutarch's *Lycurgus* XIX]
Someone asked the king why Sparta had no walls and he pointed to the armed citizens.
14 The weakest goes to the wall. [15th-century proverb]
The idea of the old saying was simply that the weak were driven to the utmost extremity, to where, in our phrase, they

had their backs against the wall.

There are later phrases, however, that speak of the quarrelsome and the overbearing "taking the wall" and the weak and the meek yielding it. This refers to the fact that in cities, until quite recently, there were no sidewalks and close to the wall of the houses was the safest place from the dangers of traffic and indignities of refuse thrown from the overhanging upper stories.

1 Walls have ears. [James Shirley: *A Bird in a Cage* I]
2 A hedge between keeps friendship green. [18th-century English proverb]
3 A wall between preserves love. [Samuel Palmer: *Moral Essays on Proverbs*]
4 Something there is that doesn't love
a wall.
[Robert Frost: *Mending Wall*]
5 Before I built a wall I'd ask to know
What I was walling in or walling out.
[Robert Frost: *Mending Wall*]

WALTZ
6 Endearing Waltz!—to thy more melting tune
Bow Irish jig and ancient rigadoon;
Scotch reels, avaunt! and country-dance, forego
Your future claims to each fantastic toe!
Waltz—Waltz alone—both legs and arms demands,
Liberal of feet and lavish of her hands;
Hands which may freely range in public sight
Where ne'er before—but—pray "put out the light."
[Byron: *The Waltz*]
Every generation seems innocently scandalized by each new dance. It is amusing that the waltz, now accepted as sedate, dignified, graceful and even a little stuffy, should have shocked Byron at its introduction. One can only assume that dancers—in their minds, at least—miss the whole point of dancing. Or, perhaps, the point of it is that under the witchery of music the body eludes the mind's censorship.

WANDERERS
7   . . . on the sea

The boldest steer but where their ports invite;
But there are wanderers o'er Eternity
Whose bark drives on and on, and anchor'd ne'er shall be.
[Byron: *Childe Harold* III.lxx.]

WANDERING
8 The wandering outlaw of his own
dark mind.
[Byron: *Childe Harold* III.iii.]
9 Wandering between two worlds, one
dead,
The other powerless to be born.
[Matthew Arnold: *Stanzas from the Grande Chartreuse*]

WANDERLUST
10 There is nothing worse for mortals than a wandering life. [Homer: *Odyssey* XV]
11 Than longen folk to goon on pilgrimages
[Chaucer: Prologue to *The Canterbury Tales*]
12   I am become a name;
. . . always roaming with a hungry heart.
[Tennyson: *Ulysses*]
13 I cannot rest from travel; I will drink
Life to the lees.
[Tennyson: *Ulysses*]
14 My soul to-day
Is far away
Sailing the Vesuvian Bay.
[Thomas Buchanan Read: *Drifting*]
15 You have heard the beat of the off-shore wind,
And the thresh of the deep-sea rain;
You have heard the song—how long? how long?
Pull out on the trail again!
[Kipling: *The Long Trail*]

WANT(S)
16 Poverty wants some, luxury many, avarice all things. [Abraham Cowley: *Essays* VII]
Poverty lacks much, avarice all.
—*Publilius Syrus:* Maxims
17 Man wants but little here below,
Nor wants that little long.
[Oliver Goldsmith: *The Hermit*]
18 "Man wants but little here below
Nor wants that little long,"
'Tis not with me exactly so;

But 'tis so in the song.
My wants are many, and, if told,
Would muster many a score;
And were each wish a mint of gold,
I still should long for more.
[John Quincy Adams: *The Wants of Man*]

1 The good want power, but to weep
barren tears.
The powerful goodness want; worse
need for them.
The wise want love; and those who
love want wisdom;
And all best things are thus confused
to ill.
Many are strong and rich, and would
be just,
But live among their suffering fellowmen
As if none felt; they know not what
they do.
[Shelley: *Prometheus Unbound* I]
want = *lack*

2 There are three wants which can
never be satisfied: that of the rich, who
wants something more; that of the sick,
who wants something different; and that
of the traveller, who says, "Anywhere but
here." [Emerson: *Considerations by the Way*]

3 As long as I have a want, I have a
reason for living. Satisfaction is death.
[G .B. Shaw: *Overruled*]

4 I want what I want when I want it.
[Henry Blossom: song title]

WAR: its appeal, excitement, glory
5 Men grow tired of sleep, love, singing
and dancing sooner than of war. [Homer: *Iliad* XIII]

6 He saith among the trumpets, Ha, ha;
and he smelleth the battle afar off, the
thunder of the captains, and the shouting. [Job 39:25]

7 Horribly stuff'd with epithets of war.
[Shakespeare: *Othello* I.i.]

8 Pride, pomp, and circumstance of
glorious war!
[Shakespeare: *Othello* III.iii.]

9 My sentence is for open war.
[John Milton: *Paradise Lost* II.51]

10 The art of war, which I take to be
the highest perfection of human knowledge. [Daniel Defoe: Introduction to
The History of Projects]

11 War, that mad game the world so
loves to play.
[Jonathan Swift: *Ode to Sir William Temple*]

12 Ancestral voices prophesying war!
[Coleridge: *Kubla Khan*]

13 Tambourgi! Tambourgi! thy 'larum
afar
Gives hope to the valiant, and promise of war.
[Byron: *Childe Harold* II.lxxii.]
tambourgi = *war drum*

14 It is well that war is so terrible—we
would grow too fond of it. [Robert E.
Lee: to James Longstreet, at Fredericks-
burg, Dec. 13, 1862]
*It is said that Louis XIV on his death-
bed confessed that he "loved war too
well."*

15 There is many a boy here today who
looks on war as all glory, but, boys, it is
all hell. [General William T. Sherman:
speaking at a G.A.R. convention at Columbus, Ohio, Aug. 11, 1880]
*This seems to be the origin of what the
public has shortened to: War is hell.*

WAR: causes of
16 In war actions of great importance
are [often] the result of trivial causes.
[Caesar: *De Bello Gallico* I.xxi.]

17 Neither are any wars so furious and
bloody, or of so long continuance, as
those occasioned by difference in opinion, especially if it be in things indifferent. [Jonathan Swift: *Gulliver's Travels*
IV.v.]

18 Hobbes clearly proves that every
creature
Lives in a state of war by nature.
[Jonathan Swift: *Poetry: A Rhapsody*]

19 In every heart
Are sown the sparks that kindle fiery
war.
[William Cowper: *The Task* V]

20 Now tell us all about the war,
And what they fought each other for.
[Robert Southey: *The Battle of Blen-
heim*]

21 War is the statesman's game, the
priest's delight,
The lawyer's jest, the hired assassin's
trade.
[Shelley: *Queen Mab* IV]

22 War is nothing more than the con-

tinuation of politics by other means. [Karl von Clausewitz: *On War*]

1 You furnish the pictures and I'll furnish the war. [Attr. William Randolph Hearst: instructions to Frederick Remington, who had been sent to Cuba to illustrate the presumedly inevitable Spanish-American war]

The story, related in several biographies of Hearst, is that Remington arrived in Cuba and wired Hearst that everything was quiet, there was no trouble there and would be no war.

See Citizen Hearst, W. A. Swanberg (1961). But see also Hearst: Lord of San Simeon, Carlson and Bates (1936), where the exact wording is doubted, though the substance is accepted.

WAR: famous utterances

2 The die is cast. [Julius Caesar; at the crossing of the Rubicon (quoted in Suetonius's *Divus Julius* XXXII)]

See also DIE and RUBICON
See also POWDER

3 The Guard dies but does not surrender! [Attr. Baron Pierre Étienne de Cambronne: commanding the Imperial Guard at Waterloo, when called on to surrender]

Although the sentence Le Garde meurt, mais ne se rend pas *is engraved on his monument at Nantes, General de Cambronne indignantly repudiated any such highflown phraseology and insisted that his answer had been the more soldierly and suitable* "Merde!"

"Merde" is frequently referred to in French as "le mot de Cambronne."

See 735:7

4 Uxbridge: "By God, sir, I've lost my leg!"

Wellington: "By God, sir, so you have!"

Whether or not this famous colloquy employs the actual words spoken when the Earl of Uxbridge was struck by a cannonball while talking to the Duke at Waterloo, it does convey the character of these two extraordinary practitioners of stiff-upper-lipmanship. Like many anecdotes, it is essentially more truthful than the truth.

For the loss of his leg, Uxbridge was awarded the Garter.

See One-Leg: The Life . . . of Henry William Paget *by the Marquess of Anglesey (1961).*

5 It is magnificent, but it isn't war! [General Pierre Bosquet: as he watched the charge of the Light Brigade at Balaclava, Oct. 28, 1854]

6 Piss when you can. [Attr. The Duke of Wellington, when asked by a young subaltern for some piece of permanent military wisdom]

Related to the editor, as "traditional in the regimental messes," by Major-General Sir Reginald Pinney, K.C.B.

7 Nuts! [General Anthony McAuliffe: in reply to a German demand for surrender of the 101st Airborne Division at Bastogne, Belgium, December 23, 1944]

General McAuliffe and his men expressed their contempt and defiance eloquently in the heroic fury of their resistance.

But in the harsh lexicon of battle, the famous rejoinder must be classified, stylistically, as weak. There is an inappropriate boy-scoutiness about it. See The Guard dies, but does not surrender! *(735:3)*

The survivors' reference to themselves as "The battered bastards of Bastogne" is a commendable attempt at redress. But the over-alliteration smacks of rear-echelon rodomontade; it is "horribly stuff'd with epithets of war" (Othello I.i.).

WAR: morality of

8 The laws are silent in time of war. [Cicero: *Pro Milone* IV.xi.]

9 The war is just which is necessary. [Machiavelli: *The Prince* XXVI]

10 The clatter of arms drowns the voice of the law. [Montaigne: *Essays* III.i.]

11 It is war's prize to take all vantage. [Shakespeare: *III Henry VI* I.iv.]

12 Force and fraud are in war the two cardinal virtues. [Hobbes: *Leviathan* I. xiii.]

13 Among the calamities of war may be justly numbered the diminution of the love of truth by the falsehoods which interest dictates and credulity encourages. [Samuel Johnson: *The Idler* No. 30]

See PROPAGANDA

14 By war's great sacrifice

The world redeems itself.
[John Davidson: *War Song*]

Many have seen virtue in war. For centuries it was a commonplace that as bleeding was good for the health of the individual, war was good for the national health. It didn't occur to anyone that bleeding wasn't good for the individual.

Nietzsche averred that "a good war halloweth every cause" (Thus Spake Zarathustra: War & Warriors). Friedrich Bernhardi saw war as "a biological necessity," "indispensable and stimulating" (Germany and the Next War).

But, as the Latin proverb has it: Dulce bellum inexpertis—sweet is war to those who have never experienced it.

1 Yes, quaint and curious war is!
   You shoot a fellow down
You'd treat if met where any bar is,
   Or help to half-a-crown.
[Thomas Hardy: *The Man He Killed*]

WAR: and peace

2 War must be for the sake of peace, business for the sake of leisure, things necessary and useful for the sake of things noble. [Aristotle: *Politics* VII. xiii.]

3 An unjust peace is better than a just war. [Cicero: *Ad Atticum* VII.xiv.]

The thought has echoed through the ages, but only philosophers have entertained it seriously; and philosophers rarely arrange truces or set the terms for the cessation of hostilities.

4 Peace makes plentie, plentie makes
                              pride,
   Pride breeds quarrell, and quarrell
                        brings warre:
   Warre brings spoile, and spoile pov-
                              ertie,
   Povertie pacience, and pacience
                              peace:
   So peace brings warre and warre
                        brings peace.
[George Puttenham: *The Art of English Poesie* (1589)]

5 In peace the sons bury their fathers and in war the fathers bury their sons. [Francis Bacon: *Apothegms*]

6 In peace there's nothing so becomes a
                              man

As modest stillness and humility:
But when the blast of war blows in
                        our ears,
Then imitate the action of the tiger,
Stiffen the sinews, summon up the
                        blood. . . .
[Shakespeare: *Henry V* III.i.]

7 Peace itself is war in masquerade.
[Dryden: *Absalom and Achitophel* I]

8 There never was a good war or a bad peace. [Benjamin Franklin: letter to Josiah Quincy, Sept. 11, 1773]

9 To be prepared for war is one of the most effectual means of preserving peace. [George Washington: Speech to Congress, Jan. 8, 1790]

10 Why do they prate of the blessings of
          Peace? we have made them a curse,
    Pickpockets, each hand lusting for all
                    that is not its own;
    The lust of gain, in the spirit of Cain,
                    is it better or worse
    Than the heart of the citizen hissing
              in war on his own hearthstone?
[Tennyson: *Maud* I.i.]

11 Ye shall love peace as a means to new wars. [Friedrich Nietzsche: *Thus Spake Zarathustra*, "War and Warriors"]

WAR: violence, danger, death, slaughter

12 We are mad, not only individually, but nationally. We check manslaughter and isolated murders; but what of war and the much vaunted crime of slaughtering whole peoples? [Seneca: *Ad Lucilium* XCV]

13 The fortunes of war are always doubtful. [Seneca: *Phoenissae*]

14   Now . . .
    Doth dogged war bristle his angry
                              crest
    And snarleth in the gentle eyes of
                              peace.
[Shakespeare: *King John* IV.iii.]

15 The purple testament of bleeding
                              war.
[Shakespeare: *Richard II* III.iii.]

16 Cry "Havoc!" and let slip the dogs of
                              war.
[Shakespeare: *Julius Caesar* III.i.]

Havok was an old military command to massacre without quarter. The origin of the word is uncertain. In the 9th year of the reign of Richard II, the cry was forbidden on pain of death.

1 Once more unto the breach, dear
friends.
[Shakespeare: *Henry V* III.i.]
2 There are few die well that die in a
battle.
[Shakespeare: *Henry V* IV.i.]
3 For I must go where lazy Peace
Will hide her drowsy head;
And, for the sport of kings, increase
The number of the dead.
[Sir William Davenant: *The Soldier Go-
ing to the Field*]
Here *"the sport of kings" is, plainly, war.
Davenant died in 1668.*

William Somerville in The Chase *I
(1735), uses the expression in its modern sense:*

My hoarse-sounding horn
Invites thee to the chase, the sport
of kings,
Image of war without its guilt.

4 Arms on armour clashing bray'd
Horrible discord, and the madding
wheels
Of brazen chariots rag'd; dire was
the noise
Of conflict.
[John Milton: *Paradise Lost* VI.209-212]
5 The brazen throat of war.
[John Milton: *Paradise Lost* XI.713]
6 Ay me! what perils do environ
The man that meddles with cold iron!
[Samuel Butler (1612-1680): *Hudibras*]
7 One to destroy, is murder by the law,
And gibbets keep the lifted hand in
awe;
To murder thousands takes a spe-
cious name,
War's glorious art, and gives immor-
tal fame.
[Edward Young: *Love of Fame* VII.lv.]
8 On Linden, when the sun was low,
All bloodless lay the untrodden snow,
And dark as winter was the flow
Of Iser, rolling rapidly.
[Thomas Campbell: *Hohenlinden*]
*Hohenlinden, in Bavaria, was the scene
of a great battle in 1800 in which the
French revolutionary general, Moreau,
defeated the Austrians.*

*Campbell's poem, long popular, cele-
brates the glory, violence and dreadful
loss of life that marked the battle.*

9 Few, few shall part where many meet!
The snow shall be their winding-sheet

And every turf beneath their feet
Shall be a soldier's sepulchre.
[Thomas Campbell: *Hohenlinden*]

WAR: miscellaneous
10 There is no discharge in that war.
[Ecclesiastes 8:8]
11 Ye shall hear of wars and rumors of
wars. [Matthew 24:6]
12 Money, the sinews of war. [Cicero:
Philippics V.ii.]
*Cicero was probably quoting a well-
known saying. The idea was expressed
before him, and many times afterwards.*

13 It is always easy to begin a war, but
very difficult to stop one, since its beginning and end are not under the control
of the same man. Anyone, even a coward, can commence a war, but it can be
brought to an end only with the consent
of the victors. [Sallust: *Jugurtha* LXXX-
VIII]
14 Just for a word—"neutrality," a word
which in war time had so often been dis-
regarded—just for a scrap of paper,
Great Britain is going to make war on a
kindred nation who desires nothing better than to be friends with her. [Theo-
bald von Bethmann-Hollweg, the Chancellor of Germany, to Sir Edward Go-
schen, the British ambassador, August 4,
1914]
*The "scrap of paper" was the treaty—to
which Germany was also a party—guar-
anteeing the neutrality of Belgium. Bethmann-Hollweg's phrase—one of the great
blunders of diplomacy—shocked the civilized world.*

WARNING
15 *Nemo me impune lacessit.* ("No man
provokes me with impunity.") [Motto
of the Order of the Thistle]

WARRIOR(S)
16 I know not how, but martial men are
given to love: I think it is but as they are
given to wine, for perils commonly ask to
be paid in pleasures. [Francis Bacon: *Of
Love*]
17 Generally all warlike people are a little idle and love danger better than travail; neither must they be too much
broken of it if they shall be preserved in
vigor. [Francis Bacon: *True Greatness
of Kingdoms*]

Ring Lardner said of a certain prize-fighter's performance in the ring that it proved that he would, literally, rather take a beating than work.

1 Little of this great world can I speak,
More than pertains to feats of broil
and battle.

[Shakespeare: *Othello* I.iii.]

2 Women adore a martial man.

[William Wycherley: *The Plain Dealer* II]

3 Who is the happy Warrior? Who is he
That every man in arms should wish
to be?
It is the generous spirit, who, when
brought
Among the tasks of real life, hath
wrought
Upon the plan that pleased his childish thought:
Whose high endeavours are an inward light
That makes the path before him always bright.

[Wordsworth: *Character of the Happy Warrior*]

4 Whose powers shed round him in the
common strife
Or mild concerns of ordinary life,
A constant influence, a peculiar grace;
But who if he be called upon to face
Some awful moment to which Heaven
has joined
Great issues, good or bad for human
kind,
Is happy as a lover; and attired
With sudden brightness, like a man
inspired;
And, through the heat of conflict,
keeps the law
In calmness made, and sees what he
foresaw.

[Wordsworth: *Character of the Happy Warrior*]

5 Home they brought her warrior dead.

[Tennyson: *The Princess* VI]

6 His nose should pant and his lip
should curl,
His cheeks should flame and his brow
should furl,
His bosom should heave and his heart
should glow,
And his fist be ever ready for a
knock-down blow.

[W. S. Gilbert: *H. M. S. Pinafore* I]

WASH(ING)

7 He took water, and washed his hands
before the multitude, saying, I am innocent of the blood of this just person: see
ye to it. [Matthew 27:24]

8 It will all come out in the wash.
[Cervantes: *Don Quixote* 1.20]

9 Seem'd washing his hands with invisible soap
In imperceptible water.

[Thomas Hood: *Miss Kilmansegg and Her Precious Leg*]

10 Earned a precarious living by taking
in one another's washing. [Attr. Mark
Twain]

WASHINGTON, GEORGE

11 A citizen, first in war, first in peace,
and first in the hearts of his countrymen.
["Light-Horse Harry" Lee: in the Resolution which Congress adopted on the
death of Washington, December 19,
1799]

Often erroneously attr. John Marshall.

12 Where may the wearied eye repose
When gazing on the great;
Where neither guilty glory glows,
Nor despicable state?
Yes—one—the first—the last—the
best—
The Cincinnatus of the West,
Whom envy dared not hate,
Bequeathed the name of Washington,
To make man blush there was but
one!

[Byron: *Ode to Napoleon Bonaparte*]

13 "George," said his father, "do you
know who killed that beautiful little
cherry tree yonder in the garden?" . . .
Looking at his father with the sweet face
of youth brightened with the inexpressible charm of all-conquering truth, he
bravely cried out, "I can't tell a lie. I did
it with my hatchet." [Mason Locke
Weems: *The Life of George Washington: with Curious Anecdotes, Equally
Honorable to Himself and Exemplary to
His Young Countrymen*]

WASTE

14 Wherefore do ye spend money for
that which is not bread? and your labour
for that which satisfieth not? [Isaiah
55:22]

15 A nice wife and a back door,

Oft do make a rich man poor.
[John Clarke: *Paroemiologia* (1639)]
nice = *finicky*
> *The back door enabled the servants to carry things off and the wife to throw things away without the master's being aware of it.*
> *The saying has been traced back to the mid-15th century.*

1 Wilful waste brings woeful want.
[Thomas Fuller (1654-1734): *Gnomologia*]

WATCH

2 Watch and pray. [Matthew 26:41]
watch = *stay awake*
> *It does not mean "keep an eye on the sinful neighbors," as many of the virtuous seem to think it does.*

3 For some must watch, while some
must sleep:
So runs the world away.
[Shakespeare: *Hamlet* III.ii.]

WATER(S)

4 Unstable as water, thou shalt not excel. [Genesis 49:4]
5 The noise of many waters. [Psalms 93:4]
6 All hands shall be feeble, and all knees shall be weak as water. [Ezekiel 7:17]
7 The fall of dropping water wears away the stone. [Lucretius: *De rerum natura* I]
> *A proverb in the first century* B.C.—*and probably before and certainly after.*

8 The deepest rivers flow with the least sound. [Quintus Curtius Rufus: *Alexander the Great* VII.iv.]
9 The ceaseless dripping of water will hollow out a stone. [Ovid: *Epistolae Ex Ponto* IV.x.]
10 Much water goeth by the mill that the miller knoweth not of. [John Heywood: *Proverbs* (1546)]
11 The same water that drives the mill, decayeth it. [Stephen Gosson: *The Schoole of Abuse*]
12 More water glideth by the mill
Than wots the miller of.
[Shakespeare: *Titus Andronicus* II.i.]
13 Smooth runs the water where the
the brook is deep.
[Shakespeare: *II Henry VI* III.i.]

14 A little water clears us of this deed.
[Shakespeare: *Macbeth* II.ii.]
15 The green mantle of the standing
pool.
[Shakespeare: *King Lear* III.iv.]
16 The waters were his winding-sheet,
the sea was made his tomb,
Yet for his fame the Ocean sea was
not sufficient room.
[Richard Barnfield: *Epitaph on Sir John Hawkins*]
17 Deep waters noiseless are; and this
we know,
That chiding streams betray small
depth below.
[Robert Herrick: *To His Mistress*]
18 As welcome as water in my shoes.
[James Howell: *English Proverbs* (1659)]
> *The earlier equivalent of the modern "hole in the head." Often used in exactly the same manner: "I need that as much as I need water in my shoes."*

19 The rising world of waters dark and
deep.
[John Milton: *Paradise Lost* III.11]
20 Liquid lapse of murmuring streams.
[John Milton: *Paradise Lost* VIII.263]
21 Water . . . doth very greatly deject the appetite, destroy the natural heat, and overthrow the strength of the stomach. [Tobias Venner: *Via recta* (1620)]
22 This business will never hold water.
[Colley Cibber: *She Wou'd and She Wou'd Not* IV]
23 These waters, rolling from their
mountain-springs
With a soft inland murmur.
[Wordsworth: *Tintern Abbey*]
24 Water, water, everywhere, nor any
drop to drink.
[Coleridge: *The Ancient Mariner* II]
25 I heard the water lapping on the
crag,
And the long ripple washing in the
reeds.
[Tennyson: *Idylls of the King*, "The Passing of Arthur"]
26 Water is the only drink for a wise man. [Thoreau: *Walden* II, "Higher Laws"]
27 Little drops of water, little grains of
sand,
Make the mighty ocean, and the
pleasant land,
So the little moments, humble though

they be,
Make the mighty ages of eternity.
[Julia Carney: *Little Things*]
1   Mother, may I go out to swim?
     Yes, my darling daughter.
     Hang your clothes on a hickory limb
     But don't go near the water.
[Anon.]
Although the earliest known appear-
ance of this famous jingle is as recent
as 1880, nothing is known for sure of its
origin. On the CBS television show "The
Last Word," in April, 1958, viewers were
invited to send in any knowledge they
might have of the rhyme. Hundreds an-
swered and scores of these stated that in
their childhood they had heard a hat-
rack or clothes tree called a "hickory
tree." If this is the reference, it adds to
the poem: the young lady was not even
to leave the house.
2   You never miss the water till the well
runs dry. [Rowland Howard: *You Never*
Miss the Water]
     See WELL
3   Little drops of water poured into the
                                           milk,
     Give the milkman's daughter lovely
                                      gowns of silk.
[Walt Mason: *Little Things*]
4   Hold me up, mighty waters,
     Keep my eye on things above.
[*Autumn*, Episcopal hymn played by the
Titanic's band as she sank. (Walter
Lord: *A Night to Remember;* Mark Sullivan: *Our Times* IV)]
The very applicability of the selection,
under the circumstances, would seem to
our—perhaps less pious—generation too
cruelly ironic.

WATERLOO
5   It has been a damned serious business.
. . . It has been a damned nice thing.
[The Duke of Wellington: referring to
the Battle of Waterloo, on June 19, 1815
(the day after the battle), quoted in *The*
Creevey Papers (1903)]
Nice did not mean pleasant, but exceed-
ingly close, touch and go, "the nearest
run thing you ever saw in your life," as
Wellington added.
6   The battle of Waterloo was won on
the playing fields of Eton. [Attr. the
Duke of Wellington]

This wholly uncharacteristic remark was
first attributed to the Duke in 1889, long
after his death. The date for the utter-
ance is fixed at "about 1825," and it is
commonly alleged that this surge of
loyalty in the Old Grad's breast was oc-
casioned by his watching a cricket match.
It is true that the Duke did attend
Eton as a boy, but, according to his
great-grandson, the seventh duke, his
career there was "short and inglorious,"
and he never had any great affection for
the place. When Wellington was at Eton
there were fields and the young gentle-
men played in them, but there were no
playing fields in the modern sense, no
organized sports, no teamwork.
H. Allen Smith's quip that the Battle
of Yorktown was lost on the playing
fields of Eton has more substance.
7   Stop!—for thy tread is on an Empire's
                                           dust!
[Byron: *Childe Harold* III.xvii.]
8   Waterloo is a battle of the first rank
won by a captain of the second. [Victor
Hugo: *Les Misérables* I.xvi.]

WATTLE, CAPTAIN
9   Did you ever hear of Captain Wattle?
     He was all for love, and a little for
                                      the bottle.
[Charles Dibdin: *Captain Wattle and*
Miss Roe]

WAVES
10 Hitherto shalt thou come, but no
further: and here shall thy proud waves
be stayed. [Job 38:11]
11   I stand as one upon a rock,
     Environ'd with a wilderness of sea,
     Who marks the waxing tide grow
                                      wave by wave.
[Shakespeare: *Titus Andronicus* III.i.]
12 What are the wild waves saying?
[J. E. Carpenter: title of a song, c.1850]
Dickens's Dombey and Son had appeared
in 1846 and the death of little Paul had
shaken the nation. The nearest Paul had
come, however, to the actual phrase was
"The sea, Floy, what is it that it keeps
on saying?" and the author added "Very
often afterwards, in the midst of their
talk, he would break off, to try to under-
stand what it was that the waves were
always saying" (VIII).

WAY

1 The next way home's the farthest way about. [Francis Quarles: *Emblems* IV. ii.]

next = *nearest*

WAYFARING

2 The wayfaring men, though fools, shall not err therein. [Isaiah 35:8]

WEAKNESS

3 To be weak is miserable,
Doing or suffering.
[John Milton: *Paradise Lost* I.157-158]

4 The greatest men are connected to their age through some weakness. [Goethe: *Sprüche in Prosa*]

Thus Donald Culross Peattie suggested that Darwin owed a great deal of his theory of sexual selection to the Victorian gentleman's idea of the courtesy due a lady.

WEALTH

5 Wealth is the parent of luxury and indolence, and poverty of meanness and viciousness, and both of discontent. [Plato: *The Republic* IV]

6 High descent and meritorious deeds, unless united to wealth, are as useless as sea-weed. [Horace: *Satires* II]

7 Nothing is more intolerable than a wealthy woman. [Juvenal: *Satires* V]

8 Cats of a good breed mouse better when they are fat than when they are starving: and likewise good men who have some talent exercise it to nobler ends when they have wealth enough to live well. [Benvenuto Cellini: *Life* I.lvi.]

9 Through tatter'd clothes small vices
do appear;
Robes and furr'd gowns hide all.
[Shakespeare: *King Lear* IV.vi.]

10 No wealth can satisfy the covetous desire of wealth. [Jeremy Taylor: *Holy Living*]

11 Wealth is crime enough to him that's poor. [Sir John Denham: *Cooper's Hill*]

12 The insolence of wealth will creep out. [Samuel Johnson: in Boswell's *Life*, April 14, 1778]

13 Ill fares the land, to hastening ills a
prey,
Where wealth accumulates and men
decay.

[Oliver Goldsmith: *The Deserted Village*]

14 As wealth is power, so all power will infallibly draw wealth to itself by some means or other. [Edmund Burke: speech (1780)]

15 Wealth is a power usurped by the few, to compel the many to labour for their benefit. [Shelley: Notes to *Queen Mab*]

16 Unearned increment. [John Stuart Mill: *Dissertations and Discussions* IV]

17 Lost wealth makes a man miserly. [Alfred de Musset: *Simone*]

No lost wealth seems more bitterly regretted than that which has never been possessed—such as might-have-been gains on the stock exchange.

18 Wealth may be an excellent thing, for it means power, it means leisure, it means liberty. [James Russell Lowell: speech at Harvard Anniversary]

19 It is not that men are ill fed, but that they have no pleasure in the work by which they make their bread, and therefore look to wealth as the only means of pleasure. [John Ruskin: *The Stones of Venice* II.vi.]

20 Malefactors of great wealth. [Theodore Roosevelt: speech, Aug. 20, 1907]

21 Wealth is now itself intrinsically honorable and confers honor on its possessor. [Thorstein Veblen: *The Theory of the Leisure Class*]

WEARINESS

22 I 'gin to be aweary of the sun. [Shakespeare: *Macbeth* V.v.]

23 Weariness
Can snore upon the flint when resty
sloth
Finds the down pillow hard.
[Shakespeare: *Cymbeline* III.vi.]

resty = *restless*

24 Let the long contention cease!
Geese are swans, and swans are geese,
Let them have it how they will!
Thou art tired; best be still.
[Matthew Arnold: *The Last Word*]

WEARY

25 I stay too long by thee, I weary thee. [Shakespeare: *II Henry IV* IV.v.]

26 How weary, stale, flat and unprofitable
Seem to me all the uses of this world.

[Shakespeare: *Hamlet* I.ii.]
uses = *customs*

1 Art thou weary, art thou languid,
Art thou sore distressed?

[John Mason Neale: *Hymn from the Greek*]

2 I have grown weary of dust and decay,
Weary of flinging my heart's wealth
away—
Weary of sowing for others to reap;
Rock me to sleep, mother, rock me to
sleep.

[Elizabeth Akers Allen: *Mother, Rock Me to Sleep*]

WEASEL

3 That's the way the money goes—
Pop goes the weasel!

[Attr. W. R. Mandale: chorus of a popular song, c.1850]

It has been suggested that weasel *was a hatter's tool and* pop *a term for pawning and the song as a whole a wrily merry reflection on the financial expedients of the poor.*

Eric Partridge thinks, "Probably erotic origin."

WEASEL WORDS

4 Weasel words are words that suck all the life out of the words next to them, just as a weasel sucks an egg and leaves the shell. [Stewart Chaplin: "The Stained-Glass Political Platform," in *Century Magazine,* June 1900]

Chaplin's phrase was popularized by Theodore Roosevelt. Chaplin illustrated what he meant by saying that a political party might consider adopting as a plank in their platform that "The Public should be protected." Before the plank is adopted, however, the word duly *would be inserted before* protected, *so that the plank reads: "The Public should be duly protected." That makes it safe, "and it will be unanimously accepted amid wild cheers."*

5 One of our defects as a nation is a tendency to use what have been called weasel words. When a weasel sucks eggs, the meat is sucked out of the egg. If you use a weasel word after another, there is nothing left of the other. [Theodore Roosevelt: in a speech in St. Louis, May 31, 1916]

WEATHER

6 Many can brook the weather that love not the wind.

[Shakespeare: *Love's Labour's Lost* IV. ii.]

7 I tax not you, you elements, with unkindness.

[Shakespeare: *King Lear* III.ii.]

8 To talk of the weather, it's nothing but folly,
For when it rains on the hill, it shines in the valley.

[Sir John Denham: *Proverbs*]

9 As the day lengthens
The cold strengthens.

[John Ray: *English Proverbs* (1670)]

10 Till April's dead
Change not a thread.

[John Ray: *English Proverbs* (1670)]
In Dorset it is: Cast not a clout/ Till May is out.

11 When two Englishmen meet, their first talk is of the weather. [Samuel Johnson: *The Idler* No. 11]

12 There is nothing more universally commended than a fine day; the reason is, that people can commend it without envy. [William Shenstone: *On Men and Manners*]

13 And finds a changing clime an happy source
Of wise reflection and well-tim'd discourse.

[William Cowper: *Conversation*]
Shelley said of his mother that "on the subject of the weather she was irresistibly eloquent."

14 Everybody talks about the weather, but nobody does anything about it.
This famous observation first appeared in an unsigned editorial in The Hartford Courant *(1890) and was attributed to "an author." It is generally believed to be by Mark Twain, though some attribute it to Charles Dudley Warner.*

15 There is a sumptuous variety about New England weather that compels the stranger's admiration. . . . In the Spring I have counted one hundred and thirty-six different kinds of weather inside of twenty-four hours. [Mark Twain: *New England Weather:* speech at a dinner of the New England Society, New York, Dec. 22, 1876]

16 This is the weather the cuckoo likes,

And so do I.
[Thomas Hardy: *Weathers*]
1 For the man sound in body and serene of mind there is no such thing as bad weather! Every sky has its beauty, and storms which whip the blood do but make it pulse more vigorously. [George Gissing: *The Private Papers of Henry Ryecroft*]
2 On the farm the weather was the great fact, and men's affairs went on underneath it, as the streams creep under the ice. [Willa Cather: *My Ántonia* II. vii.]

WEB

3 Day-long she wove at the web but by night she would unravel what she had done. [Homer: *Odyssey* XXIV]

she = *Penelope, wife of Odysseus, who would not consent to accept one of her suitors as a second husband until she had completed weaving a winding sheet for Laertes, Odysseus's aged father. For three years, she held them off with this pretext, but in the fourth her ruse was betrayed by one of her women.*

"Penelope's web" has become a term for a work that will never be completed, something that the doer really doesn't want to complete.

4 There she weaves by night and day
 A magic web with colors gay.
[Tennyson: *The Lady of Shalott*]

WEDDING

5 O come ye here to fight, young lord,
 Or come ye here to play?
 Or come ye here to drink good wine
 Upon the weddin'-day?
[Anon.: *Katharine Johnstone*]
6 Resistance on the Wedding-Night
 Is what our Maidens claim by Right.
[Jonathan Swift: *Strephon and Chloe*]
7 Same old slippers,
 Same old rice,
 Same old glimpse of
 Paradise.
[William James Lampton: *June Weddings*]

WEED(S)

8 Lilies that fester smell far worse than
 weeds.
[Shakespeare: *Sonnets* XCIV]

9 A weed is no more than a flower in disguise. [James Russell Lowell: *A Fable for Critics*]

WEEPING

10 Rachel weeping for her children, and would not be comforted, because they are not. [Matthew 2:18]
11 There shall be weeping and gnashing of teeth. [Matthew 8:12]

Matthew 13:42 reads: . . . there shall be wailing and gnashing of teeth. (Though both passages are alike in the Greek.)

The popular "weeping and wailing and gnashing of teeth" seems to be a combination of the two passages.

12 I did not weep; I had turned to stone inside. [Dante: *Inferno* XXXIII.xlix.]
13 There are three things that are not to be credited, a woman when she weeps, a merchant when he sweares, nor a drunkard when he prayes. [Barnabe Rich: *The Ladies Looking Glass*]
14 Then can I drown an eye, unused to
 flow,
 For precious friends hid in death's
 dateless night,
 And weep afresh love's long since cancell'd woe,
 And moan the expense of many a
 vanish'd sight.
[Shakespeare: *Sonnets* XXX]
15 No, I'll not weep:
 I have full cause of weeping; but this
 heart
 Shall break into a hundred thousand
 flaws
 Or ere I'll weep.
[Shakespeare: *King Lear* II.iv.]
16 As much pity is to be taken of a woman weeping, as of a goose going barefoot. [Robert Burton: *The Anatomy of Melancholy* III.2.2.5]

The idea had been proverbial for a century before Burton.

17 And weep the more because I weep in
 vain.
[Thomas Gray: *On the Death of Richard West*]
18 And if I laugh at any mortal thing,
 'Tis that I may not weep.
[Byron: *Don Juan* IV.iv.]
19 Oh! would I were dead now,
 Or up in my bed now,
 To cover my head now

And have a good cry.
[Thomas Hood: *A Table of Errata*]
1 Weep no more, my lady,
O, weep no more to-day!
We will sing one song for the old
Kentucky home,
For the old Kentucky home, far away.
[Stephen C. Foster: *My Old Kentucky Home*]
2 Crying is the refuge of plain women, but the ruin of pretty ones. [Oscar Wilde: *Lady Windermere's Fan* I]

WEE WILLIE WINKIE
3 Wee Willie Winkie rins through the toun,
Upstairs and downstairs, in his nicht-goun,
Tirlin' at the window, cryin' at the lock,
"Are the weans in their bed? for it's now ten o'clock."
[William Miller: *Willie Winkie*]

WELCOME
4 His worth is warrant for his welcome. [Shakespeare: *Two Gentlemen of Verona* II.iv.]
5 You are as welcome as the flowers in May.
[Charles Macklin: *Love à la Mode* I]
6 Come in the evening, or come in the morning,
Come when you're looked for, or come without warning.
[Thomas O. Davis: *The Welcome*]

WELL
7 'Tis not so deep as a well, nor so wide as a church-door; but 'tis enough, 'twill serve. [Shakespeare: *Romeo and Juliet* III.i.]
8 We never know the worth of water till the well runs dry. [Thomas Fuller (1654-1734): *Gnomologia*]
A proverb in Fuller's time. Now usually heard as: "You never miss the water till the well runs dry."

WELL-BRED
9 Everyone thinks himself well-bred. [Anthony Ashley Cooper (Earl of Shaftesbury): *Characteristics* I]
10 He is not well-bred that cannot bear ill-breeding in others. [Benjamin Franklin: *Poor Richard's Almanack*]

WELL-DRESSED
11 I have heard with admiring submission the experience of the lady who declared that the sense of being perfectly well-dressed gives a feeling of inward tranquillity which religion is powerless to bestow. [Emerson: *Letters and Social Aims*]

WELL ENOUGH
12 Striving to better, oft we mar what's well.
[Shakespeare: *King Lear* I.iv.]

WELLINGTON, DUKE OF
13 This is England's greatest son,
He that gained a hundred fights,
Nor ever lost an English gun.
[Tennyson: *Ode on the Death of the Duke of Wellington*]
Wellington lost many guns, but the belief that he never lost one became a myth—a myth that contributed to the insane slaughter of the Light Brigade at Balaclava.

WENCESLAS
14 Good King Wenceslas look'd out,
On the Feast of Stephen;
When the snow lay round about,
Deep and crisp and even.
[John Mason Neale: *Good King Wenceslas*]

WENCH
15 But that was in another Country: And besides, the Wench is dead. [Christopher Marlowe: *The Jew of Malta* IV.ii.]
16 O ill-starr'd wench!
Pale as thy smock! When we shall meet at compt,
This look of thine will hurl my soul from heaven,
And fiends will snatch at it.
[Shakespeare: *Othello* V.ii.]

WERTHER
17 Werther had a love for Charlotte
Such as words could never utter;
Would you know how first he met her?
She was cutting bread and butter.
[W. M. Thackeray: *Sorrows of Werther*]

WEST
18 And not by eastern windows only,

When daylight comes, comes in the
light,
In front the sun climbs slow, how
slowly.
But westward, look, the land is
bright.
[Arthur Hugh Clough: *Say Not the Struggle Naught Availeth*]

1 Westward the course of empire takes
its way;
The first four acts already past,
A fifth shall close the drama with the
day;
Time's noblest offspring is the last.
[Bishop George Berkeley: *On the Prospect of Planting Arts and Learning in America*]
Berkeley (1685-1753) hoped at one time to establish a college in Bermuda to train young Indians as missionaries. The glorious "fifth act" that he foresaw was the Christianizing of the Indians.

2 Go west, young man, go west. [John
L. B. Soule: in the *Terre Haute Express*
(1851)]
This famous admonition was early transferred in the popular mind to Horace Greeley. Greeley publicly and repeatedly disclaimed having said it. He even reprinted the article from the Terre Haute Express *in which it had first appeared. But the public will not have its ascriptions turned aside by mere fact. The phrase stuck to Greeley and he is forever stuck with it.*

3 The bountiful infinite West.
[Swinburne: *Hesperia*]

4 Out where the handclasp's a little
stronger,
Out where the smile dwells a little
longer,
That's where the West begins.
[Arthur Chapman: *Out Where the West Begins*]

5 It's a corner of heaven itself,
Though it's only a tumble-down
nest,
But with love brooding there, why,
no place can compare,
With my little grey home in the
west.
[D. Eardley Wilmot: *My Little Grey Home*]

6 The bosom of the urgent West.
[Robert Bridges: *A Passer-By*]

WHEEL(S)
7 Why tarry the wheels of his chariots?
[Judges 5:28]

8 And their appearance and their work
was as it were a wheel in the middle of a
wheel. [Ezekiel 1:16]

9 As if a wheel had been in the midst of
a wheel. [Ezekiel 10:10]
Ezekiel's vision has echoed down the corridors of our literature and speech. From the Negro spiritual based on this passage ("Ezekiel saw the wheel | 'Way up in the middle of the air") probably comes the modern slang term of big wheel *or just* wheel *for a man of power in an organization.*

10 To put a spoke in his wheel. [16th-
century saying]
Since spokes are necessary to wheels, this term for putting an obstacle in someone's way has puzzled many. But spoke here *probably means a pin used to lock the wheels—as a brake, for instance, on a steep hill. So that "to put a spoke in someone's wheel" is to apply a brake, stop him in his tracks, etc.*

11 Thou art a soul in bliss; but I am
bound
Upon a wheel of fire.
[Shakespeare: *King Lear* IV.vii.]

12 The wheel is come full circle.
[Shakespeare: *King Lear* V.iii.]

13 He . . . put his shoulder to the
wheel. [Robert Burton: *The Anatomy of Melancholy* II]

14 I want to see the wheels go round.
[John Haberton: *Helen's Babies*]
The insistent cry of a child who has been, unfortunately, allowed a glimpse of the inside of a watch.

15 But the wheel that does the squeaking
is the one that gets the grease. [Anonymous: *The Kicker*]

WHEREFORE
16 They say every why has a wherefore.
[Shakespeare: *The Comedy of Errors* II.ii.]

17 Whatever Sceptic could inquire for,
For ev'ry why he had a wherefore.
[Samuel Butler (1612-1680): *Hudibras*]

WHIMPER
18 This is the way the world ends—
Not with a bang but a whimper.
[T. S. Eliot: *The Hollow Men*]

WHIPS

1 My father hath chastised you with whips, but I will chastise you with scorpions. [I Kings 12:11]
A scorpion was a whip or scourge tipped with spikes.

WHIRLWIND

2 Rides in the whirlwind and directs the storm. [Joseph Addison: *The Campaign* (1704)]
Addison is referring to the Duke of Marlborough.
The line was borrowed by Pope and used ironically of John Rich, the manager of Covent Garden Theatre, in The Dunciad, *III (1728).*
It was this John Rich who produced John Gay's The Beggar's Opera, *one of the greatest successes ever put on the boards. It was said that it made Rich gay and Gay rich.*

3 In gallant trim the gilded vessel goes;
Youth on the prow, and Pleasure at
the Helm;
Regardless of the sweeping whirl-
wind's sway,
That, hushed in grim repose, expects
his evening prey.
[Thomas Gray: *The Bard* II.ii.]

WHISKEY

4 Freedom and Whisky gang thegither.
[Burns: *The Author's Earnest Cry and Prayer*]

WHISPERINGS

5 Foul whisperings are abroad.
[Shakespeare: *Macbeth* V.v.]

WHISTLE

6 Whistle and she'll come to you. [Beaumont and Fletcher: *Wit Without Money* IV.iv.]
The expression was proverbial. Goneril in King Lear *(IV.ii.) says, angry at her husband for not meeting her with due pomp, "I have been worth the whistle." Three hundred years later Burns used it: "Whistle and I'll come to you, lad."*

7 Whistling to keep myself from being
afraid.
[Dryden: *Amphitryon* III.i.]

WHITE

8 The weather has gone mad with
white;

The cloud, the highway touch.
White lilac is enough;
White thorn too much!
[Lizette Woodworth Reese: *Spring Ecstasy*]

9 An' for all 'is dirty 'ide
'E was white, clear white inside
When 'e went to tend the wounded
under fire.
[Kipling: *Gunga Din*]

WHITHER?

10 Whither goest thou? [John 13:36]
The Latin in the Vulgate is Quo vadis?

WHORE

11 The whore is proud her beauties are
the dread
Of peevish virtue, and the marriage-
bed.
[Edward Young: *Love of Fame* I.lxvii.]

WHORING

12 This is the fruit of whoring.
[Shakespeare: *Othello* V.i.]

WICKED

13 I have seen the wicked in great power, and spreading himself like a green bay tree. Yet he passed away, and, lo, he was not; yea, I sought him, but he could not be found. [Psalms 37:35-36]
14 The wicked flee when no man pursueth; but the righteous are bold as a lion. [Proverbs 28:1]
15 It is safer that a wicked man should not be accused than that he should be acquitted. [Livy: *Annals* XXXIV.iv.]
16 The sun also shines on the wicked. [Seneca: *De beneficiis* III]
17 No man ever became very wicked all at once. [Juvenal: *Satire* II]
There is a method in man's wickedness—
It grows up by degrees.
—Beaumont and Fletcher: A King and
No King *V.iv.*
18 Now am I, if a man should speak truly, little better than one of the wicked. [Shakespeare: *I Henry IV* I.ii.]
19 The wicked are always surprised to find ability in the good. [Vauvenargues: *Réflexions*]

WICKEDNESS

20 Though wickedness be sweet in his mouth, though he hide it under his

tongue. [Job 20:12]

1 I had rather be a doorkeeper in the house of my God, than to dwell in the tents of wickedness. [Psalms 84:10]

2 Ye have ploughed wickedness, ye have reaped iniquity. [Hosea 10:13]

3 Men are always wicked at bottom, unless they are made good by some compulsion. [Machiavelli: *The Prince* XXV]

4 As for myself, I walk abroad o' nights
   And kill sick people groaning under
          walls:
   Sometimes I go about and poison
          wells.
[Christopher Marlowe: *The Jew of Malta* II.iii]

5 By the pricking of my thumbs,
   Something wicked this way comes.
[Shakespeare: *Macbeth* IV.i.]

6 All wickedness is weakness; that plea,
          therefore,
   With God or man will gain thee no
          remission.
[John Milton: *Samson Agonistes*]

7 The world loves a spice of wickedness. [Longfellow: *Hyperion* VII.i.]

WIDOW

8 There came a certain poor widow, and she threw in two mites, which make a farthing. [Mark 12:42]

9 The welthy wythered wydow. [John Heywood: *Proverbs* (1546)]

10 He that would woo a maid must feign,
          lie, and flatter,
    But he that woos a widow must down
          with his britches and at her.
[Nathaniel Smith: *Quakers Spiritual Court* (1669)]
   This widespread and ineradicable masculine belief accounts for more failures with widows than any other illusion or tactic.

WIFE: and children

11 He that hath wife and children, hath given hostages to fortune; for they are impediments to great enterprises, either of virtue, or mischief. [Francis Bacon: *Of Marriage and Single Life*]

12 There are some that account wife and children but as bills of charges. [Francis Bacon: *Of Marriage and Single Life*]
   But Bacon regards this as miserly stupidity.

13 Certainly wife and children are a kind of discipline of humanity. [Francis Bacon: *Of Marriage and Single Life*]

14 Next to no wife and children, your own wife and children are best pastime: another's wife and your children worse: your wife and another's children worst. [Sir Henry Wotton: *Table-talk*]

15 He that loves not his wife and children, feeds a lioness at home, and broods a nest of sorrow. [Jeremy Taylor: *Sermons* I]
   broods = hatches

16 For what secures the civil life
    But pawns of children, and a wife?
    That lie, like hostages, at stake,
    To pay for all men undertake.
[Samuel Butler (1612-1680): *Hudibras*]

17 Searching auld wives' barrels—
    Ochone the day!
    That clarty barm should stain my
          laurels;
    But—what'll ye say?
    These movin' things, ca'd wives and
          weans,
    Wad move the very hearts o' stanes!
[Burns: *Extemporaneous Effusion, on Being Appointed to the Excise*]
   clarty barm = dirty yeast; weans = children
   The exciseman had to reach into barrels of home-made beer and measure how much had been sold. Furthermore, he was hated.

18 Whoever has a wife and children has given hostages to Mrs. Grundy. [J. S. Mill: *The Subjection of Women* IV]

WIFE: the dutiful wife

19 This flower of wifely patience. [Chaucer: *The Clerk's Tale*]

20 Such duty as the subject owes the
          prince
    Even such a woman oweth to her
          husband.
[Shakespeare: *The Taming of the Shrew* V.ii.]

21 My author and disposer, what thou
          bidd'st,
    Unargu'd I obey: so God ordains:
    God is thy law, thou mine: to know
          no more
    Is woman's happiest knowledge and
          her praise.
[John Milton: *Paradise Lost* IV.635-638]

1 It is a good horse that never stumbles,
And a good wife that never grumbles.
[John Ray: *English Proverbs* (1670)]

2 Be plain in dress, and sober in your
diet;
In short, my deary! kiss me, and be
quiet.
[Lady Mary Wortley Montagu: *A Summary of Lord Lyttelton's Advice*]

3 A man is in general better pleased
when he has a good dinner upon his
table, than when his wife talks Greek.
[Samuel Johnson: *Miscellanies* II.xi.]

WIFE: pro

4 Whoso findeth a wife findeth a good
thing. [Proverbs 18:22]

5 My dear, my better half. [Sir Philip
Sidney: *Arcadia* III]

6 You are my true and honourable wife,
As dear to me as are the ruddy
drops
That visit my sad heart.
[Shakespeare: *Julius Caesar* II.i.]

7 The imperial jointress to this warlike
state.
[Shakespeare: *Hamlet* I.ii.]

8 Man's best possession is a loving wife.
[Robert Burton: *The Anatomy of Melancholy* III.2.5.5]

9 The fact that Jennie was his wife
gave her quite a standing with Hiram.
He admired her for having made such a
Success of her Life. [George Ade: *The
New Fable of Susan and the Daughter*]

WIFE: con

10 The contentions of a wife are a continual dropping. [Proverbs 19:13]

11 The weaker vessel. [I Peter 3:7]

12 A light wife doth make a heavy husband.
[Shakespeare: *The Merchant of Venice*
V.i.]

13 A fellow almost damn'd in a fair wife.
[Shakespeare: *Othello* I.i.]
*Spoken of Michael Cassio. The exact
meaning of the line is puzzling. Yet it
intrigues curiosity because one feels it
comes very close to some important
meaning. Cassio is a ladies' man, a puritan, a whining moralist: he keeps company with a known prostitute, yet is
ashamed to be seen with her. Something
about his relations with women is im-*
*plied in the line, but it eludes us. The
line may be corrupted, but no one has
ever proposed a satisfactory emendation.*

14 The only comfort of my life
Is that I never yet had wife.
[Robert Herrick: *His Comfort*]

15 A Batchelour was saying, next to no
wife, a good wife is best. Nay, said a
gentlewoman, next to a good wife, no
wife is the best. [Thomas Fuller (1608-
1661): *The Holy State* III.xxii.]

16 The clog of all pleasure, the luggage
of life,
Is the best can be said for a very good
wife.
[John Wilmot, Earl of Rochester: *On a
Wife*]

17 How doth your Whither go you? Your
wife. [John Ray: *English Proverbs*
(1670)]

18 A house-wife in bed, at table a slattern;
For all 'an example, for no one a pattern.
[Jonathan Swift: *Portraits from Life*]

19 To take a wife merely as an agreeable
and rational companion will commonly
be found to be a grand mistake. [Lord
Chesterfield: *Letters to His Son*, Oct. 12,
1765]
*Yet unbeknownst to Chesterfield, that is
exactly what the son had secretly done.
And he found far more comfort in his
wife than he ever did in his father's
letters.*

20 Think you, if Laura had been Petrarch's wife,
He would have written sonnets all
his life?
[Byron: *Don Juan* III.viii.]

21 He will hold thee, when his passion
shall have spent its novel force,
Something better than his dog, a little dearer than his horse.
[Tennyson: *Locksley Hall*]

WIFE(VES): miscellaneous

22 Horses (thou say'st) and asses men
may try,
And ring suspected vessels ere they
buy:
But wives, a random choice, untried
they take,
They dream in courtship, but in wedlock wake.

[Chaucer: Prologue to *The Wife of Bath's Tale* (trans. Alexander Pope)]
1 He that will thrive must ask leave of his wife.

[15th-century proverb]
That is, a man with a thriftless wife will hardly thrive, no matter how hard he works or how carefully he saves.

2 But who may have a more ungracyous lyfe
Than a chyldes birde and a knaves wyfe?

[John Skelton: *Garlande of Laurell* (1523)]
3 Wives are young men's mistresses; companions for middle age; and old men's nurses. [Francis Bacon: *Of Marriage and Single Life*]

4 Wives may be merry and yet honest too.

[Shakespeare: *The Merry Wives of Windsor* IV.ii.]
honest = *chaste*

5   Should all despair
That have revolted wives, the tenth of mankind
Would hang themselves.

[Shakespeare: *Winter's Tale* I.ii.]
6 Good wives and private soldiers should be ignorant.

[William Wycherley: *The Country Wife* I]
7 I know not which live more unnatural lives,
Obeying husbands, or commanding wives.

[Benjamin Franklin: *Poor Richard's Almanack* (1734)]
8 What a pity it is that nobody knows how to manage a wife but a bachelor.

[George Colman the Elder: *The Jealous Wife* IV.i.]
9 "Come, come," said Tom's father, "at your time of life,
There's no longer excuse for thus playing the rake—
It is time you should think, boy, of taking a wife"—
"Why, so it is, Father—whose wife shall I take?"

[Thomas Moore: *A Joke Versified*]
10 The real business of a ball is to look out for a wife, to look after a wife, or to look after somebody else's wife. [R. S. Surtees: *Mr. Jorrocks in Paris* LVI]

11 A man may force his actual wife to share the direst poverty, but even the least vampirish woman of the third part demands to be courted in what, considering his [the average man's] station in life, is the grand manner, and the expenses of that grand manner scare off all save a minority of specialists in deception. [H. L. Menken: in *Smart Set*, December 1921]
Romanticism, gallantry and inexperience often led Mencken to unwarranted conclusions.

WILDCATS
12 He could whip his weight in wildcats. [Eugene Field: *Modjesky as Cameel*]

WILDERNESS
13 The howling wilderness. [Deuteronomy 32:10]
14 The voice of one crying in the wilderness. [Matthew 3:3; Mark 1:3; Luke 3:4]
The voice of him that crieth in the wilderness. Isaiah 40:3 (Vulgate): Vox clamantis in deserto.
15 Antres vast and deserts idle,
Rough quarries, rocks, and hills whose heads touch heaven.

[Shakespeare: *Othello* I.iii.]
antres = *caves*

WILL
16 Will is the pimp of appetite. [Lope de Vega: *Los Locos de Valencia* II.vi.]
17 Let not thy Will roar, when thy Power can but whisper. [Thomas Fuller (1608-1661): *Introductio ad Prudentiam* I.xiv.]
18 Men may be convinced, but they cannot be pleased, against their will. [Samuel Johnson: *Life of Congreve*]
19 To sleep I give my powers away;
My will is bondsman to the dark.

[Tennyson: *In Memoriam* IV]
20   Tho'
We are not now that strength which in old days
Moved earth and heaven: that which we are we are;
One equal temper of heroic hearts,
Made weak by time and fate, but strong in will
To strive, to seek, to find, and not to yield.

[Tennyson: *Ulysses*]

1 John Stuart Mill
By a mighty effort of will
Overcame his natural bonhomie
And wrote "Principles of Political
Economy."
[Edmund Clerihew Bentley: *Biography for Beginners,* "John Stuart Mill"]

WILLING
2 Barkis is willin'! [Dickens: *David Copperfield* V]

WILL-O'-THE-WISP
3 No Will-o'-the-wisp mislight thee,
Nor snake or slow-worm bite thee;
But on, on thy way
Not making a stay,
Since ghost there's none to affright thee.
[Robert Herrick: *The Night-piece, to Julia*]

WILLOW
4 All a green willow, willow,
All a green willow is my garland.
[An old ballad: printed by John Heywood (1506-1565) and appearing in Percy's *Reliques* (1764)]
5 My mother had a maid call'd Barbara:
She was in love; and he she lov'd prov'd mad,
And did forsake her: she had a song of "willow";
An old thing 'twas, but it express'd her fortune,
And she died singing it.
[Shakespeare: *Othello* IV.iii.]
6 The poor soul sat sighing by a sycamore tree,
Sing all a green willow:
Her hand on her bosom, her head on her knee,
Sing willow, willow, willow.
[Shakespeare: *Othello* IV.iii.]
7 On a tree by a river a little tom-tit
Sang "Willow, titwillow, titwillow!"
And I said to him, "Dicky-bird, why do you sit
Singing 'Willow, titwillow, titwillow!'"
[W. S. Gilbert: *The Mikado* II]

WILLS
8 Let's choose executors and talk of wills:
And yet not so, for what can we bequeath

Save our deposed bodies to the ground? . . .
Nothing can we call our own but death
And that small model of the barren earth
Which serves as paste and cover to our bones.
[Shakespeare: *Richard II* III.ii.]

WILSON, WOODROW
9 The university president who cashiered every professor unwilling to support Woodrow Wilson for the first vacancy in the Trinity . . . [H. L. Mencken: "Star-spangled Men" in the *New Republic,* Sept. 29, 1920] *See* TRINITY

WIND
10 The wings of the wind. [Psalms 18:10]
11 The wind goeth toward the south, and turneth about unto the north: it whirleth about continually, and the wind returneth again according to his circuits. [Ecclesiastes 1:6]
12 They have sown the wind, and they shall reap the whirlwind. [Hosea 8:7]
13 The wind bloweth where it listeth. [John 3:8]
14 An ill wind that bloweth no man good. [John Heywood: *Song Against Idleness* V (c.1540)]
> The thought was proverbial. Shakespeare expresses it twice (Ill blows the wind that profits nobody— III Henry VI II.v.; the ill wind which blows no man to good— II Henry IV V.iii.). And it appears in Tusser's Five Hundred Points of Good Husbandry XII (1557):
> It is an ill wind turns none to good.
> Moderns sometimes think this ancient, grim proverb a variant of the 19th-century fatuous assurance that "every cloud has a silver lining." Not so. The "silver-lining" proverb says "Buck up; there's a good time coming. So much good in the worst of us, etc. etc." The "ill-wind" proverb says that someone profits from almost every disaster or that what is a misfortune to one is a lucky break to another.

15 O western wind, when wilt thou blow
That the small rain down can rain?
Christ, that my love were in my arms

And I in my bed again!
[Anon. (16th century): *The Lover in Winter Plaineth for the Spring*]
In a 19th cent. anthology this plaintive lyric appeared as:

O western wind, when wilt thou
blow
That the small rain down can
rain?
Ah, that my love were in my
arms
Or I in my bed again.
(*Never has so little done so much!*)

1 There is something in the wind.
[Shakespeare: *The Comedy of Errors* III.i.]
2 Many can brook the weather that love not the wind.
[Shakespeare: *Love's Labour's Lost* IV. ii.]
3 The southern wind
Doth play the trumpet to his purposes,
And by his hollow whistling in the leaves
Foretells a tempest and a blustering day.
[Shakespeare: *I Henry IV* V.i.]
4 The winds with wonder whist,
Smoothly the waters kist.
[John Milton: *On the Morning of Christ's Nativity*]
5 While rocking winds are piping loud.
[John Milton: *Il Penseroso*]
6 The winds and waves are always on the side of the ablest navigators. [Edward Gibbon: *Decline and Fall of the Roman Empire* LXVIII]
7 O wild West Wind, thou breath of Autumn's being,
Thou, from whose unseen presence the leaves dead
Are driven, like ghosts from an enchanter fleeing,
Yellow, and black, and pale, and hectic red,
Pestilence-stricken multitudes.
[Shelley: *Ode to the West Wind*]
8 Wild Spirit, which art moving everywhere;
Destroyer and preserver; hear, oh, hear!
[Shelley: *Ode to the West Wind*]
9 Sweet and low, sweet and low,
Wind of the western sea,

Low, low, breathe and blow,
Wind of the western sea!
Over the rolling waters go,
Come from the dying moon, and blow,
Blow him again to me;
While my little one, while my pretty one, sleeps.
[Tennyson: *The Princess* II]
10 'Tis the old wind in the old anger.
[A. E. Housman: *On Wenlock Edge*]
11 I have forgot much, Cynara! gone with the wind,
Flung roses, roses riotously with the throng.
[Ernest Dowson: *Cynara*]
12 It's a warm wind, the west wind, full of birds' cries:
I never hear the west wind but tears are in my eyes.
For it comes from the west lands, the old brown hills,
And April's in the west wind, and daffodils.
[John Masefield: *The West Wind*]
13 The wind was a torrent of darkness among the gusty trees.
[Alfred Noyes: *The Highwayman*]
14 Vacant shuttles
Weave the wind. I have no ghosts.
[T. S. Eliot: *Gerontion*]
15 The Devil sends the wicked wind
To blow our skirts knee-high,
But God is just and sends the dust
To blind the bad man's eye.
[Anon.]

WINDMILLS
16 To tilt at windmills.
An allusion to an incident in the 8th chapter of the first book of Cervantes' Don Quixote, in which the knight mistakes windmills for giants and attacks them.

WINDOW(S)
17 "Tehee," quod she, and clapte the window to.
[Chaucer: *The Miller's Tale*]
Fair Alisoun's squeak of triumph after she has beguiled the lovesick Absalon, in the dark, into a misdirected kiss.
18 And storied windows richly dight,
Casting a dim religious light.
[John Milton: *Il Penseroso*]

WINE: its allure

1 Stay me with flagons. [Song of Solomon 2:5]

2 As with new wine intoxicated both,
They swim in mirth, and fancy that
they feel
Divinity within them breeding wings
Wherewith to scorn the earth.
[John Milton: *Paradise Lost* IX.1008-1011]

3 O, for a draught of vintage! that hath
been
Cooled a long age in the deep-delved
earth,
Tasting of Flora and the country
green,
Dance and Provençal song, and sunburnt mirth!
O, for a beaker full of the warm
South,
Full of the true, the blushful Hippocrene,
With beaded bubbles winking at the
brim,
And purple-stained mouth.
[Keats: *Ode to a Nightingale*]

4 Ah, with the Grape my fading Life
provide,
And wash the Body whence the Life
has died,
And lay me, shrouded in the living
Leaf,
By some not unfrequented Gardenside.
That even my buried Ashes such a
snare
Of Vintage shall fling up into the Air
As not a True-believer passing by
But shall be overtaken unaware.
[*Rubáiyát of Omar Khayyám* (trans. Edward FitzGerald)]

WINE: bad

5 Boys should abstain from all use of wine until their eighteenth year, for it is wrong to add fire to fire. [Plato: *Laws* II]

6 Wine is a mocker, strong drink is raging: and whosoever is deceived thereby is not wise. [Proverbs 20:1]

7 Who hath woe? who hath sorrow? who hath contentions? who hath babbling? who hath wounds without cause? who hath redness of eyes? They that tarry long at the wine. [Proverbs 23:29]

8 Look not upon the wine when it is red, when it giveth his color in the cup, when it moveth itself aright.
At the last it biteth like a serpent, and stingeth like an adder.
Thine eyes shall behold strange women, and thine heart shall utter perverse things. [Proverbs 23:31-33]

9 Wine kindles anger. [Seneca: *De ira* II.xix.]

10 O God, that men should put an enemy in their mouths to steal away their brains! [Shakespeare: *Othello* II.iii.]

11 O thou invisible spirit of wine! if thou hast no name to be known by, let us call thee devil! [Shakespeare: *Othello* II.iii.]

12 The sweet poison of misused wine. [John Milton: *Comus*]

13 Lords are lordliest in their wine. [John Milton: *Samson Agonistes*]

14 Wine gives a man nothing. It neither gives him knowledge nor wit; it only animates a man, and enables him to bring out what a dread of the company has repressed. This is one of the disadvantages of wine: it makes a man mistake words for thoughts. [Samuel Johnson: in Boswell's *Life,* April 28, 1778]

15 Wine makes a man better pleased with himself. . . . But the danger is, that while a man grows better pleased with himself, he may be growing less pleasing to others. [Samuel Johnson: in Boswell's *Life,* April 28, 1778]

WINE: good

16 Wine that maketh glad the heart of man. [Psalms 104:15]

17 Give strong drink unto him that is ready to perish, and wine unto those that be of heavy hearts. Let him drink, and forget his poverty, and remember his misery no more. [Proverbs 31:6-7]

18 Drink no longer water, but use a little wine for thy stomach's sake and thine often infirmities. [I Timothy 5:23]

19 Bacchus opens the gate of the heart. [Horace: *Satires* I.iv.]
    Ovid agrees, but wisely adds "unless you take too much." (Remediorum amoris)

20 It has become quite a common proverb that in wine there is truth. [Pliny: *Natural History* XIV.xiv.]
    The Latin: In vino veritas. *Dr. Johnson*

said that he "would not keep company with a fellow who lies as long as he's sober and whom you must make drunk before you can get a word of truth out of him." Boswell's Life of Johnson, April 15, 1772.

1 Wine is an old man's milk. [Antonio Perez: Aforismos I.clxx.]

2　　　Give me a bowl of wine:
I have not that alacrity of spirit,
Nor cheer of mind, that I was wont
　　　　　　　to have.

[Shakespeare: Richard III V.iii.]

3 Good wine needs no bush.

[Shakespeare: Epilogue to As You Like It]

The proverb is very old, going back to at least the first century of the Christian era.

A wine shop was marked by a wreath, a bush, branch or wisp of hay hanging by the door. The proverb, an ancient variant of the "better mousetrap" idea, states that if the wine is good no advertisement is needed: the merit of the product will itself draw custom. This is much doubted by the advertising profession.

4 Good wine is a good familiar creature, if it be well used.

[Shakespeare: Othello II.iii.]

5 From wine what sudden friendship springs! [John Gay: Fables II.vi.]

6 Wine gives great pleasure, and every pleasure is of itself a good. [Samuel Johnson: in Boswell's Life, April 28, 1778]

7 And much as Wine has played the Infidel,
And robbed me of my Robe of Honor
　　　　　　　—Well,
I often wonder what the Vintners
　　　　　　　buy
One half so precious as the stuff they
　　　　　　　sell.

[Rubáiyát of Omar Khayyám (trans. Edward FitzGerald)]

8 It's a Naive Domestic Burgundy without Any Breeding, But I Think You'll be Amused by its Presumption. [James Thurber: Men, Women and Dogs (caption to cartoon)]

9 This wine is too good for toast-drinking, my dear. You don't want to mix emotions up with a wine like that. You lose the taste. [Ernest Hemingway: The Sun Also Rises VII]

Count Mippipopolous speaking to Brett.

WINE: women, and song

10 Those two main plagues and common dotages of human kind, wine and women, which have infatuated and besotted myriads of people: they go commonly together. [Robert Burton: Anatomy of Melancholy I.2.3.13]

11 What fool is he that shadows seeks,
And may the substance gain!
Then if thou'lt have me love a lass,
Let it be one that's kind,
Else I'm a servant to the glass
That's with Canary lined.

[Alexander Brome: The Resolve]

12 Let us have wine and women, mirth
　　　　　　　and laughter,
Sermons and soda-water the day after.

[Byron: Don Juan II.clxxviii.]

13 Then sing as Martin Luther sang,
As Doctor Martin Luther sang:
"Who loves not wine, woman and
　　　　　　　song,
He is a fool his whole life long."

[W. M. Thackeray: A Credo]

14 In the order named these are the hardest to control: Wine, Women and Song. [Franklin P. Adams: The Ancient Three]

WINE: miscellaneous

15 Neither do men put new wine into old bottles. [Matthew 9:17]

bottles = wineskins

If they had been glass bottles, the whole meaning of the parable would have been lost.

16 If you add water to wine, it ruins it; if you don't, it ruins you. [Melchior de Santa Cruz: Floresta Española I.i.]

17 And Noah he often said to his wife
when he sat down to dine,
"I don't care where the water goes if
it doesn't get into the wine."

[G. K. Chesterton: Wine and Water]

WINEPRESS

18 I have trodden the winepress alone. [Isaiah 63:3]

WINGS

19 If I take the wings of the morning, and dwell in the uttermost parts of the sea. [Psalms 139:9]

1 At once the Four spread out their
                               starry wings
    With dreadful shade contiguous.
[John Milton: *Paradise Lost* VI.827]
    *Milton is echoing the first chapter of
    Ezekiel.*

WINTER
2 Lastly came Winter, clothed all in
                                   frieze,
    Chattering his teeth for cold that did
                                him chill,
    Whilst on his hoary beard his breath
                             did freeze,
    And the dull drops, that from his
                               purpled bill
    As from a limbeck did adown distill.
[Edmund Spenser: *Faerie Queene* VII.
    vii.31.]
        frieze = *a coarse cloth;* limbeck = *alembic*
3 When icicles hang by the wall,
    And Dick the shepherd blows his
                                   nail,
    And Tom bears logs into the hall,
    And milk comes frozen home in
                                   pail.
[Shakespeare: *Love's Labour's Lost* V.ii.]
4 Winter tames man, woman and beast.
[Shakespeare: *The Taming of the Shrew*
    IV.i.]
5 Winter's not gone yet, if the wild-
                      geese fly that way.
[Shakespeare: *King Lear* II.iv.]
6 A sad tale's best for Winter.
[Shakespeare: *The Winter's Tale* II.i.]
7 Lo, where Maeotis sleeps, and hardly
                                    flows
    The freezing Tanais thro' a waste of
                                   snows.
[Alexander Pope: *The Dunciad* III.lxxx-
    vii.]
    *Lake Maeotis is what we now call the
    Sea of Azov, and Tanais is the Don.*
8 O Winter, king of intimate delights,
    Fire-side enjoyments, home-born hap-
                                 piness,
    And all the comforts that the lowly
                                   roof
    Of undisturb'd retirement, and the
                                  hours
    Of long uninterrupted ev'ning, know.
[William Cowper: *The Task* IV]
9 The English winter—ending in July,
    To recommence in August.
[Byron: *Don Juan* XIII.xlii.]

10 St. Agnes' Eve—Ah, bitter chill it was!
    The owl, for all his feathers, was a-
                                   cold;
    The hare limp'd trembling through
                         the frozen grass,
    And silent was the flock in woolly
                                   fold.
[Keats: *The Eve of St. Agnes*]
11 Deep on the convent-roof the snows
    Are sparkling to the moon:
    My breath to heaven like vapour
                                   goes:
    May my soul follow soon!
[Tennyson: *St. Agnes' Eve*]
12 Full knee-deep lies the winter snow,
    And the winter winds are wearily
                                   sighing.
[Tennyson: *The Death of the Old Year*]

WISDOM: and folly
13 Those who wish to appear wise among
    fools, among the wise seem foolish.
[Quintillian: *Institutio Oratoria* X.vii.]
14 Wisdom cries out in the streets and
                          no man regards it.
[Shakespeare: *I Henry IV* I.ii.]
    A paraphrase of Proverbs 1:20, 21, 29, 30.
15 *Touchstone.* The more pity, that fools
    may not speak wisely, what wise men do
    foolishly.
    Celia. By my troth, thou say'st true;
    for since the little wit that fools have was
    silenced, the little foolery that wise men
    have makes a great show. [Shakespeare:
    As You Like It I.ii.]
16 Penny wise and pound foolish. [Wil-
    liam Camden: *Remains Concerning Brit-
    ain*]
17 An intelligent man on one plane can
    be a fool on others. [Albert Camus:
    Notebooks 1935-1942 I]

WISDOM: of hindsight
18 After the event even a fool is wise.
[Homer: *Iliad* XVII]
19 When the great steed is stole
    Then he taketh heed
    And maketh the stable-door fast.
[John Gower: *Confessio Amantis* IV.901
    (about 1390)]

WISDOM: and knowledge
20 Not to know certain things is a great
    part of wisdom. [Hugo Grotius: *Epi-
    grams*]

1 It is not a greater point of wisdom to discover knowledge than to hide ignorance. [Francis Quarles: *Enchiridion* III. lvii.]

2 Knowledge comes, but wisdom lingers. [Tennyson: *Locksley Hall*]

WISDOM: its limitations

3 A wise man sees as much as he ought, not as much as he can. [Montaigne: *Essays* II]

4 Wisdom sails with wind and tide. [John Florio: *Second Fruites* No. 97]
   i.e., the wise do not oppose the irresistible.

5 Our wisdom is not less at the mercy of fortune than our property. [La Rochefoucauld: *Maxims*]

6 Even the wisest show their wisdom only in indifferent matters, never in really important matters. [La Rochefoucauld: *Maxims*]

7 Wisdom is a fox, who, after long hunting, will at last cost you the pains to dig out. 'Tis a cheese, which, by how much the richer, has the thicker, the homelier, and the coarser coat; and whereof, to a judicious palate, the maggots are the best. . . . But then, lastly, 'tis a nut, which, unless you choose with judgment, may cost you a tooth and pay you with nothing but a worm. [Jonathan Swift: Introduction to *A Tale of a Tub*]

8 Wisdom makes but a slow defence against trouble, though at last a sure one. [Oliver Goldsmith: *The Vicar of Wakefield* XXI]

9 Oh, wisdom never comes when it is gold,
And the great price we pay for it full worth:
We have it only when we are half earth.
Little avails that coinage to the old!
[George Meredith: *Modern Love* IV.xiii.]

WISDOM: and sorrow

10 Wisdom cometh by suffering. [Aeschylus: *Agamemnon*]

11 Wisdom is full of pity; and thereby
   Men pay for too much wisdom with much pain.
[Euripides: *Electra* (trans. Gilbert Murray)]

12 The children of this world are in their generation wiser than the children of light. [Luke 16:8]

13 A man's wisdom is most conspicuous where he is able to distinguish among dangers and make choice of the least. [Machiavelli: *The Prince* XXI]

14 'Tis, I confess, the common fate of men of singular gifts of mind to be destitute of those of Fortune, which doth not any way deject the spirit of wiser judgments, who thoroughly understand the justice of this proceeding; and being inrich'd with higher donatives, cast a more careless eye on these vulgar parts of felicity. [Sir Thomas Browne: *Religio Medici* I.18]

15 A sadder and a wiser man,
   He rose the morrow morn.
[Coleridge: *The Ancient Mariner* VII]

16 Wisdom is early to despair. [Gerard Manley Hopkins: *The Leaden Echo*]

17 One may almost doubt if the wisest man has learned anything of absolute value by living. [Thoreau: *Walden* I]

18 The only medicine for suffering, crime, and all the other woes of mankind, is wisdom. [T. H. Huxley: *Science and Education* IV]

WISDOM: miscellaneous

19 Wisdom never lies. [Homer: *Odyssey* III.]

20 The price of wisdom is above rubies. [Job 28:18]
   See *Proverbs 3:15; 8:11.*

21 Days should speak, and multitude of years should teach wisdom. [Job 32:7]

22 The fear of the Lord is the beginning of wisdom. [Psalms 111:10]

23 Wisdom crieth without; she uttereth her voice in the streets. [Proverbs 1:20]

24 Wisdom is better than rubies. [Proverbs 8:11]

25 Wisdom hath builded her house, she hath hewn out her seven pillars. [Proverbs 9:1]

26 Wisdom is justified of her children. [Matthew 11:19]

27 Nature never says one thing and wisdom another. [Juvenal: *Satires* XIV]

28 There are two sentences inscribed upon the Delphic oracle. . . : "Know thyself" and "Nothing too much"; and

upon these all other precepts depend. [Plutarch: *Consolation to Apollonius*]
The second is more commonly expressed as "Nothing to excess."

1 The most manifest sign of wisdom is a continual cheerfulness: her state is like that of things in the regions above the moon, always clear and serene. [Montaigne: *Essays* I.xxv.]

2 And thus do we of wisdom and of reach,
With windlasses and with assays of bias,
By indirections find directions out.
[Shakespeare: *Hamlet* II.i.]
windlasses = roundabout methods; assays of bias = oblique tests and trials

3 The first and wisest of them all profess'd
To know this only, that he nothing knew.
[John Milton: *Paradise Regained* IV. 293-294]

4 Wisdom's sullen pomp. [Matthew Greene: *The Spleen*]

5 Spontaneous wisdom breathed by health,
Truth breathed by cheerfulness.
[Wordsworth: *The Tables Turned*]

6 Wisdom married to immortal verse. [Wordsworth: *The Excursion* VII]

7 I love wisdom more than she loves me.
[Byron: *Don Juan* VI.lxiii.]

8 All human wisdom is summed up in two words—wait and hope. [Alexandre Dumas, père: *The Count of Monte Cristo*]

WISE

9 How prone to doubt, how cautious are the wise!
[Homer: *Odyssey* XIII (trans. Alexander Pope)]

10 It is a high advantage for a wise man not to seem wise. [Aeschylus: *Prometheus Bound*]

11 Even a fool, when he holdeth his peace, is counted wise. [Proverbs 17:28]

12 Dare to be wise. [Horace: *Epistles* I.ii.]

13 No man is born wise. [Cervantes: *Don Quixote* II.33]

14 If any one appears wise, it is only because his follies are proportioned to his age and fortune. [La Rochefoucauld: *Maxims*]

15 It is not wise to be wiser than is necessary. [Philippe Quinault: *Armide*]

16 Deign on the passing world to turn thine eyes,
And pause awhile from letters, to be wise.
[Samuel Johnson: *Vanity of Human Wishes*]

17 Some folks are wise and some are otherwise. [Tobias Smollett: *Roderick Random* VI]
Smollett is quoting a proverb. One still hears it, usually accompanied by a complacent cackle as the speaker contemplates his own wit.

18 Type of the wise who soar, but never roam,
True to the kindred points of heaven and home.
[Wordsworth: *To a Skylark*]

19 You look wise. Pray correct that error. [Charles Lamb: *All Fools' Day*]

WISE MEN: and fools

20 How dieth the wise man? as the fool. [Ecclesiastes 2:16]

21 Among wise men, the wisest knows that he knows least; among fools, the most foolish thinks he knows most. [Antonio de Guevara: *Marco Aurelio Faustina* II]

22 Wise men ne'er sit and wail their loss,
But cheerly seek how to redress their harms.
[Shakespeare: *III Henry VI* V.iv.]

23 Well, God give them wisdom that have it; and those that are fools, let them use their talents. [Shakespeare: *Twelfth Night* I.v.]

24 The wise man profits more from the fool than the fool from the wise man; for the wise man takes warning by the fool but the wise man's sense has no value to the fool. [Melchior de Santa Cruz: *Floresta Española* I.vi.]

WISER

25 A man should never be ashamed to own he has been in the wrong, which is but saying, in other words, that he is wiser to-day than he was yesterday. [Jonathan Swift: *Thoughts on Various Subjects*]

1 It's wiser being good than bad;
It's safer being meek than fierce:
It's fitter being sane than mad.
[Robert Browning: *Apparent Failure* VII]
See SADDER

WISH(ES)
2 Thy wish was father, Harry, to that thought.
[Shakespeare: *II Henry IV* IV.v.]
3 If wishes were horses beggars would ride. [John Ray: *English Proverbs* (1670)]
4 If a man could have half his wishes he would double his Troubles. [Benjamin Franklin: *Poor Richard's Almanack* (1752)]
See DESIRES, LONGINGS

WISHERS
5 Wishers were ever fools.
[Shakespeare: *Antony and Cleopatra* IV. xv.]

WIT: its dangers
6 For when a man hath over-greet a wit,
Ful oft hym happeth to mysusen it.
[Chaucer: Prologue to *The Canon Yeoman's Tale*]
wit = *intelligence in general*
7 I shall ne'er be ware of mine own wit till I break my shins against it. [Shakespeare: *As You Like It* II.iv.]
8 The greatest fault of a penetrating wit is to go beyond the mark. [La Rochefoucauld: *Maxims*]
9 The more wit the less courage. [Thomas Fuller (1654-1734): *Gnomologia*]
wit = *intelligence*
10 For wits are treated just like common whores;
First they're enjoyed, and then kicked out of doors.
[John Wilmot, Earl of Rochester: *A Satyr Against Mankind*]
11 It is with wits as with razors, which are never so apt to cut those they are employed on as when they have lost their edges. [Jonathan Swift: Preface to *A Tale of a Tub*]
12 His wit ran him out of his money, and now his poverty has run him out of his wits. [William Congreve: *Love for Love* V.ii.]

13 Wit is so shining a quality that everybody admires it; most people aim at it, all people fear it, and few love it except in themselves. [Lord Chesterfield: *Letters to His Son*, July 21, 1752]
14 The wit we long for spoils the wit we have. [Jean Baptiste Gresset: *Le Méchant* IV.vii]
Annabelle Milbanke (later Lady Byron) said that her cousin's—Lady Caroline Lamb's—"affectation of Byronism spoiled the charm of her customary stupidity."
15 One wit, like a knuckle of ham in soup, gives a zest and flavour to the dish, but more than one serves only to spoil the pottage. [Tobias Smollett: *Humphrey Clinker*]
16 Those who cannot miss an opportunity of saying a good thing . . . are not to be trusted with the management of any great question. [William Hazlitt: *Characteristics*]
17 Professed wits, though they are generally courted for the amusement they afford, are seldom respected for the qualities they possess. [Sydney Smith: *Lectures on Wit and Humor* I]

WIT: and folly
18 Always the dulness of the fool is the whetstone of the wits. [Shakespeare: *As You Like It* I.ii.]
19 Methinks sometimes I have no more wit than a Christian or an ordinary man has; but I am a great eater of beef, and I believe that does harm to my wit. [Shakespeare: *Twelfth Night* I.iii.]
Christian = *a human being, as distinguished from a brute*
20 Better a witty fool than a foolish wit. [Shakespeare: *Twelfth Night* I.v.]
21 If it were not for the company of fools, a witty man would often be greatly at a loss. [La Rochefoucauld: *Maxims*]
22 Wit is folly unless a wise man hath the keeping of it. [John Ray: *English Proverbs* (1670)]
23 For wit and judgment often are at strife,
Tho' meant each other's aid, like man and wife.
[Alexander Pope: *An Essay on Criticism* I]
24 Fools are only laugh'd at; wits are

hated. [Alexander Pope: *Prologue to Three Hours After Marriage*]

1 You beat your pate, and fancy wit
　　　　　　　　　will come;
Knock as you please, there's nobody
　　　　　　　　　at home.
[Alexander Pope: *Epigram*]

WIT: and madness
2 There has never been great genius without an admixture of madness. [Aristotle: quoted by Seneca in *De Tranquilitate animi* I.xv.]
3 Aristotle said melancholy men of all others are most witty. [Robert Burton: *The Anatomy of Melancholy* I.3.1.2.]
So did Freud.
4 Your greatest wits have ever a touch
　　　　　　　　　of madness.
[Dryden: *Sir Martin Mar-All* V.i.]
5 Great wits are sure to madness near
　　　　　　　　　alli'd
And thin partitions do their bounds
　　　　　　　　　divide
[Dryden: *Absalom and Achitophel* I]

WIT: and malice
6 Wit is cultured insolence. [Aristotle: *Rhetoric* II.xii.]
7 Wit, like tierce claret, when 't begins
　　　　　　　　　to pall,
Neglected lies, and 's of no use at all,
But, in its full perfection of decay,
Turns vinegar, and comes again in
　　　　　　　　　play.
[Charles Sackville: *To Mr. Edward Howard*]
tierce = tierce *was an old measure of capacity, usually 42 gallons: hence a cask holding that amount: hence—as here—casked, barreled*
8 He must be a dull Fellow indeed, whom neither Love, Malice, nor Necessity, can inspire with Wit. [La Bruyère: *Les Caractères*]
9 There's no possibility of being witty without a little ill-nature; the malice of a good thing is the barb that makes it stick. [Richard Brinsley Sheridan: *The School for Scandal* I]

WIT: its power
10 I am not only witty in myself, but the cause that wit is in other men. [Shakespeare: *II Henry IV* I.ii.]

11 Wit is more necessary than beauty; and I think no young woman ugly that has it, and no handsome woman agreeable without it. [William Wycherley: *The Country Wife* I.i.]
12 A witty woman is a treasure; a witty beauty is a power. [George Meredith: *Diana of the Crossways* I]

WIT: some praises of
13 His eye begets occasion for his wit;
For every object that the one doth
　　　　　　　　　catch,
The other turns to a mirth-moving
　　　　　　　　　jest.
[Shakespeare: *Love's Labour's Lost* II.i.]
14 Sir, your wit ambles well; it goes
　　　　　　　　　easily.
[Shakespeare: *Much Ado About Nothing* V.i.]
15　　　　　　Wit will shine
Through the harsh cadence of a rugged line.
[Dryden: *To the Memory of Mr. Oldham*]
16 True wit is Nature to advantage
　　　　　　　　　dress'd,
What oft was thought, but ne'er so
　　　　　　　　　well express'd.
[Alexander Pope: *An Essay on Criticism*]

WIT: its skill and techniques
17 Rudeness is a sauce to his good wit,
Which gives men stomach to digest
　　　　　　　　　his words
With better appetite.
[Shakespeare: *Julius Caesar* I.ii.]
18 A small degree of wit, accompanied by good sense, is less tiresome in the long run than a great amount of wit without it. [La Rochefoucauld: *Maxims*]
19 How easie it is to call Rogue and Villain, and that wittily! But how hard to make a Man appear a Fool, a Blockhead, or a Knave, without using any of those opprobrious terms! . . . Yet there is still a vast difference betwixt the slovenly Butchering of a Man, and the fineness of a stroak that separates the Head from the Body, and leaves it standing in its place. [Dryden: *Discourse Concerning Satire* (Preface to the translation of the Satires of Juvenal and Persius) II]
Satire should, like polished razor
　　　　　　　　　keen,

*Wound with a touch that's scarcely
felt or seen.*

—Lady Mary Wortley Montagu: To
the Imitator of the First Satire of
Horace

1 A wit should be no more sincere than
a woman constant: one argues a decay of
the parts, as t'other of beauty. [William
Congreve: *The Way of the World* I]

2 Great wits sometimes may gloriously
offend,
And rise to faults true critics dare
not mend:
From vulgar bounds with brave dis-
order part,
And snatch a grace beyond the reach
of art.
[Alexander Pope: *An Essay on Criticism*
I]

3 As in smooth oil the razor best is
whet,
So wit is by politeness sharpest set.
[Edward Young: *Love of Fame* II.cxix.]

4 A man often runs the risk of throwing away a witticism if he admits that it
is his own. [La Bruyère: *Les Caractères*
II]

5 Surprise is so essential an ingredient
of wit that no wit will bear repetition—
at least the original electrical feeling
produced by any piece of wit can never
be renewed. [Sydney Smith: *Lectures
on Moral Philosophy* X]

WIT: miscellaneous

6 What a wit-snapper are you!
[Shakespeare: *The Merchant of Venice*
III.v.]

7 Who wears his wit in his belly, and
his guts in his head.
[Shakespeare: *Troilus and Cressida* II.i.]

8 It is wit to pick a lock and steal a
horse, but it is wisdom to let them alone.
[Thomas Fuller (1654-1734): *Gnomologia*]

9 His wit shines at the expense of his
memory. [Le Sage: *Gil Blas* III.xi.]

10 This man, I thought, had been a Lord
among wits; but, I find, he is only a wit
among Lords! [Samuel Johnson: in Boswell's *Life* (1754)]
Spoken of Lord Chesterfield.

11 Pointed axioms and acute replies fly
loose about the world, and are assigned
successively to those whom it may be the
fashion to celebrate. [Samuel Johnson:
Life of Waller]
See: *"Go West, young man" and "Everybody talks about the weather."*

12 Staircase wit.
[Denis Diderot: *The Paradox of the
Comedian*]
*Diderot's term for the witty answer that
comes too late—that comes as one is de-
scending the stairs, on his way out.*

13 Wit is the rarest quality to be met
with among people of education, and
the most common among the uneducated. [William Hazlitt: *Characteristics*]

14 The loudest wit I e'er was deafened
with.
[Byron: *Don Juan* XVI.lxxxi.]
See also APHORISM, EPIGRAM,
HUMOR, IMPROPRIETY, INTELLI-
GENCE, JEST, MALICE, RAILLERY,
SATIRE

WITCH(ES)

15 Thou shalt not suffer a witch to live.
[Exodus 22:18]

16   What are these,
So wither'd, and so wild in their
attire;
That look not like the inhabitants o'
th' earth,
And yet are on 't?
[Shakespeare: *Macbeth* I.iii.]

17 How now, you secret, black, and midnight hags!
[Shakespeare: *Macbeth* IV.i.]

18 Aroint thee, witch, aroint thee!
[Shakespeare: *King Lear* III.iv.]

19 The foul witch Sycorax, who with
age and envy
Was grown into a hoop.
[Shakespeare: *The Tempest* I.ii.]

20 For my part, I have ever believed,
and do now, that there are Witches:
they that doubt of these, do not only
deny them, but spirits; and are obliquely
and upon consequence a sort not of In-
fidels, but Atheists. [Sir Thomas Browne:
Religio Medici I.xxx.]
*Sir Thomas was not alone in this belief.
Blackstone (Commentaries IV) said that
to deny the actual existence of Witchcraft is "flatly to contradict the revealed
word of God." As it is. And John Wesley
insisted that "the giving up of witch-*

craft is in effect giving up the Bible."
(*Journal V.265, 374-5; VI.109.*) *As it is!*
A modern imagines that if he had been present at the witchcraft trials, he would have cried out against them. But the mere crying out would have been considered, in itself, conclusive evidence of atheism or witchcraft and the protestor would have been burned, as one fully guilty, along with the others. That is the essence of a witch hunt, that any questioning of the evidence or the procedures in itself constitutes proof of complicity.

1 Our witches are justly hanged because they think themselves so, and suffer deservedly for believing they did mischief, because they meant it. [Dryden: *Of Dramatic Poesy*]

2 The law against witches does not prove there be any; but it punishes the malice of those people that use such means to take away men's lives. [John Selden: *Table Talk*]

The learned Selden obviously assumed that "such means" would take away men's lives.

WITHERS
3 Let the galled jade wince, our withers are unwrung. [Shakespeare: *Hamlet* III.ii.]

WITNESSES
4 We also are compassed about with so great a cloud of witnesses. [Hebrews 12:1]

WIZARDS
5 Wizards that peep, and that mutter. [Isaiah 8:19]

WOE(S)
6 Woe unto you, when all men shall speak well of you! [Luke 6:26]

7 Small troubles may speak, great woes are silent. [Seneca: *Phaedra*]

8 For ever the latter ende of joye is wo. [Chaucer: *The Nun's Priest's Tale*]

9 O sodeyn wo, that ever art successour
To worldly blisse!
[Chaucer: *The Tale of the Man of Law*]

10 My prime of youth is but a frost of cares;
My feast of joy is but a dish of pain;
My crop of corn is but a field of tares;
And all my good is but vain hope of gain.
The day is past, and yet I saw no sun;
And now I live, and now my life is done.
[Chidiock Tichborne: *Elegy*]

Tichborne, a Roman Catholic, was hanged for his part in a plot to assassinate Queen Elizabeth. These moving lines were written in the tower before his execution. He was 28 years old.

11 All these woes shall serve
For sweet discourses in our time to come.
[Shakespeare: *Romeo and Juliet* III.v.]

12 I have that within which passeth show;
These but the trappings and the suits of woe.
[Shakespeare: *Hamlet* I.ii.]

13 One woe doth tread upon another's heel,
So fast they follow.
[Shakespeare: *Hamlet* IV.vii.]

14 The man that makes his toe
What he his heart should make
Shall of a corn cry woe,
And turn his sleep to wake.
[Shakespeare: *King Lear* III.ii.]

15 Weeping is the ease of woe.
[Richard Crashaw: *St. Mary Magdalene*]

Magdalen used to be pronounced maudlin, as it is yet in the name of the Oxford College. She was always depicted as weeping for her sins and from this came the modern meaning of maudlin.

16 Sure there's a lethargy in mighty woe,
Tears stand congeal'd and cannot flow . . .
Like Niobe we marble grow
And petrify with grief.
[Dryden: *Threnodia Augustalis*]

17 Life protracted is protracted woe.
[Samuel Johnson: *The Vanity of Human Wishes*]

18 As long as skies are blue, and fields are green,
Evening must usher night, night urge the morrow,
Month follow month with woe, and year wake year to sorrow.
[Shelley: *Adonais*]

19 The heart bow'd down by weight of

woe

To weakest hopes will cling.
[Alfred Bunn: *The Bohemian Girl* II.]
1 Unrequited affections are in youth unmitigated woes; only later on in life do we learn to appreciate the charm of these bogus heart-breaks. [Logan Pearsall Smith: *Afterthoughts*]

WOLF(VES)

2 Wolf! Wolf! [Aesop: *The Shepherd's Boy*]
In whatever form presented, the phrase goes back to Aesop's story of the shepherd boy who cried "Wolf! wolf!" as a joke and then found that, when the wolf really came, no one would pay any attention to his calls for help.
3 I have got a wolf by the ears. [Terence: *Phormio* III.ii.]
Where it is described as a saying.
4 It is hard to have wolf full and wether whole.
[Chaucer: *Troilus and Criseyde* IV]
wether = castrated male sheep
5 It is a hard winter when one wolf eats another. [John Lyly: *Euphues*]
6 It is better to keep the wolf out of the fold than to trust to drawing his teeth and talons after he shall have entered. [Thomas Jefferson: *Notes on Virginia*]
7 The pass was steep and rugged,
The wolves they howled and whined;
But he ran like a whirlwind up the pass
And he left the wolves behind.
[Thomas Macaulay: *The Battle of Lake Regillus* XXIX]
8 Who's afraid of the big bad wolf? [Ann Ronell: song, in Walt Disney's *Three Little Pigs* (1933)]

WOLSEY

9 He was a scholar, and a ripe and good one;
Exceeding wise, fair-spoken, and persuading;
Lofty and sour to them that lov'd him not;
But to those men that sought him sweet as summer.
[Shakespeare: *Henry VIII* IV.ii.]

WOMAN: and age

10 The years that a woman subtracts from her age are not lost.
They are added to the ages of other women.
[Countess Diane of Poitiers (1499-1566)]
11 Women and music should never be dated. [Oliver Goldsmith: *She Stoops to Conquer* III]

WOMAN: all alike

12 When the candles are out all women are fair. [Plutarch: *Conjugal Precepts*]
As ridicule or encouragement of the lovesick or as a consolation to the monogamous, this saying, in divers forms ("When the candles are out, all cats are gray"—Heywood's Proverbs, 1546), appears in every European language. It is neither veracious nor effective.
13 Night makes no difference 'twixt the Priest and Clerk;
Joan as my Lady is as good i' th' dark.
[Robert Herrick: *No difference i' th' Dark*]
14 Most women have no characters at all. [Alexander Pope: *Moral Essays* II]
15 Like all young men, you greatly exaggerate the difference between one young woman and another. [G. B. Shaw: *Major Barbara* III]
16 An' I learned about women from 'er. [Kipling: *The Ladies*]
17 The colonel's lady and Judy O'Grady Are sisters under their skins. [Kipling: *The Ladies*]

WOMAN: danger of her allure

18 For the lips of a strange woman drop as an honeycomb, and her mouth is smoother than oil:
But her end is bitter as wormwood, sharp as a two-edged sword. [Proverbs 5:3-4]
19 Walk with stretched forth necks and wanton eyes, walking and mincing as they go, and making a tinkling with their feet. [Isaiah 3:16]
20 Women . . . whom inhibition inciteth and restraint inviteth. [Montaigne: *Essays* III.v.]
21 Let not the creaking of shoes nor the rustling of silks betray thy poor heart to woman. [Shakespeare: *King Lear* III.iv.]

1   O why did God,
Creator wise, that peopl'd highest
                Heaven
With spirits masculine, create at last
This novelty on earth, this fair defect
Of nature, and not fill the world at
                once
With men as angels without feminine,
Or find some other way to generate
Mankind? This mischief had not then
                befall'n.
[John Milton: *Paradise Lost* X.888-895]
2 There is nothing that so much se-
duces reason from vigilance as the
thought of passing life with an amiable
woman. [Samuel Johnson: letter to Jo-
seph Baretti, Dec. 21, 1762]
3   My only books
          Were woman's looks,
And folly's all they've taught me.
[Thomas Moore: *The Time I've Lost in
Wooing*]
4 I've seen your stormy seas and stormy
                women,
And pity lovers rather more than sea-
                men.
[Byron: *Don Juan* VI.liii.]
5 Woman would be more charming if
one could fall into her arms without
falling into her hands. [Ambrose Bierce:
Epigrams]
6 Dangerous, terrible women, with
whom one's relations were liable to take
a serious turn. [Henry James: *Daisy Miller*]

WOMAN: definitions
7 Woman may be said to be an inferior
man. [Aristotle: *Poetics* XV]
    *"As regards the individual nature,
woman is defective and misbegotten."*
St. Thomas Aquinas: Summa Theologica,
Question XCII, Article i, Reply Obj. i.
8 A child of our grandmother Eve, a female; or, for thy more sweet understanding, a woman. [Shakespeare: *Love's Labour's Lost* I.i.]
9 Women are only children of a larger
growth. [Lord Chesterfield: *Letters to
His Son*, Sept. 5, 1748]
10 Woman was God's *second* mistake.
[Nietzsche: *The Antichrist* (Aphorism)]
11 Woman [is] the female of the human
species, and not a different kind of animal. [G. B. Shaw: Preface to *Saint Joan*]

12 Sphinxes without secrets. [Oscar
Wilde: *The Picture of Dorian Gray*
XVII]

WOMAN: expensive to maintain
13   Nothing agreeth worse
Than a lady's heart and a beggar's
                purse.
[John Heywood: *Proverbs* (1546)]
14 To furnish a ship requireth much
                trouble,
But to furnish a woman the charges
              are double.
[John Manningham: *Diary* (1602)]
15 A ship and a woman are ever re-
pairing. [George Herbert: *Jacula Pru-
dentum*]
16 Fire, water, woman, are man's ruin,
Says wise Professor Vander Bruin.
By flames, a house I hired was lost
Last year, and I must pay the cost.
Next year the sea o'erflow'd my
                ground,
And my best Flanders mare was
              drown'd.
A slave I am to Clara's eyes,
The gipsy knows her power and flies.
Fire, water, woman, are my ruin,
And great thy wisdom, Vander Bruin.
[Matthew Prior: *Fire, Water, Woman*]
17 Every woman who hasn't any money
is a matrimonial adventurer. [G. B.
Shaw: *Heartbreak House* II]

WOMAN: frail, shifting, treacherous
18 As a jewel of gold in a swine's snout,
so is a fair woman which is without discretion. [Proverbs 11:22]
19 I know the nature of women; they
won't when you would; when you won't
they long for it all the more. [Terence:
Eunuchus IV.vii.]
20 Woman is ever varying and change-
                able.
[Vergil: *Aeneid* IV]
21 Lo, whiche sleightes and subtilitees
    In wommen been! for ay as bisy as
                bees
Ben they, us sely men for to deceyve.
[Chaucer: Epilogue to *The Merchant's
Tale*]
22 Nature doth paint them further to be
weak, frail, impatient, feeble and foolish;
and experience hath declared them to be
unconstant, variable, cruel, and lacking
the spirit of counsel. [John Knox: *The*

Monstrous Regiment of Women]
1 Constant you are; but yet a woman.
[Shakespeare: *I Henry IV* II.iii.]
2 Frailty, thy name is woman!
[Shakespeare: *Hamlet* I.ii.]
3   You are pictures out of doors,
  Bells in your parlors, wild-cats in
          your kitchens,
  Saints in your injuries, devils being
          offended,
  Players in your housewifery, and
          housewives in your beds.
[Shakespeare: *Othello* II.i.]
*Iago's catalog was a common one, though
there were many variations. John Bercher
(1559) had a woman as "an angel in the
church, an ape in the bed."*

    *Puttenham (1589): "a shrew in the
kitchen, a saint in the church, an angel
at the board, and an ape in the bed,"
ascribing this to some "Chronicle" commenting on Jane Shore. Needless to say,
a masculine saying. But, as the Wife of
Bath demanded, "Who painted the lion?"*
4 She was false as water.
[Shakespeare: *Othello* V.ii.]
5 A very honest woman, but something
          given to lie.
[Shakespeare: *Antony and Cleopatra* V.
ii.]
6 Women, and young men, are very apt
to tell what secrets they know, from the
vanity of having been trusted. [Lord
Chesterfield: *Letters to His Son*]
7 This record will for ever stand,
  "Woman, thy vows are traced in
          sand."
[Byron: *To Woman*]
8 For study of the good and bad in
woman two women are a needless expense. [Ambrose Bierce: *Epigram*]
9 Oh the gladness of their gladness
         when they're glad,
  And the sadness of their sadness when
         they're sad;
  But the gladness of their gladness,
      and the sadness of their sadness,
  Are as nothing to their badness when
         they're bad.
[J. M. Barrie: *Rosalind*]

WOMAN: illogical and trivial
10 I have no other but a woman's reason:
  I think him so, because I think him
         so.

[Shakespeare: *The Two Gentlemen of
Verona* I.ii.]
11 Offend her, and she knows not to for-
         give;
  Oblige her, and she'll hate you while
         you live;
  But die, and she'll adore you.
[Alexander Pope: *Moral Essays* II.137]
12 Women have a great advantage, that
they may take up with little things, without disgracing themselves; a man cannot,
except with fiddling. [Samuel Johnson:
in Boswell's *Life*, April 7, 1778]
13 You sometimes have to answer a
woman according to her womanishness,
just as you have to answer a fool according to his folly. [G. B. Shaw: *An Unsocial Socialist* XVIII]
14 If men knew how women pass the
time when they are alone, they'd never
marry. [O. Henry: *Memoirs of a Yellow
Dog*]
15 Women have simple tastes. They can
get pleasure out of the conversation of
children in arms and men in love. [H. L.
Mencken: *Chrestomathy*]
16 Not huffy or stuffy, nor tiny or tall,
  But fluffy, just fluffy, with no brains
         at all.
[A. P. Herbert: *I Like Them Fluffy*]

WOMAN: and learning
17 Be to her virtues very kind;
  Be to her faults a little blind;
  Let all her ways be unconfin'd;
  And clap your padlock—on her mind.
[Matthew Prior: *An English Padlock*]
18 Men hate learned women.
[Tennyson: *The Princess* II]

WOMAN: and love
19 And in that day seven women shall
take hold of one man. [Isaiah 4:1]
  *The prophet forewarns of a day when
  the daughters of Zion shall lament for
  their men fallen by the sword.*
20 The hearts of women sicken for love
more than do the hearts of men, but
honor curbs desire. [Euripides: *Andromache*]
21 Castles that come to parlye, and
women that delight in courting, are willing to yeelde. [John Lyly: *Euphues*]
22 She's beautiful and therefore to be
         wooed,

She is a woman, and therefore to be
won.
[Shakespeare: *I Henry IV* V.iii.]
Shakespeare must have been pleased with
this couplet, since he came close to re-
peating it:
She is a woman, therefore may be woo'd;
She is a woman, therefore may be won.
—Titus Andronicus *II.i.*
1   One can find women who have never
had one love affair, but it is rare indeed
to find any who have had only one.
[La Rochefoucauld: *Maxims*]
The Kinsey Report found a great many.
2   Womankind more joy discovers
Making fools, than keeping lovers.
[John Wilmot, Earl of Rochester: *On*
the Coquetry of Women]
3   Every woman is at heart a rake.
[Alexander Pope: *Moral Essays* II]
4   In your amours you should prefer old
women to young ones. They are so grateful. [Benjamin Franklin: letter to a
young man, June 25, 1745]
5   Does the imagination dwell the most
Upon a woman won or a woman lost?
[William Butler Yeats: *The Tower*]
6   Zuleika, on a desert island, would
have spent most of her time in looking
for a man's footprint. [Max Beerbohm:
Zuleika Dobson II]

WOMAN: her malice
7   When female minds are embittered
by age or solitude their malignity is generally exerted in a rigorous and spiteful
superintendence of domestic trifles.
[Samuel Johnson: *The Rambler* No. 112]
8   A tigress robb'd of young, a lioness,
Or any interesting beast of prey,
Are similes at hand for the distress
Of ladies who cannot have their
own way.
[Byron: *Don Juan* V.cxxxii]
9   She blended in a like degree
The vixen and the devotee.
[J. G. Whittier: *Snow-Bound*]

WOMAN: man's delight in
10   There is something in a woman beyond all human delight; a magnetic
virtue, a charming quality, an occult and
powerful motive. [Robert Burton: *Anat-*
omy of Melancholy III.2.1.2]
11   She is pretty to walk with,
And witty to talk with,

And pleasant too, to think on.
[Sir John Suckling: *The Discontented*
Colonel II.i.]
12   If the heart of a man is depress'd with
cares,
The mist is dispell'd when a woman
appears.
[John Gay: *The Beggar's Opera* II.iii.]
13   Without woman the beginning of our
life would be helpless, the middle with-
out pleasure, and the end void of con-
solation. [Victor de Jouy: *Sylla* II]
14   She was a Phantom of delight
When first she gleamed upon my
sight;
A lovely Apparition sent
To be a moment's ornament.
[Wordsworth: *She Was a Phantom of*
Delight]
15   A creature not too bright or good
For human nature's daily food;
For transient sorrows, simple wiles,
Praise, blame, love, kisses, tears and
smiles.
[Wordsworth: *She Was a Phantom of*
Delight]
16   A perfect woman, nobly planned,
To warn, to comfort, and command.
[Wordsworth: *She Was a Phantom of De-*
light]
17   O woman! in our hours of ease,
Uncertain, coy, and hard to please,
And variable as the shade
By the light quivering aspen made;
When pain and anguish wring the
brow,
A ministering angel thou!
[Sir Walter Scott: *Marmion* VI.xxx.]
18   The two divinest things this world
has got,
A lovely woman in a rural spot!
[Leigh Hunt: *The Story of Rimini* III]
19   What lasting joys the man attend
Who has a polished female friend.
[Cornelius Whurr: *The Accomplished*
Female Friend]
20   Complacencies of the peignoir, and
late
Coffee and oranges in a sunny chair.
[Wallace Stevens: *Sunday Morning*]

WOMAN: man's distraction and
damnation
21   You can't live with them, you can't

live without them. [Aristophanes: *Lysis-trata*]
> *Even in 412 B.C. the aphorism was listed as a "saying."*

1 *Mulier est hominis confusio;*
Madame, the sentence of this Latine is—
Womman is mannes Ioye and al his blis.
[Chaucer: *The Nun's Priest's Tale*]
> *High on his list of reasons for admiring himself, the cock Chanticleer places what he esteems to be his vast learning. He is here condescending to his wife, Pertelote, by speaking to her in Latin and then translating for her benefit. But he is a coward and dare not really translate. For the "sentence"—the meaning—of the Latin is "Woman is man's damnation."*
>
> *Chanticleer is quoting from a dialogue ascribed to the Emperor Hadrian and Secundus, a philosopher. Hadrian asks "Quid est Mulier?" [What is woman?] and Secundus answers: "Hominis confusio, insaturabilis bestia, continua sollicitudo, indesinens pugna, viri continentis naufragium, humanum mancipium" [Man's damnation, an insatiable beast, a ceaseless fight, a continual solicitation, the shipwreck of man's virtue, the manacles of the human race (i.e., "the old ball and chain").]*

2 Lady, you are the cruell'st she alive.
[Shakespeare: *Twelfth Night* I.v.]
3 You jig, you amble, and you lisp, and nickname God's creatures, and make your wantonness your ignorance. [Shakespeare: *Hamlet* III.i.]
4 The world is full of care, much like unto a bubble,
Women and care, and care and women, and women and care and trouble.
[Nathaniel Ward: *The Simple Cobbler of Aggawam*]
5 Once a woman has given you her heart, you can never get rid of the rest of her. [Sir John Vanbrugh: *The Relapse* II]
6 Daphne knows, with equal ease,
How to vex and how to please:
But the folly of her sex
Makes her sole delight to vex.
[Jonathan Swift: *Daphne*]
7 Oh thou delicious, damned, dear, de-

structive Woman!
[William Congreve: *The Old Batchelour* III.ii.]
8 Dear, deluding Woman,
The joy of joys!
[Burns: *Epistle to James Smith*]
9 As for the women, though we scorn and flout 'em,
We may live with, but cannot live without 'em.
[Frederic Reynolds: *The Will* I.i.]
10 Look for the woman. [Alexandre Dumas, père: *Les Mohicans de Paris* II.xi.]
> *i.e., in anything mysterious in a man's behavior, look for a woman as, somehow, mixed up in it.*
>
> *Dumas' phrase is:* Cherchons la femme *(Let us look for the woman). It is usually rendered* Cherchez la femme *(Look for the woman).*

11 She like a new disease, unknown to men,
Creeps, no precaution used, among the crowd,
Makes wicked lightnings of her eyes and saps
The fealty of our friends, and stirs the pulse
With devil's leaps, and poisons half the young.
[Tennyson: *Guinevere*]
> *The more innocent among the Victorians had the most alarming notions of how a wicked woman set about her wickedness.*

12 Wicked women bother one. Good women bore one. That is the only difference between them. [Oscar Wilde: *Lady Windermere's Fan* III]
13 A fool there was and he made his prayer
(Even as you and I!)
To a rag and a bone and a hank of hair
(We called her the woman who did not care),
But the fool he called her his lady fair
(Even as you and I!)
[Kipling: *The Vampire*]

WOMAN: her power and sway
14 The First Blast of the Trumpet Against the Monstrous Regiment of Women. [John Knox (1505-1572): title

of pamphlet]

Regiment = *rule*

Mary Stuart was Queen in Scotland (1558—date of the pamphlet), and Mary Tudor had just finished her reign and Elizabeth begun hers in England.

1 What all your sex desire is Sovereignty.
[Chaucer: *The Wife of Bath's Tale* (trans. Dryden)]
2 A woman's advice has little value, but he who won't take it is a fool. [Cervantes: *Don Quixote* II.7]
3 Women wear the breeches. [Robert Burton: *Anatomy of Melancholy,* "Democritus to the Reader"]
4 Ladies, whose bright eyes
Rain influence, and judge the prize.
[John Milton: *L'Allegro*]
5 Whoe'er she be,
That not impossible She,
That shall command my heart and me.
[Richard Crashaw: *Wishes to his (Supposed) Mistress*]
6 In men we various ruling passions find;
In women two almost divide the kind;
Those only fix'd, they first or last obey,
The love of pleasure and the love of sway.
[Alexander Pope: *Moral Essays* II "Of the Characters of Women"]
7 Let men say whate'er they will,
Woman, woman, rules them still.
[Isaac Bickerstaff: *The Sultan* II.i.]
8 Disguise our bondage as we will,
'Tis woman, woman rules us still.
[Thomas Moore: *Sovereign Woman*]
9 Through all the drama—whether damn'd or not—
Love gilds the scene, and women guide the plot.
[Richard Brinsley Sheridan: Epilogue to *The Rivals*]
10 As Father Adam first was fool'd,
A case that's still too common,
Here lies a man a woman rul'd:
The Devil ruled the woman.
[Robert Burns: *Epitaph on a Hen-pecked Country Squire*]
11 Woman, wakeful woman's never weary,
Above all, when she waits to thump

her deary.
[R. H. Barham: *The Ghost*]
12 Man has his will—but woman has her way! [O. W. Holmes: *The Autocrat of the Breakfast-Table* II]

WOMAN: praise of
13 O Jupiter, sho'd I speake ill
Of woman-kind, first die I will;
Since that I know, 'mong all the rest
Of creatures, woman is the best.
[Robert Herrick: *In Praise of Women*]
14 O fairest of creation! last and best
Of all God's works!
[John Milton: *Paradise Lost* IX.896-897]
15 A bevy of fair women.
[John Milton: *Paradise Lost* XI.582]
16 Here's to the maiden of bashful fifteen;
Here's to the widow of fifty;
Here's to the flaunting, extravagant quean,
And here's to the housewife that's thrifty!
[Richard Brinsley Sheridan: *The School for Scandal* III.iii.]
17 Auld Nature swears, the lovely dears
Her noblest work she classes, O;
Her prentice han' she tried on man,
An' then she made the lasses, O.
[Burns: *Green Grow the Rashes*]
18 Glory to women! they weave and entwine
Heavenly roses into an earthly life.
[Schiller: *Würde der Frauen*]
19 The last, best work, the noblest gift of Heav'n. [Thomas Love Peacock: *The Vision of Love*]
20 The superiority of their women. [Alexis de Tocqueville (1805-1859): *Democracy in America* II.iii.]

De Tocqueville's answer to the question to what the prosperity and growing strength of the American people ought mainly to be attributed.

WOMAN: should be subject to man
21 I suffer not a woman to teach, nor to usurp authority over the man, but to be in silence. [I Timothy 2:12]
22 To promote a woman to bear rule, superiority, dominion, or empire above any realm, nation, or city, is repugnant to nature; contumely to God, a thing most contrarious to His revealed will and approved ordinances; and finally, it

is the subversion of good order, of all equity and justice. [John Knox: *The First Blast of the Trumpet Against the Monstrous Regiment of Women*]

1 Women are not altogether in the wrong when they refuse the rules of life prescribed to the World, for men only have established them and without their consent. [Montaigne: *Essays* III.v.]

Chaucer's Wife of Bath had elaborated this theme two centuries earlier.

There are a number of words in English once neuter which became attached particularly to women (harlot is an example) and then acquired an evil or much more evil connotation.

2 A woman, an ass, and a walnut tree,
Bring the more fruit, the more beaten
they be.
[George Pettie: *Civil Conversations of Stefano Guazzo* (1580)]

3 A woman, a spaniel, and a walnut tree,
The more they're beaten the better
they be.
[Thomas Fuller (1654-1734): *Gnomologia* (1732)]

The saying goes back at least two centuries before Fuller. One who quoted it in the 16th century added that it was "sung over all the entire world." One can see what was at least intended in reference to the woman and the dog, but why the walnut tree? If the proverb was universal, it must have conveyed some meaning.

4 A woman is to be from her house
three times:
When she is christened, married, and
buried.
[Thomas Fuller (1654-1734): *Gnomologia*]
from = absent from

5 God is thy law, thou mine: to know
no more
Is woman's happiest knowledge and
her praise.
[John Milton: *Paradise Lost* IV.637-638]

6 As the faculty of writing has been chiefly a masculine endowment, the reproach of making the world miserable has been always thrown upon the women. [Samuel Johnson: *The Rambler* No. 18]

7 Ah! gentle dames, it gars me greet,
To think how monie counsels sweet,
How monie lengthen'd, sage advices,

The husband frae the wife despises!
[Burns: *Tam o'Shanter*]

8 Women are called womanly only when they regard themselves as existing solely for the use of men. [G. B. Shaw: Preface to *Getting Married*]

9 I expect that Woman will be the last thing civilized by Man. [George Meredith: *The Ordeal of Richard Feverel* I]

10 Sensible and responsible women do not want to vote. The relative positions to be assumed by man and woman in the working out of our civilization were assigned long ago by a higher intelligence than ours. [Grover Cleveland: in the *Ladies' Home Journal*, April 1905]

WOMAN: and talk

11 Silence gives the proper grace to women. [Sophocles: *Ajax*]

12 'Tis woman's nature to bear her ills on lip and tongue with mournful pleasure. [Euripides: *Andromache*]

13 Let the women learn in silence with all subjection. [I Timothy 2:11]

14 Come, ladies, shall we talk a round?
As men
Do walk a mile, women should talk
an hour,
After supper: 'tis their exercise.
[Beaumont and Fletcher: *Philaster* II.iv.]

15 It is said of the horses in the vision, that "their power was in their mouths and in their tails." What is said of horses in the vision, in reality may be said of women. [Jonathan Swift: *Thoughts on Various Subjects*]

16 How a little love and conversation improve a woman! [George Farquhar: *The Beaux' Stratagem* IV.ii.]

17 Women are to be talked to as below men, and above children. [Lord Chesterfield: *Letters to His Son*, Sept. 20, 1748]

WOMAN: vices

18 If once you find a woman gluttonous, expect from her very little virtue. [Samuel Johnson: *Letters*, No. 872 (July 26, 1783)]

19 Down from the waist they are Centaurs,
Though women all above.
[Shakespeare: *King Lear* IV.vi.]

20 He seldom errs
Who thinks the worst he can of

womankind.
[John Home: *Douglas* III.iii.]
1 There are some meannesses which are too mean even for man—woman, lovely woman alone, can venture to commit them. [W. M. Thackeray: *A Shabby Genteel Story* III]

WOMAN: woes
2   Sooner would I three times
Stand in the shielded ranks than bear
                              one child.
[Euripides: *Medea*]
3 Surely of all things that have life and
                              feeling
We women are the unhappiest crea-
                              tures born.
[Euripides: *Medea*]
4 A poor lone woman.
[Shakespeare: *II Henry IV* II.i.]

WOMAN: miscellaneous
5 Women who are either indisputably beautiful, or indisputably ugly, are best flattered upon the score of their under-standings; but those who are in a state of mediocrity, are best flattered upon their beauty, for every woman who is not ab-solutely ugly thinks herself handsome. [Lord Chesterfield: *Letters to His Son*, Sept. 5, 1748]
6 . . . it was only from her French be-ing so good, that you could know she was not a born woman of fashion. [W. M. Thackeray: *Vanity Fair* XXIX]
  Spoken of Becky Sharp.
7 The happiest women, like the hap-piest nations, have no history. [George Eliot: *The Mill on the Floss* VI.iii.]
8 Has a woman who knew that she was well-dressed ever caught a cold? [Nietz-sche: *The Twilight of the Idols*]
9 A woman's mind is cleaner than a man's—she changes it oftener. [Oliver Herford: *Epigram*]
10 It's certain that fine women eat
A crazy salad with their meat.
[William Butler Yeats: *A Prayer for My Daughter*]

WONDER(S)
11 Nothing is so great or so wonderful but all men, little by little, abate their wonder. [Lucretius: *De rerum natura* II]

12 On account of that wonderful event, a nine days' solemn feast was celebrated by the Romans. [Livy: *History* I.xxxi.]
  The Roman custom may underlie the common expression "a nine-day won-der." Nine days became the proverbial length of duration of superficial fame. Chaucer says: "A wonder last but nyne nights never in toune." (Troilus and Criseyde *IV*) *and Shakespeare, Burton, Byron and G. B. Shaw all repeat the phrase.*
13   Can such things be,
And overcome us like a summer's
                              cloud,
Without our special wonder?
[Shakespeare: *Macbeth* III.iv.]
14 We carry within us the wonders we
                              seek without us:
There is all Africa and her prodigies
                              in us.
[Sir Thomas Browne: *Religio Medici* I.xv.]
15 Wonder is the daughter of ignorance.
[Thomas Fuller (1654-1734): *Gnomolo-gia*]
16 Fools admire, but men of sense ap-prove. [Alexander Pope: *An Essay on Criticism* II]
  admire = *wonder at;* approve = *commend*
17 Wonders will never cease. [Sir Henry Bate Dudley: letter to Garrick, Sept. 13, 1776]
18 Or like stout Cortez when with
                              eagle eyes
He stared at the Pacific—and all his
                              men
Look'd at each other with a wild sur-
                              mise—
Silent, upon a peak in Darien.
[Keats: *On First Looking into Chapman's Homer*]

WOODS
19 Macbeth shall never vanquish'd be
                              until
Great Birnam wood to high Dun-
                              sinane hill
Shall come against him.
[Shakespeare: *Macbeth* IV.i.]
20 Enter these enchanted woods,
You who dare.
[George Meredith: *The Woods of West-ermain* 1]
21 The woods are lovely, dark and deep.

But I have promises to keep,
And miles to go before I sleep,
And miles to go before I sleep.
[Robert Frost: *Stopping by Woods on a Snowy Evening*]

WOOING

1 A man shal winne us best with flaterye.
[Chaucer: *The Wife of Bath's Tale*]
2 Much ado there was, God wot!
He would love and she would not.
She said, Never was man true;
He said, None was false to you.
He said, He had lov'd her long;
She said, Love should have no wrong.
Coridon would kiss her then;
She said, Maids must kiss no men.
[Nicholas Breton: *Phillida and Coridon*]
3 He that after ten denials
Dares attempt no further trials,
Hath no warrant to acquire
The dainties of his chaste desire.
[Sir Philip Sidney: *Wooing Stuff*]
4 And when a woman woos, what woman's son
Will sourly leave her till she have prevailed?
[Shakespeare: *Sonnets* XLI]
5 Was ever woman in this humour woo'd?
Was ever woman in this humour won?
[Shakespeare: *Richard III* I.ii.]
6 Men are April when they woo, December when they wed.
[Shakespeare: *As You Like It* IV.i.]
7 Blessed is the wooing that is not long a-doing. [Robert Burton: *Anatomy of Melancholy* III.2.6.5]
8 To get thine ends, lay bashfulness aside;
Who fears to ask, doth teach to be deny'd.
[Robert Herrick: *No Bashfulness in Begging*]
9 The fruit that will fall without shaking,
Indeed is too mellow for me.
[Lady Mary Wortley Montagu: *To a Lady Making Love*]
10 Brisk confidence still best with woman copes;
Pique her and soothe in turns, soon passion crowns thy hopes.
[Byron: *Childe Harold* II.xxxiv.]

11 Not much he kens, I ween, of woman's breast,
Who thinks that wanton thing is won by sighs.
[Byron: *Childe Harold* XX.xxxiv.]
12 Better be courted and jilted
Than never be courted at all.
[Thomas Campbell: *The Jilted Nymph*]
13 The time I've lost in wooing,
In watching and pursuing
The light that lies
In woman's eyes,
Has been my heart's undoing.
[Thomas Moore: *The Time I've Lost in Wooing*]
14 Thrice happy's the wooing that's not long adoing,
So much time is saved in the billing and cooing.
[R. H. Barham: *Sir Rupert the Fearless*]
15 If I am not worth the wooing, I surely am not worth the winning. [Longfellow: *The Courtship of Miles Standish* III]

WOOL

16 Moche Crye and no Wull. [John Fortescue: *De laudibus legum Angliae* X]
17 Here's a great cry and but little wool (as the fellow said when he shear'd his hogs). [John Ray: *English Proverbs* (1678)]
18 "Odious! in woollen! 't would a saint provoke"
(Were the last words that poor Narcissa spoke);
"No, let a charming chintz and Brussels lace
Wrap my cold limbs, and shade my lifeless face;
One would not, sure, be frightful when one's dead—
And—Betty—give this cheek a little red."
[Alexander Pope: *Moral Essays* I]
As a subsidy and protection to the wool trade, upon which the country's prosperity depended, it was for centuries required that all shrouds be woollen.
Since Narcissa's whole concern in life has been her appearance, there is nothing surprising that it is her chief concern in death ("even in our ashes live their wonted fires"). Pope's crowning

touch—that she wanted to be rouged—is doubly ironic, since it is now customary.

WOOLGATHERING

1 His wits are woolgathering.
This fine old metaphor for absent-mindedness goes back to at least the 16th century. Literally woolgathering consisted of gathering bits of wool torn from sheep by bushes and other obstructions. Since sheep wander and such obstacles would be scattered over the fields, woolgathering could not be done systematically. Furthermore, it was an occupation for children and so usually attended with horseplay and inattention. And, to complete the metaphor, that which was gathered was of little value.

WORD: of God

2 Thy word is a lamp unto my feet, and a light unto my path. [Psalms 99:105]
3 In the beginning was the Word, and the Word was with God, and the Word was God. [John 1:1]
This verse was long regarded as the most sacred single verse in the Bible. The begging friars used the first four words of the Latin version (In principio erat verbum) as a pious salutation.
See Chaucer's Friar Hubert in the Prologue to The Canterbury Tales.
4 He was the Word that spake it:
He took the bread and brake it;
And what that word did make it
I do believe and take it.
[Donne: *On the Sacrament* (1633)]
Sometimes attr. Queen Elizabeth I.

WORD: to the wise

5 A word to the wise is sufficient. [Terence: *Phormio* III.iii., and Plautus: *Persa* IV.vii.]
The Latin: Dictum sapienti sat est.
Usually quoted as Verbum sapienti sat est and shortened humorously to verb sap.
6 To an intelligent man, there needs but a single word. [Rabelais: *Pantagruel* V.vii.]
7 Good wits jump; a word to the wise is enough. [Cervantes: *Don Quixote* II.37]
8 A word to the wise is enough, and many words won't fill a bushel. [Benja-

min Franklin: Preface to *Poor Richard Improved*]

WORDS: their futility

9 Should a wise man utter vain knowledge, and fill his belly with the east wind? [Job 15:2]
10 But words are words; I never yet did hear
That the bruis'd heart was pierced through the ear.
[Shakespeare: *Othello* I.iii.]
11 Why, what an ass am I! This is most brave
That I . . .
Must (like a whore) unpack my heart with words
And fall a-cursing like a very drab.
[Shakespeare: *Hamlet* II.ii.]
12 Few words, but to effect.
[Shakespeare: *King Lear* III.i.]
13 Words are like leaves; and where they most abound,
Much fruit of sense beneath is rarely found.
[Alexander Pope: *An Essay on Criticism* II]

WORDS: hard words

14 Few faults of style excite the malignity of a more numerous class of readers than the use of hard words. . . . But words are hard only to those who do not understand them, and the critic ought always to inquire whether he is incommoded by the fault of the writer or by his own. [Samuel Johnson: *The Idler* No. 70]
Johnson is here, of course, gratifying the prejudices of his own sesquipedality. Any reader intelligent enough to ask the question would probably have so large a vocabulary that he would not have to ask it.
15 He that thinks with more extent than another will want words of larger meaning; he that thinks with more subtlety will seek for terms of more nice discrimination. . . . Yet vanity inclines us to find faults anywhere rather than in ourselves. He that reads and grows no wiser seldom suspects his own deficiency but complains of hard words and obscure sentences and asks why books are writ-

ten which cannot be understood? [Samuel Johnson: *The Idler* No. 70]

WORDS: and meaning
1 He multiplieth words without knowledge. [Job 35:16]
2 Who is this that darkeneth counsel by words without knowledge? [Job 38:2]
3 The important thing about any word is how you understand it. [Publilius Syrus: *Maxims*]
4 I would have the matter to so surmount and fill the imagination of him that heareth that he have no remembrance at all of the words. [Montaigne: *Essays* I.xxv.]
5 The word is half his that speaks and half his that hears it. [Montaigne: *Essays* III.xiii.]
6 I understand a fury in your words,
But not the words.
[Shakespeare: *Othello* IV.ii.]
7 We should have a great many fewer disputes in the world if words were taken for what they are, the signs of our ideas only, and not for things themselves. [John Locke: *An Essay Concerning Human Understanding* III.x.]
8 "The question is," said Alice, "whether you *can* make words mean so many different things."

"The question is," said Humpty Dumpty, "which is to be master—that's all." [Lewis Carroll: *Through the Looking-Glass* VI]

WORDS: their power
9 How forcible are right words! [Job 6:25]
10 The words of the wise are as goads, and as nails fastened by the masters of assemblies. [Ecclesiastes 12:11]
11 How long a time lies in one little
word!
[Shakespeare: *Richard II* I.iii.]
King Richard had just reduced the length of Bolingbroke's banishment by four years.
12 But for your words, they rob the Hybla bees,
And leave them honeyless.
[Shakespeare: *Julius Caesar* V.i.]
13 A blow with a word strikes deeper than a blow with a sword. [Robert

Burton: *The Anatomy of Melancholy* I.2.4.4]
14 Words, when well chosen, have so great a force in them that a description often gives us more lively ideas than the sight of things themselves. [Joseph Addison: *The Spectator* No. 416]
One picture is not always worth a thousand words.
15 A good catchword can obscure analysis for fifty years. [Wendell L. Wilkie, Town Hall debate, 1938]
16 The history of our time is a history of phrases, which rise to great power and then as suddenly pass away: the "merchants of death," the "malefactors of great wealth," "monopoly," "reactionaries," "liberals," the "labor power," "America first," "cash and carry," "unconditional surrender," "peace in our time," "collective security," "bring the boys home," "disarmament," "the Red menace," "the atomic potential," etc., etc. At the time of their currency, few men have had either the courage or the resources to stand up to these tremendous shibboleths. They develop unpredictable authority.

Men are destroyed by them, and others are raised to power, and others are rallied to a fighting cause, and wars are declared, and people driven from their homes. And after all this havoc has been wreaked, suddenly the phrase disappears and is powerful no more—indeed, is lost and forgotten and replaced by something else, very likely its exact opposite. . . . It is terrifying. . . . Where, in all this, is truth? [Russell Davenport: *The Dignity of Man*]

WORDS: proper and seasonable
17 A word spoken in due season. How good is it! [Proverbs 15:23]
18 A word fitly spoken is like apples of gold in pictures of silver. [Proverbs 25:11]
19 Eek Plato seith, who-so that can him
rede,
The wordes mote be cosin to the
dede.
[Chaucer: Prologue to *The Canterbury Tales*]
mote = must
Chaucer's defense of the broad lan-

guage in some of the tales. The idea apparently appealed to him for he used it again in the Manciple's Tale:

The wyse Plato seith, as ye may rede,
The word mot nede accorde with the
dede.

1 Words borrowed of Antiquity do lend a kind of Majesty to style, and are not without their delight sometimes. For they have the authority of years, and out of their intermission do win to themselves a kind of grace-like newness. But the eldest of the present, and newest of the past Language, is the best. [Ben Jonson: *Discoveries*]
  intermission = *period of being out of common use*

WORDS: saddest of tongue or pen
2 Here are a few of the unpleasant'st words
    That ever blotted paper!
[Shakespeare: *The Merchant of Venice* III.ii.]
3 Let not your ears despise my tongue for ever,
    Which shall possess them with the heaviest sound
    That ever yet they heard.
[Shakespeare: *Macbeth* IV.iii.]
4 For of all sad words of tongue or pen,
    The saddest are these: "It might have been!"
[John Greenleaf Whittier: *Maud Muller*]
  The pronunciation of been *to rime with* pen *is still the proper pronunciation for millions of Americans—as it was for Chaucer before them.* Bin, *as also with Chaucer, is an acceptable variant. But* bee-n *is an affectation here.*
5 If, of all words of tongue and pen,
    The saddest are, "It might have been,"
    More sad are these we daily see:
    "It is, but hadn't ought to be."
[Bret Harte: *Mrs. Judge Jenkins*]
6 Of all cold words of tongue or pen
    The worst are these: "I knew him when—"
[Arthur Guiterman: *Prophets in Their Own Country*]

WORDS: use and abuse of
7 Words are the tokens current and accepted for conceits, as moneys are for values. [Francis Bacon: *The Advancement of Learning* II]
  conceits = *ideas*
8 They that dally nicely with words may quickly make them wanton. [Shakespeare: *Twelfth Night* III.i.]
9 Do not play in wench-like words with that
    Which is so serious.
[Shakespeare: *Cymbeline* IV.ii.]
10   When thou didst not, savage,
    Know thine own meaning, but wouldst gabble like
    A thing most brutish, I endow'd thy purposes
    With words that made them known.
[Shakespeare: *The Tempest* I.ii.]
11   High words, that bore
    Semblance of worth, not substance.
[John Milton: *Paradise Lost* I.528-529]
12 Words are wise men's counters, they do but reckon by them; but they are the money of fools. [Thomas Hobbes: *Leviathan* I.iv.]
  Counters were imitation coins, made of inferior metal, used as tokens.
13 He could make men laugh or cry by pronouncing the word Mesopotamia. [David Garrick, speaking of George Whitefield (1714-1770), the great Methodist preacher. See *Notes and Queries* Series XI.i.458]
14 O! many a shaft, at random sent,
    Finds mark the archer little meant!
    And many a word, at random spoken,
    May soothe or wound a heart that's broken!
[Sir Walter Scott: *The Lord of the Isles* V.xviii.]
15 I sometimes hold it half a sin
    To put in words the grief I feel;
    For words, like Nature, half reveal
    And half conceal the Soul within.
[Tennyson: *In Memoriam* V]
16 In words, like weeds, I'll wrap me o'er,
    Like coarsest clothes against the cold.
[Tennyson: *In Memoriam* V]
  weeds = *garments; cf. "widow's weeds"*

WORDS: wild, whirling and bitter
17 Winged words.
  Homer uses this expression over 100 times.
18 Some scurvy quaint collection of fus-

tian phrases, and uplandish words.
[Thomas Heywood: *Faire Maide of the Exchange* II.ii.]

1 By my troth, captain, these are very bitter words.
[Shakespeare: *II Henry IV* II.iv.]

2 Zounds! I was never so bethump'd with words,
Since I first call'd my brother's father dad.
[Shakespeare: *King John* II.i.]

3 A fine volley of words, gentlemen, and quickly shot off.
[Shakespeare: *The Two Gentlemen of Verona* II.iv.]

4 These are but wild and whirling words, my lord.
[Shakespeare: *Hamlet* I.v.]

5   I have words
That would be howl'd out in the desert air,
Where hearing should not latch them.
[Shakespeare: *Macbeth* IV.iii.]

6 What so wild as words are?
[Robert Browning: *A Woman's Last Word*]

WORDS: miscellaneous

7 The words of his mouth were smoother than butter, but war was in his heart; his words were softer than oil, yet were they drawn swords. [Psalms 55:21]

8 A glutton of words.
[Langland: *Piers Plowman* I]

9 Familiar in his mouth as household words.
[Shakespeare: *Henry V* IV.iii.]

10 His purse is empty already; all 's golden words are spent.
[Shakespeare: *Hamlet* V.ii.]

11 Fair words make me look to my purse.
[George Herbert: *Outlandish Proverbs*]

12 A man of words and not of deeds -
Is like a garden full of weeds.
And when the weeds begin to grow,
It's like a garden full of snow.
[Nursery rhyme: earliest known version 1784, but there are allusions to it more than 130 years before that]
It is one of the oldest of the songs children sing while bouncing a ball, of which probably the most popular is still One, Two, Three, O'Leary.

13 Choice word and measured phrase, above the reach

Of ordinary men.
[Wordsworth: *Resolution and Independence*]

14 Words are, of course, the most powerful drug used by mankind. [Rudyard Kipling: Speech, Feb. 14, 1923]

WORDSWORTH

15 Time may restore us in his course
Goethe's sage mind and Byron's force;
But where will Europe's latter hour
Again find Wordsworth's healing power?
[Matthew Arnold: *Memorial Verses*]

16 I firmly believe that the poetical performance of Wordsworth is, after that of Shakespeare and Milton, of which all the world now recognises the worth, undoubtedly the most considerable in our language from the Elizabethan age to the present time. [Matthew Arnold: *Essays in Criticism: Second Series,* "Wordsworth"]

17 Two voices are there: one is of the deep;
It learns the storm-cloud's thunderous melody,
Now roars, now murmurs with the changing sea,
Now bird-like pipes, now closes soft in sleep;
And one is of an old half-witted sheep
Which bleats articulate monotony,
And indicates that two and one are three,
That grass is green, lakes damp, and mountains steep:
And, Wordsworth, both are thine.
[James Kenneth Stephen: *Lapsus Calami: A Sonnet* (1891)]

WORK

18 All work and no play makes Jack a dull boy. [James Howell: *Proverbs* (1659)]

19 Let us work without theorizing; it is the only way to make life endurable. [Voltaire: *Candide* XXX]

20 Work keeps at bay three great evils: boredom, vice, and need. [Voltaire: *Candide* XXX]

21 Work while it is called Today; for the Night cometh, wherein no man can work. [Thomas Carlyle: *Sartor Resartus* II.ix.]

1 ALL work, even cotton-spinning, is noble; work is alone noble. [Thomas Carlyle: *Past and Present* III.iv.]

2 Blessed is he who has found his work; let him ask no other blessedness. [Thomas Carlyle: *Past and Present* III.xi.]

3 Most men would feel insulted if it were proposed to employ them in throwing stones over a wall, and then in throwing them back, merely that they might earn their wages. But many are no more worthily employed now. [Thoreau: *Life Without Principle*]

4 In order that people may be happy in their work, these three things are needed: They must be fit for it: They must not do too much of it: And they must have a sense of success in it. [John Ruskin: *Pre-Raphaelitism*]

5 Do the work that's nearest,
　　Though it's dull at whiles,
Helping, when you meet them,
　　Lame dogs over stiles.
[Charles Kingsley: *The Invitation*]

6 For men must work, and women must weep.
And there's little to earn, and many to keep,
Though the harbour bar be moaning.
[Charles Kingsley: *The Three Fishers*]

7 Work consists of whatever a body is *obliged* to do, and Play consists of whatever a body is not obliged to do. [Mark Twain: *Tom Sawyer* II]

8 There is dignity in work only when it is work freely accepted. [Albert Camus: *Notebooks 1935-1942*]

9 Work expands so as to fill the time available for its completion [and] the thing to be done swells in importance and complexity in a direct ratio with the time to be spent. [C. Northcote Parkinson: *Parkinson's Law and Other Studies in Administration*]
　　See PARKINSON'S LAW

WORKERS

10 Let the ruling classes tremble at a Communist revolution. The proletarians have nothing to lose but their chains. They have a world to win. Workers of the world, unite! [Karl Marx and Friedrich Engels: *The Communist Manifesto*]

11 Half of the working class is slaving away to pile up riches of which they will be plundered by the upper class. The other half is plundering the plunderers. [G. B. Shaw: *On the Rocks*]

WORKING GIRL

12 You may tempt the upper classes
　　With your villainous demi-tasses,
　　But Heaven will protect the Working Girl.
[Edgar Smith: *Heaven Will Protect the Working Girl*]

WORLD: society and its values

13 A mad world, my masters. [Nicholas Breton: title of a dialogue (1603)]
　　The phrase is probably much older. It was used as the title of a play by Thomas Middleton in 1608, and is heard today as a jocular cliché among the literary learned.

14 The more a man drinketh of the world, the more it intoxicateth. [Francis Bacon: *Of Youth and Age*]

15 In things that a man would not be seen in himself, it is a point of cunning to borrow the name of the world; as to say, "The world says," or "There is a speech abroad." [Francis Bacon: *Of Cunning*]

16 "Thus we may see," quoth he, "how the world wags."
[Shakespeare: *As You Like It* II.vii.]

17 This earthly world, where to do harm
Is often laudable, to do good sometime
Accounted dangerous folly.
[Shakespeare: *Macbeth* IV.ii.]

18 The world, as in the ark of Noah, rests,
Compos'd as then: few men and many beasts.
[Lord Herbert of Cherbury: *The State Progress of Ill*]

19 'Tis a very good world to live in,
　　To lend, or to spend, or to give in;
　　But to beg, or to borrow, or to get a man's own,
　　It's the very worst world that ever was known.
[John Wilmot, Earl of Rochester: *The World*]

20 When the world has once begun to use us ill, it afterwards continues the same treatment with less scruple or ceremony, as men do to a whore. [Jonathan Swift: *Thoughts on Various Subjects*]

1 Behold the world, how it is whirlèd
round,
And for it is so whirl'd is named so.
[Sir John Davies: *Orchestra* XXXIV]

2 The world, in its best state, is nothing more than a larger assembly of beings, combining to counterfeit happiness which they do not feel. [Samuel Johnson: *The Adventurer* No. 120]

3 This world is a comedy to those that think, a tragedy to those that feel. [Horace Walpole: letter to Sir Horace Mann, Dec. 31, 1769].

4 The world is too much with us; late
and soon,
Getting and spending, we lay waste
our powers:
Little we see in Nature that is ours;
We have given our hearts away, a sordid boon!
The Sea that bares her bosom to the
moon;
The winds that will be howling at all
hours,
And are up-gathered now like sleeping flowers;
For this, for everything, we are out of
tune;
It moves us not; Great God! I'd
rather be
A Pagan suckled in a creed outworn,
So might I, standing on this pleasant
lea,
Have glimpses that would make me
less forlorn;
Have sight of Proteus rising from the
sea,
Or hear old Triton blow his wreathèd
horn.
[Wordsworth: *The World Is Too Much With Us*]

5 I have not loved the world, nor the
world me.
[Byron: *Childe Harold* III.cxiv]

6 The world is an old woman, and mistakes any gilt farthing for a gold coin.
[Thomas Carlyle: *Sartor Resartus* II]

7 Ah! Matt.; old age has brought to me
Thy wisdom, less thy certainty;
The world's a jest, and joy's a trinket:
I knew that once: but now—I think it.
[James Stephen: *Lapsus Calami*, "Senex

to Matt. Prior"]
Stephen seems to have in mind the flippant couplet which John Gay wrote in a letter to Pope:
Life is a jest, and all things show it,
I thought so once, and now I know it—
lines which, at his own request, were put on Gay's tombstone in Westminster Abbey. The Dictionary of English Biography *feels that they "disfigure" the monument. But they are not by Matthew Prior.*

8 The world is a perpetual caricature of itself; at every moment it is the mockery and the contradiction of what it is pretending to be. [George Santayana: *Soliloquies in England*, "Dickens"]

WORLD: the terrestrial globe, man's
dwelling-place

9 The world, the flesh, and the devil.
[*Book of Common Prayer*, "The Litany"]

10 This world nis but a thurghfare ful
of wo,
And we ben pilgrimes, passinge to
and fro.
[Chaucer: *The Knight's Tale*]

11 What is this world? what asketh men
to have?
Now with his love, now in his colde
grave
Allone, with-outen any companye.
[Chaucer: *The Knight's Tale*]

12 Swich is this world; who-so it can
biholde,
In eche estat is litel hertes reste;
God leve us for to take it for the
beste.
[Chaucer: *Troilus and Criseyde* V]

13 O brave new world.
[Shakespeare: *The Tempest* V.i.]

14 For the world, I count it not an inn, but an hospital, and a place, not to live, but to die in. [Sir Thomas Browne: *Religio Medici* II]

15 The world, which took but six days to make, is like to take six thousand to make out. [Sir Thomas Browne: *Christian Morals* II.v.]

16 This visible world is but a picture of the invisible, wherein, as in a portrait, things are not truly, but in equivocal shapes. [Sir Thomas Browne: *Religio Medici* I.15]

1 This world, where much is to be done and little to be known. [Samuel Johnson: *Prayers and Meditations*]

2 To see a world in a grain of sand. [William Blake: *Auguries of Innocence*]

3 Well, well, the world must turn upon
         its axis,
And all mankind turn with it,
         heads or tails,
And live and die, make love and pay
         our taxes,
And as the veering wind shifts,
         shift our sails.
[Byron: *Don Juan* II.iv.]

4 This world, after all our science and sciences, is still a miracle; wonderful, inscrutable, *magical* and more, to whosoever will *think* of it. [Thomas Carlyle: *Heroes and Hero-Worship* I]

5 Here at the quiet limit of the world. [Tennyson: *Tithonus*]

6   This world's no blot for us,
Nor blank; it means intensely, and
         means good.
[Robert Browning: *Fra Lippo Lippi*]

7 This world is very odd we see,
    We do not comprehend it;
But in one fact we all agree,
    God won't, and we can't, mend it.
[Arthur Hugh Clough: *Dipsychus* II.ii.]

8 For every man the world is as fresh as it was at the first day, and as full of untold novelties for him who has the eyes to see them. [T. H. Huxley: *A Liberal Education*]

9 This may not be the best of all possible worlds, but to say that it is the worst is mere petulant nonsense. [T. H. Huxley: *The Struggle for Existence in Human Society*]

10 The world rolls round forever like a
         mill;
It grinds out death and life and good
         and ill;
It has no purpose, heart or mind or
         will.
[James Thomson (1834-1882): *The City of Dreadful Night*]

11 Roll on, thou ball, roll on!
Through pathless realms of space roll
         on!
What, though I'm in a sorry case?
What, though I cannot meet my bills?
What, though I suffer toothache's ills?
What, though I swallow countless
         pills?
Never *you* mind!
Roll on! [It rolls on.]
[W. S. Gilbert: *The Bab Ballads*]

12 Oh wide's the world, to rest or roam,
    With change abroad and cheer at
         home,
Fights and furloughs, talk and tale,
Company and beef and ale.
[A. E. Housman: *Last Poems* I]

13 The existence of this world—unless we lapse for a moment into an untenable scepticism—is certain, or at least, it is unquestioningly to be assumed. Experience may explore it adventurously, and science may describe it with precision, but after you have wandered up and down in it for many years, and have gathered all you could of its ways by report, this same world, because it exists substantially and is not invented, remains a foreign thing and a marvel to the spirit. [George Santayana: *Obiter Scripta*]

14 Some say the world will end in fire,
    Some say in ice.
From what I've tasted of desire
I hold with those who favor fire.
But if it had to perish twice,
I think I know enough of hate
To say that for destruction ice
Is also great
And would suffice.
[Robert Frost: *Fire and Ice*]

15   Lord, I do fear
Thou'st made the world too beautiful
         this year.
My soul is all but out of me—let fall
No burning leaf; prithee, let no bird
         call.
[Edna St. Vincent Millay: *God's World*]

WORLDLINESS

16 A seeming ignorance is often a most necessary part of worldly knowledge. [Lord Chesterfield: *Letters to His Son*, Jan. 15, 1573]

WORLDLY

17 The children of this world are in their generation wiser than the children of light. [Luke 16:8]

WORM

18 Your worm is your only emperor for diet; we fat all creatures else to fat us, and we fat ourselves for maggots.

[Shakespeare: *Hamlet* IV.iii.]
1 I wish you joy o' the worm.
[Shakespeare: *Antony and Cleopatra* V. ii.]
2 I do not want to be a fly;
I want to be a worm!
[Charlotte P. S. Gilman: *A Conservative*]

WORM WILL TURN
3 The smallest worm will turn, being trodden on.
[Shakespeare: *III Henry VI* II.ii.]
The expression was proverbial, for it also appears in Cervantes' Don Quixote, preface to Book III, Part II (1615).
Apparently the writhings of the worm were regarded as some sort of turning on its persecutor.
4 Beware the fury of a patient man.
[Dryden: *Absalom and Achitophel* I]

WORRY
5 Quod Pandarus, "Thou hast a ful gret care
Lest that the cherl may falle out of the mone!"
[Chaucer: *Troilus and Criseyde* I]
To be afraid that the man will fall out of the moon was proverbial, even in Chaucer's time, for ludicrously unnecessary worry.
6 Consider it not so deeply.
[Shakespeare: *Macbeth* II.ii.]
7 Worry, the interest paid by those who borrow trouble. [George Washington Lyon: epigram in *Judge,* March 1, 1924]

WORSE
8 I see the better course and I approve of it; but I follow the worse. [Ovid: *Metamorphoses* VII.xx.]
9 Meseems the world . . . grows daily worse and worse.
[Spenser: *The Faerie Queene* V (1596), Intro. 1]
10 Everyone is as God made him, and often much worse. [Cervantes: *Don Quixote* II.4.]
11 Though his tongue
Dropt manna, and could make the worse appear
The better reason, to perplex and dash
Maturest counsels.
[John Milton: *Paradise Lost* II.112-115]

WORSHIP
12 I bow myself in the house of Rimmon. [II Kings 5:18]
13 The first way to worship the gods is to believe in the gods.
[Seneca: *Ad Lucilium* XCV]
See RELIGION

WORST
14 Let the worst come to the worst. [Cervantes: *Don Quixote* III.v.]
15 When remedies are past, the griefs are ended
By seeing the worst, which late on hopes depended.
To mourn a mischief that is past and gone
Is the next way to draw new mischief on.
[Shakespeare: *Othello* I.iii.]
16 Things at the worst will cease, or else climb upward
To what they were before.
[Shakespeare: *Macbeth* IV.ii.]
17 The worst is not
So long as we can say "This is the worst."
[Shakespeare: *King Lear* IV.i.]
18 He that is down can fall no lower. [Samuel Butler (1612-1680): *Hudibras*]
19 No man is the worse for knowing the worst of himself. [Thomas Fuller (1654-1734): *Gnomologia*]
20 Cheer up, the worst is yet to come. [Philander Chase Johnson: *Shooting Stars*]

WORTH
21 A thing is worth whatever the buyer will pay for it. [Publilius Syrus: *Maxims*]
22 For what is worth in anything
But so much money as 'twill bring?
[Samuel Butler (1612-1680): *Hudibras*]
23 Worth makes the man, and want of it the fellow:
The rest is all but leather or prunella.
[Alexander Pope: *Essay on Man* IV]
fellow (plainly pronounced, then as now, fella) = a person of no consequence or worth, one meaning that the word held for over 400 years; prunella = a cloth material used for the uppers of women's shoes.

Pope had been saying that honor lies

in acting well your part and had been comparing the parson and the cobbler and saying that a drunken parson is no better than a drunken cobbler. Hence the image drawn from cobbling.

1 The "value" or "worth" of a man is, as of all other things, his price; that is to say, so much as would be given for the use of his power. [Thomas Hobbes: *Leviathan* I.x.]
2 The worth of a thing is known by its want. [Thomas D'Urfey: *Quixote* I.V.ii.]
3 What is the worth of anything
But for the happiness 'twill bring?
[Richard Cambridge: *Learning*]
4 You're worth what you saved, not the
million you made.
[John Boyle O'Reilly: *Rules of the Road*]
5 There's nothing worth the wear of
winning
But laughter and the love of friends.
[Hilaire Belloc: *Dedicatory Ode*]
6 These men are worth
Your tears. You are not worth their
merriment.
[Wilfred Owen: *Apologia Pro Poemate Meo*]

WOULD
7 That we would do,
We should do when we would; for
this "would" changes
And hath abatements and delays.
[Shakespeare: *Hamlet* IV.vii.]

WOUND(S)
8 The secret wound lives on within the
breast.
[Vergil: *Aeneid* IV]
9 The wound that bleedeth inwardly is
most dangerous. [John Lyly: *Euphues*]
10 Let grievous, ghastly, gaping wounds
Untwine the Sisters Three!
[Shakespeare: *II Henry IV* II.iv.]
11 What wound did ever heal but by
degrees?
[Shakespeare: *Othello* II.iii.]
12 I have yet
Room for six scotches more.
[Shakespeare: *Antony and Cleopatra* IV.vii.]
scotches = *slashes, gashes, wounds*

An amusing illustration of the pitfalls that lie in wait for the unwary reader.

WRATH
13 Let not the sun go down upon your wrath. [Ephesians 4:26]
14 I am Wrath, I had neither father nor mother: I leap'd out of a lion's mouth when I was scarce half an hour old; and ever since I have run up and down the world with this case of rapiers, wounding myself when I had nobody to fight withal. [Christopher Marlowe: *Dr. Faustus* II]
15 Nursing her wrath to keep it warm. [Burns: *Tam o'Shanter*]

WREN
16 For the poor wren,
The most diminutive of birds, will
fight,
Her young ones in her nest, against
the owl.
[Shakespeare: *Macbeth* IV.ii.]

WREN, SIR CHRISTOPHER
17 Sir Christopher Wren
Said, "I am going to dine with some
men;
If anybody calls
Say I am designing St. Paul's."
[E. C. Bentley: *Biography for Beginners*]

WRETCH(ED)
18 It is hard to be wretched, but worse to be known so. [George Herbert: *Jacula Prudentum*]
19 The wretched hasten to embrace
their miseries.
[Seneca: *Hercules Oetaeus*]
20 A needy, hollow-eyed, sharp-looking
wretch,
A living-dead man.
[Shakespeare: *The Comedy of Errors* V.i.]

WRETCHEDNESS
21 The greatness of man is so evident, that it is even proved by his wretchedness. For what in animals is nature we call in man wretchedness. [Pascal: *Pensées*]
22 It would hardly be possible to exaggerate man's wretchedness if it were not so easy to overestimate his sensibility. [George Santayana: *The Life of Reason:*

"Reason in Religion"]
> sensibility = *sensitivity*

WRINKLE

1 An old wrinkle never wears out. [Thomas Fuller (1654-1734): *Gnomologia*]

WRITER(S)

2 If you wish to be a writer, write. [Epictetus: *Discourses* II]
> *About 110* A.D.

3 He that will write well in any tongue must follow this counsel of Aristotle: to speak as the common people do, to think as wise men do. [Roger Ascham: *Toxophilus*]

4 Blot out, correct, insert, refine,
Enlarge, diminish, interline;
Be mindful, when invention fails,
To scratch your head, and bite your
> nails.

[Jonathan Swift: *On Poetry*]

5 I lisp'd in numbers, for the numbers
> came.

[Alexander Pope: *Epistle to Dr. Arbuthnot*]

6 There is nothing more dreadful to an author than neglect, compared with which reproach, hatred and opposition are names of happiness. [Samuel Johnson: *The Rambler* No. 2]

7 The writer is the Faust of modern society, the only surviving individualist in a mass age. To his orthodox contemporaries he seems a semi-madman. [Boris Pasternak, in *The Observer,* London, Dec. 20, 1959]

WRITING: the art of it

8 To be a well-favoured man is a gift of fortune: but to write and read comes by nature. [Shakespeare: *Much Ado About Nothing* III.iii.]

9 Nothing is ended with honour which does not conclude better than it began. [Samuel Johnson: *The Rambler* No. 207]

> *That is, a piece of writing worthy of honor can never let down; it must not merely maintain the pace and style with which it began but heighten it towards the end.*

10 Every author does not write for every reader; many questions are such as the illiterate part of mankind can have nei-

ther interest nor pleasure in discussing and which, therefore, it would be a useless endeavor to level with common minds by tiresome circumlocutions or laborious explanations; and many subjects of general use may be treated in a different manner, as the book is intended for the learned or the ignorant. [Samuel Johnson: *The Idler* No. 70]

11 In composition I do *not* think second thoughts are best. [Byron: Letters II]

12 Make 'em laugh; make 'em cry; make 'em wait. [Charles Reade: *Recipe for a Successful Novel*]

13 Really, universally, relations stop nowhere, and the exquisite problem of the artist is eternally but to draw, by a geometry of his own, the circle within which they shall happily *appear* to do so. [Henry James: Preface to *Roderick Hudson*]

14 The great art of writing is the art of making people real to themselves with words. [Logan Pearsall Smith: *Afterthoughts*]

15 Every fine story must leave in the mind of the sensitive reader an intangible residuum of pleasure, a cadence, a quality of voice that is exclusively the writer's own, individual, unique. [Willa Cather: *Not Under Forty,* "Miss Jewett"]

16 A writer's problem does not change. He himself changes and the world he lives in changes but his problem remains the same. It is always how to write truly and, having found what is true, to project it in such a way that it becomes a part of the experience of the person who reads it. [Ernest Hemingway: *The Problems of a Writer in War Time*]

WRITING: the itch to scribble

17 An incurable itch for scribbling [*scribendi cacoëthes*] takes possession of many and grows inveterate in their insane hearts. [Juvenal: *Satires* VII.li.]

> *A familiar taunt among those afflicted—but unknown to the fortunate many.*

18 A man starts up on a sudden, takes pen, ink, and paper, and without ever having had a thought of it before, resolves he will write a book, though he has no talent at writing. [La Bruyère: *Les Caractères* XV]

1 The desire to write grows with writing. [Erasmus: *Adagia* (1508)]

2 Things unattempted yet in prose or
rhyme.
[John Milton: *Paradise Lost* I.16]

3 Why did I write? what sin to me unknown
Dipt me in ink, my parents', or my
own?
[Alexander Pope: *Epistle to Dr. Arbuthnot*]

4 Just writes to make his barrenness
appear,
And strains from hard-bound brains,
eight lines a year.
[Alexander Pope: *Epistle to Dr. Arbuthnot*]
hard-bound = *constipated*

5 Another damned thick book! Always
scribble, scribble, scribble! Eh, Mr. Gibbon? [Affable remark of His Royal Highness, the Duke of Gloucester: on graciously accepting a copy of vol. II of the
Decline and Fall of the Roman Empire
from the dutifully kneeling author, in
1781]
So related in the Dictionary of National
Biography, *on the authority of Best's*
Memorials.

6 When once the itch of literature
comes over a man, nothing can cure it
but the scratching of a pen. [Samuel
Lover: *Handy Andy* XXXVI]

WRITING: labor and patience

7 Let your literary compositions be
kept from the public eye for nine years
at least. [Horace: *Ars poetica*]
*Probably the most unwelcome advice
ever given by a poet to poets.*
*"Nine years!" cries he, who high in
Drury Lane,*
*Lull'd by soft Zephyrs through the
broken pane,*
*Rhymes ere he wakes, and prints be-
fore Term ends,*
*Oblig'd by hunger, and request of
friends.*
Alexander Pope: Epistle to Dr. Arbuthnot

8 But words came halting forth, wanting Invention's stay.
Invention, Nature's child, fled step-
dame Study's blows;
And others' feet seemed but strangers
in my way.

Thus, great with child to speak, and
helpless in my throes,
Biting my truant pen, beating my-
self for spite:
"Fool," said my Muse to me, "look
in thy heart, and write!"
[Sir Philip Sidney: *Astrophel and Stella*,
Sonnet I]

9 True ease in writing comes from art,
not chance,
As those move easiest who have
learn'd to dance.
[Alexander Pope: *An Essay on Criticism*
II]

10 E'en copious Dryden wanted, or forgot,
The last and greatest art—the art to
blot.
[Alexander Pope: *Imitations of Horace*,
"Epistle I"]
blot = *blot out, erase, excise*

11 Composition is, for the most part, an
effort of slow diligence and steady perseverance, to which the mind is dragged
by necessity or resolution. [Samuel Johnson: *The Adventurer* No. 138]

12 A man may write at any time, if he
will set himself doggedly to it. [Samuel
Johnson: in Boswell's *Tour of the Hebrides*, Aug. 16, 1773]

13 The greatest part of a writer's time
is spent in reading, in order to write; a
man will turn over half a library to
make one book. [Samuel Johnson: in
Boswell's *Life*, April 6, 1775]

14 How can you contrive to write so
even? [Jane Austen: *Pride and Prejudice*,
Ch. 10]

15 Does he paint? he fain would write a
poem—
Does he write? he fain would paint a
picture.
[Robert Browning: *One Word More*
VIII]

16 Three hours a day will produce as
much as a man ought to write. [Anthony
Trollope: *Autobiography*, Ch. 15]

17 Most of the basic material a writer
works with is acquired before the age
of fifteen. [Willa Cather in *Willa Cather*
by René Rapin, N.Y. 1930]

WRITING: motives

18 I do not write so much from the im-

pulse of genius as to soothe the cares of love and to bewail life's unabating woe. [Propertius: *Elegies* I]

> *Compare Tennyson's:*
> *But, for the unquiet heart and brain,*
> *A use in measured language lies;*
> *The sad mechanic exercise,*
> *Like dull narcotics, numbing pain.*
>
> In Memoriam *V*

1 If it were not for a rainy day, a drunken vigil, a fit of the spleen, a course of physic, a sleepy Sunday, an ill run at dice, a long tailor's bill, a beggar's purse, a factious head, a hot sun, costive diet, want of books, and a just contempt for learning—but for these . . . the number of authors and of writing would dwindle away to a degree most woeful to behold. [Jonathan Swift: *A Tale of a Tub*, "A Farther Digression"]

2 Some write, confin'd by physic; some, by debt;
Some, for 'tis Sunday; some, because 'tis wet;

. . . .

Another writes because his father writ,
And proves himself a bastard by his wit.

[Edward Young: *Epistle to Pope* I]

3 No man but a blockhead ever wrote except for money. [Samuel Johnson: in Boswell's *Life*, April 5, 1776]

> *On another occasion Johnson said "Nothing excites a man to write but necessity."*
> *Most professional writers agree with both statements and are grateful to the old pro for making them.*

4 Writing is busy idleness. [Goethe: *Götz von Berlichingen* IV]

WRITING: miscellaneous

5 Their manner of writing is very peculiar, being neither from the left to the right, like the Europeans; nor from the right to the left, like the Arabians; from up to down, like the Chinese, nor from down to up, like the Cascagians; but a-slant from one corner of the paper to the other, like ladies in England. [Jonathan Swift: *Gulliver's Travels* I.vi.]

6 'Tis hard to say if greater want of skill

Appear in writing or in judging ill. [Alexander Pope: *An Essay on Criticism* I]

7 The only reward to be expected from the cultivation of literature is contempt if one fails and hatred if one succeeds. [Voltaire: Letter to Mlle. Quinault]

8 Tom Birch is as brisk as a bee in conversation; but no sooner does he take a pen in his hand, than it becomes a torpedo to him, and benumbs all his faculties. [Samuel Johnson: in Boswell's *Life* (1743)]

> Tom Birch = *Dr. Thomas Birch, editor of the* Biographia Britannica *and other learned works. Boswell gives the statement as one that "has been circulated." It had appeared in Hawkins's* Johnson. torpedo = *the cramp-fish or stingray, which was called the* torpedo *because it benumbed or torpefied those who touched it. The application of the word to a pen was also made by Goldsmith, who may have taken the idea from Johnson.*

9 There are two things which I am confident I can do very well: one is an introduction to any literary work, stating what it is to contain, and how it should be executed in the most perfect manner; the other is a conclusion, showing from various causes why the execution has not been equal to what the author promised to himself and to the public. [Samuel Johnson: in Boswell's *Life* (1755)]

10 Depend upon it, no man was ever written down but by himself. [Samuel Johnson: quoting "old Bentley," in Boswell's *Tour to the Hebrides*, Oct. I]

11 Write without pay until somebody offers pay. If nobody offers within three years, the candidate may look upon this circumstance with the most implicit confidence as the sign that sawing wood is what he was intended for. [Mark Twain: *A General Reply*]

12 Do right and fear no man; don't write and fear no woman. [Luke McLuke: *Epigram*]

13 The nobility of our calling will always be rooted in two commitments difficult to observe: refusal to lie about what we know, and resistance to oppression. [Albert Camus, speech accepting Nobel Prize, 1957]

WRONGS

1 The remedy for wrongs is to forget them. [Publilius Syrus: *Maxims*]

WYCLIF, JOHN

2 Thus this brook hath conveyed his ashes into Avon, Avon into Severn, Severn into the narrow seas, they into the main ocean. And thus the ashes of Wyclif are the emblem of his doctrine, which is now dispersed all the world over. [Thomas Fuller (1608-1661): *Church History* II.iv.]

> *Wyclif (waspish John Bale called him "wicked belief") was one of the precursors of the Reformation. By order of the Council of Constance, his body was dug up and thrown into a brook called the Swift.*

WYNKEN, BLYNKEN, AND NOD

3 Wynken, Blynken, and Nod one night
　Sailed off in a wooden shoe—
　Sailed on a river of crystal light
　Into a sea of dew.

[Eugene Field: *Wynken, Blynken, and Nod*]

> *This famous children's song provided Berton Braley with the rhyme and rhythm for:*
>
> 　*Mencken,*
> 　　*Nathan*
> 　　　*And God.*
> 　　　　—Three Minus One
> *And probably it lay back of Franklin Delano Roosevelt's "Martin, Barton and Fish."*

X

XANTIPPE
1 No-thing forgot he the penaunce and
   wo
   That Socrates had with his wyves
   two;
   How Xantippe caste pisse up-on his
   head;
   This sely man sat still, as he were
   deed;
   He wyped his head, namore durst he
   seyn
   But "er that thonder stinte, comth a
   reyn."

[Chaucer: Prologue to *The Wife of
   Bath's Tale*]
   he = *Jankin, the Wife of Bath's young,
   fifth husband. He continually reminds
   her, reading from his books, of what
   men have suffered at the hands of their
   wives;* sely = *silly = innocent, good,
   blameless;* seyn = *say;* stinte = *ceases
   That "before the thunder stops, there
   will be rain" was a proverb.*

Y

YARROW
1 "Whate'er betide, we'll turn aside,
And see the Braes of Yarrow."
[Wordsworth: *Yarrow Unvisited*]

YAWN(ING)
2 And heard thy everlasting yawn confess
The pains and penalties of idleness.
[Alexander Pope: *The Dunciad* IV]
3 Why doth one man's yawning make another yawn? [Robert Burton: *Anatomy of Melancholy*]
4 For ennui is a growth of English root,
Though nameless in our language: we retort
The fact for words, and let the French translate
That awful yawn which sleep can not abate.
[Byron: *Don Juan* XIII.ci.]

YEAR(S)
5 Each passing year takes something from us.
[Horace: *Epistles* II]
6 How many noble thoughts,
How many precious feelings of man's heart,
How many loves, how many gratitudes,
Do twenty years wear out, and see expire!
[Matthew Arnold: *Merope*]

YEATS, WILLIAM BUTLER
7 Earth, receive an honored guest;
William Yeats is laid to rest:
Let the Irish vessel lie
Emptied of its poetry.
[W. H. Auden: *In Memory of W. B. Yeats*]

YES
8 . . . and then I asked him with my eyes to ask again yes and then he asked me would I yes to say yes my mountain flower and first I put my arms around him yes and drew him down to me so he could feel my breasts all perfume yes and his heart was going like mad and yes I said yes I will Yes. [James Joyce: *Ulysses* (final lines)]

YES-MAN
9 A rascally yea-forsooth knave.
[Shakespeare: *II Henry IV* I.i.]
yea-forsooth = *yes indeed, yes truly*
What we would call a "yes-man." The Germans have the term Yaherr, *one who yeses you.*
Sooth = *truth. We* soothe *people by agreeing with them, telling them that everything they say is true.*

YES AND NO
10 He was like the son of the vine-dresser in the Gospel, who said No, and went; the other said Yea, and went not. [Emerson: *Character*]

YESTERDAY
11 O, call back yesterday, bid time return.
[Shakespeare: *Richard II* III.ii.]
12 And all our yesterdays have lighted fools
The way to dusty death.
[Shakespeare: *Macbeth* V.v.]
13 Do diddle di do,
Poor Jim Jay
Got stuck fast
In Yesterday.
[Walter de la Mare: *Jim Jay*]

YIELDING
14 A wise woman never yields by appointment. It should always be an unforeseen happiness. [Stendhal: *De l'Amour*]
15 A little still she strove, and much repented,
And whispering "I will ne'er consent"—consented.
[Byron: *Don Juan* I.cxvii.]

YOKE
16 My yoke is easy, and my burden is light. [Matthew 11:30]

YONGHY-BONGHY-BO
17 On the coast of Coromandel
Where the early pumpkins blow,

In the middle of the woods
Lived the Yonghy-Bonghy-Bo.
[Edward Lear: *The Courtship of the Yonghy-Bonghy-Bo*]

YORICK

1 Alas, poor Yorick! I knew him, Horatio: a fellow of infinite jest, of most excellent fancy; he hath borne me on his back a thousand times; and now, how abhorred in my imagination it is! my gorge rises at it. Here hung those lips that I have kissed I know not how oft. Where be your gibes now? your gambols? your songs? your flashes of merriment, that were wont to set the table on a roar? Not one now, to mock your own grinning? quite chap-fallen? Now get you to my lady's chamber, and tell her, let her paint an inch thick, to this favour she must come; make her laugh at that. [Shakespeare: *Hamlet* V.i.]
favour = *feature, appearance*

YOU CAN'T TAKE IT WITH YOU

2 If your riches are yours, why don't you take them with you to t'other world? [Benjamin Franklin: *Poor Richard's Almanack*]

YOUNG

3 Their mirth was without images; their laughter without motive; their pleasures were gross and sensual, in which the mind had no part. Their conduct was at once wild and mean: they laughed at order and law; but the frown of power dejected, and the eye of wisdom abashed them. [Samuel Johnson: *Rasselas* XVI]
mean = *petty, base*
Johnson is describing flaming youth.
4 Verse, a breeze mid blossoms straying,
Where Hope clung feeding, like a
bee—
Both were mine! Life went-a-maying
With Nature, Hope, and Poesy,
When I was young!
[Coleridge: *Youth and Age*]
5 In a field by the river my love and I
did stand,
And on my leaning shoulder she laid
her snow-white hand.
She bid me take life easy, as the grass
grows on the weirs;
But I was young and foolish, and

now am full of tears.
[William Butler Yeats: *Down by the Salley Gardens*]

YOUTH: its confidence and assertiveness

6 The young think they know everything and are confident in their assertions. [Aristotle: *Rhetoric* II.xii.]
7 Young men are apt to think themselves wise enough, as drunken men are apt to think themselves sober enough. [Lord Chesterfield: *Letters to His Son*, Jan. 15, 1753]
8 Towering in the confidence of twenty-one. [Samuel Johnson: letter to Bennet Langton, Jan. 9, 1758]
9 Youth enters the world with very happy prejudices in her own favour. [Samuel Johnson: *The Rambler* No. 127]
10 It is very natural for young men to be vehement, acrimonious and severe. [Samuel Johnson: *The Rambler* No. 121]
11 No young man believes he shall ever
die.
[William Hazlitt: *On the Feeling of Immortality in Youth*]
12 When one is twenty, ideas of the outside world and the effect one can have on it take precedence over everything else. [Stendhal: *The Red and the Black* I.xi.]
13 Presently the younger generation will come knocking at my door. [Henrik Ibsen: *The Master Builder* I]

YOUTH: its folly, heedlessness and illusions

14 Rashness attends youth, as prudence does old age. [Cicero: *De senectute*]
15 The majority of men employ the first part of life in making the rest miserable. [La Bruyère: *Les Caractères*]
16 Naught cared this body for wind and
weather
When Youth and I lived in 't together.
[Coleridge: *Youth and Age*]
17 Nourishing a youth sublime
With the fairy tales of science, and the
long result of Time.
[Tennyson: *Locksley Hall*]
18 O Memory, where is now my youth,
Who used to say that life was truth?
[Thomas Hardy: *Memory and I*]
19 For God's sake give me the young

man who has brains enough to make a fool of himself. [R. L. Stevenson: *Crabbed Age and Youth*]

Rarely is a wish more bountifully gratified by Fate.

1 Am I the person who used to wake in the middle of the night and laugh with the joy of living? Who worried about the existence of God, and danced with young ladies till the lark-light? Who sang "Auld Lang Syne" and howled with sentiment, and more than once gazed at the full moon through a blur of great, romantic tears? [Logan Pearsall Smith: *Afterthoughts*]

2 Everybody's youth is a dream, a form of chemical madness. [F. Scott Fitzgerald: *The Diamond as Big as the Ritz*]

YOUTH: its glory and delight

3 Youth is the best time to be rich, and the best time to be poor. [Euripides: *Heracles*]

4 The glory of young men is their strength. [Proverbs 20:29]

5 Remember now thy Creator in the days of thy youth, while the evil days come not, nor the years draw nigh, when thou shalt say, I have no pleasure in them. [Ecclesiastes 12:1]

6 We have some salt of our youth in us; we are the sons of women. [Shakespeare: *The Merry Wives of Windsor* II.iii.]

7 The morn and liquid dew of youth. [Shakespeare: *Hamlet* I.iii.]

8   He wears the rose
Of youth upon him.
[Shakespeare: *Antony and Cleopatra* III. xiii.]

9 The age is best which is the first,
When youth and blood are warmer.
[Robert Herrick: *Hesperides*]

10 Youth on the prow, and pleasure at the helm.
[Thomas Gray: *The Bard* II.ii.]

11 Bliss was it in that dawn to be alive,
But to be young was very Heaven!
[Wordsworth: *The Prelude* XI]

12 There is a feeling of Eternity in youth, which makes us amends for everything. To be young is to be as one of the Immortal Gods. [William Hazlitt: *The Feeling of Immortality in Youth*]

13 Almost everything that is great has been done by youth. [Benjamin Disraeli: *Coningsby* III]

14 When all the world is young, lad,
    And all the trees are green;
And every goose a swan, lad,
    And every lass a queen;
Then hey, for boot and horse, lad,
    And round the world away;
Young blood must have its course, lad,
    And every dog his day.
[Charles Kingsley: *The Water-Babies*]

YOUTH: inexperience, woes, problems and longings

15 Generally youth is like the first cogitations, not so wise as the second. [Francis Bacon: *Youth and Age*]

16 My salad days,
When I was green in judgment.
[Shakespeare: *Antony and Cleopatra* I.v.]

17 I would there were no age between sixteen and three-and-twenty, or that youth would sleep out the rest; for there is nothing in the between but getting wenches with child, wronging the ancientry, stealing, fighting. [Shakespeare: *The Winter's Tale* III.iii.]

18 No wise man ever wished to be younger. [Jonathan Swift: *Thoughts on Various Subjects*]

19 The atrocious crime of being a young man . . . I shall neither attempt to palliate nor deny. [William Pitt: in a speech in Parliament, March 6, 1741]

Probably written by Samuel Johnson —see Boswell's Life of Johnson, *1741. Johnson did not write the speech for Pitt, but our knowledge of it is based on Johnson's "report" which was largely made up to suit what he had been told the members discussed. He did not himself attend the debates he reported for* The Gentleman's Magazine.

20 Take her up tenderly,
    Lift her with care;
Fashioned so slenderly,
    Young, and so fair.
[Thomas Hood: *The Bridge of Sighs*]

21 A boy's will is the wind's will,
    And the thoughts of youth are long, long thoughts.
[Longfellow: *My Lost Youth*]

22 To me it seems that youth is like spring, an over-praised season—delight-

ful if it happen to be a favored one, but in practice very rarely favored and more remarkable, as a general rule, for biting east winds than genial breezes. [Samuel Butler (1835-1902): *The Way of All Flesh* VI]

1 Growing is not the easy, plain sailing business that it is commonly supposed to be: it is hard work—harder than any but a growing boy can understand; it requires attention, and you are not strong enough to attend to your bodily growth and to your lessons too. [Samuel Butler (1835-1902): *The Way of All Flesh* XXXI]

2 Youth is wasted on the young. [Attr. G. B. Shaw]

> *Probably a shortening of "Youth is a wonderful thing. What a crime to waste it on children."*

3 Don't laugh at a youth for his affectations; he's only trying on one face after another till he finds his own. [Logan Pearsall Smith: *Afterthoughts*]

4 If youth did not matter so much to itself, it would never have the heart to go on. [Willa Cather: *The Song of the Lark* I.xx.]

5 All adolescents are, in a sense, psychotic. [Fanita English: verbal comment to the editor]

> *This sums up most of what has ever been said about youth and, at the same time, explains at least half of the world's woes and worries—and more than half of its hopes.*

YOUTH: and love

6 It is natural for a young man to love, but a crime for an old one. [Publilius Syrus: *Maxims*]

7 A man can no more separate age and covetousness than 'a can part young limbs and lechery. [Shakespeare: *II Henry IV* I.ii.]

> 'a = *he*

8 Why should a man, whose blood is
warm within,
Sit like his grandsire cut in alabaster?
[Shakespeare: *The Merchant of Venice* I.i.]

> *i.e., like an alabaster effigy on a tomb.*

9 What would youth be without love? [Byron: *Beppo*]

10 Young men's eyes take in everything;

their minds fix on the glories of women, just as a plant breathes in from the air the substances necessary for its own particular nourishment. [Balzac: *Père Goriot*]

11 When the waitress puts the dinner on the table, the old men look at the dinner. The young men look at the waitress. [Gelett Burgess: *Look Eleven Years Younger*]

12 A man is still young so long as women can make him happy or unhappy. He reaches middle age when they can no longer make him unhappy. He is old when they cease to make him either happy or unhappy. [Anon.]

YOUTH: will not endure

13 And though your grene youthe floure
as yit,
In crepeth age alwey, as still as
stoon.
[Chaucer: *The Clerk's Tale*]

14 Youth's a stuff will not endure. [Shakespeare: *Twelfth Night* II.iii.]

15 I am resolved to grow fat and look young till forty, and then slip out of the world with the first wrinkle and the reputation of five-and-twenty. [Dryden: *The Maiden Queen* III.i.]

16   . . . years steal
Fire from the mind as vigor from the
limb;
And life's enchanted cup but sparkles
near the brim.
[Byron: *Childe Harold* III.viii.]

17 In fact, there's nothing that keeps its
youth,
So far as I know, but a tree and truth.
[O. W. Holmes: *The Deacon's Masterpiece*]

18 Yet Ah, that Spring should vanish
with the Rose!
That Youth's sweet-scented manuscript should close!
[*Rubáiyát of Omar Khayyám* (trans. Edward FitzGerald)]

19 Now of my threescore years and ten,
Twenty will not come again,
And take from seventy springs a score,
It only leaves me fifty more.
[A. E. Housman: *A Shropshire Lad* II]

20 Now times are altered: if I care
To buy a thing, I can;
The pence are here and here's the

fair,
But where's the lost young man?
[A. E. Housman: *Last Poems* XXXV]

YOUTH AND AGE: their conduct of affairs

1 Young men, in the conduct and management of actions, embrace more than they can hold; stir more than they can quiet; fly to the end without consideration of the means and degrees. . . . Men of age object too much, consult too long, adventure too little, repent too soon, and seldom drive business home to the full period, but content themselves with a mediocrity of success. [Francis Bacon: *Of Youth and Age*]

2 Young men are fitter to invent than to judge, fitter for execution than for counsel, and fitter for new projects than for settled business; for the experience of age, in all things that fall within the compass of it, directeth them; but in new things abuseth them. [Francis Bacon: *Of Youth and Age*]

age = *old men;* abuseth = *deceives or misleads*

That is, the very experience of old men unfits *them to deal with new things that do not accord with their experience.*

3 The errors of young men are the ruin of business; but the errors of aged men amount but to this, that more might have been done or sooner. [Francis Bacon: *Of Youth and Age*]

4 The old man trusts wholly to slow contrivance and gradual progression; the youth expects to force his way by genius, vigor, and precipitance. The old man pays regard to riches, and the youth reverences virtue. The old man deifies prudence; the youth commits himself to magnanimity and chance. The young man, who intends no ill, believes that none is intended, and therefore acts with openness and candor; but his father, having suffered the injuries of fraud, is impelled to suspect, and too often allured to practise it. Age looks with anger on the temerity of youth, and youth with contempt on the scrupulosity of age. [Samuel Johnson: *Rasselas* XXVI]

YOUTH AND AGE: their morality

5 Age is more just than youth. [Aeschylus: Fragments 228]

6 For the moral part, perhaps youth will have the preeminence, as age hath for the politic. [Francis Bacon: *Of Youth and Age*]

7 Young men have more virtue than old men; they have more generous sentiments in every respect. [Samuel Johnson: in Boswell's *Life,* July 21, 1763]

Johnson once said to Percival Stockdale: "Whenever it is the duty of a young and an old man to act with a spirit of independence and generosity, we may always have reason to hope that the young man will ardently perform—and to fear that the old man will desert his duty."

8 Youth does not dare to look at itself in the mirror of conscience when it is leaning toward injustice; maturity has already seen its image there at such a moment—in this lies all the difference between these two periods in life. [Balzac: *Père Goriot*]

9 My old age judges more charitably and thinks better of mankind than my youth ever did. [George Santayana: *Persons and Places* II]

YOUTH AND AGE: their mutual contempt

10 An old man is never welcome among the young. [Menander: *Monosticha*]

11 Young men think old men are fools; but old men *know* young men are fools. [George Chapman: *All Fools* V.i. (1605)]

Apparently a saying, because it appears elsewhere at about this time in a slightly different form.

12 Crabbed age and youth cannot live
together;
Youth is full of pleasaunce, age is
full of care;
Youth like summer morn, age like
winter weather;
Youth like summer brave, age like
winter bare.
Youth is full of sport, age's breath is
short;
Youth is nimble, age is lame;
Youth is hot and bold, age is weak
and cold;
Youth is wild, and age is tame.
Age, I do abhor thee; youth, I do
adore thee.

[Shakespeare (?): *The Passionate Pilgrim XII*]

> pleasaunce = *the condition of being pleased;* brave = *glorious, splendid, showy*

> The Passionate Pilgrim *is a collection of poems published in 1599 with "By W. Shakespeare" on the title page. But scholars now believe that only four of the poems are by Shakespeare.*

1 Every old man complains of the growing depravity of the world, of the petulance and insolence of the rising generation. [Samuel Johnson: *The Rambler* No. 50]

2 If dotards will contend with boys in those performances in which boys must always excel them; if they will dress crippled limbs in embroidery, endeavor at gaiety with faltering voices and darken assemblies of pleasure with the ghastliness of disease, they may well expect those who find their diversions obstructed will hoot them away; and that if they descend to competition with youth, they must bear the insolence of successful rivals. [Samuel Johnson: *The Rambler* No. 50]

3 The conversation of the old and the young ends generally with contempt or pity on either side. [Samuel Johnson: *The Rambler* No. 70]

4 When an old gentleman waggles his head and says: "Ah, so I thought when I was your age," it is not thought an answer at all if the young man retorts: "My venerable sir, so shall I most probably think when I am yours." And yet the one is as good as the other. [R. L. Stevenson: *Crabbed Age and Youth*]

5 The denunciation of the young is a necessary part of the hygiene of older people, and greatly assists the circulation of their blood. [Logan Pearsall Smith: *Afterthoughts*]

YOUTH AND AGE: miscellaneous

6 I shall go out with the chariots to counsel and command, for that is the privilege of the old; the young must fight in the ranks. [Homer: *Iliad* IV]

7 The young shall be silent before their elders, and give them place, and rise up before them. [Plato: *The Republic* IV]

8 If we could be twice young and twice old we could correct all our mistakes. [Euripides: *The Suppliant Women*]

9 Shame is an ornament to the young, a disgrace to the old, since an old man ought not to do anything of which he need be ashamed. [Aristotle: *Nicomachean Ethics* IV.ix.]

10 I am young, and ye are very old; wherefore I was afraid, and durst not show you mine opinion. [Job 32:6]

11 Your old men shall dream dreams, your young men shall see visions. [Joel 2:28]

12 Old men are twice boys. [Aristophanes: *The Clouds*]

13 If youth but knew; if old age could! [Henri Estienne: *Les Prémices*]

14 A man that is young in years may be old in hours, if he have lost no time; but that happeneth rarely. [Francis Bacon: *Of Youth and Age*]

15 Authority followeth old men and favor and popularity youth. [Francis Bacon: *Of Youth and Age*]

16 . . . . old men go to death, and death comes to young men. [Bacon: *Apothegms*]

17
> Thou hast nor youth nor age;
> But, as it were, an after-dinner's sleep,
> Dreaming on both; for all thy blessed
>   youth
> Becomes as aged, and doth beg the
>   alms
> Of palsied eld; and when thou art
>   old and rich,
> Thou hast neither heat, affection,
>   limb, nor beauty,
> To make thy riches pleasant. What's
>   yet in this
> That bears the name of life? Yet in
>   this life
> Lie hid moe thousand deaths; yet
>   death we fear,
> That makes these odds all even.

[Shakespeare: *Measure for Measure* III.i.]

18
> God on our Youth bestows but little
>   ease,
> But on our Age most sweet indulgences.

[Robert Herrick: *Youth and Age*]

19 And boasting youth, and narrative old age,

Their pleas were diff'rent, their request the same;
For good and bad alike are fond of fame.
[Alexander Pope: *Temple of Fame*]

1 When I was young?—Ah, woeful When!
Ah, for the change 'twixt Now and Then!
[Coleridge: *Youth and Age*]

2 O Youth! for years so many and sweet,
'Tis known that Thou and I were one.
I'll think it but a fond conceit—
It cannot be that Thou art gone!
Thy vesper-bell hath not yet tolled:—
And thou wert aye a masker bold!
What strange disguise hast now put on
To make believe that thou art gone?
I see these locks in silvery slips,
This drooping gait, this altered size:
But Springtide blossoms on thy lips,
And tears take sunshine from thine eyes!
Life is but thought: so think I will
That Youth and I are house-mates still.
[Coleridge: *Youth and Age*]

3 The excesses of our youth are drafts upon our old age, payable with interest about thirty years after date. [C. C. Colton: *Lacon*]

4 Whenever a man's friends begin to compliment him about looking young, he may be sure that they think he is growing old. [Washington Irving: *Bracebridge Hall*, "Bachelors"]

5 Youth is a blunder; manhood a struggle; old age a regret. [Benjamin Disraeli: *Coningsby* III.I.]

6 Youth longs and manhood strives, but age remembers.
[O. W. Holmes: *The Iron Gate*]

7 Therefore I summon age
To grant youth's heritage.
[Robert Browning: *Rabbi Ben Ezra*]

8 When we are at the end of life, to die means to go away; when we are at the beginning, to go away means to die. [Victor Hugo: *Les Misérables* VIII.vi.]

9 And sigh that one thing only has been lent
To youth and age in common—discontent.
[Matthew Arnold: *Youth's Agitations*]

10 Old and young, we are all on our last cruise. [R. L. Stevenson: *Crabbed Age and Youth*]

11 Young men want to be faithful and are not; Old men want to be faithless and cannot.
[Oscar Wilde: *The Picture of Dorian Gray*]

12 King David and King Solomon
Led merry, merry lives,
With many, many lady friends,
And many, many wives;
But when old age crept over them,
With many, many qualms,
King Solomon wrote the Proverbs
And King David wrote the Psalms.
[James Ball Naylor: *David and Solomon*]

Z

Z

1 Thou whoreson Zed! thou unnecessary letter!
[Shakespeare: *King Lear* II.ii.]
> zed = z, or zee, the last letter of the alphabet
> Zed was the name given to it since the Norman Conquest (1066) in England, though it has also been called Zad, Zard, Izzard ("from A to Izzard"), Ezod, Uzzard. Zee, now universal in America, was one of the English forms, though rare. It is unnecessary because it is merely a voiced s and the Elizabethans preferred to write it s.
> Whoreson was once such an indecent word that its use was punished. But it became, like bloody later, to be so overworked as to lose all meaning. The gravedigger in Hamlet speaks of a "whoreson dead body" and calls Yorick "a whoreson mad fellow." Then it became even a term of endearment. Doll Tearsheet calls Falstaff "Thou whoreson little tidy Bartholomew boar-pig."

ZEAL

2 He . . . was clad with zeal as a cloke.
[Isaiah 59:17]
> RSV: He . . . wrapped himself in fury as a mantle.

3 Th' Egyptians worshipp'd dogs, and for
Their faith made fierce and zealous war.
Others ador'd a rat, and some
For that church suffer'd martyrdom.
[Samuel Butler (1612-1680): *Hudibras*]

4 Zeal's a dreadful termagant,
That teaches saints to tear and rant.
[Samuel Butler (1612-1680): *Hudibras*]

5 Violent zeal for truth hath an hundred to one odds to be either petulancy, ambition, or pride. [Jonathan Swift: *Thoughts on Religion*]

6 I do not love a man who is zealous for nothing. [Oliver Goldsmith: in an earlier version of *The Vicar of Wakefield*]
> Samuel Johnson, in Boswell's Life (1779) quoted this line and said that Goldsmith had been "fool enough to expunge" it.

ZION

7 Woe to them that are at ease in Zion.
[Amos 6:1]

8 Glorious things of thee are spoken,
Zion, city of our God.
[John Newton: *Glorious Things of Thee Are Spoken*]
> Glorious things are spoken of thee, O city of God.
> —Psalms 87:3

ZOOS

9 All they [zoos] actually offer to the public in return for the taxes spent upon them is a form of idle and witless amusement, compared to which a visit to a penitentiary, or even to a State Legislature in session, is informing, stimulating and ennobling. [H. L. Mencken: in the *New York Evening Mail*, Feb. 2, 1918]

10 The sort of man who likes to spend his time watching a cage of monkeys chase one another, or a lion gnaw its tail, or a lizard catch flies, is precisely the sort of man whose mental weakness should be combatted at the public expense, and not fostered. [H. L. Mencken: in the *New York Evening Mail*, Feb. 2, 1918]

INDEX
OF
AUTHORS

A

B

344, 347, 349, 358, 367, 375, 376, 380,
386, 401, 403, 412, 414, 415, 426, 427,
432, 449, 467, 468, 489, 490, 501, 507,
518, 530, 534, 543, 546, 551, 584, 588,
593, 601, 608, 610, 614, 628, 655, 696,
698, 700, 730, 746, 747, 765, 766, 767,
778
Burr, Aaron (1756–1836), 557
Burton, Robert (1577–1640), 8, 20, 23,
39, 44, 60, 62, 88, 89, 118, 122, 164,
165, 176, 194, 198, 201, 223, 226, 229,
245, 260, 284, 297, 325, 337, 346, 378,
397, 403, 409, 412, 415, 418, 427, 432,
433, 440, 441, 451, 460, 463, 470, 479,
488, 499, 517, 519, 524, 526, 528, 533,
544, 554, 598, 606, 608, 616, 626, 627,
628, 638, 644, 650, 671, 691, 699, 712,
723, 743, 745, 748, 753, 758, 764, 766,
769, 771, 784
Butler, Nicholas Murray (1862–1947),
214
Butler, Samuel (1612–1680), *Hudibras*:
Part I, 1663; Part II, 1664; Part III,
1678. 17, 67, 75, 78, 99, 100, 122, 132,
144, 163, 175, 196, 221, 235, 270, 322,
323, 338, 344, 356, 373, 380, 387,
399, 408, 416, 448, 461, 465, 491, 494,
498, 501, 519, 520, 522, 526, 536, 553,
565, 584, 586, 588, 599, 611, 613, 614,
633, 687, 732, 737, 745, 747, 777, 791
Butler, Samuel (1835–1902), 12, 110, 116,
133, 147, 151, 157, 168, 173, 194, 200,

219, 229, 240, 249, 275, 281, 301, 305,
313, 316, 340, 342, 390, 391, 398, 407,
408, 409, 419, 433, 459, 460, 462, 464,
498, 507, 523, 524, 558, 567, 615, 629,
667, 699, 711, 724, 727, 786, 787
Buttes, Henry (late 16th cent.), 503, 571
Byrom, John (1692–1763), 105, 298, 655,
714
Byron, Lord George Gordon (1788–1824),
1, 7, 13, 28, 31, 34, 35, 40, 46, 49, 50,
54, 64, 66, 68, 70, 72, 73, 83, 93, 104,
107, 108, 131, 134, 149, 155, 162, 164,
165, 171, 176, 183, 199, 204, 207, 208,
209, 211, 214, 222, 223, 224, 225, 226,
234, 237, 241, 252, 263, 270, 271, 272,
283, 289, 292, 300, 301, 305, 307, 308,
310, 313, 316, 321, 339, 340, 347, 350,
353, 355, 359, 360, 368, 369, 377, 381,
382, 387, 389, 403, 404, 407, 409, 410,
411, 414, 416, 421, 422, 429, 430, 433,
435, 436, 437, 440, 441, 447, 448, 449,
450, 459, 461, 463, 467, 479, 483, 485,
486, 492, 502, 504, 508, 509, 511, 513,
515, 521, 529, 531, 533, 536, 538, 541,
566, 570, 578, 580, 584, 587, 589, 597,
598, 600, 607, 610, 611, 624, 629, 631,
635, 637, 638, 640, 642, 645, 648, 649,
650, 651, 660, 664, 677, 683, 689, 690,
693, 699, 703, 705, 707, 710, 715, 722,
726, 730, 732, 733, 734, 738, 740, 743,
748, 753, 754, 756, 759, 762, 763, 764,
769, 775, 776, 779, 784, 787

C

Cabell, James Branch (1879–1958), 312,
433, 499, 728
Cabillo de Aragon, Alvaro (1596?–1661),
245
Cadogan, William, First Earl (1675–1726),
201
Caesar, Gaius Julius (100–44 B.C.), 54,
170, 265, 597, 600, 672, 722, 734, 735
Calderón de la Barca, Pedro (1600–
1681), 2, 240, 409, 546, 717
Caligula, Gaius Caesar (12–41), 481
Calverley, Charles Stuart (1831–1884), 44,
247, 654

Cambridge, Richard (1717–1802), 778
Cambronne, General Pierre Étienne,
Comte (1770–1842), 294, 735
Camden, William (1551–1623), 53, 60, 77,
81, 131, 137, 176, 213, 251, 260, 378,
454, 498, 687, 754
Campbell, George (1719–1796), 287
Campbell, Sir John (1779–1861), 31
Campbell, Joseph (1879–1944), 11
Campbell, Roy (1901–1957), 586, 638
Campbell, Thomas (1777–1844), 24, 100,
131, 174, 233, 370, 500, 622, 737, 769
Camus, Albert (1913–1960), 40, 96, 108,

Chesterton, Gilbert Keith (1874–1936), 130, 178, 367, 395, 421, 601, 753

Chevalier, Maurice (1888–), 16

Chevalier, Sulpice-Guillaume. *See* Gauarni

Child, Lydia Maria (1802–1880), 288

Christina, Queen of Sweden (1626–1689), 443

I Chronicles, 481, 606, 622

II Chronicles, 10, 88, 523

Church, Francis (1839–1906), 605

Churchill, Charles (1731–1764), 4, 16, 18, 91, 215, 255, 356, 359, 377, 379, 516, 530, 554, 560, 652, 653, 672, 678

Churchill, Lord Randolph Spencer (1849–1895), 179

Churchill, Sir Winston (1874–1965), 66, 83, 155, 169, 189, 196, 199, 224, 233, 235, 352, 492, 553, 626, 672

Ciardi, John (1916–), 607

Cibber, Colley (1671–1757), 20, 226, 305, 328, 520, 610, 681, 690, 739

Cicero, Marcus Tullius (106–43 B.C.), 1, 8, 14, 16, 27, 47, 54, 86, 137, 140, 150, 170, 173, 179, 188, 191, 195, 198, 200, 221, 258, 278, 292, 297, 304, 316, 325, 331, 349, 377, 383, 384, 428, 454, 461, 476, 522, 524, 531, 533, 548, 557, 558, 561, 578, 597, 615, 628, 629, 671, 681, 684, 688, 709, 725, 728, 735, 736, 737, 785

Clarendon, *See* Hyde

Clark, James Beauchamp (1850–1921), 175

Clarke, John, (17th cent.), 8, 51, 318, 394, 401, 412, 739

Claudianus (fl. 4th cent. A.D.), 76

Clausewitz, Karl von (1780–1831), 734

Clay, Henry (1777–1852), 593

Cleghorn, Sarah Norcliff (1876–1959), 102, 281

Clemens, Samuel Langhorne. *See* Mark Twain

Clement of Alexandria (Titus Flavius Clemens) (150?–220?), 249

Cleveland, Grover (1837–1908), 286, 348, 767

Clive, Robert (1725–1774), 457

Clough, Arthur Hugh (1819–1861), 7, 99, 118, 235, 278, 364, 394, 459, 462, 507, 520, 531, 663, 744, 776

Cobbett, William (1763–1835), 232, 338, 545, 681

Coborn, Charles (1852–1945), 216

Cochrane, Alfred (b. 1865), 539

Cockburn, Claud (1904–), 360

Cocteau, Jean (1891–1963), 32

Cogan, Thomas (1545?–1607), 285

Cohan, George M. (1878–1942), 79

Coke, Sir Edward (1552–1634), 128, 327, 673, 689

Colbert, Jean Baptiste (1619–1683), 680

Cole, Henry (1500?–1580), 526

Coleridge, Hartley (1796–1849), 218, 252, 260, 324, 408

Coleridge, Samuel Taylor (1772–1834), 13, 17, 18, 19, 28, 36, 45, 50, 55, 58, 64, 68, 78, 79, 113, 114, 115, 124, 139, 142, 144, 159, 164, 168, 172, 180, 186, 204, 208, 213, 215, 231, 232, 245, 258, 260, 302, 319, 325, 330, 335, 336, 337, 364, 368, 382, 393, 400, 408, 414, 415, 430, 438, 463, 465, 466, 477, 478, 486, 487, 517, 531, 536, 537, 542, 549, 550, 555, 567, 599, 603, 611, 620, 623, 624, 627, 630, 631, 634, 637, 652, 655, 665, 669, 678, 686, 730, 732, 734, 739, 755, 785, 790

Collier, Jeremy (1650–1726), 2, 463

Collins, John Churton (1848–1908), 230, 555

Collins, Mortimer (1827–1876), 425

Collins, William (1721–1759), 76, 238, 311, 467

Colman, George, the Elder (1732–1794), 3, 42, 177, 400, 484, 749

Colman, George, the Younger (1762–1836), 25, 83, 237, 269, 399, 641, 701

Colossians, 651, 702

Colton, Charles Caleb (1780?–1832), 9, 28, 35, 103, 108, 211, 255, 259, 263, 285, 340, 378, 437, 455, 547, 613, 712, 790

Columella (Lucius Junius Moderatus) (1st cent. A.D.), 337

Combe, William (1741–1823), 514

Comte, Auguste (1798–1857), 540

Condell, Henry (d. 1627), 622

Congreve, William (1670–1729), 93, 131, 165, 186, 229, 245, 261, 368, 376, 407, 408, 415, 429, 433, 471, 514, 529, 604, 610, 643, 688, 716, 757, 759, 765

Connoly, Cyril (1903–), 576

Conrad, Joseph (orig: Teodor Józef Konrad Korzeniowski) (1857–1924), 146, 210, 580

Constable, Henry (1562–1613), 179

Constantine I (Flavius Valerius Aurelius Constantinus) (280?–337), 135

D

Draxe, Thomas (d. 1618), 176, 333, 456, 592

Drayton, Michael (1563–1631), 266, 359, 381, 431, 508, 534, 548, 562

Dresser, Paul (1857–1906), 732

Dryden, John (1631–1700), 14, 17, 20, 44, 51, 71, 76, 98, 124, 130, 133, 134, 142, 158, 186, 191, 193, 201, 203, 212, 224, 228, 245, 248, 254, 260, 266, 267, 270, 271, 272, 282, 297, 311, 323, 324, 327, 343, 346, 356, 382, 391, 405, 406, 414, 416, 421, 423, 424, 451, 494, 512, 527, 529, 532, 536, 537, 538, 540, 552, 565, 583, 601, 603, 607, 614, 623, 630, 645, 648, 664, 670, 691, 712, 718, 723, 727, 732, 736, 746, 758, 760, 777, 787

Du Bartas, Guillaume Salluste (1544–1590), 298, 397

Dudley, Sir Henry Bate (1745–1824), 768

Duffield, George (1818–1888), 357

Dulles, John Foster (1888–1959), 79

Dumas, Alexandre père (1802–1870), 23, 497, 717, 756, 765

Du Maurier, George (1834–1896), 393

Dumouriez, Charles François, (1739–1823), 247

Dunne, Finley Peter ("Mr. Dooley"), (1867–1936), 15, 224, 379, 511, 671, 724

Dupin, Amandine Aurore. *See* Sand, George

Durant, William James ("Will") (1885–), 332

D'Urfey, Thomas (Tom Durfey) (1653–1723), 177, 429, 520, 778

Dyer, Sir Edward (d. 1607), 452

Dyer, John (1700?–1758), 184, 389

E

Earle, Bishop John (1601?–1665), 524

Eberhart, Mignon (1900?–), 694

Ecclesiastes, 10, 56, 60, 71, 73, 74, 77, 81, 93, 120, 128, 145, 147, 176, 187, 191, 197, 247, 262, 289, 290, 298, 351, 365, 369, 371, 376, 383, 390, 393, 407, 424, 443, 460, 475, 483, 490, 496, 511, 527, 530, 545, 548, 563, 570, 571, 589, 593, 611, 612, 631, 663, 669, 682, 701, 706, 720, 731, 737, 750, 756, 771, 786

Eddington, Sir Arthur (1882–1944), 379

Eden, Anthony, Earl of Avon (1897–), 650

Edgeworth, Maria (1767–1849), 81, 101

Edison, Thomas Alva (1847–1931), 266, 649

Edward VIII (1894–). *See* Windsor, Duke of

Edwards, Jonathan (1703–1758), 604

Edwards, Oliver (1711–1791), 522

Edwards, Richard (1532?–1566), 411, 471

Einstein, Albert (1879–1955), 35, 36, 252, 283, 332, 340

Eisenhower, Dwight D. (1890–), 279

Elderton, William (d. 1592?), 131

Eliot, George (Mary Ann Evans) (1819–1880), 7, 34, 102, 103, 113, 120, 301, 338, 341, 444, 467, 508, 606, 631, 677, 701, 768

Eliot, Thomas Stearns (1888–1965), 14, 18, 29, 65, 109, 114, 128, 148, 153, 170, 187, 197, 209, 214, 231, 242, 243, 298, 325, 379, 446, 449, 576, 642, 659, 671, 672, 685, 693, 697, 698, 745, 751

Elizabeth I (1533–1603), 24, 75, 365

Elliot, Jean (1727–1805), 241

Elliot, Charlotte (1789–1871), 66

Elliott, Ebenezer (1781–1849), 217

Ellis, Havelock (1859–1939), 276, 688, 694

Emerson, Ralph Waldo (1803–1882), 11, 49, 59, 73, 78, 100, 101, 115, 117, 118, 123, 127, 130, 131, 137, 138, 145, 187, 193, 195, 196, 200, 207, 226, 232, 249, 254, 256, 262, 267, 270, 280, 282, 285, 291, 314, 323, 327, 328, 331, 338, 342, 345, 349, 350, 351, 369, 374, 386, 397, 429, 468, 473, 487, 488, 499, 528, 539,

F

G

Guazzo, Stefano (1530–1593), 51, 228, 631, 698

Guedalla, Philip (1889–1944), 100, 178, 365

Guest, Edgar A. (1881–1959), 318, 618

Guevara, Antonio de (1480?–1545), 678, 756

Guevara, Luis Velez de (1579–1644), 590

Guicciardini, Francesco (1483–1540), 172

Guillotin, Dr. Joseph Ignace (1738–1814), 295

Guinan, Texas (1884–1933), 254

Guiney, Louise Imogen (1861–1920), 493

Guiterman, Arthur (1871–1943), 21, 526, 772

Guthrie, Thomas Anstey (1856–1934), 539

H

Haberton, John (1842–1921), 745

Hadrian, Publius Aelius Hadrianus (76–138), 648

Haeckel, Ernst (1834–1919), 253, 275

Hague, Frank (1876–1956), 379

Hale, Sir Matthew (1609–1676), 134

Hale, Nathan (1755–1776), 130, 512

Hale, Sara Josepha (1788–1879), 372

Haliburton, Thomas Chandler ("Sam Slick") (1796–1865), 107, 659

Halifax, *See* Montagu, Charles, and Savile, George

Hall, Charles Sprague (fl. 1860), 80

Hall, Bishop Joseph (1574–1656), 7, 129, 265, 671

Halleck, Fitz-Greene (1790–1867), 204

Hamerton, Philip G. (1834–1894), 574

Hamilton, Alexander (1757–1804), 285

Hamilton, Edith (1867–1963), 197, 703

Hammerstein, Oscar II (1895–1960), 362

Hardenberg, Baron Friedrich von. *See* Novalis

Harding, Warren G. (1865–1923), 488

Hardy, Thomas (1840–1928), 60, 166, 168, 204, 210, 214, 276, 284, 290, 305, 352, 363, 391, 393, 412, 416, 441, 444, 445, 481, 512, 515, 520, 601, 657, 674, 685, 718, 736, 742, 785

Hare, Augustus William (1792–1834), 4, 173

Hare, Julius Charles (1795–1855), 4, 173

Harington, Sir John (1561–1612), 34, 72, 237, 251, 492, 660, 706

Harper, Robert G. (1765–1825), 160

Harrington, James (1611–1667), 378

Harris, Joel Chandler (1848–1908), 78, 586, 641, 679

Harte, Bret (Francis Brett Harte) (1836–1902), 103, 251, 288, 450, 639, 729

Harvey, Gabriel (1545?–1630), 356, 710

Haweis, Hugh R. (1838–1901), 472

Hawes, Stephen (d. c. 1523), 208

Hawker, Robert Stephen (1803–1875), 707

Hawkins, Sir Anthony Hope. *See* Hope, Anthony

Hawkins, Sir John (1719–1789), 680

Hawthorne, Alice. *See* Winner, Septimus

Hawthorne, Nathaniel (1804–1864), 98, 571, 585, 649

Hay, Lord Charles (d. 1760), 294

Hay, Ian. *See* Beith, John Hay

Hayward, Abraham (1801–1884), 604

Hazlitt, William (1778–1830), 2, 4, 9, 80, 86, 118, 127, 132, 147, 161, 194, 201, 222, 224, 226, 237, 245, 254, 255, 266, 291, 335, 343, 347, 348, 360, 380, 424, 437, 444, 453, 475, 485, 505, 516, 518, 530, 531, 553, 562, 564, 566, 583, 602, 608, 616, 623, 625, 630, 631, 662, 665, 670, 678, 679, 687, 695, 704, 711, 717, 731, 757, 759, 785, 786

Hazlitt, William Carew (1834–1913), 210, 328, 628

Hearn, Lafcadio (1850–1904), 574

Hearst, William Randolph (1863–1951), 735

Heber, Reginald (1783–1826), 207, 309, 357, 423, 561

Hebrews, 219, 277, 327, 511, 653, 760

I

J

367, 374, 375, 395, 431, 461, 483, 519,
535, 548, 577, 587, 622, 627, 632, 651,
664, 678, 689, 697, 699, 706, 727, 772

Joshua, 148, 157, 240, 620

Joubert, Joseph (1754–1824), 15, 30, 73,
102, 303, 450, 494, 667, 685

Jouy, Victor de (1764–1846), 764

Jowett, Benjamin (1817–1893), 376

Joyce, James (1882–1941), 33, 40, 214,
393, 553, 784

Joyce, John Alexander (1842–1915), 460

Judges, 83, 96, 141, 142, 276, 316, 355,
439, 521, 553, 626, 656, 689, 745

Julian (Flavius Claudius Julianus) (331–
363), 104

Julius Caesar. See Caesar, Gaius Julius

Junot, Androche, Duc D'Abrantes (1771–
1813), 22

Justinian (Flavius Anicius Justinianus)
(483–565), 658

Juvenal (Decimus Junius Juvenalis) (60–
140), 12, 60, 77, 294, 306, 321, 356,
379, 452, 457, 478, 538, 544, 545, 549,
587, 590, 616, 642, 659, 692, 696, 746,
755, 779

K

Kant, Immanuel (1724–1804), 90, 187

Kaufman, George S. (1889–1961), 460, 544

Kauffman, Reginald Wright (1877–1959),
119

Keats, John, (1795–1821), 21, 39, 44, 49,
51, 68, 93, 109, 114, 129, 149, 153,
155, 166, 172, 183, 205, 225, 231, 248,
275, 290, 300, 308, 320, 340, 341, 342,
360, 369, 371, 383, 390, 399, 406, 413,
414, 438, 441, 447, 449, 454, 465, 470,
472, 477, 487, 494, 509, 519, 523, 531,
534, 535, 537, 538, 563, 575, 597, 599,
602, 607, 611, 619, 623, 630, 631, 657,
660, 675, 702, 707, 709, 719, 729, 752,
754, 768

Keble, John (1792–1866), 192, 431, 523,
566, 730

Kelly, James (fl. 1721), 49, 52, 53, 76, 126,
434, 569

Kemble, John Philip (1757–1823), 174

Kempis, Thomas à. See Thomas à Kempis

Ken, Bishop Thomas (1637–1711), 277,
397, 548

Kennan, George (1845–1924), 314

Kennedy, John Fitzgerald (1917–1963),
260, 513, 678

Keppel, David (19th Cent.), 709

Kerr, Clark (1911–   ), 194

Kesselring, Joseph (1902–1961), 31

Key, Francis Scott (1779–1843), 91, 238,
513, 657

Key, Thomas Hewitt (1799–1875), 452

Keynes, John Maynard (1883–1946), 336,
459

Khayyám. See Omar Khayyám

Khrushchev, Nikita (1894–   ), 82

Kilmer, Joyce (1886–1918), 707

King, Benjamin Franklin (1857–1894),
489

King, Bishop Henry (1592–1669), 155,
440

King, Stoddard (1889–1933), 181

King, William (1663–1712), 500

I Kings, 10, 26, 88, 112, 157, 197, 297,
314, 352, 562, 730

II Kings, 43, 156, 176, 195, 356, 500, 514,
622, 777

Kingsley, Charles (1819–1875), 14, 90, 91,
111, 183, 242, 339, 444, 598, 694, 700,
774, 786

Kipling, Rudyard (1865–1936), 6, 19, 21,
42, 68, 73, 81, 107, 141, 144, 178, 191,
196, 199, 233, 261, 278, 280, 296, 299,
303, 307, 309, 314, 319, 330, 338, 367,
369, 373, 378, 404, 412, 426, 427,
467, 495, 528, 541, 563, 568, 570, 575,
585, 603, 607, 616, 627, 633, 634, 644,
667, 700, 713, 717, 733, 746, 761, 765,
773

Kirk, Lisa (1925–   ), 679

Kittredge, Walter (1834–1905), 685

Klopstock, Friedrich (1724–1803), 439

Knolles, Richard (1550?–1610), 20

Knowles, Frederick Lawrence (1869–1905), 731

Knox, John (1505–1572), 443, 762, 765, 766

Knox, William (1789–1825), 466, 555

Koran, The, 532

Krutch, Joseph Wood (1893–), 109, 115, 140, 393, 398, 427, 448, 464, 478, 580

L

Labouchere, Henry (1831–1912), 34

La Bruyère, Jean de (1645–1696), 20, 59, 68, 102, 126, 195, 301, 333, 376, 385, 403, 444, 530, 592, 600, 613, 651, 666, 697, 758, 759, 779, 785

La Coste, Marie R. (1849–1936), 144

Lafayette, Marie Joseph Paul, Marquis de (1757–1834), 577

La Fontaine, Jean de (1621–1695), 29, 47, 159, 273, 304, 719

Lamachus (d. 414 B.C.), 456

Lamartine, Alphonse de (1790–1869), 470, 515

Lamb, Arthur J. (1870–1928), 61, 436

Lamb, Lady Caroline (1785–1828), 420

Lamb, Charles (1775–1834), 29, 60, 70, 73, 74, 76, 119, 150, 217, 244, 264, 317, 339, 368, 436, 484, 500, 542, 565, 574, 591, 625, 682, 699, 756

Lamb, William, Viscount Melbourne (1779–1848), 265, 579

Lamentations, 647

Lampton, William James (1859–1917), 128, 743

Landor, Walter Savage (1775–1864), 20, 218, 268, 477, 580, 584, 600, 718

Lane, George Martin (1823–1897), 237

Lang, Andrew (1844–1912), 495, 729

Langbridge, Frederick (1849–1923), 499, 539

Langland, William (1332?–1400?), 185, 228, 457, 480, 773

Lardner, Ring (old) Wilmer (1885–1933), 135, 146, 168, 214, 238, 298, 416, 419, 660

La Rochefoucauld, Duc François de (1613–1680), 1, 2, 9, 13, 15, 16, 20, 39, 51, 73, 74, 98, 111, 118, 121, 126, 186, 192, 194, 210, 229, 239, 240, 244, 249, 254, 259, 288, 290, 302, 305, 314, 324, 335, 337, 347, 355, 361, 362, 385, 406, 407, 408, 410, 411, 413, 415, 421, 431, 442, 457, 467, 509, 521, 523, 527, 529, 548, 549, 554, 559, 569, 583, 592, 606, 614, 616, 617, 630, 632, 633, 642, 678, 679, 708, 711, 721, 724, 727, 755, 756, 757, 758, 764

La Sale, Antoine de (1385?–1460?), 405

Latimer, Hugh (1485?–1555), 116, 712

Lauder, Sir Harry (Harry MacLennan) (1870–1950), 30, 52, 566

Lawrence, David Herbert (1885–1930), 25, 616

Lawrence, T. E. ("Lawrence of Arabia"), changed name to T. E. Shaw (1888–1935), 320, 332, 611, 683

Lazarus, Emma (1849–1887), 386

Lean, Vincent Stuckey (1820–1899), 379, 525, 549

Lear, Edward (1812–1888), 48, 144, 244, 362, 379, 502, 516, 531, 532, 629, 653, 700, 705, 784

Lease, Mary Elizabeth ("The Kansas Pythoness") (1853–1933), 364

Lecky, William E. H. (1838–1903), 539

Lee, General Henry ("Light-Horse Harry") (1756–1818), 738

Lee, Nathaniel (1653?–1692), 292, 314, 622, 678

Lee, General Robert E. (1807–1870), 31, 734

Leigh, Henry Sambrooke (1837–1883), 183

Lenin (Vladimir Ilich Ulyanov (1870–1924), 305, 641

Leo XIII (Gioacchino Vincenzo Pecci) (1810–1903), 38, 107, 386, 700

Leon, Fray Luis de (1529–1591), 243

Leopardi, Giacomo (1798–1837), 222

Lesage, Alain René (1668–1747), 87, 648, 687, 759

Lessing, Gotthold Ephraim (1729–1781), 130, 219, 230, 377, 578

L'Estrange, Sir Roger (1616–1704), 547, 589

Leszczynski, Stanislas (1677–1766), 179, 573

Letts, Winifred Mary (1882–1962), 503

Levant, Oscar (1906–   ), 202

Leviticus, 64, 385, 482, 607

Lewes, George Henry (1817–1878), 559

Lewis, Cecil Day (1904–   ), 407

Lewis, Clive Staples (1898–   ), 509

Lewis, Sir George Cornewall (1806–1863), 531

Leybourne, George (d. 1884), 704

Lichtenberg, Georg C. (1742–1799), 63

Lillo, George (1693?–1739), 472

Lincoln, Abraham (1809–1865), 44, 95, 96, 159, 185, 214, 219, 252, 268, 328, 371, 377, 501, 518, 559, 588, 593, 618, 636, 673

Lindsay, Nicholas Vachel (1879–1931), 470, 665

Linton, William James (1812–1897), 267

Livy (Titus Livius) (50 B.C.–17 A.D.), 36, 68, 200, 209, 214, 231, 459, 573, 583, 623, 721, 746, 768

Lloyd George, David (1863–1945), 483

Locke, John (1632–1704), 5, 36, 160, 206, 213, 253, 300, 336, 452, 490, 559, 574, 579, 691, 716, 727, 771

Locker-Lampson, Frederick (1821–1895), 42, 294

Logau, Friederich von (1604–1655), 174

Lombroso, Cesare (1835–1909), 439

Longfellow, Henry Wadsworth (1807–1882), 4, 27, 31, 33, 39, 63, 76, 78, 102, 105, 146, 151, 152, 165, 173, 182, 198, 209, 211, 223, 228, 246, 247, 271, 289, 291, 292, 307, 314, 315, 318, 328, 344, 371, 392, 441, 444, 449, 451, 456, 471, 486, 487, 509, 511, 512, 515, 520, 550, 553, 558, 572, 585, 587, 588, 612, 619, 626, 637, 649, 650, 670, 697, 709, 717, 732, 747, 769, 786

Longinus, Lucius Cassius (2nd cent. B.C.), 7

Loos, Anita (1893–   ), 66

Louis XII (1462–1515), 268

Louis XIV (1638–1715), 347, 495, 658, 734

Louis XV (1710–1774), 162, 261, 541

Louis XVIII (1755–1824), 565

Lovelace, Richard (1618–1658), 322, 414, 556, 640

Lovell, Maria (1803–1877), 3

Loveman, Robert (1864–1923), 572

Lover, Samuel (1797–1868), 611, 780

Low, David (1891–1963), 205

Lowe, Robert, Viscount Sherbrooke (1811–1892), 438

Lowell, Amy (1874–1925), 3, 169, 394, 514

Lowell, James Russell (1819–1891), 30, 37, 73, 134, 142, 272, 277, 318, 350, 362, 425, 466, 513, 528, 532, 631, 658, 693, 713, 723, 741, 743

Lowry, Robert (1826–1899), 595

Lubbock, John, First Baron Avebury (1834–1913), 383

Lucan (Marcus Annaeus Lucanus) (39–65 A.D.), 39, 69, 143, 154, 231, 258, 295, 537, 561, 615

Lucas, Edward Verrall (1868–1938), 3, 359

Lucian (2nd cent. A.D.), 10, 47, 202

Luckman, Charles (1909–   ), 666

Lucretius (Titus Lucretius Carus) (96?–55 B.C.), 62, 244, 308, 373, 403, 439, 452, 489, 580, 712, 739, 768

Ludlow, Fitzhugh (1836–1870), 702

Luke, 23, 53, 77, 85, 102, 118, 149, 155, 159, 174, 208, 221, 229, 248, 295, 345, 371, 379, 423, 433, 451, 468, 482, 506, 509, 511, 514, 524, 532, 557, 583, 594, 605, 634, 680, 686, 700, 704, 749, 755, 760, 776

Luther, Martin (1483–1546), 105, 278, 297, 621, 656

Lydgate, John, (1370?–1451), 44, 65, 118, 200, 724

Lyly, John (1554?–1606), 47, 49, 102, 112, 200, 230, 245, 254, 270, 274, 284, 364, 433, 454, 463, 485, 623, 640, 712, 732, 761, 763

Lynes, Russell (1910–   ), 349, 372

Lyte, Henry Francis (1793–1847), 1, 94

Lyttelton, Lord George (1709–1773), 56

M

Massey, Gerald (1829–1907), 162, 289
Massinger, Philip (1583–1640), 157, 179, 393, 511, 673, 722
Masters, Edgar Lee (1869–1950), 464
Mather, Cotton (1663–1728), 106, 548
Matthew, 7, 8, 33, 38, 48, 65, 66, 75, 77, 81, 85, 87, 96, 99, 121, 138, 142, 145, 161, 163, 164, 167, 176, 198, 200, 207, 215, 219, 233, 237, 240, 247, 248, 250, 251, 255, 260, 265, 271, 279, 281, 282, 297, 303, 305, 308, 310, 342, 358, 359, 361, 393, 394, 401, 422, 423, 433, 437, 440, 451, 453, 459, 466, 514, 515, 523, 541, 549, 558, 560, 563, 566, 571, 585, 604, 614, 619, 620, 624, 630, 645, 648, 650, 651, 661, 662, 667, 675, 677, 678, 684, 689, 697, 700, 705, 706, 737, 738, 739, 743, 749, 753, 755, 784
Matthews, James Brander (1852–1929), 315
Maturin, Charles Robert (1782–1824), 411
Maugham, William Somerset (1874–1965), 28, 30, 32, 123, 125, 135, 140, 343, 461, 581, 667
Maupassant, Guy de (1850–1893), 317
Mayhew, Henry (1812–1887), 434
McAllister, Ward (1827–1895), 250
McAuliffe, General Anthony C. (1898–), 735
McCord, David (1897–1962), 204
McCormick, Robert Rutherford (1880–1955), 423
McCrae, John (1872–1918), 543
McGinley, Phyllis (1905–), 317
McLuke, Luke (1868–1921), 781
Mearns, Hughes (1875–1961), 298
Melchior de Santa Cruz (fl. 1574), 181, 753, 756
Melville, Herman (1819–1891), 209, 352, 649
Melville, Sir James (1535–1617), 113
Menander (343?–291? B.C.), 172, 182, 209, 433, 788
Mencken, Henry Louis (1880–1956), 7, 15, 21, 22, 30, 35, 43, 44, 46, 80, 82, 83, 85, 92, 108, 109, 110, 122, 133, 162, 180, 194, 196, 201, 210, 220, 231, 234, 258, 267, 278, 280, 286, 300, 306, 307, 322, 323, 330, 331, 334, 336, 341, 343, 348, 363, 367, 379, 388, 390, 396, 404, 406, 410, 417, 432, 445, 448, 451, 455, 462, 467, 471, 484, 493, 517, 523, 527, 535, 537, 539, 540, 541, 545, 558, 581, 584, 590, 618, 621, 652, 654, 667,

669, 682, 687, 710, 711, 717, 723, 749, 750, 763, 791
Menenius Agrippa. *See* Agrippa
Menninger, Karl (1893–1966), 350
Meredith, George (1828–1909), 55, 93, 140, 344, 392, 444, 492, 509, 551, 608, 619, 722, 755, 758, 767, 768
Meredith, Owen. *See* E. R. Bulwer-Lytton
Mermet, Claude (1550?–1605), 256
Merritt, Dixon Lanier (1879–1954), 517
Meurier, Gabriel (1530–1601), 212
Micah, 198
Middleton, Drew (1914–), 242
Middleton, Thomas (1570?–1627), 39, 381, 434
Mill, John Stuart (1806–1873), 22, 32, 283, 329, 344, 366, 386, 453, 501, 558, 614, 712, 715, 719, 747
Millay, Edna St. Vincent (1892–1950), 29, 51, 87, 148, 308, 328, 352, 404, 407, 472, 689, 694, 776
Miller, Henry (1891–), 33, 109, 255, 321, 330, 473, 507, 576, 609
Miller, Joaquin (Cincinnatus Hiner Miller) (1839–1913), 115, 591
Miller, William (1810–1872), 744
Milne, Alan Alexander (1882–1956), 80
Milnes, Richard Monckton, First Baron Houghton (1809–1885), 420
Milton, John (1608–1674), 2, 5, 6, 12, 23, 27, 31, 33, 35, 37, 44, 45, 49, 50, 56, 58, 65, 68, 70, 71, 72, 78, 86, 88, 92, 94, 95, 98, 101, 103, 106, 107, 112, 116, 120, 121, 122, 124, 131, 132, 133, 138, 139, 142, 143, 144, 145, 150, 151, 159, 160, 161, 165, 179, 181, 190, 191, 192, 195, 196, 208, 210, 212, 213, 214, 215, 216, 220, 221, 222, 223, 226, 234, 236, 238, 241, 246, 248, 252, 260, 262, 273, 277, 279, 282, 283, 284, 287, 288, 297, 303, 304, 309, 310, 311, 312, 314, 319, 324, 333, 335, 341, 347, 348, 357, 359, 369, 371, 373, 375, 382, 383, 384, 385, 387, 393, 395, 400, 402, 403, 406, 409, 410, 414, 418, 421, 422, 423, 426, 431, 439, 440, 441, 443, 452, 457, 458, 462, 463, 464, 465, 466, 468, 470, 471, 473, 479, 481, 483, 486, 487, 492, 493, 498, 499, 506, 511, 512, 514, 517, 519, 523, 528, 529, 530, 534, 535, 536, 538, 548, 549, 550, 555, 563, 571, 574, 578, 582, 587, 592, 605, 606, 610, 614, 620, 623, 624, 625, 628, 632, 634, 639, 642, 644, 646, 647, 653, 654, 656, 662, 664,

666, 669, 672, 673, 675, 678, 683, 686, 690, 691, 693, 695, 700, 701, 706, 709, 710, 711, 712, 716, 718, 720, 724, 725, 726, 727, 728, 729, 730, 732, 734, 737, 739, 741, 747, 751, 752, 754, 756, 762, 766, 767, 772, 777, 780

Miner, Charles (1780–1865), 40

Mitford, Nancy (1904—   ), 531

Mizner, Addison (1872–1933), 76

Moeller, Philip (1880–1958), 312

Moir, David (1798–1851), 52

Mola, General Emilio (1887–1937), 705

Molière (Jean Baptiste Poquelin) (1622–1673), 33, 91, 210, 257, 287, 333, 383, 409, 432, 457, 530, 561, 563, 665, 724

Monkhouse, William Cosmo (1840–1901), 541

Monroe, James (1758–1831), 462

Montagu, Charles, First Earl of Halifax (1661–1715), 8, 87

Montagu, Lady Mary Wortley (1689–1762), 9, 189, 390, 429, 460, 607, 748, 758, 769

Montague, Charles Edward (1867–1928), 108, 261

Montaigne, Michel Eyquem de (1533–1592), 2, 3, 7, 14, 16, 26, 29, 31, 37, 51, 54, 56, 57, 70, 71, 72, 87, 88, 90, 97, 102, 103, 116, 122, 125, 131, 132, 149, 155, 156, 158, 159, 178, 179, 180, 192, 195, 205, 211, 213, 214, 231, 232, 243, 244, 246, 251, 259, 277, 280, 282, 284, 287, 289, 290, 295, 297, 305, 316, 320, 329, 330, 333, 338, 360, 361, 377, 380, 381, 394, 397, 405, 407, 409, 412, 414, 419, 423, 426, 427, 428, 431, 432, 436, 439, 442, 453, 455, 457, 462, 478, 480, 481, 488, 491, 492, 494, 497, 500, 507, 511, 515, 516, 519, 523, 524, 528, 530, 532, 533, 553, 558, 563, 565, 570, 579, 583, 592, 606, 612, 615, 617, 621, 630, 632, 639, 641, 642, 651, 663, 667, 674, 679, 680, 693, 703, 710, 712, 719, 720,

725, 727, 731, 735, 755, 756, 761, 767, 771

Montemayor, Jorge de (1521?–1561), 581

Montesquieu, Charles de Secondat (1689–1755), 62, 277, 331, 349, 571, 666, 680

Montluc, Adrien de (fl. 1735), 98

Moore, Clement Clarke (1779–1863), 56, 105, 605

Moore, Edward (1712–1757), 591

Moore, George (1852–1933), 4, 103, 436, 505, 658

Moore, John (1907—1967), 225

Moore, Julia A. (1847–1920), 46, 84

Moore, Thomas (1779–1852), 18, 102, 174, 194, 215, 220, 224, 303, 309, 400, 403, 409, 442, 453, 599, 600, 670, 715, 749, 762, 766, 769

More, Sir (and Saint) Thomas (1478–1535), 48, 152, 156, 175, 232, 261, 310

Morell, Thomas (1703–1784), 314

Morin, Louis (1635–1714), 729

Morley, Christopher (1890–1957), 29, 108, 666

Morley, John, Viscount Morley of Blackburn (1838–1923), 73, 119, 128, 282, 350, 540, 580, 631, 666

Morris, George Pope (1802–1864), 707

Morris, Sir Lewis (1833–1907), 218

Morris, William (1834–1896), 182, 264, 399, 692

Morton, Thomas (1764–1838), 294, 512

Motley, John Lothrop (1814–1877), 418

Motteux, Peter (1660?–1718), 189, 237, 679

Mumford, Lewis (1895—   ), 288

Munro, Hector Hugh ("Saki") (1870–1916), 128, 143, 149, 195, 544, 556, 624

Murchison, Clint, Jr. (1895—   ), 460

Murray, William, First Earl of Mansfield (1705–1793), 363, 384

Musset, Alfred de (1810–1857), 179, 741

N

O

302, 402, 410, 452, 457, 531, 599, 695, 696, 739, 752, 777
Owen, Robert (1771–1858), 569

Owen, Wilfred (1893–1918), 296, 778
Oxenstierna, Count Axel Gustafsson (1583–1654) 286

P

Paget, Stephen (1855–1926), 392
Paine, Thomas (1737–1809), 59, 172, 252, 338, 584, 665, 687, 697
Paley, William (1743–1805), 275, 641
Palingenius Stellatus. *See* Manzolli, Pierre Angelo, 111
Palmer, John F. (late 19th cent.), 66
Palmer, Samuel (1741–1813), 194, 733
Palsgrave, John (1480?–1554), 331
Parker, Alton B. (1852–1926), 557
Parker, Dorothy (1893—1967), 78, 191, 264, 272, 384, 542, 669
Parker, Martyn (or Martin) (1600–1656), 611
Parker, Theodore (1810–1860), 269, 286
Parkinson, Cyril Northcote (1909—   ), 213, 506, 507, 774
Parton, Sara Payson ("Fanny Fern") (1811–1872), 275.
Pascal, Blaise (1623–1662), 110, 122, 139, 152, 210, 223, 257, 304, 308, 346, 362, 384, 424, 426, 488, 527, 566, 576, 580, 586, 778
Pasternak, Boris (1890–1960), 779
Pater, Walter (1839–1894), 32, 238, 519, 535, 579, 597, 665, 666
Patmore, Coventry (1823–1896), 413, 712
Payn, James (1830–1898), 698
Payne, John Howard (1791–1852), 318
Peacock, Thomas Love (1785–1866), 183, 185, 585, 766
Pearson, Hesketh (1887–1964), 131
Peel, Sir Robert (1788–1850), 267
Peele, George (1558?–1597), 31, 139, 411, 586, 598
Peirce, Charles S. (1839–1914), 464, 688, 691
Pepys, Samuel (1633–1703), 52, 100, 299, 431, 460, 471, 483, 666, 698
Percy, Bishop Thomas (1729–1811), 499
Perez, Antonio (1539–1611), 753

Perronet, Edward (1721–1792), 357
Persius (Aulus Persius Flaccus) (34–62), 222, 331
I Peter, 96, 168, 240, 748
II Peter, 176
Petrarch (Francesco Petrarca) (1304–1374), 24, 163, 632
Petronius, Gaius (surnamed Arbiter) (1st cent. A.D.), 174, 280, 524, 613
Pettie, George (1548–1589), 62, 767
Phaedrus (early 1st cent. A.D.), 135, 190, 337, 349, 493, 573, 614
Philemon (361?–263 B.C.), 524
Philippians, 56, 176, 514, 605, 726
Phillips, Wendell (1811–1884), 386, 562
Phillpotts, Eden (1862–1962), 46
Phocylides (6th cent. B.C.), 460
Pierpont, John (1785–1866), 638
Pike, Bishop James A. (1913—   ), 107
Pinckney, Charles Cotesworth (1746–1825), 160
Pindar (522?–443 B.C.), 323
Pindar, Peter. *See* Wolcot, John
Pinero, Sir Arthur Wing (1855–1934), 347, 595
Piozzi, Hester Lynch (better known, from an earlier marriage, as Mrs. Thrale) (1741–1821), 71, 95, 127, 305, 378, 435
Pirandello, Luigi (1867–1936), 122
Pitt, William ("the Elder"), First Earl of Chatham (1708–1778), 328, 481, 547, 786
Pitt, William ("the Younger") (1759–1806), 259
Pius XI (1857–1939), 114
Platen, August von (1796–1835), 717
Plato (427?–347 B.C.), 14, 16, 35, 40, 51, 75, 92, 283, 365, 376, 418, 424, 443, 444, 450, 522, 534, 535, 589, 590, 615, 621, 709, 726, 741, 752, 789
Plautus, Titus Maccius (254?–184 B.C.),

Q

Quarles, Francis (1592–1644), 25, 155, 328, 389, 421, 426, 430, 599, 741, 755
Quennell, Peter, (1905–   ), 557
Quevedo, Francisco Gómez de (1580–1645), 239, 687
Quinault, Philippe (1635–1688), 756

Quintilian (Marcus Fabius Quintilianus) (fl. 68 A.D.), 20, 31, 109, 195, 297, 416, 754
Quintus Curtius Rufus (fl. c. 2nd cent. A.D.), 231, 739

R

Rabelais, François (1494?–1553), 27, 77, 103, 133, 137, 157, 168, 176, 182, 185, 197, 250, 270, 352, 382, 383, 480, 488, 498, 502, 519, 590, 639, 679, 689, 702, 770
Raleigh, Sir Walter (1552?–1618), 154, 164, 218, 277, 316, 344, 380, 630
Raleigh, Mr. Walter (late 16th cent.), 228
Raleigh, Sir Walter Alexander (1861–1922), 211, 330
Ramsay, Allan (1686–1758), 37
Randolph, John (1773–1833), 129
Randolph, Thomas (1605–1635), 24
Rankin, Jeremiah Eames (1828–1904), 56, 508
Raspe, Rudolph Erich (1737–1794), 219
Ravenscroft, Thomas (1592?–1635), 182
Ray (or Wray), John (1627?–1705), 51, 60, 65, 66, 80, 102, 103, 114, 163, 171, 177, 194, 206, 237, 279, 303, 333, 335, 352, 376, 378, 379, 381, 395, 412, 413, 414, 435, 456, 466, 482, 487, 494, 552, 566, 597, 662, 702, 742, 748, 757, 769
Read, Thomas Buchanan (1822–1872), 401, 625, 733
Reade, Charles (1814–1884), 149, 779
Reed, Thomas B. (1839–1902), 382
Reese, Lizette Woodworth (1856–1935), 746
Reeves, Billy (1815–1892), 242
Regnier, Mathurin (1573–1613), 617
Remarque, Erich Maria (1898–   ), 570

Rexford, Eben Eugene (1848–1916), 13, 290
Reynolds, Frederic (1764–1841), 765
Revelation, 42, 54, 151, 275, 303, 326, 601
Ricardo, David (1772–1823), 371
Rich, Barnabe (1540?–1617), 743
Richard III (1452–1485), 326
Richardson, Samuel (1689–1761), 25, 561, 618, 714
Richelieu, Armand Jean du Plessis, Cardinal (1585–1642), 92, 212
Richter, Jean Paul Friedrich (1763–1825), 74, 200, 240, 276, 410, 640, 647
Riley, James Whitcomb (1849–1916), 39, 260, 275, 501, 551
Robbins, Leonard H. (1877–1947), 423
Robespierre, Maximilien (1758–1794), 194
Robinson, Clement (fl. 1566–1584), 402
Robinson, Edwin Arlington (1869–1935), 146, 184, 453, 578
Robinson, James Harvey (1863–1936), 21, 54
Roche, Sir Boyle (1743–1807), 573
Roche, James Jeffrey (1847–1908), 125
Rochester, Earl of. See Wilmot, John
Rogers, Clement F. (b. 1866), 700
Rogers, Robert Cameron (1862–1912), 599
Rogers, Samuel (1763–1855), 435, 645
Rogers, Will (1879–1935), 22
Rojas, Fernan de (1475?–1538), 232

S

T

U

V

Valerius Maximus (1st cent. A.D.), 28
Vanbrugh, Sir John (1664–1726), 106, 220, 431, 460, 765
Vanderbilt, William Henry (1821–1885), 564
Vandiver, Willard Duncan (1854–1932), 456
Van Doren, Carl (1885–1950), 121
Vaughan, Henry, (1622–1695), 206, 341, 424, 517
Vauvenargues, Marquis de (1715–1747), 112, 117, 194, 210, 283, 379, 384, 388, 397, 481, 529, 530, 548, 610, 690, 727, 746
Vaux, Thomas (1510–1556), 10
Veblen, Thorstein (1857–1929), 124, 383, 741
Vega, Lope de (1562–1635), 261, 443, 749
Venner, Tobias (1577–1660), 739
Venning, Ralph (1621?–1674), 49
Vergil (or Virgil) (Publius Vergilius Maro) (70–19 B.C.), 31, 40, 68, 76, 93, 227, 230, 263, 292, 311, 325, 371, 412, 501, 577, 582, 603, 628, 640, 675, 692, 723, 725, 762, 778
Vespasian (Titus Flavius Sabinus Vespasianus) (9–79 A.D.), 157, 461
Vest, George Graham (1830–1904), 175
Victoria (1819–1901), 22
Villiers, George, 2nd Duke of Buckingham (1628–1687), 405, 532, 628
Villon, François (b. 1431), 511
Vitellius, Aulus (15–69 A.D.), 198
Voltaire (François Marie Arouet) (1694–1778), 3, 6, 35, 46, 54, 58, 70, 71, 73, 77, 94, 106, 146, 179, 198, 199, 226, 245, 252, 270, 277, 278, 281, 316, 317, 318, 337, 338, 346, 383, 418, 431, 437, 448, 454, 472, 499, 552, 580, 591, 598, 645, 651, 665, 670, 687, 703, 727, 773, 781

W

Wace (fl. 1170), 59
Wagner, Richard (1813–1883), 167
Walker, James J. ("Jimmy") (1881–1946), 407
Wallace, William Ross (1819–1881), 298, 466
Waller, Edmund (1606–1687), 15, 50, 77, 86, 107, 188, 200, 239, 529, 532, 599, 646
Walpole, Horace (1717–1797), 285, 301, 474, 483, 533, 692, 727
Walpole, Sir Robert (1676–1745), 43, 316, 550
Walsh, William (1663–1708), 4, 165, 324
Walton, Izaak (1593–1683), 56, 82, 237, 260, 401, 454, 495, 662, 727
Warburton, Bishop William (1698–1779), 501
Ward, Artemus. See Browne, Charles Farrar
Ward, Edward ("Ned") (1667–1731), 129
Ward, Nathaniel ("The Simple Cobler of Aggawam") (1578?–1652), 700, 709, 765
Ward, Thomas (1652–1708), 317
Ware, Eugene Fitch ("Ironquill") (1841–1911), 168, 583
Warner, Charles Dudley (1829–1900), 541
Warner, Susan ("Elizabeth Wetherell") (1819–1885), 357
Warren, Earl (1891–   ), 205
Washburn, Henry Stevenson (1813–1903), 1, 402
Washington, George (1732–1799), 18, 656, 736
Wood, J. T. (late 19th cent.), 113

Y

Z

᧏ Acknowledgments ᧐

THIS BOOK IS BASED, as all such dictionaries are, on its predecessors, from Publilius Syrus to Jim Simpson. The compiler is indebted to every book he ever read and every person he ever knew.

From these latter he would like to select, for particular acknowledgment: William Abler, Mabel Burnham, Caroline Harnsberger, Dorothy Ivy, Bernice Levin, Harriet Oliver, Pamela Teichner, Albert Tricomi, Marcia Wagner and the staff of Northwestern University's Deering Library.

Special thanks must go to Richard Huett and Rosalie Barrow of the Dell Publishing Company, whose helpfulness and patience over the protracted years paragons description, excels the quirks of blazoning pens and tires the ingener. High on the list of *their* favorite quotations must be the remark of the printer of Johnson's *Dictionary* when the last sheet of that work was put in his hands: "Thank *God* I have done with him!"